THE CENTURY HISTORICAL SERIES

William E. Lingelbach, Editor

THE COURSE OF EUROPE
SINCE WATERLOO

The COURSE of EUROPE
SINCE WATERLOO

Walter Phelps Hall, Ph.D.
DODGE PROFESSOR OF HISTORY
PRINCETON UNIVERSITY

William Stearns Davis, Ph.D.
LATE PROFESSOR OF HISTORY
UNIVERSITY OF MINNESOTA

FOURTH EDITION

APPLETON-CENTURY-CROFTS, INC.
New York

PREFACE

The third edition of this book was published in 1951. Since then there have been a series of international crises. The cold war continues. Pessimists, pointing to intermittent and sporadic fighting in Kenya, Cyprus, Malaya, North Africa, and along the borders of Israel, closely followed by open war in Hungary and in Egypt, fear the worst. Optimists pin their faith on underlying Western unity (badly strained) and on mounting evidence of momentous changes taking place behind the iron curtain. Clearly, if *The Course of Europe Since Waterloo* is not to become dated, there must be some account of these new crises. To deal with them a new chapter has been added to this fourth edition.

Then, to preserve a sense of balance and to prevent overemphasis on the contemporary world, another new chapter has been written: this on the Industrial Revolution, surely the most meaningful event, or series of events, since the late eighteenth century, and a proper introduction to any history of the nineteenth and twentieth.

A further improvement may be noted. Despite two new chapters a good hundred pages has been deleted from the third edition. This has been accomplished by excising completely the chapter on nineteenth-century art; by sharply curtailing throughout descriptions of military campaigns; and by deëmphasizing the history of the Balkan states before 1914; all of which seemed desirable if proper emphasis was to be given to the twentieth century.

Numerous minor changes and corrections have been made throughout the text; twelve new maps and twenty-five new illustrations have been added; and the bibliography has been brought up to date.

These changes, I am confident, have resulted in a more useful book. Were my collaborator, the late William Stearns Davis of the University of Minnesota, alive, I feel sure he would approve. The continued popular demand for *The Course of Europe Since Waterloo*, evinced by four editions, owes much to his lively and dramatic way of presenting historical data. The author acknowledges with gratitude the kindness of Miss Florence M. Read in the careful reading of the proof.

W. P. H.

v

CONTENTS

Saves the Hapsburgs—The Revolt and Suppression of Hungary (1848-49)—Frederick William IV and the Humiliation of Olmütz (1850)

War Against Austria: Charles Albert's Failure as a National Leader—Radetzky Revives the Hapsburg Power—Renewal of the War: Abdication of Charles Albert—The Roman Republic: Garibaldi's Defense of Rome (1849): Triumph of Reaction Throughout Italy

Chartism—Corn Laws

Louis Napoleon's Intrigues to Reëstablish the Empire—The Coup d'État of December 2, 1851: Louis Napoleon Seizes Power—The Plebiscite of 1851 and the Proclamation of the "Second Empire" (December, 1852)—The Crimean War—The Siege of Sebastopol—The Peace of Paris (March, 1856): The Respite for the Sultan

Cavour's Policy in Sardinia-Piedmont (1852-56)—Cavour Makes a Secret Alliance with Napoleon: Plombières Interview (1858)—Cavour Provokes Austria to Attack Sardinia-Piedmont (April, 1859)—War Between France and Austria (1859): French Victories at Magenta and Solferino—The Agreement of Villafranca (July, 1859): The Italian Nationalist Movement Continues—Garibaldi Overthrows the Bourbons of Naples (1860)—Cavour Seizes Naples and "Makes Italy" (Autumn, 1860)—The Death of Cavour (June 6, 1861): His Achievements: Events after Him

William I's Army Reforms: Roon, His War Minister, and Moltke, Chief of Staff—The Fight with the Landtag: Defeat of the Liberals—The Schleswig-Holstein Question (1863-64)—Bismarck Against Austria—Bismarck Forces Austria into War (June, 1866)—The Austro-Prussian War (June 22-July 22, 1866)—Battle of Königgrätz (Sadowa): Decisive Prussian Victory (July 3, 1866)—The Peace of Prague (August 23, 1866): Austria Expelled from Germany—The North German Confederation (1866-67)

The Mexican Expedition (1861-67): Maximilian of Austria—Napoleon III Befooled by Bismarck in 1866-67—The "Liberal Empire" (1860-70)—The Folly of Gramont: The Ems Telegram (July 13, 1870)—German Victories: The Capitulation of Sedan—Fall of the Second Empire: "Government of the National Defense": The Siege of Paris—The Surrender of Paris (January 28, 1871): The Terms of the Treaty of Frankfort

CONTENTS

teenth there was little difference in the way in which the fields were plowed, the grain reaped, and the bread baked. Transportation on land was less rapid in 1815 than in 1 A.D.; the very carriage in which Napoleon fled the field of Waterloo more closely resembled Mark Antony's chariot than the modern automobile; and the ship which bore him to St. Helena looked more like a Viking craft than like the diesel-driven *Queen Elizabeth*.

Finally, in the mid-twentieth century came the blast at Hiroshima— atomic power, direct descendant of Prometheus, the concentrated fire of suns, the atomic bomb, the hydrogen bomb, a potential cobalt bomb, man capable of destroying man and of wiping off by fire all living things upon this planet, possibly capable of destroying even the planet itself; or, per contra, power to enrich civilization by the use of atomic energy so as to render the sum total of steam power and of machines run by it mere toys for children.

The nineteenth century is the age of steam. Toward its end electricity and oil began to supplement steam as a source of power. One continues, however, to speak of the Industrial Revolution as still with us, and the word "watt" is to be found today on every light bulb in measuring the intensity of light. Of the Industrial Revolution there is apparently no end. To what extent is it possible to say there was a beginning?

We must remember that it was not only Watt but also Boulton who made the famous engine possible. Matthew Boulton was neither scientist nor inventor. He was a Birmingham manufacturer who became wealthy by making buttons and shoe buckles, and who thereby stored up sufficient savings to risk part of them in paying for the construction of the Watt and Boulton engine.

These savings (capital) resulted from the commercial revolution of the eighteenth century, which in turn owed its origin to the Crusades, and to the opening of the New World to European settlement and of Asia to European trade. Without this new wealth there would have been no surplus to invest in experimenting with steam engines.

Watt did not, strictly speaking, invent the steam engine. What Watt did was to improve on existing models. As far back as the seventeenth century an English nobleman, Worcester, devised a contrivance whereby water could be raised to the second story of a London house to put out fires. But this was of no practical use, since it was cheaper to pass buckets of water to a man on a ladder. Then in the early eighteenth century came the Newcomen atmospheric engine, whereby water could be drained from a coal mine by a suction pump operated by steam power.

This Newcomen engine had an up-and-down motion only, and was called an atmospheric engine because the pressure of the atmosphere was relied on to force back the piston in an open cylinder, after a vacuum was created by the condensation of the steam. Unlike Worcester's engine, that of Newcomen was useful because, weak though its power might be, "if its boiler did not burst or its valves melt it could coax water out of the bottom of a coal mine."

Watt's patents improved this atmospheric engine, making it available for general use. He took out several patents and of these two were especially important, the separate condenser and the flywheel.

A major drawback to the Newcomen engine was that in order to condense the steam and make the vacuum, cold water had to be poured on the cylinder. What Watt did was to draw off the steam into a kind of box, his condenser, thus creating a vacuum under the piston without having to cool the cylinder. Watt's flywheel made possible rotary motion. A single engine now could run many other machines by means of leather belts connecting with flywheels, the number of machines thus harnessed depending on the power generated by one engine.

Running parallel with these improvements in the steam engine came certain others in the manufacture of cloth, following one another in rapid sequence until finally they conjoined with those in the steam engine in 1785.

To make cloth two processes are required—spinning and weaving. The first of these labor-saving devices concerned weaving—the flying shuttle, a kind of boomerang which enabled one man to do the work of two. This increased the demand for thread, which was met in short order by three inventions. The first was Hargreaves' spinning jenny, whereby one man by turning a crank could operate eight different spinning wheels simultaneously. This was followed by the roller-spinning frame run by water power, not useful for all kinds of thread. Finally came the spinning "mule," part jenny, part water frame, whereby both fine and coarse thread could be manufactured with equal facility.

"Now the weaver could not keep up with the spinner and invention swung back to the loom." Cartwright, a clergyman, invented one to be run by water power. But such looms could be set up only in distant valleys where there were brooks and streams, and they were not very reliable because the flow of water was uncertain. Then, in 1885, the Watt and Boulton engine was substituted for water power, and the Industrial Revolution was launched in earnest.

To place the Watt and Boulton engine on wheels was not too difficult; but to make that accomplishment economically profitable was something else again. As early as 1802 Trevithick constructed his "travelling engine" which groaned and snorted all the way from Cornwall to London. But this was no gain over travel by stagecoach. The speed was decidedly less, the cost of operation decidedly more, since there were no rails for the traveling engine to run upon.

Rail-ways had been in use in England for a long time. Over them ran

CROMPTON'S SPINNING MULE
Samuel Crompton combined previous spinning machines
in his "mule" in 1779

little wagons filled with coal, conveying it from mine to water, occasionally to rivers, for the most part to canals. They were pushed by hand,
or pulled by horses, or, when the declivity was steep, operated by inclined planes, the loaded wagon as it went down pulling up by its weight
the one that was empty. But these were short-distance hauls, not war-
ranting the use of an expensive steam engine. Already a network of
canals had been constructed for the conveyance of heavy goods, and the
stagecoach had as yet nothing to fear from competition with the stationary Watt engine.

In 1825, however, George Stephenson, an experienced workman in repairing the stationary engine, invented a new one, called by him first
the "active" and then the "locomotive." In that year enterprising Quakers
decided to build a rail-way carrying passengers over a short distance from
Stockton to Darlington. They were uncertain what power to use. Some
favored horses; others thought that stationary engines at intervals along
the route might pull the carriages by cables; Stephenson suggested his
locomotive. It was tried and proved successful. Nonetheless, the first
steam railway in existence utilized at first all three means of propulsion.

In 1829 came the opening of the Liverpool and Manchester railway, a
distance of forty miles. The directors of the company which financed it

held a competition between several different types of locomotives. Stephenson entered his "rocket," a locomotive which had tubular boilers, thus increasing the area to be heated, while at the same time by ejecting the steam through the smoke stack he increased the draught under the fire. His was an easy victory. One competing engine refused to move, another blew up, and the competition was won by the "rocket." This was the beginning of the fame and not inconsiderable wealth of George Stephenson, who never learned to read and write until he was an adult.

Within two decades these new railways were a common sight everywhere in England. In vain were new franchises sharply resisted in Parliament. Sportsmen complained that the whirr and noise of the locomotives frightened the birds they shot; scientists protested that they could not go around curves except at a snail's pace; and those who had money in toll roads, stagecoaches, and taverns asserted they would be ruined. But all to no avail: the days of the stagecoach were numbered, though for canals the end was not yet in sight. These were still useful for heavy and slow freight, and a number of them continue to be of service in our own day.

The steamboat antedated the railway, but except for river and harbor use its development was retarded. Symington's *Charlotte Dundas* was in operation in Scotland in Napoleonic days before Fulton's *Clermont* sailed from New York to Albany (despite American schoolbooks which credit Fulton with the invention of the steamboat), and the steamship *Savannah* crossed the Atlantic in 1817. But this was not much of a feat. The *Savannah*, like all early steamships, was a side-wheeler and her paddles were unshipped for most of the voyage. Only for a short time and a short distance was she propelled by steam.

Not before the formation of the Cunard line in 1840 did it prove profitable to build Atlantic liners. Coal took up so much space that room for freight and passengers was limited, and the latter continued for a long time after to prefer the spacious accommodations of the sailing packet. Then, too, the paddle wheels continued to cause trouble. If the weather was a bit rough the ship rolled and the paddle wheels were out of the water, first on one side then on the other. If storms broke they had to be unshipped and sails substituted, a laborious process.

In 1856 came something new in steamships—the Cunarder *Scotia*, made of iron. Many thought that ship an absurd experiment, for would not iron deflect from the accuracy of the compass; and would not an iron ship snap in two if run upon a reef? Experience soon proved these forebodings without substance. Came then the screw propeller, first used on the Cunarder *China*. Then followed twin screws, better engines, better boilers. The doom of the sailing ship was at hand for passenger traffic. By the twentieth century it had become an anachronism, even for freight.

Between the dates of Watt's patents in the seventeen-seventies and that of the diesel engine (1900), hundreds of inventions speeded the advance of the Industrial Revolution. Two of particular importance were Eli Whitney's cotton gin and the Bessemer process in the manufacture of steel. The first made plentiful the raw material on which the textile trade depended; the second cut the price of the all-important metal out of which were made not only the new power machines but also the tools to make them.

THE *Savannah*
THE FIRST SHIP TO CROSS THE ATLANTIC UNDER STEAM

Before Bessemer's day, three processes had been necessary in manufacturing steel. First, one made cast iron which was simply molten iron ore, too brittle to be of use in a machine age. Second came wrought iron, made by melting the cast iron and puddling it—that is, heating it and stirring it around to get rid of the carbon. This wrought iron was harder than the cast iron; ships could be made of it, iron girders and rails, cooking stoves. But it was still far inferior to steel. To manufacture the latter a third step was necessary. The wrought iron was melted and puddled all over again, and into it was introduced a quantity of carbon, approximately four per cent.

What Bessemer did was to do away altogether with making wrought iron by a process whereby the carbon could be blown out of the melted pig iron, leaving in the requisite four per cent. Down dropped the price

of steel; the iron ship gave way to the steel ship; machinery of all sorts
was cheapened; the Industrial Revolution was tremendously accelerated.

Spread of the Industrial Revolution

The start came in Britain—the reasons obvious. In part they were geographic, for the island was strategically poised for competition in transoceanic commerce, and her insular location made it possible for her to
isolate herself for the most part from wasteful Continental wars, thus
building up the essential capital for industrial development. And that
same detachment from Continental wars brought to her shores many
thousand skilled artisans, like the French Huguenots, who had fled political and religious persecution in their homelands.

There were other reasons. Britain was an old country where winters
were long and wood to burn for heat was in scant supply. This brought
about the early use of coal. To pump water from the coal mines came
the Newcomen engine, and from it the Watt and Boulton engine and the
Industrial Revolution. Then, too, Britain was abundantly blessed with
tremendous reserves of both coal and iron, in close proximity to each
other and likewise to the ocean, and so, easy to obtain.

The Industrial Revolution soon spread to other countries. Even before
the French Revolution, English capital had established the Creusot iron-
works in France operated by steam power; and in the midst of the
Napoleonic wars an English mechanic, William Cockerill, was operating
a wool-spinning factory in Belgium, to be followed by a machine shop in
Liége in 1807. Cockerill's son John, after Waterloo, became a partner
with no less a person than the King of the Netherlands, the King offering
confiscated church property, the younger Cockerill the brains, energy,
and floating capital needed. There resulted from this partnership an iron
foundry which in 1840 was the largest in the world, and the younger
Cockerill became an international capitalist, owning many Belgian factories, and establishing others in Spain, in Poland, and even in Dutch
Guiana in South America.

The Industrial Revolution first infiltrated into Belgium, then into
France and into the United States. By 1848 it was making its way into
the Rhine Valley, and by 1871 into central Europe, where ultimately in
the German Empire it was to stage its greatest triumph, the German production of steel by the opening of the First World War exceeding that
of Britain.

The spreading was done by land and by sea. Railway construction in
Belgium was as rapid as that in England, and France was only a decade
or two behind. By mid-century Stephenson was building a railway in
Egypt even before the Suez Canal was dug. By century's end, railways

EARLY STEAM LOCOMOTIVE TRANSPORTING COACHES

drove their way across continents—the Union Pacific, the Canadian Pacific, the Transcaucasian by which Russia tapped the oases north of Afghanistan, and the Trans-Siberian all the way across northern Asia to the Pacific. They passed downward on the map from Cairo to the cataracts of the Nile, thrust upward from Cape Town toward the rich minerals of South Africa, opened new lands on the pampas of South America, crisscrossed backward and forward over the vast peninsula of India, made their appearance in Chinese valleys and in the realm of the Mikado.

So likewise was it with the steamship. The dingy little "tramp," soon to be ubiquitous on all the seven seas, made its entry on history's stage, carrying steel rails to Zanzibar, the red tiles of France to Beirut, cheap hardware from Hamburg to the Celebes. The ocean lanes, meanwhile, were dotted with larger and larger liners. In the eighties frozen mutton from New Zealand made its way to England, and in another decade German ships were transporting Russian peasants from their inhospitable homelands to Canadian prairies.

And in this aspect of the Industrial Revolution Britain continued to hold her primacy but by a narrow margin. The German flag, a rarity at sea in the seventies of the nineteenth century, was everywhere in evidence in the early twentieth, the Hamburg-American Line becoming the largest single shipping company in the world, and the very steamers on the River Nile flying the ensign of the Nord Deutsche Lloyd.

Meanwhile, in European cities rose larger and ever larger industrial plants. The Ruhr Valley, stretching backward into German hills from the Rhine, became one long industrial city. North of Liverpool, one rode for mile on mile without the sight of plowed field or grazing cattle, nothing to be seen anywhere except belching smokestacks. In Belgium the hum of industrialism became a roar, and even in France, home of economic conservatism, the new "white coal" (electric power) of the Rhone Valley came into competition with the good black coal of the Saar.

Social Results of the Industrial Revolution

A hundred years ago most folk summed up these accomplishments under the blanket term "progress." In our day that word is not as popular as it was once. That important benefits followed in the wake of the Industrial Revolution none can deny. But as time passed, they seemed to be offset by results detrimental to human happiness. Just how to hold in even balance the blessings poured out by the steam cornucopia and the evils which escaped from the steam Pandora's-box is difficult.

Certainly on the credit side belongs the flood of useful articles hitherto in scant supply—houses, clothes, bed linen, and a varied diet, to say nothing of things not yet invented, such as typewriters and sewing machines. What the steam engine did for man materially may be seen at a glance if we roughly estimate horsepower in terms of human power.

The energy generated by steam was estimated in terms of horsepower and still is. And since three horses on the average have the muscular strength of twenty men it is possible to equate mathematically to some extent the power of steam with the strength of man. Suppose a certain engine generates 1,200 horsepower. If we multiply that figure by 20 over 3, we obtain the equivalent of 8,000 iron slaves. They are at man's beck and call; they are iron slaves who can be worked twenty-four hours a day; they never go on strike; the cost for food (fuel) a mere pittance per slave; and for doctor's bills (repairs) and for funeral expenses (replacement) they cost surprisingly little.

The owners of these slaves had more goods than they had ever had before. Fewer babies died in infancy, life expectancy increased, population mounted to a degree never experiencd in past history. Thanks to these slaves there was capital for new enterprises, for schools, hospitals, and churches.

Also to be included on the credit side was a reduction in the hours of labor. At first this was not the case, but as time elapsed and the trade-union movement grew in strength, work hours gradually lessened. By the end of the century the twelve-hour day had for the most part changed into one of ten hours. After the First World War eight hours became the norm, and in America the forty-hour week. Without power machinery this would have been impossible. Man lived on too narrow a margin to live at all on a forty-hour week.

Salutary in the long run were the psychological changes brought about by the migration of thousands to the city. They were far removed now from the atmosphere of traditional authority prevalent in the little village, with the squire's hall at one end of the village street and the parson's house at the other, to say nothing of the old grandfather by the chimney corner, all making it difficult for individuality to grow and expand. Coming to the city might, and frequently did, mean bad company and poorer manners. But even so, these dangers were counterbalanced and outweighed by contact with new ideas and new loyalties, revolutionary though the latter might be.

Likewise should be mentioned the substitution of the factory for the home as a work-place. Working in a factory, no matter how drab, was more sanitary than weaving cloth in a tiny cottage in the same room where meals were prepared and eaten, and occasionally where children were brought into the world.

But the Pandora's box—that too must be held in mind. Out of it flew technological unemployment. Every time a new machine was invented someone lost a job. In course of time a new job was found, for machines spawned and spawned, begetting new machines, creating new jobs, many more. But there was almost always a waiting period, sometimes protracted, for the man out of work. Oftentimes it was possible to compete for years with the new machines by increased hours of labor and decreased pay. Especially was this true of the weaving industry, where the early machines were so clumsy that it was possible to pit the human muscle against them. This was the case in England, in German Silesia, and in India, where the finer qualities of cotton cloth continued to be woven by hand for many decades.

Out of the Pandora's box flew other evils. One was a growing gulf between employer and employee. Those two words are significant. They are both modern words that came in with the Industrial Revolution, devoid of all color and warmth. The old words were *master* and *man*, indicating a personal relationship which had now faded away. Production in the old days was on a minute scale. A lad started as an apprentice. His master was personally responsible for his health and his morals; he ate with his master and was one of the family. In due course he passed a kind of examination, made with his own hands a finished product, became a master workman, and frequently after that a master in his own right with workmen and apprentices under him.

Since all workmen owned the tools of their trade the transition was easy. Enter power machinery. It was expensive and could not be had without capital. Now it became impossible for the workman to own his own tools; there was but one tool, the machine, owned by one man, the the employer. When the factory was small he might still feel some responsibility for those he employed, might still know them as Bill or Jack. But factories were not apt to stay small, and those who owned them drifted apart from those who worked in them. The ownership of tools is important, apt to become almost a part of one's personality; and to be bereft of them subtracts somewhat from individual independence and personal dignity.

The skilled craftsman in the ante-steam-engine days had few physical comforts; but the psychic satisfaction of making things for which he alone deserved the credit was his. What he produced bore the stamp of *his* work, and often bore *his* name. This was manufacture in the original sense of that word—*manus facio*, "made by hand." The Industrial Revolution changed the meaning of that word into "made by machine." When this took place, the human hand lost a certain flexibility and skill, the owner of it a certain pride and sense of accomplishment.

Then, too, power machinery introduced women and children to the factory. Their labor was cheaper, and for certain types of work more efficient than that of men, since there are many light jobs in textile factories that require quickness of eye and flexible fingers rather than physical strength. And when it came to pulling little wagons through narrow galleries far below the surface of the earth in coal mines, a child's labor was more effective than that of man.

Women have always worked, and worked hard. But before the steam age they worked in the home. The factory brought them into competition with men, broke down by degrees the barriers which custom and tradition had erected between the sexes. The results in the long run may be beneficial, but who can be sure of that? As Kipling wrote:

> But the woman that God gave him,
> Every fibre of her being,
> Proves her launched for one sole issue,
> Armed and engined for the same.

In other words woman's major physiological (possibly moral) function hitherto had been to bring babies into the world and to train them in infancy. The factory tended to subordinate this historic role of woman. As for child labor in factories, it was, of course, an unmitigated evil, perhaps the major blot upon the record of the nineteenth century, even if we remember that toward the century's end it had pretty thoroughly been legislated out of existence.

The work of women and children in factories and mines was, however, but one facet in a long indictment of power machinery. There was something even more fundamentally involved—biology. For many thousand years the human race had been conditioned for living out of doors. Now, in little more than a hundred years, old ways of living were abruptly ended in country after country. Rural areas became depopulated and the cities grew; they still do. The ultimate results of this biological uprooting to new and strange environmental surroundings can, at best, but be a matter of speculation. The Industrial Revolution—cornucopia or Pandora's box? On the threshold of the atomic age, it might be well not to dogmatize.

The Industrial Revolution: Its Impact on Classes

The nobility, the country gentry, the Junkers in Prussia, officers of armies and navies everywhere, clergymen of established churches, barristers who argued cases in court (not lawyers who drew up legal documents), judges and governmental officials who comprised the traditional upper classes—all gave way slowly before the onrush of the Industrial Revolution. They surrendered special privileges, ultimately agreed to an enlarged electorate, grumbled a good deal at the upstart bourgeoisie, but tended to profit in the pocketbook. They could not engage directly in trade without losing caste, but that did not prevent aristocrats from being sleeping partners or from serving on boards of directors. Many of their sons were poor as well as proud; but one could always marry the daughter of a wealthy man of the middle class without demeaning oneself. Furthermore, wealthy bourgeois were eager to buy land, to retire from trade, to set up as gentlemen. If not in one generation, then in two. Land had a social value altogether apart from any money to be made by cultivating the soil, as anyone can tell by reading the novels of Anthony Trollope. And those who sold it belonged to the recognized upper classes. Here and there a decayed aristocrat, long on genealogy but short in his rent roll, might lose financially. But this was the exception.

Quite the opposite was true of farm laborers and city artisans, whose lot deteriorated during the first half of the century. The cities into which they crowded lacked decent housing. Overcrowding was the norm, sanitation exiguous, the death rate appallingly high. The Industrial Revolution did not grow at a uniform rate but by fits and starts; and though demand for new products generally exceeded the supply, on occasions the reverse took place. When this happened, the steam engines came to a dead halt and unemployment brought despair to many a workman's home. A new name was applied to the factory worker to distinguish him from the bourgeoisie. He was said to belong to the *proletariat*.

Very slowly the worst of these evils were ameliorated during the middle and the latter part of the century. And the wages of the skilled artisan rose perceptibly, owing to a decline in world prices and to trade-union pressure. Some of the new wealth did flow down to him.

The moiety of it, however, went to the middle class, the bourgeoisie of the historian, to the men who made and sold goods, to manufacturers, merchants, bankers, and a host dependent on them, civil and mining engineers, chemists, doctors, and lawyers.

The bourgeoisie was no new class in British history. It had fought for Cromwell against Charles in the seventeenth century and had cheered for Wilkes in the eighteenth. But its greater glory lay ahead. This was the class that profited most from the Industrial Revolution, the hard-headed men of business (not infrequently hard-hearted), the men who saved their money, who took chances investing it, sometimes losing, more often winning, not often spending it in luxurious living but reinvesting over and over again in new industries at home or abroad. The British bourgeoisie alone built up capital funds of over $20,000,000,000 in the United States, China, India, the dominions, and elsewhere. This was "the Victorian heritage," which two world wars in the next century would exhaust. It was not static money, lying idle in banks. Without it, jobs would have been difficult to find for hundreds of thousands of emigrating citizens of the United Kingdom.

The rise to economic and political power of the bourgeoisie comprises in large measure the history of the nineteenth century, and perhaps the truest summary of what they did is to be found in this anonymous poem: [1]

> .... then came steam.
> Then came everything else. They kicked the lock off
> Pandora's box and turned it upside down.
> And they made everything right and every thing wrong:
> Machines that marched the floor with the measured precision of the
>   planetary system,
> And towns that sprawled in muddles of beastliness:
> Had hands as tender as a lover's for yarn and hard as Cain's for the
>   children they enslaved.
> Was there a bargain? They drove it. An ugliness? They made it.
> An obstacle? They cursed at it, and battered at it, and either solved it or
>   botched it.
> Being neither demigods nor heroes,
> But ingenious, hard-working descendants of *homo sapiens,*
> Who had the luck to plant their seedlings in kind weather,
> Not in the frost or the storm, but when the slow ripening of time, the
>   felicitous crossings of circumstance
> Presented unimagined opportunities,
> Which they took. And prospered. And grew tall.

[1] From the *Manchester Guardian Weekly,* November 13, 1935.

The Bourgeoisie and Liberalism

The middle-class bourgeois, the hero of this Whitmanesque poem and the man who made the Industrial Revolution click, was a staunch believer in liberalism, a key word to an understanding of nineteenth-century history.

That word is difficult to define because its contemporary meaning differs widely from its meaning in Waterloo days. A liberal then was a man who wanted the liberty to write and to read whatever he pleased; liberty to belong to any church or to none; freedom from arbitrary arrest or imprisonment; freedom from onerous and captious taxation; freedom from vexatious and arbitrary restraints on trade and commerce; the right to amass a fortune if he could do so, and protection for it if made; the right of franchise, the right to participate in the government of his country. That government, he believed, should concern itself primarily with preserving peace and enforcing contracts. The more it confined itself to these two essentials the better.

The liberal of 1815 was an optimist. With every new invention he became more so. The poor, he was apt to think, were poor because they were lazy; or because they were extravagant; or because they were improvident, particularly in having too many children. Governments should not intervene on their behalf. Keep the ring open, the rules of the game fair, and those worthy to survive and rise in the world would do so.

This was the credo of the early nineteenth-century liberal. By the middle of that century, those who held it were in the saddle in England and in France. The liberalism they professed spread eastward into Europe as the Industrial Revolution made itself felt in Germany, Austria, and Italy. There was no stopping this eastward-moving tide of the Industrial Revolution or of those liberal bourgeois ideas which went along with it. By 1904-5 they brought about a political revolution in Russia, and by 1908 another in Turkey.

By 1911 these same ideas helped to topple over the Manchu dynasty in China. But behind that revolution there were socialistic and Marxian ideas, anathema to old-fashioned liberalism. Yet liberals and socialists worked together to bring about a Chinese republic. And that demands a word of explanation.

Liberalism, as a word, was changing. A new kind of liberalism had come into being. Like traditional liberalism it was firmly anchored to faith in progress, openmindedness, and political liberty. But in important particulars, twentieth-century liberalism was the opposite of that held in the middle nineteenth century. The nineteenth-century liberal was an enthusiastic advocate of individualism, particularly in all that concerned economics. The twentieth-century liberal ordinarily does not have much to say about individualism, though he would deny that he had abandoned that doctrine. The liberalism of the past century emphasized property rights; that of the present, restrictions on them. The former found its classic expression in the French Declaration of the Rights of Man, and it is worth while to have in mind the last clause of that famous document if we would realize the originally close tie-up between liberalism and property. It reads, "Property being an inviolable and sacred right no one can be deprived of it except when public necessity, declared in the form of law, makes it clearly necessary." In other words, property is not merely that which men find useful; it is sacred, *sacra,* something to which is attached a divine sanction. Comparatively few defenders of the rights of property today would base their arguments on such grounds.

Most liberals of the present, of course, would insist that they are not socialists and that they still believe in individual enterprise; but always they would put first the necessity of curtailing its excesses for the common good. To the liberals of the early and middle nineteenth century, the less government the better; this is an idea outmoded and outworn to the contemporary liberal, who would enlarge very generously the scope of governmental functions, especially those relating to economics. The old-fashioned liberal, with whom the first half of this book is concerned, conceived of government as designed primarily to enforce contracts and to preserve peace; the man calling himself a liberal today ordinarily would scorn such a theory. To him the government must be the defender of the helpless poor against the avarice of the rich, the arbitrator between capital and labor (with a slight bias perhaps in favor of the latter), the governor of the economic engine, preventing a too rapid expansion of business but stimulating sufficient production, standing watch and guard over the distribution of economic goods, and in addition acting as a kind of moral guardian over the life of the people, both intellectually, as regards education, and physically, in respect to sanitation and public health.

Many contemporaries, of course, continue to use the label "liberal" more or less in the early nineteenth-century sense, and none can deny them that privilege. As a keen analyst of present-day problems confesses, liberalism is a word "which is now a battered armament that evokes the most equivocal sentiments." So it does: Underneath its wing both conservatives and radicals take refuge and in its name advocate diametrically opposite policies. If one chooses to define liberalism in such general terms as "the release of human energy," or as "the disestablishment of privilege," then almost every one is a liberal, at least in those countries where the democratic tradition survives. But in general the liberalism of the past has become the conservatism of the present, and the liberalism of the present has taken the form noted above. It is unfortunate that liberalism means so many different things to so many different people. In consequence one must be on guard when hearing or using that term.

Nationalism and the Bourgeoisie

Simultaneously with the spread of the Industrial Revolution and its ideological child, liberalism, a rising tide of nationalism seeped eastward across the Continent. At first European liberals applauded, since liberalism and nationalism went hand in hand. However, after 1871 and the formation of the German Empire they became doubtful; and by the time of the First World War in 1914 most thoughtful folk regarded liberalism and nationalism as opposing ideologies.

Just what is nationalism? A certain ambiguity is attached to that word because the term "state" is frequently confused with the term "nation." A state implies a government which might, like Czechoslovakia before 1938, exercise sovereignty over different nationalities, such as the Magyar, the Czech, the Slovak, the Polish, and the German. Now the question as to whether the Czechs and the Slovaks are sufficiently differentiated, one from the other, to comprise different nationalities might be disputed; but the other three groups are clearly defined and separate, although they might, in course of time, have become fused together into one nationality, as have, let us say, Frenchmen, who at one time in the past thought of themselves as Burgundians or Normans, and so on.

Originally, the word "nation," from which the word "nationality" is derived, was one with a very spacious meaning. In the Middle Ages, for instance, the students at the University of Paris were divided into the Picard, Norman, English, and French nations. Likewise, at the University of Prague there were four nations: Bavarians, Saxons, Poles, and Bohemians. Presumably, the word then applied to the locality from which they came. On the other hand we read of physicians as comprising a "nation," and in this instance the word simply implies a community of interest. Then, as time passed, one's nationality, in the sense of belonging to any given nation, became more narrowly defined and took on a political, juristic, and geographic significance as nation and country tended in most instances to become geographically identical. Nationalism as we find it today might very well be defined as the cult of glorifying and exalting the traditions, accomplishments, ideals, mission, and valor of those whom one considers his own countrymen.

As such, it has long been a characteristic of European history, predating Napoleon and the French Revolution which made him. As far back as Shakespeare's day, men were proud of being Englishmen, and Frenchmen died for France, or at least for the Valois and Bourbon families. Even earlier yet, a kind of nationalism flourished in the sense of local pride or regionalism. Bruges, Geneva, Venice, like the city-states of Greece, thought well of themselves; and it must be remembered that the Crusaders fought not only as Christians but also as Burgundians, Germans, Englishmen.

Nevertheless, prior to the French Revolution, nationalism differed from its corresponding phenomena in modern times in at least three ways: national loyalties tended to be personal (that is, attached to some leader, feudal chief, or family) rather than territorial; they were more cultural than political in character; and, until the French Revolution, they did not carry with them the totalitarian idea of a nation in arms.

Englishmen, for instance, in 1688 were as apt to debate their loyalty to King James or King William as they were to discuss the welfare of the English people. In Italy, in Dante's day, people were for pope or emperor or city—only Dante seemed to be for Italy. In the Middle Ages it was Saracen against Christian, rather than German against French, and down to the sixteenth century, both religion and education transcended nationalistic lines. Protestantism, it is true, weakened such international ties as the Roman Catholic Church had afforded and gave a decided stimulus to nationalism as we know it; but after all a great tradition of common culture remained. Latin and Greek were common denominators for the educated of all countries. Although there were no airplanes or radios to connect nations, the educated all over Europe were accustomed to think alike, for they were brought up on the same books— Virgil, Homer, Plato, Aristotle, Plutarch, and the Christian Scriptures.

In the eighteenth century there was a good deal of what has been called cultural nationalism, such, for instance, as English pride in Newton as mathematician and scientist and in Pope as poet. Frenchmen glorified Molière and Voltaire, Germans rejoiced in Mozart and Goethe, and Spaniards honored Cervantes. But Voltaire did not write patriotic essays, Mozart patriotic songs, nor Pope patriotic poetry. Goethe's fatherland was neither the first, second, nor third Reich but wherever the good and the beautiful were to be found; Voltaire's fatherland was where a man was comfortable. Neither Frenchman nor German bothered his head about inherent qualities of grandeur connected with Gallic or Teutonic traditions.

And finally there was the concept of the nation in arms. Robert the Bruce fought for an independent Scotland and William Tell for a free Switzerland, but neither conceived of such a thing as compulsory universal military service—the nation in arms of the French Revolution. Fighting in times past had been done generally by mercenary troops, or at most by volunteers. It remained for the French to give birth to the idea that old and young alike were obligated to dash to the ramparts (or trenches), there to fight for a "nation." The French Revolution popularized this doctrine; Bonaparte utilized it; the Germans copied Bonaparte and improved upon him in theory and in practice.

The French Revolution was essentially a middle-class, bourgeois revolt against time-encrusted abuses, very largely economic in character. The emergent French bourgeoisie had to fight hard for the new liberties it won, a victorious conflict which intensified French nationalism. Meanwhile, over the greater part of Europe Napoleon's armies carried with them the seeds of liberalism and nationalism. Liberty, equality, and fraternity were good for export; and most of the Continent had been inoculated with these stirring liberal slogans. Most of the Continent had also been conquered by Napoleon, and the shame and occasionally the agony thereof brought patriotic resentment to the boiling point in Germany, Italy, and Spain.

Napoleon was gone, but arbitrary feudal regimes took his place. Uniformly they were opposed to those individual liberties which liberals craved, and to the nationalistic aspirations which accompanied them. In the Hapsburg Empire the Czechs and the Magyars desperately sought to free themselves from the dynasts at Vienna and to become nations in their own right. True also was this of the Italians. In southeastern Europe Turkish tyranny brought about nationalistic revolts in Serbia, Greece, Rumania, and finally Bulgaria. Poles revolted against the overlordship of Russia in East Europe, and the Irish came close to doing so against British rule in West Europe.

British liberals were enthusiastic advocates for distressed nationalists (on the Continent) who sought independence and liberalism on the English model. So, too, were French liberals. Liberated nations would open their markets to Western goods. Furthermore, their sympathy cost the French and British liberals little, since they had no intention of going to war to help the oppressed south of the Pyrenees and Danube and east of the Rhine.

After 1871 this liberal enthusiasm for nationalism cooled perceptibly. The German Empire, founded that year, came into existence without liberal aid and in spite of liberal opposition. Liberalism and nationalism, in this instance, tugged in opposite directions.

As the decades passed, liberalism tended to fade somewhat, nationalism to grow stronger. The old nexus between the two ideologies continued with the Czechs and also with the South Slavs in Austria-Hungary, in Finland, and elsewhere. But as the nineteenth century slid into the twentieth, imperialistic nationalism became the keynote of international rivalry. Imperialism meant not freedom for Asiastics and Africans but subordination and conquest. And whether it was carried forward by Russia in Turkestan, by Britain in the Sudan, or by France in Indochina made no difference—in every instance it was the antithesis of the old-time liberalism.

The rising tide of that liberalism came to its crest somewhere between 1870 and 1900. It was checked not only by opposing nationalism but also by the spread of socialistic ideas, stronger on the Continent than in England (cradle of the Industrial Revolution), but sufficiently powerful even in the latter country to infiltrate British politics to the point of revolutionizing, by the time of the First World War (1914-1918), the very connotation of the word "liberal."

Nationalism, meanwhile, continued to spread and to become a world-wide phenomenon, planting vigorous roots in India and China, setting at naught happy prophecies of mid-century liberals that an ever increasing international trade would bind the peoples of the earth closer together. The reverse took place; and by 1914, as we shall see, nationalism was to prove a prime factor in bringing about the two catastrophic wars of the twentieth century.

The origin of those wars lies in the history of the nineteenth century. That history has running through it a common thread—the rise to power of the bourgeoisie. That social class in turn owed its vitality and strength to the Industrial Revolution.

Chapter 2

THE VIENNA CONGRESS AND
AFTERMATH

In 1815, only the visionary had any idea of the potentialities of the steam engine. As for nationalism and liberalism, both words were in ill repute, since they were associated with the French Revolution, which was too close for comfort. The upper classes of all countries could not forget that the aunt of Francis I of Austria, Marie Antoinette, had bowed her head to the guillotine. Practically every monarch on the Continent, barring the Scandinavian sovereigns, had seen his territories overrun by French armies, either chasing him from his dominions or forcing him into humiliating alliance. Every court of Europe had swarmed with French *émigrés*, people of delightful manners, unimpeachably noble lineage, and equally undeniable personal woes. Every prince in Germany who had lost his dominions; every bishop who had seen his temporal power abolished and his spiritual power assailed; every king whose land had been devastated; every rich burgher whom the moil and toil of two decades of war had reduced to penury—all saw in the Revolution only the work of the devil.

This hostile opinion was echoed by multitudes of peasants to whom the technical release from feudal burdens (brought about by French invaders), had often meant little, but to whom the ravaging of their farms and villages, the confiscation of their livestock, the debauching of their girls, the conscription and death of their tall boys, had meant much. Equally passionate, and more intelligent, was the feeling of millions of high-minded Catholics throughout Europe. The Revolution had been begun virtually, they believed, by the arch-infidel Voltaire. At its climax in France, it had revived the old Roman days of martyrdom in the treatment awarded self-respecting priests. Countless church establishments, monasteries, and nunneries had been suppressed, and their inmates insulted and scattered. In the name of a movement boasting tolerance, Christian worship had been almost abolished in France, and in 1793, a light woman had been encouraged as she screamed a ribald song from the high altar of Notre Dame in Paris, during a festival to Reason.

Therefore, for the time being, liberalism and nationalism were un-

21

popular doctrines. The entrenched traditionalism and the rotting old institutions which the French Revolution had wiped out were forgotten temporarily. Seen through the red haze of the Napoleonic wars, the Europe of 1789 seemed on the whole peaceful, honest, desirable. The peacemakers of 1815 liked that old world; they knew that some things could not come back, but the main outlines they thought hopefully to restore.

VISCOUNT CASTLEREAGH (1769-1822)

They met at the Congress of Vienna (1814-15) where, to all intents and purposes, the new map of Europe was the work of five men: Talleyrand of France, King Frederick William III of Prussia, Czar Alexander I of Russia, Castlereagh of England, and Metternich, alter ego for the Emperor of Austria.

The subtle and adroit Talleyrand, representing the Bourbon family and the brother of Louis XVI, was history's most continuously successful turncoat. A bishop of the Catholic Church in the old regime, he became a traitor to the church during the Revolution, thus saving his neck from the guillotine. He turned his back on the Revolution to follow the rising star of Bonaparte. Sensitively aware that the latter's course was doomed, he chose exactly the right moment to jump into the camp of his enemies. In 1830 he would make another *volte-face,* become a revolutionary once again, years later to die in the full odor and sanctity of the church he had abandoned, thus making the best of two worlds. Napoleon had described Talleyrand as "a silk stocking filled with mud." But he was able.

TALLEYRAND (1754-1838)

Frederick William was the least interesting and the least influential of the five men. Stupid and timorous, his only claim to glory was that he was the husband of the charming Queen Louise. His role at Vienna, in so far as he had one, was to be a follower of the Czar, whom he greatly admired.

The ruler of Russia is not easily classified. Handsome, excitable, ambitious, unstable, and a religious fanatic, he commanded the largest army in the world. Its Cossacks in 1814 had ridden down the boulevards of Paris, their first appearance in Western Europe—a dangerous omen. Temperamental Alexander held himself ordained of Heaven for a great religious mission. "The fires of Moscow," he said, "have lighted my soul.

The judgments of the Most High on the snowy battlefields have warmed the sources of my faith." Alexander fell under the power of an aristocratic charlatan, Madame de Krüdener. On the day of Waterloo, at the very moment when Blücher and Wellington were at grips with Napoleon, he had been at Heidelberg listening to her prophecies that he was the elect of God, ordained to rule the world. Mingled with all this megalomania was cloudy talk of constitutions bestowed on grateful subjects by Christian princes. The word "constitution" was in ill favor at Vienna. Sensible

PRINCE VON METTERNICH (1773-1859)

men of the world like Castlereagh and Metternich were disturbed by this human enigma in their midst.

Viscount Castlereagh, like many another Anglo-Irishman, was cold and haughty, a man of few words. But he was able, knew what England wanted, and was determined to get it. Since his country wished for no territory on the Continent, he had the great advantage of serving as a suitable arbiter between conflicting claims. "British policy," he announced, "was to bring the world back to peaceful habits." As for territorial acquisitions over seas, that was another matter. Since England ruled the seas not only in song but in fact, there were none to gainsay her should she choose to annex French colonies and Napoleonic possessions across the oceans.

Prince Clemens von Metternich was at the summit of his career. No personage in history ever understood better than he the arts of the "Old Diplomacy," of dealing out witty and plausible half-truths, of winning the promise of a province during a card party, or of confirming a coalition during a royal hunt. In his early career during the seventeen-nineties, he had visited England and had delighted the giddy circle of the Prince of Wales (later George IV) by his polite debaucheries. Later, as Austrian ambassador to France, he had won the golden opinions of Talleyrand, had flirted gracefully and profitably with Napoleon's favorite sister Caroline, and had wormed his way into the graces of "The Second Charlemagne" himself. Queens and princesses welcomed to their salons "this aristocrat, tall and graceful, with auburn curls brushed backward." He was the hero of innumerable affairs with great ladies, whereby he won much of his influence, but he never was carried away from "his own clear cold judgment."

Napoleon had complained that "Metternich mistook intrigue for statesmanship," but he certainly never swerved in his allegiance to his master and to the interests of the House of Hapsburg. Any serious break in the autocratic system in Central Europe would probably mean disaster for the Austrian monarchy. Everything else, therefore, Metternich sacrificed to this fact. Francis I recognized his worth, retained him in office, loaded him with honors, and gave him a free hand in foreign affairs.

What these five men wanted they obtained. None were to be disappointed except possibly, to a minor degree, the King of Prussia.

Talleyrand, we must remember, at the opening of the Congress was an outsider looking in; by the time it concluded he had won his major objectives, saved his defeated country from dismemberment, restored the Bourbons to the throne, escaped payment of a ruinous indemnity, and so arranged matters that in three short years the Quadruple Alliance of England, Austria, Prussia, and Russia which had driven France to her knees, was enlarged to a Quintuple Alliance, to guarantee the boundaries set by the Congress of Vienna by inviting France to join as the fifth member. When we recall that the violent eruptions which had disturbed Europe's peace ever since the fall of the Bastille had their origin in France, this was no mean accomplishment.

Talleyrand played his cards carefully. One of them was "legitimacy"— to secure tranquility, restore the old rulers.

What other solution, he suggested, was possible for France? A republic or a plebiscite of the French people was out of the question, since both were associated with the French Revolution and Napoleon. There must be a monarch; but who was eligible? To put Napoleon's child on the throne would necessitate a regency, and the boy's mother was an Austrian princess—too much influence for Austria. Bernadotte, King of Sweden, had been suggested; but Sweden was close to Russia, and no nominee of the Czar ought to become King of France. That left as the only possibility the exiled brother of France's last monarch. He was not bright; but he also was not ambitious, and no one could deny his legitimate claim to the throne. And so the Bourbons came trooping back, headed by Louis XVIII, as king of France.

A second card to play was intervention in a dispute raging between England and Austria on the one hand and Russia and Prussia on the other. The Czar, it so happened, sought to restore the old kingdom of Poland with himself at its head. He wanted all of the old Poland, and to secure it suggested that Prussia surrender her Polish lands in return for the German kingdom of Saxony, and that Austria do likewise, finding compensation for herself in Italy. This infuriated England and Austria, the former because she feared the extension of Russian power in the heart of Europe, the latter because this would make the Prussian boundary coterminous with her own, and she was determined that she, rather than Prussia, be the leading German state.

The four powers that had thrashed Bonaparte now were at loggerheads, and Talleyrand saw his chance; he allied France with England and Austria against the other two powers, thus forcing a compromise. England and Austria now were in his debt and his good friends. In consequence France regained all of her old boundaries except the Saar Valley in northeastern France, held valuable in 1815 not for coal but for strategic reasons.

To be sure, care was taken to prevent France from taking to the warpath again by creating strong buffer states on her northeastern and southeastern borders, in the former instance by annexing the Austrian Netherlands (Belgium) to The United Netherlands (Holland), and in the latter by annexing the ancient republic of Genoa to Piedmont. Aside from these precautions, France escaped all punishment for Napoleonic sins. A trifling indemnity was laid upon her for the cost to the Allies of the Waterloo campaign, and that was all. France had reason to rejoice in the diplomacy of M. Talleyrand.

Despite his setback over Saxony, Frederick William III was a substantial gainer from the Vienna pacts. He finally did obtain a part of Saxony, also the Napoleonic kingdom of Westphalia, Swedish Pomerania on the Baltic, and German lands west of the Rhine, to be known as Rhenish Prussia.

Castlereagh was the easiest man of the five to satisfy. Just so long as he could thwart Russia from her dream of European hegemony and curb Prussian ambition to annex Alsace from France, he was content. The balance of power in Europe seemed to him fairly well preserved. Of the overseas lands in the Napoleonic Empire, Britain annexed the Cape of

Good Hope and Ceylon from Holland, both excellent ports of call en route to India, also the French colony of Mauritius in the Indian Ocean for the same reason. In the Caribbean, Britain took half of Dutch Guiana away from Holland, returning to that country the other half, also a number of the French West Indies islands, but returned to France Martinique and Guadaloupe. Nothing could have prevented Castlereagh from appropriating for his country the entire Dutch East Indies, but he had sufficient wisdom not to engorge his country with more colonies than she could easily digest. A further accomplishment of Castlereagh was to persuade the Congress of Vienna to agree to a resolution condemning the slave trade.

The Czar set up his Kingdom of Poland, himself as king, shorn of certain minor parts of the old Poland retained by Prussia and Austria. Also there fell to Alexander the Grand Duchy of Finland, hitherto under Sweden. And this came about as a kind of game of musical chairs played with the Scandinavian countries, Sweden giving up rights over Finland in return for annexing Norway, formerly a possession of the King of Denmark, who gained nothing, since, like the King of Saxony, he was held worthy of punishment because he had remained loyal to Napoleon. In addition, the Czar participated in the pleasure of bestowing a new constitution on his erstwhile enemy, France.

Towering above all the other peacemakers, and map makers, was Metternich of Austria; and so successful was he that from 1815 to 1848 he was to be recognized as the most prominent figure in international politics, so much so that historians frequently refer to this period of European history as the Era of Metternich. At a mere minimum this Austrian diplomat is to be credited with devising a method of preserving European peace that was strictly enforced for at least eight years.

Metternich had three ambitions—all three accomplished. He increased tremendously the prestige and power of his country by annexations to Austria; he masterminded a constitution for the German states which guaranteed the pre-eminence of his Hapsburg master in Germany; and he succeeded so thoroughly in freezing tight the status quo on central Europe that it did not perceptibly weaken until the revolutionary year, 1848.

The annexations were in the nature of a gigantic real-estate deal by which Austria gave to Holland (the Netherlands) the legal claims of the Hapsburg family to the Austrian Netherlands (Belgium) in return for compensations in Italy. The latter were on a generous scale, Austria receiving the eastern littoral of the Adriatic, the Duchy of Milan, the Lombard Plain, the valley of the Po, and Venice. These lands she consolidated into the Lombardo-Venetian Kingdom, ruled straight from Vienna, like a Persian satrapy. To the south of this kingdom the Duchy of Modena was presented to one Austrian archduke, the Duchy of Tuscany to

EUROPE
1814–15

ORKNEY IS.

Christiania

NORTH SEA

KINGDOM OF NORWAY AND SWEDEN

KINGDOM OF DENMARK

SCHLES-WIG

HELIGO-LAND (BR.)

SCOTLAND

Glasgow

Edinburgh

Belfast

GREAT BRITAIN

IRELAND

IRISH SEA

Dublin

Liverpool

Hull

Sheffield

Birmingham

ENGLAND

London

Bristol

Dover

WALES

BOUNDARY OF GERMAN CONFEDERATION

KINGDOM OF THE NETHER-LANDS

Bremen

Ham-burg

HANOVER

Amsterdam

RHINE R.

Brussels

Cologne

Aix-la-Chapelle

Frankfurt

50°N

ATLANTIC OCEAN

CHANNEL IS. (BR.)

ENGLISH CHANNEL

Calais

Brest

SEINE R.

Paris

Versailles

LUX.

Metz

Stras-bourg

WÜRTEM-BERG

FRANCE

LOIRE R.

Nantes

Neuchatel (TO PR.)

Basel

SWITZ.

Bordeaux

RHONE R.

Lyons

Geneva

LOMBARDY

Milan

PO

Turin

Genoa

Toulouse

Nice

PARMA

MODENA

LUCCA

TUSCANY

Oporto

Burgos

EBRO R.

Zaragoza

ANDORRA

Mar-seilles

KINGDOM OF SARDINIA

CORSICA (FR.)

40°N

PORTUGAL

Lisbon

TAGUS R.

SPAIN

Madrid

Barcelona

SARDINIA

Seville

Cadiz

Tangier

GIBRALTAR (BR.)

Ceuta (SP.)

BALEARIC IS. (SP.)

MEDITERRANEA

Algiers

Bizerte

Melilla (SP.)

MOROCCO

ALGERIA

TUNIS

Tunis

TRM

AFRICA

0°F

10°E

another. Parma and Lucca, both small, were granted to Napoleon's wife, Marie Louise, an Austrian princess who had no intention of following her husband into exile.

Turning north of the Alps we come to what used to be called "the Germanies," quite properly put in the plural, since before Napoleonic conquests there were several hundred German states in what formerly was known as the Holy Roman Empire. Napoleon had abolished that shadowy ghost of an empire, and now there were thirty-nine separate sovereign German states. What should be done with them? Metternich so arranged matters that they were brought together in a Bund or federation, so loosely constituted as to be merely an alliance. This Bund was without power. There was no German king or emperor. It was specified that there should be a Diet at Frankfort; but the delegates to it were merely the ambassadors of the thirty-nine states, appointed by their legitimate rulers. In theory these ambassadors were authorized to draw up a constitution for Germany; in practice this could not be done, since a unanimous vote must first be had. The president of the Bund was to be the Emperor of Austria.

The reason why Metternich created this Bund is obvious: he did not want a united Germany. His Austria, we must remember, was not a nation in any true sense of that word but a conglomeration of peoples held together not by common nationality but by a common dynasty. Germans, Magyars, Czechs, Poles, Slovenes, Slovaks, Rumanians, and Ruthenians wore the white uniforms of the Hapsburgs and obeyed the orders of Kaiser Francis at Vienna. And now to these assorted Hapsburg subjects north of the Alps were added some 4,000,000 Italians. Outside of the Austrian Empire there were approximately 25,000,000 Germans. Austria could not have annexed them, even had she so desired. The European powers would promptly have vetoed such a proposal as upsetting the balance of powers, and North German Protestants like the Prussians would have taken up arms against it. But Metternich could and did, by the creation of this Bund, make it impossible for the Germans outside the boundaries of his Austria to combine against her.

Finally, Metternich's fine hand may be seen in an important clause in the Quadruple (later Quintuple) Alliance which guaranteed the settlements made at Vienna for twenty years. Article VI stated that the signatories pledged themselves to "reunions devoted to the great common interests, and to the examination of the measures which at any one of these periods shall be judged most salutary for the repose and prosperity of the peoples. . . ." Here in embryo was something akin to the UN of our own day, a league of five nations pledged to meet from time to time to discuss how peace might be maintained.

The major work of the Congress of Vienna was now complete, its major architect Metternich of Austria. In subsequent decades it became the fashion for historians to denounce both him and the Vienna Congress for thwarting and choking the aspirations of Germans and Italians seeking freedom and national independence. But it is necessary to remember that at the commencement of the century, apart from England, France, and to some extent Poland, nationalism in Europe practically was nonexistent.

When Napoleon rudely ended the Holy Roman Empire of the German Nation, said by Voltaire to be neither holy, Roman, nor an empire, and coalesced the West German states into the pro-French Confederation on the Rhine, Germans living there rejoiced, and that famous German marching song "Die beiden Grenadier" was written in praise of a foreign ruler, Bonaparte, not in praise of a German Fatherland. Not until Napoleon had thrust Prussia into the gutter did the poetry of Arndt, the music of Körner, and the impassioned writings of Jahn signal the birth of German nationalism.

Not otherwise was it with Italy. There, too, the soldiers of Napoleon carried in their knapsacks the seeds of Italian nationalism, above all in northern Italy where by Napoleonic fiat rose the Kingdom of Italy. But this birth of nationalism was as new to Italy as to Germany. Quite rightly did Metternich define Italy as a geographic expression. There never had been an Italy in the sense of a national state.

Italian nationalism, like German nationalism, was a product of the French Revolution and the Napoleonic wars. The purpose of the Congress of Vienna was to write "finis" to those wars, and to the broils, turmoils, and revolutions they had engendered. Since that is so, there is some excuse, if not justification, for Metternich's policy in both Germany and Italy.

Liberal historians later in the century were apt to write scornfully of human beings treated like cattle, traded from one ruler to another. But we must regard Metternich and his colleagues from the point of view of the social matrix of their own day. Finns, for instance, were not treated like cattle; the King of Sweden had been their grand duke, and now their grand duke was the Czar. They were not Swedes; they did not become Russians; they remained Finns. What took place in Italy was somewhat parallel. To erase from the map the ancient republic of Venice and to annex Venice to Austria appeared on the surface as an act of gross tyranny. But for centuries past Venice had been a decadent state, in the eighteenth century notorious as a kind of moral cesspool. Something had to be done with Venice. Napoleon had annexed it. It could not be passed back to France. To have consulted with its inhabitants as to their wishes would have set off a chain reaction throughout the Italian peninsula and in Germany, reinaugurating the political turmoil and confusion in which most of the continent had been involved ever since 1792 when the revolutionary wars had commenced.

After all, the victors over Napoleon compare favorably in some respects with those after the two World Wars of the twentieth century. The signatories at Vienna were neither knaves nor fools, nor did the leaders of the Great Powers, at least, expect to put matters back to where they had been in 1789. There was to be no return of serfdom in Prussia, no more bishop-electors along the Rhine, and Louis XVIII was to be strictly compelled to give France a recognizable constitution. The guiding formula in every transaction was not deliberate reaction, but Legitimacy, defined by Metternich as "the preservation of every legally existing institution"—notably the stabilizing power of monarchy. Without Legitimacy, he argued, there would soon be a return to "Revolution," with new ruin for everything precious in society and religion.

Europe, it must not be forgotten, was war-weary; in a terrible school she had learned that peace was more precious than certain arrangements of boundary stones or the theoretical possession of certain types of liberty.

International Government (1815-30)

The statesmen who made the Vienna settlements took steps to insure the permanence of their work, and two international organizations stood ready to guarantee it—the Holy Alliance and the Quintuple Alliance. The former, showy and theatrical, attracted much attention but otherwise did nothing. The latter put a stop to all revolutionary warfare for fifteen years.

The Holy Alliance emanated from the cloudy brain of the Czar Alexander. It was a document without precedent in European diplomacy, drawn up by Alexander, signed by him, by the Emperor Francis of Austria, and by the King of Prussia. The preamble began with an invocation to the Trinity; it recited that the three monarchs henceforth would "take for their rule of conduct only the precepts of that holy [Christian] religion, the precepts of justice, charity and peace, which far from being applicable only to private life, should, on the contrary, influence the resolutions of princes, and guide all their steps." In conformity with the order of Scripture that all men "should regard themselves as brethren, the three contracting monarchs will live united in the bonds of a true and indissoluble fraternity." They were to "consider themselves only as agents of Providence to govern three branches of the same family, thus confessing that the Christian nations, of which they and their peoples form a part, have no other sovereign but God."

This document was acceptable to the King of Prussia, a very pious Lutheran and a personal friend of Alexander. Francis of Austria said that he hesitated as to whether to refer the project to his confessor or to his minister; but he finally signed. As for Metternich, he speedily saw great advantages in the scheme: (*a*) Alexander would be under obligation to the powers accepting the alliance; (*b*) every move toward liberalism could be represented as the blow of antireligious elements against that "sovereignty of God" which Alexander was so zealous to defend. Other powers were invited to join, and Louis XVIII and other European princes consented. Alexander was worth conciliating. Britain, however, held aloof. Viscount Castlereagh likened the document to one of the fulminations of Cromwell's "Saints," and it was politely explained to the Czar that it was contrary to the English constitution to enter into such a sweeping and general alliance. Metternich quite rightly described it as "a sonorous nothing."

The Quintuple Alliance, on the other hand, in a very real sense was an experiment in international government, owing to Metternich's proviso for reunions, or congresses as they came to be called, to decide on common action to preserve tranquility and the established European order.

The first of these was at Aix-la-Chapelle, in 1818, to arrange for the evacuation of northern France by the allied troops. The congress invited France to join with Prussia, Russia, Austria, and England in a pentarchy "to preserve authority from shipwreck, and to save the peoples from their own mistakes." A protocol provided that any state or sovereign could call on the pentarchy and "receive the material help whereof it might stand in need." Metternich was delighted. "The happiest result," he wrote, "is that there is to be no change in the existing order of things."

The country that gave the first trouble to the friends of order was Germany, where zealous nationalists began to agitate close to Austria's very door (see p. 60). That, however, was but a mere flash in the pan compared with incipient revolutions breaking out in Spain and Italy.

In Spain, Ferdinand VII, restored by British bayonets and the general uprising of his people against the French, was a particularly evil and abominable despot, "devoid of all higher interests, an adept in dissimulation, distrustful even of his favorites, cowardly to servility when others had the upper hand, and cruel in the extreme when he could play the master." After the expulsion of the French in 1814, Ferdinand made haste to annul the liberal constitution proclaimed in 1812. "Whoever should maintain it," ran his proclamation, "would commit an outrage against the prerogatives of my sovereignty, and the welfare of the nation."

Soon the chiefs of the Spanish Liberal party were in dungeons or exile; the censorship and Inquisition were restored; the secularized property of the Church was handed back to the ecclesiastics without compensation to the purchasers; and exemption from taxation was granted again to nobles and clergy. Every evening, runs the tale, Ferdinand's confessors met with him, drafted decrees, and ordered arrests. Such a regime was certain to bring its own rebuke.

In 1819 the King collected an army to send to South America, to win back his almost lost colonies. The soldiers, ill-paid, ill-disciplined, barely clothed, and barely fed, were in no mood to be shipped abroad. When the force was mobilized at Cadiz, preparatory to embarking, mutiny and insurrection broke out. Disaffected colonels issued *pronunciamentos* in the south. Other disaffected elements blazed up in the northern provinces. As a result, before 1820 was over, Ferdinand VII had saved his throne and possibly his actual life by swearing allegiance again to the constitution of 1812.

For Metternich and the Czar, the plight of Ferdinand of Spain was deplorable; but the case of another Ferdinand soon seemed even more dangerous. Ferdinand IV, of the pretentious, impoverished, and bandit-infested Kingdom of Naples and Sicily, had made in 1815 a secret treaty with Austria, binding himself never to introduce a constitution into his land. Brigandage, under his misrule, so increased that in 1817 there were thousands of outlaws in the kingdom, and the government was forced to make regular treaties with their chiefs. Army officers and miscellaneous liberals now copied Spain, and the terrified Ferdinand promised to inaugurate the Spanish constitution of 1812.

To set up merely one liberal government in Italy would, in Metternich's opinion, be an incitement to revolution elsewhere in the peninsula. The restoration of absolutism, therefore, in both Spain and Naples became a life-or-death matter in Hapsburg and Czarist policy. The Czar was almost in sackcloth and ashes. "Since 1814," he asserted, "he had been deceived as to the public mind. He had wrought much evil and must bestir himself to repair it." As a consequence the great powers held congresses at Troppau, in Austrian Silesia (1820), at Laibach, in Carniola (1821), at Verona (1822), in Venetia (1822)—all, appropriately in Hapsburg territory.

The Congress of Troppau devoted itself to the affairs of Naples. It declared: "When political changes, brought about by illegal means, produce dangers to other countries by reason of proximity, and when the Allied powers can act effectively as regards these conditions, they shall, in order to bring back those countries to their allegiance, employ, first, amicable means, and then coercion."

In 1821 Ferdinand of Naples was summoned to the congress of Laibach to explain the lapse of his country from Legitimist orthodoxy. Before leaving Naples, Ferdinand swore once more to defend the constitution of his country; before he reached Laibach he was writing to the Congress imploring the powers to restore him to his autocracy. This cynical conduct disgusted even the ministers most zealous in his cause. But Ferdinand of Naples was "legitimate"; and revolt against him was an evil example for all Italy. Despite protests by England, unwilling to participate in the domestic politics of another state, an Austrian army was dispatched to restore a lawful king to his own.

The Neapolitan liberals, pitifully inexperienced in working free institutions, had squandered their opportunities. There had been an abundance of fiery oratory and of brave proclamations, but there were no effective military preparations. The swarm of corrupt officials who had battened upon the Bourbon regime; and even a large part of the idle populace of Naples, which loved an extravagant court and cared nothing for politics—all hoped to see the absolute monarchy restored. After one battle the liberals' house of cards fell. Ferdinand IV returned to his capital to put through a complete reaction. Not merely was the constitution revoked and most of its promoters exiled or sent to the galleys, but it became a capital felony for any person to possess arms or to wear the colors of the anti-monarchist society of the Carbonari. Strict censorship was the order of the day, and the books of Voltaire and Rousseau were publicly burned by the executioner.

The fate of Naples in 1821 was the fate of Spain in 1823. There again, the liberals had been strong in speech and feeble in action. The black-robed army of clericals abhorred them, and the bulk of the peasantry preferred an absolute king. In the northern provinces, a kind of civil war was raging, giving an excellent pretext for foreign intervention in the name of "order." As for Ferdinand VII, he had written personally to Louis XVIII, begging for help against his own subjects. England desired intervention in Spain even less than she had in Naples. France hesitated, distracted by internal politics and external fears, but the Czar, now even more eager than Metternich, was set on armed intervention in Spain. The result was that, at the Congress of Verona (1822), intervention was ordained in Spain, "where there was a deplorable example of the infallible consequences of any attack upon the eternal laws of the moral world." The French Chambers (at this time ultraroyalist) voted for the war, and it was undertaken by a French army.

The invaders had only a military promenade. The levies of the Spanish Liberals dispersed with astonishingly little fighting. The peasantry, to whom "The Rights of Man" and "Parliamentary Government" were as Chinese jargon, shouted to the French troops, "Death to the constitution; long live the absolute king!" Soon Ferdinand VII was on his throne again, issuing manifestos abolishing the constitution and carrying long proscription lists.

For some years Spain was in the clutches of a violent reaction. No one who had served in the Constitutionalist national guard was permitted within fifteen miles of the King's residence and purges weeded out men of character and brains in the army and learned professions. The possession of any book printed in Spain between 1820 and 1823, or of any foreign book, was sufficient cause for prosecution.

The Alliance System and the Monroe Doctrine

The Spanish revolution at least accomplished this: The final chance of reconquering the South American colonies vanished. For a time it looked as though the attempt might be made. Ever since 1818 the Czar had played with the idea of giving Spain armed help to reconquer her colonies. There had been even talk of sending twelve Russian ships of the line to South America for that purpose. North America lost to monarchy was bad enough; to surrender all of South America seemed intolerable. As the French royalist Chateaubriand wrote in 1822: "If the new world ever becomes entirely republican the monarchies of the old world will perish."

The British foreign secretary Canning, however, was loath to see the Spanish republics across the Atlantic reconquered. The great British mercantile interests would never tolerate any change in a state of affairs which had broken up the old Spanish trade monopoly and had opened the South American market to Britain. Canning was through with entangling alliances. "Britain should resume her isolation and revolve in her own orbit." An encouraging statement, to Americans. It was followed by President Monroe's message to Congress, on December 2, 1823, when he announced that doctrine which was to link his name for all time with the history of American foreign policy, and to inform the world that the extension of the Holy Alliance System to America would not be viewed "in any other light than a manifestation of an unfriendly disposition to the United States."

Invading Mexico or Peru was not invading Spain or Naples. With England applauding Monroe's warning, the zeal for intervention in the Americas died at Vienna and St. Petersburg. Already a new revolution was plaguing Metternich, and the fate of the Greeks was not to be that of the Spaniards and Neapolitans.

Greek Revolt Against the Sultan (1821)

In 1821 the Greeks revolted against the Moslem Sultan, partly because of the tyranny prevalent in the Ottoman Empire, partly because of the infusion of new ideas reaching the Levant from Western Europe. The insurgents were sorely divided and still worse led. On the mainland their chiefs were too often glorified brigands, and on the seas the daring commanders of their light brigantines were prone to pass from patriotic attacks upon the Turks to common piracy. Nevertheless, here was a

Christian people struggling desperately against a Moslem oppressor. Metternich's system was to be sorely tried.

The first Greek outbreaks had been so furious as to overpower the Turkish garrisons in the Morea (ancient Peloponnesus). Then the contest settled down to prolonged and bloodthirsty infighting. In 1821 the Greeks massacred the Moslems who had shut themselves up in Tripolitza; in 1822 the Turks answered by a wholesale massacre of nearly the entire population of the island of Chios. Finally, the Sultan, Mahmud II, invited Mehemet Ali, his nominal vassal, the great and powerful viceroy of Egypt, to conquer Greece for him. By 1827 Athens had been retaken by the Egyptians, and the Greek rebels seemed at the end of their resources.

Meanwhile in Europe, memories of Marathon, Platea, Salamis, and Thermopylae were not invoked in vain. Great scholars, poets, and men of high public leadership in Britain, France, and Germany became ardent Phil-Hellenes. Lord Byron, the first literary person in Europe, threw himself ardently into the Greek cause and died at Missolongi in 1824. Large loans were floated by Phil-Hellenes in London and Paris; gifts of cannon and munitions were sent to the rebels and many Western adventurers enlisted in their cause.

The revolt of the Greeks commanded the particular sympathies of the Russian people, for here were Orthodox Christians fighting the old enemy of the Czar. Alexander was moved by this agitation among his own people. He almost broke with the Sultan, but Metternich kept him in line. True, the Sultan was a Moslem and had not shared in the treaties of Vienna; nevertheless he was a "legitimate sovereign." If "Revolution" was given only an inch it would stretch it an ell. Therefore the Czar published to the world his disapproval of the insurrection. But in 1825 Alexander died and was succeeded by his brother Nicholas, foe of liberalism, but at the same time a passionate champion of Orthodox Christianity and the ideals of Old Russia.

So it happened that in 1826 Russia, England, and France were concerting measures for securing the autonomy of Greece. The next year, while they were still trying to persuade the Sultan to some sort of compromise, their warships entered the harbor of Navarino under orders to stop Ibrahim, the Egyptian general, from devastating the countryside. A chance shot from an Egyptian frigate precipitated a general engagement. At its close sixty Moslem ships had gone down and six thousand men with them.

A French army corps cleared the Turks out of the Morea, and an army of the Czar's forced its way over the Danube, seizing Adrianople within striking distance of Constantinople. In terror, Mahmud conceded the establishment of the independent Kingdom of Greece by the Treaty of Adrianople (1829).

Belgium Separates Itself from Holland (1830)

Metternich had watched this disturbance of "legitimate order," vainly protesting. He vaguely threatened Nicholas with the perils of a "general European war." Nicholas politely disregarded him. He knew Austria was in no condition, financial, military, or moral, for a conflict with Russia. Then, in 1830, followed an upheaval in Western Europe itself which deliberately canceled an important section of the Vienna treaties, and which Metternich was powerless to resist; Belgium tore itself loose from Holland.

The Vienna diplomats had tied together two peoples, not indeed alien in race, but differing radically in political traditions and economic interests. The Belgians were, in large measure, devoted to industry; the Dutch were equally concentrated upon commerce. Economic cross-purposes and friction, therefore, grew apace. Soon, too, there was bitterness in the Belgian provinces over the effort of the government to control education in a manner exciting the great wrath of the Catholic clergy. The result was that by 1830 there had been an intense development of local patriotism in the southern (Belgian) provinces, and an increasing demand that they should be given an administration separate from Holland. Then, suddenly, events in Paris excited the people of Brussels to anti-Dutch demonstrations which grew to riots; riots which grew to a revolution; and a revolution which led to the setting-up of an independent Belgian kingdom.

King William and the Dutch were by no means disposed to enter upon a bloody and exhausting war to hold the Belgian provinces in allegiance. They made, however, all the difficulties possible for the new state, and finally hung on with success to portions of Limburg and Luxemburg, which the Belgians vehemently claimed as their own. The break-up of the Kingdom of the Netherlands, of course, deliberately set aside a capital proviso in the Treaties of Vienna. Not merely Metternich, but the courts of Prussia and Russia, were filled with anger and talked of armed intervention; but an outbreak in Poland tied Nicholas' hands; England, on the whole, favored the Belgians; and the new king of the French, Louis Philippe, stood firmly on their side. The result was a truce imposed by the Powers upon the two parties; and it was agreed that Belgium should become an independent constitutional kingdom, with Prince Leopold of Coburg as its first sovereign.

The creation of Belgium shook the Metternich system to its foundations but it did not destroy it. After all, Poland failed completely in shaking herself free from Russia and abortive revolts in Germany and northern Italy in this year of revolutions (1830) were squelched promptly. True, France had now followed England in deserting the upholders of the status quo; but as long as Austria, Russia, and Prussia stuck together, it could not be said that *Metternichmus,* as the Germans called it, was dead.

It was, however, weakening. In Spanish America, Greece, and Belgium it had failed to function. Liberalism, nationalism, and the Industrial Revolution—all had played a part in sapping its strength. Possibly the Industrial Revolution had been the principal cause of its demise in the new world. British trade in Central and South American ports had been stimulated greatly by the advance of the steam engine in England, and the government of England, although Tory, was unwilling to have that trade endangered. Any reconquest of Spain's colonies would be detrimental to British pocketbooks, and for that reason, if for no other, Canning was willing to stand by President Monroe. Metternich, no fool, knew that intervention overseas was hopeless, and owing to his complete inertia the militant Czar was forced to give up the idea of a transatlantic expedition to reinaugurate autocracy.

The case of Greece was on somewhat different footing. As far as Russia was concerned, sympathy for Balkan nationality transcended fear of liberalism. Russia liked to consider herself the big brother of all the little Balkan peoples, and furthermore, since the Greeks were Orthodox type Catholics, rather than Roman, there was a religious bond between them and Russia. England joined with Russia in freeing Greece, partly from romantic reasons. The Greeks, no matter how debased, were descendants of the ancient Hellenes, and British aristocrats from adolescence had been taught to glorify Grecian literature. Then, too, it was felt Russia should not have all the glory of liberating Greece, for a Russian victory over Turkey might give too much prestige in the Near East to the Muscovite.

Belgian independence, meanwhile, like that of Spanish America, was due primarily to the Industrial Revolution. A great deal of British capital was invested in Belgium, and the principal friction between Belgians and Dutch had been economic in character. As long as France did not seize on Belgium, England was well pleased with the Belgian revolution. It fitted in nicely with the ideology of nationalism to welcome this newcomer, so small, so helpless, into the comity of nations. The rising bourgeoisie in both France and England, captivated with the doctrines of early nineteenth-century liberalism, were delighted with this extension of it on the Continent.

Chapter 3

BOURGEOIS VICTORY IN WESTE̲ N
EUROPE

France

FRANCE AFTER WATERLOO was, above all else, weary of war. "All the mothers are against me," Napoleon is said to have observed as he set forth on his last campaign. So in 1815 the Bourbons came back, with the Allies taking stern precautions against another disturbance of Metternich's beloved "repose."

The bulk of the French people were profoundly indifferent to politics. The country was still largely rural. The Revolution, by splitting up the great estates and multiplying landowners beyond any other country in Europe, had emphasized the essential *peasant* character of the French. The only cities besides Paris with over 100,000 inhabitants were Lyons, Marseilles, and Bordeaux. Only later, when commerce and industry expanded, was there to be a real urban development, as at Lille, Rouen, and Havre. The French peasants cared almost nothing for the franchise and felt no grievance when the Charter denied it to them. Their energies usually went into the painful hoarding of money; and the famous "stockings" were already filling with glittering louis. Their houses were still poor and filthy and their pleasures confined to very simple village dances or church processions. All they asked was to be let alone.

From the government, this peasantry, as did Metternich, made one urgent demand—"order"—to protect their painfully won property. Old soldiers of the Empire might sit around the tavern doors and recall the victories of Marengo and Austerlitz, but the bulk of the people as yet remembered the human price of these victories and hated the idea of another war. *This inherent conservatism of the French peasants was the cardinal fact in French politics from 1815 to 1914.* It brought to nought repeated revolutionary movements in Paris. Between 1914 and 1918 it supplied the granite endurance of the French nation in the struggle with Germany, and in 1919-20 it was a solid barrier upon which the wave of Bolshevism out of Russia dashed itself in vain.

Only in Paris was there political or cultural activity. The population was still barely 700,000, but the place bustled with an intense human energy, contrasting absolutely with the sleepy provincial cities. Here all was fever, the fever of a trade unsurpassed anywhere in the world, save in London; the fever of pleasure expressed by numerous theaters, great public halls, and the finest restaurants and cafés in Europe; the fever of the quest for knowledge at the great Sorbonne, and all the lesser schools. In Paris were concentrated all the omnipotent ministerial bureaus. Again, Paris was declared to be "the only spot in France where one could venture to plot, write or speak freely against the ruling powers." No newspapers worth mentioning were published outside of Paris. No instruction in any political subjects was given in all France, save in the schools and colleges of Paris; no open opposition could be voiced to the government except in the speeches of the Liberal members in the Chamber of Deputies, meeting in Paris.

The Bourbons had come back, bringing with them a great swarm of titled *émigrés*, exiled since the early seventeen-nineties and doomed thereafter to drag out weary years as shabby-genteel tutors, school-teachers, and dancing masters in England, Germany, Russia, and even America. But now the France to which they returned was completely changed. The *political* innovations of 1791, or of the Convention, Directory, or Empire could vanish overnight, but the social revolution had triumphed permanently. Not merely were the privileges of the *noblesse* gone, along with a swarm of other picturesque abuses, but the vast estates of the old nobility and of the Church had been confiscated and distributed among the peasantry. Nobody proposed to provoke the lightning by recalling the proceeding.

The Bourbons were wise enough not to upset the greater part of the internal government of France as it had been organized by Napoleon. The eighty-three departments had long since replaced the lumbering old provinces. In Paris all decisions were made; from Paris all orders were transmitted. Under ordinary conditions, through this great horde of civil servants who were at the constant beck of the Paris ministers, a government could control the country absolutely. Petty functionaries abounded and kept every hamlet tied to the central ministries. "The Restoration was the golden age of *officials*."

In justification for this system of centralized, paternal control, it could be alleged that the French people were still illiterate. Primary education, encouraged neither by the government nor by the bourgeoisie, had been amazingly neglected. In 1821 there were thousands of communes without schools. Newspapers, "expensive, empty, and monotonous," were usually under a close censorship which destroyed all their interest, and were burdened by taxes of fifteen centimes (three cents) per copy.

The Catholic Church, however, restored and encouraged by the return of its old defenders, the Royalists, was springing into new life. The nobility and all who claimed great zeal for the Bourbons were likely to be good Catholics, if only because the average liberal had read Voltaire. The clericals endeavored to control education, putting it in the hands of ecclesiastical "congregations"; and the influence of the clergy over the millions of pious women was alleged to have been always exercised on the side of the king.

So began that alliance of "the Altar and Throne"—clericalism and royalism—which was to distract and complicate French politics into the twentieth century, to the great harm of both Church and State.

Such a country, Louis XVIII (1814-24) undertook to govern by means of the Constitutional Charter. Very many of the former institutions of the First Empire were preserved—the magistrates, the law codes, the university, the titles of nobility—even the Legion of Honor. The king had general control of the administration, named the ministers, and could sanction laws passed by parliament, convoke and adjourn the latter, and dissolve its lower house (Chamber) and order a new election. Like England, France now had a Chamber of Peers, named originally by the king, but thenceforth holding office by hereditary right; and, like England, France had a Chamber of Deputies, colorably like the House of Commons. This lower Chamber, however, was chosen by a method studiously calculated to create, in the place of the old noble class privileged by birth, a new class privileged by fortune. Nobody could be an elector unless he paid direct taxes of at least 300 francs ($60). Less than 100,000 Frenchmen could do this, a fact that gave the franchise to many short-lineaged merchants and exploiters, but left the great bulk of the nation as unrepresented as before 1789.

The monarchy was indeed limited, but the real power rested with the wealthier and socially privileged classes. Unfortunately, however, this French arrangement left many important things unsettled. How must the king choose his ministers—at his own pleasure, or at the wish of the majority of the Chamber? For fifteen years, the Crown and factions of the Chamber were to clash over this main issue.

That this antidemocratic Bourbon regime lasted some fifteen years was thanks largely to the character of its first monarch, Louis XVIII (1814-24). As Comte de Provence, brother of the unfortunate Louis XVI, he had shown himself the stubborn defender of all the abuses of the Old Regime. But weary decades in exile since 1791 had taught him wisdom. It is true that as late as 1800, when a friend advised him to hasten his return to the French throne by promising representative government, he had cried with an angry shrug, "Representative government, such as in England?—better Siberia!" Nevertheless, uncomfortable wanderings through Italy, Germany, Russia, Prussia, and England had at last convinced him that heavy concessions were necessary, that the days of autocracy in France were gone forever. Said General Thiebauld of him, "He had firm desire to die *upon* the throne, and he had the intelligence and prudence not to wish this thing in vain." Between 1815 and 1824, Louis XVIII stood consistently and wisely on the side of moderation and a certain degree of liberalism.

But beside Louis XVIII there stood his brother, the Comte d'Artois (later Charles X), the evil genius of his party. Artois had learned nothing in exile. He gloried in his obstinacy, boasting that "he and Lafayette were the only men who had not changed since 1789." Every concession to liberalism, he counted a calamity; and the day the Charter was promulgated he pretended illness in order to avoid taking oath to it. "I would rather saw wood," he once avowed, "than reign in the manner of the King of England." His residence, the "Pavilion of Marsan," was the trysting spot of all the broken-down nobles who returned from exile only to breathe forth confiscations and slaughter, and of world ecclesiastics anxious to use the credulously pious Artois to advance the temporal power of the Church. Down to 1820, Louis XVIII resisted Artois's pressure. Then, growing old and weary, he began to succumb to reaction. Louis was without a son, and Artois was his heir.

The reign of Louis XVIII was largely taken up by struggles between the royal ministers (supported by the King) and the Chamber, with the latter body usually filled up with extreme Royalists ("Ultras") chosen by the limited franchise and blindly determined upon an aristocratic and clerical reaction. The Ultras hated the Charter because it sanctioned the social changes brought about by the Revolution. They were angry at the King for his moderation, and drank disloyal healths—"to the King in spite of himself." The result was that Louis XVIII, "who had found the throne the most comfortable of armchairs," also found himself sometimes in actual alliance with the decidedly weak party of Liberals, who now, in self-preservation, defended the royal power.

Louis XVIII and his first great minister, the Duc de Richelieu, were able to check some of the grosser outbreaks of the White Terror which the Ultra-Royalists directed against their opponents, although they were not able to prevent many pitiless acts as, for example, the trial and execution of Marshal Ney, "the Bravest of the Brave," for having gone over to Napoleon during the Hundred Days. The passion of the Ultras for vengeance went so far that no less personages than Czar Alexander I and the Duke of Wellington sent warnings to the King, "in the name of the tranquility of Europe," not to let the reaction go too far. The result was a dissolution of the Chamber (1816) and an election in which, even under the very limited franchise, there was a certain swing toward liberalism. But the great landowners and capitalists, who now controlled the franchise, hated anything really savoring of democracy. In 1820 a fanatical saddler stabbed the Duc de Berri, son of the Comte d'Artois, the heir presumptive to the crown, as he was leaving the Paris opera. This crime provoked an instant return to extreme royalism. The very moderate and semi-liberal prime minister was driven from office, and in his place ruled the clever reactionary Villèle, who made no concealment of his wish to undo the "Revolution."

In 1820 the censorship of the press, which had been a little relaxed, was reimposed; and the electoral law was deliberately revised so that 172 out of the 430 deputies were to be elected by the 12,000 very rich citizens paying 1,000 francs ($200) annually. This gave the control of the Chamber into the hands of the Ultras. The small Liberal element in it almost disappeared for years. The Ultras forced the King to make war on Spain, decidedly against his better judgment, and they brought about the prosecution of newspapers for mere "tendency"—for a series of articles, each one apparently innocent, which, taken all together, might be subversive.

The Ultras were thus headed directly toward a legislative program calculated to restore the old pre-Revolutionary system of class privilege and thereby to provoke the entire nation, when in 1824 Louis XVIII died. He passed away full of forebodings, having a very clear idea of his brother's incapacity. "Do not forget," he said to him, "that you have to preserve the throne to your son and grandson." Artois now became Charles X and speedily justified all his brother's pessimism.

Charles X (1824-30): His Fatuous Policy

The Bourbon monarchy, despite its sins, had still in 1824 a glorious and a proud name. It still appealed to the imagination of many Frenchmen who disliked the ragings of the Ultras. Hitherto, most of the people had submitted to the restored Royalist regime with tolerable equanimity. Their dearest interests had not been touched. Now things were suddenly changed.

Charles X began his reign by an act of clumsy stupidity; he ordered some 250 generals, veterans of the revolutionary wars and of the Empire, to be put on half pay. More stupidity followed, when in 1825, Charles was crowned at Reims. The King gave orders to "find" the Holy Ampulla (oil-flask) used at the coronation, although it was well known to have been destroyed by the Jacobins. The official *Moniteur* announced that it was "found," and it was duly used in a medieval ceremony that approached the grotesque. The poet Berenger jestingly invited the French people to help celebrate the coronation of "Charles the Simple."

Soon the Villèle ministry showed its hand by requiring a manuscript copy of newspaper articles to be deposited with the government *five days* before publication; and also by a law partially establishing noble primogeniture, by providing that the eldest son, in estates where the direct tax was over 300 francs ($60), should inherit a double portion. This was too much for the Chamber of Peers, which (less controlled by the ministry than the Deputies) threw out these two bills. Villèle and his colleagues, in anger, thereupon dissolved the Deputies, hoping to demonstrate the folly of opposition and thereby gain strength to overwhelm the upper house.

But the 300-franc electors were becoming disgusted. The Industrial Revolution was commencing in France, and the capitalists were enraged at a law recompensing the old *émigrés* for their confiscated estates with funds obtained by scaling down the interest on government bonds from five to three per cent. Many more electors were becoming disaffected by the general favor shown to the extreme clericals. The attempts to restore primogeniture, in turn, stirred the wrath of the peasants. Was it not a step toward restoring the old nobility and taking away the peasant lands? The result was an election which reflected these fears and returned a majority of deputies belonging to the left—that is, to parties more or less tinctured with liberalism.

Charles X, in angry petulance, appointed as chief minister a man after his own heart—a violent Ultra, a returned exile, the Comte de Polignac. Directed by such a minister and such a king, the Bourbon regime quickly reached the end of its tether.

The powerful and wealthy middle classes were now thoroughly aroused and strongly aided the Chamber in its effort to resist ministerial dictation. People began talking of legal resistance. Despite censorship, the *Journal des Débats* could say: "The people will pay a thousand millions to the law. They will not pay one to the ordinances of a minister. If illegal taxes are demanded a Hampden will arise to crush them. . . . Unhappy France! Unhappy King!" It was known that leagues of Constitutionalists and other defenders of the Charter were forming in Paris and the departments. Old Lafayette (lately returned from a triumphant tour of America) made a kind of progress through the South, stirring up Republican memories. The King's kinsman, Louis Philippe, Duc d'Orléans, was rumored to be intriguing with certain Liberal politicians and also with that shrewd old turncoat, Talleyrand. It seemed a time for caution—but not to Polignac and his master. They drove straight to their downfall.

In 1830 Charles X, infuriated at opposition to his policies, dissolved the Chamber. "It is not a question of the ministry but of monarchy," he avowed testily. But despite the violent appeals of the King himself to return Deputies favorable to Polignac, the electors were not to be browbeaten. In the old Chamber there had been 221 opposition members; in the new one there were now 274.

Foreign ambassadors grew alarmed, and on their reports even Czar Nicholas and the arch-Legitimist Metternich, wrote to Charles advising moderation. They wasted paper and ink. Charles had resolved upon a *coup d'etat,* and Polignac "had had a vision of the Virgin which admonished him to deliver his country from the domestic enemy."

In Africa, the royal army had just taken Algiers from the Turkish Dey, opening the prospect of a glorious expansion of French power south of the Mediterranean. This, it was assured, would give the King's cause prestige and popularity. So confident were Polignac and his master that they concentrated only a few thousand troops around Paris, and these of doubtful quality. The King's mind was fixed: "Concessions ruined Louis XVI," said he, "I have either got to mount a horse or a death-cart." On the evening of July 25, 1830, while at the pleasant suburban chateau of St. Cloud, he signed four fateful ordinances brought him by Polignac.

At eleven o'clock that night, the editor of the official *Moniteur* was summoned to the Ministry of Justice, and the ordinances were handed him to be printed. "Well," asked the Minister of Public Instruction, "what do you think of them?" "God preserve France and the King!" answered the white-lipped editor.

In substance, the four ordinances (*a*) completely abolished the freedom of the press; (*b*) dissolved the Chamber just elected, which had never met; (*c*) modified the electoral law so drastically in favor of the wealthy that only some 25,000 electors were to be left in all France; (*d*) ordered a new election to the Chamber under this revised law.

The instant these ordinances were published, the Paris journalists met at the office of the *National,* and Thiers (already famous with tongue and pen) drew up this protest: "The regime of law is interrupted; that of force has begun. The government has violated the laws; we are dispensed from obeying it." But who would put these brave words into action? The answer came from the populace of Paris.

It took only three days of street fighting to overthrow Charles X. Paris was still, as in 1789, a city of small tradesmen, journeyman workers, and loitering riffraff, with the industrial element somewhat more developed than it had been on the eve of the old Revolution. In 1789 the army had refused to side with the King, and the populace could take the offensive against the Bastille. In 1830 the troops were at first willing to fire volleys for royalty; but already the populace had learned the art of building barricades across the tortuous streets—and how a heap of paving-stones, supplemented by an overturned wagon upon the summit, with the whole crowned by a few chairs with their legs pointing outward, made an ugly obstacle for a battalion.

The ordinances were published on July 26; on the 27th, barricades began springing up, especially across the labyrinthian lanes in the eastern quarters of the city. Behind them were some 8,000 or more members of the Republican societies, now suddenly leaping into action. The leader was Cavaignac, whose father had sat in the old Convention of 1792. Against these barricades Marshal Marmont drove his regulars, but in the narrow, crooked streets the troops could not use artillery. They had only their muskets to conquer the barricades; and they struggled vainly against cross-fire and showers of tiles from the upper windows and every other impediment. Marmont dared not rout out the insurgents by burning down Paris. He was unpopular with his troops and the latter were not disposed toward reckless valor, especially as above the barricades now floated the Tricolor of the Revolution and the Empire—the flag beloved by the army. Soon the troops retreated. By the 28th, the insurgents were in possession of the Hôtel de Ville.

So far, the insurrection had been an affair of the Parisian populace; but now more responsible elements took it in charge. Members of the Assembly organized an executive committee to protect the city from anarchy. To head the movement there came forward Laffitte, the great financier, and Lafayette, the hero of 1789 and 1790, now once more the chieftain of the hastily reorganized National Guard. Not till it was too late did Charles X, comfortably playing cards at peaceful St. Cloud, realize that Marmont's men were spent and that everything was lost.

But the genteel Liberals of the executive committee did not wish for a republic as did the men of the barricades. They already had their candidate as a constitutional king, Louis Philippe, Duc d'Orléans. "He is a citizen-king," ran the manifesto. "He awaits our call. . . . He will accept the Charter as we have always wished it to be. It is at the hands of the French nation that he will receive his crown." Louis Philippe, in turn, was full of charming promises. He allowed himself to be proclaimed, at first, Lieutenant General of the Kingdom and announced, *"The Charter shall henceforth be a reality."* Charles fled to England and in Paris the Republican insurgents acquiesced in the new regime, but not gladly. "You are wrong in thanking us," said Cavaignac, "we have yielded because we are not ready for resistance." In any case, the Bourbons, protégés of the Czar and of Metternich, were out. France was now a truly constitutional monarchy.

The United Kingdom

England emerged from the Napoleonic wars with heightened prestige. British institutions had not been so much as shaken. The old unreformed Parliament, the darling of the great landowners, still met at Westminster. Lord Castlereagh, the Duke of Wellington, and the other Tory statesmen who were still guiding British policy were the incarnation of what had been during the Napoleonic wars the most intelligent, vigorous, public-spirited oligarchy ever seen since the wane of the Roman Republic and its august Senate. The new machinery—Watt's steam engines, the spinning jenny, the power loom, and the improved processes of working metals—were already transforming Britain from an agricultural country into the chief workshop of the world. The British masses, driven from the land by the inclosures of the public commons (probably a necessary movement to increase production and win the war), became effective although somewhat unruly factory operatives, in days when child-labor laws were unknown and trade unions were prohibited.

The population of the United Kingdom of Great Britain and Ireland was some 18,500,000, about one-third crowded into oppressed and impoverished Ireland. But the real strength of the realm lay not in its numbers but in its great wealth and in its incomparable sea power. Commerce and industry had made Britain the richest nation upon the planet. The old North American colonies were gone, but a second and vaster colonial empire was in the making. The Union Jack flew already at the Cape of Good Hope, at Botany Bay, and at Bombay and Calcutta. The Grand Moghul of India was sinking into a mere pensioner of the British East India Company. All this had brought Britain the wealth which enabled her to finance great coalitions against the Corsican; to keep alive the resistance of Spain and Portugal, to survive the continental blockade, and finally, when the tide turned fairly against Napoleon after Moscow, to pull him down.

Many considered this happy state of affairs to be due to the British constitution, an elastic term frequently, if loosely, applied not only to statute law but to custom and tradition. In England the framework of both government and society was aristocratic and decentralized. The House of Commons held the balance of power in Parliament, but the members of that house were not commoners, except in a legal sense. Almost exclusively they were country gentlemen and landowners who wrote "Esquire" after their names and considered none their superior except the King's Majesty. These country gentlemen did not till their own estates; rather they parceled them out to farmers who rented them. The gentry lived on the rentals and made return to society by governing the country.

They controlled the House of Commons, and their younger sons officered the navy, the army, and the Church; their first-born sons succeeded them as owners of their estates and generally became J.P.'s (justices of the peace) as their fathers before them. The J.P.'s were the local government and that was all the government that most people saw, for there was slight administrative control from London. The justices of the peace administered the law (and sometimes really made it by local ordinance), acted as local magistrates, looked after the poor, and enforced the King's peace. These country gentlemen were, with certain noticeable exceptions, poorly educated, and a great part of their day was spent frequently in hunting and over the bottle; but they were hardbitten, determined men, accustomed to power which they had no intention of losing.

Such was the British system in the eighteenth century and such it remained after Waterloo. Before the French Revolution, England had been the outstanding progressive country in Europe in all that concerned civil and political liberty. Caste was pronounced; but it was less obnoxious than on the continent, for class lines were less strictly drawn, particularly those between the wealthier middle class and the aristocracy. The Church of England held a highly favored position; but there was genuine religious liberty in practice if not in law. Freedom of speech and freedom of the press were customary. Arbitrary imprisonment without trial, manorial dues, and interior customs lines were missing. Nevertheless, many had chafed at the monopoly of government possessed by the country gentry, and in the late eighteenth century a reform of Parliament had been proposed by William Pitt. Rebellion in America, rebellion in Ireland, the searching criticism of eighteenth-century philosophers, and the emergence of a new class of capitalists whose wealth was in factories rather than in land, made its coming seem well-nigh inevitable. The French Revolution changed all that; liberalism was associated with the French Revolution, and after England fought France in 1793 it became unpatriotic to advocate French ideas.

After 1815 came grumbling. The war was over, but taxes were heavy, the national debt was huge, the psychological reaction after prolonged conflict was pronounced. Napoleon's Continental blockade was no more, and agricultural prices dropped, to the financial distress of those Englishmen who had been cultivating every possible acre for higher prices. On the other hand, an impoverished Continent could not buy English manufactured goods in large quantities. To add to the distress, the new power machinery was displacing labor for the time being, faster than new jobs could be had, and in addition there were thousands of discharged soldiers and sailors without work.

Under such circumstances the Tory party, overwhelmingly the stronghold of the country gentry and possessed of the government, was not supine. It passed, to the advantage of its own interests, Corn Laws which prohibited the importation of foreign grain below a certain price; and it repealed the income tax, to the advantage of its own members again and those of the upper middle class; but for the poorer folk it did nothing. The very force and grim determination with which it had carried on the war seemed to make it impervious to the domestic crisis.

Then came numerous popular demonstrations and not a few riots. The radicals (as the critics of the existing order were called) who got these up were not united in their criticism. Some advocated trade unions and the development of a labor movement; some urged the repudiation of the national debt and a cheapened currency; some were for land nationalization; some for a vague kind of socialism (described elsewhere; see pp. 82-84).

The best known radical of the period was a hale and hearty Englishman, William Cobbett, whose ideas were expressed in such yeasty fashion that it was not always easy to know just what he stood for. He assailed with equal vigor, in the most intemperate language, financiers, farmers, Jews, and landlords. The latter were "the most base of all the creatures that God suffered to assume human shape." The country was going to ruin fast because of the national debt which Cobbett would repudiate. The good old times were disappearing. Among other reasons which contributed to this state of affairs was the introduction of the potato, "suitable companion of misery and filth." To seek to raise the level of the people by education was "despicable cant and nonsense"; why read, he said, "the punning and smutty Shakespeare?" Cobbett gave vent to ideas such as these in his *Weekly Political Register* which, as soon as he published it as a pamphlet, ran up a circulation of 4,000 a week. Cobbett did not advocate violence directly, but because his words were so violent the possessing classes became uneasy. One way to stop his influence might be to build more churches in order that the poorer folk be made submissive to their rulers. A million pounds was devoted to this end. New churches were needed in the industrial centers if the Church of England was properly to function, but it is perfectly evident from the speeches in Parliament that their erection was primarily intended as a check on popular economic discontent due to low wages, high prices, and unemployment.

Upon one thing all radicals were agreed: the necessity of a reform of Parliament, particularly as concerned the methods in vogue for electing members of the House of Commons. There were over six hundred members, and of these well over two-thirds represented boroughs (towns), and less than one-third the counties (agricultural districts). In the latter the suffrage was uniform; it was based on the ownership of land and all forty-shilling freeholders could vote. In consequence, even the most intelligent and prosperous farmer had no vote, let alone the laborers whom he hired; for a farmer in England, by definition, was a man who rented his land. This fact gave the gentry a monopoly of the county representation. But they also, directly or indirectly, were all-powerful in selecting most of the borough representation. The classification of boroughs was very complicated. Roughly, they might be considered as of two varieties: open boroughs where many voted (very few in number), and closed boroughs with a sharply limited franchise, variously determined in accordance with certain old customs. Of this latter class, many again were known as "nomination" or "rotten" boroughs, where so few voted that the selection sometimes depended on the nomination of only one man or family. Occasionally there was not even a single resident in the borough. In the case of Old Sarum, there were five votes and no houses at all. When an election was held it was necessary to pitch a tent wherein the five votes might be recorded. Other boroughs with only a few votes each very often became the private possession of a few landed families, for most of the land upon which the small towns were built belonged to the landed gentry, and since all voting was done orally, very naturally the tenants voted as their landlord desired.

Furthermore, most of the boroughs were of great antiquity, dating back to the sixteenth century and the time of the Tudors. The Industrial Revolution was building new towns in the eighteenth and nineteenth centuries, and generally in the vicinity of water-power or coal and iron, localities where few people had lived in times past. In consequence, many of the thriving new industrial cities had no representation in Parliament at all, whereas many towns with a population under a thousand had two members apiece. This situation, so anomalous, so unfair, attracted the attention of all shades of radical thought and to remedy it the radicals were all united.

But the Tory government clamped down on their agitation with the utmost vigor, utilized soldiers to disperse meetings, suspended the writ of habeas corpus, passed stringent measures (the Six Acts) curtailing public meetings, controlling the press. A hue and cry arose that the traditional liberties of Englishmen were being trod upon; but the stiff-necked country gentlemen at the helm refused to listen, and harsh repression became the order of the day in England after Waterloo.

Fortunately for the landlords, within a few years a change for the better in world trade took much of the sharpness off economic distress, and in the House of Commons a more enlightened and intelligent attitude toward reform insured the continuation of Tory control for another decade. The old Whig party had come in the course of time to be almost as much a landlords' party as the dominant Tory group, and the Whigs had gone into an eclipse due to factional fighting among themselves. And so the Tories were all powerful. New leaders rose in their ranks, leaders known as "Liberal Tories" with intelligence sufficient to realize that certain crying abuses should be reformed.

The "Liberal Tories"

Among the leaders were Canning, Castlereagh's successor in control of foreign policy, William Huskisson, head of the Board of Trade, and Sir Robert Peel, from 1822 to 1846 forever before the public eye. Canning, never really liberal in domestic affairs, was principally occupied elsewhere as we have seen, in divorcing England from the Metternich system by standing up for Spain's revolting colonies and by assisting the Greeks in their war of independence. Huskisson may be given credit for starting a movement which, fifty years later, was to put England on a free-trade basis. South America, having escaped the clutch of Spanish mercantilism, was now an open market for English goods, and the United States, expanding rapidly westward, was another. To encourage trade with these regions and with the Continent, Huskisson reduced many tariff duties. He modified the old navigation laws which had necessitated the use of British vessels in foreign trade, opened the British colonies to the trade of other countries, and brought about the repeal of the statute which forbade the emigration of artisans. They were slipping out of England anyway, with the knowledge of the new machinery in their heads. Better to let them go and to sell the new machines openly and thus clear a profit.

More important to British history was Sir Robert Peel, a man who antecedently came from the bourgeoisie. In accordance with British tradition, however, such a one might be absorbed (as both Peel and Canning were) into the ranks of the aristocracy, that is, if the candidate had sufficient money and knew how to play his cards. Sir Robert's father, a wealthy cotton manufacturer, knew how to play his cards correctly, and the younger Peel, a graduate of Harrow and Oxford, with phlegm, coldness, hard work, ability, and commanding presence, rose to high command in the Commons and was destined in time to become the shining light of Toryism there.

Peel was interested primarily in practical government and, like a good business man, wanted to make things work efficiently and economically. As Home Secretary he found full scope for his energy in reorganizing the administration of justice, enforcing the criminal law, and making that law sufficiently rational to be enforceable. He made an end to the silly effort to suppress radical newspapers, to the employment of governmental spies among workingmen, to the old system of constables in London, where now the new "Peelers" or "Bobbies" (his policemen) kept order. Very largely owing to his efforts came the reform of the criminal law. The latter had been so long noted for the absurd multiplication of crimes for which death was the penalty that juries had grown accustomed to acquit many guilty of minor offenses, rather than accept responsibility for their deaths. Parliament, in the past, had tried to diminish crime in the most hit-and-miss fashion, simply by making the law more and more harsh. Peel saw the uselessness of this procedure, and he succeeded in having the death penalty removed from no less than a hundred minor offenses.

Nor were these the only reforms to be accredited to the Liberal Tories. They repealed the old Test and Corporation Acts, dating back over a century, which discriminated against Nonconformists, those British citizens who, though Protestant, were not members of the Church of England. These old statutes had become a dead letter, but legally it was still necessary for anyone holding office under the Crown to take Holy Communion in accordance with the Anglican rite once a year. In fact, one church in London had been set apart for that very purpose. The

Nonconformists gathered outside, and at the conclusion of the regular service the clergyman would say: "Those who want to be qualified will please step up this way." The Tories then went farther and in 1829 admitted Roman Catholics to elective office. This last they were very unwilling to do, although Canning and the wiser Tories decided they must. It was a hoary British tradition, dating back to the Spanish Armada, that Roman Catholics were not to be trusted. The Tories did not fear the Roman Catholics in England so much; they were very few in number and for the most part well-to-do and respectable. What they did fear were the Catholic Irish, among whom Daniel O'Connell, a skilled demagogue, was extraordinarily popular. The latter's constant agitation for repeal might lead to open revolt; and even if that should be squelched, a great deal of property might be destroyed. The Tories, therefore, decided to cut the ground from underneath O'Connell by rescinding the anti-Catholic laws. George IV (1820-30), the then-reigning king, a debauchee and a rake, had curious qualms of conscience and spoke feelingly of his coronation oath; but the Duke of Wellington, prime minister, insisted, and the King gave way. Catholics now were free to vote for Catholics in the United Kingdom, although in Ireland, where most of them were to be found, the property qualification was lifted to a higher level than it had been before the Catholic Emancipation Act of 1829.

Meanwhile, the demand for Parliamentary reform grew steadily. The Industrial Revolution was transforming the country, drawing more and more people from the rural districts into the cities, turning an essentially agrarian society into an industrial one. Birmingham, with 15,000 inhabitants in 1700, had 73,000 in 1801. Manchester, the center of the cotton trade, with 75,000 in 1801, was to multiply its numbers fourfold during the next fifty years. Cities like these were unrepresented in Parliament, while decayed villages elsewhere sent two members each to Westminster. Even in earlier days, before there had been a steam engine, the South of England had been heavily overrepresented, and particularly Cornwall, where the kings of England were great landlords. In the old days the Crown had determined what boroughs should be represented and what should not, and it was only natural that the Tudors should have overweighed the representation of those regions where they held property.

Nevertheless, the old Parliamentary system received staunch support. Under it, many argued. England has prospered mightily. The influence of most contemporary literary men, both indirectly and directly, was in favor of the status quo. Sir Walter Scott's indirect influence was very considerable, and that venerable knight, engrossed as he was in tales of the past which emphasized and idealized such qualities as reverence and loyalty, thought but poorly of reform movements. Southey, Wordsworth, and Coleridge, romantically and mystically inclined, emphasized the subjective nature of man, awe, mystery, and religion. It was a far cry from the practical absurdities of a bustling manufacturing city having no representation in Parliament to the *Rhyme of the Ancient Mariner* and the Romantic Movement in literature.

Furthermore, whatever might be said in favor of the rotten boroughs, they had at least been the means whereby young men of great promise had been brought early into parliamentary life. Burke, Pitt, Peel, Canning were proof; and the young man Gladstone, now entering Oxford and soon to owe his seat in the Commons to the Duke of Newcastle, was to be another. These young men were under no obligation to play politics, to scheme, and to wangle their way into the House of Commons. Do away with the rotten boroughs, it was said, and you either postpone the advent of these young geniuses into the political arena until their energies are spent, or else you keep them out of public life altogether. Finally, in the hearts of many there was still lurking the fear of the French Revolution. Once England let down the bars and went liberal, who could predict the end?

In the last analysis, however, it was neither argument nor logic that determined the issue but the steady, impressive advance of the Industrial Revolution. The ranks of the capitalists, both great and small, were swelling steadily. A few of these capitalists, socially ambitious, might intermarry with the country gentry; some, intent merely on money-making, might continue indifferent to the vote; but the majority became more and more determined to possess it, partly, perhaps, to share in passing laws which would aid their economic status, but partly also because indignant at the slight put upon them by their exclusion under the old system.

Nevertheless, the demand for the vote did not become overwhelming before 1830. The Whig party which historically opposed the Tory party in Parliament had not yet recovered from the desertion of Edmund Burke and his followers at the time of the French Revolution. It was not ill disposed to doing something for the manufacturing and commercial interests, since always in the past there had been a closer bond of sympathy between Whigs and the middle class than between the latter and the Tories. On the other hand, the Whigs were predominantly country gentry like the Tories, and many of the greatest landlords in England belonged to their party. Therefore they were not particularly enthusiastic for Parliamentary reform—that is, not before the French Revolution of 1830 showed how easy a step forward it might become.

The success of the French bourgeoisie had immediate repercussions in England. The more alert Whigs realized that a genuine opportunity was given them to drive out the Tories and to seize the government for themselves. The Duke of Wellington was very unpopular with his own Tory adherents, owing to his dictatorial manner, and in an absurd speech the Duke had praised the old British constitution with all its anomalies as perfection in government. The Whigs, on a matter of minor importance, defeated Wellington in the House and formed a ministry under Lord Grey (1830). Something would be necessary to enhance their prestige if they wanted to stay in power, and they decided that parliamentary reform would serve that purpose.

The Great Reform Bill

The intent of the elder statesmen among the Whigs had been to bring in a very moderate measure of parliamentary reform, but spurred on by a suddenly aroused public opinion, stimulated by a sharp recession in trade as well as by contemporary events in France, they quickly became more progressive than they had originally intended. In accordance with the old system, every borough had two members. Under the bill which the Whigs introduced in 1831, all rotten boroughs with a population under 2,000 were deprived entirely of their representation, and boroughs having between 2,000 and 4,000 population lost a member each. One hundred and forty-three seats were thus at the disposal of the government, for the benefit of populous counties and unrepresented industrial towns. A universal franchise yardstick was then applied to all boroughs. The vote in them was given to all adult males owning or renting a house, the rental value of which was ten pounds. In the counties (mainly agricultural districts) the franchise was also extended by admitting to the vote farmers leasing land to the rental of fifty pounds. Thus, in the boroughs practically all the middle class could vote except the poorer clerks, and in the counties the well-to-do farmers, as well as the landlords and the dwindling class of yeomen who tilled their own land and who qualified by the old franchise (not abolished) of forty-shilling freeholders.

The bill met with such obstruction in Parliament that its defeat there was certain. Thereupon, the new king, William IV (1830-37), authorized Grey to hold an election. It turned out to be the most exciting in English history. "The bill, the whole bill, and nothing but the bill," was the slogan of the middle class, aided and abetted by the rural and the urban proletariat. Ricks burned merrily in the country districts and huge demonstrations took place in the cities, occasionally leading to the destruction of property. The new Parliament had a majority in the House of Commons of two to one for the bill, but the House of Lords would have rejected the measure had it not been for the wisdom of the King and the Duke, who realized how nasty the popular temper had become and saw that a run on the Bank of England was impending. His Majesty promised Grey to appoint as many new peers as might be necessary to overcome a hostile majority in the House of Lords, and Wellington, having specialized in strategic retreats as a soldier, decided to do the same as a politician. Persuaded by him, the "diehard" peers who could not bring themselves to vote for the bill were absent in such numbers when the vote was taken that the bill passed both houses and became law in 1832.

The Reform Bill did not put the middle class completely in the saddle, by any means. In effect it meant that the middle class shared political power with the landed gentry, for the latter still controlled the county representation and that of many boroughs. In England, however, as in France, a decided step forward had been taken. The victory of the bourgeoisie in France was possibly the more clean-cut, but that in England was ultimately to prove the more important. In France peasant proprietorship was to act continuously as a brake on the progress of the Industrial Revolution, for from the time of their great Revolution in the eighteenth century even to the present, the French peasants were to cling to their land. That brake on industrialism did not exist in England where the movement toward more and more industrialization was to continue well past the first World War.

Meanwhile, in these two countries liberalism as an article of faith was gaining rapidly. France under its new king and England under its reformed Parliament both adhered to representative government in politics and to laissez faire in economics. The two countries together with Belgium were, indeed, in a separate category by themselves. More progressive, more democratic, more enlightened than the rest of Europe, freed from ungratified nationalistic aspirations, their lot seemed a happy one, particularly to patriotic Germans, Austrians, Italians, and Russians who did not enjoy similar privileges.

Chapter 4

EAST OF THE RHINE : REACTION VICTORIOUS

The German Confederation: Its Weakness

WE HAVE SEEN how the treaties of Vienna left not a German Empire but only a German Bund, a loose confederation deliberately arranged to enable Austria to check the growth of her rival, Prussia, and to dominate all Germany by bullying or cajoling the minor states. The 360 "almost independent" governments of pre-Napoleonic days had, indeed, been whittled down to 39, but the map of Germany was still a curious and bewildering patchwork. Many of the larger states had outlying possessions, "enclaves," completely surrounded by other principalities. No difference in race, cultural traditions, religion, or economic interest ordinarily separated the peoples across these narrow boundaries, but merely the fact that they were subjects of different "princely highnesses," "grand ducal highnesses," or "royal majesties."

Except in the Rhinelands, Bavaria, and Prussian Poland, the bulk of the people were Protestants. The great industrial development of Germany had not begun. The cities were small and mainly the centers of local commerce. The great masses of the population were hard-toiling peasants. The number of educated persons in Germany, however, was comparatively large—larger than in any other Continental country, barring perhaps France. It was this element in the universities and high schools, or trained therein, which viewed the Bund with the greatest disfavor.

As constituted in 1815, the Bund contained one empire—Austria; [1] five kingdoms—Prussia, Saxony, Hanover, Württemberg, and Bavaria; one electorate—Hesse-Cassel; seven grand duchies—Baden, Hesse-Darmstadt, Saxe-Weimar, and four smaller ones; twenty-one small independent states and cities. The latter (governed by merchant oligarchies) were Frankfort-on-Main, Bremen, Hamburg, and Lübeck. This heterogeneous assortment was placed in a confederacy, whereof the Emperor of Austria was the president and the King of Prussia the vice-president.

[1] Austria's Hungarian and Prussia's Polish lands were not reckoned part of the Bund.

57

The deputies for the thirty-nine sovereign members met at Frankfort. On all important questions unanimity was necessary. Each state kept its own diplomatic service, army, and supreme court. The Bund sent no envoys to foreign parts. If the Frankfort Diet (*Bundes-versammlung*) finally *did* order anything and one of the states defied it, the only means of bringing the offender to terms was by a federal execution—that is, by having all or some of the other states send armies against it.

The Bund's Diet was normally the scene of endless squabbles between the lesser states, very jealous of their sovereignty, and of interminable technicalities and lawyers' delays. For example, it took ten years to settle which should be the federal citadels—the cities to be fortified to cover Germany on the side of France.

Prussia, the strongest state barring Austria, was not political-minded. The real life of Prussia was dominated by her Junkers, the country squires of Brandenburg, Pomerania, East Prussia, and West Prussia. As a rural gentry—brave, religious, personally honorable, and with a keen sense of duty—the Junkers deserve a high place, even if they did love to cane their peasantry and to carouse coarsely in their cold gray "schlosses," upon the wind-swept mark-lands. But the great march of ideas engendered by the French Revolution had left them untouched by anything except a sense of utter aversion. Accustomed to send their sons to officer the Prussian regiments, while they themselves remained at home to cudgel and command the villagers around the castle, the last thing they desired were liberal institutions.

The Junkers were intensely proud of being *Prussians*. Their keen local patriotism hardly extended to take in Germany. Their society was still on the patriarchal basis. Assemblies, constitutions, and popular rights meant nothing. At the bottom was the peasant, good to fill the ranks in war. Then was the *gnädiger Herr*, the noble landlord; then came the *aller gnädigster Herr*, the king in Berlin; and finally, above him, was the *Herr Gott*. Autocratic monarchy seemed thus very proper. Without the Junkers' aid, Prussia (surrounded by jealous neighbors) could never have fought her way to greatness in the eighteenth century and still might be crushed between Austria and Russia. *In every estimate of Prussian policy from 1814 to 1918, this ultra-conservative (Junker) influence, applied directly upon the throne, must be reckoned with.* Presently it affected not Prussia only but all of Germany; then Europe; then the world.

In Central Germany, however, and even more decidedly in the southern Swabian lands, more liberal notions were acceptable; and in the Rhinelands, where French rule had lasted nearly two decades and had not been offensive, the population was even more liberally inclined. As the century advanced, a republican movement was to center around Baden. In this part of Germany, the pressure for nonmilitaristic democratic institutions was to be strongest. If liberalism was a thing worth striving for, it was evident that any future control of Germany must take into account the Prussian Northeast.

In the Constitution of the Bund there was a famous Article 13 which the Liberals denounced as being "Not a law but a prophecy." It ran "There will be a system of assemblies of estates" in each kingdom or principality.[2] This clause long remained for many states only a pious hope. However, most of the northern governments made the concession of convoking the old assemblies of nobles and letting them go through the form of approving the taxes. And by 1820 many of the more important states, except Prussia and Austria, possessed some kind of constitution. In the North the privileges granted were extremely limited and even the publication of the debates in the assemblies that were allowed to meet was usually prohibited. In the South, however, especially in Bavaria, Württemberg, and Baden, there were more representative assemblies; but the real power in these pretentious minor kingdoms and duchies lay with the sovereign and a very few ministers, chosen at his good pleasure. The little German courts were notoriously proud, extravagant, and more interested in questions of etiquette and punctilio than in studying the weal of their subjects. In Saxony, the king is alleged to have been so conscious of his own greatness that he never went out of the palace on foot or deigned to speak with any one in his army beneath the rank of colonel.[3]

Reaction in Prussia: The Burschenschaft Movement

So much for the minor states. The two major powers were, of course, a law unto themselves. A constitution in the Austrian lands was inconceivable while Francis I and Metternich ruled from the Hofburg palace, but for an instant Prussia gave better hopes. In 1815, under pressure from his liberal and intelligent chancellor Hardenberg, Frederick William III issued an edict ordering arrangements to be made for a national assembly "to deliberate on all subjects of legislation affecting the personal and property rights of citizens, including taxation." At last there was to be a constitution.

This promise was made only to be broken. Every pound of pressure which Metternich could exert was applied from Vienna to prevent the

[2] The first draft had run "there *must be* established within one year such a system." Metternich and his lieutenants promptly secured the altering of this dangerous concession to "Revolution."

[3] The only prince giving his subjects a genuinely liberal constitution was the Grand Duke of Saxe-Weimar, the very enlightened patron of Goethe. Many princes, especially those earlier deposed by the French and now returning to their narrow thrones, rejoiced in a policy of stark reaction. The Elector of Hesse-Cassel, driven out in 1806, treated as null everything accomplished in his absence. He restored the antiquated laws, forced labor, and medieval corporations, and even ordered the soldiers of his petty army to resume wearing the queue as in pre-Revolutionary days.

King from keeping his pledge. The Junker militarists at the court utterly disliked it; all bureaucratic elements, to whom the existing order was profitable and precious, labored to discredit the proposal. Speedily came events capable of being represented to the King as proving that a constitution was for the moment unwise, and in 1818 he issued a cabinet order declaring the times required the postponement of the project. The great reformer, Stein (who had set his heart on a constitution), wept bitterly at the news. France, the Low Countries, Sweden, Poland, all had constitutions, he said, why not Prussia? But the servile court ecclesiastic Eylert was ready with an unctuous justification: "The King had acted like a wise father, who is touched by the devoted love of his children and is in a kindly humor and consents to their wishes; but afterward upon consideration, he modifies his assent and asserts his natural authority."

What had assisted to scare the King, had been exhibitions of unrest, particularly in the universities, in forms that were easily represented to him as "dangerous movements." There were already many German student societies. In 1815 at Jena (in Saxe-Weimar and under a liberal ruler) began the most famous of them all, the *Burschenschaft*. Its members did not have a direct political aim. They were mostly tinctured with an exalted Christian faith. Duels were curtailed in number, and members were supposed to lead clean lives, free from gambling and more sordid vices. The members adopted a special costume with a high collar, "the Germanic-Christian dress," and the colors of the volunteers against France in 1813—red, black, and gold. The movement grew and it seemed to become associated, in the eyes of anxious reactionaries, with other societies of a more directly political cast. At last, in 1817, the Jena society summoned all the *Burschen* of Germany to a grand reunion and festival at the Wartburg, the castle which had once sheltered that patriotic German Martin Luther.

In the main it was a harmless if sentimental gathering. The students listened to moral and patriotic homilies from distinguished professors; Luther's hymn was sung; there was much display of animal spirits. Probably everything would have passed off quietly but for a few unwise souls who decided upon a special evening ceremony. Luther once had burned the Pope's Bull. The *Burschen* now showed their contempt for the reactionaries by lighting a grand bonfire into which an excited throng cast a pigtail, symbolic of conventionality, a corset, token of stiff-necked pedantry, a corporal's cane, and a number of books peculiarly obnoxious to the nationalist-patriotic party, including the new Prussian police code and the writings of Kotzebue, a reactionary author patronized by Czar Alexander.

Instantly this childish prank was taken up as a direct defiance of constituted authority. Metternich willfully exaggerated its significance. The Saxe-Weimar authorities were compelled to establish a strict censorship on their press, the only one hitherto that had been fairly free in all Germany. To add to the excitement, Kotzebue was assassinated by a half-lunatic student, who had conceived that he could end tyranny by killing a worthless pamphleteer. A few other isolated crimes or signs of unrest occurred and played directly into Metternich's hands. The result was a conference of the princes at Carlsbad in 1819, and the Diet at Frankfort instantly ratified their reactionary decrees.

The German princes were able to unite on no program for liberty, but at Carlsbad they easily fixed upon a general policy of repressive oversight in the universities and high schools, and of a general censorship of the press. No news or pamphlet report was to be printed before it had been officially scrutinized; while at Mainz a federal committee was to investigate "the origin and ramifications of revolutionary conspiracies and demagogic associations." The plight of the liberals was intolerable. Most of their leaders found exile the only alternative to prison. Arndt, professor of history, who had done so much to stimulate patriotic feeling against Napoleon, was held in custody three years, while his prosecutors vainly sought evidence against him. In Prussia it even became a crime to publish Fichte's memorable "Addresses to the German Nation." No public reference to "national unity" was permitted. To display the tri-color of the old Empire—black, red, and gold—was sometimes criminal, and a student who paraded the streets in a black coat, a red waist-coat, and a straw hat was sure of arrest, at least by the Prussian police. In 1821 a Prussian cabinet order actually forbade the printing of the unsettling term "Protestant," and ordered that more soothing word, "Evangelical," always to be substituted.

So the nineteenth century advanced, with intelligent Germans enjoying neither the national unity nor the political liberty which their hearts craved. The nation was weary after the desperate military struggles of 1812-14; and the peasants, country nobles, and small traders, at least, were content to let peace and autocracy alone. In consequence, the Revolution of 1830 in France met with slight repercussions in Germany, except in a few minor states. One of these was Brunswick, where Duke Charles II plundered the treasury to enrich his mistresses. His own officials connived at a comic-opera revolution as Charles fled the duchy to be replaced by his brother. In this instance even Metternich dared not intervene, so obnoxious had been the behavior of the exiled ruler.

But if political union or liberty were not for Germany in these years, in one great matter there was genuine progress. In 1819 began the famous *Zollverein,* the Prussian Customs Union, which was not to be completed until 1853. Prussia found herself after 1815 with almost impossible frontiers to patrol as customs barriers—over four thousand miles in extent, separated between the main kingdom and the Rhinelands, and with lesser states thrusting in at almost every angle. Every petty government main-

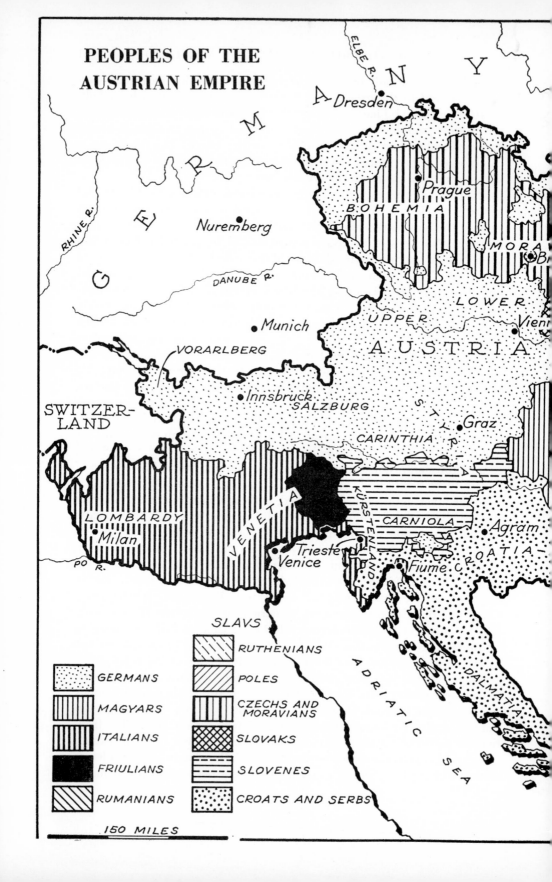

PEOPLES OF THE
AUSTRIAN EMPIRE

Dresden

GERMANY

ELBE R.

N
Y

RHINE R.

Nuremberg

DANUBE R.

Munich

VORARLBERG

SWITZER-
LAND

Innsbruck

SALZBURG

BOHEMIA

Prague

MORA

Br

LOWER

UPPER

AUSTRIA

Vienn

S
T
I
R

CARINTHIA

Graz

LOMBARDY

Milan

PO R.

VENETIA

KÜRSTENLAND

CARNIOLA

Agram

C
R
O
A
T
I
A

Venice

Trieste

Fiume

ADRIATIC

SEA

DALMATIA

SLAVS

RUTHENIANS

POLES

CZECHS AND
MORAVIANS

SLOVAKS

SLOVENES

CROATS AND SERBS

GERMANS

MAGYARS

ITALIANS

FRIULIANS

RUMANIANS

150 MILES

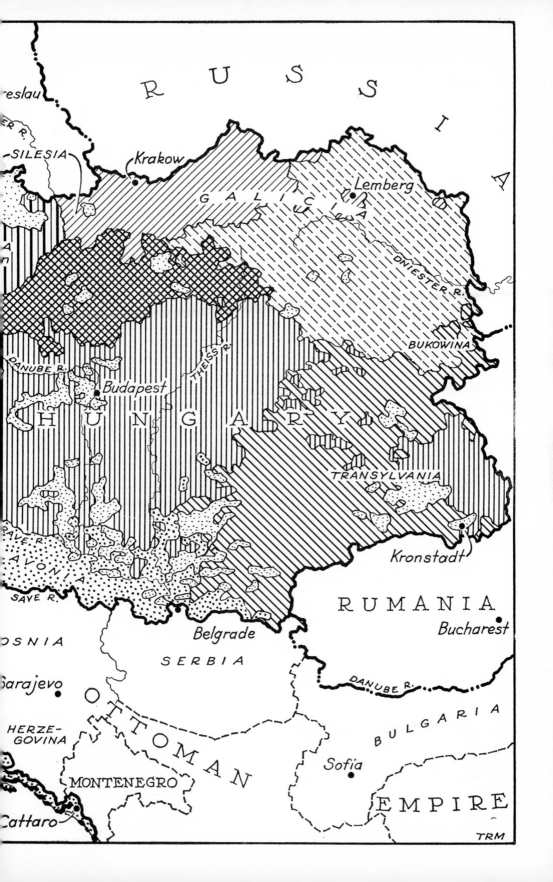

tained its own custom houses, tariffs, and vexatious exactions upon all commerce crawling across its boundaries. The situation was, of course, intolerable in the eyes of intelligent men. The great economist List (see p. 248) denounced the thirty-nine-odd tariffs "as having much the same result as if one decided to bind up the various members of the human body in order to prevent the blood from circulating from one to the other." In these local tariffs, which had no orderly "protective" principle, German "particularism" (states-rights) seemed running mad; and there was efficiency enough in Prussia to compel a drastic remedy.

In 1818 Prussia adopted a tariff scale deliberately made low and simple in order to discourage smuggling. In 1819 she induced the little principality of Schwarzburg-Sondershausen to enter her customs system. The newcomer, throwing down her customs barriers toward Prussia, accepted Prussian tariffs and customs officers, and received a share from the total customs revenues in direct proportion to her population. Down to 1828 there was much jealousy of this extension of Prussian influence on the part of the minor North German princes, but one by one many of them came into the union. In 1828 Hesse-Darmstadt (a state which because of its position was of strategic economic importance) joined this growing Zollverein, as did by 1834 even such self-sufficient kingdoms as Bavaria and Württemberg. Only Hanover and a few minor states held out in the North, and Austria, proud and distrustful, in the South.

The Austrian Lands Under the Hapsburg Autocracy

While Germany proper was thus preparing for some great political upheaval the moment that circumstances favored, the conglomerate of peoples called, for convenience, "Austria" was also infused with a new spirit. Space is lacking to tell how the national leaven was working among the Czechs of Bohemia, making them dream dreams of restoring their old independent kingdom suppressed in the Thirty Years' War; how the Croats learned to distrust their masterful neighbors, the Magyars; how the Poles of Galicia never ceased to pray for reunion with their brethren under Russia and Prussia; and how languages that seemed to have degenerated into mere local jargons or dialects were patriotically pruned, amplified, given a literature, and thus reappeared as true national tongues.

In this great, lumbering empire there were, however, two master-races —the Germans and the Magyars. They did not constitute the majority of the population, but together they could dominate it. The court, the army, the capital—bright and beautiful Vienna—were officially German. The Magyar magnates, in their turn, controlled a strategic territory upon the lower Danube and were the leaders of an extraordinarily warlike and gifted race. Every motive of interest suggested that the Hapsburgs should at all hazards conciliate both the Germans in and about Vienna and the Magyar aristocracy, which still was allowed to speak through a national Diet for "the Crown of St. Stephen"—Hungary, plus Croatia, Slavonia, and Transylvania. On the contrary, Francis I and his ministers could conceive of no such intelligent policy. They deliberately made the Hapsburg regime unpopular with Germans and Magyars alike. The result was an explosion in 1848 that would have ruined the monarchy but for the military aid of Russia.

Francis I is said to have declared that reforms were impossible in Austria, because "his Empire was an old house that would crumble away if he should try to repair it." Metternich was intelligent enough to know better, but he realized that once he asserted the need of any internal reforms, the whole corrupt camarilla of idling archdukes, greedy office-holders, inefficient militarists, and worldly ecclesiastics, who alone had political power in Austria, would see their own pet abuses threatened and cabal against him to his ruin. And Metternich loved his glory as "dictator of the foreign offices of Europe." Therefore he closed his eyes to many ugly things at home. After 1848 he once met Guizot, like him then a fallen minister in exile. "I have often governed Europe," shrewdly averred Metternich during their conversation, "but I have never governed *Austria.*"

Under such conditions the steadfast policy of the Hapsburg government was one of consistent repression. Nowhere in Christendom except Russia was there a stiffer censorship applied not merely to newspapers, but to all pamphlets and books. Every customs officer searched travelers' baggage zealously for forbidden foreign books—including the histories of Thierry, Hallam, Sismondi, and even certain disturbing medical works. Police spies infested every university professor's lecture hall to pounce upon unfortunate remarks; and librarians had to report the books borrowed by teachers to see if they were studying revolutionary doctrines. Every kind of club or association, even for the most harmless purposes, was under taboo; and Austrian subjects were permitted to quit the empire only with a passport, usually hard to obtain.

All this was going on while the Austrian nobles were given a practical monopoly of all high offices, while they were retaining seigneurial powers of police, jurisdiction, and general regulation over the peasants, while the latter were subjected to about as many imposts, corvées, and other hardships as were the peasants of pre-Revolutionary France. The civil administration was in hands of scribbling formalists, who, grimly tenacious of their salaries and prerogatives, deliberated in endless committees and councils and rarely did anything. Every measure was judged strictly from the standpoint of dynastic interest. "They call him a patriot for Austria," cried Francis I, of a person commended for promotion, "but is he also *a patriot for me?*"

Russia in 1815

Behind the blundering autocracy of Austria and the more efficient autocracy of Prussia, loomed the enormous mass of the Empire of the Czars. It had long since extended to the confines of China and the Pacific Ocean. Indeed, up to 1867, the Autocrat of All the Russias gave the law also to Alaska, in North America. In Europe and Asia, Alexander I ruled over some 8,660,000 square miles, about one-sixth of the entire land area of the planet. The measureless Siberian wilds were, of course, very thinly inhabited, but in the 2,000,000 square miles of the empire in or near Europe there were now some 50,000,000 persons, of whom the majority were of the Slavic "Great Russian" nationality.

This, the largest country in Europe, was also the most isolated. The history of Russia was profoundly affected by the fact that she had no free sea-doors. Archangel, on the White Sea, was frozen for over half of the year, and Riga and St. Petersburg on the Baltic were closed an average of 127 and 147 days per year respectively. Odessa, on the Black Sea, could be sealed at the behest of the Turks. The road system across the empire was correspondingly bad. There were times when St. Petersburg (located too far north and east to make a convenient capital) was unable to communicate with the rest of the empire. Couriers could not force their way through the spring freshets that covered the roads toward the heart of the empire.

Russia was often called *an Asiatic country with an Europeon façade.* Napoleon had said, in disgust, "Scratch a Russian and you find a Tartar." This was hardly just. The Great Russians, Little Russians, White Russians, were undeniably members of the Indo-European race. But apart from the survival in the empire of great fragments of Mongol-Turanian peoples —Lapps, Finns, Permyaks, and Ugrians in the north; Tartars of many stripes and tribes; Bushkins, Chuvashes, Mescheryaks, Khirgiz, and many others toward the south—the whole country had been brutalized by the two and a half centuries of Tartar dominion (1238 to about 1480), when the land paid tribute to the barbarous Grand Khan.

A hundred years before the settlement of Vienna, Peter the Great had, indeed, given Russia the government and organization of a Western despotism, with the royalty of Louis XIV as the present example of a perfect ruler and a perfect kingdom. Peter had been able to desert uncouth Moscow for a new "Westernized" capital upon the Neva, to force his boyars to wear French clothes and to allow their women to coquette and intrigue like French countesses instead of being mewed up in the *Terem,* to introduce among the Russian upper classes Western gallantries, luxuries, and vices; in fact he set the aristocracy of the empire in a fair way to becoming superficially Europeanized.

Between the wealthy *barins*—who officered the imperial regiments, danced at the glittering fetes at the Winter Palace, dabbled harmlessly in Voltairean infidelity, and pretended at least to keep in touch with the currents of Western thought—and the toiling "Black People," whose many millions lived in the little *izbas*, the squalid wooden houses in the innumerable villages, who groveled to their smoky ikons, and among whom literacy was a rare accomplishment, there was fixed a gulf infinitely wider than that between the silken monseigneurs and the horny-handed *routuriers* of France. In 1815 the world witnessed the extraordinary spectacle of an emperor completely Westernized, the avowed disciple of doctrines current in the most liberal circles of France and Switzerland, highly educated, and terrifying Metternich by his progressive ideas, yet who was simultaneously the actual despot over fifty million peasants, to whom he was the resistless *Gosudar*, vice-regent of the Almighty. Yet such were Alexander I and his Russia. He could make law by arbitrary fiat. The large majority of his subjects were serfs, and his father, the tactless yet sometimes brutally truthful Paul I, had said to a foreign ambassador, "Know, sir, that the only man of distinction in Russia is he whom I address, and *then* only while I am speaking to him!"

The history of Russia in the nineteenth century is in one sense the history of the struggle of her best spirits to cast off the shadow of Asia and to make Russia genuinely as well as superficially a European land. The story is one of a sustained tragedy, to be crowned by the intense miseries of the upheaval of 1917-18.

Alexander I emerged victorious over Napoleon but at a heavy price. For seventeen years his empire had not had a month of unbroken peace. The central and southern provinces had been sorely ravaged. The vast forces needed in 1812-14 had strained the national resources. A depreciated paper money crippled commerce and rendered the great horde of officials discontented because their salaries were paid in the discounted bills. The army, when peace came, seemed unnecessarily large, yet it was dangerous to disband it. The diplomatic situation was still strained, and to set loose hundreds of thousands of masterless men would have filled the country with brigandage. Considering the size of the country, the mercantile, professional, and burgher classes were dangerously small. Less than five per cent of the people dwelt in towns. St. Petersburg had only about 300,000 and Moscow 240,000 inhabitants. Between the serfs and their masters there were almost no intelligent, self-respecting intermediaries. Commerce and industry were on a primitive scale.

Two forces which should have lifted the condition of the empire seemed helpless except to obstruct natural progress. The Greek Orthodox Church, denying as it did both the possibility of altering the usages of Christianity either by papal decisions or by new personal interpretations of the Bible, held the majority of the Russians rigidly to a religion that claimed to be unchanged since the great Councils of the "Fathers" in the fourth century. Orthodoxy purported to be a complete revelation of the will of God, without the need of the slightest modification to meet new conditions. Ordinarily, its leaders opposed any political change as likely also to force religious changes. There was no central pope, and even the Patriarchate of Moscow had been suppressed; instead the czars exercised pretty complete authority over the church through the Holy Synod— practically a ministry of religion. "Cæsaro-Papism," the critics called it.

The village priests ("popes" = "fathers") were married and in close touch with their flocks, but they were charged with dense ignorance and with often catering to the peasants' crass superstitions. The bishops and their superiors, the metropolitans, were drawn from the monastic un- married clergy, which young men of family sometimes entered as the direct path to high ecclesiastical preferment. The ruling classes, tinctured with the fashionable Western infidelity, had lost belief in traditional Christianity but gladly used the church as a desirable mechanism for holding down the masses. For such a purpose, the more conservative the church, the better.

The other force for uplift ought to have been the romantic-minded Czar. But Alexander I, even if he had been a far more resolute and in- dependent character, would still have been the slave of his own isolation. At every turn his intentions were paralyzed by the passive resistance of the landed nobility. This class officered the army and supplied all the upper ranks of the *techniovniks,* the members of the great hierarchy of civil officials, whose lowest members were insignificant post-carriers and whose highest were the imperial ministers and the chancellor. Alexander I knew that the imperial ministries were so miserably organized and so poorly coördinated that even very competent high officials found their hands tied. He knew that tens of millions of serfs might become dan- gerously uneasy as the new ideas of freedom were slowly drifting east- ward even to the steppes by the Volga. All this he knew, lamented, and found himself too hampered by intrigue and circumstance to remedy.

Alexander remembered the evil fate of his father, Paul, and of his grandfather, Peter. Both had been murdered, not because they had been blundering tyrants, but because they had seemed to threaten the privi- leges of the bureaucracy. So the Czar, who in his youth had praised republican theories, who had dabbled with the idea of a constitution for Russia, and who had actually granted a constitution to Poland, in a half melancholia let himself swing back to extreme reaction and presently took as gospel all that Metternich told him. The Czar's subordinates, meanwhile, were devising censorships, knoutings, and exilings to Siberia, in the passionate desire to defend Russia against the march of time.

Alexander's Minister of Education formally denied the need for edu- cating the lower classes and affirmed that "instruction was harmful to people born to obey." Under such patronage, the curriculum of the University of Kazan was, for example, reorganized on the principles of the Holy Alliance, and the Copernican System was proscribed as "contrary to the Scripture." All professors suspected of irreligion were dismissed, and no Russian who had studied in a foreign university was appointed to the teaching staff.

Unfortunately for the repose of the empire, however, revolutionary ideas had been penetrating by another way. During the occupation of French territory, numerous young Russian officers had come in contact with influences that completely unsteadied them. They were often courted by members of the old Jacobin party, blessed now with abundant leisure, who filled them with doctrines from Rousseau and his successors. These doctrines naturally went like new wine to the heads of ardent youths, reared under a despotism, ignorant of practical politics, and prone to vague longings for the good of humanity. Many of them were of great boyar families, and they held high positions in the guard regiments at St. Petersburg, as well as in some of the southern armies. Their total number was very small, but thanks to their exalted position this influence might well have been sufficient to convulse Russia. By 1820 these young noblemen were engaged in all the excitement of organizing, at first secret societies, and then actual conspiracies for overthrowing the czardom and (for the more violent members at least) the setting-up not of a limited monarchy but of a democratic republic. Later, in 1825, the sudden death of Alexander created a situation that played directly into their hands.

Alexander had left no son. His heir, properly, would have been his oldest brother Constantine, but the latter, an unsteady and incapable man, had married a Polish noblewoman below royal rank. He therefore executed a renunciation of his rights in favor of his next brother, the far more capable Nicholas. Alexander knew and approved this, but Nicholas detested the idea of quitting the simple round of military duties in which he delighted and accepting the awful burdens of despotism. He strove desperately, therefore, to avoid having greatness thrust upon him.

The December Revolt (1825)

Alexander died in the Crimea on December 1, 1825. By frantic driving over the bad winter roads, a courier with the news reached Constantine on December 7 at Warsaw, where he was Viceroy of Poland, and it was the 9th before another messenger galloped to St. Petersburg. Instantly, Nicholas called the great officials and generals together and insisted upon their taking oath to Constantine as Czar. The various regiments were, accordingly, sworn to Constantine. Meantime, that self-abnegating prince had proclaimed Nicholas at Warsaw, but it was only on the 24th that Michael, Constantine's youngest brother, arrived in St. Petersburg from

Poland with confirmation of the fact that the Viceroy had abdicated his rights and that Nicholas was, beyond peradventure, emperor.

This delay in communications across the vast empire came near precipitating a revolution. The high-born conspirators in St. Petersburg saw their chance. The ignorant soldiers had just sworn fidelity to Constantine. Now they were being told to take a new oath to his younger brother, and the men were honestly perplexed and ready to believe that there was treason in the palace. Their noble officers cared little enough for Constantine, but he formed a convenient stalking horse. The privates of several regiments were told that Constantine was still the true Czar, and that he and his brother Michael were then in fetters in the palace. The hope of the plotters was that Nicholas, deserted and overwhelmed, would abdicate; then the Senate (council of great officials) would convene a National Assembly to make a constitution. Meantime, a Provisional Government would take charge of the empire.

Of all the many crimes committed in the name of liberty, this was among the most futile. What followed was a hideous tragedy, relieved by a few gleams of comedy.

On the morning of December 26, various St. Petersburg battalions began shouting, at the behest of their officers, "*Long live Constantine and the Constitution!*" and started for the palace. They cheered for "Constitution" gladly—the soldiers believing her to be Constantine's wife! If the insurgent leaders had kept their nerve they might then have rushed the palace and captured the Czar, for the guards on hand were too few and were not wholly reliable. But the rebels simply stood in the square before the palace and cheered for Constantine. Nicholas faced all danger coolly, announcing, "If I am to be Czar for an hour only, I will be so with dignity."

Loyal troops at length were mustered, and loyal officers remonstrated with the insurgents in the square. The instigators of the plot, convinced too late that the uprising was bound to fail, left their men in the lurch and fled. At last, after a general had been shot down by the mutineers and they still stood fast before the palace in the biting cold, Nicholas ordered their ranks to be plowed through with artillery. After a few salvos, all was over, and the "December Revolution" was at an end. It only remained to bury the dead and to hunt down the living.

This December conspiracy, famous in Russian annals, was an enormous misfortune for Slavic liberalism. The plotters had been young men of the noblest families, normally accounted the bulwarks of the czardom. To their kindred and to the government, it seemed as if they had been the victims of diabolic Western propaganda. The insanity of their attempt, which, if it could have momentarily succeeded, would only have plunged the millions of peasants into ruinous anarchy, seemed patent proof of the futility of all revolutionary doctrines. For generations, this conspiracy was to be used as evidence that Russians could not be trusted to play with free institutions. Worse still was the direct effect upon the Czar. A born believer in autocracy and never a theoretical liberal like Alexander, this uprising in which Nicholas' own life and those of his family were in extreme jeopardy and in which one of his favorite generals was shot before his eyes, confirmed him in an intense aversion to "Westernism" and to all its unsettling theories. For his entire reign (1825 to 1855), Nicholas I fought against liberalism within Russia and outside of Russia, with every means in his power.

Nicholas I's Iron Despotism: The Revolt of Poland (1830-31)

Nicholas I was no vulgar autocrat. Endowed with a magnificent height and physique, he *looked* the perfect emperor. He was a cold, reserved man, incapable of winning popularity or dropping the manners of a commanding general. But he had many noble qualities, hated flattery, was incapable of personal falsehood, loved devotedly his wife, Charlotte of Prussia, and had an intense passion for work and an exalted sense of duty. He was, in short, "the finished type of an old-world despot, the incarnation of a ceaseless struggle against thought and progress." Very illustrative was what he once told a petitioner craving his mercy: "We all expect mercy from God; but from me, the ruler of the land, my subjects must look only for justice." Such a monarch was, of course, soon destined to earn the passionate detestation of all Western liberals, especially in France and Britain, a fact which ultimately reacted upon the peace of Europe.

Under this Czar, there could be in Russia no real political history, only a succession of police repressions. Five years after the December uprising a second event strengthened Nicholas' hatred of liberalism. Poland revolted against Russian suzerainty. Alexander had given to the Russian fraction of old Poland a constitution liberal enough to permit political agitation and to encourage dreams of a completely restored Polish nationality, but not liberal enough to allow the Poles really to run their own affairs without constant friction with the Russian viceroy. Already by 1825, Alexander and the Polish Diet were at loggerheads, the Czar forbidding the Diet to publish its debates and confining the leader of the opposition to his estates. Nicholas thus inherited a situation which was fast becoming impossible. The Catholic Poles hated the Orthodox Russians as belonging to a distinctly inferior civilization. The Russian agents of the Czar at Warsaw, on their part, rode roughshod over Polish susceptibilities and talked of revoking the Constitution of 1815. "It is no longer a question," announced one high officer, "of discussion, but of obedience."

In 1830 the news of the fall of the Bourbons in France excited the

Polish nationalists, already getting beyond the control of their more moderate countrymen. It was vainly imagined that the new French ruler, Louis Philippe, would give them military aid, that the Russian troops would be chased out of Warsaw by a popular uprising, while the Polish Diet set up a provisional government and endeavored to make headway against the war power of Russia. The attempt was a gallant one in behalf of a brilliant and highly gifted people; but only a part of the Polish nation threw itself heart and soul into the struggle. The peasants had been freed from serfdom in 1807, but they were still land-less day-laborers and cared little for that liberty demanded by their noble landlords. A moderate party among the Poles vainly endeavored to get Nicholas to agree to some compromise and order the Russian army to evacuate the country. The Czar grimly demanded submission or death. He refused to receive the Polish envoys and merely sent the solemn warning: "The first cannon shot will be Poland's ruin."

Under these circumstances, the control at Warsaw soon fell to ex-tremists, who committed the great blunder of declaring that the House of Romanoff had forfeited the Polish throne. This gave to all reactionary diplomats a decent excuse for saying the Poles were violating the Treaties of Vienna, and that nothing could be done to help them. There was noisy sympathy for the patriots in London and Paris, but no desire to risk a war with the Czar. Belgium had, indeed, cut loose from Holland, in defiance of the Vienna agreement, but Holland was a weak power; Russia was very different. The Poles, therefore, were completely over-whelmed. In September, 1831, Warsaw surrendered. *"Order reigns in Warsaw,"* ran the laconic Russian dispatch to the governments of Europe.

Soon all the jails in Poland were gorged with prisoners and thousands more were plodding wearily toward Siberia. The Constitution of 1815 was suppressed. All power in Poland was entrusted to Russian officers, and for years the Poles were subjected to a military reign of terror, beside which Metternich's police censorships in Vienna seemed mild. And so again the Polish question was reported settled. "Poland (ran the Czar's ukase of 1832) shall henceforth be a part of the empire and form one nation with Russia."

Italy (1815-30)

In 1815 Italy had sunk back into the power of the dynasts assigned her by the Congress of Vienna. Nevertheless, things were not as in 1796, when the French columns had swung over the mountains. They had spread the seeds of Italian unity. A large section of the Northeast, includ-ing Lombardy, Venetia, and Umbria, had been set off as the kingdom of Italy; and in 1805 Napoleon had crowned himself in the cathedral of Milan with the famous old "Iron Crown" of Lombardy, uttering the tra-ditional formula "God gave it to me; let him beware who touches it!" In

Milan afterward, his stepson, the gifted Eugene Beauharnais, had ruled
as viceroy, proving himself not unpopular, even if once he announced to
a protesting delegation from the puppet legislature of the new kingdom,
"Your system of government is simple; the Emperor wills it to be thus."
In Naples had reigned that dashing cavalry officer, Murat, as Joachim I.
All this system, of course, vanished in the welter of 1813-15. But when
the old dynasts came back, not all of the abuses returned with them, and
all the unsettling ideas could not be quite exterminated.

Under French rule, the Italians had received *social* gains—the freedom
of all classes before the law, religious liberty, freedom in the tenure of
property and from guild restrictions in industry. The *Code Napoléon*
had brought with it a highly improved system of justice. Along with this
had come better roads, many municipal improvements, and better financial systems. Napoleon had been disliked for his remorseless conscription,
sweeping off Italian youths to fight French battles in Prussia, Spain,
Austria, and Russia; for his great financial exactions; and for his continental blockade of Britain which nearly ruined Italian commerce. Yet
his rule was not, on the whole, very unpopular. He was himself more an
Italian than a Frenchman, and he knew how to catch the Latin imagination. No such spasm of hatred for the alien swept over Italy as swept
over Germany between 1806 and 1812; and if left to themselves, the
Italians would hardly have revolted against the colossal empire that
seemed ready to absorb them.

So the French departed, and a people whose sense of nationality had
almost been crushed by Hapsburg and Bourbon oppression began to
see visions and to turn in its sleep. Once there had been a Kingdom of
Italy, an Italian flag, and an appeal, albeit somewhat perverted, to those
things which give men pride in native land. Then the French vanished;
and in place of the generals of the Corsican came the archduke from
Vienna. The peninsula cursed the change.

The various kings and princes whom Austrian bayonets had restored
in 1814-15 had only rarely learned wisdom in exile. In Piedmont all
French institutions and laws were deliberately abolished. The old caste
distinctions, and even the barbarous penalties of quartering and breaking
on the wheel, were legally restored. Suits long since settled in the French
courts were reopened—to the alarm of all men of property. The Queen
ordered that only the nobility should obtain admission to the Turin opera
house, and seats were assigned to the favored class in order of length of
pedigrees. Zealous officials threw all the new French furniture out of the
palace; the royal gardener rooted up all French plants in the botanical
gardens. It was even proposed to demolish a fine bridge over the Po because Napoleon had built it. More serious was the order that veteran
officers who had served under Napoleon could only serve now in the
lower ranks under royalist officers who had been skulking for years in the

refuge of Sardinia, and also that education should be placed absolutely in the hands of the Jesuits.

Things were not much different in the North Italian duchies. In Parma, Marie Louise (wife of Napoleon) indeed preserved many French institutions, and her small country was tolerably well governed, but the ex-empress took her ministers for her lovers and lived an abominably dissolute life. In Modena, Francis IV (son of an Austrian arch-duke) detested all liberal institutions to the point of monomania. He restored the defunct law code of 1771 and the use of judicial torture. One of the refinements of this very genuine tyrant was to administer drugs to his victims—then their ravings in delirium could serve as testimony against them. Fortunately, the larger Grand Duchy of Tuscany was under the mild and popular Ferdinand III. Sure of the loyalty of his people, this prince was able to tell the Austrians that he did not need their assistance and to maintain a very tolerable if an entirely nonliberal administration. He even admitted exiles banished from other parts of Italy. Political life in Florence, the old home of republicanism, at this time hardly existed. As Tabarrini affirmed, Tuscany was then "a country without passions or ambitions, with mild manners and an inborn sense of the beautiful."

Far less fortunate was the great diagonal of the Papal States, cutting across Italy. When Pius VII came back from exile, his zealous cardinals undertook to cancel every vestige of "French infidelity." The Congregation of the Index ordered the suppression of practically *all* political writings as a blanket precaution. All convents, mostly discouraged by the French, were reëstablished. Cardinal Pacca carried his zeal in Rome to the point of abolishing the "French institutions" of vaccination and street-lights. Simultaneously, a great increase was noticed in beggary, in robbery, and also in common murders.

The general backwardness of the Bourbon kingdom of Naples and Sicily has already been explained, as has been the evil fate of the revolution precipitated in 1820. Naples had probably been the scene of this particular uprising because there were large elements in the army who regretted the old Muratist regime, and because this southern kingdom was comparatively remote from the overshadowing power of Austria. But almost simultaneously there was a similar uprising in Piedmont. Here there was real recognition among certain chiefs of the army of the rising spirit of Italian nationalism, and in 1821 the garrison of the great fortress of Alessandria mutinied and hoisted the red, white, and green flag already recognized as the *Italian* tricolor. Count Santa Rosa took the lead in a movement "to deliver the king and the country from the Austrians," but with also a clear intention of reëstablishing the Kingdom of Italy.

The insurgents counted confidently on the assistance of Charles Albert, heir-presumptive to the throne. But Charles Albert, although he is said to have known in advance of the plot and to have sympathized with the schemes of the Carbonari, proved an uncertain reed. In the tumult, King Victor Emmanuel lost his nerve and abdicated in favor of his absent brother, Charles Felix, and Charles Albert, acting as regent, proclaimed a constitution. Instantly there was stern action in absolutist Europe. Czar Alexander ordered 100,000 men to make ready, and an Austrian corps promptly advanced from Milan. The liberals made one futile stand at Novara, and then scattered in rout. The new king disavowed the constitution; and Charles Albert, in terror lest his rights to the throne be canceled, hastily went over to the reactionaries. The only result of the movement seemed, therefore, to be a new story of exilings and executions.

Nevertheless, it was becoming clear as the nineteenth century advanced, that Piedmont was not, as was the rest of Italy, hopelessly under the heel of Austria. As early as 1814 her sagacious ambassador to the Czar, Joseph le Maistre, had written: "Sardinia [Piedmont] has no higher interest—and the interest of all Italy is the same—than that Austria should not possess one hand's breadth of land in the peninsula. *The king must make himself the head of the Italians.* He must call revolutionists to all civil and military posts in the capital itself." This was impossible doctrine for the autocratic and unoriginal Victor Emmanuel (1814-21). It was also almost equally wasted after 1821 upon Charles Felix, who was a determined despot, kindly and even generous when no question of his authority was involved, but inflexible when it was. Under him there was a general tightening of all the wretched old restrictions. For example, students at the University of Turin were compelled to observe the church fasts under official supervision, and were obliged annually to present a document showing that they had confessed and partaken of the sacrament.

In fact, in 1825 the state of Piedmont was so promising that Metternich made a personal visit to Genoa and was delighted with the result. "The King," he wrote, "is perfect, and the Prince of Carignano [Charles Albert] conducted himself very well. He uttered frankly his *pater peccavi,* and seemed firmly resolved never more to be made an instrument [of the liberals]." The Prince went so far as to promise the Austrians that he would never, after reaching the throne, grant to his people a constitution.

In 1831 when Charles Felix died, Charles Albert ruled in his stead, for some years conservative and repressive enough for even Metternich. Yet little by little Piedmont was disentangling herself from Austria. Her royal house of Savoy, if its dominions were modest, was among the oldest and most respectable dynasties of Europe; Hapsburgs, Bourbons, Hohenzollerns, and Romanoffs had hardly as lengthy pedigrees. The close proximity of Piedmont to France, furthermore, made it impossible for the latter to tolerate the idea of this country being occupied by Austria. Finally, the nationalist and liberal ideals gradually forced their way into the heart of the new king.

Charles Albert (1831-49) was a sad bundle of contradictions. Certain it is that he was terribly aware of the dangers of the situation and prone to hesitate and imagine evil whichever way he turned. "I am between the chocolate cup of the Jesuits and the stilettos of the Carbonari!" he once told a foreign visitor. But ever more clearly, he came to realize that upon him, and upon his Piedmont, the intelligent hopes of Italian nationalism were becoming concentrated. In Piedmont was perhaps the fulcrum for throwing over the crushing mass of Austrian despotism.

East of the Rhine, then, it is evident that the situation differed fundamentally from that in France and England. This was due in part to the absence of the Industrial Revolution with its attendant class of energetic entrepreneurs and capitalists. But that is not the only explanation. There had never been an Italy or a Germany in the sense that there had been a France and an England. In the former lands nationalism practically had to commence *de novo;* in the latter it was already firmly established. Furthermore, the peculiar situation of all-powerful Austria, now both a German state and an Italian one, made it impossible for Germany or for Italy to strike out on their own national careers without first eliminating the ogre (Austria) whose interests were so opposed to their nationalistic agitation. There had been, of course, a historic Russia; but that country really was so huge, so moribund, so Asiatic in tradition, that it was almost inevitable that the new liberal creed should fail of acceptance there.

Thus closed the first fifteen years after Waterloo. Reaction marked their advent, and revolution their close. War-weariness, sheer inertia, and romantic yearnings for a highly imaginative past made reaction the order of the day. In France and in England, however, where the enlightened bourgeoisie were numerous, reaction began soon to recede. In 1830 in the former country, and two years later in the latter, successful revolutions brought it to an end. In those countries men began to talk about progress once more, and soon the onrush of the Industrial Revolution found reflection in triumphant liberalism. Men also talked of progress once more in Spain, Germany, Austria, and Russia—progress in terms of liberalism and nationalism. But it all ended in talk. The Russian Decembrists proved too feeble and too doctrinaire to divert the tide of autocracy in their country. The German and Italian nationalists were too few and too divided in 1830 to make much more than a dent in the Metternich system. The dead weight of traditional authority proved too heavy for them.

Chapter 5

LOUIS PHILIPPE AND THE REVOLUTION OF 1848 IN FRANCE

IN 1830 THE EXIT of Charles X left his unloved kinsman Louis Philippe (1830-48) master of the Tuileries. In place of the Bourbons, who strove to bring back the good old days before the meeting of the States-General, there was now a "Citizen King," who talked in terms of liberalism; who called himself *"King of the French, by the grace of God and of the nation";* who supplanted the Bourbon white flag of the golden lilies with the beloved Tricolor of the Revolution; and who sent Metternich and all of his kind into spasms of fear lest France set another hideous example of a great nation ruled by democratic institutions. These fears were needless. Louis Philippe was indeed a constitutional monarch, but he had no idea of hastening history, and the liberalism which he sponsored was rather lukewarm.

In 1830 Louis Philippe was fifty-seven years old. He was the son of that Duc d'Orléans, "Philippe-Egalité," the cousin of Louis XVI, who had, as a member of the Convention, voted for the execution of the King, and then had lost his own head under the guillotine in 1793. Louis Philippe had fought for Republican France at Valmy, but presently, to escape from the guillotine, had had to flee abroad and lead a life of poverty-stricken exile. In Switzerland he had been a mathematics instructor on a salary of only 1,400 francs ($280) per year. Between 1796 and 1800 he wandered in America, traveling in the Great Lakes region and Mississippi Valley and sojourning long in Philadelphia. Then he returned to England, where the British government gave him a pension, and he lived very quietly, until in 1814 the fall of Napoleon sent him back to France.

No love had been lost between this Duke of Orleans and his Bourbon cousins. Louis Philippe was under constant suspicion with the old dynasts because of his flirting with the Liberals, and because his residence, the famous Palais Royal, was the rendezvous of those middle-class professors, bankers, manufacturers, and merchants who so quickly came to their own when the Paris multitudes chased out Charles X in the bloody

77

"July days." Now a few adroit moves, a few fine gestures toward the Republicans, such as that of publicly embracing the aged Lafayette at the Hotel de Ville, made this prince seem, for the time being, the *one* possible candidate around which all the anti-Bourbon factions could rally.

If democratic manners made a democratic ruler, Louis Philippe was an ultra-liberal. He cared nothing for the trappings of majesty. The royal lilies were erased from the panels of his carriages. He gave frequent receptions at which almost any respectable citizen was welcome to enter and not kiss hands, but *shake* hands with the head of the state. He often could be seen strolling along the sidewalks of Paris, carrying a common umbrella like any thrifty *bourgeois*. His queen seemed a perfect middle-class housewife, so very economical that it was well known that she had her dresses carefully made over to avoid buying new ones. But as soon as his position became fairly secure this citizen-king made it manifest enough that he, like his cousins, "possessed all the Bourbon tenaciousness of personal power." As his minister, Casimir-Perier, announced in 1831, *"France has desired that the monarchy should become national; it does not desire that it should be powerless."* In actual fact, the Revolution of 1830 transferred the essential control of France from the higher aristocracy and the clericals to the commercial capitalist classes, the bourgeoisie, especially to the wealthier bourgeoisie. After the aristocrats were to come the plutocrats. Charles X was the champion of the first, Louis Philippe of the second.

The Triumph of "Order" and Bourgeois Plutocracy

This transfer of power was assisted by the continuing indifference of the millions of French peasants to government changes, so long as the Paris ministers could give them order and economic stability. Very similar to the story of the St. Petersburg mutineers in 1825 is that of the Cevennes peasant woman who, in the eighteen-thirties, asked her neighbor, "What is this *Charter* people are talking about?" "Why," came the answer, "she is the wife of Louis Philippe." Even down to 1848, when violent change was in the air in Paris, the great masses of farmers remained "closely attached to the land and to their patient, humble toil, frugal and orderly, and uninterested in the Government, which, on its side, never dreamed of asking their opinions" (Emile Bourgeois). "Order," likewise, was the first demand of all the commercial-financial element, which was now becoming a great power in France. The fear lest Charles X and Polignac were about to indulge in unsettling economic innovations had been one of the prime causes of their overthrow. "*Order,*" cried a Parisian journal, soon after the Orleanist regime came in, "is the present pressing need of France. Credit is shaken; commerce is dying. *Order* can restore us to

Louis Philippe, King of the French (1773-1850)

security." Upon obtaining it, peasantry and bourgeoisie were alike determined.

With such a demand by the elements to whom he owed so much, Louis
Philippe easily put through a conservative alteration of that Charter
which he was pledged to make a reality. He desired to govern in conjunction with a Chamber of Deputies, but it must be chosen by "a limited
and enlightened body." Universal suffrage was whistled down in the new
royal circles as something even more disastrous than autocracy. By a
law of 1831, the method of voting was simplified. The qualifications for
being chosen a deputy were reduced from the payment of 1,000 to 500
francs in direct imposts and for that of being an elector (voter) from
300 to 200 francs in such taxes. Vainly was it proposed to allow the

franchise to all magistrates, university professors, and lawyers, while members of the Institute and retired field officers were only admitted within the gilded circle with great hesitancy. France had now some 240,000 electors, more than twice as many as under the Bourbons. They were proudly called the *pays légal,* the lawful country.

The franchise soon became for prosperous folk a business asset. Rich men would assign part of their property to sons or nephews in order to enable them to become electors and thereby also to be candidates for the inferior local offices. Especially, they could now become officers in the reconstituted National Guard, whose leaders were caressed and favored by the government in every possible way. This revised National Guard was, indeed, the bulwark of the Orleanist regime, having been established "to defend the Constitutional Royalty and the Charter, maintain obedience to the laws and to preserve or reestablish order and the public peace." Its officers were electors and often were men of real wealth and consequence. Its privates were less prosperous folk, but not of the lowest classes. They had to buy their own uniforms and were taught to despise the proletariat.

The 24,000 guards in Paris were the ready instruments of Louis Philippe in suppressing Republican uprisings, and could be used without awakening the same unpopularity as might come from ordering the regular troops to fire on citizens. In disgust at the turn events were now taking, the Republicans precipitated insurrections in Paris in 1832 and in Lyons in 1834; but, unsupported by either the bourgeois or the peasants, these uprisings had no chance. Presently, Guizot, a royal minister, could boast in the Chamber, "The riots are dead, the clubs are dead, revolutionary propaganda is dead."

The triumph of the middle classes seemed, indeed, complete. The noble Legitimists and the clericals groaned and intrigued in vain. The new election law had merged the interests of the landed aristocracy with those of the men of commerce, the upper tradesmen, and the manufacturers. The government had to afford to these good folk, its protectors and its patrons, every opportunity; and, as was soon angrily complained, "the bourgeois spread themselves out in France as in a conquered country." The drive for public office became irresistible, and in 1831 there were reported to have been forty thousand place-hunters in Paris alone. The old nobility usually regretted the Bourbons; the peasants were "more concerned with potatoes than politics"; but the Orleanist monarchy became the darling of the stock-jobbers, speculators, and promoters, to whom such enterprises as the new railroads presently opened a golden vista.

The Material Prosperity and Sordid Character of the July Monarchy

Undeniably, the age of Louis Philippe was the age of the Industrial Revolution in France. Railway construction began and train service was inaugurated between Paris and St. Germain. Louis Philippe wished to ride on the first train, but public opinion forbade, so strong was the belief that the passengers would be poisoned by noxious gases in going through the tunnels, or would be killed by the locomotive exploding. The Queen, however, braved public opinion and made the trip. Within a few years other railways were constructed, north to Rouen, south to Lyons. Within twenty years the consumption of coal grew from eleven to forty million hundredweight. Roubaix and Lille expanded from sleepy little towns into large, smoky cities. Paris itself increased by three hundred thousand inhabitants between 1831 and 1846. Ten years later the treasury reported a surplus of eighty million francs, despite military adventures in Algeria and an expensive new educational system. The savings-bank deposits increased steadily. The five per cent government bonds were at a premium. Great sums were set aside for permanent and very desirable public works—harbors, bridges, canals, and roads. "Modern France, the France of the nineteenth century, was growing into shape." As early as 1834 a notable industrial exposition was held in Paris, constituting a truly splendid display of those fine wares which were the glory of the French factories. The manager of the enterprise publicly thanked the King when he came to inspect the exhibitions because he, "in preserving peace with honor, had done more for France than by winning battles."

Peace and industry were in short the whole policy of Louis Philippe. The King was convinced that any policy of adventure would produce his own overthrow. His accession had been greeted with frowns and half-uttered threats by all the Legitimist courts of Europe. The King realized this better than did many of his ministers. Britain was still the jealous hereditary enemy, and there was still danger of France becoming isolated and having to fight all Europe. Louis Philippe, indeed, supported the cause of Belgian independence because it was safe to do this, but he resolutely headed off the desire of many Frenchmen to aid the Poles when they struggled for freedom against the crushing might of Nicholas (see p. 72). The King thus kept safely away from the perils and problems of foreign wars, at the same time omitting nothing to make himself a friend of those powerful wealthy classes to whom peace meant mainly the better chance for gainful exploitation.

Uneventful Years: The Advent of Socialism

Under such a regime there were for many years few exciting incidents. After 1835 the republican agitation flattened out. Its leaders were apparently dead, exiled, or in prison. Press laws punished not only attacks upon the King but also those upon the principle of private property. There was, indeed, a schism taking place between the extreme radical factions in Paris. Part of the would-be Revolutionists, led by Cavaignac, the hero of 1830, wished only for a *political* overturn, universal suffrage, the deposition of all kings, and like democratic changes. Another element, splitting away from these Republicans, began to assert that there was no real hope for the toiling masses until a *social* revolution had altered all the bases of ownership and industry. Socialism, now raising its head, was nothing new in France. Its history there went back to the French Revolution and to Gracchus Babeuf, who was guillotined in 1797. Babeuf, whose life was snuffed out in the reaction which followed the Terror, had organized a society which had placarded Paris with a manifesto proclaiming that all must work, that all had an equal right to the good things of this earth, that the Revolution was not over. At his trial he had asserted that "every person must admit that political equality is only a tantalizing illusion," an idea too radical for Jacobins to stomach, let alone the bourgeois Directory.

The idea, however, did not die. It was picked up by other socialists in the post-Napoleonic era and was widely spread in the days of the July Monarchy. Three Frenchmen, in particular, elaborated upon it—Saint-Simon, Fourier, and Blanc.

Henri Saint-Simon was an aristocrat of the Old Regime who had fought with Lafayette for America. Returning to France, he espoused the Revolutionary cause, was imprisoned and saved from death by the execution of Robespierre. Saint-Simon was a philosopher, a savant, a deeply religious person, and a romantic. He believed that society should be revolutionized, but not by a democratic revolution. The inheritance of economic goods should be abolished, and every one should work: but the formula for division should be, "from each according to his capacity, to each according to his deserts." Christianity and socialism, Saint-Simon thought, went hand in hand. He believed in both an autocratic government and an established church; but he had little use for politics or for any recognized form of either Protestantism or Catholicism. His last and best-known book, *The New Christianity* (1825), was an appeal to the rulers of Europe. "Unite," it said, "in the name of Christianity and learn to accomplish the duties which Christianity imposes on the powerful; remember that Christianity commands them to devote their energies to bettering as rapidly as possible the lot of the very poor."

Needless to say, the rulers of Europe paid scant attention to this manifesto. This was not the case, however, with many cultured Frenchmen. The followers of Saint-Simon, numerous, devoted, and romantic-minded, banded themselves into a society to bring about the acceptance of his ideas. For the most part these disciples were from the upper classes— engineers, artists, men of letters. They were responsible for initiating work on the Suez Canal; they dreamed mighty dreams of social regeneration; and they brought intense ridicule upon themselves by the quaintness of their behavior in respect both to manners and to morals.

A different kind of socialist was Charles Fourier, a romantic scientist and mathematician. Fourier came from the middle class. As a boy he had been reproved by his father for telling the truth about certain goods in the paternal shop. As a youth, at a time of great suffering, he had seen rice dumped from a ship into the harbor of Marseilles in order to keep the price of that grain high. Facts like these led him to disbelieve in economic competition, which he hoped to abolish through the agency of voluntary coöperative organizations in which people would pool their capital for the common good. Those who joined these voluntary groups were to live together in communal buildings and were to engage in both agriculture and manufacturing. Although Fourier was known as a socialist and called himself one, it must be remembered that he had no idea of abolishing private property. Production was to be carried on in common but distribution was to be made in accordance with a mathematical formula. To capital was assigned four-twelfths of the net proceeds, to management three-twelfths and to labor five-twelfths. Fourier's best known book was his *Theory of Universal Unity* (1829), a curious mixture of religion, economics, psychology, and Pythagorean belief in the magic of numbers. Mankind was influenced by nine different passions (instincts) so Fourier thought. Once bring these into harmony, one with another, and all would be well.

It is difficult to disentangle truth from absurdity in the writings of Saint-Simon and Fourier. Not so in the case of Louis Blanc. He is a kind of link between the so-called scientific socialism or materialistic socialism of Karl Marx (p. 252 et seq.) and early nineteenth-century socialism, touched as it was with the impossible romantic idea that the economic lion (capitalism) would willingly surrender his prerogatives to the gentle, hard-working lamb (proletariat) as the result of a conversion to cooperation.

Louis Blanc, son of an unimportant French official, was born in Madrid during the Napoleonic occupation of Spain. Almost all of his life, however, was spent in Paris, where he won some considerable reputation as a newspaperman and popular historian. His principal contribution to socialist theory was made in his *Organization of Labor* (1840), wherein he argued for national workshops which quietly and slowly would revolutionize production and distribution. He did not urge that government should own and operate factories and workshops, as modern socialists do; nor did he have any confidence that socialism could be brought about by purely voluntary coöperation, as did Saint-Simon and Fourier in France and Owen in England. What he wanted was to have the state lend money to coöperative groups of workingmen which would then engage in business on their own account in shops not owned but financed by the government. One part of the earnings was to be set aside for interest due the state, another for old-age pensions, for replacement of machinery, and so forth; and what was left was to be divided among the workers in accordance with a formula afterward adopted by Marx. It read: "from each according to his ability, to each according to his need."

The socialism preached by Louis Blanc met with a more hearty response in the July Monarchy than did that of Saint-Simon and Fourier. In the rabbit-warrens of Paris (a city which had grown from 780,000 in 1831 to 1,052,000 in 1846), in the caves of Lille which housed thousands of workmen, and in the other textile cities to the north and east, there was acute misery. The Industrial Revolution in France, as in England, had its seamy side—low wages, high prices, wretched housing, unemployment. The wages of French railway engineers were only three francs a day and of women and children but half of that and even less. The number of paupers doubled during the July Monarchy; there was a great increase in crimes of violence; and the physique of the city-dwellers called to the colors showed a notable decline. Once planted in such soil, revolutionary sentiment grew fast, even if underground.

Meanwhile, on the surface, parliamentary politics appeared to be a seesaw between the more liberal bourgeoisie (the party of progress) headed by Thiers, who believed that the King should reign but not govern, and the more conservative bourgeoisie (the party of resistance) headed by Guizot, who believed that the King should both reign and govern. Thiers favored a more energetic foreign policy, as well as one slightly more democratic in domestic affairs, and Guizot opposed him on both counts. In 1840 Thiers as prime minister was dismissed by the King because he seemed to be pressing a more ambitious diplomatic program in the Near East that might precipitate war with England. Guizot then succeeded him, to remain prime minister until the monarchy collapsed in 1848.

The Ministry of Guizot (1840-48): Peace and Corruption

Guizot espoused the doctrine that the control of the government ought to rest with the property-owning classes. These must elect the Chamber, but the King must select the ministers, subject, however, to approval of the Chamber. The King, by Guizot's system, was thus to have a very active share in the government. "The throne," he declared, "is not an empty armchair." Such a prime minister naturally delighted Louis Philippe. "He is my mouth!" he said of Guizot. The latter set himself resolutely to the task of holding France quiet for the benefit of "the lawful country" and believed in strong measures to insure this. "Two things," said the minister, "are needful in order to govern—common sense and cannon."

LOUIS ADOLPHE THIERS (1797-1877)

The cannon, however, were only to be used on his malcontent countrymen, for abroad Guizot pursued consistently a pacifist policy which his foes denounced as cowardly and unworthy of France. The quarrel with England over the Levant was ended with an arrangement all in favor of London. The Prime Minister frankly disclaimed any chauvinistic policies. "Let us not talk of our fellow citizens," he cried in the Chamber, "of broad lands to conquer, of great wars of revenge. If France is prosperous, if she remains free, rich, peaceful, and intelligent, we need not complain if we exercise small influence in the world abroad."

But this peace, in one sense so noble, was not accompanied by any strenuous endeavor to elevate the French masses. Firm in the support of the King, Guizot felt able to defy all opposition. All authority was soon concentrated around him, and it was said that "he had made up his mind to put an absolute veto upon all innovations in public life." Never had France seemed under a more strictly constitutional government. The Chamber was now made up of Deputies who delighted to vote confidence in the ministry at every summons. By distributing government favors and by taking advantage of the law permitting public functionaries to sit in parliament, Guizot kept a reliable majority among the Deputies. Some of his lieutenants in the ministry were adepts in the dirty work of manipulation through grants of licenses, patronage, and special legislation. State Councillors, law officers, Councillors of the Supreme Court, high university officials, heads of great public bureaus—all looked to Guizot for profit and promotion, let themselves be elected to the Chamber—and voted for the ministry. Over half of the Deputies were said to have been of this class.

There seemed, therefore, to be no means of upsetting the Prime Minister. The election of 1846 gave him over one hundred majority, and only in Paris was there a formidable opposition vote. Guizot was able to defend with eloquent language this "Regime of Electoral Corruption." Not one concession would he make to the demands for a broader franchise. "Work and grow rich," he answered to protests, "then you will become voters." And, again, "The world is no place for universal suffrage, *that absurd system* which would call all living creatures to the exercise of political right." In 1847 he delivered a very notable speech upon the unwisdom of admitting to the franchise the *Capacités,* that is, highly educated professional men, who had not the magical amount of income. The measure failed, and Guizot and his master were more self-satisfied than ever.

Yet there were warnings they might well have heeded. Men of intellectual tastes, electors or nonelectors, were becoming disgusted at this sordid sham-liberal regime. De Tocqueville published his famous books on travels in democratic America; Martin, his histories expounding the mission of France to civilization; and, above all, Michelet, whose *Histoire de la Révolution* (1847) was a glorification of the great uprising, "evoking the holy form of the People, terrible, fruitful, generous as Nature itself." The clericals hated the antireligious tendencies of the court and government and intrigued ever more vigorously, while the Bonapartists plucked up courage after 1840, when, by a serious blunder from the Orleanist viewpoint, the ashes of Napoleon were officially brought back from St. Helena and interred with pomp and ceremony in the Invalides.

There were also sordid scandals in high places, especially in 1847, when the Minister of Public Works was caught compounding through an ex-minister of war to receive a great bribe for licensing a mining company. There also were increasing rumors that some revolutionary upheaval was preparing in Paris, and there were ever louder demands and more formidable demonstrations in favor of a wider franchise. Finally the year 1848 dawned with an atmosphere charged with menace. "Do you not feel that a breath of Revolution is in the air," wrote de Tocqueville, warning Guizot to mend his policy, "that there is a storm on the horizon and that it is advancing toward you!"

Guizot and his master recognized nothing. The Prime Minister considered himself indispensable to the state: "You see I simply cannot go," he told his friends. The King also set his face like flint against any constitutional change. He would veto any reform bill from the Deputies; "I will not have it." Louis Philippe's obstinacy, in fact, rose to that point, as his years advanced, that his own sons grew anxious. "The King's will is inflexible," wrote the Duc de Nemours, "he will listen to no one. He has arrived at an age when no man accepts criticism."

Hardly had the Prince written these words, before de Tocqueville's predicted tempest broke. On February 24, 1848, Louis Philippe ceased to be king. Not merely France, but all Europe was on the verge of a general upheaval.

The Explosion of 1848 in France: Preliminaries of the Paris Uprising: February, 1848

The Revolution of 1830 in France had been almost deliberately provoked by the unconstitutional edicts of Polignac and Charles X. Such crude measures were certain to explode the magazine. The Revolution of 1848 was only vaguely sensed in advance. In January of that year, Guizot and Louis Philippe still seemed firmly intrenched in power. They were carefully governing according to the letter of the Charter. The Chamber was supporting them. The wealthy classes were on their side. A moderate enlargement of the franchise would have silenced, for the time, all dangerous opposition. Then suddenly, more by accident than design, Paris plunged herself into three days of blood and fire. When the uprising was over, Jules Simon could summarize the immediate results thus—"The agitation had been organized by the Liberals for the benefit of the Republic, which the Liberals dreaded; and at the last moment universal suffrage was put through by the Republicans for the benefit of Socialism, which the Republicans abhorred."

The Revolution of 1848 was, therefore, to a great majority of Frenchmen, not a welcome relief from intolerable oppression; it was a bewildering upheaval, far more violent than most of them desired, and it left them with institutions thrust upon the nation which few of them understood and which many of them hated.

De Tocqueville, that shrewd political thinker, who had already sniffed the storm in the air, wrote later that some "revolutions are born spontaneously, as a sort of chronic disease, suddenly made acute by an unforeseen accident." The Revolution of 1848 was precisely of this class.

The capital events were all crowded into three hectic days in February. They began thus: The Paris malcontents against the Guizot ministry—liberal monarchists, republicans, and downright socialists—had temporarily pooled their differences. Drastic social changes could wait until the franchise was enlarged and they were all rid of the detested minister. The government forbade them to hold public demonstrations, but their leaders arranged to have a great reform banquet on February 22, when speeches were to be made in favor of a wider franchise. Eighty-seven deputies (nearly the entire opposition) were to be present, and a procession of students was to march to the banquet hall. On February 21, however, the government issued a fiat forbidding the banquet. The opposition leaders believed resistance was hopeless and announced that the affair was canceled. Nevertheless, next day, the Minister of Police sent out his gendarmes to patrol the streets, and it was reported that 30,000 troops were ready to crush disorders. A great crowd of busy idlers accordingly gathered, especially at the Madeleine and the Place de la Concorde, in hopes of witnessing some harmless rioting.

The opposition chiefs were all at their homes. It was raining and very cold; but presently the crowds took to hooting and brawling with the police, and there followed a good many scuffles. As night closed down, the report spread that barricades were being thrown up across a few side streets, and that arms-dealers' shops were being forced and pillaged, but the case seemed so unpromising that even Louis Blanc, the socialist, joined with Ledru-Rollin, a Republican leader, in deciding it was useless to attempt anything that night, lest they "lead democracy to ruin and the people to the shambles." At the Tuileries, the King mocked those advisers who had told him that "concessions were necessary."

However, during the night of February 22-23, tidings came in that really formidable barricades were rising in the quarters near the center of the city, the Rue St. Denis, the Rue St. Martin, and so on, and it seemed best to call out the National Guards for the first time since 1840. Instantly, the government realized that a mistake had been made. The privates of the Guards were not electors. "Reform," as demanded by the agitators, would give them the coveted franchise. The National Guards, it soon appeared, were not, therefore, to be depended upon.

Speedily it was evident that these citizen militia would not obey orders to attack their fellow Frenchmen. When a battalion swung past the windows of the Tuileries, the men shouted, "Vive la Réforme! A bas Guizot!" so furiously that even in his cabinet the King could hear them. Louis Philippe had always considered the National Guard a true mirror of French public opinion. He was so shaken that he notified Guizot that he was no longer minister and ordered the less conservative Molé to form a cabinet. Everywhere in Paris spread the rejoicing. It was assumed that the disturbances were over. The troops marched back to their barracks. Nearly all windows were illuminated. France had apparently liberalized its monarchy with the minimum of disorder.

Noisy but harmless bands wandered toward the ministry of foreign affairs, where Guizot was still residing. A force of infantry was guarding the building, and the soldiers and the street rangers fell into a brawl. Some member of the mob fired a shot. Instantly the infantry answered with a murderous volley, apparently without orders from their commander. When the smoke cleared away, thirty-five Parisians lay dead on the pavement and fifty had been wounded. That reckless volley was the immediate cause of the fall of the Orleanists.

The Republicans now gathered courage. Sixteen bodies of the slain were loaded upon a cart and trundled down the streets, surrounded by torches and accompanied by a wild throng shouting that the government was deceiving the people and slaughtering them. The cry was no longer *"Vive la Réforme!"* It was now the terrible one of 1792, *"Vive la République!"* During the night of February 23-24, barricades were built with fury. By the next evening all was over with the King. The troops were tired of patrolling the streets; arrangements for their rations had broken down; they were even hungry. At the Tuileries, most distracted counsels prevailed. First, Molé declared himself unable to form a ministry. Then Thiers attempted the troublesome task, while the generals attempted to get the troops to storm the barricades. The soldiers, however, were half-hearted. They simply halted when faced with stiff resistance. Vainly did the King order the attack to be stayed and announce more tardy concessions. Already placards were going up around the capital: "Louis Philippe massacres us as did Charles X. Let him follow Charles X."

What shook the confidence of the King most, however, was the news that the National Guard was taking the part of the insurgents. "If I resist, blood will follow," said he "not that of professional rioters, but of the true people of the National Guard, of workers and of honest folk. Can I order the troops to fire on my own electors?" He was now an old man and perhaps weary of the game. The insurgents had seized the Palais Royal and were forcing their way nearer the Tuileries. The militia at the palace were now shouting for "Reform," and, as a last measure to save the dynasty, Louis Philippe hastily abdicated in favor of his grandson, the ten-year-old Comte de Paris, with his mother, the Duchesse d'Orléans, as Regent.

The ex-king immediately left the Tuileries and rode away toward England under a cavalry guard. It was well that he did so. Almost immediately the palace was entered. The mob had already pillaged the Palais Royal, destroying "twenty-five tons" of fine glass, porcelain, enamels, marbles, and furniture in the two residences. The Duchesse d'Orléans had rushed with the young "King" into the Chamber of Deputies to get that body to confirm her regency. Even while Ledru-Rollin, and then the poet-historian Lamartine, were demanding delay and a "provisional government," four thousand uncouth insurgents, the sweepings of the industrial quarter, surged into the Parliament building. "Away with it! Down with the Chamber!" rose their yells. The Duchesse and the King-for-an-hour fled one way; most of the deputies fled another.

A few of the extreme left members stood their ground, and were permitted by the mob to appoint a provisional government. Soon Paris, and then France, learned that the executive power rested with seven deputies, of whom the most prominent were Lamartine, Ledru-Rollin, and Louis Blanc. The logical climax came on February 25, when the new rulers issued the fiat, *"The Republic is the government of France,"* and then on March 5, ordered that an Assembly chosen by universal (manhood) suffrage should be elected to draw up a new constitution.

Thus, by one stroke, not merely was kingship abolished in France, but the total number of electors was raised without warning from 250,000 to *over nine millions.* The great majority of these new voters were entirely without political interests and were wholly untrained for the responsibility thrust upon them.

When the Republican chiefs had felt the power thrust into their hands, there had been a momentary hesitation in declaring for their full program. "You must wait until you have won the authorization of France," said the moderate Lamartine. "I've got that of the people," retorted the more radical Ledru-Rollin. "Ay," answered his colleague, "of the people of Paris." But Lamartine gave way and the Republic was proclaimed, although pretty speedily it became evident that the masses of Paris could not decree for the nation.

The Republicans: The Socialists and the Constitutional Assembly

For the moment, the hopes of the non-socialist bourgeois Republicans were high. Now they would give France a real regime of political "Liberty, Equality, and Fraternity," such as Jacobin excesses had shipwrecked in the seventeen-nineties.

They were, nevertheless, very inexperienced men. Lamartine was a distinguished author, as much a poet as a historian; Ledru-Rollin was a "rhetorician dominated by the phrases of 1793"; and associated with them in the new provisional government was Louis Blanc, who considered all political changes merely so many steps toward establishing his workshops and an entirely new organization of property and labor. Behind Blanc were vigorous socialist elements in Paris, quite ready for more barricades and street fighting, if their utopian policies were thwarted.

THE FRENCH CHAMBER OF DEPUTIES INVADED BY THE PARIS MOB (1848)

The provisional government had, therefore, to conciliate the socialists, even while Lamartine, as the new foreign minister, strove to reassure the courts of Europe that France was not to embark upon a crusade to spread republicanism and to precipitate again the great wars of the old revolution. Intimidated by the socialists, the provisional government promptly ordered that *all* citizens should join the National Guard. The industrial classes instantly obeyed, and the Paris guard thus rose from 56,000 to 190,000.

The socialists now all had muskets and a military organization. The next stage was the issuance of a decree establishing "National Workshops," and a "Government Commission for the 'Workers,'" "to undertake immediately to guarantee to the people the legitimate fruits of their labor." Under the whip and spur of the radicals, this body promptly issued an ordinance limiting the daily hours of labor to ten in Paris, and eleven in the provinces. This was followed by a demand to substitute the Red flag for the Tricolor. But here the political Republicans turned with fury. "I will reject until I die," cried Lamartine, "that flag of blood, and you should reject it more than do I. That Red flag which you bear has never made the circuit of the Champ de Mars dipped in the blood of the people of 1791 and '93, and the Tricolor has gone around the world with the name, the glory and the liberty of *la patrie*."

The socialists, however, indulged in one threatening demonstration after another. In order to get time to work up converts, they forced the ministers to change the date for electing the new Assembly from April 9 to April 23. But the provisional government was taking warning. It began organizing a special force, the *garde mobile*, from young bourgeois. When another mob invaded the Hôtel de Ville, demanding "the abolition of the exploitation of one man by another," the manifestants were expelled by a stern display of force. Obviously, the Republicans and the socialists were drifting apart.

Meantime, France was electing her Constitutional Assembly. The news had already come to Paris that the departments had received the overthrow of the Orleanists "with surprise, resignation and a vague uneasiness." There was a general feeling that the past could not be recalled and there was relief that Lamartine and his colleagues seemed to be maintaining the well-beloved "order"; but for the Republic there was little enthusiasm, and for the socialist projects very much less. However, in the election, the majority of the nine hundred representatives chosen called themselves moderate Republicans, in favor of an antisocialist democratic republic. The socialist members were very few, much fewer than the large minority that really stood for some type of monarchy.

The Assembly convened on May 4 and immediately replaced the provisional government with an executive committee of five, headed by Lamartine and Ledru-Rollin. In this group, the socialists had no power, and almost immediately their "Party of Action" endeavored to dissolve the Assembly by riotous force and to set up another provisional government, composed exclusively of extreme radicals. The bourgeois sections of the National Guard soon stamped down this uprising, and its sole result was to put the Assembly and the socialists still more at loggerheads.

The Socialist Uprisings: The "Days of June": Defeat of the Radicals

They soon came to grips over the national workshops. Other things, also, had offended the peasant and capitalist classes sorely, especially the commercial prostration caused by the disorders in Paris, and the extraordinary forty-five per cent that had been added to all direct taxes in order to meet the treasury deficit resulting from the crisis. But the national workshops had been an offense to every property owner in France. Louis Blanc claimed that they had been organized by his personal opponent, Marie, the minister of commerce, and had been deliberately arranged so as to fail. Times had been hard in Paris in 1847-48. Many artisans had been already out of employment. Now there was still greater unemployment, with tens of thousands of necessitous persons demanding work and bread. The workshops began with 6,000 persons in March; there were some 87,000 in them in May. The experiment had been thrust on the government suddenly, without adequate planning, and of course it represented so extreme an innovation that no directing skill, perhaps, could have saved it. But from the outset, the workshops were one ill-managed jumble. All the workmen, masons, textile-workers, carpenters, cabinet-workers, and the rest were put indiscriminately upon the great excavations needed for the new railway stations at St. Lazare and Montparnasse. The pay was normally two francs (forty cents) per day, but not all the men, by any means, could be kept busy. They worked in relays, and those left idle were given a franc and a half per day (thirty cents). This nonworking class, of course, swelled steadily. All the tramps and vagabonds of North France hastened to Paris to enroll for their thirty sous for doing nothing. Naturally, such arrangements demoralized the ordinary labor in private factories, and every employer and merchant was furious. When the railway excavations were finished, the men were ordered to dig up the sods in the Champs de Mars and then to put them back again—all at a charge of 150,000 francs per day upon the treasury.

Such a situation could not endure many weeks. Louis Blanc protested bitterly that here was not his system, but a hostile caricature. The Assembly, however, was only too glad to see the workshops utterly discredited. On June 21, to the great satisfaction of all property-owning France, the decree was issued closing the establishments. As for the toilers, they were invited to enroll in the army, or go out into the departments, where they could be given regular labor on the public works. This decree drove the socialists and the Parisian proletariat to desperation. The workingmen still had their muskets, and in February they had learned how to build barricades. The socialist clubs now gave them military organizations and officers.

On Friday, June 23, barricades were springing up like mushrooms all over eastern Paris. The next morning there were four hundred, many built with great skill, strongly battlemented, and rising above the first stories of the houses. The Pantheon, the quarter of the Temple, and the Place de la Bastille, were some of the insurgent centers. Behind such bulwarks were 50,000 determined men. The revolt seemed far more dangerous than those which brought an end to the rule of Charles X and Louis Philippe.

This Paris uprising of 1848, of course, has vast significance, in that it was not an attempt at a political but a social revolution. The bitterness, the wolfish enmity, the sense of inveterate wrong, which were driving the Paris workingmen in those fearful "Days of June," were precisely those motives of class hatred which were to torment Paris again in 1871, and then many another city and nation in 1918-20. The have-nots were turning upon the haves.

In 1789, the oppressors of France had seemed to be the King, the fat bishops, and the *noblesse*. Bourgeois as well as artisan had joined against them. In 1848 the oppressors of France were alleged to be the thrifty bourgeoisie, the peasant proprietors, the tradesmen, the owners of small factories. It was an attack upon the middle classes, their possessions and ideals. The precise collectivist program of the 1848 radicals is unimportant; the animus behind them can never be disregarded. Class warfare, the bloody heir of the old Jacquerie, had come into the world.

The National Assembly, however, was of stouter stuff than the two exiled kings, and its defenders more valorous. The Assembly gave dictatorial powers to General E. L. Cavaignac, younger brother of the hero of 1830. At first he had only about fifty thousand regular troops and reliable National Guardsmen, but he had organization, discipline, and artillery. Presently from all over France, even from distant Strasbourg, came strong detachments of National Guards to save the capital from destruction. The street fighting was of a terrific character. The insurgents fought with desperation from barricade to barricade. "Better to die by bullets than from hunger!" rose their cry. Cavaignac's artillery raked the streets and beat down one rebel stronghold after another. After three days of agony, the last barricade succumbed. Many prisoners were shot as soon as taken; 3,000 were deported en masse to Algeria. At last Cavaignac made his report to the Assembly: "Order has triumphed. *Vive la République!*" "The Republic is dead!" cried Lamennais, one of the few radical Deputies still keeping his seat. He was almost right, as the events of a few months were to demonstrate.

The Constitution of 1848: The New Presidency

After these hideous "Days of June" (23 to 26), the Assembly settled to its task of giving a constitution to France. The bourgeoisie and the peasants were scared and shaken. What *was* this Republic that had brought them so near to ruinous anarchy? The government bonds had fallen from 116 in February to 50. Commerce and industry were stagnant. Everybody with something to lose was terribly anxious. Opposition to monarchy was vanishing amid an intense desire for order. As for the remnants of the defeated socialists, the Republic now meant for them merely the triumph of the capitalists—they had lost all interest in it. Of the general situation, a shrewd observer, the Marquis de Circourt, wrote, "Whoever possessed anything, whoever hoped to possess anything, whoever needed to live by his own labors, begged for an authority strong and peremptory, even though it were arbitrary and crude." The Second Empire was the child of this intense craving.

The constitution of this Second French Republic, as drawn up by the Assembly, was replete with fine phrases; also, with ambiguities. There was to be a legislature of 750 elected by universal suffrage, a president similarly chosen, thus following the American precedent. But this French constitution called for a one-chamber legislature only. There was to be no Senate, no House of Peers, to act as a check on the lower house, or as in the United States, a check on presidential powers by a proviso for confirming appointments and approving treaties. Also there was no Supreme Court to act as a make-weight. The President of this short-lived republic was to appoint his own ministers, control the whole civil and military service, promulgate the laws, sign treaties—in short, exercise enormously wide powers, subject only, in extreme cases, to impeachment by the Assembly. Yet the Assembly, in turn, voted all laws and could not be prorogued or dissolved, save by its own consent. Between this very powerful president and this irresponsible legislature, there was no judge or conciliator to prevent a mortal conflict.

Louis Napoleon Elected President (December, 1848)

At last the new constitution was ready, and French manhood was summoned to the polls. If the Republic was to have a chance at all, a president must now be chosen who was devoted to its principles; a man who would appoint the 400,000 civil officials or public employees in the interests of the democratic system and use the great centralization of power at Paris to strengthen the new regime. Yet no effective candidate was forthcoming from the convinced Republicans. Lamartine, the eloquent theorist, indeed, was anxious for the honor, along with Ledru-Rollin, his more radical colleague, as well as Cavaignac, the victor in the Days of June. Cavaignac had by far the largest following of the three, but he was cursed by the Paris radicals for being a butcher and was intensely distrusted by the peasants and by men of property. The Republicans, by their blunders, had become widely unpopular. Yet the Orleanists were discredited and still more so were the old Bourbon Legitimists.

Under those circumstances, any kind of strange candidacy was possible, and fate sent to the front a personage hitherto counted little better than an adventurer—*Prince Louis Napoleon Bonaparte*, son of Louis Bonaparte, the ex-king of Holland, and therefore nephew of Napoleon the Great, who was in exile in England when the Orleanists fell. At once thrusting again into French politics, he had, on the strength of his uncle's name, been elected to the Assembly by four different departments. Certain Republicans took alarm. Might he not work against their projects? It was therefore proposed to disqualify members of former reigning families from holding office; but a Deputy objected that "a law against one man is unworthy to a great Assembly," and the project was dropped.

Louis Napoleon, therefore, remained eligible, and now he became the rallying point for all the elements that hated the regular Republicans. Very skilfully, he and his political advisers traded upon his name— "Napoleon!"—It meant something glorious to the millions of peasants who execrated the unsettling upstarts at Paris. To him rallied the royalists, who voted for him as a protest against the Republic. To him, also, came the great influence of the clericals who reckoned, not unwisely, that he

would be a better friend of the Church than either the Orleanist in-
differentists or the Republican agnostics. Men of property believed he
was at least likely to secure their beloved "order." The election results,
therefore, astonished the outside world. Lamartine was almost ignored
by the voters: Ledru-Rollin had some 370,000 ballots; Cavaignac had
1,400,000; and *Louis Napoleon had 5,400,000*. It was really the peasants
who did this. In one country district after another, the ignorant farmers
"knew but one name, that of the Emperor Napoleon—and they voted for
that name."

Very speedily, the victorious candidate (the "Prince-President" they
already called him) was ensconced in the Palais de l'Élysée and surrounded by many of the trappings of royalty. The upheaval of 1848 had
flung out the humdrum Orleanists, with their sordid pretense of liberalism. It had almost committed France to a socialist revolution. It had
finally ended by clearing the way for a military monarchy and the return
of the Man on Horseback.

Chapter 6

THE LIBERAL DEFEAT
IN CENTRAL EUROPE (1848-50)

IF THE Paris Revolution of 1848 took France by surprise, to the old monarchies of Central Europe it was a bolt from the blue. There was general fear among the old-line monarchs, lest the new French government try to preach democracy with the sword. The news from Paris reached St. Petersburg during a magnificent ball at the Winter Palace. Czar Nicholas I immediately strode into the glittering throng, shouting with excitement, "Saddle your horses, gentlemen! France is a Republic!" Any kind of blow by France seemed possible.

Gradually, however, these fears calmed. The Paris Republicans were too busy crushing the socialists and bombarding barricades to have ambitions or cannon for carrying universal suffrage beyond the Rhine. But the tidings from Paris were a spark to all that antimonarchist, nationalist gunpowder which had been gathering in the political magazines of Germany, Austria, and Italy. What the French did not do, the peoples of Central Europe at once seemed to be doing for themselves. The Hapsburg empire was soon on the edge of dissolution. Prussia was apparently liberalized. Germany and Italy seemed about to become federated nations. The repercussions of the fall of the Orleanist monarchy, therefore, touched nearly every land in Continental Europe.

In Germany its influence was profound. The Industrial Revolution, although long delayed, had gradually been seeping in. There, as in England and France, a new capitalist class was rising; there, also, a proletariat was beginning to speak. The German proletariat, however, unlike that in France, was to play a very minor role in the exciting events of 1848, and those who spoke in its name for the time being were without influence. Nevertheless, in view of the importance of socialism in European history, two of them deserve mention.

Weitling, a tailor, had been exiled for writing a book in 1845 called *The Gospel of the Poor Sinners*. His ideas roughly paralleled those of the poor German peasants whose effrontery in demanding economic liberty as a Christian right had aroused the wrath of Martin Luther in the sixteenth century. Weitling was a communist and asserted that Christ was one—in other words, he proposed the abolition of private property. His ideas in regard to sex seem to have been somewhat libertinist, and his gospel brimmed over with scurrilous attacks on the Church, both Protestant and Catholic. Weitling went to America, came back to Europe, and in 1848 had some official connection with a *liberty league* of German communists which proposed to wage war in Germany, and to compel the rich to surrender their possessions in exchange for paper money. The liberty league apparently did no fighting nor did Weitling, who later returned to the United States.

Before he left Europe he had a bitter controversy with a young Jewish journalist, Karl Marx. The latter at this time was a full-fledged revolutionary, but he did not believe that the German proletariat was either sufficiently numerous or sufficiently class-conscious to warrant any attempt to conquer Germany. Marx's role, however, in the events of 1848 was not altogether that of an outsider. As editor of the *Neue Rheinische Zeitung*, the organ of the Communist League, he participated as actively as a newspaperman might in the ordeal through which Germany was to pass. Unfortunately, the extremes of arrogant bitterness which characterized this founder of modern socialism led him viciously to assail the German bourgeoisie, a fact which ruined all chance of Dr. Karl Marx's becoming a political leader in 1848. For more about him and his ideas see Chapter 15.

It was otherwise with the German bourgeoisie—the trader, banker, and intellectual. They wanted liberalism in place of autocracy, and they passionately sought a German nation. The whole driving force of the German Revolution of 1848 came from this class, filled as it was with admiration for representative government on the English model and with loathing for the hated Bund. It was their revolution.

Had the Paris revolution been long delayed, probably some form of upheaval would have taken place ere long in Germany without any French example. Under the circumstances, the effect was almost instantaneous. Obedient to authority beyond the run of Western folk, when once the respect for government was loosed, the German people seemed to throw off all their old shackles at one stroke. "Police regulations" and "ministerial ordinances" were flung to the four winds, from the Alps to the Baltic.

The governments were demoralized and stunned. From the Austrian emperor and Prussian king, down to the least of the petty princes, the monarchs were lucky if they were not ordered to go the way of Louis Philippe. Everywhere there were public meetings, processions, demonstrations, and demands for liberal concessions, which the frightened sovereigns and ministers seemed to grant for the asking. An incredible wave of optimism swept over Germany in that deceptive spring of 1848.

It seemed as if new political heavens on earth were at hand without warfare, without hateful struggle. Trained through the ages to look toward their rulers for everything, even now the princes were bombarded with petitions trustfully proposing the instant creation of the Utopia. "Everything is being demanded of us," wrote the distracted Duke Ernest of Saxe-Coburg, "even the establishment of perfect health and the gift of long life!" Nothing but armed force could have stopped the movement, and for the moment none of the governments (particularly none of the smaller ones) could be sure of their armies.

The story of the German Revolution of 1848-50, and of its melancholy failure, falls into four subchapters, each to be read in combination with the other three. Each of the lesser states had its own special demonstrations, insurrections, and wrestlings with constitutionalism, but discarding these we may trace somewhat separately:

I. The meeting of the National Parliament at Frankfort, and its brave but ill-starred effort to give Germany a federal constitution.

II. The more local struggle for liberalism in Prussia, and how the movement failed owing to the vacillation of Frederick William IV.

III. The collapse of liberalism in Austria, and of nationalism in Hungary, thanks to the Hapsburg army and Russian bayonets.

IV. The humiliating failure of Prussia to establish a German federation of a monarchical type.

The Assembling of the Frankfort German National Parliament

Liberalism was strongest in South Germany, where already most states had tolerable constitutions. A convention of fifty-one liberals, meeting at Heidelberg (March 5, 1848), took the movement in hand. At their prompting, a "Preparatory Parliament" (*Vor-parlament*), an unofficial gathering of men who had been deputies in some kind of a German legislature, met at Frankfort. The members were nearly all South Germans, but with a fair number of Prussians and a few Austrians, so that nominally the company represented the entire nation.

Meantime, the Diet of the discredited Bund continued to sit, but its delegates were only too happy to enact into law the irresistible suggestions of the *Vor-parlament*. A national flag was proclaimed for Germany: black, red, and gold, the colors of the old patriotic *Burschenschaft;* and, of more consequence, came the order that a real national parliament was to be elected to follow the unofficial gathering. One deputy was to be chosen by universal suffrage for each 50,000 inhabitants throughout Germany. In 1815 the princes had reorganized Germany without consulting the people; now the people were to reorganize Germany without consulting the princes.

The new Parliament met, its composition overwhelmingly bourgeois, in the ugly eighteenth-century church of St. Paul in Frankfort, where through eight hectic months, beginning May 18, 1848, the German National Assembly wrought at its constitution-building. The assembly was later to be derided as a "Professors' Parliament," and gibes were thrown at the lengthy and solemn manner in which it debated the "Fundamental Rights" of German citizens, when things of far greater practical import seemed clamoring for solution. But, in truth, the Parliament faced a problem calculated to daunt the most astute politicians—*what place, if any, in the new Germany, had Austria?* The German-speaking Hapsburg lands undoubtedly had, in one sense, as good a claim to share in a new *Reich* as had Mecklenburg or Baden; but how could a modernized German federation function, if the largest partner's main strength came from Slavs, Czechs, Poles, and Croats, Latin-speaking Rumanians, and, last but not least, Turanian-descended Magyars?

The question became the more acute because, as time elapsed, the Austrian government made it increasingly evident that it would not take its exclusion from Germany passively. The other natural leader for Germany was Prussia; and despite unhappy actions in the past, the Liberals at Frankfort, on the whole, looked upon Frederick William IV as their man. Austria stood for clericalism, Metternich, and autocracy; Prussia had no such disastrous traditions. Prussia was also Protestant, as was the bulk of Liberal Germany outside of Bavaria. If Austria was to be pushed aside, the logical act, therefore, was to offer the new imperial crown to Frederick William IV. Thus, at Frankfort, there were soon two powerful opposing factions, with irreconcilable programs: the "*Great Germans,*" who deemed it impossible and abominable to omit Austria, and the "*Little Germans,*" who desired to cut off the Hapsburg lands from their scheme and to center the revived nation around Berlin.

Some of the long, weary debates at Frankfort on the "Fundamental Rights" were an excuse for postponing the day of fateful decision. Meantime, Archduke John appointed a ministry and undertook to govern Germany somewhat after the manner of a constitutional monarch.

John had no means of enforcing his orders; nevertheless his ministers directed that all soldiers in the various federated states should take an oath of allegiance to the Imperial Administrator. The larger governments quickly defied him. No armed force was at his command except the Frankfort city militia. A strong republican movement, furthermore, was showing itself in South Germany, demanding much more drastic innovations than the majority of the Parliament could possibly concede. A mob of Frankforters broke into St. Paul's church and undertook to dissolve the meeting. Prussian and Austrian troops had to be called in to restore order.

Such proceedings enabled old-line Germans to declare that the Parliament was flirting with an extreme form of social revolution, and a great number of moderates felt their ardor for the new Germany cooling. There were plenty of warnings now that Vienna and Berlin were each in the grip of a militaristic conservative reaction. As early as July, 1848, Frederick William IV, speaking at Cologne, had delivered a warning which the deputies should have heeded. He bade the Parliament "not to forget that *there are still princes* in Germany, and that I am one of them." The princes, that is, all the great influential classes, civil and military, who battened around courts, had now, in fact, recovered their courage and were biding their time.

At last the Parliament forced itself to high decisions. On March 28, 1849, a constitution grouping the German states into a federal empire was finally adopted. There was to be a popularly elected National Assembly, the "*Volkhaus*," and at the head of the state, an *Emperor of the Germans*. By this time, reaction in Austria had run so far, and the liberals at Frankfort had become so disgusted at the Hapsburg attitude, that the selection of the Austrian monarch as German emperor was out of the question. The only real issue left was whether the head of the state should be some sort of a commission (in which the Hapsburg might share), or whether his hated rival, the Hohenzollern, should receive the crown outright. By a majority of only nine was the vote creating an emperor carried. To many good Germans, it seemed outrageous to exclude Tyrol and Austria proper from the reorganized Fatherland. But by 290 votes to 248, the first great step once taken, the King of Prussia was next declared hereditary Emperor of the Germans.

The decision thus passed instantly from Frankfort to Berlin. If the King of Prussia seemed the logical choice to the majority of the delegates, to the majority of lesser German princes his election appeared a studied insult. The Hapsburgs had been Holy Roman Emperors, superior to all the little dynasts for centuries; and their great commitments toward the East forbade them to dream of actually absorbing the secondary states of Germany. The Hohenzollerns were relative upstarts among the reigning families, and their dominions spread from the Vistula to the Rhine. Very easily they might devour the lesser states and "mediatize" (strip of active power) their rulers. When the tidings of the vote at Frankfort came to the King of Württemberg, he spoke the minds of nearly all the weaker princes: "To the House of Hohenzollern I will never submit; to the Emperor of Austria had he been chosen, I would have submitted." On April 3, 1849, the plans of the Frankfort Parliament were ruined by the refusal of Frederick William IV to accept the imperial throne. It is needful to go back to events in Berlin in 1848 to understand the main causes of this shipwreck.

The Uprising in Berlin (March, 1848)

Frederick William IV disliked constitutions; and he had also a pathetic sense of loyalty to the rights of Austria, the senior member of the old German confederation, rights pretty sure to be impaired in any new arrangement. Above all, he hated the idea of revolution and of being compelled to make concessions to any popular demand.

Events, nevertheless, forced his hand immediately. By the middle of March, news came from Vienna that the Hapsburg capital had been seized by the Liberals, that Metternich had fled in disguise, and that the city was in the hands of a burgher guard. Instantly the disorderly elements in Berlin were loose. Already there had been popular petitions, processions, demonstrations, and serious clashes between the populace and the soldiery. Berlin was not yet a mighty metropolis, but it was already a capital of size, and the relations between its middle-class inhabitants and the Junker officers, especially the top-lofty officers of the royal guards, had become very bad. The Berliners hated the soldiery bitterly. The King was not personally unpopular; but he was guilty of the grievous blunder of failing to support *either* side heartily when the two came to blows, thereby largely earning the contempt and distrust of both.

On March 18, angry crowds were surging in the streets, and the military chiefs were begging their sovereign for a chance to teach the mob a lesson. The King, nevertheless, yielded so far to the public demand as to issue a proclamation promising to help in a reorganization of the old Bund, involving the granting of a constitution to all Germany. The crowds cheered the King, who appeared on a balcony before the palace to thank them for their loyal approval. But General Prittwitz, commander of the guards, mishandled a ticklish situation. The populace was allowed to throng into the square in front of the palace and then suddenly was driven out by reckless charges of dragoons, supported by a few shots from the infantry. To the excited multitude, this was sheer treachery. With cries of "Treason!" the Berliners fell back to their streets, where barricades began springing up in true Parisian manner.

The Prussian army was not the French. The officers, scions of the Junker aristocracy, were delighted to make an example of the "vile *Gesindel*" of the towns, and their peasant soldiery loyally obeyed them. The troops attacked the barricades with fury. Until midnight, the hitherto peaceful and prosaic capital was shaken with the crash of platoonfiring and artillery. Deputations of responsible citizens visited the palace and begged the King to withdraw the troops. The monarch at first refused sternly. "Not until the barricades should be pulled down!" The fighting, therefore, continued till midnight, the garrison forcing one barrier after another until resistance seemed likely to be quenched.

But the King was sorely tormented in spirit. The troops were shooting, not foreign invaders, but his own subjects, to whom he stood as a father and for whose calamities he was responsible to God. On the morning of March 19, there appeared another proclamation, "To my beloved Berliners," the King pledging his loyal subjects that, if the barricades were removed, the troops should at once evacuate all of Berlin except a few government buildings.

The Astonishing Conduct of Frederick William IV

The officers and soldiers withdrew from the city in sullen anger. They had been on the point of restoring the royal authority when, lo, the King himself had surrendered to the cursed revolutionaries! The King's brother, Prince William (later William I), the unpopular head of the military party, slipped away to temporary exile in London. The insurgents prided themselves on a complete victory. They forced their way again into the great court of the palace, and Frederick William and his Queen were compelled to show themselves upon an open gallery and salute the bodies of the slain defenders of the barricades, which were now carried into the courtyard, their gaping wounds visible and wreaths decking their heads. Finally, to quiet the throng, the King had to descend to the court and listen, bareheaded, to a hymn sung by the multitude in honor of its slain, and do them homage while veteran officers stood by weeping with rage.

Such humiliation had never been known by any Prussian monarch. It savored mightily of those wild scenes at Paris and Versailles prior to the final overthrow of Louis XVI and Marie Antoinette. It outraged all that sense of intense loyalty to the throne which prevailed throughout rural Prussia—"These were the first fruits of liberalism!" The hard-drinking, hard-riding, hard-smiting squirearchy that supplied the officer class and dominated the peasants would have none of it. Seldom was worse service done to the true cause of Liberty than during these few wild "March days" in Berlin.

But, for the nonce, Frederick William seemed rejoicing in his changed colors. A man of generous emotions, if not of steady courage, he seemed about to surrender to the new order. On March 21, robed in the black, red, and gold colors of the wars of liberation, he made a progress through Berlin upon horseback, halting at many points to assert with gushing eloquence his devotion to the national cause. The populace noisily saluted him in the streets as "*Kaiser*." Germany, he proclaimed that day, was in great peril, and "Deliverance can only come from the most intimate union of the German princes and people under a single leadership. I take this leadership upon myself in the hour of peril. Today I have assumed the old German colors, and have placed myself and my people under the venerable banner of the German Empire—*Prussia is henceforth merged in Germany!*"

Later, the King was to claim that this was "a comedy he had been forced to play." Rather, it was the impulsive action of a generous-hearted and extraordinarily unsteady man. Even the crowds that applauded his words distrusted his sudden conversion to liberalism; while to all honest conservatives he seemed a cowardly traitor to the duties of royalty. Frederick William IV had, in fact, been swept off his feet by the rush of events. He hated the idea of parting with power; and he equally hated the idea of joining in a desperate struggle with his own subjects, or with the other princes of Germany. He was incapable either of accepting the liberal program sincerely, or of fighting it manfully. As a result, he became one of the most pitiful figures in German history.

The Attempt to Establish Constitutionalism in Prussia: The Illiberal Constitution of 1850

But for the moment, while the German Parliament was being chosen and was convening at Frankfort, the "Prussian National Assembly" of 402 members was being elected in Frederick William's own kingdom and was convening at Berlin. Chosen in great haste by people with next to no political experience, it was even more of a "Professors' Parliament" than the gathering at Frankfort—with an undue proportion of learned theorists, lawyers, teachers, and pastors.

Behind the deputies, there was really only the sentiment of the middle classes and of the angry mob of Berlin. Nevertheless, a constitution, extremely liberal and heavily curtailing royal powers, was indeed drafted. But by September, 1848, its authors were already wrangling with the King. When the tidings came that the Hapsburg monarchy had recovered its grasp on the situation and had crushed the revolt of Vienna (October 31), Frederick William promptly broke with his new liberal advisers, and appointed a stiffly conservative ministry. The Assembly and the King were soon at variance over the refusal of the deputies to leave to the crown the choice of its ministers. In November, 1848, the Assembly was compelled by armed force to quit the sympathetic atmosphere of Berlin for the small city of Brandenburg, and then, in December, reaction struck another blow. The King dissolved his Assembly outright and proclaimed a constitution, grossly illiberal in form, and merely granted by the monarch to his people.

This constitution of 1850 gave Prussia, indeed, three things which Frederick William had avowedly hated—a written constitution, popular representation, and manhood suffrage; but it was a sorry travesty of those civil liberties whereof the liberals had dreamed. There was to be an Upper House (*Herrenhaus*) of royal princes, great dignitaries, and high nobles, clothed with such power as to make it the bulwark of privilege, should the Lower House ever become defiant. There was to be a Lower House ("House of Representatives"), chosen by the notorious "three-class system," whereby the electors who made the actual choice of deputies were selected, one-third by whoever paid one-third of the district taxes; one-third by those who paid the next third; and one-third by all the other local taxpayers. In addition, the voting had to be open and every vote to be publicly recorded—an admirable method for enabling landlords and employers to control the ballots of their tenants and workmen. By this system some eighty-three per cent of the voters controlled only one-third of the electors. Even this chastened and hand-picked Chamber, although it could vote the new laws and taxes, had no right to name the king's ministers, and when the Parliament (*Landtag*) was not sitting, ordinances, with the temporary force of law, could be issued by royal authority.

Frederick William IV intended to do only the best by his people. His own philosophy was expressed in his declaration, when he took oath under this wholly amended constitution: "In Prussia the king must govern. I govern not because it is my pleasure but because it is the will of God. For this cause I intend to continue to govern. There must be a free people under a free king." This constitution continued as a dangerous interrogation mark, warping Prussian politics and affecting Prussion international policy. When it disappeared in 1918, Prussian royalty was to disappear with it.

Melancholy Failure of the Frankfort Parliament (*1849*)

But the constitution of 1850 was not the worst of Frederick William's bequests to his people. Already, in 1849, the work of the Frankfort Parliament had been thrown away. The King had watched the movement to give him the imperial crown with very mixed feelings. He had great and genuine hopes for the future of Germany and for the part that Prussia should play therein. Personally, his ambition might have been satisfied if the German imperial crown had been offered to the Hapsburg, with the King of Prussia merely the "Captain General" of the united imperial army; although this was an impossible project, for the Austrian dynasts would have never accepted the shadow while the Hohenzollerns grasped the armed reality. He was painfully aware, furthermore, of his unpopularity among the lesser German princes. Archduke John of Austria had shrewdly said at the time, "If the nine Electors of the Old Empire were restored, the Prince of Reuss-Greiz would have a better chance of being chosen emperor than the King of Prussia." If, however, the princes had actually tendered the new imperial crown to him, Frederick William would probably have accepted it gladly; but now it seemed as if it were the gift of a revolution. "It was not" (so he wrote) "a crown by the Grace of God," but would "horribly pollute the bearer with the carrion smell of the Revolution of 1848."

The King, consequently, bruskly informed the official delegation from Frankfort, when it presented itself at Berlin with its splendid tender (April 3, 1849), that he would not accept what he privately called "a crown of mud and wood," and that, "If anyone is to award the crown of the German nation, it is myself and my equals who shall give it." His refusal, in substance, broke up the Parliament. Vainly, now, the disappointed delegates begged all the states to put the new federal constitution in force. Twenty-eight of the lesser ones haltingly did so, but the four "secondary" kingdoms (Bavaria, Württemberg, Saxony, and Hanover) refused; Austria, of course (excluded from the scheme), was threatening and defiant, and its deputies had quitted Frankfort.

On April 28 Frederick William definitely rejected the offer of the Empire. The Parliament strove desperately to get the constitution into action, but no other leader than the recalcitrant king was possible. In 1848 there had been petty republican revolts in Baden. Now there were more serious uprisings in the Rhinelands, in the Rhenish Palatinate, in Baden and, above all, in Saxony where the local king was fain at last to invite in Prussian troops to help fight his way back to Dresden. These events demoralized many fair-weather liberals. The Parliament had no military force behind it; and now the moral force of the nation was wavering. Nearly all the deputies except the South German radicals went home in despair and disgust.

The remnant took refuge in Stuttgart, where the Württemberg authorities, finding its presence troublesome, dispersed this melancholy "Rump" with force. Already Archduke John, the Imperial Administrator, and his helpless ministers had laid down their tinsel power. The last scenes of the German Revolution were, therefore, in Baden, where Prussian troops were stamping out a really formidable republican movement.

The causes of the momentous failure of German liberalism in 1848-49 are not hard to find. It was essentially a middle-class movement, and it was largely confined to the cities. In 1848, these German cities were neither very large nor very influential. There was no "Paris" in the center of the country, the seizure of which would have given temporary control of the nation. The revolution won over neither the armies nor the bulk of the peasants; above all it utterly failed to win over the princes. "The 'voice of the people' [at Frankfort], which at one time had seemed to shake the seats of the mighty, ceased to alarm as soon as princes and governments knew that behind it was neither national power nor national will" (Dawson). If, outside of these unarmed middle classes, there had been in Germany real leaders of courage and vision, this tragedy of disappointed national hopes would have been avoided. The deputies had striven nobly if not always wisely, and as Delbrück later wrote of the despised "Professors' Parliament," the final outcome showed that "it was more statesmanlike, and saw more clearly the needs of Germany than the sovereign who had destroyed its handiwork."

The Revolution in Austria: The Army Saves the Hapsburgs

Frederick William had been largely moved to reject the imperial crown because he knew its acceptance might involve war with Austria. At Vienna, even more than in Germany proper, the political air had been electric. When the amazing news of February came to the "Kaiser-stadt," the result was instantaneous. Political clubs, composed of students, sprang up overnight and soon were demanding every possible reform. In March, the students began active rioting. The garrison fired at them but it was not to be relied upon. Seemingly, the capital was in danger of falling into the power of a mob, and certain archdukes, in panic, demanded that Metternich resign immediately. "Forty years," declared the old man sturdily, "have I served my country. I have never yielded to an insurrection; nor will I now." But events were now too strong for him. He was forced, not merely to lay down his office, but to flee in partial disguise to England—the one sure refuge for exiles, revolutionary and absolutist alike.

Before May was over, the Emperor Ferdinand had fled from his turbulent capital to the Tyrol, and Vienna itself was in the power of the "Academic Legion" of university students and a burgher national guard; while the terrified ministry had permitted the election of a National Assembly, chosen from all parts of the empire except Hungary. The student clubs seemed, for the moment, to constitute the strongest power in Vienna. Unpopular officials were roughly handled. The uncensored press at once became violent and scurrilous. One student riot soon followed upon another, trade, of course, languished, and solid middle-class burghers began to shake their heads about the "Revolution."

The new Austrian Assembly met in July. The inexperienced deputies harangued at one another in half a dozen different languages. The meetings were very tumultuous, but at last an important decree was passed— the peasants were released from the semi-feudal control of their lords and thus became really free landowners; also the legal distinctions between nobles and common folk were abolished. This reform (which did not touch the claims of the monarchy) was permitted to endure. It was the one great gain to Austria from 1848.

But Vienna could not speak for all the Hapsburg domains. In April and May the Czechs of Bohemia were ablaze. The ideal of Pan-Slavism, the fusion of all Slavic peoples into some form of national unity, had caught the imagination of the Bohemian leaders. A kind of congress of all the

Slavs under the Hapsburgs met at Prague in June. The fiery speeches of the non-Czechish delegates were hardly understood by the Prague citizens, but the least thing expected of the movement was the granting of semi-independence to Bohemia. Then followed a riot, in which the Princess Windisch-Grätz, wife of the governor of the city, was killed by a random bullet. Prince Windisch-Grätz retaliated by bombarding the city. The Pan-Slavic projects and Bohemian patriotic hopes dissolved in the smoke from his cannon. Bohemia, at any rate, was not able to defy the monarchy, and the army was discovered to be loyal. The bombardment of Prague was really the beginning of the return everywhere of the Hapsburgs.

The Austrian army, like the Prussian army, was still a faithful instrument for despotism. In Italy, the stout old Marshal Radetzky was holding fast the Venetian fortresses for his masters, even while the Austrian ministers were willing to negotiate timorously with the very aggressive Italian nationalists. So long as the army held faithful, the Hapsburg cause was anything but lost. "In deinem Lager," said Grillparzer of Radetzky, "ist Östreich." The same might have been said of the hosts of Windisch-Grätz. The Prince was the most arrogant of aristocrats. "The human species begins with the baron," once he had asserted; but he was resolute and sure of his men.

In October, Windisch-Grätz led down his regiments from Bohemia and was before the imperial capital with 60,000 troops. The staid middle classes, in terror for life and property, were sighing for the peaceful days of Metternich. The liberals, or rather the extreme radicals, controlling the city now tried to save themselves by inviting the aid of the Magyars of Hungary, who were at this time in full revolt against the Hapsburgs; but the relieving army from Budapest was driven back. On October 31, Vienna surrendered to Windisch-Grätz, who promptly sent the insurgent chiefs to the firing squad and ruled by martial law. The once-gay metropolis was, for a long time, crushed under a regime of drill-sergeants and spies. The Hapsburgs could return to their conquered capital, there to continue their accustomed state.

While the army was doing this service to monarchy, a new minister undertook to extricate the dynasty from its political tribulations. Prince Felix Schwarzenberg was a coldly cynical blue-blood, but a man of clear judgment and strength of will. His first task was to induce the semi-imbecile Emperor Ferdinand to abdicate in favor of his nephew Francis Joseph, then a youth of eighteen. Ferdinand had sworn inconvenient oaths to give his subjects a constitution. Francis Joseph had never so sworn, and it would be a little less brazen for him to cancel all the promised liberties.

What followed might well have been expected, considering that Vienna was now helpless and the army supreme. In 1849, the Austrian National

Assembly was allowed to vote a constitution; unfortunately it was never in effect. In the opinion of leading Austrian historians, it offered a real solution of the Danube problem which might have kept the Hapsburg empire together for centuries, since at a time when nationalism among the Czechs, South Slavs, Rumanians, and others was at its beginning, the constitution offered a loose federation of nationalities on a basis of wide language and cultural autonomy and political liberalism. Nevertheless, an imperial decree in 1851 declared it void. In the interval the Hapsburgs had triumphed alike over Hungary, Prussia, and Italy. Concessions were no longer necessary.

The Revolt and Suppression of Hungary (1848-49)

The story of the revolt of Hungary is complex. Elsewhere in the Hapsburg lands, the dynasts had to deal only with insurgent *cities* (Vienna and Prague); in Hungary they had to deal with an aroused and warlike *people*. As early as March, 1848, the Hungarian Diet had declared the abolition of the feudal regime and the legal equality of all Magyars. The nobles henceforth strove for riddance of Austro-German control, which they hated, the peasants for more personal freedom.

To the first demands, the terrified Hapsburg ministers capitulated readily, but soon it was evident that the Magyars (the dominant race of Hungary) intended to win liberal institutions strictly for themselves. The great Slavic elements they intended to hold in tutelage, to force to use the Asiatic Magyar tongue and to undergo complete "Magyarization." The result was a revolt within a revolt; the South Slavs (Croats and Serbians) defied this process of absorption, stood stoutly by their local privileges, and rallied behind their *ban* (high governor) Jellachich. The Hapsburgs were quietly biding their own time. When Jellachich attacked the Magyar government, the imperial court covertly encouraged him.

The Magyars were obsessed with the fear of being overwhelmed by the Slavic folk around them. "You Magyars are an island in the ocean of Slavism," Gaï had cried in their Diet, "take heed that its waves do not overwhelm you!" Soon the control of Hungary was in the hands of a Committee of Defence headed by the ardent and highminded Kossuth. Already he had taken a bitterly anti-Austrian position. "From the charnelhouse of the Viennese system a poison-laden atmosphere steals over us!" began one of his first proclamations. Early in 1849 Kossuth had proclaimed the independence of Hungary, and the Magyar armies had flung back the first Austrian attacks.

Nevertheless, the Magyar cause was soon lost. The Italian nationalist movement had been quenched at Novara in 1849 (see p. 121), giving the Hapsburgs a free army to move northward, and, above all, Nicholas I, horrified at seeing the hated "Revolution" so near his doors, thrust upon the young Francis Joseph the services of a Russian army. Despite a gallant resistance, the Magyar generals were simply overwhelmed. Kossuth fled into exile. The Magyar leaders who could not escape were, for the most part, executed. Until 1859, Hungary, like the other Hapsburg lands, had its political life extinguished in a regime of absolutism and martial law.

So Austria, after almost vanishing from the list of Great Powers, made an astonishing recovery, thanks to the loyalty of her army and to the coarse hard genius of Radetzky and Windisch-Grätz. That army, as an instrument for fighting foreign wars, had one pronounced weakness; it was composed of too many nationalities. When, however, it was used for suppressing internal revolts, that very weakness became an advantage, since Croats could be used against Italians, and Germans against Czechs. Radetzky's troopers, for instance, had no temptation to fraternize with the Italians and had no sympathy with Italian aspirations, since they belonged to another nationality. By adopting the old Roman motto of *divide et impera,* the Hapsburgs were able to keep their ramshackle empire together. By turning the force and vigor of Croatian nationalism against Magyar nationalism they had been able not only to defeat the latter but to trample down liberalism as well. Liberalism and nationalism went hand in hand in northern Germany; but in Bohemia and in Hungary they were opposed to one another, and in consequence both suffered defeat. Of course the Austrians ran into luck; they were favored by the inability of the Italians to act as one people (as we shall note); they were abetted by the timidity and procrastination of Frederick William IV; they were aided still further by the friendship of Czar Nicholas; and their foreign affairs were in the capable hands of Schwarzenberg, no mean diplomat. But first and foremost, as an explanation of their victory, is the fact that in Austria-Hungary the forces of nationalism did not go hand in hand with those of liberalism.

Frederick William IV and the Humiliation of Olmütz (1850)

Frederick William IV had lacked high courage in 1848-49, but in his own way he wished to secure German national unity. In 1849 there was still a chance for Prussia to establish a more limited federal system than that proposed at Frankfort; therefore, in May, 1849, Prussia proposed, and most of the smaller states tentatively accepted, a "Federal German State," headed by Prussia, but to be in close alliance with Austria. There was to be a "Chamber of States," made up of delegates from the governments, and a "Chamber of the People," elected by popular vote. A meeting at Gotha of distinguished German liberals, including most of the saner leaders at Frankfort, approved the scheme as the best possible under the circumstances. For the moment, this project of "Union" appeared promising, but from the outset Bavaria and Württemberg opposed it, and, of course, Austria (again excluded) was in a fury. Saxony and Hanover pretended to join, their kings fearing the wrath of their people if they refused, but clandestinely they intrigued with Austria to bring the project to nought, and once more the intense dislike for the Hohenzollerns nursed by the petty princes became the greatest danger to German unity. Tortuous negotiations and political shuffles followed through 1849. It was becoming clear that Austria had recovered her military strength, and, confident at length in her aid, Saxony and Hanover withdrew from the Union.

Frederick William, through 1849 and 1850, continued to present a pitiful picture of indecision. He shunned the idea of war and most of his ministers were against risking it; yet he felt himself bound in personal honor to put through the project and he did not abandon the Union. As a result, one petty state after another withdrew from the undertaking, succumbing to Schwarzenberg's intrigues, and then at last, in 1850, the unscrupulous Austrian forced the issue with the King.

The Elector of Hesse-Cassel was an impossible tyrant, hated by his subjects. His chief minister, Hassenflug (popularly called *Hessenfluch* = "Hesse's Curse"), had aided his master to rule without the local parliament and to levy taxes at pleasure. Hesse belonged to the new Union, but in September, 1850, when his outraged subjects revolted against him, the Elector fled to Frankfort, where Austria had (as an anti-Prussian move) affected to restore the old Diet of the Bund. Schwarzenberg was delighted to order Austrian troops to restore the depraved Elector. It was a direct interference in what should have been strictly Prussia's sphere of influence; and by all normal reasoning, Frederick William should have risked the uttermost to resent an intolerable insult.

The King, indeed, did consent to mobilize his army, but he had no stomach for fighting. Everybody knew that Prussia was only waving a wooden sword. "I am not made of the stuff of which Frederick the Great was made," confessed the King ruefully to a confidant, "*He* would have been the man for you!" Frederick William was advised that the Prussian army, as then organized, would not prove a match for the reinvigorated Austrian hosts, plus the contingents of South Germany. Worse still, Czar Nicholas made it all too plain he would assist the Hapsburgs in behalf of Legitimacy, if the Vienna rulers were again hard pressed. The best chance for Prussia would have been an appeal to the patriotism of *all* Germany, let the little dynasts whimper as they might. Such an idea, however, was unspeakably repulsive to the sorely beset king. When the troops left for the front, the unmartial ruler frankly told the commanding general: "I hold you responsible upon your head that no blood is shed."

Schwarzenberg had grasped the situation completely and he used his opportunity ruthlessly. Shaken by the fear of a life-or-death military struggle, disgusted with his contacts with liberalism, threatened from his rear by the Czar, Frederick William IV completely betrayed the hopes of the German nationalists. The armies, faced one another. There was a skirmish between Prussian and Bavarian-Austrian troops. Five Austrians were wounded, and on the Prussian side "one white horse" was killed. But the Prussians had been ordered to fall back. On November 2, 1850, a council at Berlin resolved on peace at any price. At the Conference of Olmütz (November 29), Prussia agreed to demobilize, to let the Elector come back to Hesse, to dissolve the new Union, and to send delegates again to Frankfort to revive the old Bund of 1815.

Prussia had a real case for war in 1850; but surely it would have been inexpedient then to have risked the hazard of battle with not only a rejuvenated Austria in the field against her, but also Nicholas of Russia. Her real chance had come in 1848 and presumably at that time Frederick William IV might have become German Emperor without any war at all. It was now too late. The King's own weak and romantic character had led him straight to the "humiliation of Olmütz."

Chapter 7

NATIONALIST FAILURE IN ITALY
(1848-49)

THE LONGING of the Italian people for a nationalism all their own had not been snuffed out by the abortive revolutions in the eighteen-twenties. Despite the obscurantism of Charles Felix of Piedmont, the timidity of his successor Charles Albert, the atrocious cruelties of the Neapolitan Bourbons, and the harsh rule of the Austrians in Lombardy-Venetia, the Italian liberals had continued to work for Italian unity.

First among them was Giuseppe Mazzini (1805-72), a native of Genoa, destined at the outset for his father's profession of medicine. Conceiving a horror of "practical anatomy," he next drifted into the study of law. His bent, however, was toward literature. In 1826 he wrote his first essay, *Dante's Love of Country*. Then, by steady degrees, he developed those republican instincts which were to possess his life forever. He felt summoned to an "apostolate," namely, the winning of Italian nationalism. Soon he was a member of the Carbonari, and in 1830 he spent six months in a Piedmontese prison under political charges with "a Tacitus, a Bible and a Byron" as his chief companions; after which he fled to France, usually dwelling at Marseilles. But he kept in touch with all the crude nationalistic and liberal movements already existing in Italy, and soon he gave them what they had needed—the inspiration of a prophet who could clothe their projects with noble words and spiritualize and drama-tize their whole propaganda.

Mazzini was a republican. He disliked kings in general, and those in Italy in particular. In 1831 he founded his famous nexus for revolutionary societies, "Young Italy." Its avowed aims were, "to unite all Italy in one Republic." He hated the Church as he knew it, but he was no atheist, proclaiming as his motto "Liberty, equality, humanity, a God, a sovereign and a law of God!"

Charged with Mazzini's enthusiasm, thousands of Italy's best and bravest were to sacrifice all—were often to die. Mazzini was an inde-fatigable director of romantic conspiracies, a thing for which his people possessed peculiar genius. Unfortunately, most of his conspiracies for a long time were tragic failures. Usually they were undertaken in the pathetic belief that a few initial successes, the seizure of some fortress, the issuance of some brave proclamation, would by magic make the peasants fly to arms, pluck cannon and muskets out of the air, and rout the legions of Austria. There were a number of such risings, and they all failed. Quite otherwise was Italy to be made.

The best-known agitator during this period had been Mazzini; but there were others, men not always engaged in active conspiracy but who, by their books, their speeches, their lives, endeavored to fill the Italian people with hope, courage, and resolve to make a nation. Collectively, these agitators were so numerous and so influential that the school which they headed came to be known as the *risorgimento* (resurrection). But as to just how Italy was to be made there was no agreement.

For instance, there was Gioberti, a priest, who worked hard to persuade the Italians that the pope was the logical head of any united Italy; and when in 1846 the cardinals, defying the wishes of Austria, chose Pius IX as pontiff, there seemed to be a good chance that unity might come about in the way which Gioberti sought. Hardly, indeed, was the new pope enthroned before his pardon cleared the papal dungeons of political prisoners. The censorship of the press was partly relaxed, a council of laymen was set up in the Papal States. The hymn, "Long live Pius IX!" became a kind of political chant of the liberals. They knew that Metternich was chagrined at his election and was using every means in his power to thwart his measures. They did not know that Pius IX, although benevolent and devout and intending to do much for his people, desired to do so entirely as a free gift "from a father to his children," had no intention of ceding the essentials of political power, and that this pope would, at the first sign of popular excesses, take great alarm.

And still a third way might be for an Italian ruler to place himself at the head of Italian patriots who demanded a united Fatherland. This was the hope of another leader of the risorgimento, the liberal, D'Azeglio, who urged his own king, Charles Albert of Piedmont, to take upon himself such a dangerous task. The King, however, was hesitant, fearful about his pledge to Austria never to grant Piedmont a constitution, and fearful of the war with Austria which was sure to come if Italy endeavored to cast off her yoke. But gradually he plucked up courage. In 1845, when D'Azeglio reported to him that all Italy was working itself into a mood for a revolution and demanded a leader, Charles Albert answered him: "Let those gentlemen know that they must keep quiet at present—there is nothing to be done. But tell them that when the time *does* come, my life, the lives of my children, my army, my treasury, my all, will be spent in the Italian cause."

Unfortunately, it seemed next to impossible to bring this well-intentioned king to any important decision. He was too irresolute, prior to

1848, even to stop the active persecution of the liberals in his own dominions. When court parties pressed him to take a stand, he would take refuge in "attacks of prostration, dizziness and fainting." On the other hand, there were times when he completely underestimated the physical difficulties of the task—which was primarily that of defeating the military power of Austria. "How will Italy carry out her plans [for unification]?" a minister asked him. *"Italia fara da se"* (Italy will do it alone), the King returned boldly. Gallant words, and often quoted, but not wholly justified in the stern tests of war.

Meanwhile, the year 1847 passed in Italy with the tide of nationalism swelling ever higher and with Pius IX, the Holy Father himself, outraging all conservative sentiment by one concession after another to the liberals. The more enlightened lay sovereigns, Leopold II of Tuscany and Charles Albert of Piedmont, were doing the like, but such a loyal "Son of the Church" as Ferdinand II of the Two Sicilies was stung to anger. In his avowedly ultra-Catholic dominions, the cry "Long Live *Pio Nono!*" was punishable as seditious; persons found wearing the Pope's color or portrait were imprisoned, and the royal family deliberately instituted a *novena* (nine days of prayer) that "light might be given" to the benighted head of the Church.

Italy, no less than Germany, was ready for an explosion when Louis Philippe was quitting Paris. In Piedmont, it was generally believed that Charles Albert was ready to do great things for nationalism and liberalism. He wrote, in private letters, of intending "to give the people complete liberty except to do evil." When he visited Genoa, in 1847, he was received with a popular ovation, and "pursued with flowers and blessings," as one certain to play the hero. At his capital in Turin, even before the revolution at Paris, the demand for a constitution became irresistible.

Charles Albert, indeed, hesitated before taking the final plunge. He had solemnly promised his uncle and predecessor, Charles Felix (at Metternich's suggestion), "to govern the country even as he had found it governed." When the pressure upon him for a constitution became too great, he considered abdication, but a sagacious confessor assured him "he could break his promise without mortal sin." Therefore, on February 8, 1848, to a great council of his ministers and notables, the King presented a piece of paper at the top of which he had written "The Catholic religion, Apostolic and Roman, is the only religion of the state; all other religions are tolerated according to law." Everything besides this, the council could fill in. The result was a constitution, on the whole, singularly liberal and skilfully constructed, and destined to become the formal constitution of united Italy. On March 4, 1848, the document was promulgated. Ten days later the Pope, in his turn, proclaimed a "Fundamental Statute for the Temporal Government of the States of the Church," setting up two councils of laymen, one named by the Pope, the other elected by property-owners. Stirring days were ahead in Italy.

For Ferdinand II of Naples, the situation, alike in Palermo and Naples, had already become so dangerous that this despotic king himself promulgated a constitution (February, 1848), as did, with greater sincerity, the more benevolent Grand Duke of Tuscany; but the match which actually set Italy in a blaze was applied in the Austrian provinces.

Tobacco was an Austrian state monopoly, and the anti-Austrian elements in Lombardy undertook to show their power and to hurt the Hapsburg treasury by ordering a general boycott of all smoking. Soon any person seen in Milan with pipe, cigar, or cigarette was in danger of his life. The authorities caused gendarmes in mufti to walk the streets smoking, followed by other disguised policemen, ready to catch any who hooted or mocked those in advance. The results were, inevitably, riots in which over sixty citizens were killed or wounded. Then, in February and in March, came the great tidings from Paris and Vienna.

Instantly, Venice blazed into rebellion. The weak Austrian garrison was induced by the audacious young advocate Manin to evacuate the city. But Milan was held by the old Marshal Radetzky with 14,000 men, and for five days the Lombard capital was the scene of terrific street fighting which almost wrecked the city. The Milanese populace at first had almost no weapons; but barricades were thrown up; cannon were improvised of wood with bands of iron. The troops, charging down the narrow streets, were halted with showers of tiles, furniture, paving-stones, and boiling oil. As the struggle went on, the courage of the Milanese rose even higher, and when the Austrians proposed an armistice, the municipal council answered proudly, "The nobles of Milan know how to bury themselves under the ruins of their palaces." When the insurgent chief, Cattaneo, was told that the food supply was nearly gone, he replied "Twenty-four hours of food and twenty-four hours of fasting give us more than time in which to conquer." Soon Radetzky was compelled to lead his demoralized men out of the city, and to fling them into the fortresses of the famous *Quadrilateral*, centering around Mantua and Verona. If it had been possible to have maintained everywhere the ferocious courage of the Milanese insurgents, Italian freedom would have been won.

War Against Austria: Charles Albert's Failure as a National Leader

When the news from Milan reached Turin there seemed to be but one thing for Charles Albert and for Piedmont to do in the name of Italy. "We, men of calm minds," wrote Cavour, then merely a journalist, "accustomed to listen more to cool reason than to the impulses of the heart,

The Grand Canal, Venice

Publishers Photo Service

are bound in conscience to declare that only one path is open to the nation, the government, the king—*war, immediate war!*" Parma and Modena had just chased out their ducal tyrants; the one task remaining seemed to be to complete the expulsion of the Austrians from Lombardy-Venetia. Charles Albert declared war, announcing that he marched toward Milan and Venice, bringing, "the aid which brother extends to brother." Amid great enthusiasm, a new flag was adopted for the Piedmontese army—green, white, and red, blazoned with the arms of the House of Savoy, the Italian tricolor.

Unfortunately, Charles Albert was no Napoleon, and Austria was by no means humbled and helpless. The Italian patriots underestimated the military task. There were thunderous "*vivas!*" but there were relatively few battle-worthy volunteers. If the King had struck immediately after the evacuation of Milan, Radetzky would have been ruined. But while the Piedmontese army slowly mobilized, the Austrian pulled together his forces. The King distrusted irregular soldiery; the popular enthusiasm was not capitalized; and Charles Albert took the field with barely 25,000 poorly equipped regulars. Up to June, 1848, the King was able to win certain successes, and to keep the Austrians on the defensive, but the hour for aiming a decisive blow was now frittered away.

It was the misfortune of the Italian patriots of 1848 that generous intentions were taken for performance; and it was too lightly assumed that the masses were able to make sustained and intelligent sacrifices for liberty. Political privileges were suddenly thrust upon people trained only in the ways of despotism, with the cheerful assumption that they would now act like old Roman senators. Germany suffered from too many lecturing professors at Frankfort; Italy from too many perfervid southerners who served their country with gesticulating loquacity. Above all, there was a failure to realize that *until the military power of Austria was broken,* neither Italian liberalism nor Italian nationality could be secured. And Radetzky, clinging tenaciously to the Quadrilateral fortresses, was receiving reinforcements, biding his time.

While the war thus lagged, one blunder by untrained enthusiasts followed another. In Sicily, a separatist movement almost sundered the island from the mainland. But Ferdinand II was able to appeal to the old local pride of Naples. The army stood by him. Instead of sending effective help to Charles Albert against the Austrians, he recalled the Neapolitan troops already dispatched to the North, and the Sicilian provisional government found itself too feeble to withstand him. The result was that by May, 1849, Ferdinand had been able alike to crush Sicilian resistance and to declare the abolition of the reluctantly granted constitution for Naples itself. Of the 114 deputies who had sat in the short-lived Neapolitan parliament, presently two-thirds were condemned to death, imprisonment, or exile. Thus it was that in southern Italy "Revolution" ran its separate and disastrous course, rendering next to no aid to the general Italian cause.

In the center and North, there was also disunity. Very soon after Venice threw off the Austrian yoke, the insurgents proclaimed her a republic with Manin as president. There was historic precedent for this action, because Venice had been a republic, albeit an utterly oligarchic and illiberal one, up to its conquest by Napoleon (1797). The procedure, nevertheless, was wholly unwise. Throughout Europe, except in France, the prejudice against republican governments was very strong. More serious, however, was the fact that proclaiming a "republic" seemed a direct slap at Charles Albert and his claims to the leadership of Italy. Hearty military coöperation between Piedmont and Venice became impossible.

In the Papal States there was similar nonwisdom. The age-long repression by the clerical despots had rendered the people extraordinarily incapable of operating free institutions; now, when granted an inch they inevitably demanded an ell. Pius IX, amazed at the tempest which his few moves toward liberalism had evoked, protested furiously that he had no desire to precipitate an Italian revolution, or to face war with Austria. "His troops," he announced, "had no other duty than to defend the integrity and safety of the States of the Church." This declaration, coming at the moment when great numbers of his subjects expected him to put his forces unreservedly at the disposal of Charles Albert, with one stroke destroyed his popularity. A republican propaganda began making headway at Rome and throughout the Papal States. Pius IX seemed now revealed as indeed a devout, benevolent potentate, who might bestow many benefits upon his temporal subjects, but who would never permit them to enjoy full political rights. The anomaly of the papal position, that of the spiritual headship of Christendom, yoked with the secular headship of a sizable Italian principality, became revealed. From midsummer, 1848, the question of the *"Temporal Power"* began to stand out in all its nakedness; a question destined to divide and to harass Italy for at least two more generations.

Radetzky Revives the Hapsburg Power

While the republican flood was swelling at Rome, military events were teaching all lovers of Italy that the national cause could only be saved by the most desperate exertions. In the spring and early summer of 1848, the Hapsburg ministers had been so distracted by events in Vienna, Germany, and Hungary, that, to lessen their foes by one, they had sought English mediation to patch up a peace with Piedmont. Lombardy (but not Venetia) was offered to Charles Albert as the price of a treaty. The King was half inclined to accept, but did not accept promptly enough. While he procrastinated, Austria had plucked up courage and resolved to press the war. Meantime, dividing the bearskin before the bear was slain, Charles Albert had allowed Lombardy, Modena, Parma, and parts of Venetia to be declared annexed to Piedmont. Instantly, there were loud protests from the great republican element in central Italy, where Mazzini was assuming ever more complete leadership. It was even suggested that the Austrians had egged on the King to take this debatable action.

Joseph, Count Radetzky, was now eighty-two years old. Nothing but a soldier, grim and inflexible to civilians and devoted to the Vienna autocracy, he was idolized by his soldiers, to whom he was frank and kindly. For their "Vater Radetzky" the "White Coats" would endure much. When the storm broke he had not had over 70,000 men in Italy, but he extricated these from such wasps' nests as Milan, concentrated in the Quadrilateral, fought delaying actions, and held out until about 25,000 reinforcements reached him. When the Hapsburg ministers wrote of negotiation and compromise, Radetzky sent back imploring them not to make peace—he was confident of his ability to defeat Charles Albert.

The latter was showing himself no great captain. His strategy from the outset was timid, and he was forever changing his plans. The King's best chance would have been to force his way over the Adige, to concentrate at Vicenza and cut off reinforcements to Radetzky from the North. The Austrian marshal would then have been paralyzed, and his fortresses must have fallen one by one. On the contrary, the King marched and countermarched, avoided decisive encounters, and seemed to fear the Republicans in Venice and elsewhere quite as much as he did the Hapsburgs. Meantime, it was charged that the King yielded to a kind of personal melancholia. He "gave himself up to fasting and prayer" and was even alleged to have corresponded about his war plans with a visionary nun of Savoy.

Having thus thrown away nearly every good opportunity, Charles Albert found himself forced into the battle of Custozza, only to be routed in it by Radetzky who fell upon him like lightning from the impregnable defences of Mantua. Charles Albert was in full flight. To the wrath of the Milanese, to whom he seemed a cowardly betrayer, he hastily evacuated their city, and as hastily demanded an armistice. This was grudgingly granted, on condition that the King abandon Lombardy. For the moment it seemed as if the war in Italy was over.

Renewal of the War: Abdication of Charles Albert

But Custozza did not end the Italian uprising. Charles Albert had now been grievously discredited, and the Republicans would listen less than ever to his counsels. Venice, isolated and besieged, defended herself gallantly behind her lagoons. In Tuscany, the Republicans first forced the Grand Duke to entrust the ministry to their poet-leader, Guerazzi and then (January, 1849) to summon a Constituent Assembly. The Grand Duke, overwhelmed by the situation, took flight, and speedily, on the advice of Mazzini, Tuscany was proclaimed a republic.

Pius IX vainly strove to resist the flood of the revolution, while making concessions to the liberals. He named, as his chief minister, Rossi, former ambassador to France, a man of capacity and enlightenment, and a true friend of Italian unity. But Rossi soon earned the hatred alike of the republicans and of those red-robed reactionaries, the cardinal secretaries around the Pope. In November, 1848, on the day of the reopening of the new Chambers for the Papal States, he died from a stiletto thrust by a fanatic, and the next day the Roman republicans were thundering at the Quirinal palace, where the Pope had taken refuge, demanding "a Constituent Assembly and War with Austria."

Pius IX, cured of his last love for liberalism, yielded momentarily "in order to prevent great crimes," but protested solemnly to the ambassadors that he was under coercion. In November he fled secretly to the strong fortress of Gaeta, demanding an asylum from his old adversary, the King of Naples, and summoning the assistance of all Catholic governments. At Rome, a triumvirate headed by Mazzini was declared in power and a Constituent Assembly, hastily and tumultuously elected, proclaimed the *Roman Republic* on February 9, 1849.

The expulsion of Pius from Rome inevitably sent a thrill of horror through every clerical in Europe. It was a performance doomed to terrific requital, unless a miracle in arms protected Mazzini's new creation from the attack of Austria and (as it speedily developed) of France. The Roman republicans had little enough loyalty toward Charles Albert, but they were still expecting brave things from Piedmont, for after Custozza and the armistice, Radetzky had let his old foes off comparatively easily —he had still enough of a task hunting down nationalist bands in Lombardy and Venetia, and restoring their hated dukes to Parma and Modena.

In March, 1849, Charles Albert, backed by the demands of his parliament, undertook to reopen the war. Austria was then grappling in the East with Hungary, but Radetzky's forces were still terrible and he had lost none of his uncanny genius. The King had, nominally, 90,000 men under his colors but many were new levies who were no match for the Hapsburg "White Coats." A few days settled the revived military issue. Radetzky promptly took the offensive, and although the Italians at first gallantly repulsed many attacks, Charles Albert's host was brought to bay on the fatal field of Novara. The Italians had to fall back, with their road to Turin severed. Charles Albert had still 48,000 available men, and Radetzky had lost heavily. The King, however, had abandoned all hope of success. "All is lost, even honor," he cried, when the tide of battle turned; and to his aides who tried to keep him from peril, "It is useless—let me die. This is my last day!"

The night after the battle he called his generals around him and abdicated in favor of his eldest son, Victor Emmanuel II. Bidding an eternal farewell to his successor, who knelt weeping before him, and without revisiting Turin, he departed straight for Portugal where, four months later he died.

By his sacrifice Charles Albert cancelled many bad memories. His faults were remembered no longer. He seemed a martyr to the cause of Italy and young Victor Emmanuel inherited all the good will and sympathy which followed his father. From this time onward, the only possible head for a United Italy was the House of Savoy.

The Roman Republic: Garibaldi's Defence of Rome (1849): Triumph of Reaction Throughout Italy

But on the evening after the slaughter at Novara, "United Italy" seemed a thing very far away. The Austrian army speedily restored the Grand Duke Leopold to Tuscany, where the Constitution of 1849 was immediately cancelled, and although Venice, under Manin, held out stoutly, the city was completely isolated and at last was starved into surrender (August 22, 1849). The northern part of the "States of the Church" (Bologna, the Romagna, and the "Marches") up to Ancona was occupied by the Austrians, but Louis Napoleon was now Prince-President of France. He was in close alliance with the clericals, was very anxious to serve them, and was also very anxious to keep the Austrians from obtaining too firm a grip upon all of Italy. Therefore, when Spain, Austria, and Naples simultaneously offered military aid to the Holy Father, a French expedition obtained the pious honor of recovering for him his capital.

That a second-rate city with third-rate defences should withstand the armies of France, Spain, Austria, and the Kingdom of Naples might seem the height of absurdity. But Mazzini, literary prophet of Italian liberty and the most influential of the revolutionary leaders, did not think it so. From his point of view the prestige of Rome throughout the ages had rested on willingness to fight and to die. Ancient Rome had won imperishable renown, and so had the Rome of the popes. A third Rome now rose from the ashes and must show itself worthy of its heritage. Even if the battle was lost, Rome must go down fighting; otherwise, in the happier days to come, when Italy was united, she would not be worthy of becoming Italy's capital. Therefore, he decided to resist and persuaded his colleagues to a like resolve.

A French force of only 9,000 men were disembarked at Civita Vecchia, a convenient port near the old capital, but its general, Oudinot, imagined that he would have little fighting. He was supposed to arrange in the name of France for the preservation of liberal institutions in the Papal States, at the same time bringing back Pius IX. Oudinot's intentions were honest, but the papalists refused stiffly to make any concessions to "impious rebels," while Mazzini and his kindred spirits were resolved to hold out to the end. The Roman Republic had also found a general, who,

GIUSEPPE GARIBALDI (1807-82)

if he had earlier been given the resources of Charles Albert, might have "made" Italy.

Giuseppe Garibaldi (1807-82) was a native of Nice. He had been a conspirator in the "Young Italy" movement, had fled to South America, had fought in the navy of Uruguay, and had returned to Italy in 1848 too late to be of much service in the ill-starred Custozza campaign. Now, in the service of Mazzini, he marched to Rome his famous "volunteers," whose red shirts and Calabrian plumed hats were later to be famous in a score of battles.

Thanks to his valor and energy, the first advance of the French was thrown back with loss. Louis Napoleon now had to press the issue or suffer vast loss of prestige. Oudinot was heavily reinforced, and after a regular siege of Rome, in which Garibaldi resisted to the limits of human resources, the city at last fell, in the summer of 1849. Before it capitulated, however, Garibaldi was commissioned "dictator" of the Roman Republic; for the General thought that if he could escape, the Republic would continue to live as long as he did. Breaking through the line of besiegers with a small force, he fled to the south, thus throwing the Spaniards and Neapolitans off his trail, for they thought him headed for the heel of Italy. Then, feinting toward the northwest and the Mediterranean, he deceived the French who hurried to intercept him. Turning north he raced toward the Apennines with the Austrians at his heels. With one comrade he hid in the pine forests of Ravenna, reached Piedmont, sailed thence to Tunis, Gibraltar, Tangier, and New York, subsequently to return, to fight for Italy ten years thence.

Mazzini also escaped, and in Rome there were left to Republicans only blasted hopes and heroic memories. The clerical reaction in the Papal States was pitiless. Again laymen were excluded from nearly all forms of office, while the prisons were crammed with the most intelligent and economically efficient classes in Central Italy. The French vainly begged the Pope to show moderation; but he was now in the clutches of his Secretary of State, the pitiless Cardinal Antonelli. All liberal reforms were canceled; and when the Pope presently issued an amnesty there were few exceptions.

In the other conquered states or provinces, the plight of the nationalists was evil enough. In Naples, at one time, 20,000 persons were in dungeons for "political crimes," wedged in along with robbers and assassins. When the British government protested at the miserable condition of Sicily after the reconquest, Ferdinand II, "King Bomba," unblushingly replied that "Sicily enjoys perfect tranquillity and the inhabitants are happy to have returned to the protection of their legitimate sovereign." In Modena and Tuscany the reaction and repression was great; in Parma it was still worse. Duke Cosimo III, in that petty state, was an arbitrary and dissolute scoundrel, whose chief minister, Thomas Ward, an Englishman, had formerly been his jockey. In 1854 an officer of his household killed the Duke because of a private grudge, and Parma passed to slightly better hands. In the Austrian provinces there was a reign of terror. The Austrians were charged with flogging Italian women as a regular penalty, and General Haynau, the "hyena of Brescia" (which he had stormed), gained a horrid fame even among the military tyrants of his day.

Only in Piedmont-Sardinia was there hope. Victor Emmanuel II had rejected the broad hint that he could get better peace terms from Austria if he would cancel the new constitution. He steadfastly refused to break faith with his people. "Our endeavor," ran his first proclamation after Novara, "must now be to maintain our honor untarnished, to heal the wounds of public fortune, and to consolidate our constitution."

If the Italian revolution of 1848-49 largely failed, it at least went down fighting, which was more than could have been said of the German revolution. Charles Albert, with all his faults, had won a better place in history than Frederick William IV. The Italian movement had failed partly through inexperience, through friction between republicans and liberal monarchists, through refusal to conciliate the Pope, through the personal infirmities of Charles Albert. But the main cause had been sheer inability to create a war-machine in Italy matching that of Austria. The next time Italy drew the sword, her greatest statesmen had found her a mighty ally.

Chapter 8

ENGLAND: CHARTISM, CORN LAWS, AND THE VICTORIAN COMPROMISE

ON APRIL 10, 1848, there was shaking of heads in London as many good citizens put up the shutters of their houses and the octogenarian Duke of Wellington took council with the Whig government as to the defence of the city. All the bridges over the Thames were closely guarded, the military disposed at strategic points, and almost 170,000 special constables, including Louis Napoleon Bonaparte and W. E. Gladstone, were sworn in, to assist the soldiers against the threatened march on Parliament of supposedly determined workmen, known as Chartists and led by a fire-eating demagogue, Feargus O'Connor. But it was not necessary to use troops, nor were barricades erected in the streets. The march of the proletariat fizzed out in silly fashion. O'Connor, loud-mouthed most of the time, was meekness personified, and the petition of the Chartists to Parliament, instead of reaching that august body borne on the shoulders of angry workmen, was delivered quietly in three cabs, to be received with laughter and dismissed with derision.

How can we account for England's calm in this year of revolutions, when crown after crown was tumbling over on the Continent and the mighty Metternich fled from Vienna? Some might ascribe it to English character, to English stability, to English phlegm, and to English tradition, whereby practised statesmanship yields slowly but surely to the inevitable, thus avoiding revolution. And there is a good deal to be said for this point of view. The British bourgeoisie, it must be remembered, only won a partial victory in 1832. They shared power at last with the aristocracy; they did not control. Because they did not, they were on their good behavior; because they did not, they were held in check by the country gentry who joined with the more enlightened bourgeoisie in passing factory and mine acts which mitigated somewhat the suffering of the proletariat. And the landed aristocracy, also, on the other hand, was compelled to compromise; it was forced to give way, as we shall see, in the matter of the Corn Laws; and the result again proved beneficial in relieving economic distress.

In other words, there had been real progress in England between 1832 and 1848. Not much of it had lightened the lot of the proletariat, but even the working classes were somewhat better off than in 1815. Furthermore, in France the *Capacités*, the intellectuals of the middle class, were on the side of the proletariat in 1848; but in England the reverse was true. The bourgeoisie, the intellectuals, and the landed aristocracy all stood shoulder to shoulder there in 1848 against a mob (not very numerous at that), a mob incompetently led, divided in aim, muddle-headed in program, and in the last analysis, perhaps, not really bloodthirsty.

To explain in slightly more detail why England escaped revolution in 1848, a rough outline of British history during the thirties and forties of the last century is helpful. Such an outline would emphasize the following: the way in which the middle-class Parliament, flushed with victory in 1832, put through reform after reform, for the most part salutary in character; the way in which these reforms both aided and depressed the status of the fast-growing body of wage-earners in British factories; the way in which various remedies were suggested for the amelioration of the lot of the proletariat; the growth of Chartism (a kind of abortive labor movement); the absurdities and misfortunes of the Chartists; the fast-accelerating demand for free trade and the victory thereof in 1846; and finally, the general satisfaction expressed by most articulate British citizens in the middle of the nineteenth century as to the past, present, and future of Great Britain, and their belief that an entirely just and worthwhile political and social milieu was to be found in the Victorian Compromise.

From 1832 to 1874 the balance of power in Parliament rested pretty much with the Liberal party. The Liberals comprised on their right wing a large number of old Whig families, for the most part wealthy, rather conservative, landed gentlemen, content with the compromise of 1832. The left-wing Liberals, on the other hand, professed to be Radicals. They were not at all radical from a modern point of view. Their principal desire was to make England more democratic, to end secret voting, and to enlarge the electorate; they were "Little Englanders" and were skeptical about the continuance of the Empire; but they also belonged to the upper classes and thought little about the proletariat or landless wage-earner, except in so far as they wanted to improve him morally, to teach him how to be economical, and to make the best use of his time and opportunity.

The majority of the Liberals were middle-of-the-road bourgeoisie, whose program was peace, retrenchment, and reform. Most of them were business men, directly or indirectly profiting from the Industrial Revolution. They believed it highly desirable to save money, and one way to do that was to cut expenses. They were for reform, if it did not cost anything; but reform in their eyes was primarily concerned with ending

those privileges which had to do with social, rather than financial, inheritance. They were humanitarian also within limits, particularly in
regard to those abuses, such as Negro slavery, for which they were not
responsible.

The Liberals were opposed in Parliament by the Tory or Conservative
party, in many ways holding an ideology similar to that of the Liberals,
and from 1832 to 1846 under the acknowledged leadership of Sir Robert
Peel, the most prominent man in British politics during that period. He
was a good businessman and represented the right center of Torydom.
He and his followers differed primarily from the Liberals in that they
were less willing to abolish antiquated statutes which gave special
privileges of one kind or another to the landowning class, such as the
continuance of a protective tariff on grain (the Corn Laws) which the
Liberals were for modifying. There was, of course, an extreme right to
the Tory party, old gentlemen dreaming of the aristocratic past when the
money-mad bourgeoisie knew their place. But most Tories were not
really scornful of the middle class—the upper part, that is! Peel's money
came from cotton textiles, and the father of W. E. Gladstone, a young
Tory of prominence, derived his income from the West Indian trade. The
Tories as a group were not opposed to the Industrial Revolution. Many
of the country squires might grumble as the new railways crossed their
hunting preserves; but they sold their rights of way to the railways for
good profits, and their sons frequently rejoiced in the rich dowries which
came with their bourgeois wives. As long as the tradition held that the
ownership of an estate with its rent rolls was the sole entrée to social
preferment, the country gentlemen had little to find fault with.

For three years after 1832, reforms followed one another thick and
fast. The municipalities of Britain, great and growing cities, were democ-
ratized at one stroke to a far greater extent than the country as a whole,
in so far as all local taxpayers were now placed on an equality with
each other in the election of councilmen, who in turn elected aldermen
to determine upon such matters as light, water, sewage, and policing.
The city of London, with its curious medieval charter, alone was exempt
from these laws.

Slavery, meanwhile, came under the ban. The slave trade had been
declared illegal long before, but in 1832 there still remained to British
owners some 750,000 Negro slaves, for the most part in the West Indies
or in South Africa. These were now manumitted, that is, their status was
changed to that of apprenticeship, which meant that for seven years they
were to continue to devote part of their time to their former owners. At
the end of the seven years the slaves were to be entirely free. To com-
pensate their owners for the loss of their property, some £20,000,000 was
appropriated by Parliament.

Two other important laws were also enacted. One, the Factory Act of

1833, was of unquestionable value to the depressed classes; the other, the New Poor Law of 1834, was to some extent the opposite. The Factory Act forbade the employment of children under nine years of age in most textile mills, placed a limit of nine hours a day on the labor of children between nine and thirteen, and of twelve hours a day for young persons between thirteen and eighteen. It was evidently not a very adequate measure and was a distinct disappointment to many contemporary reformers; but it was a decided improvement upon earlier legislation, which scarcely interfered with the brutalization of children in British factories. That it was passed at all was due more to public opinion aroused by Tories than by Liberals. In Parliament the foremost agitator for the law was Lord Ashley, afterward Earl of Shaftesbury, a high Tory; and outside of Parliament credit belongs primarily to Richard Oastler, a most simple Christian gentleman, a Tory who had fought the Reform Bill and who held the antiquated point of view that it was the duty of the Crown, the Church, and the landed gentry to look out for the welfare of the children of workingmen in British cities. Most Tories, as far as this particular measure was concerned, agreed with him, the more readily perhaps because to do so would take nothing out of their own pockets, for their income came from rentals rather than from dividends.

Agitation for the welfare of children in industry now continued. Under constant pressure from Lord Shaftesbury and other reformers, Parliament took up the question of child labor in mines. Conditions were proved worse there than they had been even in the factories, boys and girls of seven and eight working twelve hours a day, stripped to the waist, hitched up like little animals, drawing diminutive wagons filled with coal through passageways too narrow for a mule to enter, the breasts of little girls frequently so hardened as to make sex almost indistinguishable from sex. After long years, Parliament in 1842 ended altogether the employment of women underground, as well as that of boys under ten. Finally in 1850, it went a step further and limited in both mines and factories the working hours of young persons under eighteen to ten hours a day. Above that age no limits were set.

The New Poor Law of 1834 was passed with somewhat less difficulty than that which the Factory Act of 1833 encountered. The object of the later statute was to make poverty so disgraceful and so uncomfortable that, rather than accept poor relief, the workman and laborer would strain his individual initiative to the utmost, be very prudent in having children, and be very careful in saving money for his old age. The law provided for one uniform system through the country, directed by three commissioners in London who were authorized to herd the poor into large workhouses (bastilles). In them there was to be a minimum of heat, a minimum of light, a minimum of clothing, and a minimum of space. Children were to be separated from parents, husbands separated from wives, and everything possible was done so as to make men and women struggle to the utmost rather than end in a "bastille."

There was, unquestionably, some excuse for this law. Before its passage, poor relief had been a charge on the local parishes, and ever since the end of the eighteenth century it had been customary to issue doles to the poor, very frequently in order to supplement starvation wages. The dole system had encouraged the poor to beget more children, for the larger the family the larger the dole; and it had encouraged factory owners constantly to cut wages, since they knew that the dole would keep their operatives alive. The weight of local taxation for poor relief thus became very onerous and some kind of reform was sadly needed. From the point of view of the English Liberals the answer was to be found in a more provident proletariat which would have fewer children and save more money. The ranks of the bourgeois Liberals were swelling fast, because hard-working, enterprising men were inventing or using new machinery whereby the sum total of wealth was increased. It would increase still further if taxes were lowered and the poor left to their own devices.

England, of course, was a Christian country and those who fell by the wayside in the economic struggle should not be permitted openly to die; on the other hand England was a country of business men and it was certainly unbusinesslike to encourage pauperism. The British Liberals who argued thus were not hard-hearted ogres; they were decent, friendly people who were hypnotized by statistics. Population was growing rapidly, and they believed it inevitable that it would press upon the food supply which they conceived of as limited in amount. The only salvation lay in keeping down the population. The Tories as a group were not very different. There was more opposition to the New Poor Law among them than among the Liberals; but after all many of the Tories were as good business men as their Liberal opponents and all Tories had to pay taxes and found them hateful. The New Poor Law certainly was inexpensive.

The four statutes which we have mentioned, the Municipality Act, the Anti-Slavery and Factory Acts, and the New Poor Law were the great basic laws passed by Parliament during the decade of the thirties. There were a number of others bringing slight reform here and there, ending certain anomalies and unfair privileges, assisting the status of Jews, reorganizing the ecclesiastical system, and commencing (very modestly) state aid for education. For the most part, however, Parliament rested on its labors. The advent of the young Victoria to the throne in 1837 found the country well advanced on the path of industrialization. Fortunes were being made at home and abroad, the prestige of Britain stood high throughout the world, and both bourgeoisie and Tories were content.

Not so with the working class, or proletariat. With every new industrial invention (and they followed one another thick and fast) there was

QUEEN VICTORIA (1819-1901)

temporary technological unemployment until newer industries, increasing the demand for labor, caught up the slack. In the interim, while waiting for this to happen, there was for many no alternative except the poorhouse or a heart-rending attempt to compete against power machinery with sheer human muscle. Furthermore, employment fluctuated for another reason, since business, then as now, tended to grow at an uneven rate, now expanding, now contracting. The first world-wide economic depression came in 1837, throwing many out of work, and this was the precursor of many such.

The proletariat, besides, lived for the most part in cities—and such cities! Jerry-built houses, built back to back, unventilated, without toilet facilities, were filled to overflowing as the tide of industrial workers swept in from rural England and from Ireland. "The town of the industrial age," it has been well put, "without beauty or method marked the spirit of this age just as truly as St. Paul's Cathedral marked the spirit of the Renaissance or the cathedral of Durham the spirit of the Crusades. It expressed a concentration in which religion, beauty, leisure, the life of the spirit, or the life of the senses were all held to be rivals to the stern life of selfish duty. The purpose of man's life was not to fight or to pray, to contemplate or to create, to enjoy or to become, but to make profits, profits for himself, if a master, profits for another, if a servant." [1]

What, then, was to be done? There were several solutions coming both from the workingclass itself and from other classes during the first ten years of Victoria's reign, and they were in hot competition for the approval of the proletariat. One solution, or rather group of solutions, came from that lovable but erratic British socialist, Robert Owen. Like the French socialists of this period, Owen was a romanticist at heart, expending much time and energy in dreaming of a future day when competition in money-making would give place to idyllic recognition of human brotherhood. Unlike Saint-Simon and Fourier, however, Owen was himself a man of business, a manufacturer and a successful one. Indeed, he had received so much flattery because of his ability to keep up dividends while abolishing the worst aspects of child labor in his factory that his head had been turned. Owen spoke and wrote at great length of "coöperative communities," where central kitchens, a central nursery, a central assembly hall, and so forth, would make for human happiness; where, forgetting the plow and returning to the spade, men could engage in both agriculture and manufacturing. These communities, once voluntarily established, would, he thought, prove so successful that they would be copied everywhere and sweet reasonableness would win the day.

Owen, also, was very keen about labor exchanges. Since, he argued, all value was determined by labor, then commodities ought to exchange for the amount of labor expended on their production. Let tags be placed on each commodity in a labor exchange expressing not their value in pounds, shillings, and pence but in days and hours of labor time. A watchmaker bringing to an exchange a watch which took five days and six hours to make should be able to exchange it for a pair of shoes with one day and four hours. If he did thus, he should get back a ticket with four days and two hours with which to make additional purchases. Also dear to the heart of Owen was a Grand Consolidated Trade Union, a kind of super-labor-organization which would knit together the scattered trade unions and make possible a general strike of all skilled workmen.

This last scheme brought the British socialist movement in contact with that of trade-unionism. The trade-unionists, however, had a much

---

[1] J. L. and Barbara Hammond, *The Rise of Modern Industry*, p. 222, quoted by permission of Harcourt, Brace and Company.

more limited objective than had Owen. From the days of their partial recognition in the late twenties they had sought primarily for the following: the organization of workmen by crafts and not by industries (that is, carpenters, masons, roofers, and so on, in separate unions, not in one big building union; the right of collective bargaining with employers; the closed shop (none to be employed except union men); shorter hours; higher wages; the limitation of apprentices (this to keep down the number of workmen in any trade in order to keep wages up); and the lengthening of the period of apprenticeship for the same purpose. The agenda of the unionists was long but the scope of their activity was somewhat narrow. It was confined to the limited welfare of small groups and never in its early days envisaged that of the proletariat as a whole, let alone that of the great mass of the unskilled.

Chartism

In addition to the socialists and the trade-unionists, there were the Chartists. Chartism, in its origin, was a working-class movement, both educational and political. It dates from the organization of the London Workingman's Association in 1836, started by certain inconspicuous cabinet-makers, compositors, and booksellers. It was tinctured by Owenism and has been well described as "a belief that democracy is a necessary preliminary to social justice and equity." The proletariat had been left out in the cold by the Reform Bill of 1832, so the London Association thought, and in the year of its birth this latter body drew up a petition to Parliament to enact a "People's Charter," whence the name "Chartists."

The petition contained the famous six points of the Charter; Parliaments elected annually; universal suffrage; the ballot (secret voting); payment of members; no property qualification for members; and equal electoral districts. On the surface, then, Chartism was entirely political in its demands, simply urging a thoroughly democratic government.

Beneath the surface, however, this was not the case. Chartism, like Owenism and trade-unionism, flowed directly out of anticapitalistic economic theory. The Chartists were convinced that something was wrong with the contemporary and dominant liberal laissez-faire organization of economic life, but that nothing could change this until free democracy should prevail in politics. What the change was to be could come later.

Chartism spread with oil-like rapidity over a great part of industrial England. Bitterness against the New Poor Law drew thousands to its support; branches were formed everywhere; and in two years it was sufficiently strong to summon and to support a convention in London, called "The People's Parliament."

The People's Parliament had an exaggerated idea of its own importance; otherwise it never would have invited Her Majesty's House of

Commons to meet in joint session with it. Unfortunate, too, was the fact that O'Connor, with his bull-like voice and empty brain, had attached himself to the Chartist cause. O'Connor talked of the possibility of using physical force and the People's Parliament rang with bold pronunciamentos. As it did so, the more timid and the more intelligent Chartists began to resign. The missionaries sent out by the People's Parliament began to return with pessimistic reports. In the country villages they were denied a hearing and in the cities they were not very successful. Evidently, the Chartists could claim no majority of the British people.

Nevertheless, their petition received a respectful hearing in the House of Commons and some few votes. The most interesting speech made there in regard to it was by a young Jewish member, Benjamin Disraeli, who displayed considerable sympathy for the Chartists, if not for Chartism. In his opinion the workingmen of England were justified in believing that they had been duped by the middle class which had advanced in power "without making simultaneous advances in the exercises of the great social duties." The aristocracy was the more natural guardian of the rights of the poor—so Disraeli asserted.

Chartism now went underground for a time. The physical-force Chartists, having frightened away the more moderate of the proletariat, actually attempted two or three minor insurrections, one of which, among the miners of the Welsh border, was sufficiently serious to produce a skirmish with soldiers, and a number of Chartists were killed.

For a year or so Chartism seemed dead. Then it mysteriously revived. "Moral-force Chartists" got the upper hand and we read of "Christian Chartists," "Temperance Chartists," and even of the "Shakespearean Association of Leicester Chartists," organized by Thomas Cooper, a shoemaker, for the education of working people. William Lovett, one of the first founders of Chartism, was released from jail. From the beginning he had insisted on the primacy of education if Chartism was to flourish. His plans were specific. By popular subscription he proposed to start 710 traveling libraries at £20 each, 4 missionaries at £200 each, and so on.

Corn Laws

Then, as Owenites, trade-unionists, and Chartists competed with one another for the support of the proletariat, a fourth contender entered the field. At the same time that the People's Parliament met and within a stone's throw of it, came the first meeting of the Anti-Corn-Law League, an organization destined to exercise more power and influence than Owenites, trade-unionists, and Chartists combined.

The Anti-Corn-Law League was the chosen instrument of the British textile manufacturers and into its coffers money literally poured. It had as principal organizer one of the ablest brains of the nineteenth century, that of Richard Cobden; it had as its foremost spokesman on the public platform possibly the finest voice to which Englishmen ever listened, that of John Bright; and its platform was so nicely adjusted to the needs of the average British citizen that its victory ultimately was assured.

The one and only purpose of the Anti-Corn-Law League was explicit in its title: The League existed to obtain free trade, particularly in food-stuffs. Its members belonged almost exclusively in the beginning to the middle class; and being a bourgeois organization through and through, it could count in advance on the hostility of the landed gentry who knew that free trade would threaten their rent rolls. The landed gentry were still very numerous in the House of Commons, and the League had no chance of a victory in Parliament without the active support of the prole-tariat. Could it succeed in winning it? Once before, in 1830-32, the middle class had enlisted the help of the proletariat in a political campaign. Now it was attempting to do it again.

The case against the Corn Laws was a strong one. However necessary they might have been in 1815, it seemed absurd that the ever growing multitude of English artisans should pay an inordinate price for bread—virtually, as it was claimed, a kind of tribute, exacted not by farm laborers and farmers but by landlords unwilling to see their rents diminish. The farm laborer could hardly be said to profit from the Corn Laws. He was living on a subsistence level anyway and was deserting the farm for the city as fast as he could. The proletarian in the city paid the piper. Often he was unemployed. Very well then, argued the missionary of the League, repeal the Corn Laws and automatically the poorer marginal land will go out of cultivation. The money invested in it will flow to the city, build new factories, and thus increase employment; and the price of wheat will drop, thus making the loaf cheaper and raising the real wages of the worker.

The Chartists did not know what to do about this new and vigorous agitation. While most of them were suspicious of honeyed words ema-nating from the middle class, many believed it a good thing to abolish the Corn Laws. On the other hand, some favored the continuance of the old protective system. They argued that the repeal of the Corn Laws would simply exchange one set of masters for another and that a "money-lord" was even worse than a "landlord." The Chartists were now divided among themselves and the Anti-Corn-Law League drove a wedge into their none-too-solid ranks.

As it did so, those Chartist leaders who hated the League and its propaganda tried to howl down the League's missionaries. The latter had better brains as well as more money than their opponents, and the rough tactics of the more extreme Chartists hurt their own cause. Little by little, in the minds of the majority of the workmen, the Charter, al-though admirable, did not seem quite as important as Corn Law repeal, for "cheap bread" was an attractive slogan and one more readily visualized than democratic vistas.

The League now proceeded to capture the Liberal party and even a few of the more enlightened Tories were willing to make a strategic retreat and abandon the Corn Laws, particularly those Tories whose income was derived from stocks and shares as well as from agricultural rents. Nevertheless, so close was the vote in Parliament that Lord John Russell, the Liberal leader, hesitated to force the issue, knowing that the House of Lords, full to overflowing with Tories, would be apt to overturn any important Liberal measure which did not have a large majority behind it. Thereupon, Russell refused to form a ministry, and Peel, who had resigned, resumed office.

At this time (1846) harvests had been poor in England and grain prices were high. In Ireland there was a nasty famine, caused by the failure of the potato crop. The rack-rented peasants of Ireland were dying by the thousand, for the Corn Laws made bread prohibitive in cost. Sir Robert Peel had to do something and he thought it best to give in and repeal the Corn Laws. To do so would not only stop the famine in Ireland but would bring an end to the pesky League which was becoming week by week very influential. Peel was both a good business man and a good politician. If the unpleasant thing had to be done by some one, the sooner the better; and his Tory party might as well receive the credit. Therefore he, with the aid of the Liberals, forced repeal through the Commons. The Duke of Wellington did likewise in the Lords. "Potatoes put Peel into his damned fright," said that aged warrior. But potatoes or no, the Queen's government had to be carried on, and the Duke had a keenly developed scent for telling when retreats were necessary. The Charter, for the time being, had dropped into the background and the stage was occupied by potential Anti-Corn-Law mobs. It would be better to give in to them and keep the Queen's government in Tory hands. Thus thought the Duke.

And so passed England's second great crisis, that of 1846—that of 1832 being the first. The country gentlemen, betrayed, never forgave Peel. Young Mr. Disraeli assailed his former Chief with venom and practically drove him out of the Tory ranks. The proud and immaculate Peel did not go unattended. Many of the brighter Tories followed him, among them young Mr. Gladstone, more scornful than ever of the upstart, Disraeli. The "Peelites," so-called, were now practically a third party in the House of Commons.

The Corn Law repeal, whatever else may be said, did have an immediate effect on lowering the price of bread, and an improvement took place in the condition of the British proletariat. It was, perhaps, only temporary, but it lasted long enough to dish the Chartist movement, which, as we have seen, showed one last spasmodic sign of life two years later, in 1848. Mobs might rage through the streets of Paris, Berlin, and Vienna, but not in England.

Most Englishmen, in the middle of the nineteenth century, felt like congratulating themselves. They had not so much deliberately worked out a satisfactory form of government as they had happened upon it. But they liked it well, this system which history knows as the Victorian Compromise. Under it the aristocracy and the middle class shared power on an approximately equal basis to the exclusion of the working class. The bourgeoisie had the more votes; but on the other hand the upper strata of it so dovetailed into the aristocracy that the latter's prestige remained enormous. Furthermore, a sufficient number of "pocket" or nomination boroughs still survived to prevent the landlord class from feeling too much outweighed. The proletariat, of course, did not share in this division of power; but on the other hand it was too humble and too divided to contend very vigorously for it. Proletarians were assured constantly that the gates of opportunity were open for them and many of them believed this true. As a matter of fact there was a certain amount of truth in this statement. Optimism was in the air, and the proletariat began to share in it to a degree. England, by 1850, "was building mills, railways, docks, harbors, waterworks, gas-works, for the whole world." British capital was everywhere. England was covered with a network of railways in the eighteen-forties; and the very railways of the Continent were built largely with English capital and by British engineers. One British contractor had enterprises under construction in five different continents, all at the same time. The sum total of British exports climbed from £40,000,000 in 1821 to £62,000,000 in 1831, to £104,000,000 in 1841, and to £188,000,000 in 1851, an unparalleled record. It was due to many causes not related to politics, to reserves of capital, to mineral wealth, to climate, to geography. But the greatest advance had taken place under that bourgeois-aristocratic alliance, the Victorian Compromise. The bourgeoisie had yielded in the matter of the Factory Acts and continued to yield in that of social prestige, willingly permitting the aristocracy to control the major offices of state, the army, the navy, the Church of England. The aristocracy, meanwhile, had made two major sacrifices, a political one in 1832, an economic one in 1846. Everything now had been compromised that needed compromise, so thought the majority in England's Parliament. That country regarded with sympathy the struggles of the poor Continental countries to secure liberalism and nationalism: but England had no intention of embroiling herself in war to aid Germans, French, or Italians—why should she?

Chapter 9

THE SECOND EMPIRE: NAPOLEON III: THE CRIMEAN WAR

On December 10, 1848, by an overwhelming majority, the people of France chose Louis Napoleon president of the Second Republic. The "Napoleonic legends" had triumphed. Very skilfully, before the election, the agents of the victorious candidate capitalized the traditions of the great Empire. "Why *shouldn't* I vote for this gentleman—" cried a veteran, approaching the ballot box, "I, whose nose was frozen near Moscow!" Similar reasoning, if not like experience, prevailed with millions of the peasants

The son of Louis Bonaparte and Hortense de Beauharnais had already crossed the public ken at a few meteoric intervals before public favor swept him in the Élysée. Born in 1808, his parents were banished from France while he was very young. He spent much of his youth in Germany and Switzerland, and he always spoke French with a marked German accent. "He is," Queen Victoria once observed shrewdly, "as little French as possible, and as much more of a German."

The Duke of Reichstadt, the "Eaglet," Napoleon II, died in 1832, and Louis Napoleon became the most eligible heir to his uncle's dubious heritage. Carefully and consciously, he began trying to impress French imagination, and create an atmosphere which would enable him to bid for power. In 1836, he undertook to raise a mutiny in the garrison of Strasbourg. The conspirators were promptly overpowered, and Louis Philippe had the young pretender placed on shipboard and landed in New York. The prince quickly slipped back first to Switzerland and then to England. In 1839 he published a book *Des Idées Napoléoniennes*, "a curious mixture of Bonapartism, socialism and pacifism." Here, as elsewhere, he promulgated his favorite theory that the ideal government was one in which the people, by democratic choice, entrusted the entire control to a great tribune of popular liberty, as he claimed (in defiance of history) Napoleon I to have been.

In 1840, with fifty-six followers, he landed at Boulogne on a second filibuster to overthrow the Orleans monarchy. This time he failed so ludi-

crously that the world ceased to regard him seriously. At his trial before
the Court of Peers he nevertheless asserted himself with boldness: "I
represent before you a principle, a cause, a defeat. The principle is the
sovereignty of the people. The cause is that of the Empire. The defeat is
Waterloo." But the unsympathetic tribunal sentenced him to life imprisonment in a fortress. He disappeared into fairly easy captivity within
the fortress of Ham. In May, 1846, he contrived to escape back to London,
and spent most of his time there "in a furious pursuit of pleasure," until
the Paris populace chased out the Orleanists. Never, however, through
all bad luck, did he lose faith in his star, in his ultimate rise to power.
"Though fortune has twice betrayed me," he would say to his intimates,
"yet my destiny will none the less be surely fulfilled. *I wait.*" But in 1848
he waited no more.

In June, 1848, four French departments elected him simultaneously to
the new National Assembly. He resigned at the first signs of opposition,
and thus had no part in the repressive measures which made the new
republic unpopular. Presently he was reëlected. His speeches in the
Assembly were so awkward that his colleagues soon held him in utter
contempt, but their opinions did not spread to the great masses of
peasants, of law-abiding bourgeois, and even of the Paris radicals, who
considered him a better choice than the "butcher" Cavaignac. The
Monarchists also looked on him as the least of evils, and the clericals
were already recognizing their man. Therefore, the election of December
10, although it astonished all Europe, was really somewhat of a foregone
conclusion.

From the moment that Louis Napoleon became president he grasped
completely that the passionate desire of the great majority of Frenchmen
was for *order,* for a public condition whereby, along with reasonable personal freedom, every man could be sure of his property rights, and could
plan with confidence his future. To this end the President exerted himself
to cause the name of his mighty uncle to be seen through a halo of
beneficence and peace. "The name of Napoleon," he announced during
1849, "is in itself a program; it stands for order, authority, religion, and
the welfare of the people in internal affairs, and in public affairs for
national dignity."

Louis Napoleon's Intrigues to Reëstablish the Empire

Many things helped Louis Napoleon in 1849: but nothing helped
more than the elections to the new Legislative Assembly provided by the
constitution. France was already swinging back towards conservatism—
no more barricades, no more public workshops, no more threats to honest
property! On May 13, 1849, there were only 250 avowed Republican
deputies elected out of a large, lumbering Chamber of 750. The avowed

Royalists were very strong; the pronounced "moderates" still stronger. The new Chamber was thus that of "a Republic without Republicanism."

There was plenty of distrust of the Prince-President's designs; yet there were no competent leaders nor projects for thwarting him. On the contrary, the ill-compacted conservative majority played directly into Louis Napoleon's hands. As the best means for attacking socialism in 1850, they carried a new electoral law, juggling the requirements as to tax-paying before voting. The practical result of this measure was to reduce the total number of voters from some nine million to six million. "The vile multitude," thus disfranchised, of course cursed the Assembly. "I cannot understand," said Mme. Cornu to the President, "how you, the offspring of universal suffrage, can defend the restricted suffrage?" "You do not understand," he answered calmly, "I am preparing the ruin of the Assembly." "But you will perish with it!" "On the contrary," he rejoined, "when the Assembly is hanging over the precipice I shall cut the rope."

The Assembly was thus deliberately undermining that republican constitution of which it was nominally the official defender. The largest faction undoubtedly desired to restore the monarchy—preferably, however, under a king very chastened and liberalized. "My conscience won't trouble me," remarked Thiers, again active in politics, "if the safety of the country requires the tearing down of the dirty poster [the constitution]." In 1850 the Orleanist and Legitimist factions in France tried to patch up a reconciliation. The only thing still needful for the project, then, would be to remove the Prince-President.

The Prince-President, however, had other plans. He was rapidly winning over the army. On the 10th of October, 1850, at a grand review, many of the troops marching past him thundered out the old cry, "Vive l'Empereur!" Louis Napoleon also made a kind of progress through Burgundy, Normandy, and other regions, evoking great popular demonstrations in his favor. It was his good fortune to be able to see beyond the mere squabbles of parties, assemblies, and ministers, and to catch the great drifts of public opinion, embodying the real wishes of the bulk of the French nation—not those of very limited classes, as had been the blunder of Guizot and Louis Philippe. He had lived long in England and had learned how much could be accomplished in English elections by small, indirect bribes, and the distribution of strong drink. While president he was not above ordering double rations of brandy for the garrison of Paris and distributing innumerable doles of half a franc (ten cents) each. Military banquets were given, at which sergeants and corporals sat beside higher officers. Promotions were skilfully granted or withheld, and generals and colonels opposed to the President were quietly superseded.

The real test was to come over the question of the reëlection of the President. Louis Napoleon's mandate expired in 1852. The constitution forbade any immediate reëlection. In 1850 he began a campaign to force a revision of the fundamental law. His friends and agents manipulated the departments so that the Assembly was bombarded with enormous petitions demanding that the president should be capable of reëlection. Did the Assembly fear to permit a free choice by the voters of France? At the same time, Louis Napoleon himself began taking the offensive: "Whatever duties," he announced, "the nation may impose upon me, she will find me ready to carry out her wishes." At other times he skilfully blew up the fears that a new socialist uprising was preparing. "A vast demagogic conspiracy is being organized in France and all over Europe," he informed the Assembly; but at the same moment he was conciliating the lower classes by demanding the repeal of the restrictive electoral law of 1850 and showing himself very zealous for universal suffrage. The deputies, broken into factions and with Republicans and Monarchists hooting one another, could unite on no protective measures. And at last the "Man of Destiny" was ready to strike.

An adventurer such as Louis Napoleon never rode to power unaided. Around him had already gathered a group of adroit, unscrupulous speculators, men capable of any major villainy in stock market, politics, or war which promised them place and profit. Chief of these was his own illegitimate half-brother, the Duc de Morny, a cool, elegant man of fashion, master of all the sordid forces in Parisian society, and never bothered by a conscience. At his elbow, too, was St. Arnaud, the new minister of war, named for the occasion. After a disreputable earlier career he had commanded successfully a brigade in Algiers, and the President knew that he would shoot down his French fellow-citizens just as readily as he had shot down Arabs. Morny was named minister of the interior just before the blow fell, and with him was also Maupas, a congenial spirit, appointed prefect of police for some very necessary work.

Louis Napoleon was intensely ambitious, and doubtless he had deceived himself into the belief that he was doing France a service by giving her stable institutions. However, when on the brink of decisive action, late in 1851, he seems to have hesitated. The always shrewd observer, de Tocqueville, said of him, "There were in him *two* men—the first the ex-conspirator, the fatalistic dreamer who believed himself summoned to be master of France [and perhaps of Europe]; the second the Epicurean, languidly enjoying an unwonted comfort and the facile pleasures that his present position afforded him, and unwilling to risk their loss by attempting to climb higher." But Morny's ambition, at least, was made of sterner stuff. Probably by December, 1851, the President had so committed himself to his itching confederates that retreat would have been impossible, and the final moves of the game were hardly in his personal hands.

During the last hectic months before the *coup,* Louis Napoleon was all things to all men. The Élysée was open to all classes, and the chief magistrate was most democratic. *"Prince, altesse, monsieur, monseigneur, citoyen"*—he smiled whatever his visitors called him. At last matters were coming to grips. A strong faction in the Assembly proposed that the president of that body should have power to call in an armed force to "protect it," very obviously from the President of the republic. The measure failed, thanks to the dissensions of the Deputies, but the warning was a plain one. The Assembly had refused to amend the election law and also had refused to make the President eligible for reëlection; and Morny, "the hero of the Bourse and a successful gambler," took his measures. No melodrama was ever better executed upon the stage than was his now in Paris.

The Coup d'État of December 2, 1851: Louis Napoleon Seizes Power

On the evening of December 1, 1851, Louis Napoleon affably "received," as was his wont every Monday night. The instant the last guests had departed, the Élysée became the scene of intense activity. Morny, St. Arnaud, and Maupas had arranged everything. Squads of police or soldiers hastened away to arrest in their beds Thiers, Changarnier, Cavaignac, and nearly all the other prominent Monarchist or Republican chiefs. The government printers were compelled, under strict guard, to set up and print two remarkable decrees and an "Appeal to the People," which the next morning were placarded over Paris. The first decree dissolved the Assembly and declared the reëstablishment of universal suffrage. The second summoned the people to the polls to accept or reject the following "plebiscite":

"The French people wish to maintain the authority of Louis Napoleon Bonaparte, and delegate to him the powers needful for making a constitution."

The appeal set forth that the public safety was in danger and that "my [Louis Napoleon's] duty is to maintain the Republic by invoking the judgment of the only sovereign I can recognize in France—the people." Such was the situation when Paris awoke on the morning of December 2, to find the garrison under arms and the hall of the Assembly crammed with soldiers.

Despite the arrest of their leaders, 217 deputies hastily gathered in a district *mairie*, and began the process provided in the constitution for deposing the president in case of a gross abuse of power. Their deliberations ended when a strong force of infantrymen appeared at the building and marched them all away to various prisons. Certain prominent Republicans, for example, Jules Favre and the famous author Victor Hugo, were still at large. They made a frantic attempt to get the industrial quarters to take up arms and to rebuild their barricades. The artisan classes, disgusted at the doings of the Assembly and now utterly bewildered, responded only very hesitantly, but the Bonapartist leaders deliberately refrained from nipping this movement in the bud. They wished, said one of their chiefs, "to give the insurrection time to develop," in order to convince France that the only choice was between Louis Napoleon and radical anarchy. On the 4th, there were enough barricades and enough insurgents behind them to suit the purpose. St. Arnaud now cleared the streets ruthlessly, shooting down (it was alleged) many innocent promenaders in relatively quiet parts of the city. Late in the evening, the "revolt" had been practically snuffed out—and the nation could be assured that it had been saved from a hideous uprising.

Morny could thus master Paris, but it was not quite so easy to win the departments. In more than twenty, the Republicans attempted local insurrections, which, with unified leadership and a little better support in the capital, might have taxed the new dynasts to control. It was now possible, however, to clamp martial law upon thirty-two departments and to set up summary courts to judge without appeal. By official documents, some 27,000 persons were lodged in prison with 4,000 pent up in the casemates of the Paris forts alone. For the crime of "belonging to a secret society" or for like offenses, 9,530 persons were transported to Algeria, and 239 to undergo the "dry guillotine" in the living death at Cayenne; while 84 of the deposed deputies, including Thiers and Victor Hugo, were banished "for the sake of general society."

Morny and his half-brother thus took pains that their speculation should not speedily come to nought. The plebiscite promised by the coup d'état took place while France was still stunned, bewildered, and bereft of any leaders except the usurpers in Paris. No time was left for any anti-Bonapartist agitation, even had it been permitted. The coup was on December 2, and the electors were summoned to the polls on the 20th. Morny had issued his orders to his henchmen, the prefects of the departments. They were to omit nothing "to secure the success of the government idea"; they were to scatter proclamations "for the guidance of right-thinking people"; and finally, they were told that "entire liberty of conscience, but a firm and persistent use of all allowable means of persuasion—*that* is what the government expects of you."

The Plebiscite of 1851 and the Proclamation of the "Second Empire" (December, 1852)

Even in those days of coercion, there were still a few brave voices raised. Jules Simon, Professor of Philosophy at the Sorbonne, informed his class: "I owe you not a lesson but an example; France is to be convoked to approve or disapprove what has just taken place. If there is going to be one word of disapproval I wish to say to you openly now, that that will be mine." Simon was, of course, immediately dismissed from his professorship. The average Frenchman must have been possessed with a great sense of helplessness. If the majority disapproved the coup, and the President suddenly resigned office, what was left for the state but sheer anarchy? Hoodwinked, hustled, coerced, intimidated as the voters were, the result was a foregone conclusion. On December 20, almost 7,500,000 Frenchmen voted "yes" on the question of approving Louis Napoleon's policy; almost 650,000 "no." The coup d'état had been a most successful speculation. The Second Empire was crossing the threshold.

There followed a year of preparatory interregnum. Louis Napoleon declared himself substantially a dictator, by means of a long series of *decrets-lois*. He was still, technically, only a "president" but all through 1852 he received the honors of a sovereign. At Bordeaux, in a famous speech, he announced to the nation the blessings which the new style of monarchy would bring to the nation. "Certain people say 'the empire is war.' I say that *the empire is peace!*" and then added to these words so flattering to the national pride, "*When France is satisfied, the world is tranquil.*"

The press was accordingly placed under a system of "administrative repression," putting every newspaper at the arbitrary mercies of a minister or even a department prefect. In November the Senate (a new body appointed by the ruler himself) proposed that its author and master should be named emperor. On November 21, 1852, yet again the French voters were summoned to the polls to confirm this proposition. The official figures were 7,800,000 "yes" and only 253,000 "no"; but over two millions had refrained from voting. On December 2 "Napoleon III" was officially proclaimed hereditary Emperor of the French. The cycle from French monarchy to democracy had thus swung back to monarchy. In 1830 the French people had refused to let Charles X rule by "ordinances." In 1848 they had condemned Louis Philippe for the abuses of personal government. Now they were permitting Louis Napoleon to erect almost a despotism. "Through dread of monarchy and of anarchy, *they were stripping themselves of liberty.*" (Emile Bourgeois)

Napoleon III was now forty-four. "The impassibility of his face and his lifeless glance" convinced observers that he was still the dreamer of his youth—full of noble ideas if also of unlimited ambitions. Events were now to prove how he would use the enormous power which fate had committed into his hands. From 1852 to 1870 the Great Adventurer was the most conspicuous man in Europe.

For almost a whole decade fortune smiled upon the Second Empire, both at home and abroad. The tempo of economic activity, stimulated by the discovery of gold in California (1848) and in Australia (1851), was accelerated throughout the whole western world in the eighteen-fifties, and France shared in the benefits which resulted. In the same way as the first Napoleon capitalized the French Revolution, his nephew capitalized the Industrial Revolution. In some respects the latter lived up to the old Saint-Simon dream that the ruler should be the first *Industriel* or business head of the state. While yet only President of the Second Republic, Louis Napoleon visited factories, pinned decorations on the blouses of old workmen, attended the baptismal ceremonies of new loco-

NAPOLEON III, EMPEROR OF THE FRENCH (1808-73)

motives, placing presidential garlands around their shining smokestacks. After he became Emperor his government did everything possible to expand business activity. It granted a charter to the *Crédit Mobilier*, a joint-stock enterprise to stimulate investment banking. The company was phenomenally successful; it extended credit to railway companies, provided funds for the transatlantic steamship service, amalgamated the gas companies of Paris, and by 1855 was paying its shareholders over 175 francs on shares issued at 500. The *Crédit Foncier*, an institution on somewhat similar lines, was organized to loan money on real estate, and from it came hundreds of millions of francs for the rebuilding of Paris.

The Bank of France grew so rapidly that it was necessary to found branches in all of the eighty-six departments. Railway mileage increased from 3,627 kilometers in 1851 to 16,207 in 1858.

French trade was booming, both internal and foreign. In 1860 a commercial treaty was struck with England which seemed to indicate that France was following that country along the path of free trade. Richard Cobden for England and Michael Chevalier for France agreed on terms whereby French wines were introduced cheaply into England in return for substantial reductions in the French tariff schedules on imported manufactured goods. The treaty, Cobden thought, not only would encourage commerce but would be an important step toward world peace which he envisaged would come from universal free trade.

In the rural districts the government encouraged horse-raising, the draining of swamps, and the formation of agricultural societies; but it was in the cities where its activities were particularly noticeable. Docks were built at Marseilles, the harbor of Havre was enlarged, and Paris was transformed. Boulevards were cut through the heart of that ancient city, the Louvre was completed, the great market halls constructed. Open spaces and squares were made around churches, barracks, and public buildings, and no longer could street fighting be carried on easily in the narrow, winding alleys which formerly had characterized Paris. The population of the city rose from 1,053,000 in 1851 to over 1,800,000 in 1866, and Paris became the foyer for the fashionable of all the world. In 1851 England had celebrated a kind of World's Fair, and Louis Napoleon, not to be outdone, ordered a finer one for Paris in 1855. Some 5,000,000 attended and gazed with wonder on splendid jewelry and superb silk, to say nothing of such new gadgets as commercialized rubber, photography, and methods of preserving food.

From the outset, Napoleon III tried to capture the French imagination. He created a magnificent court, where his new empress, Eugénie de Montijo, shone as the gracious presiding star. The imperial wedding was a dazzling display of gold lace. The Tuileries saw one colorful pageant after another. Dinners, concerts, balls were incessant: the Emperor had a civil list of $5,000,000 and used it to delight Paris with great displays. All the high officials were expected to imitate their master up to the limit of their incomes; and even the grave high judges gave pretentious banquets.

This kind of thing, of course, had its seamy side. An orgy of speculation followed in its wake, and high finance (not always reputable) was too often close to the ear of the Emperor. On the other hand, Napoleon III never failed to remember that his uncle made it a point always to look out for the welfare of the poor, and the nephew understood very clearly the great need of defending his usurpation by depriving the bulk of Frenchmen of those great non-political grievances which stir peaceful citizens to violent action. Besides, the Emperor did not lack a real humanity. "The student of Ham," who in his prison had carefully investigated the problems of pauperism, was able to do much for the betterment of the French laboring classes. During his eighteen years of power, many laws were written upon the statute books which did credit alike to the ruler's intellect and his heart. Provision was made for pauper invalids; public hospitals and convalescent homes were multiplied; self-help institutions were created for the working classes, and, above all, in 1864 the law forbidding strikes in order to obtain better labor conditions or higher wages was repealed. Despite an inevitable rise in prices, bread was kept cheap by a special fund. The swollen wealth of the House of Orleans was expropriated by the State and much of it spent on improving the dwellings of workmen. Municipal crèches were opened for poor babies, and always the Emperor's purse was available for worthy charities. "Benevolence with supervision": such was his policy toward the proletariat.

The Second Empire, up to 1860, was an autocracy under a thin democratic veneer. "Universal suffrage" was invoked to elect a Chamber of Deputies which could pass laws, but only such measures as were proposed to it by the government. No complete account of the debates could be published, and in juggling the funds from one account to another, all control of the budget disappeared. When elections were held, the government named an "official candidate"; he only could appeal to the voters on *white* posters (the color for public proclamations), and all the civil functionaries had to work for him. Opposition candidates had thus to appear as avowed opponents of the authorities. They could not even hold public meetings. As for the balloting, in many districts it lasted two days. The mayor in charge carried the box home overnight, and in that night strange things could happen. Of course, the mayors and all like functionaries were named and controlled by the imperial ministers.

Everything else was like this. The press was held under strict censorship. No press cases in the courts could go to a jury; an editor lived in the daily fear of arrest and imprisonment. Police spies were everywhere and, to justify their salaries, made constant arrests. A harmless remark on the streets, even the chatter of an old woman, could bring one before the prefect. The educational system, of course, was at the government's disposal. Unwelcomed instructors were dismissed at will; professorships in history and philosophy were repressed as "unsettling"; the clergy alone found teaching conditions tolerable.

But if political life in France seemed dead, there were plenty of elements ready to rejoice in the change. The black-gowned clericals fervently acclaimed Napoleon III as the "Second Constantine" and the Empire as a "gift of Providence." They were still more delighted when it was ordered that religious teachings should have precedence over even the classics in the schools; and when "vicious curricula" were weeded out along with "wicked teachers." There lacked not high-minded Catholics who were ashamed of the alliance! "To secure himself against the claims of Liberty," said the devout Montalembert, "he needed the support of both the guard-room and the sacristy." The Emperor, however, was quite content. For the present, both of these forces were behind him, as were great numbers of moderate men who, like the English Cobden, declared that whatever the defects of the Second Empire, it was a fine thing that "the anarchy of Utopians, Anarchists and Babblers" had terminated.

The Crimean War

Napoleon III proclaimed in 1852 that the Empire meant peace, but within four years he was taking a leading part in the Crimean War (1854-56). His allies were England, Turkey, and Piedmont, and his great opponent was Russia. This conflict, the first of any magnitude since Waterloo, raised the Second Empire to the height of its glory and reputation and indeed gave to France a kind of hegemony on the Continent, such as she had not had since the days of the first Napoleon and which she was to retain for approximately ten years.

In the background of the war was a personal quarrel between Louis Napoleon and Czar Nicholas I, and also a French tradition in regard to the Near East, dating back hundreds of years. The Czar alone of the European monarchs had snubbed Louis Napoleon when the latter became emperor. From the Czar's point of view an official recognition of the Second Empire implied a repudiation of the settlement of Vienna in 1815. Had not the four victorious powers agreed then that the Bonaparte family must never rule again in France? And so the Czar refused to address Napoleon III as "My Brother," and would only write to him as "My great and good friend." A small matter this; but it annoyed Louis Napoleon.

More important was the historic tradition of France. From the time of St. Louis and the Crusades, France had regarded herself as the special patron and protector of Roman Catholics in the Levant. Certain holy places there were sacred to Roman Catholics—the tomb of the Virgin in Gethsemane, the Church of the Holy Sepulcher at Jerusalem, and the Church of the Nativity in Bethlehem. But these places were also sacred to Greek Catholics, who quarreled with their Roman brethren as to who should control them. The Roman Catholics were backed by France, the Greek Catholics by Russia; all of which was very edifying and enjoyable to the Turks, who played one faction off against the other. The French threatened to send a fleet to enforce the rights of the Roman

Catholics. The Turks gave way and presented the Latin patriarch with the key to the main door of the Church of the Nativity. This, to the Russians, was an affront, and to counter the threat of the French fleet, the Russian army moved to the Danube.

Back of this action on the part of the Czar lay a great ambition. Early in 1853, during one of his state balls at the Winter Palace, Nicholas took the British ambassador, Sir Hamilton Seymour, aside. "We have on our hands," said the monarch, "a *sick man* (the Turkish empire), a very sick man, who can die suddenly. Well, I want to ask, won't it be better to prepare in advance for such a happening, rather than risk the chaos, and the confusion of a European war?" England, thought the Czar, could take Egypt and Crete; in European Turkey the Serbian, Rumanian, and Bulgarian lands could become "independent" under Russian protection; Constantinople, the Czar would promise "not to hold permanently"—a temporary Russian occupation might nevertheless be advisable. Let only Britain and Russia agree and "I (said Nicholas) do not care what any others may think or do."

The ambassador received this startling proposal coldly. Still more coldly and distrustfully was it received at London; but Nicholas, utterly misgaging English sentiment, and contemptuous of France, speedily forced the issue at Constantinople. To the "Sublime Porte" he sent a formidable and overweening ambassador, Prince Menchikov. At this moment the prestige of Russia was enormous, and Nicholas was assumed to be the master of an irresistible war power. He had humiliated every adversary against which he had ranged himself, and the frightened Turkish ministers quailed at the insults and demands which Menchikov now showered upon them.

The prince had a public mission and a private mission. His more open duty was to compel the Sultan to turn over to Greek Orthodox ecclesiastics the guardianship of the "Holy Places" near Jerusalem. The more secret task of the Prince was to browbeat or wheedle the Porte into granting the Czars the right of protection over all Christians within Turkey, in return for a defensive alliance. If this concession had been made, a petty anti-Christian riot in an Anatolian village would have given Russia the technical right to intervene in Ottoman affairs, and Turkish independence would have vanished.

Probably the demoralized viziers and effendis around Abdul-Medjid would have advised submission had there not been in Constantinople a great English ambassador, one of the most famous diplomats of the nineteenth century. Lord Stratford de Rêdcliffe was known as "the Voice of England in the East." This "Great Ambassador," as the Turks called him, wormed out Menchikov's intrigues and put courage and confidence into the Ottoman viziers. The Sultan refused to cancel certain concessions he

had just made in 1852 to the French as to the Holy Places; he also refused to grant Russia special privileges in "protecting" the Christians in
his dominions. Menchikov quitted Constantinople in high dudgeon (May,
1853). Nicholas now had either to eat his words or to take up arms to
rescue Christian brethren from the infidel yoke.

The Czar still believed that he could coerce Turkey without seeing
serious danger of a strong alliance in her favor. He trustingly imagined
that Austria, grateful for his repression of Hungary, would be at least
friendly. He could not persuade himself that Britain would pass to
extremities. He still despised Napoleon III. In July, 1853, he therefore
sent his troops into the Rumanian principalities without actually declaring war upon the Porte. Instantly Western opinion was inflamed.
Napoleon III was only waiting for an alliance, and an alliance was at
hand.

The Turks, encouraged, summoned the Russians to evacuate Rumania
and on refusal declared war. While the diplomats were still making a
last frantic effort to avert active hostilities, a Russian squadron met a
weaker Turkish squadron off Sinope, in the Black Sea (November 30,
1853). The Russian steamers, armed with guns hurling the new explosive
shells, annihilated their opponents. Instantly, Paris and London opinion
clamored for war—the Russians were attacking the Turks while the negotiations were still proceeding! In March, 1854, France and Britain declared war upon the Czar, and almost immediately their long columns
of battleships and troop-transports began heading toward the Black
Sea.

Nicholas met the threats of Western Europe proudly. "Russia will do
in 1854 what she did in 1812," he informed Napoleon III, but he was now
stabbed in the back by Austria. Gratitude was never a Hapsburg virtue.
The Czar now discovered that if he remained in Rumania there was
grave danger of Austria joining the coalition against him in order to
prevent the growth of Russian power in the Balkans. In great chagrin,
he therefore called back his forces over the Prut, after some very indecisive fighting with the Turks. Austrian forces then occupied the
Rumanian principalities to assure their neutrality. The war seemed over.
Nicholas could not now invade European Turkey, and his navy was pent
up in the south Russian harbors by the greater armadas of Britain and
France.

But Napoleon III required "glory"; Britain was exaltedly anxious to
come hand-to-hand with her foe; while Nicholas was in no mood for
concessions. More by accident than by design, the Allies determined to
strike the Czar at one of the few points where their forces could be used
against him. In September there began disembarking in the peninsula
of the Crimea 21,000 English, 30,000 French, and 6,000 Turks, intending
to capture Sebastopol, the great Russian harbor on the Black Sea.

The Siege of Sebastopol

To capture Sebastopol by storm proved impossible, and both sides settled down to a long gruelling siege. The Allies had the larger forces, the Russians excellent defenses augmented by the big guns of their dismantled fleet. The besiegers won all the open battles, but the Russian intrenchments continued to defy them. The besiegers had come wretchedly ill-provided with clothing and supplies for facing a northern winter. In November a storm wrecked thirty vessels loaded with camp necessities. "I have two generals who will not fail me," boasted Nicholas I, "General January and General February." Nevertheless, these adjutants could not make his foes quit. In the spring of 1855 Piedmont joined the war on the Allies' side (see p. 155) and sent a small but effective army to assist in the siege. The struggle presently came down to the attack or defense of certain key intrenchments. In June the French took the famous "Green Mamelon," but the inner defenses were still held heroically, despite a bombardment of hitherto unparalleled severity. At last, after 800 Allied cannon had pounded the Russian lines for three days, the British and French rushed to the final assault. The British attack upon the "Grand Redan" failed, despite Homeric valor and hideous losses; but French *élan* carried the even more important "Malakov" and held it, despite furious Russian counterattacks. Sebastopol was now untenable. That night Menchikov evacuated the city, and the Crimean War was over.

The Peace of Paris (March, 1856): The Respite for the Sultan

The capture of Sebastopol, an actual Russian city, was of course a blow to Muscovite prestige, but any deeper invasion of the country was out of the question. Meanwhile in the Asiatic Caucasus, the capture of Kars from the Turks gave the new Czar, Alexander II, enough of a victory slightly to heal his sorely wounded pride. The result was, therefore, the Peace Congress of Paris (February 25 to March 30, 1856), where the Russian plenipotentiaries did their best to save the honor of their country. Very briefly, the decisions at Paris were these:

I. Russia was forced to cede Bessarabia to Moldavia (Northern Rumania), in order to prevent the Czars from controlling the mouths of the Danube.

II. Russia was also forbidden to maintain warships upon the Black Sea, and she abandoned any claims to the exclusive protectorate of the Turkish Christians.

III. The Rumanian principalities and Serbia were confirmed in their rights of self-government and were placed under the protection of *all* the Great Powers.

IV. The Great Powers (including Prussia), in an exceedingly solemn fashion, "guaranteed the integrity of the Ottoman Empire," and declared that any attack upon the same constituted "a question of European interests."

Thus ended a war wholly avoidable by less truculent diplomacy, and one which gave a new lease of life to the Sick Man of Europe. For the hour, French and British statesmen congratulated themselves upon the prolonged quieting of the "Eastern Question." To imagine, however, that the Turkish Empire would reform itself (as the Sultan now solemnly promised), and that Russia would stomach the loss of Bessarabia and would refrain from building warships on the Black Sea and dismiss her dreams of possessing Constantinople, ought to have surpassed even the official credulity of the Western cabinets. Within a very short time, the needfulness, and therefore the righteousness, of this whole war were bitterly criticized. In 1870, Sir Robert Morier called the Crimean War "the one perfectly useless modern war." Indeed, the only direct, permanent gain from it was the nursing mission of Florence Nightingale, as a result of whose labors the International Red Cross was born.

In the meantime, however, Napoleon III felt quite elated. He not only was received as an equal by all European monarchs, but as an ally of Queen Victoria he had avenged the disasters which befell his famous uncle in the snows of Russia in 1812 and 1813. Furthermore, a European peace congress was now being held in Paris under his auspices, and he had secured guarantees of liberty for Rumania and Serbia. The Napoleonic tradition had been to assist the oppressed in other lands. Possibly he might do something next to help the Poles and the Italians. The Prime Minister of Piedmont, attending the peace conference as one of the Allies, quietly but effectively had made use of a chance to speak there on behalf of Italy. Might it not so happen that if Napoleon III should in the future champion Italy's cause he might augment still more the glory of France and the renown of the name "Napoleon"?

Chapter 10

THE MAKING OF ITALY

AFTER NOVARA, Italy seemed at the feet of the Hapsburg. In Lombardy and Venetia, taxes were multiplied, especially such as could hit wealthy nationalists. Never had there been more police supervision, spies, and blackmail in connection with espionage. Radetzky, governor-general, delighted in insulting Italians. Not only were nationalist agitators flogged; salt was rubbed into their bleeding backs and vinegar applied to their noses so that recovering consciousness, they might be flogged anew. And the Italians even had to pay for the salt and vinegar!

There was not much to be hoped for in old-line conspiracies. Charles Albert was dead; Manin was in Paris, Mazzini in London, and Garibaldi overseas. Nevertheless, plots went forward merrily. One after another, they were nipped in the bud. The jails were filled with conspirators and suspects and a number were executed at odd intervals, now one, now two, now in batches. The Austrians even, in one instance, sent a bill to a mother for the rope used in hanging her son. In 1853 Mazzini cooked up another revolt in Milan. It was an abortive failure, and Italians generally began to lose faith in the old conspirator. To only one part of Italy could they look for aid.

Sardinia-Piedmont still had a constitution and a hope of grasping the leadership of Italy. The new king, although not without private faults, had "the public virtues of intense patriotism, of loyalty to his engagements and to his ministers, and of devotion to a great cause." Without his homely solid qualities it is quite possible that Italian unity might have waited another decade. "King Honest-man," his subjects called him. He would not bow the knee to Austria, nor break the royal compact with his people; and presently fate sent him a great minister, possibly the greatest set over any European state all through the nineteenth century. Therefore, Victor Emmanuel had his reward. In 1849 he became king over less than 5,000,000 Piedmontese-Sardinians; in 1878 he died, king over more than 25,000,000 Italians, a fact which he owed primarily to Cavour, his prime minister.

Camillo Benso, Count of Cavour, was born at Turin in 1810. His father was of the old Piedmontese nobility, but his mother was a gentlewoman

153

of Geneva. Cavour was a good Catholic, but something of the dour, canny spirit of Calvinism entered into his veins. Only rarely did he fail to show the intellectual nonemotionalism of his more northern ancestors. His appearance was that of a commonplace, commercial bourgeois—"a stout merchant with an umbrella"—and little about him, even at the height of his career, betrayed that there was here a man scheming, ceaselessly and triumphantly, to make the Emperor of the French his instrument for driving the Hapsburg from Italy. In his youth he was sent into the army, but he hated the routine garrison work as an officer of the engineers. While in the service, he developed, furthermore, such liberal political tendencies as to make his resignation inevitable. "The most dangerous man in the kingdom," Charles Albert branded him in 1830, while he himself was only heir apparent—a true appraisal.

Fortunately, young Cavour did not ruin himself by mixing in futile republican conspiracies. For Mazzini's movements, he had always dread, if not disgust. He visited England in the eighteen-thirties, studied British liberalism at first hand, and became a passionate admirer of a strictly limited monarchy as the ideal type of government. "Milord Camillo," they presently nicknamed him in Turin for his strong English proclivities. But he held aloof from dangerous intrigues and seemed mainly zealous in improving Piedmontese agricultural methods, making his own estates into model farms, and stimulating the introduction of railroads and steamships. In 1847, while the nationalist agitation rose ever higher, he at last founded an influential paper at Turin, *Il Risorgimento* (The Resurrection), which advocated a United Italy under a liberalized Piedmont.

When the fate of Italian nationalism looked blackest, Cavour steadfastly refused to despair. "We shall begin," he declared in 1849, "and profiting by past mistakes, we shall do better *next time*." In 1850 he made in the Piedmontese Parliament a remarkable speech, which roused the doubting and enkindled the patriots. "Piedmont," he cried, "by gathering to herself all the living forces in Italy, would be in a position to lead our mother country to the high destinies whereunto she is called." This brave prophecy made Cavour a marked man. Soon thereafter he was appointed minister of commerce and agriculture. "You will see him turn you all out of your places," remarked the shrewd King to his other ministers. In 1852, Cavour was himself prime minister. From this time until 1859, all the other ministers were his mere lieutenants, and even Victor Emmanuel bowed to his dictates. The "merchant with the umbrella" *was* practically the government of Piedmont.

Cavour's Policy in Sardinia-Piedmont (1852-56)

Cavour's working theory, when he took office, held that "since it had pleased Providence that Piedmont alone of Italy should be free and independent, Piedmont was bound to make use of its freedom and independence to plead before Europe the cause of the unhappy peninsula." To do this effectively, the little kingdom must become as enlightened, progressive, and prosperous as her narrow limits could permit. Very wise measures were taken to advance agriculture and shipping and to reorganize the national finances, but, above all, it was necessary to deal firmly with the secular claims of the Church.

In 1850, Pius IX had roundly denounced Victor Emmanuel for suppressing the special courts for judging ecclesiastical offenders against the secular law, and a Piedmontese cabinet minister had been allowed to die without the sacraments because he had refused on his deathbed to profess penitence for having assisted in this suppression. Cavour, now, although always professing himself a "good Catholic," attacked the great properties and privileges of the Church. Everywhere the clergy were in politics, usually on the side of reaction. "What the nobility is to Germany," was justly said at the time, "that, the priestly caste is to Italy."

Cavour carefully let the secular clergy and the over-numerous Piedmontese bishops alone; but he dealt unrelentingly with the swarms of nuns and monks dwelling in unproductive idleness. Victor Emmanuel, it is true, hated the idea of a struggle with the Church. When his general led forth the Piedmontese troops to the Crimea the King told him openly, "You are fortunate, general, in going to fight the Russians, while I have to stay here to fight monks and nuns!" But he faithfully backed his minister, although his mother, his wife, and his brother all died in a single month, and the Pope sent him a personal letter, representing these calamities to be direct signs of the anger of God. Cavour, on his part, put through a law suppressing several hundred convents. From that time onward, the warfare between Italian liberalism and the temporal power raged more hotly than ever.

In all that he did, Cavour was a strictly constitutional minister, putting up with the petty politics of his parliament and handling unruly deputies with incomparable finesse. "Believe me," once he asserted when urged to autocratic methods, "the worst of *Chambers* is preferable to the most brilliant of *antechambers*." But he never deceived himself as to the only thing that could compass the union and liberalizing of Italy—a war power strong enough to defeat Austria. Piedmont could not supply this. No allies she could find in Italy could probably supply this. To defeat Austria, Cavour must secure a very powerful external ally. This ally, Cavour was convinced, could only be France, and to secure the armed assistance of France against Austria, the Piedmontese minister wrought with all the powers of his genius through seven intensely difficult years—with success, after agonizing delay.

In 1855, decidedly to the astonishment of many of his countrymen, Cavour caused Piedmont to join with France and Britain, to declare war on Russia, and to send a small army to reinforce the Allies before Sebastopol. What business had Piedmont in the Crimea? Cavour, however, justified himself, because Nicholas I had been very hectoring and offensive when Victor Emmanuel refused to cancel the new constitution; and because, if Austria had joined the Allies while Piedmont was neutral, the Hapsburg would be in a position to prejudice the whole position of his weak rival. The Piedmontese were a welcome reinforcement before Sebastopol. They fought well and won gratitude and recognition. The troops understood clearly why they were summoned to delve in the filthy trenches. "Never mind," said a soldier from Turin, "*out of this mud Italy will be made.*"

At the Congress of Paris (1856) Cavour, as delegate for one of the victorious powers, could not be denied a seat; and he was able (despite angry Austrian protests) to lay before the assembled diplomats "the utterly abnormal state of Italy." France, Britain, and Russia alike thought evil of the Hapsburgs, and the Austrians had to endure while Cavour recited their oppressions in Lombardy and Venetia, the Austrian occupation of part of the Papal States, and the gross misrule in Naples and Sicily. Lord Clarendon, for Britain, openly supported Cavour's arguments, and not one Power rose to second the defiance by the Austrian envoy. Of course the Congress did nothing—it could have done nothing except to arrange an armed coalition against Austria—but Cavour was content. He had seen the Italian problem formally laid before official Europe. As the meeting broke up, the Piedmontese turned to his foreign colleagues, stating his blunt opinion, "You see, there is only one solution—the cannon."

Cavour Makes a Secret Alliance with Napoleon: Plombières Interview (1858)

After the Congress of Paris, the position of Cavour as a master statesman was assured. Old Prince Metternich was still watching events from his retirement in Vienna. "There is only one diplomat in Europe," observed he, "but unfortunately he is against us—he is M. de Cavour." But the Piedmontese was still only at the beginning of his program. Very skilfully, he was convincing the republican extremists that it was better to possess a united Italy under a liberal king than a divided Italy with vague republican hopes. In 1856 Manin, the Venetian, told him, "I accept the monarchy of Savoy (Piedmont), provided it works loyally and efficiently for the making of Italy." But Cavour was seeking favor with a much greater personage than the exiled Manin. He was staking all upon winning Napoleon III.

The Man of Destiny had dabbled in Italian conspiracies in his hectic youth, and had been a member of the antimonarchist Carbonari society as an exile. A man of warm, humane impulses himself where personal ambition was not concerned, the Emperor genuinely desired to prosper the causes of two sadly oppressed peoples—the Italians and the Poles. For the latter, he was never to make more than futile gestures; for the former (thanks to Cavour) he was to do a great deal. "Poor Italy," he had remarked to Count Orloff, at the Congress at Paris, "cannot something be done for her?" The Italian radicals, however, counted the Emperor a traitor to the cause of liberty. In January of 1858, a fanatic, Orsini, attempted to assassinate Napoleon in Paris.

Orsini's bombs failed, but his attempt made a great impression upon the Emperor. Would his life be really safe if a large group of Italians really believed that he was a betrayer of their cause? Orsini was no common terrorist. A deep moral, if perverted, purpose was behind his attempt. Before execution, he sent a dying appeal to the Emperor. "I pray your Majesty to remember that so long as Italy is not independent, the tranquillity of Europe, no less than that of your Majesty, is a mere chimera." Napoleon let this letter be published, and soon after this, Prince William, the Regent of Prussia, could write, "The Italian dagger has become a fixed idea with Napoleon." Of course all this was sheer gain for Cavour. In a few months he was able to arrange a secret interview with the personage who now passed as the most powerful man in Europe.

In July, 1858, followed one of the most striking examples of the old "Secret Diplomacy," when monarchs and ministers in a few private interviews determined the fate of kingdoms.

Napoleon III was "taking the waters" at the quiet little village of Plombières in the Vosges. Here suddenly, arrived a man of "stumpy, unimpressive figure with ill-fitting spectacles and a myopic stare." The local police, suspecting another Orsini, were about to arrest him, when the stranger was identified by a member of the imperial suite. He was Cavour. Several long interviews with Napoleon followed, with no secretary or other intruder present, culminating in a lengthy drive in the Emperor's own phaëton, where the discussion could be even more informal and decisive. When Cavour slipped back across the frontier, it was with the important knowledge that Napoleon III had agreed to go to war with Austria in behalf of Italy—for a price.

In substance, the Emperor had promised that if Cavour could bring it about that Austria would appear as the aggressor, France would come to the rescue of Piedmont in war. After the Hapsburgs were beaten, Lombardy and Venetia could go to Piedmont. Some kind of central Italian kingdom could also be set up. The Pope must be left in Rome, but possibly he would not need all his old territory. Perhaps, too, His Holiness would become the titular head of an "Italian Confederation." As for France, of course she could not fight a great war without reasonable recompense. Napoleon suggested that she ought to have Savoy and Nice, the French-speaking territories of Sardinia-Piedmont west of the Alps. Also, the Emperor had a personal favor to ask. He had a "fine young cousin," Prince Napoleon Bonaparte (aged thirty-seven and a notorious rake). He must marry Victor Emmanuel's fifteen-year-old daughter Clotilde, thus uniting the upstart Bonapartes with the poor but ancient and very proud House of Savoy. At Turin, Cavour found his royal master extraordinarily unwilling to wed his child to a seasoned libertine, but the Prime Minister had his way. The princess was only another sacrifice for Italy. Before the year was over, the substance of the conversations at Plombières had been embedded in a secret treaty although during these months both Paris and Turin kept an artful silence.

Cavour Provokes Austria to Attack Sardinia-Piedmont (April, 1859)

Nevertheless, as 1858 drew towards its close, the tension in the air increased. The great composer Verdi was then at the height of his fame; but when, in Lombardy and Venetia, great crowds shouted and walls were covered with the scribbling "Viva Verdi," everybody knew what was the sentiment behind. By "*Verdi*" every Italian meant "Vittorio Emanuele *Re d-Italia*." When the Austrian emperor visited Milan in 1857, he had to drive through streets where not a head was uncovered, and in dead silence, notwithstanding the fact that, since 1856, Austrian rule in Italy had become decidedly milder, and blundering attempts had been made to conciliate native opinion. Then, on New Year's Day, 1859, Napoleon himself informed the world that a crisis was close at hand. At the diplomatic reception, before all the representatives of Europe, he said to the Austrian ambassador: "I regret that our relations with your government are not as good as they have been. I beg you to say to the emperor that my personal sentiments toward him have not been changed." Speedily thereafter, Victor Emmanuel's speech from the throne to his own Piedmontese Parliament indicated what was coming: Piedmont, he said, was only a small country but it had become potent in the councils of Europe, "because of the greatness of the ideas she represents, and the sympathies which she inspires. . . . We cannot disregard *the cry of grief* which rises to us from so many parts of Italy."

Instantly, all diplomatic Europe was in a nervous scurry. The new telegraphs were worked furiously. The English government was disturbed. Cavour had known that English liberalism yearned over Italy; but he also knew the disinclination of English statesmen to go to war out of sheer benevolence. France was more able and willing to do his business. The Piedmontese, however, by tying himself to Napoleon, awakened inevitable anxieties in London, lest the expulsion of Austria from Italy should lead to an inordinate increase of the power of France. As a result, English statesmen now exerted themselves to preserve the peace; and so, for like motives, did the Russian. Napoleon dared not stir until Austria had shown signs of attacking Piedmont.

It was, therefore, Cavour's part to become just as offensive as possible to Vienna, without giving technical provocation for war. "I shall force Austria to declare war against us!" he confidently told English visitors at Turin; and a good chance soon offered. The Austrians had ordered conscription in Lombardy-Venetia. Very well, then, Piedmont would welcome those Italians who fled from the Austrians to avoid service in the Austrian army; Austria would demand their return; Piedmont would refuse; a war would follow. The plan worked; Piedmont and Austria both glared at each other; both mobilized—Piedmont first. Napoleon III hesitated, but Cavour told him that if he backed out, he, Cavour, would resign, emigrate to America, publish to the world proof of Louis Napoleon's agreement with Piedmont. Napoleon still hesitated, but in the meanwhile Francis Joseph, Austrian emperor, was persuaded to send Piedmont an ultimatum demanding demobilization or else war. On April 28, Cavour was sitting in the Piedmontese Chamber of Deputies, when a scrap of paper was brought in by a friend. "They are here; I have seen them." "They" were two Austrian officers, bearers of the fateful demand. Cavour went out instantly to meet them. Turning to a companion, he said, smiling, "I am leaving the *last* sitting of the *last* Piedmontese Chamber."

He knew whereof he spoke. The next Chamber would be for all Italy. Austria was now the open attacker, and Napoleon was bound to assist Piedmont. Three days later Cavour dismissed Count von Kellerberg and the other Austrian politely, then said to those still present, "We have made history; now let us go to dinner."

War Between France and Austria (1859): French Victories at Magenta and Solferino

Never did a great power enter a capital war with weaker moral backing than did Austria in 1859. Liberal France and England hated her as a tyrant empire; Prussia nursed the memories of Olmütz; Russia counted her a false friend. To gross diplomatic blunders, Francis Joseph's coterie now added equally gross military blunders. War had long been brewing. Great masses of Hungarian and Austrian troops, the famous "White Coats" of the Hapsburgs, had been mustered in Lombardy. Everything called for a rapid offensive before French aid could come to the weaker armies of Piedmont.

Napoleon had, indeed, taken up the challenge promptly. Five French army corps had been mobilized; and, amid the cheers of even the few Republican Deputies, he had told his Chamber that, "Moderation has been my rule: now energy becomes my duty. If France draws the sword, it is not to conquer but to liberate." But Austria had a golden opportunity to strike while the French were still mustering and while their columns were still hastening over the Alpine passes or taking ship at Marseilles for Genoa. Radetzky, however, was in his grave. The new Austrian general had no claim to leadership except the decisive one of holding an extremely old patent of nobility. Some 100,000 Austrian troops soon violated Piedmontese territory by crossing the Ticino; but then "stood as if spellbound under their incompetent chief."

The French troops were hurried forward, ill-supplied, ill-organized, and none too competently led. Napoleon III himself undertook to play the commander, for were not his men again on soil recalling the Little Corporal of Lodi? Had the Austrian staff possessed a spark of genius, the bubble of the Second Empire might possibly have been pricked in 1859, and not in 1870. But it was a case where inefficiency in one command was out-pointed by slightly greater inefficiency in the other; and the fighting qualities of the French infantry were magnificent. Man for man, they and their Piedmontese allies outmatched the Hapsburg legions. The result was decisive for Italy.

After preliminary successes, 100,000 Frenchmen and 50,000 Piedmontese were at last in a position to push the campaign. On June 4 came the battle of Magenta. Napoleon became engaged in it with inferior forces and he was close to defeat until his General MacMahon came up with decisive reinforcements and struck the Austrian flank. Instantly, the whole Austrian line collapsed. The Hapsburg troops fell back to the Mincio, covering Venetia, while the victors swept in triumph into rejoicing Milan. Cavour (who rode in civilian clothes with the generals) was greeted with such cheering that Victor Emmanuel confessed that, "he felt himself like the tenor who leads forward the prima donna to receive the applause."

After Magenta, Napoleon promptly issued a proclamation to all Italians, which reëchoed through all the peninsula: "Animated by the sacred fire of patriotism, be soldiers today, for tomorrow you will be citizens of a great country." Addressing, in turn, the French army, he asserted, "Italy shall henceforth be mistress of her own destinies." The effect was instantaneous. From Modena, Parma, and Tuscany the local dukes, and from the Romagna the papal legates, went scurrying into exile before the spontaneous uprisings of their oppressed subjects. There was none of the disorder, extravagance, and childishness of the insurrections of 1848. Cavour had seen to that. From Turin came "suggestions" to the local nationalist committees and chiefs, which they readily received as orders. Everything, so far as Cavour could control it, went forward like clockwork—but the Austrian war power was still to be broken.

Three weeks after Magenta, the Hapsburg armies took the offensive

VICTOR EMMANUEL AND NAPOLEON III ENTER MILAN IN TRIUMPH
AFTER THE BATTLE OF MAGENTA (1859)

again, to strike the French as the latter pressed forward. At Solferino, south of Lake Garda, on June 24, the two hosts blundered into each other. Neither side had then planned for a general engagement, but presently a battle, with some 130,000 men on a side, had developed on a fourteen-mile front. On the northern end of the line, the Austrians under Benedek flung back the impetuous Italians; but on the center and south the French assaulted with better success. The "Red Pantaloons," by a small margin, outfought the "White Coats." A terrific storm put a stop to the slaughter and left the French with the honors of the field. The Franco-Piedmontese army had lost 17,500 men, but their foes had lost 22,000. The victory was supposed to give the Allies the first moves in the conquest of Venetia.

But Napoleon's nerves had been shaken by the hideous slaughter. The sight of the thousands of wounded affected him profoundly; and from France had come clear warnings that the clericals were furious at the threatened despoiling of the Pope. Above all, he was very fearful lest Prussia should attack him across the unguarded Rhine.

The Agreement of Villafranca (July, 1859): The Italian Nationalist Movement Continues

Napoleon had done for Italy perhaps everything one could expect from a man of his caliber. The Austrian army was not smashed; the next fighting would be around the powerful fortresses of the Quadrilateral, and a serious repulse might ruin the Second Empire. Therefore, to the utter astonishment and dismay of Cavour and Victor Emmanuel, thirteen days after his victory at Solferino, Napoleon opened negotiations with Francis Joseph. The Hapsburg was willing to pay heavily, although not too heavily, for peace. At Villafranca, Napoleon III presently met Francis Joseph, then "a tall young man of twenty-eight in a blue uniform," and concluded a pact which seemed, for the instant, to blast all of Cavour's larger hopes.

By the preliminary treaty of Villafranca, Lombardy, but not Venetia, was to be granted to Piedmont. The expelled dukes of Tuscany and Modena were to be restored. An Italian confederation was to be formed under the honorary presidency of the Pope, who was to be required by the two emperors to "introduce into his own states the necessary reforms." Finally, a formal congress of diplomats was to meet at Zürich to work out the details of the general agreement.

This deliberate failure of Napoleon to redeem his open promise, "Italy shall be free from the Alps to the Adriatic," was met by a burst of fury from all Italian nationalists. Cavour, for once, entirely lost his poise. He would have had Piedmont continue the war alone. Victor Emmanuel, with greater good sense, realized that he must bow to the inevitable, and accepted his great minister's resignation. Vainly did Napoleon try to sweeten the blow by telling the disappointed King: "Your government will pay me the cost of the war, and we will say no more about Nice and Savoy. *Now we will see what the Italians can do by themselves.*" For the moment, the French, so recently hailed as "Liberati," were treated by the Italians as traitors.

But when the French left off, the Italians indeed began to "do for themselves." Venetia was beyond grasp, but what of the duchies, the Papal States, Naples? The final treaty of Zürich bore this distinction among diplomatic compacts—most of its articles had been completely violated before it could be signed (November 10, 1859).

The proviso restoring the exiled dukes insulted all the liberals of Western Europe. "The disposal of the Tuscans and Modenese as if they were so many firkins of butter is somewhat too profligate," wrote Lord John Russell in September. After Villafranca, there was great confusion in northern Italy, and it was impossible to put back the old governments promptly. Speedily it was clear that only armed force could restore them at all. When, on the eve of resigning, Cavour sent *official* orders to the "Special Commissioners" in charge of the provisional governments in the revolted districts to quit their posts, *privately* he telegraphed them to hold on grimly and to watch events. They heeded the private messages.

And now events ran swiftly in the nationalists' favor. Constituent Assemblies in Tuscany, Modena, Parma, and the Romagna voted [1] to elect

---

[1] The northernmost districts of the Papal States.

Victor Emmanuel as their sovereign. The whole question soon came down to this: would France and Austria permit the agreement of Villafranca to be immediately torn to pieces? Napoleon disliked the idea of a genuinely united Italy—a rival to France. He did not love the three deposed dukes, but he dreamed of setting up his own cousin, Prince Jerome, in Tuscany. Furthermore, he greatly feared the French clericals if he continued to enrage the Pope. He was, however, in a very unfortunate position to enforce his views. How could an emperor, who ever paid lip-homage to universal suffrage and plebiscites, refuse the right of the insurgent districts to decide their destinies by popular vote—as they now did by great majorities, declaring for annexation to Piedmont? Cavour had recovered from his passion and was again his calm, decisive self. In January, 1860, he was once more Victor Emmanuel's prime minister, and to Napoleon he offered the old bribe—Nice and Savoy, if France would permit the consolidation of northern Italy. Napoleon surrendered in view of this great profit for France. "Now we are accomplices!" said Cavour to the French plenipotentiary, when they had signed the treaty of cession.

The taking of Nice and Savoy, after Villafranca, left an evil taste in the mouth of all Italians. They felt that every claim by Napoleon III to gratitude had been cancelled. He had, as the English historian Freeman put it, "for half a day's work taken two days of pay." Cavour himself spoke in the new "Italian" parliament of the cession as "the most painful duty of my life." But he was a realist, and understood the character of the Man of Destiny. Nice and Savoy were not essential parts of Italy —the duchies and the Romagna were. A dubious plebiscite in Nice and Savoy seemed to give "popular consent" to the transaction.

Garibaldi Overthrows the Bourbons of Naples (1860)

There was now a *Kingdom of Italy,* covering a large part of the peninsula. As for Austria, Francis Joseph stood sullenly aloof, glad to be sure for a while of Venetia. His treasury was nearly bankrupt. Hungary was threatening rebellion. Prussia was lifting her head. A shot fired in behalf of the exiled dukes or the Pope might tumble down the entire Hapsburg realm in ruin. So the arrangements of Villafranca went to the scrap heap, while Pius IX fulmined his anathemas in vain.

In May, 1860, Victor Emmanuel reigned from southern Tuscany to Alpine Lombardy, but Italy was not yet "made." Venetia could perhaps wait, and also Rome, but until the large, disjoined despotism of Naples-Sicily was brought within the Italian system, it was foolish for the nationalists to exult too heartily. And now, after the wars of emperors and kings in the North, came the war of a great republican partisan in the South. Garibaldi had his days of glory.

Garibaldi, the defender of Rome in 1849, had led a force of volunteers in the Piedmontese service during the campaign of 1859. Now he entered into active intrigues to conduct a filibustering expedition into Sicily. A powerful factor in arranging details was one of Mazzini's best agents, Francesco Crispi, a man destined to play a great part later in united Italy (see p. 388). Garibaldi and Cavour were in no wise friends. The great minister distrusted revolutionary conspiracies and "Republican uprisings", but he would not halt the preparations which went on at Genoa almost before his eyes. He preserved an attitude technically correct, and could presently send off his official "regrets at an attack upon a friendly kingdom," when later the powers began to question anxiously. It was reported, however, that guns from the Piedmontese arsenal found their way into Garibaldi's possession; and after the expedition sailed, Admiral Persano, commanding the North Italian fleet, received a note from Cavour, "Try to place yourself between Garibaldi and the Neapolitan cruisers. I hope you understand me," "My lord, I believe that I *do* understand you," Persano is said to have replied, "If there is need send me to the fortress prison of Fenestrella."

Nevertheless, the expedition was sufficiently desperate—1,000 daring men imperfectly armed, setting forth from Quarto, a little port near Genoa, in two small steamers to attack a sizable kingdom, whose ruler possessed a large army, as yet loyal, and where every previous anti-Bourbon attack had ended in a bloody failure. But Garibaldi was an ideal leader for such an enterprise. On the 11th of May, 1860, he landed in Sicily at Marsala, proclaiming himself dictator. The Neapolitan troops who endeavored to halt him were execrably led. A few days later Garibaldi routed his foes at Calatafimi and marched straight to Palermo.

Twenty thousand Neapolitan troops, sustained by nine frigates, held the capital of Sicily and its forts; but by a magnificent combination of bluff and audacity, Garibaldi, inferior in numbers, in munitions, in everything but courage, so fought and confounded them that on June 6 they were glad to capitulate. A few weeks later, he won at Milazzo a battle which gave him the practical control of all Sicily. His next move was, obviously, upon Naples. Victor Emmanuel kept his own official record clear by sending him a letter "dissuading" him from invading southern Italy. The Dictator replied by courteously asking "permission to disobey." After that, the stars in their courses fought against the Bourbons.

The King of Naples repented upon his political deathbed. He begged aid of Napoleon III, but the latter answered coldly: "The Italians are shrewd; they know very well that having shed the blood of my children in the cause of their nationality, I can never fire a cannon in opposition to it." Then the King, in desperation, announced he would proclaim again the Constitution of 1848, but the day for believing Bourbon promises was ended. In August, Garibaldi crossed the straits and marched steadily northward upon Naples, the whole countryside acclaiming him. Many of Francis' troops capitulated under circumstances indicating either cowardice or treachery. His naval officers emptied the boilers of his war steamers so that he could not operate his fleet, and in despair the King took refuge in the strong fortress of Gaeta. The Dictator entered Naples in triumph, and on October 1 he shattered the remnant of the Bourbon army in the hard-fought battle of the Volturno.

Cavour Seizes Naples and "Makes" Italy (Autumn, 1860)

By this time, however, Napoleon III and Cavour both were in keen anxiety about Garibaldi. Around him were many of Mazzini's republicans. Would he not now proclaim a "Neapolitan" Republic and march on Rome to chase out the Pope? Such a movement would probably bring down the armed fury of Catholic Europe and ruin Italy, ere the nation was "made." In Umbria and the Marches there were clear signs of uprising against the Papalists. If the insurgents joined Garibaldi, a war between republicans and the Vatican was inevitable.

In September, 1860, therefore, Cavour took the last great decision in his career—he ordered the North Italian troops, 35,000 strong, to cross the boundaries of Umbria, brush aside the papal levies and reach Naples, putting themselves between Garibaldi's red-shirts and Rome. He realized the seriousness of the venture. "We are touching the supreme moment," he wrote, "with God's help Italy will be *made* in three months." The papal forces resisted the Nationalists' advance, but were shattered at Castelfidardo, and Victor Emmanuel led his troops over the Neapolitan frontier. The battle of Volturno had already been won, and Garibaldi rode with the King in his solemn entry into Naples on November 7. The next day, laying down his "dictatorship," refusing all titles and public honors, and resigning his powers to Victor Emmanuel, the conqueror retired to his simple home on the island of Caprera.

This whole stroke by Cavour had been utterly perilous. Every government in Europe, except England, felt required to protest to him against this "breach of neutrality." The papacy, furious already at the loss of Romagna, now redoubled its thunders at the seizure of Umbria and the Marches. "I let them have their say," wrote Cavour to D'Azeglio, "and I go on." Napoleon III protested officially with the rest, but, more privately, he is alleged to have sent Victor Emmanuel the message, "Good luck and act promptly." When Prussia filed its warnings, Cavour prophetically told its minister, "The time will come when Prussia will follow Piedmont's example." The Austrian Emperor was in a rage. At one instant he was near ordering his troops over the Venetian frontier, but dared not—

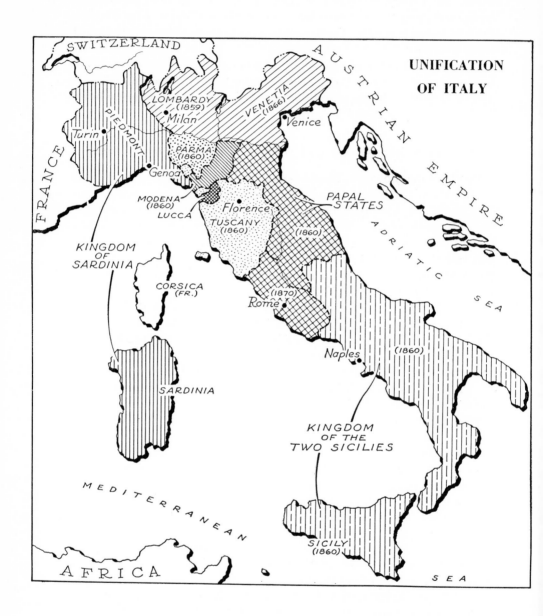

UNIFICATION OF ITALY

SWITZERLAND

FRANCE

AUSTRIAN EMPIRE

LOMBARDY
(1859)

Milan

VENETIA
(1866)

Venice

PIEDMONT

Turin

PARMA
(1860)

Genoa

MODENA
(1860)

LUCCA

Florence

TUSCANY
(1860)

PAPAL
STATES

(1860)

ADRIATIC

SEA

KINGDOM
OF
SARDINIA

CORSICA
(FR.)

Rome
(1870)

Naples
(1860)

SARDINIA

KINGDOM
OF THE
TWO SICILIES

MEDITERRANEAN

SICILY
(1860)

SEA

AFRICA

he could not be sure of the action of France and the Czar. So the suddenness of the deed and the jealousies of the powers fought on Cavour's side. On the 13th of February, 1861, Gaeta was starved into surrender, and Francis II departed into lifelong exile. Victor Emmanuel was king from the Alps to the Capes of Sicily. *Italy was made.*

On the 18th of February the first National Parliament representing North and South met at Turin. With vast enthusiasm, the King was confirmed as "Victor Emmanuel by the Grace of God and the will of the nation, King of Italy."

There still remained Venetia and Rome. Venetia could only be won after the Hapsburg had changed his heart or had lost another great war.

Rome was indeed, as Garibaldi always protested, "an Italian city," but its possession was tied up with the whole of the intricate question of the temporal power. Pius IX had lost already over half of his territories, but he was still sovereign of Rome and of most of old Latium, and Napoleon III dared not outrage the French clericals (a main prop of his throne) by handing over to Victor Emmanuel the city which all Catholics considered the sacred capital of Christendom.

Garibaldi's policy would have been to seize Rome by armed force and trust to good fortune to rescue the new Italy out of the international explosion sure then to follow. Cavour, however, recognized the necessity of temporizing—at least until there could be a change in the moods of Napoleon III. In October, 1860, he had declared in Parliament that henceforth the task of Italians was "to make the Eternal City, on which rested twenty-five hundred years of glory, the splendid capital of the Italian Kingdom." On the other hand, he realized clearly that Napoleon was assenting to the opinion of such advisers as the Duc de Gramont, "A *satisfied* pope is not an absolute necessity to France; a *free* pope is." While Pius IX had such a military protector the new Italian kingdom could not afford adventures near the Tiber.

The Death of Cavour (June 6, 1861): His Achievements: Events After Him

It was not given to the greatest statesman in Europe to see his country through the tortuous diplomacy, inevitable if Rome was to pass into Italian hands without an extreme breach with the papacy. Cavour, in the last few years, had expended a physical energy sufficient for a normal lifetime. Late in May, 1861, he became afflicted nervously, and presently was seized with a fever that defied the physicians. Soon the case was hopeless. The clericals had threatened their great adversary with refusal of the last sacraments; but a nobleminded monk, Fra Giacomo, performed his Christian duty for the dying. At the end, Cavour is said to have been tormented with the great problem of reconciling the Vatican with the new Italian nationalism, murmuring, *"Frate, frate, libera chiesa in libera stato"* ("Brother, brother, a free church in a free state!") Other accounts make him declare triumphantly, "Italy is made; all is well!"—He died thus, after a very brief illness, on June 6, 1861.

To understand the magnitude of Cavour's performance, it is needful to comprehend in detail the vast network of European intrigues and balancing forces—diplomatic, dynastic, republican, clerical—with which he had to reckon and then to become the master. The skill with which he manipulated Napoleon III and dragged France into the championship of Italy is one of the greatest achievements of diplomatic history. *"I am before all else an Italian,"* he wrote to D'Azeglio in 1860, "and it is to make my country enjoy self-government both at home and abroad, that I have undertaken the rude task of driving Austria from Italy, without substituting the domination of any other power"—a task accomplished except for Venetia.

The new Italy was yet merely a throwing-together of states, separated across the ages and now united only to a certain degree by a common language and social customs and a common desire for unity. Between Lombard peasants and Sicilian peasants there was painfully little in common. Besides the hostility of the papacy, Victor Emmanuel's enlarged kingdom was looked upon abroad as a questionable experiment, not very likely to endure. French politicians were more than skeptical of the wisdom of creating a rival nation beyond the Alps, even if Savoy and Nice were given as makeweight. "Italy is an invention of the Emperor Napoleon," patronized Rouher; while Thiers openly avowed that Italy was a "historical parasite," which lived on its past and could have no future. In Paris, in fact, it was for some time held that Victor Emmanuel would have to abandon Naples, and that young Prince Murat would be summoned thither as king. Meanwhile a French garrison held the Eternal City in the Pope's name, and greatly as the successors of Cavour longed for that city as the natural capital of the new kingdom, they dared not use force to gain it. To fight the garrison would be to fight both Napoleon III and the Catholic Church.

Cavour's creation, the Kingdom of Italy, now found a new friend in Bismarck. For the war which Bismarck planned against Austria, Italy was an ally to be had on easy terms, and he offered her Venetia. And so it happened that as the Prussians fought the Austrians at Sadowa, Italy attacked them from the south. The Italians were defeated by their old foes; but so overwhelmingly were the Prussians victorious that it made no difference; and as a result of the Austro-Prussian War of 1866 Venice became an integral part of the Italian kingdom.

Four more years, and France was at war with Prussia. The French garrison was withdrawn from Rome to protect the homeland, and the soldiers of Victor Emmanuel marched into Rome. The papal troops made a token resistance only. The Pope immured himself in the Vatican. And Rome became Italy's capital, thus fulfilling, for the time being, the nationalistic aspirations of the Italian people.

Chapter 11

BISMARCK AND THE NORTH GERMAN CONFEDERATION

THE PROBLEM of German unification in many ways paralleled that of the making of Italy; in many ways it was different. Superficially it should have been easier to solve in Germany, since there already existed the German federation drawn up in 1815, and even antecedent to that time there had been the Holy Roman Empire of the German Nation, a vague structure at best but more tangible than anything which was known to the Italians. Furthermore, the Italians were ever confronted with the fact that the Pope was a temporal ruler whose lands bisected North and South Italy. Without Rome and without the Papal States there could be no united Italy, and any attempt to force one without the consent of the Holy See inevitably would cause friction wherever devout Catholics were to be found.

On the other hand, the creation of a united Germany that included all or even most of the Germans was bound to meet with the opposition of France, diplomatic or otherwise. *Die Wacht am Rhein* was not merely a song; the Prussians stationed on the banks of that river were a constant threat to Alsace-Lorraine, the two eastern provinces of France, with their large German population. There were more Germans in Europe than Frenchmen, a fact recognized in Paris. Napoleon might aid the Italians to unite; he had nothing to fear from them. But with the Germans it was another matter; France would not willingly see them unite—not, at least, without their paying a big price in the way of territorial compensation.

Also, and more important, there were the old jealousies between the two major German states, Austria and Prussia. It was difficult to conceive of either giving in to the other without a fight. To oust Austria from Italy was difficult enough; but that, after all, was in the nature of a minor operation compared with any excision of Austria from Germany. Austria was a German land, a more thoroughly German land, racially and historically speaking, than Prussia ever had been. Yet Austria could not take the lead in any real campaign for German unity because of the Czechs, Slovaks, Slovenes, Croats, Poles, Ruthenes, Magyars, Italians, and Rumanians within the borders of Austria-Hungary. To divorce Austria from Hungary would, to be sure, rid Austria of a number of these nationalities; but even so, many others would remain, and what is more, the House of Hapsburg had no idea of surrendering the crown of St. Stephen and withdrawing from Budapest. It had no idea of surrendering any territory nor any intention whatever of permitting a Germany to exist from which it was excluded.

On the other hand, unity could not readily be achieved by the other great German power, Prussia. That country, in the first place, was Protestant, a fact which tended to line up the South German state, Catholic Bavaria, against her. Religious toleration had generally characterized the House of Hohenzollern, it is true, but it was a Lutheran house and Prussia had an established Lutheran church. Furthermore, in political and military matters, Prussia had too often offended the susceptibilities of the South German states. They had not forgotten the harsh diplomacy of Frederick the Great, and the annexation of Saxon territory after the Napoleonic wars was still remembered at Dresden. Prussia was disunited, sprawling over the map of Germany, with some of her territory west of the Rhine but most of it east of the Elbe. That she would some day try to join these lands together was highly probable, and at the expense of German princes whose territory lay between. Because of these reasons, Prussia was unpopular in Germany, particularly in that part of it which was south of the River Main, where the inhabitants, socially, culturally, racially, and religiously, felt more akin to Austrians than to Prussians.

And Prussia also was poor, attempting to support a first-class military establishment on third-rate natural resources. To the eastward of Berlin, where lay most of her land, the Industrial Revolution had scarcely penetrated. The population was a peasant one, under the strict dominance of country gentlemen known as Junkers, who resembled very much the English squirearchy of the eighteenth century. These Junkers were the main support of the Prussian monarchy; they officered the army; they filled the posts in the service of the government. They had opposed Prussia's acceptance of the Frankfort crown in 1848 and they continued to oppose any German unification by which their country (Prussia) should be submerged into a greater Germany. They were good national-ists—*Prussian nationalists;* but they sought no German nationalism unless Germany was to be swallowed by Prussia. Cavour had been faced with a slightly similar situation as far as the Piedmontese nobility was concerned, but to a much smaller degree. After all, Piedmont was a little country compared to all of Italy; but Prussia, compared to Germany, was not little, and the Prussian Junkers were a determined lot.

Soon to emerge among them as the most prominent man in Germany was Otto von Bismarck, a landed proprietor from the old "Mark," the oldest province in Brandenburg. Bismarck, a young man of great size, astonishing vitality, and extraordinary will, had dashed from his estates to defend Frederick William IV against the mob of Berliners who threatened His Majesty in the March days of 1848. "Smells of blood, will be useful later," was the secret notation then placed after his name by the Prussian police.

And Bismarck continued to smell of blood for some little time. He entered the Prussian Parliament set up in 1850 at Berlin and in it made himself conspicuous as a red-hot reactionary. He hated liberals, German nationalists, the bourgeoisie. To show his contempt for his enemies he did not hesitate to turn his back upon them while making speeches. His shrill, squeaky voice contrasted violently with his huge bulk, as he denounced those who would put German loyalty before that due his beloved Prussia. "My father's house is Prussia and I have never deserted it," he said, when some one compared him to the prodigal son in the Gospels. Prussia's honor, he declared, "meant her abstinence from any shameful union with democracy." He was friendly to Austria, and saw no shame in the capitulation of Olmütz. His narrow but very sincere Lutheranism made him believe that monarchy was ordained of God. "If I were not a Christian," he would say, "I would be a republican"; and in Christianity he always saw the best bulwark against revolution and socialism. He had been one of the Conservative deputies in the Prussian diets and assemblies of 1848-49, when he openly blamed the King for making concessions to the Liberals. "The Crown itself," he proclaimed in disgust, "has cast the earth upon its coffin." In the ensuing tumultuous debates, while German nationalism and liberalism had swelled and ebbed, he had proclaimed his contempt for the idea that bare majorities could settle the issues which seemed shattering Europe. "The decision on these principles," he had cried from the tribune in 1849, "will come, not by parliamentary debates, nor by majorities of eleven votes; sooner or later *the God who directs the battle will cast his iron dice.*"

Such was the man who was to play a role in German history comparable to that of Cavour in Italy. Liberal historians have long tended to underestimate him. They draw their picture truthfully enough of the young Bismarck; but they frequently gloss over the way in which he changed with the passing of the years. He never became a liberal, it is true; but he did cease to be a reactionary in any true sense of that word. Bismarck grew into a very practical conservative—after he had seen a little of the world. His eyes were ever on the ground, the mucky and the treacherous ground of political wire-pulling, chicanery, fraud, and pretense. Over it he was to walk warily; and very largely because of his hard work, indomitable will, and clear thinking, the German Empire (the second German Reich, if we count the old Holy Roman Empire of the German Nation as the first) was to arise in 1871. And then, for nearly twenty years after, he was to continue as Europe's greatest statesman.

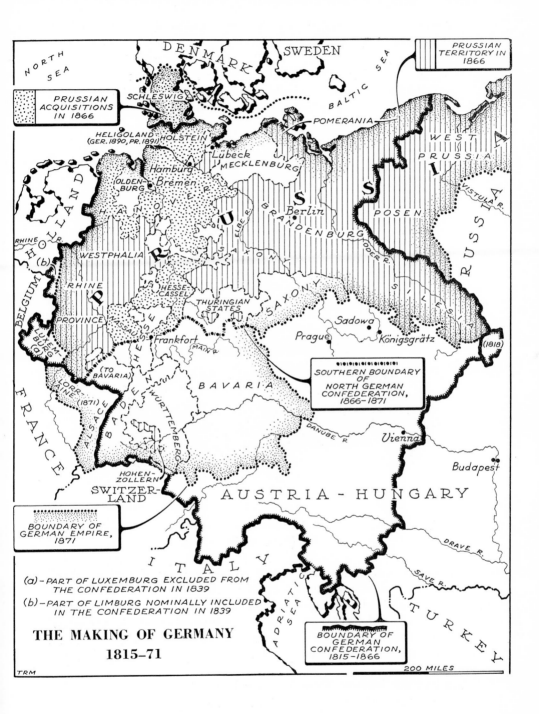

NORTH SEA

DENMARK

SWEDEN

BALTIC SEA

PRUSSIAN TERRITORY IN 1866

PRUSSIAN ACQUISITIONS IN 1866

SCHLESWIG

POMERANIA

WEST PRUSSIA

HELIGOLAND (GER.1890,PR.1891) HOLSTEIN

Lübeck MECKLENBURG

Hamburg Bremen

OLDEN-BURG

HANOVER

Berlin BRANDENBURG

POSEN

RUSSIA

VISTULA R.

HOLLAND

BELGIUM

RHINE PR.

WESTPHALIA

RHINE PROVINCE

HESSE-CASSEL

THURINGIAN STATES

SAXONY

SAXONY

SILESIA

ODER R.

ELBER R.

PRUSSIA

(1818)

LUXEM-BURG (a)

NASSAU

Frankfort (MAIN R.)

(TO BAVARIA)

Prague

Sadowa

Königsgrätz

SOUTHERN BOUNDARY OF NORTH GERMAN CONFEDERATION, 1866–1871

FRANCE

LORRAINE (1871)

ALSACE

BADEN

HESSE-D.

WÜRTTEMBERG

BAVARIA

DANUBE R.

Vienna

HOHEN-ZOLLERN

SWITZER-LAND

AUSTRIA - HUNGARY

Budapest

DRAVE R.

BOUNDARY OF GERMAN EMPIRE, 1871

SAVE R.

ITALY

(a) – PART OF LUXEMBURG EXCLUDED FROM THE CONFEDERATION IN 1839

(b) – PART OF LIMBURG NOMINALLY INCLUDED IN THE CONFEDERATION IN 1839

ADRIATIC SEA

TURKEY

BOUNDARY OF GERMAN CONFEDERATION, 1815–1866

THE MAKING OF GERMANY
1815–71

TRM

200 MILES

Bismarck's real training began in 1851 when he was sent to the old German Diet at Frankfort as the representative of the Prussian king. That congress of diplomats had resumed its empty deliberations and ceremonious dawdlings. Around them fluttered a constant attendance of financiers, idle princelets, and polite gamblers from the fashionable watering places, Homburg, Wiesbaden, and Baden-Baden near at hand. Frank-

WILLIAM I, KING OF PRUSSIA AND EMPEROR OF GERMANY
(1797-1888)

fort, in short, was "a city where intrigue took the place of statesmanship." The honest Junker from the windy Mark was at once disgusted at the atmosphere around him. Speedily he was complaining over "the petty fussiness of the delegates and friction over small points in etiquette." "Our intercourse [at the Diet]" he wrote home, "is at best nothing but a mutual suspicion and espionage—if there is anything to spy out and hide!"

He had not been at Frankfort long before he came to realize that the one use Austria had for the Diet was to manipulate the lesser states so that they would join her in curbing Prussia, and that Prussia could never be a genuinely great power, instead of only a nominally great power, until Austria had been forced to revise her attitude. The eighteen-fifties had not advanced far, therefore, before the shrewdest man in Germany had reached the fundamental conclusion that Austria, and not "the Revolution," was the greatest danger for Prussia.

OTTO VON BISMARCK, FIRST CHANCELLOR OF THE GERMAN EMPIRE (1815-98)

Meanwhile in Berlin the unstable career of his master, Frederick William IV, was about to end. In 1857 the king was pronounced hopelessly insane and his brother William ruled as regent until the king's death in 1861, when he succeeded him as King William I.

The new monarch was unlike his brother. Far less brilliant, never the victim of glowing hopes and soaring schemes, steadfast, commonplace, often (in his viewpoint) devoutly religious, as he understood Christianity, he was already known to hate liberalism and to take a passionate interest in the army. He would have abolished the constitution if he could, but

he was too honorable to repudiate a royal promise. If he was very conservative, he was never guilty of stupid obstinacy or of disastrous refusal
to accept plain facts. Above all, he was devotedly loyal to those whom he
trusted. This temperament went far to make it possible that he, who in
1858 became "Prince Regent of Prussia," in 1871 could be hailed at
Versailles as "German Emperor."

William began his reign as regent, and then as king, with the profound
conviction that the safety of Prussia required a great strengthening of
his army. His relations with his southern neighbor were uncertain. In
1859 Francis Joseph offered Alsace-Lorraine (and other things) to
William if Prussia would join Austria against France. William kept putting off the decision until Austria was beaten and in retreat. Probably
he intended to take Austria's side, but he was so slow in mobilizing that
Francis Joseph became suspicious and lost patience, ending the war with
France before faced with further losses. Both sovereigns were jealous
and suspicious of each other, and from now on enmity between Prussia
and Austria grew apace. Military weakness had been an influential
factor in inducing Prussia to kiss the rod of Olmütz and William I was
determined that there would be no Olmütz while he was king.

William I's Army Reforms: Roon, His War Minister, and Moltke, Chief of Staff

The new ruler, therefore, came to his task convinced that Prussia
needed a far superior army. As early as 1849, he said, "Whoever desires
to rule Germany must first conquer it; the thing cannot be done à la
Gagern [in parliaments]." In his first address to his ministers as regent,
he dwelt on the need of military reorganization. The army had created
Prussia's greatness, and now "the army must be strong in order that it
may be able, if necessary, to throw a heavy political weight into the
scale." Not himself a brilliant or clever man, he knew how to pick extraordinarily gifted servants. He speedily found a great war minister, Albert
von Roon, who was to put his personal stamp upon the Prussian war-
machine more definitely than any other military organizer of modern
times. Roon was devoted to his task and convinced of its importance.
The fact that for years he was intensely hated by German liberals
troubled him not one whit. Supported in office by his master, he was able
to render to Prussia a service without which all the political gifts of
Bismarck would have profited almost nothing.

Since the "War of Liberation" in 1812-13, (in theory) the Prussian
army had been "the Nation in Arms," with obligation to universal service.
Yet the population had greatly increased, although the number of troops
had remained stationary, and, as a result, a great proportion of battle-

worthy young men never were called to the colors. In addition, the organization of the *Landwehr* ("territorial army") was extremely inefficient. It compared, said Roon, sarcastically, to the regular army "as a Sunday school compares to a day school." In brief, in 1860 Prussia had a standing army of 135,000, capable of expansion to 215,000 in war. Roon and William I set their hearts upon a system giving 190,000 in peace and 450,000 soon after the outbreak of war. This change naturally involved greatly tightening the obligations to military service (a change deeply detested by the burgher liberals), and, of course, heavy expense for outfitting the new corps, and educating and maintaining the increased body of officers inevitable under the new system.

To handle this war-machine, William I also found a great general, as well as a great minister. Helmuth von Moltke was a native of Mecklenburg. He had been a cadet in the Danish army, but at twenty-two had resigned to enter the Prussian service. In the eighteen-thirties he had acted as an adviser of the Sultan in an ill-starred attempt to reorganize the Turkish armies; but in 1839 Moltke returned to Berlin in disgust. For years he remained in Prussia as a leisurely staff officer amid times of peace. About him there was nothing of the spectacular soldier.

To Moltke, the organization of armies, the handling of brigades and divisions, the accomplishment of major military problems, became the coldly intellectual work of a master chess player, or, perhaps, rather, of the great scientist moving unemotionally among his apparatus. With Moltke, *modern science,* so potent already in the peaceful life of the nineteenth century, *becomes applied to the grim purposes of war.* In 1857 he became Chief of the Prussian General Staff; and speedily both William I and Roon learned to trust him implicitly. This man, an unpretending university professor more than a Corporal of Lodi, was to direct the military overthrow of both the Hapsburg and Bonapartist empires.

With such advisers, William I flung himself into what he believed a great patriotic task, the increase of his army.

The Fight with the Landtag: Defeat of the Liberals

Now it so happened that the international tensions caused by the Franco-Austrian War of 1859 had resulted in the summoning to the colors of certain reserve regiments. The King proposed to incorporate them in the regular standing army on a permanent basis. But the Landtag, lower house of the Prussian Parliament, refused to vote credits for this addition to the army. Apparently King William must now either give up his military reforms or overthrow the constitution and revert to sheer autocracy.

From the practical standpoint the militarists had a very strong case.

Prussia was wedged between the vaster, more populous and wealthier empires of Russia, Austria, and France. "The Prussian monarchy," it was asserted, "could no more maintain itself without a large army, than the British Empire without a large navy." William, however, was discouraged. Army reform seemed required if he was to continue as a self-respecting monarch; yet his subjects apparently hated it, and his ministers told him that in the face of the vote of the Landtag they could only submit or resign. At a despairing conference, William talked of abdicating, and actually put forth his hand for the bell, to ring for a messenger to summon the Crown Prince. All the ministers leaped from their chairs, begging deliberation. Then, two days later, at Roon's advice, the King summoned to power the last hope of the conservatives—Otto von Bismarck.

Bismarck had left Frankfort in 1858 to become Prussian envoy to St. Petersburg. There he had learned thoroughly the intrigues and manners of the pretentious and quasi-Oriental court of the czars, and had won the personal friendship of Alexander II. In 1862, for a very short time, he was ambassador at Paris, but had been there only long enough to familiarize himself with the hectic atmosphere of the Second Empire, before he was summoned by wire to Berlin. *"Periculum in mora; dépêchez-vous,"* telegraphed the War Minister in a jumble of Latin and French. On September 22, Bismarck waited on the King. William's "constitutional" ministers had deserted the cause of the army as hopeless; and Bismarck found the King at Potsdam, sitting at his table, this time with an act of abdication already signed before him. He bluntly asked Bismarck if he would undertake to be minister-president, and govern even against a majority of the Landtag and without a budget. Bismarck said at once that he would do so. William tore up the abdication, and that same evening Bismarck was minister-president of Prussia, a post corresponding to that of prime minister.

From the outset the new Minister-President defied Parliament and taught the liberals their utter helplessness. The King, of course, stood loyally by him. It wounded William I grievously to seem to be thus at issue with his people, but Bismarck held him in line by representing that it was his clear duty, "as a Prussian soldier," to provide for the safety of the state. Once, when the constitutional struggle was at its height, William talked very gloomily of how he would probably lose his head on the scaffold, and Bismarck likewise. The minister replied that in a good cause such a peril should not swerve them; the examples of Charles I and Strafford were very respectable; and that "death on the scaffold under certain circumstances is as honorable as death on the field of battle."

In the contest that now ensued, Bismarck simply refused to disband the extra regiments, to cease collecting taxes, or to stop paying out funds which had not been voted. The censures of the Landtag bothered him not at all. He skilfully used a conflict upon technical points between the lower and upper houses as an excuse for saying the ministry must provide for the government and safety of the nation, while the two parts of the Parliament settled their differences. But he never forgot the real issue involved—"Which was to rule Prussia, the House of Hohenzollern or the Houses of Parliament?"

During this conflict, he carefully refrained from a coup d'état or any act of glaring violence. There was extreme discontent, but no disorders or rioting. The army was obedient; the civil officials zealously collected the taxes; and the Prussian middle classes were not adepts at passive resistance. Besides, the times were extremely prosperous. Except for the constitutional conflict, the country was well governed and personal grievances were few. There was also no interference with the liberty of individual thought and action. The result was that, after about three years of vehement protestings, petitionings, oratory, and vain threatenings, the liberal opposition flattened out. The new army had come to stay—Landtag or no Landtag.

When the world came to recognize that Bismarck was overcoming the Landtag, his position was strengthened. The King could not dismiss him —that would have meant the triumph of the liberals. He was so embroiled already with the deputies that no new censures could bother him. He could thus pursue a strictly personal policy, could do that which was right in his own eyes, without fear of home criticism; and as deliberately as Cavour had worked to get French aid for Italian nationalism, so Bismarck now worked to force a quarrel on Austria under conditions that would give Prussia the leadership of Germany. Already he was seeking friends abroad. In 1863 another insurrection blazed up in unhappy Russian Poland against czarist masters. Bismarck carefully caused the Prussian frontiers to be closed to every kind of assistance to the insurgents, and did everything except to send armies to Alexander II against them. For this the Czar was extremely grateful, the more because Austria somewhat coquetted with the insurgents. Bismarck knew how to remind Alexander later of the worth of his services. Meantime, he slowly approached his great reckoning with Austria.

The need of reorganizing the old Bund was recognized even by the most reactionary Hapsburger. In 1862, a considerable "Great German" agitation had spread over the Teutonic lands, hinting at a revival of the fine projects of 1848, and in 1863 Francis Joseph summoned at Frankfort a congress of the princes of Germany. They were to be present in person, and consider some scheme for improving the Bund. There failed to appear only three of the minor princelets—and the King of Prussia. Bismarck had been violently opposed to the conference; nothing that Austria fathered must be allowed to prosper. In vain the conference sent a personal invitation to Prussia, carried by the King of Saxony, "How can I refuse," pleaded the simple-hearted William I, "when thirty princes invite me, and their messenger is a king?" Bismarck replied that William, of course, could go, but he would himself resign immediately. The King remained away. The other princes had, it is true, a delightful time, talking at length in private conclaves with no ministers to check their indiscretions, but they accomplished nothing. Prussia was not represented. "It was Hamlet with the Prince of Denmark left out."

The Schleswig-Holstein Question (1863-64)

Bismarck was now preparing to force the issue with Austria and her German satellites by calling up one of the most complicated problems that could be thrust before Europe: the question of Schleswig-Holstein. The problem of settling who was the legitimate ruler for these two duchies, which connected Denmark with the German mainland, calls for a study of a network of dynastic history, local laws and customs, diplomatic agreements, and manifold other technicalities which would baffle the expert. Lord Palmerston said of the problem that there had been only three men who understood its intricacies: one was the Prince Consort, Albert, and he was dead; the second a certain Danish minister, and he had gone mad over it; the third was Palmerston himself, and he had forgotten it!

Stripped to its fundamentals, the Schleswig-Holstein situation was somewhat as follows: When, in 1815, the King of Denmark had been forced to abandon his rule of Norway, the Vienna diplomats awarded him, as consolation, the duchies of Schleswig and Holstein, and their small neighbor Lauenburg. The Danish king had governed these personally—that is, they did not become part of Denmark. Holstein and little Lauenburg were strictly German in speech and social connections, but there was a strong Danish element in Schleswig. Holstein became part of the German Bund; Schleswig was left in an anomalous situation, neither strictly Danish nor German. The active German party therein agitated steadily to have Schleswig added to the German confederation; and an equally active Danish party aimed at causing the direct annexation of the duchy to Denmark.

In March, 1848, this German element broke into insurrection and was aided, first, by kinsmen in Holstein, and then by public sentiment throughout Germany. The Frankfort Parliament tried, in its feeble way, to send military help to the insurgents and did actually inspire Frederick William IV to make a blundering and half-hearted attempt to assist the Schleswig-Holstein nationalists. But the Danes fought back stoutly. Their king was a legitimate ruler, and as the Frankfort Parliament waned, official zeal in Prussia for the insurgent nationalists evaporated. The latter were, therefore, overwhelmed. In 1852 a general European Treaty

to make Austria precipitate the war. He scattered incendiary utterances among all who would hear. In March the Hapsburg envoy was sent to him with the categorical question, "Do you intend to destroy the Gastein Convention and the Germanic Confederation?" "No," answered Bismarck at once, but immediately added, "If my plans were different do you think I should have answered otherwise?" This did not tend to allay Francis Joseph's fears; rather it increased them, especially when he learned of the secret Prussian-Italian alliance. He now saw himself encircled by enemies, spurred on by the master mind of Berlin. The Vienna war council realized that Prussia could mobilize in twenty-five days; Austria would take seven weeks. To prevent being overwhelmed by a sudden attack like that of Frederick the Great in 1740, Francis Joseph began to move his troops to the border. This was just what Bismarck needed to secure his own monarch's consent to mobilization. Now at last Austria was branded as the aggressor; had she not mobilized first?

From this time on, the temperature of Germany mounted higher and higher until war appeared inevitable. All throughout South Germany, if public wishes could decide battles, the Prussian cause seemed lost. Nearly all the minor states made agreements with Austria and began arming to take her side, the side of the confederation against Prussian domination. For once Francis Joseph had the fair wishes of nearly all the liberals of Germany and most of the conservatives, too. Even so good a friend of Bismarck as the Bavarian Prime Minister wrote him a moving appeal to keep the peace. War, he declared, was inevitable if Prussia insisted on keeping Schleswig-Holstein. "As a German, I adjure you," he wrote, "take counsel with your own soul ere the fateful word is spoken."

But Bismarck's tough Brandenburger soul was well content with the way things were going. By June the Prussian army was properly distributed on the chess board and Bismarck was ready to force a decision. He ordered a division of troops to occupy Holstein; the Austrian troops withdrew in order to avoid a conflict. But instantly, at Frankfort, Austria called on the old Diet to intervene against Prussia. Bismarck at once gave every German state clearly to understand that a vote for the Austrian motion meant war with Prussia. Most of the lesser states were too committed to heed the warning. By a narrow margin the Diet voted as Austria demanded and Bismarck proclaimed, amid the welter of final military preparations, that "the Federal compact is broken"; Prussia would now try to reëstablish German unity upon a better basis.

As the last reserves were rushed to the mobilization depots, William I issued a proclamation, telling his people, "I have done everything to save Prussia the cost and sacrifice of war. My folk know it, and God, who knows all hearts, knows it also." Privately, he lamented his isolation in Germany. He disliked the Italian alliance, and he said disconsolately, "I have no allies except the Duke of Mecklenburg and Mazzini"; but his Minister-President had only confidence. His great hopes seemed near fruition. "Foreign cabinets and nations underestimate our country," Bismarck told his friends, "but the world will witness with astonishment the power of despised Prussia."

The Austro-Prussian War (June 22-July 22, 1866)

Decision, however, was passing out of Bismarck's hands. Was the new Prussian war-machine equal to its builders' hopes? The Austrian army was, of course, the army that had lost, by narrow margins, Magenta and Solferino. Training and discipline, however, were very uneven, and ten different languages were spoken among the seven army corps now concentrating. The high commands were nearly all preëmpted by the six hundred families of the upper Austro-Magyar nobility. The titled officers were accounted genial, elegant, lazy, and incompetent, a very poor match for the self-sacrificing, hard-hitting, and hard-headed Junker generals and colonels, and, above all, for their coldly scientific chief-of-staff, Moltke.

Moltke could now demonstrate to astonished Europe the full effectiveness of that war-machine which Roon and he had created since 1859. With a population of thirty-five millions, Austria mobilized 540,000 men; but, out of eighteen million inhabitants, Prussia mobilized 555,000, better disciplined, better equipped, and infinitely better led. The new "needle-guns" could shoot six times as fast as the Austrian army rifles. The Prussian plans of mobilization enabled Moltke to begin the campaign with superior forces at nearly all decisive points, despite the paper equality of his foes. As for the lesser German states, their little armies lacked scientific organization and any decent system of concentration to check the Prussians. Bavarian mobilization was particularly slack and incompetent. Moltke took these lesser opponents at true measure, and told off only some 48,000 men in the west to handle them. His main effort was directed entirely against Austria.

When the first shots were fired, on June 16, Europe prepared for a long grueling war, perhaps ending in Austria's favor; and with both combatants so exhausted they would presently be glad of the very expensive mediation of Napoleon III. In five weeks all the fighting was over and the map of Germanic Europe had been utterly changed, very much to the liking of Bismarck.

In the West, there was only one important battle. When the Prussians broke into Hanover, King George and his army tried to escape to their friends in the South, but they were surrounded and forced to surrender. Hanover thus fell immediately into the hands of the Prussians, the Elector of Hesse-Cassel was carried off to Stettin a prisoner, while the King of Saxony (meeting the full brunt of the Prussian march toward Bohemia) fled hastily from Dresden. The South German armies, isolated and mishandled, were defeated separately, and the position of the lesser states was, by the second half of July, practically hopeless, even if the entire war had not been lost on July 3, upon the Austrian front.

Battle of Königgrätz (Sadowa): Decisive Prussian Victory (July 3, 1866)

The Prussians had attacked with 300,000 men, in three armies, through Saxony and Silesia, forcing their way through the mountain passes covering northern Bohemia. In a series of actions, none decisive, they mauled and hustled the Austrian generals from one position to another. The latter had depended on headlong bayonet charges in massive columns, but their men had been simply mowed down by the needle-guns. The troops now dreaded the Prussian fire, and the generals had lost confidence in their own tactics. Benedek had lost 30,000 men, although without fighting a single great battle. Profoundly discouraged, he telegraphed to Francis Joseph, "I earnestly entreat Your Majesty to conclude peace at any price. A catastrophe is inevitable." From the gray recesses of the vast Hofburg, came the reply, "Impossible to make peace. If retreat necessary, start at once. Has there been a battle?" Benedek dared not take the fearful responsibility of throwing up the campaign under the circumstances, and he arranged to fight in Bohemia, on July 3.

The battle of "Königgrätz," or "Sadowa," to use the name of another village around which the struggle raged, was a decisive Prussian victory. Benedek with the main Austrian army was at Königgrätz near the Elbe. Here the Prussian "Red Prince," Frederick Charles, attacked him. The remainder of the Prussian force, under Crown Prince Frederick, was pressing down from the north, but the battle began long before his arrival. All through the morning, Benedek more than held his own. To Bismarck, all the anxious plottings and intriguings of years seemed in jeopardy. Moltke was watching the conflict with an inscrutable face. Torn with anxiety, the Minister-President took out his cigar case and offered it to the General. Moltke looked at its contents carefully, slowly extracted the best cigar. "And then," said Bismarck afterward, "I knew we were all right."

Moltke was not mistaken. Speedily afterward, the Crown Prince's army swung into action against the Austrian right flank. By 7 p.m. the Austrian army was flying from the field. Benedek left 13,000 of his men prisoners and had lost 31,000 killed and wounded. This battle of Königgrätz practically ended the war. One more such defeat would have involved the dissolution of the ramshackle Hapsburg monarchy.

The news of Königgrätz came as a "gunpowder explosion to Europe." "The extraordinary success of Prussia," wrote Lord Malmesbury, "has alarmed all nations." It was now vastly to the advantage of Bismarck to make peace as rapidly as possible, in order to prevent combinations abroad that might threaten all that Prussia had won. On leaving the battle-field, Bismarck told King William, "The dispute with Austria is decided, we have now to win back the ancient friendship." The Minister-President, in short, had realized that Austria was not a proud, self-contained nation, whose honor had been wounded by a great defeat. She was simply a congeries of small nations under a dynasty, and her friendship could be hopefully cultivated, once she had been thrust out of Germany and taught her station.

Bismarck had to struggle hard, however, "pouring water into the flaming wine" (as he put it) of the King and his generals, and preaching thankless doctrines of moderation in the hour of victory. William seemed blind to the fact that France might intervene suddenly, and that the Austrian army had rallied in a fairly respectable manner a few days after its great defeat. It required all Bismarck's efforts to make the King accept a peace which did not strip Austria of any territory except Venetia, already ceded to France, to pass on to Italy. Outwardly, the King consented; privately, he wrote angrily that his Minister President had forced him "to bite into his sour apple and accept this shameful peace."

The peace that was actually signed seemed anything but "shameful" to most witnesses of the astonishing glory of Prussia. After the victory, Benedetti, Napoleon's envoy to Berlin, turned up in the Prussian camp. There, as he related, he found Bismarck "sitting in a deserted house, writing, with a large revolver at his side." The envoy and minister conversed until 3:30 the next morning, the Frenchman trying skilfully to feel out Bismarck's policies, and to learn what he would promise Napoleon if the latter would let him exploit the Prussian victories, but the Minister-President fended him off skilfully.

The Peace of Prague (August 23, 1866): Austria Expelled from Germany

As the Prussian troops marched rapidly toward Vienna, an armistice put a stop to the fighting. After that, the vanquished found the victors decidedly reasonable. On August 23, the Peace of Prague was signed between Prussia and Austria, and separate treaties were made between Prussia and those lesser German states that had dared to oppose her—so far as she had not devoured those lesser states outright. The cartographers could prepare their new maps of Germany.

Generally speaking, Austria escaped from the conflict remarkably well. She ceded no territory except Venetia (already lost) but she consented to the dissolution of the old German Bund, and Prussia was free to reorganize North Germany as she wished. Austria also agreed to the various annexations contemplated by Prussia and abandoned her claims to Schleswig-Holstein. Likewise, she paid the moderate indemnity of 20,000,000 thalers toward the costs of the war. By this treaty, the Hapsburgs, who since 1273 had been a German power, and who, through most of the centuries, had given emperors to Germany, ceased to rule beyond their own domains. Their German-speaking provinces were now merely a minor fraction of their dominions, with the Slav and Magyar elements ever more dominating. The future of Austria must be toward the south and east—if Austria was to have any future at all as an independent German state.

Within Germany proper, Prussia exploited her victories more ruthlessly. Schleswig-Holstein now, of course, became a province ruled from Berlin. A like fate, more unexpected, befell the kingdom of Hanover and the principalities of Hesse-Cassel and Nassau and the free city of Frankfort. The conquerors announced that these states, by rejecting neutrality, had "appealed to the arbitrament of war; [and] the issue, by the decree of God, has gone against them." The geographical position of these countries (separating the bulk of Prussia from the Rhinelands) made it necessary now to annex them. Blood and iron were consolidating Germany. By these changes, Prussia thus gained some 27,700 square miles of territory and about 4,300,000 inhabitants. She had banished Austria as a German power and had put the surviving states at her mercy, subject only to the possible veto of France.

Prussia had accomplished this by a war which, considered from twentieth-century standards, had been remarkably short and inexpensive. The struggle, after deducting the Austrian indemnity, cost Prussia only some 34,500,000 thalers (about $26,000,000); and her human toll, less than 10,000 dead, was, from a grim military standpoint, a very small price to pay for such enormous physical aggrandizement. The national economic and cultural life had not been seriously shaken. Not too many homes had been filled with bereavement. The short, inexpensive, and comparatively bloodless character of this "Five Weeks' War" went far to teach German public opinion that warfare was a prompt and desirable solvent for international bickerings. "Probably no war yielded to the conquering nation such substantial advantages at so small a cost as the campaign of 1866."

Europe was numbed by what had happened. "The world is coming to an end!" cried Cardinal Antonelli at Rome, on the news from Königgrätz. "France has sunk [by this change] to the third rank," declaimed Thiers in the French Chamber; but it was impossible to undo the startling results, the more especially as Bismarck immediately followed up the treaties of peace by putting into force his schemes for the reorganization of the nation. South Germany could wait, but North Germany was to be cast at once into a confederation, under the firm leadership of Prussia.

The North German Confederation (*1866-67*)

The triumph of the new war-machine had been almost as great a blow to the Prussian liberals as it had been to Austria. In the elections to the Landtag in 1866 the liberals sank to a feeble minority, so weak and discredited that Bismarck could venture upon an act of magnanimity and reconciliation. In the speech from the throne, King William assured the Chamber that, if required by his duty, he would again act without law, even as the crown had acted in the past. "But, gentlemen," said the King, "it will not happen again." Bismarck followed this up by demanding a bill of indemnity for the ministers' illegal acts. Vainly, certain liberal leaders stood to their guns, realizing that a great principle was at stake. There was not the least doubt that the real surrender was not by the government but by the Parliament, yet the measure carried, 230 to 75. This was really the death blow to the older type of North German liberalism. It never was to lift its head proudly again.

The lesser states which had not been suppressed outright escaped with relatively light indemnities and trifling boundary rectifications, because Bismarck was determined upon a new organization of Germany, in which Prussia would be the undoubted leader. Germany was to be divided virtually along the line of the Main. Everything *north* was to go into the "North German Confederation," everything *south* (Bavaria, Württemberg, Baden, and the southern half of Hesse-Darmstadt) was left, for the moment, independent.

Bismarck never showed his worldly wisdom more clearly than in his dealing with the lesser states. In no wise would he hurt their pride or exact any concession not absolutely needful for Prussian supremacy. Thus, they were not forbidden to have envoys at foreign courts, for he considered them "the true guardians of German unity; not the assemblies and the parties." He studiously refrained, therefore, from seeming to hustle the southern states, where there was still much bitter anti-Prussian feeling, into premature union with the rest. "It is open to these states," he said in 1867, "to join hands with the North, but they cannot be compelled." However, he disclosed to their ministers that Napoleon III had been intriguing with him for territorial readjustments in favor of France, at the expense of South Germany, and thus he terrified these southern governments into making secret alliances with Prussia—alliances which were to be used with deadly effect against France in 1870.

Undoubtedly, it lay within the military power of Prussia to have suppressed the petty North German states outright. Bismarck showed a superb moderation. "I do not wish to see 'Germany' substituted for Prussia," he had written earlier, "upon our banners, until we have brought about a closer and more practical union with our fellow countrymen." The result was an alliance between a lion and a flock of lambs, the lambs completely knowing their condition, and the lion showing himself self-restrained and benevolent.

The North German Federation now organized included all German states north of the Main. The King of Prussia was to be president, direct foreign affairs, command the army. The legislature was to consist of two houses: an upper house (*Bundesrat*) composed of envoys or ambassadors to represent the states, a lower house (*Reichstag*) to represent population. The latter was to be elected by universal suffrage, a concession to liberalism. Bismarck had no fear of universal suffrage; it would, in his opinion, have a conservative tendency in the long run, since the working class might very well side with the aristocracy against the bourgeois liberals.

There were, in all, forty-three votes in the Bundesrat—Prussia held seventeen, and Saxony, the next largest state, only four. The little states had, mostly, one apiece. Theoretically, if all the minor states stood together, they could outvote Prussia; practically they could never unite on any really important question, and by small favors Prussia could be always sure of adding enough votes to the seventeen to give her a majority. The lower house (Reichstag) consisted of 297 members, one for every 100,000 inhabitants. Four-fifths of these members came from Prussia. The Reichstag had the right to pass upon all proposed changes of law and the budget, but the members received no pay, and they had no control over naming the ministers. There was only one regular minister, the "chancellor." He "took the responsibility," but this was to the King, who named him, not to the Reichstag, whose adverse votes he could ignore. The other federal ministers were merely his subordinates—"the chancellor's clerks," not self-respecting colleagues with independent portfolios.

To this federal government were entrusted very wide powers: control of war and peace, diplomacy, army and navy, commerce, transportation, customs, the post office, money, sanitary organization, and even much power to enact civil and criminal law. The federal army was to be organized, everywhere, on the Prussian model. The federal flag—black, white, and red—was to be symbolic of Prussian leadership—the old Prussian colors had been black and white. In short, the new order practically extended Prussian control to every corner of this new Bund. The Reichstag would, indeed, serve as an escape valve for public opinion. It might sometimes check or amend unpopular legislation; but it could not repeal one unwelcome law; it could not enact an important new law that had not first run the gantlet of the chancellor and the Bundesrat.

Bismarck took vast joy in his creation. He was vindicating German nationalism, while glorifying his beloved Prussia, and that, too, without any serious surrender to liberalism. He hastened the Diet in its work, waving aside many technicalities, telling the delegates, *"Let Germany only be lifted into the saddle, and she will ride of herself!"* The grateful

William I named him at once as chancellor of the Bund. The constitution of the Federation was proclaimed in 1867, without being submitted for ratification by the Prussian Parliament, and Bismarck laughed to scorn the suggestion that the movement "when in the throw of the iron dice we played for the crowns of kings and emperors . . . could be pigeonholed by a resolution of any assembly."

Bismarck, the Chancellor, had succeeded. By two wars, brief, cheap, and successful, three-fourths of Germany had been consolidated under the domination of Prussia. Like Cavour in 1861 however, much remained for him to do. In the case of Italy, Venetia and Rome were still to be redeemed; in that of Germany, the South German states, jealous and particularistic, were yet to be won.

Chapter 12

THE SECOND EMPIRE IN COLLAPSE: THE FRANCO-PRUSSIAN WAR

In 1860 Napoleon III, the Man of Destiny, as his sycophants more than ever acclaimed him, the "Pinchbeck Napoleon," as such foes as Victor Hugo still unfalteringly denounced him, stood at the summit of his success. The two great absolutist empires of the Romanoffs and the Hapsburgs had successively measured swords with him, and each, in turn, had learned the power of France. The Kingdom of Italy had come into being largely by his agency. France assumed once more her role of the *Grande Nation.*

Both at home and abroad the Second Empire had won renown. In Africa and Asia it advanced the Tricolor. The conquest of Algeria, begun by Charles X, was completed by Louis Napoleon. His Zouaves bit deep into the heart of Northwest Africa, and one by one the native tribes behind Algiers were brought into subjection. In 1860 the Emperor went to Algiers and made a fine speech. "I am," he said, "as much the emperor of the Arabs as I am the emperor of the French." Around the African coast, meanwhile, the wretched little French port of St. Louis at the mouth of the Senegal became the foyer for a large, if not flourishing, French colony. Over five hundred miles up the Senegal the French built a fort, defended it successfully, and planned a number of treaties with natives still farther to the east, whereby they threatened to secure a footing on the upper Niger. The French empire in West Africa was rapidly taking shape.

Between 1862 and 1867 Cochin China and Cambodia were carved out of southeastern China and annexed to France. The story of how that happened and how French and British troops marched side by side in the capture of Peking in 1860 more properly belongs to the chapter on European imperialism in Asia. The fact that they did so, however, added vastly to the romantic glamor which at this time surrounded the inscrutable and sphinx-like gentleman, with stooping gait and pallid face, who was Emperor of France. After all, the great Napoleon had made no conquests in farther Asia! The nephew had surpassed the uncle.

193

The English, indeed, began to be alarmed at French success. It was all very well to assist Italy, but England did not like the way in which Napoleon secured a *pourboire* (tip) for his assistance, by annexing Nice. It was all very well to assist England with ships and soldiers in China, but the English did not welcome the hoisting of the Tricolor over various islands in the Pacific, such as Tahiti and New Caledonia. Nor were they pleased with the fact that *"Partant pour la Syrie"* was the favorite patriotic air in France. Napoleon III sent 6,000 soldiers to Syria in 1860, ostensibly to protect Christian Maronites against attack by certain Moslem tribes known as Druses. The French troops stayed too long, so the British thought, and after a year they were withdrawn. A streak of caution was noticeable in Louis Napoleon.

Despite these enumerated glories, Napoleon III began slowly but surely to lose prestige after 1860. The truth seems to have been that after the end of the Italian war of liberation the Emperor and his fellow spirits were without a fixed policy. They were bewildered at the readjustments which inevitably took place in the diplomatic world after the creation of Italy; they were perplexed at the difficult task of preserving the temporal power of the Pope and yet of retaining the friendship of the now swollen dominions of Victor Emmanuel. They found the clericals of France, hitherto the mainstay of the Second Empire, horrified and furious because Napoleon had acquiesced in depriving the Pope of the legations and Romagna, even if French troops still protected the Holy Father in Rome.

They had, furthermore, established the Empire, promising "it is peace"; now they were presently asking the nation to pay the costs, not merely of the Crimean and Italian wars, but of military expeditions of real consequence, to China, to Indo-China, to Syria, to Rome, to suppress the Algerian tribesmen, and soon they were demanding payment for an expedition to Mexico. These wars, together, cost some $720,000,000 in permanent loans and, barring Nice and Savoy, they gained practically nothing for France. The palace dynasts dared not outrage the nation by making their government still more autocratic. Indeed, to win liberal support to offset the clerical defection from 1860 onward, the government began, with halting steps, to go back toward democracy.

The Mexican Expedition (1861-67): Maximilian of Austria

Meantime, in international matters Napoleon III was committing himself to the dangerous policy of drifting. He did not want to risk another great war, but he was willing to play with many ambitious projects. Wrote Palmerston in 1860, "The emperor's mind seems as full of schemes as a warren is full of rabbits, and like rabbits his schemes go into the ground, for the moment, to avoid notice or antagonism." [1] Then, in an evil hour, he was induced to commit himself to take advantage of American preoccupation with our Civil War, and embark upon a great undertaking in Mexico. The Mexican adventure went far to destroy the Second Empire.

The American Civil War, which chiefly concerns the New World, is here dismissed with slight attention, merely pointing out how events in North America reacted upon the destinies of the Bonapartes and the Hapsburgs. In 1860 Napoleon was at the end of his systematic policy. He had nothing new wherewith to interest French public opinion. There was slowly developing a certain uneasiness about the German situation. Persigny, the Emperor's particular crony, told him flatly, "You are losing your prestige [by inaction] and discouraging your friends." His master was thus greatly tempted to attempt something new, merely because it was new.

In 1861 a sudden opportunity to fish in troubled waters developed in Mexico. That revolution-racked republic had just suspended payments on its external debt and had driven to fury the powerful elements devoted to the Catholic Church. Britain and Spain joined with France in an inglorious naval demonstration off Vera Cruz, largely to coerce the Mexican president, Juárez, into compounding with the European bond-jobbers. Vera Cruz was seized and landings were made on the Mexican coast. Juárez promised payment, then held off and made counterdemands (1862). By this time Britain and Spain were both conscious that Napoleon was acting out of ulterior political motives. Their contingents withdrew, leaving France to pursue her policy alone.

Probably, the Emperor at first had been averse to any grandiose schemes, but now, in addition to the pressure from the bondholders, came that from the vengeful Mexican clericals, Juárez' dearest enemies. At Paris they filled the Empress Eugénie with brilliant projects of a "Latin-Catholic Crusade," and of a great French dominion overseas, that should become also a far-flung bulwark for the true faith. The clericals everywhere, reasoned Napoleon, had been angered by his Italian policy; now he could conciliate them. The expedition seemed also very safe. Juárez and his "Aztecs" were weak. The United States, which cherished its Monroe Doctrine, was rent by civil war. The Southern States (Napoleon was told) were practically sure to succeed, and the protests of Lincoln and Seward could be disregarded. There was also much talk in Paris of how a splendid opportunity had come to regenerate the "Latin" races in

---

[1] As early as 1859 Tennyson in his "Riflemen, Form!" wrote in disgust at Napoleon's utterly shifting policies.

> *True we have a faithful ally—*
> *But only the devil can tell what he means!*

MAXIMILIAN, EMPEROR OF MEXICO (1832-67)

America and put a stop to "Anglo-German" supremacy. Napoleon therefore ordered his general at Vera Cruz to march inland upon Puebla.

The Mexicans, however, were no insignificant foes. The first French
attack (May, 1862) was repulsed at Puebla with loss. "The affair has
started badly," confessed Thouvenel, the imperial foreign minister, "but
we cannot now stop half-way." Heavy reënforcements were sent, at great
expense, to Vera Cruz, and in 1863 the French general Forey rode into
Mexico City. The conquerors made haste to assemble an obsequious body

CARLOTTA, EMPRESS OF MEXICO (1840-1927)

of "notables," bitter foes of Juárez, who were easily cajoled into proclaiming Mexico an "empire" and proffering the imperial crown to the Archduke Maximilian, the younger brother of Francis Joseph himself. To induce a Hapsburg to act as the official head of a French satrapy would give an air of great respectability to the whole undertaking. Napoleon used all his arts to induce a high-minded and truly capable prince to quit his life of magnificent idleness and accept a very tinsel crown. Maximilian's wife, the Belgian princess Carlotta, caught with the title of "emperor," aided in winning over her husband. Francis Joseph himself, not without worldly wisdom in dynastic matters, gave his brother many cautions, and warned him never to expect Austrian aid if things went wrong—but Maximilian listened to the glowing envoys from Paris and accepted the dubious gift of the "throne" of Mexico.

In 1864 he was in Mexico City, setting up a fair-weather court, and accepting the assurances of the French generals that the native republicans were crushed and that only a few brigands were left to be hunted down. Then, in 1865, his bubble burst. The United States had steadfastly refused to recognize the "Mexican Empire"; now the Southern Confederacy had collapsed and the Washington government, triumphant in spite of all Napoleon's reckoning, protested in terms of rising menace against the presence of French forces in Mexico. There was an ominous movement of Northern veterans into Texas, and considering the then state of American military preparedness, a struggle there between the United States and France could have only one end.

In France, the Mexican expedition, a steady drain upon the treasury was increasingly a liability to the government. "The emperor's advisers told him frankly of the unpopularity of 'The Great Speculation,' at which information the poor Emperor would mournfully shrug his shoulders." In the spring of 1867, despite the solemn pledges of support given to Maximilian, the French troops were recalled from Mexico. The unfortunate Hapsburg, overpersuaded not to desert the native clericals, nevertheless remained behind with a mere simulacrum of an army. The end came when he was captured at Querétaro, and when the brother of the Emperor of Austria was stood against a wall and shot by a file of rebels in retaliation for an order he had signed ordering the execution of "republican brigands" (June 19, 1867).

As late as 1864, however, the Ministers of the Second Empire could claim victories abroad, in China, Cochin China, Algeria, and Mexico. "In closing the Gates of the Temple of Janus," they proclaimed, "we may proudly inscribe on a new Arch of Triumph: 'To the Glory of French Arms for their victories in Europe, Asia, Africa, and America.'" But ere 1864 ended, thoughtful Frenchmen were beginning to give heed to the policies in Germany of "M. de Bismarck." The Emperor, indeed, had long considered Prussia to be a friendly power, and her new minister harmless and useful to France. "Prussia must have her place in my scheme of alliances," he said patronizingly to King William's ambassador in November, 1863. Then came the Danish War, the Convention of Gastein, and all the frantic diplomatic movements and tortuous intrigues between the two German states which preceded the war of 1866.

Napoleon III Befooled by Bismarck in 1866-67

Down to the bloody proof, however, neither Napoleon nor his French military advisers seem to have realized that the new Prussian army was formidable. The general impression in Paris was that Prussia would be defeated by Austria—in which case she would be glad of French help to save her from dismemberment; or that the Teutonic powers would exhaust one another in a long, indecisive war, in which case French intervention would be still more bloodless and decisive. Following the Biarritz interview (October, 1865) between Bismarck and Napoleon, the latter committed the crowning blunder of letting Italy enter into alliance with Prussia without any stipulation either that France should be a third member of the coalition or receive a definite reward for her neutrality.

During the actual warfare in 1866, Napoleon gave every evidence of being a man in utter perplexity. Said the Prince of Reuss, "He talks like a man who has not a clear conscience"; and Baron von der Goltz, the Prussian ambassador, wrote home directly, "The Emperor seems to have lost his head!" The moment that Austria had been brought to a really compliant mood and the little South German states had been beaten to their knees, the French politicians learned what manner of man had been playing with them. Early in August, 1866, Benedetti, Napoleon's envoy to Berlin, presented Bismarck with a practical ultimatum—France demanded Mayence [Mainz] and the whole left bank of the Rhine as "compensation" for the great gains of Prussia. Bismarck demanded that the proposal be put in writing (to use it against the Emperor), and then flatly rejected the proposition. *"Both of our armies are on a war footing; yours is not,"* he announced bruskly.

But the Emperor would not dismiss hopes of exacting some great gain for France. He endeavored to get Prussia to aid him to annex a slice of Belgium. Again the blunt German minister foiled him, and the Man of Destiny dared adventure nothing. The year 1866 closed, therefore, with the French nation profoundly conscious that directly across the Rhine had risen a Great Power, bound by its very position to be far more hostile than Austria; and that the French government had gained not the least acre or penny for a neutrality simply invaluable to Prussia. With practical truth, the Emperor's ever-watchful critics could assert that "every error that it was possible to commit, had, in the course of 1866, been committed by Napoleon III."

One last effort the Paris dynasts put forth to win a consolation prize for France. The King of the Netherlands was in financial difficulties, and he was the personal ruler of that small frontier Grand Duchy of Luxemburg, which before 1866 had been a member of the now defunct German Bund. A Prussian garrison had been allowed to occupy this old "Federal

Fortress," but there seemed no obstacle for the King to sell his unprofitable grand dukedom to France. Bismarck was sounded, and apparently
gave his consent; and the treaty conveying the thriving little territory to
France was all but signed. Suddenly Bismarck dropped words in the
North German Reichstag implying that he thought ill of the project, and
followed this by a threatening communication to The Hague. The prudent Dutch sovereign immediately threw over the bargain. The most that
France could obtain was the withdrawal of the Prussian garrison and the
pledge by the Great Powers to respect the neutrality of Luxemburg.

However, for the moment, the diplomatic tempests calmed down.
There was a steady exchange of diplomatic confidences between Vienna
and Paris. Francis Joseph was entirely willing to play with a scheme
for an Austro-French alliance to punish Prussia, with Italy as a third
member of the coalition. But Victor Emmanuel steadily demanded the
evacuation of Rome, which Napoleon as steadily refused, and Austria
was not certain about the attitude of the Czar. Would not Russia be
found on Prussia's side in event of a European war? [2] So matters drifted
through a deceptive calm in 1868-69. The French government feigned,
outwardly, to survey the North German Confederation as a fortunate development of "the sacred rights of nationality," and Bismarck was not
yet ready to force the issue along the Rhine. In the meantime, the Second
Empire underwent an amazing internal change—it became avowedly
liberal.

The "Liberal Empire" (1860-70)

The gradual shift from veiled autocracy dated back to 1859. To offset,
then, the growing clerical defection, Napoleon began to make concessions to the elements he had persecuted. A general amnesty permitted
the return of the exiles of 1851. Beginning with 1860, the debates in the
Chamber could be published in full in the official *Moniteur*. Moderate
political criticisms of the government were permitted in the press. The
Chamber was allowed a reasonable control of the budget. Since 1857,
there had been five opposition members among the deputies, "The Five,"
all chosen either by radical Paris or Lyons. One of them was Émile
Ollivier, a young advocate of very liberal tendencies, and another was
Jules Favre, one of the most distinguished orators in France. Now the
government found itself less and less able to control the electors. In 1863
there was a real anti-Bonapartist coalition in the election—the *Union
liberale*—a curiously assorted congeries of clericals and industrial workers,
Legitimists, Orleanists, and Republicans. They were able to elect, in that

[2] In 1863 Napoleon had greatly angered Alexander II by futile protests in behalf of
the Poles (then in insurrection against Russia), at a time when Bismarck won the
Czar's gratitude by doing everything possible to discourage Polish nationalism.

year, 35 deputies, as against 282 for the government. Of these 35, no less than 17 were Republicans. The spirit of 1848 was again raising its head.

After 1863, there was again, therefore, parliamentary life in France. The minority deputies indulged freely their right to scold the government; the Mexican expedition, the oppressive police system, the standing deficit in the treasury—all were under constant fire. As his situation abroad weakened, Napoleon had to make still more concessions at home. In 1869 he was obliged to take Ollivier into his confidence, and entrust him increasingly with a genuinely liberal program. The Deputies and Senators were given the valuable privilege of "interpellating" the ministry —that is, putting formal and searching questions to the government, and receiving immediate and responsible answers. Napoleon himself professed great zeal for a freer order of things. He desired (he told the Deputies) a regime "equally removed from reaction and from revolutionary theories, and based on order and on liberty. *I will answer for order; help me to save liberty.*"

Following the "Senatus Consultum" of September, 1869, France seemed again a country with fairly liberal institutions. There was a ministry, supposedly responsible to the majority of the Chamber, and bound to resign upon an adverse vote. In April, 1870, the Senate lost its right to amend the constitution and became merely a kind of House of Lords. Many of the repressive laws, dating from 1851, were swept away. Ollivier, as prime minister, declared himself publicly against the system of "official candidates." It looked as if France were being painlessly converted into a parliamentary monarchy.

Long-headed politicians, however, were not to be deceived. The Republican hopes and temper were rising. In the election of 1869, out of 7,790,000 votes cast, 3,300,000 in all had been for candidates opposed to the dynasty. It was charged that the imperialists no longer dared to put up official candidates, lest they be defeated. Paris, in particular, was showing itself intensely radical, and was competing with Marseilles for the honor of electing the fiery young Republican orator, Gambetta, to the Chamber. "I am elected," announced Gambetta, "to assert in the face of the Cæsarian Democracy, the principles, the rights, and the grievances of a true Democracy." "Every place," confirmed Jules Ferry, "is [now] full of explosives; a single spark will suffice."

Napoleon looked on the situation sadly. Sick and heavy-hearted at the rise of Bismarckian Germany, he was nevertheless very loath to make the concessions which Ollivier and his friends demanded. "You want to cut off the old lion's claws and teeth and leave him nothing but his fine mane," he protested. At length, however, he capitulated with outward grace. Ollivier had assured him that "A few months of liberty will do more to secure your dynasty than any prosecutions of the opposition"; and Napoleon dismissed any idea of bolstering up his power by force, the

Empress Eugénie herself saying, "You cannot have a coup d'état twice."

Early in May, 1870, consequently, there was held an artfully devised plebiscite which seemed to reaffirm the support of the nation to the Bonapartist empire. At the astute Rouher's prompting, the people were invited to vote upon the proposition: "The French nation approves the liberal reforms made in the constitution since 1860, by the emperor." The Republicans announced that they regarded this referendum as a subtle means of "confiscating the national will," and ordered their followers to vote "No." However, the peasants, still friends of established order, voted "Yes" almost to a man; the government agents were extraordinarily active, and many moderate liberals had been reasonably well pleased with the new arrangements. Considering the situation, therefore, it is not surprising that Napoleon's lieutenants could report to him that the new policy had been sustained by a great majority—7,350,000 to 1,570,000. The "Liberal Empire" seemed at length fairly constituted, and Ollivier and his colleagues assured the Emperor that he could count upon "a comfortable old age" and a smooth succession for the Prince Imperial. This great plebiscite was held on May 8. The Second Empire had then less than four months to live.

While French statesmen had been wrestling with the conditions of internal government, the Chancellor of the new North German Confederation had never permitted the international situation to slip out of his restless and versatile mind. He knew that France was busily negotiating with Austria; that Archduke Albrecht, victor at Custozza, visited Paris; and that the French general, Lebrun, visited Vienna. What might be the implication of these exchanges of courtesy? Bismarck knew, too, that in the South German states opinion was swinging away from Prussia as each election registered gains for the conservative, particularistic parties. Moreover, Bismarck was not sure how long his own tenure of office might last. King William was getting old; his son, the Crown Prince Frederick, was no personal friend of Bismarck. In 1871 the liberals were pretty sure to try once again to cut the German military budget, while the French army might be greatly improved. A war with France before then (provided always that France seemed the aggressor) would probably bring in the South German states in self-defense, not merely to fight on Prussia's side, but to merge later with the North German Confederation into a German Empire. All this Bismarck knew; but for the time being he was content with worrying his enemy. Since France constantly interfered in German questions, he had no scruples in making trouble for France elsewhere. He saw his chance to do so in Spain and immediately took advantage of it.

In 1868 the evil and frivolous Isabella of Spain had been chased from her throne by her disgusted subjects. The military chiefs, Serrano and

Prim, temporary dictators, were soon scouring Europe for an eligible prince to enjoy the rather tarnished glories of the Escorial. A Portuguese prince declined. A French Bourbon candidate proved impossible. Then the proffer was made to a prince of the House of Hohenzollern-Sigmaringen, the Catholic, non-reigning line of the Hohenzollern family. Here came Bismarck's opportunity.

The Spaniards seemed very much in earnest in offering the throne to Prince Leopold of Hohenzollern, and France began to take umbrage. There was already enough anxiety in Paris at the new power of Prussia. If Hohenzollerns were reigning alike at Madrid and Berlin, would not the safety and prestige of the *Grande Nation* be menaced? At first, the French opposition was politely expressed, and the Prince held back; but Bismarck took pains that the Spaniards should not be easily discouraged. No other eligible candidate seemed in sight, and early in July, 1870, it was suddenly announced that the Hohenzollern prince had accepted.

Was this a private act or an act of high Prussian policy, aimed at the encirclement of France? William I, excluded from his great minister's inner thoughts and himself a simple-minded lover of peace, stated that the other Hohenzollern branch was not under his control. It was Prince Leopold's own business either to accept or reject. In France the "Liberal Empire" had begun; the Chamber of Deputies could indulge in much irresponsible talk. Immediately a question about permitting a Hohenzollern to reign in Madrid was raised by a Deputy. The foreign minister, Gramont, answered in terms officially expressive of peace, but unnecessarily abrupt. Instantly, the Paris papers, just released from a harsh censorship, began to vindicate the "liberty of the press" by wild predictions of war.

Nevertheless, for a few days, it seemed as if peace would be preserved and that France would reap the glory. The other European powers, and notably England, scenting trouble, disapproved and discouraged the Hohenzollern candidacy. Gramont, indeed, did everything possible to bring woe to his country. He kept bombarding his ambassador to Prussia, the more sagacious Benedetti, with frantic counsels, despite the fact that Benedetti was certain that William I meant to keep the peace if not pushed too hard. "We wait only for your dispatch," wired Gramont, "to call up 300,000 men. . . . Write, telegraph something definite. If the king will not counsel the Prince of Hohenzollern to resign—well, it is immediate war." Despite such folly, there was, however, alike in France and Germany, an earnest desire to keep the peace. The Prince of Hohenzollern had hesitated too long before the Spanish proffer to have the least craving to thrust himself into a violent quarrel with France. William I had carefully refrained from urging his candidacy. Therefore, on the 12th of July, to the relief of Europe, the wires flashed the news that the Prince had refused the throne of Spain. France had won a great diplomatic victory and the crisis was over.

The Folly of Gramont: The Ems Telegram (July 13, 1870)

There was delight in the Paris ministries: "We have got our peace," cried Ollivier, the premier, "and we will not let it go again!" "We are satisfied," announced the *Constitutionnel*, an "inspired paper." "It is a great victory which has not cost a tear or a drop of blood." Political opponents, like old Guizot in his retirement, congratulated Napoleon III on the good luck of his ministers. Then Gramont, without consulting Ollivier, his superior, telegraphed to Benedetti the orders which ruined France.

Gramont was guilty of almost the grossest blunders whereof a sane politician can be capable. He knew that Francis Joseph of Austria had warned France that if war came between her and Prussia, he could not break neutrality for at least forty-two days, the time required for Austrian mobilization. He knew, also, that France had no firm alliance with Italy. The military reforms recently proposed had not been executed; nevertheless, he accepted as gospel the assurance from Leboeuf, the war minister, that the army was completely ready. He now played directly into Bismarck's hands, by making wholly unreasonable demands upon the King of Prussia.

The King was at Ems, "taking the waters," leaving his Chancellor and his Chief of Staff fuming helplessly at Berlin. To William I, while he was in the park on the morning of July 13, came Benedetti, acting under strict orders from his superior at Paris. Would the King give France a formal guarantee that the Hohenzollern candidacy would never be renewed? The demand was humiliating and needless. William answered with some directness: "You are asking a promise without limit of time and for all conditions. I cannot give it." Benedetti urged and the King firmly refused. The envoy went away. Then in the afternoon a message arrived for William from the Prussian ambassador at Paris, intimating that Napoleon III was disposed to press the matter personally. The King resolved to have an end to the incident. He sent his aide-de-camp to Benedetti to say that since the withdrawal of the candidacy was confirmed, he could not give another audience.

A telegram was now sent to Bismarck by the King (the famous "Ems dispatch"), informing the Chancellor of what had occurred and authorizing him to publish it to the world if he saw fit.

Bismarck certainly saw fit, since he knew that public opinion in both France and Germany was aroused over the question of the Spanish throne and he did not want to calm it. If the French were so foolish as to plunge into war because the King of Prussia refused to bind himself and his country for all time to a certain course of action, so much the worse for the French. In after years, Bismarck, as a garrulous old man, was to boast of this occasion and the way in which he precipitated war by editing the King's telegram so as to twist his Majesty's words out of their proper content. A careful reading, however, both of the original message and of Bismarck's version for publication will not bear out the old man's claim. The original was very long and contained much extraneous matter which was omitted by Bismarck as any intelligent editor would omit it. Perhaps on that account the refusal of the King to see the ambassador again in the matter of the Spanish throne seemed somewhat sharpened.

That refusal in no wise implied an insult, and why the French should have asserted that it did is very difficult to see. Nevertheless, they seem to have been aroused to fury, that is, at least in Paris. Napoleon III had been distracted by illness and had been going to ministerial councils more intent upon the talk of his physicians than upon issues of peace and war. He had begged his ministers to be "prudent and pacific." Now, on July 14, when the papers carried in black type the "insult to France at Ems," the Man of Destiny and his advisers hesitated pitifully upon the brink. Early in the afternoon they would mobilize; but at 6 p.m. they decided to "appeal to Europe" for an international congress to settle the Spanish question.

Then, by the evening, news of the roaring boulevards of the capital kept coming to the palace. Under the warm summer twilight, excited crowds were parading and thundering "A Berlin!" On what could the Second Empire rest if it showed itself a poltroon to the masses and to the army? The volatile Empress Eugénie was already assailing her husband and his War Minister with having "disgraced themselves." [3] There followed, accordingly, another anxious, tense meeting of ministers at St. Cloud with the voices for peace overborne. A foolish dispatch from the French chargé at Vienna, that an Austrian alliance could be relied upon, helped to turn the scales. The vote was taken for mobilization and war; and when Ollivier, the hitherto pacifist premier, went before the Chamber, the Deputies were in a white heat for action. "If ever a war was necessary," cried Ollivier from the tribune, "it is this war to which Prussia drives us"; during the friendly negotiations by France, "they announce to Europe that they have shown our envoy the door." The Chamber voted for war, 246 to 10. Soon Paris was aflame with cheers, patriotic music, Tricolor flags, and brave old tales of Jena.[4] The diplomats speedily

[3] The Empress was later charged with saying, after war was declared: "This is *my* war! With God's help we will crush those Protestant Prussians."

[4] Too late, Ollivier and his colleagues discovered that outside of Paris there was little real enthusiasm for war. The confidential official reports had it that the war was "popular" in only 16 out of 87 departments. In all the others it was accepted with hesitation or regret.

exchanged their ceremonious farewells, and the two greatest countries of Western Europe rang with the clangor of mobilization.

The die was therefore cast amid such inconceivable blunders on the French side that Bismarck could later say, with technical accuracy, that the final declaration of war was the first strictly official communication he had received from Napoleon III's ministers during the whole affair. Almost immediately, the nations were to learn what it meant to provoke the lightning—to confront, without suitable preparation, Moltke's scientifically constructed war-machine, as directed by his cold, hard genius. The soldiers of the Second Empire were just as brave, patriotic, and intelligent as their grandfathers under the Little Corporal, or their sons under Foch; but the follies of the government, denying them adequate organization or decent leadership, doomed them in advance.

Since France was technically the aggressor, the South German states, allied now to Prussia, promptly made common cause with the Hohenzollern. Moltke, this time, could assemble 500,000 men in three weeks, instead of only 250,000 in five weeks, as in 1866. The Prussian railway system had been much improved and the artillery completely rearmed with the new breech-loading cannon. The whole mobilization proceeded like clockwork; all had been prearranged. Speedily, vast hosts were pouring into the Rhinelands, ready to burst over the frontiers.

Absolute was the contrast in France. Not the least of Napoleon III's handicaps had always been that the crime of the coup d'état rendered it impossible to employ the best talent of the nation. Now he found himself with only his military satellites. Some of his generals were superannuated and incapable, others merely cheap and selfish soldiers of fortune. A real conscription had not yet been enforced on the population. The railroads were not arranged for mobilization. The French muzzle-loading field guns were very inferior to the Prussian. A thousand essential munitions seemed lacking. Above all, a competent commander-in-chief did not exist. There was a shortage in everything, except in the bravery and patriotism of the field officers and the rank and file.

Napoleon III, according to paper projects, should have assembled 750,000 men. Actually, he never mustered over 300,000 before he ceased to be emperor. The only chance for the French was through a quick dash into southern Germany, where a successful blow, before Prussia was ready, might have detached Württemberg and Bavaria from the foe, and brought in Austria as an ally. This possibility evaporated, thanks to the slow mobilization. Napoleon III reached Metz on July 28. He found there only 187,000 men, instead of the 300,000 he had expected. The remainder of his troops were spread out in a thin line, covering 240 miles of frontier. The initiative had thus slipped away at the outset, and every opportunity was in Moltke's hands. And yet, at Paris, where the ministers had jauntily asserted that "the army was ready down to the last shoe-string," there was already bitter complaint because no victories were reported.

German Victories: The Capitulation of Sedan

On August 4, 1870, the Teutonic hosts poured into Alsace where 37,000 French under MacMahon strove gallantly but vainly to drive them back. The latter's army fled westward; it was practically a rout. The same day the Germans were over the frontier in Lorraine, flinging back another French army. At Metz was the main French army under Bazaine. It was his clear duty to get his army over the Moselle and put it under the protection of the forts of Verdun, to cover the road to Paris; but procrastination and irresolution were his ruin. Almost before he knew it, Moltke had crossed the Moselle and was at his heels with 200,000 men. Bazaine had only 140,000 troops; but his position was strong and his men fought admirably. Finally, his right wing crumpled, and the French were swept back under the guns of Metz. This battle of Gravelotte (named for a village around which it raged) was really the decisive engagement of the war. The best French army was now blockaded in Metz. It never was able to escape.

Disguised messengers from Bazaine were soon making their way through the German lines, calling lustily upon his fellow-generals outside for help. Could that help reach him?

Napoleon III still possessed an army. After MacMahon fled, he rallied his remnants, gathered some heterogeneous reinforcements, and tried for a juncture with Bazaine. At Sedan, wedged between the Meuse and the Belgian frontier, the Germans closed upon him from all sides. The French were caught in a veritable pocket between hills and river, with the German cannon belching from all the heights. There was magnificent resistance, with heroic cavalry charges up to the Prussian guns, but the case was hopeless. MacMahon had been wounded, the encirclement was complete, and Napoleon hung out the white flag. Then he sent to King William I the last letter he was to write as a ruler of the France he had brought to ruin: "Monsieur my brother: Not having been able to die in the midst of my troops, it only remains for me to place my sword in the hands of your Majesty. I remain your Majesty's good brother, *Napoleon.*"

Moltke was adamant to pleas for better terms than absolute surrender. Bismarck declared it was useless to count on French gratitude for lenity, and that magnanimity was out of place. Already 37,000 French had been killed, wounded, or captured in the fighting, and on September 2d, 83,000 more, including, as the Germans gleefully reported, "one emperor," surrendered themselves prisoners. It had been less than a month since the invasion of France began.

Fall of the Second Empire: "Government of the National Defense": The Siege of Paris

Bazaine was blocked in Metz; MacMahon was a prisoner. Moltke could therefore send his hosts straight on to Paris, and on September 19 he was there. It was a new set of foes that resisted him. When the news of Sedan reached Paris the crowds on the boulevards roared, "Down with the empire; long live the republic!" A republican "Government of National Defense" seized public office. The Empress and her son, the Prince Imperial, fled post-haste to England, while on the 6th, Jules Favre, the new Foreign Minister, could proclaim that the Revolution had been consummated "without shedding a drop of blood or the loss of liberty to a single person."

The new government undertook to remain in Paris, but to send out a delegation to Tours, to rouse France against the invader. The two-weeks' interval before the Prussians came was used to rush in great quantities of provisions, and to strengthen the forts so that the defense was prolonged far beyond Moltke's calculation. Favre promptly sought an interview with Bismarck. The French, he suggested, would pay an indemnity but could not hear of ceding Alsace, as the Germans already demanded. "Not an inch of our land, not a stone of our fortresses," he declared.

It was a war in which France had no real chance to win the victory. Nearly all her regular troops left after Sedan and Metz were tied up in the Paris garrison, and these were too few to break the German blockade. Soon the great city could communicate with the outer world only by balloons or carrier pigeons. However, a magnificent attempt was made to relieve the capital. Leon Gambetta, the Republican leader, escaped by balloon on October 7, and assumed charge of the government in the departments. He had enormous energy, enthusiasm, and the power of infusing that enthusiasm in others. Soon he had called nearly all the young manhood of France to arms and was flinging large armies against the German blockades around Paris. These new armies, brave and very patriotic, were composed, however, of raw recruits. Nevertheless, the French might have succeeded, except for the demi-treason of Bazaine.

The Marshal was still detaining the best army of Germany immobilized, while it blockaded him around Metz. Instead of striving to break through, he considered the game up as soon as he got news of Sedan, and let himself be dragged into a futile and insincere political negotiation with Bismarck, which the latter spun along until the Marshal had served out his last biscuits. Then he suddenly surrendered, on October 27, with nearly 180,000 men. Traitor, coward, or incompetent, probably all of them, his deed sealed the doom of France. Some 200,000 Germans were now free to march from Metz to Paris to tighten the blockade, and the task of Gambetta's armies became impossible.

The Surrender of Paris (January 28, 1871): The Terms of the Treaty of Frankfort

The French won minor successes during the bitterly cold winter which ensued, but could never break the ring around Paris. The great city held out courageously for 130 days, while rats and cats were served in the boulevard restaurants. On January 28, 1871, Paris capitulated, agreeing to pay a special war contribution of 200,000,000 francs ($40,000,000), while an armistice was arranged to permit the election of a French National Assembly to discuss terms of peace.

Gambetta wished to fight on, but the generals pronounced the military case hopeless, and the peasantry would not make further sacrifices. The new National Assembly met in February at Bordeaux, and it sent Adolphe Thiers, the veteran Liberal statesman, as its provisional "Head of the Executive Power," to the German headquarters.

Bismarck stated his demands bluntly—a war indemnity of six billion francs ($1,200,000,000), all of Alsace, part of Lorraine, plus the fortress city of Belfort near the Swiss frontier. He had not intended to ask for so much. The city of Metz, in particular, he had wanted to return to France, and then to build with indemnity money a great fortress to the east of it. "I do not like to have so many Frenchmen in our house," he is reported as saying. But Moltke insisted that Metz was worth 100,000 men at the opening of a campaign and the King of Prussia supported him. Therefore Bismarck consented to the harsher terms.

Thiers was able to cut them down somewhat. Aided by British financial influence, which was not desirous of seeing France bankrupt, he managed to beat down the demand from six billions to five billions of francs ($1,000,000,000). He found Bismarck inexorable as to Alsace-Lorraine; but to retain Belfort the envoy made a successful stand. That fortress had held out heroically. The Germans had been unable to capture it; the place was purely French and endeared now to all Frenchmen. Thiers turned desperately at bay.

"These negotiations are nothing but a sham," he cried. "Make war then! Ravage our provinces, burn, slaughter . . . complete your work! We will fight you to our last breath. We may be defeated, but at least we will not be dishonored."

Bismarck was moved. He was not sure of how far Thiers was in earnest, but he did know that other nations were growing anxious at the swelling power of Germany and might interfere in French behalf if the war was renewed. He retired to consult Emperor William and Moltke, and came back to say that France might retain Belfort, provided Paris would consent to a triumphal march of the Prussians through her gates—something excluded by the original capitulation. Paris bowed her pride and submitted. Belfort was saved—to become, in 1914, a veritable bulwark to France in the days of a yet greater Teutonic invasion.

By the final treaty—signed at Frankfort, May 10, 1871—France was obligated to pay one billion dollars, to see a German army occupy her provinces until the debt was paid, and to submit to losing about 5,000 square miles of territory with 1,500,000 population. It was a harsh treaty, but the German annexation of Alsace-Lorraine was not without some justification. Originally, both provinces had been part of the old Holy Roman Empire of the German Nation. Little by little in centuries past, the French monarchy had absorbed these lands. The old bishoprics of Metz and Toul had been the first to go; but the annexation of Strasbourg to France had not taken place until 1697. Part of Lorraine had been joined to France even later. In both Alsace and Lorraine, German was generally spoken, and in the former province very predominantly so.

Furthermore, if there was such a thing as a natural boundary between France and Germany, it was the height of the Vosges Mountains, not the Rhine. A river is very seldom a natural boundary, since the people living on either bank are apt to see a great deal of one another, both commercially and socially. Not so with a mountain range. It may be defended more easily; it more truly divides peoples, since those who live on either side of the divide are more apt to have their social and commercial relations with the folk in the valley than with those over the mountain wall.

In addition, the retention of Alsace by the French would give them an important strategic advantage in any future war with Germany. Not far from Strasbourg was the River Main, flowing into the Rhine from the east. The French possession of Strasbourg was a pistol pointed straight at the Main Valley and the heart of Germany. True, the retention of Metz was a pistol in German hands, pointed straight at the heart of northern France. Bismarck realized this and therefore had been willing to forego Metz—only this time the militarists had their way and Bismarck suffered one of his few defeats.

The French, on the other hand, justly could object to the territorial settlements of the peace treaty. Somewhere, sometime, there must be a statute of limitations among states in regard to old territorial disputes, or else permanent peace is an idle dream. Alsace and Lorraine had at one time been part of the shadowy old German Empire; but that was not the North German Confederation, and Strasbourg had been a French city for nearly 175 years. If the distant past was always to be reopened, then Italy had a claim on Malta, Mexico on California, and Sweden on a part of Prussia. Even more to the point was the unwillingness of the Lorrainers and Alsatians in 1871 to join Germany. They had been thoroughly Gallicized, even if they tended to have blond hair, blue eyes, and continued to speak German. The French Revolution had brought them social and economic rights not enjoyed in the late eighteenth century in Prussia, and the fact that the "Marseillaise" had been written and sung first in Strasbourg was a token thereof. The deputies to the National Assembly from Alsace-Lorraine had protested bitterly against the treaty which assigned them to the conqueror. Neither Bismarck nor any one else had any intention of testing popular opinion in the two provinces. They were simply incorporated in Germany, the new German empire which was to be.

Such was the Treaty of Frankfort. It left Prussia completely victorious, France completely humiliated and thirsting for revenge. That thirst was to slacken after a decade or so: but memories lingered on, to become vivid and painful again in 1910-12, as we shall see. One root of the World War of 1914-18 was to go straight back to this Treaty of 1871.

Chapter 13

ENGLAND AT MID-CENTURY

FROM THE Chartist fiasco of 1848 to the second ministry of Disraeli in 1874, Lady Luck showered economic blessings on Britain. For more than a quarter of a century England not only ruled the waves, but in everything that concerned material power was easily first among the nations of Europe on both sea and land.

This was due in part to her immunity from the expensive wars of the mid-century, in part to her being the first country to make extensive use of the new power machinery, in part also to what took place in the United States and Australia.

In 1849 came the great California gold rush. Thousands of adventurous men, lured to the Pacific coast, had to be fed, transported, and equipped, a task assumed gladly by the British mercantile marine and the British manufacturer. The vast majority went all the way by sea, and whether they travelled by way of the Isthmus of Panama or around Cape Horn, more often than not they went in British ships, owned and operated by British capital; and the fare charged was high. The ships carried more than passengers; their holds held tools, guns, munitions, tents, and hardware made in Britain. Profits were large, profits were continuous; and profits rose higher yet with the great Australian gold discoveries in the fifties. The miners, whether American or British, intent on nuggets, whiskey, women, and gambling, spent freely. Furthermore, the very gold they dug brought mild inflation in its train, a favorable time for businessmen to borrow and pay back in cheapened currency.

Then in 1856 came the Bessemer method of making steel, already described (see p. 7), and once more Britain stood to gain added wealth.

The year 1861, and civil war in America, a local setback for the cotton spinner in Lancashire but by and large a stroke of luck for British trade and commerce, since throughout its raging the industrial expansion of the North went on unabated, both man power and capital flowing in an ever increasing stream from the British Isles.

And in addition, the American carrying trade, an active competitor of Britain on the high seas in the fifties, was badly wounded (1861-1865) by Confederate privateers, and finally stricken to death in the next decade by the gradual substitution of iron (later steel) for wood in shipbuilding—a blow to Bath, Maine, but a blessing to Clydeside.

Then too, no sooner did Lee capitulate to Grant than westward trekked many a soldier, both Confederate and Unionist. Railways rather than prairie schooners marked this migration, and both iron horses and iron rails to run them on came largely from Britain. And when in 1869 a golden spike was driven where a locomotive from the Pacific coast met one from the Atlantic, and the Union Pacific, first of the transcontinental railways, was completed, the triumph was due to British capital as well as to American enterprise.

With the coming of the seventies the American demand for British capital dwindled; but as this happened, the new German Empire for a short time took America's place. There were dark clouds rising in the economic skies by 1874, as we shall note at the end of this chapter. But prior to that, mid-Victorians had reason to rejoice, and could quote facts and figures to justify their optimism.

Thus, during the three decades from 1840 to 1870 exports of cotton goods increased three hundred per cent, exports of iron and steel eight hundred per cent. By 1870 the world's carrying trade had become practically a British monopoly. In "1844 the tonnage of ships entered and cleared from British ports in international trade was 10,300,000 tons, in 1860 it was 24,700,000 tons, and in 1870, 36,000,000 tons." [1]

The Industrial Revolution now at last was in full swing, and Britain was its favorite child. Full pocketbooks resulted for the bourgeoisie, and in general Victorian complacency and the continued success of the Victorian compromise blurred for a long time the differences between the two political parties. The Whig or aristocratic element in the Liberal Party was strong—much stronger even (if less noisy) than the radical left wing of the party. No one could tell in advance how the Peelites (see p. 136) might vote, and the Tories, or Conservatives, not yet trusting altogether young Mr. Disraeli, did little except criticize the Liberals and talk generalities. The country was interested primarily in industrial development, in balanced budgets, and in keeping a respectful distance from Continental broils, while at the same time upholding England's prestige overseas.

The country, also, was rather thoroughly given over to that general philosophy of life which is known as Benthamism. Essentially, this was a belief in pure individualism. Jeremy Bentham had argued tellingly that each individual knows best what is good for his own happiness, and that the happiness of the whole depends upon letting each individual seek his own. Since happiness (the greatest good to the greatest number) is the goal toward which society would strive, it best may be reached via the road of laissez faire—each individual out for his own advancement and

[1] F. C. Dietz, *An Economic History of England*, p. 455.

the devil take the hindmost. And this bracing creed of individualism, the intellectual foundation of British liberalism, was accepted pretty much by both Liberals and Conservatives.

Naturally there were cross-currents. A very important one was the Oxford Movement in the Church of England. The leaders of it, whose agitation dated back into the eighteen-thirties, disgusted by the complacency with which their fellow-churchmen accepted contemporary philosophy, sought to revivify the national church by a return to Catholic ideas and practices current in England before the Reformation, and, for that matter, before the Norman Conquest. These men were known as High Churchmen, since they exalted the Church of England, not as a society of individuals, but as a society of Christians who put, or who should put, the communal spirit above individualism. They were great scholars and ardent preachers, and believed thoroughly that the Church of England was just as truly Catholic as the Church of Rome. They believed in the Mass; they believed in penance; they believed in holy orders, real and not simply nominal, in other words spiritual authority distinct and separate for the clergy, coming direct from Christ. The interest which they aroused was astonishingly large; but the influence which they exerted was far less extensive than the publicity which they achieved.

Another cross-current was the Young England Movement, sponsored by certain youthful aristocrats who reacted against what seemed to them the drab bleakness of Benthamism. A prominent spokesman for "Young England" was Disraeli, better known in his early career as a novelist than as a statesman. In one of his novels, *Sybil*, he well expressed the ideas of this movement. The subtitle of the novel is, *"A Story of Two Nations,"* one of aristocratic-bourgeois complacency and success, and the other, one of proletarian misery and crime. Disraeli and his aristocratic young colleagues felt very keenly that the upper classes were responsible for this undesirable social cleavage, and they intended to bridge the gulf. Unfortunately, however, they were very hazy as to how that should be done, and they were apt to dream altogether too optimistically that it might be closed by kind condescension on the part of the well-to-do, who should rig up once more the May-pole on the village green, invite the poor to feasts of roasted ox, and visit them when old, soups and jellies being purveyed by delightfully charitable young ladies.

The main tide, however, swung the other way. Economics, then called political economy and supposedly a science, pointed straight toward laissez faire. Adam Smith, Thomas Malthus, Ricardo, James Mill, and John Stuart Mill were the gods of the new liberal dispensation. Their laissez-faire theories we shall examine more closely elsewhere (Chap. 15), but tribute should be given here to them as very substantial props indeed to mid-Victorian complacency and the consequent unreality of party strife in England between 1846 and 1865.

BENJAMIN DISRAELI, EARL OF BEACONSFIELD (1804-81)

Such conflicts as did arise had to do more particularly with the conflicting personalities of various statesmen or with foreign affairs. Certain
of the more prominent men of the period were relatively colorless, such
as the Conservative premier, Lord Derby, and his Liberal counterpart,
Lord Aberdeen, under whose rather muddled conduct of foreign affairs
the Crimean War began. But the same can not be said of Gladstone,
Disraeli, Cobden, Bright, Russell, and particularly Palmerston. The brilliant young Peelite, Gladstone, was not popular but he was able. For many
years he apparently did not know whether he belonged on the right or

left side of the political fence, a fact which made his political moves disconcerting, especially to himself, for he was a conscientious man. Just what Disraeli would do, nobody could tell exactly. That Jewish leader of the country gentry was somewhat of an enigma. Cobden and Bright worked together for the most part, but the former was more inclined to trust to the upper middle class than his more radical colleague who was building up a reputation fast among workingmen. Lord John Russell, tiny in stature, and a very opinionated Whig, was the titular leader of the Liberals and jealous of all who questioned his authority, something which Lord Palmerston was quite ready to do.

Both from the point of view of personality and from that of foreign affairs, Viscount Palmerston of the Irish peerage (therefore, politically speaking, a commoner and so not entitled to a seat in the House of Lords) was Britain's leading statesman. Palmerston, or "Pam," was both popular and able. From 1807 to his death in 1865 at the age of eighty-one, he was, with the exception of a few years, continuously in public office. He loved hard work and he loved public acclaim. His specialty was foreign affairs, and very intensive and detailed was his knowledge of all that concerned the foreign office which he ran for years very much as he saw fit, without taking the advice of his titular head, Lord John Russell, or that of the Queen and her royal consort to whom he generally was anathema. Palmerston made certain grave errors, such as recognizing prematurely the coup d'état of Louis Napoleon, and frequently he was too bellicose from the point of view of men like Cobden and Bright who were pacifists and "Little Englanders." On the other hand, he never led his country into war (if we except a brief one in China, see p. 463) and he came very decidedly to her rescue in the Crimean War, which was being conducted very inefficiently until he became prime minister in 1859, a post which he retained with the exception of one year until 1865.

The popularity of "Pam" was considerably enhanced by his buoyant self-assertiveness and bold speech. He feared no one, either great or small; and the older he grew the more determined he became. He contended vigorously, and sometimes on slight foundation, for the rights of Englishmen over all the world. He had more to do than any other man with the practical abolition of the slave traffic; he lent a sympathetic ear to the struggles of Poles, Hungarians, and Italians in their efforts to achieve national independence. He brandished a big stick but was so cautious in using it that, although always on the verge of plunging England into war, he skilfully kept her to one side. The Belgians owed much to Lord Palmerston for help in gaining their independence and so, too, the Italians, for if not willing to intervene on their behalf, he did much to keep the ring clear in Italy (1859-61).

The last five years of his life found the old gentleman more assertive than ever. He was at the helm during the American Civil War, and the stiffness of a note to the American government on the Trent affair which he approved might (conceivably) have involved England in war with the United States, had not Prince Albert managed to tone the note down. Increased French armaments, particularly naval, also upset him. His memory stretched back to the great Napoleon, and his early career had been spent in the War Office. So, at the end of his life, his mind reverted to military preparedness. England must be as ready to withstand the Third Napoleon as she had withstood the First. And the fact that W. E. Gladstone, his chancellor of the exchequer, opposed him in this program only added to Palmerston's zeal for its continuance.

The Coming of Democracy

Gladstone, meanwhile, was chafing at the bit. Palmerston, from his point of view, was altogether too old, too militant, too unprogressive to be prime minister. A change was coming over Gladstone. He no longer represented the University of Oxford (home of lost causes) in the Commons but Southeast Lancashire, a constituency which included many workmen who were beginning to clamor for the vote. The American Civil War had given a decided impetus to the cause of political democracy, for rightly or wrongly, the British visualized that conflict overseas as one in which a democratic society (the North) defeated an aristocratic society (the South). The visit of the victorious Garibaldi to England also stirred up democratic agitation. Garibaldi was a romantic figure, freshly crowned with romantic laurels. He, like Lincoln, was a plain man, a man of the people. The trade-unionists were attracted by him, and they were beginning to be aroused by Bright, who told them that they were entitled to the vote. Gladstone, ever susceptible to the changing tides of politics, realized this new drift and in his own cautious way had spoken of it with approval a year or two earlier. For doing so he had been snubbed by "Pam," whose interests lay along different lines. Gladstone resented the snub, resigned from the conservative Carlton Club in which he still held membership, and when "Pam" died in 1865 he was ready to admit that political reform was now overdue and that certain workmen at least were entitled to vote.

In the new Parliament (1866) the aged Earl Russell was prime minister and Gladstone the Liberal leader in the House of Commons. In such capacity he introduced a moderate measure of political reform, providing for a new distribution of seats more in accord with the changes in population than the old Reform Bill and also for lowering the franchise in the boroughs from £10 householders to £7 householders. By this proposal, Gladstone, the ever cautious, thought to admit to the vote the upper strata of workmen but to exclude the unskilled proletariat, for the latter occupied houses under the £7 level.

The moderateness of this change displeased Bright and the more radical Liberals; but the lowering of the franchise at all displeased the more conservative Liberals who joined forces in 1866 with the Conservatives and defeated Gladstone.

The Conservatives now took office under Lord Derby with Disraeli as their leader in the Commons. As they did so a popular clamor arose for Parliamentary reform. Bright was stirring the North to fury and a mob broke fence rails in London. Queen Victoria took alarm and brought pressure on Derby, who consulted Disraeli. The latter professed that he always had been dissatisfied with the Liberal Reform Bill of 1832 and agreed to introduce a more intelligent one. Disraeli's bill in one prospect went much farther than Gladstone's. It proposed to give the vote to every householder in the British boroughs who paid rates (taxes) for poor relief. Since every house, even a hovel, paid such taxes, this almost meant universal male suffrage. To counteract, however, that radical step, Disraeli proposed also to give additional votes (the fancy franchises) to certain classes in society, to professional men, to those who owned government securities, and so on.

It was now Gladstone's turn to attack Disraeli's bill, and he did so, laying his emphasis on the undemocratic "fancy franchises." Much to his surprise and to that of every one else, Disraeli refused to put up much of a fight for them, claiming that they were relatively unimportant: the only thing that was important, he said, was that householders paying taxes were entitled to vote. One after another of the fancy franchises were defeated by amendment and the law which finally was enacted was more radical by far than that introduced a year earlier by Gladstone and defeated by Disraeli. The new bill disenfranchised fifty-two small boroughs and gave their seats to fast-growing towns; it reduced the property qualification in the counties for farmers so low that any farmer now paying £12 a year for his farm could vote, and so could any yeoman (independent landowner, farming his own land) whose land was worth £5 a year; and it enfranchised in the towns every man who rented any kind of house. The bill did not grant complete universal suffrage, since it was not in accord with British tradition to make any reform entirely sweeping. Farm laborers were not enfranchised, nor soldiers, sailors, firemen, household servants, and certain other classes. On the other hand, the Bill of 1867 was decidedly more radical than the measure of 1832; it doubled the electorate, whereas the latter merely increased it by one-third; and it made England a genuine political democracy with the balance of power now resting securely with the working class.

By a parliamentary trick, Disraeli had outbid Gladstone and had ended the Victorian Compromise. And the Tory party, with but few exceptions, had consented thereto. To Liberals, accustomed to think of themselves as the true repository of reform, this seemed simply a cheap

Tory scheme to retain power. But from the point of view of Disraeli it must be remembered that he had constantly affirmed for many years that the natural political alliance was one between aristocracy and proletariat, not between the bourgeoisie and the aristocracy as it had been under the Victorian Compromise. He did not fear political democracy; like Bismarck he thought it might prove a useful counterweight against the bourgeoisie. Furthermore, since it was to come anyway, why should not the Tories have the credit of conferring it? The Liberals had a majority in the House of Commons and Disraeli knew they could throw him out of power any time they chose. But Derby had resigned, and he had climbed "to the top of the greasy pole" and was now prime minister. Surely the grateful proletariat would appreciate what he had done for them when a new election was held!

But it did not. The workingman was suspicious of the Tories' gift. In 1868, spurred on by Bright and Gladstone, he voted Liberal, choosing middle-class representatives and not returning a single workingman. "Shooting Niagara," as Thomas Carlyle scornfully referred to the Reform Bill of 1867, did not seem so very dangerous after all.

The Great Ministry (1868-74)

Gladstone now entered upon his "great ministry" (1868-74), and the reforms which he put on the statute books during that period throw into bold relief the distance between the Russian and the British scene in everything which has to do with political maturity.

Gladstone was now in his sixtieth year, but the years sat lightly on him, as with indomitable energy and subtle mind he attacked many an intricate problem. Certain of these had to do with implementing the political democracy granted in 1867. There was, for instance, the matter of the ballot for secret voting. Gladstone had hitherto opposed this reform on the ground that the vote was a trust, not a right, and that the public had a right to know how their trustees voted. Now that voting had become very general and was regarded as a right, he quickly recognized that workmen needed the ballot to prevent pressure being brought to bear on them by employers. The great ministry secured the ballot, but not without a tussle with the House of Lords and the threat by Gladstone to call a general election on this issue if their lordships threw out the ballot act.

To implement political democracy still further, a general educational bill was passed. "We must educate our masters," the middle class wisely thought. Before 1870 very little money had been appropriated by Parliament for schools, and half of the boys and girls in the country attended no school whatever. This disgraceful situation had been brought about partly by the prevailing laissez-faire attitude of mind, which believed in leaving everything possible to the individual, and partly by religious jealousies between the adherents of the Church of England and the Nonconformists, both factions favoring religious instruction in schools, both factions objecting to that variety taught by the other. Gladstone's political following was largely Nonconformist; on the other hand, the majority of the existing schools were controlled by the Church of England, and Gladstone, being a practical man with a strong streak of economy, could not bring himself to the point of building national schools to compete with those already in operation. Therefore, a compromise measure was enacted (Gladstone, as a good Englishman, was always making compromises), and state subsidies were granted both for building new schools, where there were insufficient facilities, and for enlarging and supporting schools already in operation (the voluntary schools). Gladstone, furthermore, agreed "to exclude from all state-built schools every catechism and formulary distinctive of denominational creed." In addition, in the School Bill there was a timetable clause which provided that such general religious instruction as should be given in schools supported by the state must be at the opening or the close of the school day, so that parents might be at liberty to excuse their children from it if they saw fit.

A democratic reorganization of governmental departments and of the army also was undertaken. Snug berths in government employ had, for time out of mind, been reserved for the relatives of important personages, and Gladstone determined to throw them open to any who should pass civil service examinations. This was done in every department except the foreign service. Then Gladstone tackled the purchase of commissions in the army. If one wanted promotion in the army in the pre-Gladstone era, up to the rank of lieutenant-colonel, one could not get it simply by professional qualifications; it was necessary to buy higher rank from some officer willing to sell his commission. The old system had not worked as badly as one might suspect: it had the advantage of making many more promotions possible, since captains and majors were continually selling their commissions to retire on the proceeds as country gentlemen. Nevertheless, the purchase of commissions meant that, without inheriting money or marrying it, no poor man could succeed in the army—an undesirable state of affairs in any country intent upon becoming more democratic. Since officers were miserably underpaid anyway and by custom kept up a fairly expensive manner of living, this reform really did not make much difference in the composition of the army's corps of officers, wherein the aristocracy remained nearly, if not quite, supreme.

Ireland proved Gladstone's greatest problem. The great ministry began with an act of justice toward that country and it went out of office in 1874 because of failure to put through another. The Irish question, indeed, has proved insoluble ever since.

Gladstone did his best to find an answer to it. Two things had always

(From the original painting by Chappel.)

W. E. GLADSTONE (1809-98)

stood uppermost in his mind—religion and economics. Because of his concern for the former he almost, as a young man, had chosen the church for his profession; because of the fascination exercised by the latter, he had built up a deservedly great reputation as a financier. Therefore, when he thought of unhappy Ireland, he envisaged her troubles as due to religious and economic oppression, and by ending these he thought that Ireland would become reconciled to her place in the United Kingdom.

Gladstone was a devout member of the Church of England, and the sister branch of that ecclesiastical organization was the Church of Ireland.

Nevertheless, Gladstone knew, as did everybody else, that the great majority of the Irish were Roman Catholics. The Anglican Church in Ireland was a wealthy and old institution, the state church of Ireland, supported by large endowments and the tithes of poor Irish peasants who never entered its doors. Congregations in the Church of Ireland frequently consisted merely of the family of the clergyman, the family of the landlord, and perhaps a land agent, or relatives of the above, whereas Roman Catholic congregations found shelter as they could in miserable little buildings where, however, there were priests and Mass was sung.

In consequence, Gladstone began his ministry with a bill to disestablish the Church of Ireland, to break its connection with the Irish government, to seize upon a large part of its endowment, and to appropriate the money taken for school and charitable institutions. The House of Lords was furious and threatened to throw out the bill; but the House of Lords was also cautious and thought it wise to bargain. Perhaps, as the price of their consent, Gladstone would leave more of the endowment to the church than he had intended. Mr. Gladstone proved not altogether unreasonable. He conceded over three-quarters of a million pounds and the bill became law.

Next came economics. The Irish peasant was a free man, neither slave nor serf. But freedom, as far as he was concerned, was a travesty; in all that had to do with food, clothes, and housing he was in as sad a plight as the Russian muzhik, and frequently in a worse one. The economic history of Ireland in the nineteenth century is a gloomy tale. There were no minerals in the country, and aside from the northeastern tip, where cheap labor and nearness to the coal and iron of Scotland made manufacturing possible, the people had to live on the land. It was vastly overcrowded and owned by landlords absent most of the time from their estates. The peasants, meanwhile, lived on land which had been divided and subdivided so often that the tiny holdings could scarcely produce even enough potatoes to nourish those dependent on them. When the potato crop was fair the peasants managed to live somehow; when it failed they died.

What could be done for these peasants? John Stuart Mill, the famous economist (see p. 249), was forced to admit that the laws of laissez faire did not apply equally to all lands. He proposed that the government should fix rents, collect them, and pay the landlords. John Bright's idea was much more radical; he urged peasant ownership. The government should buy out the landlord, providing as much as three-quarters of the money, the remainder to be extracted from the peasants. Certain Irish members of Parliament had a third proposal, and this one Gladstone adopted.

One part of Ireland and one only was an exception to the general economic blight, namely, Ulster. In that province there was a custom known as "Peasant Right," which meant that compensation had to be paid to evicted peasants, compensation of two kinds, one for improvements (such as new pig-pens) and compensation for disturbance. Gladstone now took this custom and made it legally binding throughout the length and breadth of Ireland. By it the landlord could not do just as he pleased with his land, and the peasants had a share in it.

This was the first of two Irish land acts sponsored by Gladstone; the second was to follow in 1881 (see p. 328). It accomplished some good but not nearly as much as had been hoped, as we shall see later. It was a clear break with the principles of laissez faire, that is, as far as Ireland was concerned, and it caused a number of the old Whig landlords in England and Scotland to secede from the Liberal party.

The Irish problem, as Gladstone conceived it, had three sides or facets. The two more important ones might be the religious and the economic, but there was a third which called for action—the educational. First-class educational facilities were sadly lacking in Ireland. A venerable Anglican institution was to be found at Dublin, Trinity College, with such distinguished graduates as Dean Swift and Edmund Burke. There were also a few very weak Catholic and Presbyterian institutions, but no university which might appeal to all Irishmen, irrespective of creed. Gladstone proposed to inaugurate one, to spend £5,000,000 left in the hands of the British government from the sequestration of the funds of the Church of Ireland, to invite the coöperation of existing institutions in becoming colleges in his Irish university, and thus to put university education in Ireland on a firm and secure economic foundation.

Unfortunately for the prospects of this proposal, it came toward the end of a long series of reforms and Gladstone had already lost a good deal of popular support; unfortunate, also, was a compromise which Gladstone had felt compelled to make: his new university was to have no courses in theology, philosophy, or modern history. The subcolleges, of course, would be at liberty to continue to teach them; but there would be no university instruction, as such.

There was little enthusiasm for this scheme. The Catholics, disliking mixed schools, wanted a university all their own. The Protestants feared that the university, once established, would drift into Catholic control. The radicals in the Liberal party objected to the "gagging clause." Gladstone pleaded in vain; his plan was defeated, and a few months later, January, 1874, the great ministry was at an end.

It had accomplished much, both in foreign affairs and domestic. Gladstone, unlike Palmerston, had never wrapped himself up in the Union Jack. He had agreed to settle the Alabama claims with the United States by arbitration and had, without complaint, paid over to the American government the £3,000,000 assessed against the British government for permitting the escape of Confederate privateers. During the Franco-Prussian War he had walked warily, intent mainly on securing the neutrality of Belgium, in which he succeeded. In domestic matters he had kept expenses to a minimum, had reorganized the army, had taken away from the old aristocracy certain perquisites (both ecclesiastical and political), had established a system of national schools, and for Ireland he had striven hard. Elected largely by working-class votes, he had done nothing directly to aid the economic status of the proletariat, except to aid to a very slight degree in securing protection for young workers in the coal mines.

Here lay a major blind spot in Gladstone's political vision. His motto and that of his party was "Peace, Retrenchment, and Reform." But by reform the Liberals meant the repeal of old statutes that interfered with personal liberty, not reform (except in Ireland) in the sense of new legislation aimed at improving the living conditions of the lower economic strata in British society.

By 1874 Bismarck had adopted a protective tariff, and Germany was henceforth no longer an open market for the British manufacturer. The great boom days of the fifties and sixties were gone, never again to dawn in Britain in all their pristine glory. There were men in the Liberal party who urged Gladstone boldly to face the issue of the social and economic condition of the British poor. Gladstone would not listen. All he proposed was to lower a low income tax still further. In consequence he went down to defeat in the 1874 election.

Disraeli succeeded him as prime minister. How he gave a different slant to British politics will appear in Chapter Eighteen.

Chapter 14

RUSSIA AT MID-CENTURY

BETWEEN THE Russia of Nicholas I and his successor, Alexander II, and the England of Queen Victoria, there were both contrasts and comparisons. In the tight little shires of the latter, life was peaceful and well ordered, and humming with beelike activity, as countless human beings dug deep into seemingly inexhaustible mines or covered hundreds of acres with drab factories, connecting mines and factories and harbors with a web of railways. In the broad and spacious steppes and prairies of Russia, life was peaceful but not well ordered. The Industrial Revolution was not yet in the land of the Czars and a wasteful plantation economy characterized the great, sprawling estates, whereon lazy, shiftless peasants dragged out a somnolent and sheeplike existence, and where their lords and masters, for the most part, browsed out their lives in rough abundance.

Liberalism seemingly was dead in Russia in 1850. Czar Nicholas I, the most consistently ferocious of all the Romanov family, had driven entirely underground such faint evidences of liberalism as had appeared early in the century. A sentence imposed by him upon two unfortunate Jews who tried to escape from Russia tells more about the character of his reign than any description of it. "The convicts," he wrote, "are to run the gauntlet—a thousand men—twelve times."

The death of Nicholas I, in 1855, marked the end of an era for Russia. She had been thrown back upon herself; and while France was enjoying the dubious glories of her Second Empire, while Italy and Germany were struggling successfully along the road to nationality, the enormous mass of Russia was advancing a little way along the road to Western liberalism, then halting and falling into that long era of agonizing hesitation which was to end in an enormous calamity. Externally, her power had shrunk. The military defeats before Sebastopol had not been so very serious; far more important had been the advertisement to Europe that, for offensive purposes, the Muscovite army was grievously imperfect; that it was practically helpless to impose the stern will of its autocrat upon the liberal West. Not for long years were the Czars to loom in the frightened imaginations of men as did Alexander I and his immediate successor—dispensers of thrones and defenders of established order, war-lords only a little less irresistible than Napoleon I.

Internally, Russia had also been terribly shaken. It was known in all the little wooden villages, in all the traders' taverns and peasants' *izbas*, that the enormous sacrifices of men and means in behalf of the "Little Father" had gone for nought—and that not from cowardice nor lack of fervent patriotism, but because of inefficiency, graft, and governmental incompetence, patent to the most stupid. In the cities and in the court, the result was still more immediate. "The calamities with which the reign of Nicholas closed had excited in that narrow circle of Russian society, where thought had any existence, a violent revulsion against the sterile and unchanging system of repression; the grinding servitude of the last thirty years" (Fyffe).

The one thing, in fact, which had made the old "Nicholas regime" tolerable was its corruption. As already suggested, in Russia bribery had tempered the most outrageous laws. The officials had sold liberty from prosecution to one, religious tolerance to another. Innocent and guilty could alike purchase legal immunity. Thanks to this corruption, the Raskolniks (religious dissenters) had been allowed to flourish and revolutionary books to circulate. But public corruption had also been the real cause why a small Franco-British army had been able to take Sebastopol. The situation called for desperate remedies.

The new Czar, Alexander II (1855-81), was thirty-seven years old when his father left him the throne during a disastrous war. He had been given a reasonably good education and had been instilled with a keen sense of the high responsibilities of his office. Personally, he was humane and (considering his birth and surroundings) fairly openminded; in short, he did not love to play the despot. On the other hand, he was not a man of great firmness of will or remarkable intelligence; he did not love the idea of parting with his authority; and, unlike William I of Prussia, he was unable to select a few competent ministers and to support them staunchly in office in the face of opposition. The result was that his reign was an epoch of half-measures; of imperfect reforms; of exasperating moves toward liberalism, which ended in retreat toward autocracy; of a foreign war which gained little for Russia; and, finally, of a desperate struggle, not with liberalism, but with an extreme type of revolution—which ended in a great personal tragedy.

But every monarch seems a popular deliverer upon his coronation day. The accession of Alexander II was marked with a great relaxation of that police repression which had chilled the Russian intellect. In all circles where men could read and think, the air immediately buzzed with grand schemes for reforms, political, social, and economic. The government bureaucracy stood condemned before the nation, and the censorship could not repress very violent criticisms. The Crimean War was branded openly as "the vast bankruptcy of autocracy." Change was everywhere in the air. Thus ran a pamphlet smuggled through to the very writing-desk of the new Czar, "Awake, O Russia, from thy sleep of ignorance and apathy! Too long have we been kept in serfdom by a succession of Tartar khans. Demand of the despot a reckoning for the national calamities!"

The Problem of Serfdom and "Emancipation"

Alexander II promptly did many things which justified the best hopes of the intelligentsia. The censorship of the press was relaxed; universities were opened to all classes; nearly all restrictions upon foreign travel were removed; and the inquisitorial "Third Section" was largely deprived of power and importance. The Czar also won great popularity, as well as just fame as a peace-lover, by halting recruiting for the army for three years, to the vast benefit of the treasury. These things, however, were but palliatives. What the nation was asking, with increasing anxiety, was this: How will the new regime deal with the problem of serfdom? And asking again, in some quarters quite as eagerly: Must not the emancipation of the serfs, perforce, bring with it parliamentary institutions?

By 1856 all the conscience and intelligence of Russia favored the abolition of serfdom. The institution was not defended by those selfish sophistries which were advanced in behalf of slavery in other lands, but the vastness of the task of its abolition was appalling. There were, in all, some 47,000,000 serfs. Of these, about 20,000,000 were on "crown domains"; 4,700,000 were on "appanages" reserved for the imperial family; 1,400,000 were in domestic service; and, last but not least, 21,000,000 were peasants on private estates. The "crown peasants" had the *mir* (communal village) organization and underwent tolerably good treatment; but, in the very best case, not far from five-eighths of the entire population of Russia then subsisted on land which it did not own and was denied the personal rights of freemen.

The serfs in the fields were not actually slaves. They had a prescriptive claim to the land which they and their forebears had occupied. They could only be sold with the land. "We are the lord's, but the land is ours," ran their saying. But, on the other hand, they could never quit their farms without express permission. They were liable, first, for the obligation to work certain periods on the lord's domain land (a service called the *barshchina*) and, in addition, to a direct money payment (*obrok*) which varied between five dollars and ten dollars per annum.

The law, indeed, protected the serf against certain gross outrages. He could not be punished by his master to the point of maiming, nor be forced to work more than three days per week, nor be compelled to marry a woman not of his choice. The lord, however, was, in any case, the civil judge on his estate, and only rarely could the serf invoke outside protection against him. The lord had to consent to the serf's marriage; and he had the terrible (and often cruelly exercised) power of *selecting the recruits* required for the army. On the best estates, under a good lord, the lot of the serfs was by no means very miserable; but under the poorer sort of master, only the casuist could prove that their position was a great deal better than brutal slavery.

This twilight zone between slavery and freedom in which the serfs of Russia lived is most beautifully and humorously described in Peter Kropotkin's *Memoirs of a Revolutionist.* As a boy he recalls how his Father proudly wore a medal conferred on him because one of the family serfs performed an act of bravery during the Crimean War. When teased by another nobleman for the few children born on his estates the older Kropotkin dashed out of the manor house, rang the great bell, summoned all serfs. He upbraided them for their low birth-rate, picked out all boys eighteen years old, all girls of sixteen. "Five weddings," he announced, "must take place in ten days, the next Sunday but one." John here must marry Anna, Paula will have to marry Parashla, and so on.

"A general cry of despair went up from the village. Women, young and old," Kropotkin writes, "wept in every house. Anna had hoped to marry Gregory; Paul's parents had already had a talk with the Fedotoffs about their girl who would soon be of age." All this made no difference. Orders were orders. If disobeyed, into the army the young men could be sent for eighteen years.

Serfdom was thus grievous for the serfs; but, as often enough under an evil social and economic system, it was also proving grievous for the masters. There were some 103,400 serf-owners. Of these only 1,400 owned over 1,000 "souls" (taxpaying heads of families) apiece, and 80,000 owned 100 "souls" each, or less. Two-thirds of the estates on which the serfs were located were mortgaged up to their full value. The Russian nobility, idle, dissolute, free spending, and economically of amazing inefficiency, was thus running itself straight on the rocks. On the other hand, the peasants were wildly excited by hopes that along with freedom would come the grant of wide farms, gratis, and a kind of agrarian utopia. The result, needless to say, brought heavy disappointment alike to the former "haves" and the "have-nots."

On March 3, 1861 (just as the war destined to end American slavery was about to begin) the Autocrat of All the Russians published his ukase abolishing serfdom. Already the serfs held to domestic service had been declared free; for them there had been no land problem. Now a painful and honest, if not wholly successful, attempt was made by Miliutin and his associates to deal with the vast agrarian question. The peasants, of course, became the free subjects of the Czar. The ex-serf was made the owner, personally, of his cabin and a small garden plot around; but the great reaches of arable land were divided. A considerable part was turned back to the complete and direct possession of the former serf-owner; the rest was handed over, not to the peasants individually, but to the local village community, the oft-discussed mir. This community was expected to proceed, according to rustic usage, and under an ancient form of self-government, to distribute the farm lands to each peasant family. The tiller of the soil thus had no ownership of his arable land; he had only a usufruct, with no right of sale or mortgage. Every three to twelve years, according to local custom, there was to be a redistribution. If the number of heads of families had increased in the interval, the land lots allowed to each family had perforce to be diminished. In the original scheme, the average amount of land per household was supposed to vary according to the soil, climate, and density of population in the region. Thus, in northern Russia, this average was nineteen and a quarter acres; in the excellent "Black Earth" region of the south center, it was only five and a half; in the unforested southern steppes it ran up to twenty-seven and a half.

The peasant, therefore, did not win proprietorship. He merely won equal membership in a mir, which was the common proprietor. And the mir did not get its lands for nothing; a round sum went as indemnity to the ex-landlords. Since the peasants, of course, had no free capital, the greater part of the immediate cost was assumed by the state. National bonds to the amount of $500,000,000 were floated, money raised to pay the boyars; but the peasants now owed to the tax-collector not merely the old taxes (always paid grudgingly enough), but for a period of forty-nine years, in place of the former obrok, they were held annually, for six per cent of the sum advanced for each holding.[1] This freeing of the serfs, therefore, was in no wise an agrarian revolution. The government had simply declared the peasants free, personally, and advanced them the money for redeeming their farms.

The long anticipated emancipation was pursued by anathemas alike from boyar and peasant. Vast hopes had been formed by the serfs. Now, indeed, they had personal freedom; but what, to most of them, was freedom without the land on which had toiled their fathers' fathers? It was a bitter disappointment to be told that much of their former land had been added to the domain lands of their ex-masters; and that for nearly half a century they must pay a heavy indemnity to the tax-gatherer for the rest. The upshot was that after getting freedom, the released serfs became utterly discouraged when faced with the difficulty of paying for their farms, and then flocked into the towns, where they later became exploited as working-men, swelling an ignorant and poverty-stricken proletariat. For some time, indeed, after Emancipation, many peasants used

[1] If the peasants wished to content themselves with only about one-quarter of their former farm lands, they could receive that amount gratis. All the rest, they had to redeem on the terms mentioned.

their new freedom merely in order to wander off into the country, constituting veritable armies of tramps.

As for the angry landowners, they now found their remaining estates utterly demoralized. Efficient hired labor was hard to get. The government compensation money was often enough foolishly invested or thoughtlessly squandered. Soon there were more mortgages and bankruptcies among the nobility than ever. The victims were then ready to attribute all the troubles wrought by their own prodigality and inefficiency to the Czar's flirting with liberalism. The storm, in fact, was so great that Alexander felt compelled to relegate Miliutin to "honorable obscurity" as a senator, and most of his colleagues in the great work were neglected or actually disgraced.

But the real grudge was remembered by the peasants. In every mir it was an article of faith that *all* the land belonged to those who worked it. Eyes, ever more covetous, were cast upon the reserved domain-land, especially as, with the increase of population, the land-plots assigned each member of the village community perforce grew smaller and smaller. The mirs also developed their own special evils in administration and government. This passionate desire of the Russian peasants for more land, and that land all their own, was to become a decisive factor in the year 1917 when the czardom stood at judgment bar to answer for all its sins. With every deduction, nevertheless, the emancipation of 1861 was a noble action, reflecting high credit upon Alexander II, on Miliutin, and on their host of technical coadjutors. If it failed as a final achievement, it was largely because the ills of Russia were not to be cured by declaring many millions of ignorant peasants technically "free," while at the same time making only a pretence at peasant proprietorship, and giving them a chance to redeem their farms.

If emancipation had involved merely turning the peasants loose from the soil and calling them "free citizens," the process could have been accomplished practically by unanimous consent. The ruinous complications came from the land question. To strip the peasants of their farms would create a landless, ignorant, and soon a hungry and desperate proletariat. To give them all their existing holdings, without compensation, in some form, to their ex-masters, would be the destruction of the entire *boyar* class in Russia—the one class in the empire well able to make itself heard even by the Autocrat. The provincial assemblies of nobles, when pressed upon the subject, therefore, made endless difficulties; whatever their humane theories, they were extremely anxious to keep "their peasants."

But Alexander II was genuinely determined to win the just glory of a "Czar Liberator." He was urged by not a few advisers to convoke some kind of assembly, elected by all classes of the nation, to help put through the abolition; but he was fearful that a new parliament, suddenly convened, would prove unwieldy, inexperienced, and contentious, as well as likely to drift into attacks upon his own prerogative. In addition, he believed (perhaps rightly) that the nobles would accept the loss of their serfs only at the hands of the Autocrat—himself. But on emancipation his heart was fixed. To his intimates he asserted, "Serfdom was instituted by absolute power. Only absolute power can destroy it, and to do so is my will."

Other Reforms: The Zemstvos and the New Judicial System

The Czar now threw a sop to the rising demand for a national parliament; there could be local assemblies. Two types of these *zemstvos* were created—for the district and for the province. The former was made up of deputies elected by the three classes: the nobles, the city-dwellers, and the peasants; the zemstvos of the provinces were delegates chosen by the district assemblies. These councils had fairly wide powers to deal with matters of strictly local interest—roads, bridges, poor relief, public sanitation, public buildings, and the like. To a limited extent, they had the right to impose taxes, but their authority was greatly curtailed by the permission granted the provincial governors to scrutinize their measures at every turn and, frequently enough, actually to suspend their decisions as "contrary to the good of the State." Nevertheless, for the moment, the creation of the zemstvos was hailed as a great step forward. Would not an imperial parliament follow speedily and inevitably?

Of more value, probably, to the Russian people was the sweeping *reform of the judiciary*. The old Russian legal system, indescribably technical and procrastinating, had been a perversion of common justice, even when it had not been the deliberate engine of tyranny. The bureaucrats had here nothing essential to defend; and its abolition was fairly easy. In its place, by a sweeping decree of November, 1864, was created a judicial system based avowedly on Western models and founded considerably on the French system. Henceforth, Russia had justices of the peace (somewhat after the English fashion), district courts, supreme courts, and highest of all, the Senate, the tribunal of final appeal. There were regularly qualified lawyers and public prosecutors; there were jury trials in criminal cases,[2] and, last but not least, there was a secure tenure of office for

---

[2] The Russian juries, drawn largely from peasants, speedily developed a tendency to acquit defendants under almost all circumstances. It was too often assumed that *any* alleged criminal was merely the victim of that police tyranny from which the jurymen themselves had probably suffered. Sometimes juries are said to have bawled out to a prisoner, "Will you promise not to do it again, if we let you go?" and then to have cheerfully acquitted a bloody scoundrel, merely on his nodded pledge of reformation. After political crimes multiplied, it was not surprising that acquittals were so common that the government practically suspended jury trial in all matters involving public interest.

judges.[3] On paper, judicial proceedings in Russia were, henceforth, relatively humane, speedy, and scientific; and the courts at once became a
genuine check upon the petty tyrannies of local officials. For this blessed
change, his subjects could rightly thank Alexander II.

The year 1864, however, practically saw the end of this progression of
reform. Alexander II was becoming frightened at the possibilities lurking
in further concessions. He had been especially shaken by events in
Poland in 1863.

Revolt of the Poles (1863)

Unhappy Poland had remained in the depths of despair from 1830 to
1856, when a new agitation began to give the people hope. Under the
name of an "Agricultural Society," groups of patriots began scheming and
working for a national resurrection. Alexander gave these Poles little encouragement. "Let us have no more dreams," he told the deputies of the
nobles of Warsaw. "Embrace the union with Russia and abandon all
thought of independence, now and ever more impossible." For a short
time, however, the Russian authorities followed a conciliatory policy, and
the nationalists in Poland entertained hopes that they might win a measure
of autonomy if not independence. Then, by one of those sudden shifts of
tactics common in inefficient despotisms, the czarist administrators shifted
to brutal oppression. There were wholesale arrests; murderous fusillades
were aimed at the unarmed populace of Warsaw; and finally the boys of
Poland were conscripted for the army. In the first six months of 1862 it
was estimated that one-tenth of the inhabitants of Warsaw were imprisoned, and the liberty of no educated young man of Polish blood was
safe. The Polish nobles, whose influence the Czar had determined to
break, fled to the forests. There, in 1863, they raised the banner of revolt
to fight for Poland once again.

In 1830 the Poles had had an organized government and an army; now
they had only a secret committee and irregular bands. They enjoyed very
little chance of success, consequently, unless foreign powers came to their
aid. In England, France, and Austria they had plenty of wordy unofficial
sympathy, and Napoleon III, at least, was willing to talk boldly of intervention in behalf of outraged nationalism; but he soon found that London
and Vienna were unwilling to back him up with anything more formidable
than diplomatic notes. The result was only humiliation for French prestige
and grievous disappointment for the Poles. "Napoleon's diplomacy had
sounded a charge, then his drums beat a retreat after a blank volley or
two." Foreign mutterings, therefore, made Alexander devise evil in his
heart for France, and also for Austria, while he found in Prussia under

---

[3] The government could still coerce judges by changing their place of jurisdiction.
A judge obnoxious to the ruling powers could be taught his blunders by being
ordered to hold assizes in the provinces of the Arctic North or eastern Siberia.

Bismarck a friend and near ally. The Prussian frontier was tightly closed to the Polish insurgents, and all the resources of the Hohenzollern police were utilized to head off the least assistance being smuggled to the unhappy insurgents.

In this struggle of raids, skirmishes, and forays there were no real battles. The secret committee was never able to set up a formal government. Presently its members were hunted down, and the patriot bands were destroyed one by one. Again in Poland there reigned the peace of the Muscovite sword.

This time the repression was much more complete and drastic than in 1830-32. Already in Russia was developing the doctrine of *Pan-Slavdom* —that all Slavic races required a common and distinct civilization centering around Great Russia. Alexander II gave august patronage to the movement. He allowed public addresses to be made to him, representing the Poles as worthy of condign punishment, as being traitors to Slavdom, thanks to their Western civilization and Western (Catholic) religion. The native Polish clergy were harried and placed under the control of an Ecclesiastical College at St. Petersburg, and no stone was left unturned to break their influence over their people. Most of the Catholic convents were suppressed. Catholic churches could not be built or even repaired; and all Catholic religious instruction had to be in Russian. In February, 1864, Russian was declared the only official language in all Poland; and certain impossible edicts even attempted to forbid the use of the Polish language and the Latin alphabet in the affairs of private life. In retail stores tradesmen actually were forbidden to use their native tongue in answering customers.

The real fury of the conquerors was turned, however, upon the Polish nobles who had been the backbone of the revolts both of 1830 and 1863. If the native peasantry could be won for the Czardom, would not the Russianizing process be complete? As a result, the Polish nobles lost *their* peasants and peasant-tilled lands, under conditions far more ruinous than befell their boyar contemporaries in Russia. All dues owed to them by the peasants were declared abolished, and the peasants became free *proprietors* of their entire holdings, subject to nothing but a reasonable government tax. Only a very insufficient compensation was given the nobles for this enormous loss of property. By this one stroke (1864) the Polish nobles lost half their incomes, and the Polish peasants were (presumably) lifted to the status of grateful landowners under a benevolent Autocrat.

For the moment, naturally, the illiterate toilers in the fields were happy in their new possessions and freedom; but this performance, like so many others of calculating tyranny, presently recoiled upon its authors. The Polish peasants now had a stake in their country. They were consciously part of it, as they never had been before; the next time the national consciousness awoke, they would feel a common thrill with their old oppressors, the nobles. On the other hand, Muscovite despotism, by speedily striking at all classes of Poles alike, and especially by outraging the Catholic Church (to which the peasants were almost fanatically devoted), made this nation of small landowners profoundly conscious of an enormous mass of grievances. In 1918 peasant and noble were to smite for Polish freedom together.

The suppression of the Polish revolt marked, for Alexander II, practically the end of his era of pale liberalism, and foreshadowed a gradual return to absolutism. Great interests, injured by the changes, warned the Czar that further concessions to "Westernism" would ruin the state. In 1867 a large Slavophil Congress under imperial patronage met at Moscow. The Slavs ruled by Austria, indeed, showed no signs of wishing to exchange a Hapsburg for a Romanoff yoke, but great hopes were held out for the extension of a common Slavdom among the Balkan peoples under Turkey. Russia began again to turn her eyes toward the Near East. At the same time, little groups of extreme liberals, disgusted at the denial of sweeping reforms, began dreaming more dreams of a violent revolution.

As the eighteen-seventies opened, Russia was facing new projects for an advance toward Constantinople, and also, nearer home, that lurid movement called "nihilism."

Chapter 15

ECONOMIC THOUGHT IN
THE NINETEENTH CENTURY

CHANGES IN government, nationalistic uprisings, the march of armies, and the challenge of the Industrial Revolution to the old social order have hitherto been the main topics covered in this book. Before continuing to study them country by country and analysing the international complexities and tensions which more immediately antedated the First World War, it would be well, perhaps, to stop somewhere along the line, to pry somewhat beneath the surface, and to try to discover just what was in people's minds concerning economics, science, and religion.

First of all, then, let us examine the economic ideas popular in the nineteenth century and in the first decade of the century to follow.

These ideas fall generally into either one or two channels, one flowing primarily from the theories of persons known as "classical economists," and the other derived from schools of thought roughly known as socialistic.

Adam Smith (1723-90)

The classical economists (so-called because they first were the ones to formulate certain general laws seemingly of universal application to man's economic life) primarily conceived of trade and commerce, industry and manufacture as flourishing best when let alone. Their great founder, Adam Smith, was not the first to conceive this idea—laissez faire—but he was the first to elaborate it extensively and to incorporate it in a book which, for his day and generation, was almost an exhaustive treatment of the subject of economics. Smith, like Adolf Hitler, was the son of a petty customs official. Unusually bright, he won a fellowship at Oxford. Graduated from that university, he became professor of logic at Glasgow, then tutor of the Duke of Buccleuch, with whom he traveled extensively in France. Returning, he worked ten years on his *Wealth of Nations* (1776), a book comparable in importance to Karl Marx's *Das Kapital*.

The *Wealth of Nations* provides a lucid, cogent, fair-minded and tolerant defense of economic liberty. It is a plea for individualism and laissez faire; but it is not the Bible of laissez faire in the sense that the writings of Malthus and Ricardo may be thus regarded. Adam Smith is an enthusiastic advocate of the liberty of the individual, but he is aware that limitations should be put upon it for the common good. The general tenor of his book unquestionably favors free trade, but the author realizes that there are sound arguments in certain instances for tariffs. He opposes combinations in restraint of trade, but he recognizes that the evils which they foster may be the result of capitalistic practices, as well as the result of trade union activity.

The *Wealth of Nations,* nevertheless, is a landmark in economic thought. It marks the final demise of the old mercantilist notion that the well-being of a country depended on the actual amount of bullion (gold and silver) within its borders. The victory over mercantilism had already been partly won by the French physiocrats of the late eighteenth century, and the *Wealth of Nations* may be considered as completing their work. As its author explained, "To attempt to increase the wealth of any country, either by introducing or retaining in it an unnecessary quantity of gold and silver is about as absurd as it would be to attempt to increase the good cheer of private families by obliging them to keep an unnecessary number of kitchen utensils."

But more than that: the *Wealth of Nations* marks the commencement of a new era of economic thought, summed up at its apogee by the teachings of Malthus and Ricardo, afterward explained. In accordance with it, individual initiative and prudence, probity, and self-restraint not only come first as economic virtues but also transcend other values. "The natural effort of every individual," Smith said, "to better his own condition, when suffered to exert itself with freedom and security, is so powerful a principle, that it is *alone,* and *without any assistance,* not only capable of carrying on the society to wealth and prosperity, but of surmounting a hundred impertinent obstructions with which the folly of human laws too often encumbers its operations." (The italics are the author's and have been placed in this quotation for emphasis.)

Thomas Robert Malthus (*1766-1834*)

When we come to Malthus we are much closer to the real heart of classical economics. Malthus' father was an intimate friend of Jean-Jacques Rousseau and a believer in human perfectibility. The son argued freely with his parent on that possibility and, partly as a result of opposing him, hit upon an idea which probably more than any other caused political economy (economics) to be termed "the dismal science."

The young Malthus, a brilliant student, became a clergyman in the Established Church. When he was thirty-two he published *An Essay on the Principle of Population, as It Affects the Future Improvement of*

Society (1798), which, with the possible exception of the *Communist Manifesto* of Karl Marx (see p. 255) and Darwin's *Origin of Species* (see p. 276), was the most influential book of the nineteenth century. The first edition was brief, some 50,000 words. The Essay, however, went through edition after edition, and by the time it reached the fifth it had swollen to 250,000 words. It gave Malthus a tremendous reputation and brought to him the first professorship of political economy ever established in England, namely at the East India Company's College at Haileybury, where Malthus lived a quiet and scholarly life for the rest of his days.

As has been well stated by our own contemporary economist, Keynes, "the importance of the essays consisted not in the novelty of his facts but in the smashing emphasis he placed on a simple generalization arising out of them," [1] which was that population tended to outstrip food supply.

If people multiplied more rapidly than their food, it followed that misery, poverty, starvation, and death were always around the corner, could not be dodged or evaded, and were a permanent cross to be borne by poor Christians. In the past, Malthus argued, wars, pestilence, plagues, famine had kept down human numbers. There was no other way by which they could be kept down except by voluntary continence. In his day and generation population was increasing, and the more it increased, the more poverty there would be unless food increased at an equal ratio. This he considered impossible.

The essay on population, it must be remembered, was written in the midst of the Revolutionary wars, when there was a genuine dearth of food in England. Its argument, furthermore, in later editions was supported by a wealth of statistical data. There could be no question but that numbers were increasing rapidly in the early nineteenth century. There really was no increase in the birth rate, and the augmentation of numbers was the result of better sanitation coming about from better water supply, cheap cotton clothes easily washed, to say nothing of the general use of antitoxin for smallpox. But Malthus and his friends did not realize this; they thought the birth rate had jumped. Consequently, when Malthus stated with an air of authority that babies increased at a geometrical ratio and their food only at an arithmetical one, there was just cause for alarm.

This depressing thesis fitted in nicely with the psychology of England's upper classes. They had money and the poor had none; and naturally they were pleased with a doctrine which defended the status quo and made it appear a really wicked thing to give money to the poor. If they gave the money the poor would promptly have more babies, and so there would ultimately be more misery than before. The poor were to blame for their own condition and there was nothing that could be done about it except

[1] J. M. Keynes, *Essay in Bibliography*, p. 119.

to preach continence. The rich were not to blame; they had relatively few children. Therefore they liked the book exceedingly and praised the author to the skies. His message did much to quiet many uneasy consciences.

Now, while it is true that Malthus at the beginning of the nineteenth century had no way of foretelling the incredible way in which the world's food supply was to be augmented by proper breeding methods, by scientific culture of wheat and other grains, and by the cultivation of the Canadian and American prairies, he could even then have thought of counterarguments to his thesis. Had he been as broadminded as Adam Smith, he doubtless would have done so. Malthus was a contemporary observer of the results of the English land inclosures brought about largely because of new breeding methods for both sheep and cattle. He must have heard of Jethro Tull and "Turnip" Townshend and their experiments with crop fertility. He certainly was not ignorant of the United States, with its thin population, nor of the vast hinterland of untouched acres stretching to the Mississippi Valley and beyond. Had he wanted to do so, before he died he might have read another book on population by one Michael Sadler, who logically questioned all his premises.

But Malthus did not choose to have them questioned, nor did his backers and supporters, the well-to-do of England. On that account history has heard scarcely anything of Michael Sadler, a defeated Tory who contested Leeds against Macaulay in 1832. Yet Sadler's ideas were as intelligent as those of Malthus. The former pointed out that, while famine frequently was met with in overcrowded countries like China, it also was to be encountered in underpopulated regions like North America, among the scattered Indian tribes, and in Germany when the Roman Empire was at its height. He also used statistics to show that the impoverished fishermen of North Scotland were famous for their large families, whereas the aristocracy had comparatively few children, deducing from that fact that one way to reduce a redundant population was to raise the standard of living. He also hinted at what later was scientifically demonstrated, that sheep, potatoes, beet-sugar, and other foods are far more apt to increase at a geometrical ratio than children.

Neither in Malthus' day nor our own was it possible to lay down natural laws governing human fecundity. His essay unquestionably held good both then and now, as far as certain stretches in eastern Asia were concerned, and the mere fact that he called the attention of the thoughtful to a neglected problem of importance was to his credit. Yet the historian should take note that Sadler's book was no sooner written than forgotten, whereas Malthus went through edition after edition. Could the reason be that what the former had to say was displeasing to the powerful, to those with money and education who bought books, whereas the message of the latter sounded very pleasant to that class in society?

"London Slums" by Doré

David Ricardo (1772-1823)

Closely associated with Malthus in his ideas, and equally a pillar of capitalistic thought, was Ricardo. Malthus had the honor of being the first English professor of political economy, but Ricardo had that of writing the first really definitive textbook on economics. His *Principles of Political Economy and Taxation* deserves to be considered as such, rather than the *Wealth of Nations*. Adam Smith's masterpiece, it must be remembered, in many ways was speculative and philosophical, rather than dogmatic. Ricardo's book, on the other hand, bound up economic theories into a definite system and was much more specific.

Ricardo, son of a Jewish stockbroker in London, made an independent fortune of £2,000,000 for himself by the age of forty-four. Buying an estate, he retired from business to devote his life to public affairs. He secured an Irish seat in the House of Commons in 1819 by the free use of his fortune and was unusually influential in that body, owing to his personality, and his wide knowledge.

The Principles of Political Economy, Ricardo's celebrated book, covered the whole field of economic theory. In some respects it has scarcely been superseded to this day, and in two—namely, the theory of economic rent and that of the iron law of wages—it justly deserves to be considered a classic.

So clear and seemingly irrefutable was Ricardo's theory of rent that it proved later in the century, in the British political crisis of 1846, a most useful weapon in the armory of the Anti-Corn-Law League. His argument ran as follows: "On the first settlement of a country, in which there is an abundance of rich and fertile land, a very small proportion of which is required to be cultivated—there will be no rent; for no one would pay for the use of land, when there is an abundant quantity not yet appropriated, and therefore at the disposal of whosoever might choose to cultivate it." But when population increases, land less fertile is cultivated, and as soon as this is done rent appears, and the amount of that rent will depend on the difference in the quality of the better and the poorer land. In other words, if the more valuable land with the same amount of capital and labor expended on it produces one hundred bushels of commodity X, and the poorer land ninety bushels, the rent of the former will be ten bushels, on the latter—the marginal land—nothing. Population, however, keeps on increasing and more and more marginal land is cultivated. Some land now produces one hundred bushels, some ninety bushels, and some only eighty bushels. What happens then is that the rent on the best-quality land goes higher, for it is always to be estimated at the difference between the yield of the highest and the lowest quality cultivated. Since land (1) produces one hundred bushels, land (2) ninety, and land (3) eighty bushels, the rent of land (1) doubles and becomes twenty bushels. And so on, in an indefinite series, as population rises and more and more marginal land is cultivated. The Corn Laws, according to Ricardo, made for the cultivation of still more marginal land, let us call it land (4), where it was barely possible to sustain life and only seventy bushels were produced. Repeal the Corn Laws and land (4) goes out of cultivation with two admirable results: (*a*) the labor and capital spent on land (4) flow to the cities and increase manufacturing industries; (*b*) the rents on all other agricultural lands drop, because land (3) is now marginal land, rent always remaining the difference between the product of the better land and the marginal.

The above was a capitalistic argument in favor of free trade. Another argument, however, and one more important, had to do with wages. There is a *natural* price for labor and also a *market* price. The natural price is that "which is necessary to enable the laborers, one with another, to subsist and to perpetuate their race without either increase or diminution." On the other hand there is the market price, the wages actually paid, which is the result of the law of supply and demand. "Labor," Ricardo said, "is dear when it is scarce and cheap when it is plentiful. However much the market price may deviate from its natural price, it has, like commodities, a tendency to conform to it."

Sometimes the market price, he argues, exceeds the natural price. When this happens the laborer is well off; but it could only happen when the available stock of capital was large and the supply of labor limited. Sometimes the market price goes lower than the natural price, as would occur if workingmen reproduced their numbers too rapidly, more rapidly than the increase in capital seeking investment. When this takes place the laborer's lot is very miserable.

As a result of this reasoning there developed a belief in the iron law of wages, that inevitably they tended to sink to the lowest possible level on which life might be sustained. Their tendency to drop, Ricardo maintained, could only be offset by greater supplies of free capital and by a low birth rate. He was willing to admit that "the market rate may, in an improved society, for an indefinite period, be constantly above it (the natural rate); for no sooner may the impulse which increased capital gives to a new demand for labor be obeyed, than another increase in capital may produce the same effect; and thus, if the increase in capital be gradual and constant, the demand for labor may give a continual stimulus to an increase of people." Such would be the case in new settlements where "it is probable that capital has a tendency to increase faster than mankind." But this is not true of the older and more settled regions, and in them the tendency always will be for wages to drop to the subsistence level. Even in newly developed countries there will always be a pull in the same general direction. This was a natural law and nothing could be done to stop it. "Like all other contracts, wages should be left to the fair and free competition of the market, and should never be controlled by the interference of the legislature."

Such were the teachings of Ricardo concerning wages. It is only fair to him, however, to include two apparently contradictory statements which generally have been excluded from any analysis of his wage theory. Having, early in his discussion, defined the natural price of labor as that "which is necessary to enable the laborers, one with another, to subsist," he states farther on that "it (the natural price) varies at different times in the same country, and very materially differs in different countries. It essentially depends on the habits and customs of the people. An English laborer would consider his wages under the natural rate, and too scanty to support a family, if they enabled him to purchase no other food than potatoes—." And again, "from manufactured commodities always falling and raw materials always rising, with the progress of society, such a disproportion in their relative values is at length created that in rich countries a laborer, by the sacrifice of a very small quantity only of his food, is able to provide liberally for his other wants."

Now if the natural price essentially depends on the habits and customs of the people, how can it be argued that it is merely the subsistence level? Also, if manufactured goods tend always to become cheaper and food dearer, the laborer should be in a steadily improved condition since, according to Ricardo, it is food (means of subsistence) that primarily determines his wages. If we include these qualifying statements of Ricardo, we make his general economic position much less sharp and pointed and also at the same time more humanitarian and generous.

We have thus quoted rather liberally from Ricardo because from him stem in large measure two divergent schools of economic thought. Karl Marx and the "scientific" or "materialistic" socialists were later, as we shall note in this chapter, to draw heavily on Ricardo, and so also were the capitalistic writers who were predominant throughout the first two-thirds of the century. This latter school was profoundly impressed by the pessimism latent in the idea that wages always tended to fall, unless there was more capital and fewer children. As expressed in the words of their most popular and most enthusiastic propagandist, Harriet Martineau:

The condition of laborers may be best improved:
1. By inventions and discoveries which create capital; and by husbanding instead of wasting capital, for instance by making savings instead of starting strikes.
2. By adjusting the proportion of population to capital.[2]

[2] C. R. Fay, *Great Britain from Adam Smith to the Present Day*, p. 369.

HERBERT SPENCER (1820-1903)

The stream of capitalistic thought, meanwhile, began to diverge in two directions. One, represented best by the philosopher, Herbert Spencer, continued in the straight and narrow path marked out by Malthus and Ricardo, the other, represented by Sismondi and List on the continent, and by John Stuart Mill in England, somewhat less rigid but no less logical, veered off somewhat in a less individualistic direction.

Herbert Spencer (1820-1903)

Spencer was a most extraordinary individual, whose inquiring mind never seemed to be at rest. For art, literature, religion (in any conventional sense), he cared not one whit; but to find some explanation of and solution for the complexities and social maladjustments of this world, he was most determined. By writing just one book, he leaped into fame. This was *Social Statics* (1850), which was so well thought of in America that its author was able to raise thousands of dollars for a series of books which were not yet written. From 1850 to 1896 out came the books, a synthetic philosophy of life, written by a nerve-wracked man with poor eyesight, with little cultivated background, intent on one main thesis. It calls for careful analysis, in that it concerns both this chapter and the one that follows; for Herbert Spencer's *Social Statics* may rightly be regarded as the intellectual culmination of those ideas of individualism and laissez faire made popular by Jeremy Bentham earlier and by the classical economists, Malthus and Ricardo.

"Give us a guide, cry men to the philosopher." With this sentence, the *Social Statics* commences. Spencer is not content with Bentham's "greatest good to the greatest number," which he says is simply "an enunciation of the problem to be solved." There must be some more specific key to social betterment. "Either society has laws or it has not. If it has not there can be no order, no certainty, no system in its phenomena. If it has, these are like other laws in the universe, sure, inflexible, ever active, and having no exception."

Spencer then seeks for a first principle. He finds it in individual liberty which knows just one exception: It must not infringe on the liberty of another.

First among those rights which a man must possess to have genuine liberty is private property. Personal acquisitiveness is inborn in the human animal, just as the desire for food: it is an instinct. "Whence it follows that a system affording opportunity for its exercise must be retained; which means that the system of private property must be retained. . . ."

The state, according to Spencer, exists for the sole purpose of guaranteeing individual rights. The limits of state action should be sharply defined. The state should not, for instance, spend money on general education. To do so would interfere with individual freedom and tax some, not for their own good but for the good of others, and limit the freedom of the man taxed to develop himself as he saw fit. More specifically, the state has no business to embark on sanitary supervision. "He who contaminates the atmosphere breathed by his neighbor is infringing on his neighbor's rights." The state may stop nuisances of that description but it must not extend its authority further.

For instance, the *Journal of Public Health* proposed that "every house on becoming vacant be examined by a competent person as to its being in a condition adapted for the safe indwelling of the future tenants. . . ." Spencer immediately objected. To do that involved inspectors paid for by the state, an increase in taxation, a prying into other people's affairs. Let us note, he says, how nature takes care of health. "Consumptive patients with lungs incompetent to perform the duties of lungs, people with assimilative organs that will not take up enough nutriment, people with defective hearts ... people with any constitutional flaw preventing the due fulfilment of the conditions of life, are continuously dying out, and leaving behind them those fit for the climate, food and habits to which they are born." It would be unwise to interfere with this elimination of the unfit.

What would be the result, Spencer asks, of the state insisting on ventilation and a good water supply? The first would be to lower profits. Then, "the interest on capital invested in houses no longer being so high capital would seek other investments. The building of houses would cease to keep pace with the growth of population. Hence would arise a gradual increase in the number of occupants to each house and this change in the ratio of houses to people would continue until the demand for houses had raised the profits of the landlords to what they were, and until by overcrowding new sanitary evils had been produced to parallel old ones."

Even more caustic was Spencer in dealing with the problem of poverty. He opposed all state action which involved spending money on poor relief. His argument was put so positively and was so generally accepted by nineteenth-century liberals that we quote from it *in extenso.*

Pervading all nature we may see at work a stern discipline, which is a little cruel that it may be very kind. That state of universal warfare maintained throughout the lower creation, to the great perplexity of many worthy people, is at bottom the most merciful provision which the circumstances admit of. It is much better that the ruminant animal, when deprived by age of the vigour which made its existence a pleasure, should be killed by some beast of prey, than that it should linger out a life made painful by infirmities, and eventually die of starvation. By the destruction of all such, not only is existence ended before it becomes burdensome, but room is made for a younger generation capable of the fullest enjoyment; and, moreover, out of the very act of substitution happiness is derived for a tribe of predatory creatures. Note further, that their carnivorous enemies not only remove from herbivorous herds individuals past their prime, but also weed out the sickly, the malformed, and the least fleet or powerful. By the aid of which purifying process, as well as by the fighting, so universal in the pairing season, all vitiation of the race through the multiplication of its inferior samples is prevented; and the maintenance of a constitution completely adapted to surrounding conditions, and therefore most productive of happiness, is ensured.

The development of the higher creation is a progress towards a form of being capable of a happiness undiminished by these drawbacks. It is in the human race that the consummation is to be accomplished. Civilization is the last stage of its accomplishment. And the ideal man is the man in whom all the conditions of that accomplishment are fulfilled. Meanwhile the well-being of existing humanity, and the unfolding of it into this ultimate perfection, are both secured

by that same beneficent, though severe discipline, to which the animate creation at large is subject: a discipline which is pitiless in the working out of good:
a felicity-pursuing law which never swerves for the avoidance of partial and
temporary suffering. The poverty of the incapable, the distresses that come
upon the imprudent, the starvation of the idle, and those shoulderings aside of
the weak by the strong, which leave so many "in shallows and in miseries," are
the decrees of a large, far-seeing benevolence. It seems hard that an unskilful-
ness which with all his efforts he cannot overcome, should entail hunger upon
the artizan. It seems hard that a labourer incapacitated by sickness from competing with his stronger fellows, should have to bear the resulting privations.
It seems hard that widows and orphans should be left to struggle for life or
death. Nevertheless, when regarded not separately, but in connection with the
interests of universal humanity, these harsh fatalities are seen to be full of the
highest beneficence—the same beneficence which brings to early graves the
children of diseased parents, and singles out the low-spirited, the intemperate,
and the debilitated as the victims of an epidemic.[3]

The above might seem to indicate that Herbert Spencer was a cruel
worshiper of the God of Things as They Are, and a mad devotee of the
money power. The reverse was the case. Spencer was a very fierce
democrat, whose denunciation of the idle and worthless rich fills several
hot pages of the *Social Statics*. He thought himself a radical, advocated
universal suffrage for all, including women, and was a hearty advocate
of unlimited free speech. He believed in charity, also, when it was
spontaneous and helped men to help themselves. In his personal life
he was both austere and simple, shunning decorations and honors.
Money meant nothing to him, except in so far as it enabled him to hire
more secretaries to gather data for his huge synthetic analysis of human
society. He was perhaps "mad" in the higher and more ancient sense
of that word, applicable to all great philosophers such as Rousseau,
Marx, and Spencer, who create water-tight philosophies of life. Before
evaluating him, it might be well to admit that he simply carried out to
their logical end certain implications latent in Bentham, Malthus, and
Ricardo. What the classical economists cautiously and coldly hinted, he
passionately dogmatized and confirmed. Fortunately for all concerned,
the statesmen of his day never tried to carry out his principles; unfortunately, perhaps, they were too much influenced by them.

In Spencer we find the philosophical culmination of the classical
school of economics, in its more rigorous application. There were, however, a number of distinguished economists devoted to private property,
who swung off in a different direction. Prominent among them were
Sismondi, a Swiss; List, a German; and John Stuart Mill, an Englishman.

[3] H. Spencer, *Social Statics* (London, 1868), pp. 353-54.

Sismondi (1773-1842)

John Charles Leonard Sismonde de Sismondi, of Italian and French ancestry, was an active man of letters who wrote extensively on the history of France and on that of the Italian republics. He also was a man of affairs, deeply interested in the economic problems of his own day. Intermarried with a Scottish family of distinction, he early became acquainted with the teachings of Adam Smith and originally was an enthusiastic proponent of them. In later years, however, although not abandoning capitalism, he did adversely criticize Smith, suggesting as he did so many new points of view.

The principal divergence from Smith may be found in this sentence: "In our opinion a nation does not progress in wealth merely because it accumulates more capital: it does so only if the increased capital distributes more comfort among the population which it sustains...." Wealth, according to Sismondi, must not be considered in the abstract; it always has relationship to men. These understand their own interests best, as Bentham said; but it does not inevitably follow that those interests are best for society. For instance, "the interests of a robber lie in despoiling his neighbor," and the interests of the métayer (share-cropper), who receives half the product of his land and who has lost his place and cannot find another, lie in accepting a third part of the product or less than a third, thus endangering the livelihood of other métayers.

Sismondi argued that laissez faire tended to create panics as the result of "superabundant production which outstrips consumption and is regulated not by demand but by the amount of capital seeking employment." He believed that the rapid introduction of new machines was responsible for this state of affairs; and he expressed sympathy for the social aims of the utopian socialists, while disassociating himself completely from their methods. Sismondi's own preference was for "a great number of middling capitalists" and he advocated laws which would "constantly favor the division and not the accumulation of inheritances ... the sharing of profits and the hiring of workmen for longer periods."

Friedrich List (1789-1846)

Rather different on the whole, although somewhat resembling Sismondi, was List, the most celebrated of the early German economists. A professor of political economy at Tübingen in Württemberg, he was forced to flee from Germany in 1822 because of liberal views. He came to America, edited a newspaper in Reading, Pennsylvania, made money in coal, and returned to Germany in 1830 as a United States consul. Eleven years later he published his best-known book, *The National System of Political Economy* (1841).

The book is devoted in large measure to arguments in favor of protective tariffs; they are not arguments based on mere dollars and cents but rather on broad sociological implications. List's quarrel with the classical economists was that they paid no attention to politics and consequently disregarded nationality, a living thing, for capital, an abstraction. Nationality, to List, was a kind of spiritual force which flourished or decayed in accordance with the well-being of all the people. If the economists called themselves "political economists" they had no right to ignore politics, "nor to be ignorant of it, nor misrepresent it, to sustain any cosmopolitan theory."

The individual cannot be considered apart from the group, the nation, and that nation has the best economy when it is balanced, partly agricultural, partly manufacturing. That balance can only be obtained, for countries like Germany, by protective tariffs. A tariff would stimulate German manufacturers, and the latter, in turn, would stimulate energy, enterprise, the arts, and culture. The reaction on agriculture itself would be favorable. "In no country are agricultural machines and implements more perfect, and in none is agriculture in so advanced a state as when manufacturing industry is flourishing. Under the influence of the latter husbandry becomes itself a manufacture, a science." One thinks of him as a sort of Teutonic Hamilton.

It can hardly be said of List that he was a well-rounded economist. Most of his book is devoted to the defence of tariffs and of nationalism. Nevertheless, to his credit it should be stated that he was not an advocate of economic nationalism in the narrow sense of that phrase as used today. "Free trade in agricultural products," he wrote, "is useful for nations of every degree of culture...." He was no believer in autarchy (complete economic self-sufficiency) and he was eager to encourage international trade in raw materials.

It is evident from the above that List broke away sharply from the teaching of economics as an abstract science and from that of the classical economists in the matter of free trade. On the other hand, he remained orthodox in the all-important matter of private property and the individual management of the same within limitations set by nationalism. His arguments for a protective system were based essentially, like those of Sismondi, on the welfare of the group, rather than on the abstract idea of amassing a great quantity of capital irrespective of ownership. On the other hand, he was less radical than the Swiss economist, in so far as he did not propose to split up estates and property in order to create a larger number of entrepreneurs.

John Stuart Mill (1806-73)

There remains to be considered that stalwart pillar of mid-nineteenth-century liberalism, John Stuart Mill, in whom logic and clear writing combined beautifully with breadth of view and a social conscience.

Mill is a superb example of the triumph of intelligence over environment. His father, James Mill, an economist and a philosopher in his own right, was a disciple of Jeremy Bentham, intent on educating his young son wholly and entirely in accordance with the most strict tenets of the utilitarian school. The "Benthamites," or utilitarians, scorned dreaming, detested religion and everything else that was not of practical "utility." But the intellectual curiosity of the younger Mill led him to read Wordsworth, Coleridge, and Goethe. He became an intimate friend of that arch-romanticist, Thomas Carlyle, and the latter at one time was almost convinced that in Mill he had discovered a "mystic." Mill was a long way from being one, but he did broaden immensely and learn how to regard men as human beings rather than as abstractions. A comfortable pension from the old East India Company made it unnecessary for him to earn a living during the last fifteen years of his life, and he wrote constantly, energetically, and well, finding time as he did so to sit for a while in Parliament and to give expert advice to liberal statesmen such as Gladstone.

Mill's writings are important from the points of view of philosophy, politics, and economics. However, since we are concerned here simply with the last, let us turn to his *Principles of Political Economy* (1848), a book which deserves equal rating with Smith's *Wealth of Nations,* Malthus' *Essay on Population,* and Ricardo's *Principles.*

First and foremost to be noted is that Mill's book is differentiated from earlier standard texts on economics by an attempt to draw the line sharply and clearly between production and distribution. The former, he believed, was determined by rigid, immovable natural laws beyond the power of man to change. With the latter, however, it was not so. Men are at liberty to distribute economic goods as they see proper, in any ratio they consider just or desirable, as among wage-earners, landlords, or capitalists.

The reason for this distinction may be seen in Mill's autobiography and by a study of the second half of his book, devoted to distribution. He acknowledges there that Mrs. Taylor, a woman with whom he was in love and whom he afterward married, had influenced him in writing this second half in the way he did. Mill was much troubled in conscience by the persistence of great wealth, side by side with extreme poverty. He felt very keenly that all should work. "I do not recognize," he wrote, "as either just or salutary a state of society in which there is any class which is not laboring, any human beings exempt from earning their share in the necessary labors of human life, except those unable to labor, or who have fairly earned rest by previous toil." So much for Mill's reputed radicalisms.

How to bring about this happy state of affairs? Mill never answers that question directly. He writes hopefully of the spread of education among workmen and to advance it he favors free compulsory education. Coöperative organizations, according to him, have pointed the way toward putting workingmen into business on their own account, and he believes that capitalists, in time, will be glad to lend money at low rates of interest to such groups. Mill also contends for the state protection of children in industry but not for women, who should assert their equality with men and bear equal responsibility. Water companies, railways, canals, and gasworks, he holds, are natural monopolies and should be subject to state control. The question as to whether or not the government ought to limit the hours of work in factories for adults, he examines with great care and concludes that it is impossible for him to come to any conclusion in regard to it. Mill also approves of inheritance taxes and an income tax (provided always that savings be exempt).

The above is a fair summary of Mill's practical proposals. In elucidating them he disclosed a warm current of sympathy for the proletariat not customarily found in the mid-nineteenth-century economist. This, however, must not blind us to the fact that upon most major matters Mill was severely orthodox, particularly so in respect to (a) the desirability of private property; (b) the necessity of amassing more capital; (c) the tremendous importance of limiting numbers (Malthusianism); and (d) general adhesion to the principles of laissez faire, departures from which should be few and never undertaken without very careful scrutiny.

The above thinkers and economists, while varying one from another in a number of particulars many of which are important, all were agreed in supporting the general capitalistic structure of society. They were, for the most part, orthodox; they were liberal, with the possible exception of List and his nationalist tariff. And List, it must be remembered, despite this one major heresy, approved heartily of capitalistic enterprise. The fact that he, Sismondi, and Mill wrote later than Ricardo and Malthus is significant in showing that many economists were willing to bend and to qualify when confronted with ugly reality. Nevertheless, it is evident that none of the three had any intention of assailing the inner citadel of capitalism—individual and private ownership of productive property.

There were men eager and willing to assail it. These were the socialists, of one brand or another, who kept constantly cropping up during the century. Socialism, like capitalism, is a difficult word to define, owing to the lack of common denominators among the various socialistic schools. In general, however, it would be fair to state that all varieties of socialistic thought agreed on the following: (1) that society as organized was unjust to the proletariat; (2) that it could not be made just without discovering some method of coöperative production; (3) that distribution should take place in accordance with some plan or formula.

Socialism may be said to be pre-Marxian or post-Marxian. The earlier variety, denounced by Karl Marx as "Utopian socialism," we have encountered elsewhere especially as met with in France during the forties. The later variety, of which Marx was the founder, was sometimes called "scientific socialism," sometimes "materialistic socialism," or even "dialectical materialism." Theoretically, it was all Marxian. Actually, as we shall see, this was not altogether true. Nevertheless, the socialism of the second half of the century bore heavily the Marxian imprint, and to understand its main tenets and the fundamental challenge it offered to capitalism, it is essential that Marx be studied with care.

Karl Marx (1818-83)

Marx was, perhaps, next to Charles Darwin, the most influential man of the nineteenth century. A thousand years hence, when historians look back on that day, it is not improbable that the Cavours, Palmerstons, Gladstones, and possibly even Bismarck may have faded into the shadow. But a like fate is not apt to overtake Marx and Darwin, for empires crash but thought remains.

Marx's father, a Christianized Jew with a Voltairian philosophy, was a Prussian lawyer at Treves on the Rhine. He was in relatively comfortable circumstances, for he could afford to send his son, after the German custom, to several universities in turn—Bonn, Berlin, and Jena. The young Marx was catholic in his interests, studied omnivorously, and looked forward to a professorial chair. He took his doctoral degree at Jena in Greek philosophy, but no university appointment followed. To earn a living, he then took up journalism.

Within a year Marx took charge of the *Rheinische Zeitung*, but in such capacity he found himself confronted with a world so full of complicated economic problems about which he knew next to nothing that he speedily resigned to study them intensively. He now married, moved to Paris, conversed intimately with radical agitators, read deeply, wrote critically of his native Prussia. Upon the complaint of that country, Louis Philippe's government sent him packing (1845). He went to Brussels and stayed there until the Revolution of 1848 broke out in his own country. Back he went to his native Rhineland and took part in the revolutionary movements of 1848 as we have seen in Germany. Exiled now from Prussia, he sought the hospitality of the second French Republic. Because of his radical writings he was not wanted in France. Rather than agree to live in a secluded village in Brittany, he fled, in 1849, to London, Europe's city of refuge, there to live until his death.

By this time Marx was an important figure in revolutionary circles, but he was very poor and had a growing family. His charming wife, Jennie von Westphalen, of the Prussian nobility, had long since been forced to sell what remained of the family plate, and the Marx family was driven into two small rooms, the father frequently without an overcoat, scarcely knowing where to turn for bread. Marx, throughout the rest of his life, was to find grim poverty at his door. Three of his children were to die under most depressing circumstances. As Mrs. Marx afterward wrote in regard to one of them:

> The dear child's death happened at a time when we were in direst need. Our German friends were unable to help us. . . . Ernest Jones, who paid us a visit at this time, and had promised to help, was unable to do anything. . . . In my overwhelming need, I hastened to a French refugee, who lived in the neighborhood, and had visited us not long before. At once, in the most friendly way possible, he gave me two pounds. With this sum I was able to buy the coffin in which my poor child now lies at peace. She had no cradle when she came into the world, and for a long time it was difficult to find a box for her last resting place.[4]

For many years the wolf was only kept at bay by small pittances received from the New York *Tribune* for weekly articles, and by the generosity of Friedrich Engels. The latter, a collaborator with Marx in the *Communist Manifesto,* was Marx's financial angel. Engels' father, a German manufacturer, owned a mill at Manchester which the younger Engels managed. Almost always the Marx family could expect aid from him. But not always. The father disapproved of Marx, kept close tab on his son's expenditures, and when the Engels family visited England, the younger Engels was afraid to send Marx any money. Despite these circumstances, however, he remitted small sums as he was able.

In 1856 the financial skies lifted slightly, for Mrs. Marx inherited a few hundred *thaler.* Shortly afterward they shut down again. Then, for a while, Engels was able to make Marx an allowance of £350 a year. But to the very end Marx was worried constantly by promissory notes past due, and all the troubles incidental to supporting a family whose sole reliance, practically, was the kindness of pitying friends.

Meanwhile, for years, Marx led the life of a scholarly recluse, burying himself in the British Museum. He took no part in English public life,

---

[4] From *Karl Marx* by Otto Ruhle, p. 206. Copyright, 1929. By permission of The Viking Press, Inc., New York.

KARL MARX (1818-83)

knew few Englishmen, and never even met John Stuart Mill. His acquaintanceship was limited, for the most part, to a few English trade-unionists and to a number of continental radicals. Except, indeed, for time taken out for work connected with the First International, he kept steadily at his desk until, in 1867, the first volume of *Das Kapital* (Capital) was completed.

The First International, theoretically, was a council representing the proletariat of all countries. Marx had little to do with its origin but speedily rose to high rank in its councils. This organization, the grandfather of the Third International now sitting in Moscow, lasted eleven years, holding sessions at Paris, Geneva, Brussels, The Hague, and Paris. There were many contending factions within it, and Marx succeeded in gaining and holding the mastery only by harsh domination and brutal attacks upon those who disagreed with him.

Early in the history of the International, he was able to ride roughshod over the gentle Mazzini who, with idealistic naïveté, was preaching a peculiarly romantic ideal of nationalistic unselfishness combined with nationalistic integrity. Later, Marx was confronted with the secession of the English delegates who did not like his revolutionary ideas and who conceived of the International merely as a kind of glorified super trade union. And still later he came in active conflict with the Russian revolutionary proletariat, headed by Bakunin. The latter was an anarchist who held fast to the notion of a decentralized federated movement, the reverse of what Marx wanted. In a great encounter between the Russians and the Marxians, the latter won, only to see the Italians and the Spaniards secede with their Muscovite brethren. But Bakunin and his followers continued to make trouble for Marx and his friends within the International, and Marx, in order to get rid of Russian influence, proposed its removal in 1872 to America. It met for a while in New York and died four years later at Philadelphia.

During all this time, Marx continued hard at work on the second volume of *Das Kapital*. The first volume had attracted scant notice, and the author was indignant, suspecting a conspiracy of silence. The second volume made slow progress. Marx was an ill man, suffering terribly from asthma, liver ailments, and carbuncles. When his wife died in 1881 he had neared the end of his rope. Two years later he followed her, leaving the faithful Engels to complete his masterpiece.

Concerning this man's life it is not necessary to write more. Throughout it all he acted in a most domineering and callous manner to friends and foes alike (that is, if we except his noticeable fondness for children, and kindness within the family circle). Always in ill-health and almost always poverty-stricken, he had perhaps some excuse for this behavior. His more enthusiastic followers have glorified his ruthlessness. To them it was a most fortunate circumstance that the great Marx had a bad digestion, for otherwise, they tell us, he might have compromised on certain issues and the militant socialism which he professed might have suffered. However that may be, if Marx's personality was unattractive he was at least heroic, and for better or for worse placed such a permanent stamp on socialist action as well as on socialist thought that the communists of our own day quarrel one with another as to the exact interpretation to be placed not only on the *Communist Manifesto* and *Das Kapital* but on every scrap of incidental writing (and there were many such) coming down from the great master.

The Communist Manifesto

Historians, as is quite fitting, have devoted more space to the *Communist Manifesto* than to *Das Kapital*, for the former book, although only a pamphlet, projected into the arena of the mid-nineteenth century a new philosophy of history. It finds its classic expression in the first sentence of Part I: "The history of all hitherto existing society is the history of class struggles."

This statement is the thesis upon which the *Communist Manifesto* is founded. It deserves to rank with the opening sentence of Rousseau's *Social Contract:* "Man is born free; and everywhere he is in chains." Marx and Rousseau, superficially different, in one respect are remarkably alike: they both coined sharp and epigrammatic dogmas to be swallowed lock, stock, and barrel by millions of devoted disciples.

The Marxian phrase is an unqualified affirmative declaration of the "economic" or "materialistic" interpretation of history. This can not be said to be entirely new with Marx, but if any one deserves to be known as the father of that idea, it was he. Before his day men were apt to think of history as either a personal chronicle of kings and queens and court gossip, or, less personally, as the growth and development of national states, their forms of government, their quarrels, and their wars. Voltaire, it is true, preached a history of manners and of customs—a kind of intellectual history—and Montesquieu laid considerable stress on geography. Others, interested in religion and doctrinal strife, were not adverse to pointing out with a good deal of assurance the ways of the Almighty with the children of men. But Marx brought history down to earth, showed how it had to do with the way men got food, shelter, and clothes, the way in which the great majority spent most of their days, the way in which men fought and killed one another for economic reasons. The fact that he exaggerated this idea and made the entire historic past conform to it should not blind us to the central truth that the larger part of the activities of most men have been devoted to getting a living, a fact apt to be ignored by those who are so fortunate personally as not to be at grips in their own lives with the sheer struggle for existence. From Marx's day, indeed, until the present, historical writing has been deeply influenced by this Marxian concept. Even those who detest Marx and flout his theories give nowadays far more generously of their time and space to economic forces underlying human events. The *Manifesto*, in its earlier part, narrates the continuous victories of the bourgeoisie from the late Middle Ages to the nineteenth century.

Each step [Marx tells us] in the development of the bourgeoisie was accompanied by a corresponding political advance of that class. An oppressed class under the sway of the feudal nobility, an armed and self-governing association in the medieval commune, here independent urban republic (as in Italy and Germany), there taxable third estate of the monarchy (as in France), afterwards, in the period of manufacture proper, serving either the semi-feudal or the absolute monarchy as a counterpoise against the nobility, and in fact cornerstone of the great monarchies in general, the bourgeoisie has at last, since the establishment of Modern Industry and of the world market, conquered for itself, in the modern representative State, exclusive political sway. The executive of the modern State is but a committee for managing the common affairs of the whole bourgeoisie.

This did not come about without a fight, and for hundreds of years that fight against knights, feudal lords, and country squires continued. This is the very stuff and marrow of past history; and also of present history, for during the preceding hundred years the bourgeoisie "created more massive and more colossal productive forces than have all preceding generations together. Subjection of Nature's forces to man, machinery, application of chemistry to industry and agriculture, steam navigation, railways, electric telegraphs, clearing of whole continents for cultivation, canalization of rivers, whole populations conjured out of the ground—what earlier century had even a presentiment that such productive forces slumbered in the lap of social labor."

But, behold the innumerable proletariat! "In proportion as the bourgeoisie, i.e., capital, is developed, in the same proportion is the proletariat, the modern working class, developed, a class of laborers who live only so long as they find work, and who find work only so long as their labor increases capital." The proletariat grows bigger and bigger, for into its ranks continually drop the lower bourgeoisie whose capital is insufficient "for the scale on which Modern Industry is carried on." The proletariat at first acts blindly, revolting here and there against the bourgeoisie without intelligence and leadership; but the communists will supply them with leaders and the communists are the advance guard of the revolutionary proletariat who will climb up on the back of the bourgeoisie as the latter have climbed on the backs of the feudal nobility.

This can only be done by a thoroughgoing revolution which abolishes private productive property.

You are horrified [Marx writes] at our intending to do away with private property. But in your existing society private property is already done away with for nine-tenths of the population; its existence for the few is solely due to its non-existence in the hands of those nine-tenths. You reproach us, therefore, with intending to do away with a form of property, the necessary condition for whose existence is, the non-existence of any property for the immense majority of society.

In one word you reproach us with intending to do away with your property. Precisely so; that is just what we intend.

The Communists disdain to conceal their views and aims. . . . The proletarians have nothing to lose but their chains. They have a world to win.

Workingmen of all countries, unite!

With these words the *Manifesto* ends. It is a pithy, uncompromising document, attempting to show that only by violence can the bourgeoisie be displaced by the proletariat. Openly and aboveboard does Marx teach hatred of the bourgeoisie. James Madison, in eighteenth-century America, and Guizot, in nineteenth-century France, both looked forward with dread to possible class war and did what they could to avert it. Marx looked forward with eagerness. As Mazzini said of him, "hatred outweighs love in his heart..." and this statement Marx would have approved. Only by hating the bourgeoisie could the proletariat learn to stand together.

To what extent is the *Communist Manifesto* a true analysis of historical events; what credence can be given to the materialistic interpretation of history? As is usual in propaganda books like this, the most searching criticism that can be made is to consider what facts have been ignored. Now, in so far as the Parthenon at Athens, Michelangelo's frescoes over the Sistine Chapel, Goethe's Faust, and Beethoven's symphonies are historic facts, it would be rather difficult to connect them with any outstanding struggle between classes. Garibaldi led his Thousand to Sicily and there fought very well; was that expedition an evidence of class struggle? Surely Garibaldi's exploits are history in the narrower sense of that term. The Spanish peasants rose against Napoleon. Presumably the peasants were rack-rented by callous landlords and were proletarians. Napoleon offered them economic advantages which they spurned. Was the American Civil War a class conflict? The answer is "Yes" and "No." Some economic element is very apt to be found in any mass movement in history, and thanks to Marx, we are more apt to think of such than if he had not lived. The bourgeoisie certainly did displace the feudal nobility; that we can safely grant. But from that fact does it inevitably follow that the proletariat will inevitably oust the bourgeoisie? There are many who would not be as certain as Marx.

But suppose we assume with him that victory for the proletariat in the hypothetical future, then what? According to the *Manifesto,* peace will dawn upon the earth and there will be no more class war because there will be no more classes. "In place of the old bourgeois society, with its classes and class antagonisms, we shall have an association in which the free development of each is the condition for the free development of all."

And so, as soon as we have communism, we shall have perfect freedom! That this happy state of affairs will follow is a weak assumption in so far as it is a denial of the main thesis of the *Manifesto* that all history is a class struggle; for if man throughout all his past has engaged in economic war and has thus been conditioned, is it at all likely that he will suddenly change his whole nature and immediately become friendly and well-disposed toward his fellow man?

There is a fundamental weakness in Marx's logic. It must be remembered that his early training was in philosophy and that his early intellectual life had been largely spent in revolting against Hegel, an idealistic German philosopher. The trouble with Marx is that, though he had no use for Hegel's conclusions, he did adopt his method, virtually turning Hegel upside down and trying to demonstrate the inevitability of materialism by the same means that Hegel demonstrated the inevitability of his idealism.

This Marx-Hegel method was a dangerous one called "dialectic," and involved what was called a "thesis," then portraying a conflict between that and its opposite, called an "antithesis," and then arguing that out of that conflict must emerge a "synthesis." In course of time the synthesis just established becomes a new thesis, is confronted with a new antithesis, then follows a new synthesis, and so on in an indefinite series.

What, then, is dangerous about this method? Primarily, it is apt to become too methodical, too academic, too inelastic, too abstract. It is an admirable way of thinking within limits; but those limits are always conditioned by life as it is, rather than as it is intellectually conceived of as being. It is all very well to assume with Marx the thesis (landlords), the antithesis (merchants), the synthesis (bourgeois society); and it is entirely logical to continue with him the thesis (bourgeois society), the antithesis (emergent proletariat), the synthesis (communism). But because this method is logical it does not follow that communism is inevitable. Let us not forget that Herbert Spencer was every bit as good a logician as Marx and came to quite different conclusions. Let us not forget, also, that Hegel was apt to confuse an abstract process of logical thought with the vital processes of concrete interests which do not always operate logically. Possibly the same might be true of Marx.

But even if we assume that the "dialectic materialism" of Marx, as opposed to the dialectic idealism, proves communism inevitable; then what? Suppose we stake everything on the Marxian dialectic as the only honest way of thinking, how can this dialectic process as he outlined it possibly come to an end with the classless society? Surely a new thesis, new antithesis, new synthesis, sometime, somehow must follow, if from the beginning of time man has been a depersonalized though human atom at the mercy of the blind forces of economic circumstance, as Marx seemed to think. If that is so, what becomes then of the classless society?

Das Kapital

It is a much more difficult task to analyze *Das Kapital* than the *Communist Manifesto,* for it is a huge work, written in the involved German style making constant use of intricate mathematical formulas. *Das Kapital,* it must be held in mind, has nothing in it, except by inference, about socialism. It is an analysis of the economic world as Marx found it (capitalism) and an argument to show why capitalism carries within itself the seeds of its own destruction and how that destruction will come about.

Two outstanding economic laws as defined by Marx in this book should be understood by everyone. One is that of surplus value, the other that of the concentration of capital. Of the two the former is the more important, since from it follows the latter. It is quite permissible to argue that Marx defines more economic laws than these two. For the sake of simplification, however, we shall write only of these two; and the various implications and results flowing from the law of the concentration of capital, we shall consider corollaries to that law, rather than as separate laws in themselves.

Surplus value is the difference between what it costs an entrepreneur or manufacturer to produce a commodity and what he sells it for—in other words, his profit. This surplus is wrongfully taken from the worker. Labor, alone, according to Marx, creates value, but labor only receives a fraction of the money for which goods are sold. Therefore, he asserts that labor (the workingman) is robbed by a system of industry whereby the tools of production (machinery) are owned and controlled by capitalist and entrepreneur.

How are we to prove this? Take any given number of commodities that we please—a hat, for instance, a house, a locomotive, a fountain pen. What determines the real value of these commodities? To discover it we must find a common denominator which they all possess. There is only one that can be found, namely labor. All four commodities are produced by labor and only by labor, for the very tools used in making the locomotive are the product of labor. Therefore, the value of all four is determined by labor.

A host of objections immediately arise. How about virgin soil, spring water, a diamond picked up along the wayside by an explorer; have these not value? "Certainly," Marx would admit, "they have '*value in use*'; I am talking about '*value in exchange*,' an altogether different kind of value."

Another query now rises. Suppose a magnificent carriage is manufactured, a work involving many hours of skilled labor. The carriage in our day is useless except as a model of outdated means of transportation. Can it be argued that the amount of labor used in making the carriage determines its value? "By no means," the Marxian would retort: "nothing can have value without being the object of utility."

"But," continues the objector, "suppose the hat you wear is made by a slovenly workman, whereas mine is the product of a skilled hatmaker. More work has gone into creating the inferior headpiece. Since that is so has it greater value than the other?" Again Marx's answer would be in the negative. Average labor skill and average labor time must be the yardstick, he would affirm.

Even after these various qualifications are made there still is further doubt. Granted that the only common denominator among commodities is labor, what of it? A watch certainly is an object of utility. In times of economic distress, however, its value would certainly decline in comparison with that of an overcoat. By throwing largely to one side the economic law of supply and demand and by stressing the abstract metaphysical concept of a common denominator, Marx argues his point. One doubts if it is well taken.

To put the case, however, more concretely, a Marxian would argue as follows: It costs a manufacturer $25 to produce a certain quantity of yarn, the $25 being spent on raw material, on machinery (spindles, and so forth), and on wages. The yarn is sold for $27.50, netting a gain of ten per cent. The additional $2.50 is surplus value or robbery. In other words, Marx would concede nothing to capital since he did not conceive of it as increasing production; nor anything even to management which perhaps might involve analysis of the market as to whether there was a demand at the time for the yarn.

Are we justified then in claiming that the entire Marxian concept of value is worthless? Almost. Let us trace the yarn back to its origins. Land is plowed in Alabama and planted with cotton seed; the cotton is picked, baled, placed in ships, sent to England, transported to a factory, pulled out on spindles into yarn, sold in the market place. Behind all of these operations there is labor and a great deal of it; behind them also is capital, which is the product of labor stored up for future production. Unless somebody had saved there would not be the plow for the planter, the ship for the high seas, the spindle in England. True, the plow, the ship, the spindle, were the product of labor. But at the same time their values were also created in part by capital.

"Don't stop here," cries the Marxian, "go back to the origin of all things. Labor comes first!" This, of course, is true. But it is also true that the first man who worked overtime and invented a handbarrow produced capital directly instrumental in further increasing value. As to the just share of increased value to be given those who carried the barrow (labor) and to him who made it (capitalist) there might readily be a question. Something, however, if the Ten Commandments have any meaning, should go to both participants. Marx's argument appears fallacious, both as a matter of economic theory and moral sanction.

But, fallacious or not, to simple-minded workmen it looked good. "You men make the goods—they sell for so and so. You get so and so—the capitalist gets the difference. That is surplus value. He takes it out of your pocket." How often have words similar to these been repeated on street-corner, in public square, or in saloon!

Marx's argument is not good; nevertheless, there is an important germ of truth in it, most lucidly expressed by Marx's fellow-author, Engels, in his tract, *Anti-Dühring*, which Marx corrected and approved. Wrote Engels of the economic situation after the coming of factories: [5]

Hitherto, the owner of the instruments of labor had appropriated the product because it was as a rule his own product, the auxiliary labor of other persons being the exception; now the owner of the instruments of production continue to appropriate the product, although it was no longer *his* product, but exclusively the product of *other's labor*. Thus, therefore, the products, now socially produced, were not appropriated by those who had really set the means of production in motion and really produced the products, but by the *capitalists*. Means of production, and production, had in essence become social. But they were subjected to a form of appropriation which has as its presupposition private production by individuals, with each individual owning his own product and bringing it into the market. . . . In this contraction, which gives the new mode of production its capitalistic character, *the whole conflict of today is already present in germ.*

Marx's second great law is that of the concentration of capital. The capitalists compete with one another and as a result:

One capitalist lays a number of his fellow capitalists low. Hand in hand with this centralisation, concomitantly with the expropriation of many capitalists by a few, the co-operative form of the labour process develops to an ever-increasing degree; therewith we find a growing tendency towards the purposive application of science to the improvement of technique; the land is more methodically cultivated; the instruments of labour tend to assume forms which are only utilisable by combined effort; the means of production are economised through being turned to account only by joint, by social labour; all the peoples of the world are enmeshed in the net of the world market, and therefore the capitalist régime tends more and more to assume an international character. While there is thus a progressive diminution in the number of the capitalist magnates (who usurp and monopolise all the advantages of this transformative process), there occurs a corresponding increase in the mass of poverty, oppression, enslavement, degeneration, and exploitation; but at the same time there is a steady intensification of the wrath of the working class—a class which grows ever more numerous, and is disciplined, unified, and organised by the very mechanism of the capitalist method of production. Capitalist monopoly becomes a fetter upon the method of production which has flourished with it and under it. The centralisation of the means of production and the socialisation of labour reach a point where they prove incompatible with their capitalist hulk. This bursts asunder. The knell of capitalist private property sounds. The expropriators are expropriated. [6]

This is the quintessence of the Marxian picture: fewer and fewer capitalists, more and more proletarians, bigger and more frequent commercial crises, the condition of the workers growing worse and worse, until in

---

[5] *A Handbook of Marxism*, p. 283 (New York, Random House, 1935). Reprinted by permission of the publishers.

[6] *Ibid.*, p. 554. Reprinted by permission of the publishers.

one grand catastrophe the communist spearhead of the proletarians seizes on political power, ends surplus capital, abolishes private property.

Is the picture true? The law concerning the concentration of capital is certainly on better ground than that of surplus value. On the other hand, the causes of commercial crises apparently are many, vary from crisis to crisis, and still are obscure. Surplus capital leading to overproduction may be one, but only a very dogmatic economist would assert that it was the only one, or even the leading one. As to whether the proletariat is gradually sinking to a lower and lower status, there is much to be said on both sides.

Marx, let it be said in summary, was an ingenious and fertile thinker. He conceived himself to be a kind of materialistic scientist; but that he was such is dubious. Probably it would be fairer to think of him as a kind of religious leader, a reëmbodiment of the Jewish prophets of the Old Testament, calling down the maledictions of the Most High on a wicked and adulterous generation. A genuine scientist always questions his assumptions; but Marx did not. He was sure that the world is moving forward irresistibly toward a society where man would be more kind and humane and not exploit his brother. But a true scientist would concede that we have no proof at all that the world is moving in that direction, although he might tentatively suggest one method or another by which humanity might hope to find such a desirable haven.

The religious leader, on the other hand, has faith; he is not tentative but certain. Marx had faith in the proletariat. In so far as he inspired it with indignation, with resolution, with courage, self-respect, and confidence, his religion was a good one and his influence, like that of Calvin and Rousseau, men of similar caliber, was profound and permanent.

So profound was it that ever since Marx's death almost every variety of socialistic thought has invoked the teachings of the *Manifesto* and *Das Kapital*. Five, perhaps, deserve mention here: the anarchist-socialist; the revisionary socialist; the Fabian socialist; the syndicalist socialist; and the orthodox socialist.

The Anarchist-Socialists

Most difficult of all to appraise fairly are the anarchist-socialists. Antithetical as the two words "socialism" and "anarchy" are, they may perhaps be linked, since socialists and anarchists are at one in their flat rejection of capitalism and in their acceptance of a militant revolutionary class struggle. On the other hand, from another point of view, the hyphen should be removed, in so far as socialists rejoice at the extension of state and governmental power, whereas anarchists are as bitterly opposed to the state as they are to private productive property.

Anarchists stem back to the French writer Proudhon (1809-65), whose book, *What Is Property?* (1840), stated baldly, "property is theft." The author not only wanted to abolish property but governments as well. He believed in extreme decentralization and in no compulsion whatever, holding idealistically to the theory that man, once free, would of his own nature join willingly and of his own accord with such coöperative undertakings as might prove socially useful. In one of his early writings Marx had attacked Proudhon viciously but the latter, nevertheless, found many followers, particularly among Russians, such as Peter Kropotkin (see p. 228) and Michael Bakunin.

Bakunin (1814-76), scion of the Russian aristocracy, was one of Europe's most restless and energetic radicals. Like Marx, he studied Hegel in Berlin; like Marx he took part in the German Revolution of 1848. From the latter he barely escaped with his life. Condemned to death by the government of Saxony, he was handed over to the Czar, who banished him to life imprisonment in Siberia. Escaping, he reached Europe by way of Japan and America. For a while Bakunin was as important a figure in the First International as Marx. Behind him were the Russian delegates and most of those from Latin Europe. He liked Russians, distrusted Germans, and hated Jews, so the antipathy between him and Marx was natural. It was, however, something more than personal. Bakunin had no use for political action, the Marxian principle that the proletariat should set out first to capture the machinery of the state; what he wanted was direct concentration on economics, more specifically, less work and higher wages. Socialists who fought for universal suffrage and political power he denounced as "bourgeois" socialists. Marx charged that Bakunin was a secret agent of the Czar and the latter countered by accusing Marx of being Bismarck's tool. There was a battle royal and Marx won, expelling Bakunin. From that time on there was a breach between those who sought socialism by anarchy (destruction of governments) and those who sought it by strengthening governments. In Germany and England the anarchists were negligible in numbers, but in southern Europe they comprised the majority of the class-conscious proletariat. Some of them were "philosophic anarchists," that is, not inclined to bloodshed, but a good many became terrorists and engaged in assassination, thinking that it might be possible to destroy government by shooting, stabbing, or dynamiting kings, queens, and presidents.

The Revisionary Socialists

A more important group were the so-called "revisionary socialists," who came very near capturing the socialist movement in Germany where, before the first World War, it staged its greatest success. The revisionary socialists stoutly asserted that they were good Marxians, holding the true faith in regard to the class struggle and the theory of surplus capital.

But, said they, Marx miscalculated when he assumed that the proletariat would sink into greater and greater misery until the day of revolution came. Marx also wrote: "The proletarian has no fatherland." That statement was true, so the revisionary socialists believed, when Marx wrote it. But it no longer held in Germany after the proletariat began to secure legal and political rights of value.

Edward Bernstein (1850-1932) was the leading revisionary socialist. Exiled by Bismarck, he edited a radical paper in Switzerland, visited England, and in 1899 published his *Evolutionary Socialism*. As a member of the German Reichstag, Bernstein strove for a national militia, since he held that as a German he could not support pacifism. He voted for war credits, did his best to keep Russian Bolshevism out of Germany, and retired in 1928.

A sentence or two from his book will show his point of view. "The number of members of the possessing classes is to-day not smaller but larger." And again ". . . driven by the movement of the working classes, which is daily becoming stronger, a social reaction has set in against the exploiting tendencies of capital, a counteraction which although it still proceeds timidly and feebly, yet does exist. . . ." Evidences of this reaction were factory legislation, increased power of trade unions, and co-operative trading. Socialism, perhaps, might not have to engage in open war after all, not if the intelligent capitalists gradually surrendered to it as they were doing.

Bernstein's influence in his own party was very great. In party meetings he was voted down largely because, as a matter of pure theory, the German Social Democrats did not like to think that their dogmas were being diluted. When it came to actual fact, however, this philosophy of Bernstein's pretty thoroughly permeated German socialism. By 1914 it had really ceased to be a revolutionary movement and had become "reformist," trusting that slowly and gradually Germany would become a socialist state almost before she realized it.

The Fabians

Somewhat similar to the German revisionary socialists were the Fabians in England. As the derivation of the word indicates, they believed in going slow. Their favorite slogan was "The inevitability of gradualness" and their favorite activity was to prod the British proletariat to demand very specific reforms—municipal tramways, lodging-houses, free baths, better milk, free lunch for school children and so through a long list to be undertaken by the state.

Despite the fact of Marx's long life in London, his influence on British socialism always has been relatively less than in continental countries. This was due in part to an inborn distrust in England of elaborate and closely defined dogmas, in part to a kind of indigenous socialism in England dating back hundreds of years to Sir Thomas More in the early sixteenth century and probably even earlier. That socialism did not take very kindly to the idea of class war, nor does it even yet. The English socialists, it is true, hoisted the banner of Karl Marx and chattered the phrases of *Das Kapital* and the *Communist Manifesto;* but not with enthusiasm. The Fabian Society, in particular, although calling itself socialist, was a very independent organization. How could it have been otherwise, when it contained such individualistic and non-proletarian writers as their headliners, George Bernard Shaw and H. G. Wells?

Prominent among the Fabians was Sydney Webb (1859-1947), a man inordinately acute in his observation and arrangement of minute social facts. Webb married the brilliant Beatrice Potter, a woman with enthusiasm and ability quite parallel to his own. After 1890 the two Webbs wrote constantly, in partnership, the most learned and scientific books imaginable on local government, poor laws, and trade-unionism. Webb's passion for factual knowledge proved of great assistance to the British Labor Party, of which he and his wife were distinguished members. To assist his party after it took office subsequent to the World War, he consented to enter the House of Lords as Lord Passfield.

To show how he and the other Fabians hoped to introduce piecemeal what *they* said was socialism, let us look at two or three sentences from a Fabian tract written by him in 1889.

Most of us know, [he wrote] that the local governments have assumed the care of roads, streets and bridges once entirely abandoned to individual enterprise, as well as the lighting and cleansing of all public thoroughfares, and the provision of sewers, drains ... The provision of markets, fairs, harbors, piers, docks, hospitals, cemeteries and burial grounds is still shared with private capitalists; but those in public hands absorb nearly £2,000,000 annually. Parks, pleasure grounds, libraries, museums, baths, and workhouses cost the public funds over half a million sterling ... Practically half the gas consumers in the kingdom are supplied by public gas-works ... about thirty-one towns, including nearly all the larger provincial centres, own some or all of their own tramways ... Glasgow builds and maintains seven public common lodging houses; Liverpool provides science lectures; Manchester builds and stocks an art gallery; Leeds creates extensive cattle markets and Bradford supplies water below cost price.

The socialist movement in England, as a whole, was more Marxian in tone than the Fabians. The Independent Labor Party, for instance, hewed much closer to the Marxian line. But even that left-wing organization was more Marxian in theory than in practice. A leading member of it, before the first World War, was Ramsay Macdonald, afterward Prime Minister of England. He talked bravely of the abolition of private property but stepped softly when it came to prophesying revolution. The book which he wrote on socialism, *Syndicalism: A Critical Examination* (1913), would have disgusted Karl Marx.

The Syndicalists

Still another variety of socialists called themselves "syndicalists" and found their especial habitat in France. They might best be described as a kind of cross between orthodox Marxians and anarchists, for they were thoroughgoing revolutionary socialists who thought it foolish to wait until an opportunity presented itself to overthrow the state. Their theory was to commence revolutionary violence immediately by strikes, and if possible by a general strike.

Insofar as "syndicalism" had a leader, that man was Georges Sorel (1847-1922), a civil engineer who, annoyed by revisionary and orthodox socialism alike, struck out on a line of his own. In 1908 Sorel published his *Reflections on Violence,* a book which left a permanent imprint on the mind of a young Italian journalist, Benito Mussolini. Sorel was all for instant physical action. He believed that the proletariat should organize by industries (as the C.I.O. in America), and not by trade unions. This once done, their weapon was not parliamentary action but violence. The syndicalists were to engage in "sabotage," that is, wrecking machinery; their strikes were to be violent, not peaceful. "Strikes," said Sorel, "have engendered in the proletariat the noblest, deepest and most moving sentiments they possess; the general strike groups them all in a coördinated picture and, by bringing them together, gives to each one of them its maximum of intensity. . . ."

This doctrine of the general strike had some considerable vogue in France in the early twentieth century and, as we shall see, brought about a dangerous crisis there. It also in postwar England, in 1926, produced even a more dangerous one (see p. 652), and repercussions of Sorel's teaching were also to be found in America and in Russia.

The Orthodox Socialists

Finally there were the "orthodox" socialists, namely, revolutionists who not only confessed the teachings of Marx one hundred per cent but who also held strictly to the idea not of destroying government but of capturing it and of utilizing it, by means of a dictatorship of the proletariat, in order to kill capitalistic society. Orthodox Marxians were to be found in all countries. In Germany they were particularly strong, but in Russia they were stronger yet. How the Russian Communists, loyal children of Karl Marx, thought and acted, more properly belongs to the chapter on the great Russian Revolution (see p. 372). They did not agree altogether with one another, it is true: but they were at least one in so far as they always defended their course of action by quotation from the Holy Scriptures—according to Marx.

The above analysis of economic thought is far from being inclusive. To be fair to capitalism, possibly the ideas and writings of economic theorists subsequent to Mill should have been included. Many of them humanized economics even more than Mill. They abandoned the Ricardian iron law of wages, at least in its more rigid form, arguing less from abstractions and more from a realistic standpoint. To be fair to Marx and his critique of capitalism, possibly a fuller analysis of the shortcomings of the capitalism of his day would be in order. All that has been attempted has been to throw into broad outline the major economic conflict (in books, that is) of the nineteenth century.

Chapter 16

SCIENCE AND RELIGION IN
THE NINETEENTH CENTURY

ONE OF THE most enlightened and celebrated men of the nineteenth century was Friedrich Heinrich Alexander, Baron von Humboldt (1769-1859). He was a scientist of renown, a Prussian nobleman, a friend of both Napoleon Bonaparte and Frederick William III, a famous traveler in Central and South America and Siberia, and the author of a fascinating book in four volumes, published between 1845 and 1858.

The book is entitled *Cosmos* and purports to be a description of the universe. It begins with the distant nebulæ, takes up our solar system, sun, and planets, tells us how the earth is measured and what it is composed of, tells something about earthquakes, volcanoes, different kinds of rocks, fossil animals, fossil plants, the ocean, climate, gives descriptions of nature by Persians, Finns, Arabs, Columbus, Shakespeare, and gives us the *history of the physical contemplation* of the universe by the Argonauts, Ptolemies, Pliny, Galileo, Kepler, and Newton. It was enormously popular, running through many editions and being translated into many languages. Even to-day, *Cosmos* makes fascinating reading for the layman, primarily, one suspects, for two reasons: the author was close enough to the broad philosophic climate of the eighteenth century to write in general terms; and the science of his day was still simple enough to be understood readily by the average intelligent person, even without scientific training.

There are no such general summaries of the universe available to-day. A Jeans can write an understandable book on astronomy alone; but a synthesis of all science which could be readily understood seems almost impossible; for science has become so diffused and so complicated since Humboldt wrote, as to escape the grasp of most people. It is much easier to explain the tidal influence of the moon than the first and second laws of thermodynamics; and the ways of a volcano are simplicity itself, compared with Einstein's relativity.

The nineteenth century, and particularly the last half of it, was an age wherein a tremendous enthusiasm was awakened for collecting and classifying all kinds of observable and objective facts. Add to this "the recognition of their sequence and relative significance," and we have science. In every field of human activity this scientific research was most energetically pushed—in literature, in economics, in natural science, and in religion. This chapter is concerned primarily with the last two fields.

Natural science has as its province the physical world, and customarily we are apt to think of it as divided into two main branches—"applied science" and "pure science"—the former having to do with the very practical object of making life more immediately rich in physical comfort, the latter more essentially related to the discovery of general laws which govern, or seem to govern, the world of physical nature and man's relation to it. The line between these two branches of science is, of course, somewhat difficult to draw, since pure science from time to time makes its deductions as a result of discoveries in the realm of applied science, while the latter frequently gains its inspiration from pure science. Nevertheless, the distinction is worth while in order to clarify discussion.

Slight attention will be paid in this chapter to applied science. That it made gigantic strides in the second half of the century is obvious. The telegraph, telephone, sewing machine, bicycle, and typewriter followed one another in close order. Engineers built bigger and better ships and bridges, improved and reimproved the locomotive. In 1830, thirty miles an hour was "good going" by railway. By the end of the century the speed of express trains had been doubled. The ubiquitous trolley-car appeared everywhere, as electricity was harnessed to man's will, and as early as 1885 Daimler had invented a gas engine which made the automobile possible. Chemists revolutionized the sugar industry, distilled from coal tar such diverse products as dyestuffs, antiseptics, explosives, electrode carbons, and perfumes, analyzed the soil, investigated the properties of fertilizers, discovered that light, heat, and water were not sufficient for plant life, that all plants needed ammonia, that certain plants needed calcium, and still others potassium. They also learned much about rubber, how to make raincoats, how to make pneumatic tires, and, as the result of the study of wasps' nests, how to turn wood pulp into paper. The mere listing of discoveries in applied science would fill many pages, and for that very reason we are not going to make such a list. To do so, for instance, in regard to the history of dentistry, or of photography, is merely a matter of memory at the expense of imagination and reflection. There is little more cultural value to be obtained from lists of that sort than from a complete chronology of baseball championships.

But with pure science it is a different story. The study of mathematics, physics, chemistry, and biology during the nineteenth century brought about what the Germans call a new *Weltanschauung,* in other words a new attitude toward life as a whole, which finds reflection in man's economics, literature, and religion. The seventeenth and eighteenth centuries were important eras in the history of pure science, and man felt then that he was getting somewhere; but he felt much more confident in 1900. By that date the discoveries of the preceding hundred years seemed to transcend all that had happened in the past. The infinitely great and the infinitely small had been revealed, as well as the infinite past. The nebulæ of distant solar systems, unfathomably distant even by light years; the swarming bacilli, so minute that a slight pin-prick in a piece of paper would be larger than thousands of living things: these had become matters of everyday knowledge. And the undreamed-of age of the earth and of living things on it was now a commonplace fact. High-powered lenses, photographic plates, erudite mathematical formulæ, spectroscope and microscope applied to rocks, plants, fossils, and the human blood had brought this knowledge home to man. All mysteries seemed solved or about to be solved. Matter ruled the universe and man ruled matter.

In physics and in chemistry there were revolutionary changes. Before the nineteenth century, heat was regarded as a kind of fluid. An Englishman, Joule, however, discovered that an intimate relationship was to be found between heat and energy; and a German, Helmholtz, basing his work on that of Joule and others, announced what has since been known as the law of the conservation of energy, namely, "that the sum total of the energy of the universe is a constant quantity." Joule then went further and became the founder of a kind of subscience, that of thermodynamics —"the study of the motive power of heat." From applied science (the steam engine) the physicists had gained much that aided them in their pure research; now out of the latter (thermodynamics) the applied scientist was to gather his more important data for continuous improvement in all the varieties of power machinery.

Before the nineteenth century comparatively little was known about light. Now, owing to the study of optics and advanced mathematics, the "wave theory" of light was established and placed upon a firm foundation by the study of electricity on the one hand and by the invention of the spectroscope on the other. Out of the study of light rose another subscience, that of astrophysics, which made it possible to study the chemical constituents of other worlds and to "estimate the movements and velocities of stars by studying the light they emit." Astronomy thus took on a new lease of life which was further enriched and extended by photography, the first really scientific photographic plates dating from 1878.

Back in the eighteenth century, Franklin made electricity something more than a plaything, but in the nineteenth it became an all important adjunct of pure science. Men learned how to produce it, to measure it, to utilize it, even if they did not learn just what it was. Before 1800 electricity was conceived as one thing and "magnetism" or "galvanism" as another. Subsequently, they were linked together as one phenomenon (electromagnetism). Volta, in 1800, made the first real electric battery;

Ohm and Ampère found out how to measure electric currents; eventually, as a result of research, came still more knowledge of sound and color; and soon, by the X-ray (1895), it became possible to see through some opaque substances.

In the days of Socrates it had been conjectured that everything in the world was composed of "atoms," individual and indivisible units. This was a bold guess which the English chemist, John Dalton, developed into a sound and well-substantiated atomic theory in the nineteenth century. In accordance with Dalton's ideas there were only some twenty elements in the world and everything tangible in life was composed of them. Little by little scientists have increased the number of known elements until, by the discovery of radium (1898) by Pierre and Marie Curie, there were over eighty elements listed. The Greeks had also guessed that all matter might ultimately be reduced to one atomic constituent, but Dalton did not try to investigate the interior of his atoms, believing that they were not further reducible. Gold, silver, lead, oxygen, and so forth, as atoms could be discovered, but one could not go beyond that. Meanwhile, a contemporary of the English chemist was Avogadro, an Italian, who showed that gases were composed of very minute substances which he called "molecules." For a time scientists were perplexed by these apparently conflicting discoveries. Then, in time, the term "molecule" was applied to combinations of atoms—salt, for instance, water, or carbon dioxide gas. Physicists then joined with chemists in analyzing the atoms. They were all found to be of peculiar construction, each one with a nucleus, around which revolved what were called electrons, the latter constantly in motion. Further knowledge of the electrons and their protons was a matter for the next century to investigate.

As early as the seventeenth century, Anton von Leeuwenhoeck, a janitor in Delft, Holland, had discovered the existence of tiny, invisible animals swimming around in rain water and in human saliva; but where these little animals came from and what they did was unknown. It remained for the nineteenth century to explore this invisible and mysterious world of the bacilli (microbes), and the two principal explorers thereof were Koch, a German, and Pasteur, a Frenchman.

Koch

Robert Koch (1843-1910), a poor country doctor, without time for research, mainly using homemade laboratory tools, first isolated the bacillus of anthrax, a deadly disease of cattle and of sheep, and then the bacillus of tuberculosis. Looking through his microscope at the blood of a sheep dead from anthrax, Koch saw many motionless minute rodlike structures united together as though forming a thread. He smeared the blood from this sheep on a splinter of wood, and applied it to an open cut on a mouse. Soon the mouse died of anthrax. Koch then cut out the spleen of the mouse and found in it the motionless tiny rods. Did they grow; were they alive? He took a fragment of the spleen and placed it in the eye of a freshly butchered ox. The rods then began to divide, moving in snakelike fashion across the glass on which the drop from the ox's eye rested. The bacillus which caused anthrax was now discovered, the first of many bacteriological discoveries of the utmost importance to medicine.

Koch next devoted himself to the much more difficult task of finding what caused tuberculosis. Already it was known that if one put part of the lung of a consumptive in a rabbit's eye it would produce sick tissue which would spread and kill the rabbit. Koch followed out this experiment but could discover nothing. Then it dawned on him that the bacillus he sought might be invisible even under his microscope. Therefore, he put the infected tissue from his rabbit in a strong solution of blue dye, smeared that on his glass and looked through his microscope. Forthwith bacilli appeared, much smaller than the anthrax variety, curved rather than straight, with little hooks at their ends and in size one fifteen-hundredth of an inch in length. These bacilli, placed in a blood-serum jelly of Koch's manufacture, grew and multiplied. When injected into rabbits and guinea pigs, it caused those animals to die from tuberculosis. But how was the disease transferred from animal to animal? Koch guessed that it was through the air. To prove this he put guinea pigs into an airtight box, inserted a lead pipe on one side of the box and blew dried bacilli through the tube. Soon death reigned within the box, and Koch had made one more of the great discoveries of his century.

Pasteur

In France, during this time, there lived a French chemist, Louis Pasteur (1822-95), who became even more famous than the German doctor. Pasteur, as a professor at Lille, did so much to assist the vintners and brewers of that city by studying fermentation in beer and wine that he was promoted to head the scientific teaching of the École Normale at Paris. Here he became the world's greatest authority on bacilli, a very famous savant whom even Napoleon III considered it an honor to entertain.

When Pasteur was young it was generally held that microbes were generated spontaneously, but our young chemist was determined to prove that they came from the air. He went all over France, capturing air in bottles and then analyzing it. He found that the higher he climbed the purer the air became and that the air on Mount Blanc was practically free from microbes. A balloon journey seemed desirable but Pasteur compromised: he boiled water in a clean bottle without a lid, and shortly after the water was infected with bacilli. He next boiled water in a bottle with a curved neck, and the water remained one hundred per cent clear of bacilli. From this fact he argued correctly that the bacilli, being heavier than air, dropped into his bottle with the open top but that they could not enter the other bottle. Hence the bacilli came from the air. And now Pasteur had made another of the great discoveries of the century.

Pasteur was a many-sided chemical genius. He experimented on French wines and proved that by heating them he could prevent their turning sour (pasteurization). He saved the silk industry in his native France by discovering microörganisms in the intestinal canal of silkworms. The use of aseptic methods in surgery was also due to him. Lister, in England, discovered antiseptics, but Pasteur taught a better method. He instructed surgeons to pass their instruments through a flame and to heat bandages, compresses, and other materials used in hospitals in a gas oven.

Pasteur also was able to parallel Koch in regard to anthrax. The little, unknown doctor in East Prussia first found the bacillus which killed the cattle and sheep of Europe, but the famous French chemist first found a method for immunizing sheep and cattle from that disease by inoculating them against it. But his most startling discovery had to do with hydrophobia, one of the world's most deadly and mysterious diseases. Pasteur was already about sixty and partly crippled by a paralytic stroke when he began his long campaign against hydrophobia. He commenced operations by securing a mad dog, sticking test tubes into the animal's mouth, and sucking up the saliva against a piece of cotton wool. Then he rubbed the saliva into the bloodstream of other dogs. Sometimes the latter went mad, sometimes they did not. A stronger solution evidently was necessary. Pasteur, owing to the symptoms of the disease, knew that the brain must be affected. Therefore he operated on the skulls of mad dogs, extracted a sliver from each of their brains, and injected the scrapings from it into healthy dogs. Generally this brought death to the healthy dog, inevitably so when placed on its exposed brain.

Pasteur was convinced that some live bacillus existed causing hydrophobia, but he could not see or isolate it. How, then, could it be cultivated? For experimental purposes he used the brains of living rabbits. As soon as Rabbit Number One died, he scraped a part of that rabbit's medulla and inoculated Rabbit Number Two, and so on, rabbit after rabbit. The little animals died at a faster and faster rate, so it seemed evident that the degree of virulence had been increased. Pasteur then sought to reverse the process, which he did by suspending a fragment from the medulla of a diseased rabbit in a sealed tube and letting it dry. The diseased tissue shriveled. After fourteen days what was left of the dried piece of medulla "was crushed and mixed with pure water, and injected under the skin of some dogs." Then day by day the dogs were given stronger and stronger doses, beginning with the medulla dried thirteen days, then using that dried twelve days, and finally that of a rabbit that had just died. The dogs were then exposed to the bites of mad canines. They were immune!

These experiments took years. Finally Pasteur inoculated a little boy bitten by a mad dog and saved his life. The news spread throughout the world. American children, bitten by mad dogs, were sent to Paris by popular subscription. Seven Russian peasants, badly mangled by a mad wolf, came to his laboratory. All were saved by Pasteur.

By 1887 our chemist was at the height of his glory, a world hero. The French Republic, in voting him a pension, neatly summarized the reasons for his fame. His work, it was stated, "may be classed in three series, constituting three great discoveries":

The first one may be formulated thus: *each fermentation is produced by the development of a special microbe.*

The second may be given this formula: *each infectious disease* (those at least that M. Pasteur and his immediate followers have studied) *is produced by the development within the organism of a special microbe.*

The third one may be expressed in this way: *the microbe of an infectious disease, cultivated under certain detrimental conditions, is attenuated in its pathogenic activity; from a virus it has become a vaccine.*

Money now poured in to establish in Paris the Pasteur Institute, presided over by this eminent scientist who hoped to do for diphtheria what he had done for rabies. But that task was left for other hands. Only eight more years Pasteur lived, an honored member of the French Academy, universally acclaimed as the man who had done more for France than any of her children in modern times.

Evolution

While some scientists busied themselves with the chemistry of the solar system and some devoted their labors, like Pasteur, to bacteriology, still others were trying to find out what changes had been wrought by time. Greek philosophers had speculated on this subject, and the idea of a gradually changing world with more effective and more intricate forms of life developing from those more elementary was familiar to Aristotle. The Greeks, however, had few facts upon which to base their theories, and without facts there can be no science. At the time of the Italian Renaissance that universal genius, Leonardo da Vinci, had noted that fossil plants and fossil animals were to be found in the strata of rocks, but their significance escaped him. Not until the very end of the eighteenth century was it possible to do more than vaguely guess at the age of the earth and the changes which had taken place in the life upon it.

New light began to break at this time from two different sources—one, geology; the other, biology. James Hutton (1726-90), a well-to-do Englishman, traveled widely in search of information as to how he might improve his paternal acres. He observed with great interest the stratification of rocks, changes taking place in valleys and river bottoms, the way in which new land was elevated from the sea. He perceived that all rocks were in a state of decay, that the substance out of which they were composed was steadily being conveyed to the sea. So accurate and so minute were his observations in his *Theory of the Earth* (1795) that he has since been hailed as the father of geological science. Before Hutton's day the earth, presumably, had been handed down, more or less complete, by the Almighty to man. Such changes as had taken place on it were believed to have been brought about by sudden catastrophes, such as Noah's flood. This "catastrophic theory" Hutton rejected, and in place of it he substituted "the uniformitarian theory," namely, that change was slow, that change was still going on (evolution). "In the economy of the world," he wrote, "I can find no trace of an origin or the prospect of an end."

Hutton was something of a freethinker in religious matters, and his theory was not taken very seriously until the coming of Sir Charles Lyell (1797-1875), whose *Principles of Geology* was published in three volumes (1830, 1832, 1833). This book contained a wealth of information on geological data known to Hutton only in fragmentary form, information concerning what might be called the evolution of mountains, of glaciers, and of petrified forests transformed into coal. Sir Charles was a man of wealth and diversified scientific interests. He knew a great deal about botany and paleontology, traveled widely, investigated fossils, consulted with conchologists, and supervised edition after edition of this standard book, which, by 1876, had gone through twelve editions. Reluctantly he came to Hutton's conclusion: the uniformitarian theory on the whole was correct. At first inclined to question the hypothesis of Charles Darwin concerning natural selection, Sir Charles Lyell became before his death one of Darwin's most ardent supporters.

Meanwhile, the science of biology, destined before long to become the key science of the nineteenth century, began to attract universal attention. Two Frenchmen and a German played a large part in those biological investigations which led directly to the great contests of the latter part of the century, focussing about Charles Darwin and evolution. Cuvier (1769-1832), throughout the anarchy of revolutionary France, kept aloof from politics and engaged in pure scientific research, studying extinct fossil remains, comparing them with living animal forms, noting points of likeness and of dissimilarity, proving it only reasonable to suppose that changes of some kind had been taking place in animal life. Lamarck (1744-1829), his countryman, was more specific. Appointed professor of zoology at Paris during the Revolution, he specialized in the invertebrates, and by the commencement of the nineteenth century, we find him arguing in favor of the theory of life developing constantly into more highly organized and more complex forms. At a time when Darwin was a little boy, Lamarck was already hinting that the neck of the giraffe grew longer and longer as it reached higher for its food, and that the forefeet of the kangaroo gradually atrophied as it learned to stand upright. In these ideas the work of Lamarck was paralleled by that of a German professor, Treviranus, to whom perhaps should go the credit for inventing the term "biology." Treviranus taught at the beginning of the century that the higher forms of life rose gradually from lower forms, and his *Biologie,* dating back to 1802, attempted to demonstrate this. To all practical purposes, Lamarck and Treviranus were contemporary scientists who made their discoveries independently of one another, and it is almost impossible to decide whether priority belongs to the Frenchman or to the German.

As a matter of fact, the general idea of evolutionary processes was widespread during the first half of the century. It was not simply geologists and biologists who accepted it. Nine years, indeed, before Darwin published his *Origin of Species* (1859), Herbert Spencer argued in his *Social Statics* that human life essentially was a fight in which the weaker inevitably fell by the wayside. And contemporary with Spencer was Alfred Lord Tennyson, who in the very year of the *Social Statics* published *In Memoriam,* a long poem in which doubt (created by evolutionary ideas) struggles hard with inherited Christian dogma, the victory perhaps won by neither side.

Despite these facts, Darwin deservedly is regarded as the father of the theory of evolution. He first turned hazy conjectures not only into workable but seemingly irrefutable hypotheses, producing evidence (tons of it) all pointing straight in the same direction—evidence gathered slowly and pondered over carefully before it was published. No greater scientist, indeed, ever lived, none more cautious, more painstaking, more thorough than this man whose life was devoted most unselfishly to one major end.

Darwin

Charles Darwin (1809-82), born of distinguished parentage, was very delicate as a child, so delicate that he felt compelled to give up medicine, his choice for a profession. An eager and enthusiastic naturalist, he took passage on her majesty's ship *Beagle,* which left England in 1831 on a very long voyage, primarily for purposes of oceanic surveying. The *Beagle* was gone for five years, visiting the west coast of South America, Tasmania, Australia, New Zealand, and a great many other islands in the South Seas, the Indian Ocean, and the South Atlantic. Darwin, the official

CHARLES DARWIN (1809-82)

naturalist, desperately seasick most of the time, clung to his job, and kept very full notes of both flora and fauna. He returned to England and worked hard for eight years, writing a book on barnacles. In 1859 came the most notable of his works, *The Origin of Species;* in 1868 his *Variations of Animals and Plants* (largely an elaboration and defence of *The Origin*); and in 1871 his *Descent of Man,* one of the most controversial books in human history.

The sum of these three volumes is the theory of evolution: namely, that all varieties and species of existing animal life, including man, were not created in the manner described in the book of Genesis, as separate creations brought into existence by a feat of the Almighty but that they developed out of more elementary forms of life. They did so primarily, he contended, as the result of natural selection and secondarily as the result of sexual selection. The second of these two methods, upon which Darwin laid very little stress, may be discarded, for later research has demonstrated that it is of trifling significance. Natural selection, however, sometimes called the struggle for existence, is still generally accepted by scientists. By it is meant that the weaker forms of life and those less suited to their environment disappear and give place to stronger or more adaptable forms suited to survive.

How did this theory originate? Darwin had long been puzzled over the great variety of animal life, both living and extinct. He was, of course, familiar with the ordinary classification of animals into classes, families, genera, species, and races; but what was the explanation for this great variety in the animal kingdom; how account for all extinct animals constantly being discovered; why was it that a great Dane could breed with a sheep dog and produce some kind of dog, whereas it was impossible to breed a great Dane to a sheep, an animal much nearer its size? Why should a horse and a jackass produce a mule, whereas a horse and a cow could not be mated? How account for the infinite variety of pigeons, butterflies, even worms? Was there any general secret which study might disclose?

Darwin's mind played freely over questions of this sort. He had been much impressed by reading Malthus' *Essay on Population,* and that led him to guess that possibly extinct species of animal life had been snuffed out by failure to survive in a competitive world, whereas new ones had gradually risen as slight modifications in physical structure made it possible for certain plants and animals to win out in the fight for survival and to reproduce their kind. Drawing then upon a very extensive body of material, he elaborated this theory, one also arrived at almost simultaneously by another Englishman, Alfred Wallace, as the result of studies in the East Indies.

Evolution was based on natural selection. Supplementary features were sexual selection and the inheritance of acquired characteristics. Since

Darwin's day this theory has been attacked from many angles. Sexual selection has come to be regarded by competent biologists as of slight importance, and the inheritance of acquired characteristics is now generally disbelieved. From this, however, it does not follow that two-thirds of what Darwin stood for has been exploded. Both sexual selection and the inheritance of acquired characteristics are entirely subordinate to the idea of natural selection which was Darwin's great contribution to science.

The theory of natural selection is explained in minute detail in the *Origin of Species*, a superbly written book. The author explains in it how man has artificially changed the shape of sheep and birds and plants by selective breeding, and how competition in a state of nature also brings about changes. He demonstrates pretty conclusively that all varieties of pigeons go back to one common ancestor, the rock pigeon. He makes out a strong case for the horse, the ass, the zebra, and the hemionus all having a common ancestor. The terrific competition among plants and animals for room in which to live and grow, for food to eat, for an opportunity to breed and to reproduce, is demonstrated by illustrations drawn from all sorts and varieties of plant and animal life. Variations from the normal consequently are given a decided advantage in this "struggle for existence"—words borrowed from Herbert Spencer which Darwin says are equivalent to his own phrase, natural selection. These slight variations which enable forms of life to adapt themselves better to new environments lead in turn to new varieties of plants and animals. There is, for instance, the water ouzel, a bird which has developed wings used for swimming under water; there are flying squirrels which "have their limbs and even the base of the tail united by a broad expanse of skin, which serves as a parachute"; there is that delicate instrument, the eye, which has become so highly sensitized in eagles but on the contrary has tended to atrophy in those animals which need it no longer, as the mole; there is the unique tail of the giraffe which serves its humble purpose as a fly-swatter; there is the swim-bladder in fishes which "shows us clearly the important fact that an organism originally constructed for one purpose, namely flotation, may be converted into a widely different purpose, namely respiration."

Darwin, we must remember, was first of all a botanist, and the *Origin of Species* draws most of its argument from plant life. And as an illustration of his loving and detailed study of flowers consider this description of a certain orchid which

has part of its labellum or lower lip hollowed out into a great bucket, into which drops of almost pure water continually fall from two secreting horns which stand above it; and when the bucket is half full, the water overflows by a spout on one side. The basal part of the labellum stands over the bucket, and is itself hollowed out into a sort of chamber with two lateral entrances; within this chamber there are curious fleshy ridges. The most ingenious man, if he had not witnessed what takes place, could never have imagined what purpose all these parts serve. But Dr. Crüger saw crowds of large bumble-bees visiting the gigantic flowers of this orchid, not in order to suck nectar, but to gnaw off the ridges within the chamber above the bucket; in doing this they frequently pushed each other into the bucket, and their wings being thus wetted they could not fly away, but were compelled to crawl out through the passage formed by the spout or overflow. Dr. Crüger saw a "continual procession" of bees thus crawling out of their involuntary bath. The passage is narrow, and is roofed over by the column, so that a bee, in forcing its way out, first rubs its back against the viscid stigma and then against the viscid glands of the pollen-masses. The pollen-masses are thus glued to the back of the bee which first happens to crawl out through the passage of a lately expanded flower, and are thus carried away. Dr. Crüger sent me a flower in spirits of wine, with a bee which he had killed before it had quite crawled out with a pollen-mass still fastened to its back. When the bee, thus provided, flies to another flower, or to the same flower a second time, and is pushed by its comrades into the bucket and then crawls out by the passage, the pollen-mass necessarily comes first into contact with the viscid stigma, and adheres to it, and the flower is fertilized. Now at last we see the full use of every part of the flower, of the water-secreting horns, of the bucket half full of water, which prevents the bees from flying away, and forces them to crawl out through the spout, and rub against the properly placed viscid pollen-masses and the viscid stigma.

But the man best fitted to explain Darwin was not Darwin himself but T. H. Huxley (1825-95). *The Origin of Species* is not difficult to follow, but it is difficult to compress, a fact due to the wealth of data in it and a reluctance on the part of the author boldly to generalize. Huxley was a famous scientist in his own right; but he never hesitated to generalize and he did so in such pure and limpid English that his meaning is always clear. He drew his inspiration from Darwin but his work complements rather than merely supplements that of his celebrated contemporary. Known as the "bull-dog of Darwin," Huxley speedily became the foremost champion and interpreter of his modest friend to the public. Darwin was in very fragile health and was forced to lead a retired life; Huxley, a robust fighter (very frequently, one suspects, for the love of it), made it his particular business both to defend and to explain the work of Darwin whom he always regarded as finding the key to life's mysteries in natural selection. In Huxley's *Evidence as to Man's Place in Nature*, in his *Lectures to Workingmen*, and his *Lay Sermons, Addresses and Reviews*, he tells us in a few words what Darwin was driving at. It may be understood in four paragraphs.

To a certain sheep in Massachusetts there had been born a ewe with legs shorter than customary. That biological "sport," or variant from the normal, had been kept for breeding purposes, the other sheep in the herd being sold for meat. The sheep whose life had been saved produced other sheep, and some of these were short-legged, others had normal limbs. The

THOMAS HENRY HUXLEY (1825-95)

constant killing of the normal sheep and the artificial preservation of the life of the short-legged sheep had produced a new race of sheep, the "ancon," all with short legs. This was artificial selection.

Meanwhile, there was born in Malta a man with an extra finger on one hand; he married and some of his children had the extra finger and some did not. The children married as did their children, the ultimate result being that no more babies appeared with the additional digit—the unusual biological "sport" disappeared. What was the inference? The sheep with the short legs survived; there was reason for its survival. There was, however, no advantage to be gained from having an extra finger. In fact there was a disadvantage, since the man with an additional finger might have more difficulty in obtaining a mate in comparison with one with the orthodox ten digits. Here, then, was a hint as to how nature worked; here was "natural selection." In a state of nature when a biological "sport" is born it has a better chance of surviving and reproducing its own kind of abnormality if the latter quality helps it in the competitive struggle for existence, the reverse being also true.

For instance: Paleontology fully proved that the horse originally was much smaller than at present and was equipped with several toes. As time passed the toes became one, the horse larger and swifter. What could this signify? Presumably, if a three-toed mare gave birth to a two-toed foal, a biological "sport," the foal would have a better chance of surviving than his brothers with three toes. He could run faster and thus escape his enemies; he could run faster and therefore might have a better opportunity of catching a mare and mating. Gradually, then, the three-toed horses became extinct and eventually so also the two-toed variety, until by evolution the horse with one toe—a hoof—became the standard horse.

Here at last was a hypothesis into which almost all facts fitted. The tiger and the lion, different species, both belonged to the cat family. What could be more natural than for those members of the family living in India to develop handsome stripes, for a striped cat would be concealed by the flickering light which penetrated the jungle. On the other hand, a striped cat would be noticed from afar on the open uplands of Africa, whereas one dun-colored would be less visible and therefore better suited to pounce upon prey at the water-hole. From the huge horns of the bull-moose (convenient for digging up frozen lily pads) to the most insignificant insect with protective coloration like that of the bark on which it lived, the mutabilities of all animal life could be explained.

The publication of *The Origin of Species* created a furor, particularly in the religious world. God, supposedly, had created all living creatures, each after its own kind, and evolution seemingly contradicted this special act of creation. Long before Darwin's day the multiplicity of species had thrown doubt on the story of Noah's ark; for how could the ark possibly have been the haven of refuge for so many animals? For the time being, this difficulty had been surmounted by increasing the size of the ark to incredible proportions. Even when that was done there remained the mystery of the kangaroo in Australia and the turkey in America, both far distant from Mount Ararat upon which the ark had rested. The suggestion that angels had conveyed two of each of these species to their respective habitats seemed fanciful; but how otherwise had they made the journey? The problem of extinct fossil remains also at one time had caused fluttering in ecclesiastical dovecotes. Could it have been, as some thought, that God had made the dinosaur purely for experimental purposes, afterward to throw it away in displeasure? Conjectures such as these had long been prevalent in Western Europe. *The Origin of Species* awakened them again; it did far more—it led to speculation as to whether man himself had even been the object of a special act of creation. Possibly man was but one of many animals, far removed, indeed, but none the less, blood brother to both ox and ape!

Darwin did not dodge the issue and in his third major book, *The Descent of Man,* he advanced the hypothesis that man himself had evolved out of earlier and more simple forms of life and that of all existing animals the ape was man's nearest cousin in the animal world.

The argument to prove this so was threefold:

    I. General physical structure

   II. Rudimentary survivals

   III. Embryology

Let us examine them. First, in regard to general physical structure, it was evident that man resembled the other mammals to an extraordinary degree. All mammals have two eyes, one nose, one mouth, two ears, a stomach, excretory organs, a heart, two lungs, and all in the same relative position. They all depend upon the heart to pump the blood in a circulatory fashion through the lungs, where it is revivified by oxygen. These facts seemed to argue a common origin.

Secondly, as to the survival of rudimentary organs and features. There was the appendix, a large and healthy organ in the cow, a useless and shriveled appendage in man. But the cow, a ruminating animal living on grain, has need of an appendix; man has the appendix but has no use for it. Why, then, should it be found in the human body? The presumption was clear; the appendix was a vestigial survival of man's early origins. Every human being has nerves which connect with the muscles of the abdomen. The wires, however, are down. For most humans it is impossible to twitch the abdomen; but a horse or cow can do so with ease. Why should these vestigial remains be in man?

Again, all human beings have a vestigial tail at the end of their spines.

The wires (nerves) are down but the remains of a tail exist. Why? Did our ancestors find one convenient? The human viscera are contained in a sack, apparently useless. If, however, we walked on all fours nothing would be more useful than that sack, which would act like a corset—that is, if the wires worked once more and conveyed a message from the brain which would result in the constriction of the sack.

Finally comes the argument from embryology. The history of the embryo in the human womb was carefully studied. The fœtus, soon after conception, looks very much like a fish; after some months it looks like a dog; only a month or so before birth does it take on human shape. The very womb of the mother offers corroborative evidence of evolution and of man's relationship to the lower animals.

Evolution and Religion

Such a hypothesis was infinitely more important to revealed religion than any question of Noah and his flood. The religious-minded now experienced a genuine shock, quite comparable to that produced by Galileo when he proved that the earth revolved about the sun and not vice versa. Galileo seemed to demonstrate that it was highly improbable that the earth could be the center of the universe and thereby the especially prepared stage for God's drama of redemption. But Darwin seemed to demonstrate that even on this little planet, man was not unique. He was simply *primus inter pares,* first among many animals, a kind of cousin to the dog and salamander, a slightly nearer second cousin to the monkey tribe. If this was true it certainly was very startling, also shocking, to many who were inclined to look up to their forebears with respect. It did not seem a very aristocratic theory; it might unsettle the lower classes. As one old lady in England was said to have remarked to another, "Descended from monkeys? My dear, I trust that it is not true; but if it is, let us pray that it may not become widely known."

But above all, it seemed an irreligious theory to many, since it was in flat contradiction to the story of creation as given in Genesis. The more enlightened clerics, to be sure, had long been accustomed to regard Genesis as a poetic myth, valuable as a record of the spiritual tradition of humanity, rather than as an accurate account of creation; but the average man who read his Bible had not been accustomed to think thus, and he was not inclined to surrender his beliefs offhand when challenged by a theory which he did not understand.

In the last analysis, it was not Genesis but personal immortality which was threatened. If from amœba to man it should become possible to draw a straight line of descent, what then would become of belief in life after death? No evolutionists of standing claimed that man was descended from the apes; but almost all evolutionists agreed that man and the apes had a common ancestor. Did that ancestor possess an immortal soul? If he did not, at what particular moment in the age-long upward climb of man from lower forms of animal life was the gift of this soul bestowed upon man?

The attack of the religious-minded upon evolution which followed the publication of Darwin's books was sudden, immediate, violent, and now so largely a thing of the past that books bearing upon that subject for the most part have been relegated to the more obscure corners of our libraries, where they do nothing but gather dust. The first volley asserted that Darwin did not know what he was talking about, and a number of reputable scientists sharply challenged him on a number of points. The biologist answered these questions in later editions of the Origin, courteously, fully, and for the most part satisfactorily, so that most of the scientists who had been in opposition changed their minds and accepted the main Darwinian contention of natural selection. Then came the second volley, namely, that Darwin had discovered nothing new, an accusation true up to a certain point, for it was not so much evolution which Darwin had discovered as it was a convincing hypothesis for describing how evolution worked. No single person, of course, discovered evolution.

The enemies of the new theory were not always scrupulous as to their methods, and Wilberforce, Bishop of Oxford, put himself into a very bad position by sneering at Huxley as claiming ancestry from an ape. The scientist's retort was instant: "I would rather be descended from a humble ape than to trace my ancestry to one who used his ability and power to discredit and to crush those who sought for truth." But to be fair to the churchmen, it must be admitted that they were not alone in making verbal onslaughts. The shock troops of the scientists and Huxley himself knew how to use strong language.

Curiously enough, evolution caused far less trouble among Catholics than among Protestants. It is true that the Vatican thundered immediately against the new theory and Pope Pius IX wrote: "Pride goes so far as to degrade man himself to the level of unreasoning brutes." But this reaction of the Holy Father, one suspects, was somewhat temporary, and Catholics soon ceased to contend as Catholics against Darwin. Primarily, this was due to the fact that Catholics placed less emphasis on the Old Testament than Protestants, basing authority in religion not simply on the Bible, but on the whole body of sacred literature, including the Church Fathers as interpreted by the Church. The Catholic Church, on the whole, paid very little attention to organic evolution. It regarded it somewhat askance as a doubtful theory but one which did not concern religion. The authority of the Church, it asserted, began after man was endowed by his Maker with an immortal soul, not before. If man existed prior to that date, and if he was descended from lower animals, that had no bearing on religion. To quote from an authoritative Catholic book on the subject: [1]

The Church says:

1. There is nothing in this notion intrinsically repugnant either to the Scriptures or to Faith;

2. She will not affirm it, even supposing it were true, because it is not her business to make such affirmations;

3. Since she has not yet, in her practical judgment, obtained proofs from science of a sufficiently high order of moral certitude, she will not permit any-one to assert it as a fact while speaking in her name;

4. When and if it receives physical proof as certain as (let us say) that en-joyed by the theory of gravitation when it left the hands of Newton and Kepler, it will no doubt be included in the regular programme of her scholastic establishments;

5. Taking it as a "possible hypothesis" (as derivative creation applied to animals lower than man is taken for a "probable hypothesis"), Catholics may freely work toward its establishment, by research and discussion;

6. If anyone chooses to make it a purely personal belief, he may.

The Protestants soon divided into two groups: one, composed of the stricter sects, would have nothing to do with Darwin or his theories and stuck to a literal interpretation of Holy Writ; the other, composed of those Protestant groups which were either more liberal or more Laodi-cean in their outlook (as in general was the Church of England and her sister church in America, the Protestant Episcopal), soon began to make compromises and to accept the idea that man came from lower forms of animal life. These Protestants took the point of view that there could be no real conflict ever between science and religion; that the scientists probably knew what they were talking about; that religion, after all in human history, had been a force the early manifestations of which necessarily had been crude and that it, too, had undergone evolution to blossom forth finally in Christianity. Their attitude toward organic evolu-tion (in so far as they paid any attention to it at all) was summed up rather fairly by a Scottish divine, Henry Drummond, who wrote in his *Ascent of Man* that, even as the vegetable kingdom has its roots in the mineral kingdom, so did the animals have their roots in the vegetable kingdom and man his roots in the animal kingdom. This was to man's credit, rather than otherwise, for it demonstrated that life was moving ever upward, an idea expressed by Tennyson when he wrote,

Rise upward working through the beast
And let the ape and tiger die.

[1] De Ternant, *Some Pathfinders of Organic Evolution* (1928), published by Burns, Oates & Washbourne, Ltd., London. Quoted in E. C. Messinger, *Evolution and Theology.*

Many liberal Protestants went even farther and came to regard Darwin as almost a kind of religious prophet, since he weaned man away from the cold and unattractive notion that he was a kind of fallen angel and instead made him more humble and warm-hearted by realizing "his kith and kin in Saint Francis's little birds." As for the immortality, they tended to pay very little attention to it, although some went so far as to argue that belief in personal immortality was a selfish thing anyway, that what was far more important was the future of the race, and that men should be content to find immortality in their children.

The victory of organic evolution was not due to the weight of scientific evidence alone. Darwin had simply advanced a hypothesis and had not actually proved that new species came from more simple and less generalized forms. The weight of evidence to support this hypothesis was very strong and grew cumulatively more so; but no scientist yet has even seen a true species develop out of other species. Furthermore, the overwhelming emphasis placed on environmental influences by the Darwinian theory was greatly weakened when Gregor Mendel, an Austrian monk, proved rather conclusively from long experimentation with the breeding of peas that heredity was a far more important factor in plant and animal life than Darwin had credited it with being. We must therefore look elsewhere to understand why theological resistance to organic evolution gave way so speedily.

Two reasons explain why this happened: (1) the way in which the theory of organic evolution fitted in with the psychology of the well-to-do; (2) the contemporaneous emergence of two new sciences deriving their theoretical approach to a considerable degree from evolutionary methods, namely, anthropology and biblical criticism.

Already it has been shown in this book (see p. 238) how comforting to successful and prosperous people were the conclusions of Malthus. But that philosopher and Darwin were popularly and properly linked together in the minds of most people, since organic evolution was a kind of Malthusian doctrine (survival of the fittest) applied to plants and animals. This fact instantly was made use of by the supporters of the status quo to refute sentimental social reformers who believed that modern treatment of the lame, the halt, and the blind was too unfair and cruel. If natural history taught that the big fish always swallowed the little, then it was to be expected that human history would teach the same lesson. Evolution was a two-edged sword, to be sure, as the Marxian socialists promptly noted. But this fact did not disturb the possessing classes, who realized that Darwin not only did out threaten their comfortable security but that he gave arguments (by analogy) to justify it. The enormous influence of Herbert Spencer's books is good evidence of this rapprochement between capitalistic society and the Darwinian theory. Spencer, in volume after volume, tried to demonstrate that all

life in every particular is an evolution from the simple to the heterogeneous, and that any interference therewith by society would inevitably
retard progress. The theory of evolution, it is interesting to note, met
even at the beginning with relatively little resistance in wealthy universities, a circumstance which might be interpreted as due to the encouragement given to research, and therefore to truth, by wealth; or as
due to the psychology of those groups which found support for private
property in the new doctrine.

More important, probably, was the fact that theologians soon discovered more dangerous dynamite in anthropology and in higher criticism
than ever was to be met with in organic evolution. Anthropology,
naturally, received a great stimulus from biological research. If in the
animal world the struggle for existence was the key to change, and if
men came from the animals, presumably the various races of mankind
underwent a similar competition. To prove this it was necessary to study
the various human races, which led direct to the study of "pre-history"
(history before written records) and the study of primitive races, surviving specimens of which presumably would throw light on the evolution of the more advanced races. Studies of this nature inevitably led to
theories concerning the origin of religious ideas and the significance of
myths.

A book teeming with information of this sort was written by Sir James
Frazer in 1890. His *Golden Bough,* destined to go through many editions
and to increase in size until it was swollen to twelve volumes, has much
to say about the relationship of religion to magic. Consider these two
sentences in it: "By eating the body of the god he (man) shares in the
god's attributes and powers. And when the god is a corn-god, the corn
is his proper body; when he is a wine-god, the juice of the grape is his
blood; and so, by eating the bread and drinking the blood wine, the
worshipers partake of the real body and blood of his god." The above is
but one of many illustrations which seemed to show that Christian ritual
was the outgrowth of magical practice. To many of the religious-minded,
such evidence seemed disquieting, and as the anthropologists dug up
more and more parallels between magic and religion, readjustments in
religious thought were inevitable.

More important was the application of evolutionary ideas to the Holy
Scriptures. Innumerable scholars, captivated by the general notion of
evolution, began to analyze the sources of both the Old and New Testa-
ments in order to show how these two parts of the Bible evolved from
earlier and more fragmentary sources. They began doing this before
Darwin put pen to paper, but they worked more intensively and also more
feverishly at their task after Darwin wrote than before. The new evidence
dug up by these so-called higher critics seemed to show that Moses could
not possibly have written the Pentateuch (the first five books of the Bible)

but that they were composed of three separate strands or earlier narratives woven together. The Ten Commandments, supposedly handed down from on high by Moses, seemed to have been copied from earlier codes. Certain of the prophecies in the Old Testament under scrutiny were also held to be written after and not before the events prophesied took place.

Now when we remember that the validity of the Christian religion was conceived of by many as resting on the validity of the prophecies in the Old Testament and upon the miracles of the New, the seriousness of these reputed discoveries becomes apparent.

But the scholars did not rest content with the Old Testament. Applying similar methods to the New Testament, they began to throw doubt on the validity of many miracles in it. The little star of Bethlehem, for instance, did not shine quite as bright in the imagination of many after they read of historical records antedating the New Testament sources which stated that the births of certain famous men were heralded by a star. The virgin birth of Jesus also was disputed, some scholars endeavoring to show that contradictions among the gospels as to how Jesus came into the world and as to his genealogy made this miracle doubtful. Other miracles were accounted for in part by the superstitions of the age, in part by the way in which some men by their magnetism are able to cure certain types of nervous diseases. Even the resurrection from the dead was questioned.

Prominent among these critics was David Friedrich Strauss (1808-74), a Protestant theologian who gave up lecturing at Tübingen to devote all of his time to a *Life of Jesus* which was published as early as 1835. The book created a great furor, no less in England than in Germany, and Strauss continued to be the main vortex of a great scholastic war down to the end of the century, his *Old and New Faith* (1872) going to sixteen editions. The *Life of Jesus* is both long and erudite. Probably nothing is more complicated in the world of scholarship than the reconstruction of what took place in Palestine during the days of Christ. Our historical sources are scanty and our dates uncertain. The Gospel of John is different in tone from the first three gospels, and there can be no certainty as to who wrote it or when. The other three gospels (the synoptics) are not three separate accounts of three different eye-witnesses but are composed in part of fragmentary earlier sources called "logia," or oral sayings passed down from mouth to mouth. Strauss's book deals with such matters in ways infinitesimally minute. Did Jesus rise from the dead? The choice, according to Strauss, for "the cultivated intellect" lies either upon believing that "Jesus was not really dead, or that he did not really rise again." A long and complicated argument is then given to support either thesis. Strauss did not believe in miracles, but that does not mean that his book was irreverent. Nor may he justly be accused of being shallow. His *Life of Jesus* resembles Darwin's *Origin of Species* in its careful and scrupulous reference to authorities and sources and its patient examination of facts. So anxious, however, is Strauss to discard miracles that his argument as to why certain ones could not have happened becomes almost as mysterious as the mystery he is attempting to unravel. The author, we must remember, was not trying to undermine Christianity: he was trying to purify it. "The supernatural birth of Christ, His miracles and Ascension," he assures us, "remain eternal truths whatever doubts may be cast upon their reality as facts." In these words may be found the point of view of Protestant higher critics and Catholic modernists alike.

Another writer to forward a religious revolution in the nineteenth century was Ernest Renan (1823-92). He was the author of a *Life of Jesus* (1863) which in some ways was the antithesis of that by Strauss. As a young man, Renan was an ardent and zealous Catholic whose original intention of entering the Church had been ended by disbelief in the Mosaic authorship of the Pentateuch. Sensitive, artistic, and literary, Renan was also a good scholar and for a time professor of Hebrew at the Collège de France. But there is very little pure scholarship in his brief story of Jesus' life, which is a charming psychological interpretation of the founder of Christianity. Renan is not troubled about the virgin birth, miracles, or the resurrection. More important to him is the Sea of Galilee by which Jesus taught, which he pictures to us in living words. More important yet is that we should glimpse the real Jesus. In the same way that a partly unfinished portrait may tell us more of human character than the more candid camera, so it is possible that 300 short pages of Renan may give us more of Jesus' personality than 1,000 long pages of Strauss. Renan's hero was man, not God, a man-child born to Joseph and Mary whose gospel of love and kindliness has universal application and will last forever. It is based upon "the sermon on the mount, the apotheosis of the weak, the love of the people, the taste for poverty, the renovation of all that is humble, true and simple." We must pardon Jesus, he tells us, "His expectation of an empty apocalypse, of a coming in great triumph upon the clouds of heaven. Perhaps this was the error of others rather than His own, and if it is true that He shared in the illusion of all, what matters it, since his dreams rendered him strong against death, and sustained him in a struggle without which He might have been unequal."

The spirit of Jesus' life and teachings is what Renan is concerned with. The miracles are immaterial, the mass is immaterial, the incarnation is immaterial, even the resurrection in any physical sense is immaterial. Renan says that Jesus' life came to an end with his death. The vision of the empty tomb and of the risen Christ he attributes to the overwrought imagination of Mary Magdalen. "Divine power of love, sacred moment in which the passion of a hallucinated woman gave to the world a resurrected Christ."

Since Strauss wrote long before Darwin, and Renan's *Life* came out only four years after the *Origin of Species*, it is evident that Darwin and the biologists can not be held responsible for the heretical ideas of these two scholars. The truth is that organic evolution and biblical criticism were parallel movements and were brought about by a general evolutionary attitude of mind which sought to interpret *all* ideas and *all* institutions as slowly changing and taking on new meaning. Evolution was a kind of revolution taking place in men's minds which led some to give an evolutionary interpretation to religious faith, others an evolutionary character to the forms of animal life, and still others an evolutionary explanation to political phenomena, an idea very clearly expressed in Walter Bagehot's *Physics and Politics* (1871), a book from which Woodrow Wilson was to draw much inspiration. In politics and in pure science, the opposition to evolution was not unduly prolonged. Not so, however, in regard to religion.

The Roman Catholic Church withstood the shock of new ideas in regard to the sacred writings more successfully than the Protestant bodies. In the midst of victories won all along the line by evolutionary ideas, that Church was able to rebuff all attack and to retain safe in the fold almost all of its clergy and of its laity who were inclined to stray from it. The Church, indeed, made its dogmas more affirmative rather than weakening them, and sharply defined its position on the new ideas by a number of decrees. The first, under the pontificate of Pius IX, made it obligatory among Catholics to accept the dogma of the Immaculate Conception. By this it was *not* meant that the Virgin Mary was conceived by the Holy Ghost as was her Son; rather it was affirmed that the mother of God, although having a human father, did not inherit any taint of original sin as did other human beings. Before the promulgation of this dogma in 1854 it had been optional to accept or to reject the theory of the Immaculate Conception. After this date the option no longer was permitted. In 1864 followed the far more general *Syllabus of Errors* in which Pius IX made a slashing attack on liberalism all along the line, including freemasonry, socialism, communism, naturalism, various kinds of rationalism, and the higher criticism, culminating in error number eighty which read: "The Roman Pontiff can and ought to reconcile himself to and agree with progress, liberalism and modern civilization." These eighty errors, starkly put, might appear to indicate that the Catholic Church was hostile to almost everything which had taken place in Europe since the Middle Ages. Such an interpretation would be unfair. What the Pope meant was that the Church was opposed to the idea of progress as summed up purely in terms of material achievement; that the

Church was opposed to liberalism in so far as it implied a belief in laissez-faire economics and the atomic philosophy of Jeremy Bentham whereby the good of all was considered best assured by the separate and selfish assertion of the individual will; that the Church was opposed to modern civilization in so far as the latter rested upon godlessness.

Pius IX also tightened the reins of authority still further when the Vatican Council of 1870, the first general council of the Church for hundreds of years, decided after prolonged debate to issue the decree of Papal Infallibility. By this it was *not* meant that the Pope could do no wrong, and by it was *not* meant that every time he wrote a letter or preached a sermon his utterances were binding on Catholics. What it did mean was that when the Pope spoke *ex cathedra,* formally, from St. Peter's chair, on matters of faith and morals, what he said was infallible.

Finally, higher criticism, called by Catholics "modernism," was stamped out by putting certain enumerated books on the index, by the use of ex-communication applied against certain recalcitrant Catholic modernists, and by the encyclical, *De Pascendi* (1907) of Pius X which defined in set terms the errors of modernistic thought.

These errors the Church regarded as fundamental attacks on Roman Catholicism. The Church spent no time worrying about the lack of scientific knowledge displayed by those who wrote the Bible under the inspiration of the Holy Ghost. As Pope Leo XIII stated in 1893, they "did not seek to penetrate the secrets of nature, but rather described and dealt with things in more or less figurative language, or in terms which were commonly used at the time. . . ." What did disturb the Church were the writings of Catholic priests, like the learned Loisy of France, which hinted at a slowly changing religious faith adapting itself to the needs of the hour. Loisy, for instance, argued that the Trinity and the Incarna-tion were Greek in origin, becoming attached to Christianity by a kind of syncretism, and that religious dogmas were not immutable, "applicable for all times and for all men."

Teachings such as this were regarded as "modernistic" and not to be tolerated. In accordance with Catholic theology, certain tenets of the Church are susceptible of proof, such as the existence of God, the deity of Christ, and the Petrine claim, whereas certain other tenets are to be accepted as a matter of faith, such as the Trinity and the miracle of the Mass. But in no case is religion to be considered as based simply on natural human experience, transitory or otherwise. Therefore, on that account the Church excommunicated Loisy, who refused to recant, and the heresy of modernism came practically to an end.

The various Protestant churches were much more seriously affected than the Roman Catholic by the way in which scientific scholars insisted that the Bible should be treated as other books. Holy Writ occupied a far more important position in the general Protestant scheme of things than in the Catholic, and the Protestant clergy were not subject to strict discipline, as were their Catholic brothers. It is true that, apart from the Congregationalists and Baptists, most Protestant sects had bishops, or synods, or conferences which exercised a modicum of control over ministers, particularly in licensing them to preach. But once the license was granted and the candidate admitted to Holy Orders or to the ministry, the likelihood of any trial for heresy or the formal unfrocking of a "liberal" clergyman with "liberal" ideas was slight.

Certain happenings in the Church of England during the second half of the nineteenth century illustrate this neatly. That church was rocked to its foundations by the publication in 1860 of *Essays and Reviews* written by six Anglican clergymen and one Anglican layman. It was a moderately liberal book and took the point of view that the analysis of authorship, date, and meaning of the various parts of the Bible ought to be carried on in the same way and by the same method which would apply to any other book—Homer, for instance. This idea infuriated Wilberforce, Bishop of Oxford, who made such a stir that two of the authors were suspended from their functions by their ecclesiastical superiors. Whereupon an appeal was taken to the law courts. The decision handed down by the Lord Chancellor of England was in the favor of the two authors. The Chancellor did not find, he said, "in the formularies of the English Church any such distinct declaration upon the subject as to require it to punish the expression of a hope by a clergyman that even the ultimate pardon of the wicked who are condemned in the day of judgment may be consistent with the will of Almighty God."

Now the two archbishops of the Church of England were among the judges who dissented from this opinion, and the convocation of the Church condemned it. Nevertheless, the ecclesiastics were helpless and the bishops, it is quite evident in this matter, had no authority over simple priests who appealed to Cæsar, and not in vain. "Hell dismissed with costs" was the popular version of this lawsuit.

Another interesting case arose shortly after, as the result of an effort to discipline an Anglican missionary, Bishop Colenso of Natal. Colenso found it embarrassing to explain to his Zulu converts certain statements in the Old Testament—how, for instance, a multitude of Hebrews with all their cattle could have sustained life for forty years in the little pocket-handkerchief of a desert in which they were said to have wandered, a desert only about forty square miles in area. In consequence the inquiring Zulus were told that stories like these were myths, a pronunciamento vastly annoying to the ecclesiastical authorities who, in the person of the Primate of South Africa, Bishop Gray, excommunicated Colenso. Again came an appeal to the Crown, and again a potential heretic was supported by Her Majesty's government. The judicial committee of the Privy Council set aside the excommunication and restored Colenso's salary.

Whereupon rigorous churchmen were indignant and Bishop Gray anathematized the decision as a "masterpiece of Satan." But the average Englishman, one suspects, thought the case well summarized in the contemporary limerick:

> A bishop there was of Natal,
> Who had a Zulu for a pal;
> Said the Zulu, "My dear,
> Don't you think Genesis queer?"
> Which converted my lord of Natal.

Excommunication and the spirit of Protestantism did not go very well together. The so-called "liberals" in the Protestant churches did not escape free from censure, and the battle between them and the conservatives (in America known as fundamentalists) swung back and forth as it does to this day. But whenever any considerable body of public opinion supported the radical clergyman, disciplinary measures almost always proved ineffective. Furthermore, there was always one way of escape left open for him: he might leave the denomination to which he belonged and join one more liberal, or even become the pastor of an independent church not affiliated with any denomination. In consequence the Protestant bodies, with very few exceptions, were powerless to prevent the spread of evolutionary ideas as applied to the books of the Bible.

Christianity and the Social Gospel

Christianity in the nineteenth century, meanwhile, was confronted by another problem quite as serious as that created by organic evolution, anthropology, or biblical criticism. What should be the relation of the Church to the new social order brought about by the Industrial Revolution? Did the capitalistic system of economics concern religion or not? To what extent were Christians, as such, obligated to right alleged wrongs perpetrated by imaginative entrepreneurs and far-seeing bankers on those more stupid, more careless, and more lazy, or at least less lucky, less provident, and less selfish men and women who made up the working class? And just what did Jesus mean by "Thy Kingdom come on earth..."?

Protestants and Catholics alike were perplexed by questions of this sort, and throughout the last half of the century there was a noticeable tendency among religious writers to formulate an answer. A goodly number thought that a definite stand must be taken by the churches in regard to social questions. Some of these were radicals in matters of doctrine, believing that Christianity could only conquer by the denial of such ancient dogmas as the Incarnation, the Atonement, and the Resurrection; others were of the reverse opinion, combining with strict religious orthodoxy the most unorthodox opinions concerning wages, profits, and even the taking of interest; and still others, anxious to forget or at least to minimize doctrinal disputes, simply ignored them to devote their energy to such mundane affairs as decent sanitation, good housing, employment and the lack of it.

One of the early leaders of "social Christianity" was Charles Kingsley (1819-75), an Anglican priest who championed the cause of the poor, was sympathetic toward the Chartists, and was known as a Christian socialist. Marx usually has been credited with the slogan: "Religion is the opiate of the people." But years earlier Kingsley wrote: "We have used the Bible as if it were the special constable's handbook—*an opium dose for keeping beasts of burden patient while they were being overloaded*—a mere book to keep the poor in order." Kingsley was a highly honored Englishman, a professor of history at Cambridge, a canon of Westminster, and the author of several histories and novels. As a rural clergyman he had become indignant at the wretched housing of farm laborers; as a student of Chartism he had investigated at first hand the industrial conditions in British cities, particularly those affecting the needle trades. He held that Christianity and socialism must go hand in hand. "Even the strangest and most monstrous forms of socialism," he asserted, "are at bottom but Christian heresies." And again, "every socialist system which has endeavored to stand alone has hitherto in practice been either blown up or dissolved away; whilst almost every socialist system which has maintained itself for any time has endeavored to stand, or unconsciously to itself has stood, upon those moral grounds of righteousness, self-sacrifice, mutual affection, common brotherhood which Christianity vindicates to itself for an everlasting heritage." The Gospel Kingsley held to be "incompatible with a political economy which proclaims self-interest to be the very pivot of social action."

Kingsley was nothing if not bold—that is, in theory. When it came, however, to showing just how the Kingdom of God on earth was to be brought about, he was most mild. His constructive ideas apparently went no further than to suggest that workingmen should as producers form their own coöperative associations, from which all Christians should buy, and to which wealthy and pious Christians would lend money at a low rate of interest. The clergyman apparently believed that this once done the millennium would dawn.

The social conscience of many other British clergymen was aroused. Prominent among them was William Booth (1829-1912), the founder of the Salvation Army. In 1890 Booth published *In Darkest England and the Way Out,* full of pitiful descriptions of the way in which the British poor lived. Booth suggested the founding of three colonies, one urban, one rural, and a third overseas for the rehabilitation and succor of England's poor. And another clergyman of influence whose name deserves to be linked with that of Booth and Kingsley was Bishop Gore of Oxford, a man whose doctrinal orthodoxy was unimpeachable but whose economic views the English upper class found disturbing. Gore not only had many kind things to say about socialism, but he went so far as to combine it in a mystic way with the Christian dogma of the incarnation. The bishop belonged to the High Church group of the Church of England, many of whom called themselves Anglo-Catholics. Among the latter the growth of semi-socialistic ideas toward the end of the century was pronounced. The reason therefor was evident: The Anglo-Catholics found much of their inspiration in the Middle Ages, a time when capitalism was scarcely even in bud, when craftguilds contained masters, journeymen, and apprentices, all coöperative together. The medieval notion of a "just price" a price not determined by supply and demand but by the amount of human sweat and skill that went into the making of commodities—appealed to the Anglo-Catholics, and therefore in economics their ideas were frequently as radical as they were conservative in all that concerned dogma and ritual.

This same combination of orthodox theology with a tendency to a more sympathetic attitude toward the working classes in economic matters characterized the Roman Catholic Church, even more so in fact than the Protestant bodies. Socialism was growing everywhere during the last quarter of the century, particularly among the city proletariat in France, Germany, and Belgium, a proletariat mainly Catholic in tradition. And socialists were all too apt to teach that the Christian religion, or any religion, for that matter, was opposed to the interests of the workers. To combat this idea and to deal with labor unrest everywhere, many prominent ecclesiastics of the old Church were outspoken in their views.

In England Cardinal Manning, always rigidly orthodox in dogma, openly sided with labor unions and quoted Saint Thomas Aquinas to the effect that all goods are by nature communal and that he who appropriates from the common store in time of dire need commits no sin. In Germany Bishop von Ketteler (1811-77) challenged sharply the theory that wages should be determined by supply and demand, and agreed with Manning that the rights of private property should be strictly limited.

In Italy, in 1891, the Pope himself clarified the position of the Roman Catholic Church in regard to labor and capital, and in a famous encyclical, *Rerum Novarum*, contended most vigorously against Marx. The socialist champion had denounced surplus value as wealth stolen from the worker; but Leo XIII maintained that private property could not be confiscated by the state since it was a natural right, a right which antedated human society, a right inherent in man's being something different from an unthinking and irresponsible beast. But the Pontiff also

CARDINAL MANNING (1808-92)

said that "the Church was concerned with the *material* welfare of the poor" as well as with their spiritual well-being. He said that all men are entitled to receive wages above the mere subsistence level, wages which will enable them to live in "frugal comfort," to support families, and even to save something over, with which they may hope to become property-owners.

His Holiness went further. Religion, he asserted, should extend its special protection to the weak. Children should not enter workshops "until their bodies and minds are sufficiently mature." Women are entitled to special consideration. "Those who labor in mines and quarries and who work within the bowels of the earth should have shorter hours. . . ." Adequate time must be given to all workers for rest. The latter should be encouraged to organize associations among themselves for their own protection. That these should be started under the auspices of the Church was quite in accordance with Catholic tradition.

The state [he said] should favor the multiplication of property owners. As things are at present: On the one side there is the party which holds the power because it holds the wealth; which has within its grasp all labor and all trade; which manipulates for its own benefit and its own purposes all the sources of supply, and which is powerfully represented in the councils of the state itself. On the other side there is the needy and powerless multitude, sore and suffering, always ready for disturbance. If working people can be encouraged to look forward to obtaining a share in the land, the result will be that the gulf between vast wealth and deep poverty will be bridged over, and the two orders will be brought nearer together.

Numerous clergymen, indeed, both Catholic and Protestant, recognized that Christianity could not ignore economic conditions which tended to impoverish and to degrade large numbers of men and women. The kingdom of heaven on earth, they knew, meant more than the reign of the saints after the second coming of Christ, in the future beyond the future. And to their voices was added that of one who may not properly be classified as either Catholic or Protestant, Leo Tolstoy of Russia.

Tolstoy and the Social Gospel

Among those Russian writers of the mid-nineteenth century who reflect an interest in the welfare of the downtrodden, three are pre-eminent—Turgenev, Dostoevski, and Tolstoy. In the numerous novels of Turgenev the life of the peasant is portrayed with loving care, but with the loving care of the artist, not the reformer. Turgenev is a man of letters—above the battle. Because he popularized the word "Nihilist," many have come to think of him as a radical, intent on revolution. But the truth is that he belonged neither to the right nor to the left. His novels are superb photographs of the minutiæ of Russian society, realistic certainly, but devoid of prophetic and moral fervor.

The same may not be said of Dostoevski. Most unmistakably, his novels are written with a purpose—a religious one. In his superb books, *Crime and Punishment, The Idiot,* and *The Brothers Karamazov,* the author expounds his creed of redemption through humiliation and suffering with such intensity and abandon that to the Western mind his Christianity seems unreal and distorted. There is no revolt in Dostoevski, no hint of reform apart from the mystical and subjective, no program of action. He is a Slavophil of the Slavophils, detesting Western culture and Western Christianity, implying that the latter is no more spiritual than socialism.

The approach of Tolstoy, on the other hand, to social justice is widely different from that of both Turgenev and Dostoevski. No less an artist than Turgenev, he is not content with art for art's sake. One can not imagine Tolstoy as divorcing art from morality; he earnestly longed to transform society and he believed with all his heart that the way to do this was through religion. In that respect he resembled Dostoevski. But religion, to Tolstoy, meant something more than joyous acquiescence in suffering. He was a socialist (of a kind), an advocate of vigorous and fundamental revolutionary change, not only in the human heart but likewise in economic life. No single influence was more universally felt in awakening the social conscience of Europe than that exerted by this independent genius who worked through no church and who belonged to none (after he left the Russian Orthodox), except possibly to the church universal.

Among Tolstoy's various books, one was entitled *What Shall We Do Then?* The book gave a graphic description of life at Moscow, not only among the lowly but among those wealthy ones with whom Tolstoy had hitherto been chiefly associated. In addition it advanced a program whereby, in the author's opinion, economic justice might be secured and the brotherhood of man made a reality. For three years Tolstoy worked on its composition. Troubled in heart, he thought of one solution after another whereby men might bridge the gulf between rich and poor, and all might become brothers in fact as well as brothers in name. He knew nothing about sociology or economics and cared less, but no man in modern times pondered more upon the New Testament and Christ's teachings than did Tolstoy.

The book commences with Tolstoy's hope that private charity along old-fashioned lines might solve the social problem. In order to feel in person what charity is like, he goes to a free lodginghouse in Moscow and stands in line in the snow, waiting entrance. His experience is unpleasant. One by one the guests file past, their clothes most foul, their faces emaciated and frostbitten. Tolstoy goes within, listens to their stories, and precipitates a near-riot by treating all and sundry to warm water and honey. The fetid quarters and human wreckage unnerve him. He returns to his own luxurious town house where he is served a five-course meal by footmen wearing gloves.

The sensitive man of letters is disturbed in conscience. Therefore, to pursue his investigations further, he applies for a job as a census-taker in the district occupied by prostitutes. Here he is angered by the callous conversation of those who exploit them; here also his heart is wrung by the mute appeal of the poor girls he encounters. He continues his social researches. He takes the census in factories and in the homes of factory workers; he draws comparisons between what he has discovered and the gay life of society which he knows so well—the balls and the opera, the "flowers, velvet, gloves, and perfume."

What, then, is to be done? Tolstoy concludes that charity as popularly conceived can do nothing. The trouble is too deep-rooted; for it is not merely physical wretchedness that brings ruin into the world. The poor are immoral; but the rich are no better than they, since they, too, like to get something for nothing, to live on the labor of other folk, to take advantage of someone else. The poor sense this fact and therefore have no thankfulness for any largess bestowed upon them.

There is, indeed, but one thing that can be done and that is to believe in the words of John the Baptist when he said, "He that hath two coats, let him impart to him that hath none; and he that hath meat, let him do likewise." The rich must divest themselves of their riches and earn their living by physical toil. Everyone must work. If everyone does so, the total hours of labor will be short and there will be an abundance of time remaining for literature, art, music. Rough plenty should be the lot of all men, who will be the better physically for thus living, and immeasurably the better spiritually.

Such, in rough outline, was Tolstoy's prescription for the social question. The prescriber took his own medicine, donned the smock of the peasant, plowed his own fields, made his own shoes at his own cobbler's bench. Under such circumstances he did some of his best writing. That he was a socialist of a kind it is evident; but his socialism stemmed from the four Gospels of Jesus, rather than from the *Communist Manifesto*.

Chapter 17

THE GERMAN EMPIRE, 1871-1914

On January 18, 1871, as cannon boomed about besieged and starving Paris, William I, King of Prussia, was proclaimed *German Emperor* before a brilliant assemblage of German princes and generals at Versailles. For the next forty-three years the newly created empire was to be the first land power in Europe. In place of the old disjointed German Bund, distracted by particularism, without colonies, merchant marine, or navy, in economic life far behind Britain and France, there was now a united state, more populous than France, with the most formidable army in the world, directed by an efficient government, able to build merchant ships and battleships, to seize colonies, to intervene in the affairs of Turkey, Morocco, China, and to compete with Britain for world commerce and world supremacy.

With care Bismarck had laid the foundations of the empire. After Sedan he had carried on rapid negotiations with the South German states. The latter feared their northern neighbors with their hard, masterful ways. In the pleasant Swabian lands the people were more democratic than in Prussia; while the southern princes naturally were somewhat jealous of their "brother" at Berlin. Foremost among them was the King of Bavaria.

This Louis II of Bavaria was an eccentric recluse who was quarreling incessantly with his ministers—largely because he insisted on squandering every *groschen* of his income upon extravagant palaces. Ultimately, he became insane and drowned himself (1886). In 1871 he had vainly dreamed of maintaining a genuinely independent kingdom. Circumstances were now, however, too strong for this conceited potentate. Bismarck handled him tactfully, and Louis was finally induced to send a circular letter to the other South German princes suggesting union under Prussia.

Württemberg, where there had been strong anti-union feeling, and where, as late as 1868, there had been outcries of "Better France than Prussia!" consented with unexpected readiness, thanks to the war psychosis. The Grand Duchy of Hesse was a weak state, and Baden (fearful of France) was already somewhat pro-Prussian. In the arrangement for union Bismarck was at his best, in the way of moderation and practical wisdom. To bring them within the new empire, he made very large concessions to Bavaria and to a less extent to Württemberg. Bavaria was to control her army in peacetime, as well as her posts, telegraphs, and much of her taxation. The South German states, preserving their autonomy in *civil* affairs, enjoyed local constitutions far more liberal than that of Prussia.

Down to the outbreak of the First World War, Germany was governed by a system that was merely a modification of that instituted for the North German Confederation in 1866-67. The King of Prussia now became, *ipso facto*, "German Emperor." Since the office of king and emperor were inseparable, and Prussia was a hereditary monarchy, the "kaisership" was, of course, also hereditary. The emperor could declare offensive war only after consulting the "Federal Council," but defensive war he could declare by his own personal fiat. He controlled the foreign affairs of the entire empire, was the "Supreme War Lord" of the army and navy, and appointed the chancellor.

The constitution of the new German Empire was simply that of the North German Confederation as devised by Bismarck in 1866 and now given a more resounding title. The Federal Council (*Bundesrat*) was still the mainspring of the government, enlarged now to fifty-eight members, representing not the people but the princes. Prussia kept her seventeen votes as under the old arrangement; Bavaria was given six, and the lesser states their four, three, two, or one apiece. Despite the favors that had to be granted Bavaria and Württemberg, the power of Prussia in the body was overwhelming. Thanks to this *secret*, nonparliamentary council, the emperor-king, and his one great minister, the chancellor, were able to control almost every affair of state.

The Reichstag of the North German Confederation was also increased to 397 members, chosen by manhood suffrage. Its consent was necessary for the passage of new laws and for the approval of new taxes, but not for much else. The chancellor was not responsible to the Reichstag but only to the Bundesrat, and the former body had no control over him. It was free to debate his policies; but if it disapproved it could not drive him from power, while he, on the contrary, could always force the election of a new Reichstag. Nevertheless, Bismarck and those chancellors who succeeded him took pains to have a majority of the lower house on their side, particularly when they wanted new legislation and increased expenditures.

The new empire, a federal one, comprised twenty-five states, four of which were kingdoms (Prussia, Bavaria, Saxony, and Württemberg), six grand duchies, five duchies, seven tiny principalities, and three free cities. Each state controlled its own internal affairs to a considerable degree as in the United States, the principal difference being that the German Empire had one common law code extending over the entire country. Several of these states had liberal democratic institutions, but it must be remembered that five out of every eight persons in the empire lived in Prussia and therefore continued to be influenced in their daily life quite as much by the action of the Prussian Landtag as by that of the imperial Parliament.

The general character of the Prussian constitution as granted by Frederick William IV has been sufficiently explained already. It had been originally granted by the king, out of his royal favor. It contained nowhere an admission of popular sovereignty. The king had an absolute veto upon all laws, and named and dismissed the Prussian ministers at his own good pleasure. The upper house (*Herrenhaus*—"House of Lords") was at all times the passionate defender of the rights of the "altar and the throne." The lower house (*Abgeordnetenhaus*) was still chosen upon the system of districting unrevised since 1860 until a few changes were made in 1906. Populous Berlin, up to that time, returned only 9 members; then it was allowed to have 12 out of 443. The "three-class" system, for choosing this "House of Representatives" was also still the same as in 1850. Shortly before 1914 there were 2,214 election precincts, wherein a third of the taxes were paid by *one man,* and he therefore cast the entire first-class vote for his entire precinct. Of 1,703 precincts each had only two first-class voters. The voting was still open. Any peasant or working-man consequently went to the polls in fear of his employer or landlord. Under the circumstances it was amazing that any important radical vote was cast at all. In 1907, this remarkable system registered 3 per cent of the electorate as belonging to the first class, 9.5 per cent to the second, and 87.5 per cent to the third—and *all three with precisely the same influence.* Just before the World War, the Conservatives in Prussia were electing 316 deputies out of the 443, with only 37 per cent of the total votes. The Socialists were choosing only 7 on 24 per cent of the vote.

Of course there was incessant outcry. Bismarck himself damned the arrangement as "the most miserable and absurd election law that had ever been formulated in any country." The Iron Chancellor did not love democracy, but he understood the need of controlling unwelcome agitators by subtle methods. But no change could be made in the system. The Emperor-King might be willing; there might be demonstrations in Berlin (notably in 1910) against the "three-class tyranny." These availed nothing. What the wealthy possessed, they would hold. Even very mild reform projects were steadily voted down. Prussia continued under this election system of 1850 until the monarchy perished in 1918.

The Junker Aristocracy: Its Efficiency and Its Limitations

The Prussian Junkers, moreover, could affect even the liberal South Germans. Besides giving assistance everywhere to the ultraconservatives, the Prussian aristocrats took full advantage of the fact that the imperial chancellor was also minister-president of Prussia. He had, therefore, to govern both the empire and its predominant partner simultaneously. To do the latter, he had to curry favor in his *imperial* policy with the element that held the *Prussian* government in the hollow of its hand. The Junkers exercised the standard prerogative of devoted friends of the crown—they were more autocratic than the emperor-king. As a mocking epigram said, *"They wished for an absolute kaiser, if he would do only the things which they wanted."* They provided the heads of the great civil bureaucracy, the diplomatic service, and the officer corps in the army. Thus, the three-class system really placed the grip of the rich and "well-born" elements of Prussia upon the entire German nation.

This undemocratic Prussian regime was, however, between 1871 and 1914, to exhibit an almost uncanny efficiency, else it could never have strengthened its grasp upon the empire and have become a problem for the entire world. The Junkers were coming into their own and exhibiting very many of the virtues of genuine aristocracy. They were brave, hard-hitting, devoted to duty, intensely loyal to their king, and had a keen sense of personal honor; they were, as a class, worthily exempt from sordid money-chasing; they had an intense caste pride: the professional classes, the commercial elements, and still more, the factory workers, these nobles held almost as much beneath them as the peasants, still very much under their power upon the great estates. Only with one non-noble class they made a marriage of convenience; the millionaire industrialists of the Rhine and Ruhr region found the Junker-Conservatives useful to their purpose, and the Junkers rejoiced in sustaining plebeian magnates who saw in every new regiment the contracts for more rifles and artillery.

The eldest son of such a Junker would, of course, ordinarily, inherit the *schloss,* but the rights of primogeniture were not very strict; and all sons of a nobleman wore the *von,* the prefix of nobility. For them to engage in business would be, of course, to lose caste. To supervise the family farmland was something else again, since across the ages the manure-heap has always had a fairer odor than the countinghouse. But the career par excellence for a Prussian squire still, as always, was the army.

To enter a military school, to struggle through the "glittering misery" of the rank of second lieutenant, and then, by hard and faithful work, to rise slowly to the higher grades in the army, to reinforce one's income by marriage with the daughter of a wealthy merchant whose *Mitgift* (dowry) would atone for lack of pedigree, to "turn the major's corner" and be advanced to the upper commands, to end up as an *excellenz*, general of division or corps—that was the chosen career for many a Prussian "poor but noble." The army and the landed aristocracy never lost touch.

The Material Expansion of Germany, 1871-1914

Between 1871 and 1914, the newly created German Empire enjoyed a material and economic expansion which astonished the world. Only the United States grew faster in population, wealth, and prosperity; and, in some respects, German expansion (based on limited area and long-worked soil) surpassed that of the western republic, with its virgin continent and enormous area. Great as were the Prussian military achievements in 1866 and 1870, they seemed less startling than German economic achievements thereafter. In 1871, the population of the German Empire had been barely 41,000,000. In 1890 it was 49,400,000, and in 1900 it was 56,360,000. In 1913 it was estimated at over 65,000,000. The empire, in population, was increasing more rapidly than any other country in Europe except prolific but backward Russia. This great increase in population, however, was being met by such industrial expansion, such opportunities for gainful employment, that Germans were not constrained in great numbers to emigrate beyond seas. After the disappointments of 1848, tens of thousands of virile Germans had come to America, partly, indeed, for political reasons, but a great number had emigrated solely to better their fortunes. This emigration had not ceased in 1871. Between, for example, 1880 and 1892, no less than 1,700,000 children of the Fatherland departed from their native soil for the United States alone. Others went in large numbers to Brazil, Argentina, and Canada.

But this was before the new imperial regime had caught its full stride. As the opportunities for successful industry increased at home, the stream of emigration sank to a mere trickle. In 1905, only about 40,000 Germans quitted the empire for good—26,000 of them for the United States. Just before the Great War, the numbers were even less.

Until rather shortly before the unification of the nation by Bismarck, Germany had ranked as a decidedly poor land, mainly given to agriculture. Her wealth could not compare with that of England, France, or (considering respective sizes) Belgium and Holland. Amsterdam was for a long time a much more important financial center than Berlin. As late as 1842, a German professor, discussing the rise of socialism in other countries, had declared that Germany had nothing to fear from such a movement, because the country was so completely agricultural that it did not possess any regular artisan, industrial class. Between then and

1871 the Industrial Revolution had transformed somewhat the old Germany, but not until the defeat of France was there rapid progress in industrialization.

What followed can again best be summed up in figures. In 1882 the number of Germans kept busy by manufactures and commerce was about 20,000,000; in 1910 it was 35,000,000. In 1885 less than 4,000,000 tons of pig iron were smelted in Germany; in 1913 about 15,000,000. In 1891, 73,000,000 tons of coal sufficed for the nation; in 1913, 190,000,000 tons were needed and supplied. And, to complete the story, as late as 1890 the export trade of Germany was worth only about $875,000,000. In 1913 it was not quite, $2,500,000,000. In short, the empire founded by Bismarck was second in its manufactures only to Britain, "the workshop of the world."

Furthermore, unlike the United States, which built up a world trade carried almost exclusively on foreign bottoms, the statesmen of the empire regarded the German merchant ship as the indispensable ally of the German merchant. Some steamship lines were subsidized outright; others received less direct, but nevertheless very genuine, official encouragement. In 1871 the German merchant marine had been insignificant; in 1913 it was the second greatest in ocean-going tonnage on the planet, and was giving its British rival sore anxiety as regards the supremacy in the carrying trade.

Agricultural expansion lagged somewhat. But even in agriculture the Germans worked miracles. They manufactured fertilizers from waste products at home, and imported nitrates from abroad. In beet sugar, potatoes, and hogs the German farmers held the primacy of Europe. It still seemed impossible for Germany to feed herself completely; she had to import about four-sevenths of her cereals to cover home deficiencies. This did not, however, seem to be a serious danger. The empire was not on an island. If she were at war with Russia (a great wheat country) she could still import from overseas. If she were blockaded by the naval might of England, she could still draw abundant supplies from Russia. That Russia and England would *both* unite in warfare against Germany seemed, in view of the diplomatic situation, grossly improbable—at least until 1914.

Everywhere in the empire, the cities grew by leaps and bounds—even as rapidly as in the American western states. In 1870 Hamburg possessed barely 350,000 inhabitants; in 1910 over 1,000,000. In 1870 Berlin boasted only 800,000; in 1910 over 2,000,000. As for the expansion of such "iron" towns as Essen, the seat of the famous Krupp works, it had been simply phenomenal. From about 50,000 in 1870, it had swollen to about 300,000 on the eve of the First World War. Such was the evidence, to be read by all men, of the mighty change that had come over the most powerful nation in Europe.

Parties and Politics

Meanwhile, although the Reichstag had little real power, it was consulted to some extent, and since it was elected by universal suffrage it did tend to show the drift of political thought in the country. Never at any one time did any single political party have a majority of seats in it; there were too many parties for that to happen. Therefore, majority votes had to be won by "blocs," that is, combinations of party groups. The more important parties during the empire were, from right to left, the Conservative, the National Liberal, the Centre, the Radical (Progressive), and the Social Democratic.

The strength of the Conservatives lay east of the Elbe. They were the party of the great rural landlords and of the landed nobility, favoring protective tariffs on grain and meat and the supremacy of Prussia in Germany. The Conservatives never attained even a plurality of seats; but their influence always was higher than their numerical ranking warranted, because of their social prestige. Furthermore, although their representation gradually declined with the passing of the years, it did not suffer material diminution, partly because many wealthy members of the National Liberal party joined it, partly because there was no real redistribution of seats for the Reichstag, based on population, during the history of the empire; and therefore the more thinly occupied rural districts continued to be represented out of all proportion to the number of their inhabitants.

The National Liberal party was the right, or conservative wing of what had once been the old Liberal party which fought Bismarck so bitterly before the empire was founded. Bismarck, both as Chancellor of the North German Confederation and as Chancellor of the German Empire, held out the olive branch to his old foes, and those who accepted it formed the National Liberal party. It was primarily the party of "big business," of the entrepreneurs, bankers, ship-owners, and wealthy manufacturers. For a time it had a plurality in the Reichstag but soon lost it.

The Centre party represented the Roman Catholic Church. It had very few representatives in the first Reichstag and they were present largely as South German particularists, fearful of the overshadowing power of Prussia. Then, however, the party grew rapidly as the result of Bismarck's attack on the Catholic Church. By the end of the century the Centre party had a plurality of votes and, although in the last election before the war it ceded first place to the Social Democrats, it was still very influential. The name Centre would seem to imply that this clerico-political organization was neither right nor left but occupied a center position. This would not be a fair description. The party was rigidly conservative in all that had to do with education, retaining a monopoly of the state primary schools in which Catholic youth was taught. In labor legislation, on the other hand, the Centre party was leftist, for the German Catholics for the most part came from the fast-growing industrial centers, where they met stiff opposition at the polls from the Socialists. The Pope, as we have seen, having already taken an advanced position in regard to the rights of labor the German bishops emphasized this when preaching or instructing their clergy.

Continuing to the left, we come to the Radical party which was really the left wing of the old Liberal party of the pre-empire day. The Radicals did not accept Bismarck's olive wreath. They were primarily the party of the small business man, and the reforms which they sought were for the most part political. The Radicals wanted a chancellor who would be responsible to the popularly elected Reichstag and a more democratic form of government. They were not very numerous in any of the various Reichstags elected before the First World War.

And finally there was the Social Democratic party, which began its career with two members and which grew steadily with only one setback (the election of 1907), until it had a clear plurality by 1914. The Social Democrats were a kind of hybrid group, partly socialistic, partly democratic. Their party represented the union of Ferdinand Lassalle's Workingmen's Association, which had stood mainly for complete political democracy with Marxian socialism. The party owned many presses, and the great daily newspaper, *Vorwärts*. Its program was in part political—redistribution of seats, ministerial responsibility, federal militia in place of a standing army; but it also had a big list of social and economic demands—payment of doctors and lawyers by the state, all funerals at public expense, and the wide extension of governmental ownership. Since the Social Democrats were republican and anti-Kaiser, they were an element which the Emperor and Junkers regarded with unspeakable wrath. In 1895 the socialist organization in Berlin was formally dissolved by authority; nevertheless, despite imprisonments, fines, social ostracism, and intimidation, the ultraradical vote grew apace. The socialist press took pride in barely legal innuendo, and in the Reichstag, the radical members at least used their privilege of talking freely even when they were powerless to control the government.

In 1881 the Socialists had polled 311,961 votes in a general Reichstag election. This grew steadily, year by year, until, in 1912, it reached the impressive total of 4,250,000. The unfair gerrymandering of the districts repeatedly cost the Socialists seats in the Reichstag, even when their total of votes increased, but in 1912 they not merely added 992,000 ballots to their earlier maximum, but won 67 new seats as well. They had now 110 deputies, making them the largest single party in Germany and forcing the Chancellor to depend on a jumbled coalition of "Conservatives," "Centrists," "National Liberals," "Progressives," and the like.

Socialism, however, in Germany did not imply always a strict adherence to the Marxian idea of a Communist regime. The Socialists themselves, furthermore, were seriously divided between moderate seekers for reform by evolution, and violent champions of a prompt and wholesale overturn. A large portion of its vote came really from liberal outsiders—Germans who cared little for extreme collectivism, but who were disgusted with the Hohenzollern military regime and who wanted to punish the government by "voting with the Left."

The Socialists constantly denounced militarism and voted in the Reichstag against every increase of armament. Their foes taunted them with lack of patriotism, and foreign pacifists often imagined that a great war might easily be prevented by a general refusal of the socialist conscripts to march against their "brothers," the toilers of France, Russia, and Britain. In the Reichstag, however, the Socialist orators declared that if the Fatherland should be really in danger they would "put the rifles to their shoulders." In 1914, the ruling powers knew well how to make it seem that the Fatherland *was* in danger; and, as far as we know, not one socialist soldier mutinied.

Aside from these major parties, there were a number of minor ones representing nationalist minorities in the Reich. A few deputies came from Schleswig-Holstein and capitalized the grievances of those Danes annexed to Germany; some represented the claims of Hanover (annexed by Prussia in 1866) but ceased to protest after a marriage between the former house of Hanover and the Hohenzollerns; and yet others, the most vociferous of all, spoke for the Poles.

Meanwhile, Germany was governed in accordance with Prussian theory, which required that the government should "be one of all parties," listening to their suggestions with paternal indulgence, but reserving the final decision for its own wisdom. A government, however, is after all a human institution. Between 1871 and 1914, it may be fairly said that two men dominated it: Otto von Bismarck; then, from 1890 to 1914, William II of Hohenzollern. Their personalities cannot be omitted from this history.

Bismarck's Domestic Policy After 1871

William I reigned as emperor and king down to his death in 1888. This kindly, moderate old gentleman remained entirely conscious of his own lack of genius and of the ability of his chancellor. As Bismarck said of his sovereign, he often made mistakes, "but in the end he allowed himself to be put straight again." Thanks to this one surpassing quality of being able to select and sustain great ministers, Bismarck, Moltke, and Roon, the plain, unassuming soldier ended his reign in a blaze of glory. "Kaiser Wilhelm der Gross" he was soon enrolled in the official histories by his enthusiastic grandson, as though he had been a second Charlemagne. Bismarck and William I often differed; repeatedly the Chancellor dutifully coerced his sovereign by offering to resign. "Never!" was generally the answer, and the monarch would gracefully yield. The two men were also fast personal friends; while William I lived, Bismarck was practically the dictator of Germany and without any question by far the most powerful man in all Europe.

Minister and sovereign alike had never allowed victory to turn their heads. The Iron Chancellor lived twenty-seven years after the unification of Germany, and beheld his creation advancing from strength to strength. But this was not to come about by war; he considered the empire as having become a "satiated state," needing no new conquests, and probably no colonies or large navy. During the nineteen years after 1871, while he was chancellor, he labored earnestly to maintain the peace of Europe.

The story of how he strove for the internal prosperity and stability of Germany, swings afar into many economic and political details, properly omitted here. In the eighteen-seventies, he drifted unwisely into a bitter struggle with the Catholic Church over the right of the government to control education. This *Kultur-kampf* raging until 1878, as Bismarck was suspending and even imprisoning priests and bishops, and getting himself likened to Nero and Diocletian, the persecutors. In 1878, alarmed at the growth of socialism, he felt compelled to beat a retreat, and executed a compromise with the Vatican.

Bismarck thus failed to curb the Catholics; he failed, also, to crush the Socialists, coming to the front in the eighteen-seventies and becoming formidable as the new Germany developed a great industrial class. The Socialists, of course, were not mere liberals; they praised a democratic republic and talked of a complete social revolution. Bismarck fought them unrelentingly. Two attempts to assassinate William I were utilized to enable the Chancellor, in 1878, to put through extremely severe laws against publications, meetings, and associations aiming at "the subversion of the social order." The zealous German police knew entirely how to enforce these measures, and the Socialists were driven underground. Their societies met in secret, however, and their papers were smuggled in from Switzerland. Every election saw an increased Socialist vote.

Bismarck, nevertheless, believed in making the industrial classes contented with the old order, by measures intended to remedy their condition. "Give the workingman the right to work so long as he is healthy," he said in 1884, "assure him of care when he is sick and maintenance when he is old . . . *then* if the state will show a little more Christian solicitude for him, the Socialists will sing their songs in vain."

In 1883, 1884, and 1885, laws insuring workmen against sickness and against accidents were enacted; in 1889 there followed one for insuring the aged and disabled. These laws were praised and partly imitated in England and America, while in Germany they wrought very considerable good. However, there were many complaints—the cost of the insurance was paid partly by the State, partly by the employers; but a large part was taken from the daily wages. Many of the workers, for various reasons, could not hope to enjoy the final benefit; many fraudulent sick-claims and disablements were reported. Above all, there was the sentimental objection—the laws were a mere sop thrown down from the "Above" to keep the workingmen contented.

In 1879 Bismarck swung the Germans away from the low-tariff system under which he had been working, and adopted a scheme for stiff protection. The measure undoubtedly alike helped the new class of great manufacturers, and the Prussian agriculturists, competing with Russian and American wheat. The landowners and the factory-owners were, therefore, more willing than ever to call the Chancellor blessed.

In the eighteen-eighties Bismarck likewise permitted another trend—albeit without enthusiasm. Already there were strong demands in Germany for colonies such as swelled the pride of England, of France, and even of little Holland. Germany had come very late into the colonizing field—India, Australia, and parts of Africa were pre-empted; Latin America was covered by the Monroe Doctrine. But public pressure forced Bismarck to follow up the claims staked out by certain Teutonic traders and travelers in Oceania and Africa. In this way the imperial flag presently floated over Togoland, Kamerun, German East Africa, and German Southwest Africa, jungle or desert lands mostly, and wholly unexploited; and also in the Pacific, over parts of New Guinea and the adjacent Solomon Isles, and over the greater part of the Samoan archipelago, the islands of which were divided between the United States, Britain, and Germany.

These were real achievements. The Chancellor's true greatness, of course, had been as an empire-builder. He never would have won fame simply as an economist and minister of the interior. His reputation as a diplomat, however, continued unshaken to the end. So long as William I sat on the throne, his great minister seemed one of the fixtures of Europe. By his system of alliances (see pp. 489-490) he seemed to have isolated France and secured the quiet of the Continent, and he had *almost* convinced the world that the gigantic German army was an engine solely to insure peace. But in March, 1888, William I, a hoary veteran of ninety-one, slept with his fathers. Bismarck had lost his grateful sovereign and his best personal friend.

Frederick III (1888): William II: Dismissal of Bismarck (1890)

Frederick III, husband of Victoria, the eldest daughter of Victoria of England, reigned in his father's stead. Within a few weeks he was to die from cancer of the throat. "Hail soldiers—I about to die salute you!"

is the old gladiatorial greeting which this stricken Kaiser is said to have addressed to his troops.

Thus, within ninety-nine days, the imperial army took a second oath to a new *Kaiser und König*. In place of an emperor of ninety-one, there was now a monarch of nine-and-twenty, restless, ambitious, and none too friendly to Bismarck. Within a year there was friction over renewing the antisocialist laws, and, finally, an issue over maintaining the subordination of the Prussian state ministers to their minister-president (otherwise the imperial chancellor). In 1890, came the decisive interview at the imperial *Schloss*. The Emperor explained his desire to have the ministers report direct to himself. The Chancellor objected and William insisted that his will must be carried out "if not by Bismarck then by another." Flint struck steel. *"Then I am to understand, Your Majesty,"* said the man who had saved the Hohenzollern dynasty and made the German Empire, *"that I am in your way." "Yes!"* came the firm retort of the young man before him.

In 1890 there was an open break and Bismarck resigned. Germany was stunned and, in the main, took Bismarck's side. Vainly did William shower new titles and decorations upon the man he had declared superfluous. "The dog's kick-out" Bismarck angrily called them; likening them to the boot-thrust with which Prussian squires were wont to repel the too eager attentions of devoted hounds.

No doubt Bismarck, as he aged, had become increasingly rigid and autocratic. Even William I had sometimes winced at his great minister's importance. In the eighteen-seventies, when that monarch had met Francis Joseph II at Gastein, the Austrian ruler had complained of the obtrusive curiosity of the public. "Wait a few minutes," the elder William had replied; "when Bismarck comes no one will pay any attention to *us!*" In fact, it was becoming a fair question whether the "Hohenzollern" or the "Bismarck" dynasty was ruling Germany; but now William II had "dropped the pilot," and he ruled alone.

William II of Hohenzollern (1888-1918): His Abilities and Weakness

William II was born in 1859. He was the son of the then Crown-Prince Frederick and the Princess Royal Victoria of England. He was given that severe, systematic education in things military and administrative which was one of the worthy traditions of his family. He was never cordial toward his father; his attitude toward his mother was even worse; but chilliness toward one's parents was proverbial among Prussian crown princes. He was, however, as the apple of the eye to old William I. The new monarch, in turn, was later never weary of singing the praises of "his sainted grandfather," although his father's honorable memory was seldom mentioned.

William II came to the throne at twenty-nine. When he was only twenty-three, Bismarck, who had watched him shrewdly from under his shaggy eyebrows, is alleged to have commented: "He wishes to take the government into his own hands; he is energetic and determined; not at all disposed to put up with parliamentary co-regents—a regular guardsman!" A little later, the young prince sent Bismarck his own picture with the significant words beneath it *"Cave! adsum!"* ("Look out! I'm here!") Nevertheless, at his accession, he declared himself a devoted admirer of the Chancellor. Then came the breach described already.

In 1888 William II began to reign. In 1890 he began to govern. From this time onward Germany became increasingly subject to a *strictly personal government.* Bismarck had considered it the standing duty of a good minister "not to trouble about his sovereign's favor, but to speak his mind freely." But Bismarck had been dismissed—the later chancellors were all "handy men," without his blunt speech and courage. They knew it was their main duty to take the brunt of public criticism, to work out the details of a policy decided for them, to elaborate the Emperor's ideas, and, finally, to resign gracefully when they ceased to please their master.

Eloquence, affability, and a genuine personal magnetism, it may be freely asserted, William II possessed. In the Middle Ages his versatile talents might have won him fame, like a Frederick II, "the wonder of the world." As a wealthy citizen of a republic, he would have gained just honor as philanthropist and patron of art and letters, although too unsteady for success in politics. He was also a devoutly religious man. His frequent and often patronizing references to the Deity as his constant associate sprang out of a deep, if very peculiar, piety.

William, furthermore, delighted in playing the virtuoso, in giving authoritative "hints" to authors of grand operas, to artists and sculptors, especially if their creations seemed to glorify his dynasty. He took a keen interest in education, and in 1903 publicly accepted the radical Higher Criticism of the Bible as expounded by the learned lecturer, Delitzsch. At patriotic assemblages, the launching of warships, the commemorations of great battles, he could carry his audience away by genuine flights of oratory. He understood past history, especially that of his own House, and never failed with telling historical allusions. To distinguished foreigners he could be graciousness and affability incarnate, charmingly frank and "indiscreet," given to hospitality without condescension.

But William II was also steeped in all the military traditions of the House of Hohenzollern. In 1885 he had been appointed a colonel. His teachers and companions were veteran comrades of Moltke, or young

Prussian officers who thirsted for the call to battle. Everywhere he had been taught two things:

I. The sovereign of Prussia-Germany ruled by the grace of God and all honest subjects ought to obey him.

II. Under a kindly applauding Providence he owed throne, honors, and all else, to that Prussian army without whose loyalty he would be impotent.

The circumstances of the dismissal of Bismarck rendered it impossible that his emperor could have really upstanding, forceful ministers; he could only have viziers, servants to do his business. After Bismarck came von Caprivi (1890-94), a military man of high character, but one who found the chancellorship a mere lion-skin from a deceased lion. The liberals hated him; the Junkers quarreled with him; and finally, in 1894, his master threw him over. Then came Prince von Hohenlohe (1894-1900), an elderly statesman of somewhat greater ability. He bought the support of the Conservatives by favoring the agricultural interests, but in the end the Emperor wearied of him, too. When he tactfully resigned, in 1900, he found that his successor had been chosen already by His Majesty.

The next Chancellor was a polished and astutely optimistic man of affairs, Count (and later Prince) von Bülow (1900-1909). Bismarck had declared in a famous speech, "We Germans fear God and nothing else in the world"; and a political wag now asserted "Bülow fears the Junkers and nothing else in the world." He knew better than his predecessors how to humor the Emperor and yet to retain something of his own personality. For a long time he controlled the Reichstag, thanks to skilful "deals" with the Conservatives and Catholic Centrum; but in 1909 the Junkers at last deserted him, and he found his master was again growing weary. It was painful work always trying to check William's indiscreet speeches. "You do not know how much I prevent!" Bülow had once protested, on being chided for failing to stop a glaring indiscretion. Now William allowed him to depart gracefully and Bethmann-Hollweg sat in the chair of Bismarck. This unfortunate Chancellor, destined to see the tornado loosed over Europe and to find himself a helpless victim in its path, came of a good Brandenburg family, and had worked up through all the stages of the Prussian civil service. He was technically, therefore, well qualified for office. Kindly, tactful, he would have made a good minister for a small kingdom in quiet times. He simply lacked the intellectual capacity and force of character to handle a great empire in a great crisis. Merely because he was this modest handyman, William II found him very useful, and their relations were fairly satisfactory. He was, of course, the last official possible to stand firmly against the militarists and constrain his master to peace amid the complicated international crises throughout July, 1914.

Drastic Attempts at Germanizing the Poles of Prussia: Polish Resistance

Within Germany, meanwhile, there was one problem which would not down. Advanced labor legislation, combined with economic prosperity, might and did keep the Social Democrats at bay, and the Centre was placated by the continuance of its control over religious education and by the benefits which it helped secure for workmen. But these gifts were insufficient to win over the nationalistic minorities within the country. There were Danes in Schleswig-Holstein who felt aggrieved at their forced Germanization; there were Poles, nominally German citizens, who had no loyalty for the Reich; and there were French sympathizers who never forgot 1871. Friction with these minorities was rife from 1871 to 1914.

The Danes were so few in number that no attention need to be paid to their irredentist agitation, but not so with Poles, Alsatians, and Lorrainers. By 1900, there were about 3,000,000 subjects of William II who called themselves Poles, not Prussians, and whose loyalty to the empire was under most serious suspicion.

Down to 1870, the Polish subjects of Prussia had been reasonably loyal to the king at Berlin, and friction had not been acute. Then, after 1871, while the official bureaucracy was consolidating and reorganizing the whole structure of the new German Empire with Teutonic thoroughness, the Poles were made to feel the hand of the taskmaster. In truth, the Prussians were becoming alarmed at the failure of the Poles to become peacefully Germanized, and at their steady increase in numbers. In 1886 it was found there were 200,000 more of them than twenty-five years earlier, while the Germans in the "Polish districts" had increased only 4,000—German settlers were actually succumbing to local influences and becoming "Polonized." In 1886 there were 750 children with German names in the primary schools of Posen, although members of families where nothing but Polish was spoken. The Poles were extraordinarily prolific. *"They multiply like rabbits!"* cried an angry Prussian statesman. In 1886, therefore, Bismarck and his lieutenants decided on radical remedies.

Any restoration of Polish independence was banned as impossible. It would, wrote the Iron Chancellor, mean the "breaking up and decomposition of Prussia." The only remedy, therefore, was to get rid of the Poles by a wholesale introduction of German colonists. Accordingly, a land commission was set up. Small farms were to be bought and allotted on easy terms to good German settlers. But it was no easy matter to get the land itself. Polish national consciousness was stung to the quick. Great Polish noblemen subscribed to the private loan and self-help societies which enabled the Slavic peasants to hold their own. Any Pole who sold to the government commission faced social boycott and priestly anathema. Ordinarily, the only land available for the commission was that of German estate owners, anxious to move out of a region that was growing very uncomfortable. The private Polish societies bought up German lands and assigned them to their own peasants. In 1907 it was estimated that the whole result of this policy had been *a net gain by the Poles* of 240,000 acres held by German owners before Bismarck began his campaign!

In the early nineteen-hundreds, Bülow undertook to give teeth to the land commission, stating that, "In a struggle of nationalities a nation is either hammer or anvil, either conqueror or conquered." Prussia was to play the hammer; the *compulsory expropriation* of Polish lands was authorized. But German farmers could not be compelled to quit comfortable holdings elsewhere and settle in an uncongenial "enemy's country," where police protection was often needful. The Poles clung desperately to their habits and language, and their unwelcome guests had to become "Polonized" in order to secure the least companionship.

Against the tenacious use of the native vernacular, the Prussian government fought yet again with its trusty subalterns—the schoolmasters. In 1872 German was made the sole language in the elementary schools, except that religion could still be taught (by the Catholic clergy) in Polish; but as soon as the children learned a little German they were transferred to German religion classes. Inasmuch as religion and patriotism had now, for the Poles, become practically inseparable, the resentment was widespread and intense.

Finally, in 1906, came the famous school strike in Posen and West Prussia. Some 60,000 pupils refused to answer questions on the catechism in German or to learn German hymns. The vernacular press condemned the attempt to teach religion in the language of the conquerors as "A tyranny over the conscience, in which only the devil in the gorge of hell and the Prussian government could find satisfaction." Children met their unlucky teachers of religion with Polish songs or curses, and strewed the roadside with the tatters of their German catechisms. The Prussian government struck back by refusing promotion to recalcitrant children, fining and sometimes imprisoning the parents who encouraged them.

During the three decades before the first World War, the Prussian Poles were fighting tooth and nail to preserve their language. The government police were constantly suppressing all Polish outdoor meetings and permitting Polish indoor meetings only under the strictest surveillance. Polish theatrical performances were frequently prohibited; and Polish pleadings were forbidden in the courts, even in strictly Slavic districts. No Pole was admitted to the judgeships, the postal service, the state railway service, or any other part of the great army of civil officials. A few high Polish nobles did, indeed, make their peace with Prussia, and received foreign diplomatic positions; but their own people counted them as apostates. On the other hand, year after year, a number of Polish Nationalist deputies sat in the Prussian Landtag, increasing the number of small, irresponsible factions, which were the curse of German political life.

Under alien coercion, the Prussian fraction of the Poles had come together as a people as they had never done in their days of misused independence. The peasants who had stolidly permitted Kosciusko to go down in defeat were, by 1914, joining secret societies and giving attentive ear to nationalist propaganda. Shortly before the war the Prussian police seized a prayerbook circulated among the Polish mine workers in Westphalia. Some of its invocations ran:

> Mother of God, Queen of the Poles, save Poland! . . .
> From the Muscovite and Prussian bondage, free us, O Lord!
> By the martyrdom of the soldiers murdered at Fishau free us, O Lord!
> For death on the battlefield we beseech Thee, O Lord!
> For an early universal call to arms, we beseech Thee, O Lord!

Alsace-Lorraine After Annexation to Germany (1871)

Gambetta had adjured his French countrymen concerning the loss of the two provinces, "Think of it always; speak of it never!" Every July 14, a solemn procession trailed through Paris to place a wreath of mourning upon the statue personifying Strasbourg. The story of the disaster of 1870-71 was kept alive by every veteran of the great defeat. French military men knew that a single-handed attack on Germany was madness, but political agitators and the irresponsible press often made it difficult for hard-headed statesmen to keep the peace. As time dimmed the memory of Sedan, better feeling might perhaps have developed toward Germany. French pacifists argued that this was actually the case; but the instant the First World War broke, the problem of the lost provinces once again was thrust before Europe.

If Alsace and Lorraine had seemed happy in the new connection, Frenchmen might have forgotten them; but the reverse was the case. The treatment meted out to the two conquered provinces was such that their inhabitants were kept in continuous turmoil. The majority, perhaps, grew accustomed to German citizenship, and if Alsace-Lorraine had been made as autonomous in the Reich as Bavaria, all might have been well. But Bismarck did not want to have another Roman Catholic South German state with votes in the all-powerful Bundesrat, and so the two provinces were simply made a *Reichsland,* an imperial dependency under the tutelage of Prussia. Scarcely, indeed, had the French flag been lowered, before the teaching of the French language in elementary schools was forbidden. In that Strasbourg where the Marseillaise had been written, French could not be studied save as a "foreign tongue."

But the German military conscription stirred the greatest anguish. While their slain French comrades were hardly cold, Alsatian youths were made to don the Prussian spiked helmet. Vain were protests. In 1871 a deputation expostulated with Bismarck. He told them that conscription was a school for loyalty. "Get the king's coat on a man's back and you have made both a good soldier and a good 'burgher' [for Germany] out of him." "Yes," retorted the leader of the deputation, "but you must get the coat on first—and *that* you can never do!" Twelve thousand Alsatian youths fled to France and entered the French army; the rest entered the German service so sullenly as to impair their value as soldiers.

The conquerors adhered to the policy of "thorough" with all their native tenacity. French rule had been lax, somewhat inefficient, but usually tender of local susceptibilities. Now came a swarm of Prussian officials, keyed up to more than their wonted rigidity. Down to 1879, the provinces were ruled by a military dictator sent down from Berlin. After that, they formed a *Reichsland,* with the emperor naming the governor-general and a very powerful council; but with some form of local self-government, an extremely weak elective Diet, and enough popular balloting to register protests against one ministerial ordinance after another. A really humane and enlightened governor, Baron von Manteuffel, who won much personal good will was appointed; but he was thwarted by his lesser officials, who could only bully and tyrannize, and he was compelled to enforce an impossible policy. In 1885 he died, having accomplished little.

After Manteuffel, the carpet-bagging German officials induced Berlin to attempt another regime of "proper severity." Kindness had failed; police dragooning was therefore again in order. Alsatian societies of all varieties were dissolved. Natives were forbidden to receive passports to cross the frontier, even in order to visit near relatives in France. Arrests were made for every possible cause. An Alsatian had tattooed upon his body "*Vive la France!*" When he appeared in a public bath he was seized by the police.

The Reichsland Under William II: Continued Bitterness Until 1914

William II's advent brought a little relaxation of the police regime, but his speeches were adamantine. "We would rather," said he in an oration, "sacrifice our eighteen army corps and our 42,000,000 [Prussian] inhabitants in the battlefield than yield one stone which my father and his generals have gained."

A complete lack of humor made the German administration at times a laughingstock. In 1895 there was a peasant at the village of Detwiller near Saverne. He raised a fine white cock with a lordly red crest, whereupon he dyed the bird's tail blue—making the creature a veritable emblem of the Tricolor. The imperial police pounced on the sedition-teaching fowl. The owner refused to slaughter him; at which the police saber ended the feathered traitor and avenged the Fatherland.

From this time onward, matters did not improve. The French journals in the two provinces were suppressed under every possible pretext. Passport regulations again made it difficult for a Frenchman to visit Strasbourg. A historical play requiring the display of the Tricolor was presented in that city. The police permitted only the use of the *Dutch* flag, wherein the red, white, and blue stripes ran horizontally, instead of vertically, a most absurd ruling from any psychological understanding of Alsatian sensitivity.

Finally, in 1911, the German authorities reverted again to "benevolence." The Reichsland was given a constitution with considerable autonomy, somewhat on a par with other imperial states, although the governor-general was still sent down from Berlin. But the newly elected Landtag showed its feeling by at once cutting down the governor's salary and by refusing the annual allowance for the Emperor's hunting trips to Alsace. The "All-Highest" was extremely angry and on a visit to Strasbourg in 1912 flung an open warning to the mayor: "Listen! Up to now you have only known the good side of me. You might be able to learn the other side ... If this situation lasts *we will suppress your constitution and annex you to Prussia!*"

In the Reichstag the Socialist deputies, of course, made merry over this threat. Here, vowed their spokesman, was a confession on highest authority, "that annexation to Prussia was a punishment like hard labor in the penitentiary, with the loss of civil rights." As for the Alsatian Landtag, it promptly voted that:

I. The new constitution could only be changed by the Alsatians themselves.

II. The Reichsland ought to have its own special flag.

Both propositions were, of course unacceptable at Berlin.

In 1913 came the notorious Zabern (Saverne) affair which was peculiarly exasperating to Alsace. A certain youthful garrison lieutenant of the typical Junker training, Baron von Forstner, took his epaulettes very seriously. School-children and lads had jeered at him, while he, in revenge, harangued his men, calling the Alsatians by extremely coarse names. The local papers, at length, printed caustic paragraphs. In November, 1913, a civilian crowd gathered in front of the barracks. The colonel sent a subaltern to command the burghers to go home; the latter disobeyed, whereupon the military charged into the street and arrested twenty-seven civilians, including three high judges and the state prosecuting attorney, who had got caught in the throng.

The commandant at Zabern was forthwith tried for violating the law which forbade the soldiery to interfere in civilian matters, but he was promptly acquitted by the military court on a technicality. The Governor-General of Alsace resigned in formal protest at the deeds of the military, but withdrew his action on mollifying orders from the Emperor. Almost immediately, however, Lieutenant Baron von Forstner again gave business for the telegraph under Zabern date lines.

This youthful officer had not shifted his garrison town. Very quickly he fell into a public altercation with a lame shoemaker; the latter, presuming on his infirmity, seems to have made unflattering remarks. Forstner caused two soldiers to hold the cripple, while he slashed him with his saber. Again there was public uproar. Forstner was court-martialed, sentenced to one year in custody, then speedily acquitted after an appeal to a higher tribunal, on the grounds of "self-defense."

Forstner thus vindicated the "honor" dear to every Prussian officer; but in the Reichstag civilian wrath exploded. Bethmann-Hollweg's defense of the military was feeble and evasive, but his colleague, the War Minister, poured oil on the flames by publicly stating that Forstner was a desirable and "courageous young officer." The real culprits were, of course, the army chiefs who had allowed the folly of a mere subaltern to create a great public issue. But it was far easier to bait Bethmann-Hollweg than the great General Staff, with the "Supreme War Lord" behind it. On December 6, 1913, the Reichstag overwhelmingly voted (293 to 54) a resolution of censure on the government.

In any nonautocratic government, Bethmann-Hollweg, after this, would have resigned immediately. He did nothing of the kind. Only the Socialists actually insisted that he ought to quit office. The Reichstag, legally, had merely passed a harmless resolution like a huge debating club.

Nevertheless, the Junker barons and the titled members of the great General Staff doubtless cursed Forstner and his commandant as "blockheads" and "asses." They had reason. In a most unwelcome manner, the twain had advertised the widening rift between the military and civilians. Another such incident might have found the Reichstag so angry as to refuse to vote taxes until there was a change of ministers. That would have meant a constitutional crisis of the first order, with the authority of the Kaiser at stake. That same year, the situation became so acute that Alsatian conscripts were ordered to perform their army service in distant garrisons, and not near their home towns, as were other Germans. In 1914 the friction was increasing still; distinguished Alsatian authors were fleeing to Paris to avoid punishment for publishing satires upon the German police administration.

When the European conflict began, it was manifest that, for forty-four years, the German attempt to assimilate Alsace had failed.

Pan-Germanism

Germany, thrust into the vortex of modern industrialism, did not escape the pride, conceit, and nationalistic arrogance which so frequently accompanies success. These evils were far from affecting Germany alone; they were concomitant with modern civilization. But they were more noticeable in Germany than elsewhere, for the very reason that the Germans had been so successful, not simply in piling up wealth, but in intelligently ordering their national life, so that poverty, even when severe, did not seem quite as harsh a burden as in less disciplined lands.

Primarily, this conceit took the form of intense nationalistic fervor. The Germans took pride in their accomplishments and wished to extend them. The choicest colonial prizes had been snapped by other countries before they had an opportunity to act; and this they resented. Britain they regarded as a kind of retired robber who, living comfortably on his booty, had "gone respectable" and was now reading them moral lessons. Their neighbors in the Third Republic, with a stationary population, had an extensive empire overseas without the man power to develop it; the Germans thought themselves capable of this task. They, too, wanted "a place in the sun," and they were sensitive as only the newcomer can be at the criticisms of the old residents. The wealthier they became, the less idealistic they seemed to be, and the rest of the world, partly out of jealousy, derided their pushing ways. In consequence, the Germans "tooted their own horn" all the more. The French, they said, were "degenerate" and "effeminate"; the Russians "savage"; the British "commercialized" and "sodden in repose"; the Americans "undisciplined" and "miserably governed." As early as 1897, Fritz Bley, an author of considerable acceptance, announced: "We are the most capable nation in every field of science and in every branch of the fine arts. We are the best colonists, the best mariners and even the best merchants—and yet we do not enter into our share of the heritage of the world."

It is easy to exaggerate the picture. *"Deutschland über Alles"* only means "Germany first," not "Germany over all." As a song it is no more flamboyant than "Columbia, the Gem of the Ocean" or "Rule, Britannia." Almost every chauvinistic statement emanating from German politicians could be matched by similar sentences taken from English, French, or even American sources. Even von Treitschke, the great historian, purveyor of intense German nationalism, scarcely exceeds the English historian, Seeley, in the fervor of his patriotism. The major difference is that the German, because he is a German, writes in a somewhat less restrained way.

A great to-do was made, after the First World War began, about a certain book, written by the retired general Bernhardi in 1911, entitled *Germany and the Next War,* and a certain chapter in it, headed "World Power or Downfall." The time had come, he affirmed, for Germany to try to gain world empire by one great stroke or to fall ruinously in the attempt. No mere defensive measures or defensive alliance would answer; Austria and Italy would have to be sufficiently induced to take the Fatherland's side. But it was useless to see in Russia, France, and Britain anything but formidable obstacles. There could be an armistice with them but no real peace. Russia might be kept quiet for a while, thanks to her internal troubles and the feeble character of Nicholas II, but real friendship was impossible. As for Britain, she had committed the unpardonable folly of failing to support the Southern Confederacy, and thereby to cripple her own great rival, the United States. Perhaps, if Germany and Britain went to war, America could now be induced to help Germany, but it would be unsafe to count on this. However, Canada, South Africa, and Australia were none too loyal to London, and Moslem India might revolt. In view of these facts, England was bound to be afraid of Germany and "a pacific agreement with England is, after all, a will-o'-the-wisp which no serious German statesman could follow."

As for treaties and questions of neutrality, Germans must not "allow themselves to be cramped in their freedom of action by considerations . . . which depend only on political expediency."

This book, seen in retrospect after 1914, seemed a grave indictment of the German people. But after all, military men and retired generals like Bernhardi are apt to write warlike books. Did not our own Homer Lea write one entitled *In the Days of the Saxon,* in which he portrayed the inevitable conflict with Japan and the Americans triumphant over the men of Nippon?

Pan-Germanism, or the idea that all folk of Teutonic blood like Swiss, Danes, Austrians, and Dutch should be incorporated in the Reich had few supporters in the Reichstag. It was chiefly among Conservatives and National Liberals that Pan-Germanism met with favorable response. There was a Pan-German magazine, it is true, obscure copies of which were dug up here and there in Wisconsin and other states to fool Americans during the World War into the belief that Germany sought to conquer Europe. But we know the league to sponsor Pan-Germanism was a good deal of a joke in Germany, that the greatest number of subscribers to its magazine was under 10,000 and that the high membership of the league was 21,924. Some members of the Reichstag belonged to it, either National Liberals, Conservatives, or members of small groups to the right of even the Conservatives, and bitterly anti-Semitic. But that this league had any real influence in determining German policy may safely be denied.

This was not the faith of the German people as far as counting heads was concerned. To just what extent it was the faith of the Prussian aristocracy which controlled the destiny of that people, it is impossible to say. Perhaps the fairest summary would be to state that ideas like these influenced the upper-class Junker to some degree.

The German aristocracy had much reason to feel proud of its achievements. Under its control, for the first time since the Middle Ages, the Teutonic genius for practical achievement gained full scope for its energies. The nation's rulers might be autocrats, but they committed none of the clumsy blunders of traditional despotism. School, church, factory, army, diplomatic service, university—all were articulated in the great disciplined Prussian machine, working together to make the Fatherland rich and glorious.

The German masses, naturally law-abiding, accustomed to authority, and not active politically, usually took this regime with docility, except when the government arm became exceptionally heavy. The Prussian system, indeed, fell in well with the whole German tendency to analyze, systematize, and regulate all things down to minute details. The military spirit was carried out into the civil population by a system of minute police commands and prohibitions intolerable in any less disciplined country. The cult of the infallibility of the government became a prime element in secular education and in religion. The public schools made almost every lesson in history a lesson also in loyalty to the ruling monarchies.

No country was ever more completely "governed" than Prussian-Germany. Foreign visitors called it "the land of *verboten*" ("things prohibited"). The park benches of a North German city were carefully labeled with the class and sex entitled to sit upon each one. The hours for piano-playing in flats, the number of pedestrians who might walk abreast, the size of beer-mugs, the sidewalks permissible for baby-carriages, the location of flowerpots on the window sills—all were subject to control by the ever active police. Under a corrupt and inefficient regime these regulations would have been intolerable. Fortunately, they were directed by persons usually patriotic, intelligent, self-sacrificing and, if anything, overlogical; but they tended to render the system they controlled automatic rather than human.

Everywhere else in the world, autocracy and privilege seemed on the defensive. Half consciously, in Prussianized Germany, the Junker class tried to show how much greater happiness and success they could bring to a nation than could the easygoing and sometimes blundering liberalisms of Britain, France, and America. The alliance between the Hohenzollern dynasty and the military caste ever tightened. The Junker officers hated the idea that the monarch should choose his ministers at the behest of a popularly elected parliament. This was not from any fine theory, but because the monarchy could not have two masters—the army chiefs and the people. "The dearest wish of every Prussian officer," declared Beth-mann-Hollweg as late as January, 1914, "is to see the king's army completely under the control of the king, and not becoming the army of the parliament." A little earlier, upon the very floor of the Reichstag, a spokesman for the Conservatives, a Herr von Oldenburg, had stated this view of the case with embarrassing bluntness, "The emperor ought to be in a position to say at any moment to a lieutenant 'Take ten men and shut up the Reichstag'!"

After 1871 this spirit of Prussian Junkerdom entered into increasingly close alliance with the monarchy, and held back the rising wave of liberalism by giving the German people almost everything that a proud nation could desire. The people were now to enjoy the memories of a victorious past, along with the consciousness of a prosperous present, while brilliant hopes gleamed of an even more golden future. Maximilian Harden, a bitter and often unfair critic of the Hohenzollern monarchy, wrote, this time with truth, *In order to be strong, Germany has rejected the great modern comfort of democracy.*

For a time this alliance of modern material progress and medieval political privilege affected only Germany: at length it came to affect the whole world.

Chapter 18

GREAT BRITAIN, 1874-1914

In 1874 DISRAELI became prime minister for the second time. And keynoting his ministry were two Latin words, *sanitas* and *imperium*, slogans more appropriate for Victorian Tories than for Victorian Liberals.

The new Prime Minister, in his first bid for a Parliamentary seat, had campaigned as a Radical, and a peculiar variety of radicalism did underlie the thinking of Britain's foremost Conservative champion. It was based on his romantic veneration for the past. In his novel *Sybil* he had praised a bygone England in which feudal aristocrats had ruled the country and held it their duty to preserve and to protect the health and welfare of the poor. This was a medieval idea, radically different from the viewpoint of Victorian individualism. Disraeli considered it conservative, and of course, it was both that and radical. He sought to implement this idea and succeeded by legislation for the benefit not of the middle class but of the lowly, a kind of government of the people, for the people, by British Tories.

The way to do this, he considered, was by *sanitas*—public health—and to further it Parliament passed a long series of laws, among them statutes preventing the pollution of rivers, reopening enclosed lands and heaths for public recreation, and establishing a maximum fifty-six-hour working week, anathema to Liberals devoted to laissez faire.

In one of his later novels Disraeli wrote: "Pauperism is not so much an affair of wages as it is of housing," a modernistic note that some might claim was tinged with socialism. The Artisans' Dwelling Act of 1875 incorporated this idea. By it all towns and cities of over 25,000 inhabitants were authorized to condemn and to purchase land for housing low-income groups. This was a permissive not a mandatory law; but that it passed at all is indicative that Mid-Victorian England was not wholly the slave of laissez faire.

Two other statutes marked the forward-looking character of Disraeli's second ministry. One was an act for the protection of Britain's merchant seamen, establishing specific standards as to their accommodations on shipboard and to the seaworthy character of the ships in which they sailed.

The other law was the Employers' and Workingmen's Act, a kind of omnibus measure relating primarily to trade unions, guaranteeing them not only the right to strike but the right to picket, an important landmark in the history of labor legislation.

And in this connection it is interesting to note that both Disraeli, the Tory, and that embittered German exile in London, Karl Marx, were Jews who for political and social reasons had been baptised as Christians. The father of Marx was a rabbi; the father of Disraeli a wealthy litterateur steeped in rabbinical lore. Deep in the background of their sons lay the teachings of the Hebrew prophets concerning social justice.

The details of this social legislation Disraeli left in the capable hands of Cross, home secretary in his cabinet. The older the Prime Minister grew the more he withdrew into himself. An ill man, he suffered greatly from gout and asthma, making it difficult for him to remain standing or to speak at length. The flowing locks and gay apparel of earlier years had long since disappeared. He remained a bit of a dandy, was exquisitely tailored, but clad now in somber black, his colorless face and dyed beard portraying age. Gladly in 1878 he migrated from the House of Commons to the House of Lords, made Earl of Beaconsfield by a grateful Queen. Here he stated that he was "dead, but in the Elysian fields."

Imperium now took the place of *sanitas* as interest in the expansion of the British Empire revived as in the days of Chatham and the younger Pitt. "Great Britain," to quote Beaconsfield, "is not a mere European power; she is the metropolis of a great empire."

That empire included the self-governing colonies overseas as well as India and other lands of Asia and Africa where lived alien races. Beaconsfield paid slight attention to the self-governing colonies with the exception, somewhat, of Cape Colony and Natal. What fired his imagination, dictated his policy in Egypt, the Middle East, Afghanistan, and India, was empire in the Roman rather than in the Greek sense: not so much the extension of British culture as the expansion of British prestige and power, authority emanating straight from London, insured and guaranteed by the British army and the Royal Navy.

Sweet fortune enabled the aging Beaconsfield to link the future of his beloved England with that of regions in the mystic and romantic Orient. The tale thereof relates not to this chapter but to the two chapters on imperialism and the two on the Near East. Therefore we must take leave of him.

The Second Gladstone Ministry (1880-85)

In 1880 a general election swept Disraeli (since 1876 Lord Beaconsfield) out of office and brought back Gladstone. Such a reverse had not been expected by Beaconsfield; during the campaign he had stood proudly on his record and had fancied that his triumphant return from the Berlin Congress indicated that he would win the next election. Gladstone proved this a mirage. Scotland and the industrial North swung heavily to the Liberal side; seemingly the people were willing to rebuke imperialism; they also were interested in their pocketbooks. Deficit after deficit had characterized Disraeli's ministry (he was not interested in finance), and Gladstone had no difficulty in convincing the majority that the unbalanced budget was due to the extravagance of a government which engaged in the military occupation of the South African Republic and sent armies into Afghanistan.

The new ministry was launched upon a sea of troubles. It inherited a dangerous imperial and foreign policy which it found equally impossible to reverse or to carry through; it faced an ominous economic situation which it was impossible to ignore and also impossible to remedy, at least by tried liberal principles; and finally, in Ireland it confronted opposition so bitter, so intractable, that ultimately before its weight the Liberal party all but collapsed.

Of these three problems, the one upon which Parliament focused the least attention was the depression. British economy went into a tailspin in the eighties as respects both industry and agriculture. The world demand for British manufactured goods declined sharply, and factories discharged thousands just as other thousands migrated from the farms to the cities looking for nonexistent jobs. Acute and widespread misery was quite as prevalent as in the "Hungry Forties."

But Parliament did little or nothing to alleviate it, and for three reasons: first, Gladstone and the Liberals chose to minimize and to ignore this economic blackout, insisting that it was quite temporary; secondly, the Tory party, with a very few exceptions (like Lord Randolph Churchill, father of Winston Churchill), did likewise, offering no remedial program. And finally there was Irish Nationalism.

In one respect there was a parallel between the pre-War history of the German Empire and that of Britain; if Germany was perplexed and puzzled by the growing number of restless and unreconciled Poles within her borders, the British equally were harassed by the growing unwillingness of the Irish to be reconciled to British rule.

To place one's finger on any single cause of Irish disaffection is impossible; there were too many causes. Economic distress was important; there were too many Irishmen to be supported in comfort in too small an area, even if there had been no landlordism, and Gladstone's first land act, as we have seen, only slightly mitigated that evil. But equally important, if not more so, was Irish nationalism which (as was the case with the Poles in eastern Germany) became more intense with every passing year.

Unlike the Poles, however, the Irish Nationalists had a great leader, Charles Stuart Parnell. Although a Protestant, a landlord, and an aristocrat, he was elected to Parliament in 1875, where he speedily became beloved by his Irish colleagues and hated by the English. The Commons, that first gentlemen's club of Europe, hitherto had been accustomed to free and open debate, a method only possible when every one behaves like a gentleman and obeys the rules of the game. Parnell acted otherwise. He became the leader of a small group to which most of the Irish members attached themselves. These Nationalists capitalized their nuisance value and it was considerable. By making numerous motions and countermotions, by endless debate and interruption, they made parliamentary government a farce. Gladstone at first paid scant attention to these unruly fellows; he still thought that the hearts of Irishmen could be won by religious tolerance and economic prosperity, an idea which the Parnellites ultimately forced him to realize was a delusion.

Gladstone tried kindness; a new land act was passed in 1881 (revolutionary from the point of view of laissez faire), whereby the rental of Irish farms was not left to the law of supply and demand but, whenever requested by the peasant, was to be determined by a process of judicial review, in other words set by a government commission and to stay fixed for fifteen years, after which a new review might be made. This act of rough-and-ready justice did improve the lot of many, although in view of the general decline in agricultural prices during the last two decades of the century, fifteen years was too long a time to wait for reductions in rent. But the Irish did not wait for the test of time, and Parnell denounced the law as a fraud, for he feared lest it might succeed and so injure his anti-British propaganda.

Since Parnell was president of the Irish Land League, as well as leader of his party in Parliament, and since the League was responsible for an increase in agrarian outrages, such as maiming the cattle, burning the barns, ruining the crops of men willing to take the place of evicted tenants, Gladstone decided upon different tactics.

He now tried coercion: Parnell was put in prison and civil liberties were suspended in Ireland. This but aggravated the situation. After two years Gladstone still had 25,000 redcoats in Ireland and 20,000 constabulary besides. It was an expensive business and futile. When Captain Boycott's peasants refused to cut his grain (the origin of the term "boycott") it was possible to order in troops to do it; but how long could such a procedure be kept going?

Therefore Gladstone returned to leniency. Parnell came out of prison and for a short time there was relative peace. Then followed the murder of Lord Frederic Cavendish, newly appointed Britain's viceroy in Ireland, and then more coercion. Parnell, denying responsibility for this and other murders, continued refractory; large sums of money poured into his coffers from America; his grip on the Irish Home Rule party grew tighter; and since he decided that nothing further was to be gained from Gladstone, he opened negotiations with the Tory opposition in Parliament. Gladstone, with ear ever close to the ground, began to wonder if political appeasement in the nature of an approach to Home Rule as well as economic readjustment might not be necessary.

Ireland was not the only cause of worry; there were other storms brewing in this second ministry of Gladstone's. Many of them related to foreign policy, but a number of others had to do with economic discontent within England. The Industrial Revolution had depressed the lot of the village laborers and many thought that they, as well as the crofters of Scotland, were as much deserving of state aid as Irish peasants. "Three acres and a cow" was a slogan which began to be heard on their behalf. Then, too, the slump in trade made the urban proletariat restless. What was to be done? The Liberal party was of two minds; the older members, steeped in the philosophy of laissez faire, were for doing nothing; a younger group, headed by the aggressive mayor of Birmingham, Joseph Chamberlain, were for state intervention. "What ransom will the wealthy pay for their security?" was his bold question. The words were untactful; but Chamberlain was a "stand and deliver man" and so influential in the party that Gladstone had felt compelled to retain him in his cabinet.

The Prime Minister, at this time well over seventy, sided with the older Liberals; on the other hand he was a skilled politician and had no intention of being displaced as leader by the pushing Mr. Chamberlain, whom he rather disliked. All his life he had been successful in drawing up formulas of compromise and he would try again. And so Gladstone bethought himself of Parliamentary reform, a new redistribution of seats, and an enlargement of the franchise. Here was a common platform upon which all Liberals could stand, laissez-faire men like the aged John Bright, neo-socialists like Chamberlain. The economic perplexities of the moment might be ignored if sufficient excitement could be aroused over political reform.

So it came about that a third reform bill was introduced into the House of Commons to implement that of 1867. In the same way as the former conferred the vote on the urban worker, so did the latter bestow it on the farm laborer. Naturally the result was not as revolutionary as in 1867. The Second Reform Bill, that of the earlier date, had made England to all intents and purposes a political democracy, and had passed the balance of power to the urban working classes; the third Reform Bill, that of 1884, merely added the agricultural workers, not nearly as numerous as the sum total of those employed in British factories. The Queen took alarm at these "radical" activities of her venerable prime minister; but she need not have worried. By taste and breeding

Gladstone was essentially an aristocrat, and rural laborers in England were not given to radical flights of fancy.

The second ministry was now nearing its conclusion and the fractious Irish hastened it. Parnell, to show his power, threw his Home Rulers into the opposition lobby on an inconsequential issue and Gladstone, defeated thus in 1885, resigned.

The Home Rule Bill of 1886: Third Gladstone Ministry

With the possible exception of 1832, the year 1886 was the most exciting in the annals of nineteenth-century England. Gladstone, seventy-six years old but still abounding in energy and courage, decided to end his political career with one grand, magnanimous gesture of friendship toward Ireland. Deciding that the only thing to do with the Irish Nationalists was to let them have their own way with an Irish Parliament in Dublin, he pleaded with the electorate for a majority over all in the coming election so it could not be said that the Liberals held office merely as the Irish chose. The general election was held and Gladstone obtained a mere plurality of seats, a handicap from the start. For a majority he was still dependent on the votes of the Irish members.

It was not the only handicap; Chamberlain threw his great influence in the Liberal party against the Home Rule Bill. The latter was not particularly radical, since it offered many safeguards in regard to law and order, religion and finance; but it did set up an Irish Parliament in Dublin, thus bringing the United Kingdom to an end as a legal entity. This was sufficient to stir the Tory dovecotes, always willing to be stirred against Gladstone. But this time the old Whig element in the Liberal party sided with the Tories. The English, as a people, did not trust the Irish, and religious and racial differences added to the general excitement of the parliamentary fight which followed.

It was a bitter contest and for a long time in doubt. Finally, Gladstone went down to defeat in this, one of the shortest ministries in British history. The Irish, it was evident, were not yet to find recognition of their nationality. Two reasons, perhaps, explain why. One was that, coupled with the Home Rule Bill was the promise of the Prime Minister to introduce a final land act which would buy out all Irish landlords. Such a law would be a risky venture, thought conservative Englishmen, anxious concerning the security of vast sums already invested in Ireland and dubious about the financial integrity of a Dublin Parliament. Even more influential in defeating the bill was the cry of Ulster. The majority who lived in that province were the Protestant descendants of the Protestant colony planted in North Ireland by Oliver Cromwell. Most of them were Presbyterians who, having been "top dog" for two centuries, feared inclusion in a Roman Catholic Ireland. "Ulster will fight and Ulster will be right," cried Lord Randolph Churchill, a fire-eating Tory and now political ally of Chamberlain, who was determined to defeat both Irish Home Rule and Mr. Gladstone. The Ulster men appealed to Britain for sympathy and not in vain. Memories of the Spanish Armada, never dead, were awakened. England was a Protestant country; as such could she abandon this loyal Protestant garrison of hers in Ireland? Parnell himself was a Protestant, but that fact was forgotten. The backbone of the Liberal party was composed of the middle class, largely Nonconformist in faith. Skilfully, the Tories played upon its religious prejudices. Even such a famous old radical as John Bright would not follow his friend Gladstone on this issue.

And so Home Rule was defeated and the Liberal party split into two warring factions, never to unite again. The majority followed Gladstone; the minority, calling themselves Liberal Unionists, formed a new party. They were a curious group, for the most part made up of the old Whig element surviving in the Liberal party, wealthy and conservative, joined to Chamberlain and a few of his erstwhile radical friends.

Old Grievances Continue (1886-1905)

For nearly two decades England was to be governed by the Conservatives, generally in loose alliance with the Liberal Unionists, who were destined one by one to drop into the Conservative ranks. Gladstone, half-blind, half-deaf, was destined to form a fourth ministry (1892-94) in a last effort to gain Home Rule for the Irish; but the Liberals secured only a slender grip on the government, which they lost completely in 1895. Therefore, to all intents and purposes, the two decades were to see the Conservatives in power, first under Lord Salisbury and then under his nephew, Arthur James Balfour, the two men together being spoken of as the Cecil dynasty.

The major domestic problems were, as before, Ireland and the welfare of the British proletariat. The defeat of 1886 ended for the time being all thought of concessions to Irish nationalism. The Tories, now in power, thought that Gladstone was a dreamer and that they knew what to do. They intended to give Ireland unstinted coercion on the one hand, economic rehabilitation on the other. The prescription was somewhat like that of Gladstone, but the Tories considered him a fumbling doctor who alternated back and forth at the whims of the patient. There would be no nonsense now. The younger Cecil (Balfour) was appointed doctor. Slender, versatile, but with the reputation of being a dawdling philosopher, few considered him stern enough to govern Ireland. The detractors were mistaken. Balfour's hand lay heavy on the island and soon he earned the sobriquet of "Bloody Balfour," so ruthless was he in applying coercion, in suspending legal guarantees, in rigidly applying military government. But he also sought to "kill Home Rule with kindness" (a phrase invented later) by extending land purchase, by building light railways, be erecting fishing-piers in the desolate western parts of the island, by presenting seed potatoes and trying to make Irish industry flourish. The Irish accepted the gifts and cordially hated the giver, continuing under Parnell's leadership their demand to be separated from the despised Saxon.

Soon it happened that a temporary lull came in Britain's dislike of Parnell. The London *Times,* "The Thunderer," that always respectable and reputed semi-official spokesman of the government, accused Parnell of complicity in the murder of Lord Frederic Cavendish. The newspaper, it was proved in an official investigation, had been, to say the least, very gullible; it had bought its evidence from a clumsy and discreditable forger. Meanwhile, the agents of Balfour in Ireland, the constabulary, had exceeded the bounds of decency by shooting suspects in Ireland. In consequence, British opinion began to veer; the cause of Home Rule took on new life, and Parnell found himself warmly greeted in Britain.

Followed an extraordinary affair. Parnell had lived for years with the wife of one of his nominal supporters, a certain Captain O'Shea. The captain brought suit for divorce, naming Parnell as corespondent, and the suit was undefended. Instantly the popularity of the Irish leader faded in England, and bitter were the demands of Gladstone's supporters that he denounce Parnell and renounce all alliance with the Irish Nationalists as long as they followed the adulterer. Gladstone notified Parnell that his own leadership of the Liberals would be rendered a "nullity" unless Parnell resigned that of the Nationalists.

Stormy and protracted were the meetings of the Irish Home Rulers. Parnell staved off desertion by warning his followers that before throwing him to the English wolves it would be wise first to obtain details of the Home Rule Bill which Gladstone intended to present to Parliament when returned to office. A committee of the Nationalists interviewed Gladstone but he refused to bind himself in advance of the Parliamentary elections. Parnell attacked Gladstone bitterly, saying that "the old spider" was not to be trusted, that months before, in a private interview, he had proposed unacceptable terms, particularly in regard to the land and the constabulary. Gladstone countered by denying that he had ever done so and denounced the unprincipled way in which a private conversation had been made public without permission.

The Irish members of Parliament now tore at one another's throats, dividing into Parnellites and anti-Parnellites, the latter the more numerous. Randolph Churchill's prophecy of 1886 now came to pass— Irishmen did not stick together. Gone now was the invincible phalanx of eighty-six Irish Nationalists; gone also was the feeling of good will toward Ireland which the last few years had engendered among the Nonconformists. That peculiar and especial breed of religious emotion known as the "Nonconformist conscience" was aroused. In regard to everything which touched upon sex mores it was extraordinarily sensitive. Many of the Nonconformists forgot that Parnell was a Protestant, forgot that his ancestors were British, that a whole nation can not be indicted for a single crime.

Under such disheartening circumstances Gladstone embarked on his last electoral campaign. Parnell had died from overexertion in trying to reëstablish his leadership; but Irish votes still counted in the House of Commons and Gladstone wanted above all things to be free from dependence upon them. Again he pleaded for a majority over all, and again he lost. He became prime minister in 1892 but with a plurality; only with Irish votes was a majority his. Nevertheless, he brought in a second Home Rule Bill which the Commons passed mainly out of compliment to "the grand old man," as Gladstone had come to be called. It was known in advance that the House of Lords would reject the measure, which it promptly did. Within another year Gladstone resigned, this time forever. His public life dated back to 1833 and four times he had been Prime Minister of England.

Meanwhile, the tide against laissez faire had been rising in England, and if Gladstone had only been sufficiently aware of it in his old age, he might have had his majority over all in 1892. The Liberal party was honeycombed with (for that day) radical ideas, such as a compulsory eight-hour day and the creation of small peasant proprietors in England by means of agricultural allotments. But Gladstone did not like these ideas. In regard to Ireland he was ready to advance; in regard to pure political reform, such as the abolition of plural voting, which still afforded an advantage to men possessing property in more than one Parliamentary constituency, he was also; but when it came to modifying his faith in pure individualism in economic life, he was obdurate. In consequence, he lost many votes he otherwise might have garnered during his last election.

The Conservative party, now solidly entrenched in power (1895-1905) differed very little from Gladstone in these economic ideas. Chamberlain's former radicalism sloughed off rather quickly as he and the Liberal Unionists tended toward closer and closer unity with the Conservatives. He still from time to time spoke of the desirability of old-age pensions, but frankly as an individual and not as leader of the Liberal Unionists. In the course of time "Liberal" dropped off the party title and both Conservatives and Liberal Unionists were spoken of as Unionists or Conservatives, until finally the former term was no longer used. The old traditional Tory or Conservative party was even less willing than Chamberlain to end the reign of laissez faire. It did something in the way of facilitating small allotments; it made a half-hearted gesture toward peasant proprietorship; it passed a mild workman's compensation act, applying to certain categories in specific industries; it abolished school fees for children of the poor; it extended self-government in both Britain and Ireland: but it did not recognize the necessity of regulating free competition in trade and commerce, capital and labor, nor would it follow Germany in such matters as unemployment insurance and old-age pensions.

Only in one major respect was the settled adherence of England to laissez-faire economics threatened before the great political upheaval of 1905. That was in regard to free trade. Chamberlain, as an ex-radical, as a manufacturer, and as a competitor with Balfour for the leadership of the party, did try to reverse the fiscal system of his country and to substitute protective tariffs for free trade. He argued that Germany's success was due in large measure to her tariff system; that England was foolish in upholding the cause of free trade when all the other great nations surrounded themselves with tariff walls; that England's persistence in this policy was responsible for the slowing-up of trade; that it resulted in the United States and Germany dumping down their manufactured surplus in Britain at cost or less; that a protective tariff would increase revenue, whereby social services such as old-age pensions might be made available; that a protective tariff would also tend to bind the Dominions more closely to the old country.

Chamberlain now was almost as successful in wrecking the Conservative party (1903-5) on this issue as he had been in wrecking the Liberal party in 1886. To press his fight he resigned from the ministry in 1903, and his new Conservative friends, instead of dividing into two warring camps as his old Liberal allies had done, divided into three. Some Conservatives, known as "free fooders" would have nothing to do with protective tariffs in any shape or form. Others, probably the majority, followed the subtle Balfour and were nicknamed "little piggers"—they were willing to consent to a low tariff on imported food products coming from outside the empire, provided the Dominions would raise their tariffs against manufactured goods coming from countries other than Britain, and provided a general election was held on this question before any law was passed by Parliament. The third group of Unionists or Conservatives, who followed Chamberlain wholeheartedly, asked for tariffs both on food and on manufactured products and were popularly described as "whole hoggers," willing to go the whole way.

The Advent of Labor

As the powerful Conservatives fell to fighting among themselves, a new political party was in process of formation—the Labor party. It was born in 1900, as the century opened, at a conference of various dissatisfied radical groups. Prominent among them, and predominant in the party ever since its existence, were the labor unions. The latter had been strongly entrenched in Britain for decades and their membership was now approximately one and three-quarter million. Traditionally, they had shunned politics, gaining their ends primarily by strikes and negotiation; but they were restless at the failure of the government to pass social legislation, and they were particularly indignant at the Taff Vale decision of 1901, whereby the highest court in the land decreed that trade unions were financially responsible for losses accruing to employers as the results of picketing encouraged by union officials. Allied with the trade unions in forming the new party were more radical groups. One was the Fabian Society, an organization of intellectuals and literary men who believed that socialism could and should be brought about piecemeal by incessant nibbling at the citadel of laissez faire. Another was the Social Democratic Federation, a straight Marxian organization which believed, or pretended to believe, that a revolution was imminent. And still a third was the Independent Labor party which stood for revisionary Marxism. Out of all these elements the Labor party was formed; its leadership strongly colored by socialism, its membership rather stolidly trade-unionist and somewhat suspicious of new ideas.

Then, as labor began to coalesce and as the Conservatives fought bitterly among themselves, the old Liberal party took on a new lease of life. Mr. Balfour (the younger Cecil) hung on to office as long as he could, despite many by-elections which evinced his unpopularity. The Boer War and military defeats did much to destroy the prestige of the British Conservatives in the opinion of the public (see p. 451), and their continued failure to conciliate the Irish, coupled with disputes among themselves as to free trade, added to their disrepute. Therefore, when a general election was held in 1905, a political landslide occurred toward the left, some 377 Liberals, 83 Irish Nationalists, 53 "Laborites," and 157 Conservatives being elected. Of the so-called Laborites, 29 were members of the new Labor party, the remaining 24 being workingmen, elected as Liberals, who joined labor officially two years later. Had Victoria been alive she would have been shocked beyond measure. Yet it was less than five years since the good Queen had died. The Victorian Compromise was indeed tottering.

But it did not fall. The Liberals were not obtuse; they recognized the pressure brought to bear upon them by the left and, instead of defying it, they attempted to capitalize it to their advantage. The new prime minister, Campbell-Bannerman, was an intelligent and wary Scot who knew that Gladstonian liberalism in respect to laissez faire was dead. So, too, did his successor in office, Herbert Asquith, a young lieutenant of Gladstone in 1886, who became prime minister on Campbell-Bannerman's death in 1908. There was an abundance of talent in the cabinet, men who recognized the portents of the times—David Lloyd George, Welsh lawyer and fiery radical; Winston Churchill, son of Lord Randolph, like his father brilliant and unusual; and even a self-made workingman, John Burns. Only in respect to foreign affairs did the new government honor British tradition, placing at the head of the foreign office Lord Grey, who represented both socially and intellectually the right-wing liberals.

Eight years were to elapse before the coming of the First World War, an era during which measure after measure was enacted by the British Parliament which reversed the long-settled tradition in England of "the less government the better," as far as business and the economic life of the country were concerned. No longer was government supposed to be merely an instrument for the enforcement of contracts, the maintenance of the King's peace and the defense of the country. The whole program of historic liberalism on its economic side, with the important exception of free trade, went by the board. Liberalism remained what it had been in regard to free speech, free religion, and free participation in voting (democracy); but it now was radically transformed in its economic philosophy, so much so that if Gladstone had lived another fifteen years he scarcely would have recognized the party of Palmerston, Bright, and Cobden.

Among the long list of new social and economic reforms were the following: the establishment of special boards on which both employers and employees were represented, empowered to set a minimum wage in certain underpaid industries; a workman's compensation act forcing many employers to insure wage-earners against some accidents and death; an act authorizing free meals for school-children; an act establishing labor exchanges; another which provided for better housing, giving authority to the central government to condemn old rookeries; an act establishing old age pensions; and finally a comprehensive law passed in 1911; and still more radical, the National Insurance Act providing for compulsory insurance against unemployment and sickness, the premium to be paid, in part by the employer, in part by the employee, and in part by the state.

An immediate result of these new laws was a rapid rise in governmental expenditure, and at a time, too, when the international situation (see p. 499) made it advisable for England to devote huge additional sums to the upkeep of her already large navy. Where was the money to come from? The old-age pension act alone called for the expenditure of many million pounds; for this was a noncontributory act, providing that the state should assume the entire cost, whereas the old-age pension system in Germany called in part for contributions out of wages. The followers of Chamberlain in the Commons said there was only one way to raise the money—protective tariffs. But Chamberlain was by this time a confirmed invalid and his two sons, Austen and Neville, of whom we shall hear later (see p. 654), did not as yet have much influence in the Conservative party, which was out of power anyway. The Liberals had swept into office as confirmed free-traders, therefore tariffs were taboo for money-raising. Lloyd George, chancellor of the exchequer, had to seek elsewhere.

In 1909, in a famous budget, he raised the income tax, put a supertax on large incomes, increased death duties, made tobacco and liquor pay more heavily, and attempted to tap a new source of income altogether by a twenty per cent tax on land values. The idea back of this last revolutionary impost came to Lloyd George from Henry George, an American writer, whose book, *Progress and Poverty* (1879), was extraordinarily popular in England. Henry George had argued that only one tax was necessary for governmental purposes, a single tax on land. From his point of view, the increase in the value of urban land was not due primarily to the enterprise and activity of the man who happened to own it, so much as to the joint labor of thousands of people gathered together in populous areas. He thought that a distinction should be made between a merchant or manufacturer, incessantly active, and men, more or less idle, who simply waited for land sites to go up in value as the result of the activities of other men, and he argued that the increased value belonged to society as a whole, rather than to the title-holder. Lloyd George proposed now to take one-fifth of this increase for the state, and at the same time to levy a special tax on unimproved rural property, with an eye to the breaking up of privately owned parks and hunting preserves to which the public was not admitted.

The budget brought on a first-class political fight. The House of Lords had approved the earlier measures of social reform, but the House of Lords was a house of landlords, and the income of its members would diminish sharply if the budget became law. Constitutional precedent was against the Lords refusing assent to budgets; but was this simply a revenue measure or one intended to bring on social revolution? If the latter was the case it was clearly within the constitutional rights of the Lords to refuse assent until a new Parliamentary election should decide the issue. There was a good deal to be said for this point of view as a matter of law but very little from that of policy. The Lords were unpopular in the country and the budget was popular. Any fight they might put up against the latter inevitably would be interpreted as one fought for their own pocketbooks rather than for the good of the nation. Nevertheless, the Lords threw out the budget. The Liberals appealed to the electorate and were returned again to office by a Parliamentary election in 1910, though with a sharply reduced majority. Thereupon the Lords passed the budget promptly.

This, however, did not save them from the wrath of their enemies. Ever since there had been a Liberal party, the Lords had seen fit to disapprove Liberal bills, although always approving those passed by

Conservatives, and the exasperated Liberals thought the time had come to clip their lordships' wings. This they proceeded to do by the Parliament Act, whereby any bill passed by the House of Commons became law with or without the consent of the House of Lords, provided it was passed three times by the former, and that at least two years intervened between its introduction and final passage. In addition, any bill certified by the Speaker of the Commons as a money bill became law automatically within one month after passage by the lower house. The Lords rejected this Parliament Act immediately. Again there was an election, the second within the year 1910, and again the nation supported the Liberals. Whereupon the days of 1832 were reënacted. The King gave assurance to the Prime Minister that if the Lords continued recalcitrant he would approve the appointment of a sufficient number of new peers to swamp opposition. Some "bitter-enders," rather than vote against the bill, stayed away from Westminster; and a sufficient number of peers were found to swallow officially this law which they detested so heartily. England was now more a political democracy than ever before. The House of Commons was virtually supreme, since the Lords had only a suspensive veto left. A potential veto in theory still remained with the Crown, but no ruler had exercised it for two hundred years.

Was the country apt to become a social and economic democracy as well as a political one? That lay within the bounds of possibility. The great majority who held important office under the Crown still came from the old families, still wore "the old school tie," that is, were graduates of Eton, Harrow, Rugby, and a number of other select schools. But this seemed a day of revolutionary change and who knew what might happen? The Labor party continued to grow in numbers and in influence. The social-reform measures passed by the Liberals simply whetted the appetite of the Laborites. Early in the days of the Campbell-Bannerman ministry they secured the reversal of the Taff Vale decision and then they struck hard at another legal barrier which they considered inimical to the trade unions. This was the Osborne decision, which made it illegal for trade unions to compel their members to pay an assessment for the support of the Labor members of the House of Commons. Since members of that body received no salary, the Labor men would have had a tough time if the unions had not paid them. On the other hand it seemed tyrannical that trade-unionists should be forced to contribute to their pay and the difficulty was voided by the ministry passing a law providing for a modest salary for M.P.'s. Thus one more of the old Chartist demands was victorious. Labor, however, was still not content. A flood of strikes swept the country and, unlike earlier ones, they were in certain instances nationwide. The inflammatory doctrines of Sorel, which had a contemporary vogue in France (see p. 355), and which were sinking deep into the spirit of Benito Mussolini reverberated in England.

Violence was in the air in the years immediately antecedent to the First World War. It affected women no less than men. A few decades earlier, woman's suffrage was an academic question occasionally discussed. Now it became a burning issue. Nor was it by persuasion alone that the "suffragettes" hoped to obtain the vote. They, like the more extreme labor leaders, had confidence in violence. The suffragettes broke windows, poured chemicals into letter-boxes, chained themselves to public statues and to the grill work of the Houses of Parliament, shouting "Votes for women" as they deftly concealed the keys which would loosen their chains. Placed in jail, they went on hunger strikes. The police fed them milk through tubes passed into their noses, an unpleasant affair which led to charges of cruelty; the police let them out of jail and then rearrested them in batches. One ardent suffragette set fire to houses, another threw herself before a horse at the Derby and was killed to advertise the cause. What could be done with these women?

And then, of course, there was Ireland. The Liberals did not bother much about Ireland in 1906. Their memories were acutely conscious of the way in which Ireland had once broken the unity of their party and the less said about Ireland the better. Their majority was so huge then that for the time being Ireland did not matter. But such an attitude was no longer possible in 1910. The Liberals and the Conservatives practically tied in the two elections of that year and any Liberal majority now depended on Labor and Irish support. It lay within the power of the Irish Nationalists to oust the Liberals if they pleased to do so. Apparently no bargain was struck; none was necessary. The implication was plain; if the Nationalists supported Liberals in the matter of the budget and the Parliament Act, it followed that return favors were due and that the eternal Irish question must be reopened.

From an economic point of view Ireland had not done badly during the first decade of the twentieth century. The decline of population ceased, as peasant proprietorship, financed by the British treasury which had loaned millions of pounds at very low rates of interest to the peasants, kept on increasing. The British old-age pension law also was an added blessing, especially since there were many more aged poor in Ireland than in England. A considerable amount of self-government also had been granted the Irish by the creation of county councils elected under the Parliamentary franchise, whereby administrative functions had been taken away from the grand juries consisting of landlords and placed in the hands of these popularly elected bodies.

Nevertheless at Westminster there continued to sit eighty-three to eighty-six Irish Nationalists pledged to continue the fight for Home Rule. Ireland's total representation under the Act of Union had been 103, and the difference was accounted for by the men of Ulster pledged against Home Rule. In other words, the situation had not changed appreciably in thirty years. Something more than eighty per cent of those living in Ireland continued to demand a parliament, a flag, a country of their own; something less than twenty per cent (for Ulster was split on the issue) rejoiced in British citizenship, clung close to it, and made continued unity with Britain their foremost political objective.

Out of this situation came the Third Home Rule Bill, that of 1912. It passed the Commons, was turned back by the Lords, passed the Commons twice again, became law, was suspended for the duration of the World War, and became a nullity with the revolt of the Irish in 1916. Meanwhile, it almost brought Great Britain to the verge of civil war in 1914.

The real objections to the first and second Home Rule bills of Gladstone were that the British despised the Irish Nationalists and, for military reasons, and because of religious prejudice, they could not brook the idea of a separate Parliament at Dublin. But the theoretical objections had been somewhat different and among them bulked large the fact that in the bill of 1886 all Irish representation ceased at Westminster but Ireland still was to contribute its quota for imperial defense, a fact which meant taxation without representation, and a foreign policy determined by the British Parliament which would automatically involve Ireland without Irish consent. In the case of the second bill, that of 1893, the argument was reversed. That measure proposed to continue the presence of the Irish in London, while at the same time giving them their Dublin Parliament. If this was done Irishmen would have a vote on domestic English affairs while Englishmen would have no vote on internal Irish questions. The third bill, 1912, was a compromise between bill one and bill two, for while the Irish still were to sit at Westminster, their membership in the Commons was reduced to forty-two.

This was but one of many technical difficulties brought out by the new bill. There were very many other perplexing ones, particularly those of a financial sort: What should Ireland contribute for imperial defense? What about the payment of land annuities accruing to England as the result of money advanced for the purchase of Irish land? What about the old-age pensions, a charge on the British treasury? What about the continuation of free trade between the islands? Yet in the last analysis, all of these points of difference faded into littleness compared with the question of Ulster, that hard-bitten province upon whose rock the first and second Home Rule bills had foundered.

The Protestant majority in all Ulster was slim, only fifty-five per cent; but that fifty-five per cent was wealthy, determined, powerful, and led by one of the ablest men of the British bar, Sir Edward Carson, who from the beginning had refused all compromise and who held that even the British Parliament itself had no right to exclude Ulster from union with Britain without a direct mandate to that effect.

Now there had been a Parliamentary election on the Lloyd George budget in 1910, and again in the same year on the Parliament Act. The Liberals, therefore, could fairly claim that they had a mandate to govern the country. Were they to hold a third Parliamentary election within three years on the noisy demand of the Conservatives, they would create a precedent whereby at any time it would be necessary to hold a plebiscite on almost any issue not specifically voted upon at an earlier election. Therefore they continued to ignore Carson and his friends and to press the passage of the bill.

As they did so, Carson changed the theater of his agitation from Parliament to Ulster. Thousands there took the oath upon the open Bible and the Union Jack, swore solemnly to resist by force any effort to detach them from their own country. They went further; they donned uniforms, engaged in military drill and gun-running. Armed to the teeth, they paraded up and down the countryside, prepared to prevent the enforcement of an act of the British Parliament. Yet this was only hypothetical treason; the law was not yet on the statute books.

From England there came much sympathy and encouragement, both from within the House of Commons and without. All the social bitterness that smoldered in the hearts of upper-class Englishmen as they surveyed the Liberal-Labor victories of the last few years now took fire. They did not believe that there was any majority in the United Kingdom, outside of Ireland, for Home Rule, and possibly they were right. At any rate, they were most determined to help Ulster fight the good fight of British patriotism, and as 1914 dawned it began to look like civil war. The cabinet thereupon hastily devised a compromise. Every county in Ulster (there were nine) was to vote separately as to whether it desired inclusion in the new Ireland. If it rejected union it was to stay outside of it for six years, that is, until two Parliamentary elections were held. But Carson would have none of this. "No six-years' suspension of death for Ulster," he cried. Shortly thereafter, the government ordered a detachment of the British army in Ireland north to protect his Majesty's stores. The officers resigned rather than risk firing upon Ulstermen whose sole wish was to stay British. Again the government hesitated, as every Tory newspaper and every Tory drawing room roared approval of the officers' act. The King in person took a hand; might it not be possible to divide Ulster? Might it not also be possible for George V to exercise the veto power of the Crown? Openly he was urged to do so. Meanwhile, as Ulster drilled and marched, the men of the South of Ireland began to do likewise. Almost anything might have happened in what was technically known as the United Kingdom of Great Britain and Ireland in the summer of 1914, had it not been for the hurricane of war sweeping upon Europe from the Balkan Peninsula. So both sides won a victory, and Carson the major one. Home Rule became the law; but the suspension of the operation of the act was a sentence of death to Ireland's dreams—that is, for an indefinite time.

Chapter 19

THE THIRD REPUBLIC (1871-1914)

IN 1871 FRANCE was in the depths. German Uhlans had trotted down her Champs-Élysées; two of her fairest provinces had been torn from her; and government she had none, except a hastily elected National Assembly meeting at Bordeaux. The Second Empire had faded into oblivion like the Second Republic, and what the future had in store for the "Grande Nation," none could say.

In the hastily held election for the Assembly there had been no time for campaigning. The peasants, still the great majority of the French people, wanted peace, almost at any price, and after that, a stable, conservative government. The deputies chosen were usually men of local mark with a reputation for solid capacity and experience. Bonapartists everywhere were at a discount, and so, too, were Republicans, except in the cities. As a result, about 400 of the 650 members of the Assembly called themselves Monarchists, very much divided, however, between the adherents of the old Bourbon line, the Legitimists, and the supporters of the House of Orleans who praised the happy, peaceful bourgeois days of Louis Philippe.

How peace was dictated by Bismarck, and how Belfort was wrung back from the conqueror by Thiers, has been told already (see p. 209), but a new agony almost equal to the parting with Alsace-Lorraine was soon awaiting the afflicted nation—Frenchman was again to join in death grapple with Frenchman. The spring of 1871 witnessed the bloody struggle called "The Paris Commune."

In March the Assembly quitted Bordeaux. It had named, as "Chief of the Executive Power," Thiers, then at the height of his popularity, had decreed the downfall of the Bonapartist regime, and had accepted the republic as a temporary arrangement. But the Assembly did not return to Paris. Rural France hated the city as the wicked, turbulent capital out of which had come revolutions, clamors for war, and national miseries. The Deputies, therefore, went to Versailles, twelve miles distant, alleging that the metropolis was too unsettled. "We have had enough of this Paris," they said in the lobbies, "this Paris that ten times in eighty years has sent us down a new government for France by telegraph."

The "Commune of Paris" (Spring, 1871): Its Bloody Suppression

The unfavorable reaction upon the Parisian industrial classes was now, of course, inevitable. They had suffered a long winter of famine and cold, buoyed up by a kind of "moral and physical exaltation" and the belief that they could somehow fling back the Prussian. Now, all their sacrifices had ended in defeat; their nerves were fagged, their disappointment infinite. It was impossible for the masses of the great faubourgs to believe that, after all their effort, they had been beaten by the Germans, thanks merely to superior technical preparation. The inevitable cry was, "We are betrayed"—and the traitors seemed pretty clearly those cowardly peasants who had failed to save Paris and who now had sent the arch-traitors to Versailles as their deputies.

Under such conditions, tens of thousands of workingmen, still unemployed, were easy prey to specious agitators. The old theories and programs of 1848 were spread again, while the "Monarchist" Assembly made itself still more unpopular by suppressing the pay given during the war to the National Guard (practically the whole industrial population of Paris), while simultaneously permitting landlords to begin again to collect their rents. By the middle of March, all was ready for another explosion. A "Central Committee" was virtually in control of Paris, avowedly to protect the interests of the National Guard. Soon its leaders had seized all the municipal arsenals and were masters of 450,000 muskets and some 225 cannon. On March 18, when two regiments from Versailles tried to secure these cannon, they were beset by a mob, and two generals were brutally shot. This was the beginning of civil war.

The insurgents in Paris represented a concourse of the discontented, not a well-matured attempt to put over a new utopia. A "Commune of Paris" claimed to hold power by the popular will, although, at best, its eighty-four members were chosen only by the industrial quarters. There was no common program. About seventeen of this Commune were thoroughgoing socialists of the 1848 school, the rest were rather "Jacobins," champions of the Robespierre traditions of 1793. They all wanted a "Republic"; they all hated the Versailles Assembly as the embodiment of monarchy and reaction. Beyond this, the socialists swept the Commune into declaring, practically, for a decentralization of France. Each separate commune was to possess numerous powers of local autonomy. The petty rural districts could thus hug "effete capitalism" if they wished; but Paris could set up itself as a socialist state, unvexed by the rest of France. The Commune adopted the old "Republican" calendar of the Revolution and the red flag, and defied the Assembly to do its worst. The Assembly promptly took up the gauntlet.

The story of April-May, 1871, was this: The Versailles Deputies, stung to fury by an insurrection that lifted its uncouth head while France was still bleeding from the invader, granted full powers to Thiers. He utilized more than 130,000 regular troops which had just been released from German prison camps. These beat down the Communist defenses one by one. When the Communists saw the end approaching, they tried to make Paris their funeral pyre—to burn down all the chief buildings with petroleum. The Tuileries went up in smoke, "the Seine ran down between two walls of fire." Hostages, including the Archbishop of Paris, were shot in cold blood by the Communists just before their own fate came. When all was over, some 17,000 Communists had been killed, 7,500 more were being shipped off as convicts, Paris was a shambles, and for a while the revolutionary party was no more. Frenchmen who loved their country could only survey this latest wreck, count the cost, and resolve to build a new France.

Monarchists Versus Republicans

With the Commune vanquished, France wrought zealously at the task of reconstruction. Without setting up a permanent government, the Assembly granted Thiers, in August, 1871, the title of "President of the Republic," although he could hold office only during the Deputies' good pleasure. He, himself, declared that, considering the violent rivalries of the different factions, he considered a very moderate republic the only regime possible under the circumstances. *"The Republic is the government that divides us least,"* he stated, adding the caution, *"The Republic will be conservative or it will not be!"*

In this spirit, the problem of setting up a permanent constitution was postponed. Thiers and his associates set themselves to the task of restoring the nation. The Germans were still occupying many departments, as security for the indemnity. But Thiers knew how to utilize the thrift and the equally vast reservoirs of patriotism of the French peasants. In 1872, the government called for a loan of three billion francs ($600,000,000); forty-two billions were subscribed. By 1873, the Germans had been paid off. The country bestowed on Thiers the honorable title "Liberator of the Land." In addition to this great task of financing, the drastic "military law of 1873" established obligatory army service for all male citizens.

The great loans and the military law were matters on which Republicans and Monarchists could well unite, but, by 1873, the pressure for establishing a permanent government had become irresistible. Thiers could not remain "provisional president" indefinitely. The Republicans had been greatly discredited by the Paris Commune—it had seemed the logical outgrowth of their unsettling doctrines. The Royalists were trying to compose their feuds and to bring back some kind of king. In May, 1873, this monarchist majority forced a vote which Thiers considered a censure on his policy. He resigned and the Monarchists promptly elected a new temporary president more devoted to their cause, Marshal Mac-Mahon, the gallant, if unfortunate, victim of Sedan.

For a few months, France seemed about to revert to the pomp and circumstance of a Bourbon monarchy. The Royalists had composed their feuds. The Orleanist candidate, the Count of Paris, acknowledged the Bourbon claimant, the Count of Chambord, as "Chief of the House of France" and the lawful heir.[1] Chambord himself, made all his arrangements for entering Paris in glory as Henry V. A monarchical constitution was drawn up, the torches and fireworks were ready for a grand illumination of the capital when "the King should come to his own again." Then Chambord, with the perverse genius of his house, committed political suicide.

In his exile at Frohsdorf, in Austria, he had lost nothing of his grandfather, Charles X's, obstinacy. He announced that, under no circumstances, would he become king unless for the "Republican" tricolor flag to which army and people were devoted, was substituted the old white flag of the lilies of the prerevolutionary kings. "Henry V," he wrote arrogantly, "will never abandon the flag of Henry IV." His whole attitude struck dismay into all the more reasonable royalists, who knew that only a strictly liberal parliamentary monarchy would have the least chance of surviving. "Before the white flag" avowed MacMahon (who wished Chambord well), "the chassepots [army rifles] will go off of themselves." The divine right of Kings was gone forever.

The "Constitutional Laws" of 1875

Very sorrowfully, the monarchist deputies had to postpone the coronation. But they were resolved to maintain merely a provisional government until Chambord should conveniently die, and the next heir, the Count of Paris, far more intelligent and pliable, could be thrust upon the throne.[2] However, in order to be sure of a monarchist chief of state, late in 1873, they confirmed MacMahon president for a term of seven years; by that time the royalist succession, they hoped, would be adjusted. But while the Monarchists were thus marking time, the nation was demanding action. A "Provisional Government" could not last forever. The Republicans were winning local elections and there were clear signs that the

[1] Chambord was without a son. It was arranged that the Orleanist claimant was to succeed him.

[2] In 1879 young Louis Napoleon, son of Napoleon III, the unfortunate Prince Imperial, was killed by the natives while in the British service in South Africa. The next Bonapartist pretender was an impossible individual personally. On the other hand, the Count of Chambord, despite vain and disloyal monarchist hopes that he would die, lived until 1883, when the Republic had become firmly established. In 1880, a royalist nobleman is said to have declared in disgust, "You Republicans have all the luck. The Bonapartists have just *lost* their prince; but we Royalists have *kept* ours!"

country was getting over its reaction of the Commune and was swinging against the extreme conservatives.

Early in 1875, the Assembly, with very ill grace, felt at length required to enact certain "Constitutional Laws."

Many times since 1789, France had received logically elaborated and lengthy constitutions—and all had perished. In 1875 she received three simple, and supposedly temporary, Constitutional Laws, and the Third Republic which they instituted lived. These statutes set up:

I. A president chosen for seven years by the Senate and Deputies, sitting as one body—a first magistrate surrounded with great honors, and nominally clothed with great powers, but able only to exercise authority with the countersignature of a minister who was strictly responsible to the Deputies and under political obligation to resign on an adverse vote.

II. A Senate of 300 members, chosen for nine years by the votes of the local municipal and departmental councilors or representatives in each department.

III. A Chamber of Deputies (about 576 members), chosen by universal manhood suffrage, which Chamber, of course, became the mainspring of the entire government, in view of the absolute dependence of the ministry upon its good favor. The President could not dissolve the Chamber without the consent of the Senate, and the Senate, ordinarily, hesitated to resist the Chamber on any issue where the nation had clearly spoken at a recent election of a new set of deputies.

This amazingly simple arrangement was to endure where the other fundamental laws had perished and was to see France through the unspeakable ordeal of the first World War. At the end of 1875 the Assembly at last dispersed, and early in 1876 the first elections were held for the new Senate and Chamber. The Monarchists were bitterly disappointed. They gained a small majority in the Senate, but the republican groups were nearly 200 ahead in the Chamber.

Defeat of the Monarchists (1877): The Third Republic Confirmed

MacMahon accepted, at first, only republican ministers, who could be supported by the Deputies, but around the presidential palace there still hovered a great cloud of Monarchists. To the infinite hurt of the Catholic Church, the Royalists and the clericals had now entered into a close alliance. The clericals would help back the king; the Monarchists would confirm the clergy in the control of education and use the reviving military power of France to restore the temporal power of the Pope, since 1870 held to be "imprisoned" in the Vatican by the Italian government. The President was pious and high-minded and was convinced that monarchy and Catholicism were best for France; and in 1877 he dismissed his Republican ministers and, with the consent of the royalist Senate, dissolved the Chamber of Deputies. His new ministers, headed by the royalist Broglie, now strained their official powers to secure a new Chamber of the desired stripe. Republican officials were removed, right and left; Republican newspapers were silenced on trivial charges; and Mac-Mahon, himself, openly supported the anti-Republican candidates. "The struggle is between order and disorder," announced the President, adding, "I will fulfill my mission to the end."

Against this imperfect coup d'état, the Republicans strove gallantly. Thiers was dead, but the antimonarchists had now a very effective campaigner in Gambetta, the hero of 1870. His striking personal appearance, flashing eyes, careless, joyous manner, and deep, musical oratory caught the popular imagination. Against the clerical allies of the Royalists, he struck hard. *"Le clericalisme, voila l'ennemi!"* was one of his famous battle-cries. As for MacMahon, Gambetta cried from the hustings that, after an election was held and the country had spoken, the President "must either submit or resign."

The blundering tactics of the Monarchists and clericals enabled the Republicans to pose as the champions of popular sovereignty. The Royalists were roundly defeated; the new Chamber was Republican by a heavy majority. MacMahon was too honorable and too prudent to fall back now upon his last possible weapon—the army. He dismissed Broglie and took a Republican cabinet; but his own position was impossible. His new ministers were always forcing him to measures at which he revolted. "My children would not kiss me if I did these things," he declared, and in 1879 he resigned—carrying with him (as it turned out) the last real chance of the Royalists in France. In his place, the Republicans, who had now won control also of the Senate, elected Jules Grévy, an elderly partisan who had a desirable reputation for gravity and moderation.

Thus, almost in the teeth of circumstances with a large fraction of the nation vigorously questioning its desirability, the "Third Republic" came fairly into official being in 1879. For three decades it was treated as a dubious experiment. Its downfall was steadily predicted. But it ceased to be an experiment; it gave prosperity to France.

Economic Prosperity of the Third Republic

It now seemed as though the French were destined to outlive their ill-founded reputation of being a volatile, innovating people. The Third Republic, standing for peace and firm government, and without indulging in any startling adventures, provided perhaps better than any other nation in Europe for its citizens' happiness between 1879 and 1914.

The onrush of general prosperity which characterized the Third Republic was due mainly to the advance of the Industrial Revolution in other lands. That revolution affected France directly, it is true, particularly after the commencement of the twentieth century, as hydroelectric power (white coal) was utilized in the upper valley of the Rhône. But essentially the effect of the Industrial Revolution was indirect; France became wealthy by supplying capitalistic Germany, Britain, and America with luxuries; and also by providing capital for German, British, and American entrepreneurs.

Historically, the French had specialized since the days of Louis XIV, and earlier, in the manufacture of fine rather than bulky wares, and they continued to do so. They made the best wines, the best gloves and chinaware, the finest silk cloth and other goods which commanded high prices in a luxury-loving world. Wedding-dresses for the daughters of the wealthy in both hemispheres were made of French silk, and bachelor dinners specialized in French champagne. Paris, no longer the pivot-wheel of European politics as in the days of Napoleon III, still remained the foyer of European fashion, and the wealthier Chicago, Bremen, and Manchester became, the more money there was available for Parisian luxuries.

The Third Republic, indeed, in one important respect paralleled in its development that of the July Monarchy in the heyday of its success: Its government essentially was that of the bourgeoisie, of the men of the middle class—lawyers, doctors, journalists, politicians—believing in capitalism and encouraging its growth in every possible way. True, far more men could vote than in the old days, the *Capacités* were enfranchised, and men were republican in sympathy instead of monarchical; true, also, they did not hold with laissez faire as interpreted by Guizot. Neomercantilism was what they stood for; government was to assist business; there must be a hook-up between the state and the economic life of the people. A great deal of attention was paid to agriculture. State-owned bulls and state-owned stallions improved the breed of cattle and of horses. Agricultural schools, state-supported, taught the best methods of cheese-making and of bee-culture. Public works were not neglected; harbors were deepened; new railroads and new oceanliners were subsidized; and behind the French man of business stood the French government, as firmly rooted in belief in private property as when the Declaration of the Rights of Man was drawn up in 1791.

That business man was a more cautious chap than the restless entrepreneurs of Germany and of England. He preferred to lend money rather than to risk it directly in new enterprises. The French were a frugal people, saving their surplus capital, and this they loaned out all over the world. Next to England, France became the leading banking nation in Europe. Russian and Turkish bonds were held in large amounts, and the French loaned a great deal elsewhere in Europe, as well as in both the Americas. There was much money to loan, for in the decades between the Franco-Prussian War and the World War the national wealth of France increased fifty per cent!

That wealth was widely distributed, a fact which made for general material comfort. The land policy of the French Revolution still held and peasant proprietorship continued. Industrial establishments were small, ordinarily employing but very few workmen; but there were many such establishments and petty capitalists were numerous. In fact, almost every one was a petty capitalist with some property. More than 8,000,000 French citizens held title to real estate in France. With a population of under 40,000,000, there were over 14,000,000 individual savings-bank accounts; the Bank of France had over 30,000 stockholders, a great many of whom only owned a few shares apiece. The national debt was high, but so widely scattered among Frenchmen that French credit was of the best and the government was able to borrow at three per cent at a time when five per cent was considered only a fair yield. When the Pennsylvania Railroad, in the prewar days, floated a bond issue in France, there was no trouble in getting the money provided the bonds were printed in sufficiently small denominations. Hence rose the American practice of selling "baby bonds," an idea worked out first of all to satisfy French investors who collectively possessed much but who individually insisted on having bonds in denominations of less than $1,000.

The ins and outs of French politics from 1877 to 1914 are scarcely worth remembering. Gambetta, the great Republican, died in 1882, and in his stead the antimonarchists lacked any first-class leader. After the Republic seemed reasonably secure, the deputies who favored it became split into such numerous factions that cabinet government became confused and personal. The average ministry was made up of a haphazard alliance of petty groups—the least friction or mischance would upset the combination; and a resignation, a new premier, and a new ministry became the order of the day, to so great an extent that there were no less than fifty ministries in forty-four years. Yet this was not as serious in practice as it might appear. There was continuity, for the most part, in both legislation and administration. Men shifted and changed in office but policies did so only slightly.

Four major topics of national importance absorbed public interest. The first had to do with the everspreading extent of France's colonial empire, particularly in Africa and is described elsewhere (see p. 453); the second concerned the army and its relations to the civil government; the third related to the problem of Church and State; and the fourth, largely a concern of the twentieth century, revolved about the labor question and that peculiar type of socialism known in France as syndicalism.

The Third Republic and the Army

The army situation was peculiarly intricate because it involved not only national defense but the larger issue of patriotism. Although essential to the welfare of France, the army had long been a stronghold of aristocrats and Monarchists. Even staunch Republicans, therefore, considered it desirable to treat the army with a good deal of circumspection, as may be seen by studying the Boulanger episode and the Dreyfus trial.

During the eighteen-eighties, the Republic seemed growing stronger, but in 1887 it faced a sinister danger. Relations with Germany were bad, Bismarck was hectoring, and boulevard courage cried eagerly for "revenge!" After the death of Gambetta, most of the Republican leaders were small men who could not catch the popular imagination, and in 1887 President Grévy (who had been reëlected) was forced to resign, owing to a sordid scandal in his own family. A swaggering pretender to public favor now came to the front, General Boulanger, a cheap imitator of that dubious adventurer, Napoleon III. For an anxious eighteen months, he seemed to be almost in a position to plunge France simultaneously into a domestic revolution and an unequal war with Germany.

George Ernest Boulanger, son of a Breton lawyer, was a soldier of fine military presence, an almost ideal "Man on Horseback" to win plaudits at reviews. The turn of the political wheel chanced to make him minister of war, as being one of the few generals who was considered "genuinely Republican." By 1886 he had, by relaxing discipline and by reckless talk against Germany, made himself the favorite of the privates, as well as of the café loungers along the Paris boulevards; but moderate Republicans began to suspect him. In 1887 the cabinet was at length reorganized and he lost his portfolio.

"General Revenge," as his admirers now styled him, plunged into politics and was soon put on the retired list by the government. But now the Royalists and clericals took him up—the extraordinarily light mettle of the man promised to make him their tool. A rich duchess paid much of the heavy expenses of hiring song composers to write stanzas to the burden "Death to the Prussians and hurrah for our Boulanger!" and for subsidizing newspapers to sound the hero's praises.

Boulanger himself headed a party called "Revisionists." They would destroy the laws of 1875 and, by means of a Constituent Assembly, somehow give a better government to France. This "General Revenge," nevertheless, lacked the capacity for putting over a successful revolution. In 1888 he let himself be triumphantly elected by royalist gold to the Chamber at one by-election after another, clearly with the view of securing an informal popular mandate to overthrow the government through the army. But while he was screwing his courage to the sticking point, the ministry became filled with alarm, and ordered his arrest for "offenses against the safety of the state." To the chagrin of his followers, Boulanger, so far from defying the authorities, fled to Brussels like an absconding cashier (1889). His cowardice pricked the bubble of his prestige. The danger was over instantly. The Royalists ceased to waste their money, and in 1891 Boulanger committed suicide in exile, harmless and utterly discredited.

The Dreyfus "Affair" (1898-1906)

The Republic thus had surmounted one great peril; in 1898 began the development of another which presently shook all France. In 1894, a Captain Alfred Dreyfus, a Jewish army officer, was arrested and convicted of selling military secrets to Germany. He was sent for life to the convict camp in French Guiana. It seemed an ordinary case of military crime. In 1896, however, a fearless and intelligent soldier, Colonel Picquart, upon inspecting the documents of the trial, reported to his higher officers that he was satisfied that Dreyfus was innocent and that the real offender was a dissolute Major Esterhazy. The upper officers at once showed that they considered any questioning of the Dreyfus verdict an attack upon the "honor of the army." The Monarchists and clericals promptly chimed in with them, glad to capitalize the popularity of the army. The ministry supported the generals, and Picquart was actually imprisoned for "indiscipline."

By 1898, however, the matter could not be hushed up. The novelist, Emile Zola, flew to the defense of Dreyfus with a memorable public letter *I Accuse,* in which he charged certain army chiefs with deliberately conspiring to ruin the innocent and protect the guilty. The actual fate of Dreyfus now soon became a subordinate matter in an issue convulsing the entire nation—were the army chiefs above legal process and public opinion? Esterhazy soon proved himself a pitiful scoundrel and a certain Colonel Henry committed suicide, leaving a confession that he had forged documents incriminating Dreyfus, in order to assist his superior officers.

The Monarchists and clericals still made the guilt of Dreyfus almost an article of faith and conducted a furious anti-Semitic propaganda, in order to discredit his Republican apologists, but, as Zola had written, while yet the case had seemed hopeless, "Truth was on its way." In 1899, the Supreme Court of Cassation quashed Dreyfus' sentence on technical grounds. He was then returned to France, was tried again before a military court, and again, after a trial in which passions ran exceedingly high, was found "guilty with extenuating circumstances." He was next pardoned by the then President Loubet. Outside of army circles, practically all of France was now convinced that he was innocent.

After a tactful interval, in 1906, the Court of Cassation set aside the second verdict also, and Dreyfus was restored with honor to the army. Picquart was promoted also, and presently became minister of war. It was a clear-cut victory for truth and justice, and, incidentally, beside discrediting the Royalists and clericals for supporting a very evil cause, it enabled the civil authorities to purge the army commands of a number of high officers who were not truly loyal to the Republic and whose position in time of war would have been a public danger.

The Third Republic and the Church

Just as important as the threatened domination of the Republic by the army was the controversy between Church and State. Such controversies had been chronic throughout all French history; for the Catholic Church had never won as complete supremacy in France as it had in Spain and Austria, and even in the days of that most pious potentate, Louis XIV, there had been disputes and friction. The French Revolution increased them; and ever since that event there had been constant enmity between enthusiastic Republicans and ardent Catholics, the former unwilling to forget the support given Louis XVI by the Church, the latter unwilling to condone the persecution of the clergy by the Revolution. The Church as an organization was not *now* opposed to the Republic, and Leo XIII made an official pronouncement to that effect; nor, on the other hand, did questions of church dogma concern the Republic. What caused trouble more than anything else was the fact that the Monarchists tried to use religion as a lever against a republic accused of atheism, and that certain Republicans, having no use for religion, generally agnostic at heart, and frequently so by profession, used patriotism as a weapon whereby they might destroy that which they hated, the Catholic Church.

The fight against the Church was waged on two fronts, one having to do with education, the other with the Concordat, or treaty between Church and State, dating back to the first Napoleon. At the advent of the Third Republic the Church possessed a virtual monopoly on education. It was not a legalized monopoly in the sense that non-Catholic education was prohibited; but it was a monopoly for all that, in so far as practically all schools were conducted by monastic orders which had grown numerous, wealthy, and influential during the long years of the Second Empire.

It was now charged by the anti-clerical deputies in the National Assembly that these orders stressed very old-fashioned ideas in regard to religion, science, and politics, and that they were disloyal to the Republic. There was a certain substratum of truth in these charges, for the monastic orders certainly were not teaching Darwinian ideas of evolution or the higher criticism of the Bible, and though perhaps only occasionally disloyal to the Republic, they professed no ardent faith in republican institutions.

One way to deal with this situation was to set up state schools free from tuition charges, to compete with those run by the orders. In the eighteen-eighties this was done, and in the new schools the government forbade doctrinal religious instruction. That act led prominent clerics to criticize the new schools as godless, whereupon the government countered their attack by expelling the Jesuits from France. Finally the government went further; it sponsored an Associations Act whereby all religious orders of every description had to be authorized to continue their work, that is, to be willing to submit to detailed governmental supervision.

A great hue and cry of oppression was now raised; but the radical bloc, or combination of left-wing factions in the Assembly, which favored this law, won the elections of 1901 and under Combes as premier set to work promptly to drive the religious orders out of France. A few only were authorized; the rest fled incontinently to Belgium, England, and other lands, many of them coming to America and settling in Baltimore, New York, and other places. Catholic schools as such were not closed, but teaching in them was forbidden to the members of any religious order. In consequence, state schools grew rapidly in attendance and by the commencement of the First World War, their pupils outnumbered those in Catholic schools by more than four to one.

In the state schools, meanwhile, it would be a matter of opinion as to whether the teaching was religious, antireligious, or merely nonreligious. The teachers were forbidden to teach that Christ was God; on the other hand they were compelled to teach that a benevolent Deity watched over the girls and boys of the Third Republic. Some thought this resulted in chauvinistic patriotism and that an identification, intended or otherwise, was apt to be drawn between *la patrie* and the aforementioned Deity.

Before this fight in regard to the schools had died down, Combes led another, this time against the Napoleonic Concordat of 1801, whereby the state agreed to pay the salaries of Catholic clerics and the Vatican submitted to the confiscation of Church property during the Revolution Under the Concordat there was a close tie-up between State and Church, the former nominating the French bishops, the latter confirming them; and between the Vatican and Paris there were regular diplomatic relations. Combes wanted to separate Church and State completely and to that end arranged for the President of France to visit the King of Italy, knowing that such an act would vex the Pope because of the Italian occupation of the city of Rome. The Pope made protest as Combes had hoped that he would; also it is possible that he violated the strict letter of the Concordat by sending certain directions to French bishops directly, instead of through state channels. At any rate the radical bloc in control of Parliament considered these reasons sufficient in 1905 for ending the Concordat, for separating Church and State, for ceasing to pay clerical salaries (with the exception of pensions for aged priests), and for claiming the legal ownership of all the churches in France as historical monuments.

For a time there was intense excitement. Combes, a freethinker and a bitter enemy of the Church, acted in indecent haste. Good Friday was the day appointed for inventories to be made of this *new* national property sequestrated from the Church, and that property included the sacred vessels on the altar. Irate Catholics rose here and there and were dispersed by force. The government did not go so far, however, as to close the churches; they could be used, it was said, by worship associations headed by laymen. But this was far from satisfying the Vatican, for Jews and Protestants were now on an equal footing with Catholics, apparently, as far as the use of Catholic churches was concerned; and anyhow, canon law was opposed to the use of church property by laymen. It was hard enough, from the point of view of Rome, to have the salaries of French priests stopped; must, in addition, this atheistical Republic declare itself the proprietor of the cathedrals of Notre Dame and of Chartres?

Then, in 1907, the State yielded a trifle; the separation laws still continued intact, but Catholics were permitted the use of their old churches, even if the proposed associations (forbidden by the Pope) had not been formed. The Church now submitted tacitly to the status quo and little by little this intense bitterness of the century's first decade subsided. The French Monarchists, although reprimanded by the Pope, continued to make what capital they could out of the affair; but the majority of Frenchmen, except in isolated districts, accepted the separation as a permanent settlement.

The Labor Problem

Finally, another source of discord among Frenchmen was the problem of labor. The so-called "bloc," or leftist combination in Parliament which, for the most part, governed France in the first decade of the twentieth century, consisted of a few moderates; many old-fashioned anti-clerical Republicans called "Radicals," whose major ideology dated back to the French Revolution; many Radical-Socialists with the emphasis on the hyphen (in other words they were not *radical* socialists but men devoted to private property who favored advanced labor legislation); and also various groups of more orthodox socialists, some Marxian, some not.

These leftist parties or groups constantly shifted in numerical strength, and the alliances between them were none too firm. They were willing to unite against the army; they were willing to unite against the Church;

they were also favorable to labor legislation, and as early as 1892-93 they passed acts protecting women and children in industry, establishing a maximum labor day of ten hours, and providing for employer's compulsory liability. But by 1907 not only was the army well under control but the religious program had been brought to a successful conclusion. The more radical members of the bloc wanted to keep on and to press for economic steps in the direction of socialism, a fact which led inevitably to the disintegration of this loosely associated group of parties.

French socialists never developed a party discipline comparable to that of the Social Democrats in Germany, and there were no less than three different brands of socialism in France—apart from the Radical-Socialists who really were not socialists at all. One of these varieties adhered to the straight Marxian line and its members were known as "United Socialists." Another formed the party of Independent Socialists, who believed in coöperating with bourgeois politicians, a thing abhorrent to a straight Marxian. And finally, in the early twentieth century, appeared a third group, Revolutionary Syndicalists, followers of Sorel, socialists of the extreme left wing, despairing of Parliamentary tactics and advocating direct action, strikes, and sabotage as a shortcut to a socialistic millennium.

All these three groups were displeased with the unwillingness of the more conservative members of the bloc to socialize French industry. All three, also, were growing rapidly in numbers in the early twentieth century, the United Socialists alone increasing their representation in the Chamber fifty per cent between 1906 and 1910. The Independent Socialists, fewest in number, for a time held the most strategic position. Under Briand they managed (1909) to control the government by combining left-wing Radicals with left-wing Socialists and by putting on the statute books an old-age pension law.

Then they were confronted by syndicalism. The Revolutionary Socialists, who upheld this essentially anarchistic doctrine that it was right and proper forcibly to seize power, proceeded to stage a railway strike. For a short time France seemed to be at their mercy. But Briand struck fast. He summoned to active service in the army those reservists who now were civilian strikers on the French railroads, and he ordered them, as soldiers, to man the trains. This act broke the strike and won for Briand the respect and liking of moderate Frenchmen but also the hatred of the left-wingers.

"France Herself Again"

The end of the strike brought about the end of the leftist bloc, and with the election of Poincaré, first as premier and then as president (1913), France turned her back on much of the radicalism and semi-radicalism of the preceding twenty years. A swing toward conservatism was noted. The fight against the Church had been carried too far, as had the fight against the army officers. The latter, it was said, stood no chance for promotion if seen on the way to Mass, and it was felt that constantly recurring diplomatic crises in Europe made it desirable to support rather than to weaken the army. Even while the bloc was at the height of its power, a strong nationalist, Delcassé (see p. 496) represented his country in foreign affairs; and now (1911-14) with increased tension over Morocco and also over Alsace-Lorraine (see p. 319), there was a notable revival of patriotic fervor. One form which it took was to increase the term of service in the army to three years, and another was to inquire seriously into the decline of the birthrate which made such an increase necessary. For the time being the power of the agnostic and perhaps materialistic statesmen who had ruled the country was shaken. France, as one of her leading men of letters, Abbé Dimnet, wrote of her, was becoming "France herself again."

Chapter 20

RUSSIA BETWEEN AUTOCRACY AND ANARCHY (1870-1914)

Discontent in Russia in the Eighteen-Seventies: Rise of Nihilism

DURING THE eighteen-sixties, Russia had recovered outwardly from the losses and demoralization of the Crimean War. Economically, Alexander II's empire seemed now in a relatively prosperous condition. In 1871 the imperial budgets showed a surplus of about $4,000,000; by 1875 it had risen to the unwonted figure of $17,000,000. Unfortunately, however, this remarkable state of comfort at the treasury was not matched by any corresponding degree of content in the Russian people at large. The peasants were angry and restless, thanks to the intense disappointment over the results of Emancipation. Freedom, which promised much, did little but bring mutterings and forebodings among them. The landlords had been allowed to select the portions of the estates to be assigned to their former serfs—they naturally had kept the best lands for themselves. The total acreage assigned the peasants in the great distribution was, in any case, too small for decent living. In 1877 it was estimated at about thirty-five acres per family unit. But the muzhiks formed one of the most prolific stocks in Europe. The population steadily increased, and, in direct ratio, the size of the little farms which the village communities (*mirs*) could reallot to their members shrunk steadily—by 1905 the average holding had fallen to about ten acres. All this meant discontent in good years, widespread famine and sheer starvation in bad years. Behind every picture of Russian life, from 1861 onward, must be visualized these many millions of "dark people"—the unorganized, ignorant peasants, hungry for more bread, which first, of course, meant more land.

And there was also the intelligentsia with whom to deal. The term "intelligentsia" is not one easy to define—in Russia or without. It connotes an educated class, plus an intangible something leaning toward radicalism. To write of the intelligentsia as "parlor pinks" or as "white-collared radicals" is unfair; nevertheless, in these slang expressions there is an element of truth. In general the word does imply opposition to the established order (particularly true of Russia in the nineteenth century) and an opposition on the part of a social class educated in book-learning rather than in practical experience.

Such a class was well defined in Russia. Its members came, to no inconsiderable degree, from the nobility, many of whom were detached from the actual management of their estates. Doctors, lawyers, teachers were enrolled in its ranks and later, as the Industrial Revolution began to seep into Russia, a number of the newly arisen bourgeoisie, impatient at delay and anxious to Westernize the country completely. Scientific materialism and socialism were watchwords of the members of the young Russian intelligentsia of 1870; but on the other hand they could not escape their own environment and origin, and therefore they added a distinctive Russian coloring to ideas imported from France, Germany, and England. Their socialism was not quite that of Marx; rather it was agrarian in character as befitted the Russian scene, and primarily concerned itself with the land problem—how to raise the status of the peasant. Their materialism also differed from that of the bustling, successful West, for Russia, historically speaking, had been neither bustling nor successful in a Western sense.

The Russian radical movement of the nineteenth century had its origin with such a class. In the late fifties, on the eve of emancipation, certain young writers began a violent attack on the vagueness and weakness of traditional Russian liberalism and began to demand the liberation of the individual from conventions and prejudices and from the bonds of religion and family. They believed that natural science was the best means of destroying superstition. They opposed all authority. They were not particularly interested in politics but assumed that the liberation of the personality would solve all social problems.

Those who believed this doctrine were described by the famous novelist Turgenev as Nihilists. In his superb novel, *Fathers and Children,* the hero, Bazarov, is a Nihilist; he takes nothing on faith; he has no use whatever for tradition or authority, religious, political, or otherwise; he respects nothing. Yet, paradoxical though it may seem, his creed is not merely negative, for he does believe in pure science, the laboratory, and the ultimate victory of pure reason. According to Pisarev, a youthful leader of the Nihilists, they believed at least in this: "... What can be broken we should break; whatever will stand the blow—is of use; whatever will be smashed to pieces—is rubbish; at any rate smash right and left; no harm can come out of this."

These ideas were perhaps somewhat crude and naïve; but Russia had been a crude, semi-Oriental country. A thin veneer of Western culture made it possible for a Russian intellectual of the mid-century like Herzen to boast that "an intellectual Russian is the most independent being in the world. . . . We are independent because we have nothing to lose; ail our memories are full of gall and bitterness." So also was it with Michael Bakunin, a Russian nobleman who had fled to England in 1861 after cruel imprisonment in eastern Siberia. According to him, the hope of the world lay in the destruction of every existing institution. Czar, laws, social conventions, God, everything hitherto counted worthy of reverence must be ruthlessly abolished. A free man interpreted the laws of nature by himself. Every form of human authority must be cast aside. After that the work of destruction would be succeeded by a free and happy world— but the destruction must come first.

This general attitude, which became more widespread with the disappointment over the fruits of emancipation, was reflected in several ways. It found expression in the Polish revolution of 1863, where a number of the revolutionists who were rounded up and sent to Siberia were known as Nihilists; it had much to do with numerous student demonstrations in the universities; and it permeated the beliefs of the Russian anarchist-socialists, more frequently called "Anarchists."

Many of the intelligentsia were simply Nihilists and let it go at that, taking no active part in political life. Others, however, went further and later proclaimed themselves Anarchists, eager above all things to do away with government. Anarchists, in one sense of the word, might be called socialists in reverse; in other words, instead of bringing about socialism by more and more government, as was the socialist idea in Western Europe, they sought to create a socialistic society by less and less political authority. To the Anarchist, practically all the evil that was in the world came from man-made laws which he held were invented primarily for the protection of private property. The straight Marxian socialists of later times and these anarchist-socialists of Russia both believed private property should be done away with; but the former would wipe it out through the agency of a more and more omnipotent government; the latter would destroy it simply by dissolving governmental authority altogether and by substituting in its place nothing at all except loose voluntary associations which they considered would spring up naturally and into which any one might be free to enter or to leave. If one once did away with private property and the laws which enforced it, then tyranny, crime, and disaster would vanish from human society.

Anarchists, as we have noted elsewhere (see p. 263), were not exclusively a product of Russia, and in the First International the majority of Spanish and Italian delegates were Anarchists. Nevertheless, Russia was one of their principal breeding-grounds. This was but natural: In Russia was the most despotic government to be found in Europe, and consequently it loomed larger than other European governments as the major instrument of tyranny; in Russia also the village mir, the historic coöperative village community, ruled by local custom rather than by statute law, seemed to illustrate the feasibility of untrammeled, free coöperation, once the dead hand of centralized authority was removed; and in Asiatic Russia (Siberia) apparently there were effective instances of how readily Russian immigrants could and would join forces freely and voluntarily for communal projects, and how governmental authority thwarted rather than abetted the welfare of frontier peoples, as may be seen by reading the experiences in Siberia of Russia's most distinguished Anarchist, Peter Kropotkin.

Some of the Nihilists and Anarchists were known as *Narodniks*, or "Populists," men and women advocating "populism" or the idea that the first duty of the intelligentsia was to redeem the people—the peasantry— by giving to the little wooden villages some gleam of the truth that was to make Russia free. Bakunin had passed the watchword, "Go among the people," meaning to mingle with the masses in order to excite them to revolt. As a preliminary step, thousands of students and young women, often from the best families, went out in small groups or individually and mixed with the peasants as common laborers to teach them the new doctrines. The peasants were fearfully illiterate, and their visitors became schoolmasters. To prevent their white skins from betraying them, they would expose their faces to the sun and blacken their hands with tar. All the time, they were preaching discontent and revolt and handing out subversive pamphlets to all peasants who could read.

Now it is obvious that in so far as nihilism, philosophically speaking, meant complete individualism, and populism, by the same token, implied the sacrifice of individualism for the common cause, there was a contradiction between the two terms. Contradictions in logic, however, abound everywhere, and perhaps nowhere more than in Russia; and they did not prevent Nihilists from taking part in the Populist agitation.

This was the origin of the Narodnik or Populist movement which reached its peak in the early seventies. Two tendencies developed in it. Some, following the teachings of P. L. Lavrov, believed that "the embodiment of truth and justice in social forms" could be achieved by peaceful propaganda and education of the people; others followed that notorious revolutionist, Bakunin, who called upon young revolutionists to emancipate themselves from religion, property, and family and lead the people in a great uprising to overthrow and destroy the state.

Many of the Narodniks who followed Bakunin now became "terrorists," believing necessary the assassination of notoriously brutal officials as the only effectual method of political action. The Land and Liberty Society of 1879, to which many Narodniks belonged, debated the use of terrorism in 1879 and split over the issue. Those who favored terrorism took the name *Narodnia Volia* (People's Will); those who opposed, the name *Chernyi Peredel* (Black Partition).

Both of these societies were suppressed by the government. But some of the members escaped to Western Europe. Among those who did so was a member of the Black Partition, George Plekhanov, who absorbed pure Marxian doctrine in the West and is now usually regarded as the father of doctrinaire socialism in Russia.

Left-wing Russian opinion was composed primarily of these various groups—Nihilists, Anarchists, Populists, terrorists and a few moderate liberals of some slight influence during the early years of Alexander II's reign. What now of the Russian right? In so far as it expressed any philosophy of life at all, aside from dead inertia, it may be summed up in two more or less interchangeable words, "Slavophilism" and "Pan-Slavism."

The principal literary and philosophic exponent of Slavophilism was the rising young tutor of the Czarevitch (afterward Alexander III), namely, Pobyedonostsev, professor of law at the University of Moscow and later Procurator of the Holy Synod, or head of the Greek Orthodox Church. Pobyedonostsev hated everything that haled from Western Europe in the way of liberalism. Universal education, freedom of the press, trial by jury were anathema to him. More particularly did parliamentary institutions draw his scorn. The latter, he considered, led directly to hypocrisy, nepotism, venality, and corruption. Only by resolutely closing the gates of Holy Russia to these noxious doctrines could the indigenous culture of Slavdom be protected. Slavophilism was summed up in three words, "autocracy," "orthodoxy," and "nationalism." Russia must remain frozen. The Czar was the living symbol of Slavic culture, and there must be no impairment of his prestige and authority. Warp and woof of that culture was the Russian Greek Orthodox Church, and it alone must represent the spiritual aspects of Slavic life. National minorities in the empire, whether Jewish, Polish, Finnish, or even Ukrainian (Little Russia), must be crushed, or at least compelled to adopt a culture identical with that of the Great Russians.

Pan-Slavism, somewhat narrower in its connotation that Slavophilism, was the Russian counterpart to Pan-Germanism. Its primary aim was the liberation of Slavs from Turkish and German misrule. This once accomplished, there were various ideas as to the future status of those Slavs, varying all the way from a Slavic federation under Russian hegemony (a kind of Slavic British Empire) to the political unity of all Slavic folk under the power of the Czar. Pan-Slavism was the watchword of Russian imperialists, in so far as they adopted an aggressive expansionist policy in the Balkans and endeavored to bring Bulgaria, Serbia, and Montenegro under the wing of mighty Russia. It would not be correct to state that all Slavophils were Pan-Slavists, as many of the former took little interest in the imperial expansion of Russia and sometimes even feared it. On the other hand many Pan-Slavists were captivated by the Slavophil doctrines and conceived of Russia as divinely ordained for certain services in the world, in very much the same way as did British imperialists who wrote of the "white man's burden," or Pan-Germanists like the last Kaiser who dreamed of a day when the term *"Deutscher Bürger"* would become as authoritative and as feared as *"civis romanus."*

Meanwhile, in the universities and among the Populists trying to prod the "black folk" into rebellion, the leaven was working. The universities of the seventies were rigorously policed to prevent seditious propaganda, but none the less the students, "herded in ill-warmed rooms and subsisting on Spartan fare" spent their time during the long winter evenings discussing utopia. Despite the utmost watchfulness of the authorities, the new ideas came in. The writings of Herbert Spencer and of Ralph Waldo Emerson might be confiscated as well as those of Karl Marx—that made no difference. Young men and young women suddenly disappeared, sent to Siberia without trial; but that made no difference either. Agitation still continued.

Although the work of the Populists made little headway among the peasants, a few serious riots for "more land" occurred, and the authorities began to bestir themselves. In 1875, about 770 Nihilists and Socialists were arrested, and 215 were held in prison. In 1877, there were two large-scale trials, one of 193 propagandists at Moscow, and another of 50 at St. Petersburg. At Odessa there were still more prosecutions for sedition. The educational movement was thus ruthlessly suppressed. Some of the propagandists became terrified or discouraged and dropped their activities; but a formidable remnant remained. Education and peaceful means had failed—they would fall back upon "Direct Action."

On a July night in 1877, while all Russia was on tenterhooks at the repulse of her armies before Plevna (see p. 402), fifteen young men met in the forest near Lipetsk (South Central Russia), and formed a program for waging war to the knife against existing institutions. Their periodicals, preaching assassination as a legitimate weapon of offense, were passed from hand to hand. Soon the student classes were greatly agitated. Money poured into the secret treasury. Young girls sacrificed their dowries, wealthier persons gave heavily. Blundering police prosecutions only made the cause more popular.

In February, 1878, came the first real application. General Trepov, Governor of St. Petersburg, was accused, in the press, of cruelty to a political prisoner. A young woman of noble family, Vera Zasulich, sought his presence and shot him with a pistol. Trepov survived, and his attacker was brought to trial, but a St. Petersburg jury promptly, in the face of all the formal evidence, found her "not guilty." Before the police could rearrest her, she had been hurried away by her friends, ultimately to take refuge in Switzerland. The affair struck terror into government circles—the new juries could not be relied on to convict in political cases. Military commissions had to be substituted, but direct action was only at its beginning.

The malcontents now determined to undertake to terrorize the Czarist government into granting a national parliament and liberty of the press. That would be the indispensable preliminary for further agitation, either for setting up a regime of Marxian socialism, or dissolving everything in a reign of anarchy. By thus demanding political liberty, the revolutionaries won the good graces of many liberals who abhorred socialism or anarchy; but their methods soon began turning many other would-be supporters against them. Assassination followed assassination. The revolver and the new dynamite bomb proved far more efficient than the old Greek tyrannicide's dagger. First, various obnoxious police spies were "removed"; then, in August, 1878, the hated Chief of the Third Section (secret police) was slain right before the Grand Duke Michael's palace in St. Petersburg. In February, 1879, Prince Kropotkin, Governor of Kharkov, was shot down by a masked assassin while returning from a ball. These were only a few instances. Placards announcing each "act of justice" were found posted in every city of the empire. Banishments, imprisonments, and executions failed to reach the real conspirators. Every great official, especially every high police officer, felt that he walked with a rope around his neck. The government seemed almost helpless.

During the panic the number of terrorists was greatly exaggerated. They never exceeded 10,000, but for a time they held the most absolute government in the world almost checkmated because (to quote Leroy-Beaulieu) *"they had made a pact with death."* The bureaucrats and conservatives could not realize that a relatively few decent reforms and concessions might have made the liberals turn against the terrorists. The latter were deliberately capitalizing the popular discontent.

For a time the terrorists ostentatiously refrained from attacks upon the Czar himself; then they proclaimed in their bulletins that he was incorrigible and had been "sentenced to death." Late in 1879 they almost wrecked his train when it was approaching Moscow. In February, 1880, they dynamited the dining-room of the Winter Palace—the imperial family had been delayed in entering by a petty incident, which saved them by a hair's breadth. The Czar now entrusted practically dictatorial power to an intelligent general, Loris-Melikov, of Armenian extraction.

Melikov was too wise to trust solely in repression. He released prisoners who were probably innocent; readmitted two thousand students who had been expelled from the universities, and commuted the death sentences of the less guilty Nihilists. He was a man of strong nerves, who did not waver when attacks were made upon himself. A baptized Jew strove to shoot him but failed, was arrested and hanged. "If it is not I," he boasted before execution, "it will be another. If it is not that other it will be a third. Count Melikov will be done to death by us!"

At length Melikov made a cautious proposition to the Czar—commissions were to report on the needs of the empire, and these reports would be discussed by a kind of deliberative assembly consisting of the com- missioners and various experts chosen by the city councils and the *zemstvos*. This assembly was only to "recommend." The final word lay with the Czar who was still to be Autocrat. No one proposed to take that power away from him and all that was hoped for was that some elected persons might have something to say about affairs of state. Alexander II hesitated and misdoubted. It seemed too much like partial capitulation to a band of assassins, and the Czar was no convinced liberal. Nevertheless, he gave way. In 1881 he ordered the publication of Melikov's scheme as a lawfully enacted ukase in the official gazette.

But on this very day Alexander, refusing all warnings, had insisted on taking his wonted drive through the streets of St. Petersburg. He was returning to the Winter Palace when a bomb burst, shattering the car- riage, killing guards and bystanders. The Czar was unhurt and had leaped down to assist the sufferers when a second bomb burst beside him, and he lived only long enough to be hurried to the palace. Melikov's deliber- ative parliament perished with Alexander.

Alexander III (1881-94): Pobyedonostsev and the Swing to Autocracy

The murder of the Czar swung Russia to extreme reaction. For three years the whole land had seemed in danger of anarchy. Every public servant's life was in danger. The sympathizers with the Nihilists were ever dwindling. The Czar was still the personal representative of God in the eyes of an enormous majority of his subjects, and now had come the climax; the anointed Sovereign of All the Russias had been assassinated in the name of liberalism.

Alexander III, son of the slain monarch, was temperamentally an auto- cratic conservative. He was a lover of international peace, but he hated the innovations of the West and clung, as a matter of patriotism and religion, to the good old ways of Muscovy, before the "pollutions" of liberalism. At his elbow was his tutor and confidant, Pobyedonostsev, a passionate reactionary. Alexander III indeed told Melikov, at first, that he would go ahead with the Consultative Assembly, but almost imme- diately the Czar made difficulties, the project was soon dropped, and Melikov himself, before long, was compelled to resign office.

The new sovereign now issued a proclamation announcing that he intended to maintain the autocratic power, and to "strive for the extirpa- tion of the heinous agitation which had disgraced the land." Spurred by the great assassination, the police at last grappled effectively with the Nihilists, who already had been reduced to a small band. Five regicides were caught and executed; the rest of the conspirators were rendered helpless by the national indignation. After 1881, Russia had a reasonable respite from political murders for about twenty years. They were not years of wisdom, however, for the czardom.

Alexander III deliberately worked on the theory that surrender to liberalism had cost his father his life, and that, so far as practicable, there must be a return to the iron regime of Nicholas I. The new Czar did not, indeed, regret the emancipation of the serfs; on the contrary, he considered the peasantry the one sure foundation for Russian nationality; the mischief, to his mind, had come from the more educated classes. "The peasants' Czar," he liked to call himself and, in fact, there was a good deal accomplished in an imperfect way during this reign to better the lot of the petty farmers. But against the liberals, Alexander III's attitude was one of uncompromising hostility, and in Pobyedonostsev he had an able champion of obscurantism. The Procurator of the Holy Synod told his receptive sovereign that Russia must look for salvation, not to the vaporings of a motley assembly, not to subtle attractions imported from the immoral Occident, but to the close union of the Autocrat and his people along strictly national lines. The whole empire was thus soon in the clutches of a militant reaction.

Once more, as under Nicholas I, the universities were strictly controlled; the formation of student societies, even for harmless social or benevolent purposes, became a crime; professors were again appointed by the minister of education (that is, for political reasons), and promotion went by governmental favor. The natural result of this policy was to make the students feel that their professors were merely ministerial spies, and to ignore their political instruction. On the other hand, along with this harrying of the universities, there went a calamitous failure to promote the general spread of education. In 1886, in a population of 110,000,000 in the empire, only about 2,000,000 pupils were enrolled in the primary schools; some 230,000 more were in the secondary schools; and the eight universities had only 14,027 students among them. If the imperial policy deliberately planned to ruin a mighty nation through ignorance, the Czars were laboring successfully for that end.

But Alexander III had one abiding principle, which he put through at any cost—Russification. He saw in the polyglot races of his enormous empire a menace to its safety, but he knew no method save the ukase and the knout of coercion for conforming all the alien peoples, from the uncouth Bashkirs of the Urals to cultivated Poles, to the standards and morals of Great Russia. "One Russia, one Faith, one Czar," was his favorite motto. Those Baltic provinces in which German was spoken, and the Ukraine with its Little Russians, were hardly more favored than the rest. The story of coercion, the persecution of Catholic priests and Lutheran pastors, the suppression of local autonomy, the imposition of harsh military service, the practical suppression of non-Russian printing presses, and like measures, make up a tale worthy of Spain in the sixteenth century.

Most bitter of all, however, was the struggle waged against the Jews. To the mutual unhappiness of Slav and Semite, over 5,000,000 Jews dwelt in the Russian dominions. Thanks to the constant atmosphere of despotism and oppression around them, they as a rule had clung closely to their native customs and the rabbinical law as their one national possession. Their economic efficiency had rendered them often prosperous and usually hated. Against the Jews Pobyedonostsev pursued a policy of ill-concealed extermination, running the gamut from excluding Jewish students from institutions of learning to inciting pogroms (murderous riots of the Christian proletariat against their Hebrew neighbors). He was alleged to have boasted that he would drive one-third of the Jews in the empire to emigrate, would convert one-third to Orthodox Christianity, and would harry the remaining third to destruction. This was the beginning of that great Hebrew emigration to America which was to make New York the largest Jewish center in the world. For the czardom Alexander III and his first lieutenant were laying up a legacy of hate with that clever, supple folk which was to cost the autocracy much in its hour of need.

Alexander III, however, was a conscientious, hard-working despot who, according to his understanding, toiled faithfully for his people's good. He kept out of war. He knew how to choose ministers, like the famous Sergius Witte, who labored effectively for the economic development of the empire. Across Asia the vast Trans-Siberian railway was now reaching steadily toward the Pacific at Vladivostok, and a network of other railroads spread over Russia. Metallurgical industries in the Ukraine, textiles in central Russia, and many new factories in the Petersburg area were proof of this industrial awakening, to say nothing of its concomitants—a proletariat in the cities and the growth of a small but active middle class. When the Czar died in 1894 he left Russia relatively prosperous, the liberals silenced, the conservatives and bureaucrats confident and boasting that Muscovy would never surrender to Western "heresies." If Germany seemed to deny that democracy was necessary for the highest form of modern civilization, Russia seemed to be asserting that an enormous empire could extend from Norway to Alaska and be firmly governed by institutions rooted in the Tartar vassal-state of the Principality of Moscow.

Nicholas II (1894-1917): His Infirm Character: His Empress: Russian Industrial Expansion

Nicholas II (born in 1868) reigned in his father's stead. This last Autocrat of All the Russias was a man of different stamp from his predecessor, or from the grim Nicholas I. From the outset the world rightly beheld in him a man well-intentioned, religious to the point of superstition, personally mild and gentle, and in all things pliable. His father had enjoined his tutors, "Neglect nothing that can make my son truly a man." They failed to achieve the desired result, perhaps because their task was humanly impossible. Long before his tragic downfall Nicholas II had been recognized as the victim of that evil principle of hereditary monarchy which thrusts weak men into positions of overwhelming responsibility, when heaven intended them to dwell in happy obscurity. A strong, intelligent Czar coming into power in 1894 might possibly have saved Russia. Nicholas II was probably fortunate in reigning as many as twenty-three years before catastrophe overtook him.

Nicholas married the Princess Alix of Hesse, a strong-willed German woman, clever in a limited way, but herself intensely devoted to the maintenance of imperial prerogative. Soon he was completely under her domination. Later it will be seen how this purblind empress, herself neurotic and subject to priestly control, directly hastened the fall of the czardom. For the moment, after his accession, the new emperor signalized himself merely by quenching all hopes that there would be any swing toward liberalism. To a delegation from the nobility and cities, he announced, "Let it be known that I shall maintain the autocratic system as firmly as did my father of unperishable memory." The idea of a constitution he declared to be a "senseless dream." As for Pobyedonostsev, he seemed for a time to be more potent than ever, silencing all opposition with the simple dictum, "*Thus* it was done under the late Czar."

The twentieth century dawned, therefore, with Russia seemingly more despotically governed than she had been in 1880. Pobyedonostsev, it is true, presently lost personal favor with the new monarch and shrank into retirement, but there was no change in the spirit of the government. The mild character of Nicholas II made him, however, rather less eager for violent "Russification," and Jews and Poles obtained a temporary respite. The government still clung to the policy of peace, although drifting into an attitude of steady opposition to Germany, and forming the solid Dual Alliance with France.

Since 1893 Sergius Witte had proved himself a remarkable minister of finance, a steady foe indeed to liberalism, but displaying the efficiency of an enlightened despot. The French alliance brought with it great loans of capital. Some of this went into strictly military preparations; but a large fraction enabled Russia to advance along a line of rapid industrial development, which was aimed to make her independent, especially of the manufactures of Germany. Between 1890 and 1900 production of steel and iron increased 196 per cent. Russia was still an essentially agricultural empire. Seventy-five per cent of her population were still peasants, and her main exports were wheat, rye, and oats; but the great multiplication of factories was causing not merely Moscow and St. Petersburg, but many other cities, to grow by leaps and bounds. In 1900 there were 38,000 industrial plants and 2,500,000 factory and mine workers—a real industrial "proletariat," concentrated in cities and subject to group impulses and propaganda impossible for masses of scattered peasants.

During all this time, however, no attempt had been made to adjust the institutions of this increasingly complex empire to ever changing social conditions. There was still a crushing censorship over the press. Foreign newspapers were admitted only after each copy had been scanned by the censor to "black out" unsettling paragraphs. Suspension of civil trials, "preventive arrests," arbitrary exilings to Siberia, were commonplace proceedings. The bureaucracy, including even the intelligent Witte, seems to have imagined that by giving peace and economic prosperity, the demand for political liberty could be silenced; railroads would be the substitute for ballot boxes. Then the Czar found himself drifting into a disastrous war, and out of a great military defeat Russian radicalism was born anew.

The Russo-Japanese War (1904-5): New Discontent and Agitation: "Bloody Sunday" (January 22, 1905)

The story of the Russo-Japanese War of 1904-1905 is told elsewhere (see pp. 472-473). It arose from Muscovite aggressions in Manchuria and Korea, and from the contemptuous unwillingness of the circle around Nicholas to consider the new Japan as anything more than a despicable barbarian power. Agreement upon the points at issue would have been wholly possible for a pacific diplomacy, and the Mikado's Elder Statesmen had been willing to go to great lengths ere staking their country's future upon a great war. A group of speculators and adventurers who had gained the confidence of the Czar overrode the efforts of such ministers as Witte to preserve peace. The war began in February, 1904, and at the first news of defeat the long-suffering anti-bureaucrats knew that autocracy's extremity was liberty's opportunity, and the time was ripe for revolution.

Already the peasantry had become very restless. A story had spread through the villages that the Little Father had actually issued a ukase giving the muzhiks the land of the great proprietors, and that the Grand Duke Michael, brother of the Czar, was engaged in carrying out this mandate, but was being thwarted by the clutching landlords. In 1902 it had been needful to suppress a really serious agrarian revolt. Nevertheless, the government refused to take warning. When untoward incidents in 1904 multiplied, the dynasts assumed that they had to deal with only a very small group of revived Nihilists. They could not realize that this time they confronted:

I. A truly national movement backed by practically the entire intelligentsia;

II. A movement behind which there was that which had been lacking to the liberals of Alexander II's day, the new class of factory operatives—able to strike, to riot, and even to revolt in the great cities.

In July, 1904, the ultrareactionary minister of the interior, Plehve, a promoter of Jewish pogroms and of the brutal Russification of Poland and Finland, was slain by a bomb flung under his carriage as he drove to make a report to the Czar at Peterhof. This was the beginning of "executions" of the revived revolutionists which soon almost equaled the proceedings of 1879-81. The situation grew ever more tense all through 1904. The best of the army was in Manchuria, yet the wires brought back only tidings of defeat. The Czar felt compelled to name a relatively moderate minister of the interior, and in November the Petersburg police closed their eyes when a private meeting was held of members of the provincial and municipal councils, to discuss the entire national situation. The conference agreed upon a petition to the Czar demanding a representative assembly and a reasonable bill of rights. Nicholas hesitated. An imperial ukase in December announced some desirable reforms for the peasants and local zemstvos, but said nothing about a constitution. Then, in January, came an incident which set a barrier of blood between the Czar and his people. The monarchy never recovered.

"Bloody Sunday" (January 22, 1905) was a day intensely cold, even for Russia, with a piercing wind blowing over St. Petersburg. Through the icy blasts, tens of thousands of workmen with women and children marched to the Winter Palace to present a petition to the Czar. They were led by Father Gapon, a priest of relatively conservative tendencies, whom the government had encouraged as a useful offset to the socialist agitators. The petition was simply a humble plea for humane treatment and just dealing at the hands of the officials, and stated that certain reforms, including a "national representation," could do more for Russia than the decisions of the imperial ministers.

In government circles there was hesitancy. Some ministers advised moderation, but at the last moment the police got the upper hand—a lesson must be taught the demonstrators. The procession was allowed to come near the palace, when it was dispersed by the point-blank fire of the soldiery. Some fifteen hundred dead and wounded lay reddening the snows, while the frightened multitude scattered. Henceforth it was useless to tell the masses of Russia that they were deceived by unpatriotic agitators, that the Little Father loved and cared for them. Bloody Sunday is said to have "killed the last chance of a peaceful liberation of Russia."

All through 1905 the tumults increased and the tide of revolution ran its course. More defeats by the once despised Japanese were followed by more assassinations. In February another bomb removed the Grand Duke Sergius, most pitiless of the reactionaries. Nicholas II was beginning to know fear. In June he promised to convene a National Assembly but, to the great popular wrath, when, in August, the new law was promulgated, it was found to offer only a consultive body, the real passing of laws being reserved for the Imperial Council named by the Czar. Peace was at last made with Japan on terms of sore humiliation (see p. 473), but the best corps of the army were still detained in the Far East when the final blow was struck at home.

The Great Strike of 1905: Proclamation of a Constitution (October 17, 1905)

The ministry, yielding ground little by little, had suddenly given back to the universities their autonomy. Instantly these institutions, and especially those at Moscow and St. Petersburg, became the center for intense political agitation. The police could not lawfully enter their halls. Within their precincts, therefore, any kind of revolutionary sentiment became permissible. Lectures ceased. The corridors were thronged with radical orators, singers of revolutionary songs, distributors of revolutionary pamphlets. Then, as a kind of electric impulse, in the early autumn came the most successful general strike in the history of the world. It lasted nearly two weeks. Every railroad ceased operating. Telegraph and postal service stopped. Every trade and industry ceased functioning. Lawyers refused to appear for litigation. Many towns lacked a food supply. Communication, save from house to house, almost ended. Only the revolutionary committees, with their own private intelligence systems, kept well posted as to events.

Nicholas II was in dismay but, up to the last fell instant, he hesitated. His kinsmen, however, were fearful lest all their dearest interests should perish in a general anarchy. His uncle, the Grand Duke Nicholas, at last forced his way to the Autocrat. "You see this revolver?" he had said to Baron Fredericks, a court minister, "I am now going to the Czar, and shall implore him to sign the manifesto [promising reforms]. Either he signs it or I shoot myself in his room." Nicholas signed.

On the 30th of October appeared the Czar's formal promise to his people: Russia should receive a constitution conceding wide civil rights —inviolability of person, freedom of conscience and speech, of meeting and association and a "Duma" (Assembly), chosen by a wide franchise and with full legislative authority, no law to become valid without its consent. For a few brief weeks it seemed as if the general strike had captured the Muscovite Bastille, that the struggle for Russian liberty had been won.

The Duma: Reaction Toward Autocracy

Then followed an amazing anticlimax. The Czar had virtually thrown upon his chief minister, Witte, the task of reorganizing Russia and salvaging what he could of the old autocracy. Witte did not disappoint his master. He was anything but a liberal, being a convinced believer that the Empire was unfitted for anything much beyond a firm and enlightened despotism. The October promises, however, he could not repudiate, but he did his best to refine them away; the application of the pledged reforms was delayed, and shrewd advantage was taken of the rifts soon appearing among the antimonarchists themselves. Above all, the conservatives thought the army could be relied on. If worst came to worst, it was possible to defy the soft-handed intelligentsia and the city workingmen. Louis XVI had gone down because the desertion of his army had left him helpless before the mob of Paris, but the Russian Army had not yet deserted Nicholas II.

Into the hands of the reactionaries there now played the division of their foes. The intelligentsia (milder than in the days of Alexander II and Alexander III) desired a limited monarchy or, at most, a conservative republic. Their model was Britain or France. But the masses in Moscow and St. Petersburg were surcharged with socialism. An elected legislature was to be, for them, only the prelude to a Revolution. They would not halt and consolidate their gains; they were determined to follow strike with strike, paralyze the government, and confound the whole capitalist order. In November a Council of Workingmen's Delegates ordered a second general strike, this time avowedly to establish a republic. The middle classes were unready and some of the industrial classes refused to join. The strike soon failed ingloriously. The radicals, nevertheless, refused to learn wisdom; in December they ordered a third general strike.

The government was now better prepared, and the intelligentsia with property were taking alarm; the movement was heading straight toward a crude type of socialism. In Moscow there was not a strike but downright insurrection. Armed workingmen clashed with the police and then fought the garrison. There were barricades, desperate street fighting, and avenues swept with artillery, even as once in Paris. By January 1, 1906, the outbreak was over, leaving part of Moscow in ruins and with a thousand peaceful persons slain. This uprising cost the socialists all the sympathy of the better-class liberals. Very many supporters of the first general strike were willing to avow that enough progress had been made for liberalism (some confessed "Too much!"). The swing toward revolution had been definitely halted.

The Czar could not cancel his promise of an Imperial Duma, but the ministers now left no device unused to whittle down the concessions earlier granted. "Order" was restored everywhere by ruthless military measures. Police spies abounded. Prisons were crammed, often with the wholly innocent, while thousands of alleged disturbers of the peace were executed, often without trial. Nevertheless, the new Duma was elected and convened with great pomp and ceremony in May, 1906. Witte (whom the Czar had never loved) had been already forced out of office, and the real, though not nominal, head of the government was now the shrewd Stolypin, minister of the interior. Nicholas II gave the deputies a friendly speech when he greeted them at the Winter Palace, and begged them to "work together for the love of the country," but the new parliament and old bureaucracy were soon at dagger points.

The strongest party in the Duma was the Constitutional Democratic, the "Cadets," advocates of a very limited British type of monarchy, and headed by a leader who, under happier auspices, would have proved a great constructive statesman, Paul Miliukov, one-time professor of history. To the right of the Cadets were the Octobrists, fewer in number, more conservative, willing to abide by the October Manifesto, and in favor of giving the Czar about the same powers as those possessed by the Kaiser. To the left were various radical groups, numerous if taken collectively, but torn by internal strife. Two out-and-out socialist parties were represented—the Social Democratic and the Social Revolutionary—but the Social Democrats, founded on the model of the Marxian parties of Western Europe and strong in the industrial centers, were bitterly at odds with one another, the Bolsheviki, the majority group, demanding instant and forceful action, the minority, the Mensheviki, advocating a policy of gradualism. As for the Social Revolutionary party, at that time recognized as the *Trudovik* (Labor) group, it placed most of its hopes in an appeal to the peasants, was frankly agrarian in outlook, and concerned itself far more with peasant proprietorship than with the abolition of capitalism.

This inexperienced and unwieldy Duma almost immediately tried to bring the harsh measures of the Czar's ministers under scrutiny and to establish their responsibility to the deputies, just as though Russia was a strictly constitutional country. In two months the situation was tense and Stolypin was ready to administer drastic medicine. Reliable troops were quietly moved into St. Petersburg and the first Duma was suddenly dissolved, but with no worse results than the furious protests of some two hundred Cadets who met in Viborg in Finland and drew up there a manifesto to the Russian people, summoning them to refuse to pay taxes or to serve in the army until the Duma was recalled. Stolypin acted promptly: he arrested the signatories of the manifesto, disfranchised them, and quickly suppressed all other evidence of dissent.

Stolypin's Program: The Second and Third Dumas

Stolypin now announced as his program: "First order, then reform!" Order was secured by military courts through the length and breadth of the empire. Up to May 1, 1907, six hundred persons had been hanged by these tribunals; "Stolypin's neckties" became notorious. But the minister had the wisdom to convoke another Duma, first seeing to it that, by bribery and intimidation, "safe people" were elected. The Cadets therefore lost many members, but there were still enough of them, plus the extreme radicals, to make much trouble for the ministry. This Second Duma met in March, 1907; by June 16 it had quarreled so bitterly with Stolypin that he dissolved it in turn. Then came a revision of the electoral law, giving great advantage to the rich landowners (the main prop of the government), permitting Stolypin to secure a Third Duma, more after his own heart.

The Third Duma convened in November, 1907. Thanks to the changed election laws, it contained only fifty-four Cadets or more pronounced liberals, and proved a very chastened, amenable body. For almost three years Stolypin was now the government of Russia. Opinions still differ on his career as such, but little by little he is beginning to be recognized as a real statesman who, though conservative, was enlightened. To some extent he resembled Bismarck—autocratic in temperament, chafing at constitutional restrictions, of which there were some but not many. He was highhanded in act; on the other hand he was by no means a blind reactionary. He inaugurated free primary education in Russia; he granted free civic rights to the peasants; he initiated labor legislation; he established local zemstvos where there had been none; and most important of all, he was responsible for land legislation very thoroughgoing in character.

The land laws sought to establish peasant proprietorship in Russia in place of the old communal ownership of the mirs. In accordance with the new law, any peasant was entitled to demand his individual share of the village land and to fence it about as his very own. By 1913 nearly twenty-four per cent of the peasants, as a result of this policy, owned their own farms. Meanwhile, all the peasants had one heavy burden taken off their backs, namely, the obligation to pay the remaining moneys due from the great emancipation of 1861, still a heavy debt, canceled outright in 1906.

Unfortunately for Russia, Stolypin was assassinated in 1911 and therefore had no opportunity to complete his work. Between that date, however, and the commencement of the first World War, Russia continued to make progress, though at a slower tempo. The revolutionary movement went underground, and the more radical leaders of it, like Lenin and Stalin, either sought refuge in Switzerland or were sent to Siberia. Within the realm of the Czar the old censorship, in its worst phases, disappeared, and a lively renaissance of intellectual life was noticeable. A somewhat dangerous chauvinism developed, it is true, in the rapidly rising middle class which augured no good for the future; and around the Czar and his wife there gathered certain dangerous men like the "holy man" Rasputin, a dirty and ignorant fellow, but with marked psychic powers which later he was to use somewhat devastatingly (see p. 542). But on the whole, when the First World War broke, Russia seemed on the point of taking her place with the other powers of Western Europe as a country thoroughly permeated with modern ideas and, if by no means a liberal country, by no means also a purely Asiatic despotism.

Chapter 21

AUSTRIA-HUNGARY AND ITALY

The Hapsburg Empire and Its Discordant Subjects: Francis Joseph, His Personality and Character

ACROSS THE MAP of Europe still spread the most conglomerate state in the world—Austria. Her dissolution was regularly predicted, yet as regularly postponed. The monarchy never recovered from the shock of Sadowa; Austria was the weakest of the great powers, and everybody knew that her army could not hold its own against either Prussia or Russia. After 1870 she seemed weaker still. In that year the Hapsburg ministers had been almost persuaded to take their revenge upon Bismarck by marching to the help of France, but they had waited too long; the hostile attitude of the Czar and the effect of the first French defeats froze them into anxious neutrality. With France rendered helpless, they had no real associate left in Europe. There was great relief, therefore, in Vienna when it appeared that Bismarck was resolved upon a pacific policy; and still greater relief when, in 1879, he decided that Austria would serve as a good counterpoise to Russia, and took the Hapsburgs into the Dual Alliance, after 1881 the Triple Alliance. Henceforth, Austria had a defender against the Muscovite, but at the cost of recognizing the Hohenzollern as her patron—a situation galling to the highnesses, serenities, and majesties who inhabited the wings of the colossal Hofburg.

Over the Austrian dominions, this "Slavic and Magyar house with a German façade," there still ruled Francis Joseph, white-haired now, feeble in body, but still acute in mind. *He was no longer a prince, he was becoming an institution.* It had become impossible to think of the "dual monarchy" without him. He had been proclaimed emperor amid the clatter of the abortive Revolution of 1848 in Austria; and his life was to flicker out in 1916, during the hurricane of the World War. Nobody called him "great"; not every one called him "good," but many called him "venerable" or "wise," and very few hated him deeply. He was really a cynical, good-natured opportunist, trying at every turn to conserve Hapsburg power. He had no enthusiasms. Once an ardent adviser laid before

375

him a specious scheme for reorganizing the monarchy. Francis Joseph merely smiled and said: "In theory, in theory—very good perhaps; but *in practice*—one has got to have been emperor sixty years!" He knew well the rottenness of much of the fabric under him, but he would have echoed Louis XV's comment on the Old Regime in France—"It will last my time."

Neither in private nor public life was Francis Joseph exemplary. He cared little how his ministers gained their ends, provided money and army recruits were duly obtained and politics went smoothly. Like a selfish landlord, he tolerated the petty tyranny of his "bailiffs," so long as nothing stopped his income. The Emperor was, in fact, the center for one of the most immoral and degenerate courts in the world. Constant inbreeding, intermarriage between near cousins, was ruining the Hapsburg dynasty. The sixty-odd archdukes and archduchesses were kept in a state of busy idleness by their lord and master—and uncle. Francis Joseph had to leave most affairs in his dominions to his ministers, but the enormous Hofburg was his own particular province. Here he could rule with a rod of iron. Any free conduct by an archduke meant a round lecture and probable discipline by his august kinsman.

As the years went on the Emperor became pitifully isolated. In 1889 the body of his son and heir, the Archduke Rudolf, was found in a hunting lodge, along with that of a certain baroness, with whom he had been infatuated. In 1898 the Empress Elizabeth was killed by an anarchist while sojourning at Geneva. Her husband cordially disliked his next heir, his nephew, the Archduke Francis Ferdinand, doomed to perish in 1914 at Sarajevo; but he was not much more friendly to the young Archduke Charles, next in succession. And so, cut off from nearly all that makes life dear, propping up with ceaseless expedients the power which he was intelligent enough to know must some day tumble, Francis Joseph in 1914 was eighty-four years old, "a wrinkled old man, with whiskers white as snow and blue eyes like steel."

The Austro-Hungarian Empire

Nine considerable peoples were jostling one another within Francis Joseph's territories. The core of Austria was thoroughly South German; but in the northern part were the Czechs of Bohemia, and some of the Slovaks, a kindred but differentiated Slavic folk, and still farther north and east in Galicia were Poles and Ruthenians (Little Russians), and, in the Austrian province of Bukovina, Rumanians. In the south and southwest were numerous Italians in the lower Tyrol and at the head of the Adriatic. East and northeast of the Adriatic were other Slavs, the Slovenes. So much for Austria by itself. Hungary, over which Francis Joseph also ruled, presented an equally varied picture. Again, in the center of the Hungarian plain the population was almost purely Magyar;

THE HOFBURG PALACE IN VIENNA

but in the northern part of Hungary there were also Czechs, many Ruthenians, and most of the Slovaks; in the south, the Croats, the Slovenes, and many Serbs; in the east Rumanians in great numbers and not a few islands of pure Germans.

The perennial warfare of Germans in Austria and of Magyars in Hungary against the various types of Slavs and Latins made Austrian statecraft seem a preparatory school for bedlam. Germans and Magyars, even taken together, constituted a minority; but, thanks to superior wealth, social influence, and long possession of power, so long as they were in agreement, they could ordinarily control the entire empire. Whether they liked it or not, Germans and Magyars were bound together, if not by love at least by interest. If they quarreled seriously the whole flimsy structure of Hapsburg power would come crashing down upon their heads. Germans were in a minority in Austria; the Magyars were in a minority in Hungary. Germans and Magyars had to act together. As long as they did so, they separated the North Slavs (Czechs, Slovaks, Poles, and Ruthenians) from the South Slavs (Slovenes, Croats, and Serbs). As long as they did so, they could keep open their exits to the sea—Trieste, Austria's one seaport, situated in a veritable nest of Slovenes, and also Fiume, Hungary's one seaport, although between her and it lay the Croats. Once German-Magyar unity was lost, the Germans in Austria and the Magyars in Hungary would become landlocked.

By 1866, with the cannon of Königgrätz booming in his ears, it was plain to Francis Joseph that he must reorganize his dominions still more radically if he intended to retain them. He had just been booted out of Germany. The only hope for Hapsburg recovery and expansion lay toward the East; and the best chance there was to compete with Russia for the reversion of the Balkan lands of the dying Turkish Empire. The obvious thing necessary was, therefore, to compound with the powerful Magyars, and to make them happy supporters of such new ambitions.

In 1867 and 1868 the whole empire was completely reorganized by what was known as the *Ausgleich*. Hungary was set off as a practically separate kingdom in all but a few particulars. In Vienna, Francis Joseph was still "Emperor"; in Budapest he was now "Apostolic King."

Each of these two states had its own parliament, on which, nominally, the ministers were dependent; and its own complete autonomy. Foreign affairs, the army and navy, and certain finances for the common expenses, the two realms shared. "Delegations" (equal in number) from the two parliaments met to exchange opinions in writing, and then not to debate but only vote. A bare majority settled the issue.

The Ausgleich of 1867 was an obvious makeshift. The Slavic elements, especially the Czechs under Austria and the Croats under Hungary were unhappy. Why should they not have the same favors as the Magyars? But Francis Joseph was a past master in the art of making factions fight one another. He flung concessions to the Poles of Galicia and induced them to desert their fellow-Slavs, the Czechs, and work with the ministers at Vienna. In Hungary, an unscrupulous manipulation of the election system kept the parliament in the power of the Magyars. The minorities— Czechs, Croats, Slovenes, Rumanians, Ruthenians were noisily angry, but physically helpless and the Hapsburg empire survived.

That empire was constantly on the defensive. The dynasts feared lest the German element in the old Austrian lands west of Vienna should seek union with their more numerous brethren in the new Hohenzollern realm. Italy coveted Dalmatia and the Trentino. The Serbs looked yearn- ingly upon Croatia-Slavonia and, of course, upon Bosnia. The Rumanians never forgot their brethren in Transylvania. The Czechs (Bohemians) demanded equal status with Hungary. The Poles of Galicia yearned for the hour of reunion with their brethren under the yokes of Russia and Prussia. Finally, in the northeastern background, loomed the menacing bulk of Muscovy itself—that great relentless power which marked dying empires as its prey.

But, however artificial, there was still defensive strength and much selfish wisdom in the old Hapsburg regime. It could boast of the most beautiful capital in Europe, barring, perhaps, Paris. Berlin was new, sprawling, bourgeois; Vienna, only a little smaller (1,662,000 in 1900), was elegant, cultured, leisurely. The Viennese were proud of their mag- nificent boulevards; of possibly the finest group of public buildings in the world; of their opera and music; of the grace and beauty of their women; of the southern courtesy and friendly manners and speech of all classes; of their pleasantly dawdling café life; of their bosky parks and luxuriant suburbs. Defiant of the German upstart, they still sang their proud song, "There's only one *Kaiser-stadt;* there's only one Vienna."

No European capital, it was well said, "had so imperial an air" as Vienna, and no other had such a tinge of the Orient. Learned essayists commented on the subtle change of spirit which the traveler met as he visited the Hapsburg capital and penetrated into the Austrian lands. "Austria," wrote Kürnberger in 1871, "must be comprehended as a kind of Asia. . . . Europe means law; Asia means arbitrary rule. Europe means respect for facts; Asia means the purely personal. Europe is the man. Asia is at once the old child and the man. With this key you may solve all the Austrian riddles."

Characteristics of the "Austrian" Half of the Dual Monarchy

As the twentieth century advanced, Francis Joseph found himself acclaimed "emperor-king" by a little under 50,000,000 subjects. Of these, about 28,500,000 were in the "Empire," the old Austrian lands, plus Bohemia, Galicia, and the South Slavic and Italian provinces. About

20,000,000 more, he ruled as "King of Hungary." Omitting, for the moment, the Hungarian problem, the question of nationalities, merely in the Empire, was serious enough. The Germans were in a minority, constituting less than ten million, and in them were reckoned the by no means Teutonic element of about 1,230,000 Jews. There was a perfect jargon of languages. An Austro-Hungarian bank-note was required to have, on one side, its value indicated in (1) German; (2) Czechish; (3) Polish; (4) Serbo-Croatian (in both Latin and Cyrillic—"Russian" characters); (5) Ruthene (Little Russian); (6) Slovene; (7) Italian; (8) Rumanian. On the other side, very significantly, it was only printed in Magyar—indicating how much more successful the Magyars in the "Kingdom" were than their German brethren in the "Empire" in suppressing unwelcome national aspirations.

The army was really the only factor besides the dynasty and its foreign policy which bound this "dual" realm together. There was a single minister of war for both "nations," and a single general staff. An efficient army was a life-or-death matter to the Hapsburgs and here, at least, the demands of the Magyars for a strictly separate organization were stiffly resisted. German was used as the sole "language of command and service" in the entire army; but to great bodies of the conscripts German was an utterly foreign tongue. Therefore instruction had to be given in the language of the recruit. There were thus Polish, Czechish, Ruthene, and Slavo-Croat regiments as well as German and Magyar; also many "mixed regiments," wherein any group of men amounting to twenty per cent of the entire unit was entitled to demand instruction in its mother tongue.

These curious factors in the army, of course, added nothing to military effectiveness. The Hofburg did not dare to mobilize its South Slavs with perfect confidence against the Serbians, its Italians against an Italian army, its Czechs and Poles, under all circumstances, against Slavic Russia. The Austro-German officers were men of charming social customs, far less brusque than their Prussian contemporaries, but also far more easy-going, and far less advanced in military technique. The Magyar officers, sons of a gallant, dashing race, averaged better. The army was, in any case, a great social and political institution. It was still very loyal to the dynasty; and it could be relied upon to crush any uprising of the "minorities," while the great number of upper-class families, whose sons supplied the officers corps, were held to the existing regime by a strong nexus of hopes and interests.

Certain general matters about Francis Joseph's empire deserve more than passing notice. It was a police-infested, corrupt government—not on the scale of colossal oppressions, the screwing-down of unwelcome movements by unflinching despotism, as in Russia, but a government of petty regulations, petty bribery, petty winkings at law-breaking. Along with this incessant regulating and bribe-taking, went an enormous amount of official red tape. Petty clerks, upper clerks, under-secretaries, and the like were multiplied in every government bureau. A request by a caretaker in a public school for a special payment of twenty kronen (about $4.12) had to pass through sixteen officials before it could be granted. It took eleven official signatures before a doctor could get a license to run a sanatorium.

The constitutions possessed by Austria and by Hungary, following the great settlement in 1867, were, on paper, somewhat more democratic than those enjoyed by Prussia; but the incessant clashes of the racial elements often made genuine parliamentary government, especially by the Vienna assembly, simply impossible. The imperial Reichsrat was one of the most tumultuous legislatures in the world, with Czechish and German deputies often screaming curses at one another, silencing unwelcome orators by clattering their desk covers, and even flinging inkstands at the presiding officer's head. It was easy to justify "extraordinary measures" and government by ministerial edicts, while trying to work with such a parliament. The result was that the Hapsburg monarchy averaged somewhat more autocratic than the Hohenzollern, with far less efficiency and cold intelligence. The mitigation came in the easy good-nature of the officials and the equal willingness of much of the population to jog along with a bad, but endurable government.

Indeed, the more highly industrialized Austria became, the easier, in a peculiar sense, became the retention of power by the Hapsburgs. Increased industrialization in that country, as elsewhere, led to demands for more democratic institutions, and as these were granted, the clash of contending nationalities became all the louder, especially after 1907, when a freely elected parliament for all Austria afforded an excellent sounding-board for nationalistic jealousies and sectional ambitions.

If we go back to the law of 1873, we find representation in the Reichsrat based then on four classes—landowners, chambers of commerce, cities, and peasants; and at that time the balance of control was weighted heavily in favor of the privileged few. By 1890 this system had resulted in there being one deputy for every sixty-three votes among the landlord class, to one deputy for every 11,600 peasants—and bitter was the criticism thereof. This system was modified in 1896 by establishing still a fifth class, that of all adult males over twenty-four, and to this class was awarded seventy-two seats. Over 5,000,000 Austrians now could vote; but landlords and others could vote in their own class as hitherto and also in the open class, and the latter was still in a minority in the parliament. Then, in 1907, came a revolutionary change. Austria went democratic in a big way; the class system was abolished; all adult males were given the franchise on an equal basis.

Francis Joseph, however, had no cause for worry. From 1907 to the First World War, internal dissensions in Austria grew more rather than less, and the Emperor kept his control nicely. True, there was a notable advance in social legislation, due primarily to socialistic pressure. A large, anticapitalistic Christian Socialist party, particularly strong in Vienna, had already done much to forward advanced labor legislation, and now that the franchise was thrown open to all men on an equal footing, the Social Democrats (Marxians), as well as the Christian Socialists, had an opportunity to make their influence felt. Nevertheless, these two socialist parties, together with the Liberals, elected but 264 deputies in 1907, whereas the dissenting nationalities elected 246 deputies, who fought viciously with one another and with the by-no-means united German deputies, so as virtually to disrupt parliamentary government.

These minority groups representing various nationalities had no Austrian patriotism as such; what they wanted was cultural and political autonomy. Some cultural autonomy they did obtain, such for instance as official recognition of the Czechish language; but against political autonomy the Germans in the Reichsrat set their faces sternly. There was good reason for doing so. Once autonomy of that sort was granted, it was feared that the Czechs in Bohemia would oppress Germans, that Italians in Istria would oppress Slovenes. The status quo was dangerous, but so also was change. Maintenance of the status quo, meanwhile, was abetted by universal suffrage; for, with no less than six nationalities clamoring in parliament against one another, and with the Poles of Galicia generally lined up with the Germans (these Poles being the recipients of special favors from the government), it was relatively simple to rule by the old Roman, and also old Hapsburg way: *divide et impera*.

Francis Joseph, therefore, seemed an extremely "constitutional monarch." Why otherwise? He had discovered that under the Constitution of 1867 he could exercise greater actual power over his dominions than his Prussian "brother," at Potsdam or, in a merely personal sense, than his other pliable and court-ridden "brother" at the St. Petersburg Winter Palace.

The Kingdom of Hungary: "Magyarization" of the Lesser Peoples

Nevertheless, he surely knew well that every expedient was merely staving off the evil day. In Hungary, in fact, his personal influence was considerably less than in his own loyal Vienna. In 1867 the Magyars had held the German Austrians and the dynasty completely at their mercy; a revolt would have dissolved the empire, and they had used their opportunity. They had forced the Hapsburgs to shift upon Austria an unfair share of the financial burdens, and to have the minority peoples within the "Kingdom of Hungary" put practically at their disposal. Meanwhile, at Budapest, Francis Joseph was no longer "Emperor"; he was "Apostolic King."

As such, Francis Joseph commanded the allegiance of some 20,500,000 subjects. The census listed about 8,700,000 of these as Magyars, and 5,500,000 as Slavs (Slovaks in the North, 2,000,000; Croats and Slovenes, 3,000,000; Ruthenes, 500,000; 3,000,000 as Rumanians; and 2,000,000 as Germans. The true Magyars were in a minority but the other peoples were sadly divided against themselves, and the Magyars were one of the most masterful, and political-minded nationalities in Europe. Between force and fraud, they strove, therefore, for more than forty years to crush the resistance of the Slavs and Latin peoples, and to "Magyarize" the whole mass.

The Magyars, in fact, were profoundly conscious that they were relatively few in number and of Finno-Ugrian origin, surrounded by greater Indo-European peoples, who did not love them. At any hazard, they were resolved to be complete masters of their own house. Said a one-time premier, speaking in 1908, "This country must first be preserved as a Magyar country, *then* it must be cultured, rich, enlightened, and progressive."

The "Little Peoples," inevitably, were, to a large extent, poor, ignorant, and crudely led. The Magyars justly taunted some of them with being only imperfectly civilized; and they were for the most part Slavs—of all the Western races one of the easiest to bend and yet hardest to break. The Magyars undertook to enforce "Magyarization" by a drastic elimination of alien languages. German was tabooed no less than the various forms of Slavic; in districts where only a small minority were Magyar, the Magyar tongue alone could be used for street signs, for place names, for railway timetables, and for every form of official conversation. If a non-Magyar wished to use his native tongue in the courts, it could only be through an interpreter whom he had to pay himself; if he handed in a legal petition it could be, as a great concession, written in his own language, but the reply came back in the official tongue. In Budapest no inscriptions were allowable on tombstones except in this Turanian speech, unfamiliar and uncouth to the vast majority of Europeans.

Meanwhile non-Magyar journals were oppressed and suppressed on trivial grounds—amounting to a severe police censorship. Between April, 1906, and August, 1908, sentences were passed on non-Magyars for "press offenses," totaling 181 years and three months' imprisonment. Non-Magyar schools were "supervised," harried, and often closed. In 1869 the Slovaks had 1,921 schools; in 1911 they had only 440, despite a large increase in the population and the great need of better education. It was part of the deliberate policy of Budapest to keep the "Little Peoples" ignorant and therefore helpless, unless they would give up their native tongues and their native traditions.

This system could be enforced only by a parliament wholly in the Magyar interest. The Hungarian electoral franchise was medieval, "probably the most illiberal in Europe." Great weight in awarding votes was given to property, professional, or official position, and also to ancestral privileges. Only six per cent, therefore, of the entire population actually enjoyed the right of the ballot box. This arrangement was supplemented by probably the most shameless gerrymandering, corruption, and direct intimidation at the polls known in any European country pretending to a simulacrum of "liberal" institutions. Out of the 453 deputies in the Hungarian parliament, the minor nationalities never had above 70. Under such circumstances, legal resistance to Magyarization was out of the question.

There was, nevertheless, one very obnoxious fly in the Magyar ointment. Hungary was still, after a manner, bound to the Vienna Hapsburgs, yet was almost independent; Croatia-Slavonia was, in turn, bound to Budapest, and yet also called itself a "kingdom." In 1868 the Hungarian government had been obliged to give a kind of fundamental law (*nagoda,* "agreement") to this group of South Slavs, conceding them a very large measure of local autonomy. At Agram, their capital, they had their *ban* (governor), supposedly representing the emperor-king, although actually he was the creature of the premier of Hungary. They had, likewise, their local legislature, which named the forty-three Croatian delegates to the Budapest parliament.

Fair as these paper arrangements seemed, the Magyar overlords upset them by all means fair or foul. Voting had to be done openly and orally, and the electoral machinery was controlled by the Magyars and shamelessly manipulated. The civil service was carefully filled up with Magyarizers; the Croatian-Serbian language was discouraged almost to the point of provoking an outbreak. The result was simply to goad the South Slavs under the Hapsburg rule to complete disaffection toward the whole imperial government and dynasty. True, before 1903 the South Slav movement aimed at a revival of the old triple kingdom of Croatia, Dalmatia, and Slavonia, plus Bosnia, Herzegovina, Istria, Fiume, and the Slovene area as an autonomous unit in a Hapsburg federal empire. But after that date, with a new regime in Serbia reaching out a friendly hand, they were in a mood to reëcho the angry demand of the old Italian revolutionist, Manin, in the eighteen-fifties, touching Lombardy-Venetia: "We do not want Austria to reform; we want Austria to get out." In Serbia, the brethren of these South Slavs were independent, with their own king at Belgrade. Did not Croatia-Slavonia belong under the congenial rule of Belgrade, and not that of alien, tyrannizing Budapest? This had become a very acute question by 1910; its fulfilment would wreck the Hapsburg monarchy and be a still harder blow at Hungary. Not without reason did the Magyar politicians look upon Serbia, small and feeble as she seemed, as a "natural enemy"—to be chastened, coerced, cut short at every hazard.

The Czechs of Bohemia: Growing Weakness of the "Dual Monarchy"

Within the realm of the Apostolic King, the situation therefore grew acute. It was hardly more comfortable within the dominions of his alter ego, the Austrian Emperor. A far more cultured people than the Croats was demanding its national rights more vehemently than ever. The Czechs had been the most westernized and civilized of all the Slavic races. Despite the Hapsburg oppression of the seventeenth and eighteenth centuries, they had never lost their national traditions and national character. In 1848, the Czechs had made a gallant, if premature, attempt to win back complete autonomy. When the Magyars won practical independence in 1867, the Czechs believed that Francis Joseph was on the point of coming to Prague, letting himself be crowned as "King of Bohemia," and setting up, not a "dual," but a "triple" monarchy, with Bohemia as the third partner. This was not to be. There was a strong German minority in Bohemia, which feared Czechish domination. There was also a lack of capable leadership at this epoch among the Czechs themselves. Finally, there was the determined resistance of the Magyars to any concessions within Austria to its Slavic elements; that would be a precedent for surrender to their own Slavs as well. So the Hapsburg never entered the stately Hradcany palace at Prague, above the winding Moldau, nor gave back to the Czechs that "kingdom" which had been suppressed in 1621. "Bohemia" continued merely as a province of the Austrian Empire.

The Vienna government, nevertheless, was weaker than its Magyar compeer—it dared not enforce a strict process of Germanization. On the contrary, the Czechs gained a very large local autonomy and made it a point of honor to suppress the German language wherever it proved possible. Prague became an almost purely Czechish city, with German scholars all but driven from its famous university. Only thanks to desperate efforts was the Slavic tongue kept from obtaining official recognition in the courts along with the German.

In 1914 the Czechish people were fully conscious of their proud past and present nationality. Being intelligent and cultivated, they constituted a standing menace to the integrity of the monarchy. They were simply waiting their chance to strike—a chance which all men knew must come.

As the twentieth century advanced, one phrase was increasingly on the tongue throughout the dual monarchy, "When *he* goes?" "He" was Francis Joseph I; after him all things seemed possible. The heir, Archduke Francis Ferdinand, was in very bad odor with many high politicians, especially the Hungarian magnates, because he was said to be in favor of some kind of new adjustments with the Slavs. Besides, he had contracted a morganatic marriage, and his children could not legally inherit the throne. Would there be a disputed succession? All this made the future more dubious.

The formal annexation of Bosnia in 1908 which brought another 1,600,000 South Slavs directly under the Hapsburg yoke, added more fuel to all the fires now burning fiercely along the southern marches of the monarchy.

Bosnia became more and more of a mare's nest from its annexation in 1908 to the opening of the first World War. In theory it had a constitution; but the Bosnian *Sabor*, or Parliament, was not permitted to debate legislation unless proposed by *both* Austria and Hungary, and also all laws passed by it had to be approved by both of the joint masters. The membership of this curious body was furthermore determined by religion—so many Moslem delegates, so many Greek Orthodox, so many Roman Catholic, and so on. The reason was quite plain: by perpetuating religious differences it was hoped that the growth of Bosnian nationalism would be prevented and that the desire of the Greek Orthodox Bosnians to join their fellow-Serbs in Serbia would be offset by stirring up the hatred of the Roman Catholic Croats against them. To make assurance doubly sure, however, so that nothing untoward would happen in Bosnia, twenty-eight members of the Sabor were to be nominated by the government and a tight rein was placed on the schools and a still tighter one on newspapers. Austria and Hungary, working in unison, proved a harsher taskmaster here than did the former in Bohemia, the latter in Croatia. It is not surprising that in this suppressed and alien land secret revolutionary societies flourished. How one of their members set the world aflame in 1914 will be told later.

Free Italy and Its Years of Peace: The Problems of 1870-71: The Roman Question

The history of Italy, from 1870 to 1914, suffers beyond the annals of any other great modern country from abrupt anticlimax. The struggle of Mazzini, Garibaldi, and Cavour for national unity abounds with picturesque incident. There is no such human interest in the recital of the political permutations following the "Breach in Porta Pia," during the long years of international peace which followed. Cavour, like other political paladins, had possessed efficient lieutenants, but not equal colleagues. He was followed by an era of small-calibered, if patriotic, leaders, who could advance his work only imperfectly.

Italy escaped entering the Franco-Prussian War only by a narrow margin. When the struggle began, Napoleon III appealed for aid to

Victor Emmanuel, and the Emperor was promptly informed that he could have the alliance of the King provided he would recall the French garrison from Rome. The French clericals, however, were still more terrible than the Prussians to the Man of Destiny; he refused to leave the Pope to his fate. Then, on the evening of August 6, 1870, a telegram was handed to Victor Emmanuel as he sat in the royal box in the theater at Florence. He read the dispatch with emotion. "Poor Emperor," he exclaimed on returning to the palace. "I pity him—but I've had a lucky escape!" It had been the news of the German victory at Wörth. After that, Napoleon would gladly have evacuated Rome or have done anything else to get Italian help, but Lanza, the royal prime minister, answered always emphatically, "Too late!" Italy was too experimental a nation to support an ally that was beaten already.

The Italian troops had marched into Rome on September 20, 1870, when Pius IX retired to the Vatican and began his life term of self-elected "imprisonment." In 1871 Rome became the official capital of Italy, and Victor Emmanuel made his solemn entry into the Quirinal Palace which henceforth stood as the royal residence, over against the defiant Vatican. For the first time in over eleven hundred years, the Italian peninsula was united politically. Could it become united culturally and in essential national spirit? The task was to prove slow and difficult.

Cavour had boasted, "Any one can govern in a state of siege, but I will govern in a state of liberty!" But Cavour had had no real successor, and "liberty," as Western liberals idealized it, found very rocky soil up and down much of the new kingdom. Between the Alpine lakes and the Capes of Sicily, there existed the greatest possible diversity of manners, interests, and dialects. The blond-haired Lombard peasants of the Po Valley, solid and thrifty, had little in common with the volatile, swarthy, and illiterate masses of Naples or Palermo. In 1870, seventy-three per cent of all Italians were illiterate, a greater proportion than almost anywhere else in Western Europe, except in Spain.

Italy labored under another handicap. The peninsula had for long centuries been denuded of trees and much of the soil had washed away. Also there was a ruinous absence of deposits of the two prime essentials of a modern industrial state—coal and iron. Even down to 1914, nearly all coal had to be imported from England, although "white coal"—water power from the Alps and Apennines—was developed as a considerable substitute. Considering the handicap, it speaks well for the Italian economic genius that the commerce of the kingdom grew steadily, especially in great exports of silks, cottons, and sulphur. In 1914 Italian foreign trade was substantially three times that of 1870; implying, of course, a corresponding growth of industrial and commercial cities such as Turin, Milan, and Genoa.

This difficulty of consolidating into one nation was intensified, by the

Church problem. Pius IX had interned himself in the Vatican, avowing that he could not, without peril and insult, appear in the streets of a capital no more his own. In vain in 1871 did Victor Emmanuel's government extend the olive branch, through the "Laws of Papal Guarantees." The Pope was to have complete possession of the Vatican and of its great gardens; his officials and court were to enjoy entire diplomatic immunity from Italian jurisdiction; he could also have his own uncensored telegraph offices; an income, furthermore, of 3,225,000 lire (about $620,000) was to be paid him. For a moment, it seemed as if Pius would accept these terms, but around the Pope were cardinals and secretaries to whom any composition with the hated House of Savoy was anathema. A formal encyclical speedily denounced the "Guarantees," and summoned all Catholic princes to "restore the Temporal Power."

From this time onward, the relations of Vatican and Quirinal were those of bloodless warfare. The government had to reckon on the sleepless hostility of the most powerful organization in the world. At every turn, the Italian government knew that the influence of the clerical party, in Italy and abroad, was endeavoring to thwart its projects and discredit its administration.

During the eighteen-seventies and eighteen-eighties, it mattered little whether the royal ministers called themselves "Conservatives," or one or another stripe of "Liberal." Victor Emmanuel II, who died in 1878, was not a man of genius or of absolutely unblemished personal life, but hearty, straightforward, and gifted with extraordinary common sense. The nation mourned this "master" of Cavour, as one of the supreme makers of Italy. His son and successor, Humbert I (1878-1900), was like his father, generous-hearted and open to liberal impulses, but he could do little to purify politics. By the eighteen-eighties the Socialists began to make themselves felt in the elections, while the Chamber of Deputies became more and more the prey of petty factions, fighting for office and not for principle. Although the country was supposedly organized as a democratic monarchy, as late as 1882, thanks to the heavy property qualifications, there were only 628,000 voters. Then the franchise was granted to all males who could read and write; it leaped to over 2,000,000; but for a long time, in any event, the ministers were able to cozen or manipulate the majority of the Chamber. Almost never was a cabinet overthrown by a directly adverse vote of the Deputies.

In 1887 and onward, for most of the time until 1896, the prime minister was one of the last of the old "Liberators," the Sicilian Francesco Crispi, a quondam associate of Mazzini and comrade of Garibaldi. Time had mellowed his zeal for republicanism; by 1887, he had broken with nearly all his former radical friends, and he governed very conservatively.

His foes accused him of forsaking the constitutional methods of Cavour for a kind of dictatorship, but his position seemed secure until disaster overtook an expensive and ill-considered attempt to establish an ambitious colonial empire at the mouth of the Red Sea, by forcing an Italian protectorate upon the unwilling Negus of Abyssinia. In 1896 that dusky potentate cut off and destroyed an Italian army, and this disastrous "Battle of Adowa" produced a spasm of dismay in Rome which swept Crispi out of power. There was too much common sense in his successors to renew the costly Abyssinian venture, but the home situation continued deplorable. Passions ran high, finances were disordered, North Italian hated South Italian and saw his hate returned.

The dawn of the twentieth century brought better things. Despite inefficient ministers, those constructive qualities which had made the Italian people great across the ages had been silently doing their work. A successful war had been waged against banditry and the grosser forms of beggary and ignorance. Genoa was becoming a great modern port, and Milan and other northern cities, thriving centers of modern industry. In 1900 King Humbert had perished by the pistol of an anarchist. His son and successor, Victor Emmanuel III, proved an abler man than his father, able to control bad ministers, to uphold good ministers and, in general, to stabilize and purify the national life.

Chapter 22

THE NEAR-EASTERN QUESTION FROM THE CRIMEAN WAR TO THE CONGRESS OF BERLIN

WITHIN five years after the close of the Franco-Prussian War the peace of Europe was menaced again, this time by a recrudescence of what had come to be known as "the Eastern Question." The latter was really a group of questions which had to do with the Turkish Empire: namely, the relations of the Turks to their Christian subjects, the relations of the latter to one another, and the relations of the Powers, first to the Turks, and secondly to the ever recurring crises in the Turkish Empire, particularly in the Balkan Peninsula. The World War of 1914 had many causes, but one of the most obvious was that the liquidation of the Turkish Empire in Europe was by no means complete. The Empire was still in existence; and even lands emancipated from its tyranny had not as yet established appropriate or permanent boundaries. In no instance did the old diplomacy prove more bankrupt than in attempting to deal with the Eastern Question. All Christian Europe agreed that the Turks were bloody interlopers on the Continent; and despite the bravery of the Sultan's soldiers, any one of the Great Powers might have driven the Turks back into Asia. Nevertheless, the diplomats brooded long over the fate of the Ottoman dominions, producing nothing, however, but national jealousies, internal intrigues, costly and indecisive wars, and a new lease of life for the Moslem offender.

There had been, indeed, some perfunctory and well-meant efforts by the sultans to remedy the worst abuses. In 1856 a solemn document, the once famous "Hatti-Humayoun," had promised reforms, especially for the Christian subjects. They were to have complete personal and religious liberty, equality before the laws, eligibility to public office, equality in taxation, and so on. But this went the way of countless other equally solemn documents. Practically nothing came of it. In the provinces the pashas and the beys continued to decree justice at their own sweet will, a mere sweep of the hand often being a sufficient sign for the executioner. In the Sultan's palace at Constantinople the whim of the reigning Circassian slave-girl in the harem or, more likely, of the chief black eunuch, who had purchased this slave-girl for his lord, the *Padishah,* frequently carried more weight than the remonstrances of some partly Europeanized grand vizier, who hoped to turn promised reforms into realities; or than the protests of the British ambassador, who naturally felt anxious about the conduct of the government that his nation had helped rescue from Russia.

In 1861 the Sultan of Turkey drank himself into the grave, and Abdul-Aziz reigned in his stead. He was not personally blood-thirsty, but he was weak, irresponsible, and extravagant. To satisfy the demands of his luxurious harem women and eunuchs, the treasury was sucked dry, public works were neglected, and even well-intentioned pashas were obliged to squeeze extra taxes out of their luckless provinces. As for the administration of justice, the case was pithily summed up by a British consul: "I do not hesitate to say that of all cases of justice, whether between Mussulmen solely, or Turks and Christians, ninety out of one hundred are settled by bribery alone."

To expect that, under these circumstances, Austrians would forget their longings for expansion toward Salonika and the Aegean and, still more, that the Russians would put aside old hopes for a warm-water port and Constantinople, was against human nature. The weakness of the Turkish Empire became daily more evident, and the striving of the Christian races in the Balkan Peninsula to escape from an intolerable yoke aroused the sympathies of the Russian Pan-Slavs, who demanded that Czar Alexander II intervene in the affairs of Turkey.

The Kingdom of Greece: Its Weakness and Ambitions

By the eighteen-seventies that "devil's dance" called the Eastern Question had become more complicated than ever because the various Balkan nationalities were awakening to still greater consciousness of those perplexing things called "national unity" and "national aspirations." The Serbs were becoming acutely aware that fellow South Slavs in Bosnia, Macedonia, and Croatia were under alien bondage. The Rumanians were longing for union with their Magyar-ruled fellows in Transylvania. In Macedonia, Crete, and the Aegean Islands, the Greek populations desired to become parts of the new Greek kingdom. The Bulgars (most oppressed of all) were remembering that once they had been a proud nation.

The Greek kingdom set up by the European Powers was small, poverty-stricken, disorderly, and unhappy. For fear of disintegrating Turkey, the Powers had only given it narrow boundaries—practically nothing north of the famous Pass of Thermopylae, and only a small part of the numerous Aegean islands. Fully half of the Greek-speaking peoples were still under the Ottoman yoke. In 1832 the Great Powers sent out as king, Otto, a son of the King of Bavaria. He was well-intentioned but tactless, and forced by an uprising in 1843 to grant a constitution to his subjects. Even then, he did not become popular enough to keep his throne. After another insurrection in 1862, he was compelled to abdicate, and the Greek National Assembly offered the crown to Prince Alfred, second son of Queen Victoria. England, however, dared not offend Russia, and the proffer was politely declined. An undignified canvass of all the eligible cadets of royal houses and other Highnesses and Serenities in Europe followed, until, at last, a son of the King of Denmark was proclaimed George I in 1863. He was destined to reign till 1913.

King George had a thankless task. The resources of his little kingdom were scanty; his turbulent people were always full of visions of recovering the districts still enslaved by the Turks, or even of restoring the Christian empire of Constantinople. Frequent threats and even coercion by the Great Powers were needed to keep the Greeks from flying into wars with Turkey and so destroying the general "tranquility of the East." At Athens, one ministry would succeed another in the hot strife of parties and factions. Only very gradually did the nation come to understand that, before it could make a good case for wider boundaries, it must develop peaceful industries, pay its debts, and substitute law and order for picturesque lawlessness.

The Albanians, a Survival of Barbarism: The Serbian Principality

The Albanians were a very old people, quite as old as their Greek neighbors who dwelt to the south of them. Their grandfathers had been the Illyrians of Græco-Roman times, brave, hardy barbarians who had kept their speech and native customs little spoiled by the "civilization" about them, all through the ages. The Albanians had resisted the Turks valiantly, but at last had partially succumbed. The majority had become Mohammedan, although many remained stanch Christians.

The Turks had embodied Albania nominally into their empire, but the authority of the Sultan was never taken seriously along its jagged hills and valleys. The Albanians were brave soldiers and supplied the *padishahs* with admirable regiments and generals. When, however, taxes were proposed, all the mountains blazed up in rebellion. No region of Europe was so uncivilized and backward as that which lay directly across the Adriatic from southern Italy. Travelers found it almost equal to a voyage to Africa to try to penetrate the Albanian hinterland. All that Albania asked was to be let alone by the Turkish fiscal oppressors, and to be ignored by all modern "improvements." Tribal government was the order of the day. In 1871 nobody gave Albania serious consideration, or believed that in her aspirations lay a Europeon problem.

This statement could hardly be made of the Albanians' northern and eastern neighbors, often called the Serbs, although a more proper name for this people would have been "South Slavs." In the nineteenth century their region was split into four rather distinct fragments—Serbia proper, Montenegro, Bosnia, and Croatia.

Serbia had become a semi-independent principality in 1830. Montenegro, that little pocket in the "Black Mountain," had never really been under the power of the Turks at all, but was completely separate from Serbia, under its own princes. Bosnia was a Turkish *pashalik*, Croatia-Slavonia, since 1718, had belonged to Austria and in the eighteen-seventies was a "kingdom" (imperfectly autonomous) under the power of the revived Magyar state in Hungary. The problems of "Croatia" belong to earlier and later times, but Bosnia and Serbia demand consideration at present. In Bosnia and the companion district of Herzegovina, the bulk of the nobility had apostatized and become Moslem, although the peasantry remained Christian. These Bosnian nobles became notorious for their oppression of their inferiors and also for the scant obedience they rendered their nominal lord, the Sultan.

From the Serbian principality the last Turkish garrisons had been withdrawn in 1867, but the little country was even weaker and more distracted than the Kingdom of Greece. There were no traditions of civil liberty or of fixed institutions. Belgrade, the capital, was a small, ill-built, and very filthy city situated in the extreme north of the country. Orderly government was handicapped by the existence of two rival princely houses, sprung from two leaders in the struggle for independence. The Karageorgevic dynasty had supplied Prince Alexander I, who reigned from 1842 to 1858, and was then tumultuously deposed by a popular uprising and chased into exile. In his stead reigned Milos of the Obrenovic line, who held power only until 1860. He was a very old man, having ruled once before (1817-39), and on his death his son, Michael, succeeded him. The new prince was a person of moderation and ability, and he induced the European powers to aid him in expelling the Turkish garrisons. But he was unable to get on with large factions of his unruly subjects, both those who adhered to the rival house and those who entertained a premature vision of a Greater Serbia, spreading over the whole of the Balkan Peninsula.

Michael thus became unpopular, and the Balkan countries had developed abrupt political methods. In 1868, as Michael walked in the Belgrade palace park with his betrothed princess and her mother, three men rushed from the shrubbery and fired several shots. Michael fell dead, as did the older woman. There was little doubt that these assassins (who were later caught and executed) were the tools of the exiled Karageorgevics. The plot, however, failed. Michael's friends kept their hold on the government, and Milan I, his cousin, was seated as prince.

In 1871 Serbia was a small, weak country. The Great Powers hardly took seriously her brave claims, based on her widest boundaries in the fourteenth century, to a larger share of the Balkans. Economically, thanks to the absence of any seaport for her commerce, Serbia was almost a satrapy of Austria. In Bosnia a great number of kindred Slavs were still under the heel of the Turkish oppression, and the Serbs naturally dreamed of the day when they could unite their entire people under one flag; but the statesmen at Vienna smiled at these high expectations.

The Bulgars: A Nation Returning to Self-Consciousness

Across the mountains, in the eastern Balkans, dwelt the Bulgars, a people that, in the age of Metternich, the world had practically forgotten. In no other part of their European empire had the Turks crushed out the old native liberties more completely. The Bulgars were not originally Slavs. They were originally a Finnish-Turanian-Tartar nation, with a distant kinship to the Turks themselves. They had entered the Balkan Peninsula in the seventh and eighth centuries and had founded what had been, for its day, a pretentious kingdom. Their religion and type of culture had come from the Greeks of Constantinople, but contact with the Slavs had modified their language so that it had become a Slavic tongue. While under the heel of the Turks they had, furthermore, absorbed so much Slavic blood as to change largely the original condition of their race. The conquerors had destroyed their native aristocracy, and even the control of their Orthodox Church had been grasped by the Greeks, whom the Turks regularly sustained as the most useful branch of their Christian subjects. So completely, in fact, did the identity of the Bulgarian nation seem lost, that foreign travelers in the region spoke of them as a kind of Greeks, and, down to about the time of the Crimean War, any Bulgar lucky enough to claim wealth and education was likely to describe himself as a "Greek."

In the nineteenth century, Bulgarian nationality, like so many other half-extinguished nationalities, suddenly reasserted itself. Russian diplomacy realized the value of encouraging a people who might well pass as Slavs, and who could possibly be kindled to appeal to the Czar to protect them against Islam. A movement for Bulgarian schools and the use of the native tongue in churches began, and in 1860 the Bulgarian Christians announced that they would recognize the authority of the Patriarch of Constantinople no longer. The Sultan did not enjoy this assertion, for the Patriarch had been his convenient tool. But in 1870 Russian pressure had compelled him to set up an "exarch" in Bulgaria, to rule the local Christians. This gave the awakening nation an official rallying point. The next step might be toward secular as well as religious independence. Nevertheless, in 1871 Europe hardly realized that there was a Bulgarian nation, much less a Bulgarian problem. The mountains in the eastern Balkans were still Turkish pashaliks, and no outsider bothered about them. Then suddenly, as by the wave of a magician's wand, in 1876, the name of Bulgaria was to be on every man's lips.

Rumania: The Rule of Prince Carol

One other Balkan population had been under Ottoman lordship. North of the Danube lay what long had been called "The Principalities"— Wallachia and Moldavia. In 1859 the people of these districts had insisted on uniting themselves into the single principality of Rumania. The Rumanians had a very ancient and honorable history. About 104 A.D. the Roman emperor Trajan had conquered the region (Old Dacia) and had filled it with Latinized settlers. About 256 A.D., at the advance of the barbarians, the Roman government in its turn had evacuated the country, and it lapsed back to the uncouth Goths, Huns, Avars, and other despoilers of the dying empire. But the Latin-speaking settlers had not retired with the legions. In the Carpathian mountain valleys, and in the great plains between the Prut and the Danube, they had lived on, maintaining a speech which was closer to the tongue of old Rome than any other in Europe. The great invasions and the passage of conquering races did not destroy them. They had a native proverb which time had made good, "The Rumanian never dies."

The Turks had overrun the country but had never completely conquered it. The natives kept their local institutions, including an influential nobility and the right to have a Christian hospodar to rule over each principality. After 1815, thanks to increasing Russian intervention, the suzerainty of the Sultan became little more than a name, while both Austria and Russia watched the Rumanians with a jealous eye, with a view to absorption the moment the general European situation might become such as to favor their respective dreams of imperial expansion.

During the nineteenth century the Rumanians awoke to national consciousness. In 1859 they succeeded in uniting their two principalities under a single government, and the general condition of the world was too precarious then for Austria and Russia to intervene. From 1859 to 1866, the consolidated principality was ruled by Prince Alexander Cuza, a native nobleman. He founded schools, broke up the unnecessary number of monasteries which had absorbed an absurd proportion of the land, and, greatest stroke of all, abolished serfdom among the peasantry. But Cuza's methods were those of the familiar "strong man," who rides down all opposition by setting aside paper constitutions. He made numerous enemies. In 1866 a bloodless revolution banished him.

In 1866, the Rumanians offered their throne to Prince Carol (Charles), of a side branch of the Hohenzollern family, who was also, however, connected through his mother with the dynasty of Napoleon. Austria and Russia were not enthusiastic over witnessing a Hohenzollern reigning at Bucharest, but Bismarck saw the chance to put a friend of Prussia in the Balkans and urged the young prince to accept. "Even if you fail," said he, "you will always remember with pleasure an adventure which can never be a reproach to you." Through fear of being halted by Austria, the Prince traveled down the Danube disguised as a second-class passenger, until on Rumanian soil he left the boat and was greeted by his future prime minister. Austria fumed and might have taken action, but her great war with Prussia was about to break out, and she soon had more grievous troubles. The other powers declined to intervene, and the Sultan, the Prince's nominal suzerain, confirmed the new ruler. Thus Prince Carol kept his throne.

In 1871 Rumania had laws and institutions of fairly long standing, and a reasonably well-organized army, but her problems were still many. She had not a mile of railway, and very few good roads. Bucharest was a pitiful pretense for a capital, and the Prince on his arrival "could scarcely believe that a one-storied building, looking out upon a dirty square, was the 'palace.'"

There were many Jews in Rumania. Somewhat unjustly, they were accused by their Christian neighbors of taking gross financial advantage of the ignorant peasantry, who retaliated by burning synagogues and by frequent riots. More largely to blame were the great boyars (noblemen), who not only oppressed the peasants but delighted in placing the blame on the Jews, thus escaping the blame which they themselves so richly deserved. Needless to say, the finances of the principality were in the usual Balkan tangle.

Prince Carol, however, in the early eighteen-seventies, was already showing himself a capable and tactful administrator. The native parliaments were becoming less turbulent and more responsible. The economic condition of the country was gradually improving. When, in 1877, the great storm broke over the Balkan Peninsula, Rumania was better prepared than any other of the minor countries to play an honorable part.

Such, then, were the principal actors in the new drama about to begin in the Near East: Turkey, hopelessly corrupt, medieval, and dying by inches; Greece and Serbia, both crude, restless, and seeking expansion far beyond their powers; Albania and Bulgaria, seemingly mere districts of the Turkish Empire, ignored by the outside world. Rumania alone was obviously in a fairly honorable and recognized position. As for the Great Powers of Europe: Austria and Russia were ready for any chance that would open for them the door to Constantinople and were equally ready to bar it in the face of a rival; France was too perplexed at home and too helpless; and Italy was too newly consolidated as a Great Power to become an active factor. The statesmen of England, however, were still obsessed by their old notion that any advance of Russia toward a warm-water port meant peril to their own road to India and therefore, despite its very obvious sins, "the integrity of the Ottoman Empire must be preserved." The sixth Great Power of Europe, curiously enough, seemed without interest in the Balkan problems. Bismarck considered that Germany had tasks nearer home. It was during this period that he remarked, "I never take the trouble to open the mail-bag from Constantinople," and again, "The whole of the Balkans is not worth the bones of a single Pomeranian grenadier." That German policy should ever fix its eyes upon the Sultan's palace was a thing that apparently never entered the head of the cool, practical, and eminently conservative Bismarck.

New Disorders in Turkey: The Attitude of Disraeli

In 1875 the peasants of Herzegovina, a district in Bosnia, infuriated by taxes levied by Turkish officials, rose against their oppressors and defeated a small Turkish army. Instantly, their Slavic brethren in Serbia, Montenegro, and even in the Austrian province of Dalmatia, flocked in as volunteers.

The disturbance grew so widespread that the European consuls in Bosnia stirred themselves to end the strife. The insurgents, however, were tired of Turkish promises and mollifying speeches. They demanded autonomy. The Sultan replied with glittering promises but these did not end the insurrection. Furthermore, the Turkish government at this time announced that part of the interest on its public debt would be suspended. Such an act forced the issue. Many millions' worth of Turkish bonds were held throughout Europe, and the bondholders' outcries carried farther than those of the wretched Bosnian peasants. The first fruit of their clamors was the formation of a common program by the three great imperial powers, Germany, Austria, and Russia, which were loosely allied together in what was known as the "League of the Three Emperors" (see p. 480). In their name Count Andrássy, Chancellor of Austria, addressed a solemn admonition to the Sultan, reciting his sins and specifying indispensable reforms.

The Ottomans received this "Andrássy Note" in January, 1876, with nominal acceptance; but the Bosnian insurgents were not willing to lay down their arms merely because the Austrian consuls now told them that the Sultan had promised to be good; and the Turks retaliated by saying they could not institute reforms in taxation, fair treatment of the peasantry, the administration of justice, and so forth, while their subjects were still in arms. The insurrection therefore grew. Serbia and Montenegro were on the point of declaring war in behalf of their brethren in Bosnia, and Mohammedan fanaticism became kindled. In May, 1876, a Moslem mob attacked and murdered the German and French consuls in the city of Salonica. There were riots in Constantinople. The several thousand *softas*, or Turkish theological students, rose, crying out against the Grand Vizier as being too friendly to Russia, and the weak Sultan was compelled to dismiss him.

Meanwhile, the "Three Emperors' League" was considering another attempt to calm the tempest. In May, 1876, appeared the Berlin Memorandum, a document prepared after conference with Prince Bismarck by the Russian and Austrian prime ministers. It demanded an armistice with the Bosnians and the appointment of a mixed commission of natives, with a Christian president to arrange the affairs of their country. The insurgents were to be allowed to remain in arms temporarily. To this note, France and Italy assented; but there was one power which refused—Great Britain.

Many Englishmen, since 1876, have considered this action a crowning blunder. The prime minister of Great Britain at this time was Disraeli, soon to be known as the Earl of Beaconsfield. This brilliant and versatile leader of the Conservative party may fairly be called the founder of modern British imperialism. To him England was not a "tight little island" with a thriving commerce which was somewhat helped by the possession of various colonies; she was the center of a great empire.

All English statesmen in the later nineteenth century were bred in the belief that Russia was their inveterate foe; and every move in the world's politics which seemed to Russia's advantage appeared a direct stab at their own empire. This feeling Disraeli possessed, beyond the run of his peers. He was anything but a pacifist, and repeatedly he seems to have been willing to force Russia to the breaking point. His colleagues in the ministry could usually restrain him, but to the end of his career he remained the distrustful foe of *anything* satisfactory to the Czar.

Great Britain refused to sign the Berlin Memorandum on the ground that the "Three Emperors" had formulated demands on the Ottoman Empire without her prior consent. This discordant note was happily heard at Constantinople. The Turks long had been accustomed to play one Christian empire against another and then to snap their fingers. They now reckoned that Germany, France, and Italy would never go beyond diplomatic protests; Russia and Austria could not unite in a firm agreement; and England, Disraeli's attitude seemed to indicate, might give them military and naval aid against the Czar.

The Bulgarian Massacres: War Between Serbia and Turkey

In May, 1876, the Berlin Note was presented, and almost simultaneously Great Britain, as if to show her friendship for the Turks, ordered a squadron to the mouth of the Dardanelles. In Constantinople, matters were moving briskly. The reigning sultan, Abdul-Aziz, disgusted all responsible Turks by his extravagance and gross incapacity. There was a faction in Constantinople which saw that the Empire was drifting to calamity for lack of efficient leadership. This party secured the *fetvah* (solemn decree) of the Sheik-ul-Islam (the head of the Turkish branch of Islam), authorizing the removal of the Padishah whose government was bringing ruin to the Faithful. Abdul-Aziz was easily deposed and his nephew, Murad V, was set upon the throne of Mohammed the Conqueror. Four days later it was announced that Abdul-Aziz had committed suicide by means of a pair of scissors loaned him for trimming his beard. Murad, however, soon proved to be either "feeble-minded," or possibly not sufficiently pliable for the pashas who had put him in power. In August, 1876, he, in turn, was deposed, and in his place reigned his brother, Abdul-Hamid II, who was at first too inexperienced to have a will of his own, although later he was to develop into one of the shrewdest and most bloodthirsty of all the Ottoman line.

While this national party among the beys and pashas was trying to introduce a modest degree of efficiency into the Constantinople government, their own army was making it impossible for Great Britain to aid their country against Russia. The Bosnian revolt had spread elsewhere. The Bulgarian villages had become restless. There was a feeble uprising, and about one hundred Turks were killed by Bulgar insurgents. The answer came when the government sent an army of regular troops and a still larger horde of Bashi-Bazouks—irregular soldiers under the laxest kind of discipline—into the Bulgarian mountains. The slaughter of the defenseless peasantry was terrible. In the town of Batak only two thousand of the seven thousand inhabitants escaped cold-blooded murder. The whole number of Christians thus massacred was probably over twelve thousand. Sex or age had not been spared, and a British commissioner, sent to investigate the rumors of horror, reported the whole deed as "perhaps the most heinous crime that has stained the history of the present century."

The Disraeli government committed the gross blunder of trying to minimize this deed of their announced protégés. But the English Liberal papers soon ran down the facts; Mr. Gladstone, former and succeeding prime minister and Disraeli's chief political opponent, left his theological studies on "Future Retribution" to write a famous and utterly damning pamphlet entitled *The Bulgarian Horrors*. The conscience of England was stirred by his speeches and publications. It speedily assented to his stern dictum, "Let the Turks now carry away their abuses in the only possible manner, namely, *by carrying away themselves.* . . . One and all, bag and baggage [they] shall, I hope, clear out of the province they have desolated and profaned."

It would have been folly for the Disraeli ministry to invite repudiation at home by giving further countenance to a government which could work deeds like these. "Even if Russia were to declare war against the Porte[1] [Sultan]," wrote Lord Derby to Constantinople, "Her Majesty's government would find it practically impossible to interfere."

War between Russia and Turkey was becoming every day more certain. While the Bulgarian massacres were proceeding, Serbia and Montenegro had declared war (1876) upon the Sultan. The Montenegrins won some successes, but the more ambitious Serbian campaign speedily came to grief. Once more it was disclosed that the Turks were still first-class fighting men. The Serbian army, despite large reinforcements by Russian volunteers, was defeated, and Prince Milan called lustily for an armistice. But the Powers were unable to arrange a satisfactory accommodation; every day that the quarrel continued promised new perils for the peace of the world, and the English, in turn, began to give their Ottoman protégés frank advice. It was not English admonition, however, but Russian action, which brought a momentary respite. On the 30th of October, the ambassador of the Russian Czar to Constantinople gave the Turks forty-eight hours to conclude an armistice with Serbia. With this pistol at his head, the Sultan halted. Fighting ceased. The diplomats resumed their weary efforts, making a last desperate attempt to save the Ottoman from his sins, and Turkey from Russia.

The Futile Attempt to Get the Turks to "Reform" (1876-77)

In December, 1876, a conference of the Powers met at Constantinople for the purpose of giving Abdul-Hamid II sage advice. Even as their Excellencies the ambassadors were in session, sudden salvos of artillery distracted their august deliberations. Prompt questions were raised, and an able and affable pasha announced that the Padishah, out of his vast love for his people, had bestowed upon them a liberal constitution. A nominated senate, an elected chamber of deputies, a responsible ministry, freedom of meeting and of the press, compulsory education—all these blessings, by one stroke of the pen, were to come to the fortunate subjects of the successor of the califs. The diplomats, however, were too hardheaded to be thus duped. Even the British delegates refused to take the new "liberty" seriously, and the Russian ambassador quitted Constantinople in wrath.

The Turks used their new constitution with some adroitness for further delay. How could the Powers continue to demand "reforms" when all imaginable reforms were going into effect—just as soon, of course, as the new parliament could be convened, and pass the necessary measures? And, in the meantime, how could the Padishah, now a "constitutional sovereign," enact legislation by mere fiat? As for other matters, the Turks

[1] "The Sublime Porte" was the ordinary official title for the Turkish government.

CONSTANTINOPLE, FROM AN EARLY PRINT

proved themselves to the ambassadors to be incorrigible. When the question of Bulgaria was raised, the viziers at first averred "they did not know what the word meant." They then permitted themselves to remember that it might be a "geographical term for the region north of the Balkan mountains," but that was all. In short, these "slippery barbarians, who wore tight clothes and chattered French," but who seemed to have neither honesty nor intelligence under their red fezzes, alienated their last friends and drove even England to wash her hands of them. Lord Salisbury, going home in despair, declared that "all had tried to save Turkey, but she would not allow them to save her." Thus the year 1877 opened with war between the Czar and the Sultan all but certain, and with England looking on, a neutral.

The Muscovite empire had lately been stirred by a strong Pan-Slavic movement, an agitation for the union of all Slavdom in one confederacy, under the hegemony of Russia. Meanwhile, the outraged Bulgars were counted as Slavs, too; and their woes had produced a great impression. Also, to the Muscovites, with their passionate loyalty to the Orthodox Church, the summons to rescue their fellow Christians from Turkish tyranny came as a call to a crusade. Finally, and of still keener national interest, was the fact that, in marching as the champion of Christian civilization against the Sultan, Russia was again advancing toward that outlet upon warm blue water which was a necessity for her empire. Therefore, when the Turks, in the spring of 1877, in a spirit of incredible folly, rejected the London Protocol (a last despairing proposal for reform which had been flung at them by the concert of the Powers), Russia declared war.

The Turko-Russian War of 1877

Since the Russian navy on the Black Sea could not cope with the Turkish fleet, which contained several formidable ironclads, the way to Constantinople lay across Rumania. There were divided councils at Bucharest about permitting the Russians to go through, but the Sultan committed the blunder not merely of calling on "his vassal" to preserve neutrality, but of summoning Prince Carol to take up arms against the enemies of his suzerain. The Prince was naturally anxious to become an independent sovereign, and made a treaty with Russia for full alliance. The legions of Alexander II, therefore, streamed across Wallachia, while the Prince issued a formal proclamation of Rumanian independence.

The Russians had entered into the war with enthusiasm and surpassing confidence that they could easily crush the Infidel. Their difficulties, however, were great; the railroads through southern Russia were few, and in Rumania still fewer. The hindrances to moving huge armies at a vast distance from their base proved almost unsurmountable. In the summer of 1877, the Russians forced their way over the Danube, penetrated Bulgaria, took Tirnova, the old capital of that afflicted country, and seized Shipka Pass, the best defile over the Balkan Mountains. There was panic in Constantinople. Then came a long respite. The Turks found an able general—Osman Pasha, who was able to inflict on the Czar and his grand dukes anxious nights, heavy losses, and a humiliating delay.

In their rapid advance through Bulgaria the Russians had neglected to occupy the small town of Plevna, located at the intersection of the main military roads. With some 50,000 men, Osman Pasha flung himself into Plevna, and suddenly the Russians found their whole advance menaced. Not realizing the strength of their enemies, they assaulted with inadequate force. Ten days later, a more powerful attack met with a greater disaster. The Grand Duke Nicholas must needs telegraph to Prince Carol to bring up his Rumanians to aid in the siege. The Rumanians covered themselves with glory before the bloody Turkish breastworks, but the Turks' inner lines could not be carried. The only option was to bring up reinforcements, hem Osman in, and slowly starve him out.

At last, in December, Osman served out his last biscuit and tried to cut his way through the besiegers. He was forced to surrender with 40,000 half-starved troops; but he had cost the enemy 21,000 men and five months of valuable time.

The surrender of Osman was followed by the rout of the remaining Turkish armies. One Russian army took Sofia, another reopened Shipka Pass. Serbia, too, was again in arms, likewise Montenegro; and from every quarter messengers of calamity hastened to Abdul-Hamid. The Cossacks raged and raided around Adrianople in a manner that indicated that Christians, too, understood the art of massacre. Adrianople fell in January,

1878, and the military power of Turkey collapsed. With a noose around their necks, the Ottomans accepted an armistice the end of the month, to be followed by the Treaty of San Stefano in the spring.

The Treaty of San Stefano

The Muscovites were anxious to tie their defeated foe by a hard-and-fast treaty and to confront Europe, and especially England, with a *fait accompli*. The Czar's ministers knew, however, that not merely England but Austria as well would fight, rather than see Russia in Constantinople, and they did not try to annex that city. But otherwise they dictated sweeping changes. Montenegro and Serbia were to receive appreciable increases in territory, Bosnia was to be reformed, not by promises only but by being put under the joint control of Austria and Russia. Other reforms were to be granted to oppressed minorities in Asia Minor, in which region a strip of territory (including Kars) was to be ceded outright to Russia. Rumania was to be set up as a strictly independent nation, but she was to cede Bessarabia to Russia and receive in return (at the expense of Turkey) the Dobruja, the miasmic, marshy delta of the Danube. But the most striking clause was that relating to the creation of an entirely new unit in modern Europe—*Bulgaria*. According to the terms of this treaty, a huge Bulgaria would have sprung into existence. Constantinople and its hinterland back to Adrianople, Salonika and the territory around it, and part of Albania would have been left to the Sultan; otherwise he would have been expelled from Europe.

As the Russians advanced, and still more as the full tenor of their demands became evident, the English public took ever increasing alarm. The memory of the Bulgarian massacres was already fading; the fear of the Muscovite advance toward India by way of Constantinople again gripped the British heart. Within the London cabinet, there was much difference of opinion. Disraeli himself said whimsically that "there were six parties in the ministry. The first party wanted immediate war with Russia; the second was for war in order to save Constantinople; the third was for peace at any price; the fourth would let the Russians take Constantinople and *then* turn them out; the fifth wanted to plant the cross on the dome of St. Sophia; and then there was the prime minister and the chancellor of the exchequer [Northcote], who desired to see something done, but didn't know exactly what!" It is fairly certain, however, that Disraeli was quite ready to go to war, if Russia did not knuckle under, and only the resistance of his colleagues prevented Britain from taking action bound to set cannon thundering on sea and land.

For some weeks the Muscovites and Turks confronted one another grimly at the gates of Constantinople, while a British fleet rode in the Sea of Marmora, inside the Dardanelles, ready to land men at Constantinople itself, in case the invaders showed signs of attacking the city. The situation was ticklish. The least incident would have set the Russians and British at one another's throats, despite the fact that, unless England had found a land ally, the struggle would have been, as Bismarck sarcastically declared, "a fight between an elephant and a whale."

Under these circumstances war would surely have followed, had not Russia been willing to consider the revision of the Treaty of San Stefano. There were plenty of hot-headed officers around the Czar, and plenty of ardent Pan-Slavists in the rear, quite ready to urge defiance. But Russia's hand was forced by the threatening attitude of Austria. Despite the fact that Francis Joseph had given some kind of assurances of neutrality when the attack on Turkey began, Austrian troops began to mobilize in the Carpathians, ready to make a deadly flank attack upon the Russians, strung out as they were in a long line of communication through Rumania and Bulgaria. The fear lest the proposed Bulgarian state be virtually a satrapy of Russia terrified Vienna no less than London. It would have been tempting destruction for Alexander to have fought both England and Austria simultaneously. Nevertheless, ere Alexander II could be induced to lay the settlement of the Balkans before a general congress of the Powers, there were tense moments and renewed threats of war.

Meanwhile, Disraeli gave notice that the reserves of the British army and navy would be called out. Fifteen days later he ordered eight regiments of Indian Sepoy troops to Malta. This sign of resolution brought the Czar's ministers to a more tractable mood, and they agreed to such concessions concerning the boundaries of Bulgaria as to make it likely that peace could be maintained. But Disraeli was proving to the Turks that he was not championing their integrity out of disinterested friendship. By letting them believe that Russia was likely to renew the war and that English aid would be indispensable, the Sultan was induced to promise that if Russia retained her conquests in Asia Minor (as it was perfectly certain she would do) and seemed likely to push her conquests farther, England would give armed aid to the Sultan. To enable England to defend these territories, the Ottomans gave her the occupation and administration of Cyprus.[2] The Sultan also promised to introduce the "necessary reforms" for the protection of the Armenian Christians.

The Congress of Berlin (June-July, 1878): Bismarck and Beaconsfield

Russia was thus forced to submit her entire scheme for the reconstruction of the Balkans to a congress of the Powers, which presently assembled

---

[2] The innocent Turks did not know that Britain and Russia had reached a working agreement five days before the Cyprus Convention was signed (June 4, 1878). They had bartered away a rich island for a promise to fight in behalf of the Ottomans, which England knew she would not have to redeem!

(1878) at Berlin—undoubtedly the most distinguished diplomatic gathering since the Congress of Vienna.

That Bismarck, the acknowledged center of all European diplomatic life, should preside over this assembly was only natural. He had invited the diplomats to accept the hospitality of his emperor on the ground that Germany had no selfish interests in the Balkans, and was intensely anxious to keep the general peace, offering himself to serve as an "honest broker" for his distinguished friends and clients. Nevertheless, the Russians went to Berlin with the firm expectation that the "Iron Chancellor" would prove their advocate and even their champion. The services which Russia rendered Germany in 1870, when a broad hint from the Czar possibly had prevented Austria from going to the aid of France, were admittedly very great. William I himself had written to Alexander II, "Prussia will never forget that she owes it to you that the war [with France] did not assume the most extreme dimensions; may God bless you for it." Now, surely, was the time for active gratitude.

The Russians found themselves deceived. The "Iron Chancellor" afterward said he in no wise deserved their wrath, but rather that he ought to have been decorated by the Czar for friendly services. Russian spokesmen, however, laughed him to scorn. They could point to the undeniable fact that at the Congress of Powers, Bismarck swung his influence over to the side of England and Austria, and permitted the Treaty of San Stefano to be rewritten to Russia's great hurt. The motives Bismarck had for this change of policy are explained elsewhere (see p. 489), but the accomplished results were blazoned before all Europe. In 1878 it became evident that between Berlin and St. Petersburg warm friendship had ceased.

Aside from Bismarck himself, the gathering at Berlin was notable. Seldom have more premiers or foreign ministers of Europe's nations sat around one table. France and Italy were represented, although France was still too crushed by the events of 1870 to have much influence, and Italy was hardly as yet a "Great Power," except by courtesy. Austria sent her foreign minister, the astute Count Andrássy; Russia her chancellor, Prince Gorchakov, a man of considerable ability, but on bad personal terms with Bismarck and therefore not a fortunate delegate to win the favor of the mighty Chancellor; England was represented by Lord Salisbury, and by Disraeli himself, now elevated to the peerage as the Earl of Beaconsfield.

Bismarck and the strong Austrian influence were so decidedly on Beaconsfield's side that he had little difficulty in forcing the Russians to assent to almost any terms which were not too humiliating. In fact, Beaconsfield, personally, seemed to dominate the gathering. "The old Jew—*he* is the man!" remarked Bismarck pithily; and the English Prime Minister was quite aware of his triumph. It is recorded that the Russo-

Polish Princess Radziwill met him at a brilliant reception the night that the news of the Cyprus Convention was made public. As he wandered among the throng of buzzing, criticizing, yet admiring generals and diplomats, the Princess asked the Prime Minister, "What are you thinking of?" "I am not *thinking* at all," replied Beaconsfield magnificently, "I am merely *enjoying* myself."

The Czar's ministers, in short, were soon aware that they could not fight England, with Austria as her ally, without the active help of Bismarck. There was nothing for it but to save out of the wreck of the San Stefano project whatever part they could.

The Treaty of Berlin (July, 1878)

Substantially speaking, the Treaty of San Stefano was attacked on the ground that the Great Bulgaria proposed by it denied the claims of Serbia and Greece to expansion, and unduly curtailed the Turkish dominions in Europe; for the Sultan, urged his apologists, must surely be left enough land west of the Bosporus still to be able to pass for a European power. But the readjustments at Berlin were made very unskilfully, with far greater care on the part of the opponents of Russia to prevent the wide extension of her power than to make any redistribution of the Balkan lands that would meet the reasonable demands of national hopes and international justice. The principal points in the Treaty of Berlin can be stated in summary:

I. Some extensions were given to Serbia and Montenegro, but not so great as by the San Stefano scheme; and between the two small South Slav countries was left wedged the "Sanjak of Novi-Bazar," a miserable little district now handed back to Turkey.

II. Bosnia and Herzegovina were assigned to Austria, to be "occupied and administered" by her, pending the restoration of their peace and prosperity. Theoretically, they were still part of Turkey. The Serbs and their kinsmen, the Bosnians, were angered at this evidence that Bosnia was not to escape from the moribund Sultan into the hands of Serbia, but was to become a spoil of lusty Austria. Still, the new arrangement was avowedly "temporary," and the South Slavs were to live in vain hope for thirty years, until Austria destroyed the illusion by downright annexation in 1908.

III. Greece was given a promise of an extension of her northern borders, a promise which the Sultan was very slow to fulfil. It was only reluctantly and partially executed in 1881, after severe pressure from the Powers. For the great island of Crete, with its large Hellenic population, Greece pleaded in vain. It was left to thirty-four years more of misrule and Ottoman bondage.

IV. In Asia Minor, Russia was compelled to disgorge part of her conquests, although she retained the strong fortress of Kars. The Sultan also solemnly engaged "to carry out, without further delay the improvements and reforms demanded by local requirements in the provinces [of] the Armenians, and to guarantee their security against the Circassians and Kurds." How Abdul-Hamid executed this binding promise will be told in a bloody sequel.

V. The Great Bulgaria of San Stefano was flung into the scrap heap. England would have none of it; the new state, in her opinion, would become merely a Russian protectorate. The proposed new unit was, therefore, cut into three parts, each with a different fate: (*a*) The southern region, especially Macedonia, was handed back to the Sultan, to be oppressed by his myrmidons and its own factions until 1912, with a history miserable even beyond the run of Turkish provinces. (*b*) The northern regions, a "Small Bulgaria," were formed into an "autonomous and tributary principality," practically clear of the Sultan save for an annual tribute, to have a prince and constitution of its own. (*c*) Between Bulgaria and the Turkish dominions was to be an "autonomous province under the direct political and military authority of the Sultan," but with a Christian governor named every five years. This new unit was *Eastern Rumelia.*

VI. As a sop to Russia, and as a reward to the Czar's people for their sacrifices in a victorious war, it was confirmed that Bessarabia should be detached from Rumania and given to the Muscovites. The desolate Dobruja seemed a poor enough recompense for this loss of land inhabited almost strictly by Rumanians, and Prince Carol's ministers pleaded in vain against the change. To no purpose they invoked the memories of their faithful service at Plevna. Gorchakov was inexorable, and Beaconsfield was not willing to risk a great war merely in behalf of an angry East European people.

With these results, then, the great Congress of Berlin adjourned, and Beaconsfield returned to London in fine feather, bringing, he told his applauding countrymen, "peace with honor," and also cynically asserting that he had "consolidated the Turkish Empire." The diplomatic wiseacres declared that "peace and happiness were now assured to the Balkans." On the contrary, few human arrangements were more short-sighted and transitory than this much-lauded Treaty of Berlin. The unhappy results that presently developed were these:

I. The Bosnian question, which was thrust upon Serbia and Austria, became pregnant with almost certain war.

II. Bulgaria was bound to reach out for Eastern Rumelia and then for an outlet upon the open sea—the Aegean.

III. The failure to award Crete to Greece promised hot friction and a war between Greece and Turkey.

IV. The return of Macedonia to the Turks implied that the miseries of that unhappy land would presently make it a powder factory for all Europe and indirectly for all the world.

V. The action of Bismarck in favoring England and Austria at the expense of Russia erected a barrier between Germany and Russia that was soon to develop into an enmity which, in its own turn, was likely to breed war.

VI. By exacting Cyprus from Turkey as a reward for "protection," England destroyed the claims of gratitude she might have had upon the Sultan. Abdul-Hamid bitterly resented this sharp practice. From this time onward the diplomatic influence of Britain at Constantinople waned.

VII. By helping to secure the return of Macedonia and other regions to the Ottomans, by other friendly acts, and by exacting no territorial concessions in return, Germany convinced the Turks that in *her* there was a really powerful and unselfish friend.

It is told that, on the morrow of the signature of the Treaty of Berlin, Bismarck sent for the Turkish representatives and said: "Well, gentlemen, you ought to be very much pleased. We have secured you a respite of twenty years. You have that period of grace in which to put your house in order. It is probably the last chance the Ottoman Empire will get, and of one thing I am pretty sure, *you won't take it.*"

Part of the seeds of the calamity of 1914 had been sown in 1871, when Germany dictated a humiliating peace to France. Another very large part, however, was sown in 1878, when Beaconsfield and Bismarck imposed on the Near East not a real peace, but a most unsatisfactory truce.

Chapter 23

THE NEAR-EASTERN QUESTION FROM THE CONGRESS OF BERLIN TO THE COMMENCEMENT OF THE FIRST WORLD WAR

No SOONER had the ink dried on the Treaty of Berlin than the Western world began to take note of Bulgaria. In 1870 scarcely any European knew where Bulgaria was. In 1880 her affairs were discussed even in obscure American journals.

Prince Alexander of Battenberg, a son of the Prince of Hesse and a nephew of the Czar, was chosen by the Bulgars as their first ruler (1879). He was only twenty-two years old, but he had already served as a cadet at Plevna and still later as a Prussian lieutenant. He was erect, gallant, and a man of good will; but he lacked tact, was unable to speak Bulgar, and was soon lost in a maze of intrigue. Leaning at first on his pro-Russian sponsors, he soon met with enemies in the Sobranje (Parliament), wherein the so-called Nationalists (anti-Russians) were in a majority. But the Prince was soon disgusted at the way the Czar's generals lorded it at Sofia and treated him as simply their tool. Alexander was a German and he did not mix well with the Russians. In 1883 he suddenly sent the two chief Russian ministers out of the country. From that moment, it was evident that Bulgaria was *not* to become a Muscovite satrapy, and speedily there was a great revolution in European opinion. Czar Alexander II was now dead. Czar Alexander III branded Prince Alexander as an "ingrate" and quasi-traitor to Russia (to whom he owed his crown) and began at once to undermine his authority.

Meantime, that purely artificial segment of Bulgaria, Eastern Rumelia, which had been set off as an "autonomous province of the Turkish Empire," had used its partial freedom to promote a complete union with Bulgaria proper. In 1885, at Philippopolis, the Eastern Rumelian capital, a band of Christian officers forced themselves into the Pasha's palace and informed him that his rule was at an end. The bewildered Turkish official was hustled into a carriage and paraded around the city with a Bulgarian schoolmistress flourishing a naked saber at his side, and was then shipped off to Constantinople. The Sultan, taken by surprise, did nothing. All eyes were turned toward Prince Alexander at Sofia. The Prince hesitated, but his ministers gave him the choice of advancing to Philippopolis or retiring to Darmstadt. The Prince went straight to Philippopolis and the Sobranje at once approved the union.

Then followed a strange event. In 1878, England had been willing to fight Russia to prevent Bulgaria from being made united and strong, and Russia had complained bitterly. Now in 1885 the situation was reversed. So great was Czar Alexander III's hatred of his cousin, Prince Alexander of Bulgaria, that instructions went to the Russians in Bulgaria: "Remember that the union (of the two Bulgarias) must not take place until after the abdication of Prince Alexander." Therefore it came about that England espoused Bulgaria's cause, considering that a great, strong barrier between Russia and the remnant of Turkey in Europe would be a great hindrance to the Czar. Acting mainly under British pressure, Sultan Abdul-Hamid did not resist the union of Eastern Rumelia with Bulgaria. A notable change seemed to have taken place on the map of the Balkans without a shot being fired.

The Serbian-Bulgarian War (1885): The Abdication of Alexander of Bulgaria (1886)

Meanwhile King Milan of Serbia bethought himself of how he might win inexpensive glory. The Bulgarian troops were mobilized in this year of grace (1885), facing south against the Turks. How easy to attack his neighbor from the North! And so on November 14, 1885, Serbia suddenly declared war on Bulgaria. All the cards seemed in Milan's favor. The Bulgar army was a wholly new creation, untested in battle. The Russian Czar suddenly recalled all the numerous Russian officers who acted as its instructors, and military Europe imagined that Prince Alexander was doomed utterly, for the Serbians were experienced veterans of the wars with Turkey.

Milan quitted Belgrade, acclaimed with cheers as "King of Serbia and Macedonia," but his glory was short-lived. On November 17, the Serbs met the Bulgars. There was a desperate three-day battle. The Bulgar levies, under their young officers, did not break and run away. They fought heroically and, in the end, the Serbs were flung back into their own country with the foe at their heels. Milan's troops were disgracefully routed.[1] Prince Alexander saw the road to Belgrade open before him, when Austria intervened in the name of peace and informed the victors that if they continued their march they must face the troops of Francis Joseph.

[1] The defeat of the Serbians was so complete that it became the subject for a comic opera, *The Chocolate Soldier*, well known in Europe and America.

PEOPLES OF SOUTHEASTERN EUROPE, 1878-85

TURKS
RUMANIANS
BULGARIANS
CROATS AND SERBS
GREEKS
ALBANIANS

RUSSIA

DNIESTER R.
BUG R.
PRUTH R.
BESSARABIA
Kishinev
Jassy
MOLDAVIA
Akkerman

HUNGARY

DRAVE R.
BUKOVINA
TRANSYLVANIA
Temesvar
Kronstadt
Galatz

ADMINISTRATION BY AUSTRIA-HUNGARY SINCE 1878
SAVE R.
IRON GATE
WALLACHIA
RUMANIA
Bucharest
Constantsa
DOBRUJA

BOSNIA
Sarajevo
Belgrade
SERBIA
Vidin
Rustchuk
DANUBE R.
BULGARIA
Shumla
Varna
BLACK SEA

HERZEGOVINA
NOVI-BAZAR
MORAVA R.
Nish
Sofia
EASTERN RUMELIA
Burgas

MONTENEGRO
Cattaro
Uskub (Skoplje)
Philippopolis
MARITSA R.
Adrianopolis
Constantinople
BOSPORUS

ADRIATIC SEA

ITALY

Brindisi
STRAIT OF OTRANTO
TURKEY
Monastir
MACEDONIA
Salonika
San Stefano
Gallipoli
DARDANELLES
Brusa
ASIA MINOR

CORFU
IONIAN ISLANDS
Larissa
LEMNOS
MYTILENE
Smyrna

GREECE
Patras
Athens
CHIOS
SAMOS
SPORADES

AEGEAN SEA
CYCLADES
RHODES

OTTOMAN EMPIRE
INCLUDES ALL SHADED AREAS

CRETE

MEDITERRANEAN SEA

40°N
35°N
20°E
25°E

250 MILES

TRM

The Bulgars were obliged to halt, make an armistice, and presently (1886) make a definite peace with Serbia. The war had lasted only fourteen days. "Bulgaria had gained from Serbia neither territory nor money"; but she *did* gain recognition of her right to Eastern Rumelia and, better still, consciousness of her strength and power of achievement.

One might have imagined that this victory would have assured Alexander of his throne, but in a few months he lost it. It seemed intolerable to the Russian interest that a man who had defied the Czar should be independent and prosper. After the war the Prince failed to reward certain officers as they considered their due. These discontented men were soon worked upon by Russia. A regiment mutinied at Sofia and surrounded the princely palace. The Prince escaped into the garden, but was chased back with bayonets. Having signed his abdication, Alexander was now hustled into a carriage, driven to the Danube, and thrust upon a yacht headed for Russia.

In Sofia's cathedral there was a *Te Deum* sung over "the liberation of Bulgaria from Prince Battenberg." But many officers in the garrison held aloof. Above all, Stambulov, the most influential man in the Sobranje, set his face against the conspiracy. In an amazingly short time, a revulsion of popular feeling swept the mutineers out of power and made it possible for Stambulov to telegraph Alexander to return to his people. The Prince returned in triumph, amid the plaudits of the Bulgars. But he had assured the Czar most humbly that since Russia had given him his crown, he was ready to surrender it. Therefore he persisted in abdicating. His soldiers burst into tears, crying out, "Without your Highness there is no Bulgaria." But Alexander persisted. His word was pledged to the Czar; besides, he felt that the safety of the new Bulgarian state would be compromised if he endeavored to defy his mighty neighbor. Bismarck, too, feared lest the peace of Europe be disturbed and used his influence to enforce the abdication. It was best for the Prince to go quietly, and he departed.

The Collapse of Russian Influence in Bulgaria: Ferdinand Becomes Prince (1886)

Alexander left Bulgaria in 1886, amid the lamentations of his people. But it was a pyrrhic victory for the Czar. Austria and England served notice on him that he would not be allowed to dictate the internal affairs of Bulgaria, and Stambulov, as head of the Bulgarian regents, flatly refused to be bullied by the Russian high commissioner sent "to restore order." At the election to the Sobranje, there were elected 30 pro-Russians, 20 neutral deputies, and 470 friends of Stambulov and supporters of national independence. The Russian yoke had thus been thrown off, and since Alexander III did not dare to intervene by force and fight Austria and England, the last chance of Bulgaria's becoming a mere vassal state of Muscovy vanished.

For the next eight years Stambulov, son of a poor innkeeper, was the uncrowned ruler of the principality. The majority of the nation had rallied around him, and the minority he silenced by the arbitrary imprisonment, or even by the execution of agitators. The pro-Russians intrigued incessantly against him, but he had taken their measure—the Czar would threaten, but he dared not fight—and so Stambulov went on his way.

For six months after the exit of Prince Alexander, the Bulgarian crown was hawked around Europe. But in 1886, a man of hardihood was found— Prince Ferdinand of Saxe-Coburg, a German prince who had the advantage of descent from Louis Philippe, onetime King of the French. He was also a relative of Queen Victoria. Dynastically it was a lucky choice, therefore, from every standpoint save that of Russia, and Bismarck gave this young man of twenty-six very sage advice: "Let yourself be driven gently by the stream . . . your greatest ally is time, force of habit. Avoid everything that might irritate your enemies. Unless you give them provocation they cannot do you much harm, and in the course of time the world will become accustomed to seeing you on the throne of Bulgaria."

The new prince had, of course, to face from the outset the formal protest of Russia at his accession, but this did not overthrow him. For a long time the actual government was conducted by Stambulov, while Ferdinand slowly felt his way. The great minister did notable work for Bulgaria—railroads, schools, industrial awakening, improved methods of agriculture—all these he brought to a hitherto benighted and backward land. But in the end he overplayed his part with "strong-arm" methods. The passions of his enemies rose. One of his associates in power was murdered in Sofia; one of his lesser agents was stabbed while in Constantinople. Relations between Ferdinand and Stambulov became strained. The Prince had been cannily gathering the reins into his own hands, and in 1894 he forced Stambulov to resign, while all the fallen minister's enemies rejoiced.

Prince Ferdinand was at length ruler in his own house. In 1896 he made his pact with Russia. Alexander III was dead, and Nicholas II had partly forgotten the old feud. Ferdinand himself was a Catholic, but his people were Orthodox, even as were the Russians, and now the ruler's infant son Boris was solemnly "converted" to the Greek form of Christianity and at his baptism Nicholas II acted as godfather. Ferdinand was thus formally recognized by Russia and reinstated in the good social graces of the Czar and his court. For the next decade the Western world heard comparatively little of Bulgaria, although stories were told of her steady economic development and of the creation of a formidable army.

Serbia Under Milan and Alexander

While Bulgaria thus seemed to be developing a solid prosperity, her western neighbor was less fortunate. The annals of Serbia are as troublous as those of medieval Scotland. The country was poverty-stricken, without access to the sea, and economically dependent on Austria as the sole market for its one exportable product, hogs.

King Milan was no man to rescue his country. A throne to him was not a trust but a private property. He was quite content to remain the satrap of Vienna. His queen, Natalie, however, was a Russian lady of strong anti-Austrian tendencies. This split the court asunder, and soon there came personal scandals and finally a divorce, which horrified all the prudes of Europe. The defeat by Bulgaria in 1885, of course, undermined Milan's popularity. He granted a liberal constitution in 1888, but could not make the people love him. In 1889, disgusted with the burdens of inglorious royalty, Milan abdicated, spending the remainder of his life very "unconventionally" at Paris.

In his stead ruled his son Alexander, only thirteen when he began his reign, and at first represented by three regents. But the tone of Belgrade public life did not mend. The ex-King and ex-Queen insisted on revisiting their son and aired their differences by means of bloody scuffles between their partisans. Natalie had to be escorted to the station by the police and told to leave Belgrade; Milan took the express for Paris more peaceably. At last, in 1893, Alexander suddenly threw off the restraints of boyhood and invited his three regents to a dinner party where he smilingly arrested them; he then issued a proclamation declaring himself of age and assumed the actual government. In 1894, by another stroke, he defied the "Radicals" by abolishing the liberal constitution of 1888 and restoring the far more autocratic one of 1869; then, for the next six years, he ruled with a high hand.

A woman finally undid this "Czar of the Serbians." The rulers of Belgrade did not have the status among Western princes to allow them to wed German Highnesses or Austrian archduchesses; therefore, in 1900, Alexander proceeded to marry a lady-in-waiting of his mother, a certain Madame Draga Mashin, "the widow of a Bohemian engineer" and herself of "Bohemian tendencies." No heir was born to this union, and rumors spread that the new queen was busy arranging that one of her own brothers should be declared successor to the throne.

By 1903 all Belgrade was on edge, knowing that great factions hated Queen Draga and that "action" was in the air. There were rumors of a plot to poison the royal couple by the aid of a palace cook. There was another plot to shoot the King at the door of the cathedral on Palm Sunday. But the real deed was done the night of June 10, 1903. A malcontent regiment seized the approaches to the palace. Dynamite bombs burst in the doors of the residence and, waving their revolvers, the murderers ranged through the building, hunting for their prey. Alexander, the last of the line of Obrenovic, was shot down, clasping his wife in his arms; Draga was stabbed and the two mangled corpses were then flung out the window. It was a truly "Balkan" deed, duly completed by the murder of the Queen's brothers, who were prime minister and minister of war.

The act may be justly described as "brutal but not unprovoked." Alexander and Draga had been fast becoming irresponsible tyrants, and civil war was in the air. In the morning, Belgrade rejoiced. The city was hung with flags, church bells rang, bands played, young people danced in the streets. All the papers of Europe might rage, every Great Power might threaten its condign displeasure, the British minister might quit the city; but everybody knew that the last of the line of Obrenovic was dead and that, unless the exiled house of Karageorgevic were recalled, Serbia would fall into anarchy. A national assembly, therefore, convened and proclaimed Prince Peter Karageorgevic, an elderly gentleman who had spent most of his life in exile, king. King Peter had to face bitter troubles. He was, at first, the puppet of the regicides and dared not punish them. The Great Powers all eyed him with suspicion. Indeed, the only two of them that at first recognized him were Austria and Russia. Francis Joseph denounced the murder as "a heinous and universally reprobated crime." But since he feared that if he refused recognition, the Russian influence would become all-powerful in Serbia, the Austrian minister did not depart; and little by little King Peter won back the good graces of Europe. He took oath to rule as a liberal "constitutional" monarch and he held to his promise.

Greece after 1878: The Graeco-Turkish War (1897)

While Bulgaria was defying the Czar, and Serbia scandalizing Europe, their neighbor Greece was carried away by grand memories and grandiose ambitions.

Greece had kept quiet during the Russo-Turkish War, on the strength of repeated assurances from the Powers that she could gain most by keeping still and trusting to their generosity. These promises had been very poorly kept. Especially Crete, a large island close to Greece, with the majority of its inhabitants strongly Christian and "Hellenic," had been left to the misrule of the Sultan. Between the Christian majority and the Moslem minority there had been almost chronic civil war, with the Turkish governors and garrisons giving their fellow Mohammedans just enough military aid to make the fighting odds well balanced. The "reform of Crete" had been one of those standing demands by the powers upon the Sultan, like the "reform of Macedonia" and the "reform of Armenia." The Sultan always promised reforms.

Meanwhile, in Athens, ardent patriots utterly despised the Turks and courageously ignored the military unpreparedness of Greece. The King had to choose between popular clamor and losing his throne; he preferred to keep the latter. Early in 1897 he sent a Greek torpedo flotilla and a small body of troops to Crete. The warships of the Great Powers prevented the expulsion of the Turkish garrison, but this only made national feeling burn hotter in Greece. Soon there was skirmishing on the Græco-Turkish frontier, and shortly after, in the same year (1897), Turkey declared war.

Instantly, the Greek bubble burst. The Turks, overwhelmingly victorious, speedily drove the Greeks back to the historic pass at Thermopylæ on the direct route to Athens. There was nothing for it but to ask for an armistice, and the Powers forced the Turks to grant one. The Greeks had to pay heavily for this gallant but ill-advised attempt to rescue their Christian brethren in Crete, both in land ceded to Turkey and in money paid by way of indemnity.

During the few years preceding 1908, the date which heralded a great change, Balkan affairs were comparatively quiet. Serbia, Bulgaria, and Greece, as well as Montenegro and Rumania, had recovered from their various spasms and were not intruding into the newspapers. Germany and Austria had not yet developed their Near Eastern policies. Everybody knew that Turkish misrule was creating a grievous problem in Macedonia, but that was a danger that had been many times postponed. Then, suddenly, there came an unexpected revolution in Constantinople (1908). At first it shook only the Sultan's palace; then the whole Turkish Empire; then the Balkan kingdoms; then the Great Powers of Western Europe— and behold, the face of all things was changed! From 1908 onward, the Near East beheld event crowding on event, and crisis on crisis, until the catastrophe of 1914.

To understand how this disastrous process could originate in Constantinople, one must examine the reign and evil doings of Abdul-Hamid II, "the Red Sultan."

Abdul-Hamid II

In Europe, the Treaty of Berlin left the Sultan the mere shadow of his former dominions, some 65,000 square miles, divided with rough equality between Thrace (or Rumelia proper), Macedonia, and Albania. About 6,000,000 people lived in this long, narrow, ill-compacted "Turkey in Europe." "Turkey in Asia," however, was still a sprawling empire, embracing some 700,000 square miles, without reckoning the suzerainty over the tribes of Arabia and of Tripoli in Africa. The population of Asiatic Turkey was about 17,000,000. Of this, possibly 6,000,000 were actually Turks; the remainder was rather equally divided between non-Ottoman Mohammedans (Arabs and the Kurds of the Cappadocian mountains) and various kinds of Christians—Greeks, Armenians, and Syrians.

The Christians were the leaders of the merchant and artisan classes. The Turks were settled pretty solidly in Asia Minor and were, for the most part, hard-working though unprogressive peasants. The Arabs in Syria and Mesopotamia were on very cold terms with their Ottoman fellow believers. They represented an older type of Moslem civilization and regarded the Turks as oppressive interlopers. As for the Kurds, they were such crude, unruly mountaineers that the Sultans counted themselves lucky if the Kurds were not in constant rebellion.

Over all these miscellaneous folk ruled Abdul-Hamid II, a vicious and cruel despot. The few pashas who dared to hint of reform were imprisoned or chased into exile. Liberty of the press became such a farce that virtually no one would read a Turkish newspaper, because everything of the least interest, even on very harmless subjects, was carefully excised by the censor. Indeed, certain episodes of Abdul-Hamid's government seem lifted from farce comedy. An American mission college imported some elementary chemistry textbooks from England. The consignment was held up in the customs office, and the professor in charge was informed that the volumes were "highly seditious." When he expressed surprise, he was told a dangerous cipher against the sultan had been discovered, and he was shown the familiar formula for water, H_2O. It was gravely explained to him that "H" undoubtedly indicated "Abdul-Hamid," and "2" even more clearly connoted "Second"; while "O" was a palpable covering for "nothing." The cipher therefore obviously read, "Abdul-Hamid II equals nothing"—a deliberate incitement to treason!

Another sage deduction of the Sultan affected the entire city of Constantinople. Long after the use of electric light was common elsewhere, the city of the padishahs was illuminated by gas. The reason for this was that Abdul-Hamid lived in perpetual fear of destruction by dynamite, and the difference between a "dynamo" (needful for electricity) and "dynamite" never became clear in the mind of the Commander of the Faithful. He prohibited *both* to be on the safe side.

And yet Abdul-Hamid, according to his lights, possessed a certain fearful intelligence. He detested every suggestion that the Western civilization was superior to the Oriental; his words, indeed, dropped honey to every distinguished Occidental visitor who was invited for coffee and sherbet to the palace; but any attempt to introduce changes into the "unchanging East" was met with masterly obstruction. The Sultan was frightfully extravagant in his court and harem. The revenues from the Armenian merchants and the toiling *rayahs* of Asia Minor were spent even as in the days of Solyman the Magnificent, on odalisques, Circassian beauties, the infamous boy favorites who were marshaled by the Chief of the Eunuchs. Every kind of public service was neglected. The Ottomans had possessed a fairly formidable fleet in the seventies. The ironclads were now moored along the water front at Constantinople, and were allowed to become land-locked, by the growth of seaweeds and barnacles, while their decks and turrets were covered with truck gardens profitable to their caretakers. Meanwhile, the favored "captains" and "admirals" idled ashore, squandering the upkeep money of the navy. Much of the army was miserably equipped and fed, and still worse paid. The Sultan, nevertheless, knew how to keep himself in power. Devoted adherents were seldom asked what they took from the treasury, and certain picked regiments were kept at Constantinople, their loyalty being assured by prompt and high pay and tender discipline.

Furthermore, interest on bonds held in Europe was paid promptly, a fact which kept criticism at a minimum in Paris and London. The national debt of Turkey was huge and its administration was in the hands of a European commission which collected customs dues at Turkish ports. It was an honest commission and always had a surplus on hand to turn over to Abdul-Hamid, a circumstance which led that potentate to respect its activities.

The Armenian Massacres (1894-96)

In the mountains near the southeastern coasts of the Black Sea and in the eastern part of Asia Minor, with scattered colonies elsewhere, especially in Constantinople, were the Armenians. A fraction of this nation was across the border in Russian Trans-Caucasia, but the great majority (some two million) lay under the power of Abdul-Hamid. These Armenians were an ancient and much tried people. On the sculptured slabs of hoary Nineveh the Assyrian kings had vaunted their triumphs over the men of "Urato"—the dwellers in the Armenian hill-country. Conquerors had come and gone: the Armenians were still there. They were seldom successful as soldiers. Roman, Persian, Arab, and Turk all oppressed them, but they retained tenaciously their native language and customs, and their oft-persecuted Christian faith. Many of them were peasants, but their better classes had come to supply the Turkish Empire with its business men, bankers, and merchants in their upper social strata; moneychangers and hucksters in their lower. The Ottomans often hated them because they were richer, cleverer, and more progressive than their masters. Still, for decades, there had been no grievous friction. Then suddenly, toward the end of the nineteenth century, "Armenia" became a word unwelcomely familiar to Western ears.

Abdul-Hamid had seen Serbia, Bosnia, Bulgaria, and Rumania all slip from Turkish suzerainty or direct lordship. He knew, too, that among the Armenians there was a wide circle of those who were encouraged by the success of their fellow bondsmen in the Balkans and who were ready to start, in turn, an agitation for Armenian freedom. The malcontents could adduce plenty of typically Turkish acts of oppression; the "reforms" were still merely pious wishes; and so about 1890, they organized a political society called "The Bell," and began an agitation in Western Europe for Armenian liberty.

It was not a fortunate time. Apart from the attitude of Germany, Alexander III was very unwilling to encourage a "free Armenia," fearing that the liberated folk would prove as ungrateful to Russia as in Bulgaria, and halt the Muscovite advance southward with another barrier state. Bulgaria was growing into a solid state, and her relations with Russia were not cordial. She would hardly let the Czar's troops cross her territory willingly, and if her neutrality were violated by the Russians, Austria would have much to say. England and Russia (now allied with France) were still on very bad terms. A combination of these powers against Turkey seemed, therefore, the last thing possible. Abdul-Hamid was thus growing more confident as the eighties advanced and the nineteenth century entered its last decade.

Meanwhile William II had become German Emperor, and the new master at Berlin did not hesitate to depart abruptly from old diplomatic paths. On November 1, 1889, the German imperial yacht, the *Hohenzollern*, steamed through the Dardanelles between the saluting forts. On board were William II and his empress. It was their first visit of ceremony to any great European sovereign, and it is worthy of notice that they selected for this high honor the Calif of Islam. They received an ovation at Constantinople, which was tricked out with all the pageantry and obsequiousness of the East.

Abdul-Hamid probably did not inquire the price his redoubtable new friend would ultimately ask for protection. Possibly his Oriental cunning made him believe that, if ever Berlin in turn became too domineering, he could seek defenders again from St. Petersburg or London. The important thing was that, for the moment, this informal but very real friendship with Germany made him able to defy both those capitals.

Therefore, he struck boldly at the Armenians in 1894 and let loose the fanatical Kurds of the Caucasus uplands upon them. When these brigands did not suffice, they were helped out by Turkish regulars.

The massacre began in August, 1894, in the province of Bitlis. Nine hundred Armenians there were slain in cold blood with every possible barbarity. The ambassadors of the Great Powers were horrified. Great Britain demanded a commission of inquiry. The Sultan blandly answered by ordering a commission "to inquire into the criminal conduct of the *Armenian* brigands." The Sultan refused even to admit that there had been a massacre; from his point of view there had been an Armenian revolution and it had been suppressed. There was truth in this counter-claim. Many Armenians, indeed, had long agitated for self-government, not altogether peacefully. And now the more determined among them did not hesitate to provoke bloodthirsty uprisings on their own account, with the hope that they would attract the attention of Europe to the sufferings of Armenia. The crowning exploit of this counterattack came in 1896, when in the very city of Constantinople itself, Armenian bands suc-ceeded in seizing the state bank. This particular uprising, however, was abortive, and the angry Sultan quickly got the upper hand, as six thou-sand Armenians were hunted down and clubbed to death under the noses of their Excellencies, the protesting ambassadors.

By this date, fifty thousand Armenians according to an English, seventy-five thousand by an American estimate, had perished. The consciences of very many Englishmen were stirred. There were great meetings for protest in London and Liverpool. Mr. Gladstone, now a very old man, raised his voice in angered protest, branding Abdul-Hamid as *"the Great Assassin,"* while others as pithily styled the monarch *"Abdul the Damned."* In France, too, there was fury and indignation. *"The Red Sultan,"* the Parisian journals called him. But France was still hesitant to play a bold hand for herself in foreign affairs; Russian ministers were cynically de-claring that "they did not want another Bulgaria in Asia Minor." Austria showed no interest and the diplomatic influence of Berlin was thrown in favor of ignoring the tragedies and doing nothing. Lord Salisbury, British prime minister, did urge joint action by the Powers, but when they re-fused that suggestion, no further action was taken.

Abdul-Hamid cared little for the scoldings in the Paris and London press. He had discovered his friend; he had taken the measure of his enemies; he had "quieted" the remnant of the Armenians. In 1897 came the brief war with Greece, and the Turkish army, whipped into shape by von der Goltz and other German officers, was able to give its master all the joys of a conqueror. Then came the second visit of the German Kaiser. Bismarck was out of power and dying, and the Kaiser was fain to show his whole hand. The "Red Sultan" was delighted at the cordiality of his guest. "The imperial visitor kissed him and called him brother." Proposals for the Bagdad Railroad were negotiated; and privileges were secured which opened the Turkish Empire to German concession-hunters.

The "Young Turk" Revolt Against Abdul-Hamid (1908)

Abdul-Hamid sat contentedly in the Yildiz-Kiosk and found the world going pleasantly. He had snapped his fingers at England. In 1904-1905 Russia became involved in her unlucky war with Japan; she had no strength left for another Balkan venture. Austria was engrossed with internal affairs and had agreed with Russia to "put the Balkans on ice." France was soon too embroiled with Germany over Morocco to have any plans for reforming the Levant. The desolated Armenian villages were "peaceful." In Macedonia, indeed, Greeks, Bulgars, and Serbs were reciprocally cutting throats, and the ambassadors were reminding the Padishah of the need of drastic innovations. But he no longer feared any ambassador, and the Macedonian problem for decades had been serious but never acute. The Sultan, now aging, still lived, however, in constant terror of assassination, and absurd precautions were taken at the palace to fend off any dangerous visitor. A horde of dancing girls worthy of Solomon comforted his declining days; and countless black eunuchs and ministers of pleasure assured him that he was the terror of the Christians, the hope of the Moslems, and the admiration of the entire world. Then suddenly the ground opened at Abdul-Hamid's feet. First he found his power jeopardized; then he was abruptly flung from the throne.

For a long time there had been a group of Ottomans known as the "Young Turks," a revolutionary society bent on getting rid of the Sultan and westernizing Turkey. They realized that no petty bombing or flash-in-the-pan demonstrations would overthrow the tyrant. The misrule of the Sultan was disgusting wider and wider circles of Ottomans, but he still kept around him some regiments of favored and loyal troops who guaranteed against any ordinary outbreak in the capital. At Salonika, however, lay the powerful Third Army Corps—ill-paid, restless, and good material for conspiracy. Upon this force, the Young Turks' "Committee of Union and Progress" worked from 1906 to 1908; next, with few preliminaries, at Salonika in July, 1908, they suddenly proclaimed again the constitution of 1876, then started for Constantinople with the Third and also the Second Army Corps at their backs.

Abdul-Hamid had been caught completely unawares. With astounding promptitude he seemed to throw up the struggle and transform himself into an advanced, constitutional monarch. The censorship of the press was abolished, the constitution put in full force, and a chamber of 280 deputies was ordered convened, to be elected by all the male citizens (whatever their faith) of the entire Ottoman Empire.

For a moment, it seemed as if the age of miracles had returned. In the regions of the recent massacres, Moslem *mullahs* publicly embraced and proclaimed their brotherhood with Christian priests and Jewish rabbis. Delegations of citizens called on American missionaries to request a precise meaning of the thing called "liberty," which they were about to put into effect. The Young Turks were delighted. "Henceforth," cried Enver, one of their leaders, "we are all brothers! There are no longer Bulgars, Greeks, Rumanians, Jews, Moslems; under the blue sky we are all equal; we glory in the name of being Ottomans!"

The victorious party seized at once all government offices. A new parliament was elected with a great show of zeal for liberty and equality; but naturally the Assembly was composed of men without political experience, and despite fine talk, the Christians complained that the districts had been gerrymandered in the Moslem interest. The Young Turk managing committee was the real power behind the throne. It dictated the acts of the ministers and the bills laid before the Parliament. For the moment its decisions seemed law.

But Abdul-Hamid, crafty spider, had only made concessions that he might bide his time. Against the Young Turks were rallying all the noxious elements that had battened on the fallen regime. The "Red Sultan" had still an ample privy purse and he used it. A serious massacre of the Armenians took place at Adana in Cilicia, probably in order to kindle the fanaticism of the Faithful. The eunuchs and pages of the Yildiz-Kiosk next did their master's bidding, spreading disaffection for the new regime through Constantinople. On April 13, 1909, a counter-revolution shook the capital. The Sultan's troops seized the parliament house; the liberal Grand Vizier resigned to save his life; the Minister of Justice was murdered; and Abdul-Hamid issued a pardon for all the acts of his zealous soldiery.

Those of the Young Turks who still survived fled the city for their lives, but they were not long absent. The "Committee of Union and Progress" at Salonika promptly took charge of the situation, and the entire European army, except the "Red Sultan's" corrupted regiments, obeyed its orders to march on the capital.

On April 25, the Salonika army entered Constantinople. Five hours of fierce fighting were required before the troops in some of the barracks could be bombarded into submission. Abdul the Damned had played his game, and the dice had fallen against him. All through the attack and the bombardment, the Padishah is said to have sat on his divan, pale and biting his nails, with bevies of slave-girls cowering and shrieking around him. Now the Young Turks were determined to take no chance of a second counterrevolution. On April 27, the Parliament met again to consider the question of the throne. The *fetvah* (solemn opinion) of the Sheikh-ul-Islam, declaring Abdul-Hamid unworthy to rule, was read. The Parliament unanimously voted him deposed and his younger brother, Mohammed V, was "girt with the sword of Osman" and summoned to reign.

The "Red Sultan" for hours had been in keen animal terror. Now he was greatly relieved when told he might keep his life and depart to Salonika to a comfortable villa, still solaced by a considerable number of his harem ladies. Had he stayed in Constantinople he might have seen some forty of his breeders of the recent mutiny, powerful eunuchs, or extortionate ministers, dangling from nooses as they were hanged in full view of the bridges and streets of the capital.

The new sultan was amiable and harmless. Being the presumptive heir to the throne, he had been kept in gilded imprisonment through the whole of his brother's reign, and he declared that "he had not read a newspaper for twenty years." The Young Turks, however, had found in Mohammed V precisely what they wanted—a figurehead who owed everything to their intervention.

Almost instantly the Young Turks were launched on a sea of trouble. Austria took immediate advantage of the confusion engendered by the revolution to annex Bosnia and Herzegovina, an aggression which the Young Turks were in no condition to resist; and three years later (1911) the Italians pounced on Tripoli (see p. 496), which the Young Turks were unable to defend. The latter longed for a strong, unified Turkey, controlled by Turks; but that ran counter to the nationalistic ambitions of Greeks, Arabs, Serbs, and Bulgars within their midst. It seemed obvious to the Young Turks that they could not modernize their country without a common language; but the Arabs resented steps taken in this direction, since their language was much older than Turkish—was not the Koran written in Arabic? Modern nationalism called for a common jurisprudence throughout the empire; but to have one law throughout all Turkey broke with the accepted practice whereby the Greeks had separate law courts. Universal military service also was a tenet of nationalistic creeds; but this meant that in Macedonia Greeks, Bulgars, and Serbs would have to serve in the Turkish army, a new source of tyranny to the oppressed residents of that Turkish province, and one which they had hitherto escaped. Education, the paying of taxes, good roads, and the administration of justice by regularly appointed officials: these were four concomitants of union and progress. But all four of these desiderata were heartily disliked by the fierce Albanian tribesmen, hitherto always relied on to harass on the flanks any movement for Christian autonomy in Macedonia. Nevertheless, the Young Turks endeavored to introduce into Albania taxation, army conscription, and a unified legal system which they were inflicting simultaneously on Arabs, Kurds, and Armenians. The answer was, in 1913, a violent revolt, which the Constantinople government was unable to quell. Worse still, early in June, the Turkish garrison at Monastir made common cause with the insurgents. All over Macedonia and Albania there were skirmishes, outrages, and sudden deaths.

The "Macedonian problem" had been the greatest single question left over from the miscalled Berlin "settlement." Into this unlucky territory, wedged between Greece, Albania, Serbia, Bulgaria, and Thrace, with the city of Salonika giving it an admirable frontage upon the sea, had been thrust sections of practically *all* the peoples of the Balkan Peninsula.

THE BOILING POINT.

(*Punch*, Oct. 2, 1912.)

"*Macedonia*," wrote an Italian, "*has for two thousand years been the dumping ground of different peoples and forms, indeed, a perfect ethnographic museum.*"

Naturally, the regions nearest Greece had contained many Greeks, those nearest Bulgaria, many Bulgars; but, unfortunately, Serb, Greek, Bulgar, Turkish, and often even Rumanian villages were scattered all over the picturesque hill-country. At Salonika there was, in addition, a huge colony of Jews. Nearer at hand, Greeks, Serbs, and Bulgars alike maintained an unofficial propaganda among the people of their race and faith, endeavoring, nominally by "educational" and "religious" enterprises, to make the land just as thoroughly theirs as possible, against the time when the ablest claimant could seize his own.

These three species of Christians hated one another sometimes more than they did the Infidel oppressor. Raids, feuds of village against village, wholesale banditry, abduction of travelers for ransom, and downright massacres of whole communities made Macedonia a land of brutal romance and bloody anarchy. The European Powers had addressed numerous remonstrances to Constantinople on the subject and received rather more than the usual number of promises of "reform." But to the only solution that would really have profited—namely, the setting-up of Macedonia as an autonomous province under a Christian governor—the Turks, "Old" or "Young," would never consent. Therefore they frittered away their last opportunities. In 1912, with amazing suddenness, they lost Macedonia outright.

It had been an axiom of the diplomats, Eastern and Western, that the Christian Balkan states hated one another far too cordially ever to unite for any common purpose. Serbs hated Bulgars, Greeks hated Bulgars, and Bulgars hated Greeks and Serbs impartially. On this reciprocal hate, the Turks had implicitly counted. But recent events were working a miracle. The Balkan nations were coming to realize their grievous physical limitations, that their boundaries were not to be expanded by brave hopes, fiery oratory, and patriotic pamphlets, and that to win even *part* of the coveted lands of the Turks was a major military undertaking. Then, as we shall show later, a war between Italy and Turkey in 1911 gave them a superb opportunity to make common cause against the Turks, which they did by declaring war against the Ottoman Empire in the autumn of 1912.

The Balkan Wars, 1912-13

The diplomacy of the two Balkan wars of 1912 and 1913 is so closely related to the immediate background of the great World War of 1914-18 that a consideration of it is reserved for the chapter dealing with the diplomatic antecedents of that conflict. This chapter will merely summarize the astonishing military events of these two fateful years in the Balkans.

By prearranged plan, the Montenegrins commenced the war by besieging Scutari, the strong Albanian fortress close to their frontier. The Serbs almost instantly struck southward toward Usküb in Macedonia to get in touch with the Greeks who were fighting their way north from Thessaly toward Salonika. The Bulgars, with the more serious task, flung themselves straight into Thrace, heading for Adrianople and Constantinople. The war thus had four distinct theaters. The Bulgars had about 250,000 men, the Serbs and Greeks from 150,000 to 200,000 each, and Montenegro nearly 50,000. The Turks theoretically should have assembled more than 500,000 men but, as a matter of fact, presumably never sent more than 400,000 into the field. Almost instantly the Bulgars surrounded Adrianople and within five days they struck at the main Turkish hosts near Kirk Kilisseh in Thrace. The raging Christians stormed position after position with bayonets. The victory was complete but the Bulgars did not realize their success soon enough to make proper pursuit. Their next move was to leave an army to invest Adrianople and to head straight to Constantinople. Then began the battle of Lüle-Burgas, with about 175,000 men on either side. The Turks fought better this time. For two days they flung back nearly every attack, fighting like the sons of the terrible Ottomans who had once menaced all Europe. But the French-made artillery of the Bulgars got in its deadly work. The Turkish soldiers were starving and had no strength for counterattack. At last their right wing gave way, and soon the whole army of the Sultan fled like a rabble, artillerymen forsaking cannon to ride off on the horses, infantrymen dropping rifles that they might run the faster. The flight did not cease until the Turks were behind the Chatalja forts, just beyond which lay Constantinople. It was a mighty victory.

The Turkish armies in Macedonia and Albania met with well-nigh equal losses. When the Serbs struck southward to take Usküb in Macedonia, there was a fierce battle at Kumanova, but it ended in the ignominious defeat of the Sultan's army. The Turks fled toward Monastir, the Serbs hot after them. That city surrendered and forty thousand Turks became prisoners. It was another Lüle-Burgas.

The Greeks remembered with shame their defeat of 1897. Since then they had been disciplined by French officers; and now the Turks could hardly recognize their once inefficient foes, who speedily forced their way to Salonika. The courage oozed out of the Ottoman officers holding that city. In November they surrendered to the Greek Crown Prince Constantine—and so ended their rule of a city which they had possessed before they had Constantinople.

Meanwhile, the Greek fleet was busy in the Aegean islands. With most of their warships cowering behind the Dardanelles forts, the Turks could do nothing to relieve Lesbos, which surrendered in November, or Chios, which held out till January. Samos expelled the Turks by a local uprising. The lesser islands were easily taken. The Turkish flag soon floated nowhere in the Aegean, except from the forts on the Asiatic mainland.

Turkey had been utterly beaten. Nowhere in Europe did she keep her hold, except in Constantinople, the Dardanelles forts, and the three isolated and besieged fortresses of Adrianople, Janina, and Scutari, the

last two in far Albania. For a few weeks the Christian peoples of the
Balkans forgot their miserable jealousies. In the spirit of Crusaders they
turned unitedly upon the Infidel enemy that had oppressed them so
long. Christian fanaticism struck Moslem fanaticism as in the days of
Godfrey of Bouillon.

The Sultan's situation was desperate. The treasury was empty, and at
length the more reasonable Ottoman ministers decided to accept the

THE BALKANS
1913

offered terms, grievous as they were. But the Young Turk leaders, especially Enver Bey, were enraged at the idea of throwing up the fight
without one more effort. Their methods were on the standard Levantine
model. Nasim Pasha, commander-in-chief, was assassinated. The weak
Mohammed V was then induced to make up a new cabinet of fire-eaters.
The peace conferences ceased, and the war was begun again.

Enver Bey, however, found it impossible to wage war with brave
speeches. The fighting spirit of the Turkish army was dead. The Bulgars

were still camped at the very outskirts of Constantinople and could not be dislodged. The three isolated fortresses, Janina, Adrianople, and Scutari, were, one by one, either sold out or starved out. On April 22, 1913, the last-named fortress, the longest to resist, surrendered to the Montenegrins, who had devoted practically their entire energies through the war to its investment. Already, chastened by new adversity, the Turkish envoys had resumed their conferences with the Balkan delegates. On May 30, 1913, the Treaty of London was signed, and nothing was left of Turkey in Europe except Constantinople and its immediate background.

But now the Balkan allies fell to quarreling among themselves, for it proved more difficult to divide the spoils of war than to win the victory. Italians and Austrians vetoed the expansion of Serbia to the Adriatic and Bulgars objected to Serbian and Greek annexations in Macedonia. The Bulgars swelled with pride at their victories over the main Turkish armies; they treated their allies with insulting condescension; their officers were swaggeringly confident that they could teach Serbs and Greeks, simultaneously, which was the master race of the Balkans. They had already quarreled with the Greeks over the possession of Salonika, insisting on thrusting in a garrison there to share control of the city although the Greeks had won the place unaided. As early as April, 1913, the "allies" were grievously at loggerheads, and by June the case had gone so far that the Czar issued a solemn call to the respective kings of Bulgaria and Serbia, begging them not to "dim the glory they had earned in common by a fratricidal war," offering himself as a friendly and impartial arbiter, and warning them "that the state which begins war will be held responsible before the cause of Slavdom," and that he reserved "all liberty as to the attitude which Russia will adopt in regard to the results of such a criminal struggle," a threat which the Balkan states did not take seriously.

Then, on a June evening in 1913, the Bulgar general in command ordered an attack along the whole Greek and Serbian line, for he and his lieutenants were confident that by one blow they could break the power of both enemies at once. Never were men more self-deceived. The brief "Second Balkan War" which followed was terrible for its ferocity. All the old race-hatreds of the afflicted peninsula came to the fore. Each side charged the other with gross cruelties to the civil population of Macedonia; and both sides were probably right. In any case, however, the struggle was mercifully brief. On the 29th of June it began; on the 3rd of July came the concluding armistice. Bulgaria had been utterly defeated.

The Serbs and Greeks alike had been infuriated by the suggestion that they had not done their share against the Turks. Their exasperation with their obstreperous "allies" was unspeakable. Each little nation flung itself into the new struggle with explosive energy. Greeks and Bulgars struggled in a hideously bloody battle near the Vardar. Then the Bulgars broke and retreated. The Greeks pursued. The Serbs, in turn, showed themselves anything but comic-opera fighters. Rallying from the first treacherous attack, they fought back steadily and soon had their enemy entirely on the defensive.

Bulgaria stood in a parlous way, had the war been prolonged, but fortunately for humanity's sake, it was not. Like an apparition from the North, Rumania suddenly intervened.

The Latin kingdom had remained steadily neutral during the first war, although urging on Bulgaria a rectification of her very unsatisfactory frontier on the Dobruja, as "compensation" for the great increase in territory which King Ferdinand was getting from Turkey. With ill grace, Bulgaria had agreed to make a very small and (to Rumania) inadequate concession. King Carol's government cannily bided its time. The North Balkan nation waited with masterly inactivity until Bulgaria was hopelessly involved with her old allies. Then, Rumania declared war and sent her army pouring over the Danube.

The "war" was little more than a holiday march for the Rumanians. Their foes were already so completely at grips with the Serbs and Greeks that the Rumanians could advance straight on Sofia. The military odds against King Ferdinand were so overwhelming that his generals soon gave up a hopeless struggle. On July 3d came the armistice which was followed by a peace conference at Bucharest, where the Bulgarian delegates were obliged to take the law humbly from their conquerors.

The cup of Bulgarian sorrows was, even yet, not full. Adrianople had been one of the fairest prizes just wrested from the Turk. But now, almost before the new Christian administration had settled to its task, and while the Bulgars were struggling with their Christian foes, a rehabilitated Ottoman army marched down from Constantinople and, without resistance, occupied the city.

At Bucharest, the peace delegates deliberated until August 10, 1913, when the treaty was signed which, once more, was to indicate the "final" map of the Balkans. The Bulgars had been hopelessly beaten. The Serbs and Greeks accused them of bad faith and were in no tender mood. Only the moderating influence of Rumania saved Bulgaria from a worse fate than befell her. As it was, she had to cede to Rumania a large strip of the Dobruja with the fortress city of Silistria, and she was almost expelled from Macedonia, losing, besides, her claim to many regions that would have been surely assigned her by the arbitration of Russia. All the rest of the original conquests from Turkey, less, of course, Albania, were divided between Greece, Serbia, and Montenegro, except only some districts of Thrace which were contemptuously left to King Ferdinand. So the diplomats went home, the Bulgarians dejectedly, the others joyously; and for a little while the blessing of peace seemed to rest on the blood-soaked Balkan Peninsula.

Chapter 24

IMPERIALISM IN AFRICA TO 1914

WHEN THE nineteenth century dawned, a number of ports on the African littoral flew European flags and Dutch farmers had pushed north a few miles from Capetown. Aside from Egyptian antiquities, scarcely anything was known of the Dark Continent. Almost the same could be said of Asia. Parts of the Indian peninsula had been absorbed into the British Empire, and Siberia, in a vague way, had been claimed by the Muscovite. But that was all; Persia, Afghanistan, Tibet, Siam, China, and Japan were *terra incognita* to Europeans, the subject of speculative interest alone. A hundred years later everything was different. By the commencement of the First World War almost all of Africa had been explored and partitioned among the European Powers, except the rough highlands of Abyssinia. And most of Asia, directly or indirectly, was under European guidance. Independence of a sort remained to China; but white men held her ports, dictated her economic policy. Japan alone of the Asiatic countries had succeeded in freeing herself from the meddling interference of the white nations.

The process by which these two continents were subjected to European control is known as imperialism. It was a continuous process running throughout the entire nineteenth century and beyond, gathering momentum as the years passed, attracting some considerable attention at the time of the second French empire, becoming far more important and significant in the eighties and nineties, and culminating in the decade before the First World War in such acute international ambitions and jealousies as to contribute largely to the onrush of that catastrophe.

The causes were various. Any one tempted to interpret history from the standpoint of economics would instantly point to three outstanding ones: pressure from increased population, need of raw materials, and the necessity of finding new markets. To a certain degree all three were valid. Increase in population was phenomenal, unprecedented, alarming. In European Russia it jumped from 38,000,000 to 111,000,000 between 1800 and 1900; in Germany from 21,000,000 to 56,000,000; in Italy from 18,000,000 to 32,000,000; and in Great Britain from 16,000,000 to 41,000,000. For all of Europe there was an increase in this century alone of 250 per cent—this despite emigration to the Americas and elsewhere. Here was one reason why Europe sought control over other lands. Furthermore, raw materials were in increasing demand as the Industrial Revolution spread. Iron and coal Europe had in abundance, but of the big four—cotton, rubber, oil, and copper—the first two were missing entirely and oil and copper were in scant supply. And finally there was the problem of marketing the finished goods. England produced more cotton cloth than she could sell in Europe, as did the Germans with their hardware and cutlery, and the French with their kid gloves, porcelain-tile roofing, and fine wines. If the blacks of Africa and the yellow folk of Asia could only be persuaded to wear English cloth, to shave with German razors, and to drink French wine, so much the better for those countries with surpluses of those and other commodities to sell.

But there were other causes of imperialism, among them nationalistic ambition, scientific curiosity, love of adventure, and missionary zeal. To interpret French imperialism, for instance, simply in terms of economics is fanciful. Modern French imperialism was under way early in the century, long before the Industrial Revolution created a demand for new markets; and furthermore, such goods as France did produce for international trade were articles of luxury for which neither then nor now was there any large demand in Africa, the principal area of French expansion. The Russians also did not penetrate the trans-Caucasian region north of Persia and Afghanistan primarily for economic reasons. There was no booty to be gained there commensurate with the expense; the land, aside from the oases, was desiccated and unfertile; and at the time when Russia absorbed these particular Asiatic uplands there was neither middle class nor Industrial Revolution worthy of the name in the country of the Czar. France and Russia were drawn into imperialistic enterprises, more than for any other reason, by the simple desire to dominate and to master more and more territory. Frenchmen and Russians found reflected glory for themselves in contemplating their own national glory. The English also felt this urge and so later did the Germans. The ego of many a little English boy expanded as he contemplated the red splotches in his geography, and as we near the era of the First World War there is equal evidence of Teutonic satisfaction in the conquest of a newly-won empire overseas. The economic motive is by no means to be dismissed, but alongside of it there evidently was another one, not so easy to define but none the less real. Perhaps we might call it, in psychological parlance, the power complex—sheer love of power.

Scientific curiosity also played a part in opening up new lands. What did the interior of China look like? Where were the sources of the Nile, Congo, Niger, and Zambesi? How explain the curious customs of the Japanese? What new varieties of vegetable and animal life remained to be noted by botanist and naturalist? The second half of the nineteenth century was, as we have seen, captivated by the new vistas which science disclosed. Explorers in Africa went out to see and to describe strange sights quite as much as to make treaties with simple natives whereby the latter surrendered freedom and independence for gaudy trinkets and gunpowder. Likewise, just plain love of excitement and adventure accounts in part for excursions into the heart of Africa and Asia. Particularly true was this among the English. Big-game hunters without political and economic axes to grind betook themselves into the African bush. The younger sons of the ruling class with time idle on their hands thought it more exciting to serve their country as district officers in India than to serve humanity in the counting-houses of the City of London. The Franco-Prussian War of 1870-71 ended military adventure in Western Europe for decades, and many young men found life rather tame at home. Then, too, there were the newspapers. They wanted news which, by definition, means the unusual. James Gordon Bennett of the New York *Herald* intuitively realized this when he sent his reporter Stanley in search of the lost Livingston. Here was news, both exciting and scientific, and the contemporary popularity of such books as Stanley's *In Darkest Africa* and *Through the Dark Continent* is proof of the general interest in both the scientific and what might be called the "sporting" aspects of tropical exploration which was to end, as we shall see, in the seizure of the basin of the Congo by Europeans.

And finally there was religious zeal. It permeated both Catholic and Protestant Churches. Not since the days of Francis Xavier and Marquette had the Church of Rome shown such enthusiasm for missionary work in distant lands. It was carried on by the old established orders—Franciscan, Dominican, and Jesuit, and by new orders, such as that of the "White Fathers"; and by the end of the century a million converts in China and more than twice as many in Africa gave evidence of its success. The Protestant churches before the end of the eighteenth century spent little time or energy in missionary work. Suddenly their interest, too, was aroused. German, Danish, Swedish, British, and American missionaries vied with their Roman Catholic brethren in India, Africa, and Asia in bringing the message of salvation to those who "bowed down to wood and stone." The sum total of Protestant converts was less in China than that of the Catholics, but in Japan it exceeded it, and in Africa it was about the same.

The influence of the missionaries was not simply to be measured in terms of registered converts: the missionaries did more than translate the gospel into the vernacular and preach it; they founded schools where sanitation and agriculture as well as the three R's were taught; they set up hospitals; they were the transmitters of European ways of living, and to some extent European ways of thinking. The results were not always salutary. The Chinese resented being told that chastity was a higher virtue than obedience to parents, and African bushmen found Pauline theology difficult to grasp. Yet on the whole the missionaries did good work in innumerable ways: in ending illiteracy, in elevating the status of women, in persuading the Chinese not to bind the feet of little girls, in helping to raise the status of Hindu widows, in showing Egyptian peasants how to avoid ophthalmia, in proving to African tribesmen that twin babies were not sired by the devil. The missionaries, it is true, sometimes played a double role and aided their respective governments in ways not altogether sanctioned by the Christian religion. But it was not always their fault if the authorities back home protected them by armed intervention and demanded reparation for their death at the hand of infuriated mobs. Any one inclined to cavil at their work would do well to read the life story of Mary Slessor of Calabar, a thrilling account of good work well done by a Scottish woman, or *The Edge of the Primeval Forest*, the story of how that celebrated German musician and theologian, Albert Schweitzer, gave up the amenities of cultural society to aid his fellow men.

The French in Algeria (1830-71)

The honor of commencing the partition of Africa in the nineteenth century falls to France. In the very year in which Charles X forfeited his throne, the soldiers of his army began the conquest of Algeria. They did so for two reasons: pirates and prestige. The northern shores of Africa, shut off by the Sahara from the rest of the continent, had been for centuries the happy rendezvous of Moslem pirates who picked up a tidy living by depredations on French, Italian, and Spanish fishing boats. Since England's way to India was by way of the Cape and the Indian Ocean, that country was not vexed particularly by the pirates. Anarchy in Spain and political subdivision in Italy made it difficult for Italians and Spaniards to punish the pirates. There remained France, a country ruled by a returned Bourbon exile, displeased by the unpopularity of his house and desirous of glory at small expense. Consequently it happened that when the Dey of Algiers struck the French consul with a fly-swatter, the French bombarded and occupied his capital in 1830.

By this act a new colonial empire was inaugurated which by the commencement of the First World War was to be not only second to that of England but actually to exceed it as far as African acreage was concerned.

Throughout the long and humdrum reign of Louis Philippe (1830-48) what had been simply French Algiers became French Algeria. To the east and to the west of that city and deep into the foothills of the hinterland bordering on the Sahara, the French extended their holdings. They did not do so peacefully. Frontier forays with the Arabs were numerous, and among the latter Abd-el-Kader, Emir of Mascara and chief of the

Kabyles, was a thorn in the side of the Gallic advance. The Emir made treaties and broke them; he raided French outposts, occasionally with marked success; he was driven back toward the Sahara only to escape; he was driven all the way to Morocco, only to escape again; and not until the eve of the French revolution of 1848, after fifteen years of intermittent war, did Abd-el-Kader surrender to the Gallic conqueror.

France now had a colony, but colonists were few. Unemployed workmen from Paris could not solve the problem, for the land called for farmers, not mechanics. Soil near the sea was excellent, the climate superb; only irrigation and colonists were missing. The former was supplied at slight expense but the latter were hard to find. Inducements to old soldiers to take up the land of the rebellious Kabyles brought in a few immigrants, and a matrimonial bureau to supply French soldiers in Africa with wives helped somewhat. Not, however, until after the Franco-Prussian War was there any considerable influx of Frenchmen, several thousand men of Alsace and Lorraine emigrating at that time to Algeria that they might continue to live under the Tricolor. The Second Empire made Algeria an integral part of France by dividing it into departments, each represented in Paris by deputies and senators. Napoleon III visited this new foyer of Gallic civilization to give his imperial approval to the work of civilization there carried on, and during the Third Republic Algeria was to prove, as we shall see, the entering wedge for a North African empire extending for thousands of miles south from the white houses of Algiers.

The British and the Boers in South Africa (1833-81)

Meanwhile an event occurred in England which led to imperialism in Africa on a large scale. The emancipation of the Negro throughout the British Empire in 1833 was heartily resented by the Boers, the men of mixed Dutch and Huguenot extraction who were the original white settlers at Capetown. These Boers were a scattered pastoral folk who had long chafed at the British "annexation" of Capetown after the Napoleonic wars. Negro slavery, the Boers considered, had been ordained of God and Britain had no right to end it. True, the British Parliament agreed to pay for the slaves; but payment was made in London, not in South Africa, and legal complications in getting the money were many. The Boers did not have much use for money anyway and they wanted to keep their slaves. Irritated by emancipation, and by other restrictions placed upon their freedom, some ten thousand Boers, approximately half their total number, decided to push into the interior on their own account.

Thus began what was known as the "great trek" or migration of the Boers. Begun in 1834, it continued for several years. Odd detachments or groups of Boers, a few hundred at a time or even less, would take their oxen and start forth in their wagons over the trackless uplands of South Africa, seeking new homes. They crossed the Orange River into what became known as the Orange Free State; they divided there into two streams; one, flowing north, crossed the Vaal River into what is now the Transvaal; another, crossing the Drakenburg Mountains, came to the seacoast of Natal where they speedily got in trouble with the Zulus on the one hand and the British on the other. These Boers defeated the Zulus; but the British annexed Natal and the disgusted Boers returned to the Free State, some staying there, others disappearing beyond the Vaal. The British, unwilling to assume any responsibility for the interior, acknowledged in 1852 the independence of the South African Republic (the Transvaal) and two years later that of the Orange Free State. Two Boer republics in the interior, two British colonies on the seaboard thus confronted one another in South Africa in the middle of the nineteenth century.

As far as the two British colonies were concerned there was comparative quiet for several years. Liberals in London, at this time in control of the government, had no desire to extend the empire. In fact they hoped if anything to diminish it or at least to decentralize it by bestowing self-government wherever possible. In consequence they cut the painter as far as they dared in South Africa by withdrawing troops and by ultimately conferring responsible government in 1872 on the Cape Colony, thereby outfitting that country with its own prime minister and parliament, independent of the British governor in all that concerned domestic affairs, a status which the less important colony of Natal did not reach fully until 1893. The Orange Free State likewise was relatively tranquil and undisturbed throughout these years. But not so the Transvaal! There was friction between the Boers and the British missionaries over the treatment of Negroes within the borders of the republic; there were sanguinary encounters with the wild tribesmen on the frontiers which were scarcely delimited to the north, east, and west; and there was constant internal strife among the independent liberty-loving Boers who did not like the idea of any central government, even one of their own devising. Nevertheless, even these differences might have been surmounted in the course of time had it not been for diamonds and gold.

First the diamonds. They were found in abundance at Kimberley in a rough and desolate no man's land where the southwestern boundaries of the Free State touched those of the Cape Colony. The Boers claimed the land; but the British got it and founded there in 1871 a new Crown Colony, Griqualand West. That, however, did not solve the problem created by the diamonds. Diggers flocked to this wild region from all over the world and all the "parasites of the subcontinent hastened hither to batten upon digger and native alike." The importation of both guns and whisky went on merrily; the blacks complained loudly; the neighboring Boers shoved their farms down deep into what the British said was British territory; and imperial troops kept order or quasi-order at considerable expense to the British treasury.

Whereupon Lord Carnarvon, Disraeli's secretary of state for the colonies, came to the bright conclusion in 1875 that the thing to do was to federate all of South Africa on the Canadian model under the British crown, and to make Boers and Britons alike responsible, both financially and otherwise, for the subcontinent. He met with no difficulty in Natal; that colony agreed speedily to the scheme. The Boers in the Cape Colony, and they had a numerical majority in that self-governing colony, had objections; but they might have been met. The difficulty lay with the two Boer republics.

First Carnarvon attempted to entice Brand, President of the Orange Free State, into confederation by acknowledging that England had been unjust when she annexed Griqualand West to the Cape Colony, and by offering to relinquish it and the diamond mines if Brand would federate. Without committing himself, that wily Boer succeeded in extracting some £90,000 conscience money out of England (compensation for annexing the diamond mines) and then rejected their proposed federation.

There remained the Transvaal. Into that more northern of the two republics many Englishmen had immigrated, lured by the search for gold and diamonds. The Boers of the Transvaal were disunited, their treasury empty. Burgers, their president, had floated a loan in Europe to build a railway to Delagoa Bay, a Portuguese port in East Africa; but the financial negotiations had been poorly conducted and the Boers found themselves in possession of locomotives and cars but with no money wherewith to lay rails upon which they might run. A disastrous native war had disclosed the weakness of the country, and *some* of its inhabitants would gladly have welcomed British annexation. Therefore Carnarvon took a disastrous step: he assumed that *some* meant *many*, and with his approval the Transvaal was "annexed" to England in 1877.

The hoped-for betterment of the Transvaal under the British flag failed to materialize. It requires stern sacrifice suddenly to transform a bankrupt country into a solvent one, and the Boers were not willing to make the sacrifice—not under British auspices. Her Majesty's government loaned the new colony £100,000, but unpaid bills almost instantly consumed it. On the eastern borders the Zulus threatened war. Let the British fight, said the Boers, shrugging their shoulders. The British did so; the prince imperial of France, son of Louis Napoleon Bonaparte, and a British officer, was killed by a Zulu spear and the Zulus were crushed—at the expense of the British treasury. Meanwhile, the British lieutenant-governor at Pretoria proved most untactful, and those Boers most respected by their neighbors refused to take service under him. The British high commissioner for all South Africa asserted fervently that never, never, would the British flag be lowered in the Transvaal; and the more frequently he said it the greater became the Boer wish to cut it down. The British military authorities, contemptuous of the fighting qualities of the Boer farmer, reduced their garrisons just at the time when the Boers were refusing to pay taxes and were reoccupying property sequestrated for the nonpayment of taxes. The temptation was too great for the Boers. They surprised and captured a small British detachment marching unguardedly on its way to Pretoria; they followed up this victory by storming Majuba Hill in 1881, thus routing the main British force in South Africa.

The prime minister of England was Gladstone. A year before, in his famous Midlothian campaign, he had sympathized heartily with the Boers, and now he had no intention of reconquering them. The Transvaal (South African Republic) therefore had "self-government" restored in 1881, although the British insisted in their recognition of it that foreign affairs remain under British control and that general acknowledgment be made of British suzerainty in South Africa.

Thus in this year 1881, the progress of imperialistic expansion, spreading out into a wider and wider circle since the discovery of diamonds, was temporarily checked. Now, as in 1852, there were two British colonies which confronted two Boer republics. But in two respects the situation was different. The white population of South Africa had gone up rapidly, and particularly in the Transvaal, where if immigration continued the number of adult Boer farmers soon would be exceeded by outsiders not citizens of the republic; also, what was not without significance, hastily organized groups of farmers had won a victory over her Majesty's redcoats.

England: Egypt and the Sudan (1868-1914)

In 1869 a French dream that dated back to the first Napoleon came true—a canal was cut through the Isthmus of Suez. Bonaparte had done more than dream; his engineers had actually surveyed the hundred-odd miles across the peninsula and had reported unfavorably on the projected canal. But a nineteenth-century French engineer was to report differently and was to carry forward during the time of the Second Empire the digging of this waterway. At last it had been completed, despite the constant obstruction of the British. The latter had pursued a dog-in-the-manger policy. They had everything to gain and very little to lose from the construction of the canal. Their Peninsular and Oriental steamship line already connected England with Alexandria, and Suez with Bombay; a continuous voyage through the Mediterranean would make that company even more prosperous and would shorten still further their connections with India. The redcoats were in Gibraltar and Malta, and the royal navy had no rival in sight. Nevertheless, the canal was a

French enterprise and French interests already were too powerful in Egypt to please England. That semi-independent and swashbuckling satrap of Turkey in Egypt, Mehemet Ali, had long since died, but his successors, Said (under whom the canal was started) and Ismail (under whom it was completed) were decidedly Francophil. French influence on the banks of the Nile had been paramount throughout the century. French was quite generally spoken by the upper classes; French engineers had built a network of canals in the delta of the Nile north of Cairo, and Napoleon III had been a kind of godfather to the Suez canal which had been financed largely by French funds.

Ismail Khedive was a spendthrift and an ambitious man. He prided himself on civilizing his own country, on building roads, opening schools, and redeeming for civilization the Sudan—a region of unknown extent and combative propensities to the south of Egypt. He had come to power in the days of easy money, for the American Civil War, making cotton expensive at Liverpool, had put money in the pockets of the Egyptian landlords. In consequence, the opening of the canal was a gala occasion graced by the presence of no less a personage than the Empress Eugénie, for whose special convenience a magnificent boulevard was constructed from Cairo straight to the Pyramids.

The days of affluence, however, speedily ended. Cotton went down in price and so did Egyptian land values. Ismail continued to borrow, for he had no difficulty in doing so as long as the interest rate went up. It rose steadily; before long it had reached twelve and a half per cent. Egyptian bonds, to be sure, were not twelve and a half per cent bonds; but they were sold far below par, and after subtracting the banker's commission the Egyptian treasury paid at that rate and sometimes more for what it received.

Within six years after the opening of the canal the end was in sight. Hard-pressed for money, the Khedive sold his canal shares, which had accrued to him mainly by the unpaid labor of his sweating peasants, to the British government, Benjamin Disraeli acting as broker in the deal. But the money the Khedive received was not enough to relieve the pressure. Egypt was bankrupt and the bankers, both French and British, to say nothing of the bondholders, were worried. France and England came to their assistance; they sent a joint commission to investigate; they established a joint or dual control over Egyptian finance (like referees in bankruptcy); and they persuaded Ismail to retire in favor of a most amenable nephew, Tewfik Pasha.

The dual control was highly successful—from the bondholding viewpoint. The debts of Egypt were scaled down and so, too, was the interest rate. Economy took the place of extravagance; taxes were more honestly and regularly collected; books were audited, and investors breathed easy. Not so the Egyptians, vastly annoyed at the presence of foreign officials.

Particularly was this true of Colonel Arabi Bey of the Egyptian army. That agitator (as seen by conservative Europe), that potential George Washington (as radical Europe conceived him to be), demanded the end of the dual control, an Egyptian national assembly, and Egypt for the Egyptians. The Khedive, being a puppet ruler, acted like one. Antiforeign riots broke out in Cairo and Alexandria which he was unable to suppress. Off the latter city were anchored the ironclads of France and England. Those which flew the Tricolor slipped away, leaving the British seadogs to cope with such difficulties as might arise. Arabi continued to build breastworks which the British admiral first forbade and then demolished with his naval guns. The Egyptian soldier thereupon retaliated by opening the jails, and the streets of Alexandria filled with criminals who in their rioting killed a number of Europeans. Instantly England took action; Alexandria was occupied; the Suez canal seized; and the redcoats, in a rapid surprise march on Cairo, defeated Arabi, made him prisoner, and took possession of Cairo.

All this was done in 1882 during the second ministry of Gladstone, Liberal prime minister. The action was too militant for old John Bright, but most of his party supported Gladstone. The Liberals were persuaded that Arabi was a dangerous radical, not a patriot hero; they were certain that military promptness alone had preserved not only the property but also the lives of many Europeans in Egypt, and possibly they were correct. Nevertheless, in the background of this British occupation was the Egyptian national debt, over £90,000,000, loaned at exorbitant rates of interest by bankers who demanded, and who obtained, governmental protection for risky investments.

The English were no sooner encamped in Egypt than they promised to get out—as soon as stable government could be assured. But of this there was none in sight and so Britain lingered on. It was now the turn of the French to be jealous of imperialistic practices which they had had an opportunity to share on equal terms. Therefore the French advised the Sultan of Turkey, de jure overlord of Egypt, not to compromise with England, while they themselves, rejoicing at the financial tangle in which the British found themselves, did all they could to make it more tangled yet.

Slowly, very slowly, the British began to bring order out of chaos, interrupted by a nasty outbreak of bubonic plague in Cairo, and held back even more by untoward events in the Sudan.

Egypt proper did not extend beyond the second cataract of the Nile at Wady Halfa—beyond was the Sudan. On the south it was roughly bounded by the great equatorial lakes out of which flowed the Nile; it stretched east and west from Abyssinia (if anybody knew just where the Abyssinian boundaries were) all the way into the Sahara (how far none could say). In the Sudan were wild Moslem tribesmen, partly Negro, partly Arab. They were slave dealers, miscellaneous nomads giving a restless and intermittent allegiance to their tribal chiefs. Scattered here and there in the Sudan were Egyptian garrisons, ill-paid, ill-disciplined, mutinous. They were in grave danger from a certain Mahdi ("the well-guided") claiming kinship with Allah, who promised to drive the cursed Egyptians into the sea. Was England responsible for their protection?

To evacuate the Sudan and its Egyptian garrisons, England sent General Charles George Gordon up the Nile to Khartoum with plenty of money and a dozen or so assistants, but with no redcoats. Gordon was a mystic, famous for his psychic influence on those "lesser breeds without the law" celebrated in song and story by Rudyard Kipling. The wisest of men would have failed at this task, but Gordon was not among the wisest. A sense of chivalry kept him at his post at Khartoum until he was surrounded by the Mahdi's tribesmen; a Micawber-like confidence that something would turn up restrained the idealistic government of Gladstone from sending an expedition to save him until it was too late. In the autumn of 1884 one started up the Nile and dashed madly overland beyond the third rapid to arrive in January, 1885, a few days too late. Over Khartum, at the junction of the White and Blue Niles, flew the green flag of the Mahdi. Whereupon the British speedily withdrew to the natural defenses of the second cataract, there to stay many years.

In Egypt, meanwhile, they did make progress under a quiet but most determined gentleman. That proconsul of Britain, Sir Evelyn Baring, of the great banking firm of that name, in title was simply her Majesty's consul. In fact he was Egypt's ruler. The façade of a free and independent Egypt continued; the Khedive still ruled, approved officials, made laws. But the officials were those suggested by Baring and so also the laws, since it was only necessary to point out of the palace windows to British detachments marching through the streets of Cairo to persuade the Khedive that he should accept Baring's advice. Little by little Egypt became solvent. Taxes were lowered, not raised; and now they were intelligent taxes and the money was honestly spent. Irrigation works were completed, new ones started. Under Baring, soon raised to the peerage as Earl Cromer, a well-paid, well-manned Egyptian civil service functioned smoothly and many salutary reforms were introduced, raising the economic level of the Fellahin. Education and self-government were left to the future. With almost an entire nation drawing its drinking water from one river and emptying its sewage into the same, with desperate poverty confronting 95 per cent of the people, it seemed foolish to Cromer to spend money on schools for those whose whole lives for at least a generation or two must of necessity be spent with bucket and hoe.

Meanwhile, in the Sudan the Mahdi's piles of human skulls grew larger and larger. To those of his British victims he added that of the King of Abyssinia, and of many native rebels against his authority. Peace, however, did not come to the distracted Sudan; the population diminished rapidly; and even after the original Mahdi died and another took his place, anarchy continued. To whom did the Sudan belong—to Egypt which had at one time conquered it; to Turkey, nominal overlord of Egypt; to England, actually in control of Egypt; or possibly to the Sudanese? It seemed to be a no man's land, and no country sought it until the French gave evidence of a desire to extend their African empire east and west athwart Africa. The French had a tiny colony on the Red Sea (Obok); they also were located north of the Congo. Why not then two expeditions, one from Obok to the west, the other from their holdings north of the Congo eastward until the two expeditions met, and then France could claim the Sudan by right of occupation?

This brilliant idea helped bring about a diplomatic revolution (see p. 495), and it stirred the British to the reconquest of the Sudan in the name of both England and Egypt. This time the British advanced slowly on their objective. A joint Anglo-Egyptian army commanded by General Kitchener worked its way up the Nile in 1897 and the next year smashed the army of the latest Mahdi in the Battle of Omdurman. Up the Nile then sailed Kitchener to confront the French at Fashoda with superior numbers. Thus the French were thwarted. Over the Anglo-Egyptian Sudan flew the flags of both England and Egypt, and a "condominium" or joint government was set up. Condominium was a pretty word; in theory it implied share and share alike; in practice it meant that the British governor-general of the Sudan, although appointed by the Khedive and supposedly subject to his orders, did what Cromer wanted him to do.

For in Cairo Lord Cromer continued to act as the Khedive's adviser and that monarch always took the advice proffered. Cromer remained the real ruler of Egypt until his resignation in 1907. He made that country relatively prosperous through good government. But Egypt was not content. Back in the nineteenth century a nationalistic agitation had developed which continued to grow fast. The old cry of "Egypt for the Egyptians" reëchoed again, with its demand that the British withdraw from the land of the Pharaohs or at least give Egypt self-government. The British civil servants of Cromer were efficient but not popular. They were foreigners and Christian, and the Moslem inhabitants of Egypt always disliked their presence. Cromer's successors tried unsuccessfully to cope with this agitation down to the opening of the First World War. When it broke, Egypt was already seething with rebellion, and had it not been for the immediate occupation of that land by empire troops (for the most part volunteers from Australia and New Zealand), it would have broken out openly. As it was, England deemed it wise straightway to proclaim a protectorate over Egypt and to postpone any settlement until after the world conflagration came to an end.

The Congo Basin (1878-1908)

In 1877 one of the most famous geographical expeditions in all history came to an end, as the diminutive Anglo-American, Henry M. Stanley, pushed his way from the east coast opposite Zanzibar through the rain forests of central Africa to descend the Congo River. Threading through tropical jungles, circuiting nasty rapids, losing all of his white comrades and most of his Negro porters, he emerged emaciated and half-starved on the Atlantic.

On his journey back to Europe, Stanley was met by two emissaries of King Leopold of Belgium. That monarch, at that time, had a high reputation as scientist and humanitarian. The slave trade long since had been formally abolished, but its continued existence in Central Africa was a known fact; slavers still descended on the helpless Negroes and drove a flourishing business in human flesh in North Africa and in Arabia. Leopold's heart was touched. To get rid of this curse and to add to the sum total of the world's scientific knowledge was his dearest wish. To that end he had founded an International Association for the Exploration and Civilization of Central Africa. In its name the king's agents besought Stanley to return to the Congo.

The explorer was weary; he also was a good "Britisher" and wanted his native country to annex the Congo region. But England was still somewhat skeptical concerning the Welsh orphan from North America who had risen to world-wide fame as a newspaper man, and did not encourage Stanley. And so he yielded to Leopold's enticements, going back to the Congo in 1879, the representative of a committee for the study of the upper Congo.

Very secretly he undertook this third journey into the heart of Africa. After feinting an approach from Zanzibar and the east coast, he slipped suddenly around into the South Atlantic and with five tiny steamers tried to ascend the mighty river which two years before he had had so much difficulty in descending. Leaving his boats at the great rapids of the Congo, he drove on through the rain-drenched forests overland to Stanley Pool, only to find that he had been preceded there by De Brazza, a Frenchman who had reached the river from the north and west. Stanley started a settlement on the south bank, opposite the Tricolor which flew on the north shore, and named it Leopoldville. He pressed on then for hundreds of miles, striking four hundred treaties with native chieftains and establishing some twenty-two trading posts, all in the name of the International Association of the Congo, the new name for Leopold's committee.

The Association's title now had to be ratified by the world powers. England, confident of her influence over Portugal, wished that country to control the mouth of the Congo, but France and Germany objected.

A different solution was reached. An international congress was held in Berlin in 1884 which assigned to Leopold's Association, now known as the Congo Free State, the administration of the Congo basin, approximately 900,000 square miles in area. Slavery was to be forbidden; the natives were to be educated and civilized; foreigners were to have free access; and free trade for all countries was guaranteed. Nothing was said about firearms and firewater, those two blessings of the new civilization, nor was the economic exploitation of the Congo intimated. It is significant to note, however, that the circular sent out to raise money for this third expedition of Stanley made mention not simply of humanity but also of economic opportunity.

The Congo Free State began its career auspiciously enough, but Leopold had sunk a deal of money in this humanizing project and he wanted it back. He got so much that his own character was undermined, or perhaps just revealed. From a bright young monarch interested in the march of science and in the well-being of his fellow men, Leopold became despicable. By the turn of the century he was reputed one of the most spendthrift rakes in Europe. Palatial homes and many mistresses consumed the wealth so largely created by the poor Congo Negroes, over £20,000,000 of which was estimated as accruing to Leopold alone.

For the Congo was rich in rubber! One had but to tap trees and soon buckets of latex (rubber juice) were filled. The trees were in dense forests in which, thinly scattered, were native villages. The Negroes filled the buckets—that was a tax laid upon them for roads, schools, hospitals, civilization. All unoccupied land was assigned by law to the state, and that meant all the land except the narrow confines of the villages. The state sublet this land to commercial companies who made very profitable use of it.

The Negroes did not work willingly, but they were compelled to pay taxes and there was only one way in which this could be done. That they were maltreated by the civilizing white is a fact, but the extent to which this was done remains in dispute to this day. The Belgian parliament, it must be remembered, had no control over the Congo, only the Belgian king. There was no civil service comparable to that which Cromer had set up in Egypt, and the officials of the Congo Free State were a miscellaneous group of irresponsible and underpaid adventurers, left largely to their own devices. American and British missionaries testified to their rough and brutal treatment of the Negroes whom they drove farther and farther into the jungles as the latex became more and more scarce. Unquestionably the Negroes were very lazy (everyone is in the super-heated humidity of the tropics) and much preferred to let their women-folk use the digging stick to produce a little grain, while the men gambled, hunted, and fished. But the methods used to teach habits of work were not civilized. A common one was to separate man from wife until the former brought back from the forest the required number of buckets of latex. Occasionally mutilation was resorted to, the cutting off of ears, or of hands. The police of the Free State were armed; the natives were not.

From all the civilized world a cry of protest arose in the early twentieth century concerning atrocities in the Congo. The British were particularly aroused, for a certain Irishman, Sir Roger Casement, their consul on Lake Tanganyika on the border of the Congo Free State, had been welcoming fugitives for some time from King Leopold's preserves. That Belgian sovereign at last sent a commission to report in 1904, but the evidence brought before it was never published. Reforms were suggested; no more native soldiers to be put in the villages to enforce the rubber tax, reduced now to no more than one month's labor. The Belgian parliament, however, was not satisfied. It bought out the rights of the king, assumed control over the Congo Free State, and renamed it the Belgian Congo. It was about time. The rubber was largely gone and the population had dwindled. How the Belgians gradually brought back a measure of prosperity to this desolated region, substituting copper mining and the cultivation of the palm nut for the missing rubber, and bringing decent treatment to the remaining Negroes (comparatively, that is) is another story.

The Germans in Africa (1884-1914)

The entry of Germany into the race for African territory was long delayed. Bismarck had been opposed to colonial adventures and never could it be said that he really became enthusiastic for territorial gains overseas. Nevertheless, when a merchant of Bremen did secure concessions from native chiefs on the coast of southwest Africa in 1883, Bismarck gave him diplomatic support. The land in question was a coastal strip on the Atlantic running north from the Orange River. It apparently was well-nigh worthless, a barren, hot, and dreary region which Europeans had not thought to occupy until Herr Lüderitz appeared upon the scene. His coming, however, was unwelcome to the British, of whom Bismarck had inquired as to whether they had any claim to the land or not. The British government hesitated; it did not want the Germans near one of its colonies; on the other hand it did not relish paying the slight expense involved in asserting its own responsibility for missionaries and other white men in this miserable terrain. Why should not the Cape Colony take it over? On the other hand, the Cape Colony thought that the expense of so doing should be an imperial charge. Bismarck grew tired of waiting, tired of keeping two sets of books, as he called it, one with the British foreign office and one with the colonial. And so, one year later, 1884, he proclaimed Lüderitz's settlement "under the protection of the Empire."

The settlement speedily developed into German Southwest Africa, the

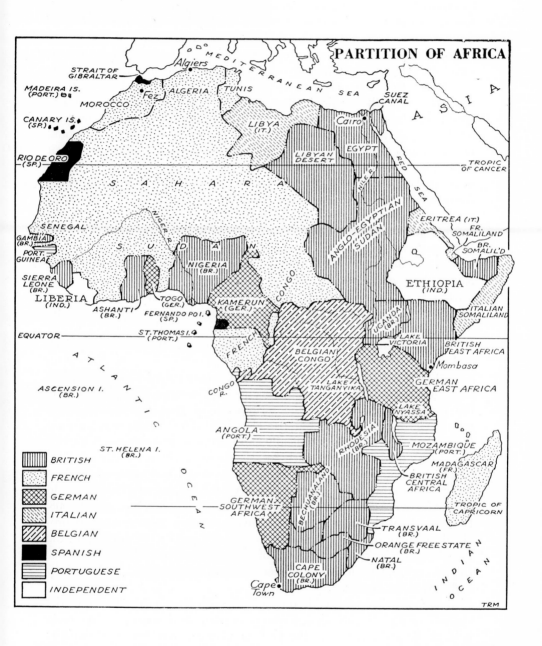

PARTITION OF AFRICA

STRAIT OF GIBRALTAR

MADEIRA IS. (PORT.)

MOROCCO

Fez

ALGERIA

TUNIS

Algiers

MEDITERRANEAN SEA

LIBYA (IT.)

EGYPT

SUEZ CANAL

Cairo

ASIA

CANARY IS. (SP.)

RIO DE ORO (SP.)

SAHARA

LIBYAN DESERT

TROPIC OF CANCER

RED SEA

NILE R.

SENEGAL

NIGER R.

ANGLO-EGYPTIAN SUDAN

ERITREA (IT.)

FR. SOMALILAND

BR. SOMALIL'D

GAMBIA (BR.)

PORT. GUINEA

SIERRA LEONE (BR.)

LIBERIA (IND.)

S U D A N

NIGERIA (BR.)

N.

ASHANTI (BR.)

TOGO (GER.)

FERNANDO PO I. (SP.)

ST. THOMAS I. (PORT.)

KAMERUN (GER.)

CONGO

FRENCH

ETHIOPIA (IND.)

ITALIAN SOMALILAND

EQUATOR

BELGIAN CONGO

UGANDA (BR.)

LAKE VICTORIA

BRITISH EAST AFRICA

Mombasa

ATLANTIC

ASCENSION I. (BR.)

CONGO R.

LAKE TANGANYIKA

GERMAN EAST AFRICA

LAKE NYASSA

ANGOLA (PORT.)

ST. HELENA I. (BR.)

OCEAN

RHODESIA (BR.)

MOZAMBIQUE (PORT.)

BRITISH CENTRAL AFRICA

MADAGASCAR (FR.)

TROPIC OF CAPRICORN

BECHUANALAND (BR.)

GERMAN SOUTHWEST AFRICA

TRANSVAAL (BR.)

ORANGE FREE STATE (BR.)

NATAL (BR.)

INDIAN OCEAN

CAPE COLONY (BR.)

Cape Town

	BRITISH
	FRENCH
	GERMAN
	ITALIAN
	BELGIAN
	SPANISH
	PORTUGUESE
	INDEPENDENT

TRM

445

first colony of the German Empire. Treaties struck with native tribes extended it north to Angola, Portugal's colony on the West African coast, and inland it reached as far as British Bechuanaland and the Kalahari desert, tapping on the northeast, by means of a narrow corridor, the upper Zambesi. German Southwest, as it came to be called, was of generous proportions, with a coast line of 800 miles and a mean depth of 400. But on all the coast there was but one natural harbor, Walfisch Bay, which the British preëmpted, and the Germans were compelled to spend very large sums in creating an artificial harbor for their colony at Swakopmund. For a long time it seemed as though cattle raising would be the only source of emolument, and the government estimate was that there was a possibility of 5,000 farms, this if every decent acre was developed—not very high return for the investment involved. In fact, German Southwest seemed destined to be a costly failure. It attracted very few immigrants, and there were less than 2,500 there in 1902 when a proposal to subsidize emigration met with bitter opposition in the Reichstag. A year later came a native revolt which spread through a good part of the new colony and was not ended until 1907. Several different Negro tribes participated in it, the principal one being the Herero. The revolt was suppressed with unusual cruelty, even for an African one, and a prominent German general incurred general odium throughout the civilized world by offering so much per capita for the death of native chiefs. By the end of the rebellion the German casualties numbered 2,500, and of the Hereros nearly half were dead.

That year, 1907, was a turning point in German colonial history—before then, general failure; after then, very general success. For the first time the Germans fully realized the seriousness of their undertakings, not only in German Southwest but also elsewhere. They began now to study their colonial problems scientifically and to copy in many respects French and British methods, particularly in substituting civilian for military rule. In German Southwest railroads were built, cables laid, wireless stations set up, and immigration financed. Even so, the colony presumably would not have flourished had it not been for the discovery of diamonds in 1908. Promptly then the mining industry saved the day. Heavy taxation provided sufficient funds for administrative needs, and by the opening of the First World War over 1,000 miles of railroad and the presence of 10,000 German settlers, exclusive of soldiers, seemed to indicate that the colony had turned the corner.

Almost simultaneous with the activities of Herr Lüderitz came the exploits of Dr. Nachtigal, a German explorer and scientist. The main field of his endeavors was the Gulf of Guinea, over the northern and northeastern shores of which the French and the British held shadowy claims—that is, more or less conflicting documents signed by native chiefs. Dr. Nachtigal obtained a few such claims for the German Empire for

Togo and Kamerun, two new German colonies. Coming late into the field, the Germans had to be content with what they could get. In both colonies the coastline was very abbreviated in comparison with the interior boundaries, Togo being squeezed in between British Ashanti and French Dahomey, and Kamerun similarly confined between British Nigeria and the French Congo. Both colonies also were located in the very worst part of Africa for the white man, being lowlands in the region of the great rain forest only a few degrees north of the equator.

Nevertheless, the Germans in Togo and Kamerun were more successful than their British and French neighbors from an economic point of view. Primarily this was due to their scientific study of colonial production and of tropical diseases. Germany, as the homeland of scientific forestry, knew how to deal with problems related to mahogany and ebony forests and rubber plantations. And the Germans also were second to none in all that concerned cleanliness and sanitation, so very important in the incessant warfare waged on tsetse fly and mosquito. In one respect, and in one only, were they not able apparently to surpass the British and French; namely, in their control of native tribes. In Togo there was not much trouble; but in Kamerun there were ugly rumors, not without foundation, of brutal oppression. The evidence was suppressed, but it proved sufficiently damaging to lead, with other things, to the resignation of Prince Hohenlohe as German chancellor. These cruelties, however, we must remember, dated back to the period before 1907 and the general overhauling of the German colonial system.

Germany's most spectacular achievement in imperialistic activity was in East Africa where a high elevation gave the Reich her only good location in the Dark Continent. Dr. Peters, a celebrated explorer, secured the necessary concessions and treaties there in 1884, resulting one year later in a charter to the German East Africa Association. The concessions came from the Sultan of Zanzibar, who claimed the ownership of all the mainland opposite his island, and four years later his Majesty granted to the German company still more land. This alarmed the British, who persuaded the Sultan not only to accept a British protectorate over his island but to grant other lands to an English company. In 1890 Germany and Great Britain made a colonial agreement. On the mainland coast, slightly to the north of Zanzibar, a line was drawn northwestward, bisecting Lake Victoria Nyanza. To the north of this line was British property; to the south, German. To the west, the new German colony was to reach inland until it bordered on Lake Tanganyika, beyond which lay the Congo Free State. On the south, the colony's borders marched side by side with those of Portuguese East Africa. There remained for the Germans a region of about the same size as German South West but infinitely superior to it in so far as it had two coastlines (one inland on Tanganyika) and a well-watered elevated plateau in the interior.

As in the case of the other African colonies, East Africa did not receive much popular support until 1907. Before that time the German East African Company had to struggle on as best it might, and at the turn of the century when the British Uganda railroad had been partially completed, the Reichstag threw out a bill appropriating a few thousand dollars for simply a railway survey. After 1907 the situation changed rapidly, the Germans taking particular pride in this, the newest of their African colonies. They constructed a railroad across it all the way to the central African lakes (completed in 1913); they built a very fine harbor on the Indian Ocean at Dar-es-Salaam; and they poured much money into East Africa. Fortunately for the native tribesmen, the development of this colony came somewhat later than that of those on the west coast where the Germans had to learn that brutal treatment of the natives did not pay. In East Africa they treated the Negroes much more leniently, so fairly, in fact, that when the First World War came the German governor of East Africa, Von Lettow-Vorbeck, was able for two years to hold off the Allies because of the loyalty of his black soldiers; and this despite a Belgian army, a British-Indian army, and a British South African army simultaneously invading his bailiwick. As a matter of fact, Von Lettow-Vorbeck never surrendered until after the war was over in Europe. Such resistance could not have been made had not the East African Negro been loyal.

Cecil Rhodes: The Boer War: The Union of South Africa (1890-1914)

The coming of the Germans to West and East Africa threatened interference with a dream which fascinated a number of imperialistic Britons, namely, the earmarking of the grassy uplands in the interior of the Dark Continent for the future use of the British peoples, and the ultimate construction of a great railroad stretching through the entire length of Africa from Capetown to Cairo. These Britons were not disturbed so much by the occupation of lowland coasts by European countries other than their own; what troubled them was the fear that Portugal or France or Germany might extend their African holdings inland from both coasts until their colonies joined hands in Central Africa, thus shutting off potential British expansion north and south through the interior.

Particularly concerned about this was Cecil Rhodes, Europe's premier capitalist toward the end of the nineteenth century. Rhodes was a keen man of business whose colossal fortune had been accumulated from diamond and gold mining in South Africa. All of his life he had been a dreamer. He wanted money, but not for its own sake. The richest man in the world, he frequently never had a penny in his pocket; he wore the roughest of clothes and cared nothing for display. His heart was set upon one thing and one alone, the expansion of the British Empire.

In order to achieve this end, he entered politics in Cape Colony and rose to be prime minister of it. He was trusted alike by Boer and Briton but distrusted somewhat by the bureaucrats of the Colonial Office who disliked his rough-and-ready ways and regarded him as too independent; for Rhodes had not hesitated vigorously to quarrel with British policy in South Africa, and particularly in Bechuanaland which lay between the Transvaal and the Germans on the South Atlantic.

Bechuanaland, Rhodes considered the *Suez Canal to the interior*. To the north of the Transvaal, he knew, lay fertile and well-watered uplands, stretching far beyond the Zambesi River and reaching all the way to the central lakes. This last frontier he coveted for Britain and there was no way to reach it except through Bechuanaland, for otherwise this modern land of Canaan (afterwards Rhodesia) was surrounded by Portuguese colonies, by German East Africa, by the Transvaal, and by the Congo Free State. When at last Britain turned southern Bechuanaland into a crown colony and declared a protectorate over the northern part, Rhodes breathed easier.

His chosen land once accessible, it now became his second objective to plant a colony there. This he did purely by his own personal initiative. The land he sought was sparsely inhabited by Negro tribes, the Matabeles and the Mashonas, the latter dominated by the former. Lobengula, King of the Matabeles, was a fierce and warlike chieftain who had to be handled with gloves. To him, Rhodes sent his friend and agent, Dr. Jameson, an English doctor of tact and cunning, who got Lobengula, in return for certain cases of champagne and the promise of many rifles and bullets, to plant his elephant-tusk seal on the necessary documents. Promptly then Rhodes hastened to London, spent money lavishly, organized a South African Company to exploit this newest venture overseas, and won his coveted charter. "Philanthropy plus five per cent" was his favorite slogan. Civilize the black brother and make a little money while so doing.

Soon after, in 1890, Rhodes gathered together his "Pioneers," first settlers of Rhodesia. For several hundred miles they trekked north from the railhead through swamp, forest, and desert, circuited around the Matabeles, reached Mashonaland, and founded the town of Salisbury. Here they met with numerous adventures, fought two wars with the Matabeles, quarreled with their Portuguese neighbors over their boundaries and even with Germans pushing south and west from German East Africa. The British were few in number, but behind them were the indomitable will and full coffers of Cecil Rhodes, as well as her Majesty's government which, in accordance with time-honored tradition, supported adventurous Britons in tight places overseas.

A third great objective now appealed to Rhodes' imagination, and hastily he grasped it, since he well knew that his huge, lumbering frame inclosed a feeble heart and that he had slight chance of living to old age. This objective was the federation of all South Africa under the Union Jack, the joining of the two Boer republics with the two British colonies of Natal and the Cape into one self-governing dominion like that of Canada. Federation, Rhodes hoped to bring about peacefully. He was friendly with the Boers and had no desire to superimpose British rule upon them. The white men of South Africa should coöperate together, he believed, irrespective of nationality, and should work for a South African nation, loosely bound to the British Empire, but entirely autonomous in all of its domestic affairs.

Had Rhodes been less impatient, it is possible that this might have happened as he hoped. The discovery of gold in the Transvaal had brought in a tremendous influx of foreigners, "Uitlanders" the Dutch called them. Some of the Boers were friendly with the Uitlanders, others were not; but had the Uitlanders bided their time, suitable adjustments might have been made between them and the citizens of the South African Republic. But in the meanwhile there was friction. The Uitlanders paid heavy taxes and obtained few benefits. They were compelled to live in the Transvaal ten years before they could enjoy the franchise, and this grievance, added to others, led them to call upon Rhodes for help.

They did not call in vain, and Rhodes most unwisely sought to force the issue. From the home government he secured permission for Dr. Jameson with the police of his South African Company to guard a narrow strip in Bechuanaland, on the western border of the Transvaal, through which a railroad ultimately was planned. He then plotted with the gold miners who were centered largely around the city of Johannesburg, not far from where his police were stationed. Rhodes sent the miners rifles and ammunition, and the plan was that they should rise in arms and start a rebellion. When this happened, Jameson and his police would rush the border and dash to Johannesburg to restore order and to prevent anarchy. After that was done Rhodes believed that the Boers could be brought to terms and that the Uitlanders' grievances would be remedied. They might then become citizens of the South African Republic on easier terms than hitherto were possible; and in that case a majority of the adult males would be of British stock. Or possibly, on the other hand, a plan might be set up for annexing the gold fields to the Cape Colony, or to Britain direct.

The plot miscarried. Jameson "upset Rhodes' applecart" in December, 1895, by a premature invasion of the Transvaal before the conspirators at Johannesburg were ready. The Boers rose in arms, but the miners did not; and the former had no trouble in capturing Jameson's tiny force. Rhodes, a British prime minister although a colonial one, had sunk to low plots

mental saddles, in gay trinkets, proved much more effective and more economical than rifles and bullets. The French knew how to give parties, how gracefully to let important chiefs win horse races, how tactfully to send the more important local potentates to Paris where, kissed on either cheek by the President of the Third Republic, they would have a decorative ribbon hung around their necks, and return to their oases, firm friends of France.

Furthermore the French were not concerned about the morals or the habits of Negro and Arab; they did not try to establish toilet conveniences in mosques as did the British; they did not try to discipline or to regiment their colored subjects as did the Germans. Their objective was different. The commercial motive with them was secondary to the political. "France," said General Mangin proudly at the time of the World War, "is not a nation of 40,000,000 people; it is one of 100,000,000." And so it was, if browns and blacks and yellows were included who knew a smattering of French and understood that la patrie was an altar of devotion belonging not simply to white folk alone.

Apart from Algeria (technically a part of France), the French empire in northern and western Africa consisted of Tunis, Senegal, Guinea, the Ivory Coast, Dahomey, Mauritania, Upper Senegal and the Niger, French Equatorial Africa, and Morocco.

The occupation of Tunis came in 1881, very much to the distress of Italy. True, Tunis bordered on Algeria and the Tunisian tribesmen were reported to have made raids in French territory; but the real reason for occupying Tunis, where Italians outnumber the French by more than two to one, was to do it before Italy did. In Tunis a greater and more rapid development took place than anywhere else under the French flag— the reasons, an abundant labor supply, mainly Italian, and the desirability of forestalling criticism by showing what might be done in the way of advancing civilization in Africa. Going from Tunis way around Morocco and to the south of it, one came on a line of desert African shore where lay the French colony of Mauretania. Beyond that and farther south was Senegal, through which flowed the river of that name. Senegal included within its borders Cape Verde, the westernmost point of Africa, and on Cape Verde is the city of Dakar, a port of considerable importance for cables, airplanes, and railroads, since it is the jumping-off place by air for Brazil, and the terminus of a railroad running five hundred miles inland to the city of Timbuktu on the Niger. Beyond Senegal and in between Portuguese Guinea and the British colony of Sierra Leone lay French Guinea, through which runs another railroad, again to tap the Niger River. Continuing eastward and this time in between the Negro republic of Liberia and the British Gold Coast was the French Ivory Coast with access to the interior rather difficult, owing to the Kong Mountains. Still farther east was Dahomey, between German Togo and

British Nigeria, Dahomey having an abbreviated coastline like its neighboring German colony but with a large island off shore in French possession. Still farther to the east in the corner of the Gulf and directly under the equator lay French Congo, since renamed French Equatorial Africa. All of these colonies apart from Tunis suffered from a miserable climate. On the other hand, all of them had one advantage over their German and British neighbors—they connected directly with French territory in the interior, whereas the German and British colonies, no matter how large, were but enclaves in the huge French empire of West Africa.

More important was Morocco, a prize which fell to France as the result of a diplomatic deal with England in 1904 (see p. 495). Morocco was not so very large, that is for Africa, since it was only about twice the area of France proper; but from any economic and political point of view its possession meant much to France. As the twentieth century opened, Morocco, together with Rhodesia, Manchuria, Persia, and Abyssinia was one of the few large areas for future settlement which had a reasonable climate and attractive economic resources. Rhodesia already was preëmpted by the British; Manchuria was a prize to be fought for by Russians and Japanese; and the highlands of Persia and Abyssinia were difficult to reach. But Morocco was different; its latitude was that of Palestine, and the great bulk of it lay north of Cairo; it fronted both on the Atlantic and the Mediterranean, making access easy; its high mountains (the Atlas) crossed it in three paralleled ranges (High Atlas, Middle Atlas, and Anti-Atlas), and in their valleys were innumerable streams providing good irrigation.

Despite these advantages, little was known of Morocco at the commencement of the twentieth century. One reason was the warlike character of its inhabitants, another was England's veto on its penetration and absorption by European powers. The population was highly mixed: pure Arab, Arab and Negro combined (Moors), and Berber. Who the Berbers were and what their origin was puzzled anthropologists; but it was generally recognized that Berbers, like Afghans, were good fighters and had to be handled gently. As for England, that country was ever mindful of Gibraltar and the entrance to the middle sea; it did not suit her purposes to have either France or Germany or Spain ensconced in the land of the peacock's tail. In consequence, ever far-distant Tibet was almost as well known to Europe as this country, so close to Europe's border.

The French were to inherit Morocco in the decade before the First World War. How they compounded their colonial differences with England over all the world in 1904, and how Morocco fell to their share, is described in a succeeding chapter dealing with international diplomacy (see p. 495). Herein we shall deal simply with how France acquired this desirable land, once England's approval was obtained.

In Morocco, society was organized on a rough sort of feudal basis. The Sultan had under him a number of semi-independent vassals whose nominal allegiance to his Majesty sat lightly on their consciences. To keep them in subjection, he maintained two capitals, one at Fez to the north and east, the other at Marakesh (Morocco City) toward the south-central part of his kingdom. The Sultan then from time to time moved back and forth between his capitals, partly for the sake of collecting revenue, partly in order to overawe his unruly subjects. Certain of the latter lived near the frontiers of Algeria and made forays, so the French asserted, into French territory, and in this fact lay a good excuse for sending punitive expeditions under the Tricolor to punish such intruders.

As the twentieth century dawned, the ruler of Morocco was Abdul-Aziz, an ambitious potentate, fond of spending money provided mainly by French bankers. He is said to have ridden the first motorcycle owned in Africa, and his fondness for European luxuries was only bounded by his knowledge of them, a fact which caused no trouble as long as Abdul-Aziz could pay interest on bonds floated in France while at the same time retaining a firm grip on his unruly tribesmen. The Sultan, however, became unpopular at home; bandit chiefs disputed his right to rule; a usurper claimed the throne; and his own brother, Hafid, started a revolt. France thereupon intervened. The process by which she absorbed the country was checked somewhat by German objections, but by 1908 she had succeeded in policing Moroccan seaports, in supplanting Abdul-Aziz by his brother Hafid, and in having her priority in Morocco recognized by a European congress.

Then came 1911 and fresh revolt of the tribesmen against Hafid, who had plunged his country up to the hilt in debt, pledging his customs receipts and even the tobacco monopoly to French bankers. Hafid was besieged in Fez, and in that city were European women and children. If Fez were captured, these innocents might be massacred. It was a *fait accompli*. The French were not supposed to own Morocco; but their troops were there and have stayed ever since. Over the country France now proclaimed a protectorate. The Spaniards were left with a section opposite Spain and certain promises were made by the French in regard to freedom of trade. General Lyautey, one of the ablest colonial administrators of France, who had won his spurs in Madagascar, was made governor-general, empowered to remove Hafid, and entrusted with reorganizing the country as he saw fit. Lyautey was a strong man, and what was more important, tactful. Only two years intervened before the First World War, but in them he not only restored order but won the hearts of the inhabitants to such a degree that he was able to denude the protectorate of its French garrisons for service in Europe without any fresh disturbances breaking out.

British Central Africa

Inferior to the French holdings in Central Africa as far as area was concerned, but equally if not more important in regard to economic exploitation and geographic location, were those over which Britain held sway. Far to the west, on the farthest fringe of the Gulf of Guinea lay Gambia and Sierra Leone, old trading posts which became crown colonies on the seaboard and protectorates in the interior with a minimum amount of supervision over the natives. Here the task was to bring an end to the society of "Human Leopards," which engaged down to very recent decades in cannibalistic orgies. Farther eastward and directly north of the Gulf of Guinea was located the Gold Coast Colony in the interior of which was Ashanti, a native kingdom. The Ashantis were troublesome and warlike; late in the nineteenth century a war with them proved very expensive. Farther east yet lay Nigeria, a very important colony, much larger in area than the other three British west-coast colonies combined, with a population of 20,000,000 blacks and containing the mouth of the Niger River. The pacification of Nigeria was primarily a twentieth-century affair and due largely to the skill and energy of Sir Frederic Lugard who, with relatively small forces, subdued the ferocious Moslem tribesmen of the interior, in part Negro and in part Arab. The interior boundaries of Nigeria were now carried all the way to Lake Chad, where they impinged on those of German Kamerun and French Equatorial Africa. Very optimistically, the British hoped to develop in the uplands of Nigeria a source of cotton supply which would make them forever independent of the United States.

In East Africa there were three colonies or protectorates that belonged to Britain—British Somaliland on the Gulf of Aden, through which the Red Sea connects with the Indian Ocean; British East Africa, directly north of "German East"; and Uganda, to the west of British East Africa (afterwards named Kenya), and between it and the Belgian Congo, with its northern boundary the Anglo-Egyptian Sudan and its southern the German East Africa Colony. Uganda and Somaliland owed their importance primarily to geography, the former essential to any control of the headwaters of the Nile, the latter a convenient buffer between the excitable Arab population of the Sudan and that of the Arabian peninsula and also a very desirable location for controlling the entrance to the Red Sea.

Of the three colonies, Kenya (British East Africa) was the choicest. Although directly under the equator, the upland plateaus here were so elevated and so extensive that they became settled by British coffee planters who soon began vociferously to demand responsible government. Their reason for so doing was not an altruistic one; they objected to such modicum of protection as the home government afforded the Negro. Since the latter did not care to work their plantations for them, and since without Negro labor it was impossible to cultivate coffee successfully, the planters insisted on a hut tax which would virtually compel work on their plantations, if the Negroes were to raise sufficient money to pay the tax. Ostensibly, and to some extent in reality, this tax was levied to pay for schools, roads, law courts, and the other paraphernalia of civilization. Nevertheless, it also served the economic purpose of providing a cheap labor supply, and because of its incidence it might well be argued that the black population of Kenya was unjustly treated by the British. The situation was further complicated by the alienation of native land reserves for white settlement, and by the presence of many thousands of Indians who had drifted in from British India. In consequence, the colonial office was subjected to a threefold pressure: from white settlers demanding still more native land, from missionaries defending the rights of Negroes, and from protests arising in India as to the treatment meted out to Indian traders and laborers.

The Portuguese and the Italians

There remain for consideration the oldest and the most recent African colonies. First of European countries in Africa was Portugal. Even before the discovery of America the Portuguese had trading posts on the West African coast, and others soon followed on the other side of the continent. The former became in the course of time Portuguese West Africa or Angola; the latter, Portuguese East Africa. These two colonies, impressively large in area, have been a source of scandal for a century and more. The helotry of the natives of the Congo Free State was duplicated in Angola, where thousands of blacks were compelled to labor on two little cocoa islands off the coast, and in the rubber plantations of the interior. The criticism of Portugal became so extensive that in 1907, on the suggestion of England, Portugal's oldest ally, reforms supposedly were inaugurated. Their effectiveness has since been severely questioned. More valuable than Angola was Portuguese East Africa, because through it railroads were constructed which connected the Transvaal and Rhodesia with the sea. Nevertheless, it remained a parasitic colony, dependent mainly upon the prosperity of the interior British possessions. More or less useless to Portugal were these two great tracts of land, except insofar as they provided jobs for officeholders and proved a happy hunting-ground for commercial companies bent on pure exploitation. That Germany would have bought them from Portugal in the era before the First World War goes without saying; but then there was France, and also England, to object.

The Italians came late on the scene. The withdrawal of the British from the Sudan in 1885 gave them their opportunity and they promptly seized it, expropriating as much of the west littoral of the Red Sea as they could, and calling it Eritrea. This new possession could not be extended inland because of Abyssinia. To the north the British blocked the way, desiring as they did to retain a reëntry to the Sudan at Port Sudan, should they ever desire to go back to Khartum. On the south the Italians were also blocked by the tiny French colony of Obok and by British Somaliland; so in order to secure more land, they went all around the northeast coast of Africa and procured a precarious foothold in that part of the Somaliland coast too sterile and too inhospitable for even the British to preëmpt. This became Italian Somaliland. Behind it lay Abyssinia, and behind Eritrea lay Abyssinia, so it was inevitable that the Italians should try to join their two colonies by annexing the land intervening between them. Abyssinia was ruled over by King Menelik, and had the Italians taken a little lesson from British history they would have thought twice before invading his wasp nest, for even the experienced British had found great difficulty in punishing that warlike Abyssinian in 1868. The Italians, however, self-confident, plunged to defeat in 1896 at Adowa and received such a thorough drubbing that their colonial ambitions cooled for a good decade.

At the commencement of the twentieth century, Italy came to an understanding with France that Italy might penetrate Tripoli with France's blessing should she care to do so in the future. There was now not much land left in Africa that could easily be taken without fighting some European power. Tripoli, in between Tunis and Egypt, with a hinterland stretching without delimitation into the interior, belonged to Turkey. But that country was weak; therefore the Italians began the invasion of Tripoli, not at first by guns and armies but by schools and banks and commercial companies. In 1908 a dramatic revolution broke out in Turkey which made that country even weaker, from a military point of view, than it had been for centuries; and so the Italians immediately found good excuses for an ultimatum to Turkey and for the invasion of Tripoli in 1911. It did not take long to conquer Tripoli, and in 1912 Turkey ceded that ancient possession to Italy. The Italians renamed it Cyrenaica (now Libya), a colony stretching far inland to the Saharan dunes, impressive on the map for size but of slight commercial value except for a narrow strip on the Mediterranean.

From 1884 to 1914 the map changes are the most impressive fact in African history. The former date shows only European fringes on the Dark Continent; the latter shows the subdivision of the entire continent among the European countries, except for the diminutive Negro republic of Liberia with a very checkered history and Abyssinia perched up so high on rough uplands that its conquest had to await the airplane. Within thirty short years Africa had become the testing ground of the new imperialism, and with results scarcely to be called satisfactory. To only a slight extent could it be said that Africa had opened up new markets for European goods; the natives did not care to purchase English cotton cloth in quantity and were too poor anyway to become general purchasers of European commodities. The Dark Continent as a home for the surplus population of Europe did not have much to offer; the climate saw to that. As the source of raw materials a higher rating could be given Africa, particularly as concerns gold, palm-nuts, oil, copper. But the sum total of these advantages seems slight when contrasted with the miserable exploitation of native tribes and the mutual jealousies, hates, and fears engendered among European countries. The invidious growth of a selfish, parochial nationalism among European countries in the latter nineteenth and early twentieth century was augmented, not diminished, by this scramble for African land—a fact not without grim significance.

Chapter 25

IMPERIALISM IN ASIA TO 1914

THE STORY OF European imperialism in Africa is relatively simple compared with the same phenomena in Asia. Africa was close at hand, scantily populated, and without resistant power; and climate rather than indigenous races stood in the way of European penetration. Asia, on the contrary, was far distant, densely populated, the home of ancient cultures too deeply rooted to be swept aside by any superficial victories which the West might win. Although European guns might breach Asiatic walls and European vigor open Asiatic markets, it was not possible in China and Japan, or even in India, to do much more than secure a good military foothold. In Asia as in Africa imperialism was rampant; but in the former continent the Europeans walked more warily, and particularly in the Far East, where they contented themselves for the most part with economic concessions, spheres of influence, and a few seaports, making, apart from Russia, no considerable effort to carry their flag inland.

China and the Powers (1842-94)

The opening of China to Western civilization (of a kind) began with the treaty of Nanking, in 1842. Before that date Jesuit missionaries had done something to acquaint the Chinese with European culture, and at Canton there had grown up a lively though restricted trade between the foreigner and the Chinese. But only at this particular Chinese port were foreigners allowed to buy and sell, and even so under strict supervision. For a few months in the year they were permitted to unload their ships and to stock their warehouses with goods; they could bring no women with them; they could carry no arms; they could not wander in the city, and on stated occasions only were they let out from their narrow confines to take walks in specified gardens. All communication with the Chinese had to be carried on through the medium of a guild of merchants, the *co-hung;* and when the buying and selling season was over all foreigners had to depart to the Portuguese port of Macao. After 1843 everything was different; the British now were in happy possession of the island of Hongkong, not far from Canton; five treaty ports now were open to the

European and American traders, and in them they enjoyed privileges which made them independent of the Chinese authorities.

These changes came about as the result of a war between England and China (1839-42), known to history as the "first opium war." In the early nineteenth century the Chinese had many commodities to sell but there were not many which they wanted to buy. Tea comprised over fifty per cent of the Chinese exports, and during the eighteen-twenties about 14,000 tons a year were shipped to England and 6,000 to the United States. Followed after that porcelain, silk, ginger, and rhubarb. The Americans could exchange their furs and cotton for these articles and the Dutch their spices, but the English would have had to pay in specie had it not been for opium. That drug came from British India, was shipped to China in British bottoms; and by 1839 the Chinese were buying, it has been estimated, some 30,000 chests a year, not far short of 200 tons.

Chinese law had forbidden for a long time the importation of opium; but nobody paid any attention to the law. The evils of the drug habit grew apace and suddenly the Emperor ordered the law enforced. Thereupon Viceroy Lin seized upon the opium stored at Canton—over 20,000 chests—and destroyed it. The enraged British refused to sign any agreement in regard to the nonimportation of opium and the Chinese refused to pay for that which they had confiscated. Certain Chinese having been killed in a fray with British and American sailors, the British were ordered to turn the guilty ones over to the Viceroy. The British said it was impossible to do this since the guilty men were unknown; the Chinese said any sailors would do, since in accordance with Chinese jurisprudence there must be life for life. When the British admiral refused to deliver anyone for punishment, the Chinese sent burning junks down the river with the hope of setting fire to the British warships. The latter thereupon opened fire on the Chinese and the war was on.

It was fought in desultory fashion. The Chinese Empire was so huge and so highly decentralized that nine-tenths of China did not know there was any war, and the British naval attacks seemed mere pinpricks. Not until a British force sailed up the Yangtse River, cut the grand canal, and appeared before Nanking did the Chinese agree to peace terms.

The treaty of Nanking which concluded the war, amplified and enlarged by other treaties made about this time by the United States and France as well as by England, established the principle of exterritoriality, in accordance with which the British, American, and French subjects in China were to be tried not in Chinese law courts and by Chinese law but in their own national courts in China presided over by their own consuls. It is evident that the Chinese had lost an integral part of their sovereignty. Originally exterritoriality had been a Moslem device contemptuously hurled at foreigners in the Levant simply because the Moslems did not care to concern themselves with their affairs, and there was much to be said for it as a temporary expedient for getting around the wide divergencies between Eastern and Western ideas of justice. Ultimately, however, exterritoriality tended to make foreign enclaves in Chinese territory and so produce an inevitable clash with Chinese nationalism.

The treaties taken as a whole were known as "the first treaty settlement." They opened to the foreigner five Chinese ports in which these special rights were held. They contained most-favored-nation clauses, which meant that privileges extended to any one foreign country having a treaty with China were extended to all, a fact which tended all the more rapidly to end historic Chinese exclusiveness. They also ceded the island of Hongkong to England.

A second "opium war" (1856-60) still further diminished Chinese prestige and gave foreigners an increased grip on her seaports. This time it was the French and English who combined forces and did the fighting, although the Russians and the Americans, noncombatants, shared equally in the spoils of victory. The French, it seems, were exacerbated by the murder of a French missionary, the British ostensibly by an insult to their flag; but what really led to war more than anything else was the refusal of the Emperor at Peking to have any dealings with Europeans, and the irritation of the latter at the constant quibblings of subordinate Chinese authorities. Canton again was bombarded and also the Taku forts in the Gulf of Pechili. Peace treaties with China were now signed; but their ratification was delayed, and the allied forces marched on China's capital where they burned the Summer Palace to the ground in retaliation for Chinese treachery in imprisoning and maltreating British envoys.

There now followed the "second treaty settlement," eight different treaties with foreign powers (1858-60), which provided for ten treaty ports, the right to send ambassadors to Peking (hitherto denied), the establishment of a Chinese foreign office at Peking to represent the Chinese Empire and to provide adequate machinery for the conduct of international relations, and a supplementary understanding in regard to a low uniform tariff on the importation of foreign goods. The treaties were with England, France, the United States, and Russia, the last-named country in addition receiving a strip of land east of the Amur River fronting on the Pacific.

For some thirty-four years after this settlement China managed to keep her house in comparative order. A nasty, long-drawn-out civil war, the Taiping rebellion, was suppressed, partly through the leadership of Frederick Ward, an American who founded the "ever victorious army," and more largely by General Charles George Gordon who succeeded him in command. The customs were thoroughly reorganized and placed under the control of Sir Robert Hart, an Englishman, whose Chinese Customs

Service became world-famous for its probity and efficiency. China even began to "go modern" in a mild sort of way. The Empress of China was a most determined old woman and a reactionary at heart, but she trusted China's foreign relations to Li Hung Chang who was so adroit as to win the reputation of being the "Bismarck of the East." Li yielded now here, now there. There were armed clashes with the French on the southeast border which resulted in the nibbling away of Chinese sovereignty in that region by the French; there was almost a war with Britain over the murder of a British consul north of the Burmese border; but Li Hung Chang made concessions and thus prevented any further war with European powers. Not, indeed, until 1894 when China and Japan ran into headlong conflict was the ancient Chinese Empire threatened seriously.

The Emergence of Japan

Even less was known about Japan in the early nineteenth century than about China. The Jesuits had carried Christianity to Japan as to China; but in the former country they had received much rougher treatment than in the latter, and the Japanese, thoroughly disgusted with Europeans, had refused to have any dealings with them, except for the Dutch, whom they permitted to land on a tiny island off the coast, shielded from sacred Nippon by a high fence.

The actual ruler of Japan in the early nineteenth century was the *Shogun.* Above him in theory was the Emperor; but that descendant of the sun god lived immured in isolation, and the shogunate, by this time hereditary in the Tokugawa clan, ruled as the government. Japan was still a feudal country of great lords (*daimyos*) under whom were knightly warriors (*samurai*). Trade and commerce were regarded as inferior occupations. The unhappy (or happy) Japanese had never heard of the word "progress." They knew there was a Europe; they knew there was an America; but they had no desire to come in contact with these distant parts of the earth; they were quite content with their own.

The honor of bringing Japan into the perimeter of Western civilization fell to Americans. In 1837 the latter tried to repatriate certain shipwrecked Japanese sailors but met with ill-luck. Their vessel was fired on and the Japanese sailors were refused admittance to their own country. Sixteen years later the Americans were more successful. In 1853 Commodore Perry of the United States navy arrived at Yedo with five steamships. He had a letter, it seemed, from the President of the United States to the Emperor. The Japanese said they could not receive the communication, but curiosity got the better of them and they took it. Perry then sailed for China to return in seven months. Weeks of negotiation followed. Perry had numerous presents which delighted the Japanese—an electric telegraph, a small-scale locomotive with rails and cars to match. The

Japanese rode around on the cars and finally signed a treaty appointing two Japanese ports at which American ships might revictual and make limited purchases.

The doors were now open. On came the Russians, the English, the French, and the Dutch, securing similar treaties, all of which contained the most-favored-nation clause giving to every signatory all privileges accorded to any other. And when a few years later the tactful Townshend Harris of the United States persuaded the Shogun to open five treaty ports to Americans, both for residence and trade, granting extraterritoriality and a limited tariff, all the European countries having treaties with Japan shared equally in these privileges.

The Tokugawa Shogun who made these treaties was unpopular in Japan and many of the great lords conspired against him. They gained the ear of the Emperor, and backed by the tacit consent of his Imperial Majesty they began a reign of terror against the foreigner. The daimyo of the Satsuma clan formed an alliance with the Choshu daimyo for the purpose of ousting both the foreigner and the Tokugawa Shogun. The Satsuma retainers murdered an Englishman; whereupon the British warships bombarded Kagoshima. Ships belonging to the lord of Choshu fired on American and Dutch steamers and a French gunboat; and this act promptly resulted in reprisals from the Americans who sank Japanese ships and from the French who bombarded villages. Finally in 1864 an allied fleet of seventeen ships (British, Dutch, French, and a chartered merchant ship with one gun to represent the American navy) forced the Straits of Shimonoseki, between the Japanese mainland and the large island of Kyushu, putting out of commission batteries erected by the Choshu clan.

The helplessness of the anti-Tokugawa clans before Western armament led to a change of policy; they became more friendly to foreigners and concentrated on getting rid of the hated Tokugawa ascendancy. In this way they were assisted by the Emperor. Daimyo after daimyo joined in the Choshu-Satsuma alliance against the Tokugawas and the latter slowly relinquished their power, a fact which led foreign governments to seek and to obtain imperial ratification for the treaties which they had originally signed simply with the Shogun. Then in 1867 the youthful Mutsuhito became Emperor, and with his advent a memorial was sent to the shogun asking him to act the patriot and to resign the shogunate for the sake of Japanese unity. The Shogun complied; his capital at Yedo was renamed Tokyo; the Emperor moved thither from Kyoto; and a new era was inaugurated in Japan known as the "meiji" or enlightened government.

The meiji was to continue forty-five years. Under it Japan leapt forward almost at a bound from feudalism to modernity. Reversing completely the time-honored Japanese idea of isolation, the Emperor proclaimed that "the uncivilized customs of former years shall be abandoned" and that "intellect and learning shall be sought throughout the world in order to establish the foundations of the empire."

The intellect and learning sought primarily was scientific and administrative. The Japanese became the eager copyists of the Industrial Revolution. Within a few years they had strung telegraph wires and had built railroads. They sent their bright young men to Europe to ferret out the secrets of European material strength, and everything which had to do with scientific and industrial production they began instantly to copy. They established military and naval academies, decreed conscription for a national army (largely under the control of the Choshu clan) and a naval establishment (similarly under the influence of the Satsuma clan). A modern banking system was inaugurated, textile manufactures started, a mercantile fleet subsidized. And finally, after much secret deliberation and care, parliamentary institutions were established in 1889.

The European model for the Japanese parliament was that of Germany. The lower house had no more power than the German Reichstag; but unlike that body a stiff suffrage requirement, gradually lessened as the years passed, acted as an additional check on precipitate democracy, if any was needed. The upper house consisted of the hereditary nobility, plus a few nominees of the Emperor and a very small group chosen by the wealthiest bourgeoisie. Supreme power continued to rest with the Emperor, in theory as well as in fact, for no monarch even in the palmiest days of the divine right of kings in Europe in the seventeenth century approached the exalted status given to the Emperor of Japan, the descendant of a God about whose worship a national religion centered. The Emperor could declare war and make peace and choose his ministers irrespective of any adverse vote in Parliament, and any time he chose he could dismiss that body and call for a new election. Japan now became a centralized state, the great daimyos becoming lords in the new order of Japanese nobility and continuing to hold important administrative posts. On the other hand, the samurai, the lesser nobility, lost caste; their privileges were taken away from them one by one. No longer could they wear the two swords characteristic of their rank; in the modern world they were expected to work and this they did not like. A sporadic revolt of the samurai was repressed in 1877 after which they no longer caused trouble.

The new Japan was soon able to make her influence felt in Far Eastern politics. The Western countries were not particularly gracious in yielding their treaty rights—exterritoriality and limitation on the Japanese tariff— but one by one they gave them up and by the end of the century practically all restrictions on Japanese sovereignty came to an end. If the Japanese were going to adopt Western customs, law codes, and ways of doing business, there was not much to be gained by exterritoriality, and

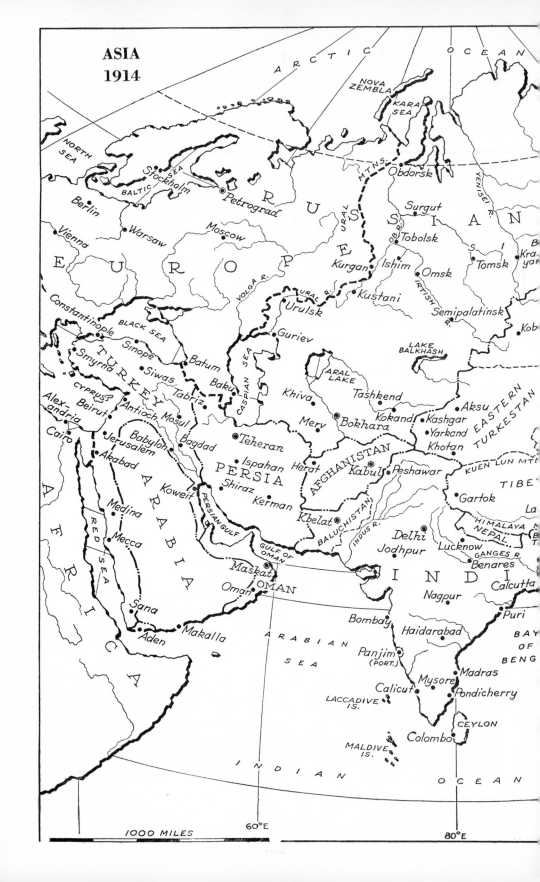

ASIA
1914

since Japan was far from being as wealthy and as valuable a market as China, there was not much to be gained by insisting that the Japanese tariff be kept low. Furthermore, it was coming to be recognized that the Japanese were potential hornets who could swarm angrily, and Europeans decided that it might be best to leave them alone.

Japan and China

It was easier for the new Japan to establish friendly relations with the old Europe than with the old China. For a long while it had been traditional with the Chinese to look down upon the *Wojins,* the black dwarfs, as they contemptuously referred to the men of Nippon. The Chinese were glad that between them and the upstart islanders Korea interposed; that country they considered a kind of self-governing cultural outpost of their own, and they were highly displeased when the Koreans opened treaty ports to Japanese trade, granted exterritoriality to Japan, and admitted a Japanese legation to Seoul.

The Chinese, taking alarm, sent a resident of their own to the Korean capital who inaugurated there a conservative, antiforeign movement directed particularly against the newcomers from Japan. So-called "progressive Koreans" sympathized with Japan and in 1884 kidnapped the King and Queen of Korea. Chinese troops sent to protect their Majesties fired upon Japanese and a war almost began. Neither China nor Japan, however, at this time was prepared to fight, the former country just emerging from the Taiping rebellion, the latter still in the throes of internal reorganization. Compromises were made which lasted ten years. Then, in 1894, when both countries had sent troops to Korea, supposedly to assist the Korean government in preserving order, Japan and China fell to blows.

The Western world expected China to win the war but it speedily was disillusioned. The Chinese warships were of greater tonnage than those of Japan, but the technical skill lay with the Japanese; the Chinese soldiers vastly outnumbered their enemies, but their equipment was miserable and their cartridges frequently contained sand rather than gunpowder. Japanese victory was quick and decisive. Out of Korea the Chinese promptly were driven, across the Yalu River, across southern Manchuria, the Japanese seizing the strategic Liaotung Peninsula, jutting down into the Gulf of Pechili from the north. That peninsula the Chinese ceded to Japan, as well as Formosa and the Pescadores Islands which were strung out in a long line from Formosa northward. China recognized also that Korea was independent, agreed to a large indemnity, and promised to open treaty ports to Japan and to accord her most-favored-nation rights.

These were the terms of the Treaty of Shimonoseki between Japan and China, 1895. But from the Japanese the fruits of victory were immediately snatched. The Russian Bear had ambitions of its own in northeastern China and did not want the Japanese in the Liaotung Peninsula. Since the Russians had a treaty with France which allied the Third Republic (see p. 489) with the government of the Czar, France and Russia together intervened; and they were joined by Germany. The three European powers in a joint note forbade the Japanese from annexing any territory on the mainland of Asia. Japan had to yield; there was nothing else she could do. The Liaotung Peninsula was deeded back to China, but Japan did not forget.

China and the Powers (1894-1904)

China's weakness in the war with Japan was a notice to all and sundry that the Celestial Empire was ripe for plucking. For some thirty years it had been popularly believed that the country was growing in strength and national unity. The cleverness of Li Hung Chang had been responsible for this impression. Under his leadership China had (supposedly) a real army, a real navy, and an efficient government; but now it was evident that reform had been on the surface alone and that China was still the huge, sprawling, disorganized land that she had been in 1840. In consequence the partition of that country in one way or another speeded up. All the great European nations now fell upon China one after another without resistance, until Italy suggested that she, too, deserved a Chinese port, a demand too much for even China to swallow.

First in the competition for Chinese loot was France. No sooner had the Treaty of Shimonoseki been concluded than the French asked and got an enlargement of their territory, the colony of Annam. Then came Russia, a country which had been extending its boundaries from the seventeenth century clear across Siberia to Alaska, sold later to the United States. The Russians were too far to the north for their own comfort, since the Amur River was their boundary, and they had coveted very much the land immediately north of Korea between the Amur and the Pacific. This they had obtained from China in 1860 and had named the Maritime Provinces, with the capital at Vladivostok. Even so they were not content. They claimed the island of Sakhalin, north of Japan, and secured title to it by a treaty with the Mikado in 1875. Continuing to press forward, they made an agreement in 1884 to train the Korean army, in return for which they were to receive a Korean port. Confronted, however, with protests from both Japan and England, Russia withdrew from this project, only to bide her time.

It came with the defeat of China by Japan. Li Hung Chang, in despair at the extent of Japanese demands in 1894, turned to Russia for help and received it—at a price. The Czar was willing to force Japan's withdrawal from the Liaotung Peninsula if China in return would grant permission for the construction of a railway across Manchuria. A few years before Russia had commenced the Trans-Siberian Railway, which was to extend all the way to Vladivostok. Its construction was expensive, and if the line was to be kept within Russian boundaries it must swing far to the north around Manchuria and then head for Vladivostok to the south. But if a railway could be built directly across the Manchurian plain the cost would be less and the economic possibilities greater. China now granted a charter for such a railway; it was to be called the Chinese Eastern and (ostensibly) was to be a joint Sino-Russian enterprise. At the end of thirty-six years China was to have the option of buying the road. If this option was not taken up at the end of eighty years the road was to revert to her free of charge. It looked like a pretty good bargain for China, but there were jokers concealed in the Sino-Russian treaty in regard to the use of land on either side of the line and the military protection which the road must have.

It was now the turn of Germany. That country, being one of the three powers to force Japan back, claimed a Chinese port as her reward. When it was not forthcoming the Germans took advantage of the murder of two German priests by brigands and occupied Kiaochow Bay on the Shantung peninsula. Result: In 1898 the port of Tsingtao on this bay was leased with its hinterland to Germany for ninety-nine years, and to Germany was promised the future economic development of all Shantung mines and railways.

Followed then Russia again and finally England. The former country got a twenty-five year lease of the Liaotung Peninsula with permission to build a railway south to it from the Russian-controlled Chinese Eastern; the latter, alarmed at Russian success (for this meant that Port Arthur at the tip of Liaotung would be a Russian port), secured a lease of Weihaiwei on the southern shores of the Gulf of Pechili, across from Port Arthur, a lease which was to be coterminous with the Russian occupation of the more northern port. This British action in turn stirred the French, who demanded and obtained a ninety-nine-year lease of 200 square miles or more of Chinese land; whereupon the British, not to be outdone, got even more land opposite Hongkong on a lease of equal length.

One result of these nibblings of Chinese territory was greatly to strengthen the hand of Tz'ŭ Hsi, the old dowager Empress, who, emerging from seclusion, took over the reins of government; another was the rapid growth of bands of "Boxers" (Fists of Righteous Harmony). The Boxers were reactionary patriots who hated missionaries and all Western ideas. Densely ignorant, they thought that magic would serve as a defense against bullets; but they were also numerous and received secret help from the Empress. The Boxers took to the warpath, burned bridges,

The Harbor of Hongkong, Developed Mainly by the British

killed missionaries, tore up the railway which ran from Taku on the Gulf of Pechili to Peking. They got control of China's capital, besieged the legations in their compounds, and killed the German ambassador. Whereupon an international army, commanded by a German general but containing soldiers or marines from all the treaty powers, marched on Peking and exacted a humiliating peace in accordance with which large indemnities were to be paid, and armed guards of all the treaty powers were to be stationed permanently in Peking.

This Boxer revolt was not displeasing to Russia; it afforded her a good excuse for moving large bodies of troops into Manchuria on the plea that they were necessary to preserve order. All the countries protested, including China, and Russia promised to withdraw her soldiers, something she had no intention of doing. The Russian lease of the Liaotung was for twenty-five years only; but the Russians fortified Port Arthur very heavily and in addition built at Dalny huge docks to make that place a commercial entrepot, and between 1900 and 1904 Manchuria, a territory of China, became to all intents and purposes a Russian protectorate, with Russia in control of the two great trunk railways which bisected it: the Chinese Eastern running east and west, and the Southern Manchurian running from Harbin on the former railway straight south to Port Arthur and Dalny.

Japan and Russia

The ominous encroachments of the Russian Bear on Chinese land did not go unnoticed in Tokyo. More particularly, the Japanese were angered by Russian gestures toward Korea, a country which the Japanese had marked for their own some day. After the Sino-Japanese war the King and Queen of Korea, that "land of the morning calm," had taken refuge in the Russian legation, there to dismiss pro-Japanese councillors and to substitute Russians in their place; mining and timber concessions were granted to Russia by Korea; and, worst of all, Russians were appointed to drill Korean recruits. Japan was willing that Russia should work her will upon Manchuria provided that Korea fell to Japan; but the Russians seemingly coveted both regions.

Japan stepped cautiously, lest she be caught again by another ultimatum from three foreign countries. Therefore, in 1902 she concluded a treaty with England whereby the signatory powers promised to remain neutral in any Far Eastern war against a single enemy, but to become allies if confronted by more than one. Then Japan tried to come to terms with Russia. Let us, she said in effect, divide Manchuria and Korea into two spheres of influence, Russia to take the first, Japan the second. St. Petersburg, however, hesitated and delayed an answer; and in the meantime men wearing the uniform of Russian reservists were operating the timber concessions along the Yalu River ceded by the Koreans. The Trans-Siberian Railway was not yet completed and Japan thought that was the reason for Russia's tardiness in answering her proposal. If Japan had to fight she might better do so before the completed railway made it possible for the Muscovites to inundate Manchuria with their troops, so thought the Mikado's statesmen.

Therefore in February, 1904, without previous declaration of war, Japan struck hard. The Czar's navy in the Far East was divided, part of it at Vladivostok, part at Port Arthur, and part at Chemulpo, Korea. A surprise torpedo attack rendered *hors de combat* the Chemulpo and Port Arthur ships; while those at Vladivostok were bottled up by a blockading fleet. The sea was clear of Russians. Soon it was black with Japanese transports. The numerical advantage for the time being was Japan's and she needed to make the most of it. Once more the enemy was driven back from the Yalu River on the boundary of Korea, this time a Russian not a Chinese enemy; and a wedge was driven in between the Russian troops in Liaotung and those farther north. Short and snappy victories were won by the Japanese. The Russians retreated along the line of their railway and dug themselves in at Port Arthur; and on both fronts the Japanese attacked with fury. For almost eleven months Port Arthur held out. So strong, indeed, was that fortress and so well stocked with munitions and food that it would not even then have fallen had the Russian general in command been as courageous and determined as his men.

Even so Japan had not won the war. From the Baltic to the Sea of Japan slowly advanced the Russian navy. On paper it looked like a goodly armament; but in the Straits of Tsushima near Korea it proved a paper fleet. The Russians could not shoot; they could not navigate; and Admiral Togo of the Rising Sun was a complete victor.

And yet the Japanese had not won the war. The Russian armies in the north grew larger daily and the Russian purse was long. Graft and drunkenness if not treachery, however, was rife in the Czar's army, and this most distant war was highly unpopular at home. Therefore Russia accepted the invitation of President Theodore Roosevelt to discuss peace terms which were drawn up in the United States and embodied in the treaty of Portsmouth (1905).

That treaty was Japan's revenge for 1894. It gave to Japan all those treaty rights in Manchuria and Liaotung of which Russia had become possessed; it recognized Korea as independent but under predominant Japanese interests; it ceded to Japan the southern half of Sakhalin; but no indemnity was paid by Russia, much to the distress of the victorious Japanese whose economic resources had been strained to the uttermost.

The repercussions of the Russo-Japanese War were profound. For the first time in modern history an Asiatic country had won a clean-cut military victory over a Western power, and the news of this event was quick to percolate not only through the Far East but also in the bazaars of crowded Indian cities, in Afghan defiles, and even on the upland plateaux of Persia. What one Oriental country had done might not another accomplish? Everywhere in Asia the stirrings of nationalistic pride were felt, even in China. As for Japan, the capitalization of her victory was immediate. Into Korea her merchants and entrepreneurs poured rapidly, and it was not long before the country in which she was recognized as having especial interests came thoroughly under the thumb of a Japanese resident-general (1907) and soon afterward was annexed to Japan (1910). Manchuria, meanwhile, more informally but none the less realistically was divided between the former enemies, Russia taking the more northern part and Japan confining herself for the time being to southern Manchuria, the Liaotung Peninsula, and the railway leading to it from its junction with the Chinese Eastern, this north and south railway (rechristened the Southern Manchurian) becoming a great commercial enterprise, owning docks, warehouses, land, and hotels. And holding a majority of the stock was the Japanese government!

In theory Manchuria remained China's; in practice it became Russian and Japanese territory with Japan holding the choicer part. This the European and American bankers speedily discovered in 1909 and again in 1910 when they endeavored to tap the resources of this underdeveloped Chinese province by the introduction of new railway lines. The veto of both Russia and Japan led to the abandonment of all such fancies. Russians and Japanese, so recently at war, now worked together in unison and seemingly were good friends as the World War broke in 1914. Japanese enterprise, courage, and ability by that date had almost if not quite raised Japan to the rank of a first-class power. Her railway mileage had increased some five hundred per cent in fifteen years, and her foreign trade at approximately the same rate. More foreign capital, indeed, was invested in Japan than in China; but there was not foreign ownership. In the island empire the foreigner owned the bonds only and had nothing to say about how business was conducted. The government of the Mikado saw to that.

China (1905-14)

As Japan advanced from glory unto glory, China went through troubled times. She was far from being mistress in her own house. In addition to extraterritorial and other privileges granted to foreigners, the Chinese were bound by the treaty of 1858 with England not to raise their tariff over five per cent. They had practically no control over concessions granted to foreign countries, and their public loans were in the hands of foreign banks which had not advanced the money without seeing to it that interest was guaranteed by stringent provisions which gave them the whip hand over the Chinese. At Canton, Shanghai, Tientsin, Hankow, and other ports European settlements to all practical purpose became independent little enclaves in Chinese territory, even in a place like Hankow, many hundred miles up the Yangtse. Huge sums of money for railways, telegraphs, war indemnities, and other purposes were owing to European syndicates. Interest rates ran from five to seven per cent, and for security not only the Chinese customs but internal taxes as well were pledged. Nor could China borrow money where she pleased and expend it as she saw fit. The valley of the Yangtse, for instance, was recognized as a British sphere of influence, and Belgian, French, or German capital was expected to refrain from building railways or developing mines in that region. Conversely, the British by courtesy held aloof from Manchuria (Russian sphere of influence), from Shantung (German sphere), and from the southeast (French sphere).

These losses in territory and humiliating concessions aroused the ire of patriotic Chinese, particularly south of the Yangtse River. A scapegoat was found in the Manchu dynasty and revolutionary clubs and societies were organized for the purpose of ousting the Manchus and establishing a Chinese republic. Chief among the conspirators was Dr. Sun Yat-sen, a much-traveled physician who had been educated in Hawaii and was as much at home in London and St. Louis as in Canton. The revolutionary movement which he headed was utterly unlike the Boxer movement of 1900; for that had aimed at restoring Chinese independence by ignoring the West. Dr. Sun was a modern of the moderns; he aimed at Chinese independence by copying the West as Japan had done. In 1911 the revolution suddenly broke, spread like wildfire, and in January, 1912, Dr. Sun found himself at Nanking, President of the Chinese Republic.

That republic was not to last long; Sun Yat-sen and his radical innovators had not counted sufficiently upon the inherent conservatism of the Chinese, and they had won the victory too easily. Within four years their republic was to be snuffed out.

When it had been proclaimed the imperial troops in North China under the able Yuan Shi-kai were still undefeated, and it was doubtful if a victory could be won over them. Dr. Sun did not welcome the continuance of civil war, and so he resigned in favor of Yuan Shi-kai who accepted the provisional presidency without any republican convictions whatever. The Chinese masses were not ready for a republic and their leaders had no first-hand experience with constitutional procedure. Consequently, the forces of privilege and reaction soon were able to bowl them over.

When the provisional parliament refused to confirm his nominees for office and rejected a foreign loan which he had negotiated, Yuan Shi-kai took the law into his own hands. Thereupon the southern representatives in parliament started civil war against Yuan. The latter crushed the rebels in a few weeks and proclaimed himself permanent president of China—this even before a constitution had been adopted. Meanwhile the members of the Kuomintang, Dr. Sun's revolutionary society which had started the original revolt, were ousted from the Chinese parliament.

China remained a republic in form, even after this event, but in practice she rapidly succumbed to a dictatorship under Yuan Shi-kai. Finally, in 1915, even the form of a republic was abolished, and Yuan, yielding reluctantly to popular will (so he said) reëstablished the empire, an act which almost instantly led to a recurrence of Chinese civil war.

The Far East Apart from China and Japan

Elsewhere in the Far East enterprising Europeans penetrated with a minimum of resistance. To the south and east of China proper lay Indo-China, comprising at one time a number of quasi-independent states over which China claimed a vague sovereignty. One by one these states—Cochin China, Cambodia, Annam, and Tonking—had fallen under French influence, and here the French between 1867 and 1896, the date of the delimitation of their hinterland by agreement with Great Britain, had carved out a colonial empire. Some 20,000,000 Asiatics, akin to the Chinese in blood, owed allegiance in these four states to the Third Republic.

Again, still farther to the south and somewhat to the west, was the long and narrow Malay Peninsula, over the greater part of which Britain exercised nominal and indirect control. The Federated Malay States of the peninsula retained their native rulers but were under his Majesty's protection, accepting the suggestion and advice of British residents appointed to their courts. Geographically and racially at one with them but juristically different was the British Crown Colony of the Straits Settlements. Located toward the end of the peninsula, it had vast strategic importance since its capital, Singapore, dominated the narrow waters between the island of Sumatra and the mainland of Asia. In the Straits Settlements, in the Federated Malay States, and in French Indo-China there was but little friction between the Western overlord and the Asiatic underdog, the former being relatively intelligent, the latter not as yet racially and patriotically conscious.

The same held true for the Dutch East Indian Empire to the south and east of Singapore. The large islands of Sumatra, Java, Celebes, and most of Borneo comprised the heart of this empire, an extraordinarily large and opulent one for any country to possess, fifty-eight times larger in area than the Netherlands, with a population seven times greater. Here, during the nineteenth century, the course of empire ran with remarkable smoothness. To some extent this was due to the wisdom of the

Dutch, who did not try to milk dry the wealth of their islands, particularly rich in sugar and tobacco, and to some extent (perhaps more) to the absence of any nationalistic fervor on the part of the preponderant Malay population.

Borneo, Sumatra, Java, and the Celebes were somewhat out of the main current of nineteenth-century affairs and the Dutch were well pleased with this fact. They did not welcome outsiders, Europeans, to their colonial preserves, and they discouraged rather than abetted the infiltration of European culture. They established schools, but in them they did not seek to introduce Western ways or ideas but rather to teach the young Malays the indigenous arts and ways of life of the East Indies. Since the latter were in no way influenced by nationalistic aspirations, and since there was no tradition of past Malay unity or grandeur, there did not develop any real agitation against the Netherlands until after the Communist revolution in Russia in 1917.

India

The same peace was not found in India. That subcontinent, numbering its peoples like China in the hundreds of millions, was not brought under British sway easily, nor once conquered did it remain as quiescent as the Dutch East Indies. The military conquest of India was in part accomplished in the second half of the eighteenth century, in part during the first half of the nineteenth; but cultural conquest there was practically none. Spain in this respect had been infinitely more successful in the New World than Britain in India. Mexico and Peru by the time of Waterloo had become thoroughly Spanish in language, literature, art and religion, whereas Bengal and Northwest India remained pretty thoroughly Hindu and Mohammedan. Railroads, taxes, forms of government—in these superficial respects India was Anglicized. But below the surface British influence seemed scarcely felt.

To speak of Indian nationalism, at least before the World War of 1914-18, is almost a misnomer. Some dozen or more nationalities rather than one found their home in India. Those who lived in the Punjab knew nothing of their fellow Indians along the Malabar coast. Neither in language, religion nor in blood was there similarity between the mild Buddhists, the sun-worshipping Parsees, and the bearded Sikhs. The men of Cashmere had no bond of union with either the mountaineers of Nepal or the plainsmen of the Central Provinces. Parsees, Hindus, Moslems, Buddhists worshipped, so they were apt to think, different gods, and a most rigorous caste system from time immemorial had made even those of the Hindu faith supremely indifferent to the fate and lives of brother Hindus who lived but across the street. The British had no easy time in conquering India, but their difficulties would have been increased tremendously had they not found it a relatively simple matter to employ native Indian troops (Sepoys) to contest the ground with their foes.

Nevertheless, despite these facts, the imperialistic activities of the British very slowly tended to create the seemingly impossible—a nationalistic movement in the Indian peninsula. For the most part it came after the World War, but the planting and inception of it came earlier, and if we are to study its gradual budding we can not do better than to turn back to the great Indian Mutiny of 1857.

That event was due to many causes, prominent among them being discontent among the Sepoys. The latter suffered from complaints both real and imaginary; they were irritated by various administrative reforms, such as new rules for paying postage instead of sending their letters under the frank of their commander; they were annoyed by changes in the regulations in regard to pensions; they were upset by many rumors (all unfounded) of Christian proselytization on the part of the government; they were angry when told that the legal obstacles in the way of Hindu widows remarrying had been removed; and particularly were they enraged at the new cartridges introduced by the army which were said to have been greased by the fat of pig or cow and which had to have the end bitten off before insertion in the rifle. Since to the Hindu the cow was sacred, and since the Moslem could eat no pork, the new cartridges patently were an untactful innovation.

There were other causes. The British had, of late decades, been introducing social reforms rather rapidly; and furthermore they had swallowed up one native state after another. In recent years they had made frequent use of the doctrine of "lapse," whereby it was claimed that the British East India Company was entitled to inherit sovereign rights in all states where the native ruler died childless. Under such pretext the British annexed in 1856 the Kingdom of Oudh, a wealthy and important state but one long given over to misrule. Many of the Sepoys came from Oudh and their revolt was in part an act of protest against the British annexation of their native land.

The mutiny, although fierce and bloody, was confined to North and Central India, the Sepoys on the east coast at Madras and on the west at Bombay remaining loyal, as did those in the Punjab. Before, however, the British could suppress them, the mutinous Sepoys had wiped out the British troops and residents at Cawnpore and had set up at Delhi, ancient center of imperial rule, a supposed heir of the Mogul emperors. At Lucknow, the capital of Oudh, the British garrison held out bravely and was relieved by the advancing troops just in the nick of time. Then followed the capture of Delhi and the dispersal of the rebels.

The mutiny never was very extensive nor for that matter very dangerous. Nevertheless, it created great excitement in England where the treachery and the brutality of the Sepoys lost nothing in the telling. The punishment meted out to the mutineers was severe, but the intelligence of the British statesmen made them realize that changes in government were desirable. Consequently, they abolished the rule of the old East India Company which was still functioning politically and annexed British India to the Crown.

The policy of associating native Indians in the government of their own country soon followed, as did the acceptance of the advice of the historian Macaulay who advocated the education of the various Indian peoples in the history, language, and culture of Englishmen. Doubtless Macaulay's idea in doing this was to make the Indians proud and grateful that they were now incorporated in the British Empire. But the results were to the contrary. All unwittingly the British, by following Macaulay's advice, created a Frankenstein for themselves. The establishment of universities in India in which Milton, Burke, and Cromwell were studied meant inevitably the start of a nationalist tide in the direction of Indian independence and unity. As a prominent British historian has written:

> The fruit of Macaulay's famous minute on Indian education is the development in India of not only an excellent official class some two million in number but of a body of educated politicians who, having been taught out of English books to admire liberty, argue that what is good for the English is good for themselves, and confront the ruling race with a challenge based upon its own doctrines of freedom and progress.[1]

The actual birth, however, of Indian nationalism was a long, slow progress. Between the mutiny of 1857 and the World War the British did not rule badly in India and opposition to their *raj* was neither immediate nor acute. During this time there never were more than five thousand British actively engaged in administering this enormous peninsula, and the morale, the discipline, and the financial honesty of those thus occupied were of high order. True, it was an expensive rule, since salaries were high in the Indian civil service and years of retirement on half-pay long; but, on the other hand, if we compare the expense of administering British India with that of the native states where there was simply a British resident to give advice, the per capita expense of government was much lighter in British India. Meanwhile, British engineers reclaimed from aridity some 20,000,000 acres; the population shot upward to over 300,000,000; the death rate shot down; malaria and the bubonic plague, if not ended, at least were combatted with some fair hope of success. The law, perhaps, was not always equitable, but it was enforced. Anarchy and domestic strife disappeared as railroads were driven back and forth across India; and a Pax Britannica, in many ways resembling the Pax Romana of classical times, was found everywhere from the snows of the Himalayas to the hot sands of the seashore.

The major objection to this system of government was its alien char-

[1] H. A. L. Fisher, *A History of Europe*, p. 1051.

acter. As far back as 1833 the British had laid down the principle that "no native of India or naturalized subject of his Majesty shall be disabled from holding any place, office, or employment by reason of his religion, place of birth, descent or color." But that was no guarantee of Indian participation in the government of India and few Indians were thus employed. As early as 1861 Indians were admitted on the nomination of the Crown to the Legislative Council of the Viceroy—an honor this but largely an empty one. They remained there in a strict minority and no Indians at all served on the higher or Executive Council. Nor did Indians obtain good posts in the civil service, examinations for which were held in London. A certain number of judgeships were given them and some ill-paid subordinate positions, and that, during the nineteenth century, was all that they obtained.

Partly because of this situation, partly because now, on Macaulay's recommendation, Indians were being educated on Western lines; and doubtless because nationalism was everywhere a world-wide phenomenon in the nineteenth century, there arose in India the "Congress Movement," an assembling of Indians seeking a common medium for expressing Indian unity.

It began in the eighties and at first was largely religious in character. Toward the beginning of the new century it veered toward politics, making demands in the direction of self-government, and debating the possibility of boycotting British goods as a means of securing it. The agitation grew rapidly after the Russo-Japanese War of 1904-1905 with its proof that Asiatics, if properly led, could withstand Europeans. It was not unnoticed in England, and after the great Liberal victory of 1906 in that country there were high hopes that England would make broad concessions to Indian nationalism. Something was, indeed, accomplished. Two Indians were invited to share in the deliberations of the Indian Council in London; an Indian was placed on the sacred Executive Council of the Viceroy in India; the number of Indians in the lower, Legislative Council was increased, and they were to be elected by their own compatriots, not to be hand-picked by the Viceroy. These concessions were not inconsiderable, even if less than those hoped for. They helped to stem the tide of dissatisfaction and would have done so even more if the nervous British authorities in India had not at this juncture expelled from British India certain fiery agitators.

Afghanistan

Going north and west from India, we come upon three other Asiatic countries which were the scene of numerous imperialistic adventures in the hundred years subsequent to Waterloo—Afghanistan, Persia, and Turkey. In the first England and Russia almost came to blows; in the second England and Russia divided the spoils of victory; and in the third Germany displaced England, Russia, and France in the imperialistic race.

Afghanistan was a wild and mountainous country which historically had played a role to India somewhat like that of Switzerland to Italy. In other words, down through the Khyber Pass and out upon the plains of India had surged wave after wave of invaders—Aryans, Greeks, Moslems. The Afghans, taken by themselves, were troublesome enough with their intermittent forays on the Indian frontier; but they were neither sufficiently numerous nor united to be a major cause of worry to the British overlords of India. What troubled the sleep of the latter was the thought of what might be going on north of Afghanistan. There, somewhere, were the Cossacks, the forerunners of Czardom.

Turkestan, the land to the north of Afghanistan, was vast, arid, and inhospitable; but it did connect by land with southern Russia and within its borders there were certain valleys, fertile, well-watered, the surviving pockets of arable land which hundreds of years earlier had been the home of important civilizations. These oases—Merv, Samarcand, Tashkent, and Khiva—might never become again what they once had been, but nevertheless they were convenient stepping-stones (somewhat far apart, it is true) for the Russian Bear to use in approaching the Afghan border. Once there it was not far to Kabul, the Afghan capital, and thence to the Khyber Pass was no great distance. Russian activity in all this region was marked during the middle third of the nineteenth century, and every British effort to ward Russia away from Constantinople served apparently as a spur to drive her forward here. There were unruly Turkoman horse thieves to punish, so said the Russians; but the British thought the Muscovites had their eyes on India.

Throughout the last century England and Russia played an ever varying game at the Amir's court at Kabul. The Afghan monarch, with superb impartiality, welcomed subsidies from both sides and kept both sides guessing. Twice during the century did England wage war on the Afghans and twice did she occupy Kabul. The first occasion was in 1839 when she dispatched six thousand men to that Afghan capital to depose a Russophil Amir. It was a disastrous expedition, since but one man of the six thousand escaped to tell the tale of treachery and woe. The next year the British came on again but did not stay. The Amir, it seemed, had decided that he loved the lion better than the bear.

Once again, in 1877, the British marched north, and for identical reasons. The second Afghan war was a tough one and the British triumph was expensive. This time Kandahar in southern Afghanistan probably would have remained in British hands after the war, had not a pacific Gladstone succeeded a warlike Disraeli. But even Gladstone had his military moments. The Russian Trans-Caucasian Railroad, hooking up the various oases with Russia, neared completion in the early eighties and threatened once more the security of the British in India. A branch line from Merv was projected south to the Afghan city of Herat, and Gladstone in 1885, for once, forgot his troubles in Egypt and threatened the Russians in most warlike tones. The dispute was compounded, neither side feeling happy. The Russians, however, compelled to suspend their railway enterprise, pushed still further west and south in Turkestan and occupied the Pamirs, a most desolate region, slightly to the east of the Khyber and only separated from India by a thin mountain wall.

Suppose they should penetrate it, jump over it, go around it? George Nathaniel Curzon, Viceroy of England in India as the twentieth century opened, proposed to take no chances. He created a new province in British India, the Northwestern. This was turned into a kind of military outpost of empire. Not far from its capital, Peshawar, and near the frontier, a kind of no man's land was made where Afghan outlaw or Russian spy might wander at will. No responsibility would Britain assume for this region, but ever did she keep her watchful eye upon it.

Persia

Nor upon it alone. There was Persia also to watch. In the eighteenth century the East India Company had made advances toward that upland plateau of Cyrus, Darius, and other mighty emperors. There was not much grandeur left in Persia now, but at least that ancient kingdom was one way by which India might be reached. Napoleon had planned it so in his day, and in the nineteenth century it was Russia who held the whip hand in Persia, always thinking of that country as an alternative route to India should the Afghan one fail. One simply reached eastward from Persia to Herat in Western Afghanistan and took the valleys to the south of Herat, thus avoiding the Khyber altogether.

At the turn of the century Russia held what almost might be called a political and economic mortgage on Persia. The Shah was heavily in debt to the Russians and had pledged the tobacco monopoly of his country to pay it back. Russians flocked to his domains in considerable numbers. Persia lay but across the Caspian Sea from Russia and access was easy. The only two cities of importance in Persia, Teheran and Tabriz, both were in the northern part of the country and both were under Russian influence. And to the east of Teheran was the tempting Herat. The British, perhaps, could be depended on to defend Herat, but that after all was not the only way to that magnet of wealth and opulence, the Indian peninsula. Persia was bordered on the south and west by the Persian Gulf and the Gulf of Oman. And directly beyond the latter body of water was Baluchistan, south of Afghanistan but also impinging on India. Why not reach the goal by way of Persian territorial waters and Baluchistan; or perhaps a railroad across Persia might lead Russia to warm waters, and at least offer a new connection between the land of the Czars and the Far East?

As far as the British were concerned, the Russians might have northern Persia and welcome. But it would not do to let them reach either of the two gulfs and so possibly intercept England's water route to India. At the mouth of the Persian Gulf lay Bundar Abbas, and when the Russians tried to establish an embryonic coaling station there, the ever watchful Curzon was quick to intervene. He sent a warship to that rough port and the Persians saw fit under the circumstances to reject the Russian request that the Cossacks might guard Russian coal deposited at Bundar Abbas. The British lion at this time was heavily engaged with the Boer republics in South Africa, but that did not spell permission for the advance of Russian imperialism, not if Curzon could prevent it.

There now broke out in Persia (1906) a nationalistic revolution against the tyranny of the Shah. Two years before the Young Turks, clamoring for liberalism and nationalism, overturned the power of Abdul-Hamid, Young Persians, fired by the same ideals, revolted against the Shah of Persia. That Asiatic despot did not have the ability of Abdul-Hamid. Completely under the thumb of the Russians, he had signed away to them monopoly after monopoly for ready cash wherewith to plunge into dissipation in Europe; and for the welfare of his people he cared nothing. Now as in Turkey, the ruler of the country first accepted and then plotted against the constitutional regime which he had sworn to defend.

In so doing he was supported secretly by the Russians, who looked askance at representative institutions in Persia. The Persian *Majliss* or Parliament was confronted by civil war but emerged victorious, the treacherous Shah seeking and finding refuge with his friends, the Russians.

These events were seized upon by Russia and by England, acting conjointly, to divide Persia between them into spheres of influence, and a general compounding of Anglo-Russian difficulties in Asia now took place in 1907, as we shall note later in more detail.

Persia, however, still remained, at least theoretically an independent country, for the spheres of influence, Russian and British, supposedly related only to the economic development of the country. Sovereignty in Persia, theoretically again, rested with the Majliss, and that assembly now tried desperately to reorganize this poverty-stricken land in which there were but fourteen miles of railroad—upon which no trains operated. The Majliss, discouraged with European interference, asked the United States to send to Persia a financial adviser, and on the recommendation of the American State Department Mr. W. Morgan Shuster was appointed to that post in 1909.

Shuster found when he reached Teheran that the British and Russian ambassadors expected to have their advice asked in all matters which concerned the administration of Persia, and Shuster from the beginning became *persona non grata* to these two officials. In almost every important respect he was thwarted in his endeavors to put Persia's house in order, and matters reached a climax when his treasury gendarmes occupied an estate belonging to the Shah's brother, which Shuster claimed was forfeited because the owner had rebelled against the constitutional authorities of his country. The Russians were very angry and, claiming that the estate had been rented to a Russian, they drove out the Persian police with a small detachment of Cossacks. The latter being evicted by a still larger body of police, the Russians occupied the city of Tabriz not far from the Caspian Sea and commenced marching toward Teheran. A Muscovite ultimatum demanded the dismissal of Shuster and the payment of an indemnity. The British, albeit somewhat reluctantly, supported the Russian demands, for the European crisis of 1911 loomed on the horizon and Britain did not dare antagonize the Russian Bear. Consequently, there was nothing for Persia to do but accept the resignation of Shuster who returned to America, not, however, until he had written a letter to the London *Times* complaining about Britain's support of Russia in this snuffing-out of Persian independence. The letter caused Sir Edward Grey some unpleasant moments in the House of Commons during the question hour.

From this date, 1911, to the outbreak of the First World War Russia remained dominant in the land of Cyrus, that is, in the only part of it of any economic value, the northern part. And as long as the Russians confined their activities to this section the British made no objection, since their principal imperialistic interest lay in preserving a no man's land in the region of the Gulf of Oman and Baluchistan.

German Exploitation of Asiatic Turkey

One reason advanced for the hasty conclusion of the 1907 Anglo-Russian treaty was fear and jealousy on the part of the signers at the fast growth of a German project in the Ottoman Empire, namely the B.B.B. or the Berlin, Byzantium, Bagdad Railroad. As far back as 1888 certain German bankers secured a franchise for a railroad in Asia Minor. But why stop with Asia Minor; why not construct the road through the mountain passes and connect Constantinople with Syria; or why not go farther yet and cross the desert all the way to Bagdad, thus reaching the Tigris and Euphrates rivers? There was much to be said for so doing. Such a railroad would give Germany an opportunity to develop the Tigris-Euphrates valley in much the same way as England had developed that of the Nile. In ancient days the former valley had been the seat of important civilizations. Now it was either swamp or desert; the canals which in ancient days had connected the two river systems, the land of Mesopotamia (between the rivers) had silted up, and this whole region, much larger than the irrigated sections of modern Egypt, now supported only a few nomads.

Many distinguished Britons agreed that the interests of civilization might best be served by having Germany assume the task of developing this region, among them Sir William Willcocks, the great irrigation engineer, who considered the proposal perfectly possible from a scientific viewpoint, and also Cecil Rhodes, who considered it politically advisable. Rhodes, of course, had an ax to grind; he wanted the Germans out of Africa and he thought that the Bagdad Railroad might serve as a lever for dislodging them from East Africa. But even so there were other advantages: the enterprising Germans would have a Herculean job on their hands which would occupy them many years; there was abundant living space in this part of Asiatic Turkey for German immigrants; and abundant employment not only for surplus German capital but for other capital as well.

Opposition, however, to the project was not lacking. If the railroad ever reached Bagdad, what would prevent its continuance to the Persian Gulf? And that would give the Germans a more direct route to India than the Suez Canal route. This thought caused consternation in English breasts. But the French also took alarm. Since the days of St. Louis and the Crusaders, France had regarded the Levant and particularly Syria as peculiarly marked out for French penetration and influence, if not politically, at least culturally and economically. The French franc and the English language predominated in Syria, and France did not relish the idea of their being supplanted by the German mark and the German tongue. But most active of all in obstruction was Russia. That country could not forget the Russo-Turkish War of 1877 and the fact that Russian victory had been achieved in part because the Turks had been unable to march an army corps from Bagdad in time to participate in the fray. A railroad to Bagdad would immeasurably strengthen Turkey from a military point of view, and the Muscovites had by no means given up their dream of supplanting the crescent by the cross in Constantinople. Also, from the Russian viewpoint, it was argued that such a railroad would augment Germany's supply of cereals, and if the latter found their way to Berlin from Mesopotamia, down would go the price of Russian grain.

Despite all opposition, however, a contract for the railroad was signed in 1903. Although the original promoters were German bankers, the railroad was to be an international enterprise, and French and British capital was sought by the entrepreneurs as well as German. Rail connection between Berlin and Constantinople already was excellent; there remained 2,400 miles between Constantinople (Byzantium of the ancients) and Bagdad. The construction would be expensive, for the railroad would have to tunnel mountains as well as cross deserts and swamps. Turkey, however, would give the right of way and assist in the finances, and the rest of the money would come from the sale of shares on the open market.

For a time the prospects seemed more than fair. The company was in the receipt of certain generous concessions; it was not to pay taxes until financially successful; numerous rights and economic privileges were granted on either side of the line (as in the case of the transcontinental railroads in the United States); the right of way was to cost nothing; and in addition a kilometric guarantee was given by the Turkish government whereby a certain sum was promised the railroad per kilometer if the earnings of the company fell below a stipulated amount. And if they rose above a certain specified sum, the company and the government would divide the profit. In consequence, both French and British investors took a warm interest in the railroad, and as it advanced from the railhead not far from Constantinople, the increase in international trade with Turkey seemed to warrant their enthusiasm.

Then, suddenly, in both France and England, opposition to the railroad took visible form. Seemingly this enterprise was devoid of imperialistic plotting on the part of Germany, for on the board of directors there were to be eight Germans, eight Frenchmen, eight Britons, and six nominees of the Turkish government, so that the French and British directors had a sheer majority. Nevertheless, a combination of political and business pressure brought about the withdrawal of Anglo-French financial assistance. Anglo-German naval rivalry presumably had something to do with it, and possibly also traditional alarm at the possibility of any European country reaching out toward India. Even if the railroad was continued beyond Bagdad all the way to the Persian Gulf and warm water, the British had bottled up already that body of water by a treaty with the Sultan of Koweit, the local sheik of the region, so there was really no cause for alarm. But after all, the city of Harun al-Rashid was 2,400 miles nearer India than was Constantinople, and it was not so difficult to raise a hue and cry against the ambitious Germans. In regard to withdrawal of French financial support the case is more cloudy. Delcassé, powerful in French politics, hated and feared the Germans. Then, too, there was Russia, an unremitting enemy, hitherto, of the B.B.B. When Russia whispered to France, the Third Republic was apt to nod acquiescence.

Nevertheless, the railroad made headway even without the help of the French and British bankers. The first section was completed in 1907, and the German bankers, following the German engineers, swarmed into Turkey, doing all kinds of business aside from pure banking, such as selling life-insurance policies to the Turks. The Germans were proud of the B.B.B., and when the Young Turks in 1908 raised 227,000,000 francs to carry construction still further, German publicists began to write of the railroad as a kind of Imperial German highway which at one and the same time threatened on the flank England's hold on Egypt while driving forward into Asia.

Suddenly, then, Russia withdrew her opposition to the B.B.B. Whether this was due to Russian pique at being unsupported by her ally France in the momentous Balkan crisis of 1908, it is impossible to say. At any rate, a bargain was struck between Russia and Germany, the former country giving up all objection to the German exploitation of the Ottoman Empire, the latter ·ountry recognizing that North Persia was for Russia alone to exploit. This Russo-German agreement immediately led France and England to reverse their policies. Both countries made good bargains. France, by agreeing to an increase in the Turkish tariff (fixed by treaty), secured the rights to build a railroad in northern Anatolia with a kilometric guarantee somewhat similar to that possessed by the Bagdad road. As for Britain, she secured Turkey's promise that the B.B.B. would not be extended beyond Bagdad, that there would be no discrimination against Britain in the matter of freight rates; that a British company would have a monopoly of navigation on the Tigris-Euphrates; and that oil rights in Mesopotamia would be controlled by a company, half the shares of which were to belong to the Anglo-Persian Oil Company (British-owned), one quarter going to the Royal Dutch Shell (partly owned in Britain), and the remaining quarter going to the Germans.

Thus plans were made and agreements struck whereby the romantic yet practical aspirations of the railroad builder might bear fruit in one of the world's great railroads. Unfortunately too late, the Anglo-German agreement, which touched on African colonies as well as on the B.B.B., was initialed in July, 1914, less than a month before the First World War.

Chapter 26

THE DIPLOMATIC BACKGROUND OF
THE FIRST WORLD WAR

THE IMPERIALISTIC adventures of the European Powers comprise a part only of the story of international politics in the decades preceding World War I (1914-18). The conflicting ambitions and mutual jealousies thereby engendered contributed their share to the amassing of armaments, the growth of tension between the powers, and their final and fatal alignment into two hostile camps; but it was not imperialism alone which did this. Smoldering nationalism throughout Europe; a longing for lost provinces on the part of France; an eagerness on the part of Italy to extend her influence; a determination on the part of England to continue mistress of the seas; Russian Pan-Slavism thrusting intermittently toward Constantinople, toward India, toward the Pacific; German uneasiness lest the Germanic folk be caught unawares by hostile armies on either flank; Pan-Germanism arrayed against Pan-Slavism; and, above all, the yeastlike budding of fervent nationalism among the various nationalities in the Balkans bursting forth in full bloom in the Balkan Wars of 1912-13—these were the imponderables which weighed quite as much with European diplomats as the planting of the flag overseas, the winning of African colonies, the earmarking of Asiatic spheres of influence. To these diplomats and to their handling of international crises in the generation before the war, this chapter is devoted.

The Bismarck Era

The story goes back to the victorious Bismarck of 1871. France for the time being lay helpless and he wanted her to remain so. Without allies the Gallic foe could not hope to cross swords with him again, and for precaution's sake he deemed it wise that Germany not France secure allies. Therefore in 1873 he organized the *Dreikaiserbund,* or Three Emperors' League—Austria, Russia, and Germany being the signatories.

This *Dreikaiserbund* was no hard and fast military alliance; there were no mutual pledges given or taken for armed assistance. All that the three

488

emperors agreed to do was to assist one another in maintaining the status quo and to consult should it be endangered. The *Dreikaiserbund* came to grief as a result of the Congress of Berlin. After its sessions Russia felt convinced that her old traditional friendship with Prussia had been betrayed by Bismarck. The Chancellor of Germany insisted that he only played the honest broker, but Russia believed herself double-crossed. What she saw was the double-eagle of Austria-Hungary in Bosnia and herself defrauded of Balkan gains. Her annexation of Bessarabia and her territorial gains east of the Black Sea hardly seemed compensation for the annulment of the Treaty of San Stefano. From this time forward Russia never again quite trusted Germany.

Bismarck may not have been responsible for Russia's failure to gain more in 1878, but he knew that Berlin had been the place where Russia's defeat had been recorded and that he had presided over the congress held there. Immediately, therefore, he sought to repair his diplomatic fences by tying up as closely with Austria as that country would permit. If he had to make a choice between Austria and Russia, he preferred the former country. Her frontier marched more closely with that of Germany; her armies held the bastions of the Carpathian Mountains from whence they could debouch upon advancing Russians; and furthermore, within Austria-Hungary were over 10,000,000 Germans who might yet be incorporated into a greater Reich.

Consequently Bismarck betook himself to Vienna. What he hoped to obtain was a hard and fast military alliance whereby Austria and Germany would bind themselves to resist with all their forces a renovated French army attacking Germany or a Russian army attacking Austria; what he did obtain was an agreement concerning Russia alone. In case of war provoked by Russia upon either signatory the other agreed to march to the defense of its ally. This was the celebrated Dual Alliance between Austria and Germany, signed in 1879 and destined to become the nucleus of a most intricate network of alliances and counter-alliances between various European states.

The Austro-German alliance worried the Czar. He began to think more kindly of his old ally, Germany, and Bismarck with an eye toward placating Russia (a characteristic of his diplomacy throughout a long lifetime) cheerfully consented in 1881 to a renewal of the *Dreikaiserbund*. The terms were more specific than those of the old agreement. All three emperors agreed to remain neutral in case one of their three countries was attacked by a fourth. In the event of Turkey in Europe being divided they were to agree in advance upon the spoils. Austria was to be permitted to annex Bosnia outright, provided she raised no objection to the union of Bulgaria with Eastern Rumelia.

The second *Dreikaiserbund* was to be wrecked, as was the first, by a renewal of Austro-Russian jealousy concerning the Balkans. This time it was Bulgaria which caused the trouble. That country (1885-87) objected vigorously to the tutelage of Russia, drove Russian officers out of her army, annexed Eastern Rumelia to Bulgaria without Russian permission. The Czar, infuriated, took steps to punish Bulgaria, Austria objecting. Bismarck cared nothing about the Balkans; what he wanted above everything else was to prevent his two allies from quarreling. Fortunately for him, a very definite stand was made unnecessary by England and Italy joining Austria in a Mediterranean agreement (1887), preserving the status quo in that sea and in the Near East.

Russia was now thoroughly angry at Austria and more suspicious than ever of Germany whom, despite professions of friendship, she suspected of conniving at her Balkan defeat. Therefore she would have no more to do with the *Dreikaiserbund*.

Bismarck's years of service were now nearly over, but before retiring he made one more desperate and successful effort to insure the eastern marches of his fatherland against Muscovite invasion. In 1887 he made a curious treaty with Russia. He called it a "reinsurance treaty" and it was to run for three years. Its provisos were three: (*a*) Germany and Russia to be neutral if either country became involved in war; (*b*) the above not to apply to a war "against Austria or France resulting from an attack upon one of these two Powers by one of the contracting powers"; (*c*) Germany "to recognize rights historically acquired by Russia in the Balkans."

A curious treaty this! Did it mean that Bismarck was double-crossing his ally, Austria? Technically, of course, the answer was in the negative. He was still pledged to assist Austria by force of arms if Russia attacked her; only in case of Austria attacking Russia was Germany to remain neutral. On the other hand, it was difficult to draw a line between offensive and defensive war. Suppose Russia should mobilize her huge strength against Austria in order to prod the latter country into fighting. Who then could be said to have started the war? Bismarck was skating on thin ice by this treaty; but all of his life he had kept some line to Russia open and he did not want to tempt the Czar into a possible French alliance, always a nightmare to him.

Meanwhile, to the dual alliance with Austria-Hungary there came in 1882 an accession of strength—or of weakness—Italy. That nation had been consumed with anger at the French occupation of Tunis one year earlier. Bismarck was largely responsible for that Gallic advance, since he had suggested after the Franco-Prussian War that the French seek compensation in Africa for the loss of Alsace-Lorraine. Then when Britain annexed Cyprus after the Congress of Berlin, Disraeli had added his advice to that of Bismarck and suggested Tunis as a proper field for French exploitation. But Tunis was less than a hundred miles from Sicily and the European population there was largely Italian in blood. Nobody had offered Italy anything after the Berlin Congress and the Italians were bitter at this French coup. Therefore they came knocking at the Berlin gate seeking allies.

Bismarck did not trust the Italians and he was not anxious to have them included in his alliance system. If a refusal, however, meant that the Italians might sign up with another group, that was another matter. Thereupon Bismarck suggested to the Italians that they approach Austria first, for owing to the inclusion of many Italians within the boundaries of Austria there had been friction between the two countries. Austria proved willing to admit Italy to the Austro-German fold, for she did not want a potential foe at her back door should she engage in war with Russia, and Bismarck was willing to have still another guarantee against France. Consequently, in 1882 the Dual Alliance between Germany and Austria was supplemented by the new Triple Alliance of Germany, Austria, and Italy.

With Italy in the bag, with Rumania part way in (that country had an alliance with Austria but not with Germany), and with his Russian reinsurance treaty, Bismarck left Germany in a secure position at the date of his retirement (1890).

William II Ruins the Work of Bismarck

She was not to stay there. One of the first acts of the melodramatic young Kaiser after forcing Bismarck's resignation was to wreak havoc with the latter's diplomacy by refusing to renew the reinsurance treaty in 1890. This act inevitably drove France and Russia together. In some respects the alliance between these two countries, the new dual alliance, was not natural. Republican France had never forgotten Alsace-Lorraine, but to autocratic Russia it made no difference who ruled those two provinces; vice versa, the Balkan jealousies of Austria and Russia in the Balkans did not interest Paris. Both France and Russia held grievances against England, the former in Egypt and the Upper Nile, the latter on the Afghan border. But it is doubtful if these alone would have brought France and Russia into an alliance. It was Germany in conjunction with England that cemented it. In the nineties there was a goodly possibility that England might become a fourth partner in the Triple Alliance, leaving France and Russia isolated and alone. In 1890 Germany and England signed a treaty liquidating certain colonial disputes, England assuming a protectorate over Zanzibar, Germany annexing Helgoland, and more agreements might follow. St. Petersburg and Paris took alarm. The Russians needed French money, the French, Russian warpower. And so in 1894 they became allied, "If France is attacked by Germany, or by Italy supported by Germany," the treaty read, "Russia shall employ all her available forces to attack Germany. If Russia is attacked by Germany or by Austria supported by Germany, France shall employ all her available forces to fight Germany." And lest there be any doubt as to just what that meant, the commitments were made quite specific. According to clause three: "The forces to be employed against Germany will be, on the part of France, 1,300,000 men, on the part of Russia 700,000 to 800,000. These forces will engage with all their might, so that Germany has to fight both on the East and West."

Thus were the rival camps established, the new dual alliance against Bismarck's Triple Alliance. The bad dreams of the Iron Chancellor had come to pass: Germany had potential foes on either flank.

There was as yet no immediate danger of war. All the alliances were said to be defensive and the two rival camps balanced off neatly against one another. The triplice had, to be sure, the advantage of interior lines, if it came to a fight; but on the other hand the nationalistic divergencies of the Austro-Hungarian peoples were a drawback and the potential manpower of Russia was enormous.

Possibly there might not have been any international war at all had it not been for Anglo-German rivalry and misunderstanding. For many decades the Germans and the British had been drifting apart. The British thought the Germans were a misguided folk who had not shown the intelligence to plan their national development along British constitutional lines. They had not forgotten that Bismarck carried through his increase in the Prussian army without pretense of popular consent, and they remembered the annexation of Schleswig-Holstein without British consent and the fact that Queen Alexandra, wife of Edward VII, was a Danish princess. They also viewed with disfavor the German tariff system, the embryonic German navy, the Teutonic demands for colonies, and the commencement of German competition overseas in steel and iron products. Always, too, the hardness of tone and vulgarity of manners of the new Germany jarred the sensibilities of the British.

Germans, on the other hand, chafed under what they considered British patronage. The complacent universality and self-assured superiority of their island neighbors in their opinion was without justification. The Germans regarded Britain as a retired robber turned pious, desirous of spending his declining years in luxury without anyone inquiring into the sources of his wealth. Von Treitschke, Germany's great historian, taught the German youth that the day of England's greatness was past and most Germans believed him.

Nevertheless, despite these facts there seemed more reasons for Britain allying herself with Germany than with any other country—if an alliance became necessary for national safety and if reliance no longer could be put on "splendid isolation," England's great tradition. To begin with there were as yet no such specific grounds for disagreement between England and Germany as existed between the latter country and France, or England and France, or England and Russia. The open sore of Alsace-Lorraine still remained unhealed. The Third Republic and the British Empire clashed at many points in Siam, in Egypt, in Oceania, north of the Gulf of Guinea, and along the headwaters of the Nile. The British Lion and the Russian Bear growled at one another across half a dozen Asiatic frontiers and the Trans-Caucasian Railway had brought Russian Cossacks within striking distance of the Khyber Pass. Furthermore, the Trans-Siberian Railway threatened to bring all North China under Russian influence, a thought most distasteful to British diplomats.

Consequently, the British toyed in the eighteen-nineties with the idea of a German-British alliance and so, too, did German statesmen. In fact, one might well have eventuated had it not been for three factors: (a) the personality of the Kaiser, (b) the belief of German diplomats that Britain ultimately would have to join the triplice, thus making it a quadruple alliance, and (c) the South African war of 1899-1902.

Kaiser William II never was able to view objectively the homeland of his mother, the British princess Victoria, favored daughter of the old British queen. This nervous, neurotic, yet frequently brilliant ruler of Germany blamed his mother for the withered arm with which he was born, hated her violently, and, through her, England. Great predecessors of his on the Prussian throne had become famous for their armies; why should he not be enrolled among the famous of Valhalla as the founder of German sea power? British newspapers mocked at his country and at him and he resented it—yet curiously enough, with all his Anglophobia there was mixed much admiration for England and what he would say about that country never could be predicted. If he had only kept silent . . . but that was one thing William II could not do. He was determined that "the old peacock," his uncle, Edward VII, should be put in his place; he always wanted to show off before the British who became alarmed that one possessed of such unquestionable power should be so irresponsible.

The German diplomats, meanwhile, overplayed their cards. They had an idea that England would come to them cap in hand and that they only had to wait long enough and England would beg to be admitted to the Triple Alliance. Now many influential British statesmen were quite willing to make a defensive treaty with Germany alone, the two countries to stand shoulder to shoulder if attacked; but they were unwilling to commit their country to any Austro-German policy in the Balkans, which might be necessary if they joined hands with Italy and Austria. Consequently, there was a great deal of smoke and but very little fire in regard to the projected alliance.

Then, too, there was the South African problem which culminated in the Boer War. The Germans were accustomed to consider the Boers as racial cousins who might form the nucleus of a potentially Teutonic nation in South Africa. German Southwest Africa was only separated from the Transvaal by the thinly populated Bechuanaland; and further-more the Transvaal abutted on Portuguese East Africa, through which ran the railway from Pretoria. Suppose that Delagoa Bay were some day to fall to Germany, or perhaps Bechuanaland? German influence was felt at Pretoria and the Germans were keenly alive to the advantages which might accrue to themselves if the two Boer republics remained inde-pendent long enough. When the Jameson Raid occurred in 1895 the Kaiser was wildly excited and insisted upon telegraphing his congratula-tions to Kruger, a fact which added to his unpopularity in Britain.

The advent of the South African war found German public opinion heavily Anglophobe, and when the British illegally stopped a German merchant ship bound for Delagoa Bay, relations between the two countries became very strained. Germany preserved neutrality throughout the war, and the Kaiser discouraged the Russians when they suggested a conti-nental front against England; but this did not discourage the German press from attacking England. Chamberlain, England's spokesman, did, it is true, continue to hold out the olive branch to Germany, suggesting an Anglo-Saxon alliance of Germany, England, and the United States; but his appeal fell upon deaf ears. The Colonial Secretary was not a tactful man. Somewhat later in the war, in defending the conduct of the British troops, he implied that their behavior was at least more exemplary than that of the Prussians in 1870-71, and as he did so the newspapers of Germany took up the challenge in no peaceful strain. Echoes of the Boer War were to continue for a good many years and as late as 1908 the Kaiser added greatly to his unpopularity in England by an interview granted to the London *Daily Telegraph* wherein he boasted that the plans of campaign used by the British armies in South Africa had been drawn up by his imperial self.

The growing animosity, however, between England and Germany did not mean that the former country was prepared to enter the Franco-Russian camp—not yet. The tradition of isolation was still strong in England, even if the Boer War did make the British feel that they were without friends on the Continent. And therefore Lord Lansdowne, foreign secretary in the Balfour government (1902-1905) contented himself with striking an alliance with Japan in 1902 whereby that distant Asiatic empire exchanged mutual guarantees with Britain, the alliance to be invoked in case either country got into a war in Far Eastern waters (1902).

Ultimately, Britain was to veer into alignment with France and Russia, but her doing so was a long and slow process. She never got all the way into the Franco-Russian tent, one foot, perhaps, being outside the flap as late as 1914. When the World War broke, the alignment of Powers quite properly was called the Triple Alliance and the Triple Entente, but even the word "entente" is a little too strong to imply Anglo-Russian relations. France and Russia were very closely allied but England was allied with neither. The truth then was that she was on something more than good terms with Russia and under very definite obligations to France.

The Entente Cordiale

The story of how that came about relates more properly to France than to England. In the former country at the turn of the century was one of Europe's cleverest diplomats, Delcassé. He had been a bitter enemy of England, and at the time of Kitchener's bloodless victory at Fashoda on the Upper Nile over Captain Marchand, Delcassé raged. But the Frenchman was a realist; he knew that overseas it was impossible to defy Britain. Why not therefore come to terms with her and extend the French colonial empire in those regions (if there were any such) to which the British laid no claims? What Delcassé had his eye on was Morocco; if the British would but give him a free hand there he felt it quite worth while to surrender French claims in the Upper Nile valley (unenforceable anyway) and in Egypt where they possessed a nuisance value only. Other outstanding rivalries in the colonial world might be compounded also, fishing disputes off the Newfoundland coast, islands in Oceania, the island of Madagascar, boundary lines and frontiers still in dispute between France and England in tropical Africa north of the Gulf of Guinea, and also in Siam, which little country was most unfortunately situated, indeed, with British Burma on the west and French Indo-China on the east.

Cautiously, Delcassé approached Lansdowne; would his lordship be agreeable to a general colonial settlement? The French suggested terms, the British counterterms, and a protracted bargain in colonial frontiers was under way. The result was almost a diplomatic revolution. Britain abandoned at this time (1904) not only her traditional anti-French policy in respect to colonial expansion but also the time-honored policy of abstention from continental commitments sponsored by Canning, Palmerston, and Salisbury, and only slightly compromised by her participation in the Crimean War. It proved the beginning of what was to England an insurance policy against an unpredictable Kaiser and an aggressive Germany; and what was to Germany the commencement of a policy of encirclement initiated by the jealous British who sought to surround Germany with an iron ring.

The Anglo-French accord looked harmless. In the more important of the treaties now signed, France acknowledged the priority of Britain's position in Egypt, the British in return recognizing that French interests in Morocco were more important than their own. But the Germans suspected secret clauses and were justified in so doing, clauses which stated that if England in the future decided to change the status quo as to

Egypt, France would support her in so doing, and that if France found it necessary to change the status quo in Morocco, Britain would support her, in the latter eventuality provision being made for Spanish annexations in Morocco, since England did not want a powerful France opposite Gibraltar.

The treaty said nothing about Italy; it did not need to, since four years earlier (1900) France had made a bargain with Italy which provided for Italian compensation in Tripoli should France decide to push westward from Algeria to Morocco. The treaty said nothing about Germany; but after all why should she be invited to share in the exploitation of Morocco; did not that region lie adjacent to French territory (Algeria), and was there not much more French money invested in Morocco than there was German?

Nevertheless, Morocco was supposed to be independent; there were German merchants there; and somewhat earlier when ambiguous Anglo-German negotiations were afoot there had been British suggestions that England would not oppose Germany gaining a foothold in Morocco. The German foreign office was indignant at this disregard of German colonial ambitions and brought pressure to bear on a very reluctant Kaiser to land at Tangier and to make a provocative speech in which he congratulated the Sultan of Morocco upon retaining his independence and assured him of German friendship.

With one of those flares of real insight which occasionally came to him the German ruler scented trouble, and he found it. The French were furious at this German intervention and the British, although more calm, aligned themselves with the French. Delcassé talked too much and too belligerently, and the French, not eager for war, dismissed him. The Germans, however, not content with getting rid of Delcassé, demanded that an international conference be held to decide Morocco's future.

The proposal was an unfortunate one for Germany, since the conference of 1906 which met at Algeciras proved a great setback for her. England supported France, as of course did Russia. But Italy supported France, too, since owing to her treaty of 1900 with that country, Tripoli was earmarked for Italy if France gained control over Morocco. The Italians now had their feet in both camps and the Germans realized as never before what an insecure hold they had on Italy. Spain also joined the anti-German group, owing to the promise of enlarged territory opposite Gibraltar, and even the United States threw the weight of her influence against Germany.

Two questions were in the foreground at Algeciras—finance and police. The finances of Morocco were as hopelessly muddled as those of Egypt in 1878, and since French bankers had loaned most of the money borrowed by the Sultan, France demanded a Bank of Morocco under a French president. This French claim was not sustained; nevertheless, the French won an indirect victory, since the international bank that was established was largely controlled by the Bank of France, the Bank of England, the Bank of Spain, and the German Imperial Bank, and the French knew that the Spaniards and the English were on their side.

But how was order to be maintained in Morocco, particularly in the seaports and along the frontier? The Germans demanded a share in policing this unruly country and they did not succeed in obtaining it. In this lay their major defeat. The conference voted that France, assisted by Spain, should officer the police, and to give an international appearance to this decision a Swiss inspector-general was appointed. Thus ended 1906. The Kaiser's intuition of the preceding year had been a good one.

In 1907 Germany was to receive a further shock in the announcement of an Anglo-Russian treaty. Like the Anglo-French treaties of 1904, it looked innocent enough, but the Germans wondered what might be behind it.

Russo-German relations since the non-renewal of Bismarck's reinsurance treaty had been unstable. When Russia and Japan fought it out in Manchuria, the Kaiser had been violently pro-Russian. To his heated imagination it was a war of East against West, of Asiatic paganism against Christian culture. He bombarded the Czar with advice as to how the war might be won; he took an active part in assisting the coaling of the Russian fleet bound to Asiatic waters; and he sent the draft of a projected treaty of alliance between Germany and Russia to the Czar for approval. Shortly after in 1905 he met the Czar off the coast of Finland and persuaded that weak monarch to sign the treaty of Björko, definitely committing himself to an alliance with Germany. The Russian foreign office was horrified; France had not been consulted. When that country resolutely refused to enter into any alliance in which Germany was a partner as long as Alsace-Lorraine remained German, the Czar backed out of the Björko treaty with what grace he could. A year later, at Algeciras, Russia voted with France against Germany, and the Kaiser and everybody else who knew anything about it realized that Björko was meaningless.

Meanwhile, Anglo-Russian relations during this same period were more unfriendly than in several decades. The Anglo-Japanese treaty of 1902 angered the Russians and prevented any hope they might have of allies in their Far Eastern adventure; and an accidental firing upon British trawlers in the North Sea by Russian warships made British public opinion even more Russophobe than it had ever been in more recent years.

It had been sufficiently so before. During the Boer War the Russians steadily encroached on the independence of Persia and endeavored as well to obtain a coaling station adjacent to the Persian Gulf over the waters of which, according to Lord Curzon, Britain exercised a kind of Monroe Doctrine. In Tibet and in Afghanistan there were Russian intrigues afoot, and any rapprochement between England and Russia seemed as remote in 1905 as one between England and France in 1904.

Nevertheless, that rapprochement took place. The treaty of 1907 between England and Russia related, it is true, entirely to Asia. By it the paramount interest of Britain in Afghanistan was recognized, Tibet was guaranteed as a no man's land, and Persia was divided by the two signatories into three zones. The first of these, the northern and most important, containing the cities of Tabriz and Teheran, went to Russia. Then came an intermediate zone in which neither Britain nor Russia claimed influence. The third zone, to the south and east, was given to Britain. These zones in theory simply marked off spheres of economic influence. Persia's independence solemnly was recognized, as was customary in treaties of this ilk.

The treaty was a blow to the Germans. England now was the friend of both Russia and France; Russia, although not anti-German, was the foe of Austria, Germany's sole dependable ally in the Balkans; Russia also was the close ally of France, still hostile to Germany because of Alsace-Lorraine. The Germans were worried and felt more need than ever of Austria.

Because of this fact Germany felt it very necessary to take a firm stand at the next international crisis which arose in the Balkans in 1908. Behind it lay the somewhat unsavory machinations of the Russian foreign secretary, Isvolski, and the Austrian foreign minister, Aerenthal. These two men concocted a secret agreement at Buchlau whereby the straits which connected the Black Sea with the Mediterranean should become open for Russian warships in return for which the Austrians should be permitted to annex Bosnia and Herzegovina, which they had been administering since 1878 in the name of the concert of Europe. A first-class diplomatic crisis now occurred when Aerenthal suddenly annexed Bosnia, despite the fact that England and France were apparently unwilling to permit the opening of the straits. Neither France nor England was disposed to back Russia in this abrupt tearing-up of the Treaty of Berlin; the Young Turks had no intention of quietly permitting Russian warships to move back and forth in front of Constantinople; and the Serbs were enraged at not being consulted and considered that the annexation of Bosnia with its large Serbian population was a direct attack on their nationalistic aspirations. Why not then another international congress to review the work done in 1878? The English and the French were agreeable to that but not the Germans or the Austrians, who had no intention of attending another Algeciras. Germany and Austria would consent, they said, only if acknowledgment were given in advance that the Bosnian annexation was accepted. Russia now was in an uncomfortable dilemma; the Serbs were pressing hard for Russian help, and French and British aid was lacking. The Kaiser saw his opportunity and brought diplomatic pressure to bear on St. Petersburg to recognize the annexation. Russia was in no condition for war; she was too exhausted after her conflict with Japan. Therefore Russia yielded: She did not get the straits but Austria did obtain Bosnia. As a distinguished historian puts it: "The weakness of Russia was revealed to the world, the Straits remained closed, the minister's prestige at home and abroad was shattered, the central empires were triumphant, the Western powers dismayed."

The German victory in the Balkans was more than counterbalanced by renewed friction with England. In the background of Anglo-German relations there always lay the naval situation, a dangerous ground for disagreement after the Germans began building rapidly in the first decade of the twentieth century. A naval race between the two countries, however, could scarcely be said to have existed until the British virtually started one by laying down in 1905 the *Dreadnought*, the first super-battleship. Whereupon the Germans followed suit. As both powers then began to construct this new type of huge battleship, Britain's superiority in naval vessels showed a relative decline since the pre-dreadnought type, in which she possessed a tremendous preponderance, became less and less important.

In England the Liberals were in office pledged to expensive social reform. They had no zest for more battleships and they hoped to set an example by only authorizing two dreadnoughts for the year 1908. A new German navy law at this same date paid no attention to this British naval move: the German law authorized four capital ships a year from 1908 to 1911, and not until after that was the rate of increase halved to two yearly. This resulted in a hasty conference in Berlin between British and German representatives which ended in recrimination. Thereupon a naval panic swept through England in 1909. "We want eight and we won't wait" was the popular slogan, as England insisted on maintaining the two-power standard, the English navy to be on a par with any two other navies in the world.

In Germany there was a hot dispute concerning this naval rivalry. Bülow, the chancellor, was for concessions and for slowing down the German rate of construction to three capital ships a year. All he wanted, he claimed, was a "risk navy," in other words, one sufficiently powerful to make it very dangerous to attack Germany. Von Tirpitz, however, head of the German admiralty, was in favor of pushing construction ahead at top speed. The Kaiser flitted from one side to the other but tended more frequently to rest on Tirpitz's perch than on that of Bülow. The British now went in for superdreadnoughts and six of their eight ships authorized in 1908 were of this variety. The result of this was to make the Germans change their plans and build superdreadnoughts also, a fact which delayed their program so that by 1912 instead of the thirteen great ships which the British had prophesied, the Germans had but nine whereas at the same date the British possessed eighteen.

This naval rivalry lay in the background of the next international crisis which arose in 1911. It came about as the result of the fast-moving Moroccan situation. Scarcely had the ink become dry on the agreement of Algeciras than the French began to strengthen their hold upon Morocco. In order to punish mutinous tribesmen near the Algerian frontier, they occupied villages in eastern Morocco; in order to quell anti-European riots at Casablanca on the Atlantic, they despatched thither an army of several thousand. Aggressive acts like the above brought about the downfall of Sultan Abdul-Aziz, a Francophil, and the elevation of his brother Mulay Hafid, a Francophobe. But Mulay Hafid now leaned like his brother upon the French for support, for they had money. The bankers at Paris paid his debts in return for new concessions, and then fresh revolts broke out, this time directed against Mulay Hafid. The capital, Fez, was said to be endangered and to protect that city the French occupied it with an army early in 1911.

How long were the French to stay in Fez? The Quai d'Orsay really could not say; evacuation would take place when order was restored. The Germans grew uneasy as the weeks passed; they recalled the British occupation of Alexandria and Cairo and came to the conclusion that the end of Moroccan independence was not far away. Should that happen the Germans felt that some colonial pickings elsewhere might as well be gathered by the Fatherland. They began a number of conferences with the French ambassador at Berlin for a quid pro quo, but the French seemed unwilling to make definite offers. The Germans then tried to force the issue. They sent a small gunboat, the *Panther,* to the Atlantic coast of Morocco and stationed it off the seaport of Agadir to protect, they said, certain German merchants, who were in danger there.

Whether this was political blackmail or not it at least hastened the willingness of the French to negotiate. The German demand was for the French Congo in return for a free hand in Morocco. The French were horrified that Germany should expect so much, and the latter country was said to have countered by offering to throw her colony of Togo into the bargain. Then came the intervention of England. That country, not having been consulted, was indignant and demanded an explanation of the *Panther's* spring. Before the German reply reached England, Lloyd George, the radical chancellor of the exchequer, made an inflammatory speech in which, in indirect fashion, he hinted at war. His words were rather strong for pre-War diplomacy, and Germany was deeply insulted when her own bad manners were imitated.

During August, 1911, peace hung in the balance. The English seemed quite willing to fight but nobody else was. The financial condition of Germany was none too pleasant; Russia warned France that she probably would not participate in a war unless France made concessions in Central Africa, and in France herself, the pacifist Caillaux was temporarily in power. In consequence France ceded Germany more than 100,000 square miles in the French Congo adjacent to the German colony of Kamerun and of very little value. Germany recognized France's right to a protectorate over Morocco. This ended the crisis of 1911, a very strange one, indeed, and only to be explained as far as England is concerned by her constant worry about Germany's fleet and her maritime ambitions. For Agadir, it must be remembered, was not inland but on the Atlantic.

One result of this crisis was a great speeding-up of the German naval program. This disturbed the British who sent their secretary of state for war, Lord Haldane, to see if something could not be done to stay the hand of the German admiralty. The Germans were not of one accord in regard to their shipbuilding program. Von Bethmann-Hollweg, the chancellor, thought it very undesirable to endanger Anglo-German relations further by still greater naval appropriations, and at times it seemed as though he had the ear of the Kaiser. But Admiral Tirpitz persuaded his Imperial Majesty that a further increase in the German fleet was imperative.

The German program primarily was directed at an enormous increase in personnel which called for four-fifths of the entire navy being permanently in commission. It meant also new battleships and new cruisers, a total by 1920 of forty-one battleships, twenty battle cruisers, and forty small cruisers. That program the Germans intimated they might modify or withdraw if a satisfactory political agreement could be had; which meant, from their point of view, an ironclad promise of neutrality on the part of England in case Germany became involved in a Continental war. This Haldane could not offer, nor would the British cabinet hear of it. The British would promise not to join in any unprovoked attack on Germany, but that was as far as they would go.

So the Haldane mission proved a fiasco with most serious results. Great Britain could and did build up her fleet against Germany's, but, expensive as that proved to be, it was not the gravest result of the Haldane failure. There was another card that Britain played at this time: she entered into a naval agreement with France. That country agreed to concentrate her fleet in the Mediterranean, there to guard British interests (by implication) while Britain moved her larger ships from the Mediterranean to the Channel and the North Sea to guard (by implication) French ports on the Channel and on the Atlantic. Accompanying this change in the location of their respective fighting craft there was an exchange of letters between Sir Edward Grey and Cambon, French ambassador at London. The letters expressly stated that this agreement in the stationing of the warships was not to be interpreted as a restriction of the freedom of either government, that it was not to bind them to come to each other's military assistance. If, however, either government had reason to suspect an unprovoked attack by a third power, then consultation in common was to be taken by England and France for the purpose of preventing aggression and preserving peace.

This was the closest that England ever came to making an alliance with France. From the point of view of the French, these letters bound England to come to France's aid if attacked by Germany. Some Englishmen were to agree to this later, some to differ.

Three Little Wars

We turn now to the Mediterranean and to the Balkan Peninsula where three little wars, of 1911, 1912, and 1913 respectively, were destined to become three little curtain raisers for the world tragedy of 1914-18.

The first of these wars was fought in 1911 by Italy against Turkey. The Italians saw their chance in 1911 and took it. In the midst of all the excitement of that year of Agadir, it seemed relatively unimportant that Italy should occupy Tripoli. There was nothing to prevent her doing so, since long ago she had secured France's blessing and that carried with it England's tacit consent. Germany and Austria were her allies and could not well object. There was, of course, Turkey, and Tripoli was a part of the Ottoman Empire. But that ancient vestige of an empire was in sorry plight with a revolution on its hands, and consequently Italy did not expect much if any resistance to her ultimatum that Tripoli be handed over to her.

The Turks, however, showed fight. Their scanty troops in Tripoli retreated to the interior oases from whence they could harass the invaders, and what was more important, Turkey refused to sue for peace. What were the Italians to do? They occupied the Turkish island of Rhodes and the Dodecanese archipelago; they bombarded the forts at the entrance of the Dardanelles: but the Turks did nothing except expel Italians from the Turkish empire and close the Dardanelles to the shipping of all nations. The mobilization of both fleet and army was proving very expensive to the Italians and the war might have dragged on indefinitely had not the whole Near Eastern Question been reopened by it. The Bulgars, Greeks, Serbs, and the men of Montenegro now saw their chance. Clever diplomacy, very largely Greek and Russian in its origin, healed for the time being ancient jealousies among these Balkan peoples and they prepared to take the warpath against the Ottomans.

Turkey, then, confronted with the likelihood of another war, and this time against the Balkan States, made peace with Italy. In the autumn of 1912 the treaty was signed. Tripoli was yielded informally to Italy, and the Italians agreed to withdraw from the islands which they had

captured, once Tripoli was completely pacified. The Italians still occupied in 1941 those islands; their promise to withdraw was but a polite
gesture, for they could always claim that any little riot anywhere in
Tripoli was evidence that pacification had not been completed.

As the Italian-Turkish War drew to a close a new one commenced,
this time between Turkey and the Balkan States. It was brief and decisive as far as its military features are concerned, and was followed in
1913 by a second war in the same area, also brief and decisive. These
two Balkan wars form an integral part of the history of the Eastern
Question; they also are intimately correlated with the diplomacy antecedent to the World War of 1914-18. Their diplomatic aspects will be
treated in this chapter; their military history is in the second chapter on
the Eastern Question.

There were a number of factors which helped bring about the united
front of the Balkan States against Turkey.

Among them were: (a) the success of Austria in annexing Bosnia,
which created fear in Bulgaria and Greece as well as in Serbia, lest it
be but the forerunner of an Austrian thrust down into Macedonia, thus
bringing an end to the territorial ambitions of all the Balkan States;
(b) the recent success of the Albanians in resisting the Turks, which indicated that the strength of the Turkish army had been overestimated;
(c) the encouragement of Russian diplomats who were striving hard to
bring about Balkan unity; and (d) the Italian attack on Tripoli which
not only gave renewed evidence of the weakness of Turkey but also
demonstrated that the European concert was either unable or unwilling
to prevent local wars. In consequence there followed a series of Balkan
alliances and understandings binding Bulgaria, Montenegro, Serbia, and
Greece together and a formal demand of these four allies upon Turkey
for drastic reforms in Macedonia.

The concert of Europe now swung into action. The Austrian and
Russian ambassadors (the latter presumably with tongue in cheek)
handed in at each of the Balkan capitals a solemn warning that the six
Great Powers would attend themselves to Macedonian reforms and if,
despite their wishes, "war did break out they would not admit at the
end of the conflict any modification of the territorial status quo of
European Turkey."

One hour after the delivery of this note the Montenegrin representative
at Constantinople asked for his passports and on his way home stated at
Bucharest: "Montenegro wants territorial increase and will not give back
whatever conquests she makes." Almost simultaneously the first Balkan
war began—Serbia, Bulgaria, Montenegro, and Greece against Turkey.

These two wars in the Balkans, 1912-13, were to hasten and in part to
cause the European holocaust of 1914-18. That, of course, had many
roots—Alsace-Lorraine, Morocco, Anglo-German commercial and indus-

trial and naval rivalry—but no single one was more important than the conflicting aims and ambitions of Austria and Russia in the Balkan Peninsula, the former country determined that come what might, Serbia should not succeed in becoming "the little Piedmont of the South Slavs," drawing into her fold the restive Slovenes and Croats of Austria-Hungary and the rebel Serbs of Bosnia, the latter country equally resolved that the Slavic folk of southeastern Europe should realize their nationalistic ambitions and that, too, with the aid and assistance of Russia. Since this was so; since Germany was tied to Austria, France to Russia, and England partially tied to France, it was evident that new and severe international crises were imminent if there should be any violent change in the territorial status quo in the Balkans.

Both Balkan wars were to result in such changes. In the first one the Bulgars, Serbs, and Greeks won amazing victories over Turkey. In fewer days than it took Moltke to burst the bubble of the Second Empire in 1870, the Balkan allies overwhelmed the Turks. Within one month the Bulgars routed the main Turkish armies twice and drove close to the defenses of Constantinople. Meanwhile, the Serbs struck south, forced the Turks out of Usküb, surrounded them at Monastir, and took 40,000 prisoners. And as they did so the triumphant Greeks not only pounced upon the Turkish islands in the Aegean, but pushing north and east captured Salonika at the mouth of the Vardar River. Turkey in Europe now practically had disappeared except for Constantinople and a few isolated fortresses, two of which in Albania were besieged by Montenegrins.

The Turk had been almost expelled from Europe. The four Balkan allies had won a smashing victory. If they avoided dissensions among themselves, and the Western Powers played them fair, their triumph meant nothing but good for the world. The Sick Man of Europe had been nearly relegated to Asia, where alone he belonged. The Macedonian problem seemed settled. Montenegro, Serbia, Bulgaria, and Greece had all received extensions of boundary which they sorely needed. The first Balkan war had appeared to justify itself by promising blessings to mankind.

This happiness was not to be; the allies had been the victims of the very magnitude of their victory. They had hoped to win a few square miles apiece and to force a Christian governor on Macedonia, after a hard, wavering war. Instead they had almost exterminated Turkey in Europe! But they did not find themselves at liberty, after their victory, to distribute their spoils according to the division compacts which they had made before commencing the joint campaign. Now, one of the prime objects of the war had been to get some kind of a fair outlet for Serbia, preferably upon salt water. The Serbs, soon after their first successes, had struck into Albania, forced their way over the mountains, and for a few proud, hopeful days their flag had floated at Durazzo beside the blue Adriatic.

Both Austria and Italy were determined that it should be hauled down; they were prepared to act in defense of an Albanian nationalist movement which Serbia was anxious to crush in the bud; they objected to a clear belt of South Slav territory reaching from the Danube to the Adriatic, for both Italy and Austria were Adriatic powers and it was not to their interest to have a Slav state perched on the eastern shores of that sea. And as a corollary Montenegro should be forced to relinquish Scutari, the Albanian fortress, on which she had set her heart. Since the Turks were now gone, an independent "Principality of Albania," they argued, should be set up under the protection of the powers, who were to provide it with a respectable sovereign.

The situation, therefore, was as follows. Bulgaria had seized most of Thrace, and by its location neither Greece nor Serbia could have that territory. But the Bulgars were also intensely interested in getting a great part of Macedonia. Here were the "unredeemed" lands of their people, and it was largely for them that King Ferdinand's armies had rushed to war. By the compacts made before the struggle began, Bulgaria was certainly to be given a great extension in Macedonia. Serbia and Greece could not deny this letter of the bond. But they could argue, with much moral emphasis, that conditions had utterly changed. *They* had expected (Greece indeed less than Serbia) to get their reward in Albania. From Albania they had been excluded by the fiat of the Great Powers. Was it just that, with Serbia denied nearly all her expected gains and Greece also part of them, Bulgaria should continue to exact her pound of flesh in Macedonia? The net result of that would have been to give Bulgaria the most of *both* Thrace and Macedonia and her allies very little new land anywhere. Obviously, here was a case which could be very dangerous if handled by the ungentle methods of Balkan diplomacy.

The European chancellories were highly exercised over this situation and urged immediate termination of the war. The Turks were agreeable, and in May, 1913, the Treaty of London ostensibly brought it to an end. Turkey ceded to the Balkan States not only all of her territory in Europe a short distance beyond Constantinople but also the island of Crete. But no proviso was drawn in this treaty as to how the spoils of war should be divided. Italy and Austria stood firm in regard to Albania, the Bulgars firm in regard to Macedonia, and none could foretell the outcome.

This situation led to the second Balkan war (June-July, 1913) in which Bulgaria fought alone against her former allies, Greece and Serbia, and a new foe, Rumania.

That war came about as follows: it was very much to the interest of Russia that her Balkan protégés should not fall to fighting among each other, and the Czar offered to arbitrate the division of land won by the first Balkan war. It was very much to the interests of Austria (the constant enemy of Serbia) that the reverse should take place and it pleased Austria highly when the Bulgars proved very truculent, threatening to seize by force Macedonian land occupied by Serbs and Greeks. The latter formed a military alliance against Bulgarian attack and just in time. Without warning the Bulgars treacherously hurled themselves on the Serbs and Greeks, only to be badly beaten, the Greeks pursuing them over the mountains into their homeland. As this happened Rumania invaded Bulgaria from the north and Turkey struck at her erstwhile foe, now helpless. The Bulgars surrendered at discretion; there was nothing else for them to do.

There followed a peace treaty, that of Bucharest (1913). Bulgaria was all but expelled from Macedonia; she lost land to Rumania on the northeast, and even most of her gains in Thrace. Rumania gained at the expense of Bulgaria 2,687 square miles and 286,000 inhabitants. Serbs and Greeks had triumphed and they did so handsomely, Serbia nearly doubling her territory, annexing 15,000 square miles in Macedonia and about 1,500,000 people, Greece gaining 18,000 square miles and an added population of about 1,700,000.

The second Balkan war was now over. In a certain sense both conflicts might be regarded as frontier wars occurring in an out-of-the-way corner of Europe, and the fact that they were concluded without any of the six Great Powers taking up arms seemed to the optimistic a hopeful sign. Europe had passed through crisis after crisis in the twentieth century successfully, two in Morocco in 1905 and 1911, and two in the Balkans in 1908, and again in 1912-13. Surely this must augur well for the future; surely those prophets of gloom who had shaken their heads at the very mention of the Balkans ever since 1878 and the Treaty of Berlin must acknowledge themselves mistaken. The errors of that treaty were now largely liquidated; the Turks had practically been expelled from Europe; Balkan nationalism had received due recognition; Bulgaria had been treated roughly, it is true, but so condign had been the punishment meted out to her that it might be many decades before she could dispute the mastery of Macedonia with Greece and Serbia.

On the other side of the ledger there were, of course, imponderables. How strong a force, for instance, was Pan-Germanism with its drive toward southeastern Europe; how strong Russian Pan-Slavism thrusting in that same direction; could a conflict between them be avoided? The defeat of Turkey was to some extent a blow at German prestige and the victory of Serbia an even greater one to Austria, Germany's ally. Austria, with Italy's help, had kept Serbia landlocked, away from the Adriatic; but she had been unable to prevent the aggrandizement of her troublesome neighbor who had never become reconciled to the Austrian annexation of Bosnia in 1908. Now, even more than before, Serbia could be counted Austria's implacable foe.

One more year of peace remained to Europe and during it the powers which were the more conciliatory were England and Germany. Neither country wanted war, and both made gestures of peace toward one another while exercising a moderating influence on the two chief trouble-makers, Russia and Austria. Anglo-German disputes of long standing concerning the building of the Berlin-Bagdad Railway were amicably settled, and finally so by a curious irony of fate in July, 1914. Russia was wildly indignant at the appointment of a German general to re-organize the Turkish army but found England unwilling to protest. The Austrians, their jails in Bosnia and Croatia overflowing with rebellious South Slavs, thought seriously of trying to annex Serbia outright, but Germany restrained them.

The French, the Austrians, and the Russians, however, all vied with one another in heating troubled waters to the boiling point. France increased her loans to Russia for military service, elected Poincaré, an intense nationalist from Lorraine, to the presidency, and started to raise the term of service of the French conscripts to three years, thereby setting the pace for Germany to follow and that, too, rapidly, for the increase in the German army occurred as France debated the issue. Meanwhile, as we have seen, Austria delivered an ultimatum to Serbia in 1913 to evacuate in eight days a part of Albania which that country had occupied in order "to preserve order." Sazonov, Russian foreign minister, journeyed among the small countries of southeastern Europe, holding forth promises of territorial enlargement at Austria's expense, and early in 1914 the Russian government held a Crown Council at which the forcing of the Straits by a military coup was seriously debated. "In the summer of 1914 peace was at the mercy of an accident."

Summer, 1914

Then, on June 28, 1914, came the assassination of the heir to the Austrian throne, the Archduke Francis Ferdinand, and within five weeks Europe was plunged into the maelstrom of World War.

The murder took place in Sarajevo, capital of Bosnia, the murderer a youthful Bosnian student who was a member of the Black Hand, a secret society of Serbian terrorists. The deed aroused the horror of the whole civilized world, and sympathy for Austria was both deep and widespread in Entente countries as well as in those of the Triple Alliance.

Nearly a month passed before Austria took public action, time spent ostensibly in ferreting out the instigators of the crime, time more largely devoted in bringing about an agreement between Tisza, Prime Minister of Hungary, and Berchtold, the Dual Monarchy's foreign secretary, for

the Magyar statesman was for caution, whereas the Austrian whose ideas prevailed was for condign punishment of Serbia and immediate aggression against that country.

On July 23, an Austrian ultimatum was delivered at Belgrade which, in addition to demanding apologies and pledges to refrain from anti-Austrian propaganda in the future, stipulated that Austrian representatives should participate in Serbian trials and that Serbia remove from her employ "all officers and functionaries guilty of propaganda against the Austro-Hungarian Monarchy whose names and deeds the Austro-Hungarian Monarchy reserve to themselves the right of communicating to the Royal Government." Forty-eight hours was given for the reply.

The Serbian reply was submissive in tone but in substance only partially so; to some of the Austrian demands it yielded and to none did it give a pointblank refusal. Nevertheless, within half an hour after the receipt of the Serbian reply the Austrian ambassador had left Belgrade, bag and baggage.

Austria and Russia now started to mobilize. On July 28, Austria declared war on Serbia; on August 1, Germany, realizing that Russia was mobilizing against her as well as Austria, declared war on the country of the Czar; on August 3, on the refusal of the French to give guarantees of neutrality, she declared war on France; on August 4, her troops invaded Belgium; and on August 4, England declared war on Germany.

How did it happen that Europe, having successfully weathered crisis after crisis in the twentieth century, succumbed to this one; what country, what government, or, indeed, what individual should be held the more largely accountable? The first question is difficult to answer; the second is impossible. Possibly in the last analysis the reason why this particular crisis became unsurmountable was because it came so quickly, without premonition. That atonement must be made by Serbia for the Archduke's murder was generally agreed, but only the general tenor of the ultimatum delivered by Austria was known by Germany, and the text was not available until it was too late to make changes. Equally unpredictable was the immediate rush of Russia to Serbia's aid. In consequence there were only a few days granted to men of good will to fight for peace. Fear paralyzed action during this last week of July, and the militarists had their way.

Nor can any single power justly be accused of bringing on the World War, or any group of powers. Beyond doubt and beyond cavil it became clear afterwards that the Serbian government was guilty of knowing in advance that there was a plot against the Archduke which it made no effort to prevent; but Serbia was not one of the European Powers. How the latter reacted to the crisis we shall now describe, since the picture may be seen better if we paint it country by country rather than day by day.

The responsibility of Austria was heavy in that she used the death of Francis Ferdinand as an excuse for destroying Serbian independence. The Austrians neither expected nor wanted their ultimatum to be accepted and they drew it up with confident hope of its rejection. They were determined, a priori, to make war on Serbia. Furthermore, the Austrians, secure in their knowledge that they could depend on Germany, refused to listen to any warnings from Russia, from England, or even from their own ally. The Germans raised very pertinent objections to what the Austrians were doing, as we shall see later, but to them the Austrians apparently were completely deaf; to the many telegrams coming from Berlin they returned the vaguest replies, and even those that they did make were frequently so belated as to be worthless. Austria may justly be accused of dragging her own ally and all of Europe into the abyss.

So also, however, does Russia stand accused; the case against her is quite as black as that against Austria. In regard to Russia there are dark surmises; there are also demonstrated facts. As an illustration of the former, let us take the activities of the Russian ambassador at Belgrade who died as the war began. He was a notorious Austrophobe and on intimate terms with various Serbian officials who were privy to the plot which killed the Archduke. Was the ambassador conversant with it also? We can prove nothing. What we can prove is that Russia first began mobilization on a big scale and that the Russians lied about it to the Germans. Sazonov, the Russian foreign minister, first suggested that mobilization be partial only and directed simply against Austria-Hungary. He was persuaded by the military men that partial mobilization was impractical, and the Czar signed an order for general mobilization on July 29. True, he shortly after cancelled this order but, owing to the pressure of the general staff, renewed it the following day. When the Bolshevists came to power in 1917 they placed on trial a number of high officials of the Czar's government, and the Russian chief of staff testified that the German ambassador at St. Petersburg protested to him against Russia adopting general mobilization in July, 1914, only to be told by the chief of staff on his honor as a gentleman that there was no truth in the rumor. "And all the time I had the order for general mobilization in my pocket," said the chief of staff.

Mobilization, it must be remembered, was considered generally by military men as tantamount to war. The Franco-Russian armies, as far as numbers went, were decidedly superior to those of the Triple Alliance. Once give Russia all the time she wanted to mobilize, and victory presumably would be hers.

Both Germany and France were less responsible for initiating the war in 1914. The old accusation against the Germans, the "Potsdam Plot," has been proved pure myth. In accordance with it the Kaiser is said to have summoned to Potsdam in July his principal military, naval, and civilian advisers together with certain key men in the world of business and finance and to have asked them if they were ready for war. They all reported that they were prepared except the financiers who asked for more time. This was given them and to allay suspicions the Kaiser went on a yachting trip to Norway. The only truth in the story is that the Kaiser took his cruise; most of the men named as participating in this plot were known to have been elsewhere. As a matter of fact it would have been decidedly better if there had been a crown council at Potsdam; in that case Germany would not have treated the entire crisis with such cavalier indifference as she did during its earlier stages. With almost criminal negligence the Germans told the Austrians to go ahead and that Germany would support them. This was the German "blank cheque" to Austria.

But on behalf of Germany it must be remembered that she tried during the last week of peace to prevent Austria from cashing that cheque. The Kaiser was pleased with the submissive character of the Serbs' reply to the Austrian ultimatum and considered it both unnecessary and unwise for Austria to proceed further. Even after Austria's declaration of war on Serbia the Kaiser urged his ally to be content with the occupation of the capital of Serbia across the Danube and to make no further conquests. "Halt in Belgrade" was the advice from Berlin.

The Austrians, however, paid no attention to these admonitions coming from Berlin, not even at the very end of July when it was almost inevitable that all Europe would be involved in disaster unless Austria was willing to delay. The German ambassador at London wired Berlin that England might become involved unless Austria's hand was stayed and Berlin relayed the warning to Vienna. And still later Berlin added: "We must earnestly and emphatically urge upon the consideration of the Vienna cabinet the adoption of mediation. . . ." The Germans now were seeking to undo the harm their careless promise of assistance had caused; but their Austrian allies refused to listen. No ultimatum from Berlin to Vienna, threatening nonsupport unless the Austrians did thus and so, was ever sent. The German chancellor was worried, but not so the German General Staff, which looked forward happily to a war for which it was well prepared.

What of France? Her responsibility for the war is less susceptible of proof than that of Germany, but possibly it may have been as great. Did the French give a blank cheque to Russia and, unlike their German neighbor, fail to protest its cashing? There is not a scintilla of documentary evidence to prove this, but there is circumstantial evidence to indicate its possibility, perhaps even probability. As far as we can judge France did very little to stop the war. A long telegram, somewhat ambiguously worded, was sent to Russia from Paris on July 30 which stated that it would be "opportune" for Russia not immediately to take steps which would give Germany a pretext for "a total or partial mobilization." In no sense of the word, however, could this message be considered a veto on Russian mobilization or even, for that matter, a solemn warning. Poincaré, the French president, does not seem to have been disturbed by the course of events and Isvolski, at that time Russian ambassador at Paris, even gloated over the situation, claiming afterward that he had brought on the war.

Isvolski's words, however, need to be discounted heavily; his previous career had not heightened his reputation for truthfulness. On the other hand, Poincaré was visiting St. Petersburg at the time of the assassination and the French president at that time had lauded the Franco-Russian alliance. Furthermore, the French ambassador at the Czar's court in his memoirs let slip a most interesting account of how the Russians informed him of their mobilization and how it made him *sursauter* (jump) with excitement since he knew this meant war. But the Frenchman warned his informant that he, Paléologue, was only the political representative of the French government and that any information concerning military matter should be reported not to himself but to the French military attaché.

To England a fairly clean bill of health may be given, up to at least Germany's declaration of war against Russia. Sir Edward Grey, foreign minister, did his best to preserve peace by suggesting first, direct mediation between Russia and Austria, and secondly, a conference of the ambassadors of Germany, Italy, France, with himself in London. The first of these proposals was unwelcome to the French who were willing enough to have mediation between Serbia and Austria but not between Russia and Austria, since they were afraid that would weaken the Triple Entente; and the second was vetoed by Germany who felt that a conference consisting of France, England, Italy, and Germany would result in a three-to-one adverse vote since the Germans had no confidence in the good faith of the Italians. Beyond this Sir Edward Grey did little; but on the other hand, what could he have done? It has been suggested that he might have stopped the war by a direct threat to involve England in it on the side of France and Russia unless Germany bridled Austria; that he might have informed the French that England would not fight unless the Russians ceased to mobilize; that he might have made a direct appeal to Austria, based on England's ancient friendship with that country. Whether any of these three lines of action would have borne fruit it is impossible to say. Sir Edward was but one member of the British cabinet and the others were only partly informed on foreign affairs. The members of the cabinet were aware of the exchange of letters between Grey and the French ambassador which had taken place two years earlier (see p. 501) but this was not true of the House of Commons, ultimate source of authority in Great Britain in which were many pacifists. Sir Edward, therefore, was no free agent.

From the first of August, however, the date of the German declaration of war against Russia, the foreign policy of England was more open to question. Was that country in honor bound to France in case of war? The French were quite certain that she was and the French ambassador at London asked Grey if England was willing to erase the word "honor" from the dictionary when he refused to commit himself. Then, on August 2, the English recognized limited liability, at any rate when they guaranteed the French coast against naval attack from Germany—the result of the exchange of letters. But beyond this was England obligated to stand by France? Nobody knew, least of all the Germans, who were very curious to discover and besought Sir Edward again and again for information but without result.

On August 4, British qualms were laid at rest by the invasion of Belgium. Here again Sir Edward refused to state in advance what England's position would be and the Germans had to guess at it. They took a chance and lost; but of course they might have gone through Belgium anyway in their desire quickly to dispose of the French.

England certainly was under treaty obligation (as was Germany) not herself to violate Belgian neutrality; but whether she was under obligation to fight other countries to prevent it is open to question. Such, presumably, had not been the belief of Gladstone when, during the Franco-Prussian War he had made supplementary treaties with France and Prussia agreeing to war against France should France violate Belgium and vice versa. England, it was noted, made no protest against the violation of Luxembourg's neutrality, yet her obligation to prevent such an act was similar to her obligation to Belgium. It is of course possible to argue that Britain interpreted her Belgian obligations purely in terms of self-interest. Belgium was on the seacoast and Luxembourg was not. In the days of Philip II of Spain, in those of Louis XIV of France, and in those of Napoleon Bonaparte she fought to prevent the Low Countries from falling completely into the maw of any great European power. Self-interest now indicated that she do likewise; that is evident. None the less, in so doing, England did support, and ultimately help to rescue, a small nation which, innocent of all warmongering, was in no way responsible for the world conflict.

Chapter 27

THE FIRST WORLD WAR (1914-16)

GERMANY WAS the foremost military power in Europe. In peace time the Kaiser had in the neighborhood of 800,000 troops actually with the colors; but owing to her reserves Germany was able to put under arms nearly 5,000,000 men and still leave a sufficient number of civilians for necessary industries, transportation, and agriculture. Her ally, Austria, was more poorly organized. At the outset she was not able to mobilize more than 2,000,000, although as time passed her large population enabled her to conscript larger numbers.

Russia, on paper, was the most important foe of the central empires. The Czar was reputed to have 1,500,000 Russians in barracks, even in days of peace. At mobilization this total was lifted to 5,000,000, and behind these were indefinite further millions if arms and officers could be found.

France, with a population two-thirds that of Germany, maintained a peace army approximately equal to that of her rival, and on paper slightly larger. Owing to rigorous conscription, trained reserves were large, and the Third Republic faced the crisis with rather more than 3,700,000 soldiers; but behind them was only two-thirds the manpower east of the Rhine.

As for the British Empire, if the continental system of conscription had been enforced, King George could have mobilized 4,000,000 or more troops. As it was, England, still clinging to her old professional army, had perhaps 250,000 regular troops in it, 160,000 of whom had been allocated for an expeditionary force.

Finally, Turkey and Italy had respectively 200,000 and 300,000 peacetime troops, and about 1,000,000 and 1,500,000 more subject to mobilization.

It thus became evident that battles in this war were apt to be unimportant unless hundreds of thousands were involved. Repeatedly in the First World War the fighting swayed continuously along enormous fronts with nearly 2,000,000 men at each other's throats. In the forty-seven days of the Argonne battle the Americans alone had over 1,000,000 engaged. By the time the war ended the British Empire had over 5,000,000 men in her armies and the United States nearly 4,000,000. And as they did so the Continental powers, except Russia, exhausted every resource to replace their war losses. The upkeep of all these soldiers required civilian armies as well as military. The railroad workers, the metal workers, the miners of coal and iron, the sailors on transports, the workers in factories were as essential as machine gunners in the trenches. Food problems became as important as those of high strategy. Economic waste was incalculable. "War" had once involved at most the hiring of a few thousand mercenaries and the devastation of a few counties. "War" now involved throwing to the winds the principles of sound finance, floating bond issue after bond issue, multiplying bank notes, spending on every conceivable object from heavy artillery to foreign press propaganda.

Everywhere it was assumed that when the war was over the foe would do the paying; everywhere, also, the working class was kept from striking by constant increase in pay as well as by promises of "a new day" after victory. The war affected the home of nearly every man and woman and the diet of nearly every child. It was to cost over seven million lives and was to spread poverty, disease, and starvation throughout most of Europe.

For the first time in history war became three-dimensional: from the air, on the land, below the surface of the sea. The airplane made its debut for scouting purposes, and as the war advanced certain other new factors came into play. In 1914 the submarine was an experiment, regarded by some as a dangerous toy, by others as an irresistible craft. In practice it proved neither. Once having learned to deal with it, warships were fairly safe from its attacks; but from 1915 on it became a matchless destroyer of commerce. The automobile and the auto truck now made their debut in war, and after two years came the armored caterpillar car, the tank, a moving fort which crossed trenches, crushed barbed wire, and drove a highway for advancing infantry. And also there was poison gas, at first sent drifting upon the wind and then later flung at great range in artillery bombs.

The Schlieffen Plan and the First Marne

The older Moltke had died in 1891, having devoted the last twenty years of his life to rendering his war machine increasingly effective, and after him Count von Schlieffen, as chief of general staff, had continued endless preparation for the next war. Under his direction a meticulously detailed plan had been made ready for the invasion of France by way of Belgium. Within forty days after the declaration of war the French armies were to be enveloped, then annihilated, and the German host was to pour into Paris. Meanwhile, the Germans would stand on the defensive in the east with about one-fourth of their troops, but the moment the French had been rendered impotent the superb German railroad system would shift most of the Kaiser's divisions to the Vistula. Deprived of her ally, feeble in her industrial development, demoralized by Czarist misrule, Russia would sue for peace. England was discounted. She might, possibly, enter the war and land 100,000 troops in France; but it was thought they would arrive too late to save Paris. After France was done for, and with Russia crying for mercy, then Germany would negotiate with the mistress of the seas, or fight her, as the occasion might warrant.

The Germans dashed to the war like salmon to the sea. For forty-three years their war machine had been perfected for this vital moment; all was ready, not merely guns and ammunition but enough field glasses for every officer, and any quantity of proclamations urging Poles to rise against their Russian oppressors, for use when the German armies turned against Warsaw. The troops left Berlin assured victors with "Pleasure trip to Paris" chalked upon their transport cars. Widely circulated was the alleged saying of the Kaiser, "By Christmas we will be home."

Belgium's turn came quickly. On the morning of August 4 the Germans swarmed across the border by horse, automobile, bicycle, and on foot. All had their weapons ready, the chauffeurs driving with one hand, a cocked revolver in the other. By night the good folk of Liége were awakened by a cannonade, the German field batteries exchanging their first salvos with the forts around the city.

The violation of Belgian neutrality was no surprise, not even to the Belgians. Their engineers had built seemingly impregnable forts around Liége, Namur, and Antwerp. Liége would halt invaders from Germany, Namur those from France, and Antwerp would be a haven of refuge for the Belgian army if overwhelmed in the field. But the German experts remembered the dictum of Clausewitz, "the pit of the stomach of the French monarchy is between Paris and Brussels." The best available military road into France lay across Liége province—therefore they would take it.

The Germans came on with the speed of the wind. Liége withstood them a few days, but the mobile howitzers of the German army pounded the Belgian forts into powder, and by the twentieth of August the invader was before Namur. Five days later this Belgian stronghold was in ruins and France lay open.

The French, meanwhile, instead of rushing to the aid of the Belgians, attacked the Germans in Alsace, captured a few villages and for a short time the city of Mulhouse. And now they were forced to confront the Teutonic tide at its crest, with only the help of some 70,000 British regulars thrown across the Channel. But the British "Tommies" and their French allies at least did not repeat the mistake of 1870; they were not surrounded. For ten sweating, bloody days they fought a rearguard action, frequently half-starved, and nearly dead with fatigue and loss of sleep. On came the Germans, too fast perhaps for their own good. By the fifth of September the First German Army under Kluck was at Meaux, fourteen miles from Paris. The French government was transferred to Bordeaux. Paris seemed doomed.

Then came the counterthrust, the first battle of the Marne. It began with a French attack on Kluck's right wing, so fierce that he was compelled to deplete his left wing to reinforce his right. By so doing, he left a gap between his left wing and the Second German Army, and into that gap drove the French and the well-nigh exhausted "old contemptibles" of England. There was now a wedge between the First and Second German Armies, and both were forced to retreat. Such, in major outline, was the turning point in the first Marne, a sanguinary battle which really stretched almost all the way from Paris to the eastern frontier. For the Germans it must be said that the Schlieffen plan never was carried out, since Kluck's army had been shorn of several divisions withdrawn for the German armies facing Russia. For the Allies, for the first time since the war started, came a taste of victory. They now pursued the enemy but could not catch him. Safe behind the Aisne River, the Germans dug themselves in.

Before the end of September the main conflict shifted to the north—to French Flanders and to Picardy. Hither dashed the British army, and as many French divisions as well, in a race to the sea, striving to crowd around the German right flank and to squeeze the Germans out of western Belgium. In this the Allies failed, and again the German artillery and superior organization stemmed retreat. King Albert, with the Belgian field army, was holding out hopefully behind the forts of Antwerp; but when the Germans fell upon him there were no troops available to help except a few brigades of British marines, and Antwerp fell. The Belgian field army retreated to the mouth of the little River Yser, to a tiny strip of Belgian land which it was to hold as long as the war lasted. The French and British meanwhile came up in time to cover the Channel ports, and as they did so the Germans tried to blast their way across the northern seacoast of France. Ypres, an old Flemish city, stood in their way. Its defense fell mainly on the British. For days the situation remained indescribably dubious as thousands fought in a mud-sea. By bulldog courage the British held on until the exhausted Germans quit. Early in November the first battle of Ypres ("Wipers," the Tommies called it) came to an end and the great deadlock on the western front began.

The War in the East

Meanwhile, across the seven thousand and more miles from Kurland to Kamchatka, millions leaped to arms at the behest of the great white Czar.

The danger to France was recognized at Petrograd, and an instant effort was made to divert Germany's attention. By the middle of August a Russian army forced the frontier and was in full advance on Königsberg. A second army struck northward from Russian Poland into East Prussia. At the very moment when the Germans rejoiced over their victories in Belgium there was a rush of terrified refugees into Berlin. The Cossacks were devastating East Prussia and alarmists were saying that the German soldiers must retreat to the line of the Vistula.

The Kaiser then summoned Hindenburg, a retired general, known to have made a close study of the system of marshes and barriers created by the Masurian lakes on the eastern frontier. While seated at a café in Hanover, he received a telegram appointing him commander-in-chief in East Prussia. His chief of staff was a younger general, Eric Ludendorff, who had already won fame before Liége. The two leaders had been placed in a partnership which was to influence the whole course of the war.

Hindenburg had inferior numbers, but he trusted to lakes and swamps to prevent the two Russian armies from joining. Within a few days after his appointment he sprung his trap. Caught in the treacherous lake district, entangled in swamps and forests, the Russians were assailed furiously on their flanks. By the end of August one army had been practically destroyed in the four-day battle of Tannenberg in which Hindenburg took 70,000 prisoners; and the other escaped only by precipitate retreat. Germany rang with the praises of Hindenburg and Ludendorff, who henceforth became the trusted heroes of the Empire.

But if Prussia flung back the Muscovites, not so with Austria. Late in August the Austrians undertook to invade Serbia and were repulsed ignominiously. And now, even as Hindenburg closed in on the Russians, two of the Czar's best commanders entered Galicia. They met with feeble resistance; Lemberg and a great part of Austrian Poland passed under the Czar's power; and in Petrograd the Russian victories caused rejoicings that effaced the mourning over Tannenberg.

Thus began the long tragedy of the campaigns on the eastern front, costing more in human loss and agony than even the wars of gods and titans in Picardy and Champagne; for here there was no long deadlock along a stabilized war zone, and enormous armies, sweeping backward and forward over wide regions, carried all the work of the devil with them.

After Tannenberg the Germans did their best to relieve the pressure on Austria by a drive on Warsaw. The Russians put up a skilful and stubborn defensive. Twice the Germans penetrated deep into Poland, but twice Russian valor and winter mud forced them back. The year 1914 closed with the Germans holding about one-quarter of Russian Poland, but with the Russians themselves holding nearly all of Galicia. They were pressing through the passes in the Carpathian Mountains and threatening the plains of Hungary; they were dangerously close to Cracow, the stronghold and key position at the western end of Austrian Poland; and they were blockading and starving out a large Hapsburg army, in a great entrenched camp around Przemysl. Germany thus defeated Russia, and Russia, Austria.

Nevertheless, by December, 1914, Russia was in dangerous plight. Nearly all the ammunition accumulated in the arsenals had been shot away, and the munition plants were inadequate for replacement. There was a growing shortage of all the tens of thousands of things which modern warfare requires and which only a great industrial country can provide. As early as October, 1914, the general at the head of the Czar's artillery is alleged to have gone weeping to the war minister: Russia, he said, would have to make peace owing to shortage of ammunition. Never before had the lack of sea doors counted so terribly against what was apparently a mighty empire. The Baltic was closed by the German fleet. Only a trickle of supplies could come in via the White Sea, frozen half the year, or via Vladivostok and the Trans-Siberian. The Black Sea route was closed by the hostility of Turkey. If, however, the water gates at Constantinople could only be opened, then Russia would be brought in contact with her allies once again; munitions would flow into Russia, and from that country would come surplus grain needed in the West. We turn now to efforts to open them.

Gallipoli

When the war clouds broke there were two German warships in the Mediterranean. The Allies assumed that they would run for shelter into the Austrian Adriatic, but instead they made for the Dardanelles. Not by accident had they steamed toward Constantinople. The Young Turk rulers had already given secret pledges to Berlin, and late in October, without any declaration of war, a combined German-Turkish fleet bombarded Odessa. The Czar replied by declaring war on Turkey, an action followed by France and England. Vast prospects were thus opened, thanks to the supposed influence of the Sultan, of an extension of the war to the east; and in Berlin there was now cheerful talk of the invasion of Egypt and even of India.

Around Turkey soon raged unlimited warfare. During the winter of 1914-15 there was fierce fighting in the Armenian mountains along the Caucasus frontiers. A Turkish attack on the Suez Canal ignominiously failed, and the British declared a direct protectorate over Egypt; but the Straits of Constantinople were, of course, now sealed to Russo-British commerce. The munition situation in Russia was already giving great anxiety in London, while on the other hand the food situation in England

From LET THERE BE SCULPTURE *by Jacob Epstein (published by G. P. Putnam's Sons, New York, 1940).*

LORD JOHN FISHER, FIRST LORD OF THE ADMIRALTY (1841-1920)

was growing uncomfortable, and the release of the great South Russian crop would assist enormously. Would not the defeat of Germany be hastened if the Dardanelles and the Bosporus were in Allied hands?

The Turkish forts at the Dardanelles were considered fairly formidable, but Liége, Namur, and Antwerp had not proved too difficult for the new artillery. In London the civilian head of the British admiralty was Winston Churchill, full of driving energy and high imagination. The British war office was under Lord Kitchener, highly honored for his victories in the Sudan, and Boer War. Kitchener was alive to the desirability of opening the Straits, but he already had promised the French heavy British reinforcements in Picardy, where there were great hopes of breaking the German front as soon as spring opened. He had no surplus troops available. Nevertheless, he let Churchill work out the problem of a British naval attack, although a land force would be needed in any case, if only to hold Constantinople after the navy had conquered it.

No enterprise that actually failed ever came nearer to justification. Its success would have convinced all the wavering Balkan kingdoms that the Allies were bound to triumph. The capture of Constantinople might have averted the agony of the Russian Revolution, might have rendered American intervention in the war unnecessary, and by ending the struggle two years earlier might have rendered a great service to Germany herself. All this hung on the razor-edge of fate during the spring and summer of 1915.

To reduce seacoast batteries by naval bombardment had hitherto been considered impractical, but the guns of the British battleships were powerful. Churchill was overwhelmingly convinced of the desirability of forcing the Straits, and although his naval experts in London questioned, they did not veto the enterprise. The older battleships of the British navy could be used, and their loss would not weaken the dreadnoughts holding the North Sea against Germany.

Turkish forces at the Straits were weak. As late as February, 1915, when the naval attack began, they numbered only 20,000, and were ill-organized, and widely scattered; and the forts were but poorly supplied with ammunition. There were 36,000 French and British troops available, and these once flung ashore, the defenders would have been demoralized and the fall of the forts well-nigh certain. But Kitchener neither sent his soldiers in time nor warned Churchill that if the British navy failed the British army could do nothing. There were orders and counterorders to the forces on the transports. There were intrigues with Greece (then neutral) to get a Greek army corps to strike a blow at its old foe, the Turk. On February 19, the British ships aided by a French squadron, attacked the outer forts of the Dardanelles and silenced them. Mine sweepers penetrated far up the waterway. In Constantinople panic reigned, and the Sultan's harem packed for a hasty trip to Asia.

The first progress was not followed up promptly. Not until March 18 did the Franco-British fleet at length attack the inner forts, the key to Constantinople. The bombardment proved less successful than was hoped; the batteries were not permanently silenced. Late in the day, two British and one French battleship struck mines in an area supposed to have been swept clear, and were sunk. Nevertheless, it was assumed everywhere that the naval attack would be renewed, and there is now competent evidence that the Turks were nearly at the end of their heavy ammunition.

But the British fleet had lost two battleships. It had been contrary to all naval axioms for ships to contend with forts. The technical heads of the admiralty had discovered that Kitchener was now willing to try to force the Dardanelles by a land attack, and were only too happy to pass the task on to the British army.

The Turkish forces were still few in number, and British troops had already been sent to the Dardanelles under Sir Ian Hamilton. But he found on arriving before the Straits that the transports had been so carelessly loaded that nearly everything needed for landing a great force and for fighting hard battles had been buried at the bottom of his transports. His ships therefore sailed away ingloriously to the nearest adequate harbor, Alexandria, to reorganize their cargoes; and the Turks had ample warning of what was coming.

A month earlier the Turks on the Gallipoli Peninsula, covering the Dardanelles, could have been defeated by a swift attack; in March they were more numerous but still outnumbered by the British. But by April, when the attack came, the Turks were equal in numbers and under the command of an experienced German, Liman von Sanders.

Despite underwater entanglements of barbed wire and shores lined with machine guns, the British threw themselves ashore near the tip of the peninsula. Their losses were terrible (nearly 19,000 in the first two weeks' fighting), but they made good their landing. To penetrate inland to the heights of Krithia was another matter, and soon the British and the Turks were looking at each other across two lines of trenches in a deadlock as complete as that in France. Hamilton nevertheless clung on, awaiting reinforcements without which nothing could be done.

Meanwhile, in London, owing to a cabinet crisis, Churchill ceased to be civilian head of the admiralty, and all projects for another naval attack lapsed. Kitchener ordered more troops to the Dardanelles, but they made haste slowly. At length, late in July, Hamilton had forces that three months earlier might have brushed the Turks aside like gossamer. But now, although he commanded 120,000, Sanders had approximately as many. The British, thanks to their command of the sea, were able to make a surprise landing at a new and unguarded point. A wholly new force was landed at Suvla Bay, up the peninsula to the north where (if success attended) the Turkish strongholds on the Straits could be over-whelmed from the rear. But it was now too late; the Turks were ready. Sanders had arrived at the scene of action together with his able lieu-tenant, Kemal Bey (later dictator of the post-War Turkish republic). The magnificent valor of the English, Australian, and New Zealand troops wore itself out against the stubborn and skilful resistance of the rein-forced enemy. By August the great attack had spent itself with none of the key positions taken. Hamilton had lost about 30,000 men in a single week and the entire campaign collapsed. Altogether the British lost at Gallipoli over 100,000 killed or wounded. The prestige of the great empire was shaken by this policy of "too little and too late."

Japan and Italy Enter the War

Meanwhile, two new allies joined the Belgians, the French, and the British. They were Japan and Italy, the former declaring war on Germany in August, 1914, the latter declaring war on Austria in May, 1915.

Concerning the entrance of Japan, little need be said. The statement of Count Okuma, head of the Japanese government, may be discounted. According to him,

not only in the Far East, but everywhere else that may be necessary, Japan is ready to lay down her life for the principles that the foremost nations will die for. It is to be in line with these nations that she is at that time opposing and fighting what she believes to be opposed to these principles. Japan's relation to the present conflict is as a defender of the things which make for higher civilization and a more lasting peace.

The real reason was quite different. Japan saw a golden opportunity to avenge herself on Germany for past wrongs and to seize the German colony of Kiauchow. It was true that Japan was bound to England by treaty, but only in case of an unprovoked attack upon either England or Japan in India or eastern Asia. Germany was making no attack there, and as Winston Churchill afterwards acknowledged, "no clauses in the Anglo-Japanese treaty entitled us to invoke the aid of Japan."

The case with Italy was much more complicated. That country was a member of the Triple Alliance; she also, as we may recall, had signed treaties with both England and France, thus having a foot in both camps. That she was entitled to remain neutral was juristically clear, since Austria had not consulted Italy in the critical June and July of 1914 in regard to her Serbian policy, thus breaking the terms of the Austro-Italian alliance. This in itself, however, scarcely justified Italy in deserting her old allies and siding with their foes; for Italy in this war simply put herself up at auction and sold herself to the highest bidder.

It was a long-drawn-out auction, lasting for months. The Germans were willing to offer Italy a good deal of Austrian territory for Italy's neutrality, and the Austrians reluctantly agreed to the cession of the South Tyrol, occupied mainly by Italians. But the Allies offered far more for Italy's active participation on their side—not only the South Tyrol but the city of Trieste, a large part of the Istrian Peninsula and of Dalmatia, Avlona in Albania, islands in the Aegean seized by Italy in her war with Turkey, and compensation in Africa if England and France annexed territory there after the war. This bargain was ratified by the Treaty of London (April, 1915), and in view of its terms it is interesting to note what Woodrow Wilson told the Italian Chamber of Deputies on his visit to Rome in 1919. "Then back of it all, and through it all," said the President of the United States, "running like the golden thread that wove it together, was our knowledge that the people of Italy had gone into this war for the same exalted principle of right and justice that moved our own people."

Italy thus projected herself into the conflict, but a great disappointment awaited her optimists. For political and sentimental reasons her campaign was directed against Trieste. Therefore her general, Cadorna, was destined to throw away his men, ultimately by hundreds of thousands, on the Austrian positions along the Isonzo and in struggling to capture the Carso plateau which commanded Trieste. All through 1915 the Italians continued this warfare, spending themselves against rock and ice with but trifling advance.

Russian Defeat, Bulgarian Entry, and Serbian Collapse (1915)

During the winter of 1914-15 the German military came to a new decision: they would stay on the defensive on the west and strike at the east on the blood-soaked plains of Poland. The German drive there in 1915 was under the command of one of William II's ablest field commanders, Mackensen, and it speaks well for the ability of the Russian generals that, despite a ruinous lack of ammunition, they were able to call back their troops involved in the Carpathian passes and to conduct an orderly and stubbornly contested retirement. No soldiers ever endured more ruthless punishment than did those of Nicholas II, last Czar of the Russias. During the first three months they fired more shells per day than their factories put out per month. They had plenty of men but no rifles to put into their hands, and only by the use of the bayonet could they halt the German advance. By September, 1915, the Russians had lost all they had gained and were driven back far beyond their own frontiers.

The Central Powers now turned their attention to the southeast. Throughout 1915 Bulgaria had been listening to offers from both sides, and had the Allies won instead of lost the Gallipoli campaign, Bulgaria would probably have yielded to their wooing. The Allies were hampered, however, by the auction held at Sophia; they had less to offer Bulgaria than the Central Powers. There was nothing, indeed, very tempting that they could offer, except Turkish territory which Bulgaria did not care for, and possibly a port on the Aegean, provided Greece might be willing to cede one in return for promises of Turkish land in Asia Minor.

What Bulgaria did want, and want very much, was Macedonian territory annexed by Serbia in 1913. Since Serbia was an ally of France and England, this land could not be decently ceded to Bulgaria without Serbian approval, and this the Serbs stanchly refused to give.

No such difficulty confronted the Germans. They were quite willing that Bulgaria should annex the Serbian conquests of 1913 in Macedonia. The Bulgars liked the German offer, and in the summer of 1915 it seemed as though Germany was winning the war. Therefore, they allied themselves with the Central Powers and agreed to hit at Serbia from the east as the Austro-Germans struck that unfortunate country from the north.

This meant the collapse of Serbia. The victorious Mackensen, in command of the Austro-German army, overran North Serbia in October, 1915, and the Bulgars almost simultaneously occupied their chosen districts in Macedonia. The Serbs, fighting bravely, retreated to Montenegro and northern Albania; but rapidly they were driven out of these mountain fastnesses. By the end of February, 1916, all that was left of the Serbian army was encamped on the Greek island of Corfu, safe for the time being because the Allies controlled the seas.

The Western Front (1915-16): Verdun

Along the western front, meanwhile, approximately four million men were deadlocked. Thousands of cannon and tens of thousands of machine guns sustained these hosts. Air combats were incessant.

At long intervals would come battles, offensives designed to master large sections of the hostile lines. These contests were usually quite alike: intense artillery fire, the rush of infantry over earthworks and barbed-wire entanglements partly destroyed by the guns, the counter-fire of the enemy, trenches won, the rush of the enemies' reserves, counter-attack, bombs, and bayonets. Then the offense would spend itself and the section of the front where it took place would settle down to standardized petty slaughter. Almost every such offense succeeded—that is, if pushed resolutely it could win a few lines of trench. Almost every such offense was defeated—never coming to a genuine breakthrough so that the enemy could be chased back into the open country. And all this went on continuously for nearly four years until new weapons and new warriors brought a return to something like a war of maneuver.

Both the French and the British tried their best in 1915 to break

through, the former in the Artois district and in Champagne, the latter
at Neuve Chapelle and at Loos. The results were disappointing. It proved
possible to demolish the German front-line trenches with comparative
ease, and even to capture parts of the second line. But behind this there
was always a third, bristling and formidable. Before the artillery could
be moved forward to destroy this barrier, the Germans were always able
to hurry forward reserves and to concentrate their own batteries on the

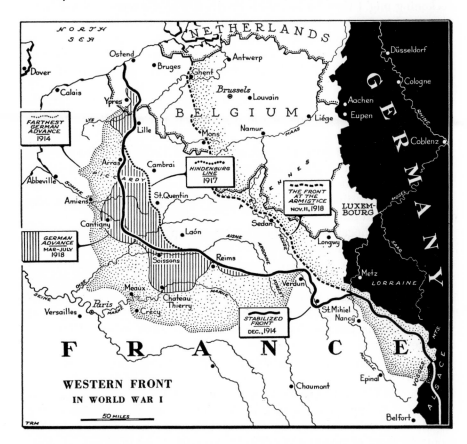

WESTERN FRONT
IN WORLD WAR I

50 MILES

chief points of danger. These inner trench lines simply could not be
stormed.

Then, as 1916 opened, the Germans in turn tried to recover the offensive on the western front. Germany had her own iron and coal; she was
also managing by desperate economies to get along with her own cereals;
nevertheless, the pressure of the British sea blockade, like the finger on
the wrestler's windpipe, was stifling the economic life of the Central
Powers. There was an especial absence of butter, lard, and all forms of
fat. Want of copper, rubber, cotton, and lubricating oils threatened. By

the end of 1915 Germany was already undergoing privation. British sea power was throttling her; what counterstroke was possible?

One possible form was the submarine, and another was a telling blow by land. Russia had been driven back about as far as it was safe to drive her. She must be left for the time being to her own miseries. Troops could be released from the eastern front for another offense against France; and if France could possibly be driven out of the war a reckoning might then be had with England. The Germans did not however, undertake a breakthrough on the main western front; they had learned the lesson of the Allies' failures of 1915. They resolved rather to win a startling success on a limited front; namely, by the capture of Verdun, the greatest of the barrier fortresses on the eastern frontier of the Third Republic.

Verdun had, indeed, been a pivotal position in the French military scheme since the beginning of the war. It was not an ordinary fortress but a vast entrenched camp, held by 175,000 men, and would never succumb to a mere park of siege-guns as did Liége and Namur. The Germans proposed to attack on a grand scale, using nineteen divisions. Preparations conducted with meticulous Prussian care were put through as secretly as possible and the French had only vague rumors as to where the blow would fall.

The attack began with a bombardment, up to that time the most severe recorded in history. It was maintained incessantly for nine hours, during which time the French trench system seemed annihilated and "the craters made by the huge shells gave all the country-side an appearance like the surface of the moon." The German infantry then went forward. But there were still Frenchmen alive in the midst of the chaos and their artillery in the rear had not been silenced. Both sides fed into the furnace of this incessant battle men, guns, and ammunition without stint, and around Verdun raged the fiercest and most sanguinary struggle of the entire war.

The great General Staff could not now break off its undertaking if it would. To relinquish the attack on Verdun meant a confession to the world of a great defeat. Every trench-line, salient, and petty hillock along the front of twenty-two miles became the scene of titanic conflict. Certain forts and important positions were taken and retaken, until their soil was drenched with blood. The famous cry of the French privates as this contest blazed hotter, *"They shall not pass!"* was more than a battle-cry; it was the expression of an inflexible will. The spirit of the defense was summed up in a scribbling found upon a wooden casing of a bomb-proof shelter in the French firing-line, near the center of the battle:

Mon corps à la terre,
Mon âme à Dieu,
Mon coeur à France.

Against this spirit, although the German Staff flung its armed men into the conflict as recklessly as it might fling coal into the furnace, victory was impossible. By sacrifices that threatened to cripple their war-machine, the Teutons, nevertheless, pressed the attack through April and May, for the prestige of Prussian militarism was at stake before its own people. By June the Germans were slowly working their way toward the inner defenses, but the French commanders were now simply sparring for time. They knew that Britain was about to make an unprecedented counterthrust. On July 1, 1916, began the Battle of the Somme, and the German lines in Picardy were in deadly peril.

The Somme

The British now came to the help of their ally. A larger part of the front was taken over from the French, and behind that sector there was an accumulation of guns and ammunition, calculated to outrival the German concentration at Verdun. The results were imposing; the country was ready for the major British offensive of 1916.

It began with the British raining shells, not on a narrow sector as at Verdun, but over a wide front, and it continued for six days. Then, on July 1, the British assaulted twenty miles of trenches just north of the Somme River while the French struck along the ten miles directly south. The artillery fire was withering, but the destruction wrought was incomplete. Much barbed wire was cut; but many machine-gun nests were still in action, and the German artillery in the rear had not been silenced. At the northern end of the battle line the British met with a stone-wall resistance and their assault there failed. On the south they made gains of one or two miles deep on a front of about seven miles. The French, under the skilful direction of Marshal Foch, met with somewhat greater success and with smaller losses—but nowhere was there a breakthrough in sight. So ended the first day of the Somme. But it was only the beginning. Haig and his men kept it up. The battle of the Somme was continued well into November, sometimes conducted fitfully, sometimes with rekindled fury. By the end of that time a wedge had been driven into the German lines along a front of over forty miles. The Allies had captured 350 guns and 65,000 prisoners, and the whole German loss was around 600,000. But the British losses had been about 450,000, the French 200,000. Technically, the Somme was an Allied victory, but it had brought no decision, and it was not able to avert one more great disaster to the Allies in the east—the overrunning of Rumania.

Russia and Rumania (1916)

Russia had been beaten in 1915, but not to her knees. In the winter of 1915-16 there was a revival of patriotic enthusiasm. The troops had kept their courage and morale, and the Czar had able generals. The result was that for the last time the war machine which Peter the Great had originally fathered went forward to new campaigns with some enthusiasm.

The Central Empires had considered the Muscovites so completely defeated that in May and June, 1916, the Austrians started an offensive from the Trentino against the Italians. But no sooner had it got under way than the Russians struck once more and the danger to Italy was averted. The troops of Francis Joseph had to be hurried back to Galicia, and even these would never have sufficed to prevent the undoing of Austria had not sixteen divisions of German veterans been withdrawn from the western front to hold back the Slavic deluge.

On June 4, 1916, all the replenished Russian cannon thundered and a few hours later their infantry charged. The brunt of the attack fell upon the Austrian armies commanded by the Archduke Joseph Ferdinand, and he, like so many Hapsburg commanders, let himself be caught unprepared. Many of his troops were Czechs with no zeal for the Vienna rulers, and they surrendered in droves. Within a few days the Russians had advanced fifty miles and had taken 70,000 prisoners. Bukovina was again overrun and the Russians seemed on the point of taking Galicia. Then German help arrived, "like lime to strengthen wet sand," and Austria was saved.

It is difficult to visualize "these dim, weird battles of the east" when, with imperfect equipment and by sheer reckless energy and disregard of sacrifices, the Russians strove to force a decision by means of a million men at constant grips with nearly as many Germans and Magyars. By August this Russian attack had spent itself; the ammunition accumulated during the winter was nearly exhausted; and within the czardom there were signs of demoralization. But the Russian successes were taken by the unfortunate Rumanians as merely an earnest of a still fiercer winter campaign, and late in August, 1916, the Rumanians forsook their neutrality and entered the war on the Allies' side.

The Rumanians, like the Bulgars and the Italians, sold themselves to the highest bidder. The Central Powers were quite willing to offer Bessarabia, Russian territory in which Rumanians were numerous; and the Allies were quite agreeable to giving away Transylvania, Hungarian territory in which Rumanians were in the majority. Of the two regions, Transylvania was by far the more valuable. But the Rumanians wanted more from the Allies; they sought the province of Bukovina, north of the Carpathians and a part of Austria; they demanded also the Banat of Temesvar, across the Danube from Belgrade in Hungary, occupied in part by Serbs as well as by Rumanians. Since the Serbs likewise desired the Banat, the Allies were unwilling to pledge it to Rumania, but they finally did so and Bukovina as well. Hungary, meanwhile, despite suggestions from Berlin, resolutely refused to cede any Hungarian land to the Rumanians, and the latter chose the side of the Allies, since their bid in the international auction was highest, and since Russian arms (temporarily) were victorious in the early part of 1916.

For a moment there was panic in Vienna and Budapest, and jumpy nerves in Berlin. For a fortnight the Rumanians advanced. Then the Germans struck hard. From the south, Mackensen, the conqueror of Serbia, drove into the delta lands of the Danube, the Dobruja, with a mixed host of Germans, Bulgars, and Turks, and the invasion of Transylvania was met by a German army after the Rumanians were fairly involved in the Carpathian passes. The invading columns were caught and routed. By gallant exertion most of the Rumanian units fought their way home again, but they were unable to save Bucharest and the national capital had to be shifted to Jassy in Moldavia. The northern third of Rumania was saved, temporarily, from the victors; but nothing could take away the effects of this new defeat of the Allies. The Central Powers, by this last success, reduced their eastern front enormously; they had access to the Black Sea; they had won in Rumania wide grain lands and great oil wells which promised to ease their famine in food and fuel.

The War in Asia Minor and Mesopotamia: Kut-el-Amara and Bagdad (1916-17)

Only in one zone did the Allies make progress—the eastern frontier of Turkey. The Caucasus armies of Russia, routed a considerable Turkish army as early as January, 1915. A year later General Yudeitch, leading 170,000 Russians on one of the most remarkable winter marches on record, forced his way through snow-blocked passes, fought a three-day battle with the Turks, and flung them back on Erzerum, key to Armenia. Within a month almost all of Armenia was in his hands. But here again advance was halted. The British attack on Gallipoli failed and Turkish reinforcements could now be hurried over from the west. The Muscovites were at the end of their lines of communication and were ill-sustained from home; to penetrate farther into Kurdistan was impossible.

The British, however, were pushing the Turks hard from the South. No sooner had Turkey entered the war than they had seized Basra at the head of the Persian Gulf. In September they were in Kut-el-Amara, chief town along the river route to Bagdad. Pressing North they collided with a superior Turkish army. Driven back on Kut, their commander, General Townshend, was besieged by the Turks. An expedition was sent up the river to succor him, but it was held up by the winter rains and floods which turned the Tigris valley into swamps. Kut held out until April, 1916, when Townshend surrendered with 9,000 starving troops. It was now necessary for the British to take Bagdad or to lose face completely throughout all Asia. Heavy reinforcements, sorely needed in other fields, were therefore hurried to the miasmic, super-heated valleys of old Babylonia. The Bedouin desert tribes, who hated Turkish misrule, were carefully conciliated, and no mistake was made a second time in despising the foe. In February, 1917, Kut was retaken, and the next month a British cavalry column swung into Bagdad.

The capture of Bagdad restored throughout the East that British prestige which Kut and Gallipoli had shaken.

The War at Sea

Hardly had the first cannon thundered in Belgium before the influence of British sea power began to tell. Like a great bunker covering the German harbors, the physical length of Great Britain lay across the path of her foe to the outer ocean. German ships could find the Atlantic only through the vigilantly guarded Straits of Dover, or by a circuitous route to northward and westward, well through the North Sea. The British "Grand Fleet," the most powerful force of dreadnoughts in the world, mobilized far to the north at Scapa Flow, an island-locked area in the windy Orkneys. Here, for years, it maintained its chief base, unseen usually, but not unfelt.

The German battleships might, indeed, have crossed the North Sea and even possibly have thrown men ashore in the southern part of England, but (irrespective of their reception on land) the Grand Fleet would have been down upon their flanks at once. Never, in the whole war, did the Germans risk such an adventure. If they had tried to reach the Atlantic by way of Norway and the Shetlands, their foes would have been on them all the more quickly. As for the Channel passage, it was not held by a great force of battleships, but by sufficient lesser craft, sustained by mines, submarines, and coast batteries, so that any attempt to seize it would have been delayed until long after the arrival of the Grand Fleet. The result was that, most of the time, Tirpitz's costly creation, the German "High Seas Fleet" never saw the high seas at all, but lay in harbor watched by British spies.

Meantime, on the distant oceans, the scattered cruisers that Germany had stationed in remote corners of the world had been chased down. For three months, the *Emden* ranged the Indian Ocean, an effective commerce ravager, until she was destroyed by the more powerful Australian cruiser *Sydney*. More dramatic was the career of the German squadron under Admiral von Spee, who found himself, with two good armored cruisers (the *Scharnhorst* and the *Gneisenau*), and several lighter vessels, on the coast of China. Japan had declared war, and was closing in upon Kiauchow; but Spee would not let himself be caught in a hopeless blockade. As became a courageous seaman, he struck out boldly across the Pacific.

The British knew that he was approaching the coast of Chile, and sent thither Sir Christopher Cradock, with a light squadron. Reinforcements were on their way to Cradock, but when he discovered the Germans off Coronel, south of Chile, he knew it was the part of English seamen to fight, and he went down with his two largest ships. The third escaped to tell the tale and London acted instantly—British prestige on the seas was at stake. Two heavy battlecruisers, and other formidable craft, were sent, full speed, to the South Atlantic.

Spee rounded Cape Horn, and endeavored to work his way northeastward. On December 8, 1914, he approached the Falkland Islands, to raid what he imagined was an unprotected British colony, when, above the headlands, he saw the tripod masts of the battlecruisers. The German admiral fled instantly towards the open sea, but his case was hopeless. The battlecruisers chased him with superior speed, then sank his ships with superior gun power. One of his light cruisers (the *Dresden*) got away but was later destroyed off Juan Fernandez in the Pacific ("Robinson Crusoe's" island). Spee himself, refusing to strike his flag, perished in the icy waters of the South Atlantic.

Jutland

On May 31, 1916, in the North Sea not far from the Danish coast came the one great naval engagement of the war—the battle of Jutland. Admiral Scheer, in command of the German "High Seas Fleet," tired of inaction and tempted by the presence in home waters of large numbers of submarines, came out from behind his mine fields sending ahead on scouting duty a squadron under Admiral Hipper, the nucleus of which were five swift battle cruisers. The British, aware that the Germans were out, steamed forth to meet them. Their "Grand Fleet" under Admiral Jellicoe was at Scapa Flow in the far north, but Admiral Beatty, with a formidable squadron of battle cruisers was at Rosyth near Edinburgh. Both fleets sailed to meet the Germans, but it was Beatty who first came in contact with them.

It was a haphazard meeting. The smoke from a Danish trader drew Beatty eastward and Hipper to the west as their two fleets joined in action early in the afternoon. In this first encounter the Germans were victorious, two large British battle cruisers being blown up and a third seriously crippled, while their foe suffered no major casualty. Nevertheless, Beatty presumably would have won the day as his heavier and relatively slower battleships swung into action, had he not suddenly found himself confronted with the main German fleet under Scheer toward which Hipper skilfully had maneuvered.

Thereupon Beatty fled north, notifying Jellicoe of his discovery. Jellicoe instantly steamed south to join Beatty who was pursued by the Germans, and about six P.M. the two main fleets met. Scheer was ignorant of Jellicoe's presence and the superiority of the British metal and speed was assured. Almost before the German admiral realized it, the shells of his enemy began to drop around him. It was now the turn of the Germans to run for safety, one of their larger ships being wounded unto death and several others being thoroughly mauled. Jellicoe, however, was cautious in pursuit. When daylight came the Germans were no longer to be seen. Skilfully, they had worked their way through the British fleet and had withdrawn to the safety of their mine fields. Britain remained the mistress of the seas.

Chapter 28

THE FIRST WORLD WAR (1917-18)

AFTER TWO and a half years there had been no decision. Except on the high seas, the Central Powers had been the more successful; but the Allies clung on doggedly and their superiority in man power and matériel sooner or later presaged triumph. In 1917 unforeseen events occurred, but fortunately enough for the Allies they counterbalanced each other; one, the entry of the United States into the war, a portent of disaster for the Germans; the other, the withdrawal of Russia from the conflict, a body blow to Allied hopes.

Public opinion in America, on the whole, sided with the Allies, a fact accounted for by sympathy for Belgium, historic friendship for France, "cultural ties" with England, and, as the war continued, by the fact that the Allies bought profusely in the United States. Certainly America did not want to see her best customers become bankrupt. On the other hand, German-Americans were numerous in the United States and so, too, Irish-Americans, traditional haters of England; those facts, together with the stretching of the laws of blockade in which England engaged, tended to neutralize pro-Ally sentiment.

The United States, however, no sooner began vigorously to contest British interference with American commerce than she faced the submarine issue. On February 4, 1915, in retaliation, it was alleged, for the British blockade on foodstuffs, a "war-zone" order appeared from Berlin: German submarines were ordered to sink enemy merchantmen, especially in the waters around the British Isles, even if their crews and passengers could not be rescued; furthermore if neutral ships entered the "blockade waters," they "could not always be prevented from suffering from attacks meant for enemy ships."

The destruction of unarmed ships without first rescuing crews and passengers was contrary to accepted doctrines and international law, and President Wilson protested formally against the German war-order zone, saying that the United States would hold Germany to "strict accountability" for harm done to American lives and property. During two months nothing serious happened. Then, in March, 1915, an American citizen perished when the British merchantman *Falaba* was torpedoed

535

by a submarine, and on May 1 the American ship *Gulflight* was torpedoed off the Scilly Isles with the loss of eleven lives. On the same day there was published in several American newspapers a formal notice warning United States citizens against traversing the war zone in ships of Britain or her allies. Within a week following came the submarining of the *Lusitania,* a British merchantman, unarmed but carrying ammunition. Upon this occasion 128 American citizens were drowned.

What would President Wilson do? He had urged his countrymen to be neutral "in both thought and deed"; he was a believer in international pacifism; and he was not particularly interested or conversant with foreign affairs. Some have thought that it was inevitable for the United States to favor the Allies because of the huge loans and credits obtained by the Allied governments in the United States with the tacit approval of the American government, and that the submarine issue raised by the sinking of the *Lusitania* was secondary in importance. This, however, remains a mere surmise. The fact remained that the Germans had violated important rights by sinking without warning an unarmed merchantship and that American lives had been lost. Clearly, action of some sort by the American President was in order.

Most German-Americans, Irish-Americans, and pacifist-Americans urged at this time, and continued to urge, that American citizens were not justified in running the risk of embroiling their country in war by insisting on their legal rights to travel on Allied merchantmen. They could either stay at home, or if business called them they could travel on such occasional liners as were entitled to fly the American flag or on ships of neutral nations—Dutch, Spanish, Danish. A compromise course of action, suggested but not followed, was for the United States to distinguish between Allied merchantmen carrying munitions and those that did not. On the former Americans should travel at their own risk; on the latter they would receive the full support of their government. The President, however, stiffly determined to stand by his original position. In his note to Germany he demanded disavowal and reparation for the sinking of the *Lusitania;* and he furthermore asserted that the United States "would omit neither word nor deed" in asserting her full rights under international law.

The Germans, on June 6, issued a formal order to U-boat commanders not to sink large passenger liners without warning; but nevertheless they had no mind to submit to Wilson's dictates and all through the summer of 1915, the sinkings by U-boats, with occasional peril to American lives, continued. As a climax, in August the British liner *Arabic* was torpedoed, and on board were Americans, of whom two perished. By this time, however, Bernstorff, German ambassador at Washington, convinced his home government that there might be limits to Wilson's patience. The submarine warfare, as then conducted, did not seem paying sufficient mili-

PRESIDENT WOODROW WILSON (1856-1924)

tary dividends to be worth braving American belligerency. The German government, therefore, gave pledge not to sink passenger liners without warning, provided they did not try to escape or resist capture.

The situation thus drifted until the spring of 1916. There were various submarine sinkings, but none sufficiently serious to cause a break. An obscure negotiation was conducted by the President's confidential agent, Colonel House, to get the Allies to enter into peace conversations with Germany; if Germany did not prove reasonable, America (the suggestion ran) would "probably" enter the war on the Allies' side. Nothing came of this, perhaps due to the word "probably." House also tells us that he got the British reluctantly to agree to take wheat off the list of contraband, provided the Germans in turn would abstain both from gas attacks and submarining merchantmen. And nothing came of this either, perhaps because of intimations to Berlin from Washington, relayed by the Austrian ambassador to the United States, who had the impression from former Secretary of State Bryan that there was no likelihood of the United States fighting over the submarine issue.

On March 24, 1916, the unarmed passenger steamer *Sussex* was sunk by a U-boat in the British Channel. Twenty-five of her passengers were Americans. On April 18, the United States reminded Germany of the *Arabic* pledge, recited how it had been broken, and warned Germany that diplomatic relations would be severed if a change of policy did not take place immediately. Severing diplomatic relationship would inevitably ere long have led to war, and Germany was not ready for that. Her U-boats were still few, and she expected to win the European contest by land battles. If her military chiefs had profound contempt for America, Bethmann-Hollweg, still clinging to office as imperial chancellor, realized something of what might come to pass. He had still strength enough in the empire's counsels to force a change of policy. A promise was given that merchant vessels "were not to be sunk without warning and without saving human lives," although the clause was added that if Britain persisted in her blockade Germany reserved "complete liberty of decision." For the time being, the crisis was ended.

During 1916, America went through the throes of a presidential election. Wilson's campaign managers capitalized the intense desire of a great part of the American people to keep if possible out of the European holocaust. "*He kept us out of war!*" was the campaign slogan with strong implications that if Wilson were reëlected he would continue the policy. In October, 1916, Bernstorff telegraphed to Berlin, begging that the U-boats conduct themselves moderately because "all Mr. Wilson's hopes of reëlection are based exclusively on the fact that, according to opinion over here, he has kept the United States out of the war."

In Germany, Wilson's reëlection was hailed as the triumph of the

pacifist party in America. Meantime, the demand for "unlimited submarine warfare" against Britain was growing. Great numbers of U-boats
had been built, and naval confidence in their efficacy was high. The food
and fuel situation was causing intense hardship to German civilians.
The army chiefs, the all-powerful circle around Ludendorff, accepted the
assurance of the admirals that the U-boats, ruthlessly used, could speedily
blockade England, create a worse food shortage than existed in Germany,
and end the war abruptly in the Teutons' favor. Public sentiment strongly
backed this opinion—if this policy angered America so much the better;
by a sham neutrality she had grown rich selling munitions to Britain—
and now let her iniquitous profits cease!

The United States Enters the War (April 6, 1917)

As 1916 approached its end, President Wilson, finding himself ever
nearer the event he dreaded, sought peace by mediation. Germany fore-
stalled him by capitalizing her Rumanian successes with a formal offer
of peace to her enemies on December 12, but in very general terms.
There was no renunciation of any claim upon Belgium; no repudiation
of schemes of annexation clamored for by the Pan-German societies and
the great Rhine industrialists.

The President, however, persisted. On December 18, he issued a formal
appeal to both coalitions to state their war objects in order to see if any
reconciliation were possible. The answers from *all* official spokesmen
were such that, from every belligerent capital, immediately came the
protest that the attitude of the foe made agreement impossible. Nevertheless, behind the scenes the President's *alter ego* and "Père Joseph,"
Colonel House and Bernstorff were striving desperately to secure some
basis for possible mediation. On January 22, Wilson addressed the United
States Senate in a somewhat mysterious speech on the necessary conditions of a "League for Peace," to be established when hostilities should
cease. The war, he declared, must first end in "peace without victory."

It was the last attempt to uphold his policy of neutrality which inexorable events were rendering impossible. Already in late December,
1916, the German admiralty had drawn up a report that if "ruthless submarine warfare" were permitted England would be starved out and
forced to capitulate. Such warfare, it held, was "the proper means of
winning the war; moreover it is the only means to this end." Bethmann-
Hollweg, German chancellor, had grave misgivings, but his objections
were overruled. "We are counting on the chances of war with the United
States," cried Hindenburg, "and have made all preparations to meet it.
Things can not be worse than they are. The war must be brought to an
end by the use of all means as soon as possible." The actual rulers of

Germany having thus spoken, a strictly secret order was issued in the Kaiser's name on January 9, 1917. "I order the unrestricted submarine warfare to be started with full energy on February 1."

On January 31, 1917, the German ambassador transmitted to the President of the United States the formal notice that, beginning the next day, in a wide ocean zone around Britain, France, and Italy, all navigation, that of neutrals included, would be "forcibly prevented." "All ships met within that zone will be sunk." A single American steamer a week was to be permitted to go to Falmouth, England, provided it was "painted with three vertical stripes, one meter wide, alternately white and red." Three days later Bernstorff received his passports and incontinently left Washington, while, simultaneously, Gerard was recalled from Berlin. In an address to Congress, Wilson, it is true, affected still to disbelieve that Germany would "pay no regard to the ancient friendship with America," but this hope died a few weeks afterward. On February 28, the war feeling was blown still hotter by the publication of a note sent in code on January 19 by Zimmermann, the imperial foreign minister, to the German minister to Mexico, proposing an alliance between that country and Germany, the latter country to finance Mexico and help her to "reconquer the lost territory in New Mexico, Texas and Arizona, taken from her by the United States."

The last stand of the pacifists in the United States Senate was to hold up by a Senatorial filibuster a bill authorizing the President to arm merchant vessels crossing the war zone; but the President, after denouncing "the little group of wilful men," armed the ships on his own authority. Followed then the Zimmermann note, seemingly a new evidence of German duplicity. On March 21 the President summoned Congress, and on April 2 he recommended it declare war. According to Wilson, Americans were to "fight for the ultimate peace of the world, and for the liberation of its peoples, the German peoples included. . . . The world must be made safe for democracy." The Congressional resolution, however, which declared war on April 6 spoke in somewhat less exalted language, reciting as grounds for action the wrongs committed on Americans by the German government.

The American entry came none too soon. On April 9, Rear-Admiral Sims of the American navy reached England to confer with Jellicoe, then first sea lord of the admiralty. The British admiral handed his American friend confidential tables showing that the U-boats had sunk of Allied and neutral shipping in February, 1917, 536,000 tons, in March 603,000 tons, and that the estimated figures for April would be in the neighborhood of 900,000 tons. Sims was astounded. "It looks," he said, "as though the Germans were winning the war."

Germany thought so, too. "Today England sees herself in a situation unparalleled in her history," announced Helfferich, imperial secretary of the.

interior. "Her food supplies across the sea disappear as a result of the blockade which our submarines are daily making more effective. We have considered, we have dared. Certain of the result, we will not allow it to be taken from us by anybody or by anything." Ludendorff, meanwhile, told Bernstorff in May, "We are going to end the business by the U-boat war inside of three months."

Fortunately the American navy was in better shape than the army, and able to help immediately. On May 4, six slim, gray destroyers glided up the Irish coast and entered Queenstown harbor. It was "the return of the Mayflower"—the first token that the United States was really in the war. By July 5 there were thirty-five American destroyers off the coast of Ireland. The American flotilla in British and French waters grew all too slowly for the anxious observers; but it grew and was of decisive use.

Prior to May, 1917, the Allied navies had fought against the submarines by means of destroyers and light patrol boats cruising wide areas of sea, and by nets and mine fields. By such means it had been possible to give heavy naval craft fairly good protection. But the merchant vessels had had to shift for themselves. Now, however, the British admiralty determined to try sending large fleets of merchantmen through the war zone under naval convoy; and it was to large extent owing to the increasing numbers of American naval craft in European waters that the convoy system became possible. Thanks to it and the devices which the naval escort could use (especially the "depth bomb") as soon as a U-boat periscope was sighted, the submarine campaign was first checked, then defeated.

The submarine danger was by no means ended; but it was held at bay. The first six destroyers at Queenstown multiplied presently into a great armada of American patrol boats; in 1918 an enormous barrier of mines was stretched across nearly the entire upper entrance to the North Sea. Without serious hindrance, vast quantities of supplies, and over 2,000,000 United States soldiers were conveyed to Europe. Months before the German chiefs called for an armistice, they knew that the "ruthless U-boat campaign" had recoiled upon their own heads; it was a failure. America was entering the war effectively and the sole hope of German victory lay in exploiting Russia and breaking the western military front before the new ally from overseas arrived in force.

But if the American navy was thus able from the outset to contribute to the Allied cause, the army was not. Volunteers could have been had in droves, but the government decided upon conscription, and machinery to enforce it had to be created. Training camps had to be constructed and civilians sent to them could not be converted into soldiers overnight. A very small expeditionary force could have been despatched to Europe immediately, but such an act would draft officers and potential non-coms out of the country at a time when they were needed desperately in the training camps. Therefore the American army did not contribute much to the cause of the Allies in 1917.

Fall of the Czardom (March, 1917)

Meanwhile, at Petrograd "dark influences" were at work. In 1916 the Czar removed his capable foreign minister, Sazonov, and in his place put the Czarina's protege, Stürmer, an arch-reactionary, suspected of being pro-German. The atmosphere was charged with intrigue, and anything seemed possible. Rasputin, "religious impostor and libertine," continued to lord it over the Czarina, and therefore over the Czar, his lodgings popularly known as "staff headquarters." The Czarina wrote constantly to her husband of "our friend," and on one occasion urged the Czar to comb his hair with Rasputin's comb in order to get strength to resist the demands of his ministers.

It proved impossible to prevent the Duma from assembling and in November, 1916, Miliukov, the liberal leader, handled Stürmer so roughly that the latter slunk out of office. Everywhere, in the army, in the navy, in the industries, in the railways, in finance, and in the food supply there was corruption. "If the German general staff," reported a commission to the Duma, "were allowed to direct our internal affairs and the conduct of the army it would do exactly what our government is doing."

But Stürmer had only been a figurehead for others more malevolent. There was Rasputin, whom the upper nobility hated, rightly fearing for the honor of their wives and daughters. They gave him a party, at which a group of princes too exalted even for the Czar to punish shot him dead. His body was flung under the ice of a canal and the slayers, not incorrectly, informed the police that they had killed a dog. But the Czarina mourned him passionately, and he had a saint's funeral.

Rasputin was a symbol, not a cause. Nicholas and his wife remained. The last Czarina had used all her influence from the commencement of the war to prevent her husband making liberal reforms. Her letters to Nicholas while he was pretending to command the army mingled personal pleadings with religious exhortations. "Don't laugh at silly old wifey; for she has trousers on unseen. Your faith has been tried and you remained firm as a rock. For that you will be blessed." She sent him holy images and ikons to strengthen his resistance to the liberals who were trying to reorganize Russia's broken war-machine. "We are living in the hardest times," she wrote late in 1916, "but God will help us through. Wifey is your staunch one, and stands as a rock behind you." And again, "Russia likes to feel the whip hand. How I wish I could pour my blood into your veins."

Thus Russia entered her year of crucifixion, 1917. The supporters of the government were growing fewer, and there was talk of deposing

Nicholas. As February advanced, the Speaker of the Duma waited on the Czar. It was time for plain speaking. Nicholas was informed that he could still save his throne if he would grant responsible ministerial government. If he did not do this, said the Speaker, there would be no further reports made by him to the Czar.

The First Revolution (March, 1917)

On Thursday, March 8, 1917, there was a gala performance in Petrograd at the Alexander Theater for the wealthy, while outside in the Russian cold long queues of women shivered before bakers' shops. In the Duma there was a perfunctory debate on the food supply and a few shops were looted. The next day the throngs in the streets were larger, angrier. Dense crowds seemed laughing, talking, always expectant. Cossacks patrolled the avenues but did not use their weapons. "You won't fire on us, brother," came from the crowds, "we want only bread." "No, we are hungry like yourselves," called back the soldiers. The city police, engaged in scuffles and arrested workingmen. On the tenth there were still greater crowds in the streets. Everybody was now asking, "What is about to happen?" The next day came street firing and some 200 were killed. A company of troops mutinied and refused to fire on the people. The Duma telegraphed a last appeal to the Czar at the front with the army. "Situation serious. Anarchy reigns in the capital. . . . It is absolutely necessary to invest someone who enjoys the confidence of the people with powers to form a new government. . . . Delay may be fatal." The Czar's ministers retaliated by ordering the Duma prorogued; but the deputies defied the order by refusing to disperse.

By dawn of March 12 the garrison of Petrograd had made up its collective mind; the troops would not obey the order to fire upon the city-folk. When certain regiments were ordered to send volleys into the crowd, they shot their own officers. Presently, many soldiers headed an unorganized mob moving straight on the public buildings, and especially on the prisons where political prisoners were held. The only government now left in Petrograd was the Duma, and it threw itself between the city and anarchy. In great haste it chose an executive committee of twelve to act in its name until a provisional government could be set up.

Nicholas had been near the front when the tempest broke at Petrograd. He started for the capital but revolting soldiers blocked the way. Two delegates from the Duma presently arrived and found the Emperor in his railroad carriage, "haggard, unwashed, and weary." The delegates informed him he must abdicate in favor of his son, with his brother Michael for regent. He demanded a sheet of paper, and drew up an abdication in favor of his brother the Grand Duke Michael. It was the last act of the czardom, for when the tidings reached Petrograd the city was in such a state that the Grand Duke, with obvious wisdom, declared that he could accept power only after it had been granted by a Constituent Assembly, elected by a plebiscite. So far as Russia had now any government at all, it was the provisional government headed by Prince Lvov, and composed of leaders among the liberal factions. The most advanced radical member was Kerensky, the new minister of justice—a "Social Revolutionary."

Simultaneous with this regime set up by the Duma, there was another power—the "Soviet (Council) of Workmen's and Soldiers' Deputies"—which desired passionately a republic, so far as it had any defined desires at all. For the moment, the "Soviet" (a roaring, gesticulating body) expressed faith in the provisional government. Nicholas II and his family faded out of view into captivity.

Russia seemed to have sloughed off the czardom without the miseries of the French Revolution and with relatively little bloodshed. The government seemed to be in the hands of moderate liberals, who would set up either a strictly limited monarchy, or, more probably, a democratic republic.

The fall of the czardom swept away those sanctions which hitherto had held together the empire. For the "Little Father," millions of peasants would fight and die; but for the provisional government there was no devotion—even though it did release political prisoners, restore autonomy to Finland, and introduce reforms. Prince Lvov and his colleagues who headed that government were convinced that a truly democratic regime could only be secured by first defeating the Prussian autocracy. But the nation had suffered terribly. The war had been the Czar's war. Now that the Czar was gone, let his war cease! The Russian people had no quarrel with the Germans. Constantinople, which had been pledged by the Allies, meant nothing to the Russian masses. Orders, issued by the Petrograd Soviet, destroyed discipline in the army, reduced officers to impotence, and practically placed the command with "Soldiers Councils"—fantastic debating clubs. Soon two slogans began to be heard in the camp, in the village, and in city soviets: (a) "self-determination," let every country decide its own future, and (b) "no annexations and no indemnities." By the middle of the summer the Russian war machine was a wreck; in the farming districts the peasants thought about one thing only—how to seize the land of the proprietors; and in the cities the workmen, sullen and discontented, spent much more time in exciting talk than in working in the factories.

And now in all the villages and the little wooden *izbas* one potent idea came home to the *muzhiks*—the chance to complete the emancipation of 1861. The former serfs and their children had never forgiven the decision to leave to their former owners a large part of the farm lands. Now was the opportunity to seize them. "It was here that they sought their annexations and indemnities!" All the peasants knew of the war was that it had sent off their sons to fight with pitchforks against machine guns and poison gas. The rural districts were soon everywhere in anarchy, the muzhiks seizing the estates of the helpless proprietors, just as all productive agriculture perishing amid rioting and confusion. From the demoralized army at the front, the soldiers (worried lest their neighbors at home take all the good land) deserted, literally, by hundreds of thousands.

In the cities, in the meantime, the workmen were for the most part socialists. They looked upon the revolution as their handiwork and they demanded drastic and immediate action toward the establishment of a socialist state. Particularly true was this of Lenin, leader of the more extreme socialists (the Bolsheviks), who had returned from exile in Switzerland in April through the kind assistance of the German authorities. Lenin was for instant peace. He had but one enemy—capitalism; he had no interest in the war, which he considered simply and solely as proof that international capitalism was in its death throes. The dawn of Messianic socialism had come and the end of the Russian bourgeois was at hand. Peace, bread, and land was his slogan, and this was the theme upon which he orated daily to the restless proletariat of Petrograd, spreading as he did so suspicion and hate of the provisional government.

As the army became more and more demoralized, and as discord grew at Petrograd, Miliukov, who had been provisional minister of foreign affairs, was forced to resign, since he had been committed to fight for Constantinople. The Duma had been elected by a very narrow franchise and carried no weight with the masses. Soon the virtual head of the government was Kerensky, hitherto counted a decided radical, but who, in any case, clearly realized the futility of trying to initiate a regime of democracy by opening the gates to the Hohenzollern.

Kerensky strove hard to combat the forces of disruption and anarchy; but he trusted too much to his eloquence and exerted no discipline over the army, where the soldiers were being taught by Bolshevik missionaries to distrust and hate their officers and to go back home and seize the old lords' acres.

The Overthrow of Kerensky: The Bolshevists Seize Power (November 7, 1917)

On July 14, the extremists tried to seize the government by force, but Kerensky had strength enough to stamp out the flames. Soon, however, the agitators were again at work; Russian industries became paralyzed; the peasants were not tilling the fields; and every wire and mail-bag brought to the distracted ministers new evidence of increasing demoralization.

In September, General Kornilov tried to force the provisional government to take round measures against the dissidents. A military coup was projected, with Kerensky himself apparently supporting the scheme. But very many around him were fearful that a bold strike would involve a return to the czardom. Kornilov was left unsupported and betrayed by men who had egged him forward. The coup failed, and this was the beginning of the end.

Kerensky was detested by the Bolshevists, and as October advanced his position grew weaker and weaker. He told the Western Powers that Russia was utterly weary and could play no active part in the war. The Bolshevists were now carrying on an active propaganda everywhere, promising universal peace and utopia. Although pledged to communism, their peace pledges pleased the peasants, who looked only for a chance to enjoy the seized lands. The crash at last came upon November 7, 1917, when the Petrograd garrison recognized the authority of the "Revolutionary Committee" of the Soviets. Kerensky issued vigorous proclamations, but found himself almost without armed supporters. Petrograd passed into the power of the Leninists with very little fighting. Kerensky fled, tried to return with the aid of a few Cossack squadrons too weak to recapture the city, and then disappeared completely. In Moscow the armed defenders of the provisional government were stronger; they yielded the Kremlin only after severe fighting, whereupon the revolutionists proclaimed: "The provisional government has been deposed. The power of the state is now in the hands of the Petrograd Soviet of Workers' and Soldiers' Deputies." And the Russian people were promised at once "the immediate offer of a democratic peace, the abolition of rights of landlordship, the workers' control of industry, and the establishment of a Soviet government."

Moves in Austria and Germany to Secure Peace (1917)

The war was now running into its third year, and another power besides Russia was becoming weary. At Vienna, the new Hapsburg emperor, the well-intentioned young Charles, was casting anxiously about him. The fate of Nicholas II afforded little lasting encouragement, even if it eased the military situation. The Vienna ministers knew that their ill-compacted government was cracking under the strain and was likely to fly asunder. "It is no good telling me," reported Czernin, Charles's foreign minister, "that the monarchical principle is too firmly rooted in Berlin and Vienna for the monarchy to be overthrown. This war has no precedent. If the monarchs do not make peace in the next few months, then the people will make peace over their heads; and then the waves of revolution will sweep away everything for which our sons are fighting today."

Charles even went so far as to negotiate with France, telling Paris that he would not sacrifice his country for the sake of a German victory, and that to get peace he would use his influence to support "the just claim of France in relation to Alsace-Lorraine." But the French promptly called attention to the claims of Italy; what concessions for her—not, of course, at Hohenzollern, but at Hapsburg expense? Charles could not bring himself to sign away Trieste and the Trentino.

Meanwhile, in Germany Matthias Erzberger, leader of the powerful Catholic Center party in the Reichstag, hitherto an advocate of wholesale annexations and exploitations, astonished a group of colleagues by telling them that "the war could not be won." His reversal of attitude caused a sensation in inner political circles; and speedily his opinions leaked out when he introduced resolutions before the Reichstag. "The Reichstag strives for a peace of understanding and the permanent reconciliation of the peoples. With such a peace, forced requisitions of territory and political, [or] economic oppressions are inconsistent."

Such resolutions the great General Staff that now ruled Germany met with unconcealed anger. Their particular rage was against Bethmann-Hollweg for having failed to maintain "the home front" against the enemy. The discredited chancellor now faded into private life. In his place the military autocrats set up a colorless Prussian official, Michaelis, who would at least do his masters' bidding. The Erzberger resolutions were passed by the Reichstag, but their effect was instantly destroyed by the announcement of the new chancellor that he accepted the proposition "as he understood it."

The French Offensive of 1917: The Pope Proposes Peace

In France, also, there was, presently, great discouragement. The war had come home to the republic as it had not to Britain, nor even to Germany. Nearly all the fighting on the western front had been on French soil. Several of the richest and most populous departments were in the clutches of the enemy, and the youth of the country seemed bleeding away. The situation was so desperate that the French decided to make one grand, furious assault on the Germans. There had been complete failure in 1915 and 1916 to accomplish this, both on the part of the Allies and on that of the Central Powers, but General Nivelle, successor to Joffre as commander-in-chief of the armies of France, was so buoyant and so optimistic that he persuaded not only his own government but that of Britain that it could be done.

Nivelle attacked in April on fifty miles of front in Champagne. He flung his main strength upon the Chemin des Dames, along the Aisne, which the Germans had been laboriously fortifying for two and half years. The first rush of the French attack enabled him to boast of taking

21,000 prisoners and 183 guns within four days; but his own losses had been appalling. The French infantry found that their artillery had failed to clear the ground properly—they were mowed down by machine guns, while they struggled with the unbroken barbed wire. Nivelle's casualties presently reached 107,000. The Germans were forced to cede valuable ground, but again no key positions were taken. There had been no break-through, and human energy could do no more. The Paris politicians were horrified at the profitless sacrifice; and on May 15, Nivelle was removed from command and replaced by the more steady Pétain. The new general had not merely to hold back the foe, but to restore the sorely shaken morale of the entire French army.

There had already been serious dissatisfaction among the French rank and file as to scanty leaves of absence, confusion in the medical service, and reports from home of how munition workers, exempted from military duty, were getting fat wages, while the women and children struggled to wrest a living from the farms of the peasant conscripts. Now, in addition to great military discouragement, there were serious mutinies. Certain divisions near Paris almost broke out into political revolution, and "de-featism"—advocacy of giving up the fight and compounding with Ger-many—spread.

The secret of the mutinies was, in fact, so well kept that not merely did the Germans fail to learn thereof, but even the British and Ameri-cans. Nevertheless, the main situation could not be concealed. Russia was falling from the war. France was temporarily unable to push any offen-sive. Italy was very tired. American troops were coming slowly. On Britain had to fall the main burden of any real pressure upon Germany during 1917.

Under such conditions, in August, Pope Benedict XV tried to mediate. A gesture during the summer to bring the warring elements together by means of a conference of socialist leaders at Stockholm had failed, partly because of the suspicion that German forces were controlling the under-taking; partly because the Allies distrusted any movement under the auspices of socialists. The attempt of the Vatican met with greater respect but no better fortune. In substance, the Pope called on the warring nations to forget their losses and wrongs and to make peace on the *status quo ante bellum*. Something ought to be done, the pontiff sug-gested, as to Armenia, Poland, and the Balkans, and occupied territory should generally be evacuated. This would have released Belgium, but would have left Alsace-Lorraine to Germany. There was much well-intentioned wisdom behind the note, but the Allied Powers were angered at the calm method with which the Pope treated both coalitions as equally innocent or culpable. The result, therefore, was foreordained. Berlin answered with apparent cordiality: they would be happy to negotiate along the suggested lines. But President Wilson was selected by the

Western Allies to be the chief spokesman. "The object of this war," he informed Pope Benedict, "was to deliver the free peoples of the world from the menace and actual power of a vast military establishment controlled by an irresponsible government which [had] secretly planned to dominate the world, and which was now in waging war stopping at no barrier of law or mercy."

Flanders and Caporetto

Despite the entrance of the United States into the war, the year 1917 was one of continued disaster for the Allies. The British were foiled in their offensives as well as the French. Twice the former tried to break through and twice they failed. Their first offensive came in Flanders, where, owing to unusual rain, the low terrain had been turned into a bog. A number of local successes were achieved, but that was all. The German grip on the Belgian coast and the coal fields around Lille had not been broken. Then, later in the year, the British made a surprise attack at Cambrai. This time there was no long artillery preparation; instead, four hundred tanks suddenly emerged from the haze of a November sunrise and went crashing through the German defenses, the infantry following. The use of tanks, begun at the Somme, was now vindicated; but unfortunately there were not nearly enough available, and a German counterattack won back most of the ground which the tanks had gained. Whereupon the western front settled down after this to another winter of local bombardments.

If the British were checked, the Italians were overwhelmed with disaster. An Austrian offensive at Caporetto, in the mountains north of the Adriatic, turned into an Italian rout. The front collapsed almost like magic. At certain points the disaffected troops greeted the enemy with white flags, while reserve battalions in the rear refused to march forward. The result was that the whole Italian front near Caporetto was broken and the Teutons poured in as through a sluice.

Despite heroic struggles, it became evident that the Italians had sustained not a defeat but a national disaster. The gains of twenty-nine months of war were gone instantly.

The crisis brought to the Italians aid which had been denied for their offensive. Six French and five British divisions were ordered entrained for cisalpine service. High French and British cabinet ministers and generals hastened to Italy, with moral support and counsel. All this, however, would have availed nothing, had the German-led forces of the Central Powers been in a position to exploit their advantage to the full.

Fortunately for Italy, this was not the case. The Germans, under whom were Magyar and Slovak troops, were delayed by the very extent of their victories, and the need of mopping up the conquered territory. They were not prepared for a headlong pursuit. Thus, the Italians, many of whose surviving troops were "disorganized, worn-out, sullen, and bewildered," were given that short breathing time, during which a truly great people can pull itself together.

The knowledge that the country was in deadly peril, that preparations were being made to evacuate Venice, that if the Piave and Adige lines went, the Teutons might soon be in Milan, united the Italian nation. The clericals became patriotic; the pacifists and socialists became silent; a "spirit of desperate devotion ran from the Alps to Sicily." When the Austro-German attacks were renewed along the Piave and downward through the Alps, they were met with determination. A little more ground had to be ceded to the attackers, but the line of the Piave was not carried. The Teutons, for one moment, had seemed on the point of driving Italy out of the struggle with one great military thrust—but that moment had passed.

Nevertheless, the disaster at Caporetto seemed, for the moment, only to add one more misery to the Allies' winter. British and French troops, sorely needed on the western front, were in Venetia assisting Italy; Russian revolutionaries were negotiating a separate truce; and submarine warfare was constantly menacing England. In France the privations of the long war were bearing hard upon the civilian population. There was, in fact, general discouragement among the Allies. Many were wondering whether the war was not likely to end with a general social revolution. The new Bolshevik dynasts in Russia were sending wholesale promises to the "have nots" throughout the world, and certain high financial groups were reported to have taken alarm.

Lloyd George's and Wilson's Peace Programs: Brest Litovsk

Early in January, 1918, Lloyd George and Wilson made clear their war aims. The British premier chose studiously moderate language: Britain was not fighting to destroy Germany, or Austria-Hungary, or those parts of Turkey which were genuinely Turkish, but Belgium and Serbia must be restored and, of course, the occupied parts of France, Italy, and Rumania. The "legitimate claims" of the Italians for union with people of their own race and tongue were to be satisfied, and "genuine self-government" must be given the Austro-Hungarian nationalities. In that event, the Hapsburgs might continue at Vienna, although no longer as the "instruments of the military autocracy of Prussia." An independent Poland was "an urgent necessity," and the Turks, although they might keep Constantinople, ought to let Armenia, Syria, Mesopotamia, and Palestine enjoy "separate national conditions." As for Alsace-Lorraine, there must be a "reconsideration of the great wrong of 1871" done to France;

but concerning Russia, since her present rulers were negotiating separately with Germany, Britain could not be responsible for unhappy
decisions.

These were carefully worded terms, skilfully calculated to drive a
wedge between the allies of Germany and the Hohenzollerns, and to
kindle all the dissident minorities, yet not to drive Germany to desperation. Wilson, a few days later, struck out somewhat more boldly. In a
well-considered statement, Wilson summarized the American position in
fourteen points. They came close to repeating the British terms in regard
to territorial settlements on the continent: but they were somewhat more
specific, and in addition called for freedom of the seas; removal of economic barriers; a treatment of colonial questions in accordance with the
best interests of native peoples; and the creation of a League of Nations.

In Austria the olive branch of the Allies was welcome, but not so in
Germany. Count Hertling, the new chancellor (replacing, in October,
1917, the feckless Michaelis), repudiated the idea that Alsace-Lorraine
could possibly be ceded back to France; and concerning every other point
he was vague and defiant. Russia must be left to the "return of order,
peace, and conditions of her welfare," which the Teutonic allies were then
arranging for her. The fate of Belgium could only be settled after elaborate negotiation, and the occupied parts of France were "valuable pawns
in our hands." Poland was to be reconstituted, as Germany and Austria
might agree among themselves—there was to be no outside interference
—and so with nearly all the other points at issue.

At the dawn of 1918, it might have been possible for Germany to have
driven a dangerous wedge between France and Britain and America by
a conciliatory peace offer. The English-speaking powers would hardly
have gone on making vast sacrifices solely to recover Strasbourg and Metz
for a sister nation. But Hertling's speech cancelled any possible effect of
Czernin's smoother platitudes, and almost convinced the most doubtful
that Germany was playing for an absolute victory and a dictated peace.
A few weeks earlier, William II, in an address to his armies, had promised
that "we must bring peace to the world by battering in with the iron
fist and shining sword the doors of those who will not have peace."

The confident tone of his Imperial Majesty was due to the collapse of
the eastern front, where the Germans had good reason to feel resistance
had vanished. In December, 1917, the Bolsheviks sent their commissars
to negotiate with the representatives of the Teutonic empires at Brest
Litovsk in Poland, where a protracted conference took place, lasting to
the March of the subsequent year, when a Russo-German treaty was
finally struck. The Bolsheviks had overwhelmed Russia with surprisingly
little fighting and they believed that a similar revolt of the proletariat in
Germany was about to send not merely the Kaiser and Junkers, but the

whole Teutonic burgher class the way of the Czar. After that, the capitalistic strongholds in France, Britain, and America must speedily crumble, and next would follow the obliteration of obsolete and oppressive nationalistic boundaries, when all peoples of the earth were fused together in the Marxian earthly paradise. The Bolsheviks were confident that their industrial "comrades" in Germany would prevent any advantage being taken of their own military helplessness. "We did not overthrow the Czar," declaimed Trotsky, "in order to fall on our knees before the Kaiser, and beg for peace." Marvelously were he and his associates to be undeceived.

The victorious Germans asked Russia to recognize the independence of all the Baltic provinces, of Poland, of the Ukraine, that vast southwestern section of Russia in Europe, occupied by the Little Russians, and stretching south and southeast of Poland to the Black Sea. Over these extensive regions, destined for the German orbit, puppet governments were to be set up by the conquerors. The vista was now opened in Berlin of the control of the routes to the oil wells of Baku, to the cotton lands of Ferghana, to the very mountain passes leading to British India. Austria received minor pickings and Turkey recovered territory on the Caucasus. Austro-German financial groups were to exploit the Rumanian oil fields.

The Bolsheviks recoiled in disgust at the German proposals. Many favored rejection and the declaration of a revolutionary war. Lenin said Soviet Russia must accept or fight; to accept meant a chance to save the revolutionary regime; to fight meant defeat and conquest by the Central Powers. Trotsky favored refusing to make peace until compelled to do so by force. On February 9, the Central Powers signed at Brest a treaty with the Ukraine, and on the following day Trotsky made his famous "no peace, no war" declaration, to the effect that Soviet Russia would neither sign an annexationist peace nor go on with the war. The Germans therefore declared the armistice at an end and sent their troops forward toward Petrograd. Some of the Bolsheviks still wanted to fight; but Lenin, now supported by Trotsky, won a majority of the party leaders for peace. When the Bolsheviks agreed to sign, the Germans presented a revised text even more severe. There were more debates and Lenin said: "It is time to put an end to revolutionary phrases and get down to real work. If this is not done I resign from the government. . . . It is a question of signing the German terms now or signing the death warrant of the Soviet government three weeks later. . . ." Lenin carried the day and the Soviet delegates signed on March 3.

This Treaty of Brest Litovsk stripped Russia of approximately forty-four per cent of her population, twenty-seven per cent of her arable land, thirty-seven per cent of her average crops, twenty-six per cent of her railroads, thirty-three per cent of her manufactures, seventy-three per cent of her iron production, seventy-five per cent of her developed coal mines.

The Western Front, March, 1918

Russia was helpless; Italy was reeling; France, despite American economic relief, was bleeding white and very tired; Britain was carrying on gallantly, but without that dauntless confidence that had inspired her sacrifices of 1915-16. America was still three thousand miles across the Atlantic.

The U-boat war had proved a disappointment to its promoters, but the surrender of Russia had restored the prestige of the great General Staff. If civilian Germany went through the winter of 1917-18, once more shivering with the cold, hungering on turnip soup in lieu of meat and potatoes, with little children nursing on thin beer in lieu of milk, and with stripling youths and middle-aged men in broken health, drafted to the trenches by a pitiless conscription, it seemed, nevertheless, that the blessed end was in sight. Given time, the wheat fields of Ukrainia and the oil fields of Rumania would feed and warm the lands of the victors, and as for the military situation, conditions were still better.

It was known that the French army was dwindling in strength through the depletion of man power. The British were paying the penalty for the awful losses on the Somme and in Flanders; and the U-boat warfare was diverting an enormous number of men into the royal navy. Vast forces under the Union Jack had also to be maintained in Mesopotamia, Palestine (where Jerusalem had been taken from the Turks on December 10, 1917), and at Salonika. Besides all these, the danger of an invasion of England across the North Sea was reckoned with, 300,000 good troops being held in Britain to meet a very improbable catastrophe. As a result, Sir Douglas Haig commanded 180,000 less fighting men in March, 1918, than in March, 1917. The German high command knew all this. They knew that by spring barely 250,000 Americans had reached France, and that the great bulk of these troops were too untrained to send to the trenches. It was time to stake everything on one great blow on the western front that could undo the work at the Marne.

In view of these facts, Ludendorff hoped to win the war by a grand final offensive on the western front. He aimed it at Amiens, since if he could take that old Picard city he would sever direct communications between the British and the French. The latter he could fling backward in demoralization upon Paris; the former he could hustle in ever increasing rout to the Channel. Former offensives had failed because waged on too narrow a front; he would succeed now by breaking through on a wide one. He would use a method of offense tried out successfully against the Russians by which, instead of an intensive bombardment followed by a rush of infantry, the artillery hardly began its work before the infantry advanced in small detachments, infiltrating the enemy's positions, concealing their advance as much as possible, and using smoke screens and mustard gas to demoralize the foe. It was now or never for the Germans; they must strike and they must win before there were too many Americans in France, and before the food shortage got too bad in Germany.

Upon the extreme south of the British line on the 21st of March, 1918, the storm broke, and before that day was spent the Germans had penetrated deep into the British positions. The British reserves were exhausted and the onslaught not stayed. The following day, as the British divisions lost contact with one another, came worse disaster and a frantic retirement to the Somme. On the 23rd the attackers swept across that stream; and as the gaps between the British units grew wider and wider, the chance of stabilizing the line grew more and more faint. Ludendorff seemingly had accomplished the impossible—a breakthrough.

Almost, but not quite. Never fought men in a manner more worthy of their inheritance than that unbowed remnant of the British army. From the south the French hurried up veteran divisions to fill the gap and to cover Amiens. The Germans still made headway but no longer rapidly, and in a few days they halted. Nevertheless, on April 1, it was possible for Ludendorff to proclaim a magnificent success—90,000 prisoners and 1,300 guns.

Amiens was saved. But Ludendorff still had power for other blows. On April 9, the Germans struck again, this time further north. Once again there was almost a breakthrough, the British forced to retreat over old battlefields, drenched now with the blood of three and a half years.

Once more the German offensive ebbed away. There had been great territorial gains for Ludendorff; but he had not forced Haig's line or put the British army out of action. By the end of April, this Battle of the Lys, as it was called, was over. Ludendorff drew back to strike again.

May, 1918, nearly passed before another great German offensive came. Meantime, the ocean was sprinkled with convoys of liners bearing the man power of America. "The Allies are very weak," General Pershing had reported to Washington as early as December, 1917, "and we must come to their relief in this year, 1918. The year after may be too late." But during the winter the ocean convoys had been slow, and even the most hopeful of the commanders overestimated the period of training needful for the American troops before they could be sent to the battle-trenches. Nevertheless, in March, 84,900 were sent across and in April, 118,600. These numbers had seemed the reasonable limit, considering the shipping available; but with the whole war now on the razor-edge of fate, the British government drafted the liners from all its great trade routes, while the process of mobilizing and organizing in America was hastened to the uttermost. In May, 246,000 Americans were destined to cross the Atlantic, in June, 278,000, in July, 306,300. The government-controlled press of Germany denounced the figures published to hearten the Allies as gross fabrications and "Yankee bluff," but the General Staff, at least, began to realize that what it would do, it must do quickly.

Late in May, Ludendorff changed his objective. Abandoning the Channel ports, he aimed at Paris. His intelligence service told him that the line of the Chemin des Dames, along the Aisne, was held by only eight divisions, four French and four British, and that these were weary from fighting elsewhere and had been sent to this supposedly "quiet sector" to reorganize. Suddenly, on May 27, Ludendorff attacked with twenty-eight divisions on a thirty-five mile line. He won immediate results. A deep zone of territory was lost to the Allies, and that, too, in the area directly covering Paris.

The Germans reported 45,000 prisoners and 400 captured guns. They were well down to the Marne, almost to the region fought over in September, 1914. One more colossal effort—and France would be as Russia; then home to the Fatherland and glory.

The Second Marne

Ludendorff knew that the deep salient or pocket he had created by his third offensive must either be enlarged or abandoned, for it was fed by but one railroad and it was open to attack from both flanks. He had tried to enlarge it on the northwest and had failed. This time he would strike to the east of Reims, to widen it on the northeast, while at the same time he would strike to the south and west of Reims toward the Marne. When the Germans rushed on this, their fifth and last offensive, they found the foe ready. Their blow struck to the east of Reims met with complete discomfiture. Twenty-five picked German divisions were shattered by the French artillery and no appreciable progress was made. Slightly better fortune attended the German attack west of Reims in the Marne salient; some ground was gained; the Marne was crossed near Château-Thierry; progress on the military maps could be noted. But the salient in the Allies' lines, though deepened, had not been widened.

Foch's hour had come. Along the thirty-five mile western flank of the great Marne salient, after a night of thunderstorms and high winds which discouraged the German airmen, there emerged 321 Allied tanks out of the shelter of the concealing woods. Behind them, striking all the way from Château-Thierry to Soissons came Mangin's forces, thirty per cent American. The advance swept through the first German defenses before the Teutons so much as realized what was happening. When night fell the Allies had taken 16,000 prisoners and had gone far beyond winning a local success. They were closing the end of the German loop or pocket which had penetrated to the Marne. If they could only close it further, thirty German divisions would be trapped within. For the next few days the Germans struggled fiercely and at last escaped north to their old battlegrounds near the Aisne. They had lost the great gains of the first of June; they had lost something more precious, confidence in victory.

Three months and three days intervened between this British drive and the end of the war, an interval filled with incessant fighting. The initiative had completely passed into the hands of Foch, now general-issimo of all the Allied armies, and never once was Ludendorff able to make a serious counteroffensive. Foch struck now here, now there. The Belgians were again in action from that little strip of their fatherland near the Yser which they had held since 1914; the British were raining blows in Flanders and Picardy; the French were beating on the German lines along the Aisne and in Champagne; and the Americans, acting as a separate army, were putting through two major operations in the Meuse Valley.

The Final Franco-British-American Attacks

The German hosts on the western front had been fed by two trunklines of railroads—that through Liége and that through Sedan. The line through Liége was relatively safe, but by itself it was totally inadequate for maintaining the German army. The line through Sedan was within thirty miles of the Allied trenches near Verdun, but those miles included the Argonne Forest, a semi-wilderness of hills, woods, and ravines, ideal for defense, almost impossible for offense. Haig and Pétain (still in command of the French armies as coadjutor to Foch) undertook to force back the Germans across Flanders, Picardy, and Champagne by incessant attacks and pressure. They each had several American divisions in their armies, but the main American effort was elsewhere. Pershing undertook to cut through the Argonne to Sedan. When its trunk railroad was under the American guns, Ludendorff's armies must either flee in rout or capitulate.

Before cutting this railroad it was considered advisable that the Germans be driven out of the Saint-Mihiel salient near Verdun, and the task of doing so was assigned to the American army. Pershing fell upon this salient, using over half a million men. He won a relatively easy victory, since the Germans were preparing to abandon the salient anyway. Pershing then started forward on the main American offense, through the Argonne in the direction of Sedan.

The battle of the Argonne lasted forty-seven days. It was begun with 450,000 men, but as it raged other troops were thrown in until the whole number of Americans engaged was over 1,000,000. The American numerical preponderance was overwhelming and it must be remembered that the war-weary enemy was in retreat. Nevertheless, the German troops knew the terrain and the Americans did not. The forest country fought over had become an almost impenetrable tangle of fallen timber, an ideal place for nests of machine guns and for labyrinths of barbed wire. It

Ewing Galloway

AMERICAN TROOPS IN ACTION ON THE WESTERN FRONT

was also cut by ravines so deep as to render tanks useless, and making it very hard for artillery to support the attackers. "It was a question of hard, slogging infantry fighting, and the American infantryman did slog hard," wrote a British general; by the middle of October "by grim, dogged effort he won his way through."

The German armies in France were caught, as it were, between enormous pincers, the Belgians and the British on one side, the Americans on the other, and the French in the center shoving their foe forward. Everywhere came the rat-tat-tat, of Foch on the retreating enemy who retired in good order, putting up everywhere a stiff rear-guard action. By the first of November the German forces were back where they had been in the summer of 1914.

Germany's Allies Surrender

As far back as September, Bulgaria had given evidence of cracking. An Allied army which had occupied Salonika after the Dardanelles defeat, forced that entire nation to remain mobilized. The Germans had handed over to Bulgaria a goodly share of the conquered Serbian lands but had exploited the supply of foodstuffs. At the very moment, furthermore, when German aid was needed most, German aid was withdrawn. Ludendorff required his men, his munitions, his money, elsewhere. Bulgaria, then, realizing that she had gambled unwisely, made peace quickly. The Bulgars agreed to demobilize their army, to evacuate all territory they had occupied, and to allow Allied armies free transit across Bulgaria to attack Turkey. The Serbs, now like raging lions, flung themselves on the small Austro-German detachments left in their country. They reëntered Nish, their ancient capital; and by the first of November they were again triumphantly in Belgrade, looking across the Danube where the first shots of the world contest had resounded fifty-one months earlier.

The collapse of Bulgaria was scarcely more rapid than that of Turkey. The Bedouin tribes of Arabia and Syria were now in full revolt against the Sultan. Jerusalem was occupied (Christmas, 1917), and during 1918 Allenby, the British commander, had pressed Liman von Sanders, the German general in command of the Turkish army, north from Nazareth to Damascus. The Sultan had hardly a single organized force to put in the field, if Allenby elected to advance across Anatolia to Stamboul. On October 25, he moved north again and took Aleppo, the great Turkish base in North Syria.

Syria was lost and Mesopotamia with it; Anatolia would soon be open and the Allies, moving across Bulgaria, would soon be pounding on the Tchalja lines behind Stamboul. Allah manifestly had spoken, and it was useless to strive against destiny. Turkish envoys, therefore, negotiated peace with the British admiral in the Aegean. The Turkish army was to be demobilized, the Turkish waterways opened; alliance with Germany was repudiated, and the whole fate of the Ottoman Empire was to be left for the final peace conference. On October 31 hostilities in the Near East ceased.

This general collapse of the allies of Austria and Germany in southeastern Europe was almost instantly followed by that of Austria. It was high time.

Czechs, Poles, Ruthenians, Slovaks, Slovenes, Croats, whom the lordly Germans and Magyars had trampled upon and despised, were turning now against the oppressor. "Self-determination" and "a world safe for democracy," supplied oil for fires of discontent already smoldering.

On October 16, the Hapsburg Empire underwent its death-bed repentance. The unfortunate Charles proclaimed his monarchy a "Federal State" in which each people could form its own government. But the Allies and the United States were now warning Vienna that there could be no peace unless the Czechs, Poles, and Yugo-Slavs were to be allowed to quit the empire outright if they so desired; and Hungary was also preparing to cut the last tie to Vienna, and set up as a completely independent government.

Austria's plight was Italy's opportunity. The Italian army, assisted by French and British units, drove in a wedge between the Austrian troops. The Austrians and the Magyars surrendered wholesale and prisoners were reckoned at more than 300,000. On November 3 Austria quit the war and a week later the Emperor Charles abdicated. German Austria became a republic; there was another republic in Hungary, a third in Czechoslovakia; Galicia was joining a revived republic of Poland; the Croats and the Slovenes were federating with the Bosnians and Serbs in the new kingdom of Yugoslavia; and Rumania had repudiated the forced Treaty of Bucharest and was seizing Transylvania. The Austrian monarchy (founded in 1272 by Rudolf of Hapsburg), that artificial but convenient makeshift and fiction which had dominated Central Europe for six hundred and forty years, was dead.

These happenings progressively heightened Germany's gloom. There was now no hope anywhere on the horizon. The army on the western front was retiring in good order and was in no immediate danger of encirclement; but even if it reached the Rhine safely there was no chance of ultimate victory. Consequently, Germany sued for peace by way of Washington. The President replied that there could be no peace unless the Allies had a representative government with which to deal, and the German militarists temporarily thought of renewing the war. But it was now known that Austria was done for and other men than Ludendorff were in charge of Germany's destinies.

The army did not finally yield, however, until socialistic revolts in the Fatherland made it inevitable that it must. The German Socialists had been wholeheartedly for the war at its commencement, only one of them, Liebknecht, voting against the first war credits. Late in 1915, however, fifteen other Socialists joined with Liebknecht, seceded from the Social Democratic party, and formed that of the Independent Socialists. They were a very weak faction and not until the treaty of Brest Litovsk in 1918 was there really any considerable revolutionary propaganda in Germany.

But as the German people became more and more hungry, revolutionary sentiment spread. And now, with Germany's allies falling away, and with Foch's legions likely to pour over the frontier any moment, a very small explosion could and did shatter the whole political structure. At Kiel the bluejackets, long disgruntled, hoisted the red flag of revolutionary socialism. This mutiny was no flash in the pan. By the 7th of November there were unkempt soviets claiming to be the government in Hamburg, Bremen, Hanover, Rostock, and lesser centers. The red flag was waving all over Germany; jails were broken open and hardened inmates released as an earnest of proletarian liberty.

Under such circumstances there was a revolution in Germany which complied completely with Wilson's demands that the Allies must deal with the representatives of the German people. The Germans not merely lost an emperor, they ceased to constitute a monarchy. On November 10 the Kaiser fled into Holland. On the same day Ebert, a journeyman saddler, accepted the chancellorship in the name of the Social Democrats, and straightway proclaimed the republic.

One day later came the armistice, the terms of which had been prepared at Paris by the Allied generals and admirals. The Germans were to surrender 5,000 cannon, 30,000 machine guns, 2,000 airplanes, and 5,000 locomotives. They were to evacuate immediately the "invaded countries" including Alsace-Lorraine, thereby automatically undoing the deed of 1871. They were to retire beyond the Rhine, and the Allied armies were to occupy not merely the western Rhinelands, but ample bridgeheads with wide radius opposite Mayence, Coblenz, and Cologne. All Allied prisoners were to be released immediately, all German mine fields to be swept; six battle cruisers, ten battleships, numerous smaller craft, and all submarines were to be interned in the ports of the victors; the remaining craft were to be disarmed and put under Allied supervision. In addition, the treaties of Brest Litovsk and Bucharest (with Rumania) were to be canceled.

At 5 A.M., at the first gray light of November 11, the German delegates, meeting Foch in his salon car, put their hands to the great surrender. Through the cold, foggy morning sometimes a shell burst, sometimes a great gun bellowed. It was said that most of the combatants were in a kind of stupor. They had fought so long, must they not fight on forever? Foch had telegraphed to his generals, "Hostilities will cease on the whole front on November 11, at eleven o'clock. The Allied troops will not, until further orders, go beyond the line reached at that hour." Suddenly, at one minute to eleven, the last "75" thundered on its carriage. The ensuing silence was more startling than even the terrible chorus of a barrage.

Presently, against the skyline, lifting themselves above the trenches, first cautiously, then bolder, were seen figures—staring, gesturing. They were Germans, gazing curiously. Americans, Frenchmen, Britons grew visible likewise. Machine-gunners unbuckled their belts, gave stiff salutes toward the opposing barbed wire, and next walked deliberately toward the rear. And then a sound "like the noise of a light wind" could be heard, whether the troops stood at Verdun or in Belgium. Across four hundred miles, millions of men were cheering from the Vosges to the sea.

Chapter 29

THE PEACE TREATIES AND THEIR AFTERMATH (1919-23)

"THE ARMISTICE has been signed this morning. Everything for which America fought has been accomplished. It will now be our fortunate duty to assist by example, by sober, friendly counsel and by material aid in the establishment of a just democracy throughout the world."

Thus President Wilson to his countrymen, November 11, 1918. In a little more than two months he was to attend the opening session of the peace conference at Paris, there to do battle for long dreary months for those ideals which he cherished so dearly.

To what extent was this venture of the American President into the maelstrom of European diplomacy a success; to what extent a failure?

Any answer to that question calls for an analysis of the handicaps under which he labored. Among them six are outstanding: a disunited country behind him; an antagonistic House of Commons in Britain; territorial ambitions of the French; secret treaties struck by his allies before the close of the war; the impossibility of applying his principle of self-determination to the closely packed yet highly differentiated nationalities in Austria-Hungary; and Wilson's own temperament.

A new Congress had been elected in the United States in November, 1918. Wilson had asked for support and it had been denied him. The Republicans controlled both houses of Congress, and Republican leaders loudly proclaimed that Wilson did not represent his own country.

In Britain there had also been an election. The facile, evasive, and slippery Lloyd George had been endorsed even more emphatically by his electorate than Wilson had been repudiated by his. A short time before, Lloyd George had signed, together with Wilson, a document limiting the amount of money the Germans must pay in reparations. He was reëlected by repudiating his word, and by promising the British people that he would extract from the surrendered foe impossibly large sums. And behind Lloyd George now stood the most hardboiled House of Commons in British history.

Clemenceau detested Wilson and his emphasis on ideals. The Premier of France was the oldest and most experienced of the peacemakers. Twice he had seen Germans marching through Paris streets. There were many more million Germans in Europe than there were Frenchmen—far too many. The peace terms could not be too harsh for Clemenceau. He favored detaching the left bank of the Rhine altogether from Germany, the annexation of the Saar Valley and of German colonies to France.

The anti-Wilson forces confronted Wilson at Paris with a number of secret treaties they had made among themselves involving annexations. Among them was a treaty with Italy which guaranteed her lands occupied by German nationals. And another was a treaty between Britain and Japan giving Japan ownership of islands in the Pacific north of the equator. Those signing these treaties said their word was pledged. Wilson dug in behind the peace terms they had accepted. It was an impasse.

Then, too, it was impossible to unscramble the different nationalities in Austria-Hungary without injustice to large minorities. Geographically and economically the Danube valley was a natural unit; ethnographically it was a hodgepodge. It was impossible to draw the boundaries of a Czechoslovakia in order to give Czechs self-determination without denying it to Germans and Magyars. An enlarged Rumania which would guarantee self-determination to Rumanians automatically would deny it to Germans and South Slavs.

And finally there was Wilson's own temperament. Intent on broad objectives, he seemingly was oblivious to those minor courtesies which help to soften disagreements. In speaking in the Guild Hall in London, it never seems to have occurred to him to say a few gracious words in praise of British sacrifices in the war; during his long stay in France, it apparently never occurred to him to visit the battlefields, close as they were to Paris. Wilson was both prophet and statesman but not a good politician. Furthermore, such politics as he was familiar with were American, not European. He was lost in a strange environment. British journalists came to think of him as a man easily deceived by specious words; more fair, perhaps, would it be to regard him as a man who really was aware of what he was doing, and who sacrificed much—possibly too much —to gain acceptance for his life's dream, the League of Nations.

Under these circumstances, it is remarkable that the President was able to accomplish as much as he did. And unfortunate as the peace treaties turned out to be, it may well be argued that they would have been more so had it not been for Woodrow Wilson.

Always it must be remembered the Germans did not surrender unconditionally. Terms were granted them. They were fair terms, even if at times ambiguously stated. And their author had been Wilson. Before the armistice was drawn up, the Germans had agreed to lay down their arms on the guarantee that the peace to follow would be based on Wilson's fourteen points and his subsequent speeches and addresses.

Here were the pre-armistice terms, accepted by the British and the French as well as by the Germans. The British and the French did not like them; but when Wilson threatened to withdraw America's armies and to make a separate peace with Germany his allies accepted his proposals with two reservations. One of these related to "freedom of the seas," now deleted because of ambiguities. The other sharpened and defined what the Germans might be charged in way of reparations. In one of the President's speeches he had stated that they were responsible for the restoration of invaded territories. The revision was made to read, "responsible for damage done to the civilian population on land, sea and from the air." Obviously unless this change had been made Britain would have received nothing, since she had not been invaded, her direct civilian losses having come from submarine sinkings and air raids.

Wilson's Victories

The President's major victories at Paris were the curbing of French expansionists and the creation of the League of Nations. The French would have liked to have detached the Rhineland, that part of the German Empire west of the Rhine, from Germany altogether, and to have made of it a neutral buffer state. And in opposing this Wilson had the support of Lloyd George. The French then proposed the occupation of the Rhineland for thirty years, and at Wilson's insistence this was cut in half to fifteen years. The French then demanded the annexation of the Saar Valley with its overwhelming German population. Here once again Wilson opposed them, but accepted a compromise whereby France was given title to the coal mines of the Saar as compensation for the destruction of coal mines in France, and the Saar was put under the jurisdiction of the proposed League of Nations for fifteen years. At the conclusion of that time a plebiscite of the inhabitants was to decide whether they desired inclusion in the French Republic, or the continued rule of the League, or return to Germany. If the third option was taken proviso was made for the repurchase of the coal mines.

The greater part of the President's time and energy at the peace conference was devoted to the formation and acceptance of the League of Nations. The idea behind it was not new, and Wilson's league was of mixed Anglo-American parentage, the American League to enforce Peace, of which William Howard Taft had been president, and the British Society of Nations, whose head, Lord Phillimore, had drawn up a form of constitution which served as the original model. But Wilson was the principal advocate of the League at Paris, and he had worked hard and long over various drafts, and was responsible for the famous article X which guaranteed the signatories against external aggression.

Serious difficulties were encountered by Wilson. Some came from the

THE BEACON LIGHT.

[Lord ROBERT CECIL is taking a leading part in the campaign for making the objects of the League of Nations better understood.   The campaign opened on the anniversary of the Armistice.]

(*Punch,* Nov. 12, 1919.)

French, some from the Japanese, some from his own Americans. The French insisted on a league "with teeth," in other words with an international army, presumably against future German attacks, presumably also with a French general in command. The Japanese were equally determined that the League should include a specific affirmation of racial equality. American opinion, which was lukewarm, was certain to oppose both these ideas; and in addition it most certainly could not be won over to approval without specific recognition of the binding character of the Monroe Doctrine and without an escalator clause permitting members to resign. Final acceptance of Wilson's covenant, as he liked to call his league, did not come until late in the sessions of the conference, and not until after he had made a special trip back to America to plead for its approval there. And it was while he was so engaged that a number of compromises were made in the peace settlement by his alter ego, Colonel House.

The League of Nations, as finally drafted, provided for an assembly representing all countries with one vote each, and for a council of nine members, five permanent and four elected by the assembly to serve for one term each. Permanent seats were to be given to the United States, Great Britain, France, Italy, and Japan. The headquarters of the League were to be at Geneva, where a secretariat or permanent board of officials was to be located. Attached to the League was to be a World Court for the settlement of international judicial disputes and an international Labor Office, which it was hoped might standardize conditions of labor throughout the world. The Assembly of the League was to meet in Geneva once a year, the Council four times a year, but not necessarily in Geneva. The latter body also could be summoned any time if danger threatened world peace. All members of the League were obligated to submit disputes between them to arbitration or to the Council for review. Decisions, to be effective, had to be unanimous.

Wilson's Defeats

Wilson's major defeats at Paris were in regard to colonies, Japanese conquests in China, and the reparation settlement to be made with Germany.

In accordance with the pre-armistice agreement there was to be "an impartial treatment of the colonial question, having in mind the best interests of native peoples." (Number 5 of Wilson's accepted fourteen points.) There should be no trouble over this, said the British Prime Minister. German Southwest Africa has been conquered by the Union of South Africa, a democracy; German Samoa has been conquered by New Zealand, a democracy; German New Guinea has been conquered by Australia, a democracy. The best interests of the native peoples is best secured by annexing them to those countries whose democratic faith is the best guarantee of fair treatment. And needless to say this British demand for outright annexation was warmly seconded by France who had her eye on Togo and Kamerun, and by Japan firmly entrenched in German-owned islands north of the equator.

But Wilson had proclaimed in his speeches that there should be no annexations, and these proposed annexations were a repudiation of the pre-armistice terms. On the other hand he was opposed to the return of her colonies to Germany since such a course of action would be prejudicial to "the best interests of the native peoples."

Wilson's high hope was that his League of Nations might first be organized before anything was done about dependent possessions. His European allies, however, pressed for an immediate colonial settlement. The President then fathered an expedient which might have functioned well had there not been crippling amendments. This was the principle of the mandate or trusteeship, whereby the country having a mandate should hold it in trust for the League and report to it annually.

The idea looked good and was accepted. There were to be three classes of mandates. Class A consisted of those regions with a fair degree of cultural advancement which might look forward in the near future to independence. Here the control of the mandatory power was slight. Falling in this category were places like Syria, Palestine, and Iraq. Class B mandates were German colonies in central Africa where there was to be more detailed supervision, but none the less a fairly long list of guarantees, such as the prohibition of slavery, freedom of trade and equality of opportunity. Class C mandates were German colonies closely adjacent to the mandatory power, and to all intent and purpose incorporated in it, since its laws became immediately applicable to the mandate and guarantees protecting the natives were fewer in number than in Class B. For instance, in Class C mandates there was nothing said about "equality of opportunity." Virtually this was veiled annexation, the only difference being the pledged word of the mandatory power to make its annual report.

The acceptance of the mandate principle, although urged by Wilson, cannot be recorded as a Wilson victory. As things worked out, it was a Wilson defeat, since in drawing up the terms of the various mandates it proved possible to insert clauses *not* in the best interest of the native peoples. As an illustration the French inserted a clause in their mandate making it legal to conscript Negroes in Africa to fight not simply there but in Europe. This caught Wilson's eye and he would have none of it. The clause was stricken out and a more general statement made whereby, by a little twist here and a little twist there, the same thing could be done.

Wilson encountered a second defeat when dealing with Japan. The Japanese not only were in actual possession of the German islands north of the equator (Class C mandates); they also had seized the German-leased port of Tsingtao on the Shantung peninsula and were busily engaged in extending their sway beyond Kiaochow Bay. Meanwhile China had entered the war on the side of the Allies, and largely through American persuasion. Wilson, therefore, argued that Japan should return to China all concessions wrested from her by the Germans.

The Japanese, unable to obtain their coveted recognition of racial equality in the League of Nations, were determined not simply to retain German concessions in China but in addition those which they had forced an impotent Chinese government to yield to them in 1915. Trifling modifications of the latter were made by Japan. But on the main issue she remained adamant. Wilson yielded. If he had not done so, Japan made it clear that she would not become a member of the League.

A third defeat was the Italian settlement. The Italian frontier was not drawn in accordance with the pre-armistice guarantee "along clearly recognizable lines of nationality," but the reverse. Somewhere between 200,000 and 250,000 Germans in the Upper Tyrol were included in Italy. About fifty-two per cent of the people in the Istrian Peninsula, now given to Italy, were of non-Italian nationality, and seventy-five per cent, if not more, of the population of the annexed regions in Dalmatia on the east coast of the Adriatic were non-Italian.

The reason for this violation of Wilsonian principles is to be found in the "secret treaties" made between the Allies during the war; and the fact that they were not abrogated upon the acceptance of Wilson's fourteen points and subsequent addresses is (the one question of reparations aside) the strongest single argument against the treaty settlement as a whole.

For purely military reasons the Allies had in their hour of great peril paid high for Italian support. The French and British now claimed that they were in honor bound to keep their word to Italy. Wilson asserted that the acceptance of his principles cancelled the secret treaties made earlier. There certainly was much to be said for this point of view. Early in the war, before American troops embarked for Europe, the Allies might logically have expected Wilson to inquire into these treaties, but apparently he did not. Now that they were brought to light he denied their validity.

The American committee of experts on Italy's frontier could find no argument in favor of taking Upper Tyrol away from Austria, but it did discover plausible reasons for the Italian annexation of the Istrian Peninsula. Population strains were so mixed in the peninsula, they said, that it was impossible to tell very much about census statistics, and after all the Austrian government before the war had iniquitously imported Slovene laborers just for the purpose of swelling the anti-Italian total. As for Dalmatia and the eastern coast of the Adriatic Wilson's advisers gave contradictory counsel. His six experts were unanimous that it would be a violation of the pre-armistice terms if any of this Slavic-held land should go to Italy. On the other hand a number of his more politically-minded councillors argued that the cities on the coast had once been Venetian outposts and the Austrians for a long time had been playing dirty politics and oppressing those of Italian blood. Dalmatia, as a whole, was Italian in culture even if not in blood, and it was absurd to expect Italy to be content with a potential enemy directly opposite her on the eastern shores of the Adriatic.

Curiously enough, the President himself took no interest in the Tyrol question where his principles were so clearly defied. What enraged him was the Italian demand for Fiume on the eastern shores of the Adriatic, the former port of Hungary, a demand not based on the Treaty of London, which had left Fiume for the Yugoslavs, but founded on his own principle of self-determination. The Italians could not have it both ways, said President Wilson, gaining certain territory because of the secret treaty and yet other territory because they invoked his principles.

Meanwhile, the Italians who had walked out of the conference rather than lose Fiume hurried back to Paris in order to sign the Treaty of Versailles, since by so doing Italy obtained what she had bargained for in 1915.

The major defeat suffered by Wilson was the reparation settlement. What it legitimately called for was simple enough: an itemized bill for damages suffered by civilians as the result of German military attack from under the water, from invasion, and from the air. This was the letter of the bond, and this and no more was to be charged against the Germans.

Keynes, British financial expert, after a careful survey, estimated the total at somewhere between ten and eleven billion dollars. And as young John Foster Dulles, a lawyer attached to Wilson's staff, stated, the victors were precluded from demanding more, no matter how just such a demand might be, because they of their own accord had placed these limitations in the pre-armistice terms.

The issue was drawn. Lloyd George had assured the British electorate that his committee of bankers had said that the Germans could pay $100,000,000,000, and that in justice they should pay the entire cost of the war. Clemenceau supported Lloyd George. Woodrow Wilson refused to budge beyond the letter of the bond.

Enter then General Smuts, prime minister of the Union of South Africa, and author of a book on holism. Smuts was quite capable of making white seem black and the reverse. He won Wilson over to his side by this argument: It was no ordinary war that had been won. The Allied soldiers were mainly civilians who had been conscripted. If wounded they would receive pensions, and if killed their widows would be entitled to them. Pensions then were payments due people who were really civilians and only temporarily soldiers. They were therefore simply compensation for losses suffered by civilians which it was legitimate to charge against the Germans. This was a specious argument. Once admit pensions as damages done to civilians and it follows logically that the same argument could be made for taxes paid by civilians for carrying on the war. And in this case, if this were done, the Germans could be assessed for the entire cost of the war. And this the pre-armistice terms very clearly forbade.

One suspects that Wilson was dimly aware of the slippery character of Smuts' proposal, but he was thoroughly exhausted physically and had never shown much interest in purely economic matters. "Logic be damned," the President was quoted as saying, "I am going to sign for pensions." And so they were embedded in the peace treaty, the bill to be determined by an international reparations commission and presented to the Germans later.

Poland

There remained one other great controversy at the peace conference as regards Germany, and that was how to draw the boundaries of the resuscitated Poland. The settlement finally reached cannot well be included as a Wilson defeat or a Wilson victory, for the President in this particular fight was largely an onlooker, the two major contestants being Lloyd George and Clemenceau.

Traditional French foreign policy for centuries had been in favor of a strong Poland to exert pressure on Germany from the East. And now the French saw their chance: they demanded that the German city of Danzig on the Baltic at the mouth of the Vistula be given to Poland; and they also proposed that the Poles annex generous areas to the south and east of Danzig which, if consummated, would have reduced East Prussia to such minimal proportions that it would probably wither on the vine.

But Lloyd George would have none of this. He insisted that Danzig be placed under the jurisdiction of the League of Nations, that plebiscites be taken in those areas adjacent to that city which the French would hand over to Poland, and furthermore that a plebiscite be held in Upper Silesia, where it was believed that Germans were more numerous than Poles. The latter had been promised access to the sea; that meant the Vistula Valley, and certainly the right to export and import through Danzig, or else the pre-armistice terms would have been meaningless. But Danzig was close to a one-hundred-per-cent German town and the British Prime Minister would not consent to Poland having it.

His action in so doing made Lloyd George the standard bearer of Wilsonian principles and not the President, a situation not easy to explain. It may partly be accounted for by Wilson's distrust of Lloyd George; by worry over the League of Nations; by personal illness; and also by ill-informed American experts who assured him that Poles were far more numerous in the localities where plebiscites were taken than they after-

wards showed themselves to be. Wilson finally threw in the weight of
his influence behind Lloyd George; Danzig went to the League with
commercial rights in its guaranteed Poland; and the plebiscites all voted
for Germany rather than for Poland.

Austria-Hungary

Of the various problems which confronted the peacemakers, one of
the most complicated was what to do with the ramshackle empire of the
Hapsburgs. By the conclusion of the war both the Czechs and the South
Slavs had been promised independence, and to bring that about meant
the dissolution of Austria-Hungary. Wilson's fourteen points had merely
promised "free development" for the various nationalities within her
borders, and presumably the better part of wisdom would have been to
compel some form of federation for lands lying in the Danube valley.
But since the publication of the fourteen points the Czechs had fought
against the Germans and the South Slavs against the Austrians.

Furthermore, long before the last stages of the war Czech leaders had already organized an independent Czech government in Paris which had obtained recognition; and as early as April, 1918, Bosnians, Slovenes, and Serbs had met in Italy, and by the Pact of Rome had proclaimed an independent South Slav nation which was to become Yugoslavia. It was now too late to insist on mere federation.

New boundaries had to be drawn for the two enemy states, Austria and Hungary; and it is evident that both must lose a great deal of territory if justice was to be done to North Slavs, Czechs, Slovaks, Poles, Ruthenians, and Slovenes in the old Austria, and also to the Rumanians and South Slavs in Hungary. For the most part this was accomplished with a rough show of justice. Austria became a puny little country comparable to Switzerland in area. This, however, was inevitable since she lost Bohemia (home of the Czechs) and Galicia (home of the Austrian Poles and Ruthenians) as well as her southern provinces occupied by Slovenes. After all, most of the German-speaking people in the old Austria were still to be found in the new. Hungary also suffered the same fate. That too was necessary, since several million Magyars woke up to find themselves citizens of Czechoslovakia, Rumania, and Yugoslavia owing to the application of Wilsonian ideas of self-determination. Nevertheless, the great majority of Magyars still found homes for themselves within the shrunken borders of the new Hungary. That there were injustices in drawing the new boundaries will be apparent as we review the Danubian settlement; but it is desirable to remember that for the most part the principle of self-determination was followed. Violations of it were numerous but in most instances unavoidable.

Taking up one after another of the countries now carved wholly or in part out of the old Hapsburg lands, we come first to Czechoslovakia. An unfortunate name was given to it, one implying the union of Czechs and Slovaks. There was really no necessity of uniting them, except that the Slovaks, formerly under Hungarian rule, were scarcely strong enough to stand by themselves unless united with the Czechs, a much more numerous and advanced people formerly under Austrian rule. By placing both Czechs and Slovaks in one country, and by joining to them the old Hungarian province of Ruthenia, a queer-shaped state was evolved, looking somewhat like a tadpole with its head in Bohemia and its tail in Ruthenia.

Bohemia, if taken by itself, was an old country not manufactured out of whole cloth to please the Czechs. Its capital, Prague, had been a foyer of Christianity and culture at a time when the Teutonic tribes to the north were semi-nomadic barbarians, and at Prague had been established the first university in Central Europe. During the sixteenth century, however, Bohemia had fallen under Hapsburg sway, and in the

seventeenth and eighteenth centuries it had become more and more
Teutonized. During the last half of the nineteenth century, the submerged Czech nationality, perhaps always in the majority, had reasserted
itself, but even as late as 1914 the predominant class in Bohemia, certainly
in wealth and possibly in culture, had been South German, looking to
Vienna.

The Czechs in Bohemia outnumbered the Germans by possibly three
to one, and to a large extent it was impossible to give Bohemia or
Czechoslovakia any reasonable boundaries at all without including in

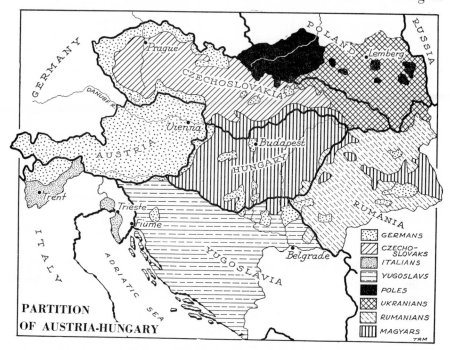

PARTITION
OF AUSTRIA-HUNGARY

GERMANS
CZECHO-
SLOVAKS
ITALIANS
YUGOSLAVS
POLES
UKRANIANS
RUMANIANS
MAGYARS

them a large part of the 3,000,000 Germans in Bohemia, for the country,
topographically, was a flat pocket or plain surrounded by mountains, and
the majority of the Germans lived on or near the border. Nevertheless,
as the Americans on the Czechoslovak committee demonstrated, some
300,000 of these Germans in Egerland and in two other border districts
might have been permitted to join the Reich without serious strategic
injuries to the boundaries of the new country.

But it was not the Germans alone who were denied in this instance the
right of self-determination. If the boundaries of Czechoslovakia had been
drawn fairly on an ethnographical basis, instead of looking like a tadpole
the country more nearly would have resembled an hourglass. Only by
including thousands of Poles on the north and possibly 750,000 Magyars

on the south was it possible to make Czechoslovakia bulge out in the middle. Furthermore, for economic reasons it was considered essential that Czechoslovakia include land where these Magyars lived, since the only railway connection between Prague and eastern Czechoslovakia went through the old city of Pressburg on the Danube in Hungary and through parts of Slovakia where there were more Magyars than Slovaks.

The Magyars suffered even greater losses elsewhere. Rumania had, as we have seen (p. 530), been bribed into the war by Allied promises of (a) Bukovina, north of the Carpathians and formerly a part of Austria—in Bukovina thirty-four per cent of the population was Magyar; (b) Transylvania, or eastern Hungary—with a population largely Rumanian, but with a large Magyar and a lesser German minority; (c) the Banat of Temesvar, across the Danube, north of Belgrade, where Serbs, Rumanians, and Magyars were hopelessly mixed. All three regions were lost to Hungary, the Rumanians receiving Bukovina and Transylvania and dividing the Banat with Yugoslavia.

To do justice to both the Magyars and the Rumanians on the basis of self-determination was impossible. A large part of the Magyar folk in Transylvania, for instance, were located well toward the Carpathian Mountains and between them and their fellow Magyars was a solid section of Rumanians. Nevertheless, the peace conference might have been much more just in regard to Hungary's eastern and southern boundaries, for at least 500,000 Magyars on the western borders of Transylvania were included in the greater Rumania, while some 250,000 odd, on the borders of the Banat, were included in Yugoslavia, the excuse in the former case being that it was essential for Rumania to have possession of the only railroad running north and south through West Transylvania.

Arguments raised at the peace conference in regard to strategic boundaries, railroads, and economic necessity were numerous, and always the French insisted that the new nations must be *viable:* these were one-way arguments, never made in behalf of Austria and Hungary, enemy states, but ever appropriate to Italy, Yugoslavia, Rumania, and Czechoslovakia. Vienna, a city of 2,000,000, former commercial and banking entrepôt of the Danube Valley, now was left to starve in the center of a tiny country, largely mountainous, where almost every boundary was but an hour distant by train or automobile. Budapest at least had food supplies from the Hungarian plain, but the city itself was much too large for the purely agricultural population left within the truncated confines of the new Hungary.

Meanwhile, Germany was to recognize the independence of Austria, a neat way of preventing the Austrian Germans from pleading self-determination and joining forces with the Germans in the Fatherland.

Herein have been described the main provisos of the so-called peace settlement. By the Treaty of Versailles, made with Germany, that country lost relatively little territory. Alsace-Lorraine, three tiny enclaves on the Belgian border, measured more readily in hundreds of yards than in miles, a part of northern Schleswig given to the Danes after a plebiscite, the city of Memel on the northeastern boundary with surrounding territory to the League of Nations (Memel's population was about 20,000, mostly Germans, but Memel and, the whole region, about half the size of Rhode Island, contained possibly as many Lithuanians as Germans); the city of Danzig to the League of Nations (some 300,000 Germans here); but Danzig was at the mouth of the Vistula and was regarded as an essential port for Poland; the district of Posen to Poland (the greater part of the population unquestionably Polish); the Polish Corridor, and a large part of Upper Silesia, also to Poland. For most of these losses of territory there was real justification; at least their cession could not be called a failure to live up to the bargain whereby Germany ceased fighting.

For the economic settlement there was no justification. The demand that the Kaiser and high German officials be tried by Allied law courts was a vindictive absurdity, and quite as absurd was the celebrated clause in the treaty, Number 231, whereby Germany acknowledged on the part of herself and her allies entire responsibility for the losses suffered by the Allies during the war. The Germans were forced to sign this untrue and humiliating statement with a pistol pointed at their head, for the economic blockade of Germany still continued and Germans starved. No clause in the entire treaty gave Hitler more of a lever when the opportunity came to denounce "the dictate of Versailles."

Separate peace treaties also were signed with the other Central Powers, that of St. Germain with Austria, Trianon with Hungary, Neuilly with Bulgaria, Sèvres with Turkey. All of these four treaties violated the Wilsonian doctrine of self-determination to a greater or less degree. Much less important than the Treaty of Versailles, they none the less were a part of the peace settlement.

On the whole, the latter was unsatisfactory. No Talleyrand had represented Germany in Paris, and the Germans had been forced to sign on the dotted line. The American President, breathing forth idealism, had put his name to a treaty which in all that concerned economics was a breach of faith with the enemy. The Prime Minister of England, on the other hand, had been responsible more than any one else for the reparations muddle, although it must be acknowledged that the French were his close second. The treaty was so bad that General Smuts thought seriously of not signing. About all that could be said in its favor is that it might have been worse; it might have annexed the Rhineland to France; it might have divided Germany again at the River Main, as she was divided in 1866; and the treaties of St. Germain and Trianon might have given the Czechs a corridor across the Hungarian plain which they asked for, thus separating Austria from Hungary and joining Czechoslovakia with Yugoslavia. These absurdities were at least avoided. It is a wild exaggeration to speak of the settlement as a Carthaginian peace, as many writers have done. Carthage was demolished and its site sown with salt. In the last analysis, the defeated Germans had received much fairer treatment than they themselves had meted out to the defeated Russians at Brest Litovsk. The men of Versailles not only did not demolish Germany but left open two ways of mitigating the harshness of their terms. There was the Reparation Commission which might show sense in tuning down the economic settlement, and there was, of course, the League of Nations, to which the idealists clung, in despair mingled with rapture.

From 1919 to the Ruhr

The four years which succeeded 1919 were full of disaster for Europe. The peace treaties seemingly settled nothing and confusion became worse confounded. Worse than that; the economic burdens borne by the European peoples became heavier and more intolerable than they had been during the war.

The first country to repudiate the Treaty of Versailles was the United States. The reasons which motivated the United States Senate were not as admirable as they might have been. The senators did not oppose the Treaty because it was unjust and a repudiation of Wilsonian promises; what they objected to was the League, the only ray of light, and a dim one at that, in a world black with angry hate. Even so, Wilson could have secured ratification had he been willing to accept drastic amendments to the League. Upon his refusal, the Treaty was rejected by the Senate and the presidential election of 1920 confirmed its rejection, the United States choosing to make its own separate treaty with Germany.

The effect of so doing was profound. It meant that the United States would not be represented either at Geneva (a term now constantly to be used as a synonym for the League of Nations), or on the Reparations Committee which was to assess the final bill against the Germans. It also served notice on the French that their concessions at Paris in return for American and British guarantees of their eastern boundary lines were useless. Even if the Senate had approved the Versailles Treaty, it is improbable that it would have accepted the additional triangular treaty between France, England, and the United States in regard to that guarantee. Now it was evident that the latter was a worthless bit of paper; for with America dropping out, England no longer was under any obligation arising from that treaty.

France, indeed, in the hour of victory felt very uneasy. Three times within one hundred years her soil had been invaded by the Germans; suppose they should come again? For the time being the French had them in the gutter; Germany was convulsed with civil strife, without allies, and defended by an army reduced to 100,000. French troops, not German, kept the "Watch on Rhine." But suppose this situation changed? There were 20,000,000 Germans too many, so the French thought. France had wanted a league of nations equipped with an international army but had given in to the British and to the Americans; she had wanted to separate the Rhineland, which lay west of the river, from the Reich, or at least to occupy it for thirty years, and again she had yielded, cutting in half the period of occupancy; and now her third bulwark against a re- vived and powerful Germany—the Anglo-American guarantee was down. Under such circumstances she not only determined to keep the German foe in economic vassalage but to surround him with a chain of states bound to herself in defensive alliance.

The French found it easy at first to secure allies. A close alliance with Belgium was consummated very soon after the Versailles Treaty, and shortly after, both Czechoslovakia and Poland joined France in a military alliance, thus surrounding Germany on three sides by prospective foes.

Czechoslovakia owed a great deal to France. That country had recog- nized and equipped the Czechoslovakian national army, had offered Paris as a temporary headquarters for the Czechoslovakian government, and had supported through thick and thin the claims of Czechoslovakia at the peace conference, ever insisting that the new nation be made *viable*, have economic resources and a creditable transportation system, whether self-determination was violated or not. In vain had the "Sudeten- deutsch," as the Germans in the old Austrian province of Bohemia were known, begged for the recognition of that principle. They were told it was impossible to employ it, that they must rest content with the promise (never fulfilled) that the Republic of Czechoslovakia would be constituted on the Swiss model as a federative rather than as a unitary state.

Nationalistic minorities in this ward of France were clearly marked and from the beginning were troublesome. About two-thirds of the popula- tion was Czech or Slovak; but a great many Slovaks liked the Poles or the Magyars better than they did the Czechs. About one-quarter of the total population was German, bitterly opposed to Czechs and Slovaks alike. The remainder, approximately 1,500,000, consisted of Magyars, Jews, Poles, and Ukrainians, not easy to handle. Nevertheless, Czecho- slovakia lay like a great bastion in Central Europe, and the French were delighted at the thought of a powerful Czechoslovakia threatening Ger- many on the south. The definite Franco-Czechoslovak alliance was not formally completed, it is true, until 1924, but from the beginning French advice, French money, and French military aid was placed freely at the disposal of this new state, the most important of all the smaller satellite nations that France hoped to attach to herself.

To the east of Germany lay Poland, another potential French ally. The Poles had been divided among themselves during the war as to how Poland might be resurrected. Some of them, among whom was the conspirator and revolutionary patriot Pilsudski, were bitterly opposed to Russia and thought it might best be accomplished through the instrumentality of Austria. Others thought the best hope lay in supporting Russia against Germany. Consequently, Poles fought on both sides in the World War. But after the victorious Austro-Germans set up a puppet state of Poland in the midst of the conflict, Pilsudski was disillusioned. Unwilling to support the Central Powers, he was thrown in prison, not to escape until after the armistice, after which he placed himself at the head of a temporary Polish government at Warsaw.

Meanwhile, a Polish army had been organized in France in 1918 and the Poles in it had fought on the western front for France. Other Poles were on the Italian front, some on the Italian side, some on the Austrian, and still other Polish troops were deep in the Ukraine. It was Pilsudski's task to get them all home, to draw up a constitution, to establish boundaries, to resurrect a nation.

In all these endeavors he received the staunch backing of France. She sent the Polish troops from the west through Germany as early as April, 1919; she assisted Pilsudski with money and munitions; she supported his demands at the peace conference fully and effectively, and if the French had not been opposed there by Britain, Poland would have dipped into former German territory even more than it actually did.

The Versailles Treaty practically determined the western boundaries of Poland, but toward the east Pilsudski's efforts practically were unchecked—except, that is, by British disapproval which the Polish chieftain ignored. He occupied Kiev in the heart of the Ukraine; he pounced upon Vilna, capital of Lithuania, to the northeast; he pressed on against the Russian Communists. The latter smote Pilsudski hip and thigh, and only through the timely arrival of a French military commission was he rescued from disaster in a battle before Moscow, which staved off communism from Poland and incidentally from Central Europe. The Treaty of Riga (1921) with Russia, which followed, extended the Polish boundaries well to the east, not so far as in 1772, the date of the first partition of Poland, but far enough to place some 4,000,000 Russians under Polish sovereignty.

Thanks also to French connivance, Pilsudski was able in 1923 to retain Vilna, in spite of the League of Nations. The French had been somewhat embarrassed when Poland and Czechoslovakia had almost come to blows over that small sector of Upper Silesia known as Teschen, for France wanted both Poles and Czechs as allies. That difficulty, however, was ironed out in 1920 by a division of Teschen between the two contestants, and now, thanks again to France, the Poles secured the better part of what was left of Upper Silesia.

The hot-headed Poles had tried to seize that rich district by a military coup in 1919 but were headed off since the great powers at Paris had provided for a plebiscite in Upper Silesia. Despite the fact that the Germans won the vote for the district as a whole, France insisted that it be divided, and in the final settlement of 1921 French aid was again given Poland. The award to that country of 53 coal mines out of 67, of 11 out of 16 zinc and lead mines, and of 21 out of 37 blast furnaces was, it is true, the award of the League of Nations. But behind the action of the League were French diplomacy and French pressure, for several months before Pilsudski had gone to Paris, there to conclude a strong military alliance with France.

To keep the Germans, however, in perpetual economic subjection, involved an inner contradiction; if this desired end was consummated, how could the Germans become sufficiently prosperous to pay for reparations? The French were in a nasty dilemma; they wanted a great deal of money from Germany but at the same time they hoped to keep their eastern neighbor poverty-stricken. No such dilemma confronted the English; they had neither fear nor memory of a German invasion of England, and they were quite willing that Germany become prosperous again, the more so that their own industrial country could not hope to prosper while Central Europe lay prostrate. The English who lived by international trade, could not afford to wait; the French, primarily agricultural in their economy, could do so. In consequence, the Treaty of Versailles was no sooner signed than dissension broke out between the British and French as to the extent of the bill to be levied against Germany, the French advocating that it be raised to a high level, the British favoring a lower amount to revive business as soon as possible.

It proved easier to decide how the receipts should be divided than what the sum total should be. In 1920 it was agreed that fifty-two per cent should go to France, twenty-two per cent to the British Empire, ten per cent to Italy, eight per cent to Belgium, and the remaining eight per cent to be divided among other countries. A year later the total was placed at $56,000,000,000; at which the Germans made a counter offer of $12,500,000,000, contingent on subtraction of $5,000,000,000 which the Germans claimed they had already paid by sequestration of property and goods. They asked also loans to Germany, her retention of Upper Silesia, and the removal of restrictions placed upon German commerce.

The Allies, duly horrified, threatened the occupation of the Ruhr Valley, the heart of industrial Germany, and the Germans made a new offer. Again it was for $12,500,000,000, but without hypothetical deduction of $5,000,000,000 and with the promise of rebuilding by German labor the destroyed villages and towns of France. This, in turn, the Reparations Committee rejected but lowered its own demands to $32,000,000,000, a figure the Germans, after vain protest, reluctantly accepted.

Did the payment of this sum lie within the bounds of possibility? It could only be paid in three ways: (*a*) by the transfer of actual gold from Germany to the Allies; (*b*) by services, the Germans repairing in person the damages they had done and delivering commodities like ships and coal, to the Allies; or (*c*) a revival of international trade whereby the Germans could build up credits throughout the world which might be assigned to the Allies.

Method (*a*) was impossible. Thirty-two billion dollars was more than twice the actual amount of all known gold in the world and but a tiny fraction of the world's gold supply was in Germany. Method (*b*) was unacceptable. The French had no intention of permitting an invasion of German carpenters, masons, and plumbers for the rebuilding of French towns, thus throwing French artisans out of work. The British already had more ships than they could find cargoes for and their own shipyards were deserted. Their coal industry also was paralyzed, injuriously affected already by reparation payments of coal made to Italy and France. There remained then method (*c*). The success of this depended on the willingness of foreign countries to lower their tariff barriers against German goods. The United States was unwilling to do this, as was also France. To the east Poland was erecting and not demolishing tariff walls, and beyond Poland lay Russia in the throes of the Communist Revolution—an old German market now almost ruined.

It is conceivable that given a sufficient length of time the Germans might have paid by method (*c*). To do so, however, meant rigid economy and continuous sacrifice for many years, so many that babies born in the midst of the war would have become old folk before the yoke was lifted from their shoulders. The Germans were not willing to put such a yoke upon themselves. They had been forced to accept responsibility for the war and had so signed on paper; but this they had done because they were strangled by the Allies' economic blockade. In the name of victorious democracy, Woodrow Wilson had made them promises which had not been fulfilled. Why then submit to economic slavery? They had signed the peace treaty rather than starve and they would accept the reparation settlement rather than starve: but they felt no responsibility for either the one or the other.

In less than two years the reparation agreement bogged down. The Germans paid the $250,000,000 due in 1921; but so swift was the decline of their mark in the money markets of the world and so swift was the flight of capital from Germany that in 1922 they asked for and received a partial moratorium. Great Britain now took alarm and Lloyd George, still prime minister, summoned an international world economic conference at Genoa. Desperately, he hoped that the United States would participate, for if that happened the obtuse Yankees might realize that one reason for making the Germans pay was to obtain the wherewithal with which the Allies might pay their war debts to America. Desperately, also, did he hope that France might rescind her announced intention not to discuss reparations at this conference. Since both hopes were entirely imaginary there was no real reason for the conference at all. The Germans came and again offered to pay in kind but not in money. The Russians came and struck a treaty with the Germans. Since neither Soviet Russia nor the German republic had funds, it was comparatively simple for them mutually to cancel each other's indebtedness. Other results Genoa had none.

On July 15, 1922, the Germans made their last cash payment; for the rest of that year they were granted a temporary moratorium. The latter was inevitable, since German currency was crashing to oblivion. Four German marks were almost equal to the American dollar in 1914; when the reparation agreement was signed the ratio was 56 to 1. But by November, 1922, it stood at 7,000 marks to the dollar, and was gone now beyond recovery.

The French were very angry. They had sunk huge sums in rebuilding their own devastated areas, and they believed that the Germans were wilfully issuing paper money to make reparations impossible. The inflation in Germany had artificially stimulated industry there and German factories were in full blast. Thereupon the French determined to seize their foes by the throat and by the hair, and in January, 1923, the forces of France marched into the Ruhr.

The valley of the Ruhr, east of the Rhine, was neither very wide nor very long; but it was the heart of industrial Germany. Nine cities with over 2,000,000 inhabitants lay within its narrow confines, as also eighty per cent of the coal and eighty per cent of the blast furnaces left to the Germans. Without the Ruhr, Germany could not exist as an industrial nation. Nevertheless the Germans decided to resist by the only means that lay within their power—the general strike. German miners refused to dig coal for the French masters, German puddlers refused to work the blast furnaces, German engineers would not operate the valley's intricate transportation system. Nothing lay before Germany but helpless poverty; but since the mark had already sunk so far, why not print more and more until the cost of the paper exceeded the value of the numerical digits put upon it? By the end of 1923 this had happened; the mark was now worth two and a half trillion to the dollar and milk was priced at 250,000,000 marks per quart.

The Germans thereupon surrendered and agreed to renew reparation payments if some new basis could be found for so doing. Their middle class had been virtually wiped out. Houses, life-insurance policies, everything that formerly had possessed monetary value was lost to millions of Germans. Almost nobody was employed in industry, practically every one had suffered except peasants and profiteers.

As for the French, their victory was tasteless. Even before the World War, their debt had been colossal and now they staggered under it. They in turn would soon have to devalue their own currency and in the meanwhile they had lost the sympathy of the British, and the Germans, putting into effect the Tolstoyan program of "non-resistance to evil by force" had not been unsuccessful in withstanding them.

All things considered, the dark clouds which hung over Europe in 1919 looked even darker in 1924. The Ruhr invasion of 1923 had seemingly crushed Germany, but without helping the French exchequer. The French still held the military hegemony of Europe, for what it was worth; they had the largest army and supporting it were the armies of Czechoslovakia and Poland, French-trained. But Russia was an imponderable factor; suppose Germany should go communist and join with Russia? Mussolini meanwhile had risen to power in Italy and was challenging both the status quo and the League of Nations. France had a permanent seat on the council of that organization and since nothing could be done without the unanimous consent of that council (and perhaps not much even with it), France had nothing to fear from the League. On the other hand, could she depend upon it in time of need? There seemed to the French but one clear line to pursue—by diplomacy and by money to secure as many allies as possible; to keep up the iron ring around Germany; to continue as she had done in the past to follow the traditional rules of power politics. How disastrous a policy this was to prove, we shall see later.

Chapter 30

THE UNION OF SOVIET SOCIALIST REPUBLICS (U.S.S.R.)

PEACE OF a kind dawned on Western Europe in November, 1918, but in Russia there was not even a semblance of peace. The Bolsheviks (the Reds) faced civil war in their own country, large sections of which were either indifferent to the Revolution or actually under control of anti-Bolshevik factions (the Whites), supported everywhere by Allied sympathy and in many cases by Allied money and Allied soldiers.

During the last stages of the war, English and American troops had occupied Murmansk, the Russian seaport on the Arctic Ocean—this to prevent the capture of war matériel by the Germans. The French, after the collapse of Germany, had landed detachments at Odessa on the Black Sea; and at Vladivostok on the Pacific the Americans and the Japanese landed forces, ostensibly to protect supplies and to guard the Trans-Siberian and Chinese Eastern railways. These various Allied interventions greatly encouraged those former adherents of the Czar who were set on reëstablishing the old regime. To their side now hastened many of the Russian Cadets (the former Constitutional Democrats), some of the Mensheviki (minority socialists), and a few of the old Social Revolutionary party. The Reds found themselves hemmed in on all sides. Allied detachments captured Archangel on the White Sea and threatened them on the north. On the west an ex-Czarist general, Yudenich, aided by White Russians and some Estonians, headed toward St. Petersburg (now Petrograd and soon to be called Leningrad). From the south a large White army under General Denikin, outfitted by Allied guns, airplanes, and tanks, was marching toward Moscow. Meanwhile, at Omsk in Siberia, an anti-Bolshevik directorate, with some claim to be the legal successor of Kerensky's deposed administration, seemed strongly entrenched. Backed by the warlike Czechoslovak troops, who had fought viciously with the Bolsheviks on their retreat toward the Pacific, and by numerous ex-Czarist officers, this directorate in western Siberia, soon to fall under the control of Admiral Kolchak, a White, apparently was quite as strong as that of the Reds centering in Moscow.

The Bolsheviks in 1919 confronted a situation somewhat parallel to that which the French Jacobins faced in 1793—disaffection from within and intervention from without. Like their radical French predecessors, they met the first with militant terrorism and the second with patriotic zeal. Trotsky, the Red commissar for war, created *de novo* a Red army which made up in morale for what it lacked in equipment. Soon it began to win victories. As in the case of the Austro-Prussian invasion of France in 1792, the Allied intervention was only half-hearted. On the former occasion the approach of the second partition of Poland in 1793 had diverted Allied interests elsewhere. Now, after the terrific strain of four years' fighting, the Allies had no stomach for adventures in Russia. The French, from a financial point of view, were likely to lose most from a Bolshevik victory, since the Russian Reds had repudiated the Czar's debts, and France had loaned more money to Russia than to any other country; but on the other hand no troops in Europe were more war-weary than those of France, and mutinies among French soldiers and sailors at the Black Sea ports made Paris hesitant to support Denikin's advance. The British were in somewhat similar case. They had a huge surplus of unsalable war supplies, speedily depreciating in value, and these they placed readily enough at the disposal of the Whites; but the lives of British soldiers were another matter. A general strike of the British trade unions was imminent if British regiments were ordered to fight the Bolsheviks, and the Lloyd George cabinet shrank back from any such commitments. Both British and French had hoped that the Americans would do something to defeat the Reds, and there had been talk at Paris of General Pershing's leading his relatively fresh forces against Trotsky. But the Americans were not interested; they withdrew their meager detachments from Vladivostok and from Murmansk and declined to participate in the anti-Bolshevik front, except to support the barrier of smaller states backed by the Allies (from Finland to Rumania), that the Bolshevik infection might be kept out of Europe.

Partly owing to these facts, Trotsky's armies proved victorious. They were led in many cases by former officers of the Imperial Russian Army, who preferred to fight for their own Russia, even if revolutionary, rather than for the Whites with their foreign support. The Whites, moreover, had no uniform command. The more they advanced into the heart of Russia, the more they embittered the peasants. Had they been willing boldly to proclaim constitutional and economic reform and formally to recognize peasant ownership of the land it is possible that the result might have been different. But even this partial acceptance of the revolution the Whites were unwilling to concede; they wanted their old rights and their former property restored. And so the peasants, at first more or less indifferent, ultimately sided with the Reds against the Whites; confronted with terrorism as practiced by both factions, they decided that the Reds were the lesser of two evils.

The civil war was over by the end of 1920. For a time it looked as though the Poles, acting on the advice of French officers and equipped with French guns, might overcome the Soviets. The Poles drove south and east from Warsaw, captured Kiev in the heart of the Ukraine; and as they did so Baron Wrangel, heading a new White army in the South, advanced north from the Crimea. Both Wrangel and the Poles, however, were routed. Wrangel followed Denikin into exile at Constantinople, and the hard-pressed Poles were in danger of losing Warsaw and would have done so, had it not been for French military assistance. Peace followed. Russia was still an "outlaw" country in the eyes of Western Europe and none of the Allied powers recognized the Soviet government; but on the other hand they took no further steps to defeat the Russian revolution by force of arms.

Left to themselves, the Bolsheviks were free to put into operation their long-cherished dream of a socialist state. They were without funds; they were inexperienced in the practical details of both government and business; and they had on their hands a backward and poverty-stricken peasantry comprising ninety per cent of the population, quite content with the individual ownership of their land, and to all intents and purposes untouched with Marxian ideas of a state-controlled economic life. So exhausted, indeed, were the Reds at the end of the civil war, that the rest of Europe confidently prophesied that their regime could not last. Trains, it was said, did not run in Russia; telephones did not operate; grass grew in the streets; all business was at a standstill; and in Moscow and Petrograd even the houses were falling to pieces. So thought the enemies of Red Russia.

But one thing they forgot—the energy and enthusiasm engendered by a blind faith in a new ideology and in Nicolai Lenin, the embodiment of it. Lenin, a conspirator for decades, came from the lesser nobility. His brother had been put to death as a university student for conspiring against Alexander III, and Lenin himself had been expelled from a Russian university for political agitation. Watched by the police, he went to St. Petersburg, advocated Marxian doctrines, was arrested and exiled for three years to Siberia. He came back, plunged into socialistic propaganda, spent much time at London, Paris, and Geneva, and was the foremost Russian delegate at the Second Congress (1903) of the Second International at Brussels. Here he led the fight of "the hards," or the Bolsheviks, against the "softs," or the Mensheviki, in other words that of the uncompromising Marxians who opposed any coöperation with bourgeois parties against their more opportunist fellows. The Bolsheviki at first won the day, hence their name, which means *majority*. But the

Mensheviki, meaning *minority*, turned the tables at last, and Lenin's group met defeat.

When the abortive revolution of 1905 broke out in Russia, Lenin slipped back to his own country. Here he again experienced defeat as he had in 1903 at the hands of the Mensheviki, since the revolutionary tempo was slowing down, the Czar winning back power and prestige. The Cadets (liberals) held the spotlight and Lenin hated all Cadets, holding that they were "vermin who take possession of the battlefield when the heroes have been defeated"—the heroes in this instance being the striking workmen of Moscow and St. Petersburg. Lenin's own liberty, if not his life, was in danger, for he was living obscurely on a false passport. There was nothing to do for the time being in Russia, and therefore he quit the country in 1907, not to return for ten years.

This second period of exile was spent for the most part in Switzerland and in secret propaganda work. Lenin remained at the head of the Bolsheviki, but the world knew nothing of them or him. In the first Russian Duma there was little talk of socialism, and what there was came from the handful of Mensheviki in it. The Bolsheviks were not even represented. Consequently, when Lenin, with the kind permission of the Germans, came back to Russia in 1917 in the midst of her new revolution, there were few to note that fact or to realize how shrewd the Germans were in importing this dynamic protagonist of proletariat revolt.

Yet this stocky, middle-aged man within three years was to become a dictator in Russia, the first of the series of twentieth-century dictators. Unlike the others Lenin was a close student of economics, had written extensively, and deservedly ranks with Marx and Engels as one of the founding fathers of communism, his most famous contribution to Communist theory being his analysis of imperialism as the last stage of capitalism. A militant of militants, he put his faith first and foremost on the seizure of power by a thoroughly disciplined and purged Communist party.

The universal acclaim with which Lenin was greeted in Russia was not due primarily to what he wrote. Other reasons help account for it. To some extent it may be credited to luck; to some extent to the complete optimism and self-confidence which made him proclaim the last battle as always the final victory. To some extent also it was due to his character. His revolutionary career had been a long one, and his reputation among revolutionaries for sincerity and determination was of the highest. He knew how to direct the energies and how to incite the loyalties of his fellows. The inflammatory but brilliant Trotsky, generally a lone hawk and a suspicious one, finally became his devoted disciple. The Georgian outlaw and ruffian, Stalin, an exile in Siberia as the revolution of 1917 broke, became another.

But in the last analysis, perhaps the major explanation of Lenin's

NIKOLAI LENIN (1870-1924)

power lay in the fact that he was the high priest of a new and virulent religious faith. Such a theory would have amused him greatly, if such a single-tracked mind could have been capable of amusement. How could anyone be said to be a religious prophet while proclaiming that his followers must be active atheists, and that religion was "the opiate of the people"? Closely examined, however, this statement is no paradox. Lenin, we must remember, had faith in one thing—the Revolution. Capitalism (the world) was at an end; communism (heaven) was at hand. It would come, to be sure, on this earth, but so rapid and so lovely would be its advent that all need for government would disappear miraculously, and justice everywhere would reign triumphant, as class ceased to struggle with class in a society in which class was nonexistent.

Lenin, like a good Communist, would object instantly to the word "miraculously," holding that there was no nexus whatever between such an objective and scientific idea as communism and the miraculous. But the real scientist ever holds his hypothesis tentative, and is constantly re-testing and reverifying not only his observed data but the hypotheses from which they are derived. It was not thus with the Marxians, to whom economic conclusions were axiomatic. As a matter of fact, the theoretical foundations of their belief—and Lenin was a convinced Marxian—rested on assumptions which were sufficiently dogmatic and all-inclusive as to become essentially a religious creed.

That creed, in summary, consisted of the following tenets: (a) all thought of a future life must be abandoned, or else it will be forever impossible to organize society upon a just and satisfactory basis; (b) the individual ownership of private property, the father of capitalism and imperialism, brought on the World War and the nemesis of the old order; (c) the communal ownership of goods and the adoption of the Marxian formula, "from each according to his capacity, to each according to his needs," is a categorical imperative; (d) that ownership can only be obtained by a dictatorship of the proletariat; (e) that in the course of time dictatorship will no longer be needed, for a classless society will not require any government; that the writings of Marx, Engels, and Lenin prove the above propositions up to the hilt and make it unnecessary and even heretical to seek elsewhere for any elucidation of human problems. The Communist explanation is inclusive, complete, final. Nothing need be added; nothing must be subtracted. All who oppose this creed, both within and without Russia, are enemies who should receive no mercy, and their defeat may be sought by utilizing any and every means available.

Such was the Communist creed, a religion held with fanatical zeal by fanatical men.

The acceptance of it, however, was not at first widespread nor was Lenin universally acclaimed as the Revolution started. It must be remembered that when he arrived back in Russia he was the accepted leader of only one of the three socialist parties and that the Mensheviki and the Social Revolutionists also were powerful, to say nothing of the Cadets. Only little by little, from the summer of 1917 to the conclusion of the civil war, did Lenin and his gospel become the accepted creed. Possibly, more than anything else, it was the man's cocksureness that insured his victory. He, almost alone among the leaders, was always utterly and completely confident that he knew exactly what should be done. At a time when the Cadets were still trying to keep Russia in the war, it was Lenin who started the cry for "peace and bread." He denounced the war as an imperialistic one in which Russia's allies were as bad as—though no worse than—the Germans. No annexations, no indemnities, Russia to quit the war and to fight one of her own against the bourgeoisie within her borders. The Cadets were traitors to the Revolution; it was not a *liberal* revolution; it was the *Communist* revolution, the greatest, and the best and the *final* revolution.

Such outspoken ideas, for the time being, meant trouble for Lenin, who was accused of being a German agent conspiring against the provisional government, and it was necessary for him frequently to take to cover. Even after the November Revolution, when the Bolsheviks seized power, the leadership of Lenin was not a certainty. When the elections for the Constituent Assembly which met in January, 1918, were held, it was found that the Social Revolutionaries were in a majority and that the Bolsheviks had only about twenty-five per cent of the membership. That assembly was given short shrift by the soviets; it held one session and then was ended by the fiat of the Petrograd soviet. Lenin's excuse was that of Robespierre or that of Cromwell—the assembly did not represent the will of the people.

What was that will? Patently it was above everything else to stop fighting. The Russian soldiers were brave; but no soldier can endure endless waiting for his comrade to be killed so that he may equip himself with that comrade's rifle. Peace and land, Lenin knew, were what the Russians wanted, and he proposed giving them both, and if necessary, peace at any price. In view of the intentions of the Germans to annex Russian provinces, it was not easy for the soviets to swallow his formula altogether, and at first Lenin was in a minority in the Council of People's Commissars, as the tentative revolutionary government was called. Some of the commissars were for further resistance, and even the realistic Trotsky preferred a Fabian plan by which there would be neither peace nor war, the Russians simply retreating before the Germans. But finally Trotsky changed his vote to Lenin's side and the latter won by a majority of one.

The peace with Germany proved popular, as did also the early legislation which the commissars favored. All non-peasant estates were immediately confiscated and placed in the hands of locally elected committees. So also was it with the homes of the wealthy nobles and bourgeois which were now open to residence for the proletariat of the cities. The banks were taken over and their funds appropriated. All debts of the former government, both national and international, were repudiated. All large factories became government property. And to suppress any objections to these stiff measures, the Cheka, or secret police, was organized and given plenary power. In the summer of 1918 the R.S.F.S.R., the Russian Socialist Federated Soviet Republic, was inaugurated and within two years, with the collapse of the Whites, it was omnipotent in Russia.

Lenin now had a few more years to live (he died in January, 1924), and during them he bent himself heroically to four major tasks: (a) the consolidation of power in the hands of the Communist party, the new name asumed by the Bolsheviks in 1918; (b) the spread of communism throughout the world by the establishment of the Third International; (c) the abolition of individualist business enterprise in Russia and the socialization in that country of all means of production; (d) the trans-formation of the entire folk psychology of the Russian people, whereby sanctions imposed by the old moralities and the old ethical conceptions shriveled up, to be supplanted by new concepts, strange and bizarre to both Asiatic and Western culture.

Ostensibly, Russia was now a republic, a word which ordinarily in the twentieth century had come to imply a certain quantum of belief in democratic or at least representative institutions. This was not true of the Russian republic; from its inception the R.S.F.S.R. was simply a mechanism through which the Communist party controlled Russia in the name of the proletariat. Therefore, it is far more important to analyze that party and its organization than the theoretical framework of the government. In theory, every Russian adult, except for certain specified social classes, like employers, men working for private gain, clergymen, former employees of the Czar's administration, and so forth, was qualified to take part in the government and to vote. In theory, also, those who voted elected freely, although indirectly through their local soviets or councils, an All-Russian Congress of Soviets, which elected an executive committee, which in turn chose the Council of People's Commissars—seventeen men at the head of the government.

But theory does not always coincide with practice, and since all voting had to be done by show of hands, and since the urban soviets, full of workmen, were heavily overweighted when it came to districting out Russia, it is easy to see how a highly disciplined group within the body of workmen, like the Communist party (it also had a number of peasant members), might readily remain master of the situation as it did.

So also was it when the government was again reorganized in 1923, as the R.S.F.S.R. gave place to the U.S.S.R. (Union of Soviet Socialist

Republics). In theory again this step was intended to demonstrate how liberal the R.S.F.S.R. could be in dealing with the various nationalistic groups remaining in the Russian Empire. The new constitution now recognized no less than nine different republics, bound together in one union, namely, the old R.S.F.S.R., the soviet republics of the Ukraine, the Transcaucasian republics (Azerbaijan, Armenia, Georgia), the White Russian republic, and three smaller ones in the eastern stretches of the empire in Asia. Each of these separate republics had a constitution like that of the original R.S.F.S.R.; each of them sent delegates to an All-Union Congress of Soviets, which again chose a central committee, as in the case of the original constitution described.

Now the idea behind this change from the R.S.F.S.R. to the U.S.S.R. was simple. Since the former constitution was socialistic, it must repudiate imperialism and all of its works. Therefore, the Russian soviet government must not tyrannize over the Ukrainian, Turkoman, and all the other peoples, or other ethnic groups which happened to be within the geographical boundaries of Russia. These other peoples had the right to enjoy their own language, culture, indigenous institutions. Thus the theory ran, and consequently each one was set up as a separate republic. But we must not be deceived by these separate republics which, though republics in name, possessed much less autonomy than the states under the American system. For instance, to the union government fell not only those functions which almost always are attached to a federal government, such as war, peace, currency, and so forth, but also such matters as health, labor laws, and even, to some extent, education.

Constitutions, however, may be one thing and realities another, and especially true was this of both the R.S.F.S.R. and the U.S.S.R. In both of them Lenin took good care to preserve the iron grip of the Communist party. It was the only party which had any legal existence. First through the Cheka and then through the G.P.U., names successively given to the secret police, the party controlled all elections, for it was very dangerous for anyone to vote against the party nominee. There was no such thing under either of these two formal Russian constitutions, it must be remembered, as independent law courts. Judges might be removed at will, and the G.P.U. could arrest and execute at will any individual without his having any recourse to such law courts as were set up. In fact, the G.P.U. was more powerful than the famous Third Section of the Czars; it had more spies; it had more money; it had a private army to enforce its bidding. Quite similar to the dreaded Gestapo (secret police) of Hitler, the G.P.U. was both whip and scorpion in the hands of first Lenin and then Stalin.

The Communist party was composed of city workmen, ex-soldiers, a few poor peasants, and (afterward) of a few professional men. From its inception, all ex-nobles, priests, traders, bankers, and all the middle-class men of every description, together with their relatives, were in theory strictly excluded. One gained admittance only after a probationary period and upon the recommendation of a number of members. Periodically, it was necessary to prove oneself worthy of membership, or else expulsion followed. Unless one was a confessed atheist, one could not join; unless one confessed the pure Marxian faith as laid down by Lenin, one could not join.

The great majority of members continued to be urban workers and soldiers. Highly organized in little groups or cells in the Russian factories, they watched and controlled local elections, reported men they disliked to the G.P.U., criticized or approved factory management, and sternly disciplined one another. Drunkenness, for instance, must never be indulged in by a Communist; he must not pay too much attention to women; he must be ever on the job as a good workman and as a good propagandist; he must not intermarry with the hated bourgeoisie (as much anathema to Communists as Jews to Nazis in Germany); he must bring up his children as good Communists; he must not let them be subject to religious instruction; he must see to it that they joined the "Young Pioneers," a youth organization attached to the Communist party; and above all things in heaven (denied existence) and on earth he must put loyalty to the party and to its principles as laid down by Lenin. For the party and the party alone was Russia's salvation.

Communism, to Lenin, was an international faith, and he set great store by the Third International, the instrumentality through which it was hoped that communism might spread throughout the world. The First International, as organized by Karl Marx, had petered out in the bloodshed at Paris in 1871, following the Franco-Prussian War, and the Second International, in existence at the outbreak of the war, and still more or less alive, was, in Lenin's opinion, hopelessly rightist in tendency, honeycombed with opportunist heresy, and impregnated with national patriotism. He would have none of this agency of Western social democracy, and therefore he promoted the Third International with headquarters at Moscow as a kind of clearinghouse for revolutionary propaganda.

The actual relations of this Third International to the U.S.S.R. have always been a matter of hot dispute. According to official statements of the Soviet authorities, the Third International, or the Comintern, as they called it, was an independent body of world Communists who simply accepted the hospitality of the U.S.S.R., held their meetings or congresses in Moscow, maintained a permanent secretariat there, and functioned independently of the Soviet government. According, however, to the enemies of Soviet Russia, this explanation was a mere blind, and the Third International or Comintern was an agency of the U.S.S.R. which found it convenient to disown the activities of the Comintern in public while supporting and directing them in private. The truth presumably lay between the two statements. There can be no question but that officials of the Comintern held important posts in the Soviet government and thus at least a kind of informal interlocking directorate existed. On the other hand the financing of the Comintern did come from dues collected from Europe, America, and Asia; and the opinions of German, American, and Chinese Communists were vented at the various congresses of the Third International and had influence in determining the policy of that organization.

The Third International was founded in 1919. Its announced aim was "to replace world Capitalism by world Communism, thus abolishing the private ownership of the means of production and with it the selfish lust for profits, exploitation of man by man, all inequalities based on sex, religion, and nationality; devastating crises and still more devastating wars." And this it hoped to do by establishing in every country a Communist party, disciplined, cohesive, and obedient to orders received from the Comintern, pledged to a revolutionary seizure of political power. At least this was true in Lenin's day. In later years the Third International became, until it was abolished in 1943, seemingly less revolutionary in act and willing, apparently, to work in harmony with "leftist" bourgeois interests.

For Lenin was a believer in the apocalyptic version of the Marxian faith. He thought the new heaven and the new earth just around the corner, that capitalism was (everywhere) on its deathbed, and that the universal revolution was imminent.

There was some excuse for this belief in 1919. In Hungary, in Germany, in Armenia, India, and China, Communist revolts either had broken out or were on the point of doing so. Particularly hopeful was Lenin of Germany. He was deceived by the semi-anarchy there into believing that Germany was on the point of going Communist, and he deserves no small amount of blame for the advent of Hitler, since his advice to the German Communists to have nothing to do with the Social Democrats, a policy followed even after his death, weakened the leftist front and made easier the advent of the Nazis.

Only as time passed did Lenin come to conceive of the world revolution as springing up first not in the highly organized capitalistic countries but rather in those regions where capitalism was weak and not yet firmly entrenched. Here, in what were called colonial or semi-colonial countries, it was held, lay the greatest hopes for immediate Communist success.

Largely on account of this theory, there was held in Baku in 1920 a congress of oppressed nationalities whom Russia and the Third International sought to rescue from their oppressors. Nearly 2,000 delegates from no less than 37 different nationalities attended the meetings. Prominent among them were the Turks, who, under Kemal Ataturk (see pp. 692-693), appealed to Russia for help and got it. Lenin surrendered to

Ataturk over 7,000 square miles, formerly part of the Czar's empire, and loaned him money and professional assistance in establishing the Turkish republic. Lenin likewise denounced the special privileges which the Czar's government had obtained at one time or another in Iran, Afghanistan, and China. He deeded land to Afghanistan, proposed that Moscow be linked to Kabul by air, offered to help the Amir in opposing Britain, "the most rapacious imperialistic government on earth." The close hookup of the Chinese Communists with Russia did not come, it is true, until after Lenin's death, but the idea of having one was his. To him Russia's influence in hastening the advent of the New Jerusalem could only come by shunning all contact with the League of Nations, a bourgeois institution controlled by capitalists, and by stirring up everywhere, but particularly in undeveloped and in semi-developed dependent countries, disorder, insurrection, and proletarian dictatorships.

The New Economic Policy

Meanwhile, neither industry nor agriculture was flourishing in Russia. The Communist leaders had no technical knowledge of business. They had been conspirators, publicists, politicians, or, if you will, statesmen. But they did not know how to manage factories, mines, and banks. In consequence, production fell off so alarmingly that in 1920 it was less than forty per cent of what it had been in 1913 and in certain lines of skilled manufacture it was way below that low level.

Nor was this the worst. There was a scarcity of food. The peasants who produced it knew nothing of Marx; they thought that the newly won land of the proprietor, the church, and the state belonged to them outright. They were willing to exchange their surplus wheat and meat for articles which they needed, like spades, and nails, and needles; but they had no intention of giving them away for paper money, rapidly depreciating in value as the articles they sought grew scarcer.

What was to be done? The dictatorship of the proletariat had seemed so simple. Its function was clear; to turn Russia into a socialist state, wherein none should work for his own gain but each for each and for his neighbor. Capitalism was the enemy; it was abolished by fiat. The bourgeoisie were the instruments of capitalism; they were abolished by fiat. "Let him not eat who does not work," was a good Marxian slogan— and also incidentally Christian, since St. Paul said it before Marx. But who was to direct how the work should be done; and how was production to be started again; and how were the people to eat? Lenin's first idea had been simply to appropriate the peasant's surplus; but the peasants saw no occasion for having any surplus. Then followed the creation of food armies, forcibly to collect food from the rural districts. The peasants hid their food, and the armed forces of the proletariat collected it with much bloodshed. Physical hardships, almost unendurable, were now met with in both town and country, and the wise shook their heads and said, "The revolution is over."

But Lenin would not have it so. Like a good soldier he decided on a strategic retreat. This was the *Nep* or new economic policy. In effect it was a partial return to capitalism. The state ownership of all the land of Russia was reaffirmed, but the peasants were no longer to have their surplus expropriated. Instead they were to pay a regular fixed tax and were free to do what they wanted with any surplus remaining. Since the land did not belong to them, they could not sell or mortgage it. But at any rate they had won a respite and were quiescent, particularly the wealthier and more ambitious ones, known as "kulaks," who received permission to rent land from their poorer neighbors.

Small industries, those employing under twenty men, were now, in accordance with the Nep, turned back to private enterprise, as was most retail trading and selling. Men thus engaged were known as "Nepmen" and were not highly regarded by the Communist party. But they were tolerated. The larger industries owned by the state were consolidated into great trusts, and foreign experts were hired at excellent salaries as advisors. These foreign experts and technicians were not desired as Russian citizens; they could not become members of the party, and had no political voice. Neither did the Russian Nepmen. One could not be a Communist and be a Nepman; one could not have the honor of voting and be a Nepman; but if one voluntarily chose to enter this humble class one could make money, always running the risk, of course, that high taxes might take it from you.

In addition to these changes, foreign corporations, as such, were invited to do business in Russia. The country stood in need of fluid capital and the best way to obtain it was to invite the foreigner in—under strict supervision. The proffered concessions promised goodly profits and many foreign capitalists took advantage of Lenin's offers. The economic tide began to turn and production reached its old level. Was this socialism or was it not? People rubbed their eyes; state socialism, or state capitalism, or call it what you will, seemingly existed side by side with individual enterprise. We keep the banks, the big industries, and the taxing power in our own hands, said the Communists, and as long as we do that we have not betrayed Marx. But seemingly they had postponed the millennium.

Yet not for long, in Lenin's opinion. All he had in mind was a brief postponement of that happy day. Very shortly it would dawn, and just as soon as the Russian proletariat could master the secrets of machinery. Motors, dynamos, tractors, electrification, power dams, hydroelectric power, technology—in this direction lay salvation. Lenin particularly was captivated by electricity. His Marxian philosophy, basing all human happiness and well-being on a materialistic accomplishment, led directly to the conviction that the machine, whether composed of flesh and blood or of copper and steel, was the only ultimate reality. He was also a Russian, as well as a Marxian, and he could not escape the tradition of Peter the Great. The great statue of that monarch in Petrograd had been hurled from its base amid the maledictions of the proletariat, for he had built his capital city by the forced labor of sweating peasants; but the tradition which he had set up of adopting Western ways of life still remained. Peter was cursed as the worst of despots, and the name of his city was changed to Leningrad; but he was none the less copied. To England, to America, to Germany, Lenin sent for chemists, agricultural experts, engineers, technicians. They would teach their secrets to his people. Then they could go back home and Russia would be a socialistic state, in fact as well as in theory. And it would not take long!

The Ideological Drive

Meanwhile, there was to be no letup in the ideological drive to use communism as the radical spearhead by which Russian life might become revolutionized. For the revolution was conceived of as something far more fundamental than a mere economic transformation of Russia. Certain ideas and predispositions had to be eradicated from the popular mind and certain others had to take their place. The family, for instance, as the unit of personal loyalty must go, and in place of it loyalty to class must come. Old ideas concerning sex, personal morality, and ethics needed uprooting; and above all it was held essential that man must believe in the ultimate validity and the ultimate victory of a materialistic conception of life.

The family in Russia, as elsewhere, had been based on differentiation of function, man the breadwinner and provider, woman the conserver and dispenser of what man provided. This conception seemed not only out of date but undesirable to the thoroughgoing Communist. Women should work as well as men in factory, field, and workshop. Children should be the wards of the state; in state nursery schools and state primary schools they must be taught that the idea of family loyalty was a selfish, restrictive influence which blinded man to the possibility of social brotherhood.

To break up the family, women were put to work. To break it up still further, free divorce was granted on the application merely of either husband or wife. This did not mean a bacchanalian orgy of sexual licentiousness. Good Communists were expected to refrain from overindulgence in sex exactly the same way as they were to refrain from drunkenness, laziness, or anything else that might lessen their value as party members. From the point of view of the Communist, sex was comparatively an unimportant matter, a question of taste rather than of morality. The

Communist did not advocate a community of women; they insisted on marriage laws and enforced them. But marriage became purely a secular affair. It was necessary to preserve it so that census statistics could be accurate, so that parents could be charged with the cost of supporting the young. If there were no children the state pretty much washed its hands of the whole affair. Even abortion in the early days was openly and legally practised. But afterwards laws were passed forbidding it as a crime against society, since it tended to reduce the birth rate.

Communism meant a complete break with the past in many other ways. Laws concerning murder, for instance, were revolutionized. In accordance with communistic philosophy it was not permitted to kill one's real or fancied enemy; but if such an act was committed as the result of sudden anger it took its place in the category of lesser crimes, as did theft when committed against the personal property of a Russian citizen. For such crimes there were jail sentences; but they were not inordinately long. What was infinitely worse in Communist eyes were offenses against the U.S.S.R. Let a man be proved guilty of petty graft and no mercy need be expected; line him up against a wall and shoot him! One real sin, as such, and one alone was recognized by Communists: the act of being "counter-revolutionary." All privileged persons under the old regime were suspected of this sin, and against them true Communists were expected to harbor bitter hate.

Favorite adjectives among Communist writers were "dialectic," "objective," "scientific," and "materialistic." Since the method of reasoning used by Marx was the dialectic, there could be no other good type of reasoning. Supposedly, Marx was also a great materialistic scientist and good Communists followed the master. Power machinery was materialistic and also something new to the Russians. From Lenin down to the humblest party member, they were fascinated by it. An early Communist poster of what a cathedral should look like represented a great dynamo in place of an altar, and above the altar, where perhaps in a Christian cathedral angels might be carved, the communist artist placed flywheels attached to the dynamo by moving belts. Chicago was hymned in Communist poetry because it was an "electromagnetic city," a true symbol of the Machine Age. All that was essential to the Communist view was to have more and more machinery, owned and operated by the people in common rather than by the individual.

It was difficult to implant such revolutionary ideals in the minds of the old; this was recognized. Consequently, it was all the more the duty of the state to capture the plastic minds of the young. As a result much emphasis was put on education. Young and old were both invited and urged to learn to read and write; but great care was taken with the texts used which centered on the teachings of Marx and explained history almost exclusively in terms of the Revolution of 1917. Competent teachers were lacking and the country was desperately poor, but none the less astonishing headway was made. Enthusiasm took the place of training, and if the pupils were shepherded rigidly into the Marxian fold, they at least learned how to read.

Since materialism and idealism are generally considered antithetical terms, it is always easy to underrate what the Communist party accomplished in the way of social amelioration. Machinery, for instance, devised to protect the workman's life and limb is materialistic, but the use thereof would seem to be idealistic, whether or not the person using it insisted that idealism was a played-out force. The Communists were keen about machinery of this description. They were prepared to do everything for labor, to take the homes of former noblemen and to turn them into sanitaria, to give vacations with pay to pregnant women for a considerable period both before and after childbirth, to provide free medical service, to lighten labor hours, to increase its rewards not merely by more pay but by encouraging cheap literature, cheap music, cheap movies, cheap education—and none of these cheap in the sense of being shoddy.

To be sure, this was all done with an eye toward propaganda, directly or indirectly. There was no freedom in Russia of any kind, except freedom to spread the new faith. The Communists pointed bravely at Pavlov and to his experiments in animal psychology to prove the contrary. But even here the reason they did not molest Pavlov is obvious: if dogs and mice are conditioned in all their acts by external influences, so also by analogy is man, and materialism scores another victory.

Therefore Pavlov the scientist they would leave alone; but not the Christian Church. The latter underwent severe oppression in all of its branches, and although the Roman Catholic Church was a distinct minority in Russia, so successfully did the Roman pontiffs raise the hue and cry against the Communists that Rome seemingly became the principal enemy of the Communist creed.

There can be no doubt that communism was a denial of historic Christianity. For one thing, it insisted that there was neither a God nor a future life; for another it regarded sex as of trifling importance; and finally it denounced as undesirable and as counterrevolutionary all ideas commonly associated with the suffering servant of Jehovah, teaching instead that humility, patience, and long-suffering were base and ignoble thoughts, not worthy ones. No doubt also that the Communists behaved very badly toward priests and monks, killing some, reducing those left alive to beggary, appropriating churches without remuneration for secular purposes, forbidding all charitable work done in the name of Christ, teaching atheism in schools, not permitting Christian schools even to be opened, turning children against their parents, and urging them as a patriotic duty to denounce their own fathers and mothers. Despite these obvious facts it is not without significance that in a curious kind of way there were points of similarity between Christianity and communism. Both religions sought the welfare of the poor. No matter how heartily the Communists might curse the otherworldliness of Christianity, it was evident that the Soviet zealots took a keen interest in social justice; no matter how heartily the Popes might berate the Communists for their materialism, it was evident that Pope Leo XIII himself had stated that the Church was concerned with the material welfare of the poor. That also in theory at least, was Lenin's business.

Trotsky Versus Stalin

In 1924 Lenin died. He had been seriously ill for two years, the result of a lifetime of overwork and constant strain. All Russia paid him honor. His body, embalmed, placed under glass, and guarded day and night by soldiers of the Red Army, was placed in a red granite mausoleum, which became a holy place, a pilgrimage center for the Communist world. More honored than Karl Marx, whose obscure grave in a London cemetery few visit, Lenin and Leninism (as his doctrine came to be known) from now on, were regarded as the ark of the covenant, the foundation of the new moral order of humanity.

For Lenin's mantle there were ultimately two main contestants, Trotsky and Stalin. Of the two, the former was by far the better known outside Russia, and at the time of Lenin's death, within that country. Jewish by birth (Lev Bronstein was his real name), Trotsky had been an intimate collaborator of Lenin's. Twice he had been exiled to Siberia before the War, and in addition he had led a wandering life among the European capitals. Driven out of Paris in 1916, he had gone to New York, whence he came back to Russia and was made commissar for war in the new Bolshevik government. The success of the Red Army in 1919 and 1920 added laurels to his fame. He both wrote and spoke brilliantly and was keenly interested in spreading communism throughout all the world with the utmost speed.

Opposed to Trotsky was Stalin, who, unlike both Lenin and Trotsky, did not hail from the upper and middle classes but from peasant stock. Stalin was a Georgian from the Caucasus, a sturdy, taciturn, and rough apostle of violence. Destined for the priesthood and trained as a boy in a theological seminary, Stalin at eighteen forswore Christianity and accepted the Marxian gospel. He became a conspirator and leader of sanguinary strikes, and very soon was constantly in trouble with the police. Twice, also, he was sent to Siberia. Escaping from there, he was deported all the way to the Arctic Circle, where he was supporting himself by hunting and trapping when the Revolution broke out.

Throughout the summer of 1917, Stalin was one of the most efficient of the Bolshevik conspirators, and with the triumph of the Soviets he became not only commissar for nationalities but also commissar of workers' and peasants' inspection, and as such took a leading rôle in bringing about the ultimate Bolshevik victory. From the very beginning he was a member of the Polit Bureau, or inner steering committee of the party, and in 1922 he became its secretary, a post which became under him the most important in all Russia. First and foremost, Stalin was a party man, and because of his long and intimate knowledge of the party's personnel, he had a certain advantage over the more versatile Trotsky, who, because of his very brilliance, was constantly making enemies.

The two men differed in policy. Trotsky was all for the world revolution, but Stalin considered that for the time being such a revolution was a dream. In his opinion communism should devote itself to perfecting the revolution within Russia. Trotsky had the greater support in the Third International, and the Chinese students at the University of Moscow paraded in his honor; but Stalin commanded the votes in the Congress of the Soviets and Trotsky was forced into exile. It was impossible, however, for Stalin to rid himself completely of Trotsky for several years or for him to entrench himself in power. According to tradition, Lenin himself had regarded Stalin as too brutal and too tough to head the party, and only slowly and by degrees was Stalin able to turn an acknowledged leadership into a dictatorship. It proved impossible permanently to expel Trotsky from the U.S.S.R. before 1929, and from Lenin's death until that year the leftist element of the party, of which Trotsky was the leading spirit, did its best to oust Stalin from the control lever. And even in that year, after Trotsky had set up his residence in Constantinople, Stalin's control was none too sure, for having defeated the left opposition, he was confronted by a new bloc on the right which thought he had gone too far in his ruthless determination to complete the work of socialism in Russia. Since that date, however, there have been few successfully to dispute in Russia with Joseph Stalin, and from 1930 to his death in 1953, to all intent and purpose, his power was absolute.

The Five-Year Plan

Victory over Trotsky once secured, the Russian Revolution entered a new phase. Lenin had driven out the old ruling class and had thoroughly liquidated it; he had socialized big business completely, whether in land, commerce, or manufacturing; and on the ideological front his success in captivating the imagination of his followers both within and without Russia had been phenomenal. But two things he had not done: he had made comparatively little headway in changing the way of living of the Russian peasants, nearly eighty-five per cent of the population; and his dream of a technological revolution in Russia had not yet passed the blueprint stage. "Communism," he had said, "is soviet government plus the electrification of the country." Substitute the word *technology,* or the word *machine* for electrification and Lenin's meaning is clarified. He dreamed of a society in which manual labor would be at a minimum. That goal was far distant when he died. Stalin made it his business to introduce the technological revolution Lenin planned. He did it so thoroughly in the decade before the Second World War that what he accomplished may justly be considered a second revolution.

In 1928 Stalin laid down a revolutionary program. It provided for the scrapping of the Nep and for a five-year plan or blueprint, whereby a tremendous speeding up in the production of capital goods was to go hand in hand with the complete socialization of the land and the substitution of farm coöperatives in place of individual enterprise. During these five years everyone in Russia was supposed to pull in his belt, to consume as little as possible, to work hard and long and scientifically in putting Russia in a place of leadership among the industrial countries of the world. Railroads, hydroelectric plants, steel mills, tractor and automobile factories, more coal, more iron; a total increase of one hundred and thirty per cent was called for in industrial production. And as this was done, agriculture was to be modernized. The state proposed to establish and manage great model farms to serve as an example of what ultimately was to be expected of the peasants. The latter were encouraged to form coöperative groups (*kolkhozes*). If they objected, they were to be forced into these groups. After five years, private enterprise would no longer be found in Russia.

The difficulties which confronted Stalin were enormous. Russia was poor, desperately poor, yet he could not carry out the five-year program without hiring expensive scientists and engineering specialists from Germany, the United States, and elsewhere. At the same time it was necessary to import machinery and tools of precision. All this would take money, and the capitalistic world was chary of granting credit to Russia. It demanded ready money and this could only be had by Russian exports, either of merchandise or gold. Then, too, laborers had to be secured from somewhere and trained as skilled workmen, millions of them. They had to be drafted from the Russian peasantry (there was no other source of supply) and this at a time when the peasants were inevitably irritated by the revolution pending in agriculture whereby they were to be ordered to give up their individual land holdings and forced to join coöperative farm groups. Compulsion would be necessary; the peasants could not be enticed by high wages, for all available money would have to be spent for materials, tools, and foreign exports. Yet economy would be impossible. The expenses of the Red army were increasing, not diminishing. Between the imminent threat of Japanese invasion in the Far East and the enmity of the capitalistic West, Stalin did not dare diminish his army. In Lenin's day there was no danger threatening from Germany; but as

Stalin came to power a wild-eyed agitator, Adolf Hitler, was inflaming his countrymen with bitter hate of Communists. Hitler might well become a serious menace. England, Italy, and the United States were hostile. There was need for haste as well as for money, so Stalin thought.

On the industrial front the principal center of activity was in the Ukraine, in the valley of the Don, in the Caucasus, the Urals, and in Western Siberia. In the Ukraine a great dam providing for the largest hydroelectric plant in Europe had already been projected. This, the Dneprostroi dam, was completed in 1932, making the Dnieper River navigable for 1,500 miles and providing 750,000 horsepower. At Kharkov, also in the Ukraine, a tractor plant was established which in short order was manufacturing 37,000 tractors a year, and near it was a plant for turbine generators and electrical equipment which by 1939 employed 40,000 men. At Rostov on the Don and at Stalingrad on the Volga mammoth steel plants, specializing in tractors and other agricultural machinery were erected.

Still further to the east were the Ural mountains and Siberia. Here lay a land, the Soviet geologists soon proved, rich in minerals and far distant from any invasion, at least 1,500 miles from any European enemy and much further from Japan. On the eastern slopes of the Urals at Magnitogorsk were two mountains so rich in iron as to be one of the principal sources of that mineral in the entire world. Coal also was to be found in the Urals, and straight east from the two mountains some 1,400 miles from Magnitogorsk where the Altai mountains separate western China from Siberia were the Kuznetz coal reserves with over 400 million tons of accessible coal. Here lay the land of Stalin's imagination; here he determined, cost what it might, to develop an industrial region to vie with Pittsburgh, Birmingham, or the Ruhr Valley.

The far northern part of this region already was traversed by the Trans-Siberian railroad. Stalin proposed to double-track it, to drive a new railroad south to Magnitogorsk, to connect that city with the Kuznetz coal, to join these new railroads to the already existing Transcaucasian railroad which linked together the oases of Turkestan, and to make western Siberia a great inland empire.

Magnitogorsk was planned as the industrial center. To create a city, several hundred engineering experts were imported from abroad, some at a salary of $100 a day. Under them was an army of many thousand laborers, most of whom were dispossessed peasants or kulaks. The latter suffered much; food shortages were chronic and such food as could be had was mostly black bread, cabbages, and potatoes. The winters were bitterly cold, the summers unbearably hot and dry. Hastily constructed, ill-heated, and overcrowded barracks housed the men. Confusion reigned. Essential tools were missing, spare parts difficult to obtain, accidents numerous. From the scaffolding "inexperienced riggers fell and untrained bricklayers laid walls which did not stand." Skilled workmen were continually deserting. One locomotive working on the mine had thirty-four engineers in one year. Only one single-track railway led to the city and soon the workmen "were faced with the necessity of supplying themselves with hammers, saws, chisels, bits, small castings and other small tools which could be made in makeshift shops. Many materials, such as copper wire for rewinding motors, simply could not be had. The workers swore at the foremen, the foremen complained to the superintendent, the supply department telegraphed to Moscow. There was no copper wire." [1] But the city was built and in less than five years was swarming with over 200,000 inhabitants.

The story of Magnitogorsk is the story of a dozen manufacturing cities with mushroom growth in eastern Russia and in western Siberia during the nineteen-thirties. The coal deposits at Kuznetz, for instance, soon proved far in excess of the Magnitogorsk demand, and smelters at Stalinsk in the Kuznetz area became busily engaged in turning Magnitogorsk ore into finished steel. Stalinsk by 1939 was a city of 220,000, connected by rail with the Russian Transcaucasian system on the south, with the Trans-Siberian system on the north and with Magnitogorsk to the west, and by 1939 the population of the surrounding district had risen to 800,000. Instead of having one Pittsburgh, Russia had two, both safe from European or Asiatic invader. There could be no doubt, on paper that is, that the first five-year drive was a success on the industrial front. No matter what the cost, both in human suffering and in money, the rails were laid, the factories built, the oil wells dug, the mines opened, the steel, the tractors (also the tanks) in operation. Officially the drive was declared closed after four and a half years—and in theory ninety-three per cent complete.

The above percentage was Stalin's estimate. It needs qualification. If measured in terms of rubles (money) the estimate is correct. But the ruble was a shifting standard, and since it had depreciated externally in value during the five years, the real increase in production was far below 93.7 per cent. Furthermore, the increase was one in industrial production only. It ignored the question of real wages, the amount of goods that might be had in terms of rubles. The available food supplies did not increase; in fact they diminished. The great industrial undertakings were only accomplished by the semistarvation of many million workingmen, who lived on black bread and cabbage soup.

Difficult as it proved to be to introduce highly specialized industrial processes among a people who by tradition were primarily agricultural, it proved even more difficult to turn these same peasants into practising socialists, willing to give up their privately owned and privately tilled acres in order to share both work and gains with their neighbors. Never-

[1] John Scott, *Behind the Urals* (Houghton Mifflin Company), p. 76. Reprinted by permission of the publishers.

theless, Stalin determined to push the agricultural offense as hard as the industrial one. It would not do, in his opinion, to have Russia half capitalist and half socialist, and unless the reluctant peasants were driven into the practice of coöperative farming, such would be the case. The peasants were stupid and the patient state would show them the way by example, by state farms, by lectures on scientific agriculture, by attractive offers and bonuses to those peasants who pooled their resources, by harsh taxes levied on the recalcitrant.

It was soon discovered that there were a great many of the latter, well-to-do peasants, or kulaks, who had prospered, partly by working hard and intelligently, partly by hiring as farm laborers their more shiftless or less fortunate neighbors. These kulaks continued to exist somehow, even though taxed unmercifully, and the soviet authorities determined to "liquidate" them. They did so thoroughly. The kulaks were driven from their homes by the hundreds of thousands; they were forced to work in the lumber-mills of the North, in the gold mines of Siberia, in the new factories. Soon there were hardly any kulaks left. By January, 1934, Stalin was able to announce that there were no less than 224,500 collective farms in Russia which, in the preceding year, sowed some 73.9 per cent of Russia's grain. Since an added ten per cent came from the state farms, the success on the agricultural front as well as on the industrial seemed assured.

Whether that success was worth the price paid for it is open to question. The forced industrial development of the country was put through by compulsory labor. The imagination of the Communists had been captivated by machinery and there can be no doubt that it was a part of their faith to work hard and long with utmost enthusiasm. But while this was true of convinced Communists who organized shock brigades in the factories to hasten production, there were not enough of them for the task in hand. If it was to be accomplished within the time limits set, forced labor was essential and Stalin did not hesitate to use it. For this the kulaks were conveniently available, as well as thousands of political prisoners. Suffering greatly from lack of decent living quarters, and half-starved, these other groups provided much of the human raw material which poured into the industrial undertakings.

Furthermore, although factories were built and filled with machinery, although mines were opened, railroads constructed, iron dug from the hillsides and turned into steel, there were many bitter criticisms of the effectiveness of the result. It was claimed that the railroads broke down continuously, that the machines were so poor in quality as to be in many instances useless, that the tractors were too heavy and too clumsy to operate. To some extent it is necessary to discount these criticisms since most of them came from European and American technicians employed by the Soviet government, and it was only natural that they should compare unfavorably the efficiency and skill of the Russian workmen with that possessed by the highly trained industrial workers of the West to which they had been accustomed. But despite all this, the cumulative evidence would seem to indicate only a partial victory as yet for this industrial revolution in Russia, brought into existence by socialistic practice. Compared with American standards, Russian factories with ten times as many workmen turned out far less per capita. Machines always seemed to be breaking down, burning out, rusting, exploding. The new dynamos, locomotives, and tractors, were there, it is true, but they did not seem to be good tractors, locomotives, and dynamos. Enthusiasm, it was found, could not take the place of mechanical skill; and the latter, it was demonstrated, could not be created overnight by fiat.

The results of the first Five-Year Plan in agriculture were more open to question. In the more advanced agricultural districts, such as the Ukraine and southern Russia, there was bitter opposition on the part of the peasants to Stalin's program. Throughout 1932 and 1933 famine raged in the Ukraine, due in part to unseasonable weather, in part to compulsory grain requisitions, in part to the unwillingness of the peasants to surrender their individual holdings. Some three or four million people lost their lives from starvation, and the country-side was well-nigh deserted. The Soviet authorities were not altogether displeased; the famine proved a convenient instrument for political policy, and after its ravages were over, there was less opposition to collective farming. Statistically, however, the official figures as released by Stalin in 1934 did not seem encouraging as far as the agricultural front went. From 1923 to 1934 the numbers of cattle, horses, sheep, and goats decreased alarmingly, and all that there were in their places were some 200,000 tractors! Theoretically, their presence on the Russian farms meant more acres cultivated and a greater consumption of cereals. Nevertheless, it is doubtful if the per capita consumption of grain at the conclusion of the Five-Year Plan was in excess of that under the Czars. The cost in terms of human suffering unquestionably was very high.

Stalin himself realized that, but like a good politician he did not acknowledge it. He made a statement called "Giddiness from Success," in which he announced certain qualifications in regard to rural coöperatives in which peasants might retain individual ownership of homes, gardens, live stock. Grain was still to be sowed and reaped by the kolkhozes, but a certain leeway was now granted to individual enterprise. Stalin likewise, and again merely by implication, toned down the harshness of the drive for industrialization by announcing a second Five-Year Plan, to be completed in 1937. Unlike the first plan, this one stressed consumers' goods. Factories were to be built for textiles, shoes, canning, candies, and no less than 350 of these factories were for food products. Prices of consumers' goods were to be lowered and the supply of them was to be augmented three hundred per cent.

Did Stalin Betray the Revolution?

Meanwhile, in certain respects, both in regard to external and internal policy, Soviet Russia became more and more conservative. As an instrument for stirring up world revolution, the Third International almost ceased to function. Lenin had hated the League of Nations but Stalin consented to enter it. The Communist parties outside of Russia were advised from the Kremlin that they should coöperate with liberal bourgeois groups against fascism, and in countries like the United States, China, France, and Spain the Communists either made common cause with such groups or tried to. Thus, in the United States, the Communists were friendly toward Roosevelt in 1936 and in instances actually supported him, adopting a stand in American politics more conservative than that of the old Social Democratic party hitherto regarded by all honest Reds as lukewarm and yellow. In China the Communists joined forces with their old enemy, Chiang Kai-shek, in opposing the Japanese advance; and in France and Spain Communists took a leading part in the organization of "popular fronts" to oppose reaction.

The same general trend to the right was noticeable also in internal affairs. In 1936 Soviet Russia adopted a new constitution which, on paper at least, seemed to denote that the U.S.S.R. was becoming both democratic and liberal. Freedom of speech and of religion was guaranteed (again on paper), and no longer was the scale weighted in favor of the more radical town and factory as against the more conservative country districts. All Russians were given the vote, even priests and kulaks, and voting was to be by ballot and not by show of hands.

Did Stalin have any real intention of going democratic? That may well be doubted. The control of the country still remained with the Communist party, the only one legally authorized, and that party remained in the hollow of his hands, as we shall note later. But perhaps Stalin did betray the Revolution, if not in whole at least in part, by drawing a line boldly between social classes in Russia, thus preventing instead of creating a classless society. Such was the argument of the exiled Trotsky who, driven out of his own country, out of Constantinople, and out of France, found a haven of refuge in Mexico. Trotsky insisted that the Russian Revolution was passing through its Thermidor, and that in the same way as the Directory, after the death of Robespierre, ended the real revolution in France, likewise was it under Stalin in Russia.

The arguments adduced by the exiled leader to prove this point were various. He pointed out that Stalin, by approving a speeding-up process in Russian factories and mines, really was paying workmen by the piece instead of by the time, the more skilful workingmen getting higher pay and receiving favors from the authorities. He also asserted that the renting of land went merrily on in Russia, some *kolkhozes* renting land at a profit to others, some even renting land to individuals. Russia, said Trotsky, was now ruled by some 400,000 bureaucrats who feathered their own nests very nicely, drew more pay than workmen, had better housing, and rapidly were becoming class-conscious. In the army the old discipline and the old caste system was said to be cropping up again. The Third International, in the interim, had been stifled and a new revolution would be necessary if ever Marxian socialism was to win. And to start this new revolution Trotsky sent out summons for a Fourth International.

The Purges

To what extent Trotsky continued from overseas to influence the course of events in Russia, it is impossible to state. Certainly many of the old Bolsheviks were discontented with Stalin's iron rule; some were of the right who disapproved of the abrupt ending of Lenin's Nep; others were of the left, in sympathy with Trotsky. Both groups plotted against Stalin; both were ruthlessly liquidated by him in thoroughgoing purges.

In 1935-37 the world made note of many curious trials for high treason in Russia. They were not conducted by Western methods, for evidence was not introduced into the court proceedings, unless wholesale confessions of willingness to sell out to the Germans and to betray the revolution be considered as evidence. Not only did almost every one put on trial freely admit guilt; the astonishing thing was that they tried to make this guilt appear as black as possible. The men placed on trial had been very high in governmental places, men like Kamenev, at one time a likely successor to Lenin; Zinoviev, former head of the Third International; a considerable number of high-ranking officers in the Red Army, among them General Tukhatchevsky, second in command; and finally numerous civil executives who were said to have wrecked railroads, trains, bridges, and to have retarded industrial production. Before he was through Stalin had gotten rid of almost every man of note who had participated in the Revolution of 1917.

Was it possible that these men were guilty? The capitalistic West was sceptical; it suspected that secret torture before trial might have caused the confessions, or that by making them the poor wretches hoped to avert the wrath of Stalin from their families. Some even suggested that the confessions were made as absurd as possible in order that the outside world might read between the lines and realize that the trials were a farce and that Stalin's regime was one of stark tyranny.

The total number of those executed by Stalin for treachery, treason,

Trotskyism, and sabotage between 1935 and 1939 is difficult to estimate, but presumably it was well over 10,000. Many were given no public trial at all, a simple announcement of their death alone being given. At the height of the executions there was a veritable reign of terror, when secret arrests were numerous and men simply disappeared. It was not healthy to inquire about their whereabouts, and few did.

Nevertheless the great body of Stalin's countrymen were prepared, it seems, to accept his word without question, and even to worship at his shrine in a way quite similar to the contemporary attitude of Germans and Italians toward Hitler and Mussolini. Stalin, indeed, became so personally identified with communism that he equalled in stature both Lenin and Marx. And this was the more noticeable in that he remained essentially a silent man, neither given to oratory as was Trotsky nor to the written amplification of the Communist scriptures as was Lenin.

Chapter 31

ITALIAN AND GERMAN FASCISM

It was just a bundle of sticks tied around an ax, but when it was borne by a lictor the mob gave way in ancient Rome. The Romans called that symbol of authority *fasces,* and from it we derive our modern word *fascism,* the answer of Italy and Germany to Russian communism, and to some extent that of other lands as well.

A strange doctrine is fascism, at once very old and very new. In so far as it concerns the dictatorship of an individual, of a Mussolini or a Hitler rising to well-nigh omnipotent power in times of anarchy, there is nothing new in Fascist doctrine, and one might as well use the term "Cæsarism" to describe it. In so far, on the other hand, as fascism is intimately correlated with capitalism, socialism, and twentieth-century nationalism, it is new, strikingly new, unlike any hitherto existing dictatorship, whether Cromwellian, Frederician, or Napoleonic.

Fascism triumphed in Italy in 1922 with Mussolini's march on Rome, and in Germany in 1933 with Adolf Hitler's appointment as chancellor of the Reich. As might be expected, its character assumed different forms in the two countries. Nevertheless, the points of likeness far exceed those of dissimilarity. What, then, is fascism, and in what respects may it be said that it is alike in all Fascist countries?

Fascism is an all-embracing doctrine which demands a one hundred per cent surrender of the individual will in the name of mystical nationalism—with ends not clearly defined. This nationalism is beyond good and evil, and thus is deified. Therefore, fascism properly should be classed as a kind of religion like communism, the latter based on class-consciousness, the former on nationalism. As such, fascism was compounded of three elements—violence, state socialism, totalitarianism. Direct and clear was its repudiation of the Sermon on the Mount, for the Fascist insists that he only is blessed who smites and smites again. Emphatic was its assertion that the economic life of the people must be controlled by governmental agencies. And furthermore, since the be all and the end all of life is the exaltation of the State, all members of it must act alike, think alike, obey alike. Such, in general outline, is the Spartan-like philosophy of twentieth-century fascism.

How explain its origin? Such an extreme reversal of the main currents of European culture, especially since the Renaissance, could only come about through revolutionary upheavals produced by disillusionment, sharp suffering, social anarchy. This was the case in both Italy and Germany. Both countries felt that they had been cheated by the peace treaties; both suffered enormously from economic maladjustment; both were at the mercy of politicians unable to bring order out of chaos; and, what is more important, in both there were large numbers of ex-soldiers, young but toughened by war, unemployed, bitter, finding after four years in the trenches that back home there was "greed in the saddle, disorder in the street, and poverty on the hearth."

The Rise of Italian Fascism

Since this greed, disorder, and poverty characterized Russia as well as Italy and Germany, the question naturally arises why those two countries did not turn toward communism. Several reasons explain why. In the first place, both in Germany and in Italy the bourgeoisie were too powerful, too numerous, to well-led to be driven to the wall by Communist uprisings. In both countries such revolts occurred; in both they were snuffed out by the enraged bourgeoisie. Secondly, in both countries, but especially in Germany, there was a tradition of discipline and order and of national cohesiveness which militated strongly against the Communist world revolution. And thirdly, one is confronted with that insoluble equation, the personal factor, the adroit cunning of Benito Mussolini in Italy, the mystical appeal to Germans latent in the raucous vocal cords of Adolf Hitler.

Of these two fiery ex-corporals, the Italian is by far the easier to understand. Benito Mussolini, ex-schoolteacher, ex-journalist, ex-laborer, and so forth, was an influential young Italian Socialist when the first World War broke. In his father's smithy he had absorbed *The Prince* of Machiavelli, with its cynical assertion that most men are "ungrateful, fickle, false, cowardly, covetous . . ." governed by fear rather than by affection. Sorel, the French syndicalist, with his philosophy of strikes and violence, had been a favorite author of his youth, and Gustave Le Bon's *Psychology of the Crowd,* with its teaching that the mob is ever unreasoning, moved hither and yon by passionate exaggeration, had left its impression upon him. Indeed, Mussolini never evinced any interest in the more scientific and theoretical aspects of socialism. He was not that kind of socialist; rather, by nature, he was inclined to masterful assertiveness, to stress will rather than reason, to frighten rather than to conciliate, to bluff and to bluster, but always with shrewd finesse and instinctive feeling as to just how far it would be safe for him to do so.

Under ordinary circumstances Mussolini would not have risen to fame;

but circumstances were not ordinary in postwar Italy. That country smarted from a sense of frustration; it had not really distinguished itself in the war; it had been saved from disaster only by Allied help and had won victory in the end only through French and British aid. Having sold herself to the highest bidder in 1915, Italy was now dissatisfied with her bargain. And she had not received all that she had bargained for! The Tyrol, Trieste, a part of the Dalmatian coast, and islands in the Adriatic and the Aegean she did obtain; but when France and England divided the German colonial empire between them, there was for Italy only the suggestion of a rectification of the boundaries of Tripoli (now Libya) and of Italian Somaliland. The Italians felt slighted. True, the German colonies were only being held in trust by France and Britain for civilization and the League of Nations. But why did Italy receive no mandates? Furthermore, in addition to the letter of the bond, the Italians had asked for Fiume at the peace conference; Fiume was not given them.

Then again, economic conditions in Italy were peculiarly distressing. Since Italy was a poor country, she had felt the strain of the war more than had France or England. Her finances after it were in terrible plight, and her currency had depreciated more than a third of its value. The well-intentioned but weak and purposeless men in charge of her government in 1919 had no plan, no program, by which the situation might be bettered. Brigandage broke out in the South, and the homes of landlords were burned; communism raised its head in the industrial North, and workingmen seized factories and announced they would operate them. Their experience was brief and unprofitable, and they gave back the factories to the former owners of their own free will. But anything might happen, apparently, in Italy, and if ever an affirmative voice was called for it was then.

Mussolini provided that voice. After the commencement of the war he had deserted his erstwhile friends, the Social Democrats, who opposed Italy's participation. Wounded, he was discharged from the army and founded in Milan a radical, pro-war newspaper. With the coming of peace he gathered around him a number of former soldiers and organized a small group, the *Fascio di combattimento*. Its program, like the original program of the Nazis, was a hybrid mixture of radical economic theory and extreme nationalism. No one thought it would amount to anything; it nominated two men for election to the Chamber of Deputies in 1919 and both were defeated. Nevertheless, when that neurotic man of letters, the poet Gabriele D'Annunzio, pounced upon Fiume with a few adventurers in the name of Italy and was shortly forced to abandon it by the Italian government, Mussolini began to gather headway by denouncing the puerile and weak-kneed authorities who interfered with Italy's destinies. And later, when the government did nothing to prevent Communist seizures of the factories, his party grew. Under his leadership, antimonarchists, antisocialists, anticlericals and antipacifists gathered, all eager to attack someone. They found the Italian Communists, who were already surrendering the commandeered factories, an easy mark; and they launched their major offensive against them, thereby delighting the wealthy bourgeoisie. Organized into squads with semimilitary discipline, they began attacking all Communists, or men suspected of being Communists, administered castor oil to their victims, and beat them up severely. Money, meanwhile, poured into the Fascist coffers and the ranks of the Black Shirts swelled with recruits.

By the spring of 1921 fascism was becoming popular in Italy with the middle and upper classes. Ostensibly, it stood for public order and the suppression of anarchy, and in the election to Parliament that year the Fascists won thirty-five seats. And along with this increase in popularity went a decrease in radicalism. Mussolini announced that he believed in monarchy, that he hated both communism and socialism, that his Black Shirts would prevent society from disintegrating as it promised to do with warring factions. In 1922 the Fascists held a grand congress in Naples which demanded either a new election or the inclusion of Fascists in the cabinet. Since the government would not listen to either alternative, a "march on Rome" began. The government offered no resistance; instead Mussolini was appointed prime minister by the King.

Parliament voted him dictatorial powers for one year and by its conclusion Mussolini was firmly seated in the saddle. To prevent ousting by subsequent parliaments, he forced through the Chamber of Deputies a law which provided that in any election the party with the biggest vote automatically should receive two-thirds of the seats. The Fascists thereupon won a majority in the election of 1924, obtained their two-thirds of the seats; and from that date on, open and organized opposition to Mussolini's dictatorship withered away. The head of the Socialist party was kidnapped and murdered under suspicious circumstances; Socialists and Liberals fled from Italy; others voluntarily retired from public life; a few, ardent nationalists, entered the Fascist ranks. Mussolini, meanwhile, by law after law, made secure his own hold on Italy; he was made head of the state; he took over several cabinet posts in person; no law could be initiated except by him; and by 1928 all elections in Italy had become a mere farce, there being but one party recognized (the Fascist) and but one list of candidates for whom it was possible to vote (the Fascist list).

In Italy, as in Germany and Russia, the new-style dictators of the twentieth century operated through the instrumentality of a political party over which they held tight rein. Again, as in Germany and Russia, the victorious political party was limited as to membership, Mussolini much preferring a party of one million to one of ten; the one million could be better organized, disciplined, watched. Entrance to the Fascist party came under ordinary circumstances entirely from below, from auxiliary youth organizations. Almost at the cradle fascism began; when eight years old, a youngster might join one of these youth groups, graduate to another at fourteen, to another at eighteen, and finally present himself as a candidate for membership in the Fascist party at twenty-one. Ostensibly, it remained a political party, not the government of Italy. But only Fascists could be elected to Parliament and the law provided that the Grand Council of the Fascist Party (presided over by Mussolini) must be consulted by Parliament on important matters. Also, the Fascist Grand Council had at its disposal a private Fascist militia and there were even special Fascist magistrates appointed. The consequence was that within ten years after the march on Rome only the shell remained of a liberal constitutional monarchy.

Fascist domestic policy, both in Italy and Germany, followed parallel lines in one respect: within both countries it aimed at the complete subordination of the individual to the will of the state. Particularly true was this of all economic activity. In Italy the Fascists took control of economic enterprise by a peculiar invention of their own, the corporative state, which reflected both the origin of Italian fascism and the method by which it had won power. Most of the early Fascists had been socialists of a sort, at least to the extent of believing in state socialism or syndicalism but, we must recall, the Fascists had risen to power by rushing to the defense of private property. They were radicals and conservatives at the same time, pledged to obtain rights for workingmen, pledged to protect private property. The corporative state combined both of these ideas. Under it the economic life of Italy was divided into six main categories: manufacturing, commerce, maritime transportation, inland transportation, agriculture, and banking. In each group there was to be a syndicate of workmen and a syndicate of employers, thus making twelve legalized syndicates; and to them a thirteenth was added, a syndicate of the learned professions. In theory the thirteen syndicates were to be autonomous. All trade unions were forbidden, and employers and employees, as represented by their respective syndicates, were to work together and engage in collective bargaining in accordance with a "Charter of Labor" granted in 1927, whereby certain rules were laid down in respect to rates of pay, old-age insurance, holidays with pay, and so forth. All syndicate members had to be in good standing with the Fascist authorities and the autonomy granted was more superficial than real.

Two years later (1929) the syndicates were fused with parliamentary representation, and Parliament was now said to be functional: in other words, to represent jobs and interests rather than districts or localities. In accordance with the new law, the thirteen syndicates selected 800 names and gave them to the Fascist Grand Council, which body also was presented with 200 additional names from other sources. Out of the

1,000 names the Council selected 400 as a Fascist list for Parliament members. An election was now held, yes or no, to this official list. No other candidate could be voted for and the ayes naturally had it. Such Parliament as Italy now had represented banking, transportation, and other interests, rather than electoral districts.

In this fashion the corporative state became identified with the national state. As an experiment in political theory it was interesting but not conclusive, for always behind the syndicates was the Fascist party and its Grand Council, the master and presiding genius of which was Mussolini. Nevertheless, for the corporative state this is to be said: The number of strikes diminished rapidly; the currency debacle was first halted, then checked, and a semblance of business recovery was noted, that is, if we judge simply from indexes of production. Excellent automobile roads were constructed by Mussolini's orders; large and spacious ocean liners owed their existence to his continued enthusiasm; and the "battle of wheat," namely, the effort to make Italy self-supporting in foodstuffs was waged strenuously and continuously by the energetic Duce, as Mussolini came to be called.

To all of this there was another side. Taxes of extreme severity were levied on the middle class, which groaned silently and paid. More serious was a decline in the standard of living of the poorer classes, already very low. There were no strikes; the workmen did not dare to strike. On the other hand they were conscious that others paid the costs as well as they. Mussolini could hardly be called a modern Robin Hood, robbing the rich to pay the poor. What he did was to exact a tremendous toll from all classes, partly to restore his country's credit, which did improve up to the great economic depression of the thirties; partly to pay for increases in armament made necessary by his determination to gain land by the sword or by threats.

The totalitarian doctrines of the Duce were less clearly defined than those of Hitler, nor did he crush out individual liberties quite as comprehensively as did his fellow dictator in Germany. There was the same talk in both countries of the decadence of liberalism and democracy, the same boasting of national solidarity and racial prowess. But with this difference: the Italians seemed disinclined to carry out their slogans to their logical conclusions. The best illustration of this fact may be found in the field of religion. As a matter of logic, pure and simple, there is no room for any religion in a totalitarian state except the religion of the State. The Germans, being logical almost to the point of the irrational, proceeded relentlessly, as we shall see, to persecute Jew, Protestant and Catholic. In Italy this was not so. The tiny group of Italian Protestants were not molested by Mussolini and with the Roman Catholic Church he made friends.

IL DUCE, WITH HONOR GUARD OF HIS YOUNGEST WARRIORS.

The Lateran treaty of 1929 with the Holy See was proof that Mussolini, the Fascist, knew how to compromise. By it the long-standing political feud between the Roman Curia and the Italian monarchy was settled amicably. The Pope recognized for the first time the legality of the Kingdom of Italy and agreed to support it. Mussolini, on the other hand, paid a handsome price for this recognition. A diminutive state of a hundred or so acres which included St. Peter's and the Vatican was ceded to the Pope, completely independent of Italy from legal code to postage stamp. In this state the Roman Pontiff was to be sole ruler. Nearly $40,000,000 in specie and an even larger sum in Italian bonds was added. The Roman Catholic religion was recognized as the religion of the State, and the canon law of the Church added to the law of Italy, Mussolini thus granting the Church privileges which had long lapsed in regard to education and marriage. Compulsory education in the Catholic faith was now prescribed for all youthful Italians.

The victory of the Church seemed very great, but Mussolini, too, secured advantages. Ecclesiastics were now called upon to support his regime. Only one source of friction between Church and State remained, the possibility of papal interference with what Mussolini considered purely political issues. A society of Catholic laymen, the Catholic Action, caused the Duce some trouble; it criticized his labor policy and he promptly abolished it. The Pope at first stood by the society; but a compromise was effected. In the future the society was to be under the direction of bishops and not of laymen; and Mussolini, on his part, agreed that the incessant drilling of small Italian youngsters in the practice of arms should not interfere, as it had been doing, with religious instruction.

For the Duce's domestic policy there was perhaps this to be said: an Italy confused, baffled, discouraged, torn by factions, and ruled by weak politicians, gave way to an Italy united, ruled by a man who knew what he wanted and knew how to obtain it. To be sure, there was a price, and a heavy one: liberties of the individual were snuffed out; newspapers printed simply what they were told; there was espionage, cruelty, and occasionally assassination of those Italians who opposed Mussolini. No mercy was shown the dissenters. Those who dared use pen or mouth in criticism either fled the country, going to France by thousands, or were rounded up and imprisoned, again by thousands. But the Duce's foreign policy was another matter. To it may be attributed the commencement of the Second World War (unless that honor be granted Japan); for the Duce established the European precedent and set the pace for Hitler to copy. When Mussolini invaded Abyssinia in 1935, fascism showed its real hand and Europe has not been at peace since. So important, indeed, was that invasion and Fascist Italy's foreign policy that its significance is left to another chapter.

The German Scene: Troubles of the Weimar Republic

Far more complicated was the picture presented by Germany after the First World War. In the spring of 1918 German hopes were high; by autumn they were shattered. A year later came Versailles and renewed disaster. That treaty had been no Carthaginian peace; but it was evident that the economic demands of the Allies could not be met without the virtual enslavement of German generations as yet unborn. The Fatherland in 1919 was in the abyss.

Under such circumstances, the constitution of the Weimar Republic was drawn up. It was a liberal, progressive, advanced constitution, and only slightly tinctured by the radicalism of the German Socialists who but one year earlier, as we have seen, administered the final blow to the Kaiser's regime. All Germans over twenty now had the ballot, and the new Reichstag which they were to elect was to govern the country through a chancellor representing a majority group or groups within it. The president of the new republic was supposedly a figurehead. The initiative, referendum, recall, proportional representation, and other up-to-date gadgets of the political scientists were included, and a gesture toward socialism was made by declarations concerning the unearned increment, condemnation of land (with indemnity), and an economic council.

This Weimar Republic was to last little more than a decade, and of its numerous elections and interminable party strife but trifling account shall be given. At no time in its history did any single party have a majority in the Reichstag. The Social Democrats, in the very first election held under the republic (1920), had by far the largest single representation; but even at the beginning they were deserted by left-wing socialists who had formed their own parties. At the extreme left were the Communists, listening to the siren voice of Lenin, confident of a second revolution which would sweep away this bourgeois republic. Other socialists to the left were the Independent Socialists, who abhorred a bloody revolution which was the dream of the Communists, but who demanded the immediate expropriation of private property throughout Germany. Had these three groups of socialists stuck together, they might have had a majority over all and Germany might have been spared Hitler; but owing to the absurd overconfidence of the Soviet authorities, constantly meddling in German affairs, this chance was lost. Meanwhile, on the extreme right, were the Nationalists, the Prussian Junkers, ex-army officers, and other defenders of the old regime. Both Communists and Nationalists, when not at each other's throats, started little civil wars of their own. For several weeks the Communists were able to hold Munich, for a short time the Nationalists were in military possession of Berlin. Both revolts were crushed; but Nationalists and Communists remained in the Reichstag, prepared to knife the republic at the slightest opportunity. Other parties of importance in the early history of the republic were the Centrists (the old Centre party of the Catholic Church); the People's party (the old National Liberal party rechristened), the stronghold of the upper bourgeoisie; and the Democratic party, a renewal of the old Radical party under the empire, drawing its membership largely from the lower bourgeoisie. There were also a few other parties of less importance; that of the National Socialists (the Nazis) did not come into prominence until 1923 and was of no special significance until late in the decade.

Who should control the destinies of the republic? For a long time the answer was an uneasy and constantly changing coalition of the more moderate groups. Sometimes a Social Democrat would be chancellor; sometimes a Centrist would be chancellor, supported in turn by Social Democrats and other factions; occasionally even a Nationalist would find his way into the cabinet. Election followed election for several highly unstable years, and the politically inexperienced Germans fought hard against terrific odds to bring some kind of order out of chaos. They were handicapped in many ways. If the Social Democrats had been somewhat more resolute, it is possible the skies might have cleared. But they had no Oliver Cromwell to lead them, nor any one else of ability, for that matter, who would dare to put through a genuine economic revolution by illegal means. The Social Democrats were democrats first and only secondarily socialists. They did not lift their little fingers against the property rights of the old nobility and the middle class; they did not even confiscate the wealth and the lands of the Hohenzollern family. The hands of the Social Democrats, and of all other parties, for that matter, were tied by proportional representation. Under it each party was represented in proportion to the number of votes which it received, and therefore the minor parties continued to live, although their existence was a continued threat against any consistent policy being carried out. Coalition government is generally weak government; and this was true of the different ministries of the Weimar Republic at the very time when Germany's principal need was for a strong government.

Then, too, from the Allies came no helping hand. They continued to treat Germany as a pariah country, whether republic or empire. She was excluded from the League of Nations; her natural resources were sadly diminished; and within four years of the signing of the peace treaty, the *poilus* were holding the Ruhr Valley by the throat. The utterly discredited Weimar Republic in 1923 suffered both from domestic malice and foreign levy.

Hitler

In that year of German crucifixion (1923) a wild-eyed, unkempt ex-corporal of the Kaiser's armies leaped on the table of the Reich commissar at Munich, fired his pistol in the air, and demanded a march on Berlin. There was no march on Berlin, but there was a parade in Munich. Headed by General Ludendorff, men known as Nazis, carrying a strange banner, forced their way through the streets of this South German city until stopped by the soldiers of the republic. Ludendorff was permitted to pass, but no others. Shots were fired; some Nazis were killed; some saved themselves by quickly dropping to the ground. Among the latter was their leading spokesman and orator, Adolf Hitler, who promptly was thrust into prison.

Before this event he was an unknown man, and for several years afterward this absurd coup d'état was regarded simply as one of the almost innumerable street brawls which desperate men had been starting in Germany ever since the defeat of the Second Marne. That this uneducated and most unprepossessing Austrian nobody should become dictator of the Reich in less than ten years, and in seven years more raise Germany to heights unknown even to Bismarck, no one dreamed.

Napoleon's origin was most respectable compared to his; the Emperor of the French at least started his career as a well-trained army officer. But in the obscurity of Hitler's early days there seemed to be no gleam of promise. The boy Adolf had some slight, very slight, artistic talent which he hoped to develop in Vienna. Poverty-stricken, a physical weakling, he only kept body and soul together in that city by accepting the hospitality of charitable institutions and by standing in bread-lines. He was not strong enough for manual labor; he was not talented enough to win more than a few miserable schillings as a decorator of gift-cards. Living from hand to mouth among the lowest of the Vienna proletariat, lazy and shiftless, he spent much of his time in the casual reading of the obscure pamphlet literature of the Pan-German expansionists and in listening, whenever chance offered, to music. In Vienna Hitler developed a bitter dislike for his companions in misery; he detested workmen, socialists, and above all else, Jews. He hated Vienna, the Hapsburg monarchy, and everything around him; and in his queer, tortured mind he found vicarious satisfaction for his own unhappiness in dreaming of a Germany which knew of no existence outside the imagination, a Germany great and glorious whose men and women, in the grandeur of their bodies, in the nobility of their souls, in the might of their wills, someday would dominate the world. He, Hitler, was a German!

In 1914 he enlisted in the German army and fought throughout the entire war. He was a brave soldier, a dispatch-bearer, who was wounded, gassed, and given the Iron Cross. When the armistice was signed he thought the end of all things had come. Germany, his one love, was broken; all that he hated was victorious—the Allies, international banking, international socialism, and the Jews.

The ex-corporal, wandering aimlessly in Munich, dropped into a beer

cellar. He listened to talk of a German Labor party, no Marxian international, bloodless and colorless, but a *pure* German party which would
repudiate such vague things as interest slavery, and would fight to the
death against such concrete actualities as the Treaty of Versailles and
the payment of reparations. Four men around a beer-stained table—and
Adolf Hitler! The party was formed, Hitler joined, and discovered that
he had a wonderful talent—his voice. The party doubled and trebled its
membership rapidly; men came to hear Hitler. Why?

The theme of his speeches was of the simplest: We did not lose the
war; the German people always win! We were betrayed, stabbed in the
back by Socialist and Jew. We have nothing to be ashamed of; we
shall yet conquer. *"Deutschland Erwache,"* Germany, awake! Down with
the international bankers, the international socialists, the evil Communists,
the "November criminals," those who signed the Treaty of Versailles. We
are not bound by that treaty; we will not be enslaved; down with Communist Russia; down with the Allies and their false promises! Throw off
the shackles. *Deutschland Erwache!*

The German Labor party soon enlarged its scope. It became the
N.S.D.A.P., the *National-sozialistische deutsche arbeiterpartei,* soon to be
called Nazi, for brevity. The emphasis from the beginning was on the
word *National,* and as the years sped on the labor aspect of the party's
program grew less and less. The party was given a flag (Hitler was not
an artist in vain), red because of its psychological stimulus, white circle
on the red background that the flag might be distinguished from the
Communist banner, and on the white circle a black, crooked cross—the
swastika—symbol of human fertility in India, of anti-Semitism in Russia.

Fortunately for the ultimate success of the Nazis, came the collapse of
the 1923 *émeute.* That failure threw Hitler into jail, thus giving him time
to formulate his dreams, and to bring to the boiling point the yeasty
depths of his subconscious. And now, a captive, he wrote *Mein Kampf!*

This Bible of the Nazi faith, calmly and objectively considered, is a
queer mélange of semitruth and unadulterated nonsense, combined with
an almost uncanny psychological insight into the mind of the mob. It is
wordy, turgid, repetitious, ill-written; but it does throw light on Hitler,
his aims, methods, character. It is easier to tell big lies than little ones, the
author tells us. The people are always gullible; they will believe anything if sufficiently repeated. Hitler is quite on a par with Mussolini in his
contempt for democracy. The Jews brought about the ruin of Germany;
they must be driven out of the country. France is pictured as the eternal
enemy, but communism as Germany's more immediate foe. The Fatherland must arouse itself, must repudiate the Versailles *diktat,* must fight,
must expand, must seize land in southern and eastern Europe. The Nazi
party will do all this.

There is not much more in *Mein Kampf.* Hitler speaks at length of his early career in Vienna and how he came to detest the Jews; he exults in the way the Nazis were able to exploit mob psychology by the use of storm troopers (hired roughnecks) instead of depending on police support. There is anticapitalistic talk of a kind; but Hitler really was not interested in economics. Where he lets himself go with feeling and abandon is when he talks about the *Volk* (people). But Volk means far more than "people" in the English sense; rather it implies an antecedent, primitive, racial throwback to a mythological German people invented during the days of the fight waged against Bonaparte by poets and philosophers and found useful by politicians. *"Blut und Boden,"* blood and soil—a sacred something in the German blood-stream, an equally sacred something in the earth on which Germans have lived. Here is nothing but a pouring forth of disjointed fragments from H. S. Chamberlain, Fichte, and Jahn, with stray bits of the Pan-German gospel picked up here and there by the casual reading of a tramp-artist in beer-cellar and public reading-room.

We are also told why Germany lost the war, what kind of government befits the longed-for volk state and what ought to be the German foreign policy of the future. The policy of the Hohenzollern regime in international affairs is adversely criticized and Austria is assailed as partly responsible for the war; but what really lost the war, according to Hitler, was (*a*) the inefficient propaganda of Germany in comparison with England; (*b*) the traitorous character of German socialism; and (*c*) the poisonous infiltration of Jewish influence in the Fatherland.

One thing Hitler instinctively grasped, the art of propaganda.

The great masses' receptive ability [he tells us], is only very limited, their understanding is small, but their forgetfulness is great. As a consequence of these facts, all effective propaganda has to limit itself only to a very few points and to use them like slogans until even the very last man is able to imagine what is intended by such a word. . . . It was completely wrong to ridicule the adversary as was done in Austrian and German propaganda in comic papers. It was basically wrong for the reason that when a man meets the adversary in reality he was bound to receive an entirely different impression; something that took its most terrible revenge; for now the German soldier, under the direct impression of the resistance of the enemy, felt himself deceived by those who were responsible for his enlightenment, and instead of strengthening his fighting spirit or even his firmness, quite the contrary occurred. The man despaired. Compared with this, the war propaganda of the British and the Americans was psychologically right. By introducing the German as a barbarian and a Hun to its own people it thus prepared the individual soldier for the terrors of war and helped guard him against disappointment . . .[1]

Concerning socialism and Jews, the future dictator of Germany was grossly partisan. There was, it is true, a socialistic revolution in the Father-

---

[1] Adolf Hitler, *Mein Kampf,* p. 234, quoted by permission of the Houghton Mifflin Company, proprietors of the basic copyrights of all American editions.

land as the war officially ended, and there was socialistic propaganda in favor of peace before that date; but the influence of the latter was very slight until late in 1918. As for the Jews, their history and their character, Hitler knew nothing. Page after page of *Mein Kampf* is devoted to their vilification. Those pages do not need examination if we remember that the ratio of casualties in the war for the German Jews was approximately the same as for the German Gentiles; that 35,000 Jews received war medals; that 23,000 Jewish soldiers were promoted to the rank of officer; that of less than 600,000 Jewish citizens of Germany, 100,000 bore arms.

The importance of *Mein Kampf* as a book is difficult to estimate. Certainly, it does not belong in the same category in the field of political science as Rousseau's *Social Contract* or the essays of John Stuart Mill. The voice, and not the pen, was the medium through which Hitler rose to power. On the other hand, it is foolish to dismiss *Mein Kampf* as simply the wild ravings of a paranoiac. After all, millions read this book, which possibly will rank in later years as the most famous or infamous production of the first quarter of the twentieth century.

Why National Socialism Continued to Grow

Hitler, once out of jail (1924), gave all his time to resuscitating the N.S.D.A.P. Only very slowly did it grow, for Locarno in 1925 (see p. 624) seemingly placed the Weimar Republic on a firmer basis, and not until as late as 1929 were Nazis much more than a joke among serious-minded Germans. Nevertheless, grow in numbers they did, and for a variety of reasons. Among them were: the peculiar appeal of the National Socialists to the lower half of the middle class, slowly slipping into the proletariat; the adroit use of propaganda; the financial assistance of wealthy Germans; and the absurd antics of the German Communists.

The middle class, particularly in the lower strata, felt the shock of Germany's financial disaster in 1923 more than any other. The peasants managed to live; they had their cattle and their gardens. The aristocrats had their rent rolls; and the wealthier bourgeoisie still owned factory and workshop which they operated as soon as the new currency, the rentenmark, was established. So also was it with the workmen who had no capital anyway to disappear with inflation and who could depend more or less on unemployment insurance. But there was no sun at all on the horizon of the little man of business, the people with money in savings banks, those with insurance, the doctors, the dentists, the professional men, and the civil servants who had saved a little for retirement or for a rainy day. All they had was wiped out overnight. Vaguely, the N.S.D.A.P. was against big business, the little people liked that; it was against war profiteers (many of them Jewish), and the little people liked that. To all baffled and defeated and discouraged men it offered two scapegoats—the Versailles *diktat* and the Jews. Those who despaired the most and who thought the least were attracted as by a magnet.

The National Socialist propaganda was unique and telling. Hitler explained in his book how meetings held at night were always more effective than those held during the day in arousing the emotions, and most of the Nazi meetings were in the evening. Nothing was omitted that might arouse passion. The Nazis made great use of huge banners borne by their separate units. These flags were consecrated by the Fuehrer by touching them with that most sacred blood-stained banner borne in the tragicomedy of 1923 in Munich. Singing and neon lights made their appeal. Hitler's advent was frequently delayed until excitement reached the fever pitch. As time wore on the Fuehrer traveled over large stretches of Germany by airplane. Searchlights would pierce the black night for his coming; bands would burst into martial music; and then the ex-corporal with magic voice would scream defiance at his various foes.

Where did the money come from to pay for uniforms, publicity, a Mercedes automobile and airplanes? In part it was derived from the sale of tickets; the Hitler shows were good ones; in part it came from the dues of party members, very considerable in the lump sum. But in addition there were contributions from the big industrialists, who contributed more or less impartially to all the anti-Marxian factions. These industrialists were not Nazis; but many of them thought the Nazis useful, since they beat up Communists in the street and demanded the rearmament of Germany, a pleasant note to the ear of the Ruhr steel men. Even the Nationalists, the Junker crowd, were sufficiently foolish to believe that Hitler, mountebank and charlatan though he might be, could be taken into camp and made a convenient tool for the reëstablishment of the monarchy. The Nationalists could not agree upon a candidate for the vacant imperial throne, some favoring Rupprecht of Bavaria, some the Hohenzollerns; but in the meanwhile a subsidy to the ex-corporal could do no harm.

Then, too, the Communist party in Germany continued through the nineteen-twenties to be a great help to Hitler. The Communists looked to Moscow for their orders and they received them. Nothing detracts more from Lenin's reputation as a statesman than his conviction that a Communist revolution was imminent in Germany, a Russian fantasy that lived long after Lenin died and still, perhaps, is cherished in Moscow. Lenin instructed his disciples in Germany to undermine the Weimar Republic; to hate and to abhor all Social Democrats, those traitors to the Marxian faith, instructions followed after Lenin's death. They fitted nicely into Hitler's hand; he denounced the Communists as base internationalists; he insisted that they went further, that they advocated loose sexual relations, free week-ends without matrimony, and so forth. The Nazis posed as the defenders of the German home. Purists of the pure (in theory), they harkened back to the folkways of the primitive Germans, their sexual cleanliness, their Spartan virtue. How these *Urdeutschers* would have revolted against the social decadence and flaunting vice of the contemporary republic in which the Communists reveled! And there is a good deal of evidence to support the Nazi claim that such conditions existed in Germany after the war, as is true more or less in all countries after the strain of war, and particularly in those where the currency depreciates so rapidly that the wise thing seems to be to spend any money available while it still has purchasing power. But to the Nazi orator the purveyors of this vice were always the Jew and the Communist!

Under such circumstances, the Weimar Republic was fortunate to survive as long as it did. Assailed from both right and left, by Nationalists, Communists, and Nazis, it kept its head well above water until the world economic crisis of 1930-31. One reason why it did so was the tactful foreign policy of Gustav Stresemann, who was Germany's foreign minister in no less than ten different ministries between 1923 and 1929. During the war Stresemann had been a violent Nationalist, and after it he was the spokesman in the Reichstag for the German People's party, the right wing of the bourgeoisie. But these facts did not prevent him from realizing the immediate necessity of placating France and England if the republic was to get on a firm basis. Within one year after the evacuation of the Ruhr by the French, the Dawes Plan for lessening the strain of the reparation problem was accepted by Stresemann, and one year later he negotiated the Treaty of Locarno with the former enemies of Germany on the basis of perfect equality.

Locarno and the Dawes Plan

That treaty guaranteed the western frontier of the Weimar Republic as drawn by the Treaty of Versailles, and the signatories—Belgium, Italy, France, England, and Germany—not only pledged themselves to respect it but also to enforce it. Thus the Germans of their own accord surrendered all claims to Alsace-Lorraine, and the French to further invasions of Germany to enforce treaty rights, such as the invasion of the Ruhr. The Germans likewise agreed to the demilitarization of Germany fifty kilometers east of the Rhine, as provided in the Versailles pact. Locarno was to go into effect with the entry of Germany into the League of Nations, which took place late in this same year, 1926.

Along with this partial settlement of political disputes and the recognition of Germany's political equality with her former enemies, came a very decided economic revival. The Reich after the war had no ruined cities to rebuild, and the very fact of inflation had enabled her to modernize her industrial machinery by borrowing huge sums which were repaid in marks which had no value. Furthermore, since the old mark now was worthless, her war loans, raised from her own citizens (domestic debt), were wiped out. There remained her debt to the Allies (reparations). This now, by the Dawes Plan, was placed upon a more intelligent basis than it had before. The Dawes Plan was still a stop-gap; it was irritating in so far as it called for a certain amount of international control over German finance; it was annoying in so far as it made the amount of the annual total due from Germany depend on an index of prosperity which meant that the more prosperous the Germans became the more they had to pay; and it was discouraging, as it set no final total of indebtedness. On the other hand, it was an improvement which worked as long as foreign loans poured into Germany. The plan called for immediate loans which were granted, and these were followed by many private ones.

Stresemann, indeed, had accomplished much, but he was heavily attacked for not doing more. The fourteen points of Wilson had called for general disarmament; but all the Germans saw was unilateral disarmament as far as they were concerned, and practically nothing accomplished by the other countries in this direction. The Dawes Plan, too, seemingly laid an almost perpetual burden on German backs, even if a slightly lighter one than that already carried. Stresemann realized this and worked hard to ease the burden still further. This he was able to accomplish by the Young Plan, 1929, which was adopted by general consent in place of the Dawes Plan. The new agreement provided a definite limit for German payment, lowering the total indebtedness. But unfortunately the agreement came too late. In this year (1929) Stresemann died and an economic blizzard began to sweep the world which transformed the situation and gave Hitler his great opportunity.

The Great Depression and the Nazis

The storm clouds burst on the New York stock exchange late in 1929 and a first-class panic followed in America. This meant not only no more loans to Germany but also the calling in of short-term credits to that country. Whereupon, in 1930, banks in Germany and Austria began to close their doors and German factories to dismiss their employees. In vain did the German chancellor appeal to the British and the French for help; the former, fearful of their own financial status, were afraid to aid; the latter were not only afraid but unwilling. A moratorium on reparation payments was, indeed, granted; but that came too late to be effective, and international trade was paralyzed.

Under such circumstances came the election of 1930. Both the German right and the German left strengthened their position against the moderate center; the Communists increased their representation at the expense of the Social Democrats, but that of the Nazis went sky-rocketing upward. Before the election the Nazis, despite their clamor, had but twelve seats in the Reichstag; after it was over they numbered 107 and were the second largest party.

The chancellor was Brüning, a Centrist. For support at home he had to depend on a slight majority made up of many different party groups and on the backing of the President of the Republic, the octogenarian Hindenburg. Support outside his country he had none. A customs union with Austria which might have helped save the day had been vetoed by the French, a veto upheld on technical grounds by the World Court at the Hague. Meanwhile, unemployment rose by leaps and bounds, and starvation threatened. The very liberalism of the Weimar Republic was telling now against it. For years the Nationalists and the Nazis had been organizing and drilling informal private armies of their own, the former the Steel Helmets, the latter the *Sturmabteilung* (Brown Shirts). Even the peaceful Social Democrats had done likewise with the *Reichsbanner* corps. Germany was seething with violent disorder. Armed bands were attacking Jews and Communists, the former not retaliating, the latter fighting back.

Between the accession of Brüning in March, 1930, and the burning of the Reichstag building in February, 1933, which threw Germany into Hitler's power, the utmost confusion reigned. Plot and counterplot followed. There were two presidential and two Reichstag elections; there were innumerable street riots and many murders; and the political balance swayed backward and forward between the defenders of Weimar and the Nationalists, the Nazis, and the Communists who hated the republic. Much is still obscure concerning these three hectic years during which the Nazis and the Nationalists, wearing their private uniforms, marched out of the Reichstag and into it again, during which Brüning, a confirmed moderate and well-wisher of the republic, was compelled to rule largely by decree until he lost the support of the President, during which also the Junker aristocracy played constantly with fire (Adolf Hitler), only in the end to be badly scorched.

The three years were full of economic misery and semistarvation, since Brüning's answer to the world depression was economy. But they were also full of betrayals of one sort or another. Hindenburg, very old and perhaps not altogether in possession of his faculties, was reëlected by the Social Democrats, the Centrists, and other moderate groups. Yet within a few weeks after the election, he seemingly betrayed his constituents by dismissing Brüning, who had at the time a majority behind him. Von Papen, a Junker, was made chancellor by Hindenburg, but he in turn was betrayed by General Schleicher and other Nationalists who intrigued against von Papen. Schleicher, von Papen, and the Nationalists (Steel Helmets) were afterward betrayed by Hitler, who played cleverly for power and only obtained it by betraying also his own leftwing followers who took their socialism seriously. Possibly the "anticapitalistic romanticism" which the coming Fuehrer had advocated hitherto, with its implied attack on land values and big business, had never been of any real significance to him; but it was imbedded in the platform of the Nazi party, and in order to obtain the support of the wealthy, Hitler threw most of it overboard, driving out of his own party many of his oldest and warmest friends.

Finally, in January, 1933, Hindenburg, field marshal, war hero, and President of the republic which he had sworn to defend, appointed ex-corporal Hitler as chancellor. This was done through the connivance of von Papen and other aristocrats, who thought Hitler would play their game. The Nazis, at the last election, had captured only thirty-two per cent of the votes and the Nationalist vote was less than one-third that of the Nazis. There was then no majority for the Nazi-Nationalist combination and another election was called, the third in one year. By the first and earlier election of 1932 the Nazis had captured thirty-seven per cent of the electorate and therefore they seemingly were declining in strength. The decline from thirty-seven to thirty-two per cent was serious; could they hope for a majority now? It looked as though they could not; but luck or treachery now stood them in good stead—the Reichstag fire!

Who destroyed the parliamentary building where the Reichstag met? "The slimy Communists did it!" shouted the Nazis, from a thousand platforms in Germany. "It was to be the signal for a Communist revolt; we and the Nationalists were in power; our General Goering nipped the plot in the bud or else there would have been a Red revolution." But that the Communists engaged in this act of arson there is no evidence, and everything points to the Nazis as having perpetrated this destruction. True, a half-witted young Dutchman, afterward executed, helped set the Reichstag on fire, and at one time he had been associated with Communists in Holland. But this fire was well planned, well executed, and required the help of several men. And there is some evidence, both direct and circumstantial, to indicate that it was done by a number of Brown Shirts, presumably under orders from that fire-eating Nazi, General Goering.

However that may be, it was the Nazis who profited. There were only three Nazis in the cabinet and they were supposedly kept well under control there by the numerical majority of Nationalists; but one of the three was Hitler, the chancellor, and they controlled the police. This latter fact really determined the result of the election in advance; Communist, Socialist, and even Centrist newspapers were suppressed and every possible hysteria was encouraged. The increase in the Nazi vote which followed brought it to forty-three and nine-tenths per cent of the total. If we add to this the eight per cent won by the Nationalists, it is evident that the coalition had fifty-two per cent, a narrow but clear majority.

The Reichstag met and the first thing done was to exclude from its meetings the 81 members elected by the Communists, an act which gave the Nazis, by themselves and for the first time, a majority over all. Followed then rapidly the abolition of the German trade unions, the abolition of the Social Democratic party, and that of all other political groups in the Reichstag except the Nazi. The Reichsbanner of the Socialists was dissolved without a fight and, unkindest cut of all, the Nationalists were forced out of the cabinet and their Stahlhelm abolished. The Centre party meanwhile voluntarily ended its own existence, and political parties, as such, were abolished in Germany with the exception of one, the N.S.D.A.P. All this took place rapidly during the year 1933 and, toward its end, Hitler, in a blaze of patriotic fervor, withdrew Germany from the "unfair" League of Nations. As he did so, he asked for a vote of the German people in approval or disapproval of his various activities. A ballot was to be cast, a curious ballot. There were Nazi names printed on it and no others were permitted. One could simply vote *"Ja"* or *"Nein"*; there was no other choice. Before the election there was to be no propaganda of any kind except Nazi propaganda. To the Nazi belonged the exclusive rights to the press, to the radio, to illuminated night meetings, and brass bands. And the S.A., the storm troopers, Brown Shirts, guarded the polls and watched the voting. The result—ninety-five per cent voted *"Ja."*

Party government now was ended, liberty vanished, democracy dead. Germany was on the verge of being a totalitarian state controlled by the will of one man, except in so far as he delegated that will to his leading subordinates like General Hermann Goering, a former aviator, now President of the Reichstag, and Joseph Paul Goebbels, the most learned of all the Nazis, a doctor of philosophy with a crippled body, whose venomous diatribes against the Jews had endeared him to Hitler. The Reichstag, it is true, continued to exist; but from now on it became merely a sounding board for Hitler's voice. Von Hindenburg still lived; but he was in his last illness and within a year was to die. Hitler did not choose to succeed him as president. That exalted title, he explained, belonged only to Hindenburg; he, Hitler, would be content to be simply *Der Fuehrer,* the man who founded the Third German Reich which would last one thousand years.

Very thoroughly now did Hitler subordinate all things in Germany to the will of the Nazi party—his will. From 1934 to the outbreak of the second World War in 1939, the Nazis proceeded (*a*) to destroy root and branch all traces of a labor party in Germany; (*b*) insanely and abominably to persecute the Jews; (*c*) to attack the Christian Church, both Catholic and Protestant; (*d*) to revolutionize education; (*e*) to cast off one by one the last remnants of the Versailles pact; (*f*) to rearm to the teeth; and (*g*) finally, to plunge Europe into another war. The first four of these seven policies of Hitler will be discussed here; the remaining three belong to the field of international relations and will be taken up later.

The Nazis and Labor

The German labor movement succumbed without a fight, whereas the churches, and the Lutheran Church in particular, seemingly weak and defenseless in the postwar period were able to withstand to some degree the will of the dictator. The German trade unions, which accepted disbandment without a murmur, were strong in numbers but weak in will. Their members were socialists who had looked forward for so long and so confidently to the time when Germany would *hineinwachsen* (grow into) socialism that they were inhibited from realizing that their cause might be lost altogether unless they were willing to meet force with force. Many of their members were led by Nazi propaganda to believe that National Socialism, as advertised, was really socialistic. The Nazis, during their first year in power, certainly succeeded in reducing unemployment. They did so by extreme economic nationalism, by starting public works, by establishing labor camps, by ordaining export subsidies, by commencing the rearmament of Germany.

Then, too, the Nazis announced a labor policy which in theory was favorable to labor. "Full authority downward, full responsibility upward," was their slogan, undemocratic, if you will, but not necessarily injurious to the material welfare of the workingman. If the latter lost his right to collective bargaining, that did not mean free competition in the labor market and the right of the employer to determine wages. Over both employer and employee now were placed fourteen labor trusts, which were to determine wages; and social honor courts with power to deal with labor disputes took the place of the old trade unions. Labor was forbidden to organize, but labor was not left completely helpless, for the Nazi party controlled the honor courts.

The historian, indeed, must walk warily in generalizing about Nazi labor policy. In certain respects it was favorable to labor. A "Strength through Joy" movement was started, whereby free vacations at state expense were provided; six months' labor service (*arbeitsdienst*) was required of all Germans irrespective of social position and rank; German peasants were protected against usury and were assured title to their holdings in perpetuity; and great care was taken to prevent the price of foodstuffs customarily used by the poor, such as potatoes, margarine, and sausages, from rising.

The Nazis did not, to be sure, satisfy their own more radical members who hoped for a genuinely socialistic revolution and the ending of capitalism in Germany. The latter were completely crushed by the bloody purge of 1934, and most of their spokesmen were killed. Just what happened behind the scenes is still obscure. There was talk of a second revolution, and Roehm, commander of the Brown Shirts, aroused the suspicions of Hitler. Just what Roehm was after it is difficult to tell; he wanted more power given the Brown Shirts and was jealous of the S.S. men, the Schutzstaffel, or private police who guarded Hitler and who seemed to the storm troopers a kind of aristocratic organization supplanting them. Roehm had been one of the more radical Nazis and he was thought to have been intriguing with von Schleicher, the ex-Nationalist chancellor and a general in the army, who might conceivably be stirring up a coup d'état against Hitler. It was also said that Roehm for a long time had been a notorious homosexual, a fact hitherto ignored by Hitler.

Suddenly now, in the summer of 1934, Hitler pounced upon Roehm and his more intimate friends and summarily put them to death. Simultaneously, Goering in Berlin slaughtered in cold blood many other Nazis, likewise General von Schleicher, his wife, and a number of other suspects. All told, upward of a thousand Germans were shot down in cold blood. "There was none of the courage of mercy. There was none of the coolness of wisdom." With berserker rage the Nazi chieftains acted, and bullets spat against cement walls as Nazi after Nazi with "Heil Hitler!" on his lips gave up his life. Hitler, in a long, rambling speech to the Reichstag, explained later that the victims of the purge were traitors, that they were dissipated, immoral, and deserved death. The world looked for some proof of the former statement; none was advanced. The immorality was nothing new, nothing hidden; it had not hitherto excited Hitler's rage. But even the sexual abnormality which characterized Roehm and certain other well-known Brown Shirts was not charged against all of those slain. A number of them, like von Schleicher, were not even Nazis. Could it be possible that von Schleicher had proof that Hitler had never received the Iron Cross for valor in the war; was he really intriguing with Roehm to overthrow the dictator; was there any significance in the fact that those Nazis employed in firing the Reichstag now were killed, thus ending any chance of their talking? Robespierre gave Danton a trial in the French Revolution; Hitler behaved otherwise to his old comrades.

The Nazis and the Jews

Possibly the single most extraordinary fact about Hitler and the Nazi victory was the anti-Semitism which characterized it. After the Nazis came to power they excluded Jews from all learned professions in Germany, forbade them to practise law, removed their physicians from state hospitals, drove Jewish judges off the bench and Jewish professors out of the universities. Jews were excluded from all governmental posts, and one by one the various economic enterprises which Jews headed were "Aryanized," placed under non-Jewish management. Jews were compelled to dispose of their large business enterprises for nominal sums, Jewish-owned department stores, banks, printing presses, manufacturing plants, were put under non-Jewish control. And finally Jews were subjected to an ever increasing flood of humiliating insults, aimed apparently at driving all Jews and those of partial Jewish blood outside the country of their birth.

Hitler himself had written "the wretched Jew, enemy of the human race, the Jew, cause of all our miseries," and Goebbels, appointed minister of propaganda by Hitler, constantly referred to Jews as beneath the contempt of all decent men. But more important, perhaps, than the statements of these two Nazi chieftains were the fulminations of Streicher, a popular Nazi propagandist, whose foul sheet *Der Stürmer*, specifically blest by Hitler, was made compulsory reading in the German schools.

Der Stürmer, by cartoon and by story, stressed one major theme—the lascivious desire of the Jewish people to contaminate the German people by sexual intercourse with it. The Jewish religion, *Der Stürmer* said, called for the spreading of the seed of Israel among non-Jews; Jewish physicians could never be trusted because they gave anesthetics in order to rape German girls. Jews must not be spoken to on the street; they must have separate benches in the schools; no German girl was to be permitted to work as a servant in a Jewish home; she must never marry a Jew; the *Protocols of Zion* (an absurd forgery) was dug up to prove that Jews conspired to rule the world; rabbis were accused of drinking Christian blood in foul rituals; and by the Nuremberg laws none could claim to be a German citizen unless he could prove that all of his four grandparents were non-Jewish. Even the non-Aryan Christians, those contaminated by having one or more Jewish grandparents, were forbidden to give the Nazi salute. They were equally guilty of belonging to an inferior race.

The situation grew worse constantly, and when a young Jewish boy assassinated an official in the German embassy at Paris in 1938, it reached its height. Mobs roamed the streets of German cities, burning synagogues, smashing the windows of Jewish stores, stealing their contents, and beating all Jews they encountered. The authorities made no effort to stop them; instead they levied a huge fine on all German Jews, so huge as virtually to wipe out all remaining Jewish wealth. Some Jews escaped from Germany, penniless; but a majority, unable to obtain visas for countries beyond the seas or in Europe, sunk back into the depths of despair as the Nazis prepared to set apart ghettos for Jews, miserable districts in the more squalid parts of German cities in which Jews must live and out of which Jews would emerge at their peril.

Why this persecution of the Jews, the most vicious, the most barbaric in modern times? It was not just the dictatorship; Frederick the Great was a dictator, but he welcomed Jews in Prussia, and Napoleon was well disposed toward them. It has been urged that Germany was always an anti-Semitic country; but the facts do not bear out this interpretation. During the period of the Second German Empire, which lasted from 1871 to the Weimar Republic, there was far more active anti-Semitism in both France and Russia than in Germany. The Germans discriminated against the Jews even then, socially, and governmental and military rank was denied them; but Jewish students were not put on a narrow quota basis in the universities as in Russia, and the learned professions in Germany were full of Jews—Jewish doctors, Jewish lawyers, Jewish professors. Important newspapers, banks, business houses, were Jewish-owned, and mixed marriages were more common in Germany than anywhere else in Europe. The very presence of the numerous non-Aryan Christians refutes this argument. The latter were more than three times as numerous as the professing Jewish people, of whom there were only some 600,000 in the Reich.

It has likewise been suggested that economic competition brought about the Jewish persecution, the Jews being held up to scorn as battening on the ills of Germany—war profiteers and usurers, prosperous while others starved. The economic level of the German Jew was, it is true, relatively high; he did own most of the department stores which took away trade from the small shopkeepers, and there were Jewish usurers. But there was nothing new about this, and all the evidence at our command goes to show that the Jew did not benefit by the war. His income declined, like that of other Germans; and as a matter of cold statistics, there were proportionately fewer Jews among the leading industrialists and bankers of Germany after the war than before.

Even less valid a reason is the assertion that the principles of National Socialism are so foreign to Jewish psychology as to make inevitable the exclusion of all Jews from a Nazi state. Jews, naturally, are opposed to anti-Semitism; but aside from that there was no proposal of the Nazis that Jews as such would automatically oppose. There are international Jews, socialist Jews, nationalist Jews, capitalistic Jews. In fact, there were certain tenets of Nazi philosophy which might be considered as rather attractive to Jews, particularly, the idea of national unity transcending all religious barriers.

What then is the explanation? Possibly the best that can be given is the racial myth that Hitler expounded, the supremacy of Aryan and particularly Teutonic blood over all other racial strains. Some reason had to be given for this superior racial strain losing the war, and the inherent wickedness of Marxian philosophy was a partial one. But Marxism could not be dramatized quite so readily as that biological absurdity of the Nazis—the poisoning of racial purity by Jewish blood. The Jews were a convenient scapegoat. Communists as scapegoats had disadvantages; they were poor and there was no booty to be gleaned from them; they were Germans, and when they transferred themselves into good Nazis, or pretended to, they had no distinguishing marks. But the Jews had money, which might come in handy; they also had distinguishing marks; their names, their physical appearance—they were Jews. As such they offered a shining mark for the attack of the bigoted, and they became the principal scapegoat upon which was loaded all the unhappiness and misery of postwar Germany.

The Nazis and the Christian Churches

The Nazis' attack on Christianity is perhaps easier to understand than their animosity toward the Jews, but the evidence of it is slightly more confusing. Whether in the long run it was more serious than the open atheism of the Russian Communists it is difficult to say, for while the Communist attack was direct and open, that of the Nazis was indirect, insidious, and therefore possibly the more dangerous. The Nazis never repudiated Christianity as a party; rather they tried to corrupt it from within, to twist and to distort its meaning.

Certain of the Nazis, to be sure, repudiated Christianity, lock, stock, and barrel. Seeking openly to reëstablish the pagan rites of their early ancestors, they resurrected Odin, Thor, and the old stone gods. By picturesque ritual and dramatic rites, they glorified bravery, loyalty, and physical force into a trinity of virtues. But these professed pagans were but a minority. What was far more characteristic of the Nazi attitude toward religion was the program of the German Christians. The latter threw out the Old Testament as a Jewish book, and many parts of the New Testament as well. They denied that Christ was Jewish and interpreted him as a kind of warrior who, by his death, had preserved the world from Jewish domination, an act of virtue duplicated by their Fuehrer, in turn a kind of second Christ. These so-called German Christians demanded that the swastika be introduced into the churches as a kind of sacred symbol, and that the church be regarded solely as a kind of adjunct to the government.

All Nazis did not go as far as these German Christians, and many of them were indifferent to the Church, whether Catholic or Protestant, as was the case, apparently, with Hitler. Nevertheless, the latter was determined to put the Lutheran Church of the country under his direct control, and appointed as head of it a reichsbishop with German Christian tendencies. This met with such stiff opposition that Hitler withdrew his appointee and selected another. Many Lutheran pastors objected to taking an oath of loyalty to Hitler which would deprive them of freedom of conscience. In consequence, a number of them were put in concentration camps.

Much to the surprise of the outside world, the Lutheran Church in Germany, hitherto considered more dead than alive as far as spiritual fervor was concerned, took on a new lease of life. Churches began to be filled, many coming, perhaps, not so much to worship the Lord as to show that they would like to voice disapproval of the Nazi tyranny in their own country. Going to church was about the only way they could show it.

The Roman Catholic Church also came in conflict with the government. It had consented to liquidate the Centre party and to retire from politics; but it would not consent to the untiring campaign of the Nazis in trying to break up all church youth organizations and compelling boys to join the Hitler *Jugend*, wherein they were taught that force alone ruled the world and that Christian ethics were better suited for a slave society than for a self-respecting Aryan nation like Germany.

Roman Catholic bishops in both Austria and Germany protested firmly in their pastoral letters against this almost complete assumption of authority by the State over the time and the activities of the young. Whereupon the Nazis fought back; they placed on trial many members of monastic orders on a variety of charges running from accusations of smuggling gold out of Germany to sexual malpractices; they banned the circulation of Catholic literature; they forbade Catholic processions; and they sternly insisted that the Church confine its activities to what the Nazis considered religious matters, education being distinctly not one.

Nazi threats on the one hand and the protest of the Pope and of Protestant pastors on the other, continued down to the commencement of the Second World War in 1939, without any final solution or compromise being reached. To claim that in this general strife the Nazis met their match would be an exaggeration; nevertheless it is evident that the Nazis did not dare go too far in their opposition to the churches. They did not, for instance, close them; they did not forbid Mass being sung. In view of the necessity of unity in foreign affairs, even Hitler refrained from a completely totalitarian policy in church affairs, and the churches retained something more than the semblance of autonomy.

Possibly in this matter the Nazis felt that time was on their side. The older generation would die before long, and boys and girls who had experienced nothing outside the Nazi fold would take its place. The same would occur in Germany as was taking place (so they thought) in Italy— the coming to maturity of youngsters trained in a new faith.

GIRLS OF THE NAZI YOUTH PARTY

Nazi Education

For the Nazis had a faith (of a kind) and they went about its indoctrination in a most thorough manner. Superficially, it copied the
Italian model. Boys and girls were expected to join the various Nazi youth
organizations appropriate for their age, there to drill, to march, to sing
the praises of the new regime, to listen to its glories, to grow accustomed
to warlike discipline, to learn in true Spartan fashion that luxury, comfort,
individualism, were not for them. But in reality this Nazi faith was much
more serious than its Italian counterpart. The Fascist teachings of Mussolini were never taken, one suspects, very seriously by him or by the
better-informed Italians. The Duce found these very useful for a clever
adventurer, but he never took pains to define them very closely. Not so
with the Nazis. Their philosophy was much more definite. To the ardent
Nazi the Fuehrer was a man sent by God, and in him were embodied
all those racial characteristics which dated from Odin, Thor, and Siegfried.
The necessity of obedience, the hatred of Jews, the substitution of the
state for the family as the social unit were encouraged and enforced.
Studies in the schools which did not serve these ends were either curtailed
or abolished. Pseudoscientific racial nonsense was given a most prominent
place; strength of body and steadiness of nerve, dangerous and arduous
physical exercise were exalted over mental acumen and ability. The
German universities became the laughingstock of the Western world.
Famous teachers were driven from them for not hewing to the party line,

standards were lowered, the course of study narrowed. Almost for the first time in German history, learning became unimportant; the duty of man was to obey, not to think.

That course of study may best be comprehended by an analysis of two books, *The Nazi Primer,* an official handbook for the young, and *The Myth of the Twentieth Century,* by Hitler's favorite philosopher, Dr. Alfred Rosenberg, a German Balt and Hitler's agent extraordinary for the promulgation of official Nazi philosophy.

In two words, *Blut* and *Boden,* blood and land, may be found the essence of Nazi educational theory. According to the primer, about seventy per cent of the German people belong to the Nordic race, which has the purest and finest blood in all the world. Most of the Nordics are in Germany. Their race, the primer assures us, "is uncommonly gifted mentally. It is outstanding for truthfulness and energy. Nordic men possess for the most part, even in regard to themselves, a great power of judgment. They incline to be taciturn and cautious. They feel instantly that too loud talking is undignified. They are persistent and stick to a purpose when once they have set themselves to it. Their energy is displayed not only in warfare but also in technology and in scientific research. They are predisposed to leadership by nature." About twenty per cent of the Germans belong to the Phalic race, second only in virtue to the Nordic. "Differences in the soul qualities of the two races are not very great." The Phalic man is less emotional than the Nordic man. He is said to be better suited for being the driving force under the leadership of Nordic men than for leadership itself. Great patience characterizes his pursuit of an aim. Never could he be as foolhardy, perhaps, as the Nordic man. He is governed by a strong feeling of loyalty toward other men. He is more good natured and more cordial than the Nordic man.

Ten per cent of the Germans belong to the other four European races, the Dinaric, the Eastern, the East Baltic, and the Western. Fortunately only two per cent belong to the Western race, which has little steadiness and is not given to reason. The man of the Western race is excitable, even passionate. The Western race with all its mental agility lacks creative power. This race has produced only a few outstanding men.

"All in all, the contrasts between the Nordic and the Phalic races and the Western race appear to be very great, but chiefly in the realm of mind and soul."

The primer describes the six European races in regard to physical appearance, shape of skull, color of hair, soul qualities, and the like. It laments the fact that great harm has come to the Fatherland by the adulteration of the pure Nordic blood-stream; but it is not too late to mend matters. The laws of heredity are then described in detail and the boys are instructed that the purification of German blood is their first duty.

The Boden, the German land: by this is not meant just the German

Fatherland as entrusted to Adolf Hitler. "By German territory," the primer informs us, "we mean every region of central Europe which is inhabited by Germans in more or less permanent settlements and has received its cultural imprint from the German people." This region of German language and cultural influence is, indeed, spacious. In area it is about three times as large as the Third Reich and for the most part stretching to the south and east. Concerning it the primer narrates much dubious history. It seems that the Germans brought about the unity of Europe between 100 A.D. and 1000 A.D., and "The Reich of the Middle Ages," we are told, "was about six times as large as it is today." Since the Thirty Years War, it appears, the Germans have been ill-treated, that is before the advent of Hitler. Their land was taken from them. "We are," laments the primer, "volk without space." [2]

What the primer states in simple language Dr. Rosenberg elaborates in sonorous and mystical praise-paeans. The lost continent of Atlantis sunk beneath the ocean the Doctor peoples with Nordic heroes. "These swarms of Atlantis men," he assures us, "went forth in their swan boats and their dragon boats" on conquest bent. They fought like heroes and they were very brave; but they were also very soulful. "Soul," the Doctor pontificates, "means race seen from within . . . ; race is the outer form of the soul." It appears that only races have souls; individuals do not. The race is immortal. A nation is simply the physical embodiment of a race.

First above all comes race! The race must be cherished, guarded, exalted, and also strengthened by the most up-to-date genetic methods, by breeding men like cattle or like plants, and especially by decontaminating the German blood-stream of Jewish blood. It also must find elbow room in crowded Europe.

In order to secure it the new German education aimed straight at preparation for inevitable war. The Nazi overlords did not intend to stop with the reëstablishment of the old frontiers of Germany, or even with inclusion within the new Germany of racial brothers excluded from the old Reich, in Austria, Hungary, or elsewhere. The intimation in *Mein Kampf* is quite clear. "The frontiers of the year 1914," wrote Hitler in that book, "signify nothing at all for the future of the German nation." His people were "penned into an impossible area." They had a right to more land and would take it.

Lebensraum, living space for eighty million cramped Germans, must be found, and preferably to the east and south where the rich soil of the Ukraine stretches down through southern Poland all the way to the Black Sea. Here was superb *Lebensraum,* closely adjacent to Germany, where also there were many settlers of Germanic blood, small islands in a sea of Slavic people. To annex it would be in line with the ancient

[2] All quotations from the Nazi primer are taken from H. L. Childs' translation, courtesy of Harper & Brothers.

tradition of civilized Germany on guard against irruptions of Asiatic barbarians. Furthermore, proposals for its annexation always could be coupled with denunciations of Communists, and so not be altogether displeasing to blind politicians in London and Paris who might congratulate themselves with the thought that they were using Hitler as their cat's-paw in attacking Russia, and her horde of hateful Communists.

The Fuehrer, to be sure, would be glad to extend his boundaries even beyond the Ukraine. "How Germany has to work," he said in 1936, "to wrest a few kilometers from the ocean and from the swamps while others are swimming in a superfluity of land! If I had the Ural Mountains with their incalculable store of treasures in raw materials, Siberia with its vast forests, and the Ukraine with its tremendous wheat fields, Germany and the National Socialist leadership would swim in plenty." [3]

In justice to Hitler it should be stated that the rest of his speech was devoted to the praise of the German worker. Nevertheless the quotation is illuminating, not only as showing the drift of the Fuehrer's mind, but also because it is in close harmony with what the Nazis liked to think was a new science, that of geopolitics.

The term *geopolitics* was invented by a Swedish professor of history and it dates back to 1916, when in the midst of the first World War he defined geopolitics as "the science which conceives the state as a geographical organism or as a phenomenon in space." The state, according to the professor, must either grow or wither, and that, too, in a geographic sense. Geographic space, and plenty of it, is politically essential. This was true, he wrote, of England and is today the position of Japan and Germany. It is clearly a case not of the lust of conquest but of "natural and necessary growth. . . ."

The ideas of the Swedish savant received a setback after the war. When it was over, however, they caught the imagination of Major General Doktor Karl Haushofer, professor of geography and military science at Munich, an intimate friend of Rudolf Hess, in turn an intimate friend of Hitler and his most trusted confidant. After Hitler became chancellor he made Haushofer president of the German Academy and set his approval on the new science of space relationship.

What the latter really amounted to was a new rationalization of an old idea—imperial conquest. The Romans never heard of geopolitics, nor did anyone else, for that matter, before the twentieth century, but they did know what conquest meant. Economics, psychology, anthropology, politics, sociology, all were lumped together by Haushofer and fused in geopolitics as a justification for the seizure of land occupied by non-Germans. Certain new and poetic expressions were coined to give an emotional overtone to these ideas. Thus Europe and Asia became the

[3] Adolf Hitler, *My New Order*, p. 400.

"Island Continent," and the central plains of Eurasia, "the Heartland." It was the destiny of the Island Continent to be dominated by one integrated racial group, presumably the German *Volk*. Once under its control, global supremacy would be within its grasp because the Island Continent, owing to its space, resources, numerous inhabitants, would easily hold the world balance of power. Land power was held more important than sea power, provided there was sufficient land.

Hitler was determined that there would be sufficient for a thousand years of his Third Reich. His early speeches stressed the sacred character of German soil; his later fulminations tended more and more to emphasize the *Lebensraum* motif, space for cheated Germans, always at a grave disadvantage because room was lacking. Thus, Hitler reasoned, "Forty-six million Britishers dominate and govern approximately 16 million square miles of the surface of the earth. Thirty-seven million Frenchmen dominate and govern a combined area of 4 million square miles. Forty-five million Italians possess, taking into consideration only those territories in any way capable of being utilized, an area of scarcely 190,000 miles. That is to say: 85 million Germans own only 232,000 square miles on which they must live their lives and 46 million Britishers possess 16 million square miles." [4]

Here was injustice which Hitler was determined to rectify. He brushed aside the fact that the greater part of Canada was frozen tundra, that the greater part of Australia was a waterless desert, that England was far more thickly populated than his own country, that Englishmen living in England had no control over the property of Englishmen living in New Zealand or South Africa. He did not stop to note that the phenomenal industrial development of the Reich necessitated the importation of Polish and Italian laborers, since there were not enough Germans available; he did not consider that the only way the land area of Germany could be increased would be by annexing lands already thickly occupied, primarily by Slavs whose increase in population per hundred thousand ran well ahead of that in Germany. The only indication of the Fuehrer's pondering upon his statistics is his obvious stacking of the cards in favor of Italy. Note the qualifying clause, "taking into consideration only those territories in any way capable of being utilized." As far as Italy was concerned Hitler was willing to subtract African deserts.

Potsdam had conquered Weimar; the Germany of Goethe and Thomas Mann was now under the heel of Prussian tradition. The Nazis brought Sparta back again; women were encouraged to become brood mares for the strengthening and augmenting of the race; and boys, trained in rough discipline, were to regard obedience to command and the fighting spirit as the culmination of German virtue. From these boys a future

[4] Adolf Hitler, *My New Order* (Reynal & Hitchcock, Inc.), p. 874.

Nazi elite was to be selected which would take over in time the work of the founder. To train this elite, a number of castles were set apart in Germany where, in strict seclusion, the rulers of the future Reich were to undergo training. Entrance requirements were strength, bravery, unquestioned and unquestioning obedience to orders, and the course of study in these Nazi nurseries was equally drastic.

Chapter 32

FRANCE AND ENGLAND
BETWEEN TWO WARS

IN CONTRADISTINCTION to the three totalitarian powers—Russia, Italy, and Germany—both France and England remained loyal in the postwar period to the democratic, liberal tradition of the nineteenth century. In both countries there was Communist agitation, more noticeable in France than in England; in both there were signs of incipient Fascist revolution, much more noticeable in France than in England; but in neither country did communism or fascism become a really serious threat.

France

The aftermath of the war, in France as elsewhere, was unpleasant. Even before the advent of that struggle the finances of the Republic were in shaky condition; for light taxes, heavy expenditure for armaments, and an unbalanced budget had created a tremendous burden of debt. That situation had caused little worry in the prewar days, for if the government was poor, the national wealth was astonishingly high; and for several decades France had become the leading banker of the Continent. After four years of war, however, there was real cause for worry; France had borrowed to the limit everywhere, both within and without her borders; the huge sums loaned to Imperial Russia had been repudiated by the Soviets; and a tenth of battle-scarred France lay in ruins.

The Republic had pledged itself early in the war to make good all damage done by the Germans in the invaded departments, and this alone was a Herculean task. Northeastern France, occupied by German armies, had been industrial France. Here had been the great textile mills, their machinery now in ruins; here had been the coal mines of France, now flooded by the Germans. Almost all of the small towns and villages in the battle zone had been wiped out by shell fire; thousands of orchards had been cut down, thousands of wells had been filled up or poisoned; the cattle and sheep had been killed or eaten, the houses destroyed.

The Germans, to be sure, in accordance with the Treaty of Versailles, were to pay for this damage; but how was France to extract money from Germany? And while the manner and method of doing it was debated, was rehabilitation to be delayed? The French said, "No!" and immediately they began, in somewhat reckless and extravagant fashion, to rebuild their factories and towns. In theory, the money thus expended was not part of the national budget but was kept in a separate account charged to the Germans. Upwards of $7,000,000,000 was thus spent; and of this sum but trifling part ever was collected from Germany.

Little wonder that the French franc could not withstand the strain. Despite the cleverest devices of clever bankers, the franc started to follow the German mark to the graveyard of repudiated currencies. And as this went on, larger and larger grew the issue of paper francs, thus hastening repudiation. The war alone had raised the national debt of France from 35,000,000,000 francs to 180,000,000,000 francs, and during the first five years of the peace that debt had nearly doubled. It was impossible even to pay interest upon it, and soon the debt was found to be maturing at the rate of 7,500,000,000 francs a month! The result was that the franc sank rapidly. In 1914 it had been quoted at slightly less than five francs to the dollar, but by 1926 forty-eight francs could be bought for that sum, and American tourists in Paris were goading the French to fury by pasting paper francs on their luggage together with hotel stickers.

There was trouble, too, in Alsace and Lorraine. Those two redeemed provinces promptly were incorporated into France proper and turned into three departments, for the Third Republic had a passion for uniformity, and all Frenchmen, it was held, should be subject to the same laws. But Alsace and Lorraine were overwhelmingly Roman Catholic. When they had been annexed by Germany in 1871 the Napoleonic Concordat with the Catholic Church still was the law of France, and the priests in Alsace and Lorraine had been supported by the State and the schools had been Catholic schools. The Germans had not changed the status of the Catholic Church in the two provinces, but when they were returned to France their inhabitants found that the Concordat had been repudiated, that the Republic no longer concerned itself with religion, that the schools were laicized. Furthermore, there was the ever important question of language bobbing up again. Most of the Alsatians used German as a primary language and the Republic changed overnight the primary instruction in the schools from German to French. No wonder, then, that protests were loud and numerous, and that agitation arose for autonomy under the Tricolor, similar to the agitation in the two provinces when ruled as a Reichsland in the German Empire.

And yet another never-ending source of worry to the French was the problem of security. The Germans still outnumbered them at the close of the war, three to two, and if Austria ever came to be included in the Reich, the disparity in numbers would be still more pronounced. The

French had surrendered at the Versailles Congress their desire for the Rhine frontier in return for guarantees from England and America, as well as from the League of Nations, guarantees which they soon discovered worthless or of slight value. The problem of French security more properly belongs to the discussion of international politics in the two postwar chapters. But it never ceased to cause friction within France herself; it was intimately correlated to the financial problem, since it contemplated construction of the expensive Maginot Line to the east, and since it further involved large loans to potential allies, such as Poland, Czechoslovakia, Yugoslavia, and so on; and it also played an important part in the constant swinging back and forth of the political pendulum between the different party groupings or blocs which controlled the government.

Party Politics in Postwar France

The Third Republic never had been blessed or cursed with the two-party system. Instead, a dozen political parties were to be met with, and the art of government, both prewar and postwar, consisted in bringing together a number of these into an alliance or bloc, whereby a majority could be secured in the Chamber of Deputies. In the period between the two World Wars, three different blocs contested political power in France, the *"bloc national,"* the *"bloc des gauches,"* and the *"front populaire."*

The first of these was generally conservative, consisting of right-wing politicians, middle-of-the-roaders, and a sufficient sprinkling of near-radicals to secure a majority. The leader of this *bloc national*, in the heyday of its triumph, was Poincaré, the hard-bitten French patriot from Lorraine who had been president during the war. The *bloc des gauches*, as its name implies, was more radical than the *bloc national*. It might properly be described as a working alliance of the center with the left-center, or the more conservative radicals. The United Socialists (orthodox Marxians) were wary of this *bloc des gauches*, and its real nucleus was the Radical-Socialist party, which, as far as tradition went, was more radical than socialistic. Its leading representatives were Herriot, popular mayor of Lyon, and Briand, now an aged radical and a broad-minded statesman who was willing to let bygones be bygones and to come to amicable understanding with the Germans. The *front populaire*, on the other hand, was a genuine combination of left-wing groups under the leadership of a cultured and wealthy Jewish citizen of the Republic, Léon Blum. The creation of this bloc was something new in French politics. It did not come into existence until 1936, and it brought together for the first time the United Socialists, of whom Blum was the titular head, and the Communists, hitherto strictly shunned as ultra-revolutionary.

The *bloc national* should be given credit for doing two things—appeasing Alsace-Lorraine and saving the franc. The Roman Catholic control of education was not restored in the two provinces, but provision was made for Catholic instruction, and great care was taken to smooth over the injured feelings of the Alsatians so that their demand for autonomy lessened.

More important was the salvaging of the franc. The *bloc national* had been responsible for the invasion of the Ruhr, and after that fiasco it was driven from power, the *bloc des gauches* taking over the government. But the latter did nothing to save the franc, and it was not until Poincaré returned to power in 1926 that financial recovery really set in. Poincaré, following a conservative course, cut expenditures to a minimum, reduced salaries and pensions, heaped on new taxes, and then stabilized the rising franc at about four cents. The instant effect of doing so was to cut down the national debt some eighty per cent in terms of the old franc. Bondholders and all others living on a fixed income suffered heavily, and the creditor classes in general had to bear the burden; but they did not object too loudly, for the franc no longer depreciated, and it was recognized that it was better to lose four-fifths of one's capital than to lose all, as would have happened if the franc had followed the mark. For the first time in many years it was now possible to balance the budget and there was an actual surplus! Promptly, Poincaré took advantage of improved credit to retire bonds paying a high rate of interest by issuing new ones at a low rate, to reduce the floating debt and to restore France's credit throughout the world. Something akin to the old prewar prosperity of the country was noted; the iron of Lorraine, the textile mills of Alsace added to it; and, had it not been for the world economic depression of 1929-33, all might have been well.

That depression, however, raised havoc in France as elsewhere. Poincaré, old and feeble, retired from politics in 1929 and with his going, French politics became very confused. Trade fell off rapidly, tourists to France were few, there was much unemployment, and the franc started to depreciate again. Royalists, Fascists, and Communists paraded in Paris; pictures of Robespierre began to appear, and there were a number of street fights. Premier followed premier in rapid succession, those between 1932 and 1934 all members of the Radical Socialist party, and all speedily thrown out of office by adverse majorities in the Deputies.

France Is Cut in Two

In 1934 a Fascist revolution threatened. Its immediate causes were unsavory revelations linking sundry conspicuous French politicians to what had come to be called "the Stavisky scandals." Stavisky, naturalized son of a Russian dentist and socially charming, had for a long time been

mysteriously protected. Moving in high circles he floated worthless securities, forged checks, gambled with marked cards, and entertained lavishly.
After he stole some 200,000,000 francs from the municipal pawnshops of
Bayonne, legal proceedings were taken against him. He fled to the French
Alps and was found dying in a hut. Rumor had it that he was murdered
by the police to prevent his talking, a rumor which met with wide
credence because of his intimacy with many cabinet members, the Minister for the Colonies having recommended his worthless securities to French
savings banks, the Minister of Justice having postponed his trial, and the
Premier himself having served at one time as legal adviser for one of
Stavisky's accomplices.

"Democracy is another name for political corruption," screamed Léon
Daudet, the royalist, and the ministry, under fire from deputies of both
right and left, resigned. Daladier, the new premier, was unable to maintain order. The Croix de Feu, a veteran and Fascist organization, marched
on the chamber, its partisans smashing windows, overturning buses and
beating up a countermob of Communists. In expectation of trouble, Daladier had stationed troops at the Palais Bourbon. Troops and police opened
fire, killing seventeen and wounding several hundred. Daladier then
resigned and Colonel La Roque, head of the Croix de Feu, announced,
"Our first objective is accomplished. Remain on duty and await further
instructions."

Paris was in an uproar. The Fascist demonstration of the extreme right
was followed at once by a drive toward the left, Radicals, Socialists and
Communists flocking to the "Popular Front" for safety from fascism. As
a well-known French woman wrote in her diary, "One feels that France
is cut in two."

This was indeed the case. Ever since the great French Revolution a
unique schism had divided France, the people never wholeheartedly
accepting that revolution as a permanent achievement. They were loyal
to France, yes; but loyalty to the government (the regime), that was
another matter.

For a time it had seemed as though that schism might heal, but the economic distress of the nineteen-thirties led both the wealthy and the
poor to distrust political democracy and to lose faith in a regime rooted
in the bourgeois ideologies of 1789. The Third Republic had survived
serious difficulties in the past, but attacks then had come mainly from
perfervid Catholics and royalists, for the most part members of the
privileged classes. Now the attack was a cross fire from two directions,
from property-owners and men of wealth who found their economic
status lowered by drastic depreciation of the franc, and from the workers
suffering grievous unemployment. French prosperity depended on luxury
trade, and economic shadows over Germany, Britain, and the United
States ruined that prosperity, for the export of fine wines and wedding

garments became negligible. Discontent grew rife, the gulf between classes opened wider, and from 1934 to the outbreak of the Second World War German Nazis and Russian Communists were only too successful in keeping it open.

The part played therein by the Nazis was the more obvious if not the more fundamental. Their instrument was a young school teacher from Karlsruhe, Otto Abetz, afterwards chosen by Hitler as his ambassador to what was left of the French Republic in 1940. Abetz residing in France became very popular there, posing as a devoted and nonpartisan friend of all young Frenchmen and all young Germans. He got them to meet together in a camp in the Black Forest and taught them to forget their differences. He became the paid agent of Von Ribbentrop, Hitler's choice to head Nazi propaganda and diplomacy outside of Germany, a man whose past career as a salesman of champagne had given him a special entrée among the wealthy and special skill in handling them. Von Ribbentrop kept in the background and entrusted Abetz with what he called "psychological soundings." Abetz had plenty of money and spent freely; he entertained French war veterans sumptuously in Berlin; he flattered French literary men by insisting that there was a large demand for German translations of their works, which he subsidized; he financed French lectures, and he never ceased to proclaim that the Fuehrer had absolutely no demands to make on France. Sensible Frenchmen, he intimated, should be suspicious of England and should hate the Soviets. Germany was their friend; political democracy was dead; Communism threatened a world upheaval which only could be averted by overthrowing corrupt and degenerate republics. The French royalists and the right in general heartily approved the two-timing Abetz, who also won many friends on the left by constantly stressing pacifism. Few suspected that he was a slick wolf in sheep's clothing.

Abetz' adroit campaign was to some degree offset by Communist borings from within; but the Communists were neither so well financed nor so clever, and for two years France drowsed toward fascism. Four premiers in these two years added to general confusion. Of the four, three were nonentities, and the fourth, Pierre Laval, since infamous at Vichy, was so underhanded and so tricky as to arouse the suspicion of all non-Fascists. Laval, posing as a pacifist in the first World War, had unquestionably aided Germany then by defeatist propaganda. Now his continuous postponement of a mutual aid treaty with Stalin, coupled with his comradely admiration for Mussolini, contributed not a little to French ills: internal strife at home and loss of influence and prestige abroad. Meanwhile, Léon Blum, leader of the popular front and of the French Socialist party, was murderously assaulted in public by members of the Action Française, a monarchist and Fascist organization, barely escaping with his life. And as this happened the government was vainly trying to curb semi-military organizations which were springing up, armed, on every hand.

Blum and the Popular Front

Finally came the national election of 1936. Thoroughly frightened by the rampant onsurge of fascism, Radicals, Socialists, and Communists buried their disagreement for once and worked together. This Popular Front was politically successful since the Socialists for the first time in French history won a plurality of seats, and, when combined with the Radicals and Communists, had a slight majority over all. It was not only slight but extraordinarily shaky, since it rested on the support of seventy-one Communists who were too suspicious to enter the cabinet, and on that of so-called radicals, wedded by tradition to property rights. Nevertheless, for the time being the advent of fascism was stayed.

Léon Blum, the new premier, was a highly cultivated and wealthy Frenchman, more at home in art and literature than in the hurly-burly of bloc politics into which he had plunged more from duty than inclination. He was too soft by nature for the crisis which confronted France.

France was economically in the doldrums, and politically torn wide open by contending factions. Blum tried to save her by inaugurating certain reforms parallel in many ways to the American "New Deal" of 1933. He started in bravely enough by establishing a forty-hour week, holidays with pay, and government ownership of munition plants. He followed the precedent of America and of England in depreciating the currency; he even tried to wrest control of the Bank of France from the exclusive group of seventy families which had long controlled it. A wave of sit-down strikes then spread through France and these Blum seemed unable to control. He was a pacifist by conviction and that made it difficult for him to deal effectively with his enemies, whether domestic or foreign. Perhaps this was his blind spot. "We do not believe," he wrote, "as did our forefathers in 1792 and 1848, that there can be any good in war, nor that war can be an instrument for liberty...." The sentiment was nicely phrased but scarcely revealed a man capable of dealing with the venomous Cagoulards, a secret Fascist society engaged in hoarding machine guns and ammunition for the coming revolution of the right.

As the Spanish Republic slowly bled to death at the hands of German and Italian Fascists, and of foreign non-interventionists, Blum hesitated, and then lost prestige both within and without France. Whether England was responsible or not for the supine foreign policy of the Popular Front is extremely difficult to fathom; but even if England had supported a firmer French attitude toward the Spanish war, it is difficult to conceive a man with Blum's pacifist psychology standing up against the fire-snorting bullies of Italy and Germany. In little over a year he resigned in disgust owing to a quarrel with the French Senate over a money bill. The Popular Front lingered on six months and then faded out. To some extent it may justly be blamed for the consequent defeat of France, soon to follow, not for its ineptitude in foreign policy alone but because it fatally slackened the production of military matériel. But on the other hand, it may have saved France from a revolution in 1936, and its leaders, though blind to fascism's menace, were less deserving of censure than those Frenchmen who preferred Hitler and his gangsters to their own radical countrymen.

France now swung to the right again; sit-down strikes and the forty-hour week led to renewed financial trouble; and the gathering of war-clouds in 1938-39 made for conservatism, the majority being of the opinion that this was no time for further social reform. When Hitler occupied Prague in March, 1939, the Chamber of Deputies did not hesitate to endow Daladier, a Radical-Socialist premier, with power to rule by decree. The city of Marseilles was deprived of its autonomy and placed directly under the national government; unemployed workers on relief could now be sent anywhere in France the government chose to send them; the forty-hour week was abandoned, and the sixty-hour week became permissible. Something approaching a government of national defense was formed under Daladier—no new election was held, but the seventy-two Communists were regarded with suspicion, as Blum and his Socialists listened to the call of patriotism and joined Daladier and the more conservative deputies of the right and center in a different kind of a united front, this time against Germany. Unfortunately the unity thus achieved was merely superficial. In 1914 the French stood united against the invaders; in 1939 they did not. During the First World War France had been bled white, losing far more lives in proportion to her population than any other country involved. Frenchmen in 1939 had no stomach for fighting; they felt they could not go through with it again. That fact alone goes far to explain the debacle that was to come in 1940. But it is not the only reason. Abetz had done his work far too well. Large numbers of Frenchmen had lost all faith in Liberty, Equality, and Fraternity, and tended to regard fascism, if not as desirable, then at least as more desir-able, more unifying than communism. As for the Communists, they followed the party line laid down in Moscow. Since Russia was not in the war they considered themselves out of it. France was half conquered before a shot was fired.

Britain

The end of the war found Britain unprepared for peace. A million soldiers came back home to wives and sweethearts, but in all too many cases there were neither homes in which to live nor jobs to work at.

No new houses had been built for years and old jobs had been discontinued or were held by women. Many discharged soldiers were shell-shocked or otherwise impaired, unfit for jobs even if these had been available. To the conservative-minded, all Britain seemed shell-shocked. The psychological rebound from the hardship of war, both civilian and military, led to a mania for dancing, jazz music, and American cocktails. The motor scooter, pogo stick and mah-jong, a complicated Chinese game, became the craze one after another. Journalism went "yellow" and university undergraduates went Bohemian; young women took to lipsticks, to stimulants, and to companionate marriage; the divorce rate doubled; and learned exponents of Freudian philosophy put all the blame for human unhappiness on "inhibitions."

The economic situation was both ominous and dolorous. England's foreign trade had fallen badly during the war and there seemed little likelihood of its recovery, not as long as Germany and Russia, two of her best customers, were too poor to buy. The British coal trade, over-expanded by the war, now came in competition with cheap German coal, turned over to the French and Italians as part payment on reparations. British shipping was surfeited with extra cargo space provided by the surrendered merchant ships of Germany just at a time when exports were falling off. British shipyards consequently became as idle as British coal mines. For a time it looked as though Britain would have to fight a war within after the war without, this time against unemployment. Her finances were in better shape than were those of her sister democracy across the Channel; but whereas France at a pinch could live largely on her agriculture, to Britain foreign trade was a necessity of life.

This explains why the British speedily sought to change those economic clauses of the peace treaty which led to Germany's default on reparation payments and to the French occupation of the Ruhr. Lloyd George, who had been more responsible than any other man for imposing the economic penalties of the peace, promptly tried to reverse himself, and at an international conference at Genoa had believed hopefully that his magnetic eloquence might win the French over to his point of view. Lloyd George failed. His successor in office, Bonar Law, tried to prevent the French from entering the Ruhr. He failed. Bonar Law even offered to remit the French debt to England if the French would cut down correspondingly on Germany's debt to France. Again he failed.

The British were in favor of letting bygones be bygones and of starting up business again. They suggested to the United States that if the latter would cancel the British debt to America of some $4,000,000,000, the British would cancel continental debts due them far greater in amount. But the Americans had the idea that the British could and would pay, and so were adamant ("They hired the money, didn't they?"—Coolidge). Thereupon the British signed a debt agreement with the Americans whereby they agreed to pay the debt in full over a period of sixty-two years but with reduced interest.

Lloyd George, meanwhile, lost his wartime popularity; he had promised to make England a land fit for heroes, and four years after the war that promise remained unfulfilled; with his usual buoyancy he had tackled the Irish problem, only to be smartly rebuffed by Sinn Fein; the French refused to take him seriously in the matter of reparations; the vigorous Turks made mincemeat of his Near Eastern policy; and the enemies within his own Liberal party, numerous and influential, awaited impatiently his downfall. He was Prime Minister of a national coalition the mainstay of which was the Tory party which detested him. His prestige once gone, the Tories inevitably would drive him out. They did so in 1923 and took over the government on a one-party basis, first under Bonar Law, the Canadian-born British statesman who died within the year, and then under Stanley Baldwin.

The First Ministries of Baldwin and MacDonald

Baldwin promptly was defeated for advocating a protective tariff and in the ensuing election he won a plurality of seats but was without a majority. To the surprise of almost everyone the historic Liberal party, torn between the followers of Lloyd George and those of H. H. Asquith, came out third in the race, second place falling to MacDonald and his Laborites.

The Labor party in theory was socialistic. During the election it had advocated the nationalization of railways and mines, and a capital levy on large fortunes. To put it in control of Britain's fortunes seemed a most dangerous procedure. Yet that is what the British Liberals did. The alternative was to support Baldwin, and they considered MacDonald the lesser of two evils; after all, they would hold the whiphand over the Socialists and forestall any danger by voting with the Conservatives! As a matter of fact, there was no trouble. The Labor party had long been committed to the truly British policy of "gradualness." The idea of revolution was repudiated and the Laborites regarded Moscow with almost as much abhorrence as did the Tories themselves.

Once in office Labor took no steps toward a capital levy; instead it contented itself with various odds and ends of amelioration, the building of inexpensive homes on a moderate scale by government subsidies, the removal of taxes on cheap movie tickets and their reduction on sugar and chocolate. The Cabinet seemed quite bent on proving itself British first and Socialist second. MacDonald was an effective worker for international peace; he promoted the inauguration of the Dawes' plans; he tried to gain the good will of the Japanese by suspending work on the great Singapore naval depot; and he even made certain friendly gestures toward Soviet Russia.

The latter brought about his downfall. Lloyd George somewhat earlier had renewed commercial relations with Russia and these MacDonald sought to implement by an Anglo-Russian treaty, a commercial, not a military or political understanding. But Russia to good Britons was still a most dangerous country, and when British Communists, supposedly under orders from the Third International in Moscow, tried to sow discontent among British workers the British Liberals joined with the Tories and voted MacDonald out. A dramatic election followed. MacDonald might have been returned to triumph had it not been for a mysterious letter (presumably forged) purporting to have been written by Zinoviev, head of the Third International, urging the revolt of British workers. Middle-class Britain saw red in reverse and middle-class Britain had belonged for the most part to the Liberal party. In fear and anger lest MacDonald win, it surged to the polls and gave Baldwin a majority over all. The Labor party lost only a few seats; but the Liberal party was reduced to a mere thirty-six and no longer held even the balance of power. From this date on it was hardly more than a cypher in British politics.

The Second Baldwin Ministry

Baldwin returned to power in 1924 to be confronted by one of the most serious crises in British history. The British coal miner during the World War had won a decent working day of seven hours and had been granted minimum wages. The wage was not high but it soon proved impossible to pay it and at the same time operate the mines at a profit. The coal trade was in the doldrums everywhere in the world in the nineteen-twenties, owing to the increased use of gasoline, oil, and hydroelectric power, and the coal trade of Britain was in even a more precarious plight than elsewhere, owing to the great depth of the mines, which made their operation expensive, and to substantial royalties paid to ground landlords like the Duke of Northumberland, who held title and merely rented coal lands to operating companies, assuming no responsibility for management.

What should be done? The miners, highly organized, adopted a slogan and clung to it desperately: "Not an hour on the day, not a penny off the pay." The operators said there was nothing to do but close the mines. The government, in desperation, subsidized miners' wages and this kept the mines in operation. They could not do this indefinitely at the expense of the nation and therefore a commission was appointed, to report in 1926 that the only salvation for the coal mining industry lay in closing certain uneconomic mines and in increasing the hours of labor in others.

Baldwin supported his commission, withdrew the subsidy, and the Trade Union Congress voted a general strike throughout Britain, all good union men, whatever their jobs, to lay down tools, certain exceptions being made for lighting, sanitary, and health services.

This was bringing revolutionary pressure to bear on Parliament, since if the Trade Union Congress could compel government to bow to its will in this matter it could do so in others and thus would become the real source of authority in the state.

The strike was badly managed. MacDonald and other leaders of the Labor party supported the miners in theory but had no stomach for a real fight on this issue; nor for that matter did the Trade Union Congress. Not so the British middle class. A vast number of amateur middle-class volunteers hastened to run the railways, to unload cargoes, to deliver food. There was little violence and the Trade Union Congress after only a few days rescinded the general strike orders. The miners, considering themselves betrayed, fought on for several months but ultimately succumbed. Parliament overwhelmingly supported Baldwin, and in 1927 passed an act curbing trade-union activities and making all general strikes illegal.

Aside from this, Baldwin resisted successfully the drive within his own party for a more authoritarian government. If he would not yield to the left, he would not give way to the right, which saw its opportunity at this time to strengthen the powers of the House of Lords. The Prime Minister, indeed, was not ill disposed toward labor; he brought about pensions for widows and he did lower the price of tea. Hopefully, he looked forward to an increase in international trade, of which there was some indication. "Safety First" was his motto; unemployment is bad, but not so bad as it was; all we need is to wait for clearer skies! This philosophy did not appeal to the impoverished electorate, and in 1929 it voted Baldwin out and MacDonald in once more.

The National Government

Again MacDonald had a plurality in the Commons, but again his total Labor strength was less than that of the Conservatives and Liberals combined. In foreign affairs this ministry was a creditable one, particularly in regard to disarmament, but at home his best efforts proved unavailing. His political dependence on the ever diminishing Liberals continued to irk him, and furthermore there was revolt within his own party. The "wild men of the Clyde," as the leftist Laborites were called, demanded a capital levy and party discipline disintegrated. Before, however, an open rupture broke out, the coming of the international trade depression of 1930-33 brought about a financial crisis in England such as that country had not experienced since the black year of 1797, when she faced Revolutionary France without allies and the Bank of England suspended specie payment.

The storm broke in 1931. Unless drastic reductions were made in relief costs, the bankers held, it would be impossible to make the necessary loans to save the pound sterling and the Bank of England. MacDonald reluctantly consented to the economies demanded, but he found it impossible to carry his party with him. Thereupon he resigned and formed a "National Government" supported by Conservatives, Liberals, and those Laborites who stayed loyal to him. Instantly, a ten per cent cut was made in all forms of individual remuneration, from the unemployed on the dole to police, admirals, generals, and cabinet ministers. The government went off the gold standard, thus depreciating the pound; the budget was balanced, the necessary loans made, and financial England weathered the worst storm encountered in over a century.

The price was heavy. MacDonald was still prime minister, at the head of a coalition. But his own Labor party, which had been steadily growing in numbers and experience ever since its creation, received as deadly a blow as the Liberal party in 1886; and in the Parliamentary election of 1931 it sank to 52 members. The Conservatives rose to 470, a signal triumph; and the Liberals, divided into warring factions (one supporting the National Government, the other opposing it), netted 70 seats.

From 1931 to 1935 MacDonald headed this National Government. It was such in name only, since the Tories had a large majority over all. The Tories now pressed for protective tariffs and this time they got them. A ten per cent levy was made on imports and some success attended the government's efforts to make reciprocal trade agreements with the Dominions. Thus unmourned and almost overnight died the free-trade dream of Cobden and of Bright. And it was not only free trade that perished. The National Government repudiated in fact, if not in theory, many other chosen tenets of laissez faire; it compelled agreements to fix prices in many industries; it granted financial aid to agriculture; it guaranteed loans to railways and built motor highways; and it heavily subsidized the building of new homes for the poor.

During this third ministry of the Scottish socialist (really but a continuation of his second), the Liberal party disintegrated rapidly. There were Liberals who supported both the National Government and the tariff; other Liberals supported the government except on the tariff issue; other Liberals kept warm the dying embers of an independent Liberal party; and a tiny group of still other Liberals held aloof under the now scarred banner of that drummer boy of the World War, David Lloyd George. The Labor party was also torn asunder; the rank and file, bitter foes of MacDonald, were bereft now, not only of his leadership, but of any leadership worth the name. MacDonald himself was saddened by the hatred of the many common people who once had trusted him and who now assailed him as a traitor to labor. A sick and disillusioned man, he gladly surrendered the reins of office in 1935 to his erstwhile political enemy, Mr. Baldwin.

The latter still kept up the pretense of a National Government. He took quick advantage of a most critical turn in international relations to hold a new parliamentary election, and the country again underwrote the Conservative control of Britain, although with a reduced majority. This third ministry of Baldwin, like the third one of MacDonald, was of the stop-gap variety. Baldwin, like his predecessor, was old, tired, discouraged. He saw the country through a temporary flurry created in 1936 by the death of George V and the unwillingness of Edward VIII to be crowned without his right to marry an American divorcée being recognized. With the coronation of Edward's younger brother as George VI in 1937, Baldwin resigned.

He was succeeded by Neville Chamberlain, second son of Joseph Chamberlain. The new Prime Minister was considered not as brilliant as his older half-brother Austen, but as one nevertheless well suited to carry on the middle-of-the-road policy of the amiable Baldwin. The Chamberlain ministry was given over largely to foreign affairs, and we shall note later in another chapter how the constant surrender of the Prime Minister to the incessant clamors of Mussolini and Hitler tended to make him unpopular, not only with the Labor opposition but with many of the abler Conservatives.

Economic Recovery

Between 1932 and the outbreak of war in 1939 there was a slow but steady economic recovery in Britain. The proud commercial hegemony of the world which was Britain's in 1914 did not come back; certain of her former leading industries, such as coal mining, shipbuilding and cotton manufacturing, remained in the doldrums; but the country as a whole did become more prosperous than at the height of the depression; unemployment was reduced and the budget was balanced.

The "New Deal" in America somewhat erroneously has been held to have copied British precedents. It did so in part; both countries went off the gold standard and depreciated their currencies; both countries developed social security programs, the British implementing what they had inaugurated before the First World War, the Americans copying British precedents; and both countries adopted complicated controls over industry. But here the general parallel comes to an end. In America the major answer to the economic black-out in the early thirties was found in public works. In Britain, as to some extent in the United States, it took the form of financial coöperation with business, provided management agreed to accept certain directions and controls.

Thus in Britain in 1932 a "Wheat Act" set standard prices for wheat and when the market price fell below that set, a subsidy was paid the wheat grower. In 1933 a "Potato Marketing Scheme" was devised. The national government established a "Milk Marketing Board" and all Britons who sold milk had to contribute to regional pools with provision made for a minimum price. Subsidies were granted for the beet sugar industry, for cattle raising; and by an intricate system of quotas what actually amounted to a protective tariff on agricultural products was enforced.

To encourage new industries a great deal of emphasis was placed upon electric power. A Central Electricity Board known as "The National Grid" was set up which subsidized 135 generating stations, and as a result power became cheaper and very many new industries were developed, particularly in the neighborhood of London.

The problem of housing was also stressed. Subsidies paid builders and home owners for new houses began as early as 1923, and the duty of the government decently to house those on the lower income level has been constantly emphasized since that date. Altogether between the two World Wars over one and a quarter million new homes were constructed in Britain by governmental aid.

It cannot be said that the problem of poverty was solved; in fact, in certain areas, particularly in South Wales, and in sections of Northern England, it continued to be very acute. In 1933 the national government flatly refused to spend money on any larger scale in public works; that method of relieving poverty it considered extravagant and wasteful. In 1934 it did appropriate some £2,000,000 for the "depressed areas," a beggarly sum in view of the distress there. But it followed this in 1935 by a so-called "Means Test," whereby the dole given to unemployed men and women for their support and that of their families was reduced to the lowest possible minimum consistent with bare existence, a direct blow at the physical well-being of the nation.

"It was all very puzzling," wrote the English novelist Priestley in his *English Journey*, published in 1934.

Was Jarrow still in England or not? Had we exiled Lancashire and the Northeast coast? Were we no longer on speaking terms with cotton weavers and miners and platers and riveters? Why had nothing been done about these decaying towns and their workless people? Was everybody waiting for a miracle to happen? I knew that doles had been given out, Means Tests applied, training places opened, socks and shirts and old books distributed by the Personal Service League and the like; but I was not thinking of feeble gestures of that kind, of the sort of charity you might extend to a drunken old ruffian begging at the back door. I meant something constructive and creative. If Germans had been threatening these towns instead of Want, Disease, Hopelessness, Misery, something would have been done quickly enough.[1]

[1] J. B. Priestley, *English Journey* (Harper and Brothers), p. 327. Reprinted by permission of the publishers.

What was the answer? The Labor party, of course, thought it knew. It wanted nationalization of railways, mines, and banking. But the Labor party was powerless, partly because a three-cornered fight in labor circles almost paralyzed that political party. The machinery of the Labor party was in the hands of conservative trade unionists who would have nothing to do with the Independent Labour party, strong in ability but weak in numbers. And neither the I.L.P. (Independent Labour Party) nor the official Labor party would have anything to do with the British Communists. In vain did Sir Stafford Cripps with his Socialist League endeavor to bring these warring elements together. Cripps, a brilliant and wealthy lawyer, was regarded with suspicion by orthodox labor and was expelled from the party. British workmen would not work together in politics. And even if they had been willing to do so, they might not have been able to carry the Parliamentary election of 1935, for the economic skies were brightening somewhat by that date and to the British poor, desiring employment above all else, half a loaf was an encouraging sign.

Pacifism Versus Preparedness

More serious in the long run for Britain was the failure of her statesmen and of her people to realize the peril which confronted her abroad. The former, perhaps, may have been blamed too much for their folly in appeasing the Axis, since for the most part they did but follow the public opinion they should have led. The average Briton was most pacifically inclined; he was fed up with war and war talk; he placed a most curious and blind trust in the League of Nations even after the impotencies of that organization were manifest to all the world; and while he was opposed to Nazi terrorism he refused to consider seriously the Nazi threat to European peace. In all this the worker believed as many of his betters did.

Pacifistic propaganda made headway everywhere. The British masses were only mildly interested in the death struggle of the Spanish Republic. The appeasement of Hitler and Mussolini which is dealt with elsewhere in this book was not cheered, but the government which indulged in it was never in danger of an adverse majority in the House. One of the most popular books of the decade was *Cry Havoc*, published in 1933. It was made compulsory reading in hundreds of schools, and overseas the Department of Education in Toronto, Canada, alone bought 7,000 copies. Pacifists in the pulpit and in the press pledged themselves to participate in no more wars, and over one thousand enthusiastic British men and women agreed to march unarmed between the ranks of future opposing armies, there to die for peace. Even at Oxford the undergraduates voted that never again would they fight for king and country.

There were, of course, countercurrents, one stirred up primarily by

Winston Churchill over air power, the other by British sea dogs concerning the American navy and Singapore. But these countercurrents carried little weight against the tide of "peace in our time."

The Singapore Naval Base

The friction between British and American admirals in regard to the size and number of cruisers made good newspaper copy, but in reality it was of no great import. Far more significant was the long-drawn-out debate over the creation of a great naval base at Singapore. The Washington Conference of 1922 once more focused attention on the Far East; it also brought an end to the Anglo-Japanese Alliance and thereby isolated the Anzac Dominions. Whereupon the British admiralty saw its chance to realize Sir Stamford Raffles' dream of the early nineteenth century—Singapore not only an entrepôt of Asiatic trade but also a naval bastion of empire. The Tory government of Baldwin backed the admiralty and in 1923 preliminary surveys were made.

Since £20,000,000 was about to be spent, an uproar arose in Labor and Liberal circles, where it was pointed out that the money might better be used to clear slums and to educate the young. Furthermore, they said, the fortification of Singapore although not technically a violation of the Washington treaty did violate its spirit and indicated a lack of faith in the League of Nations.

At this juncture MacDonald became prime minister and immediately work on the new base was suspended. And now a new uproar arose, this time in Conservative circles and in the Anzac Dominions, who felt that they were left undefended in case of future trouble with Japan.

MacDonald, as we have seen, was shortly shooed out of office and Baldwin promptly renewed the Singapore project. One main feature of it, the towing of a huge 50,000-ton drydock all the way from Britain to Singapore, was completed in 1928, much to the satisfaction of imperial-minded Britons everywhere, and much to the dissatisfaction of Japanese public opinion, highly inflamed by the jingo press of Nippon.

The British Labor party upon its return to office in 1929 was not pleased with the fortification of Singapore, but since so much money had already been spent on the enterprise they did not propose its abandonment. Work, however, on the base was retarded, so much so that the completion of what was popularly hailed as an impregnable Gibraltar of the Pacific was not attained until 1938. Nor was it then fortified against attack by land.

Churchill Sounds the Alarm

Far more significant than Singapore were the Cassandra prophecies of Winston Churchill, who, like his father before him, ever was a thorn in the side of Tory complacency. Outspoken and bulldoggish, the future war premier had no confidence whatever in disarmament proposals adumbrated in many conferences in the twenties and thirties. What dominated his imagination was the potential strength of the Third Reich and the rapid growth of the Nazi Party. He did *not* believe that *all* the Nazis wanted was equality of status, and he warned the Commons as early as 1932 that "all these bands of sturdy Teutonic youth, marching through the streets and roads of Germany, with the light of desire in their eyes to suffer for their Fatherland, are not looking for status. They are looking for weapons, and when they have weapons, believe me, they will then ask for the return of lost territories and lost colonies."

This speech was delivered in November, 1932, less than three months before Hitler was appointed Chancellor by Hindenburg. But Churchill was regarded as a firebrand who only caused trouble and MacDonald wished to make a pacifistic gesture at the coming Disarmament Conference at Geneva. Therefore, instead of increasing the appropriation for the Royal Air Force (RAF) he diminished it.

Look out, cried Churchill, we are only fifth in potential air power (France, Italy, Japan, and the United States all were rated above Britain); Germany is our nearest neighbor and Germany is rearming. But Churchill, according to Sir Herbert Samuel, Liberal leader in the Commons, used "the language of a Malay running amok," and few heeded his warning.

The skies now darkened rapidly; Germany left the League; Germany announced conscription; Germany rearmed fast. As she did so, Churchill did his best to arouse his lethargic countrymen. "It would be folly," he said in May, 1935, "for us to act as if we were swimming in a halcyon sea, as if nothing but balmy breezes and calm weather were to be expected." The British were increasing their air force at last, but the Nazis were increasing theirs at a faster tempo. Already they had surpassed Britain.

Came 1936, the abandonment of Haile Selassie in Ethiopia, the abandonment of sanctions, and Britain continued to fall farther behind. Midsummer holidays were due, but to Churchill rest and peace were illusions. "Do not forget," said he, "that all the time those remorseless hammers of which General Goering spoke are descending night and day in Germany, and that the most warlike . . . people in Europe are becoming welded into a tremendous fighting machine. . . ." "The army," he said in 1936, "lacks every weapon which is required for the latest form of modern war. Where are anti-tank guns, where are the short distance wireless sets, where are the field anti-aircraft guns. . . . ? Nothing has been done in the years the locust hath eaten, to equip the tank corps with new machines." In quality, British tanks were inferior to those of Germany, Russia, Italy, and the United States. The RAF, Churchill estimated, had 960 first-class planes, the Germans 1,500. "Owing to our past neglect," he affirmed, "in the face of the plainest warnings, we have now entered upon a period of danger greater than has befallen Britain since the U-boat campaign was crushed."

Baldwin's Parliamentary apology for this state of affairs aroused some criticism but few listened to Churchill. Not even in the year of Munich (1938) would they listen to him. "For five years," he said,

I have talked to the House on these matters—not with very great success. I have watched this famous island descending incontinently, fecklessly, the stairway which leads to a dark gulf. It is a fine broad stairway at the beginning, but after a bit the carpet ends. A little farther on there are only flagstones, and a little farther on still these break beneath your feet. Look back over the last five years. It is true that great mistakes were made in the years immediately after the War. But at Locarno we laid the foundation from which a great forward movement could have been made. Look back upon the last five years— since, that is to say, Germany began to rearm in earnest and openly to seek revenge. If we study the history of Rome and Carthage, we can understand what happened and why. It is not difficult to form an intelligent view about the three Punic Wars; but if mortal catastrophe should overtake the British Nation and the British Empire, historians a thousand years hence will still be baffled by the mystery of our affairs. They will never understand how it was that a victorious nation, with everything in hand, suffered themselves to be brought low, and to cast away all that they had gained by measureless sacrifice and absolute victory—gone with the wind!

Now the victors are the vanquished, and those who threw down their arms in the field and sued for an armistice are striding on to world mastery.

Chapter 33

THE BRITISH COMMONWEALTH

THE GREATER Britain overseas was neither commonwealth nor empire; it was both. The four Dominions, Canada, Australia, New Zealand, and the Union of South Africa, comprised the Commonwealth; all other lands over which his Majesty's government held sway, the Empire.

The First World War wrought great changes in the constitutional status of the Dominions. Not only had they raised armies and fought battles; they had been consulted openly, confidently, by Great Britain. Lloyd George's Imperial War Cabinet had been a true Commonwealth Cabinet, the premiers of the Dominions sharing in decisions of moment to the Empire, their influence and position well above that of many members of the ministry who debated on the floor of the House. The peace conference brought the premiers still greater prominence. The Dominions had separate representation, five British premiers, representing five different electorates, participating in the settlement of the war. Even if the Dominion premiers were subordinate in fact as well as in theory to their colleagues from England, their influence was felt in many ways. On the commission which dealt with Greece was Canada's representative; on that which decided Poland's boundary was Smuts of South Africa. Hughes, the Australian, was consulted about Czechoslovakia and reparations. Furthermore, in the projected League of Nations seats were duly provided for each Dominion; and at the grand conclusion of the Congress of the Nations in the Hall of Mirrors, their premiers signed the peace treaty separately on behalf of their own nations.

The Versailles treaty was ratified by all four Dominions, but not without considerable grumbling in three. In Australia, Mr. Hughes announced that his government had not been sufficiently consulted; the Americans had interfered, and German New Guinea, which otherwise would have been annexed by Australia, was now only a mandate. Besides, as a result of the treaty the Japanese were now two thousand miles nearer Australia. In Canada there was criticism of Article X of the League of Nations covenant guaranteeing each signatory its territorial integrity.

Opposition in South Africa was stronger. There were three major political groupings: the South African Party, a union of British immi-

660

grants and Dutch farmers (Boers), pledged to reduce friction between the two nationalities; the Nationalist Party, a purely Boer organization bitter against British annexation of the two Dutch republics; and the Unionist Party, purely British in membership and spirit, intent upon opposing Boer or Afrikander nationalism, as it came to be called. The Nationalists desired to repudiate the treaty, since its authors had ignored their claims. At the conclusion of the war they had betaken themselves to Paris to urge before the peace conference the cause of the Boers. This they were not permitted to do, although an audience was granted them by Lloyd George. It was easy for him to argue that, since the Nationalists were in a minority in the Union, they could not well contend that they were deprived of self-determination. He had been their friend during the South African War; but the Union constitution of 1909 had met with their approval; they could not now reverse their position. The Nationalists returned home, angry. They found nothing to praise in the work of the peace conference. "The League of Nations," said one of them in the Union legislature, "was built on a foundation of pillage and hypocrisy." "The treaty," exclaimed another, "breathes the spirit of domination, jealousy and revenge." But they were helpless to prevent its ratification. The South African Party had a plurality of votes in Parliament; when assisted by the Unionists, pro-British to a man, a safe majority was assured. The S.A.P., as it was called, found a clever leader in General Smuts. The latter had no difficulty in maintaining his liaison with the Unionists, and the treaty therefore received the imprimatur of the Union government.

The Dominions and British Foreign Policy

For decades before the War the Dominions had been self-governing except as to foreign policy, which by general consent, although not by statute, had been left to the mother country. In 1919 it became a question whether they were even thus bound. The covenant of the League gave them seats in the Assembly; were their votes there to be considered British votes as such or were the Dominions virtually independent nations, free to determine their own foreign policy? Just what was their status? The situation was anomalous, even to British statesmen not customarily troubled by want of logic in constitutional practice.

Before the War many Britons, both at home and abroad, had argued in favor of imperial federation, closer unity; but after the war there were fewer to favor it. Hughes of Australia was violently opposed. "I think," he said, "the surest way of destroying this mighty empire is to tamper with its constitution. Complete autonomy of the parts is the foundation upon which it rests." In Canada, as though it was the most casual thing in the world, the government announced that a Dominion embassy would be established at Washington. As for South Africa, General Smuts announced in Parliament that the peace conference had been a "formal recognition of the new position of the Dominions, and that in foreign relations they were to take part and speak for themselves, and that they no longer would be bound by the voice and signature of the British Parliament."

General Smuts' political position was delicate. The South African Party which he headed was composed principally of Boers, and a continuous flow of deserters constantly made its way toward Hertzog and the Nationalist tent. The very brilliance of Smuts' speeches and his unrivalled mental acumen brought him under suspicion. This philosopher-statesman, so idealized in Britain, was he true to the Afrikander? The Nationalists intimated that he was not, and as a result turned the election of 1920 against him.

The political divisions in the Assembly, after the election, show some striking changes:

	Number of seats before 1920	After 1920
South African Party	53	41
(mainly Afrikander, but friendly toward the Commonwealth)		
Unionists	38	25
(solidly British)		
Nationalists	27	44
(Boer irreconcilables)		
Labor	6	21
(Socialistic and, for the most part, indifferent toward the Commonwealth)		
Independents	6	3

For the first time in the history of the Union the extreme party of independence had a plurality of votes in the Assembly; and in order to carry on the King's government through the agency of the South African Party, Smuts had to form some kind of coalition. To do this he turned first to the Nationalists, attempting to bring the two Boer factions together. The Nationalists, however, insisted on a republic; the S.A.P. stood staunchly for Dominion nationality within the Empire. On this point there could be no compromise. The General turned now to the Unionists. The latter were willing to do anything to defeat Hertzog, even to the extent of committing political suicide. This, in effect, they did since they agreed to destroy their own political organization and to merge themselves completely in the South African Party. The political atmosphere being thus cleared, Smuts struck home and appealed to the electorate, this time winning the election for the S.A.P.

Dominion Representation

In 1921 an imperial conference between the Dominion premiers and the British ministry convened in London. Winston Churchill, the ubiquitous, was colonial secretary and the conference was ambitiously baptized by him, "Imperial Cabinet." The delegates from overseas, however, did not take to this innovation. Cabinet was synonymous with authority, and they feared centralized authority in London; that word and the word *imperial* was dropped, this meeting of British statesmen preferring the title of "Conference of the Prime Ministers of the Empire."

The program was extensive but the results meagre. The conference supposedly discussed the Pacific problem of the Anglo-Japanese treaty of 1902, and its possible renewal, the division of reparation receipts from Germany, the possibility of placating Indian opinion by alleviating the conditions under which Indians lived in the Dominions, and the possibilities of empire-settlement and migration. But the gravest question of all, that of Dominion partnership in British foreign policy, was left untouched.

Yet the problem of Dominion representation at the forthcoming disarmament conference at Washington showed the need for some common understanding in regard to that partnership. No individual invitation to attend had been given to the Dominions, since the American government thought it discourteous to the British government to issue one; whereupon the Dominions took offense. General Smuts intimated that if not invited in their own right they should ignore the proceedings; Hughes spoke of the American invitation to Great Britain alone as "slamming the door." Here was protocol with a vengeance, and Dominion sensitivity was only partially allayed by drafting an Australian, a New Zealander, and a Canadian on the British Empire delegation, Mr. Balfour signing the Washington treaty twice, once for the Empire and once for South Africa.

The ostensible object of the Washington Conference was the cutting down of naval expenditure; but this could only be obtained by abrogating or fundamentally altering the Anglo-Japanese Alliance. The treaty which inaugurated this pact, as renewed in 1905, guaranteed military aid in case "either contracting power should be involved in war in defense of its territorial rights or interests." That treaty threatened to involve Britain in war with America should the latter country come to blows with Japan. To make this impossible Britain and America had entered into special treaty obligations which provided for mutual arbitration of all difficulties. But the Senate of the United States amended this treaty in certain vital particulars and President Taft refused to accept the amendment. Thereupon the United States and Britain agreed, in 1914, to a treaty which provided for a peace commission to investigate all causes of difference between the two countries. This was not a treaty of arbitration, technically speaking; but Downing Street gave notice to Tokyo, although not to Washington, that it should so consider it, and would regard it as coming under the special clause in the second renewal of the Anglo-Japanese treaty in 1911 which excluded from the pact any country with which either signatory had a treaty of arbitration.

The Americans did not hear of this qualification until 1921, and in the meantime the race for naval supremacy in Pacific waters continued apace. British statesmen saw nightmares; they did not want to break with Japan; they did not want to antagonize America; and they must not antagonize their own Dominions. The Japanese, on the other hand, disliked the qualifications read into the treaty by the British in regard to America; the United States was ill disposed toward any Anglo-Japanese alliance; and the British Dominions, like the mother country, desired to avoid friction with America. The result was highly satisfactory to the Dominions, even if not to other participants; they at least obtained what they wanted, the abrogation of the Anglo-Japanese treaty and recognition for themselves as co-partners in the British Commonwealth.

The year of the Washington Conference was also the year of the Chanak incident, which demonstrated an unsatisfactory state of affairs as far as the relations of the Dominions to British foreign policy went. Mustapha Kemal, at the head of the Turkish Nationalists, having driven the Greeks into the sea, turned his forces against Constantinople. The porcelain treaty of Sèvres was threatened with destruction; and of the European signatories Great Britain alone gave proof of a willingness to defend it. Under Lloyd George's direction a small British force was landed at Chanak, on the Asiatic side of the Dardanelles, and an ultimatum delivered to Mustapha Kemal. The British pickets again faced those of Turkey as in 1915; war seemed imminent and the Prime Minister of England appealed by cable to the Dominions for support.

Except for New Zealand they were not as ready to give it as in 1914. The Prime Minister of the smallest Dominion cabled instantly: "Government of New Zealand desires to associate themselves with action being taken and will send contingent." Australia was less eager to offer aid. Hughes' cabinet was prepared "to associate itself with the British government," and was ready, "if circumstances required," to send an Australian contingent. Canada was even more reluctant, the Prime Minister stating, "It is for Parliament (the Canadian Parliament) to decide whether we should participate in wars in different parts of the world." South Africa aligned herself with Canada. "When the crisis in the Near East was raised," said General Smuts, "and this Government was addressed by the British government on the question of sending some contingents to take part in the operations that might take place in the Near East the Government replied that in a matter . . . of such far-reaching issues they would not commit themselves unless they consulted Parliament."

The reaction of the Dominions to the Chanak affair was disconcerting; supposing a new and more serious crisis should arise, then what? The Dominions and India had participated in the treaty of Sèvres, which broke up the old Turkey; that of Lausanne, which patched certain portions of it together again, had been negotiated and signed solely by Great Britain. Did or did not Lord Curzon's signature involve the Dominions, logically, legally, or morally, in the support of it?

The answer of the Canadian Prime Minister was an emphatic, "No!" "We take the position," he said, "that not having been invited to the Lausanne Conference, not having been represented there, not having, for the reasons which I have mentioned, signed the treaty, the treaty does not impose obligations on Canada, and those parts of the Empire on which it does impose obligations are the only parts that should be expected to sign and ratify."

Shortly after, came Locarno (see p. 624) and when Britain signed that pact she did so with the express provision that the treaty did not apply to India or to the Dominions, unless they chose to sign. From now on it was evident that a distinction must be made in the future between the foreign policy of Britain and that of the Dominions. To quote article nine of the pact: ". . . the present treaty shall impose no obligation upon any of the British Dominions or upon India, until the Government of such Dominion or of India signifies its acceptance thereof."

This was a distinct constitutional departure. At Paris and at Washington the Dominions and Great Britain had stood together. At Lausanne the Dominions were not represented and Canada had insisted that she was under no obligation to enforce that treaty. At Locarno the objections of Canada were formally recognized as valid, and upon Great Britain and Northern Ireland alone fell the onus of supporting the treaty in the name of the Empire.

In accordance with international law, when Britain was at war so also were the Dominions. But in accordance with this treaty it was evident that they might claim not to be. Suppose any Dominion should issue a declaration of neutrality in a war in which Britain was engaged in defense of this treaty of Locarno. What then would be the status of enemy aliens in Bombay, what that of a British warship at Auckland? On the other hand, why should India and the Dominions pledge themselves to Locarno and an agreement purely European in its guarantees? Were the men of West Australia concerned with the delimitation of the Rhine frontier; could one ask them to fight for it?

Immediately there was talk of yet another conference. But could it accomplish anything? Too often, it was felt, had the Dominion premiers been summoned from their own preserves for a friendly chat with the Prime Minister of Britain. Why bring men from half way round the earth for an exchange of social amenities? All vestiges of British control in

Commonwealth and Empire foreign policy had now disappeared. Such traces of subordination to Great Britain as might still be discovered were purely incidental in character: the British flag, the traditional right of veto of the Crown (as dead in the Dominions as in Britain), and the appeal to the Privy Council. Was it worth while to hold parleys over matters such as these?

Many thought that it was. In Australia and in Canada there had been agitation in favor of the appointment of native-born Australians and Canadians as governors-general. In Queensland the appointment of British-born governors had been resented. The Irish Free State had appointed a minister to Washington; why should there not be a representative of South Africa at the Hague, an Australian emissary at Tokyo? The Empire was confronted with a number of minor issues of this description which made for friction between the Dominions and the Motherland. Perhaps it would be just as well to have the Dominions understand, once and for all, that they were free in every respect to follow their own bent.

Baldwin's government wanted to make this quite clear and so it summoned still another imperial conference to meet in London in 1926.

The Imperial Conference of 1926

For the first time in history the relations of the Dominions to the mother country were now defined. The Dominions are, the conference asserted, "*autonomous Communities within the British Empire, equal in status, in no way subordinate one to another in any aspect of their domestic or external affairs, though united by a common allegiance to the Crown, and freely associated as members of the British Commonwealth of Nations.*"

There was nothing new in this pronunciamento; everybody understood before this that the Dominions were free. None the less this formal acknowledgment of equality cleared the air of any possible suspicion of imperialistic rule, and also paved the way for the construction of a true system of coördination. The committee on inter-imperial relations which drew up the above statement indicated in outline how this might be done. Treaties in the future could be signed by all the Dominions, by a number of them or even by one. All treaties were to be in the name of the King, but none were to be negotiated except by the governments concerned. In the Dominions the governors were no longer to be considered the representatives of the British government. Official communications in the future, therefore, would pass not through the governors, as representatives of the British Crown, but direct, government to government. Between the Dominions and Great Britain there was to be absolute equality.

From now on the only direct connection between Britain and the

Dominions lay through the Crown. The governor-general in each Dominion represented the Crown and had the same function in his Dominion as the King possessed in London. Since the King of England was constitutionally bound to accept the advice of his ministers it followed that the King in Canada (the governor-general) was obligated to do likewise. Theoretically, of course, this meant that the King might approve one course of action in England and a diametrically different one in Canada, where the governor-general, the King's alter ego, was equally bound to accept the opinion of the majority in the Canadian Parliament as expressed through the Canadian cabinet. It might seem illogical that the Crown could be thus split, that the King could have five different personalities, one for each Dominion (governor-general) and another as King of England. Nevertheless such was the British system as defined and practiced since 1926. The colonial office had already ceased to exist as far as the Dominions were concerned and a new cabinet officer, secretary of state for the Dominions, was one of his Majesty's ministers. But this official had no powers except to convey information from one government to another. Even the various governors-general were now selected by the Crown on the nomination of the Dominion Prime Ministers.

This curious system meant that the fiction of the Crown was maintained while the authority of the British Parliament was liquidated. There still remained even after 1926 a few who insisted that since Parliament was the source of all authority the decision of a mere imperial conference could not supersede it. To satisfy those critics Parliament passed in 1931 the Statute of Westminster which stated that no law passed by Parliament in the future had any validity in any Dominion without its express agreement. Thus a formal seal of approval was placed upon what already had become an accepted practice.

Dominion Loyalty to the Commonwealth

First and foremost in devotion to the Commonwealth stood New Zealand. Of all the Dominions it was the smallest,[1] the most isolated, the most purely British in blood, and the most closely linked of all to the mother country by commercial ties. Ninety per cent of New Zealand's exports went to Britain, and despite the efforts of her Labor party to build up home industries the one and a half million inhabitants of that country continued to rely on Britain for manufactured goods.

With Australia and Canada it was otherwise. The five million Australians and the fifteen million Canadians were more independent; their respective countries dwarfed Britain in area; their populations were more

[1] Newfoundland, Britain's oldest colony, had dominion status in 1834. Being bankrupt, she asked to be relieved of the expense of self-government. Newfoundland is now (1956) a province of Canada as the result of a plebiscite.

heterogeneous in blood, and in both instances they were more economically independent, establishing their own industries and protecting them behind tariff walls.

Australia had her own tariffs, her own army, her own navy. Betweeen the two World Wars her attention was focused on her own domestic problems, the building of a new capital in the wilderness, the financing of new railroads, the opening of her northern territory, and currency troubles resulting from overexpansion and the world depression of the early thirties.

Canada was somewhat similarly situated. The population of that Dominion was even more heterogeneous than that of Australia. The French Canadians kept aloof; the western provinces were full of immigrants from Eastern Europe and from the United States. The descendants of the old Empire Loyalists who had fled the United States after the American Revolution were more British than most Britons; but they were in a minority. Commercially and financially Canada was closely tied to Britain, but even more closely tied to the United States, the latter taking a greater volume of her exports than the mother country.

Centrifugal forces in Canada and Australia were powerful, but nonetheless the attachment of those two Dominions to the British connection was beyond cavil. Neither of them, for instance, hesitated to declare war against Germany in 1939. But the same was not true of the Union of South Africa. A change of thirteen votes in the South African legislature and the Union would have declared neutrality in the Second World War. What was the reason? The Boer War had ended in 1902 and the British had done their best to make amends for harsh treatment of the two Boer republics during that conflict by turning over the destinies of all South Africa to their keeping, for those of Boer (Afrikander) blood were in the majority in the Union. Nevertheless, memories of the old conflict stayed green and were the constant talk of the veldt. Smuts' popularity with his own people was great, but so, too, was that of General Hertzog, leader of the bitter-enders, the more intransigent Boers who composed the Nationalist Party. General Smuts had put down a strike among the gold miners and therefore was unpopular with the Labor Party. Here was Hertzog's opportunity. To maintain himself in power Smuts had brought into the fold of the South African Party the British voters. Hertzog now sought by the magic power of old association to draw out from it the Boers. "Come out of the House of the stranger," he said to them. The Boers are one in language, blood, and religion. South Africa is their first concern. The Labor and Nationalist Parties should stand as one against Smuts and his adherents, imperialists and agents of foreign capitalism.

Socialism, to the land-owning Boers, was anathema; and the Labor Party was socialistic. To the miners, on the other hand, largely of British origin, secession from the flag of their youth seemed hateful. Was it possible to make a coalition here?

Hertzog cleverly constructed it, and with Labor the South African Nationalists signed a formal pact. By it the Nationalists pledged themselves, if victorious, not to insist on secession from the Empire; by it, Labor pledged itself not to demand confiscatory legislation.

The alliance once struck moved forward to a victorious outcome. Again an election was held in South Africa and this time, to the dismay of the friends of the Commonwealth, Smuts went down to defeat. The seats held by the South African Party decreased from 72 to 53. Those in the possession of the Nationalists increased from 47 to 63. Labor enlarged its membership from 13 to 18. The alliance was victorious and the implacable Hertzog became Prime Minister.

This was in 1924, and from that date to the opening of the Second World War racial and economic strife was the norm in South Africa. Both Smuts and Hertzog were conservative at heart; both were intent upon suppressing socialist agitation among the miners and any agitation among Negroes, heavily in the majority in South Africa; both were Afrikander generals who at one time had fought against British armies; and both were Afrikander nationalists. The only real difference between them was that Smuts believed heartily in the British Commonwealth, whereas Hertzog, though seemingly appeased by the declaration of the conference of 1926, was innately suspicious of British influence and perhaps secretly hopeful that even the British Commonwealth would disintegrate. In 1932 the discreet and conciliatory Smuts went more than half way and patched up an uneasy truce with Hertzog whereby a new political party emerged, the United Party, avoiding the extremists on both sides, and this party with Hertzog as premier and with Smuts as deputy premier controlled South Africa to 1939. When war broke out then Hertzog resigned in a huff because he could not carry a neutrality resolution and Smuts became premier, supported by a very narrow majority, and then only with a promise that South African troops would not be ordered to serve beyond the confines of Africa.

Ireland or Eire

Whether Ireland or Eire should be included in a discussion of the Commonwealth was a moot question. Disaffection in South Africa was rife but it was nothing compared with that in Ireland. During the First World War there was a rebellion in South Africa, but the rebels once conquered were treated with leniency; after the 1916 Easter revolt in Dublin of Sinn Fein (the Irish Republican Party) there was bloody repression, and death by court martial.

The Irish Republicans then adopted new tactics. They boycotted the Royal Irish Constabulary, and they inaugurated Sinn Fein courts of law. Since the members of the constabulary were Irishmen, the refusal of the community round about them to engage in any form of intercourse was an effective weapon. Farmers refused to sell to the constabulary; women would not sit by the members of it in church; no good Irishman, so said Sinn Fein, should even speak to these upholders of an alien rule. Meanwhile, British judges traveled about on empty circuits and held vacant courts. From fear or preference, or both, the people made use only of the irregular and illegal tribunals set up by Sinn Fein. Within a year these were the only courts functioning over a large part of Ireland.

Came then 1920, a year so black in Irish annals that to find its counterpart one must look to the seventeenth century. And now between Irish and British an actual war arose, none the less war although there were no battles, but only raid and counterraid, murder and countermurder. For a year and a half blood was to flow freely in Ireland. The sworn servants of the Crown vied with the members of the Irish Republican army in a saturnalia of crime and cruelty. The British, to assist the fast thinning ranks of the constabulary, introduced into Ireland an auxiliary police force, clad in the old army khaki, but with black glengarry hats. To wear their uniform anywhere in Ireland soon became foolhardy; to wear it after dark or without friends at hand was to invite death. To belong to Sinn Fein, on the other hand, or to be related by marriage to Sinn Fein politician or soldier was all too often held sufficient warranty for prompt execution. Throughout all Ireland the country districts were dangerous and even in large cities the sound of the curfew bell gave warning to beware of assassins.

Between the responsibility of Sinn Fein on the one hand and Dublin Castle on the other the historian can draw no fine distinction. In the words of Mr. Griffith, Sinn Fein's founder: "The military mind is the same in every country. Our military men are as bad as the British.[2] They were. The Sinn Fein army, commanded by Michael Collins, a youthful agitator, was ill disciplined, widely scattered, and composed largely of young boys. By it many acts of vicious cruelty were perpetrated, such as dragging unarmed British officers from their beds and slaying them in cold blood. The "Black and Tans," on the other hand, well-paid, seasoned veterans in many instances of the Great War and hardened to suffering and misery, did not hesitate to burn and destroy the homes of those held suspect, and to shoot in the back prisoners whom they told to run for safety.

Lloyd George, Prime Minister, denounced the Sinn Feiners to high heaven; but after a year he changed his mind, suggested a conference, offered concessions. For weeks the delegates of Sinn Fein wrangled with

[2] P. S. O'Hegarty, *The Victory of Sinn Fein*, p. 47.

the British in London. Dominion status was offered with safeguards, mainly in regard to military and financial matters. One by one, the safeguards were surrendered by the British. The question of allegiance proved a stumbling block: The Irish would accept no allegiance to the King, but a majority of the delegates agreed "to be faithful to the King by virtue of their common citizenship" in the British Commonwealth. Even this, however, would not satisfy De Valera, the Sinn Fein president, and when he was voted down by a pro-treaty majority in the Irish Parliament, he started civil war. This came to an end by 1924, and the Irish Free State accepted dominion status.

In 1932 De Valera and his extremists carried the elections and swept into power on an anti-British platform. Promptly, De Valera began cutting such slender links as still joined Ireland to Britain; he got rid of the British governor-general; he repudiated the financial agreement whereby, in return for the cession of two strongly Roman Catholic counties in Ulster to the Free State, the latter assumed responsibility for repaying to the British treasury money advanced in the past for the purchase of Irish homesteads; and what is even more significant, the Irish Parliament passed an act defining Irish citizenship as distinct from British citizenship. Eire, or Ireland, was now regarded by De Valera as a distinct and separate country, and when England declared war on Germany in 1939, Ireland, as everyone expected her to do, proclaimed her neutrality, presumably thereby voiding her Dominion status and withdrawing from the Commonwealth.

Ulster, the northeastern province, remained aloof. The majority there so desired it, since it was Protestant in faith, largely industrial by vocation, and still in good measure descended from Cromwellian soldiers and Scottish business men. On the other hand, a very large minority in Ulster wanted union with Eire and still does. That it may some day become a majority is the lively hope of the rest of Ireland.

Chapter 34

THE LESSER STATES OF EUROPE (1919-39)

THE GROWTH of communism in Russia and of its totalitarian counterpart, fascism, in other countries was symptomatic of a general reaction throughout all Europe to the liberal ideology of the nineteenth century. Only a small part of the continent seemed immune to this general wave of discontent, namely, the four Scandinavian nations—Denmark, Norway, Sweden, and Finland, and the small democratic states of Switzerland, Holland, Belgium, and Czechoslovakia.

From 1815 to 1905 Norway had been linked to Sweden under the House of Bernadotte. For all that time there was a Norwegian Parliament, but foreign affairs were conducted under Swedish auspices. The Norwegians in their unfertile valleys would have been desperately poor, indeed, had it not been for the sea. As it was, they not only became noted fishermen but built up an excellent mercantile marine, having in the early twentieth century the largest in the world in proportion to population. Naturally, therefore, they desired their own consular service, and because King Oscar II tried to keep it in Swedish hands, the Norwegian Parliament voted to separate from Sweden and to have a King of Norway.

A prince of Denmark was selected for this honor and under him Norway became more and more democratic; the Norwegians already had universal manhood suffrage, but in 1913 they extended it to include women, and such slight power as had remained to the King in the way of vetoing legislation was abolished.

Swedish democracy, likewise, grew rapidly in strength in the years before the First World War. Until 1863 Sweden had been ranked as one of the more conservative countries in Europe, retaining a strong monarchy and being governed by a kind of medieval estates-general of four houses —nobility, clergy, burghers, and peasants. From that date onward, however, a steady and constant change in the direction of democracy took place, the result of the impact of the Industrial Revolution, for Sweden was not only rich in timber but in iron ore. Woman suffrage, old-age pensions, progressive legislation gave Sweden the reputation of being one of the most advanced democracies in Europe; and the World War seemed to strengthen rather than to weaken Sweden's devotion to democratic ways, that country becoming noted as one which kept to the "middle way," whereby capitalism was so checked and guarded by consumer co-operatives and state intervention on behalf of the poor that the latter remained content with the security which they had gained. Disparity between rich and poor was reduced to a minimum and Sweden seemingly became a kind of middleclass paradise.

It was not otherwise in Denmark. During the long reign of Christian IX (1863-1906) there was sturdy resistance on the part of the King to democratic innovation, but toward the end of his reign, and during that of his successor, particularly in 1914-15, Denmark went decidedly demo-cratic, both houses of the legislature being elected by universal suffrage, the powers of the King becoming nominal. Even before that time, the growth of coöperative agencies for the standardizing of Danish agri-cultural products had given the Danes good training in democratic practices. About one quarter of all the Danes lived in Copenhagen, one of Europe's most charming capitals, where the extremely modest royal castle of a democratic king is quite obscured by a magnificent city hall redolent with the pride of equalitarian burghers.

The fourth Scandinavian country, Finland, had lain under the heavy yoke of Russian imperialism from 1809 to the Revolution of 1917. Fin-land, soon after, jumped into popular notice as a thriving progressive democracy. The Finns paid their debts, experimented democratically with prohibition only to end it, encouraged modern architecture, turned their capital, Helsinki, into a model city, and desperately prepared to defend their hard-earned freedom from renewed Russian aggression in 1939. True, as far as blood and language are concerned, Finland belongs in a separate category from the other three Scandinavian states; but institu-tionally, as well as geographically, she justly may be considered as linked to Denmark, Norway, and Sweden.

All four of these northern countries were members of the League of Nations, and the Danes in particular took a lively interest in its work, a Dane serving on the commission on the Saar Valley, another on the high court, and Denmark herself being elected to serve a term on the council of the League. All four of these countries also have consulted together from time to time during the intervals between the two World Wars. They organized a Scandinavian bloc; they invited coöperation from other small countries, such as Holland; and within them neither fascism nor com-munism seemed to have gained a foothold.

Switzerland was another democratic country, fortunate in that her annals have been so quiet. The twenty-two states or cantons which com-pose Switzerland were bound together by a federation in 1815 and by a somewhat stronger one in 1847 after a brief civil war of three weeks. In almost all matters apart from national defense the twenty-two cantons preserved their autonomy, and six of these semi-independent cantons in this miniature country are so small that pure, unadulterated democracy is possible, voting being conducted on cantonal business directly in huge mass meetings out of doors. Universal military service holds in Switzerland, but the soldier owns his own rifle and takes it home with him. The Swiss, like the Finns, were ever careful to preserve their liberty and their democracy even if they had to fight for it.

In the Netherlands and in Belgium the picture was not radically different. In both of these lands there was much greater concentration of wealth, in the former in commerce, in the latter in manufacturing and mining. Partly because of this, partly because of surviving religious disputes, the Netherlands and Belgium can hardly be considered fully as democratic in their constitutional practice as the other democracies we have considered, for the former country did not adopt universal suffrage until 1917, and the latter not until after the war. Nevertheless, fascism and communism made relatively little headway in either land. The daughter of the Queen of Holland married a German prince, but the Queen and her country both seemed more concerned in regard to the Prince's personal behavior than for fear lest he import German ideas. A curious form of Roman Catholic fascism developed in Belgium—the Rexist movement—only to be routed at the polls. The Social Democrats still remained a powerful faction in the Belgian Parliament, but by definition they were stanch defenders of democracy; and the same also may be said for the Belgian Catholic party.

There remains the republic of Czechoslovakia. Within the borders of this new, or resurrected, country (depending on the point of view) there seemed to lie great promises for the future of democracy. The Czechs, indeed, appeared not only capable of solving those problems which confronted the other small democracies but able also to settle minority problems by democratic means. Surrounded by Fascist and semi-Fascist states, the Czechs were a beacon of light and reason until overwhelmed by the German inundation of 1938-39.

The Czechoslovak state, as set up by the Allied powers in 1919, was both republican and democratic. The legislature, elected by universal, secret, and compulsory voting, was empowered to choose a president to serve seven years. The Czechs themselves were socially democratic; there was little difference in wealth among them; until only recently the great estates and more important industries had been in German hands; the majority of the Czechs had been workmen or peasants.

There was bound to be some trouble, since one-third of the population was non-Czech. The Slovaks caused friction and so did the minority Poles and Magyars. But most troublesome of all was the German minority that lived, for the most part, toward the German border. These Sudeten Germans (a name derived from the Sudeten Mountains) had just cause for complaint. There were discriminations made against the German language; there were other grievances, mainly economic, and, above all, the sense of injustice at being included in the Czechoslovak nation against their will. But it could not be justly said that these Germans were down-trodden; politically they were on a basis of complete equality with the Czechs; they could and did have their own parties in the parliament at Prague; and, up to 1935 when the crisis came about, there were no less than three German parties—the German Agrarian, the Christian Socialist, and the Social Democratic, the three together polling sixty-five per cent of the German vote.

The Czechoslovak Republic justly can be criticized for overcentralization, and some considered that it would have been wise from the beginning to have federalized the country on the Swiss model. The Czechs were afraid to do this. Not having enjoyed freedom for centuries (it was in 1526 that the Austrian Hapsburgs absorbed the Bohemian Crown), they dared not risk the adoption of Swiss federalism. Meanwhile, secure in their military alliance with France, protected, supposedly, by a friendly Russia, the Czechs occupied what seemed to be a strongly defended bastion in Central Europe, an outpost of democracy between Nazi Germany on the north and semi-fascist Austria on the south.

Poland

Among those countries which were neither totalitarian nor democratic, Poland was the most important. That nation, resurrected from the dead by the peace treaty, full of dreams of former glory, were bent on continuing the war after the war by an aggressive anti-Russian campaign not concluded until the Treaty of Riga in 1921. By that date Pilsudski had carried the frontiers of his country eastward beyond those of 1793. Shortly afterward came the Polish occupation of Vilna, forcibly torn from Lithuania, and by 1923 Poland had become a country of 150,000 square miles, with a population of 28,000,000. In area larger than Italy, in population larger than Spain, Poland could now claim to be the sixth most important European state.

But it was a very weak state. Only on the south might it claim to have any natural boundary, the Carpathian Mountains. To the east, the north, and the west, purely artificial boundary lines were drawn, and as one approached those lines the population was of mixed nationality—Polish-German, Polish-Lithuanian, and Polish-Russian. No country in Europe had so many large minority groups within its borders. There were approximately 5,000,000 Ukrainians (Little Russians), 1,500,000 White Russians, 750,000 to 1,000,000 Germans, an indeterminate number of Lithuanians, and some 3,300,000 Jews within Poland. The country was very, very poor. During the First World War, Russian, German, and Austrian armies fiercely had swept back and forth across the Polish plain, and the subsequent two-year war against Russia had added to the devastation. Live stock had been killed, forests destroyed, towns, villages, railways, and bridges ruined. Furthermore, the Poles were without experience in self-rule. Throughout the ninetenth century they had kept alive their longing for nationality, but actual practice in free government had been denied them.

Nevertheless, in the halcyon days of 1919, with sweet freedom in the air, they did their best. The *Sejm*, or Polish Parliament, which assembled in that year was elected not only by universal suffrage but also in accordance with the principles of proportional representation. It drew up a constitution (1921), and a very liberal one, somewhat on the model of that of the Third Republic, the president possessing very limited power.

Pilsudski, Poland's strong man, considered that feature a direct slap at himself, and so he declined to accept the presidency. With Achilles sulking in his tent, Polish politics degenerated speedily into a series of factional fights which only came to an end with a coup d'état on the part of Pilsudski, who marched on Warsaw in 1926 and overthrew the government. Pilsudski, however, did not make himself dictator or establish a totalitarian regime—at least not at first. Instead, he again refused the presidency, although consenting to act as premier. From 1926 to 1935 Pilsudski's role in Polish history is difficult to disentangle. The General certainly played strong-arm politics, even at times imprisoning hostile deputies of the Sejm. Twice he resigned the premiership, only to continue to manipulate elections and parliamentary blocs; and to all intent and purpose he was about to become dictator at the time of his death in 1935, when a new constitution was adopted, one described as an "authoritarian democracy," whatever that is.

That constitution had one very unusual feature. It made an emphatic denial that a totalitarian government was desirable—did not Article 5 state: "The creative action of the individual is the lever of collective life."? On the other hand, the peculiar method adopted for selecting the president of the Polish Republic pointed in the opposite direction. He was to be chosen by a college of electors composed of high officials and members of the Sejm. If the incumbent in the presidential office approved, no further steps were necessary. If, however, he chose to nominate a candidate not approved by the electoral college then a popular vote should decide between the two nominees. Extensive additional powers were also granted the president. He was authorized to issue ordinances having the authority of law during such times as the Sejm was not in session.

In the few years remaining to the Polish Republic before its annihilation at the hands of Germany and Russia in 1939, the political pendulum swung back and forth, not between right and left but between right and center. The Communist party was forbidden and the only question was:

would Poland swing into the fascist column or continue halfway democratic? Army officers took an active part in this struggle. In the cabinets
were a number of generals and colonels, and General Smigly-Rydz,
commander-in-chief of the Polish army in the one-month war of 1939,
was made a marshal and then officially declared "first person in Poland
after the President." The marshal, in the eyes of liberals and socialists,
was a suspect; he was said to be committed to a fascist program. But this
could not be proved.

Poland, as the year of her doom drew near, was most dangerously balanced between democracy and totalitarianism. Superficially the country
seemed strong. A Polish port, Gdynia, was constructed on the sandy
wastes of the Baltic and through it flowed considerable commerce; a
Polish mercantile marine was in the making; and there were even demands
for Polish colonies. Seemingly, the government was in good position financially, with monopolies of alcohol, salt, matches, tobacco, and lotteries
to buttress up its treasury. But this was on the surface only; below was
a poverty-stricken peasantry, so poor that in eastern Poland matches were
divided four ways before being struck. The "colonels," now sitting in the
political saddle as well as in the military, did not know how to deal with
poverty, were not interested in poverty, nor were they more enlightened
in regard to the minorities.

The Germans, the Ukrainians, and the Jews in Poland continued an
outcry about the discrimination levied against them. Scattered throughout western Poland, German landlords complained that their leases were
illegally defined by Polish law courts, and that, contrary to the Treaty
of Versailles, the use of German in schools was frowned upon. The
Ukrainians asserted that they were deprived of the cultural autonomy
promised them, and that even Ukrainian Boy Scouts were disbanded by
Polish orders. The Jews, who comprised some twenty-seven per cent of
the city population, were humiliated by "ghetto benches," separate seats
assigned to Jews in university lecture halls, a practice encouraged by the
government, although not ordered by it. The treatment given minorities
in Poland was far less fair and just than that guaranteed by her sister
republic, Czechoslovakia. In fact, nowhere else in Europe were minorities
more at a disadvantage than in Poland. That country, indeed, was in
sorry plight as the German hordes drove over the western borders in
September, 1939.

Spain

The only large European state spared the horrors of the First World
War was Spain. The King, the court, the army, rumor had it, favored
the Germans; but British commercial interests were dominant and, isolated
as Spain was from the Central Powers, neutrality had been a necessity.
After the war Spain swung violently to the right under a military

dictatorship (1923-30), then violently to the left under a radical republican government, greatly influenced by communistic ideas (1930-36), then violently to the right again (1936-?) under a military dictatorship established through the active support of the Italian and German dictators.

Spain in 1919 was a constitutional monarchy, but not a well-governed one. Most of the Spanish people, however, were so long accustomed to misrule that opposition to King Alfonso and to the junta of corrupt politicians who controlled the country was not highly developed. There were, however, danger signals flying in two places—in Catalonia, the northeastern province of Spain, and in Morocco.

Catalonia was at once the most prosperous and the most radical section of the Iberian peninsula. It contained the large manufacturing city of Barcelona; it possessed a language and a literature peculiarly its own—the Catalan—for not until the nineteenth century did Catalonia cease to be at least partially autonomous. During the World War the deputies from Catalonia in the Spanish *Cortes* (parliament) had protested as a body against the weight of taxation borne by their constituents, and at the conclusion of that conflict, Catalonia demanded a revision of the Spanish constitution whereby Spain should become a federated rather than a unitary state, the various provinces having parliaments of their own.

In Spanish Morocco, meanwhile, there was active rebellion. Spanish troops sent to defeat it were badly mauled by the Moors, and King Alfonso lost such little prestige as he had managed to retain by issuing orders which resulted in further defeats, one of which resulted in the death of over 10,000 Spaniards. An investigation of these disasters was promptly suppressed (1922), and loud were the complaints in press and Parliament. Alfonso decided to abdicate, not his throne but his constitutional authority. Having made arrangements with General Primo de Rivera for a coup d'état, he left for France.

The general established himself (1923) as military dictator, brought civil liberties to an end, ruled by court martial. For a while it seemed as though Rivera might be as successful as Mussolini, since in many ways he resembled that condottiere chief. Seemingly, the general was a kind of human dynamo, very conceited, and not without ability. He ended successfully the revolt in Africa; he organized a political party, the Patriotic Union, standing ostensibly for country, religion, and monarchy; and he shared political power with it. Unlike Mussolini, however, he grew less popular with the passing years rather than more so. The Spaniards proved more fractious than the Italians; there were mutinies in the army; there were anti-Rivera demonstrations in the universities; and Rivera himself did not enjoy robust health. Suddenly in 1930 he resigned, and Alfonso immediately restored the constitution suspended in 1923 and announced the election of a new Cortes.

But it was too late to save the monarchy. Most Spaniards considered

THE VICTIM

Spain. "Whichever Wins, My Agony Endures!"

(*Punch,* Aug. 12, 1936. Reprinted by permission of the proprietors of *Punch.*)

Alfonso responsible for the late dictatorship and they did not hesitate to demand his abdication. The monarch refused to abdicate, but once again fled the country; and as he did so in 1931 the republic was proclaimed in Madrid.

The foundations upon which it rested were shaky. Few Spaniards had any use for a King who never did anything but run away from trouble; but aside from that one slender thread of unity, there was no common agreement as to the kind of government best suited to the country. On the right were those who favored a political revolution, but who looked askance upon any social revolution which might undertake a redistribution of land, and an educational program which would take away from the Catholic Church its traditional monopoly of Spanish education. On the left were innumerable grades of revolutionary sentiment, running from that professed by Social Democrats (gradualists in temperament, hoping for the piecemeal establishment of socialism) all the way to the more extreme dogmas of the Communists (some favoring Stalin, some Trotsky, but all for the red flag and immediate revolt), and to the Anarchist-Syndicalists (very strong in Barcelona), believing in no government at all and defiantly hoisting the black flag of anarchy.

Delegates drawn from these divergent groups drew up a constitution calling for a "republic of the workers of all classes," a title indicative of a certain leftist tendency in the constitution which was reflected by provisions that made for exclusively lay education and for the confiscation of large landed estates. The more conservative members of the constitutional assembly were not pleased. The more extreme right, namely, the few followers of the exiled Alfonso and those known as Carlists, who favored the pretender to the Spanish throne, began once more to plot against the republican regime, and the moderate right (much larger in numbers) became disaffected.

Shortly it became more so, as the constituent Cortes drove the Jesuits out of Spain and tried to put through an educational program without religious instruction. Under the circumstances it was perhaps foolish to act thus, for the country was over forty per cent illiterate, and to set up a sufficient number of schools to provide overnight for the 250,000 children educated by the monastic orders was impossible for such a poor country as Spain.

The Spanish republicans, indeed, fell into the same error as did the revolutionary leaders in the French Revolution: being more or less contemptuous of religion and thinking it moribund, they awoke the Catholic Church out of its lethargy. They sequestrated immediately all property of the Church not directly used for religious purposes; religious orders were forbidden to teach; the crucifix was removed from all classrooms; divorce was freely granted; and complete separation between Church and State was guaranteed.

The Pope immediately protested against these anticlerical clauses in the constitution, and many Spaniards promptly renewed their interest in a religion which lay dormant but never dead. They found themselves annoyed by the Republic in many other ways; they were angered by the success of the Catalan radicals, who were soon able to obtain a high degree of autonomy for their own province; they were worried by the confiscation (with little or no compensation) of the great estates, estimated at 50,000,000 acres, which were to be given to the peasants. These factors converging together brought about an uprising in Madrid and Seville in the name of a conservative republican dictatorship.

This revolt of the right was quickly squelched, but no sooner was that done than a rising of the left occurred, this time on the part of Anarchists who wanted no government at all and who fomented strikes to do away with it. Confronted, therefore, with revolt and counter-revolt, the constituent assembly felt far from secure as Spaniards voted in 1933 for their first national Parliament under the new constitution.

The popular vote went to the right, although the center parties in the Cortes, together with the left, could have had a small majority. The center, however, preferred the right to the left, and combining with it made possible a rightist ministry. It proved a weak one. Violence broke out on every hand. In Asturias, a mining district in northern Spain, Communists and Socialists forgot their differences and descended on the town of Oviedo. For nine days they held it, sacking banks and churches, and putting many priests to death. In Catalonia Premier Companys proclaimed Catalonia independent of Madrid. And elsewhere in Spain an organization began to be heard from known as the *Falange Española,* started ostensibly for the purpose of protecting nuns from molestation but soon to become famous as a Spanish Fascist party, bent upon the destruction of radicalism by force. The government did, indeed, succeed in crushing out the revolt in Asturias and in Catalonia, but against the incipient anarchy breaking out, now here, now there, it seemed powerless, and in a new election to the Cortes in 1936 it met with repudiation at the hands of the electorate.

This time Spain swung to the left, as the various radical groups, so frequently at each other's throats, combined in what was known as the *frente popular.* Out of 473 members chosen, the leftists now had 266, the center parties 65, and the right only 142. This was the last general election held in Spain. Civil disorder and mob violence prevailed wellnigh everywhere. The various Marxist and anarchist groups claimed that they simply countered violence by justifiable reprisals. The Falangists (Spanish Fascists), on the other hand, reversed that argument. Where the truth lay, none can tell. The facts are that nerves were frayed and patience exhausted on both sides. The conservatives claimed that the government permitted radical mobs to fire churches and to kill priests and nuns, and only intervened when conservatives tried to prevent such acts. The republican government, not communist nor socialist nor anarchist, but influenced none the less by these three groups, asserted that it had a preponderant voice in the Cortes and represented the will of the Spanish people, that the Falangists violated that will, that they took the law into their own hands, that they compelled magistrates "to sentence their opponents and acquit their members." One thing and only one is demonstrable: "the left did not know how to win, the right did not know how to lose.... Blue shirts and red shirts covered breasts in which hatred was hatching the most terrible revenge. The shadow of murder was spreading over Spain." [1] For many a year it was to remain there.

Murder is not too strong a word to use for the civil war which raged through Spain from 1936 to 1939, a vicious, cruel, and bloodthirsty war in which not Spaniards alone but many other Europeans, as well as Americans and also Moors, took active part. It began with a revolt in the army, many officers of which were enemies of the republic. Under the command of General Franco, who had been exiled to the Canaries by the republican government, a part of the army stationed in Morocco revolted and invaded Spain, accompanied by the Moors.

The revolt spread, particularly in western Spain, where a Falangist capital was set up at Burgos. Slowly the rebels in the South and West gathered strength, joined forces, and were at the very gates of Madrid. Associated with the Falangists were the Traditionalists (Carlists), and both groups from the beginning had the active sympathy and coöperation of Hitler and Mussolini. It seemed as though only a miracle could prevent the Fascist occupation of the Spanish capital.

That miracle almost occurred; the republicans matched zeal with zeal, and if they lacked military training they had numbers on their side, and also help from without. Airplanes from Russia speedily engaged in duels with Italian planes over Spain, and volunteers dashed to their assistance —exiled Germans, Italians, and radical youth from a dozen countries.

The war soon took on the aspect of a fight betwen international communism and international fascism. Hitler and Mussolini sent armed help to Franco; the former planes and many technicians, the latter doing likewise, and supplying artillery and infantry as well. The Russians soon withdrew their active support, but from England, France, and the United States several thousand individual Communists and left-wing sympathizers dashed to the rescue, forming an international brigade for the defense of the Spanish Republic. The president of the Spanish Republic was no Communist, and his premier, Caballero, was only a Social Democrat; but so loudly did Hitler and Mussolini proclaim the Holy War, and so strongly did the Holy See proclaim the conflict a crusade of Christianity against communism that a large part of the world somewhat wrongly regarded the war as purely a Communist-Fascist duel.

The Spanish Loyalists, as the republicans were called, managed to stave off the inevitable for over two years. They hung on tenaciously to Madrid, even though the Fascist forces were entrenched in the suburbs; they administered a smashing defeat to the confident Italians advancing

[1] A. Mendizabel, *The Martyrdom of Spain*, pp. 264-265.

from the north on that city. But the war in the air they could not fight. Relentlessly, the Fascists with the help of German and Italian planes swept north and west, conquering the poor Basques, who were at once both good Catholics and stanch republicans. With uncalled-for cruelty, low-flying planes carried death and destruction to innumerable small towns. The Loyalists were compelled to abandon Madrid as a capital, though they still kept military control of that city, and they moved their headquarters to Valencia. Then came Franco's drive to separate Valencia from Catalonia. It succeeded, and the Loyalists moved their capital to Barcelona, prepared to put up their last fight in the radical northeast. Soon all of Spain was lost except Madrid and Catalonia; Barcelona fell to the enemy, and the Loyalists, driven up close to the French border, crossed into France. The war was over, Madrid surrendering shortly after.

It had been fought with the utmost ferocity on both sides. The Moors in Franco's employ had been guilty of particularly abominable practices, but for that matter no mercy had been shown by either faction. Meanwhile, the conflict had important repercussions elsewhere in Europe, hastening the military advance of fascism in Italy and Germany, slowly awakening England and France to the dangers which confronted them. But these international aspects of the Spanish Civil War must be left to another chapter.

Austria

The Austrian Republic was proclaimed in Vienna on November 12, 1918, one day after the armistice. In the beginning it was quite democratic, with a constitution resembling that of the Weimar Republic. Slowly but surely, however, the democratic features gave way under the force of circumstances to a full-fledged dictatorship in 1933 under Engelbert Dollfuss, a dictatorship resembling that of Mussolini in certain respects and strikingly different in others.

From the very day of its birth the Austrian Republic was afflicted by two well-nigh incurable diseases—lack of economic self-sufficiency on the one hand and deep-rooted ideological antagonisms on the other. Austria had a large population within a very small area; worse than that, it contained within its borders a large city which once had been the commercial and banking capital of the Danube valley, and which now, having lost its economic hinterland, was in danger of starvation. The plight of Vienna, terrible beyond belief, was alleviated by the League of Nations. In 1922 Britain, France, Italy, and Czechoslovakia backed an international loan through the League for $135,000,000 and Austria struggled to her economic feet, reorganizing her currency and preserving her economic life, albeit with much difficulty, until the international financial crisis of 1929-30.

There were, however, other troubles. The majority of Austrians called themselves socialists; but between the Social Democrats of Vienna, moderate Marxists, and the Christian Socialists of the rural districts there was profound disagreement. The new constitution was federal in character, and since half the money raised by taxation had to be handed over to the particular province in which it was raised, the Social Democrats of Vienna found that they had more money to spend than had the Christian Socialists of the country districts. Vienna spent this money freely in building very decent homes for the working classes and raised increased sums for other social purposes by virtually confiscating the property of the wealthy by high taxes.

The Christian Socialists, much more conservative, disapproved of this radical procedure; they were also attached to the Roman Catholic Church and they hated the agnosticism of the city socialists. They were somewhat akin to the Centre party in Germany, although more powerful, and like that Centre party were really between two extremes, that of the Social Democrats on the left, and that of the Nationalists on the right.

The Austrian Nationalists were divided into two groups; one, under Prince von Starhemberg, was aristocratic, agrarian, Catholic, and, after the advent of Hitler to power, opposed to the submergence of Austria in Germany; the other group consisted of Pan-Germans, clamoring loudly for "*anschluss*," or union with Germany, before long virtually becoming an Austrian Nazi party taking orders from Berlin. Both sections of the Austrian Nationalists added together were in a minority in Austria; but for that matter, neither the Christian Democrats nor the Social Democrats had a majority, and since these two groups would not work in harmony, a democratic government soon became almost an impossibility. The aristocratic Nationalists founded a private army of their own, the Heimwehr, commanded by von Starhemberg; the Social Democrats countered by another private army, the Schutzbund. That of the Nationalists was not opposed to a restoration of the monarchy; it numbered some 60,000 and was better drilled. In the Schutzbund, on the other hand, there were some 100,000 men devoted to the republic; they knew less about fighting, but they did have arms and they were opposed to reaction.

For several years a rather confused political fight followed, mainly along the lines of city against country. During most of that time the Christian Socialists nominally held the reins of government; but they had little jurisdiction over Vienna; their common ground with Starhemberg was slight, and with the Austrian Nazis they had no common ground whatever.

Soon, as the Nazi propaganda spread in Austria, the Christian Socialists under Dollfuss were confronted with a grave decision. Their control of the country was extremely precarious. Dollfuss, an ardent Roman Catholic, was chancellor, and he kept his post by a temporary and tentative alliance with the Social Democrats. The Chancellor sought and obtained the warm friendship of Mussolini as insurance against Hitler and the Nazis. But for it he had to pay a heavy price. The Duce did not like Social Democrats and, to keep the Duce on his side, Dollfuss broke off his alliance with them, and with the help of von Starhemberg established a Christian Socialist dictatorship.

It was not done without severe fighting. The Social Democrats, warned by the example of what had taken place in Germany one year earlier, in 1933, went on general strike. As they did so, Dollfuss sought to disarm them. The Social Democrats thereupon barricaded themselves in the new apartment houses which they had built for the workmen of Vienna and for several days defended them against machine-gun fire. Forced to capitulate, they were disarmed and disbanded and Dollfuss ruled, a Fascist dictator.

It was a "Christian Corporate State" which Dollfuss set up in this year of 1934 with the cordial approval of Mussolini. The republic vanished and democracy vanished with it. A number of corporations with hand-picked members were organized, and these were to elect a president and to rule the country. A parliament was provided with power of veto over the acts of the corporations but with no power of initiating legislation. The real government was Dollfuss, assisted by Starhemberg.

The new Christian Corporate State, having repulsed an attack from the left (the strike of the Social Democrats), was immediately threatened from the right by the Austrian Nazis. With the backing apparently of Hitler, the Austrian Nazis now tried to destroy the Dollfuss regime. Their coup d'état almost succeeded; desperate Austrian Nazis invaded the chancellory and brutally murdered Dollfuss; the radio was about to announce the new revolution, and Austrian refugees on the border in Bavaria were ready to rush across into Austria.

But the plot failed; Mussolini was furious at the murder of his friend Dollfuss, and Hitler at this time was in no condition to oppose the Duce. Starhemberg remained loyal to his late leader and acted promptly. The ringleaders were executed and this curious Christian Fascist state survived the storm. The new chancellor of Austria was Kurt Schuschnigg, and Starhemberg became vice-chancellor.

The dictatorship continued, but it was very weak. The Social Democrats, who might have defended the country against Nazi aggression from Germany, now were no more, and their leaders were in prison or in exile. The Austrian Nazis for the time being had been dispersed or were in jail. But Schuschnigg himself was in the minority and did not dare hold an election. There had not been one since 1930; and Dollfuss, with all his personal charm, had become chancellor with a majority of only one. Schuschnigg had neither charm nor, as events were to prove, the backing of Mussolini. He might have gone ahead without the former but the latter was essential if this tiny Austria was to survive as an independent state. As soon as it suited the Duce to act in conjunction with Hitler, Austria was lost, as we shall note later.

East of Austria

East of Austria, in Hungary and the Balkan states, the general drift of political life went in the direction of totalitarianism. In Hungary, Yugoslavia, and Greece dictatorship rose in the postwar era, and in Bulgaria and Rumania representative government rested on a very shaky foundation.

The history of Hungary may be briefly noted. Here, as in Austria, a republic was proclaimed at the close of the war. Quickly it was snuffed out by a Communist dictatorship, and for nearly six months the red flag flew in Budapest. Then came a counterrevolution, this time to the right, as Admiral Horthy of the old Hapsburg navy set up a restored monarchy without a king, for Horthy ruled simply as regent in a monarchy limited by a parliament of restricted powers, chosen by a narrow suffrage by voters deprived of the protection of the secret ballot.

Hungary was a country of large estates, great landlords, illiterate peasants. The Magyar nobility, retaining its economic and social privileges, was not discontent with the new status quo, that is, within the country. It would not and could not forget the Treaty of Trianon, whereby Hungary had been so tremendously reduced in area. Irredentist ambitions to recover the lost lands showed no signs of abatement with the passing of the years. On the other hand, the government of Hungary was stable as well as arbitrary. Twice did the Magyars' former king, Charles of Hapsburg, lead an expedition to recover his lost throne; twice was he driven back, and even for a while imprisoned. Some day, the Magyars said, they would choose a king; but they were in no hurry to do so, nor were many of them enthusiastic about the House of Hapsburg.

The League of Nations was kind to Hungary, and through its agency large sums were granted to rehabilitate the country. Had it not been for two things—the economic depression of the thirties and the Nazi regime set up in Germany—domestic politics in Hungary might have remained tranquil. But like all other agricultural lands, Hungary was hard hit by the decline of grain prices which was incidental to the depression; and German Nazis, flushed with victory, lost no time in trying to stir up internal discord in Hungary as they did in Austria.

The Hungarian National Socialists (Nazis) used three arguments to good effect—anti-Semitism, revenge for Magyar territory seized by Yugoslavia, Czechoslovakia, and Rumania, and the semisocialistic plea that the big estates should be subdivided among the peasantry. Needless to say, the third of these arguments had little weight with the Magyar nobles; and furthermore, since most Magyars, poor and rich, were ardent

Catholics, the attitude of German Nazis toward the Church of Rome acted as a brake on the growth of an indigenous Nazi party in Hungary. Nevertheless, the Magyar Nazis increased rapidly in number, particularly in 1938 and 1939, as Germany swallowed up Czechoslovakia, offering as she did so tidbits of that former republic's territory to Hungary.

"The Kingdom of the Serbs, Croats, and Slovenes," or Yugoslavia, was torn by internal dissensions from the very beginning. Serbs and Croats soon found that they could not agree; and the Slovenes, by far the weakest element in this triangular grouping, took sides with the Croats. The Serbs, in the majority, were not content with having their capital, Belgrade, the capital of the new kingdom, and with the acceptance of the Serbian dynasty; they also wanted a unified rather than a federalized constitution. The Croats, proud of their culture and tradition, their use of the Latin rather than Cyrillic alphabet, their religion which was Catholic, not Orthodox, looked down upon the more numerous Serbs and were determined to preserve their own particularism.

What almost at times might be described as undeclared war was waged between Serbs and Croats from 1920 to 1939. In the course of it, King Alexander, taking advantage of the perpetual strife in the Yugoslav Parliament, took the reins in his own hands and ruled for a few years as a despot, pure and undefiled. Finally he relinquished part of his authority to a parliament organized on the model of that of Fascist Italy, in so far that whatever political party won a plurality of seats at an election was guaranteed two-thirds of the final membership. Two political assassinations bespoke the low tone of political life in this Yugoslav kingdom. One was that of the leader of the Croatian Peasant party, the spokesman of regionalism and federation; the other that of Alexander, murdered while visiting France by a member of a secret Croatian society. The Serbs thus had a taste of their own medicine, since a secret pan-Serbian society had been responsible for the murder of the Austrian Archduke in 1914. Alexander's oldest son, eleven years of age, was now proclaimed as Peter II of Yugoslavia, and the government, in the hands of a regency, nominally returned to constitutional methods. The Croats, however, were not content; and as the war clouds gathered once more over Europe in 1939, they were actively engaged in plots to disrupt by internal revolt this South Slav kingdom, so large in area, so desperately poor, so torn by internal strife.

Rumania, as far as statistics went, emerged from the First World War a European state of importance, her area doubled by the annexation of Transylvania, Bukovina, Bessarabia, and a large part of the Banat of Temesvar. She was even larger in size than Italy! But beneath the surface there was discord. Minorities were more troublesome in Rumania than in Czechoslovakia and Yugoslavia; Magyars, Jews, Germans, Ukrainians, Russians, and Bulgarians comprised a good quarter of the population; the peasantry, close to Russia and subjected to Communist propaganda, demanded the splitting up of the great landed estates; and as a further source of constant discord there were scandals in the royal family, well aired and well ventilated. When the old King Ferdinand died in 1927 his son and heir, Carol, was living in Paris with a mistress for whom he had sacrificed the throne. The latter's young son, Michael, was proclaimed king, but before long Carol returned to Bucharest to assume the throne for himself. Unsavory quarrels between the Queen Mother, Marie of Rumania, a granddaughter of Victoria of England; Helen, the queen, daughter of the King of Greece; Magda Lupescu, the mistress; and Carol II of Rumania, crowned in 1930 and a most temperamental sovereign, filled the European press and unsettled Rumania still further. As for the King, he ruled sometimes in accordance with constitutional principles and sometimes not. Between fascism, anti-Semitism (the Jews were very numerous in Rumania), communism, the "Green International," a term very loosely applied to the spasmodic efforts of landless peasants in southeastern Europe to obtain land, and the endless friction of the divergent minorities, the position of Carol was far from pleasant.

In Bulgaria the forms of constitutional government were preserved in the intervals between the two World Wars. But the reality was somewhat different from the theory: bombs were thrown, army officers cashiered, and King Boris was now about to become a dictator and now about to refrain from assuming that dangerous role. What might be called a kind of authoritarian democracy characterized the Bulgarian scene, for there continued to be a parliament and within it there were political parties. The only real authority, however, was a group of army officers who pulled the wires in the parliament, their puppet politicians voting in accordance with suggestions, gentle or forceful as the occasion dictated.

Throughout this period Greece swung backward and forward between monarchy and a reputed republicanism, ending up in 1936 under a military dictatorship with General Metaxas at the helm. King Constantine, driven out by the Allies in 1917, came back in triumph to Athens in 1920, only to lose the throne again in 1922 as the result of a disastrous campaign against the insurgent Turks. His son, George, succeeded him, only to be deposed in turn, as a republic was proclaimed in 1923. For the next twelve years there was nothing but confusion and disorder, the venerable and now aged Venizelos trying in vain to bring back some semblance of stability. Premier followed premier during this black period, when Venizelos generally was in eclipse and when it seemed at times as though he was the only patriotic Greek. Suddenly in 1935 the country swung to monarchy once more, the exiled King George returning. As far, however, as one may peer beneath the cloudy uncertainties of Greek politics, the King was but a figurehead for the very capable and conservative Metaxas, who ruled with an iron hand until his death in January, 1941.

Throughout all the Balkans there was little evidence of any progress, and none at all of stability during the postwar period. Everywhere there seemed to be a regression to some form of despotism and arbitrary rule. So was it also with various other small countries in Europe, too unimportant for detailed analysis, such as Albania, Portugal, and the tiny independent states south of the Baltic—Estonia, Latvia, and Lithuania. Dictatorships, veiled, open, semi-veiled, were the lot of all of them. Indeed, of the new countries brought into being by the peace treaties of 1919, Finland and Czechoslovakia alone showed signs of progress during these distressing times.

Chapter 35

THE MIDDLE EAST DURING TWENTY YEARS ARMISTICE (1919-39)

THE MIDDLE EAST is a blanket term covering Asia Minor, the Arabian peninsula, the Tigris-Euphrates Valley and Egypt, all formerly part of the Ottoman Empire. And probably one should also include in it Persia, directly to the east of Mesopotamia, since it too was a Moslem country, vexed by many of the same problems which confronted its neighbors: economic distress, nationalistic uprisings, xenophobia, and dictatorship.

Turkey

In 1919 the fortunes of the Ottoman Empire seemingly had reached their nadir. Continuously at war since 1911, except for a few months between the second Balkan and the first World Wars, Turkey seemed done for. The victorious Allies were in possession of Constantinople, of the Tigris-Euphrates Valley, of Palestine and Syria. It never occurred to them that they would have trouble in partitioning the Sultan's realm as they saw fit. They determined that the Turks should be excluded entirely from the Arabian peninsula, the French and the British sharing that enormous area, for the most part divided into various mandates under the League of Nations. Then, by the Treaty of Sèvres (1920) which three Turks were dragooned into signing, Greece was extended eastward to include Thrace and Adrianople so that only a tiny strip of Europe was left to the Turks behind Constantinople. Even that ancient capital of the Ottomans was not given to the Turks in full sovereignty, since a wide zone on either side of the Sea of Marmora was to be controlled by an international commission. Greece was accorded the choicest part of the western littoral of Asia Minor around Smyrna, where there were many Greeks. By an Anglo-Franco-Italian agreement, the southern coast (Adalia) was to fall to Italy, and the French were to preëmpt for themselves Cilicia, directly north of Syria. The Turks were to be pushed inland to the upland plateaus and highlands, and not even all of these inferior districts remained to them, since two republics were planned in

690

eastern Asia Minor, Kurdistan, and Armenia, it being hoped that the United States would assume responsibility for the latter as a mandate under the League of Nations.

This Treaty of Sèvres, harsher than that of Versailles, harsher even than that of Brest-Litovsk, was well-named "the porcelain treaty," for like Sèvres china it was easily shattered, and that almost immediately. Turkey, like Prussia in 1807, France in 1871, and Germany in 1919, took on a new lease of life, under the guidance of one of the most remarkable men of the twentieth century.

Mustafa Kemal, the "Ghazi," the Victorious One, or Ataturk, as he chose finally to be known, takes rank with Hitler, Mussolini, Gandhi, and Sun Yat-sen in any summary of twentieth-century nationalism. In a way his accomplishments were more notable than those of these distinguished gentlemen, since starting with nothing he accomplished well-nigh everything, not simply throwing off the yoke of the conqueror but revolutionizing the religion, the language, the very mores of his countrymen.

In 1908, as the Young Turks marched on Constantinople, Kemal was a colonel in the Turkish army. A brusque and silent man, but highly patriotic, he had long been a suspected revolutionary. Under the Young Turks he served as chief of staff against the Bulgars; before that he had fought against the Italians in Tripoli; and after that against the British in the Gallipoli campaign, against the Russians in the Caucasus, and against the British once more in Syria. At the conclusion of the First World War he did his best to persuade the Sultan not to submit to humiliating terms of peace. Failing in this, he left Constantinople to assume command of the gendarmes which the Allies permitted the Turks to maintain in Anatolia.

Mustafa Kemal put himself at the head of a Turkish nationalistic movement which defied both Sultan and Allies. The Sultan tried to break the growing influence of his general by urging the Kurds to attack him, and failed; the Allies, inviting the Turkish nationalists to a conference at Constantinople, arrested and deported many; but they also failed, since the suspicious Kemal refused to attend. Instead, he raised an army of some 25,000 ill-paid and ragged troops.

Whereupon the Allies bethought themselves of the Greeks, and the latter, encouraged by a British loan, drove inland at Kemal from Smyrna with 80,000 soldiers. In 1921, at the Sakkaria River in central Asia Minor, they were met by Kemal, and a fourteen-day battle ended such rosy dreams as King Constantine of Greece might have harbored of a restored Magna Græcia. Almost instantly the wily French saw the writing on the wall and withdrew from Cilicia, and soon afterward the Italians gave up their claims to Adalia.

The Greeks, however, still thought they had the backing of England and continued to fight. Kemal forced them back to the sea. Their retreat became a rout, and early in 1922 they evacuated Smyrna as the Turks swept into that city. England was very angry at both the French and the Turks: at the former because they had given up Cilicia without conferring with the English and because, it was rumored, the thrifty French had sold old uniforms and rifles to Kemal; at the latter because they had humiliated England's friend, Venizelos. England still held the Dardanelles and landed troops on the Asiatic side to bar the way to Kemal so that he might have no chance of pursuing the Greeks into Thrace. But Lloyd George thought better of it; the beating of the war drum in 1922 sounded but dimly in the Dominions, and England refused to enforce the Treaty of Sèvres by unilateral action. She tried to settle the Turkish problem by negotiating with the Turkish Sultan, ignoring the Turkish Nationalists led by Kemal; but the latter deposed the Sultan, who fled Constantinople on a British warship. Then England consented to confer with Kemal and his National Parliament. At Lausanne in 1923 a treaty was struck whereby all Anatolia, as well as Constantinople, Adrianople, and eastern Thrace were recognized as integral parts of an independent Turkey, and whereby, in a separate Græco-Turkish convention, all those Greeks within its borders were to be deported to Greece, in exchange for Kemal's promise to accept in Turkey all Turks still remaining in Greece. This same year Turkey became a republic. Its President was Mustafa Kemal, commander of the Turkish army, creator and master of the one political party recognized by Parliament. Thus, within five years after the great powers forced a negotiated peace, he drove out the conqueror and restored the independence of his country. A military dictatorship could have been his for the asking but he preferred one of a different sort. In the very year of Lausanne (1923) a Turkish republic was proclaimed and a constitution adopted. Under it the Ghazi was a man of unique power. He became president of the republic, president of the council of ministers, president of the assembly, and president of the people's party—the only one which the law recognized. Like Mussolini he did not hesitate to fill many offices at the same time, and like Mussolini again he took great delight in introducing startling innovations.

Only in the case of the Ghazi they were more numerous and more fundamental than those introduced in any postwar country with the possible exception of Russia. For the Ghazi was determined to "Westernize" Turkey from the very roots, not simply in laws, religion, and economics but in language, culture, and even clothes.

The sultanate had already been abolished, but the califate remained, and a relative of the ex-Sultan was calif, still holding, as representative of the Osmanli line, this ecclesiastical primacy honored by a large part of the Moslem world. Mustafa Kemal determined to divorce his country entirely from any theocratic traditions, and therefore he abolished the califate and drove into exile all remaining members of the Osmanli family. The legal code of Turkey was then transformed. All legal sanctions derived from the Koran and Moslem jurisprudence were ended; and the new Turkey took over the Swiss code as the basis of its civil law, its criminal being based on legal prescripts drawn from the Italian and German codes, and its commercial law based on the German. At this wholesale destruction of the religious foundations of Turkey, the principal Moslem state, there were loud outcries, and in the east the Kurds rose in rebellion. Speedily they were crushed by an army of 80,000 and the leader of the rebellion executed in the public square of Angora. Turkey was to be a secular state!

Its capital was placed not at Constantinople, henceforth known as Istanbul, but at Angora, renamed, Ankara. This desolate, windswept town in central Asia Minor forthwith became the center from which the ever restless and ceaselessly active Kemal spread reform after reform among his thirteen million fellow Turks.

Among these the most striking was the persistent and successful effort to change the costume of the Turks. The red fez, customary headgear, was abolished, and Turks were compelled to wear hats. First the Ghazi shocked everyone by appearing in a Panama; then he introduced the képi, or brimmed cap of the soldier, into the army; then all civil servants were ordered to wear European hats with brims; and finally, all who did not voluntarily adopt the new headgear were imprisoned. By the same method the salaam or oriental greeting was made illegal, and so also the wearing of veils by women. The personal appearance of the Turks was thus Westernized.

Turkey went Western all the way in regard to women; they were given the franchise; they were elected to Parliament; they were encouraged to enter business; they were forced out of their Eastern seclusion. And all this was done partly by example, partly by statute. The Ghazi was neither anchorite nor puritan, and was much given to cocktail parties and to dances, always, however, with women present. Those who sought his favor copied his manner. Women found it worthwhile to dress according to the latest Parisian fashion and men found that it helped advance their interests to swing their partners. "Oriental music no longer satisfies the Turkish soul," so said the Ghazi, and promptly Oriental music ceased. Soon in this land, where from time immemorial man and woman never walked together in public but always the man in advance, the woman humbly following, mixed classes of boys and girls were studying the nude of both sexes in art schools.

We must change our language, said the Ghazi, as he set the example by taking the name Kemal Ataturk. Arabic words, Greek words, French words must be exorcised from speech and pen. Turkish must be pure; Turkish must no longer be written from right to left but in the reverse or Western fashion; nor were the old characters to be used, for in the

West Latin characters were customary. There were not many printing presses in the country, and such as Turkey did possess had no Latin type; that made no difference; it must be bought. Not many Turks could read and write, and those who could found it irksome to learn the trick all over again. Nevertheless, it had to be done. First, on the postage stamps appeared the new letters; then they blossomed forth again on the paper currency; then it was announced that beginning in 1929 no printed matter might legally appear in Arabic type. Indefatigable in this reform was Ataturk; he gave lessons in the new script to all and sundry; he would stop in the middle of a state ball and with chalk in hand would explain on a blackboard how good Turks must in the future write their letters. His enthusiasm was contagious; all Turkey went to school; and soon books began to appear in purified Turkish, written with Latin characters.

Ataturk was also interested in everything that concerned economics and the physical well-being of his people. He found a country which still plowed with wooden sticks shod with iron, and harrowed with logs weighed down with stones; a country without banking facilities, or railroads worthy the name; disease-ridden, unsanitary, without irrigation, and without manufacturers. Problems like these were grist to Ataturk's mill. Olives and figs, cotton and tobacco were developed by him as staple crops; medical inspections were held; the ravages of syphilis were reduced; agricultural experts were hired; prize cattle were bought; railroads were laid; and the village of Angora grew into the avenue-lined city of Ankara. Nor was defense neglected; the straits were fortified; armaments were bought in both Germany and England with fine impartiality; and a merchant marine was started.

Ataturk planned wisely but he forgot one thing—nature. He lived not only vividly but too richly. Tobacco, wine, women, endless labor, and endless dissipation took heavy toll, and in 1938 he died in his fifty-eighth year.

Palestine

Stretching south from Turkey for thousands of miles lay Arabia, for the most part a tremendous desert, with oases here and there and certain fertile strips of land, particularly on the Mediterranean littoral and in the east where the Tigris-Euphrates Valley joined Arabia to the Asiatic mainland. Lost to the Ottoman Empire by the First World War, Arabia was in a ferment after it, the scattered nomadic tribesmen who comprised most of its population having in many instances drunk the heady wine of nationalistic aspiration and being quite uncertain what to do next.

Arabian postwar history can scarcely be taken up with the peninsula as a unit, for such a history must inevitably stress growing nationalism;

and since there never was an Arabia in the national sense, it is necessary that we turn to certain sections such as Palestine, Syria, and Iraq, and from them perhaps draw some conclusions as to the drift of affairs in the Arab world.

The history of Palestine during the twenty years' armistice between two European wars was confused, hectic, contradictory. In 1917 it was the happy thought of the British government that this ancient foyer of Jewry might become again a Jewish national home, and to make it such the British government publicly pledged itself. In doing so it forgot two important facts: first, that the Arabs in Palestine outnumbered the Jews eight or nine to one; and second, that those Arabs who had enlisted to help the British drive the Turks and Germans back through Palestine and Syria into Asia Minor during the last half of the war considered, rightly or wrongly, that Britain had promised an independent Arab state which would include Palestine. Britain, however, stuck by her word to the Jews. There had been no such formal pledge to the Arabs as there had been to the Jews; and furthermore such assurances as had been given the former were not to be interpreted, so said the British, as including Palestine. There was plenty of room in the peninsula for an independent Arab state without including Palestine, the British asserted; so they went ahead with their plans for a Jewish national home protected by Britain as a mandate under the League of Nations—Britain thus to be trustee for civilization, and incidentally for Jewish Zionists.

When the plans for this new state were published in 1922, both Jews and Arabs were dissatisfied, the former discovering that Britain, with the necessity of mollifying many million Moslems within her empire, had no intention of creating a purely Jewish state; the latter displeased that there was even the rough semblance of one and angry that Sir Herbert Samuel, an English Jew, should be the first governor.

Samuel tried to hold the balance even between Arab and Jew; to his advisory council he named four Moslems, three Christians and three Jews, a fact which pleased neither Jew nor Arab; he limited to a certain degree Jewish immigration, a fact which angered the Jews but did not satisfy the Arabs, who did not want any immigration at all. Before long the British were at their wits' end. It was not that Palestine was unprosperous. London made no charge for the imperial troops which garrisoned the mandate and defense therefore cost nothing. Meanwhile, into the country poured much Jewish money which went for power plants on the Jordan River, for building a new university at Jerusalem, for the construction of a Jewish city at Tel-Aviv on the sea coast, for the purchase of land from Arabs for Jewish agricultural colonies. What caused increased unhappiness and riots, ultimately bordering on civil war, was the conflict between Jewish and Arab nationalisms. The Jewish Zionists, enthusiastic, and well financed, looked forward to the resurrection of a

Jewish state; the Arabs, both within Palestine and without, awakening, perhaps, for the first time in their history to a sense of national conscious-ness, considered Palestine theirs, resented the presence of the Jewish interloper, and opposed all British schemes for the division of power between Jew and Arab.

Meanwhile, the immigrants, mainly from Poland and Rumania, in-creased rapidly, doubling the Jewish population by 1929. The Arabs began to fear for their land, not the wealthy Arabs who sold it to the incomer, but the Arab peasants who found themselves dispossessed by the new owners. These peasants attacked the immigrants and killed many; but the British sent reinforcements to Palestine and preserved order; and as they did so world Jewry continued to pour money into Palestine. That country scarcely felt the depression of the early thirties, so great was the influx of new capital; Haifa was made a modern port, and from it, all the way across the desert a pipe-line was laid to Mosul, thus tapping the oil fields of the upper Euphrates Valley. There was even talk of a railroad to Bagdad.

And still the Jews flocked into Palestine. The advent of Hitler in Germany stimulated their advent greatly, so much so that in 1935 no less then sixty thousand reached the land of promise, and the Jews by that date had increased to almost one-third of the entire population. Thereupon, the next year the Arabs declared a general strike in which a thousand lives were lost.

This resulted in the British sending a Royal Commission to Palestine in 1937 to investigate and to recommend. It produced a report which angered both Jew and Arab. The Commission proposed that Palestine be divided into two independent countries, one Jewish, one Arab. The mandate of the League of Nations, which Britain held, was to be ended, but the cities of Jerusalem and Bethlehem, sacred to both Jew and Arab as well as to Christian, were to continue under British protection and were to belong to neither of the two new countries.

The report was a counsel of despair. The two new states would be too small to be self-sufficient units, for the total area of even the undivided Palestine was only approximately that of Wales or Vermont. The pro-posed Jewish state, the smaller in area but with the best land, contained some 300,000 Arabs who would have to be uprooted somehow and placed elsewhere. And even into this Jewish state, immigration on any considerable scale was to be forbidden for a number of years, just at a time when Jews throughout all Central and Eastern Europe were des-perately seeking a harbor of refuge. The Arab state suggested would be larger and was promised access to the sea; but that was small comfort to Arab nationalists, who pointed to the original promises made to them by the British high commissioner to Egypt as early as 1915, when they plotted in connivance with him to revolt against Turkey. The report of the Commission glossed over these promises and did not even mention certain British guarantees to prominent Arabs in 1918, assuring them that their political and economic rights would be safeguarded in the new Palestine.

The Arabs now rose in arms and the British found it necessary to dispatch several thousand troops to Palestine. Concentration camps were established, Arabs were deported, sporadic attacks on Jews sternly punished. The partition commission, sent out in 1938 to draw up the boundaries of the two new states, gave up its task as hopeless, and a conference of Zionists and Arabs in London in 1939 accomplished just nothing at all. In view of the fast approach of world war in that year, it seemed best to the British to postpone further action, but in the meantime to close all immigration to the land of Canaan for the time being to many thousand Jews who clamored for entrance.

Lebanon and Syria

In 1916 the Russians, French, and British made a secret agreement dividing the Turkish Empire between them. The share allotted to France was generous; it included Lebanon and Syria to the north and east of Palestine, reached deep into Asia Minor still further north, and toward the east even beyond the headwaters of the Tigris. After the war the claims of the French were drastically cut, but they did receive, in the final settlement, Lebanon and Syria as a Class A mandate under the League.

For a time it appeared as though France would prove herself even more unsatisfactory as a mandate power in Lebanon and Syria than England in Palestine. There was no Jewish problem to perplex the French, but the Arab nationalism with which they had to deal was at once more vociferous and better organized than Arab nationalism in Palestine, and the French had the added necessity of stepping warily between a great variety of religious faiths, for there were numerous sects of Christians, like the Maronites, and divergent brands of Mohammedanism, such as that professed by the Druses, a warlike, schismatic Moslem tribe, in Lebanon and Syria.

For a good sixteen years after the establishment of the French mandate in 1920 there was serious trouble. Part of it may be traced to the French demand that the mandate should be in the name of two different countries rather than one, for from the beginning the French favored Lebanon, a narrow stretch of territory facing the Mediterranean, over Syria which lay behind it, although neither geographically nor racially was there good reason for so doing.

But there was a reason of another sort. Lebanon, with its capital at Beirut was for the most part Christian, and French influence there had been strong since time immemorial; Syria, on the other hand, was almost entirely Moslem. Therefore the French favored the former land at the expense of the latter, a policy which was shortsighted in the long run, for by enlarging Lebanon as they did, they brought within its boundaries a large group of hostile Moslems, while at the same time, by shutting off Syria from the sea, they antagonized the Moslems residing there and increased the xenophobia already prevalent among them.

Then, too, the French were too eager to gallicize both Lebanon and Syria. They did not realize that paternal methods which succeeded with barbaric tribes of Africa were inapplicable to this more settled and more highly developed corner of the Arabian peninsula. The French, for instance, were eager to spread their language through the schools, to teach Arab children to sing the "Marseillaise"; and the more they insisted on planting their own culture down upon the Syrians, the more restless the latter became.

Finally, by 1926, there was open rebellion. It began among the Druses in the hill country and then spread widely. There was fierce fighting in Damascus, the capital of Syria. The French bombarded its most crowded quarters both from the air and from the citadel. Thereupon the civilized world was shocked and the French high commissioner was withdrawn. From Paris came orders for a change in policy.

For the next ten years there was constant pressure put upon the French by Arab nationalities to withdraw altogether from Syria, and constant yielding of small points at issue by France. There were arrests, there were strikes, but there was no more open rebellion. Finally, in 1936, the French gave way almost entirely and signed treaties with Lebanon and Syria. In effect these recognized Syria and Lebanon as independent states which were to be admitted to the League of Nations, thus bringing the mandate to an end. The treaties were made for a duration of twenty-five years, and while they were in force France was to be permitted two airplane bases in Syria and the right to station troops in two specified areas; in Lebanon, she retained the right to station troops wherever she saw fit. The final solution, on the whole, was an Arab victory.

Iraq and Saudi Arabia

In 1920, when France received Syria as a mandate, the British obtained another on similar terms—the Tigris-Euphrates Valley with its three important cities, Mosul on the upper Tigris, Bagdad on the middle Tigris, and Basrah sixty miles above the Persian Gulf, at the confluence of the two rivers of ancient Mesopotamia. All indications pointed to a difficult and not too lucrative future for the British in this new outpost of empire. Even as they secured their mandate, a revolt of the native tribesmen kept these trustees of civilization cooped up in the cities. The Arabs had no chance of winning; the British airplanes were a guarantee against that. On the other hand, the pacification of this region, known as Iraq, was very expensive, and the British in 1920 were seeking no further expansion by land or sea. Consequently, a policy of nonintervention with strict economy was adopted.

The boundary of Iraq joined on the west that of the British mandate for Palestine and that of the French for Syria. The eastern part of their Palestine mandate the British early cut off from Palestine proper, re-naming it Transjordania—now known as Jordan. No Jews were to be ad-mitted, this a sop to Arab nationalism. Meanwhile Jordan would provide an airplane base on the way to India. Iraq's other western neighbor, Syria, was in the midst of turmoil, for the French were driving out of Damascus, Feisal, a former ally of Britain in the World War who had been chosen King of Syria by local Arabs. Why not then transfer Feisal from Damascus to Bagdad and set up a new kingdom there of Iraq? To do so would relieve the French of further trouble with Feisal, would placate the latter by giving him another throne, would put England in the good graces of the Arab world, and would bring to an end the beastly expense of governing Iraq, for the rebellion there in 1920 had cost Britain £40,000,000.

Feisal, it seemed, was willing to accept an election to the new throne, and was proclaimed king in 1921. His reign lasted twelve years, and fruitful years they turned out to be. It was a desolate region over which he governed and the three million inhabitants of this new kingdom, brutalized by Turkish misrule, occupied a region half desert, half swamp. To imbue them with patriotic spirit for an invented country called for skill, patience, and perseverance. Feisal possessed all three qualities.

Troublesome was the situation in the North, in the neighborhood of Mosul. The population here consisted largely of Kurds, a non-Arab Moslem folk whom Turkey desired to join to their fellow-Kurds in Kurdistan. But it would never do to let go the oil of Mosul, so argued the British admiralty, and Mosul was made an integral part of the new Iraq. But the British had pacified this country very largely by employing as soldiers the Assyrians, supposedly a Christian folk of Nestorian antece-dents, and Feisal had both Kurds and Assyrians, unhappy and dissatisfied.

Four different treaties were struck with Britain during Feisal's reign, all of them marking successive stages of devolution on Britain's part, until finally, in 1930, one was drawn up whereby Iraq and Britain became allies in case of future war, the former granting certain facilities in respect to air bases, the latter agreeing to provide officers to train Iraq's army. In 1933 the treaty went into effect, the mandate ended, Iraq became a member of the League of Nations, and Feisal died.

His death was a signal for renewed troubles. The poor Assyrians, having lost their protector, England, crossed the border into Syria looking for new homes. Not finding them, they tried to get back into Iraq and were massacred by the Iraqi. Feisal's young son proved less able than his father, and before long (1936) a military dictator threatened to bring an end to such trifling constitutional guarantees of liberty as Iraq had achieved. He was careful, however, not to interfere with the oil route (Mosul to Haifa via pipe-line), or with the imperial British air route, which went via Jerusalem to Jordan, through Iraq to India, Singapore, and Australia.

The greater part of Arabia lay far to the south of Palestine, Syria, and Iraq. Here stretched the inhospitable desert over which roamed bands of nomadic Bedouins, loosely—very loosely—belonging to five separate Arab kingdoms, with boundaries ill defined and political authority shifting back and forth like the sands of the desert.

Of the five kingdoms, three were particularly important—the Hedjaz to the east of the Red Sea, Nejd in the interior of the peninsula, and Yemen in the southwest corner, bordered by the Red Sea on one side, the Indian Ocean on the other.

Again, of the three kingdoms, that of the Hedjaz seemed the more likely to gain the permanent hegemony over the peninsula; within its borders were the holy places, Mecca and Medina, and over it ruled Husein, father of Feisal of Iraq.

Husein, however, ran into difficulties; he had assumed the califate over the Moslem world without due thought to the susceptibilities of other Arabs; he was blamed for French activities in Syria and for Jewish activities in Palestine; and he refused to sign a treaty with Britain because that country demanded that he acknowledge the British mandate for Palestine. Therefore, when he lost British support, he could not withstand the energetic Ibn Saud, ruler of Nejd and regions adjacent thereto.

The followers of the latter were puritanical as well as fanatical Arabs; they were Wahabis, Moslem fundamentalists who harked back to the primitive rigors of the Moslem code, and they had no use for the wine-bibbers of the Hedjaz. Under Ibn Saud they attacked Husein, captured Mecca, and annexed the entire kingdom of the Hedjaz (1926). Shortly after, Ibn Saud led his Wahabis against the Yemen. That kingdom he did not annex, although he absorbed oases adjacent to it.

Ibn Saud proved himself a decidedly efficient administrator; he obtained from England recognition of his independence; he entered into treaty relations with other states; he established permanent colonies for wandering tribesmen, trying to teach them to live in houses rather than in tents; and best of all he brought law and order to the caravan routes which traversed the desert, ending brigandage, introducing motorcars and the wireless.

Iran

Persia suffered severely during the First World War. The nationalists, annoyed for many years by Anglo-Russian control of their country, favored the Central Powers. Upon receiving encouragement from the Turks to wage a Holy War on behalf of Islam and aided by German gold, they revolted against the puppet government of Teheran and twice defeated the Russians and the British in the field. Later in the war their cause looked even brighter, when the Bolshevik Revolution of 1917 led to the withdrawal of Russian troops. But the British had their eyes not only on Iraq to the west, but on Afghanistan and Baluchistan to the east. They could not suffer a loss of prestige at this critical moment, and also they had in mind Persian oil. Troops were needed, and troops were sent, and the British were able by 1918 to sweep through Persia, all the way to the Caspian.

In 1919 Persia tried to gain admission to the Versailles Congress, but a British veto barred the way, as in the case of Egypt and Ireland. England was "top dog" and was determined to remain so, for both political and economic reasons. This same year she concluded a treaty with the de facto Persian government, whereby in return for a loan of £2,000,000 she gained the power of dictating the economic and political policies of that country to whatever extent she deemed necessary. The idea that Persia should be given to Britain as a mandate under the League was rejected; the Anglo-Persian treaty was a much simpler method of control.

This treaty was highly unpopular in Persia and almost immediately there was civil war. The Nationalists declared a provisional republic, hoping with Communist aid to drive the British out of the country. They made good headway, but their Russian allies demanded that the red flag be hoisted and the Persians refused. Russia withdrew and the revolt collapsed.

Scarcely, however, had it died down before it was renewed, this time by a nationalist coup d'état which captured Teheran and overthrew the government. The rebels lost no time; they instantly repudiated the British treaty, and they drew up a long list of social and political reforms.

Prominent among the rebels was Rheza Khan Pahlavi, commander of the Persian army and soon the most influential man in the country. As minister of war he worked in close harmony with Dr. Millspaugh, recommended by the American State Department as economic adviser. The two men achieved wonders; they unified the country, balanced the budget, opened schools, built roads. Pahlavi acted as a kind of advance agent for Millspaugh, conquering and subduing restless tribesmen, the American following after with plans of economic rehabilitation.

Meanwhile, Pahlavi grew more and more popular; in 1923 he became Prime Minister while still keeping command of the army; in 1926 he deposed the weak and useless Shah and proclaimed himself Shah-in-Shah. Pahlavi's career runs parallel in many ways to that of Ataturk: he abolished the old; he introduced the new. He changed the name of Persia to Iran; modern hats had to be worn; women were sent to schools, and coeducational ones, at that; railroads were ordered and a huge railroad station built in the capital (this before the railroads); the Persian language was purified; the priests were held in check (not to the extent that they were in Turkey, for the Persians were more religiously inclined than the Turks); the capitulations were abolished; foreigners lost all power.

Yet between the dictator of the new Iran and his Turkish counterpart one striking difference was to be noted—Pahlavi was the more Asiatic in temper; he insisted on surrounding himself with a good deal of pomp; he was difficult to meet; he always traveled in style, the roads being kept clear of all traffic when he and his retinue made royal progress in their motor cavalcade. Justice was more Oriental in Iran than in Turkey, and men critical of the Shah-in-Shah simply disappeared. Pahlavi was very sensitive to criticism; his private life was hidden; how many children he had was a matter of guesswork.

But he made Iran independent, very much so. He refused to build railroads where the British wanted them; he would not permit the latter to use Iran for their imperial air communications; and what is more he drove a sharp bargain with the Anglo-Persian Oil Company, almost an adjunct of the royal navy. That company was already paying from £1,000,000 to £2,000,000 a year to the treasury of Iran in royalties; but that was not sufficient for Pahlavi. In 1932 he threatened to close down the company altogether. The British appealed to the League of Nations; but Pahlavi was not to be moved; the company must pay a great deal more. It consented to do so, the royalty was changed from a share of the profits to a base rate per ton, and Iran's share of this new-found wealth increased promptly several hundred per cent.

Egypt

The story of England's relation to Egypt during the interval between the World Wars parallels in some ways her relation to Ireland. In the land of the Pharaohs there was seething discontent; and the rising tide of nationalism noticeable everywhere in the postwar world led to nasty riots in Cairo and other Egyptian cities, directed against the protectorate which England had proclaimed over Egypt during the war. These demonstrations Britain alternately met by stiff opposition and conciliatory concession; with the emphasis on the latter word, for military occupation of the Nile Valley was expensive and the British lion was in a generally pacifistic mood.

Three times did Britain yield to Egyptian pressure. In 1922 she announced that Egypt was "an independent national state," but coupled this declaration with the acceptance by Egypt of reservations in regard to the stationing of British troops there and the acknowledgment that foreign interests in that land were under British protection. The Egyptians, greatly irked by these "safeguards," refused to ratify the treaty which embodied them. Followed then more riots and the assassination of the British governor-general of the Sudan. Thereupon the British levied heavy fines and seized customs houses. Then, when MacDonald became Prime Minister again in 1929, the British held out the olive branch; they offered a treaty whereby their troops would be withdrawn to the canal zone, Egypt to be completely independent but joined in military alliance with Britain. Once again the Egyptian Parliament refused ratification, and a final settlement was not made until 1936. The agreement reached on that date was on the model of the British proposals of 1929. It called for a military alliance, but the Egyptians were under no obligation to fight unless Egypt was invaded. The British agreed to limit their peace-time forces to 10,000 soldiers and to station them only in the canal zone. Naval bases at Alexandria and Port Said were granted to Britain, likewise the right to move troops over Egypt in time of war. The Sudan was to remain under British control, with special rights there reserved for Egypt. In accordance with this treaty Egypt broke off relations with Germany in 1939 but did not declare war on that country.

Here were a congeries of associated problems calling for expert statesmanship. Not only did they involve self-determination for subject nationalities but also the entry of Israel on the diplomatic stage, a tiny enclave of Arabia as far as area went, but a stick of political dynamite thrust into a world of anti-Semitic Arabs who were, themselves, Semites. The results thereof we shall read later.

Chapter 36

INDIA AND THE FAR EAST (1919-39)

India

THE FIRST WORLD WAR gave a tremendous boost to Indian nationalism. The British lost a great deal of prestige when General Townshend surrendered to the Turks in 1916, and the Indians feared their overlords less than before. In addition, the winged words of President Wilson in regard to self-determination had due repercussion in India. Many thousand native Indian troops were serving on the western front, and Indians back home expected England to show her gratitude for Indian support by concessions in the way of political devolution.

They were not altogether disappointed. In 1917 the British government pledged itself to develop in India "self-governing institutions with a view to the progressive realization of responsible government in India as an integral part of the British empire." After the war in 1919 this promise was implemented by what were called the Montague-Chelmsford reforms. They did four things for India: (*a*) they decentralized the government by giving a wider degree of autonomy to the provinces; (*b*) they introduced into the provinces a new constitutional device known as the dyarchy, whereby representative government was permitted in respect to certain limited governmental functions, that is, elected legislative bodies were placed in full control of the administration of forests, sanitation, and so forth, while more important functions, such as those dealing with justice and finance, remained still under the direct supervision of the governor; (*c*) they greatly enlarged the electorate, both for the provincial and the central legislatures; (*d*) they decreased the proportion of nominated members for the upper chamber of the central legislature (the council of state) so that it was slightly under half, and of the lower chamber (the assembly) so that it was about one-third.

These reforms were not ungenerous. The viceroy still held in reserve great power, and the property qualification remained high; but it surely would have been contrary to British precedent to have gone further at this time. What really caused trouble in India was not the paucity of reform but rather the Rowlatt Bills and Mohandas Gandhi.

704

The Rowlatt Bills, in force during the war, suspended guarantees of individual liberty, such as the right of habeas corpus and trial by jury, and made it legal for the government of India to deport agitators without trial. That these bills continued to be in force after the peace aroused the antagonism of Gandhi, soon to be known as the Mahatma, or Holy One.

That emaciated little Hindu lawyer had distinguished himself many years before the war by leading a strike of Hindu coolies in South Africa to protest against racial discrimination. He was an ardent pleader for Indian nationalism, but believed that it should be won by noncoöperation and nonresistance, not by force. The foolish British forbade him to travel in certain districts of India and put him in jail when he went there. Their doing so led to instant riots, and in view of the dramatic events connected with them, the specific reforms which the British had introduced received little attention.

For Gandhi had captured the imagination of the Hindu peoples. His teachings were summed up in his doctrine of *satyagraha*, or spiritual nonresistance. To practice it, one must (*a*) boycott all government functions, government schools, and law courts; (*b*) one must boycott foreign-made goods and buy only those produced in India. Thus, and thus only, could *swaraj* (self-determination), be secured.

Now between boycott and physical violence there is no necessary connection; none the less, the two are apt to go hand in hand. So it proved in India. The followers of Gandhi were not content to shun cloth made in England; they made bonfires of it. The result was an increase in rioting. Furthermore, it now happened that the more zealous Sikhs, disciples of the Mahatma, attracted the attention of the world by an exhibition of nonviolence. Anxious to recover a certain sacred shrine which the government had decided belonged to certain other Sikhs, they advanced on their temple unarmed. Felled to the ground by the *laithis* (bamboo rods shod with iron) of the police, they continued for six weeks to practise this painful sort of martyrdom. Gandhi, reproaching himself for all acts of violence taking place in India, pleaded guilty of causing them and accepted a jail sentence of six years gratefully.

Meanwhile, the experience of the Indians with popular elections was not altogether happy. The more ardent disciples of the Mahatma boycotted the elections. Other nationalists, however, participated, and were known as Swarajists, standing for independence. For the time being they professed that they would be satisfied with dominion status; but even that was displeasing to the British, who expected a ten-year trial term of the new reforms before further devolution was demanded. The Swarajists, however, were impatient; to annoy the government they threw out the budget, and to carry on administration the viceroy was forced to certify it on his own responsibility.

India, indeed, presented a complicated and anarchic picture during the middle twenties. The Nationalists were divided among themselves as to what should be done. Friction between Hindus and Moslems was rife. The Moslems were poorer than the Hindus and also less well educated. On the other hand, they came from fighting stock; at one time they had conquered India, and they felt competent to do so again. They laughed at many of the sacred tenets of the Hindu faith. Every year they were accustomed to kill a cow to celebrate the anniversary of the sacrifice of Isaac offered by Abraham. But according to the Mahatma the cow "is the poem of pity. . . . She is the mother to millions of Indian mankind." Little wonder there was strife in "Congress," as the annual convocation of Indian nationalists was called.

Even the Hindus in that congress did not agree among themselves. Gandhi was not interested in voting and in contesting the political control of England in Indian legislatures. He put more and more emphasis on the resuscitation of ancient Hindu culture by trying to revive the spinning wheel and by manufacturing *khaddar*, home-woven cloth. The Indian peasant, he argued, was idle for many months in the year, and if he would spend his time with handloom and spinning wheel he would get rid of the moneylender, and India would become economically independent of England. He set the example by spinning virtuously, and soon it became fashionable in nationalistic circles to copy him. One could even pay one's dues to Congress by spinning a certain quantity of thread.

The British decided in 1927 to send a royal commission to India to report on progress and to make recommendations for the future. The trial period of ten years for the reforms promulgated in 1919 would soon be up and it would be well if full discussion preceded any further change. Heading the commission was Sir John Simon, an English Liberal, who with all the other members was immediately boycotted in India. The Nationalists had no grudge against Simon; the shout, "Simon, go back," simply meant that they were indignant that native-born Indians had no representation on the commission. The British were logical; they wanted a unanimous report of some kind and they knew that it would be impossible to get one if conflicting Indian opinions were represented on the board of inquiry. But there are times when tact is more important than logic, and for all the good it did, the commission might just as well never have sailed from England. Nevertheless, that commission did make a report; in guarded terms and with many qualifications, it recommended three things: (a) doing away with dyarchy, which it admitted was a failure, and the substitution for it of greater Indian responsibility in actual administration; (b) a further enlargement of the suffrage, for there had been only 5,000,000 Indians given the right to vote by the reforms of 1919, whereas there were over 250,000,000 people in British India alone; (c) decentralization, to be gained by making the provinces more autonomous and by federalizing the whole peninsula, the native princes to give up their independent status.

This was not at all what the Nationalists wanted; before the Simon Commission reported at all, most of them had approved in some degree or other of the Nehru constitution drawn up by Congress, which called for complete dominion status and universal suffrage. Until they could approximate this constitution, they were determined to make life in India unpleasant for the British; and in this they were greatly aided by the example of Gandhi, who undertook a dramatic march to the sea to make salt without the payment of the salt tax, thus symbolizing his contempt for British law. It was very little salt that Gandhi made; but the whole world watched him make it. Soon thousands refused to pay taxes and the jails overflowed with protesting Hindus. Acts of violence also took place which Gandhi repudiated; strikes were numerous; bombs were thrown; and an incipient Communist movement arose, not interested in Gandhi's *satyagraha*.

Back in England Ramsay MacDonald, former pacifist, was Prime Minister. He still had faith in conferences, and round-table discussion became the order of the day. Let the various Indian groups iron out their own difficulties, was his motto, and three of these roundtables were held in 1930, 1931, and 1932. None of them was successful. The Indian princes came, but they were unwilling to surrender the arbitrary power they still held in their own independent states. The Hindus and the Moslems were unable to agree upon any compromise in regard to the basis of representation. And to add to these dissensions, the Hindus could not agree among themselves, for the outcasts, the "Untouchables," as they were called in India, now became articulate. The Untouchables were the lowest of the low, from the Hindu point of view. They composed the proletariat in the religious and social scale, and very generally in the economic scale as well. But one of their own number had risen in the world, had been well educated at Columbia University, and had become a lawyer at Bombay. This man, Dr. Ambedekar, was now as vociferous as the Moslems in demanding separate representation for the Untouchables; for otherwise, scattered as they were throughout India, they would be at the mercy of the more numerous caste Hindus. Gandhi, recently out of jail as the result of a hunger strike (the British having made the discovery that India was generally more restless with the Mahatma in jail than out of it), came to the second round-table conference. London was intrigued by his loincloth and the fact that he brought his own goats from India; but it speedily discovered that while Indians were willing to worship him as a saint, they were unwilling to follow him as a politician. Neither Gandhi nor anyone else could bring about an agreement by general consent. All three conferences failed, and the British shrugged their shoulders. They always knew it would be so! If the Indians could not settle their own affairs then the British Parliament must decide what the government of India should be like.

Whereupon, in 1935, a new constitution was promulgated, drawn up by the British alone and certainly an advance in the direction of dominion status, but still far short of it. The new instrument of government followed along the lines suggested by the Simon report: It decentralized India; abolished dyarchy, making all the cabinet ministers in the provinces responsible to their legislatures; gave these legislatures more power, and permitted over thirty million men and women to elect their membership; reorganized the all-Indian legislature by providing for a council of state with 150 elected members chosen indirectly by the provincial legislatures, as opposed to 100 to be appointed by the native princes (should they choose to enter the Indian federation) and 10 nominated by the viceroy. The lower house was to have 250 members, 125 chosen by the princes, the balance elected by 6,000,000 electors. In both the provincial and national legislature, electoral districts were to be based partly on communal representation and partly on population, thus compromising the Hindu-Moslem impasse.

The constitution looked fair enough but there were jokers in it. These were termed, by the British, "safeguards." The lieutenant-governors, placed over the provinces, were removable by the viceroy but not by an adverse vote of their legislatures. There were other safeguards in regard to the army, foreign affairs, and finance, the viceroy possessing enormous residual powers in respect to these vital interests should he choose to exercise them.

This, Congress realized; and within that body there was a movement to boycott the new constitution. The radicals who favored this line of action were led by Nehru, a left-wing Indian Nationalist who had become almost, if not quite, as popular as Gandhi. Like the Mahatma, he was a Hindu trained in England in the law, but unlike his famous fellow Indian, he was not interested in religion, and instead of urging a return to the hallowed traditions of Hinduism as did Gandhi, he favored discarding them. Nehru came from a wealthy family on good terms with the British. Not only did he become a radical Nationalist but he persuaded his father to do likewise, and it was the father, not the son, who drew up a Nehru constitution on behalf of Congress. Both father and son suffered imprisonment for the cause. The younger Nehru served almost as many terms in prison as Gandhi himself, for whom he had intense admiration. But the Mahatma was too willing to compromise, so thought the younger Nehru, who became the recognized leader of the left center in the Congress, the extreme left position being occupied by Communists and acknowledged Socialists.

Gandhi, now approaching seventy years of age, might be regarded as the leader of the right center, then somewhat inclined to coöperate with the British. When the new constitution had first been promulgated he had been very indignant because provision had been made in it for separate communal representation of the Untouchables. His reason for so doing was that it was a disgrace for Hindus to admit that there were such people as Untouchables, that separate representation would prevent their merging with other Hindus. So keenly did he feel about this that he began one of his famous fasts. Again the British did not dare permit his death, for they feared the repercussions it might bring. Therefore they compromised once more, and Gandhi ate. Having won this victory the Mahatma was willing to permit his followers to vote, and they did so.

Nationalists won the elections in a majority of the provinces; but the constitution was only partially enforced, for to complete federation, native states containing fifty-one per cent of the population of non-British India must first ratify it. Gandhi, aroused by an act of signal injustice in a native state, began still another fast, this time he said to the death. It was a dramatic way of calling attention to conditions in the native states, for Gandhi was a clever politician as well as religious prophet. As usual the Mahatma judged rightly; this time he had to fast to dangerous lengths, for he was ninety-eight hours without nourishment. And the British gave in; the injustice was remedied by the advice of the viceroy, and all that was left of the shriveled little mystic scored another victory over the greatest empire the world has seen since Rome.

Irritation against the British in India was still profound. Half of the famous Indian Civil Service, well paid, hard-working, efficient, was to be manned by Indians not later than 1940; but Congress did not see why there should be any British on that particular payroll. They pointed to the great powers held in reserve by the British viceroy, to the British control of Indian foreign affairs, to the British control of the Indian army, and to huge sums remitted every year to Britain in return for British capital invested in India, and to high taxes. Indian taxation was very low per capita compared with other Asiatic countries; but it was a heavy burden for a teeming population on the borderline of starvation. From the point of view of the Congress, the money thus raised should go to rid the land of illiteracy rather than to support a big army.

The British had an answer. Without the investment of millions of pounds of British capital in railroads and irrigation projects, famine would be rife in the peninsula, for the railroads had made it possible to move grain to those districts where there is scarcity, and the irrigation engineer made possible a greater grain supply. The army was large; but India paid nothing for the royal navy, and a strong defense force was needed on the northwest against Afghanistan with Soviet Russia in the background. Furthermore, without the presence of British troops in that army, what chance would 250,000,000 meek Hindus have against

70,000,000 Moslems? High as taxes were in British India, they were much higher in the native states. A good deal of Hindu poverty was caused by regarding the cow as a sacred animal which can never be killed and which must be fed when worthless, as a religious duty. For the good of the Hindu *ryot* (peasant), ignorant and illiterate beyond measure, knowing nothing of Congress or of those educated Hindus who claim to represent them, the British argued that they must continue to control, in part at least, the destinies of the subcontinent.

So stood the situation as the Second World War broke. Congress immediately offered to back Britain, provided dominion status be instantly granted. The British said that was impossible during the war.

The Far East

In the Far East, meanwhile, nationalistic fervors and fevers were even more intense than in Central and Western Asia. The essentially disruptive, anarchic, and volcanic qualities of contemporary nationalism were completely unloosed in this part of the world. The xenophobia which aroused the passions of Turks, Arabs, Persians, and Indians was no less noticeable here than elsewhere; but combined with it there arose such a terrific clash between Chinese and Japanese nationalism that there resulted what the Japanese politely called "incidents" but what the historian calls "war."

The outbreak of the World War in 1914 in the West was Japan's golden opportunity in the East. Declaring war on Germany, the men of Nippon promptly captured the German colony of Kiauchow, after which they presented in 1915 an ultimatum to the weak and disorganized government of Yuan Shi-kai.

The Chinese yielded to what they considered were twenty-one Japanese demands but what the Japanese ever since have termed the Treaties of 1915, whereby China placed herself pretty thoroughly under the thumb of her island neighbor, ceding to Japan all German concessions in China proper, as well as Russian concessions in Manchuria, while agreeing to accept military and economic advisers from Japan.

The following year Yuan Shi-kai died and chaos dominated the Chinese scene. China, disgruntled at her inability to get rid of the Japanese stranglehold, refused to sign the Treaty of Versailles. Two years later at the Washington Conference which we shall discuss later, she was more fortunate; her independence was clearly guaranteed by nine different countries; she was granted the right to increase her tariff; and the Japanese agreed to restore to China the German concessions which they had secured in 1915. But these gains did not stop the spread of anarchy in China, continuous and widespread, until the Kuomintang party (southern nationalists) was able to capture Peking in 1929.

Those nationalists were ardent followers of Sun Yat-sen, a capable conspirator but no executive. Before the World War came to a conclusion, he had betaken himself to Canton in the south and had there headed a revolt against the central government. While Dr. Sun lived it met with only local successes, for its leader was more prophet than statesman. In the former role, however, he wrote a book of lasting significance to the historian, for it became the Bible of the Kuomintang, and within a decade the most authoritative written word in China.

Dr. Sun's *Three Principles of the People* tries to lay the foundations for a new Chinese society in "nationalism," "democracy," and "social welfare." Individual and family interests must be subordinated to the welfare of the nation—nationalism. The Chinese should never forget that they invented the compass, gunpowder, and a wonderful indigenous architecture of their own; they were just as strong, as intelligent as the peoples of the West, and they must be proud of their past. From the West they should learn the art of government—democracy. That word, to Dr. Sun, was an all-inclusive one, including such concepts as the separation of powers and universal suffrage, and even certain ancient Chinese practices such as civil service examinations, for the West might well profit from Chinese precedents. Then, too, the Chinese must never forget social welfare, which he defines as resting on a social and political platform evolved about one-third from Marxian socialism, one-third from Henry George's land-value theories, and one-third from economic nationalism in respect to protective tariffs. Of these three principles, which was the most important? "Nationalism," asserted the more conservative right-wing members of the Kuomintang; "social welfare," affirmed the left wing. Seemingly, Dr. Sun sympathized more with the latter, and he entered into negotiations with Soviet Russia, who sent representatives to Canton to drill the Kuomintang army and to capture the Kuomintang mind. They were more successful with the first venture than with the second, for the Kuomintang began to win victories in the field while still torn in regard to ideology.

Dr. Sun died in 1925, honored and revered as the founder of Chinese nationalism, and his mantle descended upon Chiang Kai-shek, a quiet, hard-working, abstemious young soldier, ardent disciple of Sun Yat-sen, and commander of the Kuomintang forces. He led the latter to victory after victory as Hankow, Shanghai, Nanking, and Peking fell before his troops. Peking was abandoned and the capital of China was transferred to Nanking. By the end of 1928 the government of the Kuomintang there had been recognized by all the Great Powers and had been admitted to the League of Nations. At last China's main troubles seemed to have ended, for Chiang Kai-shek was a strong and able man, moderate, liberal, devoted to the three principles which were the platform of his party.

There were, however, two obstacles to overcome before China could present a unified front against the foreign capitalist and could call her house her own: (*a*) dissensions in the ranks of the Kuomintang, and (*b*) Japanese ambitions in Manchuria. A part of the Kuomintang, led by its more radical members, among whom Dr. Sun's widow was prominent, was under Soviet influence and rejected Chiang Kai-shek's leadership. At Hankow, well up the Yangtse River it constantly stirred up trouble and virtually threw off its allegiance to Nanking. In Manchuria young Marshal Chang, governor of that province, got in hot water with the Japanese in 1931 so that the latter launched an attack on him which was to prove the beginning of a campaign to conquer a large part of China.

The Japanese were not without legal rights in Manchuria, some of them dating back to the Treaty of Portsmouth, more of them dating to the treaties (or demands?) of 1915. Manchuria had been the original home of the Manchus, who had conquered China, and legally was a part of the Celestial Empire. Nevertheless, within its borders was the Southern Manchurian Railroad, Japanese owned; and Japan had been granted the right to police that railroad and to develop the economic resources of Manchuria in its vicinity, the Chinese being forbidden to build parallel or competing lines. Japanese colonists also had been granted concessions in the country and Japan had received recognition of extra-territorial rights there which, as interpreted by her, carried with them authority not only to try cases involving Japanese citizens but also to protect the latter by Japanese police.

All these special privileges the Japanese had been able to enforce without too much difficulty after the war, because old Marshal Chang, warlord and governor, had been concilitary toward Japan. But the elder Chang died in 1928 and his son, the younger Chang, was not only a Chinese nationalist but an adherent of the Kuomintang and of Chiang Kai-shek. As such, he adopted an anti-Japanese policy, trying to prevent Japan from expanding further, interfering with Japanese colonists, and even defying the Japanese military when their activities became too pronounced.

Therefore it happened that there was an "incident." It took the form of an explosion on the Southern Manchurian Railroad, caused, so claimed the Japanese, by the soldiers of Chang. A section of track supposedly was destroyed—supposedly, because the through express passing there shortly after was only a little late at its destination. But the incident was all that was needed. Immediately, the arsenal at Mukden in which slept the soldiers of Chang was rushed by the Japanese, and the Chinese garrison made prisoners, after which Japan proceeded to flood Manchuria with her own troops.

General Chiang Kai-shek and His Wife

China appealed to the League of Nations, of which both she and Japan were members. That body investigated at length, its committees visiting China, Japan, and Manchuria, interviewing both Chinese and Japanese authorities, passing over their testimony to the opposition for rejoinders and surrejoinders, and making a unanimous report signed by a German, an Englishman, an Italian, a Frenchman, and an American, a report accepted by the League (Siam not voting).

This Lytton Report acknowledged that although China held sovereignty over Manchuria that province could not be administered as a part of China since Japan held legal rights there. On the other hand it accused Japan of violating the Nine-Power Treaty of 1921, of violating the Briand-Kellogg international peace treaty, of violating the covenant of the League of Nations.

Japan already had virtually reduced Manchuria to a Japanese dependency by setting up a puppet ruler, and now in 1932 she renounced the League and all its works, resigning from that body. Manchukuo, she claimed, was an independent country. Did it not have a flag, a capital, even an emperor—no less a person than Mr. Henry Pu-yi, the last Manchu Emperor of China, now restored to a part of his ancient heritage by popular demand? This gentleman had, indeed, been elevated to the peacock throne in Peking at the age of three, only to be driven out in a few years by the Chinese Revolution of 1911. He had lived in exile most of his life, and was a quiet, demure young man about thirty years old when luck and Nippon made him emperor again—a most convenient puppet, so the Japanese thought. Surrounded by Japanese officials and advisers, and by the Japanese army, he was circumspect in behavior.

From 1931 to the present there has not been even the semblance of order in the Far East. Russia, England, and the United States all took a hand to some extent in the devil's brew constantly boiling over in that part of the world. Russia, it must be remembered, came close to circling Manchukuo; her maritime provinces bounded that new country on the east, as did Siberia on the north and northwest. Then, too, the Soviets were deeply interested in Outer Mongolia, the northwestern part of China, due west of Manchukuo. Outer Mongolia had become virtually independent of China and established within its steppes was a semi-Communist government in close military alliance with Moscow. From 1936, the date of that alliance, there had been sporadic "incidents" on Manchukuo's western and eastern borders. To separate rumor from fact in regard to them is impossible; but armed encounters had been numerous between Japanese and Russian patrols, and occasional skirmishes at times assumed the proportion of little battles.

England, too, was concerned, primarily on account of her immense financial interests in the Yangtse Valley radiating out from Shanghai and those centering around Hongkong and Canton, further to the south.

With the United States, trade was less an issue, for American investments in China were small compared with those of Britain. On the other hand, American educational institutions had spread out across a large part of China and a great many of the leading Chinese Nationalists had been educated in the United States—facts which drew the American people much closer to the fray than they otherwise would have been.

But the protagonists have been China and Japan. A relatively weak but ever growing nationalism, that of China, was challenged in one form or another by the most virulent and most concentrated nationalism that the world has ever encountered—that of the chauvinistic Japanese Empire.

In China, Chiang Kai-shek's problem was extremely difficult; at one and the same time he was confronted with an internal Communist civil war and by incessant Japanese nibbling at the frontiers of his country. For a number of years it seemed difficult to discover which of these two dangers he considered the more serious. He was conservative by nature, and by marriage connected with the famous and wealthy Soong family, who, aside from his sister-in-law, the widow of Dr. Sun, believed that Chinese nationalism stood to gain more by accepting loans from capitalistic countries than by relying on hypothetical aid from the Soviets; on the other hand, it was impossible to contend with the Japanese without a united country behind him, and to gain that the Communists must be either conciliated or hunted down and destroyed.

The best Chinese weapon for fighting Japan at first seemed the boycott. Its inauguration in 1931 led to the death of certain Japanese citizens in Shanghai and to the bombardment of that city by the Japanese fleet, followed by a land attack of the Japanese army, said to have involved 50,000 troops. Much to the surprise of the world, the latter were withstood for several weeks by the Chinese Nineteenth Route Army. This army, however, came from South China and received no active assistance from Chiang Kai-shek, who believed it was sympathetic toward communism.

The Japanese were aroused and the militarists apparently gained the upper hand at Tokyo. Their entire country, they realized, could be tucked away in the American state of Montana with room to spare. Much of it was mountainous and could not be tilled. Of mineral wealth, oil, and iron, there was very little. The Industrial Revolution had made such rapid progress in the twentieth century that Japan inevitably would go under without raw materials and without foreign markets. And both were to be found across the narrow seas in China.

The Japanese wasted no time. In 1933 they invaded Jehol, an ancient Chinese province southwest of Manchukuo but beyond the great wall of China; it was a rich province and might open the way later to Outer Mongolia. Again Chiang Kai-shek took no active steps in opposition, and the Soviet Bear only growled.

During the next three years Japan stretched out her hand over the five northern provinces of China proper, which included Hopei, wherein Peking was located. Bit by bit these provinces were detached from Chinese sovereignty and drawn into the Japanese net. Finally, in 1937, came a new "incident." Japanese forces at the Marco Polo Bridge within ten miles of Peking lost a private (he came back the next day) and in revenge 35,000 Japanese troops advanced from the sea coast toward that city.

This time Chiang Kai-shek was ready to fight. He recently had gone through strange adventures. The Chinese Communists (frequently and erroneously held to be by many not really Communists at all, but radical democrats mainly interested in peasant proprietorship and the end of landlordism) had moved in a dangerous and courageous migration all the way across China from the low lands of the southeast to the hilly country of the northwest. Against them Chiang Kai-shek had sent an army commanded by the young Marshal Chang, late ruler of Manchuria. Then rumor had it that Chang, instead of fighting Communists, had adopted a friendly attitude toward them. Chiang Kai-shek went to investigate. No sooner did this happen than he was kidnapped by Chang, who suggested that Chiang Kai-shek treat the Communists as allies instead of enemies and join with them in driving the Japanese to the sea.

Chiang Kai-shek angrily refused. His wife flew in an airplane to his side, and he returned to Nanking with her and the apologetic Chang, having made no promises. But he had seen the light; he would forget communism for the time being and so would the Communists. Both wings of the old Kuomintang now united with one sole aim, the eviction of Japan from Chinese soil. In the summer of 1937 the Generalissimo plucked up courage; he demanded the withdrawal of the Japanese from the vicinity of Peking. The answer was the prompt occupation of that city and of Tientsin by Japan. The war was on.

It raged with unabated fury. Again the Japanese attacked Shanghai, but this time Chiang Kai-Shek's national army, German-trained, dashed to the defense, and a battle of World War dimensions followed. The Japanese ultimately won, and driving inland up the Yangtze Valley they captured Nanking, the Chinese capital, before the year was out.

The Chinese Nationalists, however, abandoned that city in time, and retreating still farther up the river established their capital at Hankow. The next year the Japanese continued the chase; they captured Hankow; they captured Canton, source of munitions for the Nationalists by way of Hongkong. According to their reckoning they had won the war.

But Chiang Kai-shek had no thought of giving over. He moved his capital still farther up the river to Chungking in western China and encouraged guerrilla warfare against the enemy from within their own lines.

SOVIET   UNION

Chita

MONGOLIAN
REPUBLIC

M A N C H U K U O
1931-33
Harbin

CHAHAR
1937-39

JEHOL

Vladivostok

SUIYUAN
1937-39

Mukden

HWANG HO

SEA   OF
JAPAN

Paotow

KOREA
1905, 1910

Peiping

C O M M U N I S T

Tientsin

Port Arthur
1905

HOPEI
1937-39

HWANG HO

SHANTUNG

A R E A S

Tsingtao

CHINA

YELLOW
SEA

Nanking

JAPAN

Hankow

Shanghai

YANGTZE

YANGTZE

Chungking

RYUKYU ISLANDS

P A C I F I C

Wenchow, 1939

Foochow, 1939

O C E A N

Amoy
1938

FORMOSA
1895

Canton
1939

Swatow
(1939)

Hongkong (BR)

JAPAN'S INVASION

S O U T H
C H I N A
S E A

OF CHINA

TO 1939

HAINAN
1939

500 MILES

TRM

The Rise of Japanese Fascism

The speedy victories won by the soldiers of the Mikado did much to speed the rise of fascism in Japan. As in Germany it was semi-socialistic in character, deriving much of its strength from army officers embittered by the hardships of the proletariat from which many of them came. As in Germany it was aided by the discovery that bluff and bluster in foreign policy bore good fruit and brought easy victory; and, as in Germany, it grew from roots deeply embedded in traditions of racial grandeur.

The world economic depression of 1930-1933 brought sharp declines in agricultural prices in Japan as elsewhere but no decline in taxation. Japanese farmers sank deeper and deeper into debt. Those who were small landlords were almost as hard hit as their tenants; they were either forced to sell their tiny estates to mortgage banks or else to raise the rent of the miniature farms which they sublet to peasants. The latter were already living on such a narrow margin as to barely keep alive; now they were driven in many instances to sell their daughters into virtual slavery by apprenticing them to mill owners in the big cities. The introduction of cheap competitive farm labor from Korea added to these troubles, and the ground was well laid for sowing seeds of discontent among the soldiers, quite willing to believe that Japan's woes were due to wealthy shipping, manufacturing and banking interests, pretending that they loved Japan and international peace, but with hearts focused on the pocketbook.

Bluff and bluster in foreign relations worked; that was Japan's experience. The world let her do what she wished in China. One country, and one only, was not easy to deal with—Soviet Russia. But when Japan demanded possession of the Chinese Eastern railroad which crossed Manchuria and was half owned by Russia, she found Stalin willing to sell out at a ridiculously low price. Twice after that she tested Stalin's willingness to fight and twice to her surprise she found him ready to do so. In 1938 the soldiers of the Mikado charged up Changkufing Hill to the south of Vladivostok and just within the borders of Russia's Maritime Province, only to be hurled back with heavy loss. One year later they invaded the Mongolian People's Republic (in military alliance with the Soviets) and after a sharp battle were defeated by the Red army. Russia patently would have to be watched.

But the British and the Americans the Japanese feared not at all; why should they? In 1937 they sunk the small American gunboat, *Panay*, in the Yangtse and shelled the survivors as they sought refuge in the reeds on the river bank. Nothing happened. True, the Japanese government promptly apologized and paid an indemnity, and the Japanese people subscribed some $2,000,000 for the survivors, money paid by us to the Japanese Red Cross. But the Japanese militarists found out what they wanted, namely that we were not greatly exercised by this act of war; and, what is more, we were utterly unwilling to take any joint action with Britain when her gunboat, the *Lady Bird,* was shelled with impunity. Roosevelt was powerless to check the rising power of the Rising Sun. He did refuse to proclaim our neutrality laws as applicable to the Far East, and this he could do since the Japanese had refused to admit that they were waging war in China. But in all other respects he was at the mercy of an isolationist Congress. Japan had violated the Nine-Power Treaty which she signed at Washington in 1922, guaranteeing the status quo in the Orient, and the Kellogg Peace Pact which she signed later, together with almost every country on the globe, outlawing war: but when our state department made the slightest move to implement these international agreements it was accused of complicity with "the international intriguers of Geneva," that is, the League of Nations. The isolationists even tried to go farther; they almost succeeded in gaining the approval of the House of Representatives for the Ludlow amendment which would have deprived Congress of the right to declare war except in case of actual invasion of the United States. This was an oblique way of hitting at the President, and was so understood not only in this country but also in Japan. It was an indirect way of saying to all and sundry that it would be fairly safe for venturesome countries to defy the warnings of our chief executive.

Meanwhile, without the support of the United States, Britain was as powerless as Roosevelt to curb the predatory Japanese, a fact which they gleefully recognized in 1939 when they blockaded and maltreated beyond the bounds of decency British nationals in Tientsin. All in all, strong-armed methods worked abroad.

And they also worked at home. In the period between the two World Wars no less than five statesmen who urged conciliatory and liberal policies were assassinated by patriotic cutthroats, members of secret Fascist societies, the best known of which was the Black Dragon; and prominent business men like Baron Dan of the House of Mitsui were either murdered or else compelled to hire bodyguards and to wear steel vests, even while playing tennis. These societies, gaining more power, were back of an open rebellion in Tokyo which, led by two young army officers, threatened in 1936 in the name of the Emperor to destroy parliamentary government completely. The mutineers surrendered and a few were punished. Nevertheless, this mutiny was only suppressed on the surface; it really won the victory, for parliamentary government (never very strong in Japan) grew steadily weaker.

A kind of fascist militarism now characterized the government of Japan, similar to German fascism in that both countries tremendous emphasis was laid on traditions of racial glory and queer hypotheses of racial purity. The Japanese claimed to be descended from the Sun Goddess who gave birth to the Japanese Islands and to a parent of the first Japanese Emperor. Since all Japanese were considered relatives of the first Emperor, all Japanese were blood brothers, and all Japanese were divine. In both Japan and Germany the sacredness of the blood has been mystically elaborated; but in the former country it has not been so essential to twist and to torture anthropological data to prove the impossible. In Japan it is a matter of faith, not one for laboratory analysis. To some historians, and particularly those who like to indict an entire nation, it has always been a matter of faith in Japan; and in a sense they are correct since the animistic aspects of Japanese tradition did not die out completely when Japan adopted western ideas in the late nineteenth century. If, however, those aspects did not die out, they did die down, so as to be to the better-educated Japanese a mere quaint survival. It suited the Japanese fascists to revive this thing, to pump fresh enthusiasm into it. They were altogether successful.

Chapter 37

FROM THE RUHR TO PRAGUE (1923-39)

FRANCE had Germany by the throat in 1923. The Ruhr was in her hands; the German mark was tumbling to destruction. It would have needed a bold prophet then to have proclaimed the resuscitation of the Reich, the challenging of the conqueror within ten years, the union of Germany and Austria within fifteen—a more powerful empire than that made by Bismarck. Nevertheless, kaleidoscopic changes in international politics brought this about, and in the autumn of 1938 a prime minister of France and a prime minister of England were to plead in vain, with a German Fuehrer that he withhold his heavy hand from a country created and guaranteed by the Versailles pacts. Roles were now quite reversed: it was Germany and not France that held the hegemony of Europe!

The factors which underlay this extraordinary reverse were these: the financial settlements made by the Dawes and Young Plans which, unintentionally and indirectly, strengthened Germany; the impotency of the League of Nations; the procrastination of the Great Powers in implementing the disarmament clauses of the Versailles treaty; American isolationists; repudiation of agreements, first by Japan and then by Italy; the superb timing of German foreign policy by Hitler; the Spanish civil war; the unwillingness of France and England to coöperate with one another until a rearmed Germany virtually had annexed Czechoslovakia, master now of Central Europe; the fact that there were approximately eighty million Germans in Europe, the largest cohesive national group to be found there if we except Russia; and the social tensions of this period, which affected not only the rise and the achievements of the Fascists and Nazis but also the attitude of the capitalistic democracies toward fascism, many leaders of the democracies shaping their policies on the belief that fascism and national socialism were simply uncouth ways of putting down communism.

Finance

The war-weary legions of the French Republic withdrew from the Ruhr Valley in 1924. Seemingly, they had won a victory; they had not been able to operate the industrial plants of Germany but they had forced that country to its knees and to an acceptance of the Dawes Plan, which, in essence, amounted to a kind of international receivership in bankruptcy. The plan and its successor, the Young Plan, have been described already. Both operated successfully for a season, but owing to one reason alone—the lending of fresh money to Germany. The loans were made partly by the English, more largely by the Americans, childishly believing the fairy stories of their bankers, who, in the lush decade of easy money in the twenties, seem to have lost their heads altogether. In addition to several hundred million dollars lent the German government, private investments amounting to some $5,000,000,000 were made in European securities, mainly German, only stopped in 1929 by the orgy of speculation on the New York Stock Market of that year and the subsequent crash. Money began to go round and round in a kind of circle, from England and America to Germany, from Germany to England and France in reparations, from England and France to America in war-debt payments. But always more money stayed in Germany that was paid out! And this money went toward building new German steamships, new German factories, new German machinery, new German homes and public buildings. From the date of the Dawes Plan, 1924, to the Hoover moratorium of 1931, Germany paid handsomely on her reparation account; but in terms of dollars she received more than she spent. Terrible as was the economic disaster which overwhelmed her in 1923, her complete bankruptcy was not without compensation. By wiping out all internal debt, the Reich was able to start afresh with a new currency, owing no money to her own citizens; but both France and England labored under colossal internal debts inherited from the First World War and before it.

The League of Nations

Meanwhile the League of Nations proved an impotent agency for world peace. In dealing with certain weak states it exerted its authority manfully. In a dispute between Turkey and Britain over the oil lands of Mosul there was a League decision in favor of Britain, and Turkey yielded. In a dispute between Sweden and Finland over the Aland Islands there was a decision in favor of Finland, and Sweden gave way. And when Yugoslavia threatened Albania in 1921, talk of sanctions at Geneva stayed the hand of Yugoslavia. The League also kept peace between Greece and Bulgaria, and did useful work in regard to international health, in codifying laws, and bringing about international agreements in regard to opium, the white-slave traffic, and the hours of labor.

But when it came to curbing the will of any Great Power, Geneva failed dismally. Poland seized Vilna in Lithuania, and despite the protests of the League nothing happened. It was not that Poland was a great power, she was not; but Poland was backed by France! Mussolini, as early as 1923, tested the temper of Geneva, and to his own satisfaction. He bombarded the Greek island of Corfu, killing many Greek citizens— this despite the fact that Greece was a member of the League. The Duce refused to acknowledge that Geneva had any right at all to intervene between Italy and Greece, the plain wording of the Covenant to the contrary.

The disabilities under which the League labored were many, but perhaps the two most prominent were that it had no way to enforce its decisions, and unanimous action on the part of the Council of the League was necessary even to obtain decisions. France was a permanent member of that Council and France was always alert lest the peace settlements of 1919 be weakened. Therefore, Geneva tended to become an agency for perpetuating those settlements rather than for readjusting them.

For two or three years after the invasion of the Ruhr it seemed possible that the machinery of the League might be so changed as to make that body a real agency to insure real peace. Scarcely had the ink dried upon the bankers' agreement (the Dawes Plan) than the French and British governments tried to fill the gaps in the Covenant and to outlaw war. They did succeed in getting the League to accept what was called the "Geneva Protocol" which gave teeth to the Council of the League, enabling it to compel arbitration, "to forbid mobilization, or to impose an armistice." This protocol defined the aggressor in specific terms and provided for outlawing him. At last France had what she wanted, security. And England agreed to give it to her.

But before Parliament ratified the protocol, Ramsay MacDonald was out as Prime Minister and Baldwin in. The British Tories would have none of the protocol. Austen Chamberlain, brother of Neville, was British foreign secretary, and he scented commitments which he was unwilling for his country to make. The chief agency for enforcing the future decisions of the League would be, in his opinion, the royal navy, for even if the method of enforcement took the mild form of economic sanctions, it would be sea power in the last analysis which would enforce them. England, therefore, decided to keep her fleet to fight her own battles, and consequently the protocol never was ratified.

Despite this drawback, the cause of international peace guaranteed by a league made headway. England, following the policy of Pitt in Napoleonic times, was willing to make local commitments, and so, too, it seems, were France and Germany. In 1925 Stresemann, the German foreign secretary, Austen Chamberlain for England, and Briand for France met at Locarno in Switzerland. From this conference emerged the Locarno treaties by which Belgium, England, France, Italy, and Germany guaranteed the existing frontiers between Belgium and Germany and those between France and Germany. The demilitarization of Germany for fifty kilometers east of the Rhine was agreed to, and a permanent place on the Council of the League of Nations was to be given Germany. That country also agreed to arbitrate any disputes she might have with Poland and Czechoslovakia. She reserved the right to seek peaceful changes in her eastern frontier, but her western one she accepted as permanent. In case there should be a flagrant violation of these sacrosanct boundaries in the West, there was to be immediate action taken by the signatories; in case of doubt the Council of the League was to determine what should be done.

With the signing of the Locarno treaties the world breathed easier. There were, of course, a number of problems yet unsolved; there was as yet no guarantee of Europe's eastern boundaries for although everyone promised not to go to war over them, that was not very specific; there was no assurance that Germany's permanent seat on the Council would carry with it colonial mandates; there was no time limit set for Germany's payments under the Dawes Plan; and, possibly even more important, there was no strengthening of the machinery of the League of Nations, aside from the presence of Germany on that body, and no indication that the pledges given and taken at Versailles in regard to future disarmament would be implemented. A local and regional pact had been drawn up, and an important one. That was all.

Within five years dark clouds settled down again upon Europe. One of them was the disastrous and complete failure of Geneva to function in a Far Eastern dispute, resulting in Japan's resignation from the League. Another was the equally disastrous and equally complete failure to bring about disarmament, resulting in Germany's withdrawing from the League, which, from now on, despite the subsequent adhesion of Russia, grew gradually less and less influential.

The sudden flooding of Manchuria in 1931 by Japanese troops inevitably had serious consequences. Almost instantly China complained to the Council of the League, which called upon both China and Japan to withdraw their soldiers from the disputed area. Japan refused, asserting that negotiations and a settlement must come first. Weeks were spent in argument and finally a suggestion of Japan's was accepted, the sending of a commission of the League to the Far East.

In the interim came the Japanese attack on Shanghai, and immediately China made a new appeal to the Council and, when that body did nothing, to the Assembly. Fifty nations attended the 1932 meeting of the Assembly which appointed a committee of nineteen to deal with the Shanghai incident. Its report called for the withdrawal of the Japanese troops from Shanghai, and Japan complied.

The commission of the League sent to the Far East reported this same year. It disputed some of the Chinese claims but leaned very heavily against those of Japan, called for the recognition of Chinese sovereignty (with limitations) in Manchuria, and for the strict enforcement of three treaties: the Covenant of the League of Nations of which both Japan and China were members, the Nine-Power Treaty of the Washington Conference of 1922, and the Kellogg-Briand Pact of 1928, whereby war was renounced by almost every country in the world as an instrument of national policy.

The Committee of Nineteen now swung into action, asking for a conciliation commission on which both Russia and the United States were to be represented. Japan refused to accept this offer, whereupon the committee reported to the Assembly against the actions of that country in the Far East in no uncertain language, recommending that all nations should refuse to recognize the Japanese puppet state of Manchukuo. The League accepted the report and Japan withdrew from Geneva. Reliance upon the Covenant of the League of Nations had proved useless in a real emergency. In the few years intervening before the Second World War it was to prove so again and again.

Disarmament

Number four of the fourteen points had been specific in regard to disarmament. "Adequate guarantees," it said, "given and taken that national armaments will be reduced to the lowest point consistent with domestic safety." But in regard to Germany alone had any such guarantees been enforced; the German army had been reduced to 100,000 men and the German navy sunk. But how about the other signatories of the Versailles Treaty?

They did do something in regard to naval disarmament in the Washington Conference of 1921-22. Britain, the United States, Japan, France, and Italy agreed there to set a ratio for their capital ships at 5: 5: 3: 1.75: 1.75—the ratio to be set in the order of countries named. There was to be no new construction of battleships for ten years, and after that date Britain and the United States were to be allowed only a total tonnage of 500,000, Japan of 300,000, and France and Italy of 175,000 respectively.

To bring about this modest limitation, all the signatory powers made sacrifices except Italy. That country was so far short of 175,000 tons and so far behind France in naval equipment that to be placed upon an equality with her Latin neighbor was no hardship for the Italians. The French, on the other hand, saw objections, and refused to agree until the conference applied the ratio only to battleships. It was very largely a matter of prestige with the French; they were not building any battleships at the time, and were not likely to exceed the 175,000-ton limit anyway. Submarines, however, were another matter; and for them and other small craft they would not accept the ratio.

For the Japanese it was likewise a matter of prestige. Their pride was hurt at accepting a lower ratio than that for the British and the Americans. On the other hand they secured some concessions. They won the right to complete a new battleship under construction; and the Americans and the British agreed not to build naval bases within striking distance of the Japanese homeland.

It was not easy for the British to yield parity to the Americans. Still, two monster British battleships were nearing completion and Britain was permitted by the treaty to finish them. With these two ships, capable of sinking anything afloat, she was still mistress of the seas. The Americans, meanwhile, offered to scrap battleships which they had commenced to build but which were far short of completion. This was their contribution to world peace.

Less successful were the conferences held at Geneva in 1927 and at London in 1930. The purpose back of the first was to extend the ratios of the Washington Conference to smaller craft, that of the second to accomplish the same end, and also to provide for the continuation of battleship limitation, the earlier treaty running out in 1931. Both conferences were failures. At the first a lively quarrel broke out between American and British admirals as to the size of cruisers. The Americans, having few naval bases, insisted on large cruisers but few in number; the British, well-equipped with naval bases but having a large mercantile marine to protect throughout all the seven seas, wanted small cruisers but many of them. The quarrel was renewed in 1930, this time primarily between France and Italy. The two countries wrangled long and loud, the Italians demanding complete equality with the French in small ships as well as large, the former country unwilling to grant it unless Britain agreed to a Mediterranean Locarno guaranteeing the status quo in that sea. This, Britain would not give unless the United States was willing to commit herself by something more than words to the cause of world peace.

The conference broke up, to meet again in 1930 in London. All that was accomplished then was a highly tentative agreement between the big three naval powers—England, Japan, and the United States—to retain the old ratio (with minor concessions to Japan) for five more years; but even this agreement was contingent upon France and Italy not exceeding their old allotment of tonnage.

Meanwhile, there had been no progress at all in disarmament on land. The League of Nations did nothing in regard to this all-important question until 1926, and then only by the appointment of a commission to consider drafts presented by the British and French governments. The commission could come to no specific agreement. Countries with conscript armies objected to counting their reserves as "effectives"; countries like Germany and England wished to have the reserves included in the total armed force allowed. Some countries, like England and France, were willing enough to reduce expenditures, but countries like the United States where the military budget was high in proportion to the number of enlisted men wanted to reduce the number of soldiers rather than lower the expense of supporting them. The French reverted time and again to the necessity of an international force to compel the observance of such disarmament as should be agreed upon, for the French did not trust the Germans, and above everything else they were concerned about their own security. The "have not" states—such as Italy, Germany, Hungary, and Bulgaria—wished to remake the map of Europe, or at least to modify existing boundaries as part of a scheme for general disarmament. The "haves"—France, Poland, Czechoslovakia, Rumania, and Yugoslavia—preferred to "freeze" European boundaries as they stood, and only to disarm with some assurance that they could retain their wartime gains. In consequence it was not until 1932, fourteen years after the war, that the League finally summoned a world conference on a vital matter which should have been tackled ten years earlier.

Some sixty nations were represented at this conference which, if we include adjournments, lasted for a year and a half. It was a heart-rending affair, since at times it almost seemed as though an agreement could be reached. The Russians professed themselves quite willing to disarm altogether, if the other nations would only do so; the Americans, first under Hoover and then under Roosevelt, withdrew to some extent from their postwar isolationist policy and said that they would be willing to consult as to violations of the Kellogg-Briand Pact, even if they would not bind themselves to enforce it. The British were eager that aerial warfare be placed under the ban, with a caveat in regard to distant and desolate regions like Afghanistan where the possession of planes made much easier their task of maintaining the Pax Britannica. The French even agreed to a German army equal to their own in Europe, with the caveat that additional troops be given to the Tricolor for service in Africa and Asia. Even the Germans finally intimated that they might be willing to wait a few years before insisting on full equality, provided they were permitted to have immediately a limited number of tanks and planes as an indication of good faith and ultimate equality. Now at last it seemed possible to rid the world of at least one nightmare.

When, indeed, the British presented a detailed plan showing how the sum total of men under arms in Europe might be reduced by 450,000, although adding to the armed force of Germany, Austria, Hungary, and Bulgaria 177,000 men, and when the Germans accepted the British plan on principle, hopes ran high.

Suddenly, then, Hitler ordered his representatives back from the conference and withdrew Germany from the League of Nations. He appealed to the German nation for a vote of confidence. He had done his best, he said, to preserve peace, but he would no longer submit to the humiliation of his country. His action was endorsed overwhelmingly at the polls in a burst of patriotic fervor, and in the next year the German budget for armaments was published—an increase of three hundred per cent for aircraft (forbidden altogether by the Versailles Treaty) and an increase of over fifty per cent for the army. Disarmament was dead in Europe!

And why? One answer may be found in a table, prepared by the Carnegie Endowment for International Peace, which shows the following figures in millions of dollars for military and naval purposes:

Country	1914	1931	Percentage
Britain	375	535	+42
France	348	455	+30
Italy	179	258	+44
Japan	95	232	+142
Russia	447	579	+30
Germany	463	170	−60

Geneva had dallied too long with this question, so the Germans thought, and perhaps Geneva really intended to continue the humiliation of Germany by insisting on a far too lengthy trial period. That such presumably was intended would seem to be a fair interpretation placed upon the legalistic phraseology of Sir John Simon, British foreign secretary. Perhaps also Hitler had secret intimation of possible support in the future from Mussolini; perhaps he realized that a quick election on this issue in Germany might endear him so greatly to his German *Volk* that it would be worth while simply from the point of view of domestic politics. At any rate, disarmament was dead; Germany was rearming.

American Isolationists

The rearmament of Germany was a danger signal and so recognized in Europe; but in America Hitler's withdrawal from the League scarcely created a ripple. The reaction against Wilsonian idealism as shown by the 1920 election of Harding grew stronger during the period between the two wars. True, in regard to the Far East we were willing to bring pressure (apart from the boycott and armed force) to preserve the open door in China, and in everything that concerned disarmament, particularly naval, we took a lively interest. We were even willing to have an "observer" present at Geneva to represent the American viewpoint. But throughout this entire period (1920-39) we refused to make any commitments which might involve us in action, and as the war clouds gathered in the late thirties the United States drew more and more within herself, absorbed in her own domestic crisis, confident that nature protected her by a broad ocean on the east and an even broader one on the west.

The indifference of the United States to the growing power of Nazi Germany was due to many causes but prominent among them were two: we felt that we had been generous and kind to our late allies both in the war and in the settlement of their war debts and we thought them ungrateful; we also harbored the naïve belief that future wars could be voted down, prevented, by merely agreeing not to fight, as though war were a kind of disease, like intemperance, and that taking the pledge might ward off its recurrence.

During the First World War and the armistice period, European governments borrowed from that of the United States $10,338,000,000, and concerning repayment there was much dispute. The British, sagacious in matters of finance, proposed a general cancellation all around. They owed us between four and five billion dollars and they offered to cancel a larger sum owed them by France, Germany, and other countries if we would cancel their indebtedness to us. We rejected their proposal. Instead, we signed a contract with the British on the basis of reducing interest from five to three per cent, payments to stretch over a period of sixty-two years, and we signed similar agreements with our other debtors, in all cases cutting the interest charges way below three per cent, but in every instance demanding and receiving (on paper) full repayment of principal.

We thought ourselves very generous; Europe thought us avaricious. There was something to be said for both points of view. Most of the money had been loaned before the armistice and when the loans were originally made they were not thought of as ordinary commercial transactions; they were popularly regarded, even in the United States, as part of our contribution to the war effort. We were at war with Germany, and until our soldiers could be trained and sent into battle the Allies would hold the line, aided by our money. Now we wanted it all back!

The only way our former allies could pay us was by gold, by goods, by services, or by getting the money out of Germany. A large share of the world's gold was already in American banks (soon to be buried in the ground in Kentucky), and it was impossible for our debtors to pay in gold. Our high tariff, raised much higher after the war, made it impossible for them to pay in goods. Payment by services rendered would have been possible had we welcomed British and French workmen in our factories; but that solution would have created unemployment in America. The only possible way remaining was to have our debtors pay over to us what they first must garner from the Germans. But we stoutly insisted that reparations from Germany were none of our affair. We not only did not ask for reparations for ourselves; we considered our former allies greedy, forcing the defeated enemy to pay unjust reparations. Our former allies said, "The money we get from Germany we pay to you. Uncle Sam is the greedy one; he insists on making the Germans sweat."

The Americans refused to acknowledge that this was so; they pointed to the secret treaties made during the War for which they were not responsible, to incessant European broils subsequent to that conflict, to huge sums wasted in rearmament, to their own modest demands made on Germany as evidence of their own moral worth.

These debt settlements made bad blood between Europe and America. Calvin Coolidge put it bluntly when he said, "They hired the money didn't they?" It was not so simple: debt contracts running for generations are apt to be voided, since grandchildren are not concerned about debts incurred by their grandfathers, and currencies are apt to fluctuate in value; thus, when the British pound dropped from $4.86 to $4 the British discovered that although they had paid us several hundred million dollars they owed us more in terms of their own currency than before they paid anything at all. To the significance of these facts we were blind, and then as the years passed and the European countries one by one defaulted (except Finland) the ire of Americans at European bad faith mounted higher and higher until in 1934 Congress passed the Johnson act forbidding American loans to foreign governments already in default on payments due the United States.

Meanwhile we celebrated the "outlawing of war" by the Kellogg-Briand Peace Pact, drawn up during the administration of President Coolidge and signed in 1929 by his successor, President Hoover. The original impetus for this unusual document came from Aristide Briand, Premier of France, who thought a public declaration of eternal peace between the United States and France might be useful. The idea was taken up with enthusiasm in the United States and enlarged so as to include all countries. As amended by us it became a general international agreement whereby the signatories (and practically every country in the world signed it) renounced war as an "instrument of national policy" and agreed that all disputes "of whatever nature and of whatever origin" were to be settled by pacific means.

This Kellogg Pact was our principal contribution to world peace during the hectic years before 1929. As a gesture of friendliness to all the world there was, perhaps, something to be said for it. Since, however, there were no provisos in the pact for its enforcement, the evangelical warmth with which we greeted it was open to question, and herein lay a genuine danger; it led too many Americans to clothe themselves and their country in the righteous garments of peace at far too easy a price.

When the world entered the depression of the thirties President Hoover, like a good business man, proposed a one-year moratorium on all international debts. One year later the Lausanne agreement virtually ended reparations. Our newspapers were delighted at this magnanimity displayed toward Germany; but when they discovered that our allies were only willing to forgive Germany provided we forgave them, they were horrified. Hoover, however, realized that there was a real connection between reparations and war debts and he was willing to reopen the debt question at a world economic conference in London. But before it met, Roosevelt succeeded Hoover, and the former commenced his long presidential career by siding with the economic isolationists, thus torpedoing the London conference in 1933. The President, hypnotized by his theory of the commodity dollar, instructed our representatives to have nothing to do with any program which led to any international stabilization of currency, a bad omen, indeed, for future relations between countries. Without such action there was no sense in holding the conference and it shortly closed its sessions.

Toward the end of his first administration the President, realizing that peace was being rapidly undermined, did his best to align the United States with those powers trying to stay the storm cloud of fascism then rising fast in both Europe and Asia. But he was blocked by an isolationist Congress. Thus, in 1935 the United States Senate refused to ratify the World Court Treaty, a most innocuous treaty whereby under carefully worded reservations the United States agreed to join the Permanent Court of International Justice. Isolationists within Congress and without beat patriotic tom-toms, chanting the Declaration of Independence and George Washington's Farewell Address. The world court, they said, was a child of the League and anything sired at Geneva in their eyes was anathema; the world court was a political, not a judicial body and had so shown itself in the decision against Germany in the matter of an Austro-German customs union (*anschluss*); and people of foreign origin with unpronounceable names (Senator Huey Long's argument) might come to sit in judgment on legal disputes concerning the United States.

An even more striking illustration of isolationist strength was the way in which Congress tied our country up in so tangled a web of neutrality legislation as to deprive the Executive of much needed liberty of action. We not only forbade the export of arms and ammunition to all nations at war, irrespective of who was the aggressor, we also turned our face completely against the historic American doctrine of the freedom of the seas, supplanting it by a new doctrine, "cash and carry." No longer did we propose to protect our American ships, our American goods, or even our American citizens upon the ocean lanes. What we fought for in the First World War we now renounced. In case of war we would sell only for money paid down and for delivery on this side of the Pacific or Atlantic.

The League of Nations was supposed to enforce peace by inaugurating sanctions, penalties laid down, economic or otherwise, against predatory powers. American foreign policy also envisaged peace, for America at least, by a theory quite different. Our position during the second half of the thirties was aptly described by Senator Thomas when he said, "The primary object of sanctions is to stop or prohibit war. The primary object of our neutrality is to keep America out of war. The sanction theory is based upon the acceptance of a moral attitude that war is bad, that it is of universal concern and therefore should be prohibited. The neutrality theory does not consider the moral question nor does it accept the idea of wars being a matter of universal concern. War is not condemned by the law; it is merely assumed to exist. Our neutrality's purpose is one of expediency."

This frank statement in some respects comes close to representing average conviction in the United States. It is somewhat unfair to the isolationist majority. They did not consider "expediency" their watchword; instead what was in their minds was the golden dream of American tradition that this country had been set apart by the Almighty as a haven of refuge from the wickedness of the old world and as a home for the free, the brave, the energetic folk who had cast off forever the effete fetters of Europe. The slogan, "The Yanks are not coming" was not yet posted on American billboards but it was deeply imbedded in the psychology of isolationist America.

Europe seemed far away to most Americans. So thoroughgoing, indeed, was reaction in this country against Woodrow Wilson's idealism that many Americans thought on the flimsiest of evidence that our entry into the First World War had been due to hard-boiled munition manufacturers, crafty bankers. Americans were interested in Europe, but at a distance. We were highly critical of the ineptitude of the League of Nations in the Ethiopian crisis, but we had no intention of doing anything ourselves; we denounced the weak-kneed acquiescence of France and England when confronted by the rape of Austria, but we did not regard that dastardly act as our affair; we were wildly indignant at Chamberlain and Bonnet for selling the Czechs down the river, but that America was in any way responsible for Munich never occurred to us. By the middle thirties most Americans were too engrossed, anyway, with the industrial depression at home, to take more than an academic interest in Europe, a fact not displeasing to those three desperado countries, Germany, Italy, and Japan.

The International Scene (1934-39)

During the next six years (1934-39), the remaining bulwarks of European peace were swept away, one by one. All the major countries of Western Europe played at cross-purposes with one another, and charges of double-dealing and treachery reverberated back and forth between Berlin, London, Rome, and Paris. "*Homo homini lupus*—man is a wolf to his fellow-man," said the cynics, pointing to treaties broken almost before the ink dried on the parchment, and to bold words no sooner spoken by bewildered statesmen than repudiated by fatuous contradictory act. With the single exception of the first year, the tide set steadily against the democratic powers, England and France, and in favor of the fascist countries, Germany and Italy. The cynical observer was prompt with his explanation: British Tories and French bourgeois, fearing above everything else the shadow of the Soviet, were willing to jettison the League of Nations and the cause of international peace in the vain hope of protecting their own pocketbooks by an ultimate war between Nazis and Russians from which they themselves would be delivered. The accusation is questionable. It can only be defended by drawing up an indictment based on a priori hypotheses, by using historical data for the purposes of a lawyer's brief. There is no such clear trail to be found in the diplomatic labyrinth of these perplexing and confused years. In summing them up, about all we may truthfully say is this: Hitler and Mussolini, leaders of the "have-not" bloc of nations, found by 1935 that they could play ball with each other by alternating pressure on the democracies. The latter, wedded to the status quo, suspicious of one another's good faith, began a disorganized and almost panic-stricken retreat before fascist advance, until Adolf Hitler, in March, 1939, entered the Czech city of Prague at the head of his armed forces, there proudly to prophesy the rebirth of the Holy Roman Empire of the German Nation, the ghost of which (supposedly) had been finally buried by Napoleon in 1806.

Only during the first year was there a temporary check to the forward march of the German Cæsar. The Nazis overreached themselves when they tried to gain Austria in 1934 by a blundering coup d'état which succeeded only in killing Dollfuss and in enraging his friend and champion Mussolini. The Duce was not yet willing to have the swastika fly in Vienna, and Hitler did not dare aid those Austrian Nazi cutthroats who broke into the chancellery and slaughtered in cold blood Austria's diminutive Christian Socialist dictator.

It is true that direct evidence is lacking that connects the German Fuehrer with that vile act. But the German Nazis could not well have been uninformed of Austrian Nazis on Bavarian soil, who had used the radio for a year past to foment revolution in Austria. They must have known of plans to invade that country from Germany at the very moment when the state radio in Vienna, which the insurgents in Vienna had captured, proclaimed the downfall of the Dollfuss regime.

In 1935 the German star was in the ascendant. In January came the plebiscite in the Saar which united that valley with the Reich. Within two months followed the proclamation of universal military service in Germany. France and England fumed at this repudiation of Versailles. The former country sounded out Russia for a mutually defensive pact and signed one in May, 1935. The latter tried to make the best of a bad situation by a unilateral bargain with Hitler. The realistic British knew a *fait accompli* when they met one. Germany had built two pocket battle-ships, as she was entitled to by the Versailles Treaty. Now Britain agreed to her repudiation of that treaty in regard to naval construction, pro-vided Hitler would promise not to build a fleet more than thirty-five per cent as strong as Britain's.

The French were not pleased by this act on the part of their sister democracy. If the Germans built to within thirty-five per cent of the British they would have a larger fleet than France, a fact not forgotten by the French when there were intimations a year or two later that France was reluctant in assisting the British to maintain sanctions against Mussolini in Abyssinia.

But Germany's greatest triumph lay ahead. On Saturday, March 7, 1936 (the Fuehrer was said always to choose Saturdays for his thunder-bolts because of the British habit of week-ending), Hitler announced that German troops were crossing the Rhine. "We have no territorial demands to make in Europe," said Hitler, "but the Russian menace is intolerable, and France has broken the Locarno treaty by making a defensive pact with that country."

France had done no such thing. There was nothing in the Locarno Treaty which forbade a defensive pact similar to that made between France and Russia in 1935; and even if there had been room for differ-ences of opinion on that point, the signatories of Locarno had pledged themselves to arbitrate questions which might arise in the future con-cerning that treaty. Locarno had been freely entered into by Germany and had been guaranteed by her as well as by France, England, Italy, and Belgium.

Hitler had no legal justification for violating this treaty, and to do so was an extremely risky act. His army was still small and not well trained; and France could easily without aid from outside have driven his troops, only 90,000 at the end of a week, back fifty kilometers east of the Rhine where the Germans had promised to keep them. Only the year before, in 1935, Italy, France, and England at a meeting at Stresa in Italy had formally rebuked Germany for rearming, and Italy was supposed to be very angry at the German threat against Austrian independence at the time of the Dollfuss murder. No wonder that Schacht, the German finance minister, Neurath, the foreign secretary, and Blomberg, commander of the German army, advised against Hitler's rash adventure.

But the Fuehrer trusted to luck. Had not the British made a bargain with Germany whereby they had insured their naval supremacy? He did not think that they would fight to keep German soldiers away from the Rhine. Italy was already in difficulties over her Abyssinian expedition and there were questions of oil sanctions aired at Geneva; he might be of use to the Duce in regard to these. There remained only France; and with the French alone he was willing to take a chance.

German Jubilation in the Saar, January, 1935

Crowds give "Heil Hitler" at announcement of result of Saar plebiscite.

France hesitated and was lost. The Czechs were in alliance with her and would have hit Germany from the south as she struck from the west. It was her golden oppportunity, and all she did was to explode verbal bombs! This grave infringement of the Locarno pact most certainly would have to be referred to Geneva, so she said, and when the League acted, then France would act. General mobilization was too expensive at this time, in the opinion of the French. Their frugality was ill timed. Needless to say, the Germans remained, and nothing happened except many and violent protests on the part of almost everybody, the Germans being loudest of all, saying that they would be perfectly willing to retire fifty kilometers east of the French boundary if the French would retire fifty kilometers west of it.

Mussolini and Abyssinia

Japan defied Geneva and departed from the League in 1933; Germany did likewise in 1934. It was now the turn of the Duce to defy that august body. He had done so in 1923 without let or hindrance, and he thought it fairly safe to do so again in regard to Abyssinia.

That country, like Italy, was a member of the League, but it was a wild, barbaric land without means of self-defense; and it was flanked besides by two low-lying coastal Italian colonies, Eritrea on the Red Sea and Italian Somaliland on the Indian Ocean. The two colonies were not worth much, but they might serve as pincers between which Abyssinia might be squeezed and conquered, and thus a sizable empire found for Italy.

Mussolini knew that the League (as such) would not be apt to prevent him. It had already been greatly weakened by the successive withdrawals of Japan and Germany, and the only interference with his schemes of conquest that he might encounter would come from Britain and France. The former country depended somewhat on the waters of the Blue Nile for the irrigation of Egypt and a British-constructed dam had been projected for Lake Tana, the headwaters of the Blue Nile, and Tana was in Abyssinia. Furthermore, the mistress of the seas was still mistress of the Mediterranean, and an Italian empire to the east of that sea might tempt the Italians to challenge Britain's control of her route to India.

France, of course, would also object, but he was not afraid of France. The tiny French colony of Obok, or French Somaliland, on the Red Sea, lay between the two Italian colonies, and from Djibouti, its capital, ran the only railway to Addis Ababa, the capital of Abyssinia. The conquest of Abyssinia might threaten the French colony and most certainly would involve readjustments in regard to the railway. Furthermore, there had been friction for many decades between France and Italy over Tunis, and a successful Italian campaign in Abyssinia might make the French fear lest the Italians, on conquest bent, might turn west from Libya as well as east, and take Tunis in their stride.

But France, the Duce knew, had her hands full with a revived Germany. So had Britain, too, for that matter, but Britain's frontier did not run side by side with that of Germany on the Rhine, and Britain had less to fear from hostile Germans in the near future than had France. The German Fuehrer had proclaimed after the return of the Saar Valley that he had no further ambitions in the west, but the French did not believe him. With the French concerned first with Germany, the Duce thought that he was fairly safe in attacking Abyssinia.

In 1934, frontier clashes occurred between the tribesmen of the Negus of Abyssinia, the King of Kings, and Italian soldiers in the hinterland of the Italian colony of Eritrea. Ethiopia (to use the new name coming into vogue for Abyssinia) appealed to the League; but Mussolini sent reinforcements to his troops. The League delayed acting on Ethiopia's complaint. An arbitration commission appointed by Geneva decreed with the wisdom of Solomon that no one was responsible for the frontier incident, since it took place in a region where both contestants believed themselves fighting on their own land. Then France and England offered financial aid to Italy in developing the economic resources of Ethiopia, and they got the ruler of that doomed country to consent to this projected exploitation. But this did not please the Duce; he said that he was going to annex part of Ethiopia and that he was determined to set up a protectorate over the rest of that country.

Committees of the League now tried to bring about a compromise of some sort; but while they talked the Duce acted. In 1935 he began an invasion of Ethiopia both from north and south, and in the autumn captured Adowa, the scene of Italy's debacle in 1896. Geneva now plucked up courage; the council of the League denounced Mussolini as the aggressor and so reported to the Assembly, where by a vote of fifty-one to three, sanctions were invoked—Austria, Hungary, and Albania alone supporting Italy. The fifty-one countries agreed that they would withhold from Italy money, munitions, and necessary raw materials, and they also would not buy from her.

For a short time it seemed as though there would be war between Britain (the foremost country urging sanctions) and Italy. A large British fleet was concentrated off Alexandria in the eastern Mediterranean to close, if necessary, the Suez Canal, thus preventing the Duce from sending any reinforcements to Ethiopia; and England's mightiest battleships lay off Gibraltar, to close the western gates of the inland sea.

But there was neither war nor Italian submission. Instead, the Italians defied the League, advanced on Addis Ababa, and finally captured it in May, 1936. The King of Italy was proclaimed Emperor of Ethiopia and the entire country was annexed to Italy. The conquest had cost that country in the neighborhood of one billion dollars and some thousands of lives. And the League of Nations once again had proved its futility. England, not Italy, had been compelled to eat humble pie. And why? Presumably the historian does not know yet what happened in the British cabinet in the late autumn of 1935. In October Mr. Baldwin was resolute enough and promised "no wavering." No sooner, however, was he safely returned to office than his foreign secretary, Sir Samuel Hoare, made an agreement with Premier Laval of France, by which England and France agreed that the Duce might annex large parts of northern Ethiopia, become entrusted with the economic exploitation of southern Ethiopia, and assume even a kind of veiled protectorate over what was left of Haile Selassie's kingdom, the League of Nations to act as "a kind of consulting specialist, or more probably as a mortician." The implication, to the British Labor party and to the Liberals, was plain: Baldwin had betrayed the cause of collective security; he had permitted himself to be reëlected on a platform supporting the League of Nations and sanctions; once in office again he had shown his real hand, and that of the class-conscious Tories who really admired Mussolini, by offering up Ethiopia as a sacrifice to the Duce and dynamiting the League. Instantly there was hue and cry raised against Baldwin, and this time not by the Laborites and Liberals alone. The Prime Minister, in evil odor with many of his own Tories, yielded before the storm. Sir Samuel Hoare resigned and Anthony Eden, a great advocate of Geneva and of sanctions, succeeded him.

The government intended to continue sanctions; so it said. But it did so half-heartedly, the necessary supply of oil not being cut off. The Duce did not worry; the Germans would soon give the British more serious things to worry about than Ethiopia, and so he pushed his soldiers forward until by the spring of 1936 Addis Ababa was in their hands.

During the interval Hitler occupied the Rhineland and unilaterally tore up Locarno, a menace which struck home to France, which had no intention whatever of risking a war with Italy over Ethiopia. The British knew that they could hold the Mediterranean against the Duce; but how about the North Sea; and the German airplanes as an additional liability if they chose to check the German Fuehrer's forward march?

The Germans were rearming with lightninglike speed. From 1933 to 1936 inclusive it was estimated that they spent some $7,500,000,000 on rearmament, and a large part of that sum on new airplanes. Britain might control the sea but she was well behind in the air race. Winston Churchill instantly sounded the alarm. The facts were that Germany was spending money on rearmament at a much faster rate than Britain, and the Prime Minister's reply to Churchill was not effective. "Supposing," said Mr. Baldwin, "I had gone to the country (1933) and said that Germany was rearming and that we must rearm, does anybody think

SWITZ. AUSTRIA HUNGARY
RUMANIA
YUGO-SLAVIA
ITALY
Nice (FR)
CORSICA (FR)
Rome
ALBANIA
SARDINIA
SICILY
BULGARIA
BLACK SEA
GREECE
TURKEY
SOVIET
UNION
CASPIAN SEA
PANTELL-ERIA (IT.)
MALTA (BR)
TUNISIA (FR)
DODECANESE IS. (ITALY)
CYPRUS (BR)
SYRIA
IRAN
IRAQ
ALGERIA (FR)
MEDITERRANEAN SEA
Tripoli
Bengazi
Alexandria
PALESTINE
SUEZ CANAL
Cairo
TRANS-JORDAN
LIBYA
EGYPT
Aswan
SAUDI
ARABIA
RED SEA
FRENCH
WEST
AFRICA
NILE
Port Sudan
ANGLO-
EGYPTIAN
SUDAN
Khartoum
BLUE NILE
Massawa
ERITREA
Adowa
YEMEN
ADEN PROT. (BR)
FRENCH SOMALILAND
FRENCH
EQUATORIAL
AFRICA
NIGERIA (BR)
LAKE TANA
Addis Ababa
ETHIOPIA
BRITISH SOMALILAND
ITALIAN SOMALILAND
BELGIAN
CONGO
UGANDA (BR)
LAKE VICTORIA
KENYA (BR)

ITALIAN EMPIRE
1939

TRM

that this pacific democracy would have rallied to that cry at that moment? I cannot think of anything that would have made the loss of the election from my point of view more certain."

Thus spoke Baldwin in November, 1936. Four months earlier Geneva had lifted sanctions and Mussolini's victory was complete.

Spain

No sooner had England and France abandoned Ethiopia to its fate than they became concerned about Spain. In the summer of 1936 General Francisco Franco raised the standard of revolt, as we have seen, and a sanguinary war commenced which was to rage with unabated fury for almost three years.

At times it almost seemed as though this civil war were an international one, or about to become so. The Italians and the Germans supported Franco, both morally and physically. They sent him supplies, munitions, airplanes, and also men—the Italians an expeditionary force, the Germans air pilots and technicians. The Russians, on the other hand, forwarded a number of planes to the hard-pressed Spanish Republicans during the first part of the conflict, and from Britain, France, the United States, and elsewhere many thousand volunteers, for the most part communist sympathizers, dashed to the fray, forming an international brigade which did yeoman service fighting against Franco and his rebels.

The Spanish Republicans (the Loyalists) fought against terrific odds, and had they received half as much assistance from the outside world as did Franco and his Fascists, they would have won. Even as it was, the medley of Spanish leftists who composed the Republican or Loyalist armies put up the only real fight waged in all Europe against triumphant fascism between Hitler's advent to power in 1933 and the Second World War of 1939. Even if the French, British, and Americans had only permitted the Loyalists to buy arms in the open market, they might still have kept the Fascists at bay. But this opportunity was denied them. A strict embargo was maintained against the Republicans, but no such embargo, except on paper, prevented the free flow of arms to Franco and the Fascists.

Why was this so? The French government was leftist under Blum, and why could not the popular front in France support the popular front in Spain? It certainly was not to the interest of any Frenchman to have Italian armies south of the Pyrenees in friendly collaboration with German airmen, nor to have Italian troops in the Balearic Islands menacing the French communication with Algeria. The British foreign policy was directed by Tories; but the latter by tradition were supposedly imperialistic, and the extension of German and Italian influence was scarcely a favorable augury for the British Empire. Presumably, both Italians and

Germans would be paid somehow by Franco. There were the Straits of Gibraltar for the British to consider, to say nothing of Port Mahon in Minorca which might readily fall into Italian hands, a *point d'appui* in the western Mediterranean similar to Malta in the eastern; there were the Spanish copper and iron mines which the British might not care to have under Hitler's control. Why, then, should England and France turn their backs on cries for aid from stricken Spain and give, as they did, a completely free hand to Hitler and to Mussolini?

Two reasons would seem to have motivated France—fear of Germany and advice from England. Blum, the premier, had just taken office. He knew that his country was far from united, that there were discordant elements in his Popular Front threatening its dissolution any moment, that his country was in no mood for challenging both Germany and Italy, that those two countries were already collaborating with each other in Spain, that France could not possibly survive another war with Germany without the active assistance of Britain, and that in this emergency it was necessary to let England take the lead. The British motivations were somewhat different. The Conservatives in control of Downing Street disliked all radicals in general and communists in particular. They considered the Spanish Civil War an ideological struggle in which there was so much to be said on both sides that there was nothing to be said for intervening on behalf of either. They wanted a stable government in Spain with which they could do business, and the various leftist alliances which formed the Loyalist majority they suspected would prove unstable. The Loyalists might claim to be merely Republicans, but the British Tories saw communists and anarchists of every stripe and description allied with them, and the fact that the Pope had publicly blessed Franco's cause made them perhaps unduly suspicious of his Spanish enemies. Then, too, Russia was supporting the Loyalists, and the British tradition, with the exception of 1907-17, had been Russophobe for over a century. Lenin and Stalin had been bitter in their jibes against British imperialism, and Russian policy had been orientated too long against the British Empire for British Tories to regard the friends of Soviet Russia with a friendly eye. Neither Hitler nor Mussolini had gone so far as the Russians in abolishing the very foundations of bourgeois society, namely, private property, and possibly they were less dangerous in the long run than Moscow. The British Tories were not prepared to sacrifice the national interests of Britain for their own class interests, but they did tend to identify their class interests with those of the nation. They longed for appeasement, the end of war, the lowering of taxes, and the unity of western Europe against the Soviets—if such were only possible. Whether they went so far as to tell Blum that England would not support him if he got in trouble with Hitler over the Spanish situation is a matter of conjecture. The facts are that Blum visited London, made a favorable impression there, returned to France, and then put on a strict embargo on all arms exported to either side in Spain.

To do so was scarcely to preserve neutrality. By international law the Loyalists, as the official government of Spain, had a right to buy arms in foreign countries, whereas Franco's regime was legally only a rebellion and was not entitled to buy arms. Consequently, the British, the French, and the Americans who placed an interdict on the sale of all arms must be said actually to have taken sides with the Spanish Fascists, no matter how far their sympathies lay with the other side.

Italy and Germany, meanwhile, recognized Franco's government as the legal government of Spain and sent him arms and men. They did, it is true, preserve a semblance of neutrality, since they agreed to join with twenty-five other nations in adopting a policy of nonintervention. All twenty-seven countries prohibited volunteering for the Spanish war, and an international committee meeting in London supported an international blockade of Spain to be carried out by the British, French, Italian, and German navies.

The blockade was a farce; neither Germany nor Italy paid any attention to it. A number of British and Russian freighters were sunk by submarines, supposedly of Italian origin, and for a brief period the international horizon looked very dark. There were threats from England and the submarining ceased. But not so the flooding of Spain by Italian volunteers. England and France tried to get Italy to withdraw her nationals, but Italy hedged, claiming that she could not enter any conference in regard to Spain without the inclusion of Germany, and that belligerent rights should first be extended to Franco. Later in the year 1937, when Franco's victories in northwestern Spain seemed indicative of ultimate conquest, Italy and Germany said they would be willing to consider "token withdrawals," provided they were made by both sides.

The fatal year 1938 dawned with democracy in retreat everywhere before advancing fascism. Baldwin had been succeeded in 1937 as prime minister by Neville Chamberlain, as prone even as his predecessor to make concessions. Chamberlain was determined to appease both Hitler and Mussolini, and this meant the sacrifice of his foreign secretary, Anthony Eden. The latter had acted reluctantly at Geneva as England's agent in removing sanctions against Italy; but he was determined that he would not give way in regard to Italian soldiers in Spain. Chamberlain thought otherwise and took Italian negotiations in his own hand. Eden resigned, a hero to Liberals and Laborites, and to many of the Tories as well, although party discipline kept them from going into the lobby with the opposition. The Duce was delighted and promptly signed an agreement with England on April 16, pledging the withdrawal of Italian troops from Spain *after* the termination of the war. One day earlier Franco reached the sea, thus cutting Loyalist Spain in two halves. That the war could continue in the Iberian peninsula for another year seemed beyond belief.

Austria

The downfall of Eden synchronized with the end of Austrian independence. Hitler's timing had been perfect. He had supported Mussolini tacitly in Ethiopia and openly in Spain; it was now his turn, and the pay and the prey was Austria. The English and the French had not been without intimation of the Fuehrer's dash to the Danube. Rapprochement between the two dictators of Central Europe had become more and more pronounced during the preceding autumn. The Duce was welcomed with pomp at Berlin. Shortly afterward he proclaimed his adherence to an anti-Comintern pact between Germany and Japan, which seemed to prophesy a political alliance between the three Fascist states. And as the year closed, Rumania seemed on the verge of joining the Fascist parade with a pro-Fascist premier. Early in 1938, Hitler announced that Germany would not forget her racial comrades who were persecuted in other lands. He mentioned 10,000,000 of them—and nearly 7,000,000 were in Austria. He then reorganized the German high command, dismissing certain conservative generals and appointing in their place officers said to be more amenable. Nazi agitation increased visibly in Austria, and a Nazi plot was unearthed whereby a legion of exiled Nazi agitators was to march on Austria from nearby Germany to save their country from the Red menace. Schuschnigg, successor to the martyred Dollfuss, feared the worst and fled to Rome to beseech the Duce to protect Austria as he had done four years earlier.

Then Schuschnigg received an invitation from Hitler to attend him at Berchtesgaden, the favorite residence of the Fuehrer, in Bavaria. Here he was berated for many hours by an angry Hitler and presented with an ultimatum. He must release all Nazi prisoners in Austria; he must give Austrian Nazis full political rights; and he must appoint two Nazis to his cabinet. These were Germany's minimum demands.

Schuschnigg hurried back to Vienna and made another desperate attempt to talk to Mussolini. The latter could not be located. The Chancellor then capitulated. With the streets full of recently imprisoned Nazis and with a Nazi in the cabinet in command of the police, it was the beginning of the end. The Chancellor made belated overtures to the Socialists shot down by Dollfuss, but it was too late. There was no help to be had from without in this month of March, 1938. France was in the midst of a ministerial crisis and had no government; in London the German ambassador, Ribbentrop, was supposedly laying the foundations for an Anglo-German entente; and in Italy the Duce had gone skiing.

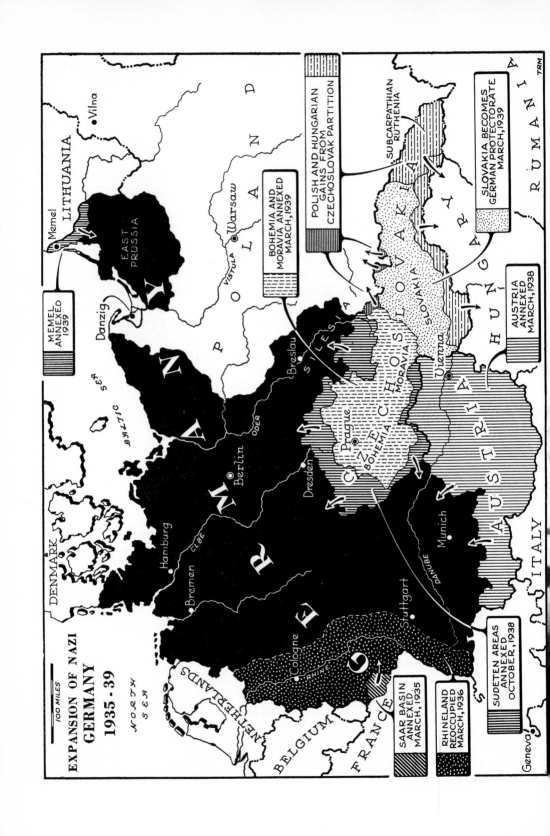

EXPANSION OF NAZI
GERMANY
1935·39

100 MILES

NORTH
SEA

MEMEL
ANNEXED
1939

DENMARK

BALTIC SEA

LITHUANIA

Vilna

Memel

EAST
PRUSSIA

Danzig

POLAND

Warsaw

VISTULA

BOHEMIA AND
MORAVIA ANNEXED
MARCH, 1939

POLISH AND HUNGARIAN
GAINS FROM
CZECHOSLOVAK PARTITION

SUBCARPATHIAN
RUTHENIA

SLOVAKIA BECOMES
GERMAN PROTECTORATE
MARCH, 1939

RUMANIA

TRM

Breslau

SILESIA

ODER

G

E

R

M

A

N

Y

Berlin

Dresden

Prague

CZECHOSLOVAKIA

BOHEMIA

MORAVIA

SLOVAKIA

Uzhorod

HUNGARY

AUSTRIA
ANNEXED
MARCH, 1938

Hamburg

ELBE

Bremen

AUSTRIA

Munich

DANUBE

Cologne

RHINE

Stuttgart

SUDETEN AREAS
ANNEXED
OCTOBER, 1938

NETHERLANDS

BELGIUM

FRANCE

SAAR BASIN
ANNEXED,
MARCH, 1935

RHINELAND
REOCCUPIED
MARCH, 1936

Geneva

ITALY

Schuschnigg resigned, as per order, but that did not stop the Germans. The new Austrian Chancellor requested Hitler to march in and restore order. The Fuehrer generously acceded. His triumph in the land of his forefathers was complete. After April, Austria no longer existed as a state, 99.75 per cent of its inhabitants approving by a popular plebiscite its incorporation into the Third Reich as the *Ostmark*.

Thus there came to an end another of the provisos of the Versailles pact—Austrian independence. And the Fuehrer had broken his word once again. In 1934 he had promised to respect Austrian independence, and in 1938 he had promised Schuschnigg that if the latter yielded to the German ultimatum he would reaffirm his promise. Both promises were broken. France and England pretended to be deeply shocked. Chamberlain said he was shocked. There were even whispers of what the half-buried League might do. In Czechoslovakia, now surrounded on three sides by Nazi Germany, there were those who recalled Hitler's words of the previous January in regard to ten million racial comrades. Seven of the ten millions had been redeemed by Austria's annexation, including those unfortunate Austrians who happened to be Jews, Slavs, and Magyars. Roughly speaking, there were three and a quarter million Germans in Czechoslovakia; could it be that they were the remaining racial comrades in captivity?

Czechoslovakia

The Czechs had watched with anxious eye, as well they might, the submergence of their southern neighbor in the German Reich. Not only did they have Nazis to the north of them and Nazis to the south of them, but within their own border was a clamorous German minority. It had received more consideration than that given to any other minority in the postwar world. It had full parliamentary representation and equal educational opportunities—in fact, there were more German secondary schools in Czechoslovakia in proportion to the population than there were schools for Czechs. On the other hand, that German minority had just cause for complaint: Public officials were generally Czechs; and minor officials, such as postmen and ticket agents, were apt to pretend that they could not understand German. The great estates in Czechoslovakia before the war had been owned by German landlords who were dissatisfied with the compensation paid them when the lands were subdivided after the war among the peasants. More important yet, the condition of the German workingmen in the industrial districts was deplorable. The Czechs were not responsible for the world economic depression of the nineteen-thirties, but they might have been more generous in the relief given to the stricken areas. At one time there were nearly a million unemployed in this little country, and over half were Germans!

Until 1935 most of the Germans in Czechoslovakia coöperated with the Czechs in carrying on parliamentary government, but in that year Konrad Henlein's *Sudetendeutsch Partei*, intransigent and disaffected, captured sixty per cent of the German vote. This party, the S.d.P., was not originally allied with the German Nazis. It did, however, stress certain German principles: hatred of democracy, devout obedience to a Fuehrer—Henlein—and racial particularism. The S.d.P.'s demands now increased, one of them being "full liberty for Germans to proclaim their Germanism and their adhesion to the ideology of Germans," and another a demand that Czechoslovakia should renounce its treaties with France and Russia, the former calling for the military support of the Third Republic should Germany threaten invasion, the latter promising Russian aid, provided France aided the threatened state first. Neither of these demands could safely be granted by the Czech majority; to accede to the first would invite open propaganda against democracy in a democratic state; to accede to the second would make Czechoslovakia defenseless in case of attack.

War was narrowly averted in the month of May, 1938. A frontier incident resulted in the death of two Germans; Hitler promptly cut off negotiations with the Czechs and hastened troops to the border. Czechoslovakia as promptly mobilized and rushed 400,000 men to the German frontier. France affirmed her support of Czechoslovakia and that meant that Russia must follow suit. Britain agreed to support France, and Hitler withdrew his troops.

But he did not change his intentions, nor did the Czechs their resolution to fight for their country. What did take place during the four succeeding months was the betrayal of Czechoslovakia by France, aided and abetted to no little degree by England.

It is very difficult to fathom what lay behind French and British policy in the crisis of September, 1938. Mile by mile the two governments gave way to Hitler's threats and bombast, until finally there was nothing left of Czechoslovakia except a completely disillusioned and discouraged little rump of a country, which could not fight if it wanted to, and which was occupied without a shot by the Fuehrer the following spring.

Czechoslovakia was by no means defenseless in the summer of 1938. She had a good army, a mountainous frontier, defended by a Maginot line reputed stronger than even the famous line of that name in France. Near Prague were the strategic Skoda munitions works, the largest in all Europe, owned by a resolute people, protected not simply by their natural frontiers but by the pledged word of France. In addition, Czechoslovakia was a member of the Little Entente, and both Yugoslavia and Rumania were sworn to aid her. True, Yugoslavia might stand aside for fear of Mussolini, and Rumania was not a dependable ally. But the Rumanians presumably would at least permit the passage of Soviet troops through their territory to aid the Czechs if they were attacked. With France, England, and Russia behind them it seemed improbable that Mussolini would give any active aid to Hitler in order that the latter might occupy Prague.

Nevertheless, the British and the French between them opened the mountain passes to the Bohemian plain, permitted Nazi troops to pass through unopposed, and thus made sure of a war in which they would not have Czechoslovakia as their ally, and Hitler would have Skoda.

The feeble and inept behavior of Britain and France during the last six months of 1938 is incredible. It began when the British sent Lord Runciman to Prague as a kind of unofficial adviser to the Czechs. The Czechs did not ask for him; they did not want him; but they were afraid that if they did not accept him Britain would wash her hands altogether and persuade France to do likewise. Chamberlain had blown neither hot nor cold. He had refused a definite guarantee of Czech independence, but at the same time he had intimated that British policy was not to be interpreted as one of non-intervention under all circumstances. Plainly, they had better accept Runciman.

The Czechs, urged on by his lordship, now offered generous concessions to the S.d.P. and Henlein. They agreed to a cantonal division of Czechoslovakia on the Swiss model. "All nationalities should share proportionately in all state offices and in state enterprises, monopolies, institutions and other organizations." Autonomy in all local matters was assured the Sudetendeutsch, and a large sum of money was to be granted for their economic relief.

This was fair enough, but not sufficiently fair for the London *Times*. It proposed that Czechoslovakia cede its border districts to Germany. The *Times*, of course, was not an official organ of the British government, but the Nazis had good reason to believe that it flew the Chamberlain kite. Hitler took the cue. A few days later, September 12, he addressed a huge meeting of Nazis and said that he intended to come instantly to the relief of his oppressed racial comrades in Czechoslovakia and announced simultaneously that the most impregnable defenses ever built by man were being rushed to completion on the western frontier of Germany.

On September 13 there were uprisings among the Sudeten Germans (acknowledged later by Runciman to have been stirred up by Nazi agitators) and the instant reply of Beneš, President of Czechoslovakia, was to proclaim martial law. One day later Chamberlain announced that he would go by airplane to consult with Hitler.

This was to be the first of three trips by air to Canossa which the Prime Minister of England was to take—successive steps, all of them, in humiliating subservience to the will of the German dictator. The first flight was to Berchtesgaden, where he was told by Hitler that Germany insisted on the instant inclusion of the Sudeten Germans in the Third Reich, even at the cost of a general war. Time would be given Chamberlain to consult with his ministers; no other concession was offered.

What was to be done? The British cabinet was divided; so was the French. The Premier of France and his foreign secretary flew to London and a decision was reached without consulting Prague. Czechoslovakia was told by England and France that she must deliver "the districts mainly inhabited by the Sudeten Germans" to Germany. If this was done there would be guarantees of her future independence.

This was selling the pass, for the districts to be ceded lay along the frontier where the Czechs had their fortifications. England and France were now offering Hitler all that he demanded. Beneš and his cabinet begged for reconsideration. Czechoslovakia had, they said, a treaty of arbitration with Germany. Why not invoke it?

Runciman, meanwhile, made his formal report. It proposed not only to give Germany all that Hitler had demanded but a little more, for he suggested not only that parts of Czechoslovakia be ceded Germany but also that the rump which remained should renounce all treaties of defense with other countries, suppress all anti-German agitation, and enter into close economic relations with the Reich.

The Runciman report was followed by sharp insistence at Prague on the part of the French and British ambassadors that Beneš agree to the Anglo-French proposals. Beneš asked that the demands be given him in writing; he was refused. Would the Czechs yield or not? If France fought on their side they had a good chance, but even so there were German divisions to the south of them in Austria and their own Maginot line was in the north. They would, in any case, be subject to a severe bombardment from the air. But France had now repudiated her word, and without France, Russia was under no obligation. Beneš and his colleagues decided to yield—with the understanding, they said, that Britain and France would guarantee the future independence of what was left of their country, and that the land transferred to Germany would not be occupied by German troops until the new frontiers had been delimited.

Whereupon followed Chamberlain's second flight to Canossa, this time to the little German town of Godesberg. To his surprise he found Hitler in a towering rage. The German army was going to march on October first, roared the Fuehrer, and nothing could stop it. There might be "subsequent corrections" in the boundaries suggested, and perhaps plebiscites. But Germany was going to take by force what was hers by right and would listen to no one. Hitler presented Chamberlain with a map showing what districts Germany was going to annex immediately, and Chamberlain received it, agreed to present it to the Czechs without recommendation, and flew back to London.

The Czechs indignantly rejected the Godesberg ultimatum, the British mobilized their fleet, the French their army. It looked like war. Trenches were dug in London streets, tanks and trucks rolled through Berlin on their way south, and gas masks were distributed in Paris. The British foreign office gave categorical assurance to France that Britain would come to her assistance if she took military action against Germany in the event of that country's invading Czechoslovakia—a much stronger guarantee than Britain gave France on August 2, 1914. Seemingly, Hitler must give way or the Second World War would break.

The Fuehrer gave no indication of yielding. Within five days his Germans were to march. He had no claims, he said, against Poland or France. "After the Sudeten German question is regulated," he asserted, "we have no further territorial claims to make in Europe." But October 1 was the deadline, and to prove that he meant business, German divisions were concentrated on the Czech frontier, and German workmen labored day and night on the "Westwall." To frighten the democracies he even took another step: "German action" (whatever that meant), he told the British ambassador, would commence the next day at 2 P.M., namely, on September 28.

The democracies, on the other hand, did give signs of yielding. The French newspapers deliberately minimized as unofficial the British guarantee of standing by France; and Chamberlain, in a most ambiguous speech, showed that he was of two minds—he spoke of Czechoslovakia as a "far-away country" for whom it seemed almost impossible that England would be fighting, the general tenor of his remarks in the House of Commons sounding more like Hamlet than Pitt or Palmerston. Then, just as the last sands were running out of the hourglass, the Fuehrer, at the request of Mussolini, postponed mobilization twenty-four hours and invited Daladier and Chamberlain to a conference with the Duce and himself at Munich.

Chamberlain accepted, and for the third time made a journey to Canossa. This Munich Conference was still another victory for the dictators. Czechoslovakia was an uninvited onlooker as the four statesmen carved up that unhappy country in accordance with the Godesberg ultimatum. Minute concessions of no importance were made by which England and France might save face. Four zones were to be occupied by the Germans "in four rapid bites instead of one." A fifth zone was created in which there were supposed to be plebiscites. "But the final result was worse for the Czechs than Godesberg would have been." The international commission supposedly in control of plebiscites was a farce. The Germans took what they wanted, marched to within forty miles of

Prague, and absorbed about 750,000 Czechs in the new Germany. As they did so the Poles invaded Teschen, annexing about 80,000 Poles and 120,000 Czechs. Hungary then advanced on the helpless Czechs from the south, crossed the Danube, took Bratislava, and would have divided Ruthenia and perhaps Slovakia with Poland had she been permitted to by the all-powerful Germans. The latter, together with the Italians, decided everything. All French and British guarantees vanished into thin air.

"I return from Germany," said Chamberlain to cheering thousands, "bringing peace with honor." He brought back neither.

Why did the British give way all along the line? Several explanations have been offered. A number of journalists asserted that the British Tories were bluffing from the beginning, that the mobilization of the fleet was a blind and a fake, carried on to deceive the simple, the real intent of the Tories being to support Hitler so that he might become strong enough to be ultimately victorious over Soviet Russia, or at least strong enough to act as their agent in staving off the Red menace. This is pure assumption and a rather silly one, for it lays too much emphasis on economic determinism and suggests an altogether too complicated and subtle a plot. The Tories, after all, were British citizens, and to impugn their patriotism and common sense without evidence is, to say the least, not being historically minded.

Another conjecture was that Britain was profoundly pacifistic, unwilling to fight in any cause which did not directly concern land over which flew the Union Jack. In this there was probably an element of truth, but not a great deal. Pacifistic or otherwise, the sons of John Bull presumably had not been transformed in less than a generation into gentle Quakers.

Two other reasons for Chamberlain's stand come closer to the truth. He knew that, arrogant and boastful though Hitler might be, he had a good talking point in demanding the inclusion of Sudeten Germans in the Reich on the grounds of self-determination. Bohemia had been a part of the old Austria, not a part of the old Germany, but that could not offset altogether the argument for self-determination. Might not Hitler be content with just annexing Germans? Perhaps there was a possibility that he would be! And finally, and perhaps most important of all, was the military argument. Russia was an uncertain factor. The Soviets were said to have promised 200 airplanes for the defense of Czechoslovakia, but on the border of that country were 1,000 German planes that probably would sweep over it before France, England, and Russia could do anything. Stalin had but recently put to death so many generals that Chamberlain might well have questioned the importance of any help Russia might provide, even if she honored her treaty with France. The French were well prepared with their Maginot line for defense, but how could they reach Czechoslovakia to rescue that country from Hitler's maw? And if the French could not, how about England? His first duty was to secure the safety of his own country. He knew that Germany was better prepared for air battles than Britain, and it is possible that he had reliable information that the Reich had a two-to-one superiority in the air. Could he afford to risk a war under such circumstances? Possibly Hitler was bluffing; but on the other hand, possibly he was not. Chamberlain's role in this affair certainly was not brilliant, but that does not necessarily mean that it was absurd. Perhaps he had some right to feel that Baldwin and MacDonald were more responsible in the long run than himself, for it was they who neglected for so many years to make ready against the day when no argument could prevail against Hitler's lawless will unless backed by superior force.

The triumphant Germans, meanwhile, had won two astonishing diplomatic victories in less than six months, since without any fighting at all not only Austria but also the mountain bastions of Bohemia lay in their hands. Hitler had solemnly pledged himself to go no farther, but he had not the slightest intention of keeping his word. Having swallowed somewhat more than one-third of the area of Czechoslovakia, and somewhat less than one-third of the population, he was still greedy for more. What was left of the Republic of Czechoslovakia soon found that it was independent in name only and that it must look to Berlin for guidance. The Germans demanded and obtained a corridor across the country for a military highway; they demanded and obtained the right to decide on the destinies of Slovakia and Ruthenia, not only in respect to government but also in respect to how much land should be ceded to Poland and Hungary. And when Hacha, the last president of the republic, protested against Germany's highhanded interference, he, like Schuschnigg, was summoned to Hitler's presence.

His going to Germany was a formality. Even before he reached Berlin, the German army had started south again. Hacha, berated and browbeaten by Hitler, signed away the independence of his country, and almost simultaneously with his so doing, the Germans entered Prague, none resisting. A few snowballs were thrown at the Teutonic invader; that was all. Czechoslovakia was made a German protectorate, and Hitler could boast of adding still more military booty, to say nothing of much needed gold, to Germany's store.

In characteristic vein, he boasted also of the first German Reich which had been born again. That German Reich had been the Holy Roman Empire, reaching far across the Rhine into France and across the Alps into the heart of Italy.

And he spoke of other things as well, this fateful month of March, 1939. It was not self-determination that Hitler emphasized now, but rather the idea of a German *Lebensraum,* a living space, which he was now in process of gaining for the Third Reich. How large was that living space to be, and where beyond Czechoslovakia was it to be extended? Always until March, 1939, there had been explanations of Nazi diplomacy based upon the iniquity of Versailles and of the violations by the Allies of the sacred right of self-determination. But the demise of Czechoslovakia could not thus be explained. Quite evident it now seemed to thoughtful men that, unless Hitler was stopped, a large part of eastern Europe would fall speedily under his control. And after that, what about Alsace-Lorraine, and French, Belgian, Dutch, and British colonies?

Chapter 38

THE SECOND WORLD WAR

THE OCCUPATION of Prague made war well nigh inevitable. Up to that event there was always a chance that Hitler would be content with his many victories; from now on it was evident that the Nazis were bent on further conquest. Always hitherto they had been able to argue that their successive victories had simply united to the Reich good Germans who longed for a common fatherland. That argument no longer held. The Czechs were not Germans, and the brutal attack on their country in March, 1939, seemed conclusive evidence that Hitler would not stop until the entire continent lay under his thumb—and perhaps not then! Presumably Poland might well be his next victim, but after Poland, what country? It might be Russia; but there were those in London fully aware that Britain administered former German colonies; and there were those in Paris who remembered the ominous words in *Mein Kampf*, "The German people's irreconcilable and mortal enemy is and remains France."

In the spring of 1939, France and England increased their military preparations, drew closer political ties, sought allies. They struck alliances with Poland and Turkey; they guaranteed to march to the aid of the former if she were invaded by Germany; they joined the latter in a mutual defense pact to preserve the status quo in the eastern Mediterranean; they promised unilateral protection to Greece and Rumania; and they invited the Soviets to join them in a defense pact against German aggression.

Joseph Stalin pondered deeply. He hated and distrusted Hitler; he also hated and distrusted Chamberlain. If the Germans drove through Poland or across the Baltic states and attacked Russia, guarantees were needed of armed support from France and Britain. But suppose those two countries failed him at the last hour; suppose they consented to a second Munich whereby Poland fell a prey to Germany and the Wehrmacht stood on the borders of the Ukraine? France and England had ignored Russia in 1938; Stalin had not been invited to Munich; the protests of his representative, Litvinoff, had been ignored at Geneva; the two western powers had abandoned, apparently, the whole idea of collective security. There seemed to be more than an even chance, so Stalin thought, that they would not be displeased at a German-Russian war from which they would stand aloof.

The inept and temporizing character of Franco-British diplomacy did much to heighten his suspicions. Chamberlain three times had flown to Germany to placate Hitler, and Chamberlain, accompanied by Lord Halifax, secretary of state for foreign affairs, had visited Mussolini; but to Moscow at the height of the crisis the British had accredited as their special envoy an under-official of the foreign office, without prestige, without authority.

Nevertheless, Stalin stood ready to make a hard-and-fast military alliance with France and Britain, provided that it included not only guarantees for Poland but for all six small countries on the western Russian frontier, Finland, Estonia, Latvia, Lithuania, Poland and Rumania; guarantees not only against external but also against internal aggression. What this latter meant was clear enough to Stalin. He proposed to ward off and to prevent Fascist propaganda and revolt from within, such as had given Hitler his excuse for invading Czechoslovakia.

These guarantees the British and French were unwilling to give. They feared, and perhaps justly, a Soviet advance in the region of the Baltic, and they argued that the Baltic countries did not want a Soviet guarantee. They would guarantee Poland and Rumania alone; but Stalin thought an attack by the Germans on Russia might readily be staged through the Baltic countries, and he held out for their inclusion in any pact.

Germany, meanwhile, claiming that she was being encircled, and flushed with her bloodless victory of March pounced upon the tiny area of Memel on her northeastern border, hitherto administered by Lithuania in the name of the League of Nations, and made demands on Poland for the return of Danzig to the Reich, together with a strip of land across the Polish Corridor. As she did so Hitler renounced his ten-year peace pact with Poland, proclaiming that the treaties just made by that country with the western democracies had broken friendly relations between Germany and Poland. Likewise for good measure he renounced Germany's naval treaty with Great Britain.

At the other end of the Axis the Duce, not to be outdone, let forth a tremendous blast against the follies of democracy and peace, invaded Albania, and annexed that country to Italy.

The spring of 1939 had been hectic, the summer more so. None could tell just what was happening in Moscow.

Then in late July the French and British sent a military commission to Moscow. Despite many clear warnings from a number of authoritative sources that Stalin might bargain with Hitler, it did not go by airplane; it took a slow steamer and did not reach Moscow until August 10th. Immediately it encountered a snag. The Russians were willing to fight the Germans in Poland provided the Red army was permitted to defend Poland's western boundary. But neither the Poles nor the western allies would accept this qualification. If the Russians were once in Poland, who could or would evict them? On the other hand, from the Russian viewpoint, if the Red army was to fight the Nazis it did not intend to wait until the latter swallowed Poland and were on the Russian border.

Stalin, in the meanwhile, determined not to be caught napping. If the anti-Nazi powers would not do business with him, he would do business with the Nazis. It would be a risky thing to do, but to wait longer was also risky. So it came about that on August 23rd the Nazi foreign minister, Von Ribbentrop, was welcomed in Moscow, and one day later a Soviet-German non-aggression pact was signed, the two contracting powers agreeing that for a period of ten years they would "refrain from any violence, from any aggressive action, and any attack against each other, individually or jointly with other powers."

The Brief Polish Campaign

This act gave the green light to the Nazis in Poland, and in Germany the government-controlled press unleashed a slashing attack on that country, accusing her not only of refusing all concessions but of maltreating Germans within her borders. The Polish question must be settled immediately, said Hitler. He would be content with the return of Danzig to the Reich and the ownership of a super-corridor across the Polish Corridor, in other words with a strip of territory one kilometer wide, sufficient for four railways or motor roads; but that strip must be German. Polish lines of communication north and south must go over or under this strip.

In the summer the skies darkened over Poland. Poles were persecuted in Germany, according to the Polish newspapers; Germans were brutalized in Poland, if the German press was to be believed. Hitler outdid himself in truculence; he would negotiate no longer with the Polish ambassador; the Poles must send a plenipotentiary to Berlin, presumably their prime minister, to accept a German ultimatum, else Germany would act.

In vain did the French and British ambassadors at Berlin assure the Fuehrer that they would investigate carefully German charges made against the Poles. Hitler would not listen, asserting that he had no quarrel with Western Europe, that England and France had no right to intervene in Polish-German controversies. German troops were concentrated on the Polish border and south of it in Slovakia, supposedly an independent country. Then, to frighten the Western democracies still further, Hitler published in triumph a ten-year non-aggression pact with Soviet Russia, his old enemy. Germany was secure now on the east; let the two democracies to the west beware!

The Germans, set on forcing the issue, on August 31 presented the British ambassador with a peace proposal in sixteen points which considerably enlarged their demands on Poland. Not only were Danzig and the extraterritorial traffic zone to be annexed, but also there were to be plebiscites whereby the Germans hoped to add the entire Polish Corridor to the Reich. The Poles, unwilling to sign on the dotted line, were not unwilling to negotiate. But Hitler refused to wait longer. On September 1, without declaration of war, the German armies invaded Poland, Hitler asserting that he had waited two days for the Poles to submit, that Germans were being mutilated by Polish mobs, and that the preceding night Polish troops had fired across the border.

Within one month Poland was conquered. England and France declared war on Germany on September 3, but did nothing to stave off annihilation of their ally. The first day of September saw Warsaw bombed three times and German armies advancing on doomed Poland from four different points. So swift was the German onrush by motorized divisions on land and by squadrons of planes in the air that the Poles never had a chance. While optimistic prophets in London and Paris predicted that French and British planes would soon be shuttling back and forth across Germany to Polish airfields to refuel and return, those very airfields were wrecked by German bombs, and Polish planes were destroyed on the ground. The famous Polish cavalry was helpless against the German *panzer* (armored) divisions. Brilliant sunshine baked the Polish plain, and the rain upon which the Poles depended to make their fields a sea of mud failed to materialize. By the middle of the month all of Poland's important cities (except Warsaw) were in German hands and the Polish government had begun its flight toward the Rumanian frontier.

The Poles fought bravely; they simply were not equipped for modern war. Here and there, scattered Polish divisions thrust vigorously at the encircling Germans. The civilian population of Warsaw turned out en masse to dig trenches around their capital, and the Warsaw radio alternated martial music, defiance of the enemy, and appeals to the world for succor as German planes droned overhead, reducing the proud city to a mass of ruins.

Then, on September 17, came an invasion of Poland by the Soviet army. The Polish government, so the Russians said, no longer existed, and Soviet forces were needed to restore order and to rescue peasants from oppression. Caught between the Germans and the Russians, Poland collapsed. Warsaw, that shell of a city, bombed and burning in a dozen places, held out until the end of the month. On October 1 the Germans occupied what was left. Russian and German armies met as Russia and Germany divided Poland between them, the lion's share of the booty in

HITLER ADDRESSING THE REICHSTAG JUST AFTER THE OUTBREAK OF WAR.

economic resources going to the Reich, the eastern marshes and the Polish Ukraine falling to Russia. Thus within one month perished Poland, a country of 50,000 square miles and 35,000,000 people.

Nazi Germany and Soviet Russia were in accord. Their non-aggression pact now was supplemented by another agreement, the opening paragraph of which struck an ominous note. "In the case of the war's being continued," it read, "joint consultations will take place between the German and Soviet governments on the subject of necessary measures." Just what did that mean? The rest of this pact simply provided for lines of demarcation in Poland and for economic coöperation between the two signatories, Russia agreeing to supply Germany with raw materials in exchange for manufactured goods. From the German point of view this economic accord by itself seemed sufficient guarantee of victory; if the Germans could depend on the Soviets for oil and food, what more was necessary!

Meanwhile, on the western front the French and British were almost immobile. The former wrested a few square miles from the enemy in the region of the Saar and the Moselle; the latter contented themselves with the worldwide seizure of German shipping and with setting up again the blockade of Germany as in 1914. During the autumn, the German submarines sank a number of British merchant vessels, also one airplane carrier and a large battleship, the *Royal Oak*. These victories were offset in December in the South Atlantic when the German pocket-battleship *Graf Spee* crept into Montevideo after an eighteen-hour engagement with three British cruisers, later to be sunk by her own crew rather than fall into British hands.

For the first six months the war in the West was remarkably quiet. The bulk of the British regular army, upward of a quarter of a million men, was transported to France without mishap and went into winter quarters. In both France and England the idea seemed to hold that the war could be won by simply exhausting the economic life of the enemy. It would not be necessary to fight; all one had to do was to wait! The Germans in turn seemed perfectly willing to wait. There were occasional flights of German planes over France and Britain, and of British and French planes over Germany; but these, primarily were for observation purposes. British children evacuated from London gradually slipped back again. Life was uncomfortable during the long, record-breaking cold winter of 1939-40, but as the months passed with little happening, the war almost seemed unreal.

Russia Attacks Finland

All but in one country—Finland. No sooner did Stalin occupy eastern Poland and agree with the Germans in regard to the Polish loot than he stretched out his hands to the Baltic states. Three of them, Estonia,

Latvia, and Lithuania, were too feeble to offer resistance and almost immediately agreed to cede land to the Soviets for naval and air bases. Not so with Finland. The Finns had fought hard for their independence and had won it in 1920 from Red Russia. Now when Stalin sought to whittle it down by demands for Finnish territory the little republic refused to accede. To fight Russia might be madness, but even that was better than surrender.

The Russians pressed the Finns hard. They asked for a rectification of their frontier at Petsamo, a port on the Arctic Ocean belonging to Finland, for six islands commanding the approaches to Leningrad, for a naval station at Hangö, and for a considerable stretch of Finnish territory on the southeastern frontier where Finland's boundary was only twenty miles away from Leningrad. That distance, so the Russians said, made it possible for the Finns to bomb a large Russian city from their own forts, an intolerable situation. If the Finns would yield to these demands, then the Soviets would be conciliatory and offer territorial compensation.

The Finns would not yield. Thereupon the Russians, asserting that they were in danger of Finnish attack (they outnumbered the Finns 50 to 1), commenced an undeclared war, dropping bombs on Helsinki, Finland's capital, on November 30.

The world expected that Finland speedily would be overrun by the Russian steamroller; but the world was mistaken. From December 1, 1939, to March 12, 1940, the Finns put up an astonishing resistance, only to capitulate when their vastly outnumbered soldiers, without ammunition and without sleep, could fight no more.

History has on record no braver epic than this. The Russians swept into Finland along several different routes. They tried to conquer north Finland near Petsamo; they tried to cut across the narrow central section or waist of that underpopulated country, thus severing the north from the south; and they advanced on both sides of huge Lake Ladoga on the southeast, endeavoring to storm the main Finnish defenses, the Mannerheim line, which stretched across the Karelian peninsula from Lake Ladoga to the Gulf of Finland.

In every direction the Finns beat them off. There was only a handful of Finns; but their country was two-thirds the size of France and was said to contain 65,000 lakes, while the land between was covered for the most part with dense forests where roads were few and poor. The athletic Finns, skilful on their skis and well-nigh invisible in their white clothing against the background of their frozen countryside, mowed down the invaders from numerous ambushes; they dug traps for Russian tanks; they set off dynamite under the ice; they broke the Russian lines of communication and captured thousands of the enemy.

Aside from the Karelian peninsula, immediately in front of Leningrad, the Russians had only one approach to Finland, a railway 800 miles long which stretched from Leningrad all the way north to the Murmansk coast and at no great distance from the Finnish frontier. This railway was easy to raid. The Finnish air force, as might have been expected, was unable to cope with the air armada let loose by the Russians; but on the other hand a number of planes were sent to Finland by France, England, Sweden, and even Italy, and the Finns were not helpless in the air. Furthermore, Finland was almost exclusively an agricultural country, and outside of Helsinki and Viborg there were few towns worth bombing.

The Soviet army during the early stages of the war was most inefficient. The army purge of 1937 had resulted in the execution of three out of five field-marshals; and all of the eight general officers who courtmartialed them had since been shot. The morale of the Russian troops was poor. So also was the equipment; the soldiers were clad in flimsy cotton uniforms and thin boots; the fighting was in subzero weather; they never had seen skis; their tanks, huge and cumbersome, broke down in swamps, were surrounded, isolated, captured. Not until Russia threw the best of her fighting men into the war in 1940 was she able to make headway.

The Finns got a great deal of sympathy from the outside world, but little else. It was impossible to reach Finland except either through the arctic wastes south of Petsamo or across Norway and Sweden; and the Germans made it abundantly clear to the Scandinavian countries that they would not permit French and British expeditionary forces to cross Scandinavia. The Germans were not sympathetic toward Russia; but the major source of iron ore for Germany came from northern Sweden and they were determined not to risk having that region overrun by Allied troops. The British had sent the Finns considerable supplies of munitions, and the volunteers also made their way thither in civilian clothes, and that was all.

Then came a final massed assault by the Russians. Throughout February an incessant rain of steel blasted away concrete forts and wave after wave of Russian tanks drove at the defenses. The number of fresh Russian troops was inexhaustible, but for the Finnish regiments no more men were available. Finland, therefore, with inevitable collapse staring her in the face, yielded to all of Russia's demands, made peace in the middle of March, and commenced evacuating the choicest part of what had been Finnish soil, the Karelian peninsula. From it some 400,000 Finns, more than one-tenth of Finland's population, packed their scanty possessions and moved westward into what was left of their country.

Thus far there had been two victors, Russia and Nazi Germany. England and France seemed semiparalyzed with inaction. In the former country Neville Chamberlain, firm in declared purpose but sluggish in act, was still prime minister. That the situation was highly critical and that his own country was well-nigh unprepared for "total war" he never

GIBRALTAR, BRITAIN'S "WESTERN KEY TO THE MEDITERRANEAN"

seemed to realize. At the very commencement of the war the Germans began strict rationing of not only food but clothing; not so in England. The British enforced a strict blackout in their cities and called to their colors their young men. But the necessity of operating their factories day and night and of throwing all they had into military preparation for total war, while there was yet time, did not dawn upon the government. Only Winston Churchill, pugnacious head of the royal navy, had sufficient imagination and foresight to know that the Germans were implacable and ferocious foes who had not yet begun to fight.

So likewise was it in France. General Gamelin, generalissimo of the Allied armies, was reputedly Europe's ablest soldier, and the French army reputedly was the best in Europe. The Maginot line, from Switzerland to the Belgian frontier, was regarded as impregnable. The Belgians, supposedly, were much better prepared for war than in 1914, and the Belgian army was mobilized and on guard. Military experts spoke of the day of offensive war being over, and the French were determined not to sacrifice their diminishing manpower by a useless and costly offense. There was the living example of what happened to Poland; but the Poles had been caught napping, so thought the French, and they were not regarded as scientific fighters anyway. And so in Paris there were even less precautions taken than in London. The French made scarcely a pretense of rationing either food or clothing. They stamped down rigorously on the Communists, established a strict censorship of the press, and increased the hours of labor. But they were as confident of ultimate victory as the British—a victory to be won without shedding much blood!

There was, of course, danger of Italian intervention on the side of Germany; but this the Allies discounted. Mussolini was constantly proclaiming that his alliance with Hitler held; but the Italians certainly hated the Russians and feared their possible advance in the Balkans. After all, Mussolini's threats might be nothing more than blackmail, a bid for concessions in return for neutrality. Italy was for many months no major problem. With the Suez Canal and Gibraltar in British hands, the Franco-British naval control of the Mediterranean secure, there was nothing Italy could do. She would scarcely risk an invasion of the Lombardy plain which might easily be launched from the French Alps. To be sure her nuisance value to Germany was considerable, since her warlike gestures made it necessary that the French keep a large army on the Franco-Italian frontier; but that was all.

The Germans Conquer Denmark, Norway, Holland, and Belgium

Of all the small states, the one which had suffered the most from the war had been Norway. Ship after ship of the Norwegian mercantile marine had been destroyed by Nazi mine and submarine while plying between British and Norwegian ports. There was nothing the Norwegians could do about it except put their shipping under the protection of the British convoy system, which the Germans claimed would be unneutral. Norway, indeed, had legitimate complaint against both Germans and British. A British destroyer boldly entered Norwegian territorial waters to rescue British seamen from a Nazi prison ship, and the British constantly interfered with German shipping threading its way down the coast of Norway with the much-prized iron ore of Sweden which, when the Baltic was frozen in winter, reached Germany via the Norwegian port of Narvik, far north within the Arctic Circle.

Then, with the coming of the spring, war came to Norway with sudden fury. On April 8 the British announced that they had mined the approaches to Narvik, despite the fact that these were within Norwegian territorial waters. One day later Germany invaded Norway.

To reach that country the Nazis were compelled to occupy Denmark, which they did in one day, the Danes offering no resistance. Less than one year earlier the Nazis had signed a nonaggression pact with Denmark. But they did not hesitate to violate it. They were eager to swallow two countries in one bite—Denmark and Norway—and they did.

The very day the Germans swept across the Danish plain, small picked detachments of the German army seized Oslo, Norway's capital, and her only important ports—Stavanger, Bergen, Trondhjem, and Narvik. Only a few thousand men proved necessary, 1,500 being sufficient to secure Oslo. By various routes the Germans came—some by sea, some by transport planes, some disembarking from German merchant ships anchored innocently alongside Norwegian wharfs, while some were already within the country in disguise.

The Norwegians, taken by complete surprise, honeycombed by Nazi propaganda, and ill equipped for war, were not able to put up much resistance. Here and there, Norwegian detachments fought bravely, and effectively. A Norwegian mine-sweeper sank a German cruiser and so did a land battery, and in the mountains hastily assembled militia (the Norwegian army was scarcely more than militia) retarded the German advance.

But there was treachery in Norway. Some Norwegians, dubbed "fifth columnists," welcomed the invaders, and among them were officers in the army. The German plans had been prepared in great detail, long before the British mine-laying at Narvik, and everything ran like clockwork. On the very first day all the Norwegian airfields were occupied by Germans and the tiny air force of Norway was useless. So completely taken by surprise were the Norwegians that their king, pursued by Nazi troopers in four autobuses, barely escaped capture.

Nevertheless, for two weeks or so it looked as though the Allies might successfully come to Norway's rescue. With Britain in command of the seas it should have been easier to land larger bodies of Allied troops in Norway than of Nazi soldiers. To many commentators Hitler's coup seemed a rash adventure, even more rash than the great Napoleon's invasion of Spain.

But the facts were that the Germans commanded the air if not the sea, that they did not need many troops, that at the start they had secured all the available ports at which any large number of troops could be disembarked easily. The British navy did score a minor success in sinking some German ships in the Skagerrak; but it proved difficult for the British to operate successfully in those nearby waters, with the German submarine beneath and the German airplane overhead, and after all it was not necessary for the Nazis to transport many men by water. Speed counted far more than numbers, and needed reinforcements were sent by passenger airplanes.

It was a difficult task to dislodge the German invader, and one beyond the none too brilliant British war office. At Narvik the British had their greatest success when their battleship *Warspite*, veteran of Jutland, did break into Narvik fiord, there to sink seven German destroyers. And this most northern port of Norway, far away from German reinforcements, ultimately was captured by the Allied besieging army, only to be evacuated in early summer, as the German advance in the Low Countries and in France made it necessary for Britain to recall all soldiers available for the defense of their island home.

The Allies could not well fight the Germans from Narvik; too many miles of well-nigh trackless forest intervened between that arctic port and the more inhabited parts of Norway. Therefore an expedition against Trondhjem was decided upon. This Norwegian port, at the head of a long and winding fiord northeast of Scotland, could not well be approached directly because of fear of German mines, even though there were only a handful of German soldiers within the city. The plan was to assault the port from the land, and for that purpose the British landed 12,000 men in two divisions, one to the north and one to the south.

These two expeditionary forces had to disembark on open beaches and were ill supported by light artillery and anti-aircraft guns. What was more serious, they were practically without planes, for the Germans had the landing fields in their possession. Nevertheless, the British advanced boldly, seeking to join their forces and encircle Trondhjem. As they did so the Germans moved swiftly to succor their detachments in that city. Scattered Norwegian units attempted to hinder the swift moving German motorized detachments, but German speed and German efficiency were at their best. On April 30 the German advance units had made contact with the German garrison of Trondhjem. Three days later the British took to their boats which lay north and south of the city.

French, a fact which impeded Allied resistance but aided the German advance, since the German *stukas,* low-flying dive-bombing planes, struck mercilessly at civilians and soldiers alike.

Speedily the German scythes swept on down the valley of the Somme toward Amiens; then cut through to Abbeville, only a few miles from the Channel, and sweeping toward the north reached Boulogne. The exultant Germans, not stopping, kept on to Calais and, finding that town stoutly defended, swept around it, almost reaching Dunkirk. A million Allied soldiers apparently had been surrounded.

There were for the latter two alternatives: to cut through the German lines of communication, not as yet very wide or strongly held; or to escape by sea to England.

On paper the first possibility seemed feasible. In less than a week the German lines had been so distended by the great, huge arc which they formed that a simultaneous thrust by the Allies on the Channel and by the main French armies before Paris might have pierced it, thus creating a pocket or pitfall whereby the German armies, which had passed the point of piercing and which had reached the Channel at Abbeville, would be severed from the main German forces and in turn be in danger of segregation and forced to surrender.

Why was this not done? Gamelin had been removed as Allied Generalissimo and Weygand, pupil of Foch and hero of the First World War, now in command, was expected any moment to commence this counterattack. Instead of doing so, he began hastily to dig trenches and to form a new line of defense. Possibly he considered that essential to protect Paris; possibly, and more likely, owing to the confusion created by the sheer audacity of the German thrust, and by the activity of German fifth columnists in France, he was unable to concentrate his troops. Yet every hour this counterattack failed to materialize saw the German lines of communication strengthened by German artillery and German infantry.

Then, whatever chance the Belgian, French, and British armies at the Channel had of piercing the German lines and joining forces with the French armies to their south went begging when the Belgian king surrendered. His army, upward of a half-million men, was in sorry plight, its ammunition spent, its food supply gone. King Leopold's men held the left wing of the Allied forces, and if they were out of the combat apparently there was nothing to prevent the Germans in Belgium from pushing on until they joined hands with the German army advancing eastward along the Channel. The French and British had come to Belgium's succor at the request of the Belgian King and he was under deep obligation to them. On the other hand, could he fight longer? To do so, he thought, would simply result in sacrifice of life.

The Belgian lines covered a distance of thirty miles which instantly had to be covered by the hard-pressed British. The result was that the latter lost contact for the time being with parts of the French army, several divisions of which were cut off by advancing German columns. What was left of the French army joined with the British, and these Allies, closing their ranks, pressed close together along the sea coast at Dunkirk, where it seemed improbable that more than a few thousand could be conveyed across the Channel.

Then out of the jaws of death and gates of hell over 335,000 French and British soldiers were rescued. From the end of May to the fourth of June the Royal Navy and the Royal Air Force, aided and abetted by all kinds of miscellaneous seafaring folk, worked at this task. The skies were darkened by planes as the RAF and German planes engaged in one unceasing duel; German artillery sprayed the beaches with its shells; German submarines and motor-launches, equipped with torpedo tubes and rapid-firing guns, swarmed out for the kill; and the German infantry threw itself "on the ever narrowing and contracting appendix within which the British and French armies fought."

The British would not use their battleships in these too-narrow waters, but every available light cruiser and destroyer was commandeered, as well as innumerable other craft. Over 200 naval warships took part, and three times as many other vessels. No one will perhaps ever know just how many, since with complete unanimity the owners of yachts, tugs, fishing smacks, motorboats, river steamers, and barges aided in it. Anything afloat that could carry men was used. Only one narrow pier at Dunkirk, constantly bombed by the Germans, was available, and over this poured a steady stream of men. Soldiers by the thousand waded into the shallow waters off the beaches and stood up to their armpits waiting for a friendly hand. Old men past sixty and young boys of fifteen worked together in hauling them into lifeboats. Almost everyone in southeastern England connected in any way with boats and shipping took part.

Day and night the work continued; back and forth the impromptu ferries plied; and on one day alone over 60,000 half-starved Soldiers of the King reached home in safety.

The evacuation was unparalleled in military annals, and the total loss to the British army was but 30,000, but little over ten per cent. Nevertheless, the very fact that there had to be evacuation made it a disastrous British defeat. Left behind in France and in the hands of the Germans were over 1,000 heavy pieces of artillery, vast stores of munitions, food, gasoline. For the time being, Britain's scarcity of war matériel was appalling, and a militant foe, flushed with victory, held Scandinavia, Holland, Belgium, and the Straits of Dover.

Not since the days of Bonaparte had Britain been in such evil case. Churchill, while praising his fighters, did not minimize the issue. Said the Prime Minister in the House of Commons: "We shall defend our island whatever the cost may be; we shall fight on the beaches, landing grounds, in fields, in streets, and on the hills. We shall never surrender, and even if, which I do not for a moment believe, this island or a large part of it were subjugated and starving then, our Empire beyond the seas, armed and guarded by the British fleet, will carry on the struggle until in God's good time the New World, with all its power and might, sets forth to the liberation of the Old."

Dark as the Allied cause was, it speedily grew darker. The Germans did not hesitate a minute. While the world wondered whether they would instantly "sail for England" or try to destroy France first, the Nazi legions embarked on the latter course. On June 5, the superbly mechanized armies of the Third Reich attacked the French in an offensive that stretched from the northern end of the Maginot line all the way to the mouth of the Somme at Abbeville—the Battle of France had begun.

Everywhere they met with victory. For a brief moment it looked as though they might be foiled by the new tactics of Weygand. That general, copying German precedents in 1918, made no attempt at holding a rigid line but let the German tanks through the first French defenses and tried to lead them into carefully concealed traps. But all that Weygand did was to retard the enemy slightly. The Germans now were using 1,500,000 men, nearly 100 divisions, and the French were outnumbered in the field two to one, since large numbers of their best troops were either isolated in the Maginot line or guarding the Italian frontier. The line of battle extended over 200 miles and so swiftly drove the Germans that the breaking French had no time to gather their forces to counterattack.

Soon it was all over. As the German armies drew close to Paris for their final battle, Italy declared war on France and England. The Duce said the time had come to break the Mediterranean prison in which Italy was confined, to strike a blow at the "pluto-democracies." On the Franco-Italian frontier were 400,000 Italian troops ready to attack France from a new quarter. Italy was to be in at the death.

The latter was not unduly prolonged. The Germans marched into an undefended Paris and three days later Marshal Pétain, at the head of the French government which was now at Bordeaux, asked for an armistice. On June 22 it was granted, and the French armies surrendered, the Germans occupying France to the Loire, the Italians having advanced a few miles in the French Alps and along the Riviera.

The Battle of France had ended. Like that of Flanders it was a quick, decisive victory for the invader. The French had been no more successful than the Poles in defending their country; and why?

Certainly one important reason was the subversive activity of the Nazi fifth column. France was betrayed as well as defeated. It had long been flooded with Nazi agents pretending to be tourists or salesmen or sometimes refugees from Nazi oppression. Now, during the war, wearing the uniform of the French staff, they gave contradictory orders, signaled German planes, aided German parachutists, spread rumors of defeat and disaster, demoralized the civilian population and paralyzed military action.

The French generals were old men, veterans of the First World War, deluded in the belief that wars of maneuvre were things of the past. They were Maginot-minded, placing all their bets on skillful defense. They laughed at young De Gaulle, a tank expert, and regarded his enthusiasm for tank divisions as fantastic dreaming. The French had tanks, good ones: but here again came the defense delusion. Tanks according to the French high command were moveable forts, serviceable for guarding bridges and fords, of auxiliary value only.

But most important of all; the French had no stomach for fighting. Their casualties in the First World War had been proportionately much higher than those of any other country. They just could not bring themselves to go through it all again.

The armistice paralleled in many ways that earlier armistice of November 11, 1918 (see p. 560). It was signed in the same railway carriage at the same spot where the Germans surrendered in the First World War. Its terms were equally harsh, and in one important respect even more so. Not only were the French to give up all their military supplies and equipment and to pay for the cost of occupation, but more than half of France was to be occupied by the triumphant Germans, including the entire Atlantic sea coast from the Belgian border to that of Spain. Concerning the ultimate disposal of this occupied territory nothing was stipulated. Even the Italians, who signed a separate armistice with France a day later, were content to wait until the war was over before receiving the jackal's share of booty.

The Germans had reason to think that the war was over. To be sure, the British had retrieved most of their troops, but the greater part of their war matériel had been left behind in France. A few days before the armistice Churchill had begged the French government to flee to North Africa, promising political union with the British Empire and a joint fight for victory. The offer had nearly been accepted; it failed by but one vote in the French cabinet. But the French, like the Germans, thought the war at an end, and the aged Marshal Pétain, who had assumed control of the government with dictatorial powers in the midst of the crisis, believed it his duty to come to such terms as he could with the enemy.

Fortunately for Britain, the Germans were in no condition to start an immediate invasion of that hated island. The disarmament of France had to be completed and vast military preparations made at the Channel ports before that happy event could be announced. Consequently there came a lull in hostilities which, apart from various intermittent air attacks on British ports and British shipping, was to last the greater part of the summer.

Britain Fights On

England was not only stunned; she was bitterly disappointed at her ally's withdrawal from the war. If Pétain had only transferred his government to Morocco it would have been safe from the Germans except for a possible air attack, so the British thought. Furthermore, the large French army in Syria would also be safe, and with the French army in Tunis threatening Italian Libya on one flank and with the British in Egypt on the other, any Italian offense in North Africa could be checked. Churchill had promised to carry on the war from Canada if England should be subjugated; why should the French be less determined?

What disturbed the British more than anything else was the future of the French fleet. The armistice terms provided that it should be interned, and the Germans promised not to make use of the French navy against France's ally. But suppose they did not keep their word? In that case German, French, and Italian navies might readily cripple British sea power, and in that eventuality the war would indeed be lost.

Thereupon the British decided they must act. The French fleet was scattered; part of it was in British harbors, part in home ports, part at Alexandria in Egypt, with the British squadron stationed there, part in the Pacific and in the West Indies. But the larger part lay off the French North African port of Oran, and to it steamed three of Britain's largest warships. Their commander delivered an ultimatum to the French admiral; he must either join forces with him against the Germans or sail to British ports or cross the Atlantic to dismantle his ships there, or else the British would use force to prevent the French ships from falling into German or Italian hands. The French elected to fight rather than yield; the British opened fire and sank or disabled three French battleships, a seaplane carrier, and two destroyers. One battleship, badly crippled, escaped, together with some lighter craft, to Toulon. The French squadron at Alexandria, meanwhile, agreed to dismantle and the French ships in British ports surrendered without much fuss, some of the sailors agreeing to continue the fight on the British side. One great French battleship stationed at Dakar was put out of action by a surprise attack, and here and overseas some French naval vessels were seized. Of the very considerable French navy, only a few scattered units remained and the British breathed easier.

This naval activity ushered in the month of July. Otherwise it was to prove a comparatively quiet month. Despite the fact that the entire coast of France was in German hands, the British managed to send their merchant ships through the Channel. There was a great increase in the number sunk, and the British lost several destroyers of which they had all too few, but they were able to keep the Channel open. What is more, they could claim by the end of the month that despite all losses since the commencement of the war the total tonnage of their mercantile marine had increased, since large numbers of Norwegian, Danish, Dutch, and Belgian ships were now under their control.

The only marked successes of July, curiously enough, were won without bloodshed by Stalin. That wily Russian seized this moment to annex to the Soviet state Lithuania, Estonia, and Latvia, the three little Baltic states which he had already cowed into granting naval bases to the Soviet. Bessarabia also was demanded from Rumania and obtained without a fight, and together with it the Russians took part of Bukovina for good measure.

Meanwhile, England girded herself for battle on her own soil. At last the British were fully awake to their own danger. They made an armed camp of their island. To its strength were added certain Polish detachments, many French soldiers under General De Gaulle, recognized by the British as the head of "Free Frenchmen" who would continue the fight, and over 100,000 soldiers as well from Canada, New Zealand, and Australia.

There were men enough, over 1,000,000 under arms, but the immediate danger lay in civilian coördination and in war matériel. Almost overnight England was transformed. Parliament placed every man and every shilling at the disposal of the government. Arrests were made of all suspects; possible landing fields for enemy planes were blocked by concrete pillars and trenches; home guards were organized to watch for parachutists; and factories worked day and night turning out planes, guns, shells.

Fortunately for the British, the Germans were so occupied in coalescing their continental gains that it was a good six weeks after the fall of France before they were able to strike at England with force. Intermittent air raids continued during that time on British seaports, and the RAF struck back as far as it was able on Nazi-controlled French air bases, but it was September before the Nazi power really showed itself.

The Nazis then struck straight at London, their bombers swooping across from Calais and swarming up the Thames Valley. Their planes came in squadrons of 100 or more at a time, first by day and then by night, and kept on doing so for weeks at a time. Occasionally there would be a lull, a day or two with scarcely an alarm. Then would follow renewed raiding. In September it was directed mainly at London, but as the autumn wore on it extended elsewhere—to Bristol, Southampton, Liverpool, and other shipping centers, to the Midland cities of Coventry, Birmingham, and Manchester.

Early in the air war the RAF was able to strike down a great many of the invading planes, for the latter flew mainly then by daylight, seeking definite targets such as docks, railway yards, manufacturing plants. But when the Germans switched to night attacks it was not so easy for the RAF or the anti-aircraft gunners to locate the foe. In the summer the British had looked forward to the short winter days as partial protection against the *Luftwaffe* (air force) of General Goering. But now with night attacks the autumn and winter season made it all the harder for the harassed islanders.

The damage done by the Luftwaffe was extensive. First would come a squadron of planes to unload incendiary bombs to start fires which would serve as beacons; and then successive waves of bombers would follow. Thousands of houses were destroyed, in many cases their inhabitants buried beneath the debris. Docks, churches, hospitals, factories, whole city blocks were left in ruins.

The Germans could report great material success, but one thing they had not been able to accomplish: they had not "softened" the fighting spirit of the British. Rather they heightened it. Crowded into congested and unsanitary bombproof shelters and in the London subway, snatching a few hours' sleep here and there, the citizens of London responded superbly to the German challenge. The killed and seriously wounded numbered several thousand a week while the raids were at their worst, but after all, this was only a very slight proportion of London's many millions of inhabitants, and the latter, regarding themselves as real soldiers (as they were), kept their thumbs up, working like beavers to clear their streets of debris and to "carry on."

As a matter of fact, serious as were the air raids over British cities, they were far less serious than the ever increased activities of the German submarine. Bad as the situation had been in 1917, it threatened to become worse in 1941. In the former year the U-boat bases were confined to the narrow shore line of Germany and of Belgium. In 1941 the sea coast of Norway, Denmark, Germany, the Netherlands, Belgium and France was now at Germany's disposal. Forth from their innumerable lairs now crept the Nazi submarines, not one at a time as formerly but hunting in packs like wolves and assisted by planes of wide cruising area, serving as eyes for the submarines.

The sinking of vessels flying the Union Jack jumped up to dangerous proportions and early optimism gave way to genuine alarm. More civilians thus far had lost their lives than had British soldiers, in England; but after all civilians could, if they must, adjust themselves to sleeping underground. But the war would be lost if cargoes could not be delivered, cargoes of food as well as of munitions. And what made the British worry more than anything else was that the Royal Navy, gravely deficient in destroyer strength at the war's commencement, had suffered severely in this category of ships, many destroyers having been sunk and many more laid up for repairs because of damage from the air.

Fortunately for the British, they had a warm friend in President Roosevelt, who did not hesitate by a stroke of the pen to deliver to the British Admiralty in September fifty over-age American destroyers in return for naval bases in the Atlantic and Caribbean.

The agreement was as follows: Great Britain presented two of the eight bases, those in Newfoundland and Bermuda, as a free gift. The other six, those in Jamaica, St. Lucia, the Bahamas, Trinidad, Antigua and British Guiana, were in payment for the destroyers. All eight bases were to be leased to the United States for a period of ninety-nine years, free from rent.

Congress was in session at the time but the President did not consult that body. Arming himself with an opinion handed down by his attorney general as to the validity of the transaction, he acted with speed and secrecy, and certain of the destroyers were already on their way to a Canadian port before America knew of their transfer to the British flag. Nevertheless, there was only scattered criticism in the United States, partly because the "destroyer deal" was an extraordinarily good bargain for the United States, partly because American public opinion was whole-heartedly on Britain's side.

The destroyers helped; but by the end of the year Britain stood in need of even more naval assistance, and particularly in need of more cargo vessels. Over 3,000,000 tons of shipping was sunk by Germany during the first fourteen months of the war, if we are to include Belgian, Dutch, and Norwegian shipping flying the Union Jack. With British yards producing less than 1,500,000 tons a year, and with small likelihood of speeding up that production, the gravity of the situation became more and more apparent.

Japan Joins the Axis (1940)

On September 27 an important victory on the diplomatic front was won for the Axis when Japan joined Germany and Italy in a triple alliance whereby Japan recognized the leadership of Germany and Italy in establishing a "new order" in Europe, in return for which Germany and Italy recognized Japan's leadership in establishing a "new order" in "Greater East Asia." In accordance with the treaty: "if one of the three contracting powers is attacked by a power at present not involved in the European war or in the Chinese-Japanese conflict" then the other two powers must assist "with all political, economic and military means."

Ostensibly this was a thrust against the United States, since that country and Russia were the only nations which could well be called powers not already engaged in the conflict, and since Article 5 in the treaty expressly stated that its terms "do not in any way affect the political status which exists at present between each of the three contracting parties and Soviet Russia."

Why this treaty? The reasons motivating Japan are easy to fathom. Angered by the Russo-German neutrality pact on the eve of the war, Japan had stood warily to one side during the first year of the conflict, waiting to see who would win. Now she felt she could wait no longer. The Japanese longed for French Indo-China; their mouths also watered at the thought of the Dutch East Indies, so ripe and so rich a prize almost within their grasp. Victorious Germany was now willing to concede to Japan the leading part in organizing a "new order in the East" in return for hypothetical aid against the United States. If the Japanese did not accept now and if Germany won the war without their aid, they might not find the Nazis quite so generous in the future. If, on the other hand, Britain won the war there would be no Indo-China and the Netherland East Indies for the Japanese Empire.

Just what Germany and Italy hoped to gain is not quite so evident. Clearly the alliance meant that Germany was now granting Japan the hegemony if not ownership of lucrative colonial pickings which the Nazis had hoped to secure for themselves in Asiatic seas. Probably it meant an insurance policy taken out against the United States, a policy which Germany might hope to cash in on later by causing the United States to keep her fleet in Pacific waters. Also, and very probably, it was a bait to the Soviet. Let the latter join the new triple alliance and there would be "new orders" and *Lebensraumen* for all the allies: the Far East for Japan; India, Afghanistan, and Iran for Russia; the Mediterranean for Italy; western Europe, central Africa, and perhaps South America for the Nazis!

If this latter was the main Nazi motive, it failed of accomplishment. The Russian foreign secretary, Molotov, came to Berlin and engaged in long conversations. But nothing apparently eventuated except protestations of neutrality and good will. The Russians were said to have advanced claims too extensive for the three allies to accept, claims which involved territorial concessions in eastern Asia at Japan's expense. What actually took place was a closely guarded secret. But Russia did not sign the pact and the three allies had to be content with the adherence, as we shall note later, of Rumania, Hungary, and that pygmy creation of Nazi Germany, Slovakia.

For the time being, the diplomatic adherence of Japan to the Axis accomplished little. It gave the Japanese an easy entrance into northern Indo-China, which they occupied with very faint protests from the defeated French government of Pétain—located at Vichy in unoccupied France, supposedly independent, but entirely at the mercy of the Nazis who had incarcerated in Germany over 1,000,000 French soldiers. But it also led to action on the part of the United States which took the form of an embargo on certain highly desired war matériel and an official warning to all Americans to withdraw from Japanese-controlled China. The United States even went further: she extended financial aid to the embattled Chinese Republic and encouraged Britain to reopen the Burma Road in order that war supplies might be rushed to Chungking and Chiang Kai-shek. The Japanese did not take these rebuffs kindly. On the other hand, there was little they could do about it. The American fleet stationed at Hawaii was superior to their own, and presumably the great British naval depôt at Singapore would be open to it in case of emergency. The Japanese army had bogged down in China, and certainly no help was immediately available from Germany and Italy. Therefore the Japanese government did nothing; but the Japanese press boasted loudly of Japan's Monroe Doctrine for eastern Asia and that the dawn of Nippon's greatness would soon come.

The Near East

Meanwhile, in 1940 the war spread to the Near East. The Balkan states had no desire to be drawn into the conflict. Nevertheless it was almost impossible for them to avoid it, partly because within their borders were raw materials much sought after by the Germans, like oil and foodstuffs, partly because they lay between the triumphant Axis and lands subject to British and French overlordship, such as Syria, Lebanon, Palestine, Egypt, and countries still farther distant, such as Iraq and Iran.

Of the five Balkan countries, three leaned toward the Allies, one might be said to be at first almost completely neutral, and one leaned somewhat toward the Axis. The Turks were both anti-German and anti-Italian. They were not, however, anti-Russian, and the defense pact which they had signed with the Allies before the war and which they had strengthened after its advent specifically excluded action against Russia. Yugoslavia and Greece also were pro-Ally in sympathy, not so much because of fair liberty as for fear of Hitler. The Yugoslavs had neither forgotten nor forgiven the unwillingness of the Italians to aid Serbia during the First World War, nor Italian determination to control the Adriatic. The same held true of Grecian memories of Mussolini's earlier bombardment of the island Corfu. To both of these Balkan countries the Italian annexation of Albania in 1939 was an ominous warning. Rumania was more or less equally poised between the conflicting powers. She asked nothing of her neighbors but she feared them all; feared Hungary lest she demand the return of Transylvania; feared Bulgaria, from whom she had taken Dobruja after the second Balkan War. She also feared Soviet Russia lest that country should invade Bessarabia, a czarist possession in 1914. What Rumania wanted was to be left alone, and therefore she played Germany and the Allies against each other, hoping for the best. Bulgaria alone somewhat favored the Axis, for the status quo displeased her mightily and she held grudges against all her neighbors.

Meanwhile, in the Near East one other country, theoretically independent, hoped against hope to stay out of the war. Egypt was an ally (as far as the law went) of England. But the alliance had been part of the bargain whereby Egypt had won recognition of her independence, and since British troops were in Egypt to guard the Suez Canal, the independent status of Egypt seemed only a nominal affair to many Egyptians.

To act as a counterweight against an Axis offensive in the Near East, and possibly to organize a thrust of their own, directed against Germany's back door, the Allies had stationed relatively large armies in that region, the British components of which were located in Egypt and Palestine, the French in Syria and French Somaliland. Before the fall of France this seemed good strategy. If the Italians should strike east from Libya against Egypt and the Suez Canal, they would be caught between two fires— between the French in Tunis and the British in Egypt. Should the Italians in Ethiopia move against the Nile Valley or the Suez, they would be exposed to a flank attack from French Somaliland. But with France out of the picture the situation was reversed. The British in Egypt now were in danger of being caught between the Italians in Ethiopia on their east and the Italians in Libya on their west.

Even before Italy was in the war she proceeded to augment her already large forces in Libya and to prepare an offensive against Egypt. During the summer of 1940 the Italians started their march against Egypt from Libya, and invaded British Somaliland from Ethiopia, easily conquering that sandy waste south of the Red Sea. And as they did so, they pushed westward from Ethiopia into the northern Sudan and southward into the outlying districts of Kenya. The hard-pressed British were indeed in danger and had, for the time at least, but one ally upon which to depend—the weather, since campaigning in Egypt and in the Egyptian Sudan is extremely difficult in the summer.

Then, as the Italians struck at the southern sections of the Near East, the Germans laid their heavy hands upon Rumania. The Russian occupation of Bessarabia and Bukovina almost instantly reverberated in Bulgaria, which threatened now to seize the Dobruja, and in Hungary, which mobilized for a thrust at Transylvania. Whereupon Germany acted, compelled the Rumanians to give up the northern half of Transylvania to Hungary and to cede the southern third of the Dobruja to Bulgaria.

This dismemberment infuriated the Rumanians who considered King Carol responsible for their calamities. That unfortunate monarch fled from his country. Young Michael, his son, became a puppet ruler, doing the bidding of the Iron Guard, a Rumanian Fascist organization. The

Germans, under pretext of preserving order and preventing the British from blowing up Rumanian oil wells, sent larger and larger bodies of troops to Rumania and finally forced that Balkan state, together with Hungary and Slovakia, to join the all-Fascist alliance of which Japan, Italy, and Germany were the charter members.

Rumania now was lost to the democracies, and with the coming of autumn Egypt was invaded by the Italians from Libya, who reached Sidi Barrani on the Mediterranean littoral without serious opposition. For some reason, perhaps the water supply, this offense bogged down, but as it did so the Italians on October 28, struck at Greece through Albania.

To the surprise of almost everyone the Greeks flew to arms with apparently all the spirit of ancient Hellas; they drove the Italians out of northern Greece; they followed after them, forced them into precipitate retreat, and by December a large part of southern Albania was in Greek hands. Throughout that month and January, 1941, Greek victories continued. The snow lay heavy on Albanian hills but the dogged Greeks continued slowly but persistently to carry hill after hill at the point of the bayonet until, by February 1, 1941, they had not only reached the Adriatic but were within seven miles of Valona, Italy's strongly fortified prized port on the Albanian coast.

The British, meanwhile, rendered the Greeks valuable assistance by air and by sea; they attacked the Italian fleet at anchor at Taranto; they steamed into the Adriatic and bombarded Albanian seaports; and they established themselves snugly on the island of Crete. Nor did this aid to the Hellenes interfere with a most dashing offense against the Italian land forces in Africa. In December the British army in Egypt, strongly reinforced by Australians and supported by "Free French" troops, swept across the desert and ferociously attacked the Italians at Sidi Barrani. That town capitulated and some 30,000 Italians surrendered. The British offense continued without letup, this time in Libya. Bardia, the Italians' strongly fortified port in eastern Libya, bombarded by land and by sea, capitulated in early January, 1941, and the British, having bagged some 40,000 additional prisoners, swooped down on Tobruk, another Libyan port still farther to the west, running up their total number of prisoners to approximately 100,000. Nor did they stop. Striking across the desert, they soon were before Derna, which they stormed as the month drew to a close. They now were no less than 145 miles west of the Egyptian frontier. Some 100 miles beyond lay Bengazi, next to Tripoli, Libya's most important city. A long way to go; but in modern warfare, tanks and planes travel fast, and fortunately for the British there was at Derna a superb water supply. If they could only capture Bengazi, all of Eastern Libya (ancient Cyrenaica) would be lost to Mussolini.

As 1941 opened, the Italian dreams of turning the Mediterranean into a *mare nostrum* seemed faint, very faint indeed, since the British kept on rolling westward, not only taking Bengazi in early February but advancing far beyond it to El Agheila, well along the sea-coast road to Tripoli. It was evident to all that Britain would soundly thrash the Italians in Libya and perhaps elsewhere unless Germany took prompt action. This Hitler realized, and soon German airmen came pouring into Italy. In January the famous *stukas* began striking at Malta and at the British convoys in the Middle Sea, doing more damage in one day than Italian planes in six months of war.

The United States on the Brink of War

The Greeks and the British had defeated the Italians, but the latter had never been anything more than the tail of the Nazi wolf. The German armies still dominated the land mass of Western Europe. Nothing could prevent their occupation of that part of France still ostensibly "free." Their legions might continue southward through the Iberian Peninsula to besiege Gibraltar or to plunge west into Portugal. Sweden and Switzerland lay at their mercy; and, if the Nazis chose to risk the enmity of Stalin, Bulgaria, Greece, and Yugoslavia might be conquered with comparative ease. Until the German armies were defeated there was scant likelihood that the Nazi grip upon conquered territory would relax. Here and there a daring Dane, Norwegian, Netherlander, Belgian, Pole, Frenchman, or Czech might try as an individual to sabotage the Nazi regime or escape to the British flag; but so long as Rumanian and Russian oil flowed to Germany, so long as Swedish and French mines produced iron ore for German smelters, and so long as the conquered peoples were compelled to share their food supply, as well as everything else, with the victors, there was no chance for revolt succeeding, within the Reich or without.

This the British fully realized. They could not by themselves defeat the Germans; their only hope of ultimate victory depended upon America. To that country Britain looked for food, munitions, planes, and shipping, since without them Britain could not survive.

And so, with the coming of 1941, it became evident to the clearsighted on both sides of the Atlantic that the United States, and the United States alone, could stave off German triumph. The Americans with their tremendous resources could, in conjunction with British efforts, surpass the German plane production by 1943—if they tried hard enough! The American mercantile marine (9,000,000 tons), plus those European vessels interned in American ports which flew the Dutch, Belgian, Norwegian, French, German, and Italian flags (158 in number), should offset submarine sinkings. Some or all of these ships Britain urgently needed. And if the Americans should be willing to turn over to the Royal Navy another fifty destroyers to guard the sea-lanes, so much the better.

What would America do? That country was closer to war in January, 1941, than most Americans realized. Informal war against Germany to all intent and purpose had seemed assured early in the contest when Congress authorized the sale of munitions; but to active armed conflict Americans were averse. The presidential election (1940) gave relatively little clue as to American opinion in this matter. Both the major candidates favored aid to Britain without stint; but both also promised that American boys would not fight in Europe. A formula, "all aid short of war," seemed to represent average American opinion.

It is, however, always easier to invent a formula than to implement it. Billions of dollars had been voted by Congress in 1940 for national defense; conscription had been adopted; and a "two-ocean navy," presumably invincible in both the Atlantic and the Pacific, had received Congressional approval. Suppose the British said their need called for every available American plane; in what situation would that leave the armed forces of the United States? This single difficulty was met by the President in assigning fifty per cent of all new government planes to Britain, thereby presumably inserting the adjective "reasonable" between the words "all" and "aid." But who was to decide on what was "reasonable," the President or Congress; and did such aid involve unlimited credit? The Johnson Act forbade loans to nations defaulting on previous loans, and Britain had defaulted. Would it be necessary to repeal the Johnson Act; was Britain's financial need really pressing; was it desirable that more naval vessels be given to Britain, with or without a quid pro quo; could the United States open its ports to British warships, take over German shipping in American ports, release these ships to Britain, and at the same time avoid war with Germany?

There was no doubt where the President stood. In December, 1940, at a press conference he suggested the possibility of a lease-lend program whereby help to Britain could be instantly granted. This he followed up by a radio address in which he suggested that in case of fire one lends one's garden hose to one's neighbor, expecting that it be returned, but not trying to sell the hose first. Satisfied with the reaction of public opinion, Roosevelt went further and in his annual message to Congress on January 6, 1941, did not hesitate to speak as follows:

Let us say to the democracies: "We Americans are vitally concerned in your defense of freedom. We are putting forth our energies, our resources and our organizing powers to give you the strength to regain and maintain a free world. We shall send you in ever-increasing numbers, ships, planes, tanks, guns. That is our purpose and our pledge."

Followed then a bill in Congress to grant to him almost unlimited, as well as unprecedented, powers in placing the material resources of the country in the scale against Germany. The bill was fought stubbornly by noninterveners, who insisted that America had little to fear from a victorious Germany; that if the Germans could not invade England across the Channel it was absurd to be alarmed at the specter of Germany invading the United States; that democracy and all that went with it would perish in this country if it became involved in the war; and finally that opening American ports for the repair of British naval vessels, the seizure of foreign shipping in American ports in order to supply British needs, and the convoying of American ships to England by the United States navy were, in fact, acts of war.

These arguments were variously met. The more intelligent interventionists did not stress the likelihood of a Nazi invasion of the United States but sketched a situation wherein South America fell under Nazi influence, thus leaving the United States isolated in a hostile world, confronted by totalitarian states across both oceans, and subjected to subversive propaganda from all sides. Democracy here, they held, stood or fell with democracy elsewhere: the Fascist-molded states had won hitherto because the democracies had failed to support one another. As to whether such support as they proposed to give Britain was an act of war or not, that was an academic matter. The Nazis, in the President's words, "did not wait for Norway or Belgium or the Netherlands to commit an act of war. Their only interest is in a new one-way international law which lacks mutuality in its observance and therefore becomes an instrument of oppression." The United States, by implication, then, was under no obligation to regard "international law" as binding in dealing with an outlaw nation such as Hitler's Germany. The case for intervention was tersely put by Roosevelt in one sentence: "Those who would give up essential liberty to purchase a little temporary safety deserve neither liberty nor safety."

The bill, introduced into Congress on January 10, 1941, became law on March 11. To many it meant a last desperate effort to keep America out of the conflict by turning that country into an arsenal for Great Britain; to others it meant that the full military and naval strength of the United States would inevitably be used to destroy the armed strength of Germany; and that, as in 1918, America would arrive like Blücher at Waterloo before the coming of the night.

Chapter 39

FROM LEND-LEASE TO TUNISIA

In 1941 the long shadow of Nazi enslavement darkened Balkan skies, and by midsummer a series of German victories carried the swastika to the Aegean and came close to driving Britain out of the Mediterranean.

The Germans cared nothing for the Italians; but it did not suit their purpose to let them be exterminated by British and Greek armies in Libya and Albania. A blitzkrieg in the Balkans against the Greeks not only would rescue the Italians but also might pay good dividends, both economic and psychological. Perhaps the threat of war, combined with economic and diplomatic pressure, might enclose the entire Balkan Peninsula in the Nazi net. If Britain chose to jeopardize her army by assisting Greeks, so much the worse for her; a British expeditionary force in the Balkans would drain England's strength in Libya and in Egypt, and if this happened it might prove possible to drive the British not only out of Greece but also out of Africa.

For months past, Nazi troops had poured into Rumania. On March 1, 1941, they crossed from it into Bulgaria and within one day clicked their heels in the streets of Sofia. Thus two out of five Balkan states went down without a fight. Beyond Bulgaria lay Turkey and Greece. Both countries threatened to resist, but British troops already had landed in Greece and the Germans decided to leave Turkey alone for the time being. How to get at the Greeks? The frontier between Greece and Bulgaria was mountainous and the Germans hesitated. They could hit at Greece more readily through Turkey in Europe but they did not want to put the Turk to the test, not yet. Better to engulf Yugoslavia first, and then to flow through the Vardar Valley to inundate both Greeks and Britons from the north.

Yugoslavia, that triune kingdom of Croats, Serbs, and Slovenes, was in a serious dilemma. Prince Paul, the regent, signed a pact with Germany which admitted German technicians to Yugoslavia and gave to Hitler the right of transit across his country to munition and hospital trains. But now the Yugoslavian army under Serbian officers revolted, overturned the government of the regent, raised young King Peter, not yet eighteen, to the throne, and defied the Germans. The latter did not hesitate: they invaded both Yugoslavia and Greece.

The Balkan Campaign of 1941

The campaign thus initiated was to last less than a month. A German arc of 1,000 miles stretching from Austria through Hungary, Rumania, and Bulgaria ran parallel with two-thirds of the Yugoslav frontier. All the Nazis had to do was to keep the Greeks and British occupied on the Bulgar-Greek frontier while they launched several convergent attacks on Yugoslavia. The most important struck like lightning at the Vardar Valley from Bulgaria, thus cutting off the greater part of Yugoslavia from her allies. The German wedge now fanned out north and south, while units of it going west joined hands with the harassed Italians in Albania. Meanwhile, Belgrade fell before a German rush from the north. The oncoming Germans, with new light-built tanks for mountain warfare, with trained parachute troops supported by two of Germany's six air fleets and some 3,000 planes, were irresistible. At Sarajevo the Yugoslav army made its last stand. Here it was trapped, in part by aid given the enemy by treacherous Croats. On April 16th, it laid down its arms. There was nothing left of Yugoslavia now unless scattered bands of guerilla fighters in remote valleys could be said to represent her.

The Greeks were next on the German slaughter list. Although they held the Wehrmacht back on the Bulgarian frontier by furious fighting, they could do nothing to stem the Nazi offensive down the valley of the Vardar. Germans, streaming down that spacious valley, captured Salonika, where the Vardar flows into the sea, and thus the Greeks in the east were isolated from their main army. As this happened, the 57,000 British troops sent to their assistance, for the most part Australian and New Zealand Anzacs, retreated across the flat Thessalian plain, harassed by a murderous assault from the Luftwaffe which the feeble squadrons of the RAF could do little to check. The Anzacs kept their ranks intact and managed for three days to hold the pass at Thermopylae against six German divisions. But this they did, not so much to help the Greeks, who had already told them that nothing more could be done, as to make possible their own debarkation. Again, the Royal Navy did its part, and from tiny ports and scattered beaches it managed to rescue 44,000 exhausted British soldiers. A second Dunkirk.

By May 1st all was over. The Greeks who had fought to the last ounce of endurance lay prostrate under German and Italian rule, for Mussolini, Hitler's lackey, claiming his share of victory, was permitted to police Athens. Yugoslavia was hung, drawn, and quartered. Croatia fell to Italy, the Banat to Hungary, and that part of Macedonia formerly in Yugoslavia was thrown to the Bulgars. The Germans took what was left.

A German army rested on its laurels in Belgrade. As for Britain, this was just one more disaster.

Crete and Libya

There were others to follow in this spring of 1941. Both in Libya and in Crete the British were to undergo defeat, and at home to stave off starvation and destruction by the narrowest of margins.

The Nazis had their eye on Africa as well as on the Balkans. For a long time they had been training men in Germany for desert warfare, conditioning them to excessive heat, preparing them with Teutonic thoroughness for what they must contend against in Africa. This German Afrika Korps, commanded by General Rommel, they despatched to Tripoli. With its armored tanks it became the spearhead of the Axis army, the Italians under Rommel's orders being left the minor function of consolidating land won by the more warlike Nazis.

Rommel struck out at El Agheila in March; and then and there began the retreat of Wavell's Britishers all along the weary, dusty coastline of Cyrenaica over which they had so recently driven the Italians. The British had advanced rapidly; their retreat was even more rapid; past Benghazi, past Derna, all the way to Tobruk. They clung so doggedly to that wretched seaport that the Afrika Korps was not able to dislodge them. Leaving it besieged, Rommel drove the British further east, past Bardia and into Egypt. He then halted to capture Tobruk, for he did not dare leave his flank exposed. In vain, however, did the Germans roll their tanks forward against the British lines. Reinforced constantly by sea, the tenacious Britons retained their toehold on the African coast, and Rommel, far now from his base, was compelled to give over further advance.

The greater part of the British expeditionary force rescued from the Grecian fiasco fled to Crete. That island protected both Palestine and the Suez; it threatened Italian communication with the Dodecanese Islands. It should and could be defended; so thought the British.

But once again they underestimated Hitler's men. Before they knew it, German paratroopers began dropping from the skies all over Crete, thousands of them. They came by air, in transport planes, in gliders towed by transport planes, ten or twelve men to a glider, equipped with radio sets and machine guns. The Nazi air superiority was marked; the British had no fighter planes competent to drive off the Nazis; bombers flying at low levels raked the British with machine guns and soon rendered untenable their hold on Crete. Within ten days, evacuation became inevitable. It was a third Dunkirk. Nearly half the British troops were killed or taken prisoner. Four cruisers and six destroyers were sunk, a battleship crippled. It was a sad day for Britain. What now could stop victorious Nazidom from spreading further east, to Syria, to Palestine, to Iraq?

Iraq and Syria

As the Nazis drove the British out of Grecian valleys and pried loose their grip on Crete, they noted with great glee events in Baghdad. Rashid Ali Beg Gailani, former premier of Iraq, a disgruntled Anglophobe, deposed by force the pro-British regent who acted for the six-year-old king. Britain had secured the admission of Iraq in 1930 to the League of Nations and Britain had recognized the independence of Iraq; nevertheless by treaty she was authorized to maintain troops in Iraq, to guard imperial communications, and more especially the precious oil fields. And now, as Britain reinforced her slender garrison at Basra at the head of the Persian gulf, Rashid Ali besieged a large British airport at Habbaniah. That airport was unfortified, and to defend it the British had to fly both men and artillery in from Basra. If the Iraqi won, if they once succeeded in cutting the pipeline to Haifa in Palestine, the plight of the royal navy and of the RAF in the eastern Mediterranean would be serious. Fortunately the Germans were so heavily engaged this month in Crete that they were unable to help Rashid Ali except by flying in a few planes from Syria; fortunately, also, many Arabs revolted against Rashid Ali. By the end of the month his inglorious rule was over and the former regent was back on the throne.

The planes which the Germans sent to Iraq had been flown from French bases in Syria, and the excuses offered by the French governor there, who had been appointed by Vichy, were very flimsy. The British felt they could take no chances; a German occupation of Syria was by no means impossible, and once nested there the Nazis could put pressure on Turkey from the south, on Palestine from the north, and on Iraq from the west. Only part of the oil from Mosul went to Haifa; the pipeline bifurcated and a great part of it flowed to the sea at Tripoli in Syria, an invaluable source for the Luftwaffe. The British decided to strike. Conjointly with the Free French troops of General De Gaulle they crossed from Palestine into Syria. By June 28th, Damascus fell and immediate danger was over.

The Threat Nearer Home

Clearly it had been an Axis spring; and not in the Near East alone. The Luftwaffe had been turned loose once more on Britain, this time to focus primarily on British ports. Eight raids on Plymouth left that city a smoldering mass of ruins, more battered in 1941 than Coventry in 1940. Eight nights in succession the Nazis blasted at Liverpool's docks. Hull, Newcastle, Bristol, Portsmouth, and even Belfast were visited by Nazi airmen who also were not forgetful of London, giving that city the most savage pounding it received during the entire war.

Upon the high seas the U-boats took heavier and heavier toll of British shipping. In April 589,273 tons were sunk, this the peak month since the war commenced. Ships were lost at three times the rate of construction in British and American shipyards; and food and war matériel piled higher and higher on American and Australian docks. The food ration was cut in Britain and her margin of safety grew appreciably less. The German subs were prowling further and further afield, far south of the equator and up and down the coast lines of the Americas and Africa.

The picture was not altogether one-sided. In the Mediterranean the Italians felt the weight of British armor when three of their heavy cruisers and presumably a battleship were sunk. Moreover throughout the spring their Ethiopian empire faded into dust when Addis Ababa fell. Also German victories of April and May were marred somewhat by the sinking of their finest battleship, the *Bismarck*, after a long and exciting chase by the most powerful units of the British fleet. Nonetheless, the over-all picture was highly favorable to the Axis. The Balkan Peninsula was under their thumb, to do with as they wished. The southeastern door to Europe was shut and bolted. There would be no second front there to worry about for months or years to come.

Hitler Invades Russia

When German armies invaded France in 1940 Russia saw her chance and took it; she ordered Rumania to cede to her Bessarabia and northern Bukovina. The former province had been Russian territory before the First World War and Russia had never acquiesced in its loss. Bukovina had been part of the old Austrian empire and never had been Russian. Its population, however, was predominantly Ukrainian and Stalin thought there was no time like the present for uniting all Ukrainians under the Soviets. In 1940 he gauged the situation correctly: the Nazis were not consulted about this enlargement of the Russian frontiers and the Nazis were sulky; but the Nazis did not interfere.

A month or two later, after France had fallen and England seemed about to fall, the Nazis were not so conciliatory toward Soviet ambitions in the southeast. So Stalin discovered when he put renewed pressure on Rumania. This time the Nazis took action in a supposedly Russian sphere of influence without consulting him. They carved Rumania according to their own plans, presenting part of Transylvania to Hungary, the Dobrudja (formerly Bulgarian territory) to Bulgaria, granting what was left a guarantee of territorial integrity backed by the immediate presence of German troops.

It was now Stalin's turn to be conciliatory; he had miscalculated German strength and had neither wished nor expected such a speedy and overwhelming German triumph in the west. With Germany supplying the Finns with numerous planes and fresh ammunition in the autumn of 1940, the Russians decided to be circumspect; they scrupulously delivered to Germany the goods called for by their trade agreement of 1939; they sent Premier Molotov to Berlin late in 1940. It was not a pleasant visit for the Russian, since he discovered that his country was expected to join the Axis, as had Rumania and Slovakia. This Stalin would not do; he had no intention of duplicating Mussolini's fateful career and playing second fiddle to Hitler.

Stalin knew Russia was ill prepared for war; he also knew that Hitler distrusted him as much as he did Hitler. And so he made his preparations. He signed a peace pact with Japan, thus insuring Russia against war on two fronts; he lengthened the work-day from seven to eight hours; he made it a crime against the state to be more than twenty minutes tardy at the factories; he shunted nearly a million boys and girls into trade schools for special training in mechanical pursuits; he speeded production in war matériel; and he gave orders that many vital war industries in Moscow, Leningrad, and elsewhere should dismantle their machinery and reassemble it east of the Urals.

Meantime the Soviet chieftain tried by diplomacy to stave off Nazi attack. To curry favor with the Germans he refused recognition any longer to the Belgian and Norwegian embassies and he gave it to the pro-German rebels in Baghdad. And finally in May, 1941, he dismissed the ministers of Greece and Yugoslavia.

All this to no avail. By June Hitler had determined to smite the Russians, if troop concentrations have any meaning. The Rumanians mobilized on the Russian border; Nazi storm troopers who had conquered Greece were ordered to the Polish frontier; to Finland the Nazis dispatched German units; and the Luftwaffe, withdrawn largely from the West, was concentrated in the East, its squadrons flying over Russian territory on reconnaissance flights.

Then without warning on June 22 the Nazi legions crossed the border and there was war with Russia! The most gigantic duel in recorded history now had opened. Never before had so many million men been hurled so savagely at one another; never before had there been a battle line of 1,800 miles across which so many armies lunged. Tanks ripped holes in opposing lines and syphoned through to widen salients. And then, the pincer movements; planes droning overhead and dropping death amid the ack, ack of the anti-aircraft guns; pockets of resistance, now large, now small, contracting, expanding; encirclements, escapes, the trapper sometimes trapped; a constant fluid war of movement; a ruinous scene of hell on earth which Lucifer himself could not surpass.

The Germans had a plan of campaign, brilliant in design, brilliant in execution, which suited well their temperament and their superb military skill. The "Blitzkrieg" tactics so successfully applied two years earlier in Flanders were repeated. The Nazis aimed at Moscow, but it was neither this river nor that town that was their main objective. The Russian armies were their quarry, and these they proposed to run down and to exterminate before cold weather came, by wide open maneuvres across wide, level plains. Dive bombers and tanks, speed and force would encircle the Slav, enfold him in unexpected pockets, and then crush and slay the ponderous red giant. And this the Germans almost did in 1941, but not quite; and once again in 1942, but not quite.

For the Russians, too, had a plan, one suited to their temperament, their tradition, their climate. It was very simple; to keep their armies intact no matter how much ground they yielded. A hundred thousand square miles was less important to them than their armies. Space, time, and winter weather, Russia's ancient allies, had served her well against the Swedes in the eighteenth century, against the French in the nineteenth. The Russian defense was one in depth, not ordinary depth but Russian depth. Stalin proposed to contest the frontier lightly, to lure on the enemy, to depend on guerilla action to harass his communications, to hammer away at his flanks, and above all to be patient under defeat, conscious that new Russian armies, and still more new Russian armies, given time, would hurl themselves at the Hitlerites, expel them from Sovietland.

As might have been predicted, 1941 was a year of German victory. In little more than three weeks the Luftwaffe destroyed a considerable part of the Russian planes before they even left the ground, the German tanks penetrated the Stalin line of frontier defense, and the German infantry was in Smolensk with Moscow only two hundred miles away. To have covered two-thirds of the distance to the Russian capital in twenty-six days was good going. Nevertheless, the war was still young and the road to Moscow was no open highway.

It was now midsummer and the Nazis looked forward hopefully to the conquest of Moscow. But the Russians had just begun to fight. Already they had ruined by fire and by dynamite their bridges, railways, power houses, water mains, dwellings; and now they counterattacked all along the line, warily, intermittently, avoiding encirclement. The series of sanguine battles which followed one another in quick succession in central Russia are known collectively as the Battle of Smolensk, although for the most part they took place to the east of that strategic rail center and at some distance from it. The spearhead of the German advance reached Vyazma, northeast of Smolensk and only one hundred miles from Moscow; it penetrated to Bryansk to the southeast, athwart the Moscow-

Kiev-Odessa railroad. But the Russian lines were elastic; they bent but did not break.

Long before German pressure on the central front slowed down it was felt in the Ukraine in southern Russia and at Leningrad in the north. The black earth of the Ukraine, the mineral wealth of the Donets basin, and the rich oil-fields of the Caucasus lured on the Nazis. From early August to late November they kept advancing. Bypassing Kiev, they raced for the Black Sea coast and reached it; they then dived at Kiev from the east, and that capital of the Ukraine fell into their hands. All through October Teutonic victory-waves flowed east and south. They swept to the Sea of Azov; they submerged Stalino on the Don and Kharkov, the Ukraine's second largest city. Then they abated somewhat, finally seeping into Rostov at the mouth of the Don, a good eight hundred miles from the old Russian frontier. The Ukraine, Russia's granary and main center of heavy industry was now entirely in German hands. The blow was heavy but the Red armies remained intact.

Almost simultaneously came a dash for Leningrad. That city once captured, the Nazis would touch hands around the eastern shores of the Baltic with the Finns, who had renewed their war with Russia. Victorious to the far north of Moscow as well as to the far south, the Nazis could then initiate a gigantic pincer movement, which closing in on the Soviet capital could choke and end the Bolshevik menace.

Leningrad the Germans failed to capture. No matter how hard they tried; no matter how heavy and sustained their air bombardment; no matter how powerful their siege guns, the Russians still withstood them. A great part of the city was pulverized from the air, and so close did the Germans come that the noise of battle echoed in the streets. The civilian population worked day and night upon the fortifications which ringed their city. And since the Nazis could not break them they settled down on November 1 to a long siege.

Meanwhile the hard-hitting Germans decided to wait no longer in subduing Moscow. On October 2 Hitler told his troops, "To-day begins the last great decisive battle of this year"—a true statement, but not in the sense intended. This time the swastika came close to floating over the Kremlin. The German tanks tore vicious gaps in the Russian lines and in less than three weeks Moscow was nearly encircled. On came the Germans, from north and west and south. The fall of Moscow seemed inevitable. But fate and weather ruled it otherwise. In November came welcome snow and ice. The Nazi tide had reached its perigee but could not rise above it. Then on December 6, eve of Pearl Harbor, the Red armies launched a counterattack against the half-frozen German tank formations. The surprised Nazis were forced back; two days later they announced the suspension of major activities on the eastern front, due to the weather.

The United States Closer to the Brink

"Give us the tools and we will finish the job," thus spoke Churchill in 1941 as the American public debated the pros and cons of lend-lease. But did "give us the tools" mean give them to us in America, or deliver them to us in England?

The majority of Americans would avoid "a shooting war," yet that same majority was determined that the Nazis must not win. To find an intermediate way between lend-lease and war was difficult, but the President found it. To order the American navy to convoy transatlantic cargoes meant "shooting"; but how about patrols instead of convoys? To use the President's analogy, a patrol on the high seas had the same function as a scout on the western plains: not to fight but warily to watch, and instantly to report the presence of hostile Indians. Warships on patrol would do the same, would look for submarines, those "rattlesnakes of the ocean," and send word by wireless of their whereabouts. If British naval units picked up said messages and acted thereon, that did not mean war, or did it?

By April 11 our navy was on patrol duty and on April 25 the President said that patrol would be extended, if necessary, to "all the Seven Seas." Two days after, the day the Germans entered Athens, Churchill addressed his faithful House of Commons. "When you come to think of it," he said, "the United States are very closely bound up with us now.... When I said ten weeks ago: give us the tools and we will finish the job, I meant, *give* them to us: put them within our reach—and that is what it now seems the Americans are going to do." The situation in the Near East is perilous but what of it? "Nothing that can happen in the east is comparable with what is happening in the west." And Churchill ended, quoting Clough:

> And not by eastern windows only,
> When daylight comes, comes in the light;
> In front the sun climbs slow; how slowly!
> But westward, look, the land is bright.

Through the spring we drifted toward war with Nazi Germany; we occupied Greenland to forestall Hitler; British warships limped into our drydocks to have their war wounds treated, unquestionably an unneutral act on our part; and, May 21, the *Robin Moor*, an American ship far from the prescribed war zone, was sunk in the South Atlantic, unquestionably an act of war on the part of the Reich. Technically we were still at peace, but more thoughtful isolationists, realizing the inevitable, were resigning from America First Committees, and more did so when President Roosevelt announced July 7th that our troops had landed in Iceland.

The Atlantic Charter

On August 16, the President of the United States and the Prime Minister of England made rendezvous off Newfoundland. While their naval and military staffs took common council the two chief magistrates signed the Atlantic Charter, a document reminiscent of Wilson's fourteen points. Both statesmen proclaimed that they opposed "aggression, territorial or otherwise"; that "they desired to see no territorial changes that do not accord with the expressed wishes of the people concerned"; that "they respect the right of all peoples to choose the form of government under which they will live"; that they favored "access on equal terms to the trade and to the raw materials of the world"; that they wished to secure for all nations "improved labor standards, economic advancement and social security"; that "after the destruction of Nazi tyranny" a peace should be established which would guarantee "to all men, in all lands" the chance to live "in freedom from want and fear"; that the high seas be free for all; that the use of force be abandoned; and that "a permanent system of general security is essential."

This charter was not binding; it was not an alliance; it stated the ideal goal toward which both countries meant to strive. British public opinion was disappointed that the Atlantic Charter did not go farther. But would an alliance have been ratified by the United States Senate? Roosevelt and Churchill were practical and experienced politicians; and both were confident that time, tide, and Nazi Germany would soon bring such hopes to happy fruition.

Nor were they disappointed. On September 4th the United States destroyer *Greer* was fired on by a German submarine. The *Greer* escaped, but promptly the President stated that henceforth the navy "would shoot on sight." On October 17 the U.S. destroyer *Kearney* was badly mauled in fighting a German submarine, and shortly after, the destroyer *Reuben James* was sunk. These acts of war brought congressional repeal of neutrality legislation which had forbidden the arming of merchant vessels and their entry into combatant harbors. But the vote in the House of Representatives was only 212 to 194 in favor of such repeal, and this was on November 13, less than a month before Pearl Harbor. Pacifists and noninterventionists were still numerous in America. Yet to many it seemed that we had been at war since the sinking of the *Robin Moor,* or at least since the "shoot on sight" order.

The United States Enters the War

December 7, 1941. All doubts were removed; America was in the war.

Relations between the United States and Japan had been increasingly strained since 1931. Our refusal to recognize the Japanese puppet state of Manchukuo and our steadfast sympathy with China led the militarist statesmen of Japan to conclude that they must either abandon their ambition to rule East Asia or fight the United States.

In July, 1939, the United States gave the requisite six months' notice that it intended to denounce its commercial treaty with Japan, due to expire in January, 1940. The Japanese were furious, also somewhat alarmed. The United States was their best customer and from us they imported much war material, particularly scrap iron and high octane gas. Why should America act thus? Our ambassador at Tokyo, Mr. Grew, told them the blunt truth. "The people of the United States," he said, "resent the methods which the Japanese armed forces employ in China today and what appears to be their objective."

Meanwhile we advanced loans and credits to the Chinese whereby they could purchase tools of war. But how could these be imported? There were only two feasible routes—one by rail through French Indo-China; the other by the Burma Road, a steep and twisting motor high-way from railhead in Burma to Chungking in far western China, a road handmade by Chiang Kai-shek's people with pick-axe, crow bar and wheelbarrow. The first route the French promptly sealed, for impotent Vichy dared not defy a Japanese ultimatum to do so. Britain in 1940 knew she had no chance to defend Hongkong without aid from America, and very little with it. Therefore she, too, gave way, and that summer agreed to close the Burma Road for three months.

The British held no cards and could not do otherwise; but this was not true for the Americans. We could stop shipment of vital war matériel to Japan, and this we gingerly began to do by restricting export of scrap iron and gasoline. In September, Japan joined the Axis and shortly after the United States advised her citizens in Japan to return home. Whether this act of ours stayed Japan's hand, or whether the cautious Nipponese were waiting the results of German air assault on Britain one cannot say.

For some months Japanese policy remained uncertain. Japan might sail south and seize the Dutch East Indies, taking French Indo-China, Hongkong, Malaya, Singapore, and the Philippines en route. But Japan was not sure of Russia; and with that traditional foe on friendly terms with Germany and snugly dug in at Vladivostok, perhaps it was as well to see what diplomacy might win.

And so Matsuoka, secretary for foreign affairs, visited first Berlin, then Moscow, signing a nonaggression pact with Stalin. The absorption of French Indo-China followed, the French, in June, 1941, granting military bases and the right to troop transit. Thereupon soldiers of Japan were rushed to the Thai border, thus putting pressure on Thailand to accept Japanese domination, or else! As Churchill broadcast in August, "They stretch their grasping hand into the southern seas of China. They snatch Indo-China from the wretched Vichy French. They menace by their movements Siam. They menace Singapore, the British link with Australasia, and they menace the Philippine Islands under the protection of the United States. It is certain that this has got to stop."

Who was to stop it, and when? Both Britain and the United States froze Japanese credits this fateful summer of 1941, thus ending trade relations with Nippon; the Dutch East Indies, absorbing courage from the two democracies, grew recalcitrant about selling Tokyo more oil; and there was talk of the A.B.C.D. powers (America, Britain, China, and the Dutch East Indies) acting in unison: but China was otherwise engaged and so was Britain; only a handful of Netherlanders were in the East Indies; the native peoples were not organized for defense; and that left the United States as the solitary lion in the path of aggressive Japan.

The American public had been so engrossed with the European drama that it had not paid much attention to the Far East, and President Roosevelt had been careful since the outbreak of the war scarcely to mention Japan in his public addresses. With one war menacing us in the Atlantic we preferred avoiding another in the Pacific, and the state department did its best to delay an outbreak there. But our government remained adamant in helping China; it extended lend-lease to that country; it permitted an American officer to organize a Chinese air service; it dispatched a military mission to Chungking; and it continued to protest the boa-constrictor engorgement of Indo-China.

Few dreamed the Japanese might attack us. After three years invasion of China and with a million soldiers stationed there, it surely would be the height of folly for Japan to engage America. We little realized the bitter hate and scorn with which we were regarded in Tokyo, or how the war lords had hypnotized their people in regard to the divine mission of Japan. What we thought was that Tokyo probably intended to absorb Thailand; and few Americans cared much about that remote nation. Once secure in Thailand Japan might then invade Burma to close the Burma Road. But why cross that bridge until we came to it; it was not nearly as exciting a topic as Mr. Roosevelt's Atlantic patrols.

And so when the Konoye cabinet fell in October, 1941, and militarist General Tojo became premier, Americans were not much concerned. On November 5 Tojo announced that he was sending Kurusu as a special envoy to the United States. His *peace* mission was but a screen behind which Japan made ready her lightning stroke of December 7, and so Churchill saw it when he warned Tokyo on November 12 that if war came between Japan and the United States, Britain would be at war with Japan "within the hour." Americans, however, were more optimistic. Kurusu doubtless would tempt us to abandon the Chinese, and this we would not do; but possibly he had some compromise to offer.

Kurusu suggested a modus vivendi, with the United States acting as mediator in the Sino-Japanese War. The President agreed under certain conditions to act as "introducer" but not as "mediator"—a subtle distinction to avoid offending China. Kurusu then proposed on November 20 to evacuate southern Indo-China as soon as an agreement was signed with the United States, and all of Indo-China on the conclusion of general peace in the Far East. We were to cease our aid to China and withdraw our economic sanctions against Japan.

We countered with a note withdrawing the President's offer to act as introducer, reaffirming continued aid to China and proposing that Japan withdraw from China and resign from the Axis. If Japan would do this we would remove all restrictions on exports to Japan and help that country stabilize its currency. The Japanese reply was handed to Mr. Hull on the afternoon of December 7. All this was superfluous; torpedo planes and fighter escorts blazoned with the Rising Sun of Japan were already dropping bombs on our naval base at Pearl Harbor.

Japanese Victories

Our carelessness in Hawaii was inexcusable. More than ten days before, our commanders there had been advised that war might break at any instant, yet few precautions were taken. The navy took it for granted that the aircraft warning system operated by the army was functioning all the time, and would give adequate advance notice of the approach of enemy planes; but the army only operated this system three hours a day. The army took it for granted that the navy kept constant watch by long-distance reconnaissance flights; but the navy patrolled to the south only, and the Japanese came from the north. The army had one chance to save the day and muffed it; a soldier experimenting after hours with the aircraft detector heard the approaching Japanese planes only to be told by his superior that they were American flying fortresses. The navy also had its chance; a full hour before the attack it sank an enemy submarine just off Pearl Harbor but gave no general alarm.

Down swooped Japanese planes upon motionless aircraft, lined up in close formation, wing to wing. Having destroyed at one blow most of our planes the Japanese airmen made for our warships and caught them at anchor. The crews did what they could with their anti-aircraft batteries, but a battleship at anchor, unsupported by planes, is helpless, and in a few minutes five battle-wagons were either sunk or badly crippled.

Three days later the *Prince of Wales* and the *Repulse*, two of the royal navy's best and biggest ships, were sent to the bottom off the coast of Malaya. The British admiral in command took a chance, and lost. Without air escort he steamed north to intercept a Japanese convoy, trusting to murky weather to screen him from air attack. The weather suddenly cleared and down upon the huge ships swept the Japanese planes. The

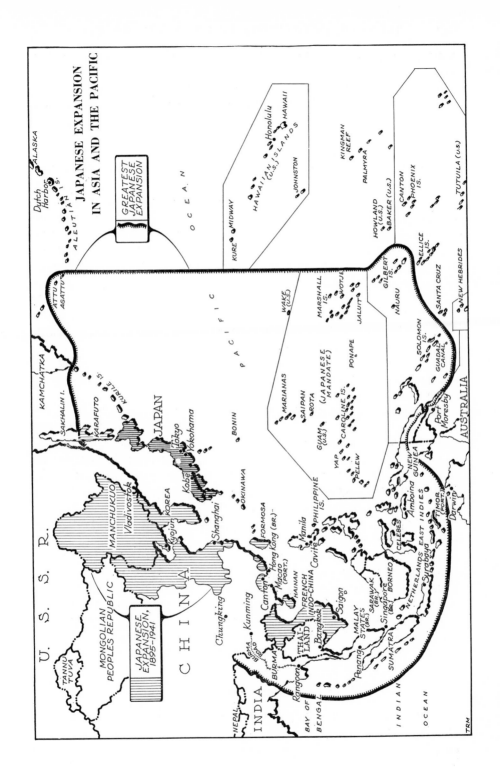

JAPANESE EXPANSION
IN ASIA AND THE PACIFIC

GREATEST
JAPANESE
EXPANSION

JAPANESE
EXPANSION,
1895–1941

British put up a stiff fight for three hours; but the Japanese got their quarry.

These two naval disasters were catastrophic. The Japanese army was well trained, needing little food, fanatically patriotic, hardened by years of war in China; but without command of the sea even that army could not approach the Philippines or the Dutch East Indies, much less Singapore. United, the Anglo-American fleets would have controlled the seas off Asia; but now the Rising Sun of Japan shone far and wide across those waters.

Almost simultaneously the enemy struck at Singapore, Hongkong, Guam, Wake Island, and Philippines. We had recently sent to Manila many new planes. Parked in rows, wing to wing, precisely as at Pearl Harbor, most of them were caught on the ground before dropping a bomb. Guam, located in a veritable nest of Japanese islands and (thanks to Congress) still unfortified, succumbed after four days. The 378 marines on Wake held out heroically until December 23, sinking with their light shore batteries two destroyers and a cruiser. Two days later Hongkong, battered by artillery and dive bombing, surrendered to Japan. Within one week after Pearl Harbor the Japanese army had landed in force in Luzon. Our army retreated with its Philippine allies into the wild and mountainous peninsula of Bataan, to fight on for months, hoping for succor that could not come.

If the Japanese had struck only at the Philippines we would, of course, have gone to war, for we had pledged the independence of those islands. But the voices of isolationist and pacifist would have risen high in lamentations for the death of our soldiers, sailors, and marines in lands far away. Now all such internal wrangling ceased. The Americans were angry; all of them. And as the casualty list lengthened they became more so.

The United States declared war on Japan; Germany and Italy declared war on us; Churchill flew the Atlantic to consult with Roosevelt. The world-wide issue now was joined. The United Nations (in 1917 it had been the Allies) signed on January 1, 1942, a military alliance. The Chinese Republic, Britain, and the United States, in addition governments in exile Luxemburg, Holland, Belgium, Norway, Greece, and Yugoslavia, as also the Central American and Caribbean republics and India, made up the original list. Russia remained at peace with Japan. But the "phoney war" of 1939 was global war in 1942.

The Swarming Japanese: Bataan

The American garrison in the Philippines was well situated for defense. Corregidor in Manila Bay was strongly fortified; it could be approached only by sea or air, and deep within its bowels was a huge tunnel the length of a city block, sufficiently wide to permit two ambulances to pass abreast, and with lateral tunnels on either side. Corregidor seemed a safe refuge from Japanese bombing and artillery fire. So long as our flag flew over it the enemy was not safe in Manila; and so long as our artillery could fire from it we could protect to some extent our troops on Bataan, only four miles away. Bataan was a natural fortress; its precipitous hills and deep ravines, covered by jungle growth, and its relatively narrow neck made penetration difficult.

Equally important was the loyal support of our Filipino allies. The Filipino Scouts, hardy, agile, well disciplined, proved themselves as good as any soldiers; and the regular Filipino army, largely without training, acquitted itself with distinction. Even the aboriginal Negritos joined in lustily, capturing Japanese stragglers and bringing them into the American lines in bamboo cages. The wise policy of Philippine independence bore good fruit; had it not been for these allies we could have done little to stave off the enemy.

In mid-January, 1942, the Japanese made a major assault on the American lines, and again in early February. And on both occasions they were driven back. None could gainsay their reckless courage: they charged into nests of machine guns without faltering; they hurled themselves on barbed wire, electrically charged, and stuck there, making of themselves a living bridge over which poured their reserves; they dangled like monkeys from tree tops; they fought by night and day. Death had no terrors for the men of Nippon.

Even so, Bataan's 40,000 defenders, mostly Filipinos, could have held out had it not been for lack of air support, food, and matériel. After January 1, MacArthur never had more than five military planes, all old models, continuously damaged and repaired with great difficulty. Four antique civilian planes, called "the bamboo fleet," because held together by splicing them with bamboo and bits of wire, were his service of supply, and the Bamboo Fleet could do little to replenish drugs, spare parts, and food, even if Corregidor could have spared them its stores. The defense grew weaker from malnutrition, malaria, dysentery, beriberi, and hookworm. Soon our outnumbered men could get no sleep. There was no intermission, no relief, for there were not soldiers enough to spell the half-starved malaria-stricken men in the front-line fox holes. Driven back to the sea some few were evacuated to Corregidor by motor torpedo boats, and some, challenging the sharks, swam four miles to the island where the flag still flew. What remained of the ammunition was destroyed and the flag of Nippon flew over the peninsula of Bataan.

General MacArthur, complying with the command of the President, had left by motor boat and submarine to renew the war as commander-in-chief of the United Nations in Australia. General Wainwright, his successor, continued American resistance on Corregidor until May. His men were sick, half-starved, cooped up underground, their island refuge shaken day in and day out by Japanese bombs. Before long the enemy made good a landing. Resistance futile, Wainwright surrendered.

Malaya and Singapore

The British had over 70,000 troops to defend Malaya and Singapore, but their naval strength was puny, their air force utterly inadequate. Even so, if their troops had been trained for jungle fighting (which was not the case) and if the Malays had been given Commonwealth citizenship (or even the promise of it) and trained to fight, the story of Singapore might have been different.

At Singapore there were British regiments famous for tropical warfare of the nineteenth-century variety celebrated by Kipling, the hollow square beating off the Fuzzy-Wuzzies. In all the Far East the British had nothing comparable to our Filipino Scouts. The Malays were not treacherous, nor had they been ill treated by the British raj, which had left them under their native sultans. But the Malays simply did not consider it their war.

The Japanese fought this brief, incisive, and completely victorious campaign with astonishing skill and foresight. Their shock troops, carefully selected and better paid than the average soldier, were snipers. Especially trained in tree climbing, in remaining motionless for hours, in camouflaging themselves to look like leaves, the snipers dropped hand grenades on the British by day and, to give the illusion of attack, set off firecrackers by night. Japanese troops were everywhere; they were lightly clad and carried no heavy equipment; they lived on hard rice cake impregnated with meat; they needed no fire; they were prepared for every emergency, with rubber sneakers in place of shoes, with bicycles for jungle paths, with collapsible boats for jungle streams, with chemicals to purify muddy water.

The British army was a land force; that of the Japanese was amphibious, traveling by boat and barge, sometimes by river, sometimes by sea, forcing its way along roads or through rubber plantations, forever getting in the rear of the baffled British and cutting off detachments. The Japanese tanks were light but far superior to the British armored cars, some of which dated from 1918. Excellent, too, were the Japanese paratroopers, skilled in signaling with the radio, adept at ambush. And so the British land army never had a chance. Defeated in skirmish after skirmish, in foray after foray, it staggered back to the tip of Malaya, crossed the causeway to Singapore, blew up the bridge behind it, and thought to hold Singapore until help came.

The Americans still held Corregidor; the British still held Malta; but Singapore was too big; there were forty miles of coastline and the Straits of Johore were easy to cross, particularly in the west where the water was shallow and where reedy swamps and shallow streams on the Singapore side invited Japanese infiltration. There were no underground caverns as on Malta or man-made tunnels as on Corregidor. Fighting was in the open, and from the pitiless skies poured down the Japanese bombs. The British did their best to send reinforcements, even endangering their Eighth Army in Egypt by so doing. Planes arrived, but too late, for the Japanese had already infiltrated through the marshy shorelands of the west and had repaired the dynamited causeway. With the enemy in command of both sea and air a Dunkirk was impossible. After a thirty-day siege came the surrender—the most humiliating in British army annals and, historically speaking, the most significant since Saratoga.

Burma

Burma in many ways repeated Malaya and Singapore, the soldiers of the Rising Sun bobbing up where least expected; the Imperials baffled and confused, fighting back blindly, strafed from the air, losing contact with their own detachments, cut off from retreat, poorly led by officers whose ingrained contempt for "natives" was costly.

The Burma campaign synchronized with Malaya and Singapore and lasted longer, but only because Burma was of large area and it was impossible to push all the British to the sea. Nevertheless, the outcome was soon a foregone conclusion.

For a long time Burma had been a neglected ward of the Empire, the Burmese complaining that they had no land communication with India, owing to the pull of shipping interests, and that their pleas for self-government were without effect. The Japanese took full advantage of this disaffection; their spy system in Burma was well organized, their promises of independence for Burma loud and emphatic. British propaganda could hardly have been worse; it promised nothing apart from protection; it did not even try to enlist the Burmese to defend their own country. Keep cool and trust us, was the British slogan; and in consequence as fast as the Japanese won victories just so rapidly did the Burmese lose their respect for British arms.

The main Japanese objective was Rangoon at the mouth of the Irrawaddy. Once Rangoon fell the Burma Road would be bottled up, the Chinese lifeline severed, and the Japanese could attack the oil fields far up the Irrawaddy.

January 15 the invasion started, and it took the Japanese over two weeks to cut through the tangled jungles on the Thailand border, to capture Moulmein opposite Rangoon on the Gulf of Martaban. Once there they fanned out, crossed the broad and shallow Salween (three miles wide at its mouth), and circled around to the north of Rangoon. Meanwhile, detachments slipped across the Gulf in small boats to strike at Rangoon from the south and west. The city became impossible to hold and its evacuation in early March was a military necessity.

During the next two months the Japanese swarmed north up the Irrawaddy, the Sittang, and the Salween, driving before them the British and the Chinese, who had finally been welcomed as allies. Numerous and isolated engagements took place between invaders and defenders; the former, wary in frontal attack but swift in movement, appeared with monotonous regularity from nowhere to block roads, to bomb tanks, and to worry and harass the exhausted soldiers of Britain and China; the latter kept on retreating toward the borders of India, the foothills of the Himalayas, and to the far southeastern corner of China, dynamiting oil wells and burning lend-lease matériel as opportunity offered.

The retreat became a rout. The British, burdened with mechanized equipment utterly unsuitable for a terrain of interlaced swamps and forest, abandoned their tanks and scurried on toward India. Most of them made it. The Chinese under the American General Stilwell came near being caught. They had stayed, perhaps, too long in central Burma and the Japanese had already cut off their retreat over the Burma Road by penetrating northeast from Thailand. The problem which confronted this fifty-nine-year-old American general was to press north faster than the Japanese could outflank him. Radio communication with Chungking was interrupted, and the Chinese forces in Burma widely scattered. Stilwell succeeded in extricating some Chinese and British soldiers and miscellaneous civilians by a march of wild adventure and diversified hardship which deserves well the attention of future historians.

For months to come refugees straggled into India. Fed from the skies by British planes, with swamps under their feet as often as dry land, plunging blindly where trails were not even blazed, many lost their way and perished; how many died will be forever unknown.

Java and Australia

"The fall of Singapore opened the battle for Australia," thus spoke the Prime Minister of Australia in the middle of February, 1942. But the battle for Java had first to be fought. Java was the key island of the East Indies. Although not the largest, it was, owing to its tea and coffee, rice, quinine, manganese, and oil, the most prosperous. To defend it the Dutch had a hastily drilled army of 100,000 natives, not too reliable, some 400 planes, mostly obsolete, a few cruisers, none very large, and a number of destroyers and submarines. Add to this our own Asiatic squadron (which had left the Philippines in the nick of time) of one heavy cruiser together with a number of destroyers and submarines, a British cruiser, an Australian cruiser, and some lesser British craft, all under the command of a Dutch admiral.

The Japanese took few chances; their game was to isolate prey before devouring it. In December, 1941, British North Borneo with its oil fields fell to their attack, and in January the eastern coast of Borneo and the island of Celebes. Delayed by continued British resistance at Singapore, the Japanese spread further east, taking the northern coastline of New Guinea in their stride and landing a force at Rabaul in New Britain, thus planting the flag of the Rising Sun well to the northeast of Australia. Then came direct action toward Java down through the Macassar Straits. This time the Japanese were driven back, American and Dutch submarines dealing heavy damage to their destroyers and transports.

The check was momentary; no sooner did Singapore fall than the Japanese made good their conquest of Sumatra, thus closing off Java to the west; and as they did so they occupied Portuguese Timor to the east, and after that Bali on Java's eastern tip. It was now late in February, and as the invaders prepared their armada for Java the United Nations' motley fleet boldly challenged the navy of Japan.

The ensuing naval Battle of Macassar Straits sealed the fate of Java. Only a few Allied ships survived this two-day sea fight, and when these tried later to escape almost all were sunk.

On now came the Japanese hitting at Java from east, west, and center. Their transports drew close to shore, and then, just above the water line great doors opened and out came motored barges. On reaching shore these barges dropped gangways, and dashing pell-mell over them came the little yellow men with bicycles, motorcycles, the lightest of tommy-guns and artillery. It was Bataan, Singapore, and Burma over again, with one difference. In Java were many well-paved roads over which the Japanese scooted so rapidly that their conquest made record time. They landed on February 28 and by March 9, aside from isolated fighting in the mountains, it was all over.

Then began the battle for Australia, an island-continent in area approaching the United States and with population centered in the far south and southeast. There were Australian air bases on the southeastern shores of New Guinea (Papua) at Port Moresby, and also at Darwin in north Australia. In 1940 the Australians had rushed a railroad to Darwin, and that city and Port Moresby, with the help of the Americans, they determined to hold.

The Japanese though persistent were cautious. Before trying invasion they tried to soften Port Moresby and Darwin by air raids. Perhaps they were not even certain whether to keep on to the southeast or to advance westward. During April they attacked Ceylon and sank British ships in the Indian Ocean. Possibly the course of empire ran that way; and having Vichy under the yoke they might try the same manoeuvre in Madagascar. While they were making up their minds, the British landed in Madagascar and American planes bombed Tokyo from carriers. This challenge to their homeland may have decided the Japanese to veer to the southeast against both Australia and America, for the Americans were now rushing to help their allies "down under."

So it happened that during the first week in May a great concentration of Japanese shipping was seen in the Coral Sea, which separated Australia from the Solomon Islands. The Japanese objective was plain: abandonment of the invasion of North Australia and a bold bid toward Sydney and Melbourne, heartland of the continent. Could the Japanese land near those cities in force and hold their lines of communication, Australia would be lost. And not Australia alone. Going further east they could pounce upon New Caledonia where we had a base, and this meant severing the American-Australian life lines. South of New Caledonia was New Zealand. The prospects for Japan were truly imperial.

But now Japan met her first reverse in six months of war. A task force of the United States navy met the oncoming Japanese in the Battle of the Coral Sea. It was a fight unparalleled in naval history, a battle not only at huge distances but also by planes. No battleship, apparently, was engaged by either side: but Japan did lose two airplane carriers to one of ours, and her loss in cruisers and destroyers was heavier. For the time being the Japanese would have to be content with their enormous and swiftly won conquests of millions of square miles, millions of people across 3,000 miles of ocean.

Rommel Routs the British

The Allies fared no better amid the sand dunes of Libya than in the archipelagoes of the South Seas. Their African prospects in December, 1941, were bright; but so alarming was the tale of disaster from the Far East that few rejoiced over British advance in Africa. Nevertheless the Eighth Army was repeating in late 1941 its victories of 1940, covering the old ground once more, bypassing thousands of Axis troops in Halfaya Pass and compelling them to surrender, hoisting the Union Jack again over Bengazi, driving back the Axis forces even farther than the Italians in the earlier year, this time one hundred miles beyond Bengazi, all the way to El Agheila, where Rommel, protected by the sea on one flank and by salt marshes on the other, stayed his retreat. But 1942 reversed all this; and disaster so serious overtook the overconfident Britons that as fast as their sun of empire sunk in the Far East almost as rapidly did it sink in North Africa.

January, 1942, and thousands of fresh troops were added to the Italo-German army in Libya under that wolf of desert warfare, General Rommel, also many new high-powered field guns, self-propelling, which could outshoot the light British field artillery, and many new tanks of the Mark IV model, a better tank than any thus far shipped to Egypt from America or England.

Rommel struck so hard, and so skilfully, at the end of January, that he threw the British back 360 miles to the Egyptian border and, breaking through, kept on halfway to Alexandria.

His campaign was superb; he not only had better tanks but knew how to concentrate them to best advantage; he caught the British off center by feints to the wasteland in the south as he kept on with his main offense along the seacoast; he outflanked and outwitted his enemy so fast that over and over again their food, their oil, their ammunition, their tanks fell into his hands; and in odd moments he delivered lectures on desert strategy and tactics to captured British officers.

The British, exhausted by their rush from east to west, now had no time to rest as they were rushed back faster than they had come. For a brief season in May it looked as though Rommel might be held; he was far from his supply line and every week that passed the British came closer to their own. Thanks to American and British matériel rushed around to Egypt through the Red Sea they were now nearly equal to the Germans in tanks and probably superior in the air: but Rommel was a genius in the art of war and he led the overconfident British into ambush. Out of 300 tanks, 230 were lost. And without tanks one does not win desert battles.

Tobruk had been reinforced and had withstood one long siege. So long as the Union Jack flew above its low ramparts Rommel's advance would be endangered. But now before the garrison could sow mines properly the German panzer divisions were upon them. In some ways what followed was even worse than Dunkirk, Crete, Greece, or Singapore. A very few managed to escape by sea; the remainder died or were made prisoners; and the piled-up war matériel came in very handy for Rommel.

That master of war gave his enemy no breathing space; by the end of June he was deep in Egypt. If he once reached Alexandria, then Cairo and the Suez were at his mercy. Once at Suez, the shadow of the swastika would darken the entire Middle East. At this very moment the Wehrmacht was striking across the Ukraine toward the Caucasus. Rommel's army was the southern prong of a gigantic pincer, the northern prong of which was approaching the Volga and the Caspian. The two prongs might close in northern Persia.

To throw Rommel back the British put in everything they had: soldiers from Iraq, Palestine, and Syria, green troops from England, and equally green Americans handling a few American lend-lease tanks. The RAF flew to the rescue, aided and abetted by American airmen. It was nip and go: but much Nazi matériel en route to Rommel was reported sabotaged in the Balkans, and he was held at El Alamein, seventy miles west of Alexandria. El Alamein was on the sea and forty miles inland was the

Quattara Depression of sand so soft as to make tank warfare impossible. But forty miles left ample room to manoeuvre, and on July 1 a panzer spearhead broke through the British lines. It was driven back by almost superhuman counterattack, and Rommel stopped. The Nazi tide in the Near East had reached its perigee; but who could then be sure of that?

Russia: The Second Nazi Offensive, 1942

Throughout the winter of 1941-42 the Nazis went defensive in Russia, depending on strategic fortresses to hold the furious Russians back. Out around these fortresses were fortified villages like the quills of the hedgehog, and to strike through to the center of a hedgehog or to encircle it point by point and compel surrender was costly business. All winter long that was the main Soviet endeavor.

The Red army fought through long winter months with abandon; its soldiers endured subzero weather better than did the enemy; they were better clad; and the Russian inferiority in tanks, noticeable in the summer of 1941, was now ended. From their factories beyond the Urals came new tanks, "white mammoths," as they were called by the Germans, huge brutes of fifty tons, which the Red tankmen drove at the Germans with ferocious skill through great snowbanks, across frozen lakes and rivers. The ice groaned and bent beneath their weight but the winter-wise Red soldiers put down timbers, covered them with water so they froze, and made precarious roadways like frozen pontoons. Time and again they surprised startled Nazis, cut deep behind German lines, and looked forward hopefully to a major German defeat. It never came. "Hedgehogs" might be surrounded, but their garrisons were supplied with food by plane. There were not enough of the white mammoths, not enough of their "little brothers," English tanks sent to Russia and manned by Russians. The Red cavalry performed prodigies of valor; so did the Red ski troops; so did the Red paratroopers. The Nazis suffered horribly, as Hitler acknowledged. But reinforced in February they held most of their hedgehogs. Staraya Russia, Vyazma, Bryansk, Orel, Kursk, Kharkov were still in their hands by the spring of 1942. The Russians at most had retaken but 20 per cent of the invaded lands, and the invaders were in good shape to try again.

This time the Nazis must not fail. They had now been at war two years and a half, and now with the United States a foe, with the RAF hampering their production, it was essential that 1942 see all Europe under their yoke. They had underestimated Red armies once; they would not do so again.

Very carefully they made ready a concentrated drive south and east, a surge to carry the swastika to the Black Sea, the Caucasus, and to the Volga. If Germany held Stalingrad on the Volga, lend-lease matériel

500 MILES

RUSSIAN FRONT
1941 - 42

RUSSIAN AREAS
HELD BY AXIS,
NOV., 1942

OTHER
AXIS-DOMINATED
AREAS

•••••• DEC., 1941
FARTHEST AXIS
ADVANCE
------- NOV., 1942

ARCTIC OCEAN

ALLIED SUPPLY LINES

NORTH CAPE

NORWAY

Murmansk

WHITE SEA

SWEDEN

FINLAND

Archangel

LAKE LADOGA

BALTIC SEA

ESTONIA

Leningrad

SOVIET

LATVIA

VOLGA

LITHUANIA

Rzhev   Moscow   Gorki

EAST PRUSSIA

Smolensk

"GREATER"
GERMANY

BYELO-RUSSIA

Orel

Kuibyshev

P O L A N D

Voronezh   Saratov

Kiev

UNION

SLOVAKIA

U K R A I N E

Kharkov

Stalingrad

HUNGARY

BESSARABIA

Rostov   DON   VOLGA

Odessa

Astrakhan

SERBIA

RUMANIA

Kerch

Maikop

CASPIAN SEA

BULGARIA

Sevastopol Yalta

Mozdok

ALLIED SUPPLY LINE

B L A C K   S E A

Grozny

Istanbul

Batum   Tiflis   TRANSCAUCASIA   Baku

GREECE

DARDANELLES

Ankara

Izmir

TURKEY

Tabriz

IRAN

SYRIA   IRAQ

TRM

which was seeping into Russia via Persia and the Caspian would be blocked. If once she dominated the Black Sea she would have the Turks at her mercy. With Bulgar-German forces close to Istanbul, and with a victorious German army on their eastern frontier, the Turks could be persuaded (or compelled) to open the gates of Anatolia. What chance then of Syria or Palestine remaining under British occupation?

For many months, beginning in May, 1942, German victories came in such quick succession that almost every day fresh disaster overwhelmed the Red armies. Within two weeks the Wehrmacht penetrated 150 miles further east than in 1941. Sebastopol, under siege all winter, resisted stubbornly. But the Germans were not to be denied. They could not use their tanks effectively among the jagged hills which ringed that seaport but their artillery and their Luftwaffe blasted the city into ruins. It took three weeks of hand-to-hand fighting before they forced their way into the town, and even after that the Russians did not give over. They fought from street to street, from house to house, retreating to their few ships gathered in the harbor. It was a kind of Russian Dunkirk.

Meanwhile in the eastern Crimea the Kerch peninsula had already fallen to the Nazis and just beyond the narrow straits lay the Caucasus. The Nazis were not quite ready for adventure there; an army of several hundred thousand needs room in which to operate, and to secure it the German steamroller moved steadily and relentlessly in June across the eastern Ukraine, pushing the Russians back beyond the Donetz River.

Then at the end of June, 1942, came the final rush for oil and glory. Behind the Donetz lay the Don, sweeping in a majestic arc far to the east before flowing into the sea at Rostov. To force a crossing of the Don, to seep through the rich lands of the Don basin, to conquer Rostov at the river's mouth, to cross the Kerch Straits and invade the Caucasus took the greater part of the summer.

Early in July the Germans were across the Don; by the middle of the month they had cut the railroad from between Stalingrad and the Donetz, thus severing the northern from the southern Russian armies; and by the end of the month they were attacking Rostov at the Don's mouth from the east. Early in August the Maikop oil fields which produced seven per cent of Russia's oil fell to the invader, whose rate of advance in the Caucasus was rapidly accelerated as the Russians withdrew their tanks and depended for defense on cavalry. Meanwhile by the middle of August the entire Don Bend was in German hands and by the 31st a Nazi panzer division shoved into the outskirts of Stalingrad.

Unlike Bataan or Sebastopol, Stalingrad had no natural defenses. It stretched north and south along the west bank of the Volga for twenty straggling miles, and between it and the victorious Germans was open steppe with a few low-lying hills. The Nazis had superiority in numbers, in tanks, and especially in the air, assailing the city with a thousand planes. They held the west bank of the Volga both north and south of Stalingrad; they had cut all rail communications; no reinforcements could reach the Russians except by water; and German planes hovered over the river. The prospects of making Mother Volga the eastern boundary of Hitler's Thousand Year Reich seemed excellent.

Nevertheless, as week followed week and the war swung into its fourth year the Nazis failed to nail their conquest down. They drove their tanks again and again into the heart of the city; they blasted tall new factories and turned residential quarters into shambles; they took house after house, street after street, and even reached the Volga. But always the Red army fought back. Houses and factories became debris; but behind crumbling walls and shattered cement crawled Red army men with machine guns, bayonets and knives, careless of death. The very destruction the Germans wrought helped the defense against them, for the streets of Stalingrad choked with collapsed buildings stopped the ingress of German tanks. Sometimes the Nazis would clear an entire city block, but always was there danger of losing it next day. Yet the Germans dared not lift the siege. So long as the Soviets held here on the western bank of Russia's greatest river any further drive to the Caspian would fail by a Soviet flank attack.

As for the Russians, their Stalingrad was the sign and symbol of the 1917 revolution. Stalin had ordered it defended to the death and so long as their flotilla on the Volga could shell Nazi outposts, so long as fresh troops could seep into their city across Mother Volga under friendly shelter of the night, the cursed Nazis were deprived of their prey and Red Russia lived.

Midway, the Aleutians, and Guadalcanal

In the summer of 1942 the outlook for the United Nations would have been bleak indeed but for the Pacific. There, in the far North among the fogbound Aleutians, in the central Pacific at Midway, as also at Guadalcanal in the Solomon Islands in the South Pacific, the Americans took the war to their foes.

The most important of these engagements was the Midway battle. As in that of the Coral Sea opposing warships never sighted one another and offensive fighting was entirely by plane. Early in June some eighty vessels under the Rising Sun ensign—battleships, carriers, cruisers, destroyers, transports—converged on American-held Midway. This was no reconnaissance in force. Clearly the Japanese intended, if victorious here, to attack Hawaii. But the Mikado's soldiers never landed on Midway. Land-based bombers of the army, navy planes from carriers, navy flying boats intercepted the Japanese fleet and it sought safety in flight. Action continued for four days. The loss of American planes was heavy, five out of six in one sortie, eight out of sixteen in another, and fifteen out of fifteen in a third. The Japanese also sank our carrier, the *Yorktown*. But their own losses were far more serious, four carriers, two battleships, two heavy cruisers, three destroyers and transports. Midway was a happy augury for the future, particularly heartening in the destruction of carriers, a type of craft in which the enemy's navy hitherto had been predominant.

Along with the raid on Midway came a Japanese thrust at Dutch Harbor in the eastern Aleutians. Planes based there could easily raid Alaska, make possible an invasion of continental America.

Sixty miles west of Dutch Harbor lies Umnak Island, and upon it two months earlier had been laid steel landing mats for planes. From this secret base in the fog our army Warhawks swooped down upon the foe—and from west of them. Confused by this attack, the invaders fled. They stopped in retreat to capture Kiska, 672 miles from Dutch Harbor, and Attu, still further distant at the Aleutians' western tip. Hence our North Pacific victory was incomplete. But for the time being Alaska, Canada, and our northwestern states were clear of enemy bombers. Conversely, as long as Kiska and Attu remained in their hands, Nippon was similarly protected.

Despite the Battle of the Coral Sea the Japanese were still set upon the conquest of Australia. They strove persistently to capture Port Moresby on the southeastern side of New Guinea; their forces fanned out steadily from the northern Solomons southeastward along the thousand-mile length of that archipelago and built an airfield on the large island of Guadalcanal in the southern Solomons. Their objective was evident—cutting the American lifeline to Australia. And this we had to protect by an offensive-defensive at Guadalcanal.

On August 7 American marines, protected by a naval air task force, landed on Guadalcanal and on the nearby islands of Tulagi and Gavutu. They surprised the enemy on Guadalcanal, captured the airfield, re-naming it Henderson Field. On Gavutu they ran into a hornet's nest, the Japanese defending their caves with reckless courage, dying to a man. On Guadalcanal the surprised Nipponese rallied to the attack. So did the Japanese navy. Smashing into our task force on August 8, it sank three heavy American cruisers and one Australian. Our transports, how-ever, escaped destruction, and our marines, heavily reinforced, beat off the Japanese on land.

Throughout August and September the enemy did its best to dislodge the marines, strafing from the air and shelling from the sea the narrow and confined area which they had won, only about seven miles along the coast by four or five in depth. On the island there was endless fight-ing. Japanese troops, continuously reinforced at night by fast destroyers, proved worthy antagonists. Few were captured; many died. So also was it with the marines, who found the hot miasmic air, the malaria, and insect life of Guadalcanal quite as unpleasant as the soldiers of the Mikado. Time after time the latter returned to the fray, supported by naval carriers, destroyers, and battleships; time after time they were repulsed. The flag still flew over Henderson Field, and from it rose American bombers to harry Japanese ships and bomb Japanese installations. The yellow tide of conquest still lapped these shores, but whether it had passed its peak and was now receding was anybody's guess.

Air Raids and Submarines

In 1942 the war in the air encouraged the United Nations. There was no proof as yet that the Luftwaffe was outclassed in Europe, since a large part of Goering's fleet was heavily engaged on the eastern front; but German assaults on Britain did peter out, while British attacks on Germany, and upon armament factories, docks, and railroads in the German occupied lands began to tell heavily against the Nazis.

There were more allied raids than before; there were many more planes to each raid; and the bombers were much heavier, huge Stirlings, great four-motored Lancasters, and 300 planes often in a single raid. The British focussed on the Ruhr and on industrial Germany; they lambasted Cologne in one night with 3,000 tons of bombs carried by over 1,000 planes; they spread afield; they flew to Augsburg in southern Germany and destroyed Diesel engines being fabricated for submarines; they flew to the distant Baltic ports of Rostock and Lübeck, wiped out docks, shipbuilding yards, aircraft factories, doing more damage to those ancient cities than the Germans ever did to Coventry. And they found time to smash as well at French factories.

Autumn, 1942

The war swung into its fourth year, and almost everywhere the Axis still was winning. The Hitlerites had one foot in Stalingrad and looked hopefully to sweeping up the Volga valley to roll in on Moscow from the east. They were already deep within the Caucasus, the Maikop oilfields had been won, and Nazi advance units were progressing steadily along the western shoreline of the Black Sea toward Batum. On the east the Axis' chances of forcing its way through Daghestan to Baku were slight, but the Nazis might slip around the snow-clad mountains of that wild and sparsely settled province and following the shoreline of the Caspian penetrate to Baku, there to quench the thirst of their war machines with endless Soviet oil. Over the Caspian, then, soon would fly the Nazi banner, and the southern supply line from the United States to Russia would be severed. If necessary, northern Persia could be taken, and Turkestan. Perhaps a junction could be effected with Japan in Afghanistan or in the Pamirs. The prospects were enticing.

In Egypt, Rommel was halted at El Alamein. But Alexandria was only sixty miles away, a glittering prize. Nothing favored the British except terrain, and their badly battered Eighth Army only recently had been outwitted and outflanked by military wizardry which might well outwit and outflank them again. One more deceptive infiltration, one more successful ruse, and the entire delta of the Nile with Cairo at its apex was at Rommel's mercy.

India, meanwhile, seethed with rebellious unrest and the victorious Japanese, engorged with Burma, were at her borders. The leaders of the Indian National Congress, exasperated by the evident unwillingness of British authority to implement promises of self-government after the war by trusting Congress with any important share in the prosecution of it, actively engaged in fermenting "non-violent resistance," that is, promoting strikes, discouraging enlistment, spreading defeatism. Gandhi, whether prophet, saint, or politician, implied that he was not unwilling to negotiate with Japan. And communication between China and India was now ended except for a trickle by transport plane over high mountains.

The entire East Indies lay quiescent under Japanese authority. The northern coastline of New Guinea was in Japanese hands and Port Moresby on the southern shore in grave danger. Everywhere north of Australia the Japanese swarmed. The Americans, it is true, had won a great mid-Pacific victory at Midway and had driven back an armada aimed at Hawaii and Alaska, had won a toehold on Guadalcanal. But this was most precarious, a single airfield only, surrounded by a jungle infested with Japanese soldiers, constantly under attack from their landbased planes in the northern Solomons and at Rabaul, still further north in New Britain Island. The southward expansion of Japan toward Australia and New Zealand was blocked for the time being, and that was all.

In Western Europe, meanwhile, there was no second front, nor any near prospect of one. In August a reconnaissance in force met with bloody rebuff at Dieppe on the French coast. After this, it seemed obvious that no second front could be established in 1942. Yet Stalin kept on insisting that there must be one. Churchill flew to Moscow to pacify him. The British are sea animals, he explained, the Russians land animals. The latter must be patient. But still the Russian chieftain was dissatisfied; he did not think the British and Americans were doing their fair share to win the war.

The United Nations fought for time as well as victory; time to convert America into the arsenal of democracy promised by Roosevelt; time to make the tools with which to make the ships, the planes, the tanks that would beat Hitler down; time to build factories, and homes for men and

The "Big Three" at Teheran Conference (December, 1943)

Acme Photo

women to work in them; time to assemble raw materials, to train crafts-men, chemists, soldiers, technicians; time to transport overseas millions of men from Canada and the United States with arms and food; time to equip and drill these forces, and to pile up in Britain vast reservoirs of all things necessary for offensive war.

If America was the arsenal of democracy, Britain was its warehouse. The average Englishman ate less now than formerly, but his health was better; his house, if he had one, was damp and cold, but his spirits were high. He knew it was not so bad as in 1940 when England faced the Nazi storm alone; his island now was an armed camp, and with every passing month became more crowded with fighting men. The worst, he sensed, was over. Sometime, somewhere, somehow, the measure of the Axis would be taken.

The Axis, on the other hand, was not so confident as in 1940. The English were still in the war, and now there were Russians and Ameri-cans in as well! The conquered countries would not support the new order. The name of Hitler's Norwegian viceroy, Major Quisling, was a hissing and a byword to all the world. Norwegians refused to enlist for the crusade against bolshevism; they turned their backs on German soldiers, put poison in fish canned for the German army, stood by their bishops, ministers, and teachers who refused to follow Quisling's orders, and escaped when possible to England.

So likewise was it in Denmark, the Netherlands, Belgium, Luxemburg, France, Czechoslovakia, Poland. Fines, exactions, court-martials, starva-tion, death—they made no difference. The terrorism of the gestapo met with sullen bitterness, secret sabotage, sporadic assassination. When "Hitler's hangman," Heydrich, was killed in Czechoslovakia and the Nazis slew every male adult in Lidice, the wrath of the Czechs but mounted higher. In Yugoslavia's mountains the breath of freedom never died, and every outlying German garrison knew it must keep constant watch or else, perchance, be slaughtered. In London, General de Gaulle still kept the Tricolor flying, and by ones and twos and threes his Free French forces were augmented, as young lads slipped through the German lines to join him. There were many accidents in French factories; trains were derailed, bridges mysteriously blew up, cars were set afire, and German soldiers died. The French respected old Marshal Pétain, who had signed the armistice with Hitler, but Pierre Laval, the Nazi stooge, was anathema in France as was Quisling in Norway. A scattering few were found to fight bolshevism, and Frenchmen agreed to work in Germany that French prisoners of war might be delivered from German concentration camps; but the great majority watched dumbly as their goods and chattels, machinery, horses, cattle, even grain were passed over the border into Germany. They were helpless and knew it; but collaborate with Hitler they would not.

Three years of war had not turned Nazi victims into Nazi slaves, nor had it convinced Chinese that Japan was sincere in her grandiloquent proclamation of the "Great East Asia Co-Prosperity Sphere." In this, and in their fast accumulating stores of war matériel, lay the major hope of the United Nations.

November Victories

The autumn of 1942 was to bring sweet revenge for 1940, for 1941, for 1942. In Africa, Europe, and in the South Seas the United Nations could list these victories: Rommel routed in Egypt and in Cyrenaica; French Morocco and Algeria occupied by British and American troops; the collapse of the German offense in Russia; and a new defeat of the Japanese navy in the South Seas, together with the drowning of thousands of soldiers headed for the reconquest of Guadalcanal.

General Montgomery and his British Eighth Army struck at El Alamein at the end of October, with superb superiority of artillery, tanks, planes. Most of his new matériel had reached Egypt via the long sea route around Africa, much of it American. Montgomery's army was mixed, pure British units, New Zealanders, men of Australia, long accustomed to desert war, men of South Africa, Punjabis, Sikhs, and other Indian warriors, a few Americans, most of them tankmen or airmen. It was a clear-cut British victory.

The Afrika Korps withdrew swiftly but with skill. Past all the old landmarks flowed the retreating German tide, past Tobruk, Derna, Bengazi with its useful harbor, around the bend of Cyrenaica, back to the salt marshes of El Agheila. For the first time since the war began the church bells pealed in England. As Churchill told his public: "We have now 100 Italian generals and 300,000 of his (Mussolini's) soldiers in our hands as prisoners of war."

As Montgomery's artillery barked at El Alamein an Anglo-American expeditionary force bound for Northwest Africa was on the high seas. It was hoped that the French garrisons there, upwards of 100,000 men, would welcome our arrival. For the most part they did so. At Algiers only a few shots were fired. At Oran, 130 miles west, there was more serious resistance. And at Casablanca on the Atlantic coast of Morocco there was, for a time, stiff fighting. It was necessary to land tanks both east and west of that city and begin siege operations. Fortunately the mysterious Admiral Darlan in Algiers, the North African representative of Marshal Pétain, gave orders to end resistance.

The American general, Eisenhower, commander-in-chief of the expeditionary force, immediately recognized Darlan as head of the civil administration and for this was violently criticized. Darlan's previous career had been that of a bitter Anglophobe, and since he had yielded from time to time to Nazi pressure most Englishmen and many Americans considered it undesirable that we should have any dealings with him. But Darlan, as our enemy, could cause us no end of trouble; and as our friend he could, and did, render possible our occupation of a great empire in record-making time.

His collaboration gave Hitler an excuse for occupying all France and for seizing the French ships at Toulon. The French army did not resist but Hitler lost the fleet. As the Nazis reached Toulon, their planes filling the skies, the French blew up their vessels! Meanwhile the British First Army, along with American detachments raced for Bizerte and Tunis. These two seaports in the French Protectorate of Tunisia were five hundred miles from Algiers and less than a hundred from Sicily, too great a handicap. The Germans got there first by air and sea, and in superior numbers. The Allies, within twelve miles of their goal, were driven back.

The redoubtable Russians also took the offensive this month of November, all the way from Leningrad to Stalingrad. Instead of capturing Stalingrad before snowfall, as Hitler had promised his people, 300,000 desperate Germans and Rumanians before and within that ruined city found Russian forces slowly closing in around them from north and south. Besiegers became the besieged. Farther south in the Caucasus trapped and widely scattered divisions of the mighty German host now sought safety in retreat. Back in Germany dreams of the gushing oil from Baku faded fast; instead came memory of last year's trials on Russian steppes and forebodings lest another and a worse year be in store.

Nor was this all! The Japanese suffered a double setback in the South Seas. Just as Hitler prophesied the fall of Stalingrad to his own men and the capture of Port Moresby in Papua by his yellow allies, the nimble Nipponese infiltrating through the jungle and over the Owen Stanley range of mountains were driven back by MacArthur's Australian-American fighters. And better yet, the American Admiral, Halsey, won in mid-November a victory at Guadalcanal, sinking many Japanese transports heavily loaded with troops.

Winter, 1942-43

In all three major theatres of war, in the Asiatic and Pacific area, in Africa, and in Russia the United Nations kept on winning. The Japanese made little headway in China and were subject there to continuous and effective, if somewhat meagre, air raiding; a Japanese army in Papua (eastern New Guinea) was exterminated and Papua cleansed of the invader; in Africa the British Eighth Army, still in pursuit of Rommel, this time went beyond El Agheila, captured Tripoli, cleared the Axis entirely out of Libya, penetrated southern Tunisia; and in Russia the greatest victory thus far of the United Nations was won at Stalingrad.

The major fighting in the Southwest Pacific took place in Papua, where some 1,500 Japanese troops tried to force their way across high mountains to attack Port Moresby. Soon they were in full retreat as a somewhat larger force of Americans and Australians drove them back to their base at Buna on the northern shore of Papua. Absence of roads and the necessity of transporting all food, ammunition, and supplies by hand or by airplane made progress slow; and the further our soldiers dipped north over the Owen Stanley mountains and the closer they got to Buna the slower the drive became. Slowly we closed in on the trapped Japanese. Reinforcements were sent them from their island bases farther north; but these were wiped out by our airmen. The fighting was carried on by every ruse known to the jungle. Thick undergrowth made visibility only possible a few feet ahead, and underneath was soggy ground in which fox-holes filled with water. We inched forward; we drove wedges in between Japanese detachments; we isolated them in pockets; and these one by one we exterminated. To do this was the work of weeks. Not until January 3rd did Buna fall.

The North African winter campaign would have ended in stalemate had it not been for General Montgomery and his British Eighth Army. Early in the winter it was at El Agheila, still in pursuit of Italians and Germans. The closer the latter got to their main base at Tripoli the shorter became their lines of communications; conversely the further the British shoved ahead the more difficult became theirs. Nevertheless, the British were not held up long at El Agheila. By the time their artillery was ready to clear a passage, and their engineers had exploded mines and booby traps, the Afrika Korps was in full retreat. Montgomery pushed on. Beyond lay Tripoli, capital of Libya, a good seaport, well defended from encircling hills. But the Germans did not choose to hold it, and Italians could not. A brief skirmish and Italy's African empire had fallen. In thirteen weeks the Eighth Army had chased the enemy 1,300 miles, the longest drive in history. On went Montgomery. The retreating Germans panted after the security of the Mareth line in French Tunisia, and Montgomery followed them there. To breach these strong fortifications was a first-class military action as Montgomery well knew, and the Eighth Army halted.

Elsewhere in North Africa the situation was more complicated. There was the problem of logistics, how to supply an army of approximately 200,000 with food and guns, tanks and planes, from bases as far distant as England and the United States, with submarines lurking in the ocean pathways; how after the matériel once reached Africa to distribute it to fighting men often hundreds of miles from the port of debarkation. Railways in North Africa were few and in disrepair; in some instances they had to be rebuilt and locomotives and freight cars imported from America.

Then, too, there was the political problem; who was to govern the restless, seething population, part French, part Arab. It had been solved temporarily by putting Darlan in authority; but Darlan was promptly assassinated. The men under him had been of Vichy and in consequence were anti-British. Though not pro-German they were undemocratic, loyal to Pétain alone. They hated de Gaulle and his "Free French" who had done so much to keep alive the fires of French resistance; and the Free French replied in kind.

The only common denominator available seemed to be General Giraud, an officer reputed as patriotic as de Gaulle himself. Giraud had not been a party to the fall of France. Imprisoned by the Germans in 1940, he had escaped from Germany and been taken to North Africa by a British submarine. Giraud succeeded Darlan as the head of French administration in North Africa; but the Free French would not acknowledge his leadership and bitter feud continued.

And finally there was the military problem. Germans and Italians had entrenched at Bizerte and Tunis and behind these two cities were fortifying a range of hills from which it would be difficult to oust them. They had already forced back the British First Army, and American and French contingents. If we were not careful we might be caught between Axis troops rolling down from Tunis and the Afrika Korps, rolling up from the Mareth line.

Meanwhile Hitler insisted that his bridgehead in Africa be held, and Axis reinforcements flowed into Tunis and Bizerte. All over Tunisia the weather was atrociously bad and for a large part of the winter the war was reduced to patrol action. Then it flared up suddenly and with startling reverses for the Americans.

On February 11 the Nazi army poured through Faid Pass at the eastern end of the American sector. Tanks and dive bombers seemed to come from everywhere, and all at once. We took quite a beating, retreating to Kasserine Pass, surrendering some 4,000 square miles of territory. We were even driven out of the Kasserine, and that meant serious business, for if the Germans gained control of the plateau region beyond, they might encircle the British First Army to the north and drive the United Nations back into Algeria. This was our baptism of fire, and apparently we were caught with equipment too light, with poor air support, and inferior tactics. We tried to rescue detachments which could not be rescued; we fell into traps and got what was coming to us.

Then the very next week we held and defeated the Wehrmacht. That drubbing had served us well. Our army functioned like a well-oiled machine. Stuka bombers were something to laugh at; our artillery fire was excellent; and the hitherto triumphant Nazis retreated through the

Kasserine Pass with their tails between their legs. Eisenhower was quoted after our initial defeat as saying, "Our boys will fight better now they are mad."

Stalingrad

The Fuehrer's New Year's message to his folk was not cheerful. The best he could say about the eastern front was that the winter there could not be worse than the preceding one. He erred. In January and February, Stalin's armies hurled themselves with such terrific and unrelenting force upon the discouraged Nazis as to free Leningrad from its besiegers, draw tighter and tighter the noose around twenty German divisions trapped at Stalingrad, and on February 2nd to compel the half-starved and abandoned soldiers left there to surrender.

There had been time enough to withdraw these divisions and sufficient warning during the autumn that fatal consequences would follow if they were not withdrawn. Only the conceit of a paranoiac would have abandoned them to their fate. Early in January they were cut off completely by a ring of Red armies, and beyond that ring a second was in process of formation, and beyond that a third. And now as the Red soldiers closed in for the kill it was the turn of the Nazis to dig for shelter in the ruined cellars of Stalingrad and to feed as the Russians had on horse meat, when and if it could be found. Their only contact with the outside world was by plane, and that too intermittent to provide sufficient food and ammunition, much less reinforcements. Nevertheless they stuck it out, and did so until over half had been exterminated.

Germany was thrown into consternation. "Europe is in mortal peril," cried Goebbels. "Only Germany can save Europe now. The onrush of the steppes against our venerable continent has broken out this winter with a violence overshadowing all human imagination." European civilization would be defended in total war which the Nazis would wage. If they were to do the fighting the least the rest of Europe could do was to labor in the common cause. His words speak volumes.

The Axis Expelled from Africa

Autumn victories over the Axis had cautiously been hailed by Churchill as "the end of the beginning." And now as winter turned to spring one could somewhat confidently write of "the beginning of the end." The tide had been slow in turning but by the middle of May it had run out a good six months, and there was rejoicing in the camp of the United Nations.

A second front clearly was impossible until Tunisia was won, and as winter ended that task seemed formidable. In northern Tunisia the Germans and Italians were safe behind a range of jagged hills and in the south they held the Mareth line against Montgomery. Their weakest point was the elongated corridor which led to the Mareth line, but it was protected by the sea on one side and by deep gorges and ravines on the other. Both French and Americans had tried to break through here in the neighborhood of Faid Pass and had been rolled back. Could they have done so they would have split the Axis forces in two. Conversely, so long as Montgomery's Eighth Army was on the other side of the Mareth line the United Nations' armies remained split.

Montgomery tried to crack the Mareth line, failed, then deployed his New Zealanders and the Free French who had crossed the Sahara to join him, into the desert at his left. These sturdy warriors circled around the Mareth line way to the northeast thus compelling the outflanked Afrika Korps to abandon their fortifications and to follow the coastal plain toward Tunis. Montgomery lunged after them as fast as his engineers could dig up land mines left by the capable Germans, who now had steadily retreated some 1,600 miles from El Alamein.

By these manoeuvres the Axis armies were forced back into northern Tunisia in an area somewhat smaller than Connecticut. They could not adopt defense in depth, for they were held too close to the Mediterranean; yet they had a long line to defend, well over one hundred miles. Their front wound like a snake around mountainous crags which their artillery commanded, and it was thought they might hold out many weeks, perhaps longer, if reinforcements could be gotten in from Sicily.

In less than a fortnight, however, the Italians and Germans were surrendering in tens of thousands. What took place was roughly as follows. As Montgomery swept north along the seacoast the British First Army, the Americans, and the French closed in on the now shrinking Axis lines. As formed now the Allied line ran from northwest to southeast thus: French Moroccan troops faced Bizerte on the Mediterranean, then came the Americans, the British First Army, the main body of the French, and the British Eighth Army.

The American assignment was to pry open the mountain gateway at Mateur, leading to Bizerte. To do this it was necessary to storm three hills, the key one, Hill 609, defended by as good troops as Germany had, and in a region so rough that mules were used for trucks. In the face of heavy machine-gun fire the Americans stormed this hill with hand grenades and at the point of the bayonet. Beyond they could see Mateur, now defenseless, and farther beyond shimmering in the sunshine the white houses of Bizerte and the blue Mediterranean Sea.

Our men streamed down toward Bizerte, cut the road to Tunis, captured Bizerte without further fighting. An hour or two later the British First Army was in Tunis, likewise meeting no resistance. In almost every direction German and Italian detachments threw down their arms. Some took refuge on Cape Bon but soon surrendered. Part of the famous

Afrika Korps, bypassed by the quick dash of the Allies, fought for a few days in the hills. By May 8 victory was assured; by May 15, 1943, the African resistance ended everywhere.

This Tunisian campaign cost the Axis dear. It lost over 300,000 men, among whom were 266,000 prisoners; it also lost its last outpost in Africa. More than that: it proved that the U-boat campaign, however successful, had not prevented the enemy conveying and supplying large armies overseas; it proved that air supremacy had at last shifted from the Luftwaffe to the United Nations; that Axis naval supremacy in the Mediterranean was a dream, that the soft under-belly of the continent was now open to invasion.

Italians became jittery and talked alternately of peace and of fighting to the bitter end. The Nazis belittled what had occurred and explained to their people that they had fought in Tunisia merely to gain time to make invincible their Europa fortress. The Maginot line psychology of defensive warfare which bedeviled the French in 1940 had in turn infected the Nazis, an augury of good fortune for the United Nations.

Was this battle for Bizerte and Tunis to be *the* turning point of the second World War? Churchill at once flew to Washington, where final plans were in process for insuring and for speeding campaigns to follow. The Prime Minister's address in Congress late in May compared Bizerte-Tunis of 1943 to Gettysburg of 1863, but warned that though the grey tide of the Confederate army never rose so high again, two years passed and thousands died before the victors came to Appomattox.

Chapter 40

STORMING FORTRESS EUROPA

Summer, 1943, and Fortress Europa seemingly was as strong as ever. The central keep was Germany; the outer bulwarks, Norway, Denmark, Holland, Belgium, the Channel and Biscayan ports, Spain, Italy, the Balkans, Crete, the Crimea, and bristling Nazi hedgehogs firmly planted in the heart of western Russia, from the Baltic south to the Black Sea.

There were many countries, but there was one sole command, not only military but also economic. Manufacturing centered in the greater Germany. Other areas supplied raw materials: wheat from France; iron ore, timber, and fish from Norway and Sweden; butter, eggs, and bacon from Denmark; fruits, copper, minerals from Spain and Italy; cereals, meat, bauxite, and oil from the Balkans. Such a fortress could not be starved into submission nor could the siege safely be delayed, since every month that passed without assault the Nazi screws on Europe's economy tightened and hope of succor for many millions under the Nazi yoke grew dim.

Since these things were so, it was the better part of wisdom to give *priority* to the European war, to defeat first the major enemy, Germany, and to regard Japan the lesser foe. Stalin called loudly for an invasion of the French coast. To launch one in 1943 was impossible. But there were two other ways whereby the Anglo-Americans might strike at Germany—by air and by way of Italy, and both were tried.

Air Blitz in Reverse

Some Allied experts were certain of knocking out Germany from the air alone, but Churchill was as ever conservative. "The experiment," he prudently told Congress in May, "is well worth trying so long as other methods are not excluded." The plane did not knock out Germany, but it did severely weaken military power there. The RAF, numerically stronger in 1943 than the American air arm in Europe, concentrated on the Ruhr, pounding congested areas in that industrial valley over and over again, blowing up houses, railroads and dams, flooding towns, pulverizing factories, killing unknown numbers of persons, reducing German steel production perhaps thirty per cent.

Hamburg in particular took heavy punishment, more severe than that inflicted on London. Night after night British bombers blasted docks, shipping, and factories. Their raids were costly, the defense desperate; but there was precious little left of Hamburg, second city of the Reich.

Far and wide through occupied France and Belgium scoured the Allied planes, ripping up airfields, smashing railroad trains, destroying coastal installations, and focusing on German submarine bases at Lorient and St. Nazaire. The damage done the submarine pens, those cement caverns reinforced with steel of which one at Lorient was spacious enough to stable thirty U-boats, was disappointing; but the ruin inflicted on shipyards, repair depots, and transportation facilities which the U-boats used, was held worth the sacrifice of Allied planes and airmen.

For this harassing from the west the Germans had small answers—the U-boat and the Luftwaffe. In 1943 the Reich navy concentrated exclusively on the U-boat, and for awhile sinkings rose rapidly. But there were Allied answers for the new U-boats. One of them was the frigate, easily constructed in great numbers, somewhat smaller than a destroyer, but capable of convoy duty; another smaller ship was the destroyer escort, and finally there was the patrol plane, weighed down with gas rather than with armament, good for long-distance aërial convoy work. There were ups and downs this year in the U-boat war but gradually its menace faded, particularly in the North Atlantic where the Canadian navy specialized in convoy duty, with some five hundred ships flying the Canadian flag by 1944.

The Luftwaffe also failed as signally as did the U-boat. It was not that German science fell behind; it was German production and German manpower that failed to keep pace. The Germans simply did not have the trained pilots, the trained mechanics, factory facilities, aluminum, and oil necessary in 1943 to meet what was thrown at the Reich by Allied air raiders. Top priorities went to fighter planes so that German bombing of Britain dwindled. Goering's organization for air mastery had planned too small and could not catch up.

Meanwhile production in the United States was swelling into incredible torrents of matériel. The Americans and Britons lost 335 heavy bombers in June alone, but British plane production had quadrupled and that of the United States had doubled, and redoubled and redoubled again. The new type planes carried four-ton bombs, later to be six- and even eight-ton "block busters." Over Coventry the Germans had strewed 450 tons of small stuff; now in 1943, many a German city was plastered four times that heavily.

The Sicilian and Italian Campaign, 1943

On July 9, 1943, two allied armies landed on the Sicilian coast, the American Seventh and the British Eighth, some thirteen divisions in all.

To conquer Sicily took thirty-nine days. The fighting, comparatively light in the earlier stages, became heavy and bitter, Allied casualties in dead and wounded going over the 20,000 mark, the Axis somewhat more.

The American Seventh Army encircled the western shore; its tanks rolled overland to Palermo, capital of Sicily on the Tyrrhenian Sea; the greater part of the island's 9,000-odd square miles was overrun; Italian garrisons surrendered after token resistance; and villagers with smiling faces offered fruit and flowers.

The British Eighth Army had a harder task. The eastern shore up which it slowly pried its way was precipitous, and close to the sea in the northeast towered Mount Etna, 10,000 feet in elevation. To its protecting security the Germans withdrew their three and one-half divisions; their temper was excellent; their courage beyond question; their defense position superb.

The terrain was so rugged and the ravines cut by swift streams so deep that any breakthrough by tanks was impossible. Tanks were used for brief snorting charges but the battles, or rather the incessant series of little local battles, were for the artillery and infantry. Slowly the British and Canadians won through the foothills to the west of Mount Etna, where they linked up with the Americans. From one strategic height after another the united Allies pressed the foe. Ferociously fighting and with great skill, the Germans withdrew by August 16. Almost all their troops were ferried over the narrow straits by plane or in small craft. There was no big bag of German prisoners as in Tunis; this time the booty consisted of Italians and German tanks. The underbelly of the Axis thus far was not so soft.

Then on September 3 the British Eighth crossed the straits to romp over the toe and heel of Italy, Italian garrisons surrendering with abandon. The more forehanded and more treacherous of the Fascist leaders, among whom Dino Grandi, the obsolete Marshal Badoglio, and Count Ciano, the Duce's infamous son-in-law, were notorious, having determined that the ship of state was sinking, decided to desert it. At a ten-hour session of the Fascist Grand Council at which Mussolini presided they somewhat disclosed their hand. A motion was made and carried calling upon the king to take the leadership of the nation. Mussolini sped to Victor Emmanuel, was arrested and sneaked away to prison, and Badoglio was asked by the king to form a "new" government.

Ruin came over Italy like some great pestilential fog; Italian armies were in full retreat; the civil population was semi-starved; the lynx-eyed Gestapo watched Badoglio; and the German forces in Italy were enlarged.

Victor Emmanuel and Badoglio played their cards with treacherous cunning. They were between three fires, the jittery mobs in Italian cities, the coldly suspicious Germans, and the overwhelming Allies. Crookedly

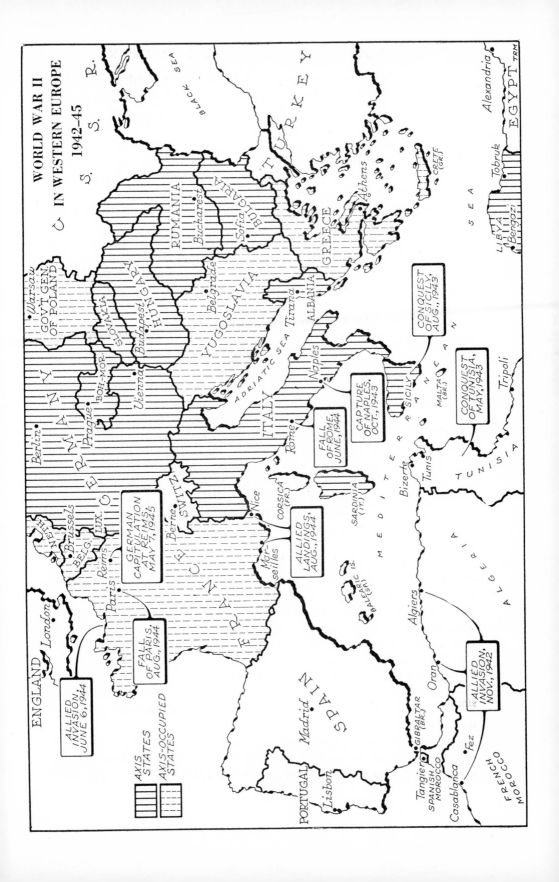

WORLD WAR II
IN WESTERN EUROPE
1942-45

S. S. R.

AXIS
STATES

AXIS-OCCUPIED
STATES

ENGLAND

London

ALLIED
INVASION,
JUNE 6, 1944

NETH.

Brussels

BELG.

Reims

LUX.

Paris

FALL
OF PARIS,
AUG., 1944

GERMAN
CAPITULATION
AT REIMS,
MAY 7, 1945

Berlin

GERMANY

Berne

SWITZ.

FRANCE

Nice

Marseilles

ALLIED
LANDINGS,
AUG., 1944

PORTUGAL

Lisbon

Madrid

SPAIN

Tangier

SPANISH
MOROCCO

GIBRALTAR
(BR.)

Oran

Algiers

ALLIED
INVASION,
NOV., 1942

Fez

Casablanca

FRENCH
MOROCCO

ALGERIA

BALEARIC IS.
(SP.)

CORSICA
(FR.)

SARDINIA
(IT.)

MEDITERRANEAN

Bizerte

Tunis

TUNISIA

Tripoli

CONQUEST
OF TUNISIA,
MAY, 1943

MALTA
(BR.)

ITALY

Rome

FALL
OF ROME,
JUNE, 1944

CAPTURE
OF NAPLES,
OCT., 1943

Naples

SICILY

CONQUEST
OF SICILY,
AUG., 1943

SEA

LIBYA

Bengazi

Tobruk

Alexandria

EGYPT

GOV'T GEN.
OF POLAND

Warsaw

BOH-MOR-

Prague

SLOVAKIA

Vienna

Budapest

HUNGARY

RUMANIA

Bucharest

Belgrade

YUGOSLAVIA

BULGARIA

Sofia

ADRIATIC SEA

Tirana

ALBANIA

GREECE

Athens

CRETE
(GR.)

TURKEY

BLACK SEA

TRM

willing to double-cross anyone or everybody, they played possum. The Allies gave Badoglio a brief thinking spell, suspected that he still fancied the Hitlerites, then enforced on him a rough reminder of their power by renewed air raids. The effect was instant and salutary. Through devious channels Badoglio intimated that he wished to join the Allies.

The terms offered were harsh, or would have been had Italy had anything to lose, unconditional surrender, demobilization of the Italian forces, surrender of the fleet—what was left of it. Badoglio agreed, begging that negotiations be kept secret lest his German friends and masters get wind of his spoor.

With one tremendous military stroke the Allies now planned to bring the fighting in southern Italy to a quick conclusion. Their strategy called for a landing in force on the beaches of Salerno just south of the Bay of Naples and Mount Vesuvius; for the withholding of the news of Italy's surrender until just before disembarking; for a rapid and more or less unimpeded march inland to join forces with British troops advancing north from the heel of Italy. They would then be in position to strike for Naples and Rome, cities which they thought would fall like apples ready for the plucking.

But the Germans were not caught napping. Two days before General Clark led his men ashore on September 9, approximately half from the British Eighth Army and half from the American Fifth, the Germans had cleared the beaches of Italians, armed the hills with Germans, and were at the ready. The Battle of the Beaches swung first this way, then that, for several days. The Germans held high ground north, south, and east of the dried mud flats and pebbly shores on which the landing barges grated. They strafed the barges, the beaches, and the thin line of soldiers in their foxholes, by artillery and from the air; they came so close to driving them into the sea that the German radio blared "another Dunkirk."

It almost was one. What saved the day was Allied fire power. Salerno was the outside limit for land-based planes operating from captured Sicilian airfields. Fighter aircraft, as it was, could not stay more than fifteen minutes over the front without running short of gas. But there were thousands of them, and frequently they made two trips a day. It was no longer necessary to give any thought to Italian warships, for they had surrendered, and the British brought up their largest battle-wagons to pour withering fire on German batteries. Meanwhile on the beaches the LCTs (landing craft tanks) were close-packed together like monster whales. And out of them came tanks to crash incessantly into the enemy's lines.

The British Eighth Army was 150 miles to the south when Clark landed at Salerno, but it came on with astonishing speed, leap-frogging forward by the use of planes and parachutists. Within ten days the Allied forces joined, and the Germans, in danger of being outflanked, retired to Naples.

That Italian seaport they thoroughly wrecked. Out of what seems pure malice, and aimless vengeance they burned libraries, plundered art treasures, dynamited the water system as well as gas and electrical services, and set time bombs in hotels and post offices which exploded later and brought death to civilians. After this joint work of coverage and sadism they retired north to strong entrenchments beyond the Volturno River.

From Naples two historic highways led north toward Rome, the Via Appia, across Pontine marshes near the sea, and the Via Latina, often known as the Via Casalina, which wound its way around craggy little mountains through the town of Cassino. By this route the Allies hoped to force their way into Rome before 1943 came to an end.

They were doomed to disappointment. The Germans held savagely all along the Volturno, scene of Garibaldi's victory over the Neapolitans in 1860, and when driven back entrenched themselves anew on the Liri River flowing by Cassino. As the year ended the British Eighth Army on the Adriatic was still short of reaching Pescara, east of Rome and the terminal of the only decent route from the Adriatic to that city. And the American Fifth Army under Clark, to which were attached British, New Zealand, French, and Indian troops, had only begun to claw its way through the tangled mountain heights around Cassino.

Russian Victories of 1943

From every side the storm clouds of 1943 converged on Fortress Europa. From the south, so far distant were their thunders echoing in the Apennines that they scarce were heard north of the Alps. Block-busters on German cities were devastating proof of very present foul weather, but, after all, such bomb smashes were intermittent, and though black nimbus clouds in westward Britain piled higher with every convoy and transport from America, the continent still seemed immune from invasion out of the west. Not so on the east! There through all this ghastly year raged a war storm, more widespread, more violent than any on record in German history.

It bore some resemblance to that of 1941 and 1942, but this time the all-conquering Germans were in retreat. From river to river, from city to city they were crushed back toward their Fatherland. The gains of two superhuman years were erased, the brags of Hitler and Goebbels now proved a mockery by German dead, the flower of the Wehrmacht scorched beneath the smoldering ruins of a dozen Russian cities, drowned in swamps, strewn carelessly by indifferent death in forests or on wind-swept steppes.

Rostov, on the Sea of Azov, was in Soviet hands by February 14, and German threats to Soviet oil ended. Equal success crowned Red army campaigns in the Donetz and the Ukraine, and all the way north to Leningrad. Kharkov was taken and the Russians pressed beyond it toward Poltava, where Charles XII of Sweden had had his greatness crushed in the seventeenth century. The battle line in three months had been pushed four hundred miles west of Stalingrad.

As shadows deepened over the Reich, Hitler spoke less frequently and in different strain. No longer did he boast of coming conquests but dwelt rather on how long Germany could withstand her enemies. All that was necessary was for her to hold out staunchly and her foes would tire. Had this not happened in the Seven Years War? Was it not obvious that the great Frederick had emerged triumphant even after the Russians had stormed Berlin? That, too, was Goebbels' theme. But he had others; bombed out civilians would have no chance to get their property restored if the Allies won the war; an American book had urged that Germans be made eunuchs; the "grey wolves" (U-boats) were being steadily improved and would yet starve England; new secret weapons in the blueprint stage would revolutionize the art of war.

The approaching winter found Germany jittery. There was plenty of money but nothing to buy with it. Shops were closing all over the Reich and general trade was reduced to barter, a baby carriage for a frying pan, shoes for furniture. Everything was scarce. In May, 1943, some 30,000,000 persons were employed in field, factory, and workshop, a larger number than in time of peace; but of these 12,000,000 were foreigners and of the Germans more than half were women and children. The output of the foreigners was estimated at only 65 per cent by prewar standards and that of the German workers at only 80 per cent, facts which indicated a lowered war potential at a time when the demand for war matériel was at its peak.

Without setting enemies and foreigners to work, outnumbered Germany could not survive; on the other hand, their presence caused uneasiness. A few came more or less willingly to the Reich and relative freedom of movement was granted them. But the great majority were either prisoners of war or deportees from the conquered areas. These had to be watched, confined in barracks. Armed guards and machine guns could and did prevent their rioting, but sloppy work is not easily proved, prevented, or punished.

On the surface, discipline in the Reich was excellent. The only approach to disorder was at the University of Munich where some students were executed for advocating Hitler's overthrow. But there was much grumbling and latent fear, as was shown by party members ducking for safety.

What kept all this rebelliousness from organizing and breaking out into the open was the appointment of Heinrich Himmler, on August 25, as home secretary. Most criminal in act and in nature of all the Nazis was this Gestapo chieftain, a specialist in low cunning and sadistic cruelty, as well as in devilish insight and mastery of police work. His elevation to dictatorial authority over civilians, and the favors showered on his instrument, the SS forces, were proof that Hitler would stop at nothing to hold Germany to the war. If love of Fuehrer and Fatherland could not do it, then fear and tyranny would. The SS numbered in the summer of 1943 some 1,000,000 men. Himmler enlarged it. Its functions were military and political; it had its own uniform and its own officers, answerable not to German generals but to Himmler; its purpose was terrorism; its political agencies the headsman's axe, the torture chamber, and the concentration camp. The SS received higher pay than the Wehrmacht; promotion, was more rapid; its picked divisions fought to the last man, stiffening resistance on every front; and to its sponsor, Heinrich Himmler, now master of German destiny, it gave unswerving obedience.

And so approached the fifth winter of the war. From Narvik in Norway to Bordeaux, France; from Finland to Odessa still flew the Nazi flag. There was as yet no second front, and the Atlantic Wall, reinforced by heavy guns dragged from the Maginot line, seemed an insuperable obstacle to Anglo-American armies beyond the Channel moat; German armies held Rome and the war-worthy part of Italy. Except for a few guerrilla partisans in Yugoslavia, the entire Balkan Peninsula was under German domination, as well as Crete and the islands of the Aegean Sea.

Seen from without, the *Festung Europa* was impressive in its massive strength.

Prospects of 1944

Nineteen forty-four, and at long last the Russians, the British, and the Americans had the men, the weapons, the will, and the skill to blast Germany back into the homeland. Now coördinated strategy toward that end could be and was perfected. This meant the Second Front, attack from the west and south, for which Stalin had long clamored; it meant threefold hammer blows upon the German anvil for the first time in this war; it meant grimly crashing through to victory. Most of all, it meant that for the first time in history the superlative technology and exhaustless resources of the twentieth-century United States were to be hurled against the newest of empire imperialisms.

The United States had close to 4,000,000 men overseas, and Britain was rapidly turning into our armed camp against Hitler, soon to have more GIs than British Tommies stationed there. There was less and less to fear from U-boats. The last German battleship available to threaten sea lanes, the *Scharnhorst,* had been sunk by the Royal Navy the day after Christmas. That great battlewagon *Tirpitz*, sister ship of the *Bismarck*, lay bottled up, in a Norwegian fiord. The Red armies, driving hard on a winter offensive, were already west of Kiev and in January had planted the hammer and sickle flag within ten miles of the Polish-Latvian border. In Yugoslavia, Marshal Tito and his slashing partisans had tied up several more divisions which the Germans needed in Italy. Rome was only seventy miles from the American Fifth and the British Eighth Armies. Few Italians had any notion of fighting further. Finland, Rumania, and even Hungary showed no interest in anti-Bolshevism but a great deal in their own safety. German civilians and German industry were being smashed and destroyed by the merciless downpouring of bombs. The conquest of the Hitler lands might be delayed but it could not be stopped.

The Eastern Front Before D-Day

By the first week in January the Red army had crossed the Polish border of 1939 and was threatening Sarny on the main north-south route from the Baltic states to southern Poland. The Russian steamroller was grinding westward on the road to conquest, hoisting a red warning to the Polish "government" in London, acutely conscious as these exiles were that Stalin's announcement spoke of "Poland" as still 200 miles to the west, and therefore that much west of the 1939 line between Poles and Russians!

That same month Red armies hit the German forces elsewhere; across the frozen Pripet marshes toward Pinsk in what had once been eastern Poland; south and southeast of Kiev in the Ukraine, thus continuing the vast encircling movement earlier begun to cut off Hitler's divisions in the deep bend of the Dnieper north and east of Odessa.

The eastern battles raged with mounting fury. Whenever, it was noted, the Nazis suffered reverses anywhere, whether the *Scharnhorst* was sunk or a defeat inflicted in the Ukraine, they speeded up shelling Leningrad, under siege now two and one-half years. That city was not in as dire peril as formerly, for rail connection of a kind had been opened with Moscow. It was no longer necessary to fend off scurvy with a brew of pine needles, nor for women and young girls to shovel earth into their aprons and carry it to desperately driven earthworks. Yet Germans pumped shells into the city, and some thirty German divisions were still involved in what looked like a lunar landscape but was called the Leningrad front.

They could not retreat, partly because it would isolate their ally Finland, partly because of pride in their huge, ingenious "Leningrad Padlock," an inferno of mine fields, booby traps, and underground pill boxes or "wells" strung on deep trenches. But the Russians whanged away at the Germans with artillery and dropped hand grenades down into the German wells. By the end of January the padlock was broken.

It was in the milder Ukraine, however, not in the bleak far north that the startling victory march was staged. Here in midwinter (January 24-February 3, 1944) the First and Second Red Ukrainian Armies encircled and all but annihilated some ten German divisions in the Upper Dnieper Bend southeast of Kiev where the Eighth German Army held a front of fifty miles. The Russians threw round their motorized divisions in two great sweeping arcs, forming the aptly named "Russian rat trap." The area, at first broad and spacious, was soon squeezed tight as Don Cossacks and Russian tankmen pared it down into small and smaller pockets, until the last was but a few kilometers across.

The cornered Germans, told by radio that help was near, and fed by parachutes, milled round in these battle pens, stacking their dead like cordwood, as they fought off Russian blows. A few escaped, more were taken prisoner, most died, and ten divisions were lost to the Reich.

Wiped out on the Upper Dnieper, the Germans soon were hard pressed near its estuary. The Germans backed up steadily westward all through March. To the west of the Dnieper and somewhat parallel with it flows the Bug River, a strong defensive barrier. The Russians forced passage March 15. Another and a greater river, the Dniester, was sixty miles farther west. In four days the Red army was on the east bank and Stalin's men surged over to invade Bessarabia, from 1919 to 1939 a province of Rumania but not by any means Russia's frontier as now seen by Stalin. Not until the Red flag waved along the east bank of the Pruth, some seventy miles farther west on March 26, had Soviet forces reached what the Kremlin promptly called "The Soviet State frontier." The Germans were back where they started from in 1941. In 1,009 days, to be exact, they had made the round trip of 1,700 miles from the Pruth to the Volga and return—tidal waves of war unique in history.

Odessa, Russia's largest port on the Black Sea and the only bit of Ukraine left in the Nazi grip, fell on April 10. Five days later Red soldiers overran the Crimea to rebesiege Sebastopol. Nature had made that town of more strength than Gibraltar, as French and British found in 1854 and Germans in 1942, when they were kept at bay a good six months. The fighting ended this time in four weeks, as the garrison was mainly Rumanian. The Black Sea was once more a Soviet lake.

All southern Russia and more, too, had been "redeemed." Russian armies marched into Bukovina, another long disputed and lately Rumanian province northeast of the Carpathians. Here they were within rifle shot of the old Mongol conquerors' Tatar Pass leading into Czechoslovakia. They could turn at will north to Poland or south to the Balkans, and the Germans could only reinforce their Balkan forces through Hungary.

Italy Before D-Day

Nineteen forty-four opened with French, Polish, Brazilian, Indian, Dominion, British, and American troops slowly hacking and edging their way to Rome. From Ortona on the Adriatic to just south of Gaeta on the Mediterranean, the Gustav line wound its way in and out among the mountains; and behind it was the pick of the German Army, SS troops and paratroopers, amply supplied with the best of artillery.

To reach Rome one must either breach the Gustav line at the town of Cassino through which ran Route VI, the Via Casalina, the only adequate highway leading north to the goal, or else make amphibious landings on the seacoast nearer the Eternal City, thus outflanking the Germans behind the Gustav line and compelling their withdrawal. Ultimately the Allies were successful in doing both, but it took all they had, and nearly five months hard hand fighting.

The Liri Valley, in which Cassino nestled, was flanked by commanding hills on either side, and through the town ran not only the Via Casalina but also the Rapido River, in winter a raging torrent. We tried to wipe out Cassino from the air and apparently did so, as far as reconnaissance photographs showed. But the more the ruins, the harder the fighting, as Spanish Alcazar and Russian Stalingrad had proved. New Zealanders did pry open doors with bayonets, killed Germans, and in turn were killed by them; Indian Gurkhas did gain the summit of Hangman's Hill; and Germans did surrender in what had once been the Hotel Continental. But fresh waves of German paratroopers recovered much the New Zealanders had won; the Gurkhas on their hill were isolated and had to be fed by parachute; the hotel filled up again with German warriors as though by magic, and German tanks dashed in and out the ruined lobby. By April, after three months' attack, Cassino was only cellar holes and roofless houses, but in there with machine guns the Germans held fast, and their artillery on nearby hills still commanded the Via Casalina.

If the Gustav line could not be breached, why not outflank it? This, the Fifth Army, under our General Mark Clark, tried to do in January by a surprise landing above and below the shore village of Anzio on the Mediterranean, some thirty miles south of Rome.

The beachhead was relatively long, fourteen miles, and much too shallow, only eight miles. The land Clark's men squatted on was low and marshy, cut up by numerous drainage ditches in many of which our infantry stood waist-deep. Down from the high ground of the hinterland the enemy soon poured a murderous fire on Anglo-Americans closely packed together, the British to the north, the Americans to the south. Ten days later the rosy prospects of a quick breakthrough had faded into lurking fear lest another Dunkirk loom ahead.

United States Troops Landing on the Normandy Beachhead

Meanwhile, sixty miles to the south lay Cassino. A breakthrough there would save the beachhead; conversely a successfully widened beachhead would disrupt the enemy's communications, cut the Via Casalina north of Cassino, compel its evacuation. But could the Yanks and Tommies do either?

From January 22, through the whole infernal winter until well into spring, day followed day and week followed week at Anzio, a few yards gained, a few yards lost. The Anglo-Americans by day were hammered by German tanks, at night bombed by German planes, soaked by blinding rain, and stuck fast in bogs and mud. Only by the narrowest margin did the Fifth Army stick it out. After a month it was stalemate both at Anzio and at Cassino. In London Churchill sounded his usual cheery note, and American war correspondents praised the grim humorous staying quality of the Yanks. But facts are facts: the casualty lists were much too long, and "half a year had gone by since the Salerno landing and the Allies had pushed forward less than a hundred miles."

April wore by, and then with May our air-blasting of the Reich began to tell on its war power, so that a strong thrust forward opened the road to Rome. Although formally under over-all command of a British general, it truly was an international fracas in which roles were played by Free French under General Juin and even by Poles fighting under their own flag. The French contingent opened the attack by storming Mt. Faito to the south of Cassino; the British, Canadians, and Indians swept forward across the Rapido River and circled toward a junction with the Polish detachment; the Americans, posted between the French and the sea, scored the largest gains in mileage but over easier terrain; on the Adriatic the Eighth Army made good headway, while at Anzio both British and Americans at last secured needed headroom, pressed close on German communications between Rome and Cassino.

May 11 the Allied offensive began and within a week the Germans were in retreat, neatly and quickly abandoning also the Hitler line which lay behind the Gustav barrier. June 4, 1944, and Rome fell. Barring slight skirmishes in the suburbs, the Allied occupation of their first Axis capital was bloodless. Taking such small loot as they had a fancy to, the invaders made their way north to the hills surrounding Florence.

D-Day

In 1915 a younger Churchill had fathered an impromptu and risky invasion of the Dardanelles; it failed and stunted his career for twenty years. Now an older Churchill was Prime Minister of England, a Churchill stubbornly refusing to take chances. It might have been possible to gain a beachhead on the French coast in 1943, but the cost seemed too frightful, and the question then would have arisen how to enlarge it. The Russians had been indignant because the hazard was not put to the test, also some Americans. But Churchill preferred the slow and sure, an African landing and flank attack on Fortress Europe from the south. He had to wait while Germany was softened up as much as possible from the air before making the grand attack through France, a truly Allied enterprise, though one in fact in which the Americans, as much the greater power, must, of necessity, play the larger role.

The Americans had certainly been speeded fast to the battle lines. June 1, 1944, Secretary Stimson stated that there were 5,223,000 Americans in our armed forces overseas, 3,300,000 of them soldiers, the great bulk in Britain. Many had only recently been inducted and these reserves must undergo severe training before action or else incur ghastly losses. In the initial stages it was planned to deploy in approximately equal numbers Americans and British Imperial troops.

And behind all these fighting men, both Yanks and Tommies, were the factories, workshops, shipyards, and spacious farmlands of the entire Allied world. There were in Britain 33,000,000 men and women between fourteen and sixty-four, and of these no less than 23,000,000 were in war work of all sorts. To Britain fell the major task of conveying and convoying the Yanks to Europe. The British had to house them, for the most part to feed them, and also to build new port facilities for their landings in England. All this in addition to piling up munitions and to expanding the tonnage of bombs dropped on Germany (48,200 tons, for instance, for the first quarter of 1944 as opposed to 34,075 for the entire year 1943). And as they did this, it must be remembered that during the one month of May, 1944, British and American ships moved almost 4,000,000 tons of cargo from American ports to Britain. Into one gigantic pool the industrial products of the whole English-speaking world and their allies were poured to feed the flaming maw of war. A magnificent testimony to the loyal sweat of men and women in overalls making possible the deeds of those obedient in khaki.

June came. Behind their Atlantic Wall the Germans prepared more sites for the rocket bomb. Shabby and half-starved French of all ages and both sexes drilled in secret for guerrilla war. And in millions of homes all over the earth there were high-strung nerves and anxious worry, for all knew D-Day was near.

Tuesday, June 6, and D-Day. From six minutes past midnight paratroopers in long trains of gliders hopped the Channel to drop down in Normandy before daybreak behind the German lines. And as they did so, landing craft drew near the hostile shore. All night they had worked twisting passage through the choppy seas, keeping lookout for the well-marked buoys, close-convoyed by destroyer watchdogs and corvettes, the GIs and the Bors (British other ranks, the British equivalent for GI) channel-sick, half-frozen, conscious that for many life was a matter of hours or minutes.

The landing was hard. Barely beneath the surface of the water the Germans had driven down six-pronged iron spikes upon which many a landing craft was impaled; and in the same deadly fashion anchored logs lay hidden to which mines were attached. As stumbling soldiers and lumbering tanks hit their beach, the Germans shot into them with enfilading fire from machine-gun nests and from heavy artillery deep-sunk in concrete emplacements up on banks which must be stormed, and that right speedily, lest the successive waves of ground troops find no standing room on the crowded beaches. No time to dig foxholes. Up the narrow ravines toward the cliffs they charged, ravines and gullies filled with murderous booby traps, barbed wire, the German fire-storm and death.

Four landings came on in one great drive, two British, two American. They were spaced widely over sixty miles of the northern shore line of Normandy. The British Second Army, soon to have Rommel's tanks launched against it, had a relatively easy time at the start. So likewise was it with the Canadian First Army, the men of Canada penetrating seven miles in one day to Bayeux. Lady Luck also smiled on those Yanks who landed farthest west, for swamp rather than frowning cliff confronted them, and they were able to drive inland and make speedy contact with the airborne forces.

But it was nip and tuck for those Americans who stormed ashore east of the Vire River. All D-Day the GIs there clung desperately to shallow beachheads, suffering most grievous casualties, and not until late afternoon were they out of deadly peril. On D-Day plus one came reinforcements and with them America's beloved correspondent, Ernie Pyle, who described the scene: "Submerged tanks and overturned boats and burned trucks and shell-shattered jeeps and sad little personal belongings were strewn all over those bitter sands...bodies of soldiers lying in rows covered with blankets, the toes of their shoes sticking up in a line as though on drill." [1]

Victory in Normandy

Six weeks' grueling battle came and went before the northwestern corner of France was wrested from the foe. The Allies were held back by execrable weather, high seas, and the lack of harbor facilities; by the deep-ditched Norman hedgerows, dense thickets lining roadsides, "horse-high, bull-strong, hog-tight"; by the counterattack of German rocket guns on London and by German panzer divisions in France. Had it not been for their overlordship of the air, our forces would have had a far tougher time of it. As it was, British and American planes rode high, wide, and handsome over northern France, demolishing rocket gun em-

[1] Ernie Pyle, *Brave Men* (New York, Henry Holt and Company, Inc., 1944), p. 360.

placements, smashing bridges as far south as the Loire, strafing locomotives, stations, railway lines, and motor roads so that the Germans had to move troops by night or else detour them long distances.

A united front once achieved, the first task of the Americans was to push on to Cherbourg. Elements of four German divisions within put up one of the hottest defenses of the war; they knew how imperative it was for the Allies to have a harbor; and if there was no chance of holding Cherbourg for the Reich, time might be won in which to ruin it for the Allies. And so for five days the Stalingrad and Cassino scene was reënacted, fighting through house by house, cellar by cellar, street by street, tanks versus tanks, tanks versus pill boxes, tight little pill boxes of reinforced concrete with wicked slits through which machine guns spit, while the heavens were dark with our droning planes. Caveman war worsened by all modern science.

A ding-dong fight for Caen followed, the Tommies driving hard at that Norman city time after time from different angles, the German panzers strongly beating them back and for two weeks with considerable success. But the British finally took Caen. Plunging forward through a sea of mud, they even got four miles beyond. Here they were held down by anti-tank fire and heavy German artillery (July 19).

The Americans, after taking Cherbourg, wheeled south heading for the rail junction of St. Lô which, if taken, would serve to seal off German forces in Brittany and on the Atlantic seaboard from potential reinforcement from those major German armies based elsewhere in France.

The approaches to St. Lô had to be fought for inch by inch, almost every farmhouse (and they were all made of stone) had been converted into a fortress; and in the omnipresent hedgerows, lining all roads, dividing all fields, the Germans had their machine guns. Out of these hedges they had to be driven, flushed like so many human partridges, by tanks equipped with side-cutters which split the path open for the advancing Yanks. St. Lô was one of the nastiest fights of the entire war. It took us a good month to take the place, a month of heavy casualties, 7,944 American boys being killed and 39,549 wounded. It was worse than D-Day itself.

But by late July, the Americans, the British, and the Canadians between them had accounted for 156,000 Germans, of whom 60,000 were prisoners. And, what is more, the Allies held half of Normandy and, out from ruined Caen and blasted St. Lô, were in position to strike hard.

The Rush for Paris

General Patton in command, driving incessantly full speed ahead, sent probing thrusts of Sherman tanks both north and south as he sped toward the French metropolis. His dirty, sweating, sleep-short tankmen were soon in the streets of Orléans, cutting off German forces in the south of France; almost simultaneously they appeared north of the Seine; one day later the Eiffel Tower was in view of Patton's outposts twenty miles away.

And as this happened the Canadians sweeping eastward toward Rouen, another ancient capital of Normandy, cut off the Germans at Le Havre on the coast; the British Second Army also crossed the Seine and pushed on to the Somme, thirty-four miles distant; and on August 15 an entirely new American army, the Seventh, broke in on the coast of the Riviera.

This new menace to the Germans was made up of troops withdrawn from Italy, some American, some French. Aided by British paratroopers and with strong naval backing, it struck at the Riviera coast. The Seventh was soon in position to roll back on Italy from the northwest, or to plunge toward Toulon and Marseilles, or to hit north up the valley of the Rhône. And wherever it was ordered to go, it was sure of the assistance of the FFIs (French Forces of the Interior), the Maquis, guerrilla bands of young Frenchmen, poorly armed but knowing well the countryside, enraged by subjection, spoiling for a fight, eager to trap and to kill.

In three short weeks the outlook in the west was revolutionized. In what had been a bare two months earlier a prostrate France, everywhere the Germans were on the way out, their convoys, tanks, and ground troops constantly strafed from the air, escaping over bridgeless rivers as best they might. On August 19 some 50,000 FFIs revolted in the invader-emptied Paris. A remnant garrison resisted until advance units of Patton's army dashed into that city, then surrendered on August 25. In Paris there had been much loose looting, but of dynamite and destruction there was none, of real damage very little. These were surrender times for invaders.

In Paris the American GIs were kissed freely but their effective pursuit of the Germans never let up. From twenty to fifty miles a day it raced along in a dozen different sectors. The Canadians took Rouen and went past it to the Channel to sew up the German garrison at Dieppe. The British, somewhat farther to the south, recovered Amiens, their headquarters in World War I, continued eastward, eager to seize the launching platforms of rocket guns if they could find them; the American First Army kept rolling along without meeting a foe, past Château Thierry, Soissons, and Rheims of the old war, all the way to an older Sedan. Patton's Third Army, farther south, surged on through Châlons, Verdun, St. Mihiel, and approached Metz; while the American Seventh, advancing up the Rhône, took Grenoble and was fast nearing Alsace, ready for its part on the southern flank of the vast Allied drive for the Rhine. As the crow flies, our tanks were now 350 miles from Cherbourg and close to the German frontier, less than forty days after pouring through the St. Lô funnel, less than three months after "D" Day itself. As for the enemy, his overall picture September 1 was summarized by General Eisenhower: "The equivalent of five panzer divisions have been destroyed and a further six badly mauled.... The equivalent of twenty infantry divisions have been eliminated and a further twelve very badly cut up.... Total enemy casualties amount to more than 400,000 killed, wounded and prisoners." The war seemed certain to end in Europe before Christmas.

Italian Front of 1944

Allied invaders were weaker in Italy than elsewhere. Soon after Rome was taken they had reason to feel that they were the forgotten front. Black death was just as hard to meet in Italy as in Normandy, and the foe confronting us was relatively stronger in numbers and morale, his dislodgement in some ways more difficult. Nevertheless all summer the American Fifth Army and the British Eighth plugged away at the German defenses in Italy, the Americans to the west, mainly along the Tyrrhenian coast, the British at the center and along the Adriatic side. For a short time after passing Rome the pursuit of fleeing German forces was relatively rapid, as the foe was retreating fast to newer and even stronger positions than the Gustav line; once there, it was a different story. The Apennines in northern Italy run south and east of the Po, and that valley the Germans tried to hold to the bitter end, and did. Its fields are one of Europe's major granaries and, with the swastika waving there, Nazi rule could endure in Bavaria, Czechoslovakia, Austria, and north Italy, though all the rest of the Reich surrendered. The Po Valley was vital to this citadel of the inner Fortress-Germania, sometimes called "The National Redoubt," and the Gothic line which defended it on the south was defense in depth from Pisa on the Tyrrhenian Sea to Rimini on the Adriatic. At all hazards it must remain German.

The American Fifth had a tough time of it; the British Eighth had one even tougher. The little mountains fringing Florence vied with those around Cassino in height and number, and the confusedly protracted siege-battling in and around Florence sadly battered Italy's loveliest city. British troops forced an entry there August 4, the Germans clinging still to strong points within and just north of Florence until August 10. Meanwhile other elements of the Eighth Army, some Polish, some Indian, and in 1945 some Greek, paralleled the American advance on the Tyrrhenian flank by taking Pesaro on the Adriatic Sea, and finally Rimini, baffled this time not by mountains but by swamps, canals, and drainage ditches. The Gothic line bent back a little at both ends, but held in the middle. Whenever the Allies made gains fierce counterattacks threw them back. Owing to the Anglo-American rush past Paris in the west and the vast Russian tornado roaring down on Berlin from the East, the world paid little attention to Italy during the second half of 1944. The black eagles of the Teutonic North had been her curse a good fifteen hundred years, and their talon clutch still dug deep in her fairest provinces.

The Red Russian Storm

As the western Allies swarmed into Normandy, the Russians were making good their grasp on the Karelian Peninsula, forcing Finland out of the war. Then, with the opening of the summer offensives, the Red armies struck first and hardest against the Baltic states and East Prussia; for so long as the Wehrmacht held on there in strength it was impregnably placed for outflanking any direct Soviet drive on Warsaw and Berlin.

Soon, then, the whole eastern front was ablaze. The First, Second, and Third Baltic Armies were out to trap and to destroy thirty German divisions in Lithuania, Latvia, and Estonia. Consummation of this project took months but the shadow of coming Baltic events was clear when Soviet forces reached that sea on August 4. Meanwhile, three other Russian armies hurtled at the Germans farther west, the First and Second White Russian Armies rushing on into Poland, the Third plunging for East Prussia, cradle of the Teutonic knights of old. Inside of six weeks eastern Poland was taken, the fortress of Brest-Litovsk fell once more, the Reds reached the Vistula both north and south of Warsaw, and its suburbs could be bombed from Russian lines. The Third White Army struck harder going, but it made headway, and pressed now against the East Prussian defenses.

As the Baltic lines bent back and German Poland caved in, the omnipresent Russians opened yet another offensive, this time in the south. All the way from the Carpathians to the Black Sea, the Ukrainian Red armies rolled into action. It was Rumania's turn. By August 29 the Russians were at the Danube's mouth. In two more days they pierced the Galati Gap, pounced on the Ploesti oil fields, broke into Bucharest, the second Axis capital to capitulate. There a palace coup d'état "headed" by boy-king Michael drove the pro-German premier, Antonescu, from office and the bewildered Rumanian army, what was left of it, got orders to turn and fight, not Russians but Germans and Hungarians.

With Rumania reversing sides, fifteen German divisions were stuck in the Balkans in ever worse plight than those foundered in Finland. Before long all Balkan Nazis were cut off from the Reich except for circuitous routes through Yugoslavia where pro-Russian Marshal Tito was rapidly gaining the upper hand. On September 6 the Red Army hit the Yugoslav border and two days later broke into Bulgaria. Politically-minded Bulgar colonels rapidly followed Rumanian precedents, and Bulgaria was at war against Germany by September 9. Lost now to the Reich's power was the entire Near East, apart from various garrisons stranded on cut-off Greek islands, elsewhere in Greece, and in isolated German enclaves of Yugoslavia. Of all the satellites, Hungary alone stood faithful as conquering Russia kicked in the gates of Fortress Europa from north, east, and south.

Why the Germans Kept On Fighting

In September the front caved in on every side, and from the air augmenting death came showering down on German cities, factories, and airfields. Plainly the Reich must yield. But she would not; and why? Three reasons tell the story; hope, not altogether fanciful, of secret weapons; hope, more illusory, that Allied dissensions might split and unbalance their enemies, lead perhaps to German victory in the field, and win some sort of compromise peace; and finally not hope but fear; fear of Allied vengeance and extermination, particularly Russian, and what the Cossack East might do when once within the Reich; fear at home of Heinrich Himmler's gestapo, prison camps, and Nazi superthugs.

Rumors of secret weapons were now running wild in Naziland. "Within six months," said an SS propagandist, "all Germans will know something which for the time being must be kept secret. You will wake from the dark depressive night. Tomorrow will be very calm and clear. Everything that threatened and terrified you will have vanished."

The Allied press sneered at these rumors of secret weapons, but the British and American governments, knowing full well what their own scientists hard at work were developing in new techniques, were fairly certain that the Germans were doing likewise. As early as April, 1943, the British secret service heard of strange events taking place on a tiny island in the Baltic, and the RAF promptly photographed that island. It was well for Britain that they did so, for the Germans were experimenting with Hitler's *Vergeltungswaffe*, vengeance weapon, the rocket bomb.

That same month the RAF heavily attacked that island, but a month later British reconnaissance planes discovered a whole series of launching platforms or ramps similar to the Baltic specimen. All pointed toward London, and all that were visible the RAF and the AAF bombed, an action which cost the Allies 450 planes and nearly 3,000 aviators. That attack slowed up the German program which was to start New Year's Day, 1944, with 1,000 rocket bombs, but had to be postponed until June 15 when the first "buzz" shells were launched on the British capital. They came fast and furiously at five to seven miles per minute.

Through June and July some two hundred a day came hurtling down the war-torn air. In some ways it was worse than Goering's great 1940 blitz. Then, at any rate, there was siren warning, bombs came mostly at night with comparative immunity in daytime. Now no one could tell what second of day or night the robot death might strike, or where, for these lethal missives could be aimed only in the general direction of London. Only a few planes had speed enough to overtake the rockets, the new Tempests, Spitfires, and Mustangs. Had it not been for radar and innumerable anti-aircraft guns, both British and American, lined thick along the coasts, London would have been pulverized.

There was still hope of a super-robot launched from farther away and flying at greater speed and higher altitude, a promise actually fulfilled by autumn with the V-2, launched out of occupied Holland. But Germany then was being so rapidly submerged that the V-2, looking for all the world like a flying telegraph pole, did not get any real testing. The sites were taken too soon.

Always there was a chance for a rift between the Allies, and the Nazis looked for one in Yugoslavia and Poland. In Yugoslavia, any dreams of Allied discord that the Germans might fancy vanished into thin mist as Anglo-American aid shifted from General Mihailovich, Commander-in-chief of the Yugoslav Army under the direction of the exiled Yugoslav government in London, to Marshal Tito, victorious Communist-sponsored patriot and partisan. Tito might be a deep, dark Red but he fought Germans with vim, vigor, and velocity, which no one could say for the royalist Mihailovich.

The Polish problem was more complicated. The exiled Polish government in London was recognized by Britain and America; Polish soldiers fought in Italy. But Stalin condemned that Polish government as a clique of landlords and loan sharks. He knew what he wanted and would take nothing else, the Polish frontier of 1921 and the establishment of a Communist Polish government in which Communist influence would be dominant.

Stalin had early broken relations with that exiled Polish regime in London, and as his armies scorched Warsaw he set up in Lublin a committee of Polish Communists to whom he proposed to turn over a liberated Poland, which distressed his democratic allies, Britain and the United States.

Then in midsummer, 1944, as the Russians reached the Vistula, General Bor of the Warsaw underground revolted and defended part of that city for weeks. Fighting the Germans, he clamored for Russian aid. It was not given. The Russians said the rising had been premature; it had been done without Russian approval or knowledge; the Red army for the time being had other objectives than the taking of Warsaw. And so, although it pushed both north and south of Warsaw, it did nothing to relieve General Bor.

Britain was particularly upset. The London Poles had urged Bor to fight on; they had sent Poles to fight for Britain in Italy, and the British in turn sent Bor supplies all the way by air from the Mediterranean.

The Germans let Poles out of German prisons; they urged Poles to enlist in the Wehrmacht to save Poland from Bolshevism.

Between the intransigent Polish government in exile and the stubborn Stalin, Britain was on the horns of a dilemma and was to stay so. The best Churchill could do was to ask Stalin to receive Mikolajczyk, their Polish premier, in Moscow and persuade the London Poles to despatch their premier to Stalin. Mikolajczyk made the trip twice without result, except that the Polish question was left on ice. It remained a thorny one, and Churchill pleaded with the House of Commons "not to engage in language which would make our task harder." That task was to let Russia have her way and to save face if possible. There was still a war to win and we were winning it, so the Germans gained little from these Polish quarrels.

Last but not least, fear gripped the German heart, sheer terror of what might be if they lay their weapons down. It was not now so much the shrill voice of Goebbels but the black deeds of Himmler which sent shivers down the German spine. A mighty weapon his SS troopers and his gestapo, but a mightier one yet in Germany after July 20, 1944, the day on which the army plot to kill the Fuehrer failed. From that date forward the world heard little that was authentic of Adolf Hitler, for in his name Himmler now ruled the Reich. "The blueblooded swine," the Prussian aristocrats who had tried to save something of Germany by a revolution from within, not only lost their lives, as did those remotely associated with them, but, as matters worsened, a fresh twist was given to the strangler's noose which tightened around the neck of every German who gave voice to doubts about the war or who even was caught with a Swiss or Swedish newspaper.

This terror from within transcended the terror from without. With the foes' forces on all German frontiers, children were ordered out of school, the old out of their armchairs, marched, drilled, put in uniform. The *Volksturm* of Napoleonic days was revived to include all Germans from sixteen to sixty. The last man and boy were rallied that ditches might be dug, mines laid, cities and towns fortified for street-to-street and house-to-house defense. *Festung Europa* was out. The ungrateful continent could look out for itself. Germany would defend her own. If the flat plains of northern Germany were foe-engulfed, then retreat to the stark citadel of Nazidom, the Bavarian Alps! Here, flanked on every side by close-linked mountains, ringed by set defenses, would come the last fight of those to whom death was infinitely better than defeat.

Hitler's Last Stand

The Nazi Inner Fortress was shrinking day by day, must be weakening, must be bleeding from every vein of war-power, yet in the northern mists and from out of the chemical fogs of airborne ruin it loomed grim, grey, and evil as some great, gaunt timber wolf, cornered for the kill in the last of his granite holds, death in its fangs still.

That autumn German resistance hardened—east, south, and west. In the far northeast the Russians did not cross East Prussian frontiers until October 18, and then in that lake-studded land of swamp and forest they made but slow headway. Red armies had forced the Vistula barrier but Warsaw was German still, as was Cracow in southern Poland, and as long as the latter city held out the approaches to industrial Silesia were relatively safe. Once having cracked the Carpathian defenses, it would seem as though nothing could withstand the sweep of Red armor across flat Hungarian plains, but though Szeged, Hungary's second largest city, fell October 11 it proved impossible in 1944 to capture Budapest, no great distance away.

From Italy, that forgotten front, came word that the Gothic line was being pierced, that Americans soon would reach Bologna, that the British were rounding the foe's eastern flank at Rimini. But prophecies are not facts, and the truth was that the Gothic line stymied the Allies; their victories were rather patrol actions, so minor as hardly to be noted on an ordinary map.

So, too, was it in the west. The German frontier once passed, the Canadians, British, and Americans found the going much rougher. The British captured Antwerp September 4, but since German forces still blocked the exits from the Scheldt, the occupation of Belgium's great seaport was not much help. Almost everything the Allied armies used had to be carried by motor or be flown from a few congested ports hundreds of miles west, and even after British engineers sank a gasoline pipeline across and under Channel waters the fuel still was far from thirsty tanks. Hitler's Westwall was far more a defense to the Reich than the Maginot line ever could have been to France. It might be, and was, bent in spots by tank rushes, but a defense in depth cannot readily be broken or surmounted.

The Allies were too confident too long of having the Germans on the run; they underestimated the foe's resiliency; the war, they thought, might be forced to a swift finish by outflanking the Westwall far to the north, where the Rhine River flows sluggishly across Holland through several branches. To strike the enemy in this supposedly weak sector the British First Airborne Division parachuted to earth beyond the Lek River, a tributary of the Rhine. Instantly it was encircled by Nazi forces swarming in like angry wasps. For over a week the Tommies, reinforced constantly by air, put up a heartrending fight. The British Second Army did its best to rescue them and almost succeeded. But only some 1,800 British paratroopers fought their way back across the Lek.

This was discouraging, but the steady though costly Allied gains of the autumn might well restore the balance by December. The Canadians, clearing the Channel ports, had conquered Nazi garrisons at Boulogne and Calais, as had the Americans at Brest. British marines, His Majesty's Jollies, had forced a landing on Walcheren Island at the mouth of the Scheldt in a daring exploit. The British Second made good its hold on Belgium, and had swept on into Holland. The American First Army, bypassing Aachen, capital of Charlemagne, was well over the frontier, pressing toward Cologne. Patton's Third, retarded by a distinguished defense of an old French fort at Metz by German military cadets, had edged toward the Saar. And the American Seventh, together with a fully equipped French army, had got within striking distance of Belfort near the Swiss corner.

November passed. Still the German lines bent backward. The Tricolor flew again over Strasbourg and the upper Rhine was tapped. Patch's Seventh was forcing its way through Alsace. Patton's Third was at the Saar, one bridge across it, with German blast furnaces under American fire. Hodges' First U. S. Army surged forward to the west bank of the Rohr, the only sizable stream between it and Cologne, less than thirty miles away. Farther north Simpson's Ninth U. S. Army and the British Second clawed their way into German areas, and to the far north the Canadians swung up forward ready for a second shot at outflanking the Siegfried line.

Winter was now at hand and the war would not end in 1944. The Allies had moved forward; but the most successful of their armies, the American First, had taken four weeks to go twelve miles. Some months earlier Churchill had prophesied that the war would be won by the early spring or early summer of 1945. He now suggested eliminating the adjective "early."

Battle of the Bulge

Then, December 16, to the amazement of all and to the consternation of many, the Wehrmacht lashed out at the Americans in one great burst of flame and fury. Behind German lines, unseen by Allied intelligence, the German commander, Von Rundstedt, had gathered his strength, fused a mass of his best fighters, concentrated motorized divisions with new tanks better for this last battle than any of the British or American armies had.

Out from their Westwall leaped the Germans on a sixty-mile front from south of Aachen into northern Luxembourg, and on they plunged into the Ardennes Forest, the old, old bloody trail which led toward Liége in Belgium, Sedan in France.

The Battle of the Bulge was on, and it raged for weeks, Von Rundstedt caught the Americans off balance. The Allies were hammering hard on a 450-mile front; he hammered harder and hammered through on one of sixty. Once reach Liége on the Meuse, he might strike at Antwerp, drive a wedge between British and Americans, roll back our forces, and fuel his thirsty Tiger tanks with American oil, so tantalizingly near at hand.

As it was, he unhinged the American line, isolated and pulverized American regiments, destroyed thousands of our men in the thick, snow-covered forestland of the Argonne; and his armor forced its way fifty miles in, rushing to probe either side of the deep bulge thus created to mark a further breakthrough.

At Christmas the German flood reached its crest, and soon thereafter subsided. Many German tanks stalled for lack of gas. Time was lost trying to wipe out American enclaves of resistance enclosed by the greater German pocket. Of these, Bastogne has a place in American history. Completely circled by the surging German tide, our men fought round the whole front and held out as aid and munitions reached them by air, and finally paratroopers, without whom they would have died.

From the south Patton dashed with his armor to the rescue of this pocket, as from the north Montgomery came on with the Second British Army. Placed by Eisenhower in command of American troops on the northern side of the bulge, Montgomery hooked up Yanks and Tommies to press on against the German area from that side, as did Patton from the south, and between them they narrowed the base slightly, but enough to be dangerous for the Germans within. An old rule of warfare decrees that a penetration must not exceed one-half the base from which it starts. That base in early January was only the same as the farthest depth, around fifty-five miles. The danger point for Von Rundstedt clearly had been reached. There was even talk of the hunter being hunted, of trapping the Germans, forcing their surrender. The wary Von Rundstedt was not to be caught thus. He extricated both men and armor and by January's end the British and American forces were back pretty much where they had been in early December.

Once again we had underestimated the adversary. GIs cursed loud and long when they found our vaunted General Sherman no match for the German King Tiger tank of sixty-seven tons and eight-inch armor. Having learned their lesson, our generals went more cautiously with their march on Rhine.

Ebb Tide Speeds Up

That the Germans hung on thereafter for three months and more was little short of a miracle. Fortress Germania was shrinking now as fast as Fortress Europa had six months before. Finland took her peace from Russia, pledged to intern German divisions left within her lines. The Red armies drove across Finland to attack Germans in northern Norway; they captured Riga and were cutting up the Wehrmacht isolated in the northeast; they commenced the invasion of East Prussia after long probing the frontiers of that iron homeland of iron men; they rolled into Warsaw and were well on the way to Berlin across western Poland; and reaching the banks of the Oder opposite Frankfort they came at long last within striking distance of the Nazi capital. Farther south, after bypassing beleaguered Budapest, Soviet armor drew near Vienna.

Only in Italy did Germans really withstand the adversary. Northern Italy, all but the tip of Norway, Denmark, parts of Finland, Holland, and a few French ports still were held by German soldiers needed for that last-ditch fight at home, if there was to be one. No hope gleamed on any horizon. But many were yet to die before Russians joined hands with Yanks across the Oder.

Futile though further war was, the Nazis kept on with it all through February, March, April, and into May. At ever accelerated pace the Allies closed and drove in on the doomed Reich. In February closely coordinated blows struck at its heart from both west and east. The Allies had long been stalled by the little Rohr River flowing parallel to the Rhine. They were on its banks, but dared not force a crossing since they knew there were huge dams on its upper reaches still in enemy hands, and these, once dynamited, would flood the lower Rohr to a good 1,000 yards in width. The Germans clung desperately to their dams, their single ace in hole, and the greater part of February was consumed in mastering the Rohr Valley. Once done, progress became rapid, German resistance spotty. Hodges' First Army took Cologne March 6; the American Ninth, arriving at the Rhine a few days earlier, turned north to meet Canadians coming south, both armies now behind the Westwall, and by their junction cutting off the retreat of thousands of Germans. And meanwhile the British Second, storming into Cleves in the lower Rhineland, headed toward Westphalia.

The west bank of the Rhine was now taken from Cologne north through Holland, but the Allies had yet to cross the river. The American First then got a toehold on its eastern shore north of Cologne March 8, by a rapid dash up the Rhine for the Ludendorff bridge at Remagen. Patton with the American Third now swept down the Moselle Valley and, whirling round to his right, drove in behind German forces which had held him at bay in the Saar. Patton going south met the advancing U. S. Seventh coming from that direction and the Germans thus cut off surrendered in droves; the Saar was lost; so, too, the Palatinate west of the Rhine; the Westwall ceased to exist and became mere history.

Far north the British fought their way out of Holland onto the Westphalian plain; in the south the French redeemed all Alsace; and now along the whole Rhine River's length British, Americans, Canadians, and French threw new bridgeheads over, to cross the swift and beautiful Rhine in almost every conceivable way, using parachutes, pontoons,

Bailey bridges, ferrying over in barges, motor boats, "buffaloes," "ducks," and other special craft, many manned by U. S. naval forces. Before March turned to April, Germany collapsed in the west.

So also in the east, and in the south. By early February the Russians were at Frankfort-on-Oder, a city they had taken twice before, once in Frederick the Great's time, once toward the close of Napoleonic days in 1813. The battered rubble of Hitler's capital was fifty miles away. Berliners saw the flares by night and heard by day the clamor of the guns. But the Red army paused. In its rapid leap from Warsaw to the Oder, it left behind strong enemy pockets; like Von Rundstedt's bulge, the base of Russia's holding in Germany was too narrow for the depth of penetration. Fifty miles to go, but these fierce with German fortifications. The Russians wanted no Stalingrad in reverse, took no chances. And so, through February and March they widened their base, struck north in East Prussia against Königsberg, hit against Danzig and Stettin, overran Pomerania, drove south to Breslau, and even farther south in Hungary and Austria. Budapest, with more than half its buildings wrecked, surrendered February 13, the third Axis capital to succumb; Vienna, the fourth, held out until April 13.

That same month the end came in Italy. American Mountain Infantry (ski troops long trained in Colorado) at last accomplished what American armor and the Brazilians had been unable to do. By a brilliant demonstration of highly specialized mountain warfare our ski fighters drove out the Germans from their fortified nests on 3,760-foot Mt. Belvedere where they outflanked the only good road from Florence north to Bologna. The British Eighth, meanwhile, came circling in from the Adriatic. The Gothic line was erased, the Germans beaten down, a signal for partisans in Genoa, Venice, Turin, Milan, to rise and throw out the Germans. All German troops in Italy and in southwest Austria as well surrendered. One day earlier Mussolini was taken near the Swiss frontier, shot, his body and that of a woman hung up by the heels in Milan.

Curtain Falls

Everywhere the twilight of the end was dusking down on Europe's tragedy. The German armies in the west were gone, British and American armies driving at will over Adolf Hitler's super-highways, the British to the north, Americans to the center, and in the south Americans and French. Over half a million war captives were locked in prison pens during the first two weeks of April, and on the 24th Himmler tried to surrender exclusively to the British and Americans. His offer was refused.

May, and in one week more it was over. American armies near Berlin were halted by Eisenhower's orders. It would have been easy for us to have marched straight into the Nazi capital, for our arrival would have been greeted with joy by defenders who dreaded Red devastation. But Hodges' First rested on Elbe bank, leaving, as was right, the war's major honors to the men of the Soviets, who had done most to merit those dread laurels.

Why the German High Command strove still for another week is hard to fathom; the last chance of a last stand had faded with Italian surrender as the American First struck fast across central Germany and two southern American armies and the French forces drove ahead toward Bavaria and Czechoslovakia. No union of last-ditch fighters was possible. All plans were useless, even "planned chaos" was now impossible for the Nazis. Adolf Hitler was perhaps somewhere in Berlin. Power was gone and leadership also.

Berlin was a city dying. Their air ministry, the opera house, the vast chancellery of the thousand-year-old Reich-to-be, a blasted shambles. Riots at soup kitchens. Huddled civilians in cellars. The streets a terror by night. The city plastered with Russian shells, British and American bombs. The probing, implacable Red army crept north and south around the city. Russian tanks crashed through barricaded streets. From subways SS men dashed out at them from the rear, the death gasp of men already dead.

May 2 the Russians had Berlin, all of it; and farther south where a bridge spanned the Elbe Red army men and Yanks on April 26 shook hands, drank together. The European war was at an end. The Hitler Empire, Europe's most terrific adventure in militarism, in twelve years had run its course.

Chapter 41

JAPAN OVERWHELMED

THE SURRENDER OF Germany in 1945 set free the British and the Americans to complete the conquest of Japan, clearly foreshadowed in the not too distant future by British victories in Burma and American victories on the High Seas.

As 1943 opened all of Burma, except the northern tip, lay quiescent under the flag of the Rising Sun, and an invasion of India impended. In less than two years such detachments of the Japanese army as remained in Burma were in full flight. In January, 1943, the long march of the American navy across the Pacific had not yet begun, and the land approach of MacArthur along the northern coastline of New Guinea toward the Philippines was still in the blueprint stage. By the time the Yanks were swinging over the Rhine in 1945, all this had changed. The Japanese inner defense line had been breached: the marines held Iwo Jima in the Bonins and leathernecks and G.I.'s in Okinawa were driving Hirohito's men to cover. Meanwhile MacArthur was on shore at Leyte, back in the Philippines.

These American victories were slow in starting, had to be since the European war held precedence over that in the Pacific. But the date of their commencement stands out clearly, the Battle of Midway, June 4–5, 1942, only seven months less two days since Pearl Harbor. Fought and won by carrier planes against carrier planes, "it permanently crippled Japan's naval power by reducing her carrier strength to so low a level that she never was able to catch up with American production." [1] First and foremost factor in the Pacific war was the carrier plane.

Tough fighting lay ahead for the Americans. Japan's geographical isolation was superb. North and east of her homeland were the Kuriles, island wardens along the inner moat of Hirohito's hidden country. And to the south and southeast was the farflung shield of the Ryukyu and Bonin islands. Beyond the Ryukyus was Taiwan (Formosa) and far beyond Taiwan were Hainan, the Philippines, Borneo, Sumatra, Java, the Malay states, and French Indo-China, to enclose the whole China Sea with the arrayed imperial outposts of Japan. And still farther, barrier be-

[1] Major General J. F. C. Fuller, *The Second World War*, p. 152.

848

yond barrier, the mandated islands in the Marianas, the Carolines, the Marshalls. Here were stationary aircraft carriers past which, if unconquered, it would not be safe for us to venture. Nor was this all. South and east of the Marshalls our foe's talons clutched the once British-owned Gilberts, a threat to Fiji and to the Australian-American life-line, clutched also at the northern coastline of New Guinea, New Britain, and all the Solomons except for one airstrip on Guadalcanal fiercely held by too few American marines.

To break through these barriers was America's business. These Japanese islands must be conquered or immunized. It was a large order. To the north it meant dislodging the enemy from the American-owned Aleutians; in the mid-Pacific it meant driving out the Japanese from their strongly fortified mandated islands, the Marshall Islands, the Caroline Islands, and the Marianas; and to the south and southwest it meant the recovery of the British Gilberts and the Solomon Islands, occupied by Japan after Pearl Harbor, and the approach to the Philippines by way of New Guinea.

American action in the Pacific theatre in 1943-44 falls under two general heads, mopping up operations in regard to these islands, and MacArthur's slower but none the less dramatic approach to the quarry from Australian waters.

The Aleutians

First, then, the Aleutians in the spring of 1943. The main Japanese base there was Kiska, halfway between Kamchatka and Alaska. The American command decided to crack down on fog-shrouded Kiska by encirclement. Some 170 miles west of Kiska was Attu, upon which we landed in force during mid-May.

Our landings both to the north and to the south were unopposed; but when it came to pushing inland through the deep ravines and being ambushed by snipers hidden on the mountain slopes, then death took a hand. Five days passed before the two American expeditions met, only to find their hardest work still ahead. The soldiers of Nippon were most excellently screened in their base at Chichagov Harbor. Between them and the Americans were mountains 2,000 feet high, swept by snowstorms and thick fogs, and between the mountains were precipitous winding passes of over 800-foot elevation. The Japanese had dug in skilfully; their final defenses could only be reached along a ridge so narrow that two men could not walk abreast thereon, a treacherous ridge, half the time from fog and with a sheer drop 200 feet down on both sides. Manpower lugged up the ammunition in this campaign; soldiers fought, ate, and slept in wet snow, or on stones, or on soggy, treacherous tundra; Japs and Yanks stumbled into each other's mist-hidden fox holes; and a hundred miniature mêlées between half-seen combatants scattered by fog and wind made up the summary of the Attu adventure. May 30, and that island, not good for much but still American terrain, had been gripped and firmly held by our forces.

The wind-up of the Aleutian campaign came quickly. The Attu conquest had enabled us to dig in well to the west of the chief enemy base at Kiska; we had that island at our mercy; all that remained necessary was to soften it by intense bombardment from the air and from the sea, and then move in on foot as before. But to our surprise and even to our annoyance, Kiska proved to be quite empty. Some 10,000 Mikado soldiers had slipped through our fog-bedeviled blockade and had betaken themselves elsewhere.

Tarawa

The American occupation of Kiska sealed off Alaska from any would-be conquerors. The Aleutians gave us a springboard from whence to bomb the Kuriles and we did so (intermittently); but the game was scarcely worth the candle. Distances, even for our new planes, were phenomenally long; williwaws, terrific and sudden storms characteristic of the North Pacific, were frequent; and the Kuriles were far distant from Hokkaido, northernmost of the Japanese home islands, mountainous, underpopulated, far from the heart of the enemy's empire. Not by attack from the north could the foe's lifeblood be drained.

The major American offensive thus far had been directed against the Solomons and the great enemy base at Rabaul on New Britain to the north. But the way thither was long, some 7,200 miles of circuitous steaming from Hawaii to Port Moresby. The route lay almost due south from Honolulu to Samoa, then curved westward to Fiji and New Caledonia, then north by west to the Solomons, and the Japanese-held Gilberts lay athwart any direct approach. The task of wresting them from Japan fell mainly to the navy and marines. Sixteen island groupings comprise the archipelago, about equal in area to one-half of New York City. None were as mountainous as the Carolines, and granted East Pacific naval supremacy, which was ours by November, 1943, their conquest seemingly should have been easier than that of Attu.

But it did not prove so, our four-day fight for Tarawa, keystone of the Gilbert area, being the most costly thus far experienced in the war against Japan. Tarawa was a typical atoll, a cluster of some twenty-five islands grouped in a ragged circle around a lagoon, the islands only a few feet in elevation, most of them joined together at low water by a coral barrier reef. On one, Betio, less than one square mile of land was a Japanese garrison, the American objective.

As the U. S. marines set out in their landing barges it seemed as though most of the island's defenders must be dead, for hour after hour our battlewagons, cruisers, and destroyers had been lobbing shells on Betio;

hour after hour American planes had filled the sky, dropping thousands of their smashing eggs on this narrowly constricted target; hour after hour dense smoke had risen from Betio. But our landing barges could not get near shore. A reef far from land obstructed the way and the marines had to be transferred from barges to amphtracks, amphibious contrivances capable of carrying a few men on either land or water. This led to much confusion; the defending garrison, far from dead, strafed both barges and amphtracks; of the latter there were an insufficient number, and our men got ashore as best they could, many of them wading two or three hundred yards waist-high in water, carrying full equipment, many of them dying without touching land.

After one day of fighting they held only a few yards of narrow beachhead. On Betio the enemy had constructed some 500 pill boxes, most of them made of a double section of palmetto logs, filled with sand, covered with sand, almost impossible to destroy by shell fire, impossible to locate with precision from the air or the sea. Here, dug in and armed to the teeth, the Imperial Japanese marines fought to the last man, taking their own lives by hugging exploding hand grenades to their chests rather than surrender. Of our first men ashore almost all died, and in many of the pill boxes were found later two or three dead marines, six or seven dead Japanese. The American dead had given a good account of themselves; they had to die so that their comrades might conquer, for we were in haste to take Tarawa.

Betio once won, and Abemama and Makin, also atolls, the two former by marines, the latter by the army, and the Gilberts by the end of November were ours. The long process of leap-frogging across the far Pacific waters had really begun. And the annals of the United States Marine Corps had another name, Tarawa, as illustrious in their history as Tripoli in North Africa, Fisher's Island, North Carolina, or Château Thierry in 1918, or Guadalcanal of the Solomons.

The story of Tarawa was to be repeated over and over again with variations for the next year and a half. Northwest of the Gilberts were the Marshalls, another and larger archipelago, Japanese mandated-island areas, *terra incognita,* and forbidden to foreigners for many years. There were thirty-two islands in the Marshalls, spaced out over hundreds of ocean miles, most of them enclosing spacious lagoons. The Marshalls lay across the direct line between the Gilberts and Japan, and were much closer to the all-important Carolines, northeast of New Guinea, than the Gilberts. Quite evidently the Americans had to nail down a few of the Marshalls. And this the American navy did, capturing Kwajalein, a Marshall Island atoll, and shortly after Eniwetok, some 340 miles beyond it.

Victory followed victory. The navy swept on westward, bypassed the eastern Carolines and by the middle of the month was close enough to

Truk, the vaunted secret Gibraltar of Japan in the mandated South Pacific, to attack it and the Japanese ships there from American plane carriers. Our planes sank twenty-three hostile vessels and wiped out 201 planes. We had hoped for more, since Truk was reputed to be the rendezvous of Tokyo's main fleet. But the cruisers, destroyers, and auxiliary craft we did sink made up in part for Pearl Harbor and gave a sad shock to Japan's pride, as shown by the immediate dismissal of her naval chief of staff. This fortress, Truk, was no ordinary atoll. Within its spacious lagoon were several volcanic islands and many airfields, and from its supposedly impregnable isolation the Japanese had sent reinforcements to New Britain, New Guinea, and the Solomons.

Saipan and Guam

The American navy meanwhile roamed the East Pacific, seeking a battered foe not any too anxious to do battle, launching attacks from carrier planes at Palau in the Western Carolines, less than 600 miles from the Philippines and over 2,200 miles from the Marshalls, paying reconnaissance calls in force on the Marianas, Guam, Tinian, and Saipan. Whether we were headed straight west via Palau to the Philippines, or northwest from New Guinea to the same goal, or straight toward Tokyo by the Marianas route, was anybody's guess.

The last proved the choice of our strategists, and of the three largest islands in the Marianas they selected the most northern, Saipan, in distance 3,800 miles west of Pearl Harbor, about 1,500 miles from either the Philippines or Japan, 110 miles north of Guam, still in hostile hands.

American strategy was on the scale of our strength. Simultaneously it planned to feint south from the Aleutians with bombers and cruisers against the Kuriles, to assail the Japanese homeland with the new B-29 superforts now based on Chinese airfields, to strike north from New Guinea at Yap, Palau, and the Philippines, to bomb Truk, Nauru, and Ponape in the Carolines, as well as to land on Saipan. Coördination was not perfect but it was pretty good, and though the Japanese got wind of our main objective before our marines were ashore another victory was won, both by land and by sea.

The fight for Saipan was more deadly than that at Tarawa, far more protracted than that at Kwajalein, for the island was long and tapering with a curving mountainous spine well suited for defense. In, under, and behind every possible barrier the hostile snipers were located and their fire was deadly. The center of the battle line was reported as safe as anywhere else. First a hundred yards here and a hundred yards there, until finally the foe were forced back into a narrow pocket at the north. Here they re-formed and at last dashed out to destruction in a frenetic banzai charge. Some 22,000 dead soldiers of Nippon lay upon the ground.

Shortly after came the reconquest of Guam. Once more there was a stiff workout against mountain terrain, resistance to the death. Early in August it was all over and the Marianas, all three, were added to the American string of Pacific islands. In Tokyo the loss of Saipan had forced the resignation of Premier Tojo. In his own oblique way he stated the facts of disaster. "Japan," he said, "has come to face an unprecedentedly great national crisis.... The situation now approaches when the opportunity will occur to crack the enemy and to win the victory." Alarm in Tokyo was well founded. Between that city and our men lay only the Bonin and Volcanic Islands; between them and the Chinese coast but one island, Formosa.

These quick-paced American victories were won by a type of amphibious warfare hitherto unknown to history. Admiral Nimitz needed no base west of Honolulu to range over the vast Pacific because he carried his base with him. "Each class of warship—battleship, cruiser, destroyer, aircraft carrier and submarine—had a special type of supply and repair ship...." It was not necessary to send disabled ships back to America to be repaired. In almost every instance the work was done by floating workshops. And no sooner was an island atoll wrested from the Japanese than in moved the Seabees (U. S. Naval Construction Battalions) who, with utmost speed, built hospitals, roads, docks, redeemed ripped-up jungles and made them useful for further advance.

Then, too, the landing barges, many thousands of them. They ranged from the LCRS (landing craft, rubber, small) holding half a dozen men, to the LSD (landing ship dock) a dry dock over 450 feet in length crammed with power vehicles and manned by a crew of more than two hundred. In between was every conceivable type the ingenuity of man could devise. There was the "buffalo," an amphibious tank mounting several guns. There was the LCVP (landing craft, vehicles and personnel); the LCM (landing craft medium), to take either sixty soldiers or thirty tons of supplies; the LCT (landing craft, tanks); the LST (landing ship, tanks) with a complement of 132 men and officers, a cavernous vessel so large that it tucked away in its bowels several smaller type of landing craft filled with still other devices; and the LCIL (landing craft, infantry, large) each capable of putting on shore more than two hundred troops and equipped with machinery to pull itself from a beach back to the open sea. These were the principal American types. The British had still others, as for instance, the LBK (landing barge, kitchen) and the LBF (landing barge, flak). These ships, if they may be called such, were to play as important a role in the war as even the submarine or the destroyer. Thanks to our resources, our workers, and our vast experience in mass production of machinery, autos, and so forth, the American navy really had the tools to do the job.

By 1945 our sea power, in this ultra-modern guise, had grown to such colossal proportions that it was ready to clear the ocean paths all across the Pacific. Never in all history could there possibly have been any enterprise remotely resembling this, a giant-size transoceanic offense over waterways three times any Atlantic distances, involving conquest en route of desperately defended enemy islands; and all the complexities of it concurrent with an even vaster amphibious task in conjunction with Britain, off Normandy beaches, at the opposite end of the world.

Yanks and Aussies, 1943

February, 1943, and the half-starved Japanese garrison on Guadalcanal withdrew. Thus ended the fight for the southern Solomons. The Japanese had need for all the ships, the planes, and men they could muster to defend the northern Solomons and to reinforce their troops in northern Papua at Lae. On March 3–4 came the Battle of the Bismarck Sea in which an entire Japanese division bound for Lae was annihilated by American air power.

With the coming of the spring in 1943 the tempo of the South Pacific campaign rose rapidly. Tokyo's strategists concentrated troops and shipping at their great base of Truk in the Carolines, so far north of Rabaul that it could not be reached effectively. From there they could and did add constantly to their garrisons in New Guinea and the Solomons. The Yanks and Aussies, however, under command of MacArthur took the offensive and were not to lose it again in this war; they skirted along the coast of New Guinea to lay siege to Lae and Salamaua; they repeated all over again their experiences in the swamps of Papua; and as this happened the Americans made it their particular business to rout enemy elements out of the central Solomons.

It was mid-September before Lae and Salamaua fell. The Japanese there strove desperately to hang on to their airfields, to reinforce their garrisons. They had the manpower to do so, but not the transportation. Meanwhile, by landing craft and by parachute the Allies drove in for the kill. With Aussies pressing from one side and Yanks from another, the Japanese were caught. A few escaped to the jungle, the rest died. The Aussies kept right on. In October they took Finschhafen, in November, Satelburg, and were advancing overland toward Madang on the north coast. By the end of 1943 the tedious process of digging out the Japanese from their nests in New Guinea was well under way.

Thus also in the Solomons. At Munda in New Georgia the enemy had an air base much closer to Guadalcanal than Rabaul in New Britain, and Munda we decided to take. The operation proved long and costly. Before New Georgia could be invaded outlying islands must first be occupied, the Russells, Rendova, and Woodlark. Even after we landed on New Georgia, the advance was yard by yard. Despite bulldozers, tanks, and flame throwers, the defenders stuck to their posts until late in August, large numbers escaping then by air. We were now halfway "up the ladder" from the southern Solomons. Still further north lay Bougainville, bigger than New Georgia. Our marines rolled ashore at Empress Augusta Bay in November but the Japanese took to the hills and we did not follow them; instead we isolated their airfields by the seizure of key islands farther north. By the end of 1943 the Solomons were no longer a menace to our march ahead.

The tempo and the tension of the Pacific war tended to heighten. September to September, 1943-1944, MacArthur's campaign in New Guinea slogged out a glorious conclusion. Seven enemy-held airfields were strewn out at irregular intervals along the malarial lowlands of that infernal island, and to have taken them one by one would have involved incommensurate sacrifice. Better to smash steadily at the airfields until the Japanese air force was pulverized there and then leapfrog westward along the coast. For that purpose the American general had at his command sixteen divisions, eight U. S. army, two U. S. marines, five Australian, one New Zealand. By the end of April, 1944, MacArthur had jumped 500 miles to the west to Hollandia in Dutch New Guinea. Two landings here, a pincer-closing movement, a march inland through crocodile-infested swamps, U. S. Hellcats, Avengers, Douglas dive-bombers in the air; buffalos, half-tracks, jeeps, bulldozers vomited out of a U. S. LSD (landing ship dock) on land, and very shortly Hollandia was ours. June 20, and Biak Island off the northwestern tip of New Guinea was taken; another month and we had gone one hundred miles farther to the west. Within three hours thanks to our paratroopers Numfor Island was occupied, and the Philippines were now but 800 miles away.

On went MacArthur, all the way to Sansapor at the furthest northwestern tip of New Guinea. He had reached it by his famous leapfrogging tactics, having bypassed the headquarters of the Second Japanese Army, now 120 miles eastward. Between him and the Philippines there was now but 600 miles. He did not stop. The Halmahera islands were between him and his goal. Leapfrogging once more, he landed on the most northern of that group, Molotai, the Philippines 300 miles away.

"Thus," as General Fuller states, "in a little over twelve months, the Allies had advanced one thousand, three hundred miles and cut off no less than 135,000 Japanese beyond all hope of rescue." [2]

And the very day MacArthur landed on Molotai, September 15, 1944, saw the U. S. Third Amphibious Force (marines) ashore on Peleliu Island on MacArthur's right flank.

[2] Fuller, *op. cit.,* p. 202.

Reconquest of the Philippines

The war with Japan was still two months short of three years, and American planes were soaring again over the Philippines, knocking out of the skies in one day more enemy aircraft than we lost in the Bataan fighting, and sinking in Manila Bay no less than forty Japanese ships. We were coming back.

The Yanks arrived October 20 in the central Philippines on the eastern side of Leyte Island. It had been generally assumed that MacArthur would first invade Mindanao in the south, since to bypass that large island with its excellent airstrips would be risky. But the American armed forces had long since proved that leapfrogging was the best of tactics; and so the Americans jumped clear to the heart of the Philippines, 600 ships convoying and transporting some 250,000 men, a sea invasion of tremendous magnitude, more dangerous than the Anglo-American invasion of North Africa nearly two years earlier.

The total enemy forces in the Philippines were about equal to our own but widely scattered, while ours were concentrated. On the other hand, the enemy's navy, though somewhat battered and deficient in light craft and carriers, had a major advantage. It could menace our fleet of transports by any one of three different routes: across the Sulu Sea, south of Leyte; from the direction of Singapore; across the China Sea through the San Bernardino Straits north of Leyte; and from farther north, skirting the eastern shores of Luzon and Samar, to hit our transports from the east. It was now or never for Japan, and she must strike quickly before our shore footing was secure. She did her best to do so, and from all three directions. Those were anxious days late in October as we divided our naval strength to face this triple threat, for none could tell which one of the three enemy task forces packed the greater punch. We met all three and drove them back. At one time the defenseless transports were stripped of naval coverage and severe, even catastrophic, damage might have overtaken them had it not been for the audacity, courage, and skill of motor torpedo boats, destroyers, light craft, and airmen. But the final results were more than satisfactory. In three crucial engagements the enemy naval power was crippled, three of their battleships and six heavy cruisers being sunk, also one large carrier and several small ones, to say nothing of lighter craft and not far short of 700 planes. Out of a total of some sixty hostile ships, only a few destroyers escaped undamaged. Thus by "Navy Day," T. R.'s birthday, October 27, 1944, the sea power of Tokyo was, as Admiral Halsey reported, "beaten, routed and broken." It was our own American Trafalgar.

The American navy reported the loss of the carrier *Princeton* and that of a few destroyers and escort carriers. "The ghastly annihilation of Allied naval units," said the Tokyo radio, "resulted in forty-five ships sunk"—a cryptic statement in view of the fact that there were left only remnants of their three fleets, and that these were never again to trouble us in Philippine waters during this war.

The Mikado's army, however, could dig in on land and so put up much more of a fight; it constantly brought fresh forces into Leyte from the neighboring islands; it slipped them in by night as on Guadalcanal; it contested every swamp and hilltop. Incessant rain, knee-deep mud, last-ditch warriors in multitudinous caves—it was the old, hard story of a dozen islands. An invasion of Leyte's west coast, paralleling the main attack on the east, finally cut the Japanese forces into segments as our planes time and time again flattened down their dwindling air strength throughout all the Philippines. On the third anniversary of Pearl Harbor the red and white flag of the Sun Goddess still waved over a corner of Leyte, but with the United States navy master of the sea and our planes darkening the skies, our ultimate recapture of the Philippines was assured. By January 1, 1945, no less than 50,000 Japanese dead had been counted on Leyte and resistance there reduced to patrol action. But enemy forces numbering some 50,000 more still remained in Luzon, and no one knew how many more menaced Mindanao, Panay, and the other islands of the archipelago. Our Philippine campaign had just begun.

It had for its next phase the retaking of Luzon. Most fortunately for the United States, enemy air power based there had dwindled steadily, for the Japanese had played it all out and for keeps during the Leyte campaign, with swarms of Manila-based planes hurtling south to dash at reckless odds and in vain against Liberators, Warhawks, Black Widows, navy Hellcats, and marine Corsairs. Luzon was strongly held, and should General Yamashita, Singapore's conqueror, hold out in Luzon in 1945 as MacArthur and Wainwright did in Bataan in 1942, a year or more might pass before the mainland of Japan felt the tread of Yank leather.

Since the Rising Sun flag flew over Corregidor, frontal attack on Manila was out. We had the choice of driving from the south—best as far as distance went and best, too, for air coverage; or, on the other hand, we could strike in at the Lingayen Gulf and assault Manila from the north—at greater distance but mostly along a broad, flat valley with excellent motor roads. We chose the Gulf, conveyed thither seven convoys without the loss of a transport, clear proof that Japanese air power and Japanese sea power fast were waning.

Yamashita did not set up battle on the open beaches nor in the broad valley; presumably he had neither planes, nor tanks, nor enough matériel to do so. Only when we probed inland to the hills on either side did we meet stiff resistance. On February 4, with little loss of life, we were back in the capital of the Philippines.

Burma in 1943

In 1943 the Japanese surging across Burma were at the gates of India. They expected easy entrance, perhaps a junction with victorious Nazis in Persia.

India, seething with rebellion, was but lightly garrisoned. Wavell, the viceroy, however, did not hesitate. He clapped Gandhi, Nehru, and all leading members of the Indian National Congress in jail, reorganized his Anglo-Indian forces, prepared to take the offensive. It was on a limited scale but won its objectives, largely because of the ability and courage of Major Charles Wingate, an outstanding hero of this war.

Wingate's career paralleled in many ways that of Chinese Gordon, England's roving soldier of the later nineteenth century. Both were masters of the unexpected, scornful of brass hats, distinguished for exploits in frontier warfare, famous for winning the friendship of rough tribesmen, and assiduous in their study of the Old Testament. As a young officer in Palestine, Wingate had won his spurs by capturing Arab guerrillas; as a major in the British army his exploits in Ethiopia with a rickety plane, camels, and native warriors had become legendary; and now Wavell gave him a free hand in Burma.

He introduced something new in warfare. The long protracted hardening of average raw recruits into tough, resilient units was not new, nor was the painstakingly minute drill in geographic lore upon which Wingate insisted: what he did that was novel was to plan a campaign in all its details and involving several thousand men, in which commissariat and munitions were to be transported entirely by plane. Food had been dropped from the air to succor the fleeing remnants of British troops in Burma. Now Wingate proposed to articulate the plane so closely to his projected offense that it would replace railroads, motor trucks, bullock trains, and make possible a victorious rapidity of movement despite rain, forest, and jungle.

Early in February, 1943, Major, now General Wingate, led his troops over the Indian border. He called them "Chindits," a name derived from the curious carvings, part lion, part griffin, which protected Burmese temples from the devil. For over two months the Chindits were to emulate on Asiatic land what Elizabeth's sea dogs did to Spain on oceanic waters, to harass and wear down an enemy too potent to challenge face to face.

The immediate task was to sever hostile communication lines. These ran north and south following the valley of the Chindwin, the Irrawaddy, and the Salween rivers. Most important of all was the north-south railway line from Mandalay to Myitkyina. To get there, the Chindits must drive east-west over high mountains, chain after chain of jumbled ranges, down through deep valleys, roughing it over bridle paths or no paths at all.

By the time Wingate's roughies won back to India they had raided on foot over 1,000 miles, penetrated to the east of the Irrawaddy River, disrupted communications over a strategic area of 10,000 square miles in North Burma, killed several thousand foemen, proved that a small army could be fed, clothed, and armed, even in the tropics, by air.

Britain, however, had little to spare for such costly fighting in Burma. Until new airfields in great number were built and equipped in India, both for the RAF and the United States Tenth Air Force, no large-scale offense could be launched against our implacable enemy in that humid-hot malarial jungle of a dysentery-ridden land.

China in 1943 and 1944

After endless years of anarchy and grueling war, China was played out and bogged down. Financial inflation was rampant; lend-lease aid came dribbling in but slowly, all of it borne by air from India; a dubiously pro-Japanese government, presided over by a Chinese carpetbagger, functioned after the fashion of such rascals at Nanking; in North China Communists had their own regime, bitterly oppressed by and opposed to the landlords and loan sharks of the Kuomintang party who ruled what it could reach of China from air-battered Chungking; and Chiang Kai-shek, the generalissimo, rapidly aging, always supersensitive, sur-rounded by politicians of Asiatic craft and greed, did not take kindly to relentless pressure applied by our own high-octane general, Joseph Stilwell (Vinegar Joe), chief-of-staff for the Burma theater.

In China there were wars within wars, in particular that between the Chinese Communists and the Kuomintang, occasionally breaking out in open strife, soldier against soldier, gun against gun, more often smoulder-ing under cover, a feud of factions contending for the loyalty of starving men and for the lordship of wasted lands.

This internecine strife had long been far from new, and the quarrels it engendered dated back to the twenties. In 1937 the breach was par-tially healed; but old sores festered, to break out with renewed fury by the forties, and in 1944 there were two distinct regimes in China, united only by hatred of Tokyo, in all other ways mutually distrustful and hostile.

The Chinese Communists, said to number around 80,000,000, were located mainly in the northwest provinces with their capital at Yenan. Here they had a government of their own, with separate currency, sep-arate taxes, and a separate army which they said existed to fight Japan, which the Kuomintang said was for the purpose of spreading Commu-nism. Several of Chiang Kai-shek's advisers, if not the generalissimo him-self, were so inclined to this view that many of his Chinese troops, which should have been used against invading Japan, were deployed north to ride herd on the Communists and to keep their power from spreading further.

Meanwhile, the military situation worsened. Beginning in the spring of 1944 and continuing at rapid and accelerating tempo, the Japanese made good their project to cut and to control a wide swathe through all China from Peiping in the north to Canton and Nan-ning in the south, thus bringing their conquests in overland contact with French Indochina, a *fait accompli* which made it possible not simply to sever the coastal plains of East China from Chungking but also to reinforce Japanese troops in Thailand and Burma by land.

Week by week and month by month the somber news of Chinese defeat kept leaking out. The foe long since had controlled the Yangtze Valley beyond Hankow. They now pressed north from Hankow and south from Peiping across the wheat belt of Hanoi to capture Chengchow and Loyang farther west; they drove south from Hankow and north from Canton, taking en route the important city of Chang-sha, making good their rail connections from Korea to Canton; they forced the hasty abandonment of many of the Fourteenth American Air Force bases; and as this happened they occupied one after another Chinese coastal ports between Canton and Shanghai, thus sealing off potential landing sites for an American army invading China by sea.

Burma and India in 1944

Farther to the west in Burma and in one small pocket of northeastern India, the Japanese were defeated. In this remote and pestilential corner, Chinese, Americans, Britons, East Africans, and Indians, together with sundry local hill tribes, reconquered about one-fifth of all Burma and made possible the linking up of the Ledo Road with the Burma Road in order to reopen a back door into China. This was a truly international achievement but credit primarily should go to the Chinese and to the Indians, the former serving under General Stilwell, the latter under British high command. Aside from American aviators, engineers, and a handful of picked raiders and machine gunners, few Americans took part in the obscure campaign which by the end of 1944 had carried Allied arms as far south as Bhamo, eighty miles beyond Myitkyina.

Divergencies of viewpoint, logistical problems, the truly infernal terrain, and the down-streaming monsoon combined to complicate military problems in Burma-India. The Allied commander-in-chief in Southeast Asia, Lieutenant General Mountbatten, was more interested in Central and Southern Burma than in various inaccessible upper valleys; more concerned about the recovery of Rangoon, Mandalay, and ultimately Singapore for the British Empire than about what many considered so hair-brained a scheme as building an impossible highway across impassable mountains. Deputy commander under Mountbatten was our own Vinegar Joe, whose pet project was the Ledo Road. Stilwell did not get on well with either Mountbatten or with Chiang Kai-shek, upon whom he had to depend for ninety per cent or more of his soldiers. But what Stilwell lacked in tact he much more than made up in brains and energy. Furthermore, until the end of the year, he had the backing of Washington.

Many thought Ledo a fantastic idea. It would be necessary to transport bulldozers, trucks, workmen, and all their impedimenta hundreds of miles from Calcutta over a twisting narrow gauge railway to the extreme upper corner of Northeast India before even a yard could be constructed. After that, one was confronted with engineering problems more difficult by far than those encountered in the Alaska highway, dense forests to be felled, zigzagging corkscrew curves to be constructed down precipitous mountain slopes and up steep ridges, and this in the face of determined enemy resistance and the worst climate in the world, with a monsoon arriving in May to terminate operations if not to wash out with torrential floods everything thus far accomplished. But Stilwell clung to his plans; he had the money, the equipment, the engineers, the manpower, and the soldiers to clear the path; and he was going to do just that.

The Sino-British-American objective (for Mountbatten did finally and generously assist his hard-bitten American deputy) was Myitkyina, railhead of Japanese communications in north Burma. That town and its airfield once occupied, hostile detachments on the north could be cut off and the Ledo enterprise once reaching Myitkyina could be continued eastward, despite very bad terrain, so as ultimately to link up with the Burma Road in the Chinese province of Yün-nan. The British said it would be "impossible" to take Myitkyina before 1945; Stilwell arrived there, aided greatly by the British, and did so by converging attacks on the eve of the 1944 monsoon season. His Chinese troops, whom he had trained and equipped, and whom he considered second to none, headed for Myitkyina from northeast and southeast. From the southwest came Wingate's raiders, soon to have over them another commander, owing to the untimely death of General Wingate who was killed before he could know how well Americans could carry out the methods he improved and often originated. And from the northwest, like scouts searching out the ways for the Ledo engineers, came Merrill's marauders, the Yankee counterpart to Wingate's men. And now for the first time in Asiatic jungle war gliders were used to convey troops. The commando fighters of Merrill were joined by Indian troops, coming in glider transports, towed off the ground by planes and landing in the jungle. British and American airplane power was making victory possible in North Burma even as it was doing in western Europe and at Saipan.

The Japanese this spring of 1944 meanwhile launched an offense of their own, and in two directions; one, the lesser, in the Arakan region of the Burma-Indian frontier east of the Bay of Bengal, aimed at the conquest of Chittagong, an important seaport and British air base, the other, more important, directed at Imphal, capital of the little Indian state of Manipur, tucked away amid the Naga Hills on the borders of North Burma and India. North of Imphal for some 174 miles a highway led to Dimapur on the Calcutta-Ledo railway. Once the Rising Sun reached Dimapur, Stilwell's way to China would revert to the jungle and the Sino-American-British forces in North Burma would be isolated. All that would be necessary then would be a holding action while Japanese troops, assisted, it was hoped, by revolting Indians, swung down the Brahmaputra Valley into Bengal, perhaps to stage another Singapore at Calcutta.

This was the Japanese plan. Thanks to General Slim and his Fourteenth British Army, it was thwarted, the Japanese soundly thrashed, all that they gained lost, and by the third anniversary of Pearl Harbor the foundations laid for the reconquest of Burma in 1945.

"The march on Delhi has begun, the Fourteenth British Army is destroyed," thus the Tokyo radio in the first week of February, 1944, as General Tenashi trapped the Fifteenth Corps of that army in the Arakan area. The general's plans were excellent but he had forgotten that Britain, not Japan, had air supremacy over Burma and that the British now were operating on Wingate's advice, "Have no lines of communication on the jungle floor. Bring the goods like Father Christmas down the chimney." The airmen came to the rescue, flew 400 sorties, fed food and munitions to the trapped Imperials, even brought them beer and mail. The foe had rations for ten days only. They stayed too long. Counterattacks sent them reeling eastward, leaving in the jungle 7,000 dead.

The real march on Delhi, however, was by way of Imphal. Against that fourth-rate Indian town the Japanese hurled 80,000 picked troops, besieged it for over two months, surged on north, surrounded for eighteen days another British force at Kohima which if they had only by-passed might have brought them to the strategic railroad. But the Jap orders were: "First take Kohima, then the railroad"; and Japanese soldiers always obey orders, which is not always the way to win.

Time now pressed; the monsoon was not far distant; the Japanese made one final try for Manipur. "You will take Manipur," said their commander, "or the division will be annihilated." The second part of his statement time verified. It was now Slim's turn. Like thistledown before the wind the Imperials drove the adversary south, counting more than 50,000 Japanese dead. How many more of the original 80,000 perished in the jungle of sickness or by knives of irate hillmen there is no record.

The Fourteenth Army, too, had suffered heavily; but Slim was back at Kalewa on the frontier where he had buried his guns on his retreat in 1942. Now he could, and did, dig them up again. From now on it was the British Empire, not Japan, that took the offensive in Burma.

Burma Won Back

The Japanese were already on their way out of Burma. The colossal and catastrophic defeat in 1942 of the British Empire there had been well advertised; but the return in triumph of Imperial forces in 1944 and 1945 attracted little notice. The American press, as was natural, laid such emphasis as it gave to the Allied campaign in Burma on the dramatic achievements of our own General Stilwell and his Chinese troops in taking Myitkyina, in effect minimizing rather unduly the assistance rendered by British penetration forces, and underestimating, very decidedly, the stress and strain imposed upon the British Fourteenth Army which had to drive back the main Japanese invaders. That army, during the first half of 1944, not only suffered over 40,000 casualties, but, according to Churchill, "sustained no fewer than 237,000 cases of sickness which had to be evacuated to the rear over the long, difficult communications, and tended in hospitals."

That army, nevertheless, during the first five months of 1945 "liberated" Burma, retook Mandalay, chased the enemy from Rangoon, killed them by the thousands, drove the rest in full retreat toward the Siamese border. And Burma, it is worth remembering, was as large as Germany, with a fighting front in 1945 of 700 miles, and exceeded in World War II only by the Russian. Here was a country with two enemies to fight— Japan and the climate. Sodden wet, choking dust, malaria, jaundice, dysentery, mud, ticks, a humidity of 95 per cent, and Hirohito's desperate soldiers—a bad land to win.

The American contribution to this Southern Pacific victory of 1945 was relatively small. Our concern, and quite rightly, had been with northern Burma, to open there communication lines with China. Lend-lease had helped make possible the British comeback of 1945; but planning the final campaign, and the execution of it, was a British Imperial achievement. Statistics tell the tale. Of the ground troops in Burma in 1945, about 250,000 came from Britain, some 470,000 were Indian, 30,000 were from British East Africa, 30,000 from British West Africa. Chinese forces engaged were approximately 125,000, and American troops, 25,000. A total of 900,000, possibly more.

Kipling's Mandalay was Japan's main base in Burma, and the attack on it had priority for the 1945 campaign which burst forth with speed and fury late in February. General Slim, commander of the Fourteenth British Army, drove at Mandalay from the north and simultaneously rushed a mechanized force south and east for a surprise assault on Meiktila, eighty miles south of Mandalay. While a Sino-American force assisted by British troops drove down from Lashio in the northeast to assist in the siege of Fort Dufferin, an additional brigade was flown intact to support the troops who had won through to Meiktila. Thus it was that when Fort Dufferin fell, May 8, and the Japanese were forced to evacuate the capital city, they found themselves outflanked in the south and overwhelmed in the north. The most severe fighting in Burma ensued, as the Mikado's men tried fanatically to break through to the south. But the line held, and in little over a week Slim's men had killed over ten thousand of the best Japanese troops in Burma, acquired six airstrips in the arid zone about Meiktila, far from mud and monsoons, tons of Japanese war matériel, the top of the railroad corridor, and Burma's main auto routes, and most important of all, a springboard from which to drive south to the sea.

There was still Rangoon to capture, 700 miles down the pestilent valley of the Irrawaddy. Time was precious, for unless Slim took Rangoon before the middle of May the monsoon would block land operations, write finis to war work in the skies. He therefore took the long chance and disregarded his flanks to speed his truck-bearing infantry and tanks on south. All April the adversary did his best to stay that onward rush, but so fast did it crash through that frequently Japanese headquarters only heard of British victories days after they had occurred, and in one instance Slim's tanks "ran down Jap policemen directing traffic at the crossroads."

The terrain now was flat and open, well suited for rapid movement. May 1, and Rangoon was close at hand. From the sea amphibious British landings drove ashore, and British paratroopers dropped down on the lowlands of the Irrawaddy delta. Rangoon was surrounded, north, south, and west. The foe had had enough and too much; May 3 he fled. "Slim had beaten the enemy and the monsoon."

China Revived

Even before Rangoon's fall and the taking of Okinawa, the resilient and tough Chinese were turning past defeat into present victory. Chinese morale was on the upgrade throughout 1945. There had been a noticeable increase in airborne freight from India, and soon American trucks began to squirm their way through north Burma hills over the Ledo-Burma highway, rechristened "Stilwell Road" in honor of the man whose imagination, grit, and perseverance had made it possible. "Welcome Honorable Truck Convoy," the banners said, as this new stream of matériel-in-aid trickled in over the thirsty desert of a half-starved land.

Also instrumental in reviving China's strength was the reorganization of her army, to a considerable degree "U. S. trained, U. S. supplied, U. S. supported." General Stilwell and the Generalissimo did not see eye to eye; both were touchy men and coöperation lagged. Stilwell's dual job as commander of U. S. troops in China and as chief of staff of Chiang Kai-shek was taken by General Wedemeyer, who made himself *persona grata* to that Chinese chief of state, so that Chinese soldiers were now better fed, better clothed, better disciplined, and consequently better fighters.

The Chinese took the offensive in the late spring and summer of 1945. One by one the American airfields in China were won back and the conqueror's corridor to Indochina, Thailand, and Malaya, for which he had fought so long, was so narrowed by mid-June that he withdrew from it to avoid capture.

Iwo Jima

Nineteen forty-five and Japan's brief day of glory ended. As Slim's Fourteenth British Army drove the foe out of Burma, the American army and navy were delivering a frontal attack that could not be withstood.

The American bases in the Marianas—Saipan, Tinian, and Guam—were a good thirteen hundred miles from Tokyo. Round trips to the targets took sixteen hours in good weather, leaving for emergencies less than one hour's margin on gas supply. If the weather was bad, the superfortress was out of luck and out of the war; and even if the weather was fair, there was always danger of attack by Japanese bombers based on Iwo Jima, 600 miles from Tokyo, 700 from Saipan, and on a direct line between them.

Once the United States had Iwo Jima the picture would shift radically; the Americans then would have a fueling depot for returning B-29s; and, what is more, American fighter planes based on Iwo could escort our superforts to the Japanese mainland and thus enable them to fly at low altitudes, engage in precision bombing. Clearly this miserable excrescence of volcanic rock, Iwo Jima, was an American must, "a good rock to have on our side."

Iwo was bare of vegetation, was crusted and heaped with volcanic ash along the beaches, soft, miry, and treacherous. At the southern end rose 556 feet of rocky Mt. Suribachi, an extinct volcano; at its northern end were cliffs and caves, many of the latter steaming sulphurously from latent subterranean fires; and upon this island battlefield of only eight square miles 23,000 Japanese soldiers held three airfields that meant much both to Nippon and to America. It was a nasty little place for even marines to tackle and, as one remarked, "It ain't like Brooklyn."

The barrage the navy threw up on Iwo was thick enough and black enough to screen the landing. None the less our landing losses were heavy, some twenty per cent, and worse to follow.

To reach the base of Suribachi and scale it took the leathernecks four days. And even then Iwo was far from won. The Japs still held two of the three airfields. Pillboxes and blockhouses of steel-reinforced concrete covered deep with volcanic ash and sand had to be reduced one after another. The foe made full use of his innumerable underground passages; the nasty weather grew nastier; the surf ran high; reinforcements of both men and matériel were hard to get ashore. And even after all three airfields were won, there were thousands of enemy soldiers holed up in the northern cliffs of Iwo. They died in the last ditch and almost to the last man. There were some suicides and but few prisoners. General H. M. Smith, our marine commander on Iwo, said grimly, "This is the toughest fight we've run across in 168 years." In the American cemetery 4,300 marines are buried.

Okinawa

On the last lap of his long outward voyage to Japan in 1853, Commodore Perry, U. S. N., paid an extensive visit to the Lew Chew islands (the Ryukyus of the present day), staying several weeks on Great Lew Chew, the Okinawa of our Pacific war.

Unlike Iwo, Okinawa is a large island, sixty miles long and varying in width from two to twenty miles. It lies half again as close to the two southern islands of Japan as Iwo Jima, and has the further advantage of being only 400 miles from China. Formosa is even nearer to the latter country than Okinawa, but 365 miles south of the Ryukyus. If our strategy called first for an invasion of China and subsequently that of Japan, then Formosa would be our best bet. Reverse this, however, and invade Japan first, then Okinawa, quite evidently would be the prize capture. Planes based on it were within easy range of Shanghai in China, Kyushu, and southern Honshu in Japan. And furthermore, the B-29, if based on Okinawa, could skim the Yellow Sea and the Straits of Shimonoseki and return in safety with fuel to spare.

Easter morning, 1945, and the newly formed Tenth American Army, convoyed and protected by some 1,400 ships and commanded by General Simon Bolivar Buckner III, landed on Okinawa. It looked easy. We had 100,000 men, and we spread across the island to bisect it, scarce hearing a hostile shot. Few suspected then what was to happen, the bloodiest campaign of the whole Pacific war. Eighty-two furious days were consumed to complete it, total American casualties, army and navy together, running to no less than 45,029; while on the other side 90,000 soldiers of Hirohito were killed, 4,000 taken prisoner.

The Japanese had no illusions as to the significance of Okinawa. If they lost that island they lost the war. It was bad enough to lose Iwo Jima; but that infernal pinpoint in the ocean had only three airfields, and was much too small to be made our major base. This was not true of Okinawa, much closer to Japan, upon which endless airfields might be built to harbor thousands of the dreaded B-29s. Okinawa was built by nature for rugged defense; the southern half was rough and mountainous land, and cut in through its hills wound fortifications with interlocking and inter-communicating tunnels, caves, and pillboxes. So now it was share and share alike for GIs and Leathernecks, who faced daily withering fire whenever and wherever they tried to gain a few yards. And there were many more yards to cover than on Iwo.

This time, too, the American navy felt the death-sting of Nippon's wasp-men. The Japanese had a dangerous threat in reserve, the *Kamikaze*, which translated means "divine wind."

Centuries before, Japan, as tradition holds, had been kept inviolate by a divine wind or kamikaze sent by the Sun Goddess, a wind which wrecked the navies of the Mongol conqueror, and now there would be a divine wind, man-contrived, thousands of suicide planes launched at the great American fleet spaced out for miles off Okinawa, an armada inevitably huge in view of the multifarious need of 100,000 men and all the cumbrous implements of our modern war. The Kamikaze planes were of minimum construction, each pilot locked in his cockpit, no armor for the plane, no parachute for the pilot, only brief specific training. Neither pilot nor plane was expected to survive.

The Kamikaze concept fitted well that older medieval psychology which the Japanese inherit—also their more modern theology. For them, as for Moslems of the earlier centuries, paradise was close at hand; before setting one's course of death, a wonderful party, many drinks, pre-Lethean honors. Kamikaze tactics were an improvement on the banzai charge, for the suicide planes did reach their mark on over 200 of our vessels, sank many a destroyer and small craft, and crippled badly two of our biggest carriers, killing so many bluejackets that in some weeks navy casualties exceeded both those of marines and army.

"One hundred million countrymen: the enemy now stands at our front gate. It is the gravest moment in our country's history." Thus Koiso, Japan's premier, on the eve of Okinawa. But he could do nothing to shake off the black hand of fate that smote Nippon's fighting men. As they lost ground yard by yard, a ministerial crisis ensued at Tokyo and Koiso resigned. His desperate successors ordered the remnants of Japan's navy to Okinawa. Let the Kamikaze attack once more with all it had, and in the midst of hoped-for confusion there might be one last chance for Hirohito's war-craft. But the ships of Japan never got to Okinawa. Our fighter bombers shot out from their flattops to the kill, sank two light cruisers, three destroyers, and the battleship *Yamato* of 45,000 tons, Japan's finest. Meanwhile, Russia denounced her ten-year neutrality pact with Japan, ominous indication that the Soviets would attack in Manchuria as soon as they considered it to their interests so to do.

The European war ended in May but on Okinawa war continued well into June. Through May the dwindling beleaguered garrison fought grimly as our Tenth Army and the marines edged it back to Shuri Castle, pivotal point in the last defense line. Slowly we were winning because we were killing foes who could not be replaced, some 80,000 of the original 90,000 now being dead. We ruled sea and air. On this island they could only die.

On the Eve of Hiroshima

Summer, 1945, and Japan was mortally stricken. Her death throes were those of Germany in February, March, and April, but with this difference: no hostile armies had as yet set foot upon her homeland.

Yet she was done for: her continental conquests were shrinking fast; her scattered garrisons over widespread Oceania were completely useless; the Australians were depriving her of the oil of Borneo; the converging aircraft of the United States were destroying her cities; the American navy conjointly with the planes of the American army were cutting the lifelines to Korea and Manchuria, without which she could not live; and the most imposing armada ever seen on any ocean, mostly American, but joined now by a powerful British squadron, paraded up and down, and down and up her now defenseless coasts, pouring floods of shells on helpless targets.

Invaded Nippon had more to die of and less to fight with than invaded Germany six months earlier. Even before Pearl Harbor, Japan's industrial potential was insufficient for large-scale war; now it was almost nonexistent. Unlike Germany, her domestic resources were few. Much of the food she ate came from out the sea. It now was death to her, the fishing boats sunk or driven to hiding.

Even more than Britain, Japan's life depended on ships, and where were they now? Tiny craft still stole stealthily at night Korea-bound, slunk along the China coast, slid slyly into Singapore, or rusted at the wharves of Shanghai and Batavia; but the navy which so proudly shattered Imperial Russia's fleet in 1905 was to all intents and purposes erased from this war.

During the nine months before Hiroshima our B-29s alone flew over 30,000 sorties, dropped over 169,000 crushing tons on shipyards, airfields, factories, cities. And this does not count the planes catapulted from our carriers against the enemy, or the four-engined bombers based on Iwo and Okinawa. Now, as resistance dwindled, our bombers flew at low levels, used jellied petroleum to start quenchless fires, and sent scurrying to rural hideouts the remnant millions of homeless Japan. And even so, we had not reached the peak of this cosmic destruction, for redeploy-

The Japanese Surrender Aboard the U.S.S. Missouri

ment of the European air forces had scarce begun, and Okinawa airfields still under construction would launch a thousand more planes per day.

This air assault was deadlier on Japan than on Germany, for the former's economic arteries were more exposed, her far flimsier cities more congested. Almost to the war's end, the German radar and German áck-áck kept functioning. Not so with Japan. She did not have the mechanics, the laboratories, the reserve of technological skill, nor the space that the Nazis could command; her citizens had neither the material nor the skill to make artificial gasoline and synthetic rubber.

In August the end was near. Japan turned to Russia, besought her aid to approach Britain and the United States. But Stalin, secretly committed to join in Japan's destruction, refused. The United States and Britain dictated unconditional surrender, and to this the Japanese were not willing to subscribe. And so they husbanded their dwindling planes, hid them as best they might, refused combat in the air to the swarming air fleets of the United States, which now struck at rail communications, bridges, and ferries rather than at burnt-out factories and slain cities. Bracing themselves against our infantry, soon to storm Nippon's shores, they planned then to bring out their last planes, to renew Kamikaze tactics, to kill many thousand Yankees. And they hoped that time soon would come.

Invasion in force had been set for November. It was not necessary, for Hiroshima came first.

Hiroshima

On July 16, some 300 picked scientists assembled in the New Mexico desert. An experiment was up for testing, the fruit of many years of research, and at a cost of $2,000,000,000.

And this is what the scientists, huddled at safe distance, saw: a great green light, changing color, now purple, now orange, instantaneously expanding, shooting upward in a fifth of a second, higher than Mt. Everest. Then came unbearable thunder. Here at long last was total power, total war, which man himself could wield—"the first cry of the newborn world."

This was the atomic bomb, man-made but of the very stuff of the suns, a bomb equal to 20,000 tons of TNT and with the fullest destructive power of 2,000 B-29s. Prometheus in Greek legend had stolen for us fire from the gods, and for that and other presumptions had been chained to a rock by Father Zeus. Man now, for weal or woe, Prometheus-like, was chained to his own full knowledge of this central secret of the universe.

On August 6 an American plane dropped a single atomic bomb on Hiroshima, a Japanese city and army base with a population upwards of

350,000. Sixty per cent of Hiroshima immediately was no more, dead instantly all those in the doomed area, dying those on the perimeter, "a death no men ever died before."

Two days later Russia declared war on Japan. Stalin had previously agreed to do so. And promptly Russian armies now crossed Manchurian borders.

Three days later a second and deadlier bomb was dropped, this time on the port of Nagasaki, and over an area even larger than at Hiroshima.

On the fourth day of this new world, August 10, Japan offered to surrender and accepted terms four days later.

Before our synthetic Sun-Fire destroyed Hiroshima and Nagasaki so utterly, Soviet entrance on the Far East's last act of world tragedy would have been news of great moment, and Japan's acknowledged defeat would have roused joy entire all through the United Nations. But epoch-making though these facts were, the ghost-shadow of Hiroshima and of Nagasaki eclipsed the Soviet act, damped our joy.

It was not that most men opposed the bomb's use; no doubt it shortened the war, saved many lives. Nor was it horror at what we had done to men that tempered rejoicing among those still capable of thought. There had been too much horror during ten years past for numbed nerves to respond in shock to any new ghastliness. Rather it was a profound sense of awe and fear. Against the energy released by split atoms, how piffling now inventions like gunpowder, the compass, the steam engine! Out of the laboratory of the chemist-physicist had come this miracled genie, his birth hurried by the clash of arms, the mad roar of battle. His future, what? And our own?

Chapter 42

THE POSTWAR WORLD

WORLD WAR II was over, and victors as well as vanquished licked their wounds. Millions had died, millions were in prison, millions were homeless, millions were hungry, and many millions more were numbed by toil, fagged out by nervous strain. To revive and to arouse them to thought and act, to beat swords into ploughshares, to rebuild cities, to restore trade and commerce, to blueprint peace treaties, would have been a staggering task even had the victors stood shoulder to shoulder in peace as in war. But such was not to be, and in five short years a third World War loomed on the horizon.

United Nations Charter

Permanent peace on earth had been one of the ideals of the United Nations. But swaddling clothes bound that infant very tightly as Britain, the United States, and Soviet Russia carefully guarded the cradle, admitting later as subordinate and part-time nurses Chungking China and the Free France of De Gaulle. Not, indeed, until the San Francisco Conference of April, 1945, was that organization much more than window dressing.

Not that history's pages were blank between 1942 and 1945 in the matter of conferences. There were many—Casablanca, Cairo, Moscow, Teheran, Yalta in the Crimea, and two at Quebec; conferences at Hot Springs, Virginia (food and agriculture), at Bretton Woods, New Hampshire (international finance), at Chicago (aviation), at Philadelphia (ILO—International Labor Office), at Atlantic City, New Jersey (UNRRA —United Nations Relief and Rehabilitation Administration), and at Dumbarton Oaks, Washington (preparatory for the San Francisco meeting). Many of these conferences were but consultations of two or three larger states on how to win the war. This was true of Casablanca (January, 1943), a meeting held between Roosevelt and Churchill with their military and naval staffs, in which mention was made of Stalin's inability to attend and assurances given that he had been fully informed of military proposals. It was also true of the first Quebec Conference

(August, 1943), which was concerned primarily with matters of military strategy in Europe and Asia. In the Cairo Conference (November, 1943), Chiang Kai-shek joined Roosevelt and Churchill, and the agenda was confined to war against Japan and how that country was to be stripped after its conclusion, not only of conquests made in the twentieth century but also of those made in the nineteenth. There was nothing here, certainly, of any United Nations machinery for governing the postwar world. So likewise was it with the second Quebec Conference (September, 1944), exclusively devoted to considering Anglo-American political and military interests in eastern Asia.

More important was the conference at Teheran, Iran (December, 1943) at which Roosevelt, Stalin, and Churchill signed a declaration calling for a "world family of democratic nations." So much for press release. What was not made public was a blueprint for Russian expansion (indirect of course) in eastern and southeastern Europe. Greece was exempted from it, and recognition was made of preponderant Russian influence in eastern Asia—a predated check which Russia was to cash a year and a half later at Yalta.

Much more important was the Yalta Conference on the Russian coast of the Black Sea, held in February, 1945. At it Stalin, Roosevelt, and Churchill agreed on joint military action to win the war and ways in which the world might be reconstructed after it was over. The victor was Stalin. Practically everything he wanted he obtained: Soviet control of Manchurian ports and railroads; Communist preponderance in Poland, Yugoslavia, Bulgaria, Rumania, and Hungary; the greater share of German reparations from Germany yet to be conquered; and membership in the projected United Nations not only for Russia but also for Byelorussia and the Ukraine, thus guaranteeing three votes to the Soviet Union. In return for these concessions Stalin promised an early entry by Russia into the war against Japan.

Why did Roosevelt and Churchill concede so much? One reason was that they considered Russian help against Japan highly desirable. Yalta preceded Hiroshima and the mainland of Japan had not yet been invaded. In Manchuria there was a large Japanese army which Russia could immobilize. Furthermore, Roosevelt and Churchill were powerless to stay Stalin's hand in eastern Europe anyway, and they thought it better to obtain certain Soviet pledges for decency and democracy in that part of Europe, flimsy though they might be, rather than do nothing at all to check unbridled Soviet aggression. As for the additional seats in the United Nations for Byelorussia and the Ukraine, Stalin had an argument: from his point of view granting seats to the Commonwealth countries, such as Canada and Australia, added to Britain's prestige, and the bloc of Central American countries he considered added to American influence.

Publicly the three signatories at Yalta agreed to set countries free from the German yoke, to institute democratic regimes, and to hold free elections. Secretly, although indirectly, however, Roosevelt and Churchill suborned if not betrayed a Poland they had fought to save, while at the same time handing over to Stalin an integral part of China, their ally in the war against Japan. The *quid pro quo* looked good, a Russian declaration of war against Japan and relinquishment on Stalin's part of Soviet interference in Italy and Greece. But however Yalta may be regarded, the decisions taken there were unquestionably in Stalin's favor and later were to embarrass both Britain and the United States in dealing with the Russian dictator.

We come now to Dumbarton Oaks at Washington, where for seven weeks ending October 7, 1944, the representatives of the Big Three, plus China, threshed out a specific program in accordance with the Teheran pledge.

What emerged bore striking resemblance to the 1919 League of Nations, a General Assembly in which each state admitted to the privileges of the United Nations should have one vote and a Security Council of eleven members, the Big Three, enlarged to the "Big Five" by the inclusion of China and France with permanent membership, and six other members to be chosen by the Assembly.

Born in San Francisco, April, 1945, the infant United Nations came close to dying. Molotov of Russia and Evatt of Australia, the two protagonists at this full-dress gala event, clashed again and again, the former generally winning, holding better cards, playing them relentlessly; the latter generally losing, but putting up a dogged fight on behalf of real democracy and the lesser nations.

The Russian got what he wanted; he lost two or three minor contests which he could well afford, since he was the victor in major ones, although not because a majority—or anything like it—of the smaller countries favored the Russian demand, but because Britain and the United States yielded their influence to Molotov's side and persuaded many to vote against their real desire, if not against their convictions. For Britain and America were determined at all cost that their ideological baby, the United Nations, must not perish.

Minor combats were over Poland and the Argentine Republic. Molotov asked admittance for the Moscow-trained Lublin Poles as representatives of Poland. To have acceded would have broken the Yalta agreement so barefacedly that the request was refused. He then tried to have the Argentine excluded, on the logical ground that she was a Fascist state. Once more he lost, not because his argument was poor, but because Britain was concerned about her meat deliveries and the United States supported the Argentine to placate our string of South American republics.

The Russian victories, however, were outstanding. That country got three votes in the Assembly instead of one, by insisting on and obtaining additional seats for the Ukraine and for Byelorussia. And, much more important yet, by the Constitution of the United Nations as finally adopted, each one of the five permanent members of the Security Council was acknowledged as having a right of absolute veto, not simply in regard to economic sanctions and the use of troops to coerce warlike nations, but even in regard to the peaceful settlement of international disputes.

Potsdam

Two months later in July came still another meeting of the Big Three in Prussian Potsdam—the three big states, that is, not the three big men of whom the world had long been so aware.

Roosevelt was dead. Organizer and architect of victory, F.D.R. would be sadly missed, his dauntless smile no longer seen, his adroit, uncanny political perception no longer discovering a way out of every conceivable impasse, no longer able to turn enemies into fellow workers if not always into friends. His place was taken by our new President, Harry Truman of Missouri, living embodiment of that commonwealth as popularly conceived in these United States.

And before Potsdam was over Winston Churchill, supreme orator of the Anglo-Americas, also departed, victim of a parliamentary revolution, his place taken by Clement Attlee, quiet-spoken chieftain of the British Labour party.

The Potsdam agreement was as follows: it provided for an interim government of Germany until peace treaties were drawn; it divided that country into four zones for administrative purposes (the largest, if we include that part of the Reich temporarily assigned to Poland, to be occupied by Russian troops, the smallest by the French); it subdivided the city of Berlin administratively among the four allies and provided for joint consultations there; it recognized Russian rights to Königsberg and the region around it and Polish administration of eastern Germany as far west as the rivers Oder and Neisse, but subject to later ratification; it promised Russia immediate reparations, giving her the right to dismantle German factories in her own zone, and in addition a goodly share of such reparations as might be extracted from the rest of Germany; it agreed to the forcible removal of German nationals from the Baltic states, the enlarged Poland, and from Czechoslovakia, and their lodgement in the truncated Reich; and it provided for the trial of German warmongers.

Berlin, meanwhile, lay far within the Russian zone, and by inexcusable oversight there was no proviso made at Potsdam for free access to that city for British, French, and American troops needed to garrison their respective zones in the German capital. Those zones were little islands in a Soviet sea and could only be reached by crossing Soviet-held lands. What if Stalin should withhold permission? Like Yalta, Potsdam was a Soviet victory.

In September, 1945, the representatives of Russia, Britain, and America met in London. It was a disappointing conference. At Potsdam the Russians had agreed to enlarge the Big Three—Russia, Britain, and the United States—by the inclusion of France and China. Now they insisted that the two latter countries be excluded from voting on the terms of peace. Britain and the United States stood out for their inclusion. Neither side would yield and the conference adjourned to meet again in December, 1945, at Moscow. This time the Russians were more tractable; they no longer insisted that the Big Three alone determine the peace. The United States also made concessions. MacArthur's rule in Japan was subjected to distant control by a board sitting in Washington on which Russia was to be represented, and in Tokyo an Allied council was set up to advise the American general. It was likewise determined that there would be an atomic energy commission, responsible to the council of the United Nations, and by the month of May, 1946, all preliminaries were to be completed and the peace treaties made ready for general acceptance.

The Allies Drift Apart

In January, 1946, the United Nations was to make its first official debut in London. Would that infant organization grow in strength and power, develop into a genuine agency for world government, or would it slowly atrophy into impotence as was the fate of the League of Nations? That was the open question of the New Year.

The omens were none too propitious since within a year there was evidence of ill-feeling between Britain and America, and much more serious, a rift between Soviet Russia and the West, soon to result in what became known as "the cold war."

Britain, more than any other country in the world, lived by international trade. For her it literally was necessary to export or die. Yet in January, 1946, her trade was but one-third of its prewar level; her foreign investments were for the most part liquidated; her mercantile marine was shattered; and her factories, machine shops, and general economy had been geared for war production rather than for peace. For the winning of the war she had made every sacrifice and during the last stages of it had relied heavily on lend-lease. The conclusion of the war in the Pacific brought that to an abrupt end. No longer was it possible for the British to obtain even powdered eggs from the United States, and they soon found that their food supply instead of becoming more plentiful tended to become less.

AN EARLY SESSION OF THE UNITED NATIONS

Left to Right: Gromyko, Cadogan, Stettinius, Byrnes

Under these circumstances they turned to us, asking for a loan of $4,000,000,000. They were reluctant to do so, for they were a proud people. But there was no other feasible alternative. The Americans, on occasions, generous to a fault, prided themselves on their acumen. What security had Britain to offer; what interest would she pay; what economic concessions would she make?

In regard to these and other questions there was protracted debate and unfortunately some display of temper on both sides. The British reluctantly agreed to pay two per cent interest beginning in 1951, to end certain economic practices which gave them trade advantages in a number of countries tied to the pound sterling, known as the sterling bloc, and to let the loan be reduced to $3,750,000,000. Nevertheless Congress hung fire, could not make up its collective mind, and delayed action on this essential gesture of friendship to our best customer and most important potential ally for many months, deferring ratification of the loan until July, 1946.

Why? One reason was the lurking suspicion, endemic in certain quarters, that our foreign policy was too closely linked with Britain's, that the latter country was far more concerned with oil concessions and her imperial lifeline in the Near East than with problems of world peace, and that as long as we continued to line up with Britain against Russia in international conferences so long would it be impossible to establish friendly relations with the latter.

Another factor operating against the loan was the political turnover in Britain of August, 1945, that brought the British Labor party to power. There had been no Parliamentary election for ten years and one was overdue. Churchill would have postponed it until after Japan was crushed, but with Berlin's occupation the Labor party seceded from the coalition government which had won the war, and Churchill agreed to an early election, expecting, as did most people, that he would be returned to office.

The British electorate, however, reversed its precedent of 1919 and voted so heavily in favor of the Labor party that for the first time in its history it not only had a majority but a very substantial one, returning to the House of Commons 390 out of a total membership of 640. The victorious Laborites, it must be remembered, were pledged to socialism. They proposed to nationalize the Bank of England, mining, transportation, steel, and other industries, a very decidedly leftward swing from the point of view of American public opinion, which looked askance at the use of American capital to buttress even mild socialism abroad.

Palestine, also, was a source of friction between the two great branches of the English-speaking world. Millions of Jews had been slaughtered in Europe during the war, but there still remained approximately 1,500,000, most of whom were homeless and stateless, barely kept alive by British and American aid. Desperately anxious to leave Europe forever, the majority cast a wistful eye on Palestine as a potential Jewish state as well as a Jewish homeland.

The British Labor party, out of office, had been bitterly critical of the policy of the British government whereby immigration to Palestine had been reduced to a mere trickle, but once in office it found itself enmeshed in traditional British foreign policy: to admit more Jews to Palestine would not only antagonize the indigenous Arabs, still a considerable majority there, but also the Arab League, a loose federation of five Moslem states hitherto well disposed toward Britain. There were anti-Jewish riots in Palestine; Jews were killed and Jews began to arm themselves, many of them already having been armed by the British. Most of these armed Jews became embittered by the unwillingness of the British to admit the refugee Jews, and a few of them, active terrorists, slew a prominent British official. The British began to disarm the Palestinian Jews, an act widely protested in the United States where anti-British mass meetings demanded the free entry of dispossessed Jews into the Holy Land.

A joint Anglo-American commission recommended the admission of 100,000 immigrants and at the same time the continuation of the British mandate, a solution satisfactory to neither Jew nor Arab, the former insisting on free immigration and the setting up of a Jewish state, the latter proclaiming resistance by force to those two proposals.

President Truman urged the prompt admission of the 100,000 in the name of humanity, promising financial aid in transporting them to their new home; but Britain insisted that the United States should join with her in offering them protection once there, an implication of American military action which found no favor in Congress.

Meanwhile tension increased in Palestine. The Jews refused to give up their arms and a few considered that they were at war with Britain, fighting for their independence. Bridges were dynamited, British officers kidnapped, concentration camps established for Jewish agitators and for several thousand Jews smuggled into the country. In Congress violent anti-British speeches were delivered and threats made to defeat the British loan.

Much more alarming, however, than any friction between Britain and America was the rift gradually widening between the Soviet Union on the one hand and the Western democracies on the other. To the West it looked as though Russian imperialism was on the march. The unilateral Russian annexations of the Baltic states and the extension of Poland deep into Germany, with new boundaries far to the west of those she had enjoyed at the height of her power in the Middle Ages, aroused the fears of the West. In Poland, Rumania, Bulgaria, and Yugoslavia the Russians had promised free elections, promises they ignored. Despite the fact that China had suffered grievously at the hands of Japan, and Russia not at all, the Big Three ceded the Soviets economic and strategic rights in Manchuria such as Russia had not enjoyed since the Russo-Japanese war of 1904-5. Russia likewise annexed the Kuriles and the southern half of Sakhalin; she demanded and obtained control over the northern half of Korea; and she stripped Manchurian factories of machinery under the guise of reparations from Japan, machinery which rightfully should have gone to China. Nor was this all; she invaded an oil-rich province of Iran, despite promises to the contrary; she set up claims to the Dodecanese Islands, the population of which was Greek; she demanded of Turkey territorial concessions in eastern Asia Minor; she asked for control of one of the Italian colonies; she cruelly and abruptly drove into Germany German nationals forced out of Poland, the Baltic states, and Czechoslovakia, in violation of her agreement that such compulsory migrations be conducted in an orderly manner; she forcibly compelled German Social Democrats in her half of occupied Germany to amalgamate with German Communists by methods quite comparable to those used by the Gestapo; and, as Churchill was to assert later, she drew an iron curtain from Stettin on the Baltic to the head of the Adriatic Sea behind which the correspondents of the Western world were forbidden entry. Because of these facts suspicion of future Russian aims was inevitable.

Seen from the Soviet angle, of course, the world of the capitalistic West would stand watching. Americans were seemingly determined to control Japan entirely as they saw fit; they supported the Kuomintang in its perennial strife with the Chinese Communists; they were as deeply involved in oil concessions, so the Russians thought, in Southern Arabia as was Russia in Northern Iran; and what is more, the American President by his very presence on the same platform with Churchill in March, 1946, at Fulton, Missouri, was held to have endorsed that Briton's plea for Anglo-American unity to confront the menace of Russian ideology. As for the British, how could they legitimately complain of Russian garrisons in the Balkans while they kept an army in Greece, ruled Palestine with an iron hand, and, it was darkly hinted, retained Polish forces in Italy in British uniforms, potential mercenary troops for future wars?

Nearly a year after Hiroshima and no action taken in regard to the Danube Valley, the Russians refusing all overtures opening it to world trade. No action yet in regard to Austria, that country still occupied by British, American, and Russian armies. No action yet in regard to Europe's major problem—Germany. As long as that country remained divided into four distinct zones with four distinct administrations, Russian, British, French, and American, its political future was unsettled, its economic life stifled. The Russians accused the British of keeping intact large units of the former Wehrmacht under the guise of labor battalions but really for the purpose of using them at some future day against Moscow. The British accused the Russians of dumping down in the British zone thousands of Germans who would have to be fed by Britain. The French accused the British of utilizing the slowly recovering Ruhr mines for the rehabilitation of German industry rather than for supplying France with needed coal. The Americans in their southern zone, like the British to the north, were confronted with well-nigh insuperable problems, among which bulked large the feeding of huge numbers of dispossessed persons flocking in from Russian-occupied Germany and Poland.

And as for the atomic bomb, no action yet! The Americans were prepared to share its secrets, provided that ironclad agreements were first ratified providing for international inspection and control. To this Russia would be no means agree. She demanded first that all atomic bombs be destroyed and after that an international treaty be drawn, guaranteeing that no more bombs be manufactured. The fulfillment of the treaty would depend on the word of the signatory alone.

Only on relatively minor issues did international agreement prove possible. In July, 1946, an international peace conference, to which twenty-one nations were invited, was held in Paris, and it did, after months of labor, hammer out five peace treaties: with Bulgaria, Rumania, Hungary, Finland, and Italy. Bulgaria, owing to Russian friendship, got off very lightly, being assessed but a few million dollars payable to Yugoslavia and Greece. Rumania formally ceded Bukovina and Bessarabia to Russia and agreed to pay that country $300,000,000 in reparations. Hungary ceded minor regions to Rumania and Czechoslovakia and agreed to pay $300,000,000, mostly to Russia. Harsher treatment was accorded Finland. Not only did Russia extract $300,000,000 from that small country but received in addition the northern province of Petsamo (thus making the Russian and the Norwegian boundaries coterminous), and most of the Karelian peninsula in southern Finland with its large population, including the city of Viborg.

Of the five treaties that with Italy was the only one of much importance. The terms were these: Russia yielded all claims to the Dodecanese and to the Italian colonies; she agreed to limit her reparation bill from Italy to $100,000,000, an estimate of one-twentieth the damage done in invaded Russia by Italian soldiers; France won certain minor rectifications along the Franco-Italian frontier; Italy retained South Tyrol, to which she was not entitled, and almost lost Trieste, which should have gone to her—this owing to Russian insistence that Trieste at the head of the Adriatic go to Yugoslavia. Britain and the United States resisted that Russian demand; and Trieste was placed under international control, a compromise agreeable to no one, unless possibly France who proposed it. Final settlement of colonial questions in Africa was postponed.

The Star of Israel

Despite these treaties, shadows of approaching doom gathered headway almost everywhere in Asia and in Europe. Never perhaps in recorded history had there been at any one single time such a widespread area of social and political upheaval. Italy, France, and to a lesser degree Britain faced economic hardships of the first magnitude; Germany, bisected by the Russian iron curtain, lived from hand to mouth, the western half dependent in large measure on food imported from America; Czechoslovakia, Poland, Hungary, and the Balkan countries, succumbing in various degrees and at various rates of speed to communist pressure, were full of turmoil and dissension; the Arab lands of western Asia could not unite even for the purpose of knifing Israel during its birth pangs; India, freed from the British raj, was split in twain by religious fanaticism and intermittent bloodletting; unhappy Chinese Nationalists and Communists were at each other's throats; and in the islands of the South Seas the feeble Republic of Indonesia strove to become viable in a world semiparalyzed with torpor, hunger, and despair.

About the only ray of sunshine in the storm-tossed Eastern Hemisphere shone from the star of Israel in Vermont-sized, sterile Palestine, where in a short time indomitable courage, pertinacity, and vigor made clear what human brain and brawn might do.

In 1947, the United Nations decreed that Palestine be partitioned. Their decision was ignored by Jew and Arab, and Britain, weary of her thankless task, renounced her mandate and withdrew her garrison the following spring. Forthwith the Jews, in quick defiance of the United Nations, proclaimed the new state of Israel.

That act looked like madness. The Jews were outnumbered two to one in Palestine by the Arabs, and on the borders of that land to the north, east, and south were the armies of the Arab League, Lebanon, Syria, Iraq, Transjordan, and Egypt. The Jews were widely scattered. The majority were huddled on the long and pitifully narrow coastal plain, while the hill towns to the east were held by the Arabs. A large minority dwelt in isolated colonies surrounded by a sea of Arabs—north near Lake Galilee, far south in the windswept Negeb, and in the Jewish quarter of Jerusalem. What chance Israel? Little wonder "it was predicted that when King Farouk's Egyptian army marched the 650,000 Jews who occupied the coastal plain would be hurled into the sea." [1]

The Jews, however, with their backs to the sea, fought like wildcats. The Arabs only pretended to fight. Speedily the Israelis, as they choose to be called, were in possession of all Galilee. They soon opened a wide corridor from Tel Aviv to Jerusalem, occupying the greater part of that city; they drove the boastful Egyptians far to the south, and they struck

[1] K. W. Bilby, *New Star in the Near East*, p. 8.

THE INAUGURATION OF CHAIM WEIZMANN AS FIRST PRESIDENT OF ISRAEL

through the Negeb all the way to the Red Sea, thus making possible a new port for Israel and cutting off Jordan from Egypt.

Hailed as a miracle, it was not exactly one. Bad blood among the members of the Arab League accounted in part for the Israeli triumph. The Hasamite (heretical) kingdom of Jordan east of the Dead Sea and the Jordan River had a wily ruler, Abdullah, suspected by the other Arab lands of treachery and of being willing to sell out his fellow league members to further his ambition to become King of Palestine. Then, too, the Israeli were the better armed; from America came money to buy arms and from Czechoslovakia came most of the war matériel which it bought.

Nevertheless the Israeli victory was astonishing evidence that men fresh from the ghettos and concentration camps of Europe, who had never held a gun in their hands, could fight—and women too, for the Israeli forces of from 25,000 to 40,000 contained women in large numbers.

But it was not the victory in the field that made the birth of Israel (admitted to the United Nations as the fifty-ninth member in May, 1949) so noteworthy as it was the ordered discipline and self-sacrificing cohesiveness of the Israeli people under their Prime Minister, Ben-Gurion. Pipe lines were laid for irrigation across the desert Negeb, bedraggled Arab villages turned almost overnight into prosperous communities, orange groves sprung up in place of sand dunes. The hearty welcome given to Jews of every age, nationality, class, and degree of infirmity from all over the known world (many of them too weak and too old ever to be capable of earning their own sustenance) and the vigorous give-and-take of parliamentary debate in the Knesset, Israeli's Parliament: these were encouraging proofs of what democracy, energy, and good will can accomplish.

Good will, unfortunately, for Jews but not for Arabs, some 800,000 in number, exiles from their old home, without hope and for the most part without shelter or sufficient food, eking out a miserable existence on the borders of Israel. Yet in that country, it must be remembered, in three short years the population had shot up from 650,000 to over 1,000,000, and the immigrants were still arriving at the rate of from 15,000 to 16,000 a month. The resources of the Israeli were stretched to the limit. That is one reason why they refuse to accept more than 100,000 of the displaced Arabs.

The Peoples Democracies

Slowly but with ever increasing momentum the greater part of the world gravitated into two antagonistic camps, one under the somewhat hesitant leadership of the United States, the other under the domination of Soviet Russia. Well within the Russian camp were those countries called, in the well-known upside-down logic of Soviet semantics, "Peoples

Democracies." They were: Albania, Yugoslavia, Bulgaria, Rumania, Poland, Czechoslovakia, Hungary, North Korea, and somewhat later China.

These Peoples Democracies, or Russian satellites, were not fully developed communist states like Russia, nor were their political and economic systems completely uniform. The one common denominator which they all had with one another and with Russia was that they were all police states in which minority groups of disciplined communists seized power by force and violence, intimidating, imprisoning, and sometimes torturing all whom they suspected of opposing their tyrannical will.

The process by which this was brought about was fourfold: first came infiltration, communists posing as simply desirous of forming Popular Front governments; second, the securing of certain key posts in the government, such as minister of justice, and minister of the interior, to whom generally was entrusted the police power; third, an election in which there would be but one ticket, that of the Popular Front; and finally, the expelling from office of all non-communist officials, thus creating a monolithic communist regime.

Of these Peoples Democracies in Eastern Europe four deserve special mention: Poland, to show how expediency triumphed over justice at Yalta; Czechoslovakia, because the brutal communist coup d'état by which she lost her freedom should have demonstrated long before the Korean War that Communists would stop at nothing to gain their objective; Hungary, as an illustration of how communism can vary from place to place in choice of methods; and Yugoslavia, as proof that Russian threats sometimes backfire.

At its onset the Second World War was fought by the West on behalf of Polish independence. The Polish government in exile was recognized by Britain and the United States as an ally, and a Polish army assembled by it, and under its orders, fought bravely in North Africa and in Italy. Nevertheless both Roosevelt and Churchill turned their back on the London Poles. Victorious Russia placed in authority in Poland a committee of Communist Poles and Russian stooges. Russia, Britain, and the United States then agreed at Yalta that Poland was to be governed by a provisional government composed of the Russian-backed Lublin Poles, with the addition of a number of democratic and non-Communist Poles, thus broadening the provisional government so that all parties would be represented in it until democratic elections could be held.

Soon it happened that Russia vetoed the appointment of men from the government-in-exile in London, even that of Mikolajczyk, Prime Minister. Followed then the mysterious disappearance in Sovietland of sixteen prominent non-Communist Poles invited to Moscow to talk over plans for the enlarged provisional government.

At Yalta it was also promised that there would be free elections. To guarantee their freedom some supervision was essential. None was permitted. At Yalta, Molotov assured Roosevelt and Churchill that the elections would be held in a few months. They were postponed a year and a half by the new Polish government, the time set being midwinter, 1947, when, owing to inclement weather and impassable roads, thousands of peasants could not vote. The elections were a farce. Mikolajczyk, head of the Peasant's Party, largest in prewar Poland, was pressured to join the so-called Popular Front set up by the Communists but refused. The pro-Communist provisional government then saw to it that his followers were refused UNRRA relief, that they were dismissed from all government jobs, that they were imprisoned on absurd charges, that neither radio time nor newspaper space was afforded them, that government agents alone corrected the ballots.

Thus the Popular Front won the election, and almost instantly shed its sheep's clothing and transformed itself into a purely Communist regime, recognized now as the government of Poland by Britain and the United States. The latter, against the earnest solicitation of the American ambassador, granted a $70,000,000 credit to the Communist Poles.

In Czechoslovakia the story was somewhat different. The Czechs, the only truly democratic people in Eastern Europe, believed Russia their friend. It was not Russia but England and France that sold them down the river at Munich and there had been no instance in the past of bad faith on the part of the Russians. Then, too, it was the Red army that liberated Prague in 1945 from the hated Germans. True, General Patton with his tank-men could have done it sooner had his army not been halted, a fact which we may well regret now.

Czechoslovakia was a democracy from its birth after World War I until February, 1948, when within one month it became a Moscow satellite. The story runs as follows: in Czechoslovakia there were several political parties, that of the Communists in 1947 being the largest. The government was a coalition and Beneš had appointed a Communist to head the police. The cabinet voted to reprimand that latter official for filling his ranks with Communists. He refused to heed their warning. Several members of the cabinet resigned in protest. Instantly armed Communists seized the party headquarters of the resigning ministers, purged the parliament of non-Communist deputies, purged the press, purged the university, purged even the numerous athletic associations of anti-Communist critics. Czechoslovakia became a police state and a Peoples Democracy at one and the same time that unhappy spring of 1948, as a new constitution based on that of Russia was adopted and an election was held in which the Czechs were presented with a list of hand-picked delegates to their parliament, the only ones for whom they could vote.

In Hungary, again, procedure differed. In that country a radical agrarian party, that of the Small Landowners, had carried the elections in

1945, Communists gaining but seventeen per cent of the votes. From the Communist point of view peasant proprietorship was anathema and it would never do to have socialistic reforms carried out by democratic parliament. To get rid of Nagy, Prime Minister, was their first aim, and this they succeeded in doing by economic threats in regard to reparations and by military threats from the occupying Red army. Nagy in Switzerland hesitated to return to Budapest. At the same time he also feared for the safety of his small son in that city. A bargain was struck: the boy was delivered to the father and the latter resigned.

The Communists now persuaded parliament to expel some twenty members. The purged parliament quietly submitted, and another Peoples Republic was born. It ran head on into a fight with the Roman Catholic Church. The head of the Catholic hierarchy in Hungary, Cardinal Mindszenty, fought vigorously for the retention of religious education and the property rights of monastic orders. He was arrested and tried for high treason in 1949 with the results quite typical of such trials behind the iron curtain—in other words, the Cardinal pleaded guilty and confessed that he had plotted against the state. There can be little doubt but that his confession was forced from him by torture of one kind or another. He was sentenced to life imprisonment. Not quite so fortunate was Rajk, Nagy's successor as prime minister. Although a Communist he indulged in that dangerous pastime of having ideas of his own. Rajk, tried as an agent of Western imperialism, was promptly executed the same year.

One Peoples Republic, that of Yugoslavia, revolted against the rule of the Kremlin. For a good two years after Potsdam, Yugoslavia was at one with the Soviet Union in both ideology and practice. Mammoth portraits of Stalin the Great hung side by side with those of Tito, the Yugoslav dictator, and the harsh and brutal treatment accorded to all nonconformists in the Peoples Democracies was as pronounced in Yugoslavia as elsewhere behind the iron curtain. The Yugoslavs, however, were a proud people. From their point of view Bulgars, Rumanians, Albanians, and Poles might feel they owed their liberation to the Red army if they wanted to. Not so the Yugoslavs! Never throughout the war had they bent their knee to the German invader, who already was in swift retreat by the time the Russians came. Yugoslavs regarded Stalin with awe as head of the Soviet family; but Tito was quite on a par with the Russian in their esteem and far closer to their hearts as their own Yugoslav deliverer. Therefore, although willing to join the Cominform and to uphold the doctrines of Marx-Leninism, the Yugoslavs would do so as Russia's ally, not as a Russian satellite.

There was no open break with Moscow until 1948, for Marshal Tito needed Russian help in his demands for Trieste and Carinthia which he hoped to detach from Austria, but he had nevertheless been irritated by increasing Soviet pressure similar to that used in Bulgaria and Rumania.

This took the form primarily of Russian interference with Tito's control of his own army, and a demand that Yugoslavia submit her economy to Russian supervision and provide raw materials in return for manufactured goods to be delivered from behind the iron curtain.

Tito balked: he drove out of his country Russian officers who dared interfere with his army; he would brook no interruption of his own five-year plan to make Yugoslavia economically independent. The result was a complete break with Moscow and her satellites. Anti-Tito Soviet agents swarmed into Yugoslavia and were arrested and imprisoned by the proud Tito. Poland and Czechoslovakia now cancelled their commercial treaties with Yugoslavia. Hungarian, Rumanian, Bulgarian, and Albanian armies gathered on her borders. Tito vied now with British and American imperialism as a favorite object of Pravda's vituperation, and Titoism became a deep, dark heresy.

Tito breathed defiance. He built up his army half a million strong; purged it of all disaffected pro-Soviet officers; proclaimed that he, not Stalin, wore the true Marx-Lenin mantle; held Stalin a Russian national-ist, intent on conquering her small neighbor. Tito's military chances seemed none too good, and his likelihood of economic survival slim. His country, about the size of Oregon, had mineral wealth in abundance, but with trade behind the iron curtain prohibited and with no credits with the capitalistic West how was he to survive? Furthermore, fierce and protracted guerrilla war waged against the German invader had ruined cities, bridges, railways.

And so Marshal Tito, still a convinced Communist, turned west for aid. He showed his *bona fides* by evicting Greek Communist bands from his country and so gained commercial credits from England and America; he supported the United Nations in the Korean war as far as he dared, and so American money, earmarked for Marshall aid, was diverted toward Yugoslavia. It came just in time. A crop failure in Yugoslavia of mammoth proportions in 1950 threatened. But as this happened at the very end of that year the American Congress voted a free gift of $37,500,000. If war broke between Russia and the United States, Tito at least might be depended on to immobilize many a Russian division.

Shortly after the conclusion of the war it looked as though two other countries in Eastern Europe might become Peoples Democracies, Greece and Turkey. In Greece, civil war followed in the wake of the retreating Germans. The National Liberation Front (EAM), Greek irregulars, detested the absentee King and refused to surrender their arms to the small British army in Greece representing him. The EAM, radical from the outset, became more and more communist as time passed, and between it, the British army, and those Greeks loyal to the King a sporadic war followed. Greek politics, at no time easy to follow, were in this instance extraordinarily complicated. Unsavory scandals had brought the prestige of the official Greek government, never at a high level, to one even lower. The British, exhausted nervously and financially from the long bitter war, now found themselves embroiled in a nasty minute one, extremely unpopular in England. In 1946, an Allied commission of French, American, and British observers supervised a Greek election. It gave a clear conservative majority; but the EAM, boycotting the election, claimed that it did not represent a majority of the Greek people, a claim disavowed by the neutral observers who asserted that not more than fifteen per cent of the registered voters kept away from the polls. Another plebiscite taken shortly afterwards invited the King to return to Greece. He was an unpopular ruler but still a symbol of anti-Communism. The EAM refused to acknowledge his authority, took to the hills, and continued to fight.

In March, 1947, a bankrupt and shaky Greek government appealed to President Truman for succor. The British, tired of the weary Titan role, intimated they were going to withdraw from Greece altogether. Action on the part of the United Nations proved impossible because of the Russian veto. Whereupon the United States proved to all the world that it had no intention of following the precedent of 1920 and withdrawing into its own shell. By what became known as the Truman Doctrine, Congress voted $400,000,000 for Greek rehabilitation and included Turkey as well as a recipient of American aid.

Most of the money went to Greece. It was spent in building up and equipping the Greek army, bolstering the feeble Greek economy, repairing roads and bridges, digging canals, making war-racked Greece viable. A handful of American officers advised the Greek soldiers on how best to fight the Communist guerrillas; a handful of American civilians, by keeping a tight grip on the expenditure of funds and by threats of withdrawing them altogether, reduced corruption in the Greek government and compelled it to lay heavier taxes on wealthy Greek civilians.

For two years it proved well-nigh impossible to keep Greeks away from one another's throats. Guerrillas burned villages, destroyed crops, terrorized the countryside, kidnapped young boys and took them to neighboring Yugoslavia for indoctrination into Communism. The Greek government rounded up groups of Communists, or suspected Communists, and slew them more or less off hand with but slight attention to judicial decorum. Ultimately, however, when Tito closed his borders to hunted guerrilla bands, it proved possible to wipe them out and by 1950 the semblance of order was restored.

Turkey needed less money and got less, since she had preserved an uneasy neutrality during the war to the last possible moment before declaring for the Allies. But Turkish economy had been rudely undermined during the long conflict, and Russia, once Potsdam was over, made threatening demands for a share in policing the Straits. Therefore, in accordance with the Truman Doctrine of fending off Russian aggression in the Middle East, military and naval equipment was sent by the United States, together with a military commission to help organize Turkish defense.

Western Europe

Of the three major powers in Western Europe—Britain, France, and Italy—only the first managed to avoid internal schism and to keep clear of Communist infiltration. Parliamentary elections in 1945 had put the Labor party firmly in the saddle; but that party had had many a bitter experience with Communists during the period between the two World Wars, and although committed to democratic socialism the right-wing socialists in the British cabinet held a firm grip on governmental policies. The Labor party, busily engaged in nationalizing banks, mines, and railways, regarded with disdain any suggestion that capitalism must be overthrown with force. They were already doing this by sheer weight of votes. Communists in Britain there were; but they buzzed around the fringe of the Labor party and presented no imminent threat.

The British government, to be sure, was confronted with economic problems almost unsolvable. Three and a half million houses had been damaged or destroyed by German bombs, half of Britain's mercantile marine had been sunk by German submarines, export trade had declined nearly a third, and the war debt exceeded £22,000,000,000. Under circumstances such as these how could Britain extend her social services at home, lengthen the age for leaving school, provide free medical care for every citizen, and continue to play an important role in international affairs, supported by an army and a navy?

Nevertheless these things were accomplished, primarily by the highest taxes levied anywhere in the world, and by retaining strict controls over food, clothes, and housing, reducing the standard of living of the upper and middle class, raising that of working folk; and also by the timely assistance of the United States not only by the loan of $2,750,000,000 granted in 1946 but by a large share of the Marshall aid money (known as the ERP, the European Relief Program). For five years after the war everything was in short supply in Britain, more so in fact than during the war years. Nevertheless in the Parliamentary elections of 1950, which the Labor party won by the narrowest of margins, not a single Communist was elected to the House of Commons, even Battersea and the Red Clyde turning their back on Moscow propaganda.

In comparison with Britain, confusion, disillusionment, and despair were widespread in both France and Italy after the war, and to a certain extent still are, despite American intervention (Marshall aid) bringing with it a real degree of economic recovery, and assurance of future military assistance.

The aftermath of the war left France not simply wrecked economically but thoroughly confused, discouraged, and disunited. France, indeed, seemed split three ways, as during the period between the two World Wars: a Communist France, a Social Democratic France, and a relatively conservative France, the latter group attracting more votes than either of the other two but lacking in leadership, unless of course De Gaulle be considered its leader.

That patriotic, Catholic, authoritarian general, accused by his critics as semifascist, was not content with any of the three parties above mentioned. He wanted to stand above party and to that end launched his *Reassemblement du Peuple Français* (Reunion of the French People), calling for a strong France under a strong leader—De Gaulle by implication, since its principal slogan was "De Gaulle to power."

It was difficult to say just where France stood. Cabinets rose and fell with even more than usual French rapidity. Prime ministers shifted back and forth, and in general what was known as "The Third Force," a rather loose combination of Socialist groups in collaboration with the MRP, (*Mouvement Republicain Populaire*), a Roman Catholic party, mildly liberal and opposed to both De Gaulle and to the Communists, retained an uneasy balance of power. Inflation, meanwhile, ran ragged through France; expenditures continued to exceed income; strikes, not all Communist inspired, were numerous; and not until Marshall aid money began pouring into France, 1948-51, was there any indication of economic and industrial recovery.

In Italy the picture was somewhat clearer despite the fact that Italy had suffered far more from the ravages of war than had France. This was due to three factors; the able leadership of De Gasperi, most adroit of all postwar statesmen; the active intervention of the Catholic Church on his behalf; and the vigorous and sustained economic aid reaching Italy from the United States.

The election to the Constituent Assembly to provide a constitution for the new Italian republic showed the Christian Democrats under the Catholic-inspired De Gasperi well in the lead with 207 deputies elected. Communist and Socialist united however, slightly overtopped them in number, and Italian Socialists were decidedly less vigorously opposed to communism than their Social Democratic counterparts in France and Britain.

In 1948 came the first election under the new constitution. It was contested with great bitterness and accompanied by riots which, after the Italian fashion, were more noisy than bloodthirsty. The Catholic Church now entered the fray, threatening excommunication to all who professed communism. The United States having already paid for the greater part of UNRRA relief given Italy, some $450,000,000 for food, now promised further assistance. Italian-born citizens in America were asked to write relatives in Italy counselling against Communists. The U.S. government presented Italy with twenty-nine ships as a token of regard, and both the United States and Britain placed themselves on record as favoring the return of Trieste to Italy.

On the surface the results of the election were a blow to communism. De Gasperi and his Christian Democrats now had a majority over all though a slight one. Nevertheless the Communists polled within a fraction of as many votes as they did in 1946, and were now with 132 seats in parliament the second largest party. It was the Socialists who lost this election rather than the Communists, their deputies being reduced to 82 and badly split at that between right- and left-wing factions. De Gasperi had need for all possible wisdom and acuteness. In his parliament the Communist minority staged nerve-wracking demonstrations; in the countryside the splitting up of the big estates, promised the peasantry, proceeded but at a snail's pace. Italy was a far poorer country than her neighbor, but unlike France had a rapidly increasing population.

Germany

Germany after Potsdam lay prostrate. Four powers—Britain, France, the United States, and Russia—were in complete control. They could agree upon but one thing: prominent Nazi leaders should be tried for crimes against humanity and for plotting war. Twenty-two were brought to trial; three were acquitted; four were sentenced to prison for terms ranging from ten years to life; and twelve received the death penalty. The defendants did plot war; they also were responsible for revolting acts of inhuman cruelty. But did the victors act wisely in this *ex post facto* procedure of defining crimes after and not before the acts perpetrated had been committed? To many a good lawyer it seemed a dubious procedure to invoke the hazy Kellogg-Briand peace pacts as a precedent. Furthermore, one of the judges was a Russian, and it was a known fact that the Russians had murdered some 1,500 Polish officers and men in 1943. The court sternly refused to permit any evidence of this mass murder to be introduced into court—quite naturally, since a Russian judge sat on the bench.

Concerning practically all other matters it proved impossible to agree. The Russians demanded harsher treatment of the enemy than the British and Americans would permit. The Americans brought more Nazis to trial than did the British and objected vigorously to Britain employing Nazis in operating the Ruhr mines. In fact we were so enthusiastic about our denazification program that we jailed little Nazis in droves and so well-nigh crippled German elementary education, for practically all German teachers had been compelled, at least outwardly, to public support of Nazi ideology. Meanwhile the Russians ripped from their zones almost everything moveable, demanded the delivery of more and more machinery from West Germany as reparations due Russia under the Potsdam agreement. They refused admittance of their former allies to their zone refused to make any audit of reparations they had taken from it, refused to give any accounting of the German prisoners of war, and so maltreated the civilian population in their zone and in the Baltic states that a steady stream of exiles from the east added so to the overcrowded western zones that West Germany had as large a population as all of Germany before the war.

Slowly the four former allies drifted into two camps: France, Britain, and America more or less in harmony in one; unyielding and suspicious Russia in the other, objecting to any German peace treaty except on its own terms, equally recalcitrant as regards the revival of German trade and industry.

In the west by 1946, free elections were held to provide for local self-government, and in them the Communist vote averaged about 10 per cent. By the same year elections were held in East Germany, but there Social Democrats were forced to amalgamate with the Communists forming the S.E.D. (Social Unity Party) thus making a farce of political freedom. The Allied Control Council sitting in Berlin was completely stymied by Russian obstruction in all that concerned economic reorganization. Whereupon it happened that the Americans and the British joined their two zones into one in matters economic (Bizonia), a union which the French later joined.

Economic unity necessitated a common currency, and since Russia would not coöperate in any agreement regulating paper money in circulation, the three Western powers printed their own paper money, which speedily became worth far more than that printed by the Russians. As a result of this currency debate the Russians started a blockade of all trains and trucks entering Berlin from the west. But air at least was free, and in 1948 for month after month the citizens of West Berlin, and the French, British, and American troops stationed there, received by air lift not simply the food they ate but also the coal essential for heating and lighting. It proved enormously expensive but it was a boon to the airplane industry in both Britain and America. Possibly that was the reason why Russia dropped her blockade as speedily as she began it.

The split between East and West Germany widened. In 1949 in the west the Länder (the local governments) sent representatives to Bonn to draw up a constitution for a Federal German Republic, so constituted that the Eastern German Länder might later adhere to it. As they did this a Russian-sponsored German state was set up in East Germany.

Elections were now in order, both west and east. In the Bonn elections the Christian Democrats headed the polls with a slight lead over the Social Democrats and were able to organize a majority government by combining their strength with a few minority groups. Out of 432 deputies in the Bonn parliament the Communists elected but 15. The East German elections ran true to form. One voted S.E.D. or else. Many did not vote at all.

Austria meanwhile like Germany was divided into four zones. The course of events, however, ran in smoother channels than in Germany. Time after time it seemed possible that Austria might be confirmed in her independence and that all occupation troops might be withdrawn. Always, however, there stood in the way Russian insistence that Austrian property appropriated by the Nazis should be regarded as reparations due from Germany. Compromise on this point proved impossible.

Western Upswing

Beginning in the summer of 1947 the international skies lightened in one respect—economic recovery. The impetus for this came from the United States where Secretary of State Marshall suggested extensive American assistance for all Europe, both east and west. In one respect this was nothing new. UNRRA, mostly American financed, had already fed millions on both sides of the iron curtain, but UNRRA had at best been but an emergency measure. This time it was suggested that America would grant money on a very large scale, not just for food but to purchase machinery, set up power plants, build factories, and reinvigorate the economic life of the entire continent.

The proposal was scornfully rejected by Russia and her satellites, despite many a wistful glance westward on the part of industrial Czechoslovakia. But the other countries went ahead with implementing the plan with the exception of Franco Spain which was not invited to participate. A bill of particulars was drawn up by sixteen nations at Paris. Their total needs for four years they estimated at $22,440,000,000, a figure reduced by President Truman in presenting the plan to Congress to $17,000,000,000. The latter accepted the plan in principle but did not commit this country to any final figure. Congress said the money should be voted in allotments and a preliminary appropriation for fifteen months of $6,800,000,000 was voted, the spending to be under the directions of an American administrator, Europe coöperating by lowering tariffs between European states and by currency stabilization. This Marshall Plan proved unquestionably a success to all countries participating in it, the United States included. Everywhere it was in operation the standard of living was higher in 1950 than in 1947. The Russians called the plan American imperialism. That it reduced Communist influence in France and Italy and western Germany cannot be doubted.

As in economics so too in political coöperation the West began to draw together. In consequence of a widespread demand a "Council of Europe" opened its doors at Strasbourg. Ten countries participated, Italy, France, and Britain having 18 delegates each in the descending scale to Luxembourg with 3. The powers of the Council were strictly limited, the delegates for the most part but puppets of their home governments.

Italy and a few other countries sought vigorously to enlarge the scope of this pan-European council but without much success.

More important by far than the Council of Europe was the signing at Washington in 1949 of an Atlantic Defense Pact. It was in the nature of an enlarged Western Union, since in addition to the members of that Union now were added Iceland, Denmark, Norway, Canada, Italy, Portugal, and the United States, all pledged to go to war should their forces be attacked in Europe, North Africa, or on the Atlantic. How they would fight, however, and whether they would combine their forces under a joint commander or not were questions left for future negotiation.

Asiatic Problems

As far as all surface indications went the entire structure of Japanese society, political, economic, educational, and cultural, was revolutionized during the five years subsequent to Japan's surrender. In theory Japan was put under a Far Eastern Commission meeting in Washington, consisting of representatives of the eleven countries which declared war on Japan; in practice her destiny was determined by SCAP, another name for Supreme Commander Allied Powers, otherwise our own General of the Army, Douglas MacArthur. Most Japanese seemingly were greatly pleased with the reforms dictated by that American officer. The country was said to have gone democratic almost overnight, Hirohito merely retaining his title of Emperor as titular head of a people who, under a brand-new democratic constitution, were supposed to govern themselves. This meant they followed rather closely MacArthur's advice. Big business in Japan as represented by financial magnates of the old regime was dissolved, land reform inaugurated, the great estates broken up, peasant proprietorship established, shintoism discouraged in religion, education made over so that children might be indoctrinated with democratic theories of life.

Elsewhere in Asia the very ease with which the Japanese during World War II flung down the flimsy structure of Dutch rule in the East Indies made it forever impossible to restore it; in Burma and India the prestige of the British had been so jolted by years of war that even final victory could not bring it back; and in China, Chiang Kai-shek's regime, honeycombed with corruption, accused of capitalism and Western orientation, fell with a thud heard throughout all Asia as Chinese Communists crashed through to victory in 1949.

World War II commenced with India heavily in debt to Britain; it concluded with Britain heavily in debt to India, for the cost of defending India had not been paid by that country but by the British treasury. The British possessed neither the will nor the power to govern India any more. Nothing stood in the way of complete independence except the problem of finding some agency to which the government of India could be entrusted. And so, in 1946, the British sought desperately for some kind of compromise between Moslem and Hindu factions so that a stable government might succeed them.

Ever fertile in political expedients the British proposed a curious three-tiered constitution. The idea was as follows: tier A would be a central government for all of India with very limited powers; tier B would consist of such regional groupings as the various provinces might choose to make; tier C would be the individual provinces and the native states. Little was done to implement this proposed compromise. A constitutional convention was elected but the Moslems boycotted it; they stood out for Pakistan—entire separation from India of the Moslem peoples. Britain decided she could do no more, and in 1947 announced that by June 1, 1948, she would quit India altogether, no matter what the situation might be by that date.

Reaction in India to this announcement was immediate. Rather than risk war, the Indian Congress (Hindu-controlled) agreed to Pakistan, a separate Moslem state, but located in two different regions where there was a Moslem majority, one in the northwest, the other in the northeast. Before the year closed two new dominions were added to the Commonwealth (the adjective British being deleted from it). Pakistan established its capital at Karachi; India, its capital at New Delhi.

Misery and bloodshed followed as Hindus migrated from Pakistan to India and as Moslems migrated from India to Pakistan. Some 4,000,000 people lost their old homes and journeyed to strange lands where no new homes were to be had; very bloody communal riots took heavy toll of human life, and rival armed forces knifed one another in Kashmir, a province claimed both by India and Pakistan. None could dispute but that the population of Kashmir as a whole was Moslem. On the other hand certain sections had a Hindu majority, and over all Kashmir ruled an hereditary Hindu prince. It did not prove easy to enforce an effective cease-fire among hillsmen. Pakistan offered to let the impasse be settled by the collective action of the Commonwealth premiers, an offer rejected by Prime Minister Nehru in January, 1951.

Burma, meanwhile, abandoning all ties with Britain, preferred to go it alone and declared its independence. Ceylon chose dominion status. And so it happened that by the middle of the twentieth century nothing remained of British imperial rule in central and eastern Asia except a tenuous hold on the Federated Malay States and Singapore, and the equally tenuous hold on Hong Kong off the Chinese coast.

Even more complete than the ending of British imperialism in Asia was the death of Dutch imperialism in the East Indies. After the defeat of Japan in 1945 sporadic and indecisive fighting took place there between the Dutch and the native Indonesians on the one hand, and between pro-Communist Indonesians and those opposed to communism on the other. The Dutch did not surrender their control without a token fight and

JAWAHARLAL NEHRU
DISCIPLE OF GANDHI AND PRIME MINISTER
OF THE DOMINION OF INDIA

three times the Council of the United Nations tried to secure a cease-fire agreement between the Dutch and Indonesian republicans. Finally in 1950 Indonesia was recognized as an independent country.

The withdrawal of the Japanese from China marked the commencement of civil war there in deadly earnest. For three years, 1946-48, it raged fiercely, first Nationalist China (Chiang and the Kuomintang), then Communist China having the upper hand. Beneath the surface, however, a steady deterioration of the morale of the Chinese Nationalist party was taking place while that of Mao and his Communists grew stronger.

The United States government, with the best of intentions, intervened between the contestants and lost the good will of both. We tried to force the Nationalists to coöperate with the Communists and to inaugurate reforms—a policy which angered the Nationalists. We gave arms and ammunition to the Nationalists—a policy which angered the Communists, who asserted that our frequent ultimatums to Chiang were meaningless. Corruption, incompetence, wildcat inflation, and ruinous taxation sapped the will of the Nationalists to resist. Nineteen-hundred and forty-nine, and the collapse came. The Communists crossed the Yangtse and Chiang changed his capital from Nanking to Canton; the Communists advanced south and Chiang changed to Chungking; the Communists drove west and Chiang flew to Taiwan (Formosa) where such few troops as remained loyal to him had already gathered. October, 1949, at Peking the Peoples Republic of China was founded, with Mao at its head—as Chairman of the Peoples Revolutionary Committee, the same Mao who had led the long march of the Chinese Communists in the early thirties from southeast China to the semi-barren northwest, Chiang's armies in close pursuit. Now the tables were reversed.

Mao's victory gave rise to a host of new problems. China, together with England, France, Russia, and the United States, was one of the permanent members of the Council of the United Nations. Somewhat over forty vetoes of Soviet Russia had already done much to retard the usefulness of the UN, and if the vote of Communist China were added to that of the Soviets, it is evident that Stalin's power to hold up the pressing demand for world government would be strengthened. Nevertheless Mao's government was the *de facto* government of China, and in accordance with international practice, American as well as European, it should receive recognition. Logically it followed then that Nationalist China should lose her seat in the Council and that Communist China should inherit it.

Almost immediately England, India, and a number of other countries recognized Mao's China. American recognition of Mao's government hung fire. What should we do? The answer came on June 26, 1950, when the Communist government of North Korea flung its troops across the 38th parallel.

Chapter 43

KOREAN WAR AND AFTERMATH

KOREA, AN INDEPENDENT country before the Russo-Japanese War of 1904-5, fell under Japanese control, and a few years later was officially annexed to Japan. At Potsdam, Korea was bisected at the 38th parallel, to be occupied north of that line by the Russian army, to the south by the American, until such time as Korea might become a self-governing democratic country.

Within a year it was painfully evident that there could be no agreement as to how this was to be done. In the north the Russians promptly set up a Peoples Democracy on the customary lines, armed the Koreans in their zone heavily, closed the frontier to all non-Communist visitors. In the south the Americans encouraged free democratic elections, and as a result there sprang up a plethora of political parties which called for a convention of all Korean factions to establish a constitution for the whole of Korea. North Korea sent no delegates but the South Koreans went ahead and inaugurated a government of their own. A committee of the United Nations authorized to investigate the situation was refused admission to North Korea, and in the meantime the United States Army evacuated South Korea, leaving behind a few score of military personnel to assist the South Koreans in organizing their own army.

The invasion of South Korea by the armies of the North Korean Peoples Republic, reactivated the semi-paralysed United Nations. The Council (Russia being absent) authorized armed aid for the South Koreans. General MacArthur, our proconsul in Japan, on the order of President Truman, immediately sent such few American troops as were available. On came the North Koreans, amply supplied with tanks but with few planes. Seoul fell before their onslaught, and by midsummer the Americans and their South Korean allies were driven to the southeast corner of the peninsula with its excellent port of Pusan within easy reach of Japan.

Russia now hurried back to the Council of the UN. It was too late for her to veto the action of the Council; but she could and did denounce the United States for what the Russians termed the American invasion of Korea and Formosa. The South Koreans were about to attack the North

Koreans, so said the Russians, and the latter were but defending their homeland. At best it was only a civil war which was no concern of the United States. As for Formosa, there was no invasion; but it was true that President Truman had ordered the immunization of that island for the time being by the Seventh Fleet to prevent the war from spreading. Meanwhile American reinforcements poured into Korea.

In the autumn the UN forces struck back. An American army transported by sea landed at Inchon on the west coast near Seoul. Thanks to superb naval coöperation and brilliant tactics Seoul was recaptured and the North Korean Army outflanked, caught now between two fires, one from the south from the Pusan area, the other from the north and east from that of Seoul.

The North Korean forces surrendered in droves and melted away into the hills. MacArthur in hot pursuit did not stop at the 38th parallel, but, armed with a UN mandate to restore order in Korea, speeded his men north so rapidly that in a few weeks some of his detachments had reached the Yalu River, boundary between Korea and Manchuria. Quickly then the wheels of fate reversed. Out from their lairs in Manchuria poured Chinese Communist troops outnumbering the UN forces ten to one. MacArthur ordered retreat. Skilfully it was conducted. The victorious Chinese soon were in the capital of North Korea; they crossed the 38th parallel; they entered Seoul; they drove south from that ruined city, boasting that their enemy soon would be back at Pusan, ultimately forced to evacuate all Korean soil.

Then, in this seesaw conflict the fortunes of war suddenly were reversed. United Nations troops, heavily reinforced, drove north again. In March, 1951, they recaptured Seoul for the second time. In April, they were surging over the 38th parallel once more.

As this happened General MacArthur, demanding that the war be pushed to a victorious conclusion and that the invading Chinese be driven out of Korea, was removed from his command by President Truman. The presidential reasons as given were that the General disobeyed orders and criticized his commander-in-chief by corresponding with hostile politicians. But in the background, and supporting the President, were the chiefs of staff, inclined to agree with General Bradley that this was the wrong war and in the wrong place, and might lead to a third World War with a large American army tied down in a mountainous Asiatic country.

This also was the opinion of our allies in the United Nations. MacArthur was an American general, but he commanded United Nations troops. Serving under him in 1951 were British, Australian, New Zealand, South African, Canadian, Ethiopian, French, Turkish, Greek, and Filipino detachments, with Denmark, Italy, Sweden, and India providing

UNITED NATIONS TROOPS IN KOREA

hospital facilities. The brunt of the fighting was done by South Koreans and Americans, their total casualties running over ninety-five per cent of the United Nations total. Even so it was a United Nations army, and to continue the war without the backing of that organization would have had a deleterious effect on its power to preserve peace and to combat communism, not only in Asia but throughout the world.

"There is no substitute for victory," said MacArthur. We have attained victory, said his critics in the United States and in Europe. A Communist coup d'état has failed. The Communist world has learned a lesson. Aggression does not pay.

And so Washington agreed to negotiate an armistice with the North Koreans and the Chinese invaders. It took two years, from July, 1951, to July, 1953, to do so, while by mutual understanding military operations came almost to a standstill. When finally signed, the armistice established a boundary line between North and South Korea, roughly along the 38th parallel, thus bringing back the *status quo ante* of 1950. Neither side was to reinforce its troops, no new airfields were to be built, prisoners were to be repatriated, or if they refused to return whence they had come, they were to be set free, and an international committee was to see to it that the armistice was observed. The future status of Korea was to be determined by an international conference to be held in Geneva in 1954.

It met that year and promptly deadlocked. The North Koreans proposed elections in which they, with twenty-five per cent of the population, were to have equal weight with South Koreans with seventy-five per cent. In this they were supported by the Chinese, and the Russians who had been invited to attend. The sixteen nations which had repelled aggression supported a settlement which called for elections under UN supervision to elect an assembly chosen by equal electoral districts throughout all Korea. To this the Communist bloc would not agree.

The Chinese Nationalists in Formosa also came into the picture. They continued to hold China's seat in the council of the United Nations, and the Seventh U.S. fleet continued to protect them against attack from the Communist mainland. The Americans were publicly committed to defend Formosa and the Pescadores Islands close to Formosa. But what if the Chinese Communists should try to conquer off-shore islands close to the mainland, held by the Nationalists; would America fight to protect them? No one knew what would happen in such a contingency, since Washington simply reserved freedom of action.

In Korea, meanwhile, the South Koreans complained justly that the Chinese and the North Koreans did not adhere to the armistice but kept on preparing for another round. Only by the United States imposing strict limitations on the gasoline and munitions available were the South Koreans restrained from hurling themselves on the foe.

Indochina

As these events took place another civil war in Eastern Asia, intermittently raging for seven years, approached a climax. After the Second World War French Indochina had been reorganized into three states, Laos, Cambodia, and Vietnam. The last was the largest and most populous. And here an anti-French, pro-nationalist and pro-communist revolt had broken out as early as 1942.

It was led by Ho Chi Minh and was fought, ostensibly to make Vietnam independent of France. The French made concession after concession, but unfortunately the puppet emperor they set up in Vietnam, Bao-Dai, was more playboy than statesman, and what at first was considered a minor rebellion drifted into full-fledged civil war, Vietminh (the nationalist rebels) against Vietnam (pro-French loyalists), supported by a French army of 100,000 and by war material supplied by the United States.

As fighting died down in Korea it became accentuated in Indochina. United States rifles, lend-leased to Chiang Kai-shek before he was driven from the Chinese mainland, were used by the Vietminh rebels, and Mao,

Communist ruler of China, proclaimed the Indochina war another evidence of United States plotting against Asiatic freedom. By 1954 it was evident that Vietminh was winning. In May of that year Dien Bien Phu, a strong fortress in North Vietnam, capitulated after a long siege, and the Red River delta, including the important port of Hanoi, fell to the rebels.

Again, as in Korea, peace of a kind was patched up between two contending factions. Once more a country was bisected, in this instance by a line drawn at the 17th parallel. North of it Ho Chi Minh set up a Communist government. To the South there was to be a democratic regime, France assenting to its independence. Finally, in 1956, elections were to be held in both North and South to determine the future of Vietnam.

Nato, Seato, and Bandung

The Chinese revolution which put communism in the saddle, and the subsequent events in Korea and Indochina were striking proof of the effectiveness of Communist propaganda. Repercussion in the West was immediate. The democratic countries had no time to waste. They must unite in fact as well as in spirit if they were to withstand communism. Temporarily they had stopped it seeping westward. But now all Asia was in danger.

Preliminary steps toward Western unity had been taken in 1947 by the formation of a North Atlantic Treaty Organization (NATO). But thus far it had been a gesture, a statement of policy, no muscle or sinew to it.

The Korean War changed all that. In 1950 the United States voted $3,500,000,000 to supply NATO with arms. Eisenhower was appointed supreme commander, and SHAPE (Staff Headquarters Allied Powers in Europe) became a physical fact. Some 28 divisions were immediately available on the continent with more to follow. This was not much against 100 Russian divisions; but NATO was armed with atomic artillery, and it was felt that this army, small as it was, could prevent any sudden engulfment of Western Europe by the Soviets. Meanwhile a semicircle of NATO airfields stretching from England through North Africa to Iraq threatened instant retaliation—if Russia started war. With Greece and Turkey joining NATO some fourteen countries were thus united in a grand alliance.

Germany was the unknown factor. Unless and until German support was assured NATO could not long withstand a Soviet march to the Atlantic. But to admit the German Federal Republic (West Germany)

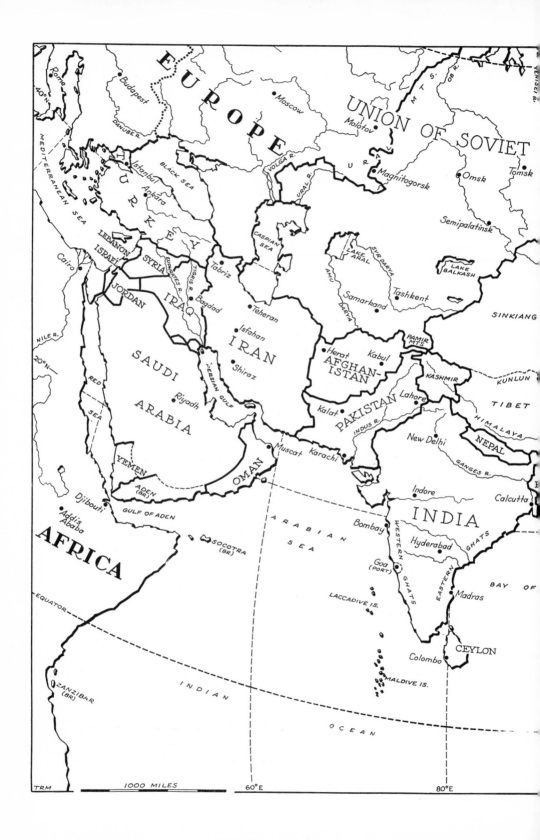

ASIA
1954

ARCTIC CIRCLE   LENA R.

SEA OF OKHOTSK   KAMCHATKA

SAKHALIN I. (USSR)

KURILE IS. (USSR)

OCIALIST REPUBLICS

S I B E R I A

40° N

LAKE BAIKAL

Khabarovsk

NORTH PACIFIC OCEAN

Irkutsk   Chita

KHINGAN

AMUR R.

MANCHURIA

Harbin

Vladivostok

JAPAN

Ulan Bator

MONGOLIAN PEOPLE'S REPUBLIC

Mukden

PEOPLE'S REP. OF NORTH KOREA

SEA OF JAPAN

Tokyo

Yokohama

MTS.

GOBI DESERT

Peking

Dairen

REP. OF SOUTH KOREA

Seoul

Osaka

BONIN IS.

HWANG R.

Tientsin

YELLOW SEA

IWO JIMA

CHINESE

Lanchow

Nagasaki

EAST CHINA SEA

20° N

PEOPLE'S REP.

Nanking

Shanghai

Hankow

Changsha

Foochow

RYUKYU ISLANDS

OKINAWA

MARIANAS

SAIPAN

Chungking

YANGTSE

Amoy

Taipei

FORMOSA (NAT. CHINA)

GUAM (USA)

Canton

Macao (PORT)

Hong Kong (BR)

CAROLINE IS.

BURMA

MAPUTRA R.

MEKONG R.

Hanoi

Kwangchowan (FR)

HAINAN

LUZON

PHILIPPINE REPUBLIC

PALAU I.

Mandalay

IRRAWADDY R.

SALWEEN R.

LAOS

VIET NAM

Hué

Manila

Rangoon

THAILAND

FRENCH INDO-CHINA

LEYTE

SOUTH PACIFIC OCEAN

NGAL

ANDAMAN IS.

Bangkok

CAMBODIA

SOUTH CHINA SEA

Iloilo

MINDANAO

BAR IS.

GULF OF THAILAND

Saigon

SPRATLEY I.

Zamboanga

Sandakan

MOROTAI

EQUATOR

Brunei

MALAYA

SARAWAK (BR)

Hollandia

DUTCH NEW GUINEA

STR. OF MALACCA

Singapore (BR)

BORNEO

MOLUCCAS

CERAM

CELEBES

I N D O N E S I A

SUMATRA

(PORT)

Darwin

AUSTRALIA

Jogjakarta

JAVA

TIMOR

100° E

120° E

140° E

to NATO meant a German army, and it seemed incongruous that a war to disarm Germans should be followed by rearming them. The French opposed doing so. There were 50,000,000 Germans in West Germany and France feared them quite as much as Communist armies. On the other hand, if the Germans were rebuffed by the democracies there was always a chance that they might be cajoled by the Russians to join their side; and that would make matters even worse.

Followed then the compromise plan of Premier Faure of France. This was the EDC (European Defense Community), an army organized on a purely international basis but subject to orders from NATO. Conscripts from West Germany, France, Italy, Belgium and the Netherlands would compose this international army which would wear its own uniform. In its divisions the various nationalities would be mixed. This scheme, it was thought, would prevent the recrudescence of a German national army, as such, with German divisions taking orders from a German general staff.

The French National Assembly, however, voted down the EDC, and hope for the alignment of the German republic with the West diminished. Whereupon a new French premier, Mendès-France, with the help of Britain secured membership for Germany in NATO. A principal objection to EDC was that Britain had refused to join. Now, to save the day for European unity, she pledged herself not to withdraw her forces from Germany without the consent of the Western Union (see p. 895). This promise led France to consent to a German army of 500,000 and to Germany joining NATO. And by doing so the German Federal Republic won recognition at last as an independent national state, the only limitation on her sovereignty being the right of Britain, France, and the United States to retain troops in Germany until a final peace treaty was signed, together with certain restrictions on the type of weapons Germans might manufacture.

The German people were far from enthusiastic about this new army. To most of them it was only the lesser of two evils. What they wanted first of all was the unity of all Germany, and since Soviet Russia was adamant against having this brought about by free elections there seemed no way of obtaining their heart's desire except to join NATO and so bring pressure against Russia. Very slowly and cautiously they set about creating this new army. It must be a democratic army and as unlike the late Wehrmacht as possible. By 1956 but a mere handful of recruits had been sworn in.

NATO might offer protection to the West against Communist aggression; but how about Southeast Asia? The Indochina settlement had been a Communist victory. In northern Vietnam was the rich rice-producing valley of the Red River, the important city of Hanoi, and

Eastfoto

PREMIER CHOU EN-LAI DELIVERS A SPEECH AT THE BANDUNG CONFERENCE (APRIL, 1955)

far more than half the population of Vietnam was now securely within the Communist orbit. Furthermore, France was utterly discredited as a colonial power in Asia, and the United States, supplier of arms to the French, apparently was unable to stem the Communist tide.

Communism was on the march, south and east. To build a bulwark against its further spreading, a meeting of anti-communist states was held at Manila. Thus was born SEATO (Southeast Asia Security Organization) intended as a kind of NATO for the Far East. Australia, New Zealand, Britain, France, and the United States were the non-Asiatic countries. Pakistan, Thailand and the Philippines represented the non-communist nations in Asia. India, Burma, and Ceylon were all invited. All three refused to join, the first two because they preferred to remain neutral in the cold war, Ceylon on the plea that her primary interest lay in the Colombo Plan which proposed to set up on a very modest scale, a kind of Marshall Plan for Asia.

Whether SEATO was more than a gesture remains to be seen. Its program for holding back communism expressly excluded Formosa, and there was no proviso, as with NATO, for a SEATO army with a commander-in-chief. In 1956 it did give a demonstration as to how it might aid Thailand in case of attack. Manoeuvres of a kind were held there. They were not impressive. Pakistan refused to join them on the ground that she had not been properly notified. A task force of American marines and Filipino troops paraded in Thailand, supported by British and American warships. That was all.

Meanwhile an Afro-Asiatic conference was held at Bandung, Indonesia, presumably inspired by Communists although that was not openly stated. Bandung was attended by Chou En-lai, foreign minister of Communist China, Nehru of India, Nu of Burma, Nasser, prime minister of Egypt, the President of Liberia, and a few other Africans, mainly Arabs. The keynotes struck were anti-imperialism, anti-colonialism, and Asiatic and African nationalism. Bandung did not formally organize for future activity as did SEATO. It refused to take any direct stand in a world conflict arising over communism. But it did serve as a platform for Chinese Communists to denounce American imperialism and for Nehru to put India in the category of neutralist states along with Burma and Indonesia. Israel, although an Asiatic country, was not invited. To have asked her would have angered the Arab world.

African Nationalism

The end of French rule in Indochina was not simply a Communist victory; it also was one for Asiatic nationalism. And the latter in turn was symbolic of worldwide antagonism to white domination over all colored races and in all continents.

This was as true of Africa as of Asia, the main difference being that African nationalism was a more recent phenomenon and seemingly immune to communist ideology until the middle of this century.

With the crushing defeat of France in Indochina Arab nationalism in Morocco, long simmering, broke out in menacing riots, bloodshed, and petty war.

Hitherto it had been relatively easy to suppress. In the ancient practice of *divide et impera* the French had been greatly aided by El Glaoui, a mighty feudal lord with a private army of his own of Berber tribesmen who hated the Arab folk in Moroccan cities. The Istaqulil, party of independence, had been driven to cover. The Sultan, said to favor it, had been exiled to Madagascar, and a Moroccan stooge exalted to the Peacock's Throne. Furthermore, the French Foreign Legion, composed largely of former German soldiers, hitherto had made physical revolt hazardous.

But that same legion had been defeated in Indochina and its prestige was shattered. Mendès-France, engineer of French withdrawal from Asia, now had a new problem—how was the French Empire to be rescued in Morocco?

Mendès-France was conciliatory. He promised reform and ultimate freedom for Morocco. But he had no intention of repealing the laws against the Istaqulil or of recalling the exiled Sultan. Whereupon violence erupted into the open. The Nationalists took to the sword, slaying many French *coloni*, Frenchmen who had settled permanently in Morocco, of whom there were a half million. The Foreign Legion tried to protect them and many died on both sides. To prevent this petty war from spreading, the old Sultan was brought back and reinstated. The prestige of El Glaoui was destroyed. He crawled on his hands and knees before the Sultan he had driven out of Morocco, but received no forgiveness. In 1956 he died just as an important election was held in France that left no man and no party to deal firmly with a crisis which threatened not merely Morocco but Algeria and Tunisia.

Algeria by law was Metropolitan France, an integral part of France itself, sending representatives to the National Assembly at Paris. But in the critical years 1955-56, elections were postponed owing to anarchy and bloodshed in Algeria. Formidable Arab revolts and the murder of the French coloni brought about a situation far beyond the control of the Foreign Legion, and many thousand French troops had to be flown in from France.

The Arab world, stirred up by the Cairo radio, took up the hue and cry of anti-colonialism, and temporarily the Arab delegates at the United Nations won a majority to put Algeria on the agenda. The French in high dudgeon left the UN but decided to return.

In Tunisia the situation was roughly parallel. Here nationalistic demonstrations had been suppressed, the Neo-Destour Party sponsoring them declared illegal, its founder exiled. Tunisia was not pacified. The slaying of French coloni continued. Mendès-France flew to Tunis. Complete autonomy was promised, the ban on Neo-Destour removed, its founder returned in triumph as premier.

Everywhere in North Africa the story was the same. The victorious Nationalists were Arab Moslems, not Communists, and their revolt was as much religious and racist as economic. But in the background lay great poverty and the fact that a few thousand French coloni owned most of the land that was fertile.

Within a year everything drifted from bad to worse. France was unable to withdraw with dignity and prestige from North Africa as had Britain from India. The weak coalition government of Mendès-France gave way to one still weaker under Faure, and that to one weaker yet under Mollet.

The parliamentary election of 1956 brought despair to all friends of France. Now there was not only no majority for any party but seemingly no possible coalition. The old Radical party, which hitherto had served as a rallying ground for men of moderate opinion, was split in two, to the advantage of the Communists, who won the greatest number of seats. A new party in this land of splinter groups appeared on the extreme right composed of reactionary shopkeepers called Poujadists. The Socialists came in second. But they hated Communists and were hated by them. And even if these two parties had united they would have been short of a majority.

Only by adding together Communists, Socialists, and the Radicals who swore by Mendès-France would it be possible to form a government. But Mendès-France had little use for Socialists and hated all Communists. If the men who followed him had been willing to join forces with those Radicals under Faure they might have formed a government with the help of the moderate MRP and certain splinter groups. But Mendès-France and Faure were at swords' points, and both were antagonistic to the MRP.

There was thus almost a complete deadlock. Temporarily it was solved by electing Mollet, a Socialist, premier. At any moment the Communists had it in their power to oust him; so also could Mendès-France with his assorted Radicals, who chose for the time being only to back Mollet.

France no longer, except by courtesy, could be called a first-class power. With Indochina lost, Morocco and Tunis declared independent, and an insurrection in Algeria rapidly assuming the gravity of civil war she was in sorry plight.

Desperately France tried to hold Algeria. Some 1,000,000 Europeans had their homes there, most of them Frenchmen, confronted by 9,000,000 restive Arabs inflamed by the heady wine of Arab Nationalism. Mollet offered olive branches, suggested partial autonomy; all in vain, the insurrection became more ominous. To defeat it 100,000 French troops were detached from French NATO forces sent to Algeria. They proved insufficient. Another 100,000 reservists were summoned to the colors. And as this happened a sharp Parliamentary battle followed between Mendès-France, demanding fresh concessions to the rebels, and Mollet, asserting that the preservation of order must have precedence. All this Moscow noted without disfavor, knowing full well that a telegram sent to Paris would spell Mollet's downfall.

Vigorous demonstrations on behalf of African nationalism were not confined to northwest Africa. To a greater or less degree nationalistic tomtoms reverberated throughout the entire dark continent.

Particularly true was this in Egypt and in the Sudan. Its more recent development in Egypt may be dated to a revolt of Egyptian army officers in 1952 against a corrupt and most noisome Khedive, Farouk, which drove him into exile and proceeded to govern Egypt with an iron hand. One of these officers, Nasser, became Prime Minister. He was a staunch nationalist and as such demanded that Britain abandon the Suez Canal zone and withdraw from the Anglo-Egyptian Sudan.

The British had occupied the Suez Canal zone since 1882, and by their treaty recognizing Egyptian independence (1926) they were authorized to retain a garrison there. Sporadic attacks by inflamed Egyptian nationalists took place and the garrison had been increased to 80,000 men.

Historically the Suez Canal had been a place of great strategic importance, but the advent of the atom bomb changed all that. To remain had become merely a matter of prestige, not worth fighting about. And so Britain yielded to Nasser, began the withdrawal of her troops, promising to have them all out by 1956.

Egyptian nationalists, meanwhile, sought to annex the Sudan, claiming that it was imperative to do so since Egypt was dependent for its existence on Nile water, and was justly concerned about its sources. The British preferred the status quo of joint ownership with Egypt, since much British capital was invested in Sudanese cotton, and since they considered it unwise to turn over the 9,000,000 inhabitants of mixed Arab and Negro blood that inhabited the Sudan to politicians at Cairo.

Followed then an Anglo-Egyptian agreement in 1953 that elections be held in the Sudan so that the Sudanese might determine their own future. A long and confused campaign followed with the upshot that a Sudanese parliament meeting at Khartum in 1956 declared the Sudan an independent country, and applied for admission to the United Nations —a triumph for African nationalism.

The cry of Africa for the Africans resounded in other parts of Africa. Particularly was this true of Nigeria, largest dependency under the British Crown, and in the Gold Coast, north of the Gulf of Guinea.

Nigeria was a federated state, its three component parts known as East, West, and Northern Nigeria, the two former well advanced toward self-government, with the last more backward, more illiterate, still governed by native chiefs under the guidance of the British.

A legislature with limited powers represented all Nigeria, and as successive changes were made in the constitution more and more power was given to it. A further revision is promised for 1956, and in this year Nigerians are to decide for themselves whether they opt for three separate autonomous parliaments for the three states in question, or for a more unified country with a greater concentration of power. The two southern states already are equipped with legislatures and are largely self-governing. In them the clamor for Nigerian independence is loud and persistent. The main trouble is what can be done with the more backward North.

Further along the road to complete autonomy within the Commonwealth, or to independence without it, was the Gold Coast. Here African nationalism had won a great victory with the approval of local British officials, who appear quite willing to turn over the Gold Coast completely to its prosperous cocoa-growing Negro population.

In the Gold Coast there is a popularly elected legislature with an all Negro cabinet—the first in any British dependency—and a Negro premier, Dr. Nkrumah.

The latter was first educated by Roman Catholic missionaries, then graduated from Lincoln University in the United States, and as a graduate student in London much befriended by British Communists.

The doctor describes himself as a Marxian Christian, and has been for many years the leader of a party pledged to secure independence for the Gold Coast. Jailed by the governor for left-wing agitation, he was set free after his party won a decisive victory at the polls in 1951. Ever since then, Nkrumah has been a national hero. Opposed by Communists in the legislature, he acted promptly and expelled them from his party. The British look forward not only to the Gold Coast as becoming her Majesty's first Negro dominion but also as the nucleus around which may develop a larger Negro dominion, including Nigeria.

Uganda and Kenya

Meanwhile, south of the Sudan and athwart the great lakes lay Britain's model African colony, Uganda. Prosperous and well-governed by its local chiefs, with a modicum of authority exercised over them by the colonial office, Uganda was slow to catch the contemporary fever of nationalism. Suddenly it became mildly infected. The most important of the chiefs was the Kabarka of Buganda, a Cambridge university graduate and very popular in high British society. In 1953 the Kabarka opposed the British governor of Uganda who favored uniting Kenya, Tanganyika, and Uganda into a North African federation. The Kabarka refused his consent. The governor exiled him. The Kabarka appealed to Parliament, which upheld the governor. Violent was the wave of protest which swept Buganda. For three years it continued to rise. Britain yielded. The Kabarka returned to his throne in triumph in 1956.

East of Uganda lay Kenya, Britain's worst trouble spot in all Africa. Approximately one quarter of its total acreage, some 16,000 square miles, was known as the Highlands. Within it gathered most of Kenya's 40,000 Whites, for the land was very fertile and the climate salubrious. All land in the Highlands was owned by the Whites, who depended on Negro labor for the cultivation of their coffee plantations. The tribe which provided most of it was the Kikuyu.

Now it happened that a young Kikuyu boy, Jomo Kenyatta, educated by Scottish missionaries, went to London, studied at the London School of Economics, became an anthropologist, spent some time at the university of Moscow, returned to his people, became an agitator among them for self-government. He it was who was arrested in 1952 as responsible for abetting the Mau Mau rebellion of certain Kikuyus.

Mau Mau was a secret terrorist society. A most bloodthirsty and obscene oath was required of all members. Mau Mau was organized to rid Kenya of all Whites and to frighten all Kikuyus into joining it. Murders were perpetrated in an orgiastic ritual. The Mau Mau terror spread rapidly. The Whites were infuriated, the Kikuyus panic-stricken. Mau Mau spared neither age nor sex, killing secretly, slashing its victims until they died, defiling their bodies. It slew relatively few Whites, about sixty, since the latter all carried arms. Among the Kikuyus, death stalked everywhere, Mau Mau slaying thousands, either for betraying the oath or for refusing to take it.

Paratroopers were flown in from Britain and the manhunt began. Thousands of Kikuyus were rounded up, stuck in stockades, screened. Jomo Kenyatta was sentenced to serve a prison term of seven years after a trial scarcely in accordance with the fine record of British law courts. Order was restored, Mau Mau stamped out. To the displeasure of the white settlers the British government revised the constitution of Kenya and insisted that some Negroes be elected to the legislature. Educational and other requirements were high and the number chosen but a handful. White settlers were angry, their country bankrupt, their future uncertain.

The Gold Coast and Kenya are in stark contrast. In the former there is no color bar, and the British regard with approval the approach there to dominion status. In the latter Whites and Blacks do not associate with one another and demonstrations in favor of self-government are sternly suppressed. In the Gold Coast the number of Whites is exiguous. The opposite is true of Kenya where Whites are relatively numerous. For many decades they have been entrenched in the Highlands, accustomed to governing themselves through their own legislature, and therefore largely free from the Colonial Office in London with its long and distinguished record of protecting black folk.

Nationalism is far less an acute problem in Africa than it is in Asia. Negroes are as yet too ignorant, too conditioned by long habit and custom to submissiveness, to be profoundly stirred by it. The Afrikander Whites in the saddle in the Union of South Africa are a powerful and determined people, and Negro nationalism in their midst is nipped in the bud. In the new British federation of the two Rhodesias and Nyassaland the color bar is as strictly enforced as in the Union of South Africa. Negroes may apply for British citizenship, and so have the right to vote for a very few selected men of their own race in the legislature. But the qualifications of becoming a British citizen in this almost wholly illiterate land are high, and to retain the status of "protected person" provides a certain security.

Hitherto Communist propaganda in Africa south of the equator has been slight. It may spread rapidly, however, where people are miserable and have a sense of injustice. There is in Moscow no color bar, a fact that gives Communism an entering wedge.

The Meeting at the Summit (Geneva, 1955)

March, 1953, Stalin died. Taking his place as premier was Malenkov, presumably a stooge for others, since he resigned within a year. Bulganin and Khrushchev took over, the first as premier, the second as secretary of the Communist party. In the interim, Beria, all-powerful head of the secret police, was executed as a traitor. The West looked forward with some hope to what might happen next.

Early omens were propitious. The British, the French, the Americans, and the Russians signed a treaty restoring independence to Austria, a boon which that country had not enjoyed since Hitler's invasion seventeen years earlier. Austria gladly accepted the status of Switzerland, that of a country pledged to perpetual neutrality.

Followed then what was known as a meeting at the summit, not of foreign secretaries but of chiefs of state. It was held in Geneva in 1955. Present were President Eisenhower, Sir Anthony Eden, the new British Prime Minister, Faure of France, and the two new joint rulers of Russia.

Upon the surface there was little wrangling. In the open meetings everyone was smiling; everyone agreed on the necessity of universal peace, the necessity of world disarmament. No tempers were lost. The three men who represented the West asked that the problem of Germany be first on the agenda. They were willing, they said, to give guarantees to Russia if that country would consent to free elections in Eastern Germany, and Eden for Britain suggested a demilitarized buffer state between Russia and a united Germany if Russia would agree to those free elections. But the Russians asserted that the Germans were not yet ready for unification and that there was but one way to achieve it, namely, for the West Germans and the East Germans to negotiate on a basis of complete equality, despite the fact that the West Germans outnumbered the East German Communists by a good three to one.

As for disarmament Russia said she had already reduced her army by 640,000 men and the West should do likewise. But how large was that army before the reduction? Russia would not say, and as a matter of statistics the Americans had reduced their army twice since the armistice in Korea. The two Russians once again pleaded for the destruction of all nuclear weapons but remained adamant on international inspection. Eisenhower offered free aerial inspection in the United States to the Russian air force if Bulganin and Khrushchev would permit UN aerial inspection of Russian plants and military installations. This they would not concede. So the meeting at the summit amounted to little, except that both sides agreed that their conversations had been productive of an excellent spirit of friendliness, and that another meeting should be held later in the year of the foreign ministers of the four countries concerned to hammer out something specific whereby world tensions might be lessened. This very small mouse was termed, "the spirit of Geneva."

When the four lesser statesmen met, that spirit completely evaporated. In the interval the Russians had exploded a hydrogen bomb, and this proof that both sides now had it within their power to wipe civilization off this terrestrial globe apparently hardened the Soviet heart. Once again the conference was completely blocked. In the middle of it Molotov went back to Russia. He returned saying he had brought something nice in his baggage. What he brought was a bitter denunciation of the West and a refusal to yield an inch.

Middle East, 1955-56

In 1948, as we have seen, the state of Israel unexpectedly emerged. Attacked north, east, and south by her Arab neighbors, Israel emerged triumphant. There was, however, no peace treaty, only an armistice, and that none too well observed.

Between 1948 and 1955 an intermittent, informal kind of war continued between Arabs and Israelis. There were only 1,500,000 Israelis as opposed to 40,000,000 Arabs. But the Israelis were united and their enemies, jealous of one another, were without common purpose or leadership, ill prepared for war.

Bitterness grew steadily in intensity, border raids in number, some 1,200 reported during these seven years. Syria and Jordan clashed with

Israel over the diversion of the waters of the Jordan River for irrigation purposes, Egypt and Jordan over the right of some 900,000 Arab refugees driven from their home in Palestine in 1948, barely kept alive by UNRRA waiting to return to their former homes in Palestine. The frontiers drawn by the uneasy truce of 1948 stretched far beyond those proposed by the United Nations partition plan. And the Arabs made much of this, asserting that the Israelis plotted a greater Israel, all the way to the Suez Canal and to the Tigris River. But, according to the Israelis, the Egyptians, spurred on by Nasser's nationalists, plotted a joint Arab attack that would wipe Israel from the map.

Then suddenly, in September, 1955, the Russians and the Czecho-slovaks promised to supply Egypt with heavy armament, jet planes, tanks, and submarines, and some ten ships conveying them shortly after landed at Alexandria.

This presented the Israelis with a serious problem. Their tiny country, only some 8,000 square miles, had a frontier 591 miles in length fronting on four Arab states, Lebanon, Syria, Jordan, and Egypt. Tel Aviv, their principal city, was but a few miles from the Gaza strip and the Egyptians. The average distance from the Mediterranean to the Jordan frontier was only twelve miles. In this narrow space there was no opportunity for manoeuvre should war occur. Israel had no submarines; she also had no heavy armament with which to ward off Arab attack. Therefore she appealed to the United States to sell her arms to offset those sold her potential enemies by the Communist states.

The United States, England, and France had promised action to prevent the status quo from being upset by war. But in case of quick Arab action would these friendly countries have time to implement their promise, and would they really do it?

The United States, Britain, France, all three, were caught in a network of conflicting interests. For Washington to sell the Israelis the arms they desired would have resulted in Czechoslovakia, Moscow's cat's-paw, selling the Arabs more, and an arms race would follow, bringing war closer. To refuse to sell to Israel might result in its destruction, and to prevent this America had pledged its word. Furthermore, the United States at this very time was dickering with the Egyptians over the construction of a great dam over the Nile; and certainly it was to our interest to avoid angering Saudi Arabia from whence came much of our oil.

Britain was even more worried. She had just completed a defensive alliance, the Bagdad Pact, with Turkey, Iran, Iraq, and Pakistan. Jordan, an Arab state, was expected to join. That state owed its birth to British diplomacy, had been and still is (1956), subsidized by the British treasury with an army trained by a British general. But Jordan refused to join the Bagdad Pact and dismissed Glubb Pasha, the general. The

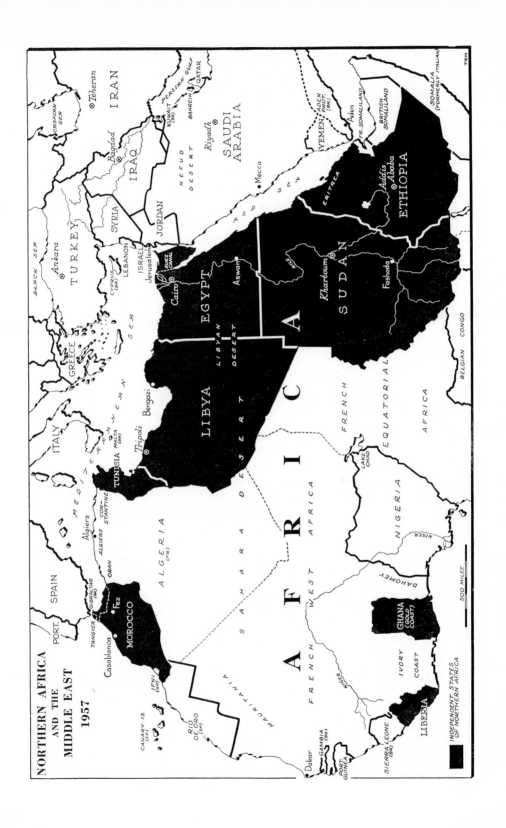

NORTHERN AFRICA
AND THE
MIDDLE EAST
1957

INDEPENDENT STATES
OF NORTHERN AFRICA

500 MILES

reason was fairly obvious. Ibn Saud, luxury-enveloped and enormously wealthy ruler of Saudi Arabia, showered his American dollars and British pounds on Jordan mobs to stage anti-British riots. Without oil Britain could not live. Most of it came from Saudi Arabia, South Arabia, Iran and Iraq.

France, too, needed oil from Arab lands. And with civil war on her hands with Algerian Arabs she must necessarily step cautiously, lest Nasser of Egypt put himself at the head of a belligerent pan-Arab and pan-Moslem group whose influence would extend throughout all the Moslem world from Casablanca on the Atlantic to the gates of India.

It looked like war, so much so that the United Nations sent its secretary to the Middle East to plead with Israelis and Arabs alike to abstain from incessant frontier raids. As he did so the Russians shifted their ground from a pro-Arab position to one of professed neutrality, agreeing that no arms should be sent to either side, pledging Russia to the support of a United Nations program which would prevent any outbreak of war in the disturbed Middle East.

The Dethronement of Stalin

In 1956 the inexplicable Russians seemingly made a complete ideological somersault. At the conference of the Russian Communist Congress Khrushchev announced that Russia and her allies, the Peoples Democracies, had suffered long from one-man rule. Stalin's self-glorification had resulted in spreading a *cult of personality*. This was a grievous error. Leadership must be collective. Furthermore the coming world victory of communism did not necessarily have to be accompanied by force and bloodshed. Under certain circumstances it might be won by democratic majorities secured by peaceful means.

Followed then a secret speech made by Khrushchev in the congress, in which he accused Stalin of gross neglect of duty in not readying Russia against Hitler's attack, of cowardice during the war, of absurd boasting, and of heinous crimes: the murder of old Bolshevik heroes in the amazing and phoney treason trials of 1917, and the appalling slaughter of 5,000 Red army officers.

This philippic was not released either in full or at once to the public, as though it was first necessary to test the reception it would meet with in the Communist world. For a moment the latter was stunned at this denegation of the accepted hero. It recovered very quickly; was not this pronunciamento official, and from the head of the party? And soon, not only in Russia but in all satellite countries, profuse were the apologies for past errors and loud the lamentations for the death by Stalin's orders of good Communists whose only blame was to incur Stalin's displeasure.

Even thus did communism about-face, making Stalin the scapegoat for all tyrannical and brutish acts, "a blundering paranoid murderer whose stupidity and obstinacy almost destroyed the Soviet Union."

Why this speech of Khrushchev? It is possible that he, Bulganin, and their associates suspected a new purge that might include themselves, and so, to save their necks, murdered Stalin. It is possible that they sensed such deep hatred of Stalin in Russia that an internal revolution threatened the downfall of the party unless they took action first. Another explanation might be that they hoped to cozen the European Socialists into the old united-front trap into which Czechoslovak Socialists had fallen, and by so doing destroy the unity of the West.

The significance of Stalin's repudiation is difficult to gauge. The conspirators who had brought it about had been obedient henchmen of the dead tyrant. They had shared in his crimes; could they now repudiate him without self-incrimination? Did their *volte-face* imply fundamental changes in Soviet policy; or was it simply the result of a cutthroat squabble among gangsters, motivated by hate, fear, and cupidity, to substitute the rule of several for that of one, because no one was sufficiently powerful as yet to impose his single will upon all?

However that may be a certain easement in Soviet propaganda occurred. The iron curtain was raised slightly. It became easier to secure Russian passports; newspaper men were given more freedom; Russian officials became more friendly. The advantages of trade were stressed rather than military might. There was less emphasis on Marxian theories concerning the inner contradictions of capitalism, that doomed it to destruction, and more on the beauties of coöperation.

The Russians even proposed to adopt a kind of Marshall Plan of their own for economic aid and technological assistance to impoverished folk in Asia and Africa, with yellow, brown, and black skins. War was still war; but an economic one with the West was more desirable than one waged with guns.

To further this new approach Bulganin and Khrushchev embarked on a pilgrimage to India, Burma, and Afghanistan, traveling troubadours of sweetness and light, praising fulsomely the lands they visited, promising the friendship of Big Brother Russia, commenting freely on Asiatic struggles for freedom from British, French, and even Portuguese imperialism, covertly supported by capitalistic America. Peace, nationalism, and coexistence was the burden of their song.

Just what, specifically, did coexistence mean? Were the traveling Russians sincere in implying that the cold war was over? Would they really do anything comparable to what the West had done to make the depressed areas of the world more viable by economic aid? Was this a Communist subterfuge beneath which the Soviets intended to plant further seeds of discord among those nations endeavoring to maintain a common front against world communism? Did the Russians really intend to do anything at all to solve Europe's major problems—German unification and world disarmament?

In the great international chess game it was now the West's turn to play. It was ill prepared to do so. It had trusted too much to NATO. That organization was perceptibly weakening. The reasons were numerous. Among them were: the withdrawal of more than half of the French NATO divisions from Europe to Africa; the collapse of NATO's Eastern defense line, since Greece and Turkey, admitted to defend it, were now at cross-purposes over Cyprus, the Greeks intent on integrating that island into Greece, the Turks and the British determined that this should not be done; the weakening of the British Commonwealth by the deflection of Ceylon from a pro-Western orientation to neutralism; the failure of France and Germany to compound their differences over the Saar; and finally, lessened support in Germany for aged Chancellor Adenauer and NATO which he had done so much to create.

Prospects for world peace were dark. Both sides now had the hydrogen bomb. Eleven years had passed since the atom bomb had been dropped on Hiroshima with its equivalent of 20,000 tons of TNT. The hydrogen bomb packed an explosive power of 2,000,000 tons. The testing of the first one at Bikini atoll in 1954 led Field Marshal Montgomery to say one year later: "win or lose is no longer applicable to contests between nations which have nuclear power of any magnitude . . . Man will have it in his power in the future to destroy himself and every living thing upon this planet."

Suddenly, in the summer of 1956, came a new international crisis, possibly worse in its implications than the Berlin airlift of 1948 and the Korean War of 1950.

Nasser of Egypt, piqued by American and British withdrawal of aid in the building of the High Aswan Dam, declared the Suez Canal nationalized, under the exclusive control of Egypt. Through this waterway passed the tankers which carried the oil of Arabian lands and Iran upon which the economic life of Western Europe depended. Clearly it was intolerable that the power to open or to shut it should depend on the ruler of Egypt. In consequence, Britain and France began to concentrate air, naval, and military strength in the Eastern Mediterranean.

An international conference in London proved disappointing. Egypt refused to attend, but Soviet Russia went and spoke in approval of Nasser's coup. Three other nations also supported the Egyptian—Indonesia, India, and Ceylon—the last two being members of the Commonwealth. They and Soviet Russia were in agreement; the canal was Egyptian property over which no international control was warranted.

Eighteen of the twenty-two nations attending adhered to the principle that world peace depended on at least a modicum of international administration of the canal. They appointed a committee of five, headed by the Prime Minister of Australia, to confer with Nasser. He received them but would not compromise the main issue—Egyptian not international management.

The United States now proposed an Association of Canal Users to test the right of Egypt to refuse passage to its ships, free passage to all nations being guaranteed by the treaty of 1888. A second conference was held in London of the eighteen nations who did approve of international supervision. It was presented with the American proposal. A few nations refused to join the proposed Users Association. Others were lukewarm, even after the original proposal was watered down. Whereupon Britain and France appealed to the United Nations, where their resolution to condemn Egypt was promptly vetoed by Russia.

Summer slid into autumn. Nasser remained master of the Suez. Along the winding Israeli-Jordan frontier bloody forays were increasingly frequent. Jordan was Britain's ally, and a British subsidy paid for Jordan's army. But a parliamentary election in that country favored Egypt over Britain, and Jordan put an Egyptian general in command of her army. This made no sense to Englishmen who paid for it, and who kept an expensive garrison in Cyprus to ride herd over Nasser and the Near East.

And now, from behind the iron curtain, came explosions. In Poland half-starved and frantic Poles demonstrated so vigorously against Moscow that war threatened. For the nonce it was stayed by Soviet concessions that implied that Poland was semi-independent.

This Polish explosion set off another and a greater one in Hungary. In that unhappy land desperate Magyars rose in arms against their own Communist government. The latter called in the Russian army. Soon Russian tanks were roaming the streets of Budapest and blood flowed freely. The Peoples Democracies of Eastern Europe and the countries of the Near East boiled with eruptive violence.

As this happened, the Israeli army stabbed southward into the Sinai peninsula and swung westward toward the Suez Canal. As they did so, France and Britain demanded from Nasser the right to protect the Canal. This demand being instantly rebuffed by Nasser, their bombers attacked Egyptian airfields, their parachutists capturing Port Said at the Canal's northern end.

At this act of war the world stood aghast. The world was angry; and a majority in the Security Council of the United Nations, including the United States and Russia (for once in agreement), censured the Franco-British action, referred the matter to the Assembly of the United Nations. That body with practical unanimity called for the withdrawal of French, British, and Israeli troops from Egyptian territory.

Gone was western unity; NATO became a joke; Nasser and his Russian backers were triumphant.

But the Russians played their cards badly. About to withdraw from Hungary and to leave that land free from Communist dominance, the Russians promised free elections to the Magyars. Suddenly they changed their minds. Fearing an anti-Soviet Magyar regime they brought back their armor. For a few days the Magyars fought the Russian tanks and their own security police. With ammunition spent and food gone they had no chance. By November 11, the armistice day of the First World War, thousands of Magyars lay dead.

The United Nations was now as indignant against Russia as it was against Israel, France, and Britain. Just as its Assembly unanimously condemned Russian aggression in Hungary, from Moscow came threats of intervention in Egypt. These acts, together with the knowledge that they could expect no support from the United States or the United Nations, led Israel, France, and Britain to sign a cease-fire agreement and to consent to a conditional withdrawal of their forces from Egyptian soil, provided that detachments of United Nations forces were to stand guard in Egypt. Several of the smaller nations, among them Denmark, Norway, Sweden, Finland, Colombia, and Canada, agreed to send them.

What chance now, peace? The free world was bitter at Russia for the barbarous behavior of her troops in Hungary: but so was most of it at France, Britain, and Israel for flouting the charter of the United Nations. In Russia, army officers rushed to enlist as volunteers to defend Egypt, an action parallel to that in China as MacArthur rolled northward in Korea. If Russia intervened directly, or indirectly by sending volunteers to fight in Arab lands, what would America do? and could the United Nations do anything? Would November, 1956, go down in history as such a fatal month as July, 1914, or August, 1939?

READING LIST

The purpose of this reading list is to offer suggestions for students desiring to read more widely in the history of Europe since 1815. For this reason, the suggestions are restricted to books in the English language, and an effort has been made to indicate those volumes which are most suitable for undergraduate reading. While the bibliography follows the general arrangement of the material in the text, the books are listed by topic rather than by chapter.

I. GENERAL WORKS

BIBLIOGRAPHIES AND ENCYCLOPEDIAS: The most useful general bibliographies are W. H. Allison and others, eds., *A Guide to Historical Literature* (1931), which provides a convenient starting point for any historical investigation; L. J. Ragatz, *A Bibliography for the Study of European History, 1815-1939* (1942), with two supplements (1943 and 1945); W. L. Langer and H. F. Armstrong, *Foreign Affairs Bibliography, 1919-1932* (1933); R. G. Woolbert, *Foreign Affairs Bibliography, 1932-1942* (1945); and A. Bullock and A. J. P. Taylor, *Select List of Books on European History, 1815-1914* (1944). For current publications, these guides may be supplemented by the bibliographies in the *American Historical Review* and the *Journal of Modern History*. Biographical sketches and special articles on a wide variety of subjects will be found in the *Encyclopoedia Britannica* and the *Encyclopedia of the Social Sciences*. W. L. Langer, ed., *An Encyclopedia of World History* (1940) offers a compact factual survey. For maps, see W. R. Shepherd, *Historical Atlas* (7th ed., 1929); I. Bowman, *The New World: Problems in Political Geography* (1928); J. F. Horrabin, *An Atlas of Current Affairs* (6th ed., 1939); *Hammond's Historical Atlas* (1953); and H. L. Roberts, assisted by J. Gunther and J. A. Kreslins, *Foreign Affairs Bibliography* (1955).

SOURCE COLLECTIONS: For the consultation of the original texts of treaties, speeches, and other documents in English translation, the following collections may be recommended: A. Oakes and R. B. Mowat, *Great European Treaties of the Nineteenth Century* (1918), which deals with the period from 1815 to 1878; W. P. Hall and E. A. Beller, *Historical Readings in Nineteenth-Century Thought* (1928), and D. O. Wagner, *Social Reformers* (1934), for intellectual documents; J. H. Robinson and C. A. Beard, *Readings in Modern European History* (2 vols., 1908-09), Vol. II; J. F. Scott and A. Baltzly, *Readings in*

i

European History Since 1814 (1934); A. N. Cook, *Readings in Modern and Contemporary History* (1937); W. C. Langsam, *Documents and Readings in the History of Europe Since 1918* (1939); Columbia University, *Introduction to Contemporary Civilization in the West* (2 vols., 1954); G. H. Knoles and R. K. Snyder, *Readings in Western Civilization* (1954).

EUROPE SINCE 1815: The best extended treatment of the period will be found in the relevant volumes of the two leading coöperative works on modern European history: A. W. Ward, G. W. Prothero, and S. Leathes, eds., *The Cambridge Modern History;* and W. L. Langer, ed., *The Rise of Modern Europe.* For briefer recent surveys of the whole period, see: E. Fueter, *World History, 1815-1920* (1922); B. Croce, *History of Europe in the Nineteenth Century* (1933); C. J. H. Hayes, *A Political and Cultural History of Modern Europe* (2 vols., 1933-36), Vol. II; J. S. Schapiro, *Modern and Contemporary European History, 1815-1940* (1940); F. L. Benns, *European History Since 1870* (1955); and A. J. Grant and H. Temperley, *Europe in the Nineteenth and Twentieth Centuries, 1789-1938* (1939). A general survey of the diplomacy of the period is offered in R. B. Mowat, *A History of European Diplomacy, 1815-1914* (1922).

II. GENERAL WORKS IN SPECIAL TOPICS

GREAT BRITAIN: Detailed accounts of England since 1815 are given in two of the coöperative histories: J. A. R. Marriott, *England Since Waterloo* (1913), and *Modern England, 1885-1932* (1934); in C. W. C. Oman, ed., *A History of England* (8 vols., 1904-34); and, more recently, E. L. Woodward, *The Age of Reform, 1815-1870* (1938); R. C. K. Ensor, *England, 1870-1914* (1936); and in G. N. Clark, ed., *Oxford History of England* (14 vols., 1934 ff.). Briefer accounts of the same period are to be had in W. L. Blease, *Short History of English Liberalism* (1913); E. Halevy, *History of the English People* (5 vols., 1924-34), for the years 1815-41 and 1895-1915; G. M. Trevelyan, *British History in the Nineteenth Century and After, 1782-1919* (1937); A. Bryant, *The Pageant of England, 1840-1940* (1941); and J. B. Brebner and A. Nevins, *The Makings of Modern Britain* (1943). For foreign policy, the standard general treatment is A. W. Ward and G. P. Gooch, eds., *Cambridge History of British Foreign Policy, 1783-1919* (3 vols., 1922-23); briefer studies are G. P. Gooch and J. H. B. Masterman, *Century of British Foreign Policy* (1917); and R. W. Seton-Watson, *Britain in Europe, 1789-1914: A Survey of Foreign Policy* (1937). The social and economic aspects of modern England are ably presented in C. R. Fay, *Great Britain from Adam Smith to the Present Day* (1928), and *Life and Labour in the Nineteenth Century* (1933); E. Lipson, *The Economic History of England* (3 vols., 1920-31); J. H. Clapham, *An Economic History of Modern Britain* (3 vols., 1926-28); T. C. Ashton, *The Industrial Revolution, 1760-1830* (1948); A. Redford, *An Economic History of England, 1760-1860* (1947); S. and B. Webb, *History of Trade Unionism* (rev. ed., 1920); and G. D. H. Cole, *A Short History of the British Working Class Movement, 1789-1927* (3 vols., 1925-27), and *The British Common People, 1746-1938* (1938). The standard treatment of the English political system is A. L. Lowell, *Government of England* (2 vols., 2nd ed., 1912);

special aspects of the subject are discussed in W. Bagehot, *The English Constitution* (rev. ed., 1872); J. A. Thomas, *The House of Commons, 1832-1901* (1939); D. L. Keir, *The Constitutional History of Modern Britain, 1485-1937* (1938); and A. B. Keith, *The Constitution of England, from Queen Victoria to George VI* (2 vols., 1940). Recent surveys of English thought are F. J. C. Hearnshaw, ed., *The Social and Political Ideas of Some Representative Thinkers of the Victorian Age* (1923); D. C. Somervell, *English Thought in the Nineteenth Century* (1929); C. C. Brinton, *English Political Thought in the Nineteenth Century* (1933); and D. Thompson, *England in the Nineteenth Century* (1950).

FRANCE, SWITZERLAND, BELGIUM, AND THE NETHERLANDS: Good general histories of modern France are those of E. Bourgeois, *History of Modern France, 1815-1913* (2 vols., 1919); M. O. Davis, *Political History of France, 1789-1910* (1916); J. G. Coulter, *The Story of Modern France, 1610-1914* (1939); J. B. Wolf, *A History of France Since 1815* (1940); J. A. R. Marriott, *A Short History of France* (1944); A. L. Guerard, *France, a Short History* (1946); J. P. T. Bury, *France, 1814-1940* (1949); J. H. Clapham, *Economic Development of France and Germany, 1815-1914* (4th ed., 1936); and S. B. Clough, *France: A History of National Economics, 1789-1939* (1939). Special topics are considered in L. Levine (L. L. Lorwin), *Syndicalism in France* (2nd ed., 1914); and A. Girault, *The Colonial Tariff Policy in France* (1916). Several studies of French intellectual life may be cited: A. Tilley, *Modern France, a Companion to French Studies* (1922); A. L. Guerard, *French Civilization in the Nineteenth Century* (1914); L. Levy-Bruhl, *History of Modern Philosophy in France* (1899); R. Soltau, *French Political Thought in the Nineteenth Century* (1931); and J. P. Mayer, *Political Thought in France from Sieyes to Sorel* (1943). On Switzerland: W. D. McCracken, *The Rise of the Swiss Republic* (1901); W. Oechsli, *History of Switzerland, 1499-1914* (1922); and W. Martin, *A History of Switzerland* (1931). On Belgium: H. V. Linden, *Belgium, the Making of a Nation* (1920); and L. van der Essen, *Short History of Belgium* (2nd ed., 1920). And more recently H. Gibson, *Belgium* (1939); and E. Cammaerts, *The Keystone of Europe: History of the Belgian Dynasty, 1830-1939* (1939). On the Netherlands: G. Edmundson, *History of Holland* (1922); A. C. J. Jitta, *Holland's Modern Renascence* (1930); and A. J. Barnouw, *The Dutch* (1940); and the problems of the Dutch empire are treated in E. S. de Klerck, *History of the Netherlands East Indies* (1938); and A. Vandenbosch, *The Dutch East Indies* (1941).

GERMANY: Reliable general histories of Germany are E. F. Henderson, *A Short History of Germany* (rev. ed., 1928); H. Pinnow, *History of Germany* (rev. ed., 1939); A. Ramos Oliveira, *A People's History of Germany* (1942); G. Shuster and A. Bergstraesser, *Germany: A Short History* (1944); A. J. P. Taylor, *The Course of German History* (1945); V. Valentin, *The German People: Their History and Civilization from the Holy Roman Empire to the Third Reich* (1946); R. Flenley, *Modern German History* (1953); G. A. Craig, *The Politics of the Prussian Army, 1640-1945* (1955). The social and economic development of Germany is described in J. H. Clapham, *Economic Develop-*

ment of France and Germany, 1815-1914 (4th ed., 1936); W. F. Bruck, *Social and Economic History of Germany from William II to Hitler, 1888-1938* (1938); G. Stolper, *German Economy, 1870-1940* (1940); and E. Kohn-Bramstedt, *Aristocracy and the Middle Classes in Germany*, or *Social Types in German Literature, 1830-1900* (1937).

ITALY, SPAIN, AND PORTUGAL: L. Salvatorelli, *A Concise History of Italy* (1940) offers the best general survey of Italian history in one volume. The nineteenth century is treated in more detail in W. J. Stillman, *The Union of Italy, 1815-1895* (rev. ed., 1909); B. King, *History of Italy* (2 vols., 2nd ed., 1912), covering the period 1814-1871; A. Solmi, *The Making of Modern Italy* (1925); J. A. R. Marriott, *The Makers of Modern Italy* (1931); C. J. S. Sprigge, *The Development of Modern Italy* (1944); C. Sforza, *Contemporary Italy: Its Intellectual and Moral Origins* (1944); G. B. McClellan, *Modern Italy* (1933); and R. Albrecht Carrie, *Italy from Napoleon to Mussolini* (1950). And for the countries of the Iberian Peninsula: G. F. White, *A Century of Spain and Portugal, 1788-1898* (1909); M. A. S. Hume, *Modern Spain, 1788-1898* (2nd ed., 1909); W. C. Atkinson, *Spain, a Brief History* (1934); R. Sencourt (R. E. G. George), *The Spanish Crown, 1808-1931* (1932); A. R. Verduin, *A Manual of Spanish Constitutions, 1808-1931* (1941); N. B. Adams, *The Heritage of Spain* (1944); J. B. Trend, *The Civilization of Spain* (1944); H. M. Stephens, *Portugal* (4th ed., 1908); and G. Young, *Portugal Old and Young* (1917).

AUSTRIA AND HUNGARY: The best general account in English of Austria-Hungary since the Napoleonic wars is A. J. P. Taylor, *The Hapsburg Monarchy, 1815-1918* (1941); A. J. May, *The Hapsburg Monarchy, 1867-1914* (1951); J. S. C. Abbott, *The Empire of Austria* (1902); and L. P. M. Leger, *History of Austria-Hungary* (2nd ed., 1907). The Hungarian lands of the Hapsburgs are adequately treated in C. M. Knatchbull-Hugessen, *The Political Evolution of the Hungarian Nation* (1908); A. Vambery, *The Story of Hungary* (1922); J. Horvath, *Modern Hungary, 1660-1920* (1922); F. Eckhart, *A Short History of the Hungarian People* (1931); O. Zarek, *The History of Hungary* (1939); and D. G. Kosary, *A History of Hungary* (1941).

RUSSIA AND POLAND: The best accounts of Russia since 1815 are to be found in the revelant chapters of the following works: A. Kornilov, *Modern Russian History* (1924); S. F. Platonov, *History of Russia* (1925); G. V. Vernadsky, *Political and Diplomatic History of Russia* (1936); R. S. Tompkins, *Russia Through the Ages* (1940); B. Pares, *A History of Russia* (rev. ed., 1944); and G. V. Vernadsky, *A History of Russia* (rev. ed., 1944). Briefer periods and individual interpretations are handled in M. Karpovich, *Imperial Russia, 1801-1917* (1932); W. A. Gerhardi, *The Romanovs* (1939); B. Pares, *Russia* (1940); R. J. Kerner, *The Urge to the Sea* (1942); B. H. Sumner, *A Short History of Russia* (1943); and A. Howard, *Pictorial History of Russia from Rurik to Stalin* (1944). A colorful account of the ruling dynasty during the last three centuries is given in W. A. Gerhardi, *The Romanovs* (1939). Social and economic matters are ably treated in T. G. Masaryk, *The Spirit of Russia*

(2 vols., 1919), a classic treatise by the great Czech scholar and statesman;
D. S. Mirsky, *Russia, a Social History* (1931); J. Mavor, *An Economic History
of Russia* (2nd ed., 2 vols., 1925); A. Raffalovitch, ed., *Russia: Its Trade and
Commerce* (1918); and S. P. Turin, *From Peter the Great to Lenin: a History
of the Russian Labor Movement* (1935). The territorial growth of Russia is
discussed in F. H. Skrine, *Expansion of Russia, 1815-1900* (1915); F. A.
Golder, *Russian Expansion on the Pacific, 1641-1850* (1914); and A. Lobanov-
Rostovsky, *Russia and Asia* (1933).

For Poland: E. H. Lewinski-Corwin, *Political History of Poland* (1917);
R. Dyboski, *Outlines of Polish History* (1931); O. Gorka, *An Outline of Polish
History, Past and Present* (1942); and O. Halecki, *The History of Poland*
(1942).

SOUTHEASTERN EUROPE AND THE EASTERN QUESTION: General histories are N.
Forbes and others, *The Balkans* (1919); W. S. Davis, *A Short History of the
Near East (A.D. 330-1922)* (1922); F. Schevill, *The History of the Balkan
Peninsula* (2nd ed., 1933); W. Miller, *The Ottoman Empire and Its Successors,
1801-1927* (4th ed., 1936); and, in brief outline, W. M. Gewehr, *The Rise of
Nationalism in the Balkans, 1800-1930* (1931). A popular recent account is
that of S. Pribichevich, *World Without End: the Saga of Southeastern Europe*
(1939). Special aspects of the history of this area are handled in R. W. Seton-
Watson, *Rise of Nationality in the Balkans* (1917); H. Kohn, *A History of
Nationalism in the Near East* (1929); and W. W. White, *The Process of
Change in the Ottoman Empire* (1937), which deals with the legal aspects of
the changes in territory and national sovereignty. For a survey of the diplo-
matic history, see J. A. R. Marriott, *The Eastern Question: an Historical Study
in European Diplomacy* (4th ed., 1940); P. P. Graves, *The Question of the
Straits* (1931); and J. T. Shotwell and F. Deak, *Turkey at the Straits: a Short
History* (1940). Useful histories of the individual countries are also available:
G. J. S. L. Eversley, *The Turkish Empire from 1288 to 1914* (2nd ed., 1923);
H. C. J. Luke, *The Making of Modern Turkey* (1936); H. W. V. Temperley,
History of Serbia (1917); F. S. Stevenson, *History of Montenegro* (1912); W.
Miller, *A History of the Greek People, 1821-1921* (1922); J. Mavrogordato,
Modern Greece, 1800-1931 (1931); N. S. Kaltchas, *Introduction to the Con-
stitutional History of Modern Greece* (1940); N. Iorga, *A History of Roumania*
(1925); and especially R. W. Seton-Watson, *A History of the Roumanians*
(1934); J. Samuelson, *Bulgaria, Past and Present* (1888); C. A. Chekrezi, *Albania, Past and Present* (1919); and Federal Writers' Project, *The Albanian
Struggle in the Old World and New* (1939). On the knotty Macedonian question, H. N. Brailsford, *Macedonia, Its Races and Their Future* (1906) is still
the most satisfactory book in English; C. Anastasoff, *The Tragic Peninsula*
(1938) treats the question from a partisan point of view.

INDUSTRIAL REVOLUTION AND ECONOMIC HISTORY: A. P. Usher, *A History of
Mechanical Inventions* (1954); T. S. Ashton, *The Industrial Revolution, 1760-
1830* (1948); S. Chase, *Men and Machines* (1929); J. Clapham, *An Economic
History of Modern Britain* (1938); F. C. Bowen, *A Century of Atlantic Travel*
(1930); S. C. Gilfillian, *Inventing the Ship* (1935); F. A. Talbot, *Railway*

Conquest of the World (1911); A. Birnie, *Economic History of Europe, 1760-1930* (1930); H. Heaton, *Economic History of Europe* (1936); W. W. Jennings, *A History of the Economic and Social Progress of European Peoples* (1936); and especially W. Bowden, M. Karpovich and A. P. Usher, *The Economic History of Europe Since 1750* (1937); S. B. Clough and C. W. Cole, *An Economic History of Europe* (1941); and E. L. Bogart, *An Economic History of Europe, 1760-1939* (1942). One of the most characteristic phases of modern economic history is the predominance of financial institutions, which may be studied in J. A. Hobson, *The Evolution of Modern Capitalism* (rev. ed., 1926); H. E. See, *Modern Capitalism, Its Origins and Evolution* (1928); F. L. Nussbaum, *A History of the Economic Institutions of Modern Europe* (1933); P. H. Emden, *Money Power of Europe in the Nineteenth and Twentieth Centuries* (1938); G. W. Edwards, *The Evolution of Finance Capitalism* (1938); and for an interesting account of one of the most prominent banking houses, E. C. Corti, *The Rise of the House of Rothschild* (1928), and *The Reign of the House of Rothschild* (1928). Special aspects are treated in: L. C. A. Knowles, *Industrial and Commercial Revolutions During the Nineteenth Century* (1928); R. Piotrowski, *Cartels and Trusts; Their Origins and Historical Development from the Economic and Legal Aspects* (1933); J. L. and B. Hammond, *The Rise of Modern Industry* (1925); I. Lippincott, *The Development of Modern World Trade* (1936); J. Kuczynski, *Labour Conditions in Western Europe, 1820 to 1935* (1937); and F. A. Von Hayek, *Capitalism and the Historian* (1954).

ECONOMIC THOUGHT: Of the general treaties, the following may be cited: C. Gide and C. Rist, *A History of Economic Doctrines* (1915); J. M. Keynes, *Essays in Biography* (1933); H. W. Peck, *Economic Thought and Its Institutional Background* (1935); L. H. Haney, *History of Economic Thought* (3rd ed., 1936); and E. Whittaker, *History of Economic Ideas* (1940). For a more detailed exposition of the classical economic doctrines, the original works should be consulted: A. Smith, *The Wealth of Nations* (1776); T. R. Malthus, *An Essay on the Principles of Population As It Affects the Future Improvement of Society* (1798); D. Ricardo, *Principles of Political Economy and Taxation* (1817); F. List, *The National System of Political Economy* (1841); J. S. Mill, *Principles of Political Economy* (1848); and H. Spencer, *Social Statics* (1851). And for the socialist writers: A. Shadwell, *The Socialist Movement, 1824-1924* (2 vols., 1925); C. J. Sprigge, *Karl Marx* (1949); O. Rühle, *Karl Marx* (1929); and E. Wilson, *To the Finland Station* (1940); P. J. Proudhon, *What Is Property?* (1840); Karl Marx, *Capital: A Critique of Political Economy* (1887); E. Bernstein, *Evolutionary Socialism* (1899); G. Sorel, *Reflections on Violence* (1908); and E. Roll, *A History of Economic Thought* (1955).

CULTURAL HISTORY: The new contributions to philosophy in modern Europe may be followed in H. Höffding, *A History of Modern Philosophy* (2 vols., 1908), Vol. II; J. Royce, *The Spirit of Modern Philosophy* (1924); R. B. Perry, *Philosophy of the Recent Past* (1926); and G. Boas, *The Major Traditions of European Philosophy* (1929). The broader aspects of European thought are

treated in J. T. Merz, *History of European Thought in the Nineteenth Century*
(4 vols., 1897-1914); J. M. Robertson, *History of Free Thought in the Nineteenth Century* (1929); E. Friedell, *Cultural History of the Modern Age*
(3 vols., 1930-32); G. H. Mead, *Movements of Thought in the Nineteenth
Century* (1936); F. S. Marvin, ed., *Recent Developments in European Thought*
(1920); P. Viereck, *Metapolitics: From the Romantics to Hitler* (1941). Political
ideas are stressed in J. H. Randall, *The Making of the Modern Mind* (rev. ed.,
1940); G. de Ruggiero, *History of European Liberalism* (1927); H. J. Laski,
The Rise of Liberalism: the Philosophy of a Business Civilization (1936); and
E. Wilson, *To the Finland Station* (1940). For a discussion of some aspects of
modern European literature: G. Brandes, *Main Currents in Nineteenth Century
Literature* (6 vols., 1901-06); F. L. Lucas, *The Decline and Fall of the
Romantic Ideal* (1936); M. M. Colum, *From These Roots: the Ideas That
Have Made Modern Literature* (1937); and H. V. Routh, *Towards the
Twentieth Century: Essays in the Spiritual History of the Nineteenth* (1937).
The following books may be cited in the recent history of religious ideas and
institutions: C. MacCaffrey, *History of the Catholic Church ... 1789-1908*
(2 vols., 1910); W. Barry, *The Papacy in Modern Times* (1911); and A. C.
McGiffert, *The Rise of Modern Religious Ideas* (1915). Particular aspects of
religious history are discussed in A. Lunn and C. E. M. Joad, *Is Christianity
True?* (1933); E. C. Messenger, *Evolution and Theology* (1931), from the
Catholic viewpoint; and C. C. Eckhart, *The Papacy and World Affairs* (1937).
Several recent texts offer a very adequate survey of modern science: W. T.
Sedgwick and H. W. Tyler, *A Short History of Science* (rev. ed., 1939); H.
Levy, *Modern Science* (1939); and F. S. Taylor, *The March of Mind: a Short
History of Science* (1939). Certain important topics in the history of science
are treated in: A. N. Whitehead, *Science and the Modern World* (1925); R.
Valery-Radot, *The Life of Pasteur* (1926); J. H. Jeans, *The World Around Us*
(1930), dealing with astronomy; R. H. Shryock, *The Development of Modern
Medicine* (1936); L. H. Hogben, *Mathematics for the Millions* (1937); and
J. G. Frazer, *Golden Bough; a Study in Magic and Religion* (12 vols., 3rd ed.,
1935; 1 vol. ed., 1940). Of the original milestones of modern science, the
following may be noted: J. Hutton, *The Theory of the Earth* (1795); C. Lyell,
Principles of Geology (3 vols., 1830-33); C. Darwin, *The Origin of the Species*
(1859), *The Variation of Animals and Plants Under Domestication* (1868), and
The Descent of Man (1871); and T. H. Huxley, *Evidence as to Man's Place
in Nature* (1864), and *Lay Sermons, Addresses, and Reviews* (1870). The
history of art is covered in several recent compends: D. M. Robb, *Art in the
Western World* (1935); N. Pevsner, *Pioneers of the Modern Movement from
William Morris to Walter Gropius* (1936); and E. P. Richardson, *The Way of
Western Art, 1776-1914* (1939). And for music, see: P. C. Buck, *The Oxford
History of Music* (7 vols., 2nd ed., 1929-38); A. Einstein, *A Short History of
Music* (1938); and H. D. McKinney, *Music in History* (1940). The general
characteristics of modern nationalism are discussed in C. J. H. Hayes, *Essays on
Nationalism* (1926), and *Historical Evolution of Modern Nationalism* (1931);
and, more recently, Royal Institute of International Affairs, *Nationalism* (1940).
Particular aspects of nationalism are reflected in J. A. de Gobineau, *Moral and*

Intellectual Diversity of Races (1856); and H. S. Chamberlain, *Foundations of the Nineteenth Century* (2 vols., 1913).

III. SPECIAL WORKS

1. 1815 TO 1848

GENERAL: F. B. Artz, *Reaction and Revolution, 1814-1832* (1934 offers an excellent general survey of the earlier part of this period. The whole period is treated in briefer scope in A. May, *The Age of Metternich, 1814-1848* (1933); L. Woolf, *After the Deluge; a Study of Communal Psychology* (2 vols., 1931-40); and P. Viereck, *Conservatism Revisited: the Revolt against Revolt, 1815-1849* (1949).

ENGLAND: The political life is best reflected in a number of distinguished biographies, notably: S. Walpole, *The Life of Lord John Russell* (2 vols., 2nd ed., 1889); J. A. Hobson, *Richard Cobden, the International Man* (1919); G. M. Trevelyan, *Lord Grey of the Reform Bill* (1920); B. Blackburn, *Noble Lord, the Seventh Earl of Shaftesbury* (1949); G. M. Trevelyan, *Life of John Bright* (1925); A. Aspinwall, *Lord Brougham and the Whig Party* (1927); P. Guedalla, *Palmerston* (1927), and *Wellington* (1931); and H. C. F. Bell, *Lord Palmerston* (2 vols., 1936). There are good biographies of Queen Victoria by G. L. Strachey (1921); G. D. H. Cole, *William Cobbet* (1924), and *Robert Owen* (1930); G. Wallas, *Life of Francis Place, 1771-1854* (1925); C. Driver, *Tory Radical, the Life of Richard Oastler* (1946); E. F. Benson (1935), and E. Sitwell (1936), good biographies of Queen Victoria; A. C. Benson, G. E. Buckle, and Lord Esher, eds., *The Letters of Queen Victoria* (9 vols., 1908-32). Special topics are treated in F. J. F. Jackson, *Social Life of England, 1750-1850* (1916); M. Hovell, *The Chartist Movement* (1925); J. L. and B. Hammond, *The Age of the Chartists, 1832-1854* (1930); R. J. Cruikshank, *Charles Dickens and Early Victorian England* (1949); C. K. Webster, *Foreign Policy of Castlereagh, 1815-1822* (1925); and H. W. V. Temperley, *Foreign Policy of Canning, 1822-1827* (1925).

FRANCE: The best general studies are those of J. Lucas-Dubreton, *The Restoration and the July Monarchy* (1929); and F. B. Artz, *France Under the Bourbon Restoration, 1814-1830* (1931). There are also several biographies in English: F. A. Simpson, *Rise of Louis Napoleon* (rev. ed., 1925); J. M. S. Allison, *Thiers and the French Monarchy, 1797-1848* (1926); and E. P. Brush, *Guizot in the Early Years of the Orleanist Monarchy* (1929). And for the July Monarchy, J. M. S. Allison, *Church and State in the Reign of Louis Philippe, 1830-1848* (1926); S. Kent, *Electoral Procedure Under Louis Philippe* (1937); G. Elton, *The Revolutionary Idea in France, 1789-1871* (1923); J. Plamenatz, *The Revolutionary Movement in France, 1815-1871* (1952); C. T. Muret, *French Royalist Doctrines Since the Revolution* (1933); and N. E. Hudson, *Ultraroyalism and the French Restoration* (1936).

GERMANY: H. G. von Treitschke, *History of Germany in the Nineteenth Century* (7 vols., 1915-19), which stops in 1848, is the classic work in this period;

the same ground is covered more briefly in J. G. Legge, *Rhyme and Revolution in Germany, 1813-1850* (1918).

ITALY AND SPAIN: This period in Italian history is covered in detail by G. F. H. and J. Berkeley, *Italy in the Making* (3 vols., 1932-40). This may be supplemented by P. Colletta, *History of the Kingdom of Naples, 1734-1825* (2 vols., 1858); J. H. Brady, *Rome and the Neapolitan Revolution of 1820-1821* (1937); M. W. Wicks, *The Italian Exiles in London, 1816-1848* (1937); A. J. P. Taylor, *The Italian Problem in European Diplomacy, 1847-1849* (1934); A. J. Whyte, *Early Life and Letters of Cavour, 1810-1848* (1925); and S. Barr, *Mazzini, Portrait of an Exile* (1935).

For Spain: E. J. Parry, *The Spanish Marriages, 1841-1846* (1936).

AUSTRIA: *The Memoirs of Prince Metternich* (5 vols., 1880-82) are an important source, and may be supplemented by the biographies of the chancellor by A. Herman (1932), H. Du Coudray (1936), and A. Cecil (1943); and J. Blum, *Noble Landowners and Agriculture in Austria, 1815-1848* (1948).

RUSSIA: There are two recent lives of Alexander I, both unsatisfactory, by F. H. Gribble (1931) and M. Paleologue (1938). An important episode in his career is treated in E. J. Knapton, *The Lady of the Holy Alliance, the Life of Julie de Krudener* (1939). Other aspects of his reign are discussed in H. B. George, *Napoleon's Invasion of Russia* (1899); E. V. Tarle, *Napoleon's Invasion of Russia, 1812* (1942); and A. G. Mazour, *The First Russian Revolution, 1825* (1937).

SOUTHEASTERN EUROPE AND THE EASTERN QUESTION: Various aspects of the Eastern Question are treated in P. F. Shupp, *The European Powers and the Near Eastern Question, 1806-1807* (1931); F. S. Rodkey, *The Turco-Egyptian Question in the Relations of England, France and Russia, 1832-1841* (1924); and P. E. Mosely, *Russian Diplomacy and the Opening of the Eastern Question in 1838 and 1839* (1934). W. A. Phillips, *The War of Greek Independence, 1821 to 1833* (1897) is still the best account of the Greek struggle, the diplomatic aspects of which are discussed in some detail in C. W. Crawley, *The Question of Greek Independence: a Study of British Policy in the Near East, 1821-1833* (1930). The only full account in English of the Serbian uprising is L. von Ranke, *History of Servia and the Servian Revolution* (1847).

2. 1848 TO 1870

GENERAL: F. Fejeto, *The Opening of an Era: 1848, an Historical Symposium* (1949); P. Robertson, *Revolutions of 1848: a Social History* (1952); R. C. Binkley, *Realism and Nationalism, 1852-1871* (1935) is the only survey of this period. On the Franco-Prussian War: R. H. Lord, *Origins of the War of 1870* (1924), and H. Oncken, *Napoleon III and the Rhine: Origin of the War of 1870-71* (1928).

ENGLAND: For domestic history, see: E. L. Woodward, *The Age of Reform, 1815-1870* (1938); G. M. Young, ed., *Early Victorian England, 1830-1865*

(1935); S. Maccoby, *English Radicalism, 1853-1886* (1938); and the biographies of Queen Elizabeth, Palmerston, Gladstone, and Disraeli cited in the previous and the following sections. Foreign affairs are discussed in E. D. Adams, *Great Britain and the American Civil War* (2 vols., 1925); W. P. Morrell, *British Colonial Policy in the Age of Peel and Russell* (1930); and R. J. Sontag, *Germany and England: Background of Conflict, 1848-1894* (1938).

FRANCE: R. Arnaud, *The Second Republic and Napoleon III* (1930) offers a general survey of the whole period. Two excellent accounts of the Second Empire are those of P. Guedalla (1937) and O. Aubry (1940). The earlier part of the emperor's reign is described in F. A. Simpson, *Louis Napoleon and the Recovery of France, 1848-1856* (1923). Among the most interesting of the personal accounts of the Revolution of 1948 are A. de Lamartine, *History of the French Revolution of 1848* (1852), and A. de Tocqueville, *Recollections* (1896); D. C. McKay, *The National Workshops: a Study of the French Revolution of 1848* (1933).

GERMANY: The standard account of the unification of Germany is H. von Sybel, *Founding of the German Empire* (7 vols., 1890-98); the period to 1866 is treated more briefly in H. Friedjung, *The Struggle for Supremacy in Germany* (1935). V. Valentin, *1848, Chapters of German History* (1940) gives an account of the German share of the general European disturbance. Bismarck's memoirs have been translated under the title *Bismarck, the Man and the Statesman* (2 vols., 1899); a good biography is C. G. Robertson, *Bismarck* (1919); see also G. B. Smith, *William I and the German Empire* (1888); and F. E. Whitton, *Moltke* (1921). And for one aspect of foreign relations, R. J. Sontag, *Germany and England: Background of Conflict, 1848-1894* (1938).

ITALY: For the unification of Italy, see G. M. Trevelyan, *Garibaldi's Defence of the Roman Republic* (1907), *Garibaldi and the Thousand* (1909), and *Garibaldi and the Making of Italy* (1911). Other biographies are W. R. Thayer, *Life and Times of Cavour* (2 vols., 1911); E. K. Hancock, *Bettino Ricasoli and the Risorgimento in Italy* (1926); C. S. Forester, *Victor Emmanuel II and the Union of Italy* (1927); P. Frischauer, *Garibaldi: the Man and the Nation* (1935); and S. Barr, *Mazzini, Portrait of an Exile* (1935). K. R. Greenfield, *Economics and Nationalism in the Risorgimento; a Study of Nationalism in Lombardy* (1934) is a recent study in this period.

AUSTRIA-HUNGARY: The standard biography of the emperor is J. Redlich, *Emperor Francis Joseph of Austria* (1929); see also E. Bagger, *Francis Joseph* (1927); K. Tschuppik, *The Reign of the Emperor Francis Joseph, 1848-1916* (1930); and E. Corti, *Elizabeth, Empress of Austria* (1936). A thorough treatment of Austrian diplomacy is to be found in C. W. Clark, *Franz Joseph and Bismarck: the Diplomacy of Austria Before the War of 1866* (1934).

RUSSIA: A. von Haxthausen, *The Russian Empire, Its People, Institutions and Resources* (2 vols., 1856) emphasizes the agrarian problem, which has been analyzed more recently in G. T. Robinson, *Rural Russia Under the Old Regime* (1932). A recent biography of the reform emperor is S. Graham, *Tsar of Freedom; the Life and Reign of Alexander II* (1935).

SOUTHEASTERN EUROPE AND THE EASTERN QUESTION: The classic account of the Crimean War in English is A. W. Kinglake, *The Invasion of the Crimea* (8 vols., 1863-87); briefer accounts are E. B. Hamley, *The War in the Crimea* (2nd ed., 1910); and G. F. MacMunn, *Crimea in Perspective* (1935). V. J. Puryear, *England, Russia and the Straits Question, 1844-1856* (1931) deals with an important aspect of the diplomacy, and H. W. V. Temperley, *England and the Near East: the Crimea* (1936), is broader in scope than its title implies. The unification of Rumania is treated in W. G. East, *The Union of Moldavia and Wallachia* (1927); and T. W. Riker, *The Making of Roumania* (1931).

3. 1870 TO 1914

GENERAL: For a good general treatment of the period see F. L. Benns, *European History Since 1870* (1955); and V. L. and E. M. Albjerg, *From Sedan to Stresa: Europe Since 1870* (1937). New interpretations of this period are D. C. Somervell, *Modern Europe, 1871-1939* (1940); and C. J. Hayes, *A Generation of Materialism, 1871-1900* (1941). On nationalism: L. L. Snyder, *The Meaning of Nationalism* (1954); and B. C. Shafer, *Nationalism: Myth and Reality* (1955). On liberalism: H. J. Laski, *The Rise of European Liberalism* (1947).

ENGLAND: General surveys of this period are R. H. Gretton, *A Modern History of the English People, 1880-1922* (1930); J. A. R. Marriott, *Modern England, 1885-1932* (1934); R. C. K. Ensor, *England, 1870-1914* (1936); and D. C. Somervell, *Modern Britain, 1870-1939* (1941). Many of the best treatments of this period are to be found in such biographies as W. F. Monypenny and G. E. Buckle, *Life of Benjamin Disraeli* (6 vols., 1910-20); C. Roth, *Benjamin Disraeli, Earl of Beaconsfield* (1952), and a popular interpretation by A. Maurois (1928); J. Morley, *Life of William Edward Gladstone* (new ed., 1921); W. P. Hall, *Mr. Gladstone* (1931); P. Magnus, *Gladstone: a Biography* (1956); P. Guedalla, *The Queen and Mr. Gladstone* (1933); P. Knaplund, *Gladstone's Foreign Policy* (1935); G. Cecil, *Life of Robert, Marquis of Salisbury* (4 vols., 1921-32); J. L. Garvin, *Life of Joseph Chamberlain* (3 vols., 1932-34); S. Lee, *King Edward VII* (2 vols., 1925-27); J. Spender and C. Asquith, *The Life of Herbert Henry Asquith, Lord Oxford and Asquith* (2 vols., 1932); Lord Haldane, *Autobiography* (1929); Earl Grey, *Twenty-five Years* (2 vols., 1925), and G. M. Trevelyan, *Grey of Fallodon* (1937); and, for one of the best general surveys of British pre-war diplomacy, H. Nicolson, *Portrait of a Diplomatist* (1930). The problems facing the British Navy are carefully analyzed in E. L. Woodward, *Great Britain and the German Navy* (1935); and A. J. Marder, *The Anatomy of British Sea Power: a History of British Naval Power in the Pre-Dreadnought Era, 1880-1905* (1940). The most thorough treatment of the empire as a whole is J. H. Rose, A. P. Newton and E. A. Benians, eds., *The Cambridge History of the British Empire* (8 vols.,

1929-36); other surveys are C. W. Dilke, *Problems of Greater Britain* (4th ed., 1890); J. A. Hobson, *Imperialism, a Study* (3rd ed., 1938); P. Knaplund, *Gladstone and Britain's Imperial Policy* (1927); and, for the later period, W. P. Hall, *Empire to Commonwealth: Thirty Years of British Imperial History* (1928); W. Y. Elliott, *The New British Empire* (1932); and J. E. Tyler, *The Struggle for Imperial Unity, 1868-1895* (1938). And for the Irish Question: J. O'Connor, *History of Ireland, 1790-1924* (2 vols., 1925); J. E. Pomfret, *The Struggle for Land in Ireland, 1800-1923* (1930); and St. J. G. Ervine, *Parnell* (1925).

FRANCE: The outstanding history of France since 1870 is D. W. Brogan, *The Development of Modern France (1870-1939)* (1940); a briefer account is R. Recouly, *The Third Republic* (1928). The first years of the Third Republic have been considered in detail in several valuable books: G. Hanotaux, *Contemporary France* (4 vols., 1903-09), dealing with the years from 1870 to 1882; L. A. Thiers, *Memoirs, 1870-1873* (1915); J. M. S. Allison, *Monsieur Thiers* (1932); H. M. Stannard, *Gambetta and the Foundation of the Third French Republic* (1921); J. P. T. Bury, *France, 1814-1940: A History* (1949); E. S. Mason, *The Paris Commune, an Episode in the History of the Socialist Movement* (1930); F. Jellinek, *The Paris Commune of 1871* (1937); and F. H. Brabant, *The Beginning of the Third Republic in France: a History of the National Assembly, February–September, 1871* (1940. Other studies in this period are: J. Kayser, *The Dreyfus Affair* (1931); A. and P. Dreyfus, *The Dreyfus Case* (1937); L. M. Friedman, *Zola and the Dreyfus Case* (1937); C. W. Porter, *The Career of Théophile Delcassé* (1936); H. R. Weinstein, *Jean Jaurès, a Study of Patriotism in the French Socialist Movement* (1936); E. M. Sait, *Government and Politics in France* (1921); R. H. Soltau, *French Parties and Politics, 1871-1921* (rev. ed., 1930); W. L. Middleton, *The French Political System* (1932); S. Bernstein, *The Beginnings of Marxian Socialism in France* (1933); F. L. Schuman, *War and Diplomacy in the French Republic* (1931); E. M. Carroll, *French Public Opinion and Foreign Affairs, 1870-1914* (1931); T. F. Power, Jr., *Jules Ferry and the Renaissance of French Imperialism* (1944); and W. Williams, *The Tiger of France* (1949).

GERMANY: Good general accounts of Germany during this period are: R. H. Fife, *The German Empire Between Two Wars* (1916); W. H. Dawson, *The German Empire, 1867-1914* (2 vols., 1919); G. P. Gooch, *Germany* (1925); and, in many ways the most satisfactory treatment, A. Rosenberg, *The Birth of the German Republic, 1871-1918* (1931). For biographies of Bismarck, see the previous section. For the Kaiser: Wilhelm II, *My Memoirs, 1878-1918* (1922); E. Ludwig, *Kaiser Wilhelm II* (1926); G. S. Viereck, *The Kaiser on Trial* (1937); and, on a broader canvas, K. F. Nowak, *Kaiser, and Chancellor* (1930), and *Germany's Road to Ruin* (1932). Other biographies are: F. E. Whitton, *Moltke* (1922); C. Hohenlohe-Schillingsfürst, *Memoirs* (2 vols., 1906); A. von Waldersee, *A Field-Marshal's Memoirs* (1924); A. von Tirpitz, *My Memoirs* (2 vols., 1919); and the *Memoirs of Prince von Bülow* (4 vols., 1931-33). M. S. Wertheimer, *Pan-German League, 1890-1914* (1924) discusses one aspect of German nationalism which found expression in such volumes as F. von Bernhardi, *Germany and the Next War* (1914); and F. Naumann, *Central Europe* (1917). The story of Germany's rapid economic development is told in: W. F. Bruck, *Social and Economic History of Germany from William II to Hitler, 1888-1938* (1938); G. Stolper, *German Economy, 1870-1940* (1940); W. H. Dawson, *Protection in Germany; a History of German Fiscal Policy During the Nineteenth Century* (1904); E. D. Howard, *The Cause and Extent of the Recent Industrial Progress of Germany* (1907); and T. Veblen, *Imperial Germany and the Industrial Revolution* (1915). The best survey of foreign policy is E. Brandenburg, *From Bismarck to the World War, 1890-1914* (1927), and various aspects of it are discussed in M. E. Townsend, *The Rise and Fall of Germany's Colonial Empire, 1884-1918* (1930); R. J. Sontag, *Germany and England: Background of Conflict, 1848-1894* (1938); and E. M. Carroll, *Germany and the Great Powers, 1866-1914: a Study in Public Opinion and Foreign Policy* (1938). A special topic of great importance is considered in A. S. Hurd and H. Castle, *German Sea Power* (1913); and R. J. S. Hoffman, *Great Britain and the German Trade Rivalry, 1875-1914* (1933). W. L. Langer, *European Alliances and Alignments* (1950).

ITALY AND SPAIN: B. Croce, *A History of Italy, 1871-1915* (1929) gives an excellent general account, which may be supplemented by the *Memoirs of Francesco Crispi* (3 vols., 1912-14); and R. Albrecht-Carrie, *Italy from Napoleon to Mussolini* (1950). Special topics are presented by T. Tittoni, *Italy's Foreign and Colonial Policy* (1914), the speeches of a prominent statesman; S. W. Halperin, *Italy and the Vatican at War* (1939), dealing with the period from 1870 to 1878; and *The Separation of Church and State in Italian Thought From Cavour to Mussolini* (1937). J. B. Trend, *The Origins of Modern Spain* (1934), emphasizes the intellectual development since 1868.

AUSTRIA-HUNGARY: The best analysis of Hapsburg problems is to be found in O. Jaszi, *The Dissolution of the Hapsburg Monarchy* (1929), which may be supplemented by R. W. Seton-Watson, *Racial Problems in Hungary* (1908), and *The Southern Slav Question and the Hapsburg Monarchy* (1911). Biographies of Francis Joseph are given in the previous section. Foreign affairs are discussed in A. F. Pribram, *Austrian Foreign Policy, 1908-1918* (1923).

RUSSIA: While there is no general history of Russia dealing with this particular period, there are a number of valuable volumes dealing with various aspects of it. Biographies of Alexander II are cited in the previous section; the life of his successor is treated in C. Lowe, *Alexander III of Russia* (1895); and an interesting light is thrown on the last emperor in *The Letters of Tsar Nicholas and Empress Marie* (1937); and E. J. Bing, ed., *The Secret Letters of the Last Tsar* (1938). Further biographical material includes: S. Witte, *The Memoirs of Count Witte* (1921); V. N. Kokovtsev, *Out of My Past* (1933); and V. I. Gurko, *Features and Figures of the Past* (1939). A full picture of Russian life is presented in D. M. Wallace, *Russia* (2 vols., 1905); and B. Pares, *Russia and Reform* (1905). Foreign and military affairs are treated in S. A. Korff, *Russia's Foreign Relations During the Last Half Century* (1922), a conventional account; B. H. Sumner, *Russia and the Balkans, 1870-1880* (1937); F. V. Greene, *The Russian Campaign in Turkey, 1877-78* (1908); A. Novikoff-Priboy, *Tsushima* (1937). For social and economic questions: G. T. Robinson, *Rural Russia Under the Old Regime* (1932); M. S. Miller, *The Economic Development of Russia, 1905-1914* (1926); G. A. Pavlovski, *Agricultural Russia on the Eve of the Revolution* (1930); L. A. Owen, *The Russian Peasant Movement, 1906-1917* (1937); and J. S. Curtiss, *State and Church in Russia: the Last Years of the Empire, 1900-1917* (1940).

SOUTHEASTERN EUROPE AND THE EASTERN QUESTION: A general survey of the period is offered in M. W. Tyler, *The Great Powers and the Near East, 1878-1908* (1925). Special aspects of the Eastern Question are considered in: D. Harris, *A Diplomatic History of the Balkan Crisis of 1875-1878; the First Year* (1936); M. D. Stojanovic, *The Great Powers and the Balkans, 1875-1878* (1939); W. N. Medlicott, *The Congress of Berlin and After, 1878-1880* (1938); R. W. Seton-Watson, *Disraeli, Gladstone and the Eastern Question* (1935); D. Harris, *Britain and the Bulgarian Horrors of 1876* (1939); L. Villari, ed., *The Balkan Question* (1905); H. N. Brailsford, *Macedonia, Its Races and Their Future* (1906); C. Anastasoff, *The Tragic Peninsula* (1938); E. M. Earle, *Turkey, the Great Powers, and the Bagdad Railway* (1923); and J. B. Wolf, *The Diplomatic History of the Bagdad Railroad* (1936). And for the individual countries:

Turkey: E. F. Knight, *The Awakening of Turkey* (1909); A. H. Midhat, *The Life of Midhat Pasha* (1903); E. Pears, *Life of Abdul-Hamid* (1917); Djemal Pasha, *Memories of a Turkish Statesman, 1913-1919* (1922); and D. C. Blaisdell, *European Financial Control in the Ottoman Empire* (1929).

Bulgaria: A. von Huhn, *The Struggle of the Bulgarians for National Independence under Prince Alexander* (1886), and *The Kidnapping of Prince Alexander* (1887); A. H. Beaman, *M. Stambuloff* (1895); E. Dicey, *The Peasant State* (1894); J. Macdonald, *Czar Ferdinand and His People* (1913); W. S. Monroe, *Bulgaria and Her People* (1914); and C. E. Black, *The Establishment of Constitutional Government in Bulgaria* (1943).

Serbia: C. Mijatovich, *The Memoirs of a Balkan Diplomatist* (1917); H. Baerlein, *The Birth of Yugoslavia* (2 vols., 1922); and R. W. Seton-Watson, *Serajevo* (1926).

Greece: R. A. H. Bickford-Smith, *Greece under King George* (1893); C. Bigham, *With the Turkish Army in Thessaly* (1897); W. K. Rose, *With the Greeks in Thessaly* (1897); P. F. Martin, *Greece of the Twentieth Century* (1913); and W. Christmas, *King George of Greece* (1914).

The Balkan Wars are discussed in E. C. Helmreich, *The Diplomacy of the Balkan Wars, 1912-1913* (1938); I. E. Gueshoff, *The Balkan League* (1915); and D. J. Cassavetti, *Hellas and the Balkan Wars* (1914).

INTERNATIONAL RELATIONS: Of the many accounts dealing with European diplomacy since 1870, the following may be cited: W. S. Davis, *The Roots of the War* (1919); H. E. Barnes, *The Genesis of the World War* (1926), one of the first attempts to present a balanced view; S. B. Fay, *The Origins of the World War* (2 vols. in 1, 2nd ed., 1931), the standard account; R. B. Mowat,

The Concert of Europe (1931). In briefer scope N. Mansergh, *The Coming of the First World War: a Study of the European Balance, 1878-1914* (1949); R. J. Sontag, *European Diplomatic History, 1871-1932* (1933); and G. P. Gooch, *Before the War; Studies in Diplomacy* (2 vols., 1936-38). Limited periods and special topics are discussed, for the earlier period, in W. L. Langer, *European Alliances and Alignments, 1871-1890* (1931), and *The Diplomacy of Imperialism, 1890-1902* (2 vols., 1935); the period of the formation of the alliances is discussed in G. L. Dickinson, *The International Anarchy, 1904-1914* (1926); E. N. Anderson, *The First Moroccan Crisis, 1904-1906* (1930); O. J. Hale, *Germany and the Diplomatic Revolution: a Study in the Diplomacy of the Press, 1904-1906* (1931); B. E. Schmitt, *Triple Alliance and Triple Entente* (1934), a brief servey, and *The Annexation of Bosnia, 1908-1909* (1937); R. P. Churchill, *The Anglo-Russian Convention of 1907* (1939); W. C. Askew, *Europe and Italy's Acquisition of Libya, 1911-1912* (1942); and E. C. Helmreich, *The Diplomacy of the Balkan Wars, 1912-1913* (1938). A number of important volumes have also been devoted to the diplomatic maneuvers during the last year of peace: P. Renouvin, *The Immediate Origins of the War* (1928); B. E. Schmitt, *The Coming of the War: 1914* (2 vols., 1930); A. von Wegerer, *A Refutation of the Versailles War Guilt Thesis* (1930); and T. Wolff, *The Eve of 1914* (1935). For other aspects of the problem, see: A. F. Pribram, *England and the International Policy of the European Great Powers, 1871-1914* (1931); R. J. Sontag, *Germany and England: Background of Conflict, 1848-1894* (1938); E. M. Carroll, *French Public Opinion and Foreign Affairs, 1870-1914* (1930), and *Germany and the Great Powers, 1866-1914: a Study in Public Opinion and Foreign Policy* (1938); O. J. Hale, *Publicity and Diplomacy, With Special Reference to England and Germany, 1890-1914* (1940); and L. Albertini, *The Origins of the War of 1914* (2 vols. in translation, 1952-53).

The problem of European imperialism during this period is one of the most important aspects of international relations; in addition to the general histories of diplomacy cited above, the following books deal more specifically with this problem: L. Woolf, *Economic Imperialism* (1921), and *Imperialism and Civilization* (1928); P. T. Moon, *Imperialism and World Politics* (1926), a general text; N. Lenin, *Imperialism, the Last Stage of Capitalism* (1937), representing the Marxist viewpoint; G. Clark, *A Place in the Sun* (1936), and *The Balance Sheets of Imperialism* (1936); and J. A. Hobson, *Imperialism, A Study* (3rd ed., 1938); L. C. Robbins, *The Economic Causes of War* (1939); E. M. Winslow, *The Pattern of Imperialism: a Study in the Theories of Power* (1948); R. Maunier, *The Sociology of Colonies: an Introduction to the Study of Race Conduct* (2 vols., 1949); and J. A. Schumpter, *Imperialism and Social Classes* (1955).

For imperialism in Asia, see: N. D. Harris, *Europe and the East* (1926); G. W. Keeton, *The Development of Extraterritoriality in China* (2 vols., 1928); H. B. Morse and H. F. MacNair, *Far Eastern International Relations* (1928); G. H. Blakeslee, *The Pacific Area* (1929); D. E. Owen, *Imperialism and Nationalism in the Far East* (1929); G. Bienstock, *The Struggle for the Pacific* (1937); and E. R. Hughes, *The Invasion of China by the Western World* (1938). Special aspects of Far Eastern imperialism are treated in E. S.

Tai, *Treaty Ports in China* (1918); T. W. Overlach, *Foreign Financial Control in China* (1919); A. Vandenbosch, *Dutch East Indies* (1934); D. E. Owen, *British Opium Policy in China and India* (1934); W. C. Costin, Great Britain and China, *1833-1860* (1937); J. Pratt, *The Expansion of Europe in the Far East* (1947); B. H. Sumner, *Tsardom and Imperialism in the Far East and the Middle East* (1944); J. F. Cady, *The Roots of French Imperialism in Eastern Asia* (1954).

For imperialism in Africa, see: C. P. Lucas, *The Partition and Colonization of Africa* (1922); N. D. Harris, *Europe and Africa* (1927); H. L. Hoskins, *European Imperialism in Africa* (1930); L. A. C. Raphael, *The Cape to Cairo Dream: a Study in British Imperialism* (1936); and Lord Hailey, *An African Survey* (1938). Special studies in African imperialism are: E. B. Cromer, *Modern Egypt* (2 vols., 1908); L. Mitchell, *The Life of the Rt. Hon. Cecil John Rhodes, 1853-1902* (2 vols., 1910); L. S. Woolf, *Empire and Commerce in Africa* (1919); A. Schweitzer, *On the Edge of the Primeval Forest* (1922); W. P. Livingstone, *Mary Slessor of Calabar* (1925); R. L. Buell, *The Native Problems in Africa* (2 vols., 1928); R. Coupland, *The Exploitation of East Africa, 1856-1890* (1939); J. A. Noon, *Labor Problems of Africa* (1944); R. Rudin, *Germans in the Cameroons, 1884-1914; a Study in Modern Imperialism* (1938); and M. M. Knight, *Morocco as a French Economic Venture: a Study of Open-Door Imperialism* (1937).

IV. WORLD WAR I

THE FIRST WORLD WAR: The best volume on the war is C. R. M. F. Cruttwell, *History of the Great War* (1934); B. H. L. Hart, *A History of the World War, 1914-1918* (1934), and *The War in Outline, 1914-1918* (1936) are somewhat narrower in scope. Some of the most valuable accounts of the war are to be found in the memoirs. For the British: J. French (1919); J. R. Jellicoe (1919); I. Hamilton (2 vols., 1920); W. Churchill (5 vols., 1923-29); and T. E. Lawrence (1927). For the Germans: E. Ludendorff (2 vols., 1919); A. P. F. von Tirpitz (2 vols., 1919); E. von Falkenhayn (1920); A. H. R. von Kluck (1920); R. Scheer (1920); P. von Hindenburg (2 vols., 1921); and L. von Sanders (1927). For the French: H. P. Petain (1929); F. Foch (1931); and J. J. C. Joffre (2 vols., 1932). There are also a number of interesting biographies, of which the following may be noted: C. R. Ballard, *Kitchener* (1930); B. H. L. Hart, *Foch* (1931); R. Recouly, *Joffre* (1931); and K. Tschuppik, *Ludendorff* (1932). See also: Abbott, G. F., *Greece and the Allies, 1914-1922* (1922); A. Emin, *Turkey in the World War* (1930); R. Graves, *Lawrence and the Arabian Adventure* (1928); E. Ironside, *Tannenberg: the First Thirty Days in East Prussia* (1935); J. C. Adams, *Flight in Winter* (1942), a fine account of the martyrdom of Serbia; S. Tyng, *The Campaign of the Marne, 1914* (1935); L. Villari, *The War on the Italian Front* (1932); C. Domville, *Submarines and Sea Power* (1919); and J. R. Jellicoe, *The Grand Fleet, 1914-1916* (1922).

ENGLAND: Perhaps the best general account of England at war is W. S. Churchill, *The World Crisis* (5 vols., 1923-29; 1 vol. condensed ed., 1931); *The War Memoirs of David Lloyd George* (5 vols., 1933-36) is of similar scope. Special topics are discussed in H. L. Gray, *War Time Control of Industry: the Experience of England* (1918); and C. R. M. F. Cruttwell, *The Role of British Strategy in the Great War* (1936).

FRANCE AND BELGIUM: H. M. Hyndman, *The Man and His Time* (1919); G. Clemenceau, *Grandeur and Misery of Victory* (1930); G. G. Aston, *The Biography of the Late Marshal Foch* (1929); F. Foch, *Memoirs* (1931); R. Recouly, *Joffre* (1931); E. J. Galet, *Albert, King of the Belgians in the Great War* (1931); and *Cardinal Mercier's Own Story* (1920).

UNITED STATES: N. D. Baker, *Why We Went to War* (1936); B. J. Hendrick, *Life and Letters of Walter H. Page* (1922); W. Millis, *The Road to War: America, 1914-1917* (1935); C. Seymour, *Woodrow Wilson and the World War* (1922); and J. G. Harbord, *The American Army in France* (1936).

GERMANY: E. Bevan, *German Social Democracy During the War* (1919); R. H. Lutz, *The Causes of the German Collapse in 1919* (1934); A. Rosenberg, *The Birth of the German Republic* (1931); and M. Baumont, *The Fall of the Kaiser* (1931).

AUSTRIA-HUNGARY: E. Glaise Von Hostenau, *The Collapse of the Austro-Hungarian Empire* (1930); Nowak, K. F., *The Collapse of Central Europe* (1924); T. G. Masaryk, *The Making of a State* (1921); S. Burian, *Austria in Dissolution* (1925); Jas. O. Jaszi, *The Dissolution of the Hapsburg Monarchy* (1929); and J. Pilsudski, *The Memories of a Polish Revolutionary and Soldier* (1931).

RUSSIA: W. H. Chamberlin, *The Russian Revolution, 1917-1918* (2 vols., 1934); V. Chernov, *The Great Russian Revolution* (1936); M. T. Florinsky, *The End of the Russian Empire* (1931); R. Fulop-Miller, *Rasputin: the Holy Devil* (1928); E. H. Carr, *The Bolshevik Revolution, 1917-1923* (3 vols., 1951-1953); P. Kirby, *The Russian Revolution* (1940); P. Miliukov, *History of the Second Russian Revolution* (1920); N. Lenin, *Preparing for Revolt* (1929); N. Lenin, *Toward the Seizure of Power* (2 vols., 1932); D. Shub, *Lenin, a Biography* (1948); L. Trotsky, *The History of the Russian Revolution* (1934), and *My Life* (1940); and J. W. Wheeler-Bennett, *Brest-litovsk: the Forgotten Peace*, March 1918 (1939).

PEACE TREATIES: The most useful accounts of the Paris Peace Conference are: H. W. V. Temperley, *A History of the Peace Conferences of Paris* (6 vols., 1920-1924); H. Nicholson, *Peacemaking, 1919* (1933); P. Birdsal, *Versailles Twenty Years Afterward* (1941); J. M. Keynes, *Economic Consequences of the Peace* (1921); and J. M. Keynes, *A Revision of the Treaty* (1922). For a reply see: E. Mantoux, *The Carthaginian Peace, or the Economic Consequences of Mr. Keynes* (1946); H. R. Rudin, *Armistice, 1918;* G. B. Noble, *Policies and Opinions at Paris, 1919* (1935); and A. Cobben, *National Self-determination* (1944).

V. TWENTY YEARS' TRUCE

1919 TO 1939

ENGLAND: C. F. G. Masterman, *England After the War* (1923); A. Siegfried, *Post-War Britain* (1924); W. Dibelius, *England* (1930); D. C. Somervell, *The Reign of George V* (1935); and R. Graves and A. Hodge, *The Long Week-End; A Social History of Great Britain, 1918-1939* (1941). J. Buchan, *The People's King* (1935); H. Bolitho, *King George VI* (1938); and M. Thomson, *David Lloyd George, The Official Biography* (1948), are interesting biographies. The economic crisis is dicussed in H. Heaton, *The British Way to Recovery* (1934); and the problems of post-war diplomacy are treated in: H. Nicolson, *Curzon: the Last Phase, 1919-1925: a Study in Post-War Diplomacy* (1934); R. W. Seton-Watson, *Britain and the Dictators, a Survey of Post-War British Policy* (1938), and *From Munich to Danzig* (1939); W. S. Churchill, *While England Slept; a Survey of World Affairs, 1932-1938* (1938), and *Step by Step, 1936-1939* (1939); N. Chamberlain, *The Struggle for Peace* (1939); N. Henderson, *Failure of a Mission* (1940); A. Wolfers, *Britain and France Between Two Wars* (1940); C. F. Brand, *British Labour's Rise to Power* (1941); H. Dalton, *Practical Socialism in England* (1935); G. A. Greenwood, *England Today: a Social History of Our Own Time* (1926); J. A. R. Marriott, *A History of My Own Time* (1943); J. B. Priestley, *An English Journey* (1934); and K. Feiling, *The Life of Neville Chamberlain* (1946).

FRANCE: The best general account is D. W. Brogan, *The Development of Modern France, 1870-1939* (1940). P. Vaucher, *Post-War France* (1934); A. Werth, *France in Ferment* (1935), and *Which Way France?* (1937); M. Thorez, *France To-Day and the People's Front* (1936); G. Bruun, *Clemenceau* (1943); G. Wright, *Raymond Poincaré and the French Presidency* (1942); S. Huddleston, *Poincaré: a Biographical Portrait* (1924); and V. Thompson, *Briand, Man of Peace* (1930). For internal affairs: R. L. Buell, *Contemporary French Politics* (1920); W. Macdonald, *Reconstruction in France* (1922); J. Barthelemy, *Government of France* (1924); W. F. Ogburn, *The Economic Development of Post-War France* (1929); and D. J. Saposs, *The Labor Movement in Post-War France* (1931). And for foreign affairs: H. I. Priestley, *France Overseas: A Study of Modern Imperialism* (1938); and A. Wolfers, *Britain and France Between Two Wars* (1940); R. W. Fox, *France Faces the Future* (1936); C. J. H. Hayes, *France: a Nation of Patriots* (1930); G. Peel, *The Economic Policy of France* (1937); A. Siegfried, *France: a Study in Nationality* (1930); J. J. Spengler, *France Faces Depopulation* (1938); R. L. Stokes, *Leon Blum: Poet to Premier* (1937); and A. Werth, *France in Ferment* (1935).

BELGIUM AND THE NETHERLANDS: L. Pierard, *Belgian Problems Since the War* (1929); A. J. Barnouw, *The Making of Modern Holland* (1944); B. Landleer, ed., *The Netherlands* (1944); and H. Riemus, *The Netherlands* (1944).

GERMANY: Of the numerous discussions of post-war Germany, the following may be cited: H. Quigley and R. T. Clark, *Republican Germany* (1928); E. Luehr, *The New German Republic* (1929); R. T. Clark, *The Fall of the Ger-*

man Republic (1935); A. Rosenberg, *A History of the German Republic* (1936); and, in briefer summary, F. L. Schuman, *Germany Since 1918* (1937). Special aspects of the period are treated in: R. H. Lutz, *The German Revolution, 1918-1919* (1922); R. von Kühlmann, *Thoughts on Germany* (1932); H. Kraus, *The Crisis of German Democracy* (1932); C. B. Hoover, *Germany Enters the Third Reich* (1933); J. W. Angell, *The Recovery of Germany* (2nd. ed., 1932); and A. Mendelssohn-Bartholdy, *The War and German Society* (1937). Memoirs: M. von Baden, *Memoirs* (2 vols., 1928); P. Scheidemann, *Memoirs: the Making of New Germany* (2 vols., 1929); and E. Sutton, ed., *Gustav Stresemann: His Diaries, Letters, and Papers* (3 vols., 1935-40). And biographies: R. Olden, *Stresemann* (1930); J. W. Wheeler-Bennet, *Wooden Titan* (1936), for the career of Hindenburg; R. Olden, *Hitler* (1936); and K. Heiden, *Hitler: a Biography* (1936).

The emergence of National Socialism has given rise to a great flood of controversial literature. The German views are presented in A. Hitler, *Mein Kampf* (American ed., 1939); H. Goering, *Germany Reborn* (1934); and J. Goebbels, *My Part in Germany's Fight* (1935). For critical studies of the Nazi regime, see: K. Heiden, *A History of National Socialism* (1935); F. L. Schuman, *The Nazi Dictatorship* (1935); S. H. Roberts, *The House That Hitler Built* (1937); P. F. Drucker, *The End of Economic Man: a Study of the New Totalitarianism* (1939); H. Rauschning, *The Revolution of Nihilism* (1939), and *Hitler Speaks* (1939); O. Strasser, *Hitler and I* (1940); O. D. Tolischus, *They Wanted War* (1940); and G. Stolper, *German Economy, 1870-1940* (1940). Of the volumes published more recently, W. M. McGovern, *From Luther to Hitler* (1941); S. D. Stirk, *The Prussian Spirit, 1914-1940* (1941); and R. D'O. Butler, *The Roots of National Socialism* (1941), deal with the ideological aspects of Nazism; K. Loewenstein, *Hitler's Germany: the Nazi Background to War* (1940); and F. Neumann, *Behemoth: the Structure and Practice of National Socialism* (1942). W. E., Jr., and M. Dodd, eds., *Ambassador Dodd's Diary* (1941), by an American liberal; H. zu Lowenstein, *The Germans in History* (1945), by a German Catholic; G. Eisler and others, *The Lesson of Germany: a Guide to her History* (1945); H. Rothfels, *The German Opposition to Hitler* (1948); F. Brennecke, *The Nazi Primer*, read by all Hitler youth (1945); A. Frey, *Cross and Swastika; the Ordeal of the German Church* (1938); E. Winkler, *Four Years of Nazi Torture* (1942); and A. Wolf, *Higher Education in Nazi Germany* (1944).

ITALY, SPAIN, AND PORTUGAL: Mussolini's Fascist regime is sympathetically described in: E. W. Hulinger, *The New Fascist State* (1928); B. Mussolini, *My Autobiography* (1928); L. Villari, *The Expansion of Italy* (1930); M. I. Currey, *Italian Foreign Policy, 1918-1932* (1932); and C. Pellizzi, *Italy* (1939). Critical accounts from the democratic point of view are: G. Salvemini, *The Fascist Dictatorship in Italy* (1927), and *Under the Axe of Fascism* (1936); H. Finer, *Mussolini's Italy* (1935); G. A. Borgese, *Goliath; the March of Fascism* (1937); G. Megaro, *Italy in the Making* (1938); M. H. H. Macartney and P. Cremona, *Italy's Foreign and Colonial Policy, 1914-1937* (1938); G. T. Garratt, *Mussolini's Roman Empire* (1938); I. Silone, *The School for Dictators* (1938); and M. W. Rader, *No Compromise* (1939). Recent studies of Mussolini's Italy are: A. Rossi, *The Rise of Italian Fascism* (1938); M. Hentze, *Pre-Fascist Italy: the*

Rise and Fall of the Parliamentary Regime (1939); S. W. Halperin, *Italy and the Vatican at War* (1939); and R. and E. Packard, *Balcony Empire: Italy Under Mussolini* (1942).

On Spain: E. A. Peers, *The Spanish Tragedy, 1930-1936* (1936); H. Gannes and T. Repard, *Spain in Revolt* (1936); J. Castillejo, *Wars of Ideas in Spain* (1937); F. E. Manuel, *The Politics of Modern Spain* (1938); R. Sencourt (R. E. G. George), *Spain's Ordeal* (1940); R. M. Smith, *The Day of the Liberals in Spain* (1938); E. A. Peers, *Spain in Eclipse, 1937-1943* (1943); F. J. Hamilton, *Appeasement's Child: the Franco Regime in Spain* (1943); S. de Madariaga, *Spain* (1943).

On Portugal: G. de Reynold, *Portugal* (1936); V. de Bragança-Cunha, *Revolutionary Portugal, 1910-1936* (1938); A. Ferro, *Salazar; Portugal and Her Leader* (1939); M. Derrick, *The Portugal of Salazar* (1939); and F. C. Egerton, *Salazar, Rebuilder of Portugal* (1943).

CENTRAL EUROPE: C. A. Macartney, *The Social Revolution in Austria* (1926); D. F. Strong, *Austria, October 1918-March 1919: Transition From Empire to Republic* (1939). The general problems of the heirs of the Hapsburgs are presented in: L. Pasvolsky, *Economic Nationalism in the Danubian States* (1926); R. Machray, *The Little Entente* (1929), and *The Struggle for the Danube and the Little Entente, 1929-1938* (1938); J. O. Crane, *The Little Entente* (1931); and G. E. R. Gedye, *Betrayal in Central Europe* (1939), a journalistic account. The tragic story of Austria after the war is told in: V. W. Germains, *Austria of To-Day* (1932); C. Hamilton, *Modern Austria* (1935); J. D. Gregory, *Dollfuss and His Times* (1935); J. Messner, *Dollfuss, an Austrian Patriot* (1935); M. Bullock, *Austria, 1918-1938: A Study in Failure* (1939); K. Schuschnigg, *My Austria* (1938); O. Dutch, *Thus Died Austria* (1938); and M. Fuchs, *Showdown in Vienna: The Death of Austria* (1939); K. Schuschnigg, *Austrian Requiem* (1946); R. K. Sheridan, *Kurt Von Schuschnigg* (1942).

On Hungary: P. Teleki, *The Evolution of Hungary and Its Place in European Politics* (1923), dealing with the period since 1867; O. Jászi, *Revolution and Counter-Revolution in Hungary* (1924); A. Apponyi, and others, *Justice for Hungary* (1928); *The Memoirs of Count Apponyi* (1935); C. A. Macartney, *Hungary and Her Successors: the Treaty of Trianon and Its Consequences, 1919-1937* (1937); M. A. Kobr, *Hungary's War* (1943); T. Mende, *Hungary* (1944); and G. Pálóczy-Horváth, *In Darkest Hungary* (1945).

On Czechoslovakia: F. von Lützow and H. A. Piehler, *Bohemia, an Historical Sketch* (1939), for the historical background; E. Wiskemann, *Czechs and Germans* (1938); T. G. Masaryk, *The Making of a State* (1927); A. Werner, *T. G. Masaryk* (1934); P. Crabitès, *Beneš* (1934); K. Krofta, *A Short History of Czechoslovakia* (1934); F. J. Vondracek, *The Foreign Policy of Czechoslovakia, 1918-1935* (1937); D. A. Lowrie, *Masaryk of Czechoslovakia* (1938); E. B. Hitchcock, *"I Built a Temple for Peace." The Life of Eduard Beneš* (1940); R. Freund, *Watch Czechoslovakia!* (1938). Recent books on Czechoslovakia are: E. P. Young, *Czechoslovakia: Keystone of Peace and Democracy* (1938); R. J. Kerner, ed., *Czechoslovakia* (1940), an important collection of essays; W. P. Warren, *Masaryk's Democracy* (1941); R. W. Seton-Watson, *A History of the*

Czechs and Slovaks (1943); S. H. Thomson, *Czechoslovakia in European History* (1943); and E. Tabórsky, *Czechoslovak Democracy at Work* (1945).

On Poland: G. Slocombe, *History of Poland* (rev. ed., 1940); J. Pilsudski, *The Memories of a Polish Revolutionary and Soldier* (1931); E. J. Patterson, *Poland* (1934), and *Pilsudski* (1935); R. Machray, *The Poland of Pilsudski* (1937); G. Humphrey, *Pilsudski: Builder of Poland* (1936); R. Gorecki, *Poland and Her Economic Development* (1935); R. L. Buell, *Poland: Key to Europe* (1939); W. J. Rose, *Poland* (1939); and P. Super, *The Polish Tradition* (1939). The following are more recent books: W. F. Reddaway, ed., *The Cambridge History of Poland, 1697-1935* (1941); S. Segal, *The New Order in Poland* (1942); B. E. Schmitt, ed., *Poland* (1945); and K. Symonolewicz, *Studies in Nationality and Nationalism in Poland Between the Two Wars* (1944).

NORTHERN EUROPE: For the Scandinavian countries as a group, see: R. N. Bain, *Scandinavia: a Political History of Denmark, Norway and Sweden from 1513 to 1900* (1905); J. Stefansson, *Denmark and Sweden, with Iceland and Finland* (1917); B. A. Arneson, *The Democratic Monarchies of Scandinavia* (1939); K. Singer, *Duel for the Northland* (1943); and also G. Bach, *A History of Scandinavian Literature* (1932). On Sweden: C. Hallendorff and A. Schück, *History of Sweden* (1929); R. Svanström and C. Palmstierna, *A Short History of Sweden* (1934); C. Grimberg, *A History of Sweden* (1935); N. Herlitz, *Sweden: a Modern Democracy on Ancient Foundations* (1939); B. Braatoy, *The New Sweden* (1939); M. M. Cole and C. Smith, eds., *Democratic Sweden* (1939); and A. Myrdal, *Nation and Family: the Swedish Experiment in Democratic Family and Population Policy* (1941).

On Norway: G. M. Gathorne-Hardy, *Norway* (1925); A. Rothery, *Norway: Changing and Changeless* (1939); and G. R. Harris, *Progressive Norway* (1939).

On Denmark: A. Rothery, *Denmark, Kingdom of Reason* (1937); J. H. S. Birch, *Denmark in History* (1938); and P. Manniche, *Denmark, a Social Laboratory* (1939).

On Finland: T. W. Atchley, *Finland* (1931); J. H. Wuorinen, *Nationalism in Modern Finland* (1931); A. E. Rothery, *Finland, the New Nation* (1936); J. H. Jackson, *Finland* (1938); H. B. Elliston, *Finland Fights* (1940); J. Langdon-Davies, *Finland: the First Total War* (1940). *The Finnish Blue Book* (1940) and *Finland Reveals Her Secret Documents* (1941) give the Finnish point of view, while the Soviet position is presented in A. Brody and others, eds., *War and Peace in Finland* (1940); and W. P. and Z. Coates, *The Soviet-Finnish Campaign: Military and Political, 1939-1940* (1942).

On Iceland: K. Gjerset, *History of Iceland* (1924); H. Lindroth, *Iceland: a Land of Contrasts* (1937); and V. Stefansson, *Iceland, the First American Republic* (1939).

RUSSIA: The controversial history of the Soviet regime is treated from different points of view in: C. B. Hoover, *The Economic Life of Soviet Russia* (1931); L. Lawton, *An Economic History of Soviet Russia* (2 vols., 1932); W. H. Chamberlin, *Soviet Russia* (1931), and *Russia's Iron Age* (1934); S. and B. Webb, *Soviet Communism: a New Civilization?* (2 vols., 1936); V. M. Dean, *Soviet*

Russia: 1917-1936 (1936); M. T. Florinsky, *Toward an Understanding of the U. S. S. R.* (1939); L. Fischer, *The Soviets in World Affairs* (2 vols., 1930); T. A. Taracouzio, *War and Peace in Soviet Diplomacy* (1940); F. L. Schuman, *Soviet Politics at Home and Abroad* (1946); B. Pares, *Russia and the Peace* (1944); K. Gibberd, *Soviet Russia: an Interpretation* (1943); W. Duranty, *USSR: the Story of Soviet Russia* (1944); and R. E. Lauterbach, *These Are the Russians* (1945). In a more critical tone are L. Fischer, *Men and Politics* (1941), D. J. Dallin, *Soviet Russia's Foreign Policy* (1942), *Russia and Postwar Europe* (1943), and *The Real Soviet Russia* (1944); W. H. Chamberlin, *The Russian Enigma* (1943); W. L. White, *Report on the Russians* (1945); and L. Trotsky, *Stalin* (1946). The Soviet viewpoint is presented in S. and B. Webb, *The Truth About Russia* (1942); A. L. Strong, *Peoples of the USSR* (1944); and N. Mikhailov, *The Russian Story* (1945). See also: S. N. Harper, *The Government of the Soviet Union* (1949); A. Rosenberg, *A History of Bolshevism from Marx to the First Five-Year Plan* (1934); B. Moore, Jr., *Soviet Politics: the Dilemma of Power* (1950); M. Fainsod, *How Russia Is Ruled* (1953); H. Schwartz, *Russia's Soviet Economy* (1954); N. Jasny, *The Socialized Agriculture of the U. S. S. R.* (1949); A. Arakelian, *Industrial Management in the U. S. S. R.* (1949); P. F. Anderson, *People, Church and State in Modern Russia* (1944); J. Somerville, *Soviet Philosophy: a Study of Theory and Practice* (1946); G. S. V. Counts and N. Lodge, *The Country of the Blind: the Soviet System of Mind Control* (1949); F. Borkenau, *The Communist International* (1938); and F. Borkenau, *European Communism* (1953). On Lenin: V. Marcu, *Lenin: Thirty Years of Russia* (1928); D. S. Mirsky, *Lenin* (1931); D. Shub, *Lenin: a Biography* (1948); H. Barbusse, *Stalin: a New World Seen Through One Man* (1935); and B. Souvarine, *Stalin, a Critical Survey of Bolshevism* (1939).

SOUTHEASTERN EUROPE AND THE EASTERN QUESTION: Many aspects of the recent history of this area have been studied: H. F. Armstrong, *The New Balkans* (1926), and *Where the East Begins* (1929); H. Kohn, *Nationalism and Imperialism in the Hither East* (1932); G. Antonious, *The Arab Awakening* (1939); D. Mitrany, *The Effect of the War in Southeastern Europe* (1936); N. J. Padelford, *Peace in the Balkans* (1935); R. J. Kerner and H. N. Howard, *The Balkan Conferences and the Balkan Entente, 1930-1935* (1936); J. S. Roucek, *Politics of the Balkans* (1939); Royal Institute of International Affairs, *South-Eastern Europe: a Political and Economic Survey* (1939); and T. I. Geshkoff, *Balkan Union: a Road to Peace in Southeastern Europe* (1940). And, more recently, H. G. Wanklyn, *The Eastern Marchlands of Europe* (1941); C. A. Macartney, *Problems of the Danubian Basin* (1942); L. S. Stavrianos, *Balkan Federation* (1944); B. Newman, *Balkan Background* (1945); and, most important of all, H. Seton-Watson, *Eastern Europe Between the Wars, 1918-1941* (1945).

On Turkey: G. F. Abbott, *Turkey, Greece, and the Great Powers* (1917); A. J. Toynbee, *The Western Question in Greece and Turkey* (1922); S. P. Ladas, *The Exchange of Minorities—Bulgaria, Greece and Turkey* (1932); G. F. Hudson, *Turkey, Greece and the Eastern Mediterranean* (1939); H. N. Howard, *The Partition of Turkey: a Diplomatic History, 1913-1923* (1931); A. J. Toynbee and K. P. Kirkwood, *Turkey* (1927); T. L. Jarman, *Turkey* (1935); H. E. Allen, *The Turkish Transformation* (1935); H. Luke, *The Making of Modern Turkey* (1936); D. von Mikusch, *Mustapha Kemal* (1931); D. E. Webster, *The Turkey of Ataturk* (1939); and J. Parker and C. Smith, *Modern Turkey* (1940).

On Greece: G. F. Abbott, *Greece and the Allies, 1914-1922* (1923); P. Hibben, *Constantine I and the Greek People* (1920); H. A. Gibbons, *Venizelos* (2nd ed., 1923); S. P. P. Cosmetatos, *The Tragedy of Greece* (1928); E. G. Mears, *Greece Today* (1929); A. A. Pallis, *Greece's Anatolian Adventure and After* (1937); E. S. Forster, *A Short History of Modern Greece, 1821-1940* (1941); D. Alastos, *Venizelos* (1942); and D. Caclamanos, *Greece: the Whole Story* (1946).

On Yugoslavia: H. Baerlein, *The Birth of Yugoslavia* (2 vols., 1922); W. H. C. Price, *Serbia's Part in the War* (1918); J. Buchan, ed., *Yugoslavia* (1923); C. A. Beard and G. Radin, *Balkan Pivot: Yugoslavia* (1929); R. G. D. Laffan, *Yugoslavia Since 1918* (1929); E. J. Patterson, *Yugoslavia* (1936); and S. Graham, *Alexander of Yugoslavia* (1939); R. West, *Black Lamb and Grey Falcon* (1941); H. D. Harrison, *The Soul of Yugoslavia* (1941); L. Adamic, *My Native Land* (1943).

On Rumania: C. U. Clark, *United Roumania* (1932); J. S. Roucek, *Contemporary Roumania and Her Problems* (1932); D. Mitrany, *The Land and Peasant in Roumania* (1930); Marie, Queen of Roumania, *The Story of My Life* (1934), and *Ordeal: the Story of My Life* (1935); A. L. Easterman, *King Carol, Hitler and Lupescu* (1942); C. Kormos, *Rumania* (1944); and P. Pavel, *Why Rumania Failed* (1944).

On Bulgaria: L. Pasvolsky, *Bulgaria's Economic Position* (1930); R. H. Markham, *Meet Bulgaria* (1931); G. C. Logio, *Bulgaria, Past and Present* (1936); J. Swire, *Bulgarian Conspiracy* (1939); M. Padev, *Escape From the Balkans* (1943); and K. Todorov, *Balkan Firebrand* (1943).

On Albania: E. P. Stickney, *Southern Albania or Northern Epirus in European International Affairs, 1912-1923* (1926); J. Swire, *Albania: the Rise of a Kingdom* (1929), and *King Zog's Albania* (1937); and V. Robinson, *Albania's Road to Freedom* (1942).

THE FAR EAST: P. J. Treat, *The Far East* (1934); H. M. Vinacke, *History of the Far East in Modern Times* (2nd ed., 1936); G. N. Steiger, *A History of the Far East* (1936); P. H. Clyde, *A History of the Modern and Contemporary Far East* (1937); W. W. Willoughby, *The Sino-Japanese Controversy and the League of Nations* (1935); S. King-Hall, *Western Civilization in the Far East* (1924); E. Snow, *The Battle for Asia* (1941); H. S. Quigley, *Far Eastern War, 1937-1941* (1942); O. Lattimore, *Solution in Asia* (1945); and P. Jaffe, *New Frontiers in Asia* (1945).

On China: K. S. Latourette, *The Chinese, Their History and Culture* (2 vols., 1934), and *Development of China* (5th ed., 1937); H. M. Vinacke, *Modern Constitutional Development in China* (1920); T. T. C. Woo, *The Kuomintang and the Future of the Chinese Revolution* (1928); H. A. Van Dorn, *Twenty Years of the Chinese Republic* (1932); O. Lattimore, *Manchuria, Cradle of Conflict* (1932); T. E. LaFargue, *China and the World War* (1937); L. Sharman, *Sun Yat-Sen* (1934); P. M. Anthony, *The Political Doctrines of Sun Yat-Sen* (1937); R. Berkov, *Strong Man of China: the Story of Chiang Kai-Shek* (1938); H. K. Tong, *Chiang Kai-Shek: Soldier and Statesman* (2 vols., 1938); E. Snow, *Red Star over China* (1938); and R. T. Pollard, *China's Foreign Relations, 1917-1931* (1933). Recent books on China are: A. Clegg, *The Birth of New China, 1842-1942* (1943); G. W. Keeton, *China, the Far East and the Future* (1943); O. Lattimore, *The Making of Modern China* (1944); D. N. Rowe, *China Among the Powers* (1945); and L. K. Rosinger, *China's Crisis* (1945).

On Japan: H. Kara, *Introduction to the History of Japan* (1920); H. H. Gowen, *An Outline History of Japan* (1927); J. I. Bryan, *The Civilization of Japan* (1927); G. C. Allen, *Modern Japan and Its Problems* (1928); A. J. Brown, *Japan in the World of Today* (1928); J. E. Orchard, *Japan's Economic Position* (1930); R. H. Akazi, *Japan's Foreign Relations* (1936); A. E. Hindmarch, *The Basis of Japanese Policy* (1936); A. M. Young, *Imperial Japan, 1926-1938* (1938); H. Borton, *Japan Since 1931* (1940); and J. C. Grew, *Ten Years in Japan, 1932-1942* (1944).

INTERNATIONAL RELATIONS: The inter-war period is discussed in F. H. Simonds and B. Emeny, *The Great Powers in World Politics* (1937); W. A. Orton, *Twenty Years' Armistice, 1918-1938* (1938); R. S. Kain, *Europe: Versailles to Warsaw* (1939); G. M. Gathorne-Hardy, *A Short History of International Affairs, 1920-1938* (1939); E. H. Carr, *The Twenty Years' Crisis, 1919-1939* (1939); R. M. Rayner, *The Twenty Years' Truce, 1919-1939* (1943); A. F. Sturmthal, *The Tragedy of European Labor, 1918-1939* (1943); and, in a somewhat lighter vein, D. Low, *Europe Since Versailles: a History in One Hundred Cartoons* (1940). The immediate background of the war is treated in F. L. Schuman, *Europe on the Eve: the Crisis of Diplomacy, 1933-1939* (1939), and *Night over Europe; the Diplomacy of Nemesis, 1939-1940* (1941); D. E. Lee, *Ten Years: the World on the Way to War, 1930-1940* (1942); and C. G. Haines and R. J. S. Hoffman, *The Origins and Background of the Second World War* (1943). The attempt to establish a permanent system of international peace is described in A. E. Zimmern, *The League of Nations and the Rule of Law, 1918-1935* (1936); J. I. Knudson, *A History of the League of Nations* (1938); M. O. Hudson, *The World Court, 1921-1938* (1938); and W. E. Rappard, *The Quest for Peace Since the World War* (1940).

The problems involved in establishing a new international system are discussed in: E. H. Carr, *Conditions of Peace* (1942); L. W. Holborn, *War and Peace Aims of the United Nations, 1939-1942* (1943); *The United Nations in the Making: Basic Documents* (1945); L. M. Goodrich and E. Hambro, *Charter of the United Nations: Commentary and Documents* (1946); and V. M. Dean, *The Four Cornerstones of Peace* (1946).

The attempt to establish a permanent system of international peace is described in: A. E. Zimmern, *The League of Nations and the Rule of Law, 1918-1935* (1936); J. I. Knudson, *A History of the League of Nations* (1938); M. O. Hudson, *The World Court, 1921-1938* (1938); W. E. Rappard, *The Quest for Peace Since the World War* (1940). Special aspects of the problem are treated in: F. W. Foster, *Europe and the German Question* (1940); A. Wolfers, *Britain and France Between Two Wars* (1940); P. Birdsall, *Versailles Twenty Years After* (1941); I. Silone, *The School for Dictators* (1938); C. K. Streit, *Union Now* (1939); M. M. Rader, *No Compromise* (1939); C. B. Hoover, *Dictators and Democracies* (1937); H. Kohn, *Revolutions and Dictatorships* (1939); E. Beneš, *Democracy Today and Tomorrow* (1939); R. B. Perry, *Shall Not Perish From the Earth* (1940); and G. A. Craig, *The Politics of the Prussian Army 1640-1945* (1955).

VI. WORLD WAR II.

GENERAL: W. S. Churchill, *The Gathering Storm, Their Finest Hour, The Grand Alliance, Closing the Ring,* and *Triumph Through Tragedy* (1948-1953). See also, W. P. Hall, *Iron Out of Calvary, an Interpretative History of the Second World War* (1950); H. C. O'Neill, *A Short History of the Second World War* (1951); C. Wilmot, *The Struggle for Europe* (1952); and A. Van Sinderen, *The Story of Six Years of Global Conflict* (1946).

EARLY STAGES OF THE WAR: W. Anders, *An Army in Exile: the Story of the Second Polish Corps* (1949); J. Bryan, *Siege of Warsaw* (1940); K. Wierzynski, *The Forgotten Battlefield; the Story of Finland* (1944); C. J. Hambro, *I Saw It Happen in Norway* (1940); A. Johnson, *Norway, Her Invasion and Occupation* (1948); *Belgian-American Educational Foundation: the Belgian Campaign and the Surrender of the Belgian Army* (1940).

FRANCE: H. F. Armstrong, *Chronology of Failure: the Last Days of the French Republic* (1940); P. J. Philip, *France in Defeat* (1941); A. Werth, *The Twilight of France* (1942); A. Géraud (Pertinax), *The Gravediggers of France* (1944); *For All Mankind* (1946), a socialist explains France's defeat; P. Cot, *Triumph of Treason* (1944); A. Maurois, *Why France Fell* (1941); M. Weygand, *Recalled to Service* (1952); J. Flanner, *Petain: the Old Man of France* (1944); S. Huddleston, *Petain: Patriot or Traitor* (1951); C. de Gaulle, *War Memoirs, Vol. 1, 1940-1942* (1955); J. Lorraine, *Behind the Battle of France* (1943); and R. Aglion, *The Fighting French* (1943).

BRITAIN: Defense by air and by sea; K. Ayling, *The Story of a British Pilot Fighter* (1941); A. A. Michie and W. Graebner, *Their Finest Hour* (1941); W. Churchill, *The War Speeches of the Rt. Hon. Winston Churchill* (1953); R. Carse, *Lifeline: the Ships and Men of Our Merchant Marine at War* (1944); R. Grenfell, *The Bismarck Episode* (1949); N. Monsanirat, *Corvette Command* (1944); I. Halstead, *Heroes of the Atlantic* (1942); and F. Herman, *Dynamite Cargo* (1943).

WAR IN AFRICA AND THE BALKANS: R. Aglion, *War in the Desert: the Battle for Africa* (1941); A. G. Clifford, *The Conquest of North Africa, 1940-1943* (1943); R. Hill, *Desert Conquest* (1943); B. H. Liddell Hart, *The Rommel Papers* (1953); Viscount Montgomery, *El Alamein to the River Sangro* (1949); D. Young, *Rommel, the Desert Fox* (1950); L. White, *The Long Balkan Night* (1943); R. Mitchel, *The Serbs Chose War* (1943); B. Wason, *Miracle in*

Hellas: the Greeks Fight On (1943); E. L. Easterman, *King Carol, Hitler and Lupescu* (1942); J. Hetherington, *Airborne Invasion* (1943); and T. H. Wisdom, *Wings Over Olympus: the Story of the Royal Air Force in Libya and Greece* (1942).

WAR IN THE WEST AND IN ITALY: L. E. O. Charlton, *The Royal Air Force and the U. S. A. A. F. from July 1943 to September 1945* (2 vols., 1946-1947); W. F. Craven and J. L. Cates, eds., *The Army Air Forces in World War II* (4 vols., 1948-1951); A. O. Pollard, *Bombers over the Reich* (1941); C. C. Wertenbaker, *Invasion* (1944); J. D'Arcy-Dawson, *European Victory* (1945); D. D. Eisenhower, *Crusade in Europe* (1948); J. Gunther, *D-Day: What Preceded It; What Followed It* (1944); Viscount Montgomery, *Normandy to the Baltic* (1947); G. S. Patton, Jr., *War as I Knew It* (1947); E. Pyle, *Brave Men* (1944); H. Speidel, *Rommel and the Normandy Campaign* (1950); P. Badoglio, *Italy in the Second World War* (1948); E. Linklater, *The Campaign in Italy* (1951); and R. Tregaskis, *Invasion Diary* (1944).

WAR AND AMERICA: C. Hull, *The Memoirs of Cordell Hull* (2 vols., 1948); W. Johnson, *The Battle Against Isolation* (1944); W. S. Cole, *America First: the Battle Against Intervention, 1940-1941* (1953); T. Sherwood, *Roosevelt and Hopkins* (1951); D. M. Nelson, *Arsenal of Democracy* (1946); H. V. Morton, *Atlantic Meeting* (1943); E. R. Stettinius, *Lend Lease: Weapons for Victory* (1944); S. Wells, *Seven Decisions That Shaped History* (1951); and E. L. Stimson, *On Active Service in Peace and War* (1948).

WAR IN EASTERN EUROPE: I. Ehrenburg, *The Tempering of Russia* (1944); W. E. D. Allen and P. Muratoff, *The Russian Campaigns of 1944-1945* (1946); A. Fadeev, *Leningrad in the Days of the Blockade* (1946); S. A. Kovpak, *Our Partisan Course* (1947); L. Lesueur, *Twelve Months That Changed the World* (1943); T. Plievier, *Stalingrad* (1948); A. Poliakov, *White Mammoths: the Dramatic Story of Russian Tanks in Action* (1943); B. Voyetekhov, *The Last Days of Sevastopol* (1953); and W. Anders, *Hitler's Defeat in Russia* (1953).

NAZI GERMANY AND OCCUPIED EUROPE: M. Berg, *Warsaw Ghetto* (1945); S. Christensen, *Norway Is My Country* (1943); J. A. Goris, *Belgium in Bondage* (1944); S. Gudme, *Denmark, Hitler's Model Protectorate* (1942); R. Lemkin, *Axis Rule in Occupied Europe* (1945); B. Shub, *Starvation over Europe: Made in Germany* (1943); J. Karski, *Story of a Secret State* (1943); B. Hoye and T. M. Ager, *The Fight of the Norwegian Church Against Nazism* (1943); W. Jones, *Twelve Months with Tito's Partisans* (1946); A. J. Liebling, *The Republic of Silence* (1947); and R. B. Nyquist, *Sons of the Vikings* (1943).

WAR IN THE PACIFIC: H. Abend, *Chaos in Asia* (1940); K. Matsuo, *How Japan Plans to Win* (1942); H. S. Quigley, *Far Eastern War, 1937-1941* (1942); T. A. Bisson, *America's Far Eastern Policy* (1942); H. Feis, *The Road to Pearl Harbor: the Coming of the War Between Japan and the United States* (1950); W. Millis, *This is Pearl! The United States and Japan, 1941* (1947); G. Morganstern, *Pearl Harbor: the Story of the Secret War* (1947); W. L. J. Bayler, *Last*

Man off Wake Island (1943); J. Hersey, *Men on Bataan* (1942); E. B. Miller, *Bataan Uncensored* (1949); E. M. Glover, *In 70 Days: the Story of the Japanese Campaign in British Malaya* (1944); C. P. Romulo, *I Saw the Fall of the Philippines* (1943); J. Stilwell, *The Stilwell Papers* (1948); J. Wainwright, *General Wainwright's Story* (1946); J. Iseley and P. J. Crowl, *The United States Marines and the Amphibious War* (1951); R. L. Eichelberger, *Our Jungle Road to Tokio* (1950); S. Morrison, *History of United States Naval Operations in World War II* (7 vols., 1948-1953); R. Sherrod, *Tarawa: the Story of a Battle* (1944); R. Tregaskis, *Guadalcanal Diary* (1943); C. V. Woodward, *The Battle for Leyte Gulf* (1947); J. Belden, *Retreat with Stilwell* (1943); F. Owen, *The Campaign in Burma* (1946); and J. Hersey, *Hiroshima* (1946).

VII. POST WORLD WAR II

PROBLEMS OF WORLD PEACE: A. Vanderbosch and W. N. Hogan, *The United Nations: Background, Organization, Functions, Activities* (1952); L. Holborn, *War and Peace Aims of the United Nations* (2 vols., 1934-1948); F. W. Pick, *Peacemaking in Perspective* (1950); S. E. Harris, *The European Recovery Program* (1948); C. P. Kindleberger, *The Dollar Shortage* (1951); I. Burnham, *The Struggle for the World* (1947); E. H. Carr, *The Soviet Impact on the Rest of the World* (1947); G. Stopler, *German Realities* (1948); S. Glueck, *The Nuremberg Trial and Aggressive War* (1946); R. H. Jackson, *The Case Against the Nazi War Criminals* (1946); C. Bowles, *The New Dimensions of Peace* (1955); L. B. Pearson, *Democracy in World Politics* (1955); G. L. Arnold, *The Pattern of World Conflict* (1955); and A. and V. Toynbee, *The Realignment of Europe* (1955).

POSTWAR WESTERN EUROPE: C. P. O. Clarke, *Britain Today: a Review of Current Political and Social Trends* (1951); H. Morrison, *The Peaceful Revolution* (1949); V. Cowles, *Winston Churchill: the Era and the Man* (1953); E. Watkins, *The Cautious Revolution: Britain Today and Tomorrow* (1950); F. Goguel, *France under the Fourth Republic* (1952); D. Pickles, *French Politics: the First Years of the Fourth Republic* (1953); M. Einaudi, *Christian Democracy in Italy and France* (1952); H. S. Hughes, *The United States and Italy* (1953); and M. Grinbod, *The Rebuilding of Italy* (1955).

POSTWAR CENTRAL EUROPE: W. Byford-Jones, *Berlin Twilight* (1947); F. Howley, *Berlin Command* (1950); M. Klemme, *The Inside Story of U.N.R.R.A.: an Experiment in Internationalism* (1949); D. Middleton, *The Struggle for Germany* (1949); N. Muhlen, *The Return of Germany: a Tale of Two Countries (Federal and Communist Germany)* (1953); U. S. Department of State, *East Germany under Soviet Control* (1952); K. Gruber, *Between Liberation and Liberty* (1955); and G. Bolton, *Czech Tragedy* (1955).

POSTWAR COMMUNIST LANDS: G. Counts and N. Lodge, *The Country of the Blind: the Soviet System of Mind Control* (1949); E. Crankshaw, *Cracks in the Kremlin Wall* (1951); A. K. Herling, *The Soviet Slave Empire* (1951); G.

Schueller, *The Politburo* (1951); F. Rounds, Jr., *A Window on Red Square* (1953); S. M. Schwartz, *Labor in the Soviet Union* (1951); J. S. Curtiss, *The Russian Church and the Soviet State, 1917-1950* (1953); M. Fainsod, *How Russia Is Ruled* (1953); W. O. Douglas, *Russian Journey* (1956); D. D. Dallin, *The Changing World of Soviet Russia* (1956); V. Bartlett, *East of the Iron Curtain* (1950); L. Stowe, *Conquest by Terror* (1952); H. Tennyson, *Tito Lifts the Curtain* (1955).

CONTEMPORARY AFRICA: J. Gunther, *Inside Africa* (1955); S. Cloete, *African Giant* (1955); M. Slater, *The Trial of Jomo Kenyatta* (1955); A. Campbell. *The Heart of Africa* (1955); C. Dundas, *African Crossroads* (1955); A. Paton, *Cry the Beloved Country* (1950); L. Van Der Post, *Dark Eye in Africa* (1955); J. H. Oldham, *New Hope in Africa* (1955); J. Seymour, *One Man's Africa* (1955); J. F. Macdonald, *Zambesi River* (1955); and H. Tingsten, *The Problem of South Africa* (1955).

CONTEMPORARY ASIA: K. W. Bilby, *New Star in the East* (1951); G. Hoffman, *The Land and People of Israel* (1950); U. Heyd, *Foundations of Turkish National* (1950); J. Nehru, *Independence and After* (1950); J. B. Schechtman, *Population Transfers in Asia* (1949); V. Sheean, *Lead, Kindly Light* (1949); S. Hsiung, *The Life of Chiang Kai-shek* (1948); D. Wehe, *The Birth of Indonesia* (1948); P. Spear, *India, Pakistan and the West* (1949); J. F. Muehl, *Interview with India* (1950); G. F. Eliot, *Hate, Hope and High Explosives: a Report on the Middle East* (1948); G. Moorad, *Lost Peace in China* (1948); O. Lattimore, *Pivot in Asia* (1950), and *the Situation in Asia* (1949); D. Warriner, *Land and Poverty in the Middle East* (1948); E. Hunter, *Brainwashing: the Story of the Men Who Defied It* (1956); F. Hunt, *The Untold Story of General MacArthur* (1954); C. Turner, *How Communists Negotiate* (1956); K. M. Pannikar, *In Two Chinas* (1955); F. W. Fernan, *Moslems on the March* (1955); L. P. Elwell-Sutten, *Persian Oil* (1955); D. G. E. Hall, *A History of Southeast Asia* (1955); D. Woodman, *The Republic of Indonesia* (1955); J. Cameron, *Mandarin Red* (1955); M. Lindsay, *China and the Cold War* (1955); R. T. Oliver, *Syngman Rhee* (1955); and R. L. Walker, *China Under Communism* (1956).

GENERAL READING: E. H. Carr, *Studies in Revolution* (1950); G. C. D. Cole, *Meaning of Marxism* (1948); G. Hoover, *Twentieth-Century Economic Thought* (1950); and A. J. Toynbee, *War and Civilization* (1950).

Current events may best be studied in *The Annual Register, The Survey of International Affairs* (annual), *Foreign Affairs* (quarterly), and the weekly edition of *The Manchester Guardian*.

INDEX